D0635581

f life

Collins
Italian
Dictionary

HarperCollins Publishers
Westerhill Road
Bishopbriggs
Glasgow
G64 2QT
Great Britain

Second Edition 2009

Reprint 10 9 8 7 6 5 4 3 2 1 0

© HarperCollins Publishers 2006, 2009

ISBN 978-0-00-729885-3

Collins® is a registered trademark of
HarperCollins Publishers Limited

www.collinslanguage.com

A catalogue record for this book is
available from the British Library

Typeset by Wordcraft, Glasgow

Printed and bound in Great Britain by
Clays Ltd, St Ives, plc

Acknowledgements
We would like to thank those authors
and publishers who kindly gave
permission for copyright material
to be used in the Collins Word Web.
We would also like to thank Times
Newspapers Ltd for providing
valuable data.

When you buy a Collins dictionary
or thesaurus and register on
www.collinslanguage.com for the
free online and digital services, you
will not be charged by HarperCollins
for access to Collins free Online
Dictionary content or Collins free
Online Thesaurus content on that
website. However, your operator's
charges for using the internet on
your computer will apply. Costs
vary from operator to operator.
HarperCollins is not responsible
for any charges levied by online
service providers for accessing
Collins free Online Dictionary or
Collins free Online Thesaurus on
www.collinslanguage.com using
these services

MANAGING EDITOR
Gaëlle Amiot-Cadey

CONTRIBUTORS
G Bacchelli

EDITORIAL COORDINATION
Susie Beattie

SERIES EDITOR
Rob Scriven

BASED ON THE COLLINS ITALIAN GEM
Catherine E Love
P L Rossi
D M Chaplin
F Villa
E Bilucaglia

INDICE CONTENTS

William Collins' dream of knowledge for all began with the publication of his first book in 1819. A self-educated mill worker, he not only enriched millions of lives, but also founded a flourishing publishing house. Today, staying true to this spirit, Collins books are packed with inspiration, innovation, and practical expertise. They place you at the centre of a world of possibility and give you exactly what you need to explore it.

Language is the key to this exploration, and at the heart of Collins Dictionaries is language as it is really used. New words, phrases, and meanings spring up every day, and all of them are captured and analysed by the Collins Word Web. Constantly updated, and with over 2.5 billion entries, this living language resource is unique to our dictionaries.

Words are tools for life. And a Collins Dictionary makes them work for you.

Collins. Do more

INTRODUZIONE

Vi ringraziamo di aver scelto il Dizionario inglese Collins e ci auguriamo che esso si riveli uno strumento utile e piacevole da usare nello studio, in vacanza e sul lavoro.

INTRODUCTION

We are delighted that you have decided to buy the Collins Italian Dictionary and hope you will enjoy and benefit from using it at school, at home, on holiday or at work.

ABBREVIAZIONI

ABBREVIATIONS

abbreviazione	*abbr*	abbreviation
aggettivo	*adj*	adjective
amministrazione	*Admin*	administration
avverbio	*adv*	adverb
aeronautica, viaggi aerei	*Aer*	flying, air travel
aggettivo	*ag*	adjective
agricoltura	*Agr*	agriculture
amministrazione	*Amm*	administration
anatomia	*Anat*	anatomy
architettura	*Archit*	architecture
articolo determinativo	*art def*	definite article
articolo indeterminativo	*art indef*	indefinite article
attributivo	*attrib*	attributive
ausiliare	*aus, aux*	auxiliary
automobile	*Aut*	motor car and motoring
avverbio	*av*	adverb
aeronautica, viaggi aerei	*Aviat*	flying, air travel
biologia	*Biol*	biology
botanica	*Bot*	botany
inglese britannico	*BRIT*	British English
consonante	C	consonant
chimica	*Chim, Chem*	chemistry
commercio, finanza	*Comm*	commerce, finance
comparativo	*compar*	comparative
informatica	*Comput*	computing
congiunzione	*cong, conj*	conjunction
edilizia	*Constr*	building
sostantivo usato come aggettivo, ma mai con funzione predicativa	*cpd*	compound element: noun used as adjective and which cannot follow the noun it qualifies
cucina	*Cuc, Culin*	cookery
davanti a	*dav*	before

ABBREVIAZIONI		ABBREVIATIONS
articolo determinativo	*def art*	definite article
determinativo; articolo, aggettivo dimostrativo o indefinito ecc	*det*	determiner: article, demonstrative etc
diminutivo	*dimin*	diminutive
diritto	*Dir*	law
economia	*Econ*	economics
edilizia	*Edil*	building
elettricità, elettronica	*Elettr, Elec*	electricity, electronics
esclamazione	*escl, excl*	exclamation
femminile	*f*	feminine
familiare (! da evitare)	*fam(!)*	colloquial usage (! particularly offensive)
ferrovia	*Ferr*	railways
senso figurato	*fig*	figurative use
fisiologia	*Fisiol*	physiology
fotografia	*Fot*	photography
verbo inglese la cui particella è inseparabile dal verbo	*fus*	(phrasal verb) where the particle cannot be separated from the main verb
nella maggior parte dei sensi; generalmente	*gen*	in most or all senses; generally
geografia, geologia	*Geo*	geography, geology
geometria	*Geom*	geometry
storia, storico	*Hist*	history, historical
impersonale	*impers*	impersonal
articolo indeterminativo	*indef art*	indefinite article
familiare (! da evitare)	*inf(!)*	colloquial usage (! particularly offensive)
infinito	*infin*	infinitive
informatica	*Inform*	computing

ABBREVIAZIONI

		ABBREVIATIONS
insegnamento, sistema scolastico e universitario	*Ins*	schooling, schools and universities
invariabile	*inv*	invariable
irregolare	*irreg*	irregular
grammatica, linguistica	*Ling*	grammar, linguistics
maschile	*m*	masculine
matematica	*Mat(h)*	mathematics
termine medico, medicina	*Med*	medical term, medicine
il tempo, meteorologia	*Meteor*	the weather, meteorology
maschile o femminile	*m/f*	masculine or feminine
esercito, linguaggio militare	*Mil*	military matters
musica	*Mus*	music
sostantivo	*n*	noun
nautica	*Naut*	sailing, navigation
numerale (aggettivo, sostantivo)	*num*	numeral adjective or noun
	o.s.	oneself
peggiorativo	*peg, pej*	derogatory, pejorative
fotografia	*Phot*	photography
fisiologia	*Physiol*	physiology
plurale	*pl*	plural
politica	*Pol*	politics
participio passato	*pp*	past participle
preposizione	*prep*	preposition
pronome	*pron*	pronoun
psicologia, psichiatria	*Psic, Psych*	psychology, psychiatry
tempo passato	*pt*	past tense
qualcosa	*qc*	
qualcuno	*qn*	
religione, liturgia	*Rel*	religions, church service
sostantivo	*s*	noun
	sb	somebody

ABBREVIAZIONI		ABBREVIATIONS
insegnamento, sistema scolastico e universitario	*Scol*	schooling, schools and universities
singolare	*sg*	singular
soggetto (grammaticale)	*sog*	(grammatical) subject
	sth	something
congiuntivo	*sub*	subjunctive
soggetto (grammaticale)	*subj*	(grammatical) subject
superlativo	*superl*	superlative
termine tecnico, tecnologia	*Tecn, Tech*	technical term, technology
telecomunicazioni	*Tel*	telecommunications
tipografia	*Tip*	typography, printing
televisione	*TV*	television
tipografia	*Typ*	typography, printing
università	*Univ*	university
inglese americano	*US*	American English
vocale	*V*	vowel
verbo	*vb*	verb
verbo o gruppo verbale con funzione intransitiva	*vi*	verb or phrasal verb used intransitively
verbo pronominale o riflessivo	*vpr*	pronominal or reflexive verb
verbo o gruppo verbale con funzione transitiva	*vt*	verb or phrasal verb used transitively
zoologia	*Zool*	zoology
marchio registrato	®	registered trademark
introduce un'equivalenza culturale	≈	introduces a cultural equivalent

TRASCRIZIONE FONETICA

Consonanti		Consonants
padre	p	puppy
bambino	b	baby
tutto	t	tent
dado	d	daddy
cane che	k	cork kiss chord
gola ghiro	g	gag guess
sano	s	so rice kiss
svago esame	z	cousin buzz
scena	ʃ	sheep sugar
	ʒ	pleasure beige
pece lanciare	tʃ	church
giro gioco	dʒ	judge general
afa faro	f	farm raffle
vero bravo	v	very rev
	θ	thin maths
	ð	that other
letto ala	l	little ball
gli	ʎ	million
rete arco	r	rat rare
ramo madre	m	mummy comb
no fumante	n	no ran
gnomo	ɲ	canyon
	ŋ	singing bank
	h	hat reheat
buio piacere	j	yet
uomo guaio	w	wall bewail
	x	loch

Varie		Miscellaneous
per l'inglese: la "r" finale viene pronunciata se seguita da una vocale	r	
precede la sillaba accentata	'	precedes the stressed syllable

NB p, b, t, d, k, g sono seguite da un'aspirazione in inglese.

NB p, b, t, d, k, g are not aspirated in Italian.

PHONETIC TRANSCRIPTION

Vocali		Vowels

NB La messa in equivalenza di certi suoni indica solo una rassomiglianza approssimativa.

NB The pairing of some vowel sounds only indicates approximate equivalence.

Vocali		Vowels
vino idea	i iː	heel bead
	ɪ	hit pity
stella edera	e	
epoca eccetto	ɛ	set tent
mamma amore	a æ	bat apple
	ɑː	after car calm
	ã	fiancé
	ʌ	fun cousin
müsli	y	
	ə	over above
	əː	urn fern work
rosa occhio	ɔ	wash pot
	ɔː	born cork
ponte ognuno	o	
föhn	ø	
utile zucca	u	full soot
	uː	boon lewd

Dittonghi		Diphthongs
	ɪə	beer tier
	ɛə	tear fair there
	eɪ	date plaice day
	aɪ	life buy cry
	au	owl foul now
	əu	low no
	ɔɪ	boil boy oily
	uə	poor tour

ITALIAN PRONUNCIATION

Vowels

Where the vowel **e** or the vowel **o** appears in a stressed syllable it can be either open [ɛ], [ɔ] or closed [e], [o]. As the open or closed pronunciation of these vowels is subject to regional variation, the distinction is of little importance to the user of this dictionary. Phonetic transcription for headwords containing these vowels will therefore only appear where other pronunciation difficulties are present.

Consonants

c before "e" or "i" is pronounced like the *"tch"* in match.
ch is pronounced like the *"k"* in "kit".
g before "e" or "i" is pronounced like the *"j"* in "jet".
gh is pronounced like the *"g"* in "get".
gl before "e" or "i" is normally pronounced like the *"lli"* in "million", and in a few cases only like the *"gl"* in "glove".
gn is pronounced like the *"ny"* in "canyon"
sc before "e" or "i" is pronounced *"sh"*.
z is pronounced like the *"ts"* in "stetson", or like the *"d's"* in "bird's-eye".

Headwords containing the above consonants and consonantal groups have been given full phonetic transcription in this dictionary.

NB All double written consonants in Italian are fully sounded: e.g. the *tt* in "tutto" is pronounced as in "hat trick".

ITALIAN VERB FORMS

1 Gerundio **2** Participio passato **3** Presente **4** Imperfetto **5** Passato remoto **6** Futuro **7** Condizionale **8** Congiuntivo presente **9** Congiuntivo passato **10** Imperativo

andare 3 vado, vai, va, andiamo, andate, vanno **6** andrò *ecc.* **8** vada **10** va'!, vada!, andate!, vadano!

apparire 2 apparso **3** appaio, appari *o* apparisci, appare *o* apparisce, appaiono *o* appariscono **5** apparvi *o* apparsi, apparisti, apparve *o* apparì *o* apparse, apparvero *o* apparirono *o* apparsero **8** appaia *o* apparisca

aprire 2 aperto **3** apro **5** aprii, apristi **8** apra

AVERE 3 ho, hai, ha, abbiamo, avete, hanno **5** ebbi, avesti, ebbe, avemmo, aveste, ebbero **6** avrò *ecc.* **8** abbia *ecc.* **10** abbi!, abbia!, abbiate!, abbiano!

bere 1 bevendo **2** bevuto **3** bevo *ecc.* **4** bevevo *ecc.* **5** bevvi *o* bevetti, bevesti **6** berrò *ecc.* **8** beva *ecc.* **9** bevessi *ecc.*

cadere 5 caddi, cadesti **6** cadrò *ecc.*

cogliere 2 colto **3** colgo, colgono **5** colsi, cogliesti **8** colga

correre 2 corso **5** corsi, corresti

cuocere 2 cotto **3** cuocio, cociamo, cuociono **5** cossi, cocesti

dare 3 do, dai, dà, diamo, date, danno **5** diedi *o* detti, desti **6** darò *ecc.* **8** dia *ecc.* **9** dessi *ecc.* **10** da'!, dai!, date!, diano!

dire 1 dicendo **2** detto **3** dico, dici, dice, diciamo, dite, dicono **4** dicevo *ecc.* **5** dissi, dicesti **6** dirò *ecc.* **8** dica, diciamo, diciate, dicano **9** dicessi *ecc.* **10** di'!, dica!, dite!, dicano!

dolere 3 dolgo, duoli, duole, dolgono **5** dolsi, dolesti **6** dorrò *ecc.* **8** dolga

dovere 3 devo *o* debbo, devi, deve, dobbiamo, dovete, devono *o* debbono **6** dovrò *ecc.* **8** debba, dobbiamo, dobbiate, devano *o* debbano

ESSERE 2 stato **3** sono, sei, è, siamo, siete, sono **4** ero, eri, era, eravamo, eravate, erano **5** fui, fosti, fu, fummo, foste, furono **6** sarò *ecc.* **8** sia *ecc.* **9** fossi, fossi, fosse, fossimo, foste, fossero **10** sii!, sia!, siate!, siano!

fare 1 facendo **2** fatto **3** faccio, fai, fa, facciamo, fate, fanno **4** facevo *ecc.* **5** feci, facesti **6** farò *ecc.* **8** faccia *ecc.* **9** facessi *ecc.* **10** fa'!, faccia!, fate!, facciano!

FINIRE 1 finendo **2** finito **3** finisco, finisci, finisce, finiamo, finite, finiscono **4** finivo, finivi, finiva, finivamo, finivate, finivano **5** finii, finisti, finì, finimmo, finiste, finirono **6** finirò, finirai, finirà, finiremo, finirete, finiranno **7** finirei, finiresti, finirebbe, finiremmo, finireste, finirebbero **8** finisca, finisca, finisca, finiamo, finiate, finiscano **9** finissi, finissi, finisse, finissimo, finiste, finissero **10** finisci!, finisca!, finite!, finiscano!

giungere 2 giunto **5** giunsi, giungesti

leggere 2 letto **5** lessi, leggesti

mettere 2 messo **5** misi, mettesti

morire 2 morto **3** muoio, muori, muore, moriamo, morite, muoiono **6** morirò *o* morrò *ecc.* **8** muoia

muovere 2 mosso **5** mossi, movesti

nascere 2 nato **5** nacqui, nascesti

nuocere 2 nuociuto **3** nuoccio, nuoci, nuoce, nociamo *o* nuociamo, nuocete, nuocciono **4** nuocevo *ecc.* **5** nocqui, nuocesti **6** nuocerò *ecc.* **7** nuoccia

offrire 2 offerto **5** offersi *o* offrii, offristi **8** offra

parere 2 parso **3** paio, paiamo, paiono **5** parvi *o* parsi, paresti **6** parrò *ecc.* **8** paia, paiamo, paiate, paiano

PARLARE 1 parlando **2** parlato **3** parlo, parli, parla, parliamo, parlate, parlano **4** parlavo, parlavi, parlava, parlavamo, parlavate, parlavano **5** parlai, parlasti, parlò, parlammo, parlaste, parlarono **6** parlerò, parlerai, parlerà, parleremo, parlerete, parleranno **7** parlerei, parleresti, parlerebbe, parleremmo, parlereste, parlerebbero **8** parli, parli, parli, parliamo, parliate, parlino **9** parlassi, parlassi, parlasse, parlassimo, parlaste, parlassero **10** parla!, parli!, parlate!, parlino!

piacere 2 piaciuto **3** piaccio, piacciamo, piacciono **5** piacqui, piacesti **8** piacci *ecc.*

porre 1 ponendo **2** posto **3** pongo, poni, pone, poniamo, ponete, pongono **4** ponevo *ecc.* **5** posi, ponesti **6** porrò *ecc.* **8** ponga, poniamo, poniate, pongano **9** ponessi *ecc.*

potere 3 posso, puoi, può, possiamo, potete, possono **6** potrò *ecc.* **8** possa, possiamo, possiate, possano

prendere 2 preso **5** presi, prendesti

ridurre 1 riducendo **2** ridotto **3** riduco *ecc.* **4** riducevo *ecc.* **5** ridussi, riducesti **6** ridurrò *ecc.* **8** riduca *ecc.* **9** riducessi *ecc.*

riempire 1 riempiendo **3** riempio, riempi, riempie, riempiono

rimanere 2 rimasto **3** rimango, rimangono **5** rimasi, rimanesti **6** rimarrò *ecc.* **8** rimanga

rispondere 2 risposto **5** risposi, rispondesti

salire 3 salgo, sali, salgono **8** salga

sapere 3 so, sai, sa, sappiamo, sapete, sanno **5** seppi, sapesti **6** saprò *ecc.* **8** sappia *ecc.* **10** sappi!, sappia!, sappiate!, sappiano!

scrivere 2 scritto **5** scrissi, scrivesti

sedere 3 siedo, siedi, siede, siedono **8** sieda

spegnere 2 spento **3** spengo, spengono **5** spensi, spegnesti **8** spenga

stare 2 stato **3** sto, stai, sta, stiamo, state, stanno **5** stetti, stesti **6** starò *ecc.* **8** stia *ecc.* **9** stessi *ecc.* **10** sta'!, stia!, state!, stiano!

tacere 2 taciuto **3** taccio, tacciono **5** tacqui, tacesti **8** taccia

tenere 3 tengo, tieni, tiene, tengono **5** tenni, tenesti **6** terrò *ecc.* **8** tenga

trarre 1 traendo **2** tratto **3** traggo, trai, trae, traiamo, traete, traggono **4** traevo *ecc.* **5** trassi, traesti **6** trarrò *ecc.* **8** tragga **9** traessi *ecc.*

udire 3 odo, odi, ode, odono **8** oda

uscire 3 esco, esci, esce, escono **8** esca

valere 2 valso **3** valgo, valgono **5** valsi, valesti **6** varrò *ecc.* **8** valga

vedere 2 visto *o* veduto **5** vidi, vedesti **6** vedrò *ecc.*

VENDERE 1 vendendo **2** venduto **3** vendo, vendi, vende, vendiamo, vendete, vendono **4** vendevo, vendevi, vendeva, vendevamo, vendevate, vendevano **5** vendei *o* vendetti, vendesti, vendé *o* vendette, vendemmo, vendeste, venderono *o* vendettero **6** venderò, venderai, venderà, venderemo, venderete, venderanno **7** venderei, venderesti, venderebbe, venderemmo, vendereste, venderebbero **8** venda, venda, venda, vendiamo, vendiate, vendano **9** vendessi, vendessi, vendesse, vendessimo, vendeste, vendessero **10** vendi!, venda!, vendete!, vendano!

venire 2 venuto **3** vengo, vieni, viene, vengono **5** venni, venisti **6** verrò *ecc.* **8** venga

vivere 2 vissuto **5** vissi, vivesti

volere 3 voglio, vuoi, vuole, vogliamo, volete, vogliono **5** volli, volesti **6** vorrò *ecc.* **8** voglia *ecc.* **10** vogli!, voglia!, vogliate!, vogliano!

ENGLISH VERB FORMS

present	pt	pp	present	pt	pp
arise	arose	arisen	feed	fed	fed
awake	awoke	awoken	feel	felt	felt
be (am, is, are; being)	was, were	been	fight	fought	fought
			find	found	found
bear	bore	born(e)	flee	fled	fled
beat	beat	beaten	fling	flung	flung
become	became	become	fly	flew	flown
begin	began	begun	forbid	forbade	forbidden
bend	bent	bent	forecast	forecast	forecast
bet	bet, betted	bet, betted	forget	forgot	forgotten
			forgive	forgave	forgiven
bid (at auction, cards)	bid	bid	forsake	forsook	forsaken
			freeze	froze	frozen
bid (say)	bade	bidden	get	got	got, (US) gotten
bind	bound	bound			
bite	bit	bitten	give	gave	given
bleed	bled	bled	go (goes)	went	gone
blow	blew	blown	grind	ground	ground
break	broke	broken	grow	grew	grown
breed	bred	bred	hang	hung	hung
bring	brought	brought	hang (execute)	hanged	hanged
build	built	built	have (has; having)	had	had
burn	burnt, burned	burnt, burned			
burst	burst	burst	hear	heard	heard
buy	bought	bought	hide	hid	hidden
can	could	(been able)	hit	hit	hit
cast	cast	cast	hold	held	held
catch	caught	caught	hurt	hurt	hurt
choose	chose	chosen	keep	kept	kept
cling	clung	clung	kneel	knelt, kneeled	knelt, kneeled
come	came	come			
cost	cost	cost	know	knew	known
cost (work out price of)	costed	costed	lay	laid	laid
			lead	led	led
creep	crept	crept	lean	leant, leaned	leant, leaned
cut	cut	cut			
deal	dealt	dealt	leap	leapt, leaped	leapt, leaped
dig	dug	dug	learn	learnt, learned	learnt, learned
do (does)	did	done			
draw	drew	drawn	leave	left	left
dream	dreamed, dreamt	dreamed, dreamt	lend	lent	lent
			let	let	let
drink	drank	drunk	lie (lying)	lay	lain
drive	drove	driven	light	lit, lighted	lit, lighted
dwell	dwelt	dwelt			
eat	ate	eaten	lose	lost	lost
fall	fell	fallen	make	made	made

present	pt	pp	present	pt	pp
may	might	—	spell	spelt, spelled	spelt, spelled
mean	meant	meant	spend	spent	spent
meet	met	met	spill	spilt, spilled	spilt, spilled
mistake	mistook	mistaken			
mow	mowed	mown, mowed	spin	spun	spun
			spit	spat	spat
must	(had to)	(had to)	split	split	split
pay	paid	paid	spoil	spoiled, spoilt	spoiled, spoilt
put	put	put			
quit	quit, quitted	quit, quitted	spread	spread	spread
			spring	sprang	sprung
read	read	read	stand	stood	stood
rid	rid	rid	steal	stole	stolen
ride	rode	ridden	stick	stuck	stuck
ring	rang	rung	sting	stung	stung
rise	rose	risen	stink	stank	stunk
run	ran	run	stride	strode	stridden
saw	sawed	sawed, sawn	strike	struck	struck, stricken
say	said	said			
see	saw	seen	strive	strove	striven
seek	sought	sought	swear	swore	sworn
sell	sold	sold	sweep	swept	swept
send	sent	sent	swell	swelled	swollen, swelled
set	set	set			
sew	sewed	sewn	swim	swam	swum
shake	shook	shaken	swing	swung	swung
shear	sheared	shorn, sheared	take	took	taken
			teach	taught	taught
shed	shed	shed	tear	tore	torn
shine	shone	shone	tell	told	told
shoot	shot	shot	think	thought	thought
show	showed	shown	throw	threw	thrown
shrink	shrank	shrunk	thrust	thrust	thrust
shut	shut	shut	tread	trod	trodden
sing	sang	sung	wake	woke, waked	woken, waked
sink	sank	sunk			
sit	sat	sat	wear	wore	worn
slay	slew	slain	weave	wove, weaved	woven, weaved
sleep	slept	slept			
slide	slid	slid	wed	wedded, wed	wedded, wed
sling	slung	slung			
slit	slit	slit			
smell	smelt, smelled	smelt, smelled	weep	wept	wept
			win	won	won
sow	sowed	sown, sowed	wind	wound	wound
			wring	wrung	wrung
speak	spoke	spoken	write	wrote	written
speed	sped, speeded	sped, speeded			

a

A *abbr* (= *autostrada*) ≈ M (*motorway*)

🔘 **PAROLA CHIAVE**

a (*a* + *il* = **al**, *a* + *lo* = **allo**, *a* + *l'* = **all'**, *a* + *la* = **alla**, *a* + *i* = **ai**, *a* + *gli* = **agli**, *a* + *le* = **alle**) *prep*
1 (*stato in luogo*) at; (: *in*) in; **essere alla stazione** to be at the station; **essere a casa/a scuola/a Roma** to be at home/at school/in Rome; **è a 10 km da qui** it's 10 km from here, it's 10 km away
2 (*moto a luogo*) to; **andare a casa/a scuola** to go home/to school
3 (*tempo*) at; (*epoca, stagione*) in; **alle cinque** at five (o'clock); **a mezzanotte/ Natale** at midnight/Christmas; **al mattino** in the morning; **a maggio/primavera** in May/spring; **a cinquant'anni** at fifty (years of age); **a domani!** see you tomorrow!
4 (*complemento di termine*) to; **dare qc a qn** to give sth to sb
5 (*mezzo, modo*) with, by, **a piedi/cavallo** on foot/horseback; **fatto a mano** made by hand, handmade; **una barca a motore** a motorboat; **a uno a uno** one by one; **all'italiana** the Italian way, in the Italian fashion
6 (*rapporto*) a, per; (: *con prezzi*) at; **prendo 850 euro al mese** I get 850 euros a *o* per month; **pagato a ore** paid by the hour; **vendere qc a 2 euro il chilo** to sell sth at 2 euros a *o* per kilo

abbagli'ante [abbaʎ'ʎante] *ag* dazzling; **abbaglianti** *smpl* (*Aut*): **accendere gli abbaglianti** to put one's headlights on full (*BRIT*) *o* high (*US*) beam
abbagli'are [abbaʎ'ʎare] *vt* to dazzle; (*illudere*) to delude
abbai'are *vi* to bark
abbando'nare *vt* to leave, abandon, desert; (*trascurare*) to neglect; (*rinunciare a*) to abandon, give up; **abbandonarsi** *vpr* to let o.s. go; **abbandonarsi a** (*ricordi, vizio*) to give o.s. up to
abbas'sare *vt* to lower; (*radio*) to turn down; **abbassarsi** *vpr* (*chinarsi*) to stoop; (*livello, sole*) to go down; (*fig: umiliarsi*) to demean o.s.; **~ i fari** (*Aut*) to dip *o* dim (*US*) one's lights
ab'basso *escl* **~ il re!** down with the king!
abbas'tanza [abbas'tantsa] *av* (*a sufficienza*) enough; (*alquanto*) quite, rather, fairly; **non è ~ furbo** he's not shrewd enough; **un vino ~ dolce** quite a sweet wine; **averne ~ di qn/qc** to have had enough of sb/sth
ab'battere *vt* (*muro, casa*) to pull down; (*ostacolo*) to knock down; (*albero*) to fell; (: *vento*) to bring down; (*bestie da macello*) to slaughter; (*cane, cavallo*) to destroy, put down; (*selvaggina, aereo*) to shoot down; (*fig: malattia, disgrazia*) to lay low; **abbattersi** *vpr* (*avvilirsi*) to lose heart; **abbat'tuto, -a** *ag* (*fig*) depressed
abba'zia [abbat'tsia] *sf* abbey
'abbia *vb vedi* **avere**
abbi'ente *ag* well-to-do, well-off; **abbienti** *smpl* **gli abbienti** the well-to-do
abbiglia'mento [abbiʎʎa'mento] *sm* dress *no pl*; (*indumenti*) clothes *pl*; (*industria*) clothing industry
abbi'nare *vt* **~ (a)** to combine (with)
abboc'care *vi* (*pesce*) to bite; (*tubi*) to join; **~ (all'amo)** (*fig*) to swallow the bait
abbona'mento *sm* subscription; (*alle ferrovie ecc*) season ticket; **fare l'~** to take out a subscription (*o* season ticket)
abbo'narsi *vpr* **~ a un giornale** to take out a subscription to a newspaper; **~ al teatro/alle ferrovie** to take out a season ticket for the theatre/the train
abbon'dante *ag* abundant, plentiful; (*giacca*) roomy
abbon'danza [abbon'dantsa] *sf* abundance; plenty
abbor'dabile *ag* (*persona*) approachable; (*prezzo*) reasonable

abbotto'nare vt to button up, do up

abbracci'are [abbrat't∫are] vt to embrace; (persona) to hug, embrace; (professione) to take up; (contenere) to include; **abbracciarsi** vpr to hug o embrace (one another); **ab'braccio** sm hug, embrace

abbrevi'are vt to shorten; (parola) to abbreviate

abbreviazi'one [abbrevjat'tsjone] sf abbreviation

abbron'zante [abbron'dzante] ag tanning, sun cpd

abbronzarsi vpr to tan, get a tan

abbron'zato, -a [abbron'dzato] ag (sun)tanned

abbrusto'lire vt (pane) to toast; (caffè) to roast; **abbrustolirsi** vpr to toast; (fig: al sole) to soak up the sun

abbuf'farsi vpr (fam): ~ (di qc) to stuff o.s. (with sth)

abdi'care vi to abdicate; ~ **a** to give up, renounce

a'bete sm fir (tree); **abete rosso** spruce

'abile ag (idoneo): ~ **(a qc/a fare qc)** fit (for sth/to do sth); (capace) able; (astuto) clever; (accorto) skilful; ~ **al servizio militare** fit for military service; **abilità** sf inv ability; cleverness; skill

a'bisso sm abyss, gulf

abi'tante sm/f inhabitant

abi'tare vt to live in, dwell in ▷ vi ~ **in campagna/a Roma** to live in the country/in Rome; **dove abita?** where do you live?; **abitazi'one** sf residence; house

'abito sm dress no pl; (da uomo) suit; (da donna) dress; (abitudine, disposizione, Rel) habit; **abiti** smpl (vestiti) clothes; **in ~ da sera** in evening dress

abitu'ale ag usual, habitual; (cliente) regular

abitual'mente av usually, normally

abitu'are vt ~ **qn a** to get sb used o accustomed to; **abituarsi a** to get used to, accustom o.s. to

abitudi'nario, -a ag of fixed habits ▷ sm/f regular customer

abi'tudine sf habit; **aver l'~ di fare qc** to be in the habit of doing sth; **d'~** usually; **per ~** from o out of habit

abo'lire vt to abolish; (Dir) to repeal

abor'tire vi (Med) to miscarry, have a miscarriage; (: deliberatamente) to have an abortion; (fig) to miscarry, fail; **a'borto** sm miscarriage; abortion

ABS [abiεsε] sigla m (= Anti-Blockier System) ABS

'abside sf apse

abu'sare vi ~ **di** to abuse, misuse; (alcool) to take to excess; (approfittare, violare) to take advantage of

abu'sivo, -a ag unauthorized, unlawful; **(occupante)** ~ (di una casa) squatter

Attenzione! In inglese esiste la parola abusive che però vuol dire ingiurioso.

a.C. av abbr (= avanti Cristo) B.C.

a'cacia, -cie [a'kat∫a] sf (Bot) acacia

ac'cadde vb vedi **accadere**

acca'demia sf (società) learned society; (scuola: d'arte, militare) academy

acca'dere vb impers to happen, occur

accal'dato ag hot

accalo'rarsi vpr (fig) to get excited

accampa'mento sm camp

accamparsi vpr to camp

acca'nirsi vpr (infierire) to rage; (ostinarsi) to persist; **acca'nito, -a** ag (odio, gelosia) fierce, bitter; (lavoratore) assiduous, dogged; (fumatore) inveterate

ac'canto av near, nearby; ~ **a** prep near, beside, close to

accanto'nare vt (problema) to shelve; (somma) to set aside

accappa'toio sm bathrobe

accarez'zare [akkaret'tsare] vt to caress, stroke, fondle; (fig) to toy with

acca'sarsi vpr to set up house; to get married

accasci'arsi [akka∫'∫arsi] vpr to collapse; (fig) to lose heart

accat'tone, -a sm/f beggar

accaval'lare vt (gambe) to cross

acce'care [att∫e'kare] vt to blind ▷ vi to go blind

ac'cedere [at't∫edere] vi ~ **a** to enter; (richiesta) to grant, accede to

accele'rare [att∫ele'rare] vt to speed up ▷ vi (Aut) to accelerate; ~ **il passo** to quicken one's pace; **accelera'tore** sm (Aut) accelerator

ac'cendere [at't∫endere] vt (fuoco, sigaretta) to light; (luce, televisione) to put on, switch on, turn on; (Aut: motore) to switch on; (Comm: conto) to open; (fig: suscitare) to inflame, stir up; **ha da ~?** have you got a light?; **non riesco ad ~ il riscaldamento** I can't turn the heating on; **accen'dino, accendi'sigaro** sm (cigarette) lighter

accen'nare [att∫en'nare] vt (Mus) to pick out the notes of; to hum ▷ vi ~ **a** (fig: alludere a) to hint at; (: far atto di) to make as if; ~ **un saluto** (con la mano) to make as if to wave; (col capo) to half nod; **accenna a piovere** it looks as if it's going to rain

ac'cenno [at't∫enno] sm (cenno) sign; nod; (allusione) hint

accensi'one [att∫en'sjone] sf (vedi verbo) lighting; switching on; opening; (Aut) ignition

ac'cento [at'tʃɛnto] sm accent; (Fonetica, fig) stress; (inflessione) tone (of voice)

accentu'are [attʃentu'are] vt to stress, emphasize; **accentuarsi** vpr to become more noticeable

accerchi'are [attʃer'kjare] vt to surround, encircle

accerta'mento [attʃerta'mento] sm check; assessment

accer'tare [attʃer'tare] vt to ascertain; (verificare) to check; (reddito) to assess; **accertarsi** vpr **accertarsi (di)** to make sure (of)

ac'ceso, -a [at'tʃeso] pp di **accendere** ▷ ag lit; on; open; (colore) bright

acces'sibile [attʃes'sibile] ag (luogo) accessible; (persona) approachable, (prezzo) reasonable

ac'cesso [at'tʃɛsso] sm (anche Inform) access; (Med) attack, fit; (impulso violento) fit, outburst

accessori smpl accessories

ac'cetta [at'tʃetta] sf hatchet

accet'tabile [attʃet'tabile] ag acceptable

accet'tare [attʃet'tare] vt to accept; **accettate carte di credito?** do you accept credit cards?; **~ di fare qc** to agree to do sth; **accettazi'one** sf acceptance; (locale di servizio pubblico) reception; **accettazione bagagli** (Aer) check-in (desk)

acchiap'pare [akkjap'pare] vt to catch

acciaie'ria [attʃaje'ria] sf steelworks sg

acci'aio [at'tʃajo] sm steel

acciden'tato, -a [attʃiden'tato] ag (terreno ecc) uneven

accigli'ato, -a [attʃiʎ'ʎato] ag frowning

ac'cingersi [at'tʃindʒersi] vpr **~ a fare qc** to be about to do sth

acciuf'fare [attʃuf'fare] vt to seize, catch

acci'uga, -ghe [at'tʃuga] sf anchovy

ac'cludere vt to enclose

accocco'larsi vpr to crouch

accogli'ente [akkoʎ'ʎente] ag welcoming, friendly

ac'cogliere [ak'kɔʎʎere] vt (ricevere) to receive; (dare il benvenuto) to welcome; (approvare) to agree to, accept; (contenere) to hold, accommodate

ac'colgo ecc vb vedi **accogliere**

ac'colsi ecc vb vedi **accogliere**

accoltel'lare vt to knife, stab

accomoda'mento sm agreement, settlement

accomo'dante ag accommodating

accomodarsi vpr (sedersi) to sit down; (entrare) to come in; **s'accomodi!** (venga avanti) come in!; (si sieda) take a seat!

accompagna'mento [akkompaɲɲa'mento] sm (Mus) accompaniment

accompa'gnare [akkompaɲ'ɲare] vt to accompany, come o go with; (Mus) to accompany; (unire) to couple; **~ la porta** to close the door gently

accompagna'tore, -trice sm/f companion; **~ turistico** courier

acconcia'tura [akkontʃa'tura] sf hairstyle

accondiscen'dente [akkondiʃʃen'dɛnte] ag affable

acconsen'tire vi **~ (a)** to agree o consent (to)

acconten'tare vt to satisfy; **accontentarsi** vpr **accontentarsi di** to be satisfied with, content o.s. with

ac'conto sm part payment; **pagare una somma in ~** to pay a sum of money as a deposit

acco'rato, -a ag heartfelt

accorci'are [akkor'tʃare] vt to shorten; **accorciarsi** vpr to become shorter

accor'dare vt to reconcile; (colori) to match; (Mus) to tune; (Ling): **~ qc con qc** to make sth agree with sth; (Dir) to grant; **accordarsi** vpr to agree, come to an agreement; (colori) to match

ac'cordo sm agreement; (armonia) harmony; (Mus) chord; **essere d'~** to agree; **andare d'~** to get on well together; **d'~!** all right!, agreed!; **accordo commerciale** trade agreement

ac'corgersi [ak'kordʒersi] vpr **~ di** to notice; (fig) to realize

ac'correre vi to run up

ac'corto, -a pp di **accorgersi** ▷ ag shrewd; **stare ~** to be on one's guard

accos'tare vt (avvicinare): **~ qc a** to bring sth near to, put sth near to; (avvicinarsi a) to approach; (socchiudere: imposte) to half-close; (: porta) to leave ajar ▷ vi (Naut) to come alongside; **accostarsi** vpr **accostarsi a** to draw near, approach; (fig) to support

accredi'tare vt (notizia) to confirm the truth of; (Comm) to credit; (diplomatico) to accredit

ac'credito sm (Comm: atto) crediting; (: effetto) credit

accucci'arsi [akkut'tʃarsi] vpr (cane) to lie down

accu'dire vt (anche: vi **~ a**) to attend to

accumu'lare vt to accumulate; **accumularsi** vpr to accumulate; (Finanza) to accrue

accu'rato, -a ag (diligente) careful; (preciso) accurate

ac'cusa *sf* accusation; (*Dir*) charge; **la pubblica ~** the prosecution

accu'sare *vt* **~ qn di qc** to accuse sb of sth; (*Dir*) to charge sb with sth; **~ ricevuta di** (*Comm*) to acknowledge receipt of

accusa'tore, -'trice *sm/f* accuser ▷ *sm* (*Dir*) prosecutor

a'cerbo, -a [a'tʃerbo] *ag* bitter; (*frutta*) sour, unripe; (*persona*) immature

'acero ['atʃero] *sm* maple

a'cerrimo, -a [a'tʃerrimo] *ag* very fierce

a'ceto [a'tʃeto] *sm* vinegar

ace'tone [atʃe'tone] *sm* nail varnish remover

A.C.I. ['atʃi] *sigla m* = **Automobile Club d'Italia**

'acido, -a ['atʃido] *ag* (*sapore*) acid, sour; (*Chim*) acid ▷ *sm* (*Chim*) acid

'acino ['atʃino] *sm* berry; **acino d'uva** grape

'acne *sf* acne

'acqua *sf* water; (*pioggia*) rain; **acque** *sfpl* (*di mare, fiume ecc*) waters; **fare ~** (*Naut*) to leak, take in water; **~ in bocca!** mum's the word!; **acqua corrente** running water; **acqua dolce/salata** fresh/salt water; **acqua minerale/potabile/tonica** mineral/drinking/tonic water; **acque termali** thermal waters

a'cquaio *sm* sink

acqua'ragia [akkwa'radʒa] *sf* turpentine

a'cquario *sm* aquarium; (*dello zodiaco*): **A~** Aquarius

acquascooter [akkwas'kuter] *sm inv* Jet Ski®

ac'quatico, -a, -ci, -che *ag* aquatic; (*Sport, Scienza*) water *cpd*

acqua'vite *sf* brandy

acquaz'zone [akkwat'tsone] *sm* cloudburst, heavy shower

acque'dotto *sm* aqueduct; waterworks *pl*, water system

acque'rello *sm* watercolour

acqui'rente *sm/f* purchaser, buyer

acquis'tare *vt* to purchase, buy; (*fig*) to gain; **a'cquisto** *sm* purchase; **fare acquisti** to go shopping

acquo'lina *sf* **far venire l'~ in bocca a qn** to make sb's mouth water

a'crobata, -i, -e *sm/f* acrobat

a'culeo *sm* (*Zool*) sting; (*Bot*) prickle

a'cume *sm* acumen, perspicacity

a'custico, -a, ci, che *ag* acoustic ▷ *sf* (*scienza*) acoustics *sg*; (*di una sala*) acoustics *pl*; **cornetto ~** ear trumpet; **apparecchio ~** hearing aid

a'cuto, -a *ag* (*appuntito*) sharp, pointed; (*suono, voce*) shrill, piercing; (*Mat, Ling, Med*) acute; (*Mus*) high-pitched; (*fig: dolore,*

desiderio) intense; (*: perspicace*) acute, keen

a'dagio [a'dadʒo] *av* slowly ▷ *sm* (*Mus*) adagio; (*proverbio*) adage, saying

adatta'mento *sm* adaptation

adat'tare *vt* to adapt; (*sistemare*) to fit; **adattarsi** *vpr* **adattarsi (a)** (*ambiente, tempi*) to adapt (to); (*essere adatto*) to be suitable (for)

a'datto, -a *ag* **~ (a)** suitable (for), right (for)

addebi'tare *vt* **~ qc a qn** to debit sb with sth

ad'debito *sm* (*Comm*) debit

adden'tare *vt* to bite into

adden'trarsi *vpr* **~ in** to penetrate, go into

addestra'mento *sm* training

addes'trare *vt* to train

ad'detto, -a *ag* **~ a** (*persona*) assigned to; (*oggetto*) intended for ▷ *sm* employee; (*funzionario*) attaché; **gli addetti ai lavori** authorized personnel; (*fig*) those in the know; **addetto commerciale** commercial attaché; **addetto stampa** press attaché

ad'dio *sm, escl* goodbye, farewell

addirit'tura *av* (*veramente*) really, absolutely; (*perfino*) even; (*direttamente*) directly, right away

addi'tare *vt* to point out; (*fig*) to expose

addi'tivo *sm* additive

addizi'one *sf* addition

addob'bare *vt* to decorate; **ad'dobbo** *sm* decoration

addolo'rare *vt* to pain, grieve; **addolorarsi (per)** to be distressed (by)

addolo'rato, -a *ag* distressed, upset; **l'Addolorata** (*Rel*) Our Lady of Sorrows

ad'dome *sm* abdomen

addomesti'care *vt* to tame

addomi'nale *ag* abdominal; **(muscoli mpl) addominali** stomach muscles

addormen'tare *vt* to put to sleep; **addormentarsi** *vpr* to fall asleep, go to sleep

ad'dosso *av* on; **mettersi ~ il cappotto** to put one's coat on; **~ a** (*sopra*) on; (*molto vicino*) right next to; **stare ~ a qn** (*fig*) to breathe down sb's neck; **dare ~ a qn** (*fig*) to attack sb

adeguarsi *vpr* to adapt

adegu'ato, -a *ag* adequate; (*conveniente*) suitable; (*equo*) fair

a'dempiere *vt* to fulfil, carry out

ade'rente *ag* adhesive; (*vestito*) close-fitting ▷ *sm/f* follower

ade'rire *vi* (*stare attaccato*) to adhere, stick; **~ a** to adhere to, stick to; (*fig: società, partito*) to join; (*: opinione*) to support; (*richiesta*) to agree to

adesi'one *sf* adhesion; (*fig*) agreement,

acceptance; **ade'sivo, -a** *ag, sm* adhesive
a'desso *av (ora)* now; *(or ora, poco fa)* just
now; *(tra poco)* any moment now
adia'cente [adja'tʃɛnte] *ag* adjacent
adi'bire *vt (usare)*: **~ qc a** to turn sth into
adole'scente [adoleʃ'ʃɛnte] *ag, sm/f*
adolescent
adope'rare *vt* to use
ado'rare *vt* to adore; *(Rel)* to adore,
worship
adot'tare *vt* to adopt; *(decisione,
provvedimenti)* to pass; **adot'tivo, -a** *ag
(genitori)* adoptive; *(figlio, patria)* adopted;
adozi'one *sf* adoption; **adozione a
distanza** child sponsorship
adri'atico, -a, -ci, -che *ag* Adriatic ▷ *sm*
l'A~, il mare A~ the Adriatic, the Adriatic
Sea
adu'lare *vt* to adulate, flatter
a'dultero, -a *ag* adulterous ▷ *sm/f*
adulterer (adulteress)
a'dulto, -a *ag* adult; *(fig)* mature ▷ *sm*
adult, grown-up
a'ereo, -a *ag* air *cpd*; *(radice)* aerial ▷ *sm*
aerial; *(aeroplano)* plane; **aereo da caccia**
fighter (plane); **aereo di linea** airliner;
aereo a reazione jet (plane); **ae'robica**
sf aerobics *sg*; **aero'nautica** *sf (scienza)*
aeronautics *sg*; **aeronautica militare**
air force
aero'porto *sm* airport; **all'~ per favore** to
the airport, please
aero'sol *sm inv* aerosol
'afa *sf* sultriness
af'fabile *ag* affable
affaccen'dato, -a [affattʃen'dato] *ag
(persona)* busy
affacci'arsi [affat'tʃarsi] *vpr* **~ (a)** to
appear (at)
affa'mato, -a *ag* starving; *(fig)*: **~ (di)**
eager (for)
affan'noso, -a *ag (respiro)* difficult; *(fig)*
troubled, anxious
af'fare *sm (faccenda)* matter, affair;
(Comm) piece of business, (business) deal;
(occasione) bargain; *(Dir)* case; *(fam: cosa)*
thing; **affari** *smpl (Comm)* business *sg*;
Ministro degli Affari esteri Foreign
Secretary (BRIT), Secretary of State (US)
affasci'nante [affaʃʃi'nante] *ag*
fascinating
affasci'nare [affaʃʃi'nare] *vt* to bewitch;
(fig) to charm, fascinate
affati'care *vt* to tire; **affaticarsi** *vpr (durar
fatica)* to tire o.s. out; **affati'cato, -a** *ag*
tired
af'fatto *av* completely; **non ... ~** not ... at
all; **niente ~** not at all
affer'mare *vt (dichiarare)* to maintain,

affirm; **affermarsi** *vpr* to assert o.s., make
one's name known; **affer'mato, -a** *ag*
established, well-known; **affermazi'one**
sf affirmation, assertion; *(successo)*
achievement
affer'rare *vt* to seize, grasp; *(fig: idea)*
to grasp; **afferrarsi** *vpr* **afferrarsi a** to
cling to
affet'tare *vt (tagliare a fette)* to slice;
(ostentare) to affect
affetta'trice [affetta'tritʃe] *sf* meat slicer
affet'tivo, -a *ag* emotional, affective
af'fetto *sm* affection; **affettu'oso, -a** *ag*
affectionate
affezio'narsi [affettsjo'narsi] *vpr* **~ a** to
grow fond of
affezio'nato, -a [affettsjo'nato] *ag* **~ a**
qn/qc fond of sb/sth; *(attaccato)* attached
to sb/sth
affia'tato, -a *ag* **essere molto affiatati**
to get on very well
affibbi'are *vt (fig: dare)* to give
affi'dabile *ag* reliable
affida'mento *sm (Dir: di bambino)*
custody; *(fiducia)*: **fare ~ su qn** to rely on
sb; **non dà nessun ~** he's not to be trusted
affi'dare *vt* **~ qc o qn a qn** to entrust sth o
sb to sb; **affidarsi** *vpr* **affidarsi a** to place
one's trust in
affi'lare *vt* to sharpen
affi'lato, -a *ag (gen)* sharp; *(volto, naso)*
thin
affinché [affin'ke] *cong* in order that, so
that
affit'tare *vt (dare in affitto)* to let, rent
(out); *(prendere in affitto)* to rent; **af'fitto**
sm rent; *(contratto)* lease
af'fliggere [af'fliddʒere] *vt* to torment;
affliggersi *vpr* to grieve
af'flissi *ecc vb vedi* **affliggere**
afflosci'arsi [affloʃ'ʃarsi] *vpr* to go limp
afflu'ente *sm* tributary
affo'gare *vt, vi* to drown
affol'lare *vt* to crowd; **affollarsi** *vpr* to
crowd; **affol'lato, -a** *ag* crowded
affon'dare *vt* to sink
affran'care *vt* to free, liberate;
(Amm) to redeem; *(lettera)* to stamp;
(: meccanicamente) to frank (BRIT), meter
(US)
af'fresco, -schi *sm* fresco
affrettarsi *vpr* to hurry; **~ a fare qc** to
hurry o hasten to do sth
affret'tato, -a *ag (veloce: passo, ritmo)*
quick, fast; *(frettoloso: decisione)* hurried,
hasty; *(: lavoro)* rushed
affron'tare *vt (pericolo ecc)* to face;
(nemico) to confront; **affrontarsi** *vpr
(reciproco)* to come to blows

affumi'cato, -a *ag* (*prosciutto, aringa ecc*) smoked

affuso'lato, -a *ag* tapering

Af'ganistan *sm* l'~ Afghanistan

a'foso, -a *ag* sultry, close

'Africa *sf* l'~ Africa; **afri'cano, -a** *ag, sm/f* African

a'genda [a'dʒɛnda] *sf* diary

Attenzione! In inglese esiste la parola *agenda* che però vuol dire *ordine del giorno*.

a'gente [a'dʒɛnte] *sm* agent; **agente di cambio** stockbroker; **agente di polizia** police officer; **agente segreto** secret agent; **agen'zia** *sf* agency; (*succursale*) branch; **agenzia immobiliare** estate agent's (office) (BRIT), real estate office (US); **agenzia di collocamento/stampa** employment/press agency; **agenzia viaggi** travel agency

agevo'lare [adʒevo'lare] *vt* to facilitate, make easy

agevolazi'one [adʒevolat'tsjone] *sf* (*facilitazione economica*) facility; **agevolazione di pagamento** payment on easy terms; **agevolazioni creditizie** credit facilities; **agevolazioni fiscali** tax concessions

a'gevole [a'dʒevole] *ag* easy; (*strada*) smooth

agganci'are [aggan'tʃare] *vt* to hook up; (*Ferr*) to couple

ag'geggio [ad'dʒeddʒo] *sm* gadget, contraption

agget'tivo [addʒet'tivo] *sm* adjective

agghiacci'ante [aggjat'tʃante] *ag* chilling

aggior'nare [addʒor'nare] *vt* (*opera, manuale*) to bring up-to-date; (*seduta ecc*) to postpone; **aggiornarsi** *vpr* to bring (*o* keep) o.s. up-to-date; **aggior'nato, -a** *ag* up-to-date

aggi'rare [addʒi'rare] *vt* to go round; (*fig: ingannare*) to trick; **aggirarsi** *vpr* to wander about; **il prezzo s'aggira sul milione** the price is around the million mark

aggi'ungere [ad'dʒundʒere] *vt* to add

aggi'unsi *ecc* [ad'dʒunsi] *vb vedi* **aggiungere**

aggius'tare [addʒus'tare] *vt* (*accomodare*) to mend, repair; (*riassettare*) to adjust; (*fig: lite*) to settle

aggrap'parsi *vpr* ~ **a** to cling to

aggra'vare *vt* (*aumentare*) to increase; (*appesantire: anche fig*) to weigh down, make heavy; (*pena*) to make worse; **aggravarsi** *vpr* to worsen, become worse

aggre'dire *vt* to attack, assault

aggressi'one *sf* aggression; (*atto*) attack, assault

aggres'sivo, -a *ag* aggressive

aggres'sore *sm* aggressor, attacker

aggrot'tare *vt* ~ **le sopracciglia** to frown

aggrovigli'arsi *vpr* (*fig*) to become complicated

aggu'ato *sm* trap; (*imboscata*) ambush; **tendere un** ~ **a qn** to set a trap for sb

agguer'rito, -a *ag* fierce

agi'ato, -a [a'dʒato] *ag* (*vita*) easy; (*persona*) well-off, well-to-do

'agile ['adʒile] *ag* agile, nimble

'agio ['adʒo] *sm* ease, comfort; **mettersi a proprio** ~ to make o.s. at home *o* comfortable; **agi** *smpl* comforts; **mettersi a proprio** ~ to make o.s. at home *o* comfortable; **dare** ~ **a qn di fare qc** to give sb the chance of doing sth

a'gire [a'dʒire] *vi* to act; (*esercitare un'azione*) to take effect; (*Tecn*) to work, function; ~ **contro qn** (*Dir*) to take action against sb

agi'tare [adʒi'tare] *vt* (*bottiglia*) to shake; (*mano, fazzoletto*) to wave; (*fig: turbare*) to disturb; (*: incitare*) to stir (up); (*: dibattere*) to discuss; **agitarsi** *vpr* (*mare*) to be rough; (*malato, dormitore*) to toss and turn; (*bambino*) to fidget; (*emozionarsi*) to get upset; (*Pol*) to agitate; **agi'tato, -a** *ag* rough; restless; fidgety; upset, perturbed

'aglio ['aʎʎo] *sm* garlic

a'gnello [aɲ'nɛllo] *sm* lamb

'ago (*pl* '**aghi**) *sm* needle

ago'nistico, -a, -ci, -che *ag* athletic; (*fig*) competitive

agopun'tura *sf* acupuncture

a'gosto *sm* August

a'grario, -a *ag* agrarian, agricultural; (*riforma*) land *cpd*

a'gricolo, -a *ag* agricultural, farm *cpd*; **agricol'tore** *sm* farmer; **agricol'tura** *sf* agriculture, farming

agri'foglio [agri'fɔʎʎo] *sm* holly

agritu'rismo *sm* farm holidays *pl*

agrodolce *ag* bittersweet; (*salsa*) sweet and sour

a'grume *sm* (*spesso al pl: pianta*) citrus; (*: frutto*) citrus fruit

a'guzzo, -a [a'guttso] *ag* sharp

'ahi *escl* (*dolore*) ouch!

'Aia *sf* l'~ the Hague

'aids *abbr m o f* Aids

airbag *sm inv* air bag

ai'rone *sm* heron

aiu'ola *sf* flower bed

aiu'tante *sm/f* assistant ▷ *sm* (*Mil*) adjutant; (*Naut*) master-at-arms; **aiutante di campo** aide-de-camp

aiu'tare *vt* to help; ~ **qn (a fare)** to help sb

(to do); **aiutarsi** *vpr* to help each other; **~ qn ln qc/a fare qc** to help sb with sth/to do sth; **può aiutarmi?** can you help me?

ai'uto *sm* help, assistance, aid; *(aiutante)* assistant; **venire in ~ di qn** to come to sb's aid; **aiuto chirurgo** assistant surgeon

'ala *(pl* **'ali)** *sf* wing; **fare ~** to fall back, make way; **ala destra/sinistra** *(Sport)* right/left wing

ala'bastro *sm* alabaster

a'lano *sm* Great Dane

'alba *sf* dawn

alba'nese *ag, sm/f, sm* Albanian

Alba'nia *sf* **l'~** Albania

albe'rato, -a *ag (viale, piazza)* lined with trees, tree-lined

al'bergo, -ghi *sm* hotel; **albergo della gioventù** youth hostel

'albero *sm* tree; *(Naut)* mast; *(Tecn)* shaft; **albero genealogico** family tree; **albero a gomiti** crankshaft; **albero maestro** mainmast; **albero di Natale** Christmas tree; **albero di trasmissione** transmission shaft

albi'cocca, -che *sf* apricot

'album *sm* album; **album da disegno** sketch book

al'bume *sm* albumen

'alce ['altʃe] *sm* elk

'alcol *sm inv* = **alcool**

al'colico, -a, -ci, -che *ag* alcoholic ▷ *sm* alcoholic drink

alcoliz'zato, -a [alkolid'dzato] *sm/f* alcoholic

'alcool *sm inv* alcohol

al'cuno, -a *(det: dav sm:* **alcun** + *C, V,* **alcuno** + *s impura, gn, pn, ps, x, z; dav sf:* **alcuna** + *C,* **alcun'** +*V) det (nessuno):* **non ... ~** no, not any; **alcuni, e** *det pl* some, a few; **non c'è alcuna fretta** there's no hurry, there isn't any hurry; **senza alcun riguardo** without any consideration ▷ *pron pl* **alcuni, e** some, a few

alfa'betico, -a, ci, che *ag* alphabetical

alfa'beto *sm* alphabet

'alga, -ghe *sf* seaweed *no pl,* alga

'algebra ['aldʒebra] *sf* algebra

Alge'ria [aldʒe'ria] *sf* **l'~** Algeria

alge'rino, -a [aldʒe'rino] *ag, sm/f* Algerian

ali'ante *sm (Aer)* glider

'alibi *sm inv* alibi

a'lice [a'litʃe] *sf* anchovy

ali'eno, -a *ag (avverso):* **~ (da)** opposed (to), averse (to) ▷ *sm/f* alien

alimen'tare *vt* to feed; *(Tecn)* to feed; to supply; *(fig)* to sustain ▷ *ag* food *cpd;* **alimentari** *smpl* foodstuffs; *(anche:*

negozio di alimentari) grocer's shop; **alimentazi'one** *sf* feeding; supplying; sustaining; *(gll alimenti)* diet

a'liquota *sf* share; *(d'imposta)* rate; **aliquota d'imposta** tax rate

alis'cafo *sm* hydrofoil

'alito *sm* breath

all. *abbr* (= *allegato*) encl.

allaccia'mento [allattʃa'mento] *sm* *(Tecn)* connection

allacci'are [allat'tʃare] *vt (scarpe)* to tie, lace (up); *(cintura)* to do up, fasten; *(luce, gas)* to connect; *(amicizia)* to form

allaccia'tura [allattʃa'tura] *sf* fastening

alla'gare *vt* to flood; **allagarsi** *vpr* to flood

allar'gare *vt* to widen; *(vestito)* to let out; *(aprire)* to open; *(fig: dilatare)* to extend; **allargarsi** *vpr (gen)* to widen; *(scarpe, pantaloni)* to stretch; *(fig: problema, fenomeno)* to spread

allar'mare *vt* to alarm

al'larme *sm* alarm; **allarme aereo** air-raid warning

allat'tare *vt* to feed

alle'anza [alle'antsa] *sf* alliance

alle'arsi *vpr* to form an alliance; **alle'ato, -a** *ag* allied ▷ *sm/f* ally

alle'gare *vt (accludere)* to enclose; *(Dir: citare)* to cite, adduce; *(denti)* to set on edge; **alle'gato, -a** *ag* enclosed ▷ *sm* enclosure; *(di e-mail)* attachment; **in allegato** enclosed

allegge'rire [alleddʒe'rire] *vt* to lighten, make lighter; *(fig: lavoro, tasse)* to reduce

alle'gria *sf* gaiety, cheerfulness

al'legro, -a *ag* cheerful, merry; *(un po' brillo)* merry, tipsy; *(vivace: colore)* bright ▷ *sm (Mus)* allegro

allena'mento *sm* training

alle'nare *vt* to train; **allenarsi** *vpr* to train; **allena'tore** *sm (Sport)* trainer, coach

allen'tare *vt* to slacken; *(disciplina)* to relax; **allentarsi** *vpr* to become slack; *(ingranaggio)* to work loose

aller'gia, -'gie [aller'dʒia] *sf* allergy; **al'lergico, -a, -ci, -che** *ag* allergic; **sono allergico alla penicillina** I'm allergic to penicillin

alles'tire *vt (cena)* to prepare; *(esercito, nave)* to equip, fit out; *(spettacolo)* to stage

allet'tante *ag* attractive, alluring

alle'vare *vt (animale)* to breed, rear; *(bambino)* to bring up

allevi'are *vt* to alleviate

alli'bito, -a *ag* astounded

alli'evo *sm* pupil; *(apprendista)* apprentice; *(Mil)* cadet

alliga'tore *sm* alligator

alline'are vt (persone, cose) to line up; (Tip) to align; (fig: economia, salari) to adjust, align; **allinearsi** vpr to line up; (fig: a idee): **allinearsi a** to come into line with

al'lodola sf (sky)lark

alloggi'are [allod'dʒare] vt to accommodate ▷ vi to live; **al'loggio** sm lodging, accommodation (BRIT), accommodations (US)

allonta'nare vt to send away, send off; (impiegato) to dismiss; (pericolo) to avert, remove; (estraniare) to alienate; **allontanarsi** vpr **allontanarsi (da)** to go away (from); (estraniarsi) to become estranged (from)

al'lora av (in quel momento) then ▷ cong (in questo caso) well then; (dunque) well then, so; **la gente d'~** people then o in those days; **da ~ in poi** from then on

al'loro sm laurel

'alluce ['allutʃe] sm big toe

alluci'nante [allutʃi'nante] ag awful; (fam) amazing

allucinazi'one [allutʃinat'tsjone] sf hallucination

al'ludere vi **~ a** to allude to, hint at

allu'minio sm aluminium (BRIT), aluminum (US)

allun'gare vt to lengthen; (distendere) to prolong, extend; (diluire) to water down; **allungarsi** vpr to lengthen; (ragazzo) to stretch, grow taller; (sdraiarsi) to lie down, stretch out

al'lusi ecc vb vedi **alludere**

allusi'one sf hint, allusion

alluvi'one sf flood

al'meno av at least ▷ cong (se) **~** if only; **(se) ~ piovesse!** if only it would rain!

a'logeno, -a [a'lɔdʒeno] ag **lampada alogena** halogen lamp

a'lone sm halo

'Alpi sfpl **le ~** the Alps

alpi'nismo sm mountaineering, climbing; **alpi'nista, -i, -e** sm/f mountaineer, climber

al'pino, -a ag Alpine; mountain cpd; **alpini** smpl (Mil) Italian Alpine troops

alt escl halt!, stop!

alta'lena sf (a funi) swing; (in bilico) seesaw

al'tare sm altar

alter'nare vt to alternate; **alternarsi** vpr to alternate; **alterna'tiva** sf alternative; **alterna'tivo, -a** ag alternative

al'terno, -a ag alternate; **a giorni alterni** on alternate days, every other day

al'tero, -a ag proud

al'tezza [al'tettsa] sf height; width, breadth; depth; pitch; (Geo) latitude;

(titolo) highness; (fig: nobiltà) greatness; **essere all'~ di** to be on a level with; (fig) to be up to o equal to

al'ticcio, -a, -ci, -ce [al'tittʃo] ag tipsy

alti'tudine sf altitude

'alto, -a ag high; (persona) tall; (tessuto) wide, broad; (sonno, acque) deep; (suono) high(-pitched); (Geo) upper; (settentrionale) northern ▷ sm top (part) ▷ av high; (parlare) aloud, loudly; **il palazzo è ~ 20 metri** the building is 20 metres high; **ad alta voce** aloud; **a notte alta** in the dead of night; **in ~** up, upwards; at the top; **dall'~ in o al basso** up and down; **degli alti e bassi** (fig) ups and downs; **alta fedeltà** high fidelity, hi-fi; **alta finanza/società** high finance/society; **alta moda** haute couture

altopar'lante sm loudspeaker

altopi'ano (pl altipi'ani) sm plateau, upland plain

altret'tanto, -a ag, pron as much; (pl) as many ▷ av equally; **tanti auguri! — grazie, ~** all the best! — thank you, the same to you

altri'menti av otherwise

PAROLA CHIAVE

'altro, -a det **1** (diverso) other, different; **questa è un'altra cosa** that's another o a different thing

2 (supplementare) other; **prendi un altro cioccolatino** have another chocolate; **hai avuto altre notizie?** have you had any more o any other news?

3 (nel tempo): **l'altro giorno** the other day; **l'altr'anno** last year; **l'altro ieri** the day before yesterday; **domani l'altro** the day after tomorrow; **quest'altro mese** next month

4: **d'altra parte** on the other hand ▷ pron **1** (persona, cosa diversa o supplementare): **un altro, un'altra** another (one); **lo farà un altro** someone else will do it; **altri, e** others; **gli altri** (la gente) others, other people; **l'uno e l'altro** both (of them); **aiutarsi l'un l'altro** to help one another; **da un giorno all'altro** from day to day; (nel giro di 24 ore) from one day to the next; (da un momento all'altro) any day now

2 (sostantivato: solo maschile) something else; (: in espressioni interrogative) anything else; **non ho altro da dire** I have nothing else to say o I don't have anything else to say; **più che altro** above all; **se non altro** at least; **tra l'altro** among other things; **ci mancherebbe altro!** that's all we need!; **non faccio altro che lavorare** I do nothing but work; **contento? — altro che!** are you pleased? — and how!; *vedi* **senza**; **noialtri**; **voialtri**; **tutto**

al'trove *av* elsewhere, somewhere else
altru'ista, -i, -e *ag* altruistic
a'lunno, -a *sm/f* pupil
alve'are *sm* hive
al'zare [al'tsare] *vt* to raise, lift; (*issare*) to hoist; (*costruire*) to build, erect; **alzarsi** *vpr* to rise; (*dal letto*) to get up; (*crescere*) to grow tall (*o* taller); **~ le spalle** to shrug one's shoulders; **alzarsi in piedi** to stand up, get to one's feet
a'maca, -che *sf* hammock
amalga'mare *vt* to amalgamate; **amalgamarsi** *vpr* to amalgamate
a'mante *ag* **~ di** (*musica ecc*) fond of ▷ *sm/f* lover/mistress
a'mare *vt* to love; (*amico, musica, sport*) to like; **amarsi** *vpr* to love each other
amareggi'ato, -a [amared'dʒato] *ag* upset, saddened
ama'rena *sf* sour black cherry
ama'rezza [ama'rettsa] *sf* bitterness
a'maro, -a *ag* bitter ▷ *sm* bitterness; (*liquore*) bitters *pl*
amaz'zonico, -a, ci, che [amad'dzɔniko] *ag* Amazonian; Amazon *cpd*
ambasci'ata [ambaʃ'ʃata] *sf* embassy; (*messaggio*) message; **ambascia'tore, -'trice** *sm/f* ambassador/ambassadress
ambe'due *ag inv* **~ i ragazzi** both boys ▷ *pron inv* both
ambienta'lista, -i, e *ag* environmental ▷ *sm/f* environmentalist
ambien'tare *vt* to acclimatize; (*romanzo, film*) to set; **ambientarsi** *vpr* to get used to one's surroundings
ambi'ente *sm* environment; (*fig: insieme di persone*) milieu; (*stanza*) room
am'biguo, -a *ag* ambiguous
ambizi'one [ambit'tsjone] *sf* ambition; **ambizi'oso, -a** *ag* ambitious
'ambo *ag inv* both ▷ *sm* (*al gioco*) double
'ambra *sf* amber; **ambra grigia** ambergris
ambu'lante *ag* itinerant ▷ *sm* peddler
ambu'lanza [ambu'lantsa] *sf* ambulance; **chiamate un ~** call an ambulance
ambula'torio *sm* (*studio medico*) surgery
A'merica *sf* l'**~** America; l'**~ latina** Latin America; **ameri'cano, -a** *ag, sm/f* American
ami'anto *sm* asbestos
ami'chevole [ami'kevole] *ag* friendly
ami'cizia [ami'tʃittsja] *sf* friendship; **amicizie** *sfpl* (*amici*) friends
a'mico, -a, -ci, -che *sm/f* friend;

(*fidanzato*) boyfriend/girlfriend; **amico del cuore** bosom friend
'amido *sm* starch
ammac'care *vt* (*pentola*) to dent; (*persona*) to bruise
ammacca'tura *sf* dent; bruise
ammaes'trare *vt* (*animale*) to train
ammai'nare *vt* to lower, haul down
amma'larsi *vpr* to fall ill; **amma'lato, -a** *ag* ill, sick ▷ *sm/f* sick person; (*paziente*) patient
ammanet'tare *vt* to handcuff
ammas'sare *vt* (*ammucchiare*) to amass; (*raccogliere*) to gather together; **ammassarsi** *vpr* to pile up; to gather
ammat'tire *vi* to go mad
ammaz'zare [ammat'tsare] *vt* to kill; **ammazzarsi** *vpr* (*uccidersi*) to kill o.s.; (*rimanere ucciso*) to be killed; **ammazzarsi di lavoro** to work o.s. to death
am'mettere *vt* to admit; (*riconoscere: fatto*) to acknowledge, admit; (*permettere*) to allow, accept; (*supporre*) to suppose
amminis'trare *vt* to run, manage; (*Rel, Dir*) to administer; **amministra'tore** *sm* administrator; (*di condominio*) flats manager; **amministratore delegato** managing director; **amministrazi'one** *sf* management; administration
ammi'raglio [ammi'raʎʎo] *sm* admiral
ammi'rare *vt* to admire; **ammirazi'one** *sf* admiration
am'misi *ecc vb vedi* **ammettere**
ammobili'ato, -a *ag* furnished
am'mollo *sm* **lasciare in ~** to leave to soak
ammo'niaca *sf* ammonia
ammo'nire *vt* (*avvertire*) to warn; (*rimproverare*) to admonish; (*Dir*) to caution
ammonizi'one [ammonit'tsjone] *sf* (*monito: anche Sport*) warning; (*rimprovero*) reprimand; (*Dir*) caution
ammon'tare *vi* **~ a** to amount to ▷ *sm* (*total*) amount
ammorbi'dente *sm* fabric conditioner
ammorbi'dire *vt* to soften
ammortizza'tore *sm* (*Aut, Tecn*) shock-absorber
ammucchi'are [ammuk'kjare] *vt* to pile up, accumulate
ammuf'fire *vi* to go mouldy (*BRIT*) *o* moldy (*US*)
ammuto'lire *vi* to be struck dumb
amne'sia *sf* amnesia
amnis'tia *sf* amnesty
'amo *sm* (*Pesca*) hook; (*fig*) bait
a'more *sm* love; **amori** *smpl* love affairs; **il tuo bambino è un ~** your baby's a darling; **fare l'~** *o* **all'~** to make love; **per ~ o per forza** by hook or by crook; **amor proprio**

self-esteem, pride

amo'roso, -a *ag* (*affettuoso*) loving, affectionate; (*d'amore: sguardo*) amorous; (: *poesia, relazione*) love *cpd*

'**ampio, -a** *ag* wide, broad; (*spazioso*) spacious; (*abbondante: vestito*) loose; (: *gonna*) full; (: *spiegazione*) ample, full

am'plesso *sm* intercourse

ampli'are *vt* (*ingrandire*) to enlarge; (*allargare*) to widen; **ampliarsi** *vpr* to grow, increase

amplifica'tore *sm* (*Tecn, Mus*) amplifier

ampu'tare *vt* (*Med*) to amputate

A.N. *sigla f* (= *Alleanza Nazionale*) Italian right-wing party

anabbaglianti *smpl* dipped (BRIT) o dimmed (US) headlights

anaboliz'zante *ag* anabolic ▷ *sm* anabolic steroid

anal'colico, -a, -ci, -che *ag* non-alcoholic ▷ *sm* soft drink

analfa'beta, -i, -e *ag, sm/f* illiterate

anal'gesico, -a, -ci, -che [anal'dʒɛziko] *ag, sm* analgesic

a'nalisi *sf inv* analysis; (*Med: esame*) test; **analisi del sangue** blood test *sg*

analiz'zare [analid'dzare] *vt* to analyse; (*Med*) to test

a'nalogo, -a, -ghi, -ghe *ag* analogous

'**ananas** *sm inv* pineapple

anar'chia [anar'kia] *sf* anarchy; **a'narchico, -a, -ci, -che** *ag* anarchic(al) ▷ *sm/f* anarchist

anarco-insurreziona'lista *ag* anarcho-revolutionary

'**A.N.A.S.** *sigla f* (= *Azienda Nazionale Autonoma delle Strade*) national roads department

anato'mia *sf* anatomy

'**anatra** *sf* duck

'**anca, -che** *sf* (*Anat*) hip

'**anche** ['anke] *cong* (*inoltre, pure*) also, too; (*perfino*) even; **vengo anch'io** I'm coming too; ~ **se** even if

an'cora *av* still; (*di nuovo*) again; (*di più*) some more; (*persino*): ~ **più forte** even stronger; **non** ~ not yet; ~ **una volta** once more, once again; ~ **un po'** a little more; (*di tempo*) a little longer

an'dare *sm* **a lungo** ~ in the long run ▷ *vi* to go; (*essere adatto*): ~ **a** to suit; (*piacere*): **il suo comportamento non mi va** I don't like the way he behaves; **ti va di** ~ **al cinema?** do you feel like going to the cinema?; **andarsene** to go away; **questa camicia va lavata** this shirt needs a wash o should be washed; ~ **in macchina/aereo** to go by car/plane; ~ **a fare qc** to go and do sth; ~ **a pescare/**

sciare to go fishing/skiing; ~ **a male** to go bad; **come va?** (*lavoro, progetto*) how are things?; **come va? — bene, grazie!** how are you? — fine, thanks!; **va fatto entro oggi** it's got to be done today; **ne va della nostra vita** our lives are at stake; **an'data** *sf* going; (*viaggio*) outward journey; **biglietto di sola andata** single (BRIT) o one-way ticket; **biglietto di andata e ritorno** return (BRIT) o round-trip (US) ticket

andrò *ecc vb vedi* **andare**

a'neddoto *sm* anecdote

a'nello *sm* ring; (*di catena*) link; **anelli** *smpl* (*Ginnastica*) rings

a'nemico, -a, -ci, -che *ag* anaemic

aneste'sia *sf* anaesthesia

'**angelo** ['andʒelo] *sm* angel; **angelo custode** guardian angel

anghe'ria [ange'ria] *sf* vexation

angli'cano, -a *ag* Anglican

anglo'sassone *ag* Anglo-Saxon

'**angolo** *sm* corner; (*Mat*) angle; **angolo cottura** (*di appartamento ecc*) cooking area

an'goscia, -sce [an'goʃʃa] *sf* deep anxiety, anguish *no pl*

angu'illa *sf* eel

an'guria *sf* watermelon

'**anice** ['anitʃe] *sm* (*Cuc*) aniseed; (*Bot*) anise

'**anima** *sf* soul; (*abitante*) inhabitant; **non c'era** ~ **viva** there wasn't a living soul; **anima gemella** soul mate

ani'male *sm, ag* animal; **animale domestico** pet

anna'cquare *vt* to water down, dilute

annaffi'are *vt* to water; **annaffia'toio** *sm* watering can

an'nata *sf* year; (*importo annuo*) annual amount; **vino d'**~ vintage wine

anne'gare *vt, vi* to drown

anne'rire *vt* to blacken ▷ *vi* to become black

annien'tare *vt* to annihilate, destroy

anniver'sario *sm* anniversary; **anniversario di matrimonio** wedding anniversary

'**anno** *sm* year; **ha 8 anni** he's 8 (years old)

anno'dare *vt* to knot, tie; (*fig: rapporto*) to form

annoi'are *vt* to bore; **annoiarsi** *vpr* to be bored

> Attenzione! In inglese esiste il verbo *to annoy* che però vuol dire *dare fastidio a*.

anno'tare *vt* (*registrare*) to note, note down; (*commentare*) to annotate

annu'ale *ag* annual

annu'ire *vi* to nod; (*acconsentire*) to agree

annul'lare *vt* to annihilate, destroy;

(*contratto, francobollo*) to cancel; (*matrimonio*) to annul; (*sentenza*) to quash; (*risultati*) to declare void

annunci'are [annun'tʃare] *vt* to announce; (*dar segni rivelatori*) to herald

an'nuncio [an'nuntʃo] *sm* announcement; (*fig*) sign; **annunci economici** classified advertisements, small ads; **annunci mortuari** (*colonna*) obituary column; **annuncio pubblicitario** advertisement

'**annuo, -a** *ag* annual, yearly

annu'sare *vt* to sniff, smell; **~ tabacco** to take snuff

a'nomalo, -a *ag* anomalous

a'nonimo, -a *ag* anonymous ▷ *sm* (*autore*) anonymous writer (*o painter ecc*); **società anonima** (*Comm*) joint stock company

anores'sia *sf* anorexia

ano'ressico, -a, ci, che *ag* anorexic

anor'male *ag* abnormal ▷ *sm/f* subnormal person

ANSA *sigla f* (= *Agenzia Nazionale Stampa Associata*) press agency

'**ansia** *sf* anxiety

ansi'mare *vi* to pant

ansi'oso, -a *ag* anxious

'**anta** *sf* (*di finestra*) shutter; (*di armadio*) door

An'tartide *sf* l'~ Antarctica

an'tenna *sf* (*Radio, TV*) aerial; (*Zool*) antenna, feeler; (*Naut*) yard; **antenna parabolica** satellite dish

ante'prima *sf* preview; **anteprima di stampa** (*Inform*) print preview

anteri'ore *ag* (*ruota, zampa*) front; (*fatti*) previous, preceding

antiade'rente *ag* non-stick

antibi'otico, -a, -ci, -che *ag, sm* antibiotic

anti'camera *sf* anteroom; **fare ~** to wait (for an audience)

antici'pare [antitʃi'pare] *vt* (*consegna, visita*) to bring forward, anticipate; (*somma di denaro*) to pay in advance; (*notizia*) to disclose ▷ *vi* to be ahead of time; **an'ticipo** *sm* anticipation; (*di denaro*) advance; **in anticipo** early, in advance; **occorre che prenoti in anticipo?** do I need to book in advance?

an'tico, -a, -chi, -che *ag* (*quadro, mobili*) antique; (*dell'antichità*) ancient; **all'antica** old-fashioned

anticoncezio'nale [antikontʃettsjo'nale] *sm* contraceptive

anticonfor'mista, -i, -e *ag, sm/f* nonconformist

anti'corpo *sm* antibody

antidolo'rifico, -ci *sm* painkiller

anti'doping *sm* drug testing ▷ *ag inv* **test ~ drugs** (BRIT) o **drug** (US) **test**

an'tifona *sf* (*Mus, Rel*) antiphon; **capire l'~** (*fig*) to take the hint

anti'forfora *ag inv* anti-dandruff

anti'furto *sm* anti-theft device

anti'gelo [anti'dʒelo] *ag inv* (**liquido**) **~** (*per motore*) antifreeze; (*per cristalli*) de-icer

antiglobalizzazione [antiglobalidd zat'tsjone] *ag inv* **movimento ~** anti-globalization movement

An'tille *sfpl* **le ~** the West Indies

antin'cendio [antin'tʃendjo] *ag inv* fire *cpd*

anti'nebbia *sm inv* (*anche*: **faro ~**: *Aut*) fog lamp

antinfiamma'torio, -a *ag, sm* anti-inflammatory

antio'rario [antio'rarjo] *ag* **in senso ~** anticlockwise

anti'pasto *sm* hors d'œuvre

antipa'tia *sf* antipathy, dislike; **anti'patico, -a, -ci, -che** *ag* unpleasant, disagreeable

antiproi'ettile *ag inv* bulletproof

antiquari'ato *sm* antique trade; **un oggetto d'~** an antique

anti'quario *sm* antique dealer

anti'quato, -a *ag* antiquated, old-fashioned

anti'rughe *ag inv* (*crema, prodotto*) anti-wrinkle

antitraspi'rante *ag* antiperspirant

anti'vipera *ag inv* **siero ~** remedy for snake bites

antivirus [anti'virus] *sm inv* antivirus software *no pl* ▷ *ag inv* antivirus

antolo'gia, -'gie [antolo'dʒia] *sf* anthology

anu'lare *ag* ring *cpd* ▷ *sm* third finger

'**anzi** ['antsi] *av* (*invece*) on the contrary; (*o meglio*) or rather, or better still

anzi'ano, -a [an'tsjano] *ag* old; (*Amm*) senior ▷ *sm/f* old person; senior member

anziché [antsi'ke] *cong* rather than

a'patico, -a, -ci, -che *ag* apathetic

'**ape** *sf* bee

aperi'tivo *sm* apéritif

aperta'mente *av* openly

a'perto, -a *pp di* **aprire** ▷ *ag* open; **all'~** in the open (air); **è ~ al pubblico?** is it open to the public?; **quando è ~ il museo?** when is the museum open?

aper'tura *sf* opening; (*ampiezza*) width; (*Fot*) aperture; **apertura alare** wing span; **apertura mentale** open-mindedness

ap'nea *sf* **immergersi in ~** to dive without breathing apparatus

a'postrofo *sm* apostrophe

ap'paio *ecc vb vedi* **apparire**

ap'palto *sm* (*Comm*) contract; **dare/ prendere in ~ un lavoro** to let out/ undertake a job on contract

appannarsi *vpr* to mist over; to grow dim

apparecchi'are [apparek'kjare] *vt* to prepare; (*tavola*) to set ▷ *vi* to set the table

appa'recchio [appa'rekkjo] *sm* piece of apparatus, device; (*aeroplano*) aircraft *inv*; **apparecchio acustico** hearing aid; **apparecchio telefonico** telephone; **apparecchio televisivo** television set

appa'rente *ag* apparent

appa'rire *vi* to appear; (*sembrare*) to seem, appear

apparta'mento *sm* flat (*BRIT*), apartment (*US*)

appar'tarsi *vpr* to withdraw

apparte'nere *vi* **~ a** to belong to

ap'parvi *ecc vb vedi* **apparire**

appassio'nare *vt* to thrill; (*commuovere*) to move; **appassionarsi** *vpr* **appassionarsi a qc** to take a great interest in sth; **appassio'nato, -a** *ag* passionate; (*entusiasta*): **appassionato (di)** keen (on)

appas'sire *vi* to wither

appas'sito, -a *ag* dead

ap'pello *sm* roll-call; (*implorazione, Dir*) appeal; **fare ~ a** to appeal to

ap'pena *av* (*a stento*) hardly, scarcely; (*solamente, da poco*) just ▷ *cong* as soon as; **(non) ~ furono arrivati ... appena** as soon as they had arrived ...; **~ ... che** *o* **quando** no sooner ... than

ap'pendere *vt* to hang (up)

appen'dice [appen'ditʃe] *sf* appendix; **romanzo d'~** popular serial

appendi'cite [appendi'tʃite] *sf* appendicitis

Appen'nini *smpl* **gli ~** the Apennines

appesan'tire *vt* to make heavy; **appesantirsi** *vpr* to grow stout

appe'tito *sm* appetite

appic'care *vt* **~ il fuoco a** to set fire to, set on fire

appicci'care [appittʃi'kare] *vt* to stick; **appiccicarsi** *vpr* to stick; (*fig: persona*) to cling

appiso'larsi *vpr* to doze off

applau'dire *vt, vi* to applaud; **ap'plauso** *sm* applause

appli'care *vt* to apply; (*regolamento*) to enforce; **applicarsi** *vpr* to apply o.s.

appoggi'are [appod'dʒare] *vt* (*mettere contro*): **~ qc a qc** to lean *o* rest sth against sth; (*fig: sostenere*) to support; **appoggiarsi** *vpr* **appoggiarsi a** to lean against; (*fig*) to rely upon; **ap'poggio** *sm* support

apposita'mente *av* specially; (*apposta*) on purpose

ap'posito, -a *ag* appropriate

ap'posta *av* on purpose, deliberately

appos'tarsi *vpr* to lie in wait

ap'prendere *vt* (*imparare*) to learn

appren'dista, -i, -e *sm/f* apprentice

apprensi'one *sf* apprehension

apprez'zare [appret'tsare] *vt* to appreciate

appro'dare *vi* (*Naut*) to land; (*fig*): **non ~ a nulla** to come to nothing

approfit'tare *vi* **~ di** to make the most of; (*peg*) to take advantage of

approfon'dire *vt* to deepen; (*fig*) to study in depth

appropri'ato, -a *ag* appropriate

approssima'tivo, -a *ag* approximate, rough; (*impreciso*) inexact, imprecise

appro'vare *vt* (*condotta, azione*) to approve of; (*candidato*) to pass; (*progetto di legge*) to approve

appunta'mento *sm* appointment; (*amoroso*) date; **darsi ~** to arrange to meet (one another); **ho un ~ con...** I have an appointment with ...; **vorrei prendere un ~** I'd like to make an appointment

ap'punto *sm* note; (*rimprovero*) reproach ▷ *av* (*proprio*) exactly, just; **per l'~!, ~!** exactly!

apribot'tiglie [apribot'tiʎʎe] *sm inv* bottle opener

a'prile *sm* April

a'prire *vt* to open; (*via, cadavere*) to open up; (*gas, luce, acqua*) to turn on ▷ *vi* to open; **aprirsi** *vpr* to open; **aprirsi a qn** to confide in sb, open one's heart to sb; **a che ora aprite?** what time do you open?

apris'catole *sm inv* tin (*BRIT*) *o* can opener

APT *sigla f* (= *Azienda di Promozione*) ≈ tourist board

aquagym [akkwa'dʒim] *sf* aquaerobics

'aquila *sf* (*Zool*) eagle; (*fig*) genius

aqui'lone *sm* (*giocattolo*) kite; (*vento*) North wind

A/R *abbr* = **andata e ritorno** (*biglietto*) return ticket (*BRIT*), round-trip ticket (*US*)

A'rabia Sau'dita *sf* **l'~** Saudi Arabia

'arabo, -a *ag, sm/f* Arab ▷ *sm* (*Ling*) Arabic

a'rachide [a'rakide] *sf* peanut

ara'gosta *sf* crayfish; lobster

a'rancia, -ce [a'rantʃa] *sf* orange; **aranci'ata** *sf* orangeade; **aranci'one** *ag inv* (*color*) **arancione** bright orange

a'rare *vt* to plough (*BRIT*), plow (*US*)

a'ratro *sm* plough (*BRIT*), plow (*US*)

a'razzo [a'rattso] *sm* tapestry

arbi'trare *vt* (*Sport*) to referee; to umpire; (*Dir*) to arbitrate

arbi'trario, -a ag arbitrary

'arbitro sm arbiter, judge; (Dir) arbitrator; (Sport) referee; (: Tennis, Cricket) umpire

ar'busto sm shrub

archeolo'gia [arkeolo'dʒia] sf arch(a)eology; **arche'ologo, -a, -gi, -ghe** sm/f arch(a)eologist

architet'tare [arkitet'tare] vt (fig: ideare) to devise; (: macchinare) to plan, concoct

archi'tetto [arki'tetto] sm architect; **architet'tura** sf architecture

ar'chivio [ar'kivjo] sm archives pl; (Inform) file

'arco sm (arma, Mus) bow; (Archit) arch; (Mat) arc

arcoba'leno sm rainbow

arcu'ato, -a ag curved, bent

'ardere vt, vi to burn

ar'desia sf slate

'area sf area; (Edil) land, ground; **area di rigore** (Sport) penalty area; **area di servizio** (Aut) service area

a'rena sf arena; (per corride) bullring; (sabbia) sand

are'narsi vpr to run aground

argente'ria [ardʒente'ria] sf silverware, silver

Argen'tina [ardʒen'tina] sf l'~ Argentina; **argen'tino, -a** ag, sm/f Argentinian

ar'gento [ar'dʒɛnto] sm silver; **argento vivo** quicksilver

ar'gilla [ar'dʒilla] sf clay

'argine [ar'dʒine] sm embankment, bank; (diga) dyke, dike

argo'mento sm argument; (motivo) motive; (materia, tema) subject

'aria sf air; (espressione, aspetto) air, look; (Mus: melodia) tune; (di opera) aria; **mandare all'~ qc** to ruin o upset sth; **all'~ aperta** in the open (air)

'arido, -a ag arid

arieggi'are [arjed'dʒare] vt (cambiare aria) to air; (imitare) to imitate

ari'ete sm ram; (Mil) battering ram; (dello zodiaco): **A~** Aries

a'ringa, -ghe sf herring inv

arit'metica sf arithmetic

'arma, -i sf weapon, arm; (parte dell'esercito) arm; **chiamare alle armi** to call up (BRIT), draft (US); **sotto le armi** in the army (o forces); **alle armi!** to arms!; **arma atomica/nucleare** atomic/nuclear weapon; **arma da fuoco** firearm; **armi di distruzione di massa** weapons of mass destruction

arma'dietto sm (di medicinali) medicine cabinet; (in palestra ecc) locker; (in cucina) (kitchen) cupboard

ar'madio sm cupboard; (per abiti) wardrobe; **armadio a muro** built-in cupboard

ar'mato, -a ag ~ **(di)** (anche fig) armed (with) ▷ sf (Mil) army; (Naut) fleet; **rapina a mano armata** armed robbery

arma'tura sf (struttura di sostegno) framework; (impalcatura) scaffolding; (Storia) armour no pl, suit of armour

armis'tizio [armis'tittsjo] sm armistice

armo'nia sf harmony

ar'nese sm tool, implement; (oggetto indeterminato) thing, contraption; **male in ~** (malvestito) badly dressed; (di salute malferma) in poor health; (povero) down-at-heel

'arnia sf hive

a'roma, -i sm aroma; fragrance; **aromi** smpl (Cuc) herbs and spices; **aromatera'pia** sf aromatherapy

'arpa sf (Mus) harp

arrabbi'are vi (cane) to be affected with rabies; **arrabbiarsi** vpr (essere preso dall'ira) to get angry, fly into a rage; **arrabbi'ato, -a** ag rabid, with rabies; furious, angry

arrampi'carsi vpr to climb (up)

arrangiarsi vpr to manage, do the best one can

arreda'mento sm (studio) interior design; (mobili ecc) furnishings pl

arre'dare vt to furnish

ar'rendersi vpr to surrender

arres'tare vt (fermare) to stop, halt; (catturare) to arrest; **arrestarsi** vpr (fermarsi) to stop; **ar'resto** sm (cessazione) stopping; (fermata) stop; (cattura, Med) arrest; **subire un arresto** to come to a stop o standstill; **mettere agli arresti** to place under arrest; **arresti domiciliari** house arrest sg

arre'trare vt, vi to withdraw; **arre'trato, -a** ag (lavoro) behind schedule; (paese, bambino) backward; (numero di giornale) back cpd; **arretrati** smpl arrears

arric'chire [arrik'kire] vt to enrich; **arricchirsi** vpr to become rich

arri'vare vi to arrive; (accadere) to happen, occur; ~ **a** (livello, grado ecc) to reach; **a che ora arriva il treno da Londra?** what time does the train from London arrive?; **non ci arrivo** I can't reach it; (fig: non capisco) I can't understand it

arrive'derci [arrive'dertʃi] escl goodbye!

arri'vista, -i, -e sm/f go-getter

ar'rivo sm arrival; (Sport) finish, finishing line

arro'gante ag arrogant

arros'sire vi (per vergogna, timidezza) to blush, flush; (per gioia, rabbia) to flush

arros'tire vt to roast; (pane) to toast; (ai

ferri) to grill
ar'rosto *sm, ag inv* roast
arroto'lare *vt* to roll up
arroton'dare *vt* (*forma, oggetto*) to round;
(*stipendio*) to add to; (*somma*) to round off
arrugginito, -a [arrudʒin'ito] *ag* rusty
'arsi *vb vedi* **ardere**
'arte *sf* art; (*abilità*) skill
ar'teria *sf* artery; **arteria stradale** main
road
'artico, -a, -ci, -che *ag* Arctic
articolazi'one *sf* articulation; (*Anat,
Tecn*) joint
ar'ticolo *sm* article; **articolo di fondo**
(*Stampa*) leader, leading article
artifici'ale [artifi'tʃale] *ag* artificial
artigia'nato [artidʒa'nato] *sm*
craftsmanship; craftsmen *pl*
artigi'ano, -a [arti'dʒano] *sm/f*
craftsman/woman
ar'tista, -i, -e *sm/f* artist; **ar'tistico, -a,
-ci, -che** *ag* artistic
ar'trite *sf* (*Med*) arthritis
a'scella [aʃ'ʃella] *sf* (*Anat*) armpit
ascen'dente [aʃʃen'dɛnte] *sm* ancestor;
(*fig*) ascendancy; (*Astr*) ascendant
ascen'sore [aʃʃen'sore] *sm* lift
a'scesso [aʃ'ʃesso] *sm* (*Med*) abscess
asciugaca'pelli [aʃʃugaka'pelli] *sm*
hair-drier
asciuga'mano [aʃʃuga'mano] *sm* towel
asciu'gare [aʃʃu'gare] *vt* to dry;
asciugarsi *vpr* to dry o.s.; (*diventare
asciutto*) to dry
asci'utto, -a [aʃ'ʃutto] *ag* dry; (*fig: magro*)
lean; (*: burbero*) curt; **restare a bocca
asciutta** (*fig*) to be disappointed
ascol'tare *vt* to listen to
as'falto *sm* asphalt
'Asia *sf* l'~ Asia; **asi'atico, -a, -ci, -che** *ag,
sm/f* Asiatic, Asian
a'silo *sm* refuge, sanctuary; **~ (d'infanzia)**
nursery(-school); **asilo nido** crèche; **asilo
politico** political asylum
'asino *sm* donkey, ass
ASL *sigla f* (= *Azienda Sanitaria Locale*) local
health centre
'asma *sf* asthma
as'parago, -gi *sm* asparagus *no pl*
aspet'tare *vt* to wait for; (*anche Comm*)
to await; (*aspettarsi*) to expect ▷ *vi* to
wait; **aspettami, per favore** wait for me,
please
as'petto *sm* (*apparenza*) aspect,
appearance, look; (*punto di vista*) point of
view; **di bell'~** good-looking
aspira'polvere *sm inv* vacuum cleaner
aspi'rare *vt* (*respirare*) to breathe in,
inhale; (*apparecchi*) to suck (up) ▷ *vi* **~ a** to

aspire to
aspi'rina *sf* aspirin
'aspro, -a *ag* (*sapore*) sour, tart; (*odore*)
acrid, pungent; (*voce, clima, fig*) harsh;
(*superficie*) rough; (*paesaggio*) rugged
assaggi'are [assad'dʒare] *vt* to taste;
posso assaggiarlo? can I have a taste?;
assaggino [assad'dʒino] *sm* **assaggini**
(*Cuc*) selection of first courses; **solo un
assaggino** just a little
as'sai *av* (*molto*) a lot, much; (*: con ag*) very;
(*a sufficienza*) enough ▷ *ag inv* (*quantità*)
a lot of, much; (*numero*) a lot of, many; **~
contento** very pleased
as'salgo *ecc vb vedi* **assalire**
assa'lire *vt* to attack, assail
assal'tare *vt* (*Mil*) to storm; (*banca*) to raid;
(*treno, diligenza*) to hold up
as'salto *sm* attack, assault
assassi'nare *vt* to murder; to assassinate;
(*fig*) to ruin; **assas'sino, -a** *ag* murderous
▷ *sm/f* murderer; assassin
'asse *sm* (*Tecn*) axle; (*Mat*) axis ▷ *sf* board;
asse *sf* **da stiro** ironing board
assedi'are *vt* to besiege
asse'gnare [asseɲ'ɲare] *vt* to assign,
allot; (*premio*) to award
as'segno [as'seɲɲo] *sm* allowance; (*anche:
~ bancario) cheque (BRIT), check (US);
contro ~ cash on delivery; **posso pagare
con un ~?** can I pay by cheque?; **assegno
circolare** bank draft; **assegni familiari**
≈ child benefit *no pl*; **assegno sbarrato**
crossed cheque; **assegno di viaggio**
traveller's cheque; **assegno a vuoto**
dud cheque; **assegno di malattia/di
invalidità** sick pay/disability benefit
assem'blea *sf* assembly
assen'tarsi *vpr* to go out
as'sente *ag* absent; (*fig*) faraway, vacant;
as'senza *sf* absence
asse'tato, -a *ag* thirsty, parched
assicu'rare *vt* (*accertare*) to ensure;
(*infondere certezza*) to assure; (*fermare,
legare*) to make fast, secure; (*fare un
contratto di assicurazione*) to insure;
assicurarsi *vpr* (*accertarsi*): **assicurarsi
(di)** to make sure (of); (*contro il furto
ecc*): **assicurarsi (contro)** to insure o.s.
(against); **assicurazi'one** *sf* assurance;
insurance
assi'eme *av* (*insieme*) together; **~ a**
(together) with
assil'lare *vt* to pester, torment
assis'tente *sm/f* assistant; **assistente
sociale** social worker; **assistente di volo**
(*Aer*) steward/stewardess
assis'tenza [assis'tɛntsa] *sf* assistance;
~ ospedaliera free hospital treatment;

~ sociale welfare services pl; **assistenza sanitaria** health service

as'sistere vt (aiutare) to assist, help; (curare) to treat ▷ vi **~ (a qc)** (essere presente) to be present (at sth), to attend (sth)

'asso sm ace; **piantare qn in ~** to leave sb in the lurch

associ'are [asso'tʃare] vt to associate; **associarsi** vpr to enter into partnership; **associarsi a** to become a member of, join; (dolori, gioie) to share in; **~ qn alle carceri** to take sb to prison

associazi'one [assotʃat'tsjone] sf association; (Comm) association, society; **~ a delinquere** (Dir) criminal association

as'solsi ecc vb vedi **assolvere**

assoluta'mente av absolutely

asso'luto, -a ag absolute

assoluzi'one [assolut'tsjone] sf (Dir) acquittal; (Rel) absolution

as'solvere vt (Dir) to acquit; (Rel) to absolve; (adempiere) to carry out, perform

assomigli'are [assomiʎ'ʎare] vi **~ a** to resemble, look like; **assomigliarsi** vpr to look alike; (nel carattere) to be alike

asson'nato, -a ag sleepy

asso'pirsi vpr to doze off

assor'bente ag absorbent ▷ sm: **assorbente interno** tampon; **assorbente esterno/igienico** sanitary towel

assor'bire vt to absorb

assor'dare vt to deafen

assorti'mento sm assortment

assor'tito, -a ag assorted; matched, matching

assuefazi'one [assuefat'tsjone] sf (Med) addiction

as'sumere vt (impiegato) to take on, engage; (responsabilità) to assume, take upon o.s.; (contegno, espressione) to assume, put on; (droga) to consume

as'sunsi ecc vb vedi **assumere**

assurdità sf inv absurdity; **dire delle ~** to talk nonsense

as'surdo, -a ag absurd

'asta sf pole; (vendita) auction

as'temio, -a ag teetotal ▷ sm/f teetotaller

Attenzione! In inglese esiste la parola *abstemious* che però vuol dire *moderato*.

aste'nersi vpr **~ (da)** to abstain (from), refrain (from); (Pol) to abstain (from)

aste'risco, -schi sm asterisk

'astice ['astitʃe] sm lobster

astig'matico, -a, ci, che ag astigmatic

asti'nenza [asti'nɛntsa] sf abstinence; **essere in crisi di ~** to suffer from withdrawal symptoms

as'tratto, -a ag abstract

'astro... prefisso; **astrolo'gia** [astrolo'dʒia] sf astrology; **astro'nauta, -i, -e** sm/f astronaut; **astro'nave** sf space ship; **astrono'mia** sf astronomy; **astro'nomico, -a, -ci, -che** ag astronomic(al)

as'tuccio [as'tuttʃo] sm case, box, holder

as'tuto, -a ag astute, cunning, shrewd

A'tene sf Athens

'ateo, -a ag, sm/f atheist

at'lante sm atlas

at'lantico, -a, -ci, -che ag Atlantic ▷ sm: **l'A~, l'Oceano A~** the Atlantic, the Atlantic Ocean

at'leta, -i, -e sm/f athlete; **at'letica** sf athletics sg; **atletica leggera** track and field events pl; **atletica pesante** weightlifting and wrestling

atmos'fera sf atmosphere

a'tomico, -a, -ci, -che ag atomic; (nucleare) atomic, atom cpd, nuclear

'atomo sm atom

'atrio sm entrance hall, lobby

a'troce [a'trotʃe] ag (che provoca orrore) dreadful; (terribile) atrocious

attac'cante sm/f (Sport) forward

attacca'panni sm hook, peg; (mobile) hall stand

attac'care vt (unire) to attach; (cucendo) to sew on; (far aderire) to stick (on); (appendere) to hang (up); (assalire: anche fig) to attack; (iniziare) to begin, start; (fig: contagiare) to pass on ▷ vi to stick, adhere; **attaccarsi** vpr to stick, adhere; (trasmettersi per contagio) to be contagious; (afferrarsi): **attaccarsi (a)** to cling (to); (fig: affezionarsi): **attaccarsi (a)** to become attached (to); **~ discorso** to start a conversation; **at'tacco, -chi** sm (azione offensiva: anche fig) attack; (Med) attack, fit; (Sci) binding; (Elettr) socket

attegia'mento [atteddʒa'mento] sm attitude

at'tendere vt to wait for, await ▷ vi **~ a** to attend to

atten'dibile ag (storia) credible; (testimone) reliable

atten'tato sm attack; **~ alla vita di qn** attempt on sb's life

at'tento, -a ag attentive; (accurato) careful, thorough; **stare ~ a qc** to pay attention to sth; **~!** be careful!

attenzi'one [atten'tsjone] sf attention; **~!** watch out!, be careful!; **attenzioni** sfpl (premure) attentions; **fare ~ a** to watch out for; **coprire qn di attenzioni** to lavish attentions on sb

atter'raggio [atter'raddʒo] sm landing

atter'rare *vt* to bring down ▷ *vi* to land
at'tesa *sf* waiting; (*tempo trascorso aspettando*) wait; **essere in ~ di qc** to be waiting for sth
at'tesi *ecc vb vedi* **attendere**
at'teso, -a *pp di* **attendere**
'attico, -ci *sm* attic
attil'lato, -a *ag* (*vestito*) close-fitting
'attimo *sm* moment; **in un ~** in a moment
atti'rare *vt* to attract
atti'tudine *sf* (*disposizione*) aptitude; (*atteggiamento*) attitude
attività *sf inv* activity; (*Comm*) assets *pl*
at'tivo, -a *ag* active; (*Comm*) profit-making, credit *cpd* ▷ *sm* (*Comm*) assets *pl*; **in ~** in credit
'atto *sm* act; (*azione, gesto*) action, act, deed; (*Dir: documento*) deed, document; **atti** *smpl* (*di congressi ecc*) proceedings; **mettere in ~** to put into action; **fare ~ di fare qc** to make as if to do sth; **atto di morte/di nascita** death/birth certificate
at'tore, -'trice *sm/f* actor/actress
at'torno *av* round, around, about; **~ a** round, around, about
attrac'care *vt, vi* (*Naut*) to dock, berth
at'tracco, -chi *sm* (*Naut*) docking *no pl*; berth
at'trae *ecc vb vedi* **attrarre**
attra'ente *ag* attractive
at'traggo *ecc vb vedi* **attrarre**
at'trarre *vt* to attract
at'trassi *ecc vb vedi* **attrarre**
attraver'sare *vt* to cross; (*città, bosco, fig: periodo*) to go through; (*fiume*) to run through
attra'verso *prep* through; (*da una parte all'altra*) across
attrazi'one [attrat'tsjone] *sf* attraction
at'trezzo *sm* tool, instrument; (*Sport*) piece of equipment
at'trice [at'tritʃe] *sf vedi* **attore**
attu'ale *ag* (*presente*) present; (*di attualità*) topical

> ▌Attenzione! In inglese esiste la parola *actual* che però vuol dire *effettivo*.

attualità *sf inv* topicality; (*avvenimento*) current event
attual'mente *av* at the moment, at present

> ▌Attenzione! In inglese esiste la parola *actually* che però vuol dire *effettivamente* oppure *veramente*.

attu'are *vt* to carry out
attu'tire *vt* to deaden, reduce
'audio *sm* (*TV, Radio, Cine*) sound
audiovi'sivo, -a *ag* audiovisual
audizi'one [audit'tsjone] *sf* hearing; (*Mus*) audition

augu'rare *vt* to wish; **augurarsi qc** to hope for sth
au'guri *smpl* best wishes; **fare gli ~ a qn** to give sb one's best wishes; **tanti ~!** best wishes!; (*per compleanno*) happy birthday!
'aula *sf* (*scolastica*) classroom; (*universitaria*) lecture theatre; (*di edificio pubblico*) hall
aumen'tare *vt, vi* to increase; **au'mento** *sm* increase
au'rora *sf* dawn
ausili'are *ag, sm, sm/f* auxiliary
Aus'tralia *sf* l'~ Australia; **australi'ano, -a** *ag, sm/f* Australian
'Austria *sf* l'~ Austria; **aus'triaco, -a, -ci, -che** *ag, sm/f* Austrian
au'tentico, -a, -ci, -che *ag* authentic, genuine
au'tista, -i *sm* driver
'auto *sf inv* car
autoabbron'zante *sm, ag* self-tan
autoade'sivo, -a *ag* self-adhesive ▷ *sm* sticker
autobio'grafico, -a, ci, che *ag* autobiographic(al)
'autobus *sm inv* bus
auto'carro *sm* lorry (BRIT), truck
autocertificazi'one [autotʃertifikat'tsjone] *sf* self-declaration
autodistrut'tivo, -a *ag* self-destructive
auto'gol *sm inv* own goal
au'tografo, -a *ag, sm* autograph
auto'grill® *sm inv* motorway restaurant
auto'matico, -a, -ci, -che *ag* automatic ▷ *sm* (*bottone*) snap fastener; (*fucile*) automatic
auto'mobile *sf* (motor) car
automobi'lista, -i, -e *sm/f* motorist
autono'leggio *sm* car hire
autono'mia *sf* autonomy; (*di volo*) range
au'tonomo, -a *ag* autonomous, independent
autop'sia *sf* post-mortem, autopsy
auto'radio *sf inv* (*apparecchio*) car radio; (*autoveicolo*) radio car
au'tore, -'trice *sm/f* author
autoreggente [autored'dʒɛnte] *ag* **calze autoreggenti** hold ups
auto'revole *ag* authoritative; (*persona*) influential
autoricari'cabile *ag* **scheda ~** top-up card
autori'messa *sf* garage
autorità *sf inv* authority
autoriz'zare [autorid'dzare] *vt* (*permettere*) to authorize; (*giustificare*) to allow, sanction
autos'contro *sm* dodgem car (BRIT), bumper car (US)

autoscu'ola *sf* driving school

autos'tima *sf* self-esteem

autos'top *sm* hitchhiking;
autostop'pista, -i, -e *sm/f* hitchhiker

autos'trada *sf* motorway (BRIT),
highway (US); **autostrada informatica**
information superhighway

● **AUTOSTRADE**
●
● You have to pay to use Italian
● motorways. They are indicated by an "A"
● followed by a number on a green sign.
● The speed limit on Italian motorways
● is 130 kph.

auto'velox® *sm inv* (police) speed camera

autovet'tura *sf* (motor) car

au'tunno *sm* autumn

avam'braccio [avam'brattʃo] (*pl* (*f*) **-cia**)
sm forearm

avangu'ardia *sf* vanguard

a'vanti *av* (*stato in luogo*) in front; (*moto:
andare, venire*) forward; (*tempo: prima*)
before ▷ *prep* (*luogo*): ~ **a** before, in front
of; (*tempo*): ~ **Cristo** before Christ ▷ *escl*
(*entrate*) come (*o* go) in!; (*Mil*) forward!;
(*coraggio*) come on! ▷ *sm inv* (*Sport*)
forward; ~ **e indietro** backwards and
forwards; **andare** ~ to go forward;
(*continuare*) to go on; (*precedere*) to go
(on) ahead; (*orologio*) to be fast; **essere** ~
negli studi to be well advanced with one's
studies

avan'zare [avan'tsare] *vt* (*spostare
in avanti*) to move forward, advance;
(*domanda*) to put forward; (*promuovere*) to
promote; (*essere creditore*): ~ **qc da qn** to be
owed sth by sb ▷ *vi* (*andare avanti*) to move
forward, advance; (*progredire*) to make
progress; (*essere d'avanzo*) to be left, remain

ava'ria *sf* (*guasto*) damage; (: *meccanico*)
breakdown

a'varo, -a *ag* avaricious, miserly ▷ *sm*
miser

○ **PAROLA CHIAVE**

a'vere *sm* (*Comm*) credit; **gli averi** (*ricchezze*)
wealth *sg*
▷ *vt* **1** (*possedere*) to have; **ha due
bambini/una bella casa** she has (got)
two children/a lovely house; **ha i capelli
lunghi** he has (got) long hair; **non ho da
mangiare/bere** I've (got) nothing to eat/
drink, I don't have anything to eat/drink
2 (*indossare*) to wear, have on; **aveva una
maglietta rossa** he was wearing *o* he had
on a red tee-shirt; **ha gli occhiali** he wears

o has glasses
3 (*ricevere*) to get; **hai avuto l'assegno?**
did you get *o* have you had the cheque?
4 (*età, dimensione*) to be; **ha 9 anni** he
is 9 (years old); **la stanza ha 3 metri di
lunghezza** the room is 3 metres in length;
vedi **fame**; **paura** *ecc*
5 (*tempo*): **quanti ne abbiamo oggi?**
what's the date today?; **ne hai per molto?**
will you be long?
6 (*fraseologia*): **avercela con qn** to be
angry with sb; **cos'hai?** what's wrong *o*
what's the matter (with you)?; **non ha
niente a che vedere** *o* **fare con me** it's
got nothing to do with me
▷ *vb aus* **1** to have; **aver bevuto/
mangiato** to have drunk/eaten
2 (+ *da* + *infinito*): **avere da fare qc** to have
to do sth; **non hai che da chiederlo** you
only have to ask him

aviazi'one [avjat'tsjone] *sf* aviation; (*Mil*)
air force

'avido, -a *ag* eager; (*peg*) greedy

avo'cado *sm* avocado

a'vorio *sm* ivory

Avv. *abbr* = **avvocato**

avvantaggi'are [avvantad'dʒare]
vt to favour; **avvantaggiarsi** *vpr*
**avvantaggiarsi negli affari/sui
concorrenti** to get ahead in business/of
one's competitors

avvele'nare *vt* to poison

av'vengo *ecc vb vedi* **avvenire**

avveni'mento *sm* event

avve'nire *vi*, *vb impers* to happen, occur
▷ *sm* future

av'venni *ecc vb vedi* **avvenire**

avven'tato, -a *ag* rash, reckless

avven'tura *sf* adventure; (*amorosa*) affair

avventu'rarsi *vpr* to venture

avventu'roso, -a *ag* adventurous

avve'rarsi *vpr* to come true

av'verbio *sm* adverb

avverrò *ecc vb vedi* **avvenire**

avver'sario, -a *ag* opposing ▷ *sm*
opponent, adversary

avver'tenza [avver'tentsa] *sf*
(*ammonimento*) warning; (*cautela*) care;
(*premessa*) foreword; **avvertenze** *sfpl*
(*istruzioni per l'uso*) instructions

avverti'mento *sm* warning

avver'tire *vt* (*avvisare*) to warn; (*rendere
consapevole*) to inform, notify; (*percepire*)
to feel

avvi'are *vt* (*mettere sul cammino*) to direct;
(*impresa, trattative*) to begin, start; (*motore*)
to start; **avviarsi** *vpr* to set off, set out

avvici'nare [avvitʃi'nare] *vt* to bring

near; (*trattare con: persona*) to approach;
avvicinarsi *vpr* **avvicinarsi (a qn/qc)** to
approach (sb/sth), draw near (to sb/sth)
avvi'lito, -a *ag* discouraged
avvin'cente *ag* captivating
avvi'sare *vt* (*far sapere*) to inform;
(*mettere in guardia*) to warn; **av'viso** *sm*
warning; (*annuncio*) announcement;
(: *affisso*) notice; (*inserzione pubblicitaria*)
advertisement; **a mio avviso** in my
opinion; **avviso di chiamata** (*servizio*)
call waiting; (*segnale*) call waiting signal;
avviso di garanzia (*Dir*) notification (*of
impending investigation and of the right to
name a defence lawyer*)

▮ Attenzione! In inglese esiste la parola
advice che però vuol dire *consiglio*.

avvis'tare *vt* to sight
avvi'tare *vt* to screw down (*o* in)
avvo'cato, -'essa *sm/f* (*Dir*) barrister
(BRIT), lawyer; (*fig*) defender, advocate
av'volgere [av'voldʒere] *vt* to roll up;
(*avviluppare*) to wrap up; **avvolgersi** *vpr*
(*avvilupparsi*) to wrap o.s. up; **avvol'gibile**
sm roller blind (BRIT), blind
av'volsi *ecc vb vedi* **avvolgere**
avvol'toio *sm* vulture
aza'lea [addza'lɛa] *sf* azalea
azi'enda [ad'dzjɛnda] *sf* business, firm,
concern; **azienda agricola** farm
azi'one [at'tsjone] *sf* action; (*Comm*) share
a'zoto [ad'dzɔto] *sm* nitrogen
azzar'dare [addzar'dare] *vt* (*soldi, vita*) to
risk, hazard; (*domanda, ipotesi*) to hazard,
venture; **azzardarsi** *vpr* **azzardarsi a fare**
to dare (to) do
az'zardo [ad'dzardo] *sm* risk
azzec'care [attsek'kare] *vt* (*risposta ecc*)
to get right
azzuf'farsi [attsuf'farsi] *vpr* to come to
blows
az'zurro, -a [ad'dzurro] *ag* blue ▷ *sm*
(*colore*) blue; **gli azzurri** (*Sport*) the Italian
national team

'babbo *sm* (*fam*) dad, daddy; **Babbo
Natale** Father Christmas
baby'sitter ['beɪbɪsɪtəʳ] *sm/f inv* baby-
sitter
'bacca, -che *sf* berry
baccalà *sm* dried salted cod; (*fig: peg*)
dummy
bac'chetta [bak'ketta] *sf* (*verga*) stick, rod;
(*di direttore d'orchestra*) baton; (*di tamburo*)
drumstick; **~ magica** magic wand
ba'checa, -che [ba'kɛka] *sf* (*mobile*)
showcase, display case; (*Univ, in ufficio*)
notice board (BRIT), bulletin board (US)
baci'are [ba'tʃare] *vt* to kiss; **baciarsi** *vpr*
to kiss (one another)
baci'nella [batʃi'nɛlla] *sf* basin
ba'cino [ba'tʃino] *sm* basin; (*Mineralogia*)
field, bed; (*Anat*) pelvis; (*Naut*) dock
'bacio ['batʃo] *sm* kiss
'baco, -chi *sm* worm; **baco da seta**
silkworm
ba'dare *vi* (*fare attenzione*) to take care, be
careful; (*occuparsi di*): **~ a** to look after, take
care of; (*dar ascolto*): **~ a** to pay attention
to; **bada ai fatti tuoi!** mind your own
business!
'baffi *smpl* moustache *sg*; (*di animale*)
whiskers; **ridere sotto i ~** to laugh up
one's sleeve; **leccarsi i ~** to lick one's lips
bagagli'aio [bagaʎ'ʎajo] *sm* luggage van

(BRIT) o car (US); (Aut) boot (BRIT), trunk (US)

ba'gaglio [ba'gaʎʎo] sm luggage no pl, baggage no pl; **fare/disfare i bagagli** to pack/unpack; **i nostri bagagli non sono arrivati** our luggage has not arrived; **può mandare qualcuno a prendere i nostri bagagli?** could you send someone to collect our luggage?; **bagaglio a mano** hand luggage

bagli'ore [baʎ'ʎore] sm flash, dazzling light; **un ~ di speranza** a ray of hope

ba'gnante [baɲ'ɲante] sm/f bather

ba'gnare [baɲ'ɲare] vt to wet; (inzuppare) to soak; (innaffiare) to water; (fiume) to flow through; (: mare) to wash, bathe; **bagnarsi** vpr to get wet; (al mare) to go swimming o bathing; (in vasca) to have a bath

ba'gnato, -a [baɲ'ɲato] ag wet

ba'gnino [baɲ'ɲino] sm lifeguard

'bagno ['baɲɲo] sm bath; (stanza) bathroom; (toilette) toilet; **bagni** smpl (stabilimento) baths; **fare il ~** to have a bath; (nel mare) to go swimming o bathing; **dov'è il ~?** where's the toilet?; **fare il ~ a qn** to give sb a bath; **mettere a ~** to soak; **~ schiuma** bubble bath

bagnoma'ria [baɲɲoma'ria] sm **cuocere a ~** to cook in a double saucepan

bagnoschi'uma [baɲɲoskj'uma] sm inv bubble bath

'baia sf bay

balbet'tare vi to stutter, stammer; (bimbo) to babble ▷ vt to stammer out

bal'canico, -a, ci, che ag Balkan

bal'cone sm balcony; **avete una camera con ~?** do you have a room with a balcony?

bal'doria sf **fare ~** to have a riotous time

ba'lena sf whale

ba'leno sm flash of lightning; **in un ~** in a flash

bal'lare vt, vi to dance

balle'rina sf dancer; ballet dancer; (scarpa) ballet shoe

balle'rino sm dancer; ballet dancer

bal'letto sm ballet

'ballo sm dance; (azione) dancing no pl; **essere in ~** (fig: persona) to be involved; (: cosa) to be at stake

balne'are ag seaside cpd; (stagione) bathing

'balsamo sm (aroma) balsam; (lenimento, fig) balm

bal'zare [bal'tsare] vi to bounce; (lanciarsi) to jump, leap; **'balzo** sm bounce; jump, leap; (del terreno) crag

bam'bina ag, sf vedi **bambino**

bam'bino, -a sm/f child

'bambola sf doll

bambù sm bamboo

ba'nale ag banal, commonplace

ba'nana sf banana

'banca, -che sf bank; **banca dati** data bank

banca'rella sf stall

banca'rotta sf bankruptcy; **fare ~** to go bankrupt

ban'chetto [ban'ketto] sm banquet

banchi'ere [ban'kjɛre] sm banker

ban'china [ban'kina] sf (di porto) quay; (per pedoni, ciclisti) path; (di stazione) platform; **~ cedevole** (Aut) soft verge (BRIT) o shoulder (US)

'banco, -chi sm bench; (di negozio) counter; (di mercato) stall; (di officina) (work-)bench; (Geo, banca) bank; **banco di corallo** coral reef; **banco degli imputati** dock; **banco di prova** (fig) testing ground; **banco dei testimoni** witness box; **banco dei pegni** pawnshop; **banco di nebbia** bank of fog

'Bancomat® sm inv automated banking; (tessera) cash card

banco'nota sf banknote

'banda sf band; (di stoffa) band, stripe; (lato, parte) side; **~ perforata** punch tape

bandi'era sf flag, banner

ban'dito sm outlaw, bandit

'bando sm proclamation; (esilio) exile, banishment; **~ alle chiacchiere!** that's enough talk!; **bando di concorso** announcement of a competition

bar sm inv bar

'bara sf coffin

ba'racca, -che sf shed, hut; (peg) hovel; **mandare avanti la ~** to keep things going

ba'rare vi to cheat

ba'ratro sm abyss

ba'ratto sm barter

ba'rattolo sm (di latta) tin; (di vetro) jar; (di coccio) pot

'barba sf beard; **farsi la ~** to shave; **farla in ~ a qn** (fig) to do sth to sb's face; **che ~!** what a bore!

barbabi'etola sf beetroot (BRIT), beet (US); **barbabietola da zucchero** sugar beet

barbi'ere sm barber

bar'bone sm (cane) poodle; (vagabondo) tramp

'barca, -che sf boat; **barca a motore** motorboat; **barca a remi** rowing boat; **barca a vela** sail(ing) boat

barcol'lare vi to stagger

ba'rella sf (lettiga) stretcher

ba'rile sm barrel, cask

ba'rista, -i, -e sm/f barman/maid; (proprietario) bar owner

ba'rocco, -a, -chi, -che *ag, sm* baroque
ba'rometro *sm* barometer
ba'rone *sm* baron; **baro'nessa** *sf* baroness
'barra *sf* bar; (*Naut*) helm; (*linea grafica*) line, stroke
bar'rare *vt* to bar
barri'carsi *vpr* to barricade o.s.
barri'era *sf* barrier; (*Geo*) reef
ba'ruffa *sf* scuffle
barzel'letta [bardzel'letta] *sf* joke, funny story
ba'sare *vt* to base, found; **basarsi** *vpr* **basarsi su** (*fatti, prove*) to be based *o* founded on; (: *persona*) to base one's arguments on
'basco, -a, -schi, -sche *ag* Basque ▷ *sm* (*copricapo*) beret
'base *sf* base; (*fig: fondamento*) basis; (*Pol*) rank and file; **di ~** basic; **in ~ a** on the basis of, according to; **a ~ di caffè** coffee-based
'baseball ['beisbɔːl] *sm* baseball
ba'sette *sfpl* sideburns
ba'silica, -che *sf* basilica
ba'silico *sm* basil
basket ['basket] *sm* basketball
bas'sista, -i, -e *sm/f* bass player
'basso, -a *ag* low; (*di statura*) short; (*meridionale*) southern ▷ *sm* bottom, lower part; (*Mus*) bass; **la bassa Italia** southern Italy
bassorili'evo *sm* bas-relief
bas'sotto, -a *ag* squat ▷ *sm* (*cane*) dachshund
'basta *escl* (that's) enough!, that will do!
bas'tardo, -a *ag* (*animale, pianta*) hybrid, crossbreed; (*persona*) illegitimate, bastard; (*peg*) ▷ *sm/f* illegitimate child, bastard (*peg*)
bas'tare *vi, vb impers* to be enough, be sufficient; **~ a qn** to be enough for sb; **basta chiedere** *o* **che chieda a un vigile** you have only to *o* need only ask a policeman; **basta così, grazie** that's enough, thanks
basto'nare *vt* to beat, thrash
baston'cino [baston'tʃino] *sm* (*Sci*) ski pole; **bastoncini di pesce** fish fingers
bas'tone *sm* stick; **~ da passeggio** walking stick
bat'taglia [bat'taʎʎa] *sf* battle; fight
bat'tello *sm* boat
bat'tente *sm* (*imposta: di porta*) wing, flap; (: *di finestra*) shutter; (*batacchio: di porta*) knocker; (: *di orologio*) hammer; **chiudere i battenti** (*fig*) to shut up shop
'battere *vt* to beat; (*grano*) to thresh; (*percorrere*) to scour ▷ *vi* (*bussare*) to knock; (*urtare*): **~ contro** to hit *o* strike against;

(*pioggia, sole*) to beat down; (*cuore*) to beat; (*Tennis*) to serve; **battersi** *vpr* to fight; **~ le mani** to clap; **~ i piedi** to stamp one's feet; **~ a macchina** to type; **~ bandiera italiana** to fly the Italian flag; **~ in testa** (*Aut*) to knock; **in un batter d'occhio** in the twinkling of an eye
batte'ria *sf* battery; (*Mus*) drums *pl*
bat'terio *sm* bacterium
batte'rista, -i, -e *sm/f* drummer
bat'tesimo *sm* (*rito*) baptism; christening
battez'zare [batted'dzare] *vt* to baptize; to christen
batti'panni *sm inv* carpet-beater
battis'trada *sm inv* (*di pneumatico*) tread; (*di gara*) pacemaker
'battito *sm* beat, throb; **battito cardiaco** heartbeat
bat'tuta *sf* blow; (*di macchina da scrivere*) stroke; (*Mus*) bar; beat; (*Teatro*) cue; (*frase spiritosa*) witty remark; (*di caccia*) beating; (*Polizia*) combing, scouring; (*Tennis*) service
ba'tuffolo *sm* wad
ba'ule *sm* trunk; (*Aut*) boot (BRIT), trunk (US)
'bava *sf* (*di animale*) slaver, slobber; (*di lumaca*) slime; (*di vento*) breath
bava'glino [bavaʎ'ʎino] *sm* bib
ba'vaglio [ba'vaʎʎo] *sm* gag
'bavero *sm* collar
ba'zar [bad'dzar] *sm inv* bazaar
BCE *sigla f* (= *Banca centrale europea*) ECB
be'ato, -a *ag* blessed; (*fig*) happy; **~ te!** lucky you!
bec'care *vt* to peck; (*fig: raffreddore*) to catch; **beccarsi** *vpr* (*fig*) to squabble; **beccarsi qc** to catch sth
beccherò *ecc* [bekke'rɔ] *vb vedi* **beccare**
'becco, -chi *sm* beak, bill; (*di caffettiera ecc*) spout; lip
be'fana *sf* hag, witch; **la B~** old woman who, according to legend, brings children their presents at the Epiphany; (*Epifania*) Epiphany

bef'fardo, -a *ag* scornful, mocking
'begli ['beʎʎi] *ag vedi* **bello**
'bei *ag vedi* **bello**

beige [bɛʒ] *ag inv* beige
bel *ag vedi* **bello**
be'lare *vi* to bleat
'belga, -gi, -ghe *ag, sm/f* Belgian
'Belgio ['bɛldʒo] *sm* **il ~** Belgium
'bella *sf* (*Sport*) decider; *vedi anche* **bello**
bel'lezza [bel'lettsa] *sf* beauty

🔵 **PAROLA CHIAVE**

'bello, -a (*ag: dav sm* **bel** + *C,* **bell'** + *V,*
bello + *s impura, gn, pn, ps, x, z, pl* **bei** +
C, **begli** + *s impura ecc o* V) *ag* **1** (*oggetto,*
donna, paesaggio) beautiful, lovely; (*uomo*)
handsome; (*tempo*) beautiful, fine, lovely;
le belle arti fine arts
2 (*quantità*): **una bella cifra** a considerable
sum of money; **un bel niente** absolutely
nothing
3 (*rafforzativo*): **è una truffa bella e**
buona! it's a real fraud!; **è bell'e finito** it's
already finished
▷ *sm* **1** (*bellezza*) beauty; (*tempo*) fine
weather
2: **adesso viene il bello** now comes the
best bit; **sul più bello** at the crucial point;
cosa fai di bello? are you doing anything
interesting?
▷ *av* **fa bello** the weather is fine, it's fine

'belva *sf* wild animal
belve'dere *sm inv* panoramic viewpoint
benché [ben'ke] *cong* although
'benda *sf* bandage; (*per gli occhi*) blindfold;
ben'dare *vt* to bandage; to blindfold
'bene *av* well; (*completamente, affatto*):
è ben difficile it's very difficult ▷ *ag inv*
gente ~ well-to-do people ▷ *sm* good;
beni *smpl* (*averi*) property sg, estate sg;
io sto ~/poco ~ I'm well/not very well;
va ~ all right; **volere un ~ dell'anima a**
qn to love sb very much; **un uomo per ~**
a respectable man; **fare ~** to do the right
thing; **fare ~ a** (*salute*) to be good for; **fare**
del ~ a qn to do sb a good turn; **beni di**
consumo consumer goods
bene'detto, -a *pp di* **benedire** ▷ *ag*
blessed, holy
bene'dire *vt* to bless; to consecrate
benedu'cato, -a *ag* well-mannered
benefi'cenza [benefi'tʃentsa] *sf* charity
bene'ficio [bene'fitʃo] *sm* benefit; **con ~**
d'inventario (*fig*) with reservations
be'nessere *sm* well-being
benes'tante *ag* well-to-do
be'nigno, -a [be'niɲɲo] *ag* kind, kindly;
(*critica ecc*) favourable; (*Med*) benign
benve'nuto, -a *ag, sm* welcome; **dare il ~**
a qn to welcome sb

ben'zina [ben'dzina] *sf* petrol (BRIT), gas
(US); **fare ~** to get petrol (BRIT) o gas (US);
sono rimasto senza ~ I have run out of
petrol (BRIT) o gas (US); **benzina verde**
unleaded (petrol); **benzi'naio** *sm* petrol
(BRIT) o gas (US) pump attendant
'bere *vt* to drink; **darla a ~ a qn** (*fig*) to fool
sb; **vuoi qualcosa da ~?** would you like
a drink?
ber'lina *sf* (*Aut*) saloon (car) (BRIT), sedan
(US)
Ber'lino *sf* Berlin
ber'muda *smpl* (*calzoncini*) Bermuda
shorts
ber'noccolo *sm* bump; (*inclinazione*) flair
ber'retto *sm* cap
berrò *ecc vb vedi* **bere**
ber'saglio [ber'saʎʎo] *sm* target
besciamella [beʃʃa'mɛlla] *sf* béchamel
sauce
bes'temmia *sf* curse; (*Rel*) blasphemy
bestemmi'are *vi* to curse, swear; to
blaspheme ▷ *vt* to curse, swear at; to
blaspheme
'bestia *sf* animal; **andare in ~** (*fig*) to fly
into a rage; **besti'ale** *ag* beastly; animal
cpd; (*fam*): **fa un freddo bestiale** it's
bitterly cold; **besti'ame** *sm* livestock;
(*bovino*) cattle *pl*
be'tulla *sf* birch
be'vanda *sf* drink, beverage
'bevo *ecc vb vedi* **bere**
be'vuto, -a *pp di* **bere**
'bevvi *ecc vb vedi* **bere**
bianche'ria [bjanke'ria] *sf* linen; **~**
da donna ladies' underwear, lingerie;
biancheria femminile lingerie;
biancheria intima underwear
bi'anco, -a, -chi, -che *ag* white; (*non*
scritto) blank ▷ *sm* white; (*intonaco*)
whitewash ▷ *sm/f* white, white man/
woman; **in ~** (*foglio, assegno*) blank; (*notte*)
sleepless; **in bianco e nero** (TV, Fot) black and
white; **mangiare in ~** to follow a bland
diet; **pesce in ~** boiled fish; **andare in**
~ (*non riuscire*) to fail; **bianco dell'uovo**
egg-white
biasi'mare *vt* to disapprove of, censure
'Bibbia *sf* (*anche fig*) bible
bibe'ron *sm inv* feeding bottle
'bibita *sf* (soft) drink
biblio'teca, -che *sf* library; (*mobile*)
bookcase
bicarbo'nato *sm* **~ (di sodio)** bicarbonate
(of soda)
bicchi'ere [bik'kjɛre] *sm* glass
bici'cletta [bitʃi'kletta] *sf* bicycle; **andare**
in ~ to cycle
bidè *sm inv* bidet

bi'dello, -a sm/f (Ins) janitor
bi'done sm drum, can; (anche: ~ **dell'immondizia**) (dust)bin; (fam: truffa) swindle; **fare un ~ a qn** (fam) to let sb down; to cheat sb
bien'nale ag biennial

⬤ **BIENNALE DI VENEZIA**
⬤
⬤ The **Biennale di Venezia** is an
⬤ international contemporary art festival,
⬤ which takes place every two years at
⬤ Giardini in Venice. In its current form,
⬤ it includes exhibits by artists from the
⬤ many countries taking part, a thematic
⬤ exhibition and a section for young
⬤ artists.

bifamili'are sf ≈ semi-detached house
bifor'carsi vpr to fork
bigiotte'ria [bidʒotte'ria] sf costume jewellery; (negozio) jeweller's (selling only costume jewellery)
bigliet'taio, -a sm/f (in treno) ticket inspector; (in autobus) conductor
bigliette'ria [biʎʎette'ria] sf (di stazione) ticket office; booking office; (di teatro) box office
bigli'etto [biʎ'ʎetto] sm (per viaggi, spettacoli ecc) ticket; (cartoncino) card; (anche: ~ **di banca**) (bank)note; **biglietto d'auguri** greetings card; **biglietto da visita** visiting card; **biglietto d'andata e ritorno** return (ticket), round-trip ticket (us); **biglietto di sola andata** single (ticket)
bignè [biɲ'ɲe] sm inv cream puff
bigo'dino sm roller, curler
bi'gotto, -a ag over-pious ▷ sm/f church fiend
bi'kini sm inv bikini
bi'lancia, -ce [bi'lantʃa] sf (pesa) scales pl; (: di precisione) balance; (dello zodiaco) **B~** Libra; **bilancia commerciale** balance of trade; **bilancia dei pagamenti** balance of payments
bi'lancio [bi'lantʃo] sm (Comm) balance(-sheet); (statale) budget; **fare il ~ di** (fig) to assess; **bilancio consuntivo** (final) balance; **bilancio preventivo** budget
bili'ardo sm billiards sg; billiard table
bi'lingue ag bilingual
bilo'cale sm two-room flat (Brit) o apartment (us)
bi'nario, -a ag (sistema) binary ▷ sm (railway) track o line; (piattaforma) platform; **da che ~ parte il treno per Londra?** which platform does the train for

London go from?; **binario morto** dead-end track
bi'nocolo sm binoculars pl
bio... prefisso **biodegra'dabile** ag biodegradable; **biodi'namico, -a, -ci, -che** ag biodynamic; **biogra'fia** sf biography; **biolo'gia** sf biology
bio'logico, -a, -ci, -che ag (scienze, fenomeni ecc)) biological; (agricoltura, prodotti) organic; **guerra biologica** biological warfare
bi'ondo, -a ag blond, fair
biotecnologia [bioteknolo'dʒia] sf biotechnology
biri'chino, -a [biri'kino] ag mischievous ▷ sm/f scamp, little rascal
bi'rillo sm skittle (BRIT), pin (us)
'biro® sf inv biro®
'birra sf beer; **a tutta ~** (fig) at top speed; **birra chiara/scura** ≈ lager/stout; **birre'ria** sf ≈ bierkeller
bis escl, sm inv encore
bis'betico, -a, -ci, -che ag ill-tempered, crabby
bisbigli'are [bisbiʎ'ʎare] vt, vi to whisper
'bisca, -sche sf gambling-house
'biscia, -sce ['biʃʃa] sf snake; **biscia d'acqua** grass snake
biscot'tato, -a ag crisp; **fette biscottate** rusks
bis'cotto sm biscuit
bisessu'ale ag, sm/f bisexual
bises'tile ag anno ~ leap year
bis'nonno, -a sm/f great grandfather/grandmother
biso'gnare [bizoɲ'ɲare] vb impers **bisogna che tu parta/lo faccia** you'll have to go/do it; **bisogna parlargli** we'll (o I'll) have to talk to him
bi'sogno [bi'zoɲɲo] sm need; **ha ~ di qualcosa?** do you need anything?
bis'tecca, -che sf steak, beefsteak
bisticci'are [bistit'tʃare] vi to quarrel, bicker; **bisticciarsi** vpr to quarrel, bicker
'bisturi sm scalpel
'bivio sm fork; (fig) dilemma
biz'zarro, -a [bid'dzarro] ag bizarre, strange
blate'rare vi to chatter
blin'dato, -a ag armoured
bloc'care vt to block; (isolare) to isolate, cut off; (porto) to blockade; (prezzi, beni) to freeze; (meccanismo) to jam; **bloccarsi** vpr (motore) to stall; (freni, porta) to jam, stick; (ascensore) to stop, get stuck
bloccherò ecc [blokke'rɔ] vb vedi **bloccare**
bloc'chetto [blok'ketto] sm notebook; (di biglietti) book

'blocco, -chi sm block; (Mil) blockade; (dei fitti) restriction; (quadernetto) pad; (fig: unione) coalition; (il bloccare) blocking; isolating, cutting-off; blockading; freezing; jamming; **in ~** (nell'insieme) as a whole; (Comm) in bulk; **blocco cardiaco** cardiac arrest; **blocco stradale** road block

blu ag inv, sm dark blue

'blusa sf (camiciotto) smock; (camicetta) blouse

'boa sm inv (Zool) boa constrictor; (sciarpa) feather boa ▷ sf buoy

bo'ato sm rumble, roar

bob [bɔb] sm inv bobsleigh

'bocca, -che sf mouth; **in ~ al lupo!** good luck!

boc'caccia, -ce [bok'kattʃa] sf (malalingua) gossip; **fare le boccacce** to pull faces

boc'cale sm jug; **boccale da birra** tankard

boc'cetta [bot'tʃetta] sf small bottle

'boccia, -ce ['bɔttʃa] sf bottle; (da vino) decanter, carafe; (palla) bowl; **gioco delle bocce** bowls sg

bocci'are [bot'tʃare] vt (proposta, progetto) to reject; (Ins) to fail; (Bocce) to hit

bocci'olo [bot'tʃɔlo] sm bud

boc'cone sm mouthful, morsel

boicot'tare vt to boycott

'bolla sf bubble; (Med) blister; **bolla di consegna** (Comm) delivery note; **bolla papale** papal bull

bol'lente ag boiling; boiling hot

bol'letta sf bill; (ricevuta) receipt; **essere in ~** to be hard up

bollet'tino sm bulletin; (Comm) note; **bollettino meteorologico** weather report; **bollettino di spedizione** consignment note

bollicina [bolli'tʃina] sf bubble

bol'lire vt, vi to boil

bolli'tore sm (Cuc) kettle; (per riscaldamento) boiler

'bollo sm stamp; **bollo per patente** driving licence tax; **bollo postale** postmark

'bomba sf bomb; **bomba atomica** atom bomb; **bomba a mano** hand grenade; **bomba ad orologeria** time bomb

bombarda'mento sm bombardment; bombing

bombar'dare vt to bombard; (da aereo) to bomb

'bombola sf cylinder

bombo'letta sf aerosol

bomboni'era sf box of sweets (as souvenir at weddings, first communions etc)

bo'nifico, -ci sm (riduzione, abbuono) discount; (versamento a terzi) credit transfer

bontà sf goodness; (cortesia) kindness; **aver la ~ di fare qc** to be good o kind enough to do sth

borbot'tare vi to mumble

'borchia ['bɔrkja] sf stud

bor'deaux [bor'dɔ] ag inv, sm inv maroon

'bordo sm (Naut) ship's side; (orlo) edge; (striscia di guarnizione) border, trim; **a ~ di** (nave, aereo) aboard, on board; (macchina) in

bor'ghese [bor'geze] ag (spesso peg) middle-class; bourgeois; **abito ~** civilian dress

'borgo, -ghi sm (paesino) village; (quartiere) district; (sobborgo) suburb

boro'talco sm talcum powder

bor'raccia, -ce [bor'rattʃa] sf canteen, water-bottle

'borsa sf bag; (anche: ~ da signora) handbag; (Econ) **la B~ (valori)** the Stock Exchange; **borsa dell'acqua calda** hot-water bottle; **borsa nera** black market; **borsa della spesa** shopping bag; **borsa di studio** grant; **borsel'lino** sm purse; **bor'setta** sf handbag

'bosco, -schi sm wood

bos'niaco, -a, ci, che ag, sm/f Bosnian

'Bosnia Erze'govina ['bɔsnja erdze'govina] sf **la ~** Bosnia Herzegovina

Bot, bot sigla m inv (= buono ordinario del Tesoro) short-term Treasury bond

bo'tanica sf botany

bo'tanico, -a, -ci, -che ag botanical ▷ sm botanist

'botola sf trap door

'botta sf blow; (rumore) bang

'botte sf barrel, cask

bot'tega, -ghe sf shop; (officina) workshop

bot'tiglia [bot'tiʎʎa] sf bottle; **bottiglie'ria** sf wine shop

bot'tino sm (di guerra) booty; (di rapina, furto) loot

'botto sm bang; crash; **di ~** suddenly

bot'tone sm button; **attaccare ~ a qn** (fig) to buttonhole sb

bo'vino, -a ag bovine; **bovini** smpl cattle

box [bɔks] sm inv (per cavalli) horsebox; (per macchina) lock-up; (per macchina da corsa) pit; (per bambini) playpen

boxe [bɔks] sf boxing

'boxer ['bɔkser] sm inv (cane) boxer ▷ smpl (mutande): **un paio di ~** a pair of boxer shorts

BR sigla fpl = **Brigate Rosse**

brac'cetto [brat'tʃetto] sm **a ~** arm in arm

braccia'letto sm bracelet; bangle

bracci'ata [brat'tʃata] sf (nel nuoto) stroke
'braccio ['brattʃo] (pl(f) **braccia**) sm (Anat)
arm; (pl(m) **bracci**: di gru, fiume) arm; (: di
edificio) wing; **braccio di mare** sound;
bracci'olo sm (appoggio) arm
'bracco, -chi sm hound
'brace ['bratʃe] sf embers pl
braci'ola [bra'tʃola] sf (Cuc) chop
'branca, -che sf branch
'branchia ['brankja] sf (Zool) gill
'branco, -chi sm (di cani, lupi) pack; (di
pecore) flock; (peg: di persone) gang, pack
bran'dina sf camp bed (BRIT), cot (US)
'brano sm piece; (di libro) passage
Bra'sile sm **il ~** Brazil; **brasili'ano, -a** ag,
sm/f Brazilian
'bravo, -a ag (abile) clever, capable, skilful;
(buono) good, honest; (: bambino) good;
(coraggioso) brave; **~!** well done!; (a teatro)
bravo!
bra'vura sf cleverness, skill
Bre'tagna [bre'taɲɲa] sf **la ~** Brittany
bre'tella sf (Aut) link; **bretelle** sfpl (di
calzoni) braces
'bretone ag, sm/f Breton
'breve ag brief, short; **in ~** in short
brevet'tare vt to patent
bre'vetto sm patent; **brevetto di
pilotaggio** pilot's licence (BRIT) o license
(US)
'bricco, -chi sm jug; **bricco del caffè**
coffeepot
'briciola ['britʃola] sf crumb
'briciolo ['britʃolo] sm (specie fig) bit
'briga, -ghe sf (fastidio) trouble, bother;
pigliarsi la ~ di fare qc to take the trouble
to do sth
bri'gata sf (Mil) brigade; (gruppo) group,
party; **Brigate Rosse** (Pol) Red Brigades
'briglia ['briʎʎa] sf rein; **a ~ sciolta** at full
gallop; (fig) at full speed
bril'lante ag bright; (anche fig) brilliant;
(che luccica) shining ▷ sm diamond
bril'lare vi to shine; (mina) to blow up ▷ vt
(mina) to set off
'brillo, -a ag merry, tipsy
'brina sf hoarfrost
brin'dare vi **~ a qn/qc** to drink to o toast
sb/sth
'brindisi sm inv toast
bri'oche [bri'ɔʃ] sf inv brioche
bri'tannico, -a, -ci, -che ag British
'brivido sm shiver; (di ribrezzo) shudder;
(fig) thrill
brizzo'lato, -a [brittso'lato] ag (persona)
going grey; (barba, capelli) greying
'brocca, -che sf jug
'broccoli smpl broccoli sg
'brodo sm broth; (per cucinare) stock;

brodo ristretto consommé
bron'chite [bron'kite] sf (Med) bronchitis
bronto'lare vi to grumble; (tuono, stomaco)
to rumble
'bronzo ['brondzo] sm bronze
'browser ['brauzer] sm inv (Inform)
browser
brucia'pelo [brutʃa'pelo]: **a ~** av point-
blank
bruci'are [bru'tʃare] vt to burn; (scottare)
to scald ▷ vi to burn; **bruciarsi** vpr to
burn o.s.; (fallire) to ruin one's chances; **~
le tappe** (fig) to shoot ahead; **bruciarsi la
carriera** to ruin one's career
'bruco, -chi sm caterpillar; grub
'brufolo sm pimple, spot
'brullo, -a ag bare, bleak
'bruno, -a ag brown, dark; (persona)
dark(-haired)
'brusco, -a, -schi, -sche ag (sapore)
sharp; (modi, persona) brusque, abrupt;
(movimento) abrupt, sudden
bru'sio sm buzz, buzzing
bru'tale ag brutal
'brutto, -a ag ugly; (cattivo) bad; (malattia,
strada, affare) nasty, bad; **~ tempo** bad
weather
Bru'xelles [bry'sɛl] sf Brussels
BSE [biesse'e] sigla f (= encefalopatia
spongiforme bovina) BSE
'buca, -che sf hole; (avvallamento) hollow;
buca delle lettere letterbox
buca'neve sm inv snowdrop
bu'care vt (forare) to make a hole (o holes)
in; (pungere) to pierce; (biglietto) to punch;
bucarsi vpr (di eroina) to mainline; **~ una
gomma** to have a puncture
bu'cato sm (operazione) washing; (panni)
wash, washing
'buccia, -ce ['buttʃa] sf skin, peel
bucherò ecc [buke'rɔ] vb vedi **bucare**
'buco, -chi sm hole
bud'dismo sm Buddhism
bu'dino sm pudding
'bue sm ox; **carne di ~** beef
bu'fera sf storm
'buffo, -a ag funny; (Teatro) comic
bu'gia, -'gie [bu'dʒia] sf lie; **dire una ~** to
tell a lie; **bugi'ardo, -a** ag lying, deceitful
▷ sm/f liar
'buio, -a ag dark ▷ sm dark, darkness
'bulbo sm (Bot) bulb; **bulbo oculare**
eyeball
Bulga'ria sf **la ~** Bulgaria
'bulgaro, -a ag, sm/f, sm Bulgarian
buli'mia sf bulimia; **bu'limico, -a, -ci, -che**
ag bulimic
bul'lone sm bolt
buona'notte escl good night! ▷ sf **dare la**

~ **a** to say good night to

buona'sera *escl* good evening!

buongi'orno [bwon'dʒorno] *escl* good morning (*o* afternoon)!

buongus'taio, -a *sm/f* gourmet

○ **PAROLA CHIAVE**

bu'ono, -a (*ag*: *dav sm* **buon** + *C o V,* **buono** + *s impura, gn, pn, ps, x, z; dav sf* **buon'** +*V*) *ag*
1 (*gen*) good; **un buon pranzo/ristorante** a good lunch/restaurant; **(stai) buono!** behave!
2 (*benevolo*): **buono (con)** good (to), kind (to)
3 (*giusto, valido*) right; **al momento buono** at the right moment
4 (*adatto*): **buono a/da** fit for/to; **essere buono a nulla** to be no good *o* use at anything
5 (*auguri*): **buon anno!** happy New Year!; **buon appetito!** enjoy your meal!; **buon compleanno!** happy birthday!; **buon divertimento!** have a nice time!; **buona fortuna!** good luck!; **buon riposo!** sleep well!; **buon viaggio!** bon voyage!, have a good trip!
6: **a buon mercato** cheap; **di buon'ora** early; **buon senso** common sense; **alla buona** *ag* simple
▷ *av* in a simple way, without any fuss ▷ *sm*
1 (*bontà*) goodness, good
2 (*Comm*) voucher, coupon; **buono di cassa** cash voucher; **buono di consegna** delivery note; **buono del Tesoro** Treasury bill

buon'senso *sm* = **buon senso**

burat'tino *sm* puppet

'burbero, -a *ag* surly, gruff

buro'cratico, -a, ci, che *ag* bureaucratic

burocra'zia [burokrat'tsia] *sf* bureaucracy

bur'rasca, -sche *sf* storm

'burro *sm* butter

bur'rone *sm* ravine

bus'sare *vi* to knock

'bussola *sf* compass

'busta *sf* (*da lettera*) envelope; (*astuccio*) case; **in ~ aperta/chiusa** in an unsealed/ sealed envelope; **busta paga** pay packet

busta'rella *sf* bribe, backhander

bus'tina *sf* (*piccola busta*) envelope; (*di cibi, farmaci*) sachet; (*Mil*) forage cap; **bustina di tè** tea bag

'busto *sm* bust; (*indumento*) corset, girdle; **a mezzo ~** (*foto*) half-length

but'tare *vt* to throw; (*anche:* **~ via**) to throw away; **~ giù** (*scritto*) to scribble down; (*cibo*) to gulp down; (*edificio*) to pull down, demolish; (*pasta, verdura*) to put into boiling water; **buttarsi** *vpr* (*saltare*) to jump; **buttarsi dalla finestra** to jump out of the window

byte ['bait] *sm inv* byte

C

to drop; (*anche*: **~ dal sonno**) to be falling asleep on one's feet; **~ dalle nuvole** (*fig*) to be taken aback

cadrò *ecc vb vedi* **cadere**

ca'duta *sf* fall; **la ~ dei capelli** hair loss

caffè *sm inv* coffee; (*locale*) café; **caffè corretto** espresso coffee with a shot of spirits; **caffè macchiato** coffee with a dash of milk; **caffè macinato** ground coffee

caffel'latte *sm inv* white coffee

caffetti'era *sf* coffeepot

'cagna ['kaɲɲa] *sf* (*Zool, peg*) bitch

CAI *sigla m* = **Club Alpino Italiano**

cala'brone *sm* hornet

cala'maro *sm* squid

cala'mita *sf* magnet

calamità *sf inv* calamity, disaster

ca'lare *vt* (*far discendere*) to lower; (*Maglia*) to decrease ▷ *vi* (*discendere*) to go (*o come*) down; (*tramontare*) to set, go down; **~ di peso** to lose weight

cal'cagno [kal'kaɲɲo] *sm* heel

cal'care *sm* (*incrostazione*) (lime)scale

'calce ['kaltʃe] *sm* **in ~** at the foot of the page ▷ *sf* lime; **calce viva** quicklime

calci'are [kal'tʃare] *vt, vi* to kick; **calcia'tore** *sm* footballer

'calcio ['kaltʃo] *sm* (*pedata*) kick; (*sport*) football, soccer; (*di pistola, fucile*) butt; (*Chim*) calcium; **calcio d'angolo** (*Sport*) corner (kick); **calcio di punizione** (*Sport*) free kick; **calcio di rigore** penalty

calco'lare *vt* to calculate, work out, reckon; (*ponderare*) to weigh (up); **calcola'tore, -'trice** *ag* calculating ▷ *sm* calculator; (*fig*) calculating person; **calcolatore elettronico** computer; **calcola'trice** *sf* calculator

'calcolo *sm* (*anche Mat*) calculation; (*infinitesimale ecc*) calculus; (*Med*) stone; **fare i propri calcoli** (*fig*) to weigh the pros and cons; **per ~** out of self-interest

cal'daia *sf* boiler

'caldo, -a *ag* warm; (*molto caldo*) hot; (*fig: appassionato*) keen; hearty ▷ *sm* heat; **ho ~** I'm warm; I'm hot; **fa ~** it's warm; it's hot

caleidos'copio *sm* kaleidoscope

calen'dario *sm* calendar

'calibro *sm* (*di arma*) calibre, bore; (*Tecn*) callipers *pl*; (*fig*) calibre; **di grosso ~** (*fig*) prominent

'calice ['kalitʃe] *sm* goblet; (*Rel*) chalice

Cali'fornia *sf* California

californi'ano, -a *ag* Californian

calligra'fia *sf* (*scrittura*) handwriting; (*arte*) calligraphy

'callo *sm* callus; (*ai piedi*) corn

'calma *sf* calm

ca'bina *sf* (*di nave*) cabin; (*da spiaggia*) beach hut; (*di autocarro, treno*) cab; (*di aereo*) cockpit; (*di ascensore*) cage; **cabi'nato** *sm* cabin cruiser; **cabina di pilotaggio** cockpit; **cabina telefonica** call *o* (tele)phone box

ca'cao *sm* cocoa

'caccia ['kattʃa] *sf* hunting; (*con fucile*) shooting; (*inseguimento*) chase; (*cacciagione*) game ▷ *sm inv* (*aereo*) fighter; (*nave*) destroyer; **caccia grossa** big-game hunting; **caccia all'uomo** manhunt

cacci'are [kat'tʃare] *vt* to hunt; (*mandar via*) to chase away; (*ficcare*) to shove, stick ▷ *vi* to hunt; **cacciarsi** *vpr* **dove s'è cacciata la mia borsa?** where has my bag got to?; **cacciarsi nei guai** to get into trouble; **~ fuori qc** to whip *o* pull sth out; **~ un urlo** to let out a yell; **caccia'tore** *sm* hunter; **cacciatore di frodo** poacher

caccia'vite [kattʃa'vite] *sm inv* screwdriver

'cactus *sm inv* cactus

ca'davere *sm* (dead) body, corpse

'caddi *ecc vb vedi* **cadere**

ca'denza [ka'dɛntsa] *sf* cadence; (*ritmo*) rhythm; (*Mus*) cadenza

ca'dere *vi* to fall; (*denti, capelli*) to fall out; (*tetto*) to fall in; **questa gonna cade bene** this skirt hangs well; **lasciar ~** (*anche fig*)

cal'mante sm tranquillizer

cal'mare vt to calm; (lenire) to soothe; **calmarsi** vpr to grow calm, calm down; (vento) to abate; (dolori) to ease

'**calmo, -a** ag calm, quiet

'**calo** sm (Comm: di prezzi) fall; (: di volume) shrinkage; (: di peso) loss

ca'lore sm warmth; heat; **in ~** (Zool) on heat

calo'ria sf calorie

calo'rifero sm radiator

calo'roso, -a ag warm

calpes'tare vt to tread on, trample on; "**è vietato ~ l'erba**" "keep off the grass"

ca'lunnia sf slander; (scritta) libel

cal'vizie [kal'vittsje] sf baldness

'**calvo, -a** ag bald

'**calza** ['kaltsa] sf (da donna) stocking; (da uomo) sock; **fare la ~** to knit; **calze di nailon** nylons, (nylon) stockings

calza'maglia [kaltsa'maʎʎa] sf tights pl; (per danza, ginnastica) leotard

calzet'tone [kaltset'tone] sm heavy knee-length sock

cal'zino [kal'tsino] sm sock

calzo'laio [kaltso'lajo] sm shoemaker; (che ripara scarpe) cobbler

calzon'cini [kaltson'tʃini] smpl shorts; **calzoncini da bagno** (swimming) trunks

cal'zone [kal'tsone] sm trouser leg; (Cuc) savoury turnover made with pizza dough; **calzoni** smpl (pantaloni) trousers (BRIT), pants (US)

camale'onte sm chameleon

cambia'mento sm change

cambi'are vt to change; (modificare) to alter, change; (barattare): **~ (qc con qn/qc)** to exchange (sth with sb/for sth) ▷ vi to change, alter; **cambiarsi** vpr (d'abito) to change; **~ casa** to move (house); **~ idea** to change one's mind; **~ treno** to change trains; **dove posso ~ dei soldi?** where can I change some money?; **ha da ~?** have you got any change?; **posso cambiarlo, per favore?** could I exchange this, please?

cambia'lute sm inv exchange office

'**cambio** sm change; (modifica) alteration, change; (scambio, Comm) exchange; (corso dei cambi) rate (of exchange); (Tecn, Aut) gears pl; **in ~ di** in exchange for; **dare il ~ a qn** to take over from sb

'**camera** sf room; (anche: ~ da letto) bedroom; (Pol) chamber, house; **camera ardente** mortuary chapel; **camera d'aria** inner tube; (di pallone) bladder; **camera di commercio** Chamber of Commerce; **Camera dei Deputati** Chamber of Deputies, ≈ House of Commons (BRIT),

≈ House of Representatives (US); **camera a gas** gas chamber; **camera a un letto/due letti** single/twin-bedded room; **camera matrimoniale** double room; **camera oscura** (Fot) dark room

> Attenzione! In inglese esiste la parola **camera**, che però significa macchina fotografica.

came'rata, -i, -e sm/f companion, mate ▷ sf dormitory

cameri'era sf (domestica) maid; (che serve a tavola) waitress; (che fa le camere) chambermaid

cameri'ere sm (man)servant; (di ristorante) waiter

came'rino sm (Teatro) dressing room

'**camice** ['kamitʃe] sm (Rel) alb; (per medici ecc) white coat

cami'cetta [kami'tʃetta] sf blouse

ca'micia, -cie [ka'mitʃa] sf (da uomo) shirt; (da donna) blouse; **camicia di forza** straitjacket; **camicia di notte** (da donna) nightdress; (da uomo) nightshirt

cami'netto sm hearth, fireplace

ca'mino sm chimney; (focolare) fireplace, hearth

'**camion** sm inv lorry (BRIT), truck (US)

camio'nista, -i sm lorry driver (BRIT), truck driver (US)

cam'mello sm (Zool) camel; (tessuto) camel hair

cammi'nare vi to walk; (funzionare) to work, go

cam'mino sm walk; (sentiero) path; (itinerario, direzione, tragitto) way; **mettersi in ~** to set o start off

camo'milla sf camomile; (infuso) camomile tea

ca'moscio [ka'moʃʃo] sm chamois; **di ~** (scarpe, borsa) suede cpd

cam'pagna [kam'paɲɲa] sf country, countryside; (Pol, Comm, Mil) campaign; **in ~** in the country; **andare in ~** to go to the country; **fare una ~** to campaign; **campagna pubblicitaria** advertising campaign

cam'pana sf bell; (anche: ~ di vetro) bell jar; **campa'nello** sm (all'uscio, da tavola) bell

campa'nile sm bell tower, belfry

cam'peggio sm camping; (terreno) camp site; **fare (del) ~** to go camping

camper ['kamper] sm inv motor caravan (BRIT), motor home (US)

campio'nario, -a ag **fiera campionaria** trade fair ▷ sm collection of samples

campio'nato sm championship

campi'one, -'essa sm/f (Sport) champion ▷ sm (Comm) sample

campo *sm* field; (*Mil*) field; (*accampamento*) camp; (*spazio delimitato: sportivo ecc*) ground; field; (*di quadro*) background; **i campi** (*campagna*) the countryside; **campo da aviazione** airfield; **campo di battaglia** (*Mil*, *fig*) battlefield; **campo di concentramento** concentration camp; **campo da golf** golf course; **campo profughi** refugee camp; **campo sportivo** sports ground; **campo da tennis** tennis court; **campo visivo** field of vision

Canada *sm* **il ~** Canada; **cana'dese** *ag*, *sm/f* Canadian ▷ *sf* (*anche*: **tenda canadese**) ridge tent

ca'naglia [ka'naʎʎa] *sf* rabble, mob; (*persona*) scoundrel, rogue

ca'nale *sm* (*anche fig*) channel; (*artificiale*) canal

canapa *sf* hemp; **canapa indiana** (*droga*) cannabis

cana'rino *sm* canary

cancel'lare [kantʃel'lare] *vt* (*con la gomma*) to rub out, erase; (*con la penna*) to strike out; (*annullare*) to annul, cancel; (*disdire*) to cancel

cancelle'ria [kantʃelle'ria] *sf* chancery; (*materiale per scrivere*) stationery

can'cello [kan'tʃello] *sm* gate

cancro *sm* (*Med*) cancer; (*dello zodiaco*): **C~** Cancer

candeg'gina [kanded'dʒina] *sf* bleach

can'dela *sf* candle; **candela (di accensione)** (*Aut*) spark(ing) plug

cande'labro *sm* candelabra

candeli'ere *sm* candlestick

candi'dare *vt* to present as candidate; **candidarsi** *vpr* to present o.s. as candidate

candi'dato, -a *sm/f* candidate; (*aspirante a una carica*) applicant

candido, -a *ag* white as snow; (*puro*) pure; (*sincero*) sincere, candid

can'dito, -a *ag* candied

cane *sm* dog; (*di pistola, fucile*) cock; **fa un freddo ~** it's bitterly cold; **non c'era un ~** there wasn't a soul; **cane da caccia/da guardia** hunting/guard dog; **cane lupo** Alsatian; **cane pastore** sheepdog

ca'nestro *sm* basket

can'guro *sm* kangaroo

ca'nile *sm* kennel; (*di allevamento*) kennels *pl*; **canile municipale** dog pound

canna *sf* (*pianta*) reed; (: *indica, da zucchero*) cane; (*bastone*) stick, cane; (*di fucile*) barrel; (*di organo*) pipe; (*fam: droga*) joint; **canna fumaria** chimney flue; **canna da pesca** (fishing) rod; **canna da zucchero** sugar cane

cannel'loni *smpl pasta tubes stuffed with sauce and baked*

cannocchi'ale [kannok'kjale] *sm* telescope

can'none *sm* (*Mil*) gun; (*Storia*) cannon; (*tubo*) pipe, tube; (*piega*) box pleat; (*fig*) ace

can'nuccia, -ce [kan'nuttʃa] *sf* (drinking) straw

ca'noa *sf* canoe

canone *sm* canon, criterion; (*mensile, annuo*) rent; fee

canot'taggio [kanot'taddʒo] *sm* rowing

canotti'era *sf* vest

ca'notto *sm* small boat, dinghy; canoe

can'tante *sm/f* singer

can'tare *vt*, *vi* to sing; **cantau'tore, -'trice** *sm/f* singer-composer

canti'ere *sm* (*Edil*) (building) site; (*cantiere navale*) shipyard

can'tina *sf* cellar; (*bottega*) wine shop; **cantina sociale** cooperative winegrowers' association

> Attenzione! In inglese esiste la parola *canteen*, che però significa *mensa*.

canto *sm* song; (*arte*) singing; (*Rel*) chant; chanting; (*poesia*) poem, lyric; (*parte di una poesia*) canto; (*parte, lato*): **da un ~** on the one hand; **d'altro ~** on the other hand

canzo'nare [kantso'nare] *vt* to tease

can'zone [kan'tsone] *sf* song; (*Poesia*) canzone

caos *sm inv* chaos; **ca'otico, -a, -ci, -che** *ag* chaotic

CAP *sigla m* = **codice di avviamento postale**

ca'pace [ka'patʃe] *ag* able, capable; (*ampio, vasto*) large, capacious; **sei ~ di farlo?** can you *o* are you able to do it?; **capacità** *sf inv* ability; (*Dir, di recipiente*) capacity

ca'panna *sf* hut

capan'none *sm* (*Agr*) barn; (*fabbricato industriale*) (factory) shed

ca'parbio, -a *ag* stubborn

ca'parra *sf* deposit, down payment

ca'pello *sm* hair; **capelli** *smpl* (*capigliatura*) hair *sg*

ca'pezzolo [ka'pettsolo] *sm* nipple

ca'pire *vt* to understand; **non capisco** I don't understand

capi'tale *ag* (*mortale*) capital; (*fondamentale*) main, chief ▷ *sf* (*città*) capital ▷ *sm* (*Econ*) capital

capi'tano *sm* captain

capi'tare *vi* (*giungere casualmente*) to happen to go, find o.s.; (*accadere*) to happen; (*presentarsi: cosa*) to turn up, present itself ▷ *vb impers* to happen; **mi è capitato un guaio** I've had a spot of trouble

capi'tello *sm* (*Archit*) capital

ca'pitolo *sm* chapter

capi'tombolo *sm* headlong fall, tumble

'capo *sm* head; (*persona*) head, leader; (: *in ufficio*) head, boss; (: *in tribù*) chief; (*di oggetti*) head; top; end; (*Geo*) cape; **andare a ~** to start a new paragraph; **da ~** over again; **capo di bestiame** head *inv* of cattle; **capo di vestiario** item of clothing; **Capo'danno** *sm* New Year; **capo'giro** *sm* dizziness *no pl*; **capola'voro, -i** *sm* masterpiece; **capo'linea** (*pl* **capi'linea**) *sm* terminus; **capostazi'one** (*pl* **capistazi'one**) *sm* station master

capo'tavola (*pl*(*m*) **capi'tavola**) *pl*(*f*) *inv sm/f* (*persona*) head of the table; **sedere a ~** to sit at the head of the table

capo'volgere [kapo'voldʒere] *vt* to overturn; (*fig*) to reverse; **capovolgersi** *vpr* to overturn; (*barca*) to capsize; (*fig*) to be reversed

'cappa *sf* (*mantello*) cape, cloak; (*del camino*) hood

cap'pella *sf* (*Rel*) chapel

cap'pello *sm* hat

'cappero *sm* caper

cap'pone *sm* capon

cap'potto *sm* (over)coat

cappuc'cino [kapput'tʃino] *sm* (*frate*) Capuchin monk; (*bevanda*) cappuccino, frothy white coffee

cap'puccio [kap'puttʃo] *sm* (*copricapo*) hood; (*della biro*) cap

'capra *sf* (she-)goat

ca'priccio [ka'prittʃo] *sm* caprice, whim; (*bizza*) tantrum; **fare i capricci** to be very naughty; **capricci'oso, -a** *ag* capricious, whimsical; naughty

Capri'corno *sm* Capricorn

capri'ola *sf* somersault

capri'olo *sm* roe deer

'capro *sm* **~ espiatorio** scapegoat

ca'prone *sm* billy-goat

'capsula *sf* capsule; (*di arma, per bottiglie*) cap

cap'tare *vt* (*Radio, TV*) to pick up; (*cattivarsi*) to gain, win

carabini'ere *sm* member of Italian military police force

ca'raffa *sf* carafe

Ca'raibi *smpl* **il mar dei ~** the Caribbean (Sea)

cara'mella *sf* sweet

ca'rattere *sm* character; (*caratteristica*) characteristic, trait; **avere un buon ~** to be good-natured; **carattere jolly** wild card; **caratte'ristica, -che** *sf* characteristic, trait, peculiarity; **caratte'ristico, -a, -ci, -che** *ag* characteristic

car'bone *sm* coal

carbu'rante *sm* (*motor*) fuel

carbura'tore *sm* carburettor

carce'rato, -a [kartʃe'rato] *sm/f* prisoner

'carcere ['kartʃere] *sm* prison; (*pena*) imprisonment

carci'ofo [kar'tʃɔfo] *sm* artichoke

cardel'lino *sm* goldfinch

car'diaco, -a, -ci, -che *ag* cardiac, heart *cpd*

cardi'nale *ag, sm* cardinal

'cardine *sm* hinge

'cardo *sm* thistle

ca'rente *ag* **~ di** lacking in

cares'tia *sf* famine; (*penuria*) scarcity, dearth

ca'rezza [ka'rettsa] *sf* caress

'carica, -che *sf* (*mansione ufficiale*) office, position; (*Mil, Tecn, Elettr*) charge; **ha una forte ~ di simpatia** he's very likeable; *vedi anche* **carico**

caricabatte'ria *sm inv* battery charger

cari'care *vt* (*merce, Inform*) to load; (*orologio*) to wind up; (*batteria, Mil*) to charge

'carico, -a, -chi, -che *ag* (*che porta un peso*): **~ di** loaded o laden with; (*fucile*) loaded; (*orologio*) wound up; (*batteria*) charged; (*colore*) deep; (*caffè, tè*) strong ▷ *sm* (*il caricare*) loading; (*ciò che si carica*) load; (*fig: peso*) burden, weight; **persona a ~ dependent**; **essere a ~ di qn** (*spese ecc*) to be charged to sb

'carie *sf* (*dentaria*) decay

ca'rino, -a *ag* (*grazioso*) lovely, pretty, nice; (*riferito a uomo, anche simpatico*) nice

carità *sf* charity; **per ~!** (*escl di rifiuto*) good heavens, no!

carnagi'one [karna'dʒone] *sf* complexion

'carne *sf* flesh; (*bovina, ovina ecc*) meat; **non mangio ~** I don't eat meat; **carne di maiale/manzo/pecora** pork/beef/mutton; **carne in scatola** tinned o canned meat; **carne tritata** o **macinata** mince (*BRIT*), hamburger meat (*US*), minced (*BRIT*) o ground (*US*) meat

carne'vale *sm* carnival

'**caro, -a** *ag* (*amato*) dear; (*costóso*) dear,
expensive; **è troppo ~** it's too expensive

ca'rogna [ka'roɲɲa] *sf* carrion; (*anche: fig:
fam*) swine

ca'rota *sf* carrot

caro'vana *sf* caravan

car'poni *av* on all fours

car'rabile *ag* suitable for vehicles; **"passo
~"** "keep clear"

carreggi'ata [karred'dʒata] *sf*
carriageway (BRIT), (road)way

car'rello *sm* trolley; (Aer) undercarriage;
(Cinema) dolly; (*di macchina da scrivere*)
carriage

carri'era *sf* career; **fare ~** to get on; **a gran
~** at full speed

carri'ola *sf* wheelbarrow

'**carro** *sm* cart, wagon; **carro armato**
tank; **carro attrezzi** breakdown van

car'rozza [kar'rɔttsa] *sf* carriage, coach

carrozze'ria [karrottse'ria] *sf* body,
coachwork (BRIT); (*officina*) coachbuilder's
workshop (BRIT), body shop

carroz'zina [karrot'tsina] *sf* pram (BRIT),
baby carriage (US)

'**carta** *sf* paper; (*al ristorante*) menu; (Geo)
map; plan; (*documento*) card; (*costituzione*)
charter; **carte** *sfpl* (*documenti*) papers,
documents; **alla ~** (*al ristorante*) à la
carte; **carta assegni** bank card; **carta
assorbente** blotting paper; **carta bollata**
o **da bollo** official stamped paper; **carta
(da gioco)** playing card; **carta di credito**
credit card; **carta (geografica)** map;
carta d'identità identity card; **carta
igienica** toilet paper; **carta d'imbarco**
(Aer, Naut) boarding card; **carta da lettere**
writing paper; **carta da pacchi** wrapping
paper; **carta da parati** wallpaper; **carta
libera** (Amm) unstamped paper; **carta
stradale** road map; **carta verde** (Aut)
green card; **carta vetrata** sandpaper;
carta da visita visiting card

car'taccia, -ce [kar'tattʃa] *sf* waste paper

carta'pesta *sf* papier-mâché

car'tella *sf* (*scheda*) card; (*Inform, custodia:
di cartone*) folder; (: *di uomo d'affari ecc*)
briefcase; (: *di scolaro*) schoolbag, satchel;
cartella clinica (Med) case sheet

cartel'lino *sm* (*etichetta*) label; (*su porta*)
notice; (*scheda*) card; **timbrare il ~**
(*all'entrata*) to clock in; (*all'uscita*) to clock
out; **cartellino di presenza** clock card,
timecard

car'tello *sm* sign; (*pubblicitario*) poster;
(*stradale*) sign, signpost; (Econ) cartel; (*in
dimostrazioni*) placard; **cartello stradale**
sign; **cartel'lone** *sm* (*della tombola*)
scoring frame; (Teatro) playbill; **tenere il
cartellone** (*spettacolo*) to have a long run;
cartellone pubblicitario advertising
poster

car'tina *sf* (Aut, Geo) map; **può
indicarmelo sulla ~?** can you show it to
me on the map?

car'toccio [kar'tɔttʃo] *sm* paper bag

cartole'ria *sf* stationer's (shop)

carto'lina *sf* postcard; **cartolina postale**
ready-stamped postcard

car'tone *sm* cardboard; (Arte) cartoon;
cartoni animati (Cinema) cartoons

car'tuccia, -ce [kar'tuttʃa] *sf* cartridge

'**casa** *sf* house; (*in senso astratto*) home;
(Comm) firm, house; **essere a ~** to be at
home; **vado a ~ mia/tua** I'm going home/
to your house; **vino della ~** house wine;
casa di cura nursing home; **casa editrice**
publishing house; **Casa delle Libertà**
centre-right coalition; **casa di riposo** (old
people's) home, care home; **case popolari**
≈ council houses (o flats) (BRIT), ≈ public
housing units (US); **casa dello studente**
student hostel

ca'sacca, -che *sf* military coat; (*di fantino*)
blouse

casa'linga, -ghe *sf* housewife

casa'lingo, -a, -ghi, -ghe *ag* household,
domestic; (*fatto a casa*) home-made;
(*semplice*) homely; (*amante della casa*)
home-loving

cas'care *vi* to fall; **cas'cata** *sf* fall;
(*d'acqua*) cascade, waterfall

cascherò *ecc* [kaske'rɔ] *vb vedi* **cascare**

'**casco, -schi** *sm* helmet; (*del parrucchiere*)
hair-drier; (*di banane*) bunch; **casco blu**
(Mil) blue helmet (UN soldier)

casei'ficio [kazei'fitʃo] *sm* creamery

ca'sella *sf* pigeon-hole; **casella postale**
post office box

ca'sello *sm* (*di autostrada*) toll-house

ca'serma *sf* barracks *pl*

ca'sino (*fam*) *sm* brothel; (*confusione*) row,
racket

casinò *sm inv* casino

'**caso** *sm* chance; (*fatto, vicenda*) event,
incident; (*possibilità*) possibility; (Med,

Ling) case; **a ~** at random; **per ~** by chance, by accident; **in ogni ~, in tutti i casi** in any case, at any rate; **al ~** should the opportunity arise; **nel ~ che** in case; **~ mai** if by chance; **caso limite** borderline case

caso'lare *sm* cottage

'caspita *escl* (*di sorpresa*) good heavens!; (*di impazienza*) for goodness' sake!

'cassa *sf* case, crate, box; (*bara*) coffin; (*mobile*) chest; (*involucro: di orologio ecc*) case; (*macchina*) cash register, till; (*luogo di pagamento*) checkout (counter); (*fondo*) fund; (*istituto bancario*) bank; **cassa automatica prelievi** cash dispenser; **cassa continua** night safe; **cassa mutua** *o* **malattia** health insurance scheme; **cassa integrazione: mettere in cassa integrazione** = to lay off; **cassa di risparmio** savings bank; **cassa toracica** (*Anat*) chest

cassa'forte (*pl* **casse'forti**) *sf* safe; **lo potrebbe mettere nella ~?** could you put this in the safe, please?

cassa'panca (*pl* **cassa'panche** *o* **casse'panche**) *sf* settle

casseru'ola *sf* saucepan

cas'setta *sf* box; (*per registratore*) cassette; (*Cinema, Teatro*) box-office takings *pl*; **film di ~** box-office draw; **cassetta di sicurezza** strongbox; **cassetta delle lettere** letterbox

cas'setto *sm* drawer

cassi'ere, -a *sm/f* cashier; (*di banca*) teller

casso'netto *sm* wheelie-bin

cas'tagna [kas'taɲɲa] *sf* chestnut

cas'tagno [kas'taɲɲo] *sm* chestnut (tree)

cas'tano, -a *ag* chestnut (brown)

cas'tello *sm* castle; (*Tecn*) scaffolding

casti'gare *vt* to punish; **cas'tigo, -ghi** *sm* punishment

cas'toro *sm* beaver

casu'ale *ag* chance *cpd*; (*Inform*) random *cpd*

catalizza'tore [kataliddza'tore] *sm* (*anche fig*) catalyst; (*Aut*) catalytic converter

ca'talogo, -ghi *sm* catalogue

catarifran'gente [katarifran'dʒɛnte] *sm* (*Aut*) reflector

ca'tarro *sm* catarrh

ca'tastrofe *sf* catastrophe, disaster

catego'ria *sf* category

ca'tena *sf* chain; **catena di montaggio** assembly line; **catene da neve** (*Aut*) snow chains; **cate'nina** *sf* (*gioiello*) (thin) chain

cate'ratta *sf* cataract; (*chiusa*) sluice-gate

ca'tino *sm* basin

ca'trame *sm* tar

'cattedra *sf* teacher's desk; (*di docente*) chair

catte'drale *sf* cathedral

catti'veria *sf* malice, spite; naughtiness; (*atto*) spiteful act; (*parole*) malicious *o* spiteful remark

cat'tivo, -a *ag* bad; (*malvagio*) bad, wicked; (*turbolento: bambino*) bad, naughty; (*: mare*) rough; (*odore, sapore*) nasty, bad

cat'tolico, -a, -ci, -che *ag, sm/f* (Roman) Catholic

cattu'rare *vt* to capture

'causa *sf* cause; (*Dir*) lawsuit, case, action; **a ~ di, per ~ di** because of; **fare** *o* **muovere ~ a qn** to take legal action against sb

cau'sare *vt* to cause

cau'tela *sf* caution, prudence

'cauto, -a *ag* cautious, prudent

cauzi'one [kaut'tsjone] *sf* security; (*Dir*) bail

'cava *sf* quarry

caval'care *vt* (*cavallo*) to ride; (*muro*) to sit astride; (*ponte*) to span; **caval'cata** *sf* ride; (*gruppo di persone*) riding party

cavalca'via *sm inv* flyover

cavalci'oni [kaval'tʃoni]: **a ~ di** *prep* astride

cavali'ere *sm* rider; (*feudale, titolo*) knight; (*soldato*) cavalryman; (*al ballo*) partner

caval'letta *sf* grasshopper

caval'letto *sm* (*Fot*) tripod; (*da pittore*) easel

ca'vallo *sm* horse; (*Scacchi*) knight; (*Aut: anche: ~ vapore*) horsepower; (*dei pantaloni*) crotch; **a ~** on horseback; **a ~ di** astride, straddling; **cavallo di battaglia** (*fig*) hobby-horse; **cavallo di corsa** racehorse; **cavallo a dondolo** rocking horse

ca'vare *vt* (*togliere*) to draw out, extract, take out; (*: giacca, scarpe*) to take off; (*: fame, sete, voglia*) to satisfy; **cavarsela** to manage, get on all right; (*scamparla*) to get away with it

cava'tappi *sm inv* corkscrew

ca'verna *sf* cave

'cavia *sf* guinea pig

cavi'ale *sm* caviar

ca'viglia [ka'viʎʎa] *sf* ankle

'cavo, -a *ag* hollow ▷ *sm* (*Anat*) cavity; (*corda, Elettr, Tel*) cable

cavo'letto *sm* **~ di Bruxelles** Brussels sprout

cavolfi'ore *sm* cauliflower

'cavolo *sm* cabbage; (*fam*): **non m'importa un ~** I don't give a damn

'cazzo ['kattso] *sm* (*fam!: pene*) prick (!); **non gliene importa un ~** (*fig fam!*) he doesn't give a damn about it; **fatti i**

cazzi tuoi (*fig fam!*) mind your own damn business

C.C.D. *sigla m* (= *Centro Cristiano Democratico*) Italian political party of the centre

CD *sm inv* CD; (*lettore*) CD player

CD-Rom [tʃidi'rom] *sm inv* CD-ROM

C.D.U. *sigla m* (= *Cristiano Democratici Uniti*) Italian centre-right political party

ce [tʃe] *pron*, *av vedi* **ci**

Ce'cenia [tʃe'tʃenja] *sf* **la ~** Chechnya

ce'ceno, -a [tʃe'tʃeno] *sm/f*, *ag* Chechen

'ceco, -a, -chi, -che ['tʃɛko] *ag*, *sm/f* Czech; **la Repubblica Ceca** the Czech Republic

'cedere ['tʃedere] *vt* (*concedere posto*) to give up; (*Dir*) to transfer, make over ▷ *vi* (*cadere*) to give way, subside; **~ (a)** to surrender (to), yield (to), give in (to)

'cedola ['tʃedola] *sf* (*Comm*) coupon; voucher

'ceffo ['tʃeffo] (*peg*) *sm* ugly mug

cef'fone [tʃef'fone] *sm* slap, smack

cele'brare [tʃele'brare] *vt* to celebrate

'celebre ['tʃelebre] *ag* famous, celebrated

ce'leste [tʃe'lɛste] *ag* celestial; heavenly; (*colore*) sky-blue

'celibe ['tʃelibe] *ag* single, unmarried

'cella ['tʃɛlla] *sf* cell; **cella frigorifera** cold store

'cellula ['tʃɛllula] *sf* (*Biol, Elettr, Pol*) cell; **cellu'lare** *sm* cellphone

cellu'lite [tʃellu'lite] *sf* cellulite

cemen'tare [tʃemen'tare] *vt* (*anche fig*) to cement

ce'mento [tʃe'mento] *sm* cement; **cemento armato** reinforced concrete

'cena ['tʃena] *sf* dinner; (*leggera*) supper

ce'nare [tʃe'nare] *vi* to dine, have dinner

'cenere ['tʃenere] *sf* ash

'cenno ['tʃenno] *sm* (*segno*) sign, signal; (*gesto*) gesture; (*col capo*) nod; (*con la mano*) wave; (*allusione*) hint, mention; (*breve esposizione*) short account; **far ~ di sì/no** to nod (one's head)/shake one's head

censi'mento [tʃensi'mento] *sm* census

cen'sura [tʃen'sura] *sf* censorship; censor's office; (*fig*) censure

cente'nario, -a [tʃente'narjo] *ag* (*che ha cento anni*) hundred-year-old; (*che ricorre ogni cento anni*) centennial, centenary *cpd* ▷ *sm/f* centenarian ▷ *sm* centenary

cen'tesimo, -a [tʃen'tezimo] *ag*, *sm* hundredth; (*di euro, dollaro*) cent

cen'tigrado, -a [tʃen'tigrado] *ag* centigrade; **20 gradi centigradi** 20 degrees centigrade

cen'timetro [tʃen'timetro] *sm* centimetre

centi'naio [tʃenti'najo] (*pl(f)* **-aia**) *sm* **un ~ (di)** a hundred; about a hundred

'cento ['tʃento] *num* a hundred, one hundred

cento'mila [tʃento'mila] *num* a o one hundred thousand; **te l'ho detto ~ volte** (*fig*) I've told you a thousand times

cen'trale [tʃen'trale] *ag* central ▷ *sf*: **centrale telefonica** (telephone) exchange; **centrale elettrica** electric power station; **centrali'nista** *sm/f* operator; **centra'lino** *sm* (telephone) exchange; (*di albergo ecc*) switchboard; **centralizzato, -a** [tʃentralid'dzato] *ag* central

cen'trare [tʃen'trare] *vt* to hit the centre of; (*Tecn*) to centre

cen'trifuga [tʃen'trifuga] *sf* spin-drier

'centro ['tʃentro] *sm* centre; **centro civico** civic centre; **centro commerciale** shopping centre; (*città*) commercial centre

'ceppo ['tʃeppo] *sm* (*di albero*) stump; (*pezzo di legno*) log

'cera ['tʃera] *sf* wax; (*aspetto*) appearance

ce'ramica, -che [tʃe'ramika] *sf* ceramic; (*Arte*) ceramics *sg*

cerbi'atto [tʃer'bjatto] *sm* (*Zool*) fawn

cer'care [tʃer'kare] *vt* to look for, search for ▷ *vi* **~ di fare qc** to try to do sth; **stiamo cercando un albergo/ristorante** we're looking for a hotel/restaurant

cercherò ecc [tʃerke'rɔ] *vb vedi* **cercare**

'cerchia ['tʃerkja] *sf* circle

cerchietto [tʃer'kjetto] *sm* (*per capelli*) hairband

'cerchio ['tʃerkjo] *sm* circle; (*giocattolo, di botte*) hoop

cereali [tʃere'ali] *smpl* cereal *sg*

ceri'monia [tʃeri'mɔnja] *sf* ceremony

ce'rino [tʃe'rino] *sm* wax match

'cernia ['tʃernja] *sf* (*Zool*) stone bass

cerni'era [tʃer'njera] *sf* hinge; **cerniera lampo** zip (fastener) (*BRIT*), zipper (*US*)

'cero ['tʃero] *sm* (church) candle

ce'rotto [tʃe'rɔtto] *sm* sticking plaster

certa'mente [tʃerta'mente] *av* certainly

certifi'cato *sm* certificate; **certificato medico** medical certificate; **certificato di nascita/di morte** birth/death certificate

○ **PAROLA CHIAVE**

'certo, -a ['tʃerto] *ag* (*sicuro*): **certo (di/che)** certain o sure (of/that) ▷ *det* **1** (*tale*) certain; **un certo signor Smith** a (certain) Mr Smith

2 (*qualche: con valore intensivo*) some; **dopo un certo tempo** after some time; **un fatto di una certa importanza** a matter of some importance; **di una certa età**

past one's prime, not so young
▷ pron **certi, e** pl some ▷ av (certamente)
certainly; (senz'altro) of course; **di certo**
certainly; **no (di) certo!, certo che**
no! certainly not!; **sì certo** yes indeed,
certainly

cer'vello, -i [tʃer'vɛllo] (Anat) (pl(f) **-a**) sm
brain; **cervello elettronico** computer
'cervo, -a ['tʃɛrvo] sm/f stag/doe ▷ sm
deer; **cervo volante** stag beetle
ces'puglio [tʃes'puʎʎo] sm bush
ces'sare [tʃes'sare] vi, vt to stop, cease; **~ di**
fare qc to stop doing sth
ces'tino [tʃes'tino] sm basket; (per la carta
straccia) wastepaper basket; **cestino da**
viaggio (Ferr) packed lunch (o dinner)
'cesto ['tʃesto] sm basket
'ceto ['tʃeto] sm (social) class
cetrio'lino [tʃetrio'lino] sm gherkin
cetri'olo [tʃetri'ɔlo] sm cucumber
Cfr. abbr (= confronta) cf.
CGIL sigla f (= Confederazione Generale
Italiana del Lavoro) trades union organization
chat line [tʃæt'laen] sf inv chat room
chattare [tʃat'tare] vi (Inform) to chat
online

🔘 **PAROLA CHIAVE**

che [ke] pron **1** (relativo: persona: soggetto)
who; (: oggetto) whom, that; (: cosa,
animale) which, that; **il ragazzo che è**
venuto the boy who came; **l'uomo che io**
vedo the man (whom) I see; **il libro che è**
sul tavolo the book which o that is on the
table; **il libro che vedi** the book (which o
that) you see; **la sera che ti ho visto** the
evening I saw you
2 (interrogativo, esclamativo) what; **che**
(cosa) fai? what are you doing?; **a che**
(cosa) pensi? what are you thinking
about?; **non sa che (cosa) fare** he doesn't
know what to do; **ma che dici!** what are
you saying!
3 (indefinito): **quell'uomo ha un che**
di losco there's something suspicious
about that man; **un certo non so che** an
indefinable something
▷ det **1** (interrogativo: tra tanti) what; (: tra
pochi) which; **che tipo di film preferisci?**
what sort of film do you prefer?; **che**
vestito ti vuoi mettere? what (o which)
dress do you want to put on?
2 (esclamativo: seguito da aggettivo) how;
(: seguito da sostantivo) what; **che buono!**
how delicious!; **che bel vestito!** what a
lovely dress!
▷ cong **1** (con proposizioni subordinate) that;

credo che verrà I think he'll come; **voglio**
che tu studi I want you to study; **so che**
tu c'eri I know (that) you were there; **non**
che, non che sia sbagliato, ma ... not
that it's wrong, but ...
2 (finale) so that; **vieni qua, che ti veda**
come here, so (that) I can see you
3 (temporale): **arrivai che eri già partito**
you had already left when I arrived; **sono**
anni che non lo vedo I haven't seen him
for years
4 (in frasi imperative, concessive): **che venga**
pure! let him come by all means!; **che tu**
sia benedetto! may God bless you!
5 (comparativo: con più, meno) than; vedi
anche **più**; **meno**; **così** ecc

chemiotera'pia [kemjotera'pia] sf
chemotherapy
chero'sene [kero'zɛne] sm kerosene

🔘 **PAROLA CHIAVE**

chi [ki] pron **1** (interrogativo: soggetto) who;
(: oggetto) who, whom; **chi è?** who is it?; **di**
chi è questo libro? whose book is this?,
whose is this book?; **con chi parli?** who are
you talking to?; **a chi pensi?** who are you
thinking about?; **chi di voi?** which of you?;
non so a chi rivolgermi I don't know who
to ask
2 (relativo) whoever, anyone who; **dillo a**
chi vuoi tell whoever you like
3 (indefinito): **chi ... chi ...** some ...
others ...; **chi dice una cosa, chi dice**
un'altra some say one thing, others say
another

chiacchie'rare [kjakkje'rare] vi to chat;
(discorrere futilmente) to chatter; (far
pettegolezzi) to gossip; **chi'acchiere** sfpl
fare due o quattro chiacchiere to have
a chat
chia'mare [kja'mare] vt to call; (rivolgersi
a qn) to call (in), send for; **chiamarsi** vpr
(aver nome) to be called; **come ti chiami?**
what's your name?; **mi chiamo Paolo**
my name is Paolo, I'm called Paolo; **~ alle**
armi to call up; **~ in giudizio** to summon;
chia'mata sf (Tel) call; (Mil) call-up
chia'rezza [kja'rettsa] sf clearness; clarity
chia'rire [kja'rire] vt to make clear; (fig:
spiegare) to clear up, explain
chi'aro, -a ['kjaro] ag clear; (luminoso)
clear, bright; (colore) pale, light
chi'asso ['kjasso] sm uproar, row
chi'ave ['kjave] sf key ▷ ag inv key cpd;
posso avere la mia ~? can I have my key?;
chiave d'accensione (Aut) ignition key;

chiave di volta keystone; **chiave inglese** monkey wrench

chi'azza ['kjattsa] sf stain; splash

'chicco, -chi ['kikko] sm grain; (di caffè) bean; **chicco d'uva** grape

chi'edere ['kjɛdere] vt (per sapere) to ask; (per avere) to ask for ▷ **~ di qn** to ask after sb; (al telefono) to ask for o want sb; **~ qc a qn** to ask sb sth; to ask sb for sth; **chiedersi** vpr **chiedersi (se)** to wonder (whether)

chi'esa ['kjɛza] sf church

chi'esi ecc ['kjɛzi] vb vedi **chiedere**

'chiglia ['kiʎʎa] sf keel

'chilo ['kilo] sm kilo; **chi'lometro** sm kilometre

'chimica ['kimika] sf chemistry

'chimico, -a, -ci, -che ['kimiko] ag chemical ▷ sm/f chemist

chi'nare [ki'nare] vt to lower, bend; **chinarsi** vpr to stoop, bend

chi'occiola ['kjɔttʃola] sf snail; (di indirizzo e-mail) at sign, @; **scala a ~** spiral staircase

chi'odo ['kjɔdo] sm nail; (fig) obsession; **chiodo di garofano** (Cuc) clove

chi'osco, -schi ['kjɔsko] sm kiosk, stall

chi'ostro ['kjɔstro] sm cloister

chiro'mante [kiro'mante] sm/f palmist

chirur'gia [kirur'dʒia] sf surgery; **chirurgia estetica** cosmetic surgery; **chi'rurgo, -ghi** o gi sm surgeon

chissà [kis'sa] av who knows, I wonder

chi'tarra [ki'tarra] sf guitar

chitar'rista, -i, e [kitar'rista] sm/f guitarist, guitar player

chi'udere ['kjudere] vt to close, shut; (luce, acqua) to put off, turn off; (definitivamente: fabbrica) to close down, shut down; (strada) to close; (recingere) to enclose; (porre termine a) to end ▷ vi to close, shut; to close down, shut down; to end; **chiudersi** vpr to shut, close; (ritirarsi: anche fig) to shut o.s. away; (ferita) to close up; **a che ora chiudete?** what time do you close?

chi'unque [ki'unkwe] pron (relativo) whoever; (indefinito) anyone, anybody; **~ sia** whoever it is

chi'usi ecc ['kjusi] vb vedi **chiudere**

chi'uso, -a ['kjuso] pp di **chiudere** ▷ sf (di corso d'acqua) sluice, lock; (recinto) enclosure; (di discorso ecc) conclusion, ending; **chiu'sura** sf (vedi **chiudere**) closing; shutting; closing o shutting down; enclosing; putting o turning off; ending; (dispositivo) catch; fastening; fastener; **chiusura lampo®** zip (fastener) (BRIT), zipper (US)

C.I. abbr = **carta d'identità**

PAROLA CHIAVE

ci [tʃi] (dav lo, la, li, le, ne diventa **ce**) pron **1** (personale: complemento oggetto) us; (: a noi: complemento di termine) (to) us; (: riflessivo) ourselves; (: reciproco) each other, one another; (impersonale): **ci si veste** we get dressed; **ci ha visti** he's seen us; **non ci ha dato niente** he gave us nothing; **ci vestiamo** we get dressed; **ci amiamo** we love one another o each other

2 (dimostrativo: di ciò, su ciò, in ciò ecc) about (o on o of) it; **non so cosa farci** I don't know what to do about it; **che c'entro io?** what have I got to do with it?
▷ av (qui) here; (lì) there; (moto attraverso luogo): **ci passa sopra un ponte** a bridge passes over it; **non ci passa più nessuno** nobody comes this way any more; **esserci** vedi **essere**

cia'batta [tʃa'batta] sf slipper; (pane) ciabatta

ciam'bella [tʃam'bɛlla] sf (Cuc) ring-shaped cake; (salvagente) rubber ring

ci'ao ['tʃao] escl (all'arrivo) hello!; (alla partenza) cheerio! (BRIT), bye!

cias'cuno, -a [tʃas'kuno] (det: dav sm: **ciascun** +C, V, **ciascuno** +s impura, gn, pn, ps, x, z; dav sf: **ciascuna** +C, **ciascun'** +V) det every, each; (ogni) every ▷ pron each (one); (tutti) everyone, everybody

ci'barie [tʃi'barje] sfpl foodstuffs

cibernauta, -i, -e [tʃiber'nauta] sm/f Internet surfer

ciberspazio [tʃiber'spattsjo] sm cyberspace

'cibo ['tʃibo] sm food

ci'cala [tʃi'kala] sf cicada

cica'trice [tʃika'tritʃe] sf scar

'cicca ['tʃikka] sf cigarette end

'ciccia ['tʃittʃa] sf (fam) fat

cicci'one, -a [tʃit'tʃone] sm/f (fam) fatty

cicla'mino [tʃikla'mino] sm cyclamen

ci'clismo [tʃi'klizmo] sm cycling; **ci'clista, -i, -e** sm/f cyclist

'ciclo ['tʃiklo] sm cycle; (di malattia) course

ciclomo'tore [tʃiklomo'tore] sm moped

ci'clone [tʃi'klone] sm cyclone

ci'cogna [tʃi'koɲɲa] sf stork

ci'eco, -a, -chi, -che ['tʃɛko] ag blind ▷ sm/f blind man/woman

ci'elo ['tʃɛlo] sm sky; (Rel) heaven

'cifra ['tʃifra] sf (numero) figure; numeral; (somma di denaro) sum, figure; (monogramma) monogram, initials pl; (codice) code, cipher

'ciglio, -i ['tʃiʎʎo] *(delle palpebre)* *(pl(f)* **ciglia)** *sm (margine)* edge, verge; *(eye)*lash; *(eye)*lid; *(sopracciglio)* eyebrow

'cigno ['tʃiɲɲo] *sm* swan

cigo'lare [tʃigo'lare] *vi* to squeak, creak

'Cile ['tʃile] *sm* **il ~** Chile

ci'leno, -a [tʃi'lɛno] *ag, sm/f* Chilean

cili'egia, -gie o **ge** [tʃi'ljɛdʒa] *sf* cherry

ciliegina [tʃilje'dʒina] *sf* glacé cherry

cilin'drata [tʃilin'drata] *sf (Aut)* (cubic) capacity; **una macchina di grossa ~** a big-engined car

ci'lindro [tʃi'lindro] *sm* cylinder; *(cappello)* top hat

'cima ['tʃima] *sf (sommità)* top; *(di monte)* top, summit; *(estremità)* end; **in ~ a** at the top of; **da ~ a fondo** from top to bottom; *(fig)* from beginning to end

'cimice ['tʃimitʃe] *sf (Zool)* bug; *(puntina)* drawing pin *(BRIT)*, thumbtack *(US)*

cimini'era [tʃimi'njɛra] *sf* chimney; *(di nave)* funnel

cimi'tero [tʃimi'tɛro] *sm* cemetery

'Cina ['tʃina] *sf* **la ~** China

cin'cin [tʃin'tʃin] *escl* cheers!

'cinema ['tʃinema] *sm inv* cinema

ci'nese [tʃi'nese] *ag, sm/f, sm* Chinese *inv*

'cinghia ['tʃingja] *sf* strap; *(cintura, Tecn)* belt

cinghi'ale [tʃin'gjale] *sm* wild boar

cinguet'tare [tʃingwet'tare] *vi* to twitter

'cinico, -a, -ci, -che ['tʃiniko] *ag* cynical ▷ *sm/f* cynic

cin'quanta [tʃin'kwanta] *num* fifty; **cinquan'tesimo, -a** *num* fiftieth

cinquan'tina [tʃinkwan'tina] *sf (serie)*: **una ~ (di)** about fifty; *(età)*: **essere sulla ~** to be about fifty

'cinque ['tʃinkwe] *num* five; **avere ~ anni** to be five (years old); **il ~ dicembre 1998** the fifth of December 1998; **alle ~ (ora)** at five (o'clock)

cinque'cento [tʃinkwe'tʃɛnto] *num* five hundred ▷ *sm* **il C~** the sixteenth century

cin'tura [tʃin'tura] *sf* belt; **cintura di salvataggio** lifebelt *(BRIT)*, life preserver *(US)*; **cintura di sicurezza** *(Aut, Aer)* safety o seat belt

cintu'rino [tʃintu'rino] *sm* strap; **~ dell'orologio** watch strap

ciò [tʃɔ] *pron* this; that; **~ che** what; **~ nonostante** o **nondimeno** nevertheless, in spite of that

ci'occa, -che ['tʃɔkka] *sf (di capelli)* lock

ciocco'lata [tʃokko'lata] *sf* chocolate; *(bevanda)* (hot) chocolate; **cioccola'tino** *sm* chocolate

cioè [tʃo'ɛ] *av* that is (to say)

ci'otola ['tʃɔtola] *sf* bowl

ci'ottolo ['tʃɔttolo] *sm* pebble; *(di strada)* cobble(stone)

ci'polla [tʃi'polla] *sf* onion; *(di tulipano ecc)* bulb

cipol'lina [tʃipol'lina] *sf* **cipolline sottaceto** pickled onions

ci'presso [tʃi'presso] *sm* cypress (tree)

'cipria ['tʃiprja] *sf* (face) powder

'Cipro ['tʃipro] *sm* Cyprus

'circa ['tʃirka] *av* about, roughly ▷ *prep* about, concerning; **a mezzogiorno ~** about midday

'circo, -chi ['tʃirko] *sm* circus

circo'lare [tʃirko'lare] *vi* to circulate; *(Aut)* to drive (along), move (along) ▷ *ag* circular ▷ *sf (Amm)* circular; *(di autobus)* circle (line)

'circolo ['tʃirkolo] *sm* circle

circon'dare [tʃirkon'dare] *vt* to surround; **circondarsi** *vpr* **circondarsi di** to surround o.s. with

circonvallazi'one [tʃirkonvallat'tsjone] *sf* ring road *(BRIT)*, beltway *(US)*; *(per evitare una città)* by-pass

circos'petto, -a [tʃirkos'pɛtto] *ag* circumspect, cautious

circos'tante [tʃirkos'tante] *ag* surrounding, neighbouring

circos'tanza [tʃirkos'tantsa] *sf* circumstance; *(occasione)* occasion

cir'cuito [tʃir'kuito] *sm* circuit

CISL *sigla f* (= *Confederazione Italiana Sindacati Lavoratori*) *trades union organization*

cis'terna [tʃis'tɛrna] *sf* tank, cistern

'cisti ['tʃisti] *sf* cyst

cis'tite [tʃis'tite] *sf* cystitis

ci'tare [tʃi'tare] *vt (Dir)* to summon; *(autore)* to quote; *(a esempio, modello)* to cite

ci'tofono [tʃi'tɔfono] *sm* entry phone; *(in uffici)* intercom

città [tʃit'ta] *sf inv* town; *(importante)* city; **città universitaria** university campus

cittadi'nanza [tʃittadi'nantsa] *sf* citizens *pl*; *(Dir)* citizenship

citta'dino, -a [tʃitta'dino] *ag* town *cpd*; city *cpd* ▷ *sm/f (di uno Stato)* citizen; *(abitante di città)* townsman, city dweller

ci'uccio ['tʃuttʃo] *sm (fam)* comforter, dummy *(BRIT)*, pacifier *(US)*

ci'uffo ['tʃuffo] *sm* tuft

ci'vetta [tʃi'vetta] *sf (Zool)* owl; *(fig: donna)* coquette, flirt ▷ *ag inv* **auto/nave ~** decoy car/ship

'civico, -a, -ci, -che ['tʃiviko] *ag* civic; *(museo)* municipal, town *cpd*; city *cpd*

ci'vile [tʃi'vile] *ag* civil; *(non militare)* civilian; *(nazione)* civilized ▷ *sm* civilian

civiltà [tʃivil'ta] *sf* civilization; (*cortesia*) civility

'clacson *sm inv* (Aut) horn

clandes'tino, -a *ag* clandestine; (*Pol*) underground, clandestine; (*immigrato*) illegal ▷ *sm/f* stowaway; (*anche*: **immigrato ~**) illegal immigrant

'classe *sf* class; **di ~** (*fig*) with class; of excellent quality; **classe operaia** working class; **classe turistica** (Aer) economy class

'classico, -a, -ci, -che *ag* classical; (*tradizionale: moda*) classic(al) ▷ *sm* classic; classical author

clas'sifica *sf* classification; (*Sport*) placings *pl*

classifi'care *vt* to classify; (*candidato, compito*) to grade; **classificarsi** *vpr* to be placed

'clausola *sf* (Dir) clause

clavi'cembalo [klavi'tʃembalo] *sm* harpsichord

cla'vicola *sf* (Anat) collar bone

clic'care *vi* (Inform): **~ su** to click on

cli'ente *sm/f* customer, client

'clima, -i *sm* climate; **climatizzatore** *sm* air conditioning system

'clinica, -che *sf* (*scienza*) clinical medicine; (*casa di cura*) clinic, nursing home; (*settore d'ospedale*) clinic

clo'nare *vt* to clone; **clonazione** [klona'tsjone] *sf* cloning

'cloro *sm* chlorine

club *sm inv* club

c.m. *abbr* = **corrente mese**

cm *abbr* (= *centimetro*) cm

coalizi'one [koalit'tsjone] *sf* coalition

'COBAS *sigla mpl* (= *Comitati di base*) independent trades unions

'coca *sf* (*bibita*) Coke®; (*droga*) cocaine

coca'ina *sf* cocaine

cocci'nella [kottʃi'nɛlla] *sf* ladybird (BRIT), ladybug (US)

cocci'uto, -a [kot'tʃuto] *ag* stubborn, pigheaded

'cocco, -chi *sm* (*pianta*) coconut palm; (*frutto*): **noce di ~** coconut ▷ *sm/f* (*fam*) darling

cocco'drillo *sm* crocodile

cocco'lare *vt* to cuddle, fondle

cocerò *ecc* [kotʃe'rɔ] *vb vedi* **cuocere**

co'comero *sm* watermelon

'coda *sf* tail; (*fila di persone, auto*) queue (BRIT), line (US); (*di abiti*) train; **con la ~ dell'occhio** out of the corner of one's eye; **mettersi in ~** to queue (up) (BRIT), line up (US); to join the queue (BRIT) o line (US); **coda di cavallo** (*acconciatura*) ponytail

co'dardo, -a *ag* cowardly ▷ *sm/f* coward

'codice ['koditʃe] *sm* code; **codice di avviamento postale** postcode (BRIT), zip code (US); **codice a barre** bar code; **codice civile** civil code; **codice fiscale** tax code; **codice penale** penal code; **codice segreto** (*di tessera magnetica*) PIN (number); **codice della strada** highway code

coe'rente *ag* coherent

coe'taneo, -a *ag, sm/f* contemporary

'cofano *sm* (Aut) bonnet (BRIT), hood (US); (*forziere*) chest

'cogliere ['kɔʎʎere] *vt* (*fiore: frutto*) to pick, gather; (*sorprendere*) to catch, surprise; (*bersaglio*) to hit; (*fig: momento opportuno ecc*) to grasp, seize, take; (: *capire*) to grasp; **~ qn in flagrante** *o* **in fallo** to catch sb red-handed

co'gnato, -a [koɲ'ɲato] *sm/f* brother-/sister-in-law

co'gnome [koɲ'ɲome] *sm* surname

coinci'denza [kointʃi'dɛntsa] *sf* coincidence; (Ferr, Aer, *di autobus*) connection

coin'cidere [koin'tʃidere] *vi* to coincide

coin'volgere [koin'vɔldʒere] *vt* **~ in** to involve in

cola'pasta *sm inv* colander

co'lare *vt* (*liquido*) to strain; (*pasta*) to drain; (*oro fuso*) to pour ▷ *vi* (*sudore*) to drip; (*botte*) to leak; (*cera*) to melt; **~ a picco** *vt, vi* (*nave*) to sink

colazi'one [kolat'tsjone] *sf* breakfast; **fare ~** to have breakfast; **a che ora è servita la ~?** what time is breakfast?

co'lera *sm* (Med) cholera

'colgo *ecc* *vb vedi* **cogliere**

'colica *sf* (Med) colic

co'lino *sm* strainer

'colla *sf* glue; (*di farina*) paste

collabo'rare *vi* to collaborate; **~ a** to collaborate on; (*giornale*) to contribute to; **collabora'tore, -'trice** *sm/f* collaborator; contributor; **collaboratore esterno** freelance; **collaboratrice familiare** home help

col'lana *sf* necklace; (*collezione*) collection, series

col'lant [kɔ'lã] *sm inv* tights *pl*

col'lare *sm* collar

col'lasso *sm* (Med) collapse

collau'dare *vt* to test, try out

col'lega, -ghi, -ghe *sm/f* colleague

collega'mento *sm* connection; (*Mil*) liaison

colle'gare *vt* to connect, join, link; **collegarsi** *vpr* (Radio, TV) to link up; **collegarsi con** (Tel) to get through to

col'legio [kol'lɛdʒo] *sm* college; (*convitto*)

boarding school; **collegio elettorale** (*Pol*) constituency

'**collera** *sf* anger

col'**lerico, -a, -ci, -che** *ag* quick-tempered, irascible

col'**letta** *sf* collection

col'**letto** *sm* collar

collezio'**nare** [kollettsjo'nare] *vt* to collect

collezi'**one** [kollet'tsjone] *sf* collection

col'**lina** *sf* hill

col'**lirio** *sm* eyewash

'**collo** *sm* neck; (*di abito*) neck, collar; (*pacco*) parcel; **collo del piede** instep

colloca'**mento** *sm* (*impiego*) employment; (*disposizione*) placing, arrangement

collo'**care** *vt* (*libri, mobili*) to place; (*Comm: merce*) to find a market for

collocazi'**one** [kollokat'tsjone] *sf* placing; (*di libro*) classification

col'**loquio** *sm* conversation, talk; (*ufficiale, per un lavoro*) interview; (*Ins*) preliminary oral exam

col'**mare** *vt* ~ **di** (*anche fig*) to fill with; (*dare in abbondanza*) to load o overwhelm with

co'**lombo, -a** *sm/f* dove; pigeon

co'**lonia** *sf* colony; (*per bambini*) holiday camp; (**acqua di**) ~ (eau de) cologne

co'**lonna** *sf* column; **colonna sonora** (*Cinema*) sound track; **colonna vertebrale** spine, spinal column

colon'**nello** *sm* colonel

colo'**rante** *sm* colouring

colo'**rare** *vt* to colour; (*disegno*) to colour in

co'**lore** *sm* colour; **a colori** in colour, colour *cpd*; **farne di tutti i colori** to get up to all sorts of mischief; **vorrei un ~ diverso** I'd like a different colour

colo'**rito, -a** *ag* coloured; (*viso*) rosy, pink; (*linguaggio*) colourful ▷ *sm* (*tinta*) colour; (*carnagione*) complexion

'**colpa** *sf* fault; (*biasimo*) blame; (*colpevolezza*) guilt; (*azione colpevole*) offence; (*peccato*) sin; **di chi è la ~?** whose fault is it?; **è ~ sua** it's his fault; **per ~ di** through, owing to; **col'pevole** *ag* guilty

col'**pire** *vt* to hit, strike; (*fig*) to strike; **rimanere colpito da qc** to be amazed o struck by sth

'**colpo** *sm* (*urto*) knock; (: *affettivo*) blow, shock; (: *aggressivo*) blow; (*di pistola*) shot; (*Med*) stroke; (*rapina*) raid; **di ~** suddenly; **fare ~** to make a strong impression; **colpo d'aria** chill; **colpo in banca** bank job o raid; **colpo basso** (*Pugilato, fig*) punch below the belt; **colpo di fulmine** love at first sight; **colpo di grazia** coup de grâce; **colpo di scena** (*Teatro*) coup de théâtre; (*fig*) dramatic turn of events; **colpo di sole** sunstroke; **colpo di Stato** coup d'état; **colpo di telefono** phone call; **colpo di testa** (sudden) impulse o whim; **colpo di vento** gust (of wind); **colpi di sole** (*nei capelli*) highlights

'**colsi** *ecc vb vedi* **cogliere**

coltel'**lata** *sf* stab

col'**tello** *sm* knife; **coltello a serramanico** clasp knife

colti'**vare** *vt* to cultivate; (*verdura*) to grow, cultivate

'**colto, -a** *pp di* **cogliere** ▷ *ag* (*istruito*) cultured, educated

'**coma** *sm inv* coma

comanda'**mento** *sm* (*Rel*) commandment

coman'**dante** *sm* (*Mil*) commander, commandant; (*di reggimento*) commanding officer; (*Naut, Aer*) captain

coman'**dare** *vi* to be in command ▷ *vt* to command; (*imporre*) to order, command; ~ **a qn di fare** to order sb to do

combaci'**are** [komba'tʃare] *vi* to meet; (*fig: coincidere*) to coincide

com'**battere** *vt, vi* to fight

combi'**nare** *vt* to combine; (*organizzare*) to arrange; (*fam: fare*) to make, cause; **combinazi'one** *sf* combination; (*caso fortuito*) coincidence; **per combinazione** by chance

combus'**tibile** *ag* combustible ▷ *sm* fuel

○ **PAROLA CHIAVE**

'**come** *av* 1 (*alla maniera di*) like; **ti comporti come lui** you behave like him o like he does; **bianco come la neve** (as) white as snow; **come se** as if, as though

2 (*in qualità di*) as a; **lavora come autista** he works as a driver

3 (*interrogativo*) how; **come ti chiami?** what's your name?; **come sta?** how are you?; **com'è il tuo amico?** what is your friend like?; **come?** (*prego?*) pardon?, sorry?; **come mai?** how come?; **come mai non ci hai avvertiti?** why on earth didn't you warn us?

4 (*esclamativo*): **come sei bravo!** how clever you are!; **come mi dispiace!** I'm terribly sorry!

▷ *cong* 1 (*in che modo*) how; **mi ha spiegato come l'ha conosciuto** he told me how he met him

2 (*correlativo*) as; (*con comparativi di maggioranza*) than; **non è bravo come pensavo** he isn't as clever as I thought; **è**

meglio di come pensassi it's better than I thought

3 (*appena che, quando*) as soon as; **come arrivò, iniziò a lavorare** as soon as he arrived, he set to work; *vedi* **così**; **tanto**

'comico, -a, -ci, -che *ag* (*Teatro*) comic; (*buffo*) comical ▷ *sm* (*attore*) comedian, comic actor

cominci'are [komin'tʃare] *vt, vi* to begin, start; **~ a fare/col fare** to begin to do/by doing; **a che ora comincia il film?** when does the film start?

comi'tato *sm* committee

comi'tiva *sf* party, group

co'mizio [ko'mittsjo] *sm* (*Pol*) meeting, assembly

com'media *sf* comedy; (*opera teatrale*) play; (: *che fa ridere*) comedy; (*fig*) playacting *no pl*

commemo'rare *vt* to commemorate

commen'tare *vt* to comment on; (*testo*) to annotate; (*Radio, TV*) to give a commentary on

commerci'ale [kommer'tʃale] *ag* commercial, trading; (*peg*) commercial

commercia'lista, -i, e [kommertʃa'lista] *sm/f* (*laureato*) graduate in economics and commerce; (*consulente*) business consultant

commerci'ante [kommer'tʃante] *sm/f* trader, dealer; (*negoziante*) shopkeeper

commerci'are [kommer'tʃare] *vt, vi* **~ in** to deal *o* trade in

com'mercio [kom'mertʃo] *sm* trade, commerce; **essere in ~** (*prodotto*) to be on the market *o* on sale; **essere nel ~** (*persona*) to be in business; **commercio al dettaglio/all'ingrosso** retail/wholesale trade; **commercio elettronico** e-commerce

com'messo, -a *pp di* **commettere** ▷ *sm/f* shop assistant (BRIT), sales clerk (US) ▷ *sm* (*impiegato*) clerk; **commesso viaggiatore** commercial traveller

commes'tibile *ag* edible

com'mettere *vt* to commit

com'misi *ecc vb vedi* **commettere**

commissari'ato *sm* (*Amm*) commissionership; (: *sede*) commissioner's office; **commissariato di polizia** police station

commis'sario *sm* commissioner; (*di pubblica sicurezza*) ≈ (police) superintendent (BRIT), ≈ (police) captain (US); (*Sport*) steward; (*membro di commissione*) member of a committee *o* board

commissi'one *sf* (*incarico*) errand;

(*comitato, percentuale*) commission; (*Comm: ordinazione*) order; **commissioni** *sfpl* (*acquisti*) shopping *sg*; **commissioni bancarie** bank charges; **commissione d'esame** examining board

com'mosso, -a *pp di* **commuovere**

commo'vente *ag* moving

commozi'one [kommot'tsjone] *sf* emotion, deep feeling; **commozione cerebrale** (*Med*) concussion

commu'overe *vt* to move, affect; **commuoversi** *vpr* to be moved

como'dino *sm* bedside table

comodità *sf inv* comfort; convenience

'comodo, -a *ag* comfortable; (*facile*) easy; (*conveniente*) convenient; (*utile*) useful, handy ▷ *sm* comfort; convenience; **con ~** at one's convenience *o* leisure; **fare il proprio ~** to do as one pleases; **far ~** to be useful *o* handy

compa'gnia [kompaɲ'ɲia] *sf* company; (*gruppo*) gathering

com'pagno, -a [kom'paɲɲo] *sm/f* (*di classe, gioco*) companion; (*Pol*) comrade

com'paio *ecc vb vedi* **comparire**

compa'rare *vt* to compare

compara'tivo, -a *ag, sm* comparative

compa'rire *vi* to appear

com'parvi *ecc vb vedi* **comparire**

compassi'one *sf* compassion, pity; **avere ~ di qn** to feel sorry for sb, to pity sb

com'passo *sm* (pair of) compasses *pl*; callipers *pl*

compa'tibile *ag* (*scusabile*) excusable; (*conciliabile, Inform*) compatible

compa'tire *vt* (*aver compassione di*) to sympathize with, feel sorry for; (*scusare*) to make allowances for

com'patto, -a *ag* compact; (*roccia*) solid; (*folla*) dense; (*fig: gruppo, partito*) united

compen'sare *vt* (*equilibrare*) to compensate for, make up for; **~ qn di** (*rimunerare*) to pay *o* remunerate sb for; (*risarcire*) to pay compensation to sb for; (*fig: fatiche, dolori*) to reward sb for; **com'penso** *sm* compensation payment, remuneration; reward; **in compenso** (*d'altra parte*) on the other hand

compe'rare *vt* = **comprare**

'compere *sfpl* **fare ~** to do the shopping

compe'tente *ag* competent; (*mancia*) apt, suitable

com'petere *vi* to compete, vie; (*Dir: spettare*): **~ a** to lie within the competence of; **competizi'one** *sf* competition

compi'angere [kom'pjandʒere] *vt* to sympathize with, feel sorry for

'compiere *vt* (*concludere*) to finish, complete; (*adempiere*) to carry out, fulfil;

compiersi vpr (avverarsi) to be fulfilled, come true; ~ **gli anni** to have one's birthday

compi'lare vt (modulo) to fill in; (dizionario, elenco) to compile

'**compito** sm (incarico) task, duty; (dovere) duty; (Ins) exercise; (: a casa) piece of homework; **fare i compiti** to do one's homework

comple'anno sm birthday

complessità sf complexity

comples'sivo, -a ag (globale) comprehensive, overall; (totale: cifra) total

com'plesso, -a ag complex ▷ sm (Psic, Edil) complex; (Mus: corale) ensemble; (: orchestrina) band; (: di musica pop) group; **in** o **nel ~** on the whole; **complesso alberghiero** hotel complex; **complesso edilizio** building complex; **complesso vitaminico** vitamin complex

completa'mente av completely

comple'tare vt to complete

com'pleto, -a ag complete; (teatro, autobus) full ▷ sm suit; **al ~** full; (tutti presenti) all present; **completo da sci** ski suit

compli'care vt to complicate; **complicarsi** vpr to become complicated

'**complice** ['kɔmplitʃe] sm/f accomplice

complicità [komplitʃi'ta] sf inv complicity; **un sorriso/uno sguardo di ~** a knowing smile/look

complimen'tarsi vpr ~ **con** to congratulate

compli'mento sm compliment; **complimenti** smpl (cortesia eccessiva) ceremony sg; (ossequi) regards, compliments; **complimenti!** congratulations!; **senza complimenti!** don't stand on ceremony!; make yourself at home!; help yourself!

complot'tare vi to plot, conspire

com'plotto sm plot, conspiracy

com'pone ecc vb vedi **comporre**

compo'nente sm/f member ▷ sm component

com'pongo ecc vb vedi **comporre**

componi'mento sm (Dir) settlement; (Ins) composition; (poetico, teatrale) work

com'porre vt (musica, testo) to compose; (mettere in ordine) to arrange; (Dir: lite) to settle; (Tip) to set; (Tel) to dial; **comporsi** vpr **comporsi di** to consist of, be composed of

comporta'mento sm behaviour

compor'tare vt (implicare) to involve; **comportarsi** vpr to behave

com'posi ecc vb vedi **comporre**

composi'tore, -'trice sm/f composer;

(Tip) compositor, typesetter

com'posto, -a pp di **comporre** ▷ ag (persona) composed, self-possessed; (: decoroso) dignified; (formato da più elementi) compound cpd ▷ sm compound

com'prare vt to buy; **dove posso ~ delle cartoline?** where can I buy some postcards?

com'prendere vt (contenere) to comprise, consist of; (capire) to understand

compren'sibile ag understandable

comprensi'one sf understanding

compren'sivo, -a ag (prezzo): ~ **di** inclusive of; (indulgente) understanding

> Attenzione! In inglese esiste la parola *comprehensive*, che però in genere significa *completo*.

com'preso, -a pp di **comprendere** ▷ ag (incluso) included; **il servizio è ~?** is service included?

com'pressa sf (Med: garza) compress; (: pastiglia) tablet; vedi anche **compresso**

com'primere vt (premere) to press; (Fisica) to compress; (fig) to repress

compro'messo, -a pp di **compromettere** ▷ sm compromise

compro'mettere vt to compromise; **compromettersi** vpr to compromise o.s.

com'puter sm inv computer

comu'nale ag municipal, town cpd, ≈ borough cpd

co'mune ag common; (consueto) common, everyday; (di livello medio) average; (ordinario) ordinary ▷ sm (Amm) town council; (: sede) town hall ▷ sf (di persone) commune; **fuori del ~** out of the ordinary; **avere in ~** to have in common, share; **mettere in ~** to share

comuni'care vt (notizia) to pass on, convey; (malattia) to pass on; (ansia ecc) to communicate; (trasmettere: calore ecc) to transmit, communicate; (Rel) to administer communion to ▷ vi to communicate

comuni'cato sm communiqué; **comunicato stampa** press release

comunicazi'one [komunikat'tsjone] sf communication; (annuncio) announcement; (Tel): **dare la ~ a qn** to put sb through; **ottenere la ~** to get through; **comunicazione (telefonica)** (telephone) call

comuni'one sf communion; **comunione di beni** (Dir) joint ownership of property

comu'nismo sm communism

comunità sf inv community; **Comunità Europea** European Community

co'munque cong however, no matter how ▷ av (in ogni modo) in any case; (tuttavia) however, nevertheless

con *prep* with; **partire col treno** to leave by train; **~ mio grande stupore** to my great astonishment; **~ tutto ciò** for all that

con'cedere [kon'tʃɛdere] *vt* (*accordare*) to grant; (*ammettere*) to admit, concede; **concedersi qc** to treat o.s. to sth, to allow o.s. sth

concentrarsi *vpr* to concentrate

concentrazi'one *sf* concentration

conce'pire [kontʃe'pire] *vt* (*bambino*) to conceive; (*progetto, idea*) to conceive (of); (*metodo, piano*) to devise

con'certo [kon'tʃɛrto] *sm* (*Mus*) concert; (: *componimento*) concerto

con'cessi *ecc* [kon'tʃɛssi] *vb vedi* **concedere**

con'cetto [kon'tʃɛtto] *sm* (*pensiero, idea*) concept; (*opinione*) opinion

concezi'one [kontʃet'tsjone] *sf* conception

con'chiglia [kon'kiʎʎa] *sf* shell

conci'are [kon'tʃare] *vt* (*pelli*) to tan; (*tabacco*) to cure; (*fig: ridurre in cattivo stato*) to beat up; **conciarsi** *vpr* (*sporcarsi*) to get in a mess; (*vestirsi male*) to dress badly

concili'are [kontʃi'ljare] *vt* to reconcile; (*contravvenzione*) to pay on the spot; (*sonno*) to be conducive to, induce; **conciliarsi qc** to gain o win sth (for o.s.); **conciliarsi qn** to win sb over; **conciliarsi con** to be reconciled with

con'cime [kon'tʃime] *sm* manure; (*chimico*) fertilizer

con'ciso, -a [kon'tʃizo] *ag* concise, succinct

concitta'dino, -a [kontʃitta'dino] *sm/f* fellow citizen

con'cludere *vt* to conclude; (*portare a compimento*) to conclude, finish, bring to an end; (*operare positivamente*) to achieve ▷ *vi* (*essere convincente*) to be conclusive; **concludersi** *vpr* to come to an end, close

concor'dare *vt* (*tregua, prezzo*) to agree on; (*Ling*) to make agree ▷ *vi* to agree

con'corde *ag* (*d'accordo*) in agreement; (*simultaneo*) simultaneous

concor'rente *sm/f* competitor; (*Ins*) candidate; **concor'renza** *sf* competition

concorrenzi'ale [konkorren'tsjale] *ag* competitive

con'correre *vi* **~ (in)** (*Mat*) to converge o meet (in); **~ (a)** (*competere*) to compete (for); (: *Ins: a una cattedra*) to apply (for); (*partecipare: a un'impresa*) to take part (in), contribute (to); **con'corso, -a** *pp di* **concorrere** ▷ *sm* competition; (*Ins*) competitive examination; **concorso di colpa** (*Dir*) contributory negligence

con'creto, -a *ag* concrete

con'danna *sf* sentence; conviction; condemnation

condan'nare *vt* (*Dir*): **~ a** to sentence to; **~ per** to convict of; (*disapprovare*) to condemn

conden'sare *vt* to condense

condi'mento *sm* seasoning; dressing

con'dire *vt* to season; (*insalata*) to dress

condi'videre *vt* to share

condizio'nale [kondittsjo'nale] *ag* conditional ▷ *sm* (*Ling*) conditional ▷ *sf* (*Dir*) suspended sentence

condizio'nare [kondittsjo'nare] *vt* to condition; **ad aria condizionata** air-conditioned; **condiziona'tore** *sm* air conditioner

condizi'one [kondit'tsjone] *sf* condition

condogli'anze [kondoʎ'ʎantse] *sfpl* condolences

condo'minio *sm* joint ownership; (*edificio*) jointly-owned building

con'dotta *sf* (*modo di comportarsi*) conduct, behaviour; (*di un affare ecc*) handling; (*di acqua*) piping; (*incarico sanitario*) country medical practice controlled by a local authority

condu'cente [kondu'tʃɛnte] *sm* driver

con'duco *ecc* *vb vedi* **condurre**

con'durre *vt* to conduct; (*azienda*) to manage; (*accompagnare: bambino*) to take; (*automobile*) to drive; (*trasportare: acqua, gas*) to convey, conduct; (*fig*) to lead ▷ *vi* to lead

con'dussi *ecc* *vb vedi* **condurre**

confe'renza [konfe'rentsa] *sf* (*discorso*) lecture; (*riunione*) conference; **conferenza stampa** press conference

con'ferma *sf* confirmation

confer'mare *vt* to confirm

confes'sare *vt* to confess; **confessarsi** *vpr* to confess; **andare a confessarsi** (*Rel*) to go to confession

con'fetto *sm* sugared almond; (*Med*) pill

> ▨ Attenzione! In inglese esiste la parola *confetti*, che però significa *coriandoli*.

confet'tura *sf* (*gen*) jam; (*di arance*) marmalade

confezio'nare [konfettsjo'nare] *vt* (*vestito*) to make (up); (*merci, pacchi*) to package

confezi'one [konfet'tsjone] *sf* (*di abiti: da uomo*) tailoring; (: *da donna*) dressmaking; (*imballaggio*) packaging; **confezioni per signora** ladies' wear; **confezioni da uomo** menswear; **confezione regalo** gift pack

confic'care *vt* **~ qc in** to hammer o drive sth into; **conficcarsi** *vpr* to stick

confi'dare *vi* **~ in** to confide in, rely on ▷ *vt* to confide; **confidarsi con qn** to confide in sb

configu'rare vt (Inform) to set

configurazi'one [konfigurat'tsjone] sf configuration; (Inform) setting

confi'nare vi ~ **con** to border on ▷ vt (Pol) to intern; (fig) to confine

Confin'dustria sigla f (= Confederazione Generale dell'Industria Italiana) employers' association; ≈ CBI (BRIT)

con'fine sm boundary; (di paese) border, frontier

confis'care vt to confiscate

con'flitto sm conflict

conflu'enza [konflu'entsa] sf (di fiumi) confluence; (di strade) junction

con'fondere vt to mix up, confuse; (imbarazzare) to embarrass; **confondersi** vpr (mescolarsi) to mingle; (turbarsi) to be confused; (sbagliare) to get mixed up

confor'tare vt to comfort, console

confron'tare vt to compare

con'fronto sm comparison; **in** o **a ~ di** in comparison with, compared to; **nei miei** (o **tuoi** ecc) **confronti** towards me (o you ecc)

con'fusi ecc vb vedi **confondere**

confusi'one sf confusion; (chiasso) racket, noise; (imbarazzo) embarrassment

con'fuso, -a pp di **confondere** ▷ ag (vedi confondere) confused; embarrassed

conge'dare [kondʒe'dare] vt to dismiss; (Mil) to demobilize; **congedarsi** vpr to take one's leave

con'gegno sm device, mechanism

conge'lare [kondʒe'lare] vt to freeze; **congelarsi** vpr to freeze; **congela'tore** sm freezer

congesti'one [kondʒes'tjone] sf congestion

conget'tura [kondʒet'tura] sf conjecture

con'giungere [kon'dʒundʒere] vt to join (together); **congiungersi** vpr to join (together)

congiunti'vite [kondʒunti'vite] sf conjunctivitis

congiun'tivo [kondʒun'tivo] sm (Ling) subjunctive

congi'unto, -a [kon'dʒunto] pp di **congiungere** ▷ ag (unito) joined ▷ sm/f relative

congiunzi'one [kondʒun'tsjone] sf (Ling) conjunction

congi'ura [kon'dʒura] sf conspiracy

congratu'larsi vpr ~ **con qn per qc** to congratulate sb on sth

congratulazi'oni [kongratulat'tsjoni] sfpl congratulations

con'gresso sm congress

C.O.N.I. sigla m (= Comitato Olimpico Nazionale Italiano) Italian Olympic Games Committee

coni'are vt to mint, coin; (fig) to coin

co'niglio [ko'niʎʎo] sm rabbit

coniu'gare vt (Ling) to conjugate; **coniugarsi** vpr to get married

'coniuge ['kɔnjudʒe] sm/f spouse

connazio'nale [konnattsjo'nale] sm/f fellow-countryman/woman

connessi'one sf connection

con'nettere vt to connect, join ▷ vi (fig) to think straight

'cono sm cone; **cono gelato** ice-cream cone

co'nobbi ecc vb vedi **conoscere**

cono'scente [konoʃ'ʃente] sm/f acquaintance

cono'scenza [konoʃ'ʃentsa] sf (il sapere) knowledge no pl; (persona) acquaintance; (facoltà sensoriale) consciousness no pl; **perdere ~** to lose consciousness

co'noscere [ko'noʃʃere] vt to know; **ci siamo conosciuti a Firenze** we (first) met in Florence; **conoscersi** vpr to know o.s.; (reciproco) to know each other; (incontrarsi) to meet; ~ **qn di vista** to know sb by sight; **farsi ~** (fig) to make a name for o.s.; **conosci'uto, -a** pp di **conoscere** ▷ ag well-known

con'quista sf conquest

conquis'tare vt to conquer; (fig) to gain, win

consa'pevole ag ~ **di** aware o conscious of

'conscio, -a, -sci, -sce ['kɔnʃo] ag ~ **di** aware o conscious of

consecu'tivo, -a ag consecutive; (successivo: giorno) following, next

con'segna [kon'seɲɲa] sf delivery; (merce consegnata) consignment; (custodia) care, custody; (Mil: ordine) orders pl; (: punizione) confinement to barracks; **pagamento alla ~** cash on delivery; **dare qc in ~ a qn** to entrust sth to sb

conse'gnare [konseɲ'ɲare] vt to deliver; (affidare) to entrust, hand over; (Mil) to confine to barracks

consegu'enza [konse'gwentsa] sf consequence; **per** o **di ~** consequently

con'senso sm approval, consent; **consenso informato** informed consent

consen'tire vi ~ **a** to consent o agree to ▷ vt to allow, permit

con'serva sf (Cuc) preserve; **conserva di frutta** jam; **conserva di pomodoro** tomato purée

conser'vante sm (per alimenti) preservative

conser'vare vt (Cuc) to preserve; (custodire) to keep; (: dalla distruzione ecc) to preserve, conserve

conserva'tore, -'trice *sm/f* (*Pol*) conservative

conserva'torio *sm* (*di musica*) conservatory

conservazi'one [konservat'tsjone] *sf* preservation; conservation

conside'rare *vt* to consider; (*reputare*) to consider, regard; **considerarsi** *vpr* to consider o.s.

consigli'are [konsiʎ'ʎare] *vt* (*persona*) to advise; (*metodo, azione*) to recommend, advise, suggest; **mi può ~ un buon ristorante?** can you recommend a good restaurant?; **con'siglio** *sm* (*suggerimento*) advice *no pl*, piece of advice; (*assemblea*) council; **consiglio d'amministrazione** board; **Consiglio d'Europa** Council of Europe; **Consiglio dei Ministri** (*Pol*): **il Consiglio dei Ministri** ≈ the Cabinet

consis'tente *ag* thick; solid; (*fig*) sound, valid

con'sistere *vi* **~ in** to consist of

conso'lare *ag* consular ▷ *vt* (*confortare*) to console, comfort; (*rallegrare*) to cheer up; **consolarsi** *vpr* to be comforted; to cheer up

conso'lato *sm* consulate

consolazi'one [konsolat'tsjone] *sf* consolation, comfort

'console *sm* consul

conso'nante *sf* consonant

'consono, -a *ag* **~ a** consistent with, consonant with

con'sorte *sm/f* consort

consta'tare *vt* to establish, verify

consu'eto, -a *ag* habitual, usual

consu'lente *sm/f* consultant

consul'tare *vt* to consult; **consultarsi** *vpr* **consultarsi con qn** to seek the advice of sb

consul'torio *sm* **~ familiare** family planning clinic

consu'mare *vt* (*logorare: abiti, scarpe*) to wear out; (*usare*) to consume, use up; (*mangiare, bere*) to consume; (*Dir*) to consummate; **consumarsi** *vpr* to wear out; to be used up; (*anche fig*) to be consumed; (*combustibile*) to burn out

con'tabile *ag* accounts *cpd*, accounting ▷ *sm/f* accountant

contachi'lometri [kontaki'lɔmetri] *sm inv* ≈ mileometer

conta'dino, -a *sm/f* countryman/ woman, farm worker; (*peg*) peasant

contagi'are [konta'dʒare] *vt* to infect

contagi'oso, -a *ag* infectious; contagious

conta'gocce [konta'gottʃe] *sm inv* (*Med*) dropper

contami'nare *vt* to contaminate

con'tante *sm* cash; **pagare in contanti** to pay cash; **non ho contanti** I haven't got any cash

con'tare *vt* to count; (*considerare*) to consider ▷ *vi* to count, be of importance; **~ su qn** to count o rely on sb; **~ di fare qc** to intend to do sth; **conta'tore** *sm* meter

contat'tare *vt* to contact

con'tatto *sm* contact

'conte *sm* count

conteggi'are [konted'dʒare] *vt* to charge, put on the bill

con'tegno [kon'teɲɲo] *sm* (*comportamento*) behaviour; (*atteggiamento*) attitude; **darsi un ~** to act nonchalant; to pull o.s. together

contemporanea'mente *av* simultaneously; at the same time

contempo'raneo, -a *ag, sm/f* contemporary

conten'dente *sm/f* opponent, adversary

conte'nere *vt* to contain; **conteni'tore** *sm* container

conten'tezza [konten'tettsa] *sf* contentment

con'tento, -a *ag* pleased, glad; **~ di** pleased with

conte'nuto *sm* contents *pl*; (*argomento*) content

con'tessa *sf* countess

contes'tare *vt* (*Dir*) to notify; (*fig*) to dispute

con'testo *sm* context

continen'tale *ag, sm/f* continental

conti'nente *ag* continent ▷ *sm* (*Geo*) continent; (: *terra ferma*) mainland

contin'gente [kontin'dʒɛnte] *ag* contingent ▷ *sm* (*Comm*) quota; (*Mil*) contingent

continua'mente *av* (*senza interruzione*) continuously, nonstop; (*ripetutamente*) continually

continu'are *vt* to continue (with), go on with ▷ *vi* to continue, go on; **~ a fare qc** to go on o continue doing sth

continuità *sf* continuity

con'tinuo, -a *ag* (*numerazione*) continuous; (*pioggia*) continual, constant; (*Elettr*): **corrente continua** direct current; **di ~** continually

'conto *sm* (*calcolo*) calculation; (*Comm, Econ*) account; (*di ristorante, albergo*) bill; (*fig: stima*) consideration, esteem; **il ~, per favore** can I have the bill, please?; **lo metta sul mio ~** put it on my bill; **fare i conti con qn** to settle one's account with sb; **fare ~ su qn/qc** to count o rely on sb; **rendere ~ a qn di qc** to be accountable to sb for sth; **tener ~ di qn/qc** to take sb/sth into account; **per ~ di** on behalf of; **per ~ mio** as far as I'm concerned; **a conti fatti, in fin dei conti** all things considered; **conto corrente** current account; **conto alla rovescia** countdown

con'torno sm (linea) outline, contour; (ornamento) border; (Cuc) vegetables pl

con'torto, -a pp di **contorcere**

contrabbandi'ere, -a sm/f smuggler

contrab'bando sm smuggling, contraband; **merce di ~** contraband, smuggled goods pl

contrab'basso sm (Mus) (double) bass

contraccambi'are vt (favore ecc) to return

contraccet'tivo, -a [kontrattʃet'tivo] ag, sm contraceptive

contrac'colpo sm rebound; (di arma da fuoco) recoil; (fig) repercussion

contrad'dire vt to contradict; **contraddirsi** vpr to contradict o.s.; (uso reciproco: persone) to contradict each other o one another; (: testimonianze ecc) to be contradictory

contraf'fare vt (persona) to mimic; (alterare: voce) to disguise; (firma) to forge, counterfeit

contraria'mente av **~ a** contrary to

contrari'are vt (contrastare) to thwart, oppose; (irritare) to annoy, bother

con'trario, -a ag opposite; (sfavorevole) unfavourable ▷ sm opposite; **essere ~ a qc** (persona) to be against sth; **in caso ~** otherwise; **avere qc in ~** to have some objection; **al ~** on the contrary

contrasse'gnare [kontrasseɲ'ɲare] vt to mark

contras'tare vt (avversare) to oppose; (impedire) to bar; (negare: diritto) to contest, dispute ▷ vi **~ (con)** (essere in disaccordo) to contrast (with), (lottare) to struggle (with)

contrat'tacco sm counterattack

contrat'tare vt, vi to negotiate

contrat'tempo sm hitch

con'tratto, -a pp di **contrarre** ▷ sm contract

contravvenzi'one [kontravven'tsjone] sf contravention; (ammenda) fine

contrazi'one [kontrat'tsjone] sf contraction; (di prezzi ecc) reduction

contribu'ente sm/f taxpayer; ratepayer (BRIT), property tax payer (US)

contribu'ire vi to contribute

'contro prep against; **~ di me/lui** against me/him; **pastiglie ~ la tosse** throat lozenges; **~ pagamento** (Comm) on payment ▷ prefisso: **controfi'gura** sf (Cinema) double

control'lare vt (accertare) to check; (sorvegliare) to watch, control; (tenere nel proprio potere, fig: dominare) to control; **controllarsi** vpr to control o.s.; **con'trollo** sm check; watch; control; **controllo delle nascite** birth control; **control'lore** sm (Ferr, Autobus) (ticket) inspector

contro'luce [kontro'lutʃe] sf inv (Fot) backlit shot ▷ av **(in) ~** against the light; (fotografare) into the light

contro'mano av **guidare ~** to drive on the wrong side of the road; (in un senso unico) to drive the wrong way up a one-way street

controprodu'cente [kontroprodu'tʃente] ag counterproductive

contro'senso sm (contraddizione) contradiction in terms; (assurdità) nonsense

controspio'naggio [kontrospio'naddʒo] sm counterespionage

contro'versia sf controversy; (Dir) dispute

contro'verso, -a ag controversial

contro'voglia [kontro'vɔʎʎa] av unwillingly

contusi'one sf (Med) bruise

convale'scente [konvaleʃ'ʃente] ag, sm/f convalescent

convali'dare vt (Amm) to validate; (fig: sospetto, dubbio) to confirm

con'vegno [kon'veɲɲo] sm (incontro) meeting; (congresso) convention, congress; (luogo) meeting place

conve'nevoli smpl civilities

conveni'ente ag suitable; (vantaggioso) profitable; (: prezzo) cheap

> Attenzione! In inglese esiste la parola convenient, che però significa comodo.

conve'nire vi (riunirsi) to gather, assemble; (concordare) to agree; (tornare utile) to be worthwhile ▷ vb impers **conviene fare questo** it is advisable to do this; **conviene andarsene** we should go; **ne convengo** I agree

con'vento sm (di frati) monastery; (di suore) convent

convenzio'nale [konventsjo'nale] ag conventional

convenzi'one [konven'tsjone] sf (Dir) agreement; (nella società) convention

conver'sare vi to have a conversation, converse

conversazi'one [konversat'tsjone] sf conversation; **fare ~** to chat, have a chat

conversi'one sf conversion; **conversione ad U** (Aut) U-turn

conver'tire vt (trasformare) to change; (Pol, Rel) to convert; **convertirsi** vpr **convertirsi (a)** to be converted (to)

con'vesso, -a ag convex

convin'cente [konvin'tʃɛnte] *ag* convincing

con'vincere [kon'vintʃere] *vt* to convince; **~ qn di qc** to convince sb of sth; **~ qn a fare qc** to persuade sb to do sth; **convincersi** *vpr* **convincersi (di qc)** to convince o.s. (of sth); **~ qn di qc** to convince sb of sth; **~ qn a fare qc** to convince sb to do sth

convi'vente *sm/f* common-law husband/ wife

con'vivere *vi* to live together

convo'care *vt* to call, convene; (*Dir*) to summon

convulsi'one *sf* convulsion

coope'rare *vi* **~ (a)** to cooperate (in); **coopera'tiva** *sf* cooperative

coordi'nare *vt* to coordinate

co'perchio [ko'perkjo] *sm* cover; (*di pentola*) lid

co'perta *sf* cover; (*di lana*) blanket; (*da viaggio*) rug; (*Naut*) deck

coper'tina *sf* (*Stampa*) cover, jacket

co'perto, -a *pp di* **coprire** ▷ *ag* covered; (*cielo*) overcast ▷ *sm* place setting; (*posto a tavola*) place; (*al ristorante*) cover charge; **~ di** covered in *o* with

coper'tone *sm* (*Aut*) rubber tyre

coper'tura *sf* (*anche Econ, Mil*) cover; (*di edificio*) roofing

'copia *sf* copy; **brutta/bella ~** rough/final copy

copi'are *vt* to copy

copi'one *sm* (*Cinema, Teatro*) script

'coppa *sf* (*bicchiere*) goblet; (*per frutta, gelato*) dish; (*trofeo*) cup, trophy; **coppa dell'olio** oil sump (BRIT) *o* pan (US)

'coppia *sf* (*di persone*) couple; (*di animali, Sport*) pair

coprifu'oco, -chi *sm* curfew

copri'letto *sm* bedspread

copripiu'mino *sm* duvet cover

co'prire *vt* to cover; (*occupare: carica, posto*) to hold; **coprirsi** *vpr* (*cielo*) to cloud over; (*vestirsi*) to wrap up, cover up; (*Econ*) to cover o.s.; **coprirsi di** (*macchie, muffa*) to become covered in

coque [kɔk] *sf* **uovo alla ~** boiled egg

co'raggio [ko'raddʒo] *sm* courage, bravery; **~!** (*forza!*) come on!; (*animo!*) cheer up!

co'rallo *sm* coral

Co'rano *sm* (*Rel*) Koran

co'razza [ko'rattsa] *sf* armour; (*di animali*) carapace, shell; (*Mil*) armour(-plating)

'corda *sf* cord; (*fune*) rope; (*spago, Mus*) string; **dare ~ a qn** to let sb have his (*o* her) way; **tenere sulla ~ qn** to keep sb on tenterhooks; **tagliare la ~** to slip away, sneak off; **corda vocale** vocal cords

cordi'ale *ag* cordial, warm ▷ *sm* (*bevanda*) cordial

'cordless ['kɔːdlɪs] *sm inv* cordless phone

cor'done *sm* cord, string; (*linea: di polizia*) cordon; **cordone ombelicale** umbilical cord

Co'rea *sf* **la ~** Korea

coreogra'fia *sf* choreography

cori'andolo *sm* (*Bot*) coriander; **coriandoli** *smpl* confetti *sg*

cor'nacchia [kor'nakkja] *sf* crow

corna'musa *sf* bagpipes *pl*

cor'netta *sf* (*Mus*) cornet; (*Tel*) receiver

cor'netto *sm* (*Cuc*) croissant; (*gelato*) cone

cor'nice [kor'nitʃe] *sf* frame; (*fig*) setting, background

cornici'one [korni'tʃone] *sm* (*di edificio*) ledge; (*Archit*) cornice

'corno (*pl(f)* **-a**) *sm* (*Zool*) horn; (*pl(m)* **-i**: *Mus*) horn; **fare le corna a qn** to be unfaithful to sb

Corno'vaglia [korno'vaʎʎa] *sf* **la ~** Cornwall

cor'nuto, -a *ag* (*con corna*) horned; (*fam!*: *marito*) cuckolded ▷ *sm* (*fam!*) cuckold; (: *insulto*) bastard (!)

'coro *sm* chorus; (*Rel*) choir

co'rona *sf* crown; (*di fiori*) wreath

'corpo *sm* body; (*militare, diplomatico*) corps *inv*; **prendere ~** to take shape; **a ~ ~** hand-to-hand; **corpo di ballo** corps de ballet; **corpo insegnante** teaching staff

corpora'tura *sf* build, physique

cor'reggere [kor'reddʒere] *vt* to correct; (*compiti*) to correct, mark

cor'rente *ag* (*acqua: di fiume*) flowing; (: *di rubinetto*) running; (*moneta, prezzo*) current; (*comune*) everyday ▷ *sm* **essere al ~ (di)** to be well-informed (about); **mettere al ~ (di)** to inform (of) ▷ *sf* (*d'acqua*) current, stream; (*spiffero*) draught; (*Elettr, Meteor*) current; (*fig*) trend, tendency; **la vostra lettera del 5 ~ mese** (*Comm*) your letter of the 5th of this month; **corrente alternata/continua** alternate/direct current; **corrente'mente** *av* commonly; **parlare una lingua correntemente** to speak a language fluently

'correre *vi* to run; (*precipitarsi*) to rush; (*partecipare a una gara*) to race, run; (*fig: diffondersi*) to go round ▷ *vt* (*Sport: gara*) to compete in; (*rischio*) to run; (*pericolo*) to face; **~ dietro a qn** to run after sb; **corre voce che …** it is rumoured that …

cor'ressi *ecc vb vedi* **correggere**

correzi'one [korret'tsjone] *sf* correction; marking; **correzione di bozze** proofreading

corri'doio *sm* corridor; (*in aereo, al cinema*)

aisle; **vorrei un posto sul ~** I'd like an aisle seat

corri'dore sm (Sport) runner; (: su veicolo) racer

corri'era sf coach (BRIT), bus

corri'ere sm (diplomatico, di guerra, postale) courier; (Comm) carrier

corri'mano sm handrail

corrispon'dente ag corresponding ▷ sm/f correspondent

corrispon'denza [korrispon'dɛntsa] sf correspondence

corris'pondere vi (equivalere): **~ (a)** to correspond (to) ▷ vt (stipendio) to pay; (fig: amore) to return

cor'rodere vt to corrode

cor'rompere vt to corrupt; (comprare) to bribe

cor'roso, -a pp di **corrodere**

cor'rotto, -a pp di **corrompere** ▷ ag corrupt

corru'gare vt to wrinkle; **~ la fronte** to knit one's brows

cor'ruppi ecc vb vedi **corrompere**

corruzi'one [korrut'tsjone] sf corruption; bribery

'corsa sf running no pl; (gara) race; (di autobus, taxi) journey, trip; **fare una ~** to run, dash; (Sport) to run a race; **corsa campestre** cross-country race

'corsi ecc vb vedi **correre**

cor'sia sf (Aut, Sport) lane; (di ospedale) ward

'Corsica sf **la ~** Corsica

cor'sivo sm cursive (writing); (Tip) italics pl

'corso, -a pp di **correre** ▷ sm course; (strada cittadina) main street; (di unità monetaria) circulation; (di titoli, valori) rate, price; **in ~** in progress, under way; (annata) current; **corso d'acqua** river, stream; (artificiale) waterway; **corso d'aggiornamento** refresher course; **corso serale** evening class

'corte sf (court)yard; (Dir, regale) court; **fare la ~ a qn** to court sb; **corte marziale** court-martial

cor'teccia, -ce [kor'tettʃa] sf bark

corteggi'are [korted'dʒare] vt to court

cor'teo sm procession

cor'tese ag courteous; **corte'sia** sf courtesy; **per cortesia ...** excuse me, please ...

cor'tile sm (court)yard

cor'tina sf curtain; (anche fig) screen

'corto, -a ag short; **essere a ~ di qc** to be short of sth; **corto circuito** short-circuit

'corvo sm raven

'cosa sf thing; (faccenda) affair, matter, business no pl; **(che) ~?** what?; **(che)**

cos'è? what is it?; **a ~ pensi?** what are you thinking about?

'coscia, -sce ['kɔʃʃa] sf thigh; **coscia di pollo** (Cuc) chicken leg

cosci'ente [koʃʃɛnte] ag conscious; **~ di** conscious o aware of

PAROLA CHIAVE

così av **1** (in questo modo) like this, (in) this way; (in tal modo) so; **le cose stanno così** this is the way things stand; **non ho detto così!** I didn't say that!; **come stai? — (e) così** how are you? — so-so; **e così via** and so on; **per così dire** so to speak

2 (tanto) so; **così lontano** so far away; **un ragazzo così intelligente** such an intelligent boy

▷ ag inv (tale): **non ho mai visto un film così** I've never seen such a film ▷ cong **1** (perciò) so, therefore

2: così ... come as ... as; **non è così bravo come te** he's not as good as you; **così ... che** so ... that

cosid'detto, -a ag so-called

cos'metico, -a, -ci, -che ag, sm cosmetic

cos'pargere [kos'pardʒere] vt **~ di** to sprinkle with

cos'picuo, -a ag considerable, large

cospi'rare vi to conspire

'cossi ecc vb vedi **cuocere**

'costa sf (tra terra e mare) coast(line); (litorale) shore; (Anat) rib; **la C~ Azzurra** the French Riviera

cos'tante ag constant; (persona) steadfast ▷ sf constant

cos'tare vi, vt to cost; **quanto costa?** how much does it cost?; **~ caro** to be expensive, cost a lot

cos'tata sf (Cuc) large chop

costeggi'are [kosted'dʒare] vt to be close to; to run alongside

costi'ero, -a ag coastal, coast cpd

costitu'ire vt (comitato, gruppo) to set up, form; (elementi, parti: comporre) to make up, constitute; (rappresentare) to constitute; (Dir) to appoint; **costituirsi** vpr **costituirsi alla polizia** to give o.s. up to the police

costituzi'one [kostitut'tsjone] sf setting up; building up; constitution

'costo sm cost; **a ogni o qualunque ~, a tutti i costi** at all costs

'costola sf (Anat) rib

cos'toso, -a ag expensive, costly

cos'tringere [kos'trindʒere] vt **~ qn a fare qc** to force sb to do sth

costru'ire vt to construct, build;

costruzi'one sf construction, building

cos'tume sm (uso) custom; (foggia di vestire, indumento) costume; **costume da bagno** bathing o swimming costume (BRIT), swimsuit; (da uomo) bathing o swimming trunks pl

co'tenna sf bacon rind

coto'letta sf (di maiale, montone) chop; (di vitello, agnello) cutlet

co'tone sm cotton; **cotone idrofilo** cotton wool (BRIT), absorbent cotton (US)

'cotta sf (fam: innamoramento) crush

'cottimo sm **lavorare a ~** to do piecework

'cotto, -a pp di **cuocere** ▷ ag cooked; (fam: innamorato) head-over-heels in love; **ben ~** (carne) well done

cot'tura sf cooking; (in forno) baking; (in umido) stewing

co'vare vt to hatch; (fig: malattia) to be sickening for; (: odio, rancore) to nurse ▷ vi (fuoco, fig) to smoulder

'covo sm den

co'vone sm sheaf

'cozza ['kɔttsa] sf mussel

coz'zare [kot'tsare] vi **~ contro** to bang into, collide with

'crampo sm cramp; **ho un ~ alla gamba** I've got cramp in my leg

'cranio sm skull

cra'tere sm crater

cra'vatta sf tie

cre'are vt to create

'crebbi ecc vb vedi **crescere**

cre'dente sm/f (Rel) believer

cre'denza [kre'dɛntsa] sf belief; (armadio) sideboard

'credere vt to believe ▷ vi **~ in, ~ a** to believe in; **~ qn onesto** to believe sb (to be) honest; **~ che** to believe o think that; **credersi furbo** to think one is clever

'credito sm (anche Comm) credit; (reputazione) esteem, repute; **comprare a ~** to buy on credit

'crema sf cream; (con uova, zucchero ecc) custard; **crema pasticciera** confectioner's custard; **crema solare** sun cream

cre'mare vt to cremate

'crepa sf crack

cre'paccio [kre'pattʃo] sm large crack, fissure; (di ghiacciaio) crevasse

crepacu'ore sm broken heart

cre'pare vi (fam: morire) to snuff it, kick the bucket; **~ dalle risa** to split one's sides laughing

crêpe [krɛp] sf inv pancake

cre'puscolo sm twilight, dusk

'crescere ['kreʃʃere] vi to grow ▷ vt (figli) to raise

'cresima sf (Rel) confirmation

'crespo, -a ag (capelli) frizzy; (tessuto) puckered ▷ sm crêpe

'cresta sf crest; (di polli, uccelli) crest, comb

'creta sf chalk; clay

creti'nata sf (fam): **dire/fare una ~** to say/do a stupid thing

cre'tino, -a ag stupid ▷ sm/f idiot, fool

CRI sigla f = **Croce Rossa Italiana**

cric sm inv (Tecn) jack

cri'ceto [kri'tʃeto] sm hamster

crimi'nale ag, sm/f criminal

criminalità sf crime; **criminalità organizzata** organized crime

'crimine sm (Dir) crime

crip'tare vt (TV: programma) to encrypt

crisan'temo sm chrysanthemum

'crisi sf inv crisis; (Med) attack, fit; **crisi di nervi** attack o fit of nerves

cris'tallo sm crystal; **cristalli liquidi** liquid crystals

cristia'nesimo sm Christianity

cristi'ano, -a ag, sm/f Christian

'Cristo sm Christ

cri'terio sm criterion; (buon senso) (common) sense

'critica, -che sf criticism; **la ~** (attività) criticism; (persone) the critics pl; vedi anche **critico**

criti'care vt to criticize

'critico, -a, -ci, -che ag critical ▷ sm critic

cro'ato, -a ag, sm/f Croatian, Croat

Croa'zia [kroa'ttsja] sf Croatia

croc'cante ag crisp, crunchy

'croce ['krotʃe] sf cross; **in ~** (di traverso) crosswise; (fig) on tenterhooks; **Croce Rossa** Red Cross

croci'ata [kro'tʃata] sf crusade

croci'era [kro'tʃera] sf (viaggio) cruise; (Archit) transept

croci'fisso, -a pp di **crocifiggere**

crol'lare vi to collapse; **'crollo** sm collapse; (di prezzi) slump, sudden fall; **crollo in Borsa** slump in prices on the Stock Exchange

cro'mato, -a ag chromium-plated

'cromo sm chrome, chromium

'cronaca, -che sf (Stampa) news sg; (: rubrica) column; (TV, Radio) commentary; **fatto o episodio di ~** news item; **cronaca nera** crime news sg; crime column

'cronico, -a, -ci, -che ag chronic

cro'nista, -i sm (Stampa) reporter

cro'nometro sm chronometer; (a scatto) stopwatch

'crosta sf crust

cros'tacei [kros'tatʃei] smpl shellfish

cros'tata sf (Cuc) tart

cros'tino sm (Cuc) crouton; (: da antipasto) canapé

cruci'ale [kru'tʃale] ag crucial
cruci'verba sm inv crossword (puzzle)
cru'dele ag cruel
'crudo, -a ag (non cotto) raw; (aspro) harsh, severe
cru'miro (peg) sm blackleg (BRIT), scab
'crusca sf bran
crus'cotto sm (Aut) dashboard
CSI sigla f inv (= Comunità Stati Indipendenti) CIS
CSM [tʃiɛsse'ɛmme] sigla m (= consiglio superiore della magistratura) Magistrates' Board of Supervisors
'Cuba sf Cuba
cu'bano, -a ag, sm/f Cuban
cu'betto sm; **cubetto di ghiaccio** ice cube
'cubico, -a, -ci, -che ag cubic
cu'bista, -i, -e (Arte) Cubist ▷ sf (in discoteca) podium dancer
'cubo, -a ag cubic ▷ sm cube; **elevare al ~** (Mat) to cube
cuc'cagna [kuk'kaɲɲa] sf **paese della ~** land of plenty; **albero della ~** greasy pole (fig)
cuc'cetta [kut'tʃetta] sf (Ferr) couchette; (Naut) berth
cucchiai'ata [kukja'jata] sf spoonful
cucchia'ino [kukkja'ino] sm teaspoon; coffee spoon
cucchi'aio [kuk'kjajo] sm spoon
'cuccia, -ce ['kuttʃa] sf dog's bed; **a ~!** down!
'cucciolo ['kuttʃolo] sm cub; (di cane) puppy
cu'cina [ku'tʃina] sf (locale) kitchen; (arte culinaria) cooking, cookery; (le vivande) food, cooking; (apparecchio) cooker; **cucina componibile** fitted kitchen; **cuci'nare** vt to cook
cu'cire [ku'tʃire] vt to sew, stitch; **cuci'trice** sf stapler
cucù sm inv cuckoo
'cuffia sf bonnet, cap; (da infermiera) cap; (da bagno) (bathing) cap; (per ascoltare) headphones pl, headset
cu'gino, -a [ku'dʒino] sm/f cousin

PAROLA CHIAVE

'cui pron **1** (nei complementi indiretti: persona) whom; (: oggetto, animale) which; **la persona/le persone a cui accennavi** the person/people you were referring to o to whom you were referring; **i libri di cui parlavo** the books I was talking about o about which I was talking; **il quartiere in cui abito** the district where I live; **la ragione per cui** the reason why
2 (inserito tra articolo e sostantivo) whose;

la donna i cui figli sono scomparsi the woman whose children have disappeared; **il signore, dal cui figlio ho avuto il libro** the man from whose son I got the book

culi'naria sf cookery
'culla sf cradle
cul'lare vt to rock
'culmine sm top, summit
'culo (fam!) sm arse (BRIT!), ass (US!); (fig: fortuna): **aver ~** to have the luck of the devil
'culto sm (religione) religion; (adorazione) worship, adoration; (venerazione: anche fig) cult
cul'tura sf culture; education, learning; **cultu'rale** ag cultural
cultu'rismo sm body-building
cumula'tivo, -a ag cumulative; (prezzo) inclusive; (biglietto) group cpd
'cumulo sm (mucchio) pile, heap; (Meteor) cumulus
cu'netta sf (avvallamento) dip; (di scolo) gutter
cu'ocere ['kwɔtʃere] vt (alimenti) to cook; (mattoni ecc) to fire ▷ vi to cook; **~ al forno** (pane) to bake; (arrosto) to roast; **cu'oco, -a, -chi, -che** sm/f cook; (di ristorante) chef
cu'oio sm leather; **cuoio capelluto** scalp
cu'ore sm heart; **cuori** smpl (Carte) hearts; **avere buon ~** to be kind-hearted; **stare a ~ a qn** to be important to sb
'cupo, -a ag dark; (suono) dull; (fig) gloomy, dismal
'cupola sf dome; cupola
'cura sf care; (Med: trattamento) (course of) treatment; **aver ~ di** (occuparsi di) to look after; **a ~ di** (libro) edited by; **cura dimagrante** diet
cu'rare vt (malato, malattia) to treat; (: guarire) to cure; (aver cura di) to take care of; (testo) to edit; **curarsi** vpr to take care of o.s.; (Med) to follow a course of treatment; **curarsi di** to pay attention to
curio'sare vi to look round, wander round; (tra libri) to browse; **~ nei negozi** to look o wander round the shops
curiosità sf inv curiosity; (cosa rara) curio, curiosity
curi'oso, -a ag curious; **essere ~ di** to be curious about
cur'sore sm (Inform) cursor
'curva sf curve; (stradale) bend, curve
cur'vare vt to bend ▷ vi (veicolo) to take a bend; (strada) to bend, curve; **curvarsi** vpr to bend; (legno) to warp
'curvo, -a ag curved; (piegato) bent
cusci'netto [kuʃʃi'netto] sm pad; (Tecn) bearing ▷ ag inv **stato ~** buffer state; **cuscinetto a sfere** ball bearing

cu'scino [kuʃˈʃino] *sm* cushion; (*guanciale*) pillow

cus'tode *sm/f* keeper, custodian

cus'todia *sf* care; (*Dir*) custody; (*astuccio*) case, holder

custo'dire *vt* (*conservare*) to keep; (*assistere*) to look after, take care of; (*fare la guardia*) to guard

CV *abbr* (= *cavallo vapore*) h.p.

cybercaffè [tʃiberkaˈfe] *sm inv* cybercafé

cybernauta, -i, -e *sm/f* Internet surfer

cyberspazio *sm* cyberspace

○ **PAROLA CHIAVE**

da (*da+il* = **dal**, *da+lo* = **dallo**, *da+l'* = **dall'**, *da+la* = **dalla**, *da+i* = **dai**, *da+gli* = **dagli**, *da+le* = **dalle**) *prep* **1** (*agente*) by; **dipinto da un grande artista** painted by a great artist

2 (*causa*) with; **tremare dalla paura** to tremble with fear

3 (*stato in luogo*) at; **abito da lui** I'm living at his house *o* with him; **sono dal giornalaio/da Francesco** I'm at the newsagent's/Francesco's (house) ·

4 (*moto a luogo*) to; (*moto per luogo*) through; **vado da Pietro/dal giornalaio** I'm going to Pietro's (house)/to the newsagent's; **sono passati dalla finestra** they came in through the window

5 (*provenienza, allontanamento*) from; **arrivare/partire da Milano** to arrive/ depart from Milan; **scendere dal treno/ dalla macchina** to get off the train/out of the car; **si trova a 5 km da qui** it's 5 km from here

6 (*tempo: durata*) for; (: *a partire da: nel passato*) since; (: *nel futuro*) from; **vivo qui da un anno** I've been living here for a year; **è dalle 3 che ti aspetto** I've been waiting for you since 3 (o'clock); **da oggi in poi** from today onwards; **da bambino** as a

child, when I (*o* he *ecc*) was a child
7 (*modo, maniera*) like; **comportarsi da uomo** to behave like a man; **l'ho fatto da me** I did it (by) myself
8 (*descrittivo*): **una macchina da corsa** a racing car; **una ragazza dai capelli biondi** a girl with blonde hair; **un vestito da 60 euro** a 60 euros dress

dà *vb vedi* **dare**
dac'capo *av* (*di nuovo*) (once) again; (*dal principio*) all over again, from the beginning
'dado *sm* (*da gioco*) dice *o* die; (*Cuc*) stock (BRIT) *o* bouillon (US) cube; (*Tecn*) (screw)nut; **dadi** *smpl* (*game of*) dice; **giocare a dadi** to play dice
'daino *sm* (fallow) deer *inv*; (*pelle*) buckskin
dal'tonico, -a, -ci, -che *ag* colour-blind
'dama *sf* lady; (*nei balli*) partner; (*gioco*) draughts *sg* (BRIT), checkers *sg* (US)
damigi'ana [dami'dʒana] *sf* demijohn
da'nese *ag* Danish ▷ *sm/f* Dane ▷ *sm* (*Ling*) Danish
Dani'marca *sf* **la ~** Denmark
dannazi'one *sf* damnation
danneggi'are [danned'dʒare] *vt* to damage; (*rovinare*) to spoil; (*nuocere*) to harm
'danno *sm* damage; (*a persona*) harm, injury; **danni** *smpl* (*Dir*) damages; **dan'noso, -a** *ag* **dannoso (a, per)** harmful (to), bad (for)
Da'nubio *sm* **il ~** the Danube
'danza ['dantsa] *sf* **la ~** dancing; **una ~** a dance
dan'zare [dan'tsare] *vt, vi* to dance
dapper'tutto *av* everywhere
dap'prima *av* at first
'dare *sm* (*Comm*) debit ▷ *vt* to give; (*produrre: frutti, suono*) to produce ▷ *vi* (*guardare*): **~ su** to look (out) onto; **darsi** *vpr* **darsi a** to dedicate o.s. to; **darsi al commercio** to go into business; **darsi al bere** to take to drink; **~ da mangiare a qn** to give sb sth to eat; **~ per certo qc** to consider sth certain; **~ per morto qn** to give sb up for dead; **darsi per vinto** to give in
'data *sf* date; **~ limite d'utilizzo** *or* **di consumo** best-before date; **data di nascita** date of birth; **data di scadenza** expiry date
'dato, -a *ag* (*stabilito*) given ▷ *sm* datum; **dati** *smpl* data *pl*; **un ~ di fatto** a fact; **dati sensibili** personal information
da'tore, -'trice *sm/f*; **datore di lavoro** employer
'dattero *sm* date

dattilogra'fia *sf* typing
datti'lografo, -a *sm/f* typist
da'vanti *av* in front; (*dirimpetto*) opposite ▷ *ag inv* front ▷ *sm* front; **~ a** in front of; facing, opposite; (*in presenza di*) before, in front of
davan'zale [davan'tsale] *sm* windowsill
dav'vero *av* really, indeed
d.C. *adv abbr* (= *dopo Cristo*) A.D.
'dea *sf* goddess
'debbo *ecc vb vedi* **dovere**
'debito, -a *ag* due, proper ▷ *sm* debt; (*Comm: dare*) debit; **a tempo ~** at the right time
'debole *ag* weak, feeble; (*suono*) faint; (*luce*) dim ▷ *sm* weakness; **debo'lezza** *sf* weakness
debut'tare *vi* to make one's debut
deca'denza [deka'dɛntsa] *sf* decline; (*Dir*) loss, forfeiture
decaffei'nato, -a *ag* decaffeinated
decapi'tare *vt* to decapitate, behead
decappot'tabile *ag, sf* convertible
de'cennio [de'tʃɛnnjo] *sm* decade
de'cente [de'tʃɛnte] *ag* decent, respectable, proper; (*accettabile*) satisfactory, decent
de'cesso [de'tʃɛsso] *sm* death
de'cidere [de'tʃidere] *vt* **~ qc** to decide on sth; (*questione, lite*) to settle sth; **~ di fare/ che** to decide to do/that; **~ di qc** (*cosa*) to determine sth; **decidersi (a fare)** to decide (to do), make up one's mind (to do)
deci'frare [detʃi'frare] *vt* to decode; (*fig*) to decipher, make out
deci'male [detʃi'male] *ag* decimal
'decimo, -a ['dɛtʃimo] *num* tenth
de'cina [de'tʃina] *sf* ten; (*circa dieci*): **una ~ (di)** about ten
de'cisi *ecc* [de'tʃizi] *vb vedi* **decidere**
decisi'one [detʃi'zjone] *sf* decision; **prendere una ~** to make a decision
deci'sivo, -a [detʃi'zivo] *ag* (*gen*) decisive; (*fattore*) deciding
de'ciso, -a [de'tʃizo] *pp di* **decidere**
decli'nare *vi* (*pendio*) to slope down; (*fig: diminuire*) to decline ▷ *vt* to decline
declinazi'one *sf* (*Ling*) declension
de'clino *sm* decline
decodifica'tore *sm* (*Tel*) decoder
decol'lare *vi* (*Aer*) to take off; **de'collo** *sm* take-off
deco'rare *vt* to decorate; **decorazi'one** *sf* decoration
de'creto *sm* decree; **decreto legge** *decree with the force of law*
'dedica, -che *sf* dedication
dedi'care *vt* to dedicate; **dedicarsi** *vpr* **dedicarsi a** to devote o.s. to

dedicherò ecc [dedike'rɔ] vb vedi **dedicare**

'dedito, -a ag ~ **a** (studio ecc) dedicated o devoted to; (vizio) addicted to

de'duco ecc vb vedi **dedurre**

de'durre vt (concludere) to deduce; (defalcare) to deduct

de'dussi ecc vb vedi **dedurre**

defici'ente [defi'tʃɛnte] ag (mancante): ~ **di** deficient in; (insufficiente) insufficient ▷ sm/f mental defective; (peg: cretino) idiot

'deficit ['dɛfitʃit] sm inv (Econ) deficit

defi'nire vt to define; (risolvere) to settle; **defini'tiva** sf **in** ~ (dopotutto) in the end; (dunque) hence; **defini'tivo, -a** ag definitive, final; **definizi'one** sf definition; settlement

defor'mare vt (alterare) to put out of shape; (corpo) to deform; (pensiero, fatto) to distort; **deformarsi** vpr to lose its shape

de'forme ag deformed; disfigured

de'funto, -a ag late cpd ▷ sm/f deceased

degene'rare [dedʒene'rare] vi to degenerate

de'gente [de'dʒɛnte] sm/f (in ospedale) in-patient

deglu'tire vt to swallow

de'gnare [deɲ'ɲare] vt ~ **qn della propria presenza** to honour sb with one's presence; **degnarsi** vpr **degnarsi di fare qc** to deign o condescend to do sth

'degno, -a ag dignified; ~ **di** worthy of; ~ **di lode** praiseworthy

de'grado sm; **degrado urbano** urban decline

'delega, -ghe sf (procura) proxy

dele'terio, -a ag damaging; (per salute ecc) harmful

del'fino sm (Zool) dolphin; (Storia) dauphin; (fig) probable successor

deli'cato, -a ag delicate; (salute) delicate, frail; (fig: gentile) thoughtful, considerate; (: che dimostra tatto) tactful

delin'quente sm/f criminal, delinquent; **delinquente abituale** regular offender, habitual offender; **delin'quenza** sf criminality, delinquency; **delinquenza minorile** juvenile delinquency

deli'rare vi to be delirious, rave; (fig) to rave

de'lirio sm delirium; (ragionamento insensato) raving; (fig): **andare/mandare in** ~ to go/send into a frenzy

de'litto sm crime

delizi'oso, -a ag delightful; (cibi) delicious

delta'plano sm hang-glider; **volo col** ~ hang-gliding

delu'dente ag disappointing

de'ludere vt to disappoint; **delusi'one** sf disappointment; **de'luso, -a** pp di

deludere

'demmo vb vedi **dare**

demo'cratico, -a, -ci, -che ag democratic

democra'zia [demokrat'tsia] sf democracy

demo'lire vt to demolish

de'monio sm demon, devil; **il D~** the Devil

de'naro sm money

densità sf inv density

'denso, -a ag thick, dense

den'tale ag dental

'dente sm tooth; (di forchetta) prong; **al** ~ (Cuc: pasta) al dente; **denti del giudizio** wisdom teeth; **denti da latte** milk teeth; **denti'era** sf (set of) false teeth pl

denti'fricio [denti'fritʃo] sm toothpaste

den'tista, -i, -e sm/f dentist

'dentro av inside; (in casa) indoors; (fig: nell'intimo) inwardly ▷ prep ~ **(a)** in; **piegato in** ~ folded over; **qui/là** ~ in here/ there; ~ **di sé** (pensare, brontolare) to oneself

de'nuncia, -ce o **cie** [de'nuntʃa] sf denunciation; declaration; **denuncia dei redditi** (income) tax return

denunci'are [denun'tʃare] vt to denounce; (dichiarare) to declare; (persona, smarrimento ecc) report; **vorrei** ~ **un furto** I'd like to report a theft

denu'trito, -a ag undernourished

denutrizi'one [denutrit'tsjone] sf malnutrition

deodo'rante sm deodorant

depe'rire vi to waste away

depi'larsi vpr ~ **(le gambe)** (con rasoio) to shave (one's legs); (con ceretta) to wax (one's legs)

depila'torio, -a ag hair-removing cpd, depilatory

dépli'ant [depli'ã] sm inv leaflet; (opuscolo) brochure

deplo'revole ag deplorable

de'pone, de'pongo ecc vb vedi **deporre**

de'porre vt (depositare) to put down; (rimuovere: da una carica) to remove; (: re) to depose; (Dir) to testify

depor'tare vt to deport

de'posi ecc vb vedi **deporre**

deposi'tare vt (gen, Geo, Econ) to deposit; (lasciare) to leave; (merci) to store; **depositarsi** vpr (sabbia, polvere) to settle

de'posito sm deposit; (luogo) warehouse; depot; (: Mil) depot; **deposito bagagli** left-luggage office

deposizi'one [depozit'tsjone] sf deposition; (da una carica) removal

depra'vato, -a ag depraved ▷ sm/f degenerate

depre'dare vt to rob, plunder

depressi'one *sf* depression

de'presso, -a *pp di* **deprimere** ▷ *ag* depressed

deprez'zare [depret'tsare] *vt* (*Econ*) to depreciate

depri'mente *ag* depressing

de'primere *vt* to depress

depu'rare *vt* to purify

depu'tato *sm* (*Pol*) deputy, ≈ Member of Parliament (BRIT), ≈ Member of Congress (US)

deragli'are [deraʎ'ʎare] *vi* to be derailed; **far ~** to derail

de'ridere *vt* to mock, deride

de'risi *ecc vb vedi* **deridere**

de'riva *sf* (*Naut, Aer*) drift; **andare alla ~** (*anche fig*) to drift

deri'vare *vi* **~ da** to derive from ▷ *vt* to derive; (*corso d'acqua*) to divert

derma'tologo, -a, -gi, -ghe *sm/f* dermatologist

deru'bare *vt* to rob

des'crivere *vt* to describe; **descrizi'one** *sf* description

de'serto, -a *ag* deserted ▷ *sm* (*Geo*) desert; **isola deserta** desert island

deside'rare *vt* to want, wish for; (*sessualmente*) to desire; **~ fare/che qn faccia** to want o wish to do/sb to do; **desidera fare una passeggiata?** would you like to go for a walk?

desi'derio *sm* wish; (*più intenso, carnale*) desire

deside'roso, -a *ag* **~ di** longing o eager for

desi'nenza [dezi'nɛntsa] *sf* (*Ling*) ending, inflexion

de'sistere *vi* **~ da** to give up, desist from

deso'lato, -a *ag* (*paesaggio*) desolate; (*persona: spiacente*) sorry

'dessi *ecc vb vedi* **dare**

'deste *ecc vb vedi* **dare**

desti'nare *vt* to destine; (*assegnare*) to appoint, assign; (*indirizzare*) to address; **~ qc a qn** to intend to give sth to sb, intend sb to have sth; **destina'tario, -a** *sm/f* (*di lettera*) addressee

destinazi'one [destinat'tsjone] *sf* destination; (*uso*) purpose

des'tino *sm* destiny, fate

destitu'ire *vt* to dismiss, remove

'destra *sf* (*mano*) right hand; (*parte*) right (side); (*Pol*): **la ~** the Right; **a ~** (*essere*) on the right; (*andare*) to the right

destreggi'arsi [destred'dʒarsi] *vpr* to manoeuvre (BRIT), maneuver (US)

des'trezza [des'trettsa] *sf* skill, dexterity

'destro, -a *ag* right, right-hand

dete'nuto, -a *sm/f* prisoner

deter'gente [deter'dʒɛnte] *ag* (*crema, latte*) cleansing ▷ *sm* cleanser

▌ Attenzione! In inglese esiste la parola *detergent* che però significa *detersivo*.

determi'nare *vt* to determine

determina'tivo, -a *ag* determining; **articolo ~** (*Ling*) definite article

determi'nato, -a *ag* (*gen*) certain; (*particolare*) specific; (*risoluto*) determined, resolute

deter'sivo *sm* detergent

detes'tare *vt* to detest, hate

de'trae, de'traggo *ecc vb vedi* **detrarre**

de'trarre *vt* **~ (da)** to deduct (from), take away (from)

de'trassi *ecc vb vedi* **detrarre**

'detta *sf* **a ~ di** according to

det'taglio [det'taʎʎo] *sm* detail; (*Comm*): **il ~** retail; **al ~** (*Comm*) retail; separately

det'tare *vt* to dictate; **~ legge** (*fig*) to lay down the law; **det'tato** *sm* dictation

'detto, -a *pp di* **dire** ▷ *ag* (*soprannominato*) called, known as; (*già nominato*) above-mentioned ▷ *sm* saying; **~ fatto** no sooner said than done

devas'tare *vt* to devastate; (*fig*) to ravage

devi'are *vi* **~ (da)** to turn off (from) ▷ *vt* to divert; **deviazi'one** *sf* (*anche Aut*) diversion

'devo *ecc vb vedi* **dovere**

de'volvere *vt* (*Dir*) to transfer, devolve

de'voto, -a *ag* (*Rel*) devout, pious; (*affezionato*) devoted

devozi'one [devot'tsjone] *sf* devoutness; (*anche Rel*) devotion

🔵 **PAROLA CHIAVE**

di (*di+il* = **del**, *di+lo* = **dello**, *di+l'* = **dell'**, *di+la* = **della**, *di+i* = **dei**, *di+gli* = **degli**, *di+le* = **delle**) *prep* **1** (*possesso, specificazione*) of; (*composto da, scritto da*) by; **la macchina di Paolo/mio fratello** Paolo's/my brother's car; **un amico di mio fratello** a friend of my brother's, one of my brother's friends; **un quadro di Botticelli** a painting by Botticelli

2 (*caratterizzazione, misura*) of; **una casa di mattoni** a brick house, a house made of bricks; **un orologio d'oro** a gold watch; **un bimbo di 3 anni** a child of 3, a 3-year-old child

3 (*causa, mezzo, modo*) with; **tremare di paura** to tremble with fear; **morire di cancro** to die of cancer; **spalmare di burro** to spread with butter

4 (*argomento*) about, of; **discutere di sport** to talk about sport

5 (*luogo: provenienza*) from; out of; **essere**

di Roma to be from Rome; **uscire di casa** to come out of o leave the house **6** (*tempo*) in; **d'estate/d'inverno** in (the) summer/winter; **di notte** by night, at night; **di mattina/sera** in the morning/ evening; **di lunedì** on Mondays ▷ *det* (*una certa quantità di*) some; (: *negativo*) any; (*interrogativo*) any; some; **del pane** (some) bread; **delle caramelle** (some) sweets; **degli amici miei** some friends of mine; **vuoi del vino?** do you want some o any wine?

dia'bete *sm* diabetes *sg*
dia'betico, -a, ci, che *ag, sm/f* diabetic
dia'framma, -i *sm* (*divisione*) screen; (*Anat, Fot, contraccettivo*) diaphragm
di'agnosi [di'aɲɲozi] *sf* diagnosis *sg*
diago'nale *ag, sf* diagonal
dia'gramma, -i *sm* diagram
dia'letto *sm* dialect
di'alisi *sf* dialysis *sg*
di'alogo, -ghi *sm* dialogue
dia'mante *sm* diamond
di'ametro *sm* diameter
diaposi'tiva *sf* transparency, slide
di'ario *sm* diary
diar'rea *sf* diarrhoea
di'avolo *sm* devil
di'battito *sm* debate, discussion
'dice ['ditʃe] *vb vedi* **dire**
di'cembre [di'tʃɛmbre] *sm* December
dice'ria [ditʃe'ria] *sf* rumour, piece of gossip
dichia'rare [dikja'rare] *vt* to declare; **dichiararsi** *vpr* to declare o.s.; (*innamorato*) to declare one's love; **dichiararsi vinto** to acknowledge defeat; **dichiarazi'one** *sf* declaration; **dichiarazione dei redditi** statement of income; (*modulo*) tax return
dician'nove [ditʃan'nɔve] *num* nineteen
dicias'sette [ditʃas'sɛtte] *num* seventeen
dici'otto [di'tʃɔtto] *num* eighteen
dici'tura [ditʃi'tura] *sf* words *pl*, wording
'dico *ecc vb vedi* **dire**
didasca'lia *sf* (*di illustrazione*) caption; (*Cine*) subtitle; (*Teatro*) stage directions *pl*
di'eci ['djɛtʃi] *num* ten
di'edi *ecc vb vedi* **dare**
'diesel ['dizəl] *sm inv* diesel engine
dies'sino, -a *sm/f* member of the DS political party
di'eta *sf* diet; **essere a ~ to** be on a diet
di'etro *av* behind; (*in fondo*) at the back ▷ *prep* behind; (*tempo: dopo*) after ▷ *sm* back, rear ▷ *ag inv* back *cpd*; **le zampe di ~** the hind legs; **~ richiesta** on demand; (*scritta*) on application

di'fendere *vt* to defend; **difendersi** *vpr* (*cavarsela*) to get by; **difendersi da/contro** to defend o.s. from/against; **difendersi dal freddo** to protect o.s. from the cold; **difen'sore, -a** *sm/f* defender; **avvocato difensore** counsel for the defence; **di'fesa** *sf* defence
di'fesi *ecc vb vedi* **difendere**
di'fetto *sm* (*mancanza*): **~ di** lack of; shortage of; (*di fabbricazione*) fault, flaw, defect; (*morale*) fault, failing, defect; (*fisico*) defect; **far ~** to be lacking; **in ~** at fault; in the wrong; **difet'toso, -a** *ag* defective, faulty
diffe'rente *ag* different
diffe'renza [diffe'rɛntsa] *sf* difference; **a ~ di** unlike
diffe'rire *vt* to postpone, defer ▷ *vi* to be different
diffe'rita *sf* **in ~** (*trasmettere*) prerecorded
dif'ficile [dif'fitʃile] *ag* difficult; (*persona*) hard to please, difficult (to please); (*poco probabile*): **è ~ che sia libero** it is unlikely that he'll be free ▷ *sm* difficult part; difficulty; **difficoltà** *sf inv* difficulty
diffi'dente *ag* suspicious, distrustful
diffi'denza *sf* suspicion, distrust
dif'fondere *vt* (*luce, calore*) to diffuse; (*notizie*) to spread, circulate; **diffondersi** *vpr* to spread
dif'fusi *ecc vb vedi* **diffondere**
dif'fuso, -a *pp di* **diffondere** ▷ *ag* (*malattia, fenomeno*) widespread
'diga, -ghe *sf* dam; (*portuale*) breakwater
dige'rente [didʒe'rɛnte] *ag* (*apparato*) digestive
dige'rire [didʒe'rire] *vt* to digest; **digesti'one** *sf* digestion; **diges'tivo, -a** *ag* digestive ▷ *sm* (*after-dinner*) liqueur
digi'tale [didʒi'tale] *ag* digital; (*delle dita*) finger *cpd*, digital ▷ *sf* (*Bot*) foxglove
digi'tare [didʒi'tare] *vt, vi* (*Inform*) to key (in)
digiu'nare [didʒu'nare] *vi* to starve o.s.; (*Rel*) to fast; **digi'uno, -a** *ag* **essere digiuno** not to have eaten ▷ *sm* fast; **a digiuno** on an empty stomach
dignità [diɲɲi'ta] *sf inv* dignity
'DIGOS ['digos] *sigla f* (= *Divisione Investigazioni Generali e Operazioni Speciali*) police department dealing with political security
digri'gnare [digriɲ'ɲare] *vt* **~ i denti** to grind one's teeth
dilapi'dare *vt* to squander, waste
dila'tare *vt* to dilate; (*gas*) to cause to expand; (*passaggio, cavità*) to open (up); **dilatarsi** *vpr* to dilate; (*Fisica*) to expand
dilazio'nare [dilattsjo'nare] *vt* to delay,

defer
di'lemma, -i sm dilemma
dilet'tante sm/f dilettante; (anche Sport) amateur
dili'gente [dili'dʒɛnte] ag (scrupoloso) diligent; (accurato) careful, accurate
dilu'ire vt to dilute
dilun'garsi vpr (fig): **~ su** to talk at length on o about
diluvi'are vb impers to pour (down)
di'luvio sm downpour; (inondazione, fig) flood
dima'grante ag slimming cpd
dima'grire vi to get thinner, lose weight
dime'nare vt to wave, shake; **dimenarsi** vpr to toss and turn; (fig) to struggle; **~ la coda** (cane) to wag its tail
dimensi'one sf dimension; (grandezza) size
dimenti'canza [dimenti'kantsa] sf forgetfulness; (errore) oversight, slip; **per ~** inadvertently
dimenti'care vt to forget; **ho dimenticato la chiave/il passaporto** I forgot the key/my passport; **dimenticarsi** vpr **dimenticarsi di qc** to forget sth
dimesti'chezza [dimesti'kettsa] sf familiarity
di'mettere vt **~ qn da** to dismiss sb from; (dall'ospedale) to discharge sb from; **dimettersi** vpr **dimettersi (da)** to resign (from)
dimez'zare [dimed'dzare] vt to halve
diminu'ire vt to reduce, diminish; (prezzi) to bring down, reduce ▷ vi to decrease, diminish; (rumore) to die down, die away; (prezzi) to fall, go down
diminu'tivo, -a ag, sm diminutive
dimlnuzi'one sf decreasing, diminishing
di'misi ecc vb vedi **dimettere**
dimissi'oni sfpl resignation sg; **dare** o **presentare le ~** to resign, hand in one's resignation
dimos'trare vt to demonstrate, show; (provare) to prove, demonstrate; **dimostrarsi** vpr **dimostrarsi molto abile** to show o.s. o prove to be very clever; **dimostra 30 anni** he looks about 30 (years old); **dimostrazi'one** sf demonstration; proof
di'namica sf dynamics sg
di'namico, -a, -ci, -che ag dynamic
dina'mite sf dynamite
'dinamo sf inv dynamo
dino'sauro sm dinosaur
din'torni smpl outskirts; **nei ~ di** in the vicinity o neighbourhood of
'dio (pl **'dei**) sm god; **D~** God; **gli dei** the gods; **D~ mio!** my goodness!, my God!

diparti'mento sm department
dipen'dente ag dependent ▷ sm/f employee; **dipendente statale** state employee
di'pendere vi **~ da** to depend on; (finanziariamente) to be dependent on; (derivare) to come from, be due to
di'pesi ecc vb vedi **dipendere**
di'pingere [di'pindʒere] vt to paint
di'pinsi ecc vb vedi **dipingere**
di'pinto, -a pp di **dipingere** ▷ sm painting
diplo'ma, -i sm diploma
diplo'matico, -a, -ci, -che ag diplomatic ▷ sm diplomat
diploma'zia [diplomat'tsia] sf diplomacy
di'porto: imbarcazione da ~ sf pleasure craft
dira'dare vt to thin (out); (visite) to reduce, make less frequent; **diradarsi** vpr to disperse; (nebbia) to clear (up)
'dire vt to say; (segreto, fatto) to tell; **~ qc a qn** to tell sb sth; **~ a qn di fare qc** to tell sb to do sth; **~ di sì/no** to say yes/no; **si dice che ...** they say that ...; **si ~bbe che ...** it looks (o sounds) as though ...; **dica, signora?** (in un negozio) yes, Madam, can I help you?; **come si dice in inglese...?** what's the English (word) for ...?
di'ressi ecc vb vedi **dirigere**
di'retta sf vedi **diretto**
di'retto, -a pp di **dirigere** ▷ ag direct ▷ sm (Ferr) through train
diret'tore, -'trice sm/f (di azienda) director: manager/ess; (di scuola elementare) head (teacher) (BRIT), principal (US); **direttore d'orchestra** conductor; **direttore vendite** sales director o manager
direzi'one [diret'tsjone] sf board of directors; management; (senso di movimento) direction; **in ~ di** in the direction of, towards
diri'gente [diri'dʒɛnte] sm/f executive; (Pol) leader ▷ ag **classe ~** ruling class
di'rigere [di'ridʒere] vt to direct; (impresa) to run, manage; (Mus) to conduct; **dirigersi** vpr **dirigersi verso** o **a** to make o head for
dirim'petto av opposite; **~ a** opposite, facing
di'ritto, -a ag straight; (onesto) straight, upright ▷ av straight, directly; **andare ~** to go straight on ▷ sm right side; (Tennis) forehand; (Maglia) plain stitch; (prerogativa) right; (leggi, scienza) **il ~** law; **diritti** smpl (tasse) duty sg; **stare ~** to stand up straight; **aver ~ a qc** to be entitled to sth; **diritti d'autore** royalties
dirotta'mento sm; **dirottamento**

(aereo) hijack

dirot'tare vt (nave, aereo) to change the course of; (aereo sotto minaccia) to hijack; (traffico) to divert ▷ vi (nave, aereo) to change course; **dirotta'tore, -'trice** sm/f hijacker

di'rotto, -a ag (pioggia) torrential; (pianto) unrestrained; **piovere a ~** to pour; **piangere a ~** to cry one's heart out

di'rupo sm crag, precipice

di'sabile sm/f disabled person ▷ ag disabled; **i disabili** the disabled

disabi'tato, -a ag uninhabited

disabitu'arsi vpr **~ a** to get out of the habit of

disac'cordo sm disagreement

disadat'tato, -a ag (Psic) maladjusted

disa'dorno, -a ag plain, unadorned

disagi'ato, -a [diza'dʒato] ag poor, needy; (vita) hard

di'sagio [di'zadʒo] sm discomfort; (disturbo) inconvenience; (fig: imbarazzo) embarrassment; **essere a ~** to be ill at ease

disappro'vare vt to disapprove of; **disapprovazi'one** sf disapproval

disap'punto sm disappointment

disar'mare vt, vi to disarm; **di'sarmo** sm (Mil) disarmament

di'sastro sm disaster

disas'troso, -a ag disastrous

disat'tento, -a ag inattentive; **disattenzi'one** sf carelessness, lack of attention

disavven'tura sf misadventure, mishap

dis'capito sm **a ~ di** to the detriment of

dis'carica, -che sf (di rifiuti) rubbish tip o dump

di'scendere [diʃ'ʃendere] vt to go (o come) down ▷ vi to go (o come) down; (strada) to go down; (smontare) to get off; **~ da** (famiglia) to be descended from; **~ dalla macchina/dal treno** to get out of the car/out of o off the train; **~ da cavallo** to dismount, get off one's horse

di'scesa [diʃ'ʃesa] sf descent; (pendio) slope; **in ~** (strada) downhill cpd, sloping; **discesa libera** (Sci) downhill (race)

disci'plina [diʃʃi'plina] sf discipline

'disco, -schi sm disc; (Sport) discus; (fonografico) record; (Inform) disk; **disco orario** (Aut) parking disc; **disco rigido** (Inform) hard disk; **disco volante** flying saucer

disco'grafico, -a, ci, che ag record cpd, recording cpd ▷ sm record producer; **casa discografica** record(ing) company

dis'correre vi **~ (di)** to talk (about)

dis'corso, -a pp di **discorrere** ▷ sm speech; (conversazione) conversation, talk

disco'teca, -che sf (raccolta) record library; (locale) disco

discre'panza [diskre'pantsa] sf disagreement

dis'creto, -a ag discreet; (abbastanza buono) reasonable, fair

discriminazi'one [diskriminat'tsjone] sf discrimination

dis'cussi ecc vb vedi **discutere**

discussi'one sf discussion; (litigio) argument; **fuori ~** out of the question

dis'cutere vt to discuss, debate; (contestare) to question ▷ vi (conversare): **~ (di)** to discuss; (litigare) to argue

dis'detta sf (di prenotazione ecc) cancellation; (sfortuna) bad luck

dis'dire vt (prenotazione) to cancel; (Dir): **~ un contratto d'affitto** to give notice (to quit); **vorrei ~ la mia prenotazione** I want to cancel my booking

dise'gnare [diseɲ'ɲare] vt to draw; (progettare) to design; (fig) to outline

disegna'tore, -'trice sm/f designer

di'segno [di'seɲɲo] sm drawing; design; outline; **disegno di legge** (Dir) bill

diser'bante sm weed-killer

diser'tare vt, vi to desert

dis'fare vt to undo; (valigie) to unpack; (meccanismo) to take to pieces; (neve) to melt; **disfarsi** vpr to come undone; (neve) to melt; **~ il letto** to strip the bed; **disfarsi di qn** (liberarsi) to get rid of sb; **dis'fatto, -a** pp di **disfare**

dis'gelo [diz'dʒelo] sm thaw

dis'grazia [diz'grattsja] sf (sventura) misfortune; (incidente) accident, mishap

disgu'ido sm hitch; **disguido postale** error in postal delivery

disgus'tare vt to disgust

dis'gusto sm disgust; **disgus'toso, -a** ag disgusting

disidra'tare vt to dehydrate

disimpa'rare vt to forget

disinfet'tante ag, sm disinfectant

disinfet'tare vt to disinfect

disini'bito, -a ag uninhibited

disinstal'lare vt (software) to uninstall

disinte'grare vt, vi to disintegrate; **disintegrarsi** vpr to disintegrate

disinteres'sarsi vpr **~ di** to take no interest in

disinte'resse sm indifference; (generosità) unselfishness

disintossi'carsi vpr to clear out one's system; (alcolizzato, drogato) to be treated for alcoholism (o drug addiction)

disin'volto, -a ag casual, free and easy

dismi'sura sf excess; **a ~** to excess, excessively

disoccu'pato, -a *ag* unemployed ▷ *sm/f*
unemployed person; **disoccupazi'one** *sf*
unemployment

diso'nesto, -a *ag* dishonest

disordi'nato, -a *ag* untidy; (*privo di misura*)
irregular, wild

di'sordine *sm* (*confusione*) disorder,
confusion; (*sregolatezza*) debauchery;
disordini *smpl* (*Pol ecc*) disorder *sg*;
(*tumulti*) riots

disorien'tare *vt* to disorientate

disorien'tato, -a *ag* disorientated

'**dispari** *ag inv* odd, uneven

dis'parte: **in ~** *av* (*da lato*) aside, apart;
tenersi *o* **starsene in ~** to keep to o.s.,
hold o.s. aloof

dispendi'oso, -a *ag* expensive

dis'pensa *sf* pantry, larder; (*mobile*)
sideboard; (*Dir*) exemption; (*Rel*)
dispensation; (*fascicolo*) number, issue

dispe'rato, -a *ag* (*persona*) in despair;
(*caso, tentativo*) desperate

disperazi'one *sf* despair

dis'perdere *vt* (*disseminare*) to disperse;
(*Mil*) to scatter, rout; (*fig: consumare*) to
waste, squander; **disperdersi** *vpr* to
disperse; to scatter; **dis'perso, -a** *pp di*
disperdere ▷ *sm/f* missing person

dis'petto *sm* spite *no pl*, spitefulness *no
pl*; **fare un ~ a qn** to play a (nasty) trick on
sb; **a ~ di** in spite of; **dispet'toso, -a** *ag*
spiteful

dispia'cere [dispja'tʃere] *sm* (*rammarico*)
regret, sorrow; (*dolore*) grief; **dispiaceri**
smpl (*preoccupazioni*) troubles, worries *vi ~*
a to displease *vb impers* **mi dispiace (che)**
I am sorry (that); **le dispiace se...?** do you
mind if ...?

dis'pone, dis'pongo *ecc vb vedi* **disporre**

dispo'nibile *ag* available

dis'porre *vt* (*sistemare*) to arrange;
(*preparare*) to prepare; (*Dir*) to order;
(*persuadere*): **~ qn a** to incline *o* dispose
sb towards ▷ *vi* (*decidere*) to decide;
(*usufruire*): **~ di** to use, have at one's
disposal; (*essere dotato*): **~ di** to have

dis'posi *ecc vb vedi* **disporre**

disposi'tivo *sm* (*meccanismo*) device

disposizi'one [dispozit'tsjone] *sf*
arrangement, layout; (*stato d'animo*) mood;
(*tendenza*) bent, inclination; (*comando*)
order; (*Dir*) provision, regulation; **a ~ di qn**
at sb's disposal

dis'posto, -a *pp di* **disporre**

disprez'zare [dispret'tsare] *vt* to despise

dis'prezzo [dis'prettso] *sm* contempt

'**disputa** *sf* dispute, quarrel

dispu'tare *vt* (*contendere*) to dispute,
contest; (*gara*) to take part in ▷ *vi* to

quarrel; **~ di** to discuss; **disputarsi qc** to
fight for sth

'**disse** *vb vedi* **dire**

dissente'ria *sf* dysentery

dissen'tire *vi* **~ (da)** to disagree (with)

disse'tante *ag* refreshing

'**dissi** *vb vedi* **dire**

dissimu'lare *vt* (*fingere*) to dissemble;
(*nascondere*) to conceal

dissi'pare *vt* to dissipate; (*scialacquare*) to
squander, waste

dissu'adere *vt* **~ qn da** to dissuade sb
from

distac'care *vt* to detach, separate; (*Sport*)
to leave behind; **distaccarsi** *vpr* to be
detached; (*fig*) to stand out; **distaccarsi
da** (*fig: allontanarsi*) to grow away from

dis'tacco, -chi *sm* (*separazione*)
separation; (*fig: indifferenza*) detachment;
(*Sport*): **vincere con un ~ di ...** to win by a
distance of ...

dis'tante *av* far away ▷ *ag* **~ (da)** distant
(from), far away (from)

dis'tanza [dis'tantsa] *sf* distance

distanzi'are [distan'tsjare] *vt* to
space out, place at intervals; (*Sport*) to
outdistance; (*fig: superare*) to outstrip,
surpass

dis'tare *vi* **distiamo pochi chilometri da
Roma** we are only a few kilometres (away)
from Rome; **quanto dista il centro da
qui?** how far is the town centre?

dis'tendere *vt* (*coperta*) to spread out;
(*gambe*) to stretch (out); (*mettere a giacere*)
to lay; (*rilassare: muscoli, nervi*) to relax;
distendersi *vpr* (*rilassarsi*) to relax;
(*sdraiarsi*) to lie down

dis'tesa *sf* expanse, stretch

dis'teso, -a *pp di* **distendere**

distil'lare *vt* to distil

distille'ria *sf* distillery

dis'tinguere *vt* to distinguish;
distinguersi *vpr* (*essere riconoscibile*) to be
distinguished; (*emergere*) to stand out, be
conspicuous, distinguish o.s.

dis'tinta *sf* (*nota*) note; (*elenco*) list;
distinta di versamento pay-in slip

distin'tivo, -a *ag* distinctive;
distinguishing ▷ *sm* badge

dis'tinto, -a *pp di* **distinguere** ▷ *ag*
(*dignitoso ed elegante*) distinguished;
"distinti saluti" (*in lettera*) yours faithfully

distinzi'one [distin'tsjone] *sf* distinction

dis'togliere [dis'tɔʎʎere] *vt* **~ da** to take
away from; (*fig*) to dissuade from

distorsi'one *sf* (*Med*) sprain; (*Fisica, Ottica*)
distortion

dis'trarre *vt* to distract; (*divertire*) to
entertain, amuse; **distrarsi** *vpr* (*non*

fare attenzione) to be distracted, let one's mind wander; (*svagarsi*) to amuse o enjoy o.s.; **dis'tratto, -a** *pp di* **distrarre** ▷ *ag* absent-minded; (*disattento*) inattentive; **distrazi'one** *sf* absent-mindedness; inattention; (*svago*) distraction, entertainment

dis'tretto *sm* district

distribu'ire *vt* to distribute; (*Carte*) to deal (out); (*posta*) to deliver; (*lavoro*) to allocate, assign; (*ripartire*) to share out; **distribu'tore** *sm* (*di benzina*) petrol (BRIT) o gas (US) pump; (*Aut, Elettr*) distributor; **distributore automatico** vending machine

distri'care *vt* to disentangle, unravel; **districarsi** *vpr* (*tirarsi fuori*): **districarsi da** to get out of, disentangle o.s. from

dis'truggere [dis'truddʒere] *vt* to destroy; **distruzi'one** *sf* destruction

distur'bare *vt* to disturb, trouble; (*sonno, lezioni*) to disturb, interrupt; **disturbarsi** *vpr* to put o.s. out

dis'turbo *sm* trouble, bother, inconvenience; (*indisposizione*) (slight) disorder, ailment; **scusi il ~** I'm sorry to trouble you

disubbidi'ente *ag* disobedient

disubbi'dire *vi* **~ (a qn)** to disobey (sb)

disu'mano, -a *ag* inhuman

di'tale *sm* thimble

'dito (*pl(f)* **'dita**) *sm* finger; (*misura*) finger, finger's breadth; **dito (del piede)** toe

'ditta *sf* firm, business

ditta'tore *sm* dictator

ditta'tura *sf* dictatorship

dit'tongo, -ghi *sm* diphthong

di'urno, -a *ag* day *cpd*, daytime *cpd*

'diva *sf vedi* **divo**

di'vano *sm* sofa; divan; **divano letto** bed settee, sofa bed

divari'care *vt* to open wide

di'vario *sm* difference

diven'tare *vi* to become; **~ famoso/ professore** to become famous/a teacher

diversifi'care *vt* to diversify, vary; to differentiate; **diversificarsi** *vpr* **diversificarsi (per)** to differ (in)

diversità *sf inv* difference, diversity; (*varietà*) variety

diver'sivo *sm* diversion, distraction

di'verso, -a *ag* (*differente*): **~ (da)** different (from); **diversi, -e** *det pl* several, various; (*Comm*) sundry *pron pl* several (people), many (people)

diver'tente *ag* amusing

diverti'mento *sm* amusement, pleasure; (*passatempo*) pastime, recreation

diver'tire *vt* to amuse, entertain;

divertirsi *vpr* to amuse o enjoy o.s.

di'videre *vt* (*anche Mat*) to divide; (*distribuire, ripartire*) to divide (up), split (up); **dividersi** *vpr* (*separarsi*) to separate; (*strade*) to fork

divi'eto *sm* prohibition; **"~ di sosta"** (Aut) "no parking"

divinco'larsi *vpr* to wriggle, writhe

di'vino, -a *ag* divine

di'visa *sf* (*Mil ecc*) uniform; (*Comm*) foreign currency

di'visi *ecc vb vedi* **dividere**

divisi'one *sf* division

'divo, -a *sm/f* star

divo'rare *vt* to devour

divorzi'are [divor'tsjare] *vi* **~ (da qn)** to divorce (sb)

di'vorzio [di'vortsjo] *sm* divorce

divul'gare *vt* to divulge, disclose; (*rendere comprensibile*) to popularize

dizio'nario [ditsjo'narjo] *sm* dictionary

DJ [di'dʒei] *sigla m/f* (= Disk Jockey) DJ

do *sm* (Mus) C; (: *solfeggiando*) do(h)

dobbi'amo *vb vedi* **dovere**

D.O.C. [dɔk] *abbr* (= *denominazione di origine controllata*) label guaranteeing the quality of wine

'doccia, -ce ['dottʃa] *sf* (*bagno*) shower; **fare la ~** to have a shower

do'cente [do'tʃɛnte] *ag* teaching ▷ *sm/f* teacher; (*di università*) lecturer

'docile ['dɔtʃile] *ag* docile

documen'tario *sm* documentary

documentarsi *vpr* **~ (su)** to gather information o material (about)

docu'mento *sm* document; **documenti** *smpl* (*d'identità ecc*) papers

dodi'cesimo, -a [dodi'tʃɛzimo] *num* twelfth

'dodici ['doditʃi] *num* twelve

do'gana *sf* (*ufficio*) customs *pl*; (*tassa*) (customs) duty; **passare la ~** to go through customs; **dogani'ere** *sm* customs officer

'doglie ['dɔʎʎe] *sfpl* (Med) labour *sg*, labour pains

'dolce ['doltʃe] *ag* sweet; (*carattere, persona*) gentle, mild; (*fig: mite: clima*) mild; (*non ripido: pendio*) gentle ▷ *sm* (*sapore dolce*) sweetness, sweet taste; (Cuc: *portata*) sweet, dessert; (: *torta*) cake; **dolcifi'cante** *sm* sweetener

'dollaro *sm* dollar

Dolo'miti *sfpl* **le ~** the Dolomites

do'lore *sm* (*fisico*) pain; (*morale*) sorrow, grief; **dolo'roso, -a** *ag* painful; sorrowful, sad

do'manda *sf* (*interrogazione*) question; (*richiesta*) demand; (: *cortese*) request;

(*Dir: richiesta scritta*) application; (*Econ*):
la ~ demand; **fare una ~ a qn** to ask sb a
question; **fare ~ (per un lavoro)** to apply
(for a job)

doman'dare *vt* (*per avere*) to ask for;
(*per sapere*) to ask; (*esigere*) to demand;
domandarsi *vpr* to wonder; to ask o.s.; **~
qc a qn** to ask sb for sth; to ask sb sth

do'mani *av* tomorrow ▷ *sm* **il ~** (*il futuro*)
the future; (*il giorno successivo*) the next
day; **~ l'altro** the day after tomorrow

do'mare *vt* to tame

doma'tore, -'trice *sm/f* (*gen*) tamer;
domatore di cavalli horsebreaker;
domatore di leoni lion tamer

domat'tina *av* tomorrow morning

do'menica, -che *sf* Sunday; **di** *o* **la ~** on
Sundays

do'mestico, -a, -ci, -che *ag* domestic
▷ *sm/f* servant, domestic

domi'cilio [domi'tʃiljo] *sm* (*Dir*) domicile,
place of residence

domi'nare *vt* to dominate; (*fig: sentimenti*)
to control, master ▷ *vi* to be in the
dominant position

do'nare *vt* to give, present; (*per
beneficenza ecc*) to donate ▷ *vi* (*fig*): **~ a**
to suit, become; **~ sangue** to give blood;
dona'tore, -'trice *sm/f* donor; **donatore
di sangue/di organi** blood/organ donor

dondo'lare *vt* (*cullare*) to rock; **dondolarsi**
vpr to swing, sway; **'dondolo** *sm* **sedia/
cavallo a dondolo** rocking chair/horse

'donna *sf* woman; **donna di casa**
housewife; home-loving woman; **donna
di servizio** maid

donnai'olo *sm* ladykiller

'donnola *sf* weasel

'dono *sm* gift

doping ['dopiŋ] *sm* doping

'dopo *av* (*tempo*) afterwards; (*più tardi*)
later; (*luogo*) after, next ▷ *prep* after ▷ *cong*
(*temporale*): **~ aver studiato** after having
studied; **~ mangiato va a dormire** after
having eaten *o* after a meal he goes for a
sleep ▷ *ag inv* **il giorno ~** the following
day; **un anno ~** a year later; **~ di me/lui**
after me/him; **~, a ~!** see you later!

dopo'barba *sm inv* after-shave

dopodo'mani *av* the day after tomorrow

doposcì [dopoʃʃi] *sm inv* après-ski outfit

dopo'sole *sm inv* aftersun (lotion)

dopo'tutto *av* (*tutto considerato*) after all

doppi'aggio [dop'pjaddʒo] *sm* (*Cinema*)
dubbing

doppi'are *vt* (*Naut*) to round; (*Sport*) to lap;
(*Cinema*) to dub

'doppio, -a *ag* double; (*fig: falso*) double-
dealing, deceitful ▷ *sm* (*quantità*): **il ~**

(*di*) twice as much (*o* many), double the
amount (*o* number) of; (*Sport*) doubles *pl*
▷ *av* double

doppi'one *sm* duplicate (copy)

doppio'petto *sm* double-breasted jacket

dormicch'iare [dormik'kjare] *vi* to doze

dormigli'one, -a [dormiʎ'ʎone] *sm/f*
sleepyhead

dor'mire *vt*, *vi* to sleep; **andare a ~** to go
to bed; **dor'mita** *sf* **farsi una dormita** to
have a good sleep

dormi'torio *sm* dormitory

dormi'veglia [dormi'veʎʎa] *sm*
drowsiness

'dorso *sm* back; (*di montagna*) ridge, crest;
(*di libro*) spine; **a ~ di cavallo** on horseback

do'sare *vt* to measure out; (*Med*) to dose

'dose *sf* quantity, amount; (*Med*) dose

do'tato, -a *ag* **~ di** (*attrezzature*) equipped
with; (*bellezza, intelligenza*) endowed with;
un uomo ~ a gifted man

'dote *sf* (*di sposa*) dowry; (*assegnata a un
ente*) endowment; (*fig*) gift, talent

Dott. *abbr* (= *dottore*) Dr.

dotto'rato *sm* degree; **dottorato di
ricerca** doctorate, doctor's degree

dot'tore, -essa *sm/f* doctor; **chiamate
un ~** call a doctor

● **DOTTORE**
●
● In Italy, anyone who has a degree in any
● subject can use the title **dottore**. Thus
● a person who is addressed as **dottore** is
● not necessarily a doctor of medicine.

dot'trina *sf* doctrine

Dott.ssa *abbr* (= *dottoressa*) Dr.

'dove *av* (*gen*) where; (*in cui*) where,
in which; (*dovunque*) wherever ▷ *cong*
(*mentre, laddove*) whereas; **~ sei?/vai?**
where are you?/are you going?; **dimmi
dov'è** tell me where it is; **di ~ sei?** where
are you from?; **per ~ si passa?** which way
should we go?; **la città ~ abito** the town
where *o* in which I live; **siediti ~ vuoi** sit
wherever you like

do'vere *sm* (*obbligo*) duty ▷ *vt* (*essere
debitore*): **~ qc (a qn)** to owe (sb) sth
▷ *vi* (*seguito dall'infinito: obbligo*) to
have to; **rivolgersi a chi di ~** to apply
to the appropriate authority *o* person;
lui deve farlo he has to do it, he must
do it; **quanto le devo?** how much do I
owe you?; **è dovuto partire** he had to
leave; **ha dovuto pagare** he had to pay;
(: *intenzione*): **devo partire domani** I'm
(due) to leave tomorrow; (: *probabilità*):
dev'essere tardi it must be late; **come**

si deve (*lavorare, comportarsi*) properly;
una persona come si deve a respectable
person

dove'roso, -a *ag* (right and) proper

dovrò *ecc vb vedi* **dovere**

do'vunque *av* (*in qualunque luogo*)
wherever; (*dappertutto*) everywhere; **~ io
vada** wherever I go

do'vuto, -a *ag* (*causato*): **~ a** due to

doz'zina [dod'dzina] *sf* dozen; **una ~ di
uova** a dozen eggs

dozzi'nale [doddzi'nale] *ag* cheap,
second-rate

'drago, -ghi *sm* dragon

'dramma, -i *sm* drama; **dram'matico, -a,
-ci, -che** *ag* dramatic

'drastico, -a, -ci, -che *ag* drastic

'dritto, -a *ag, av* = **diritto**

'droga, -ghe *sf* (*sostanza aromatica*) spice;
(*stupefacente*) drug; **droghe leggere/
pesanti** soft/hard drugs

drogarsi *vpr* to take drugs

dro'gato, -a *sm/f* drug addict

droghe'ria [droge'ria] *sf* grocer's shop
(BRIT), grocery (store) (US)

drome'dario *sm* dromedary

DS [di'esse] *sigla mpl* (= *Democratici di
Sinistra*) *Italian left-wing party*

'dubbio, -a *ag* (*incerto*) doubtful, dubious;
(*ambiguo*) dubious ▷ *sm* (*incertezza*) doubt;
avere il ~ che to be afraid that, suspect
that; **mettere in ~ qc** to question sth

dubi'tare *vi* **~ di** to doubt; (*risultato*) to be
doubtful of

Dub'lino *sf* Dublin

'duca, -chi *sm* duke

du'chessa [du'kessa] *sf* duchess

'due *num* two

due'cento [due'tʃɛnto] *num* two hundred
▷ *sm* **il D~** the thirteenth century

due'pezzi [due'pɛttsi] *sm* (*costume
da bagno*) two-piece swimsuit; (*abito
femminile*) two-piece suit

'dunque *cong* (*perciò*) so, therefore;
(*riprendendo il discorso*) well (then) ▷ *sm inv*
venire al ~ to come to the point

du'omo *sm* cathedral

Attenzione! In inglese esiste la parola
dome, che però significa *cupola*.

dupli'cato *sm* duplicate

'duplice ['duplitʃe] *ag* double, twofold; **in
~ copia** in duplicate

du'rante *prep* during

du'rare *vi* to last; **~ fatica a** to have
difficulty in

du'rezza [du'rettsa] *sf* hardness;
stubbornness; harshness; toughness

'duro, -a *ag* (*pietra, lavoro, materasso,
problema*) hard; (*persona: ostinato*)
stubborn, obstinate; (*severo*) harsh, hard;
(*voce*) harsh; (*carne*) tough ▷ *sm* hardness;
(*difficoltà*) hard part; (*persona*) tough
guy; **tener ~** to stand firm, hold out; **~
d'orecchi** hard of hearing

DVD [divu'di] *sigla m* (= *digital versatile (or)
video disc*) DVD; (*lettore*) DVD player

e

e (dav V spesso **ed**) cong and; **e lui?** what about him?; **e compralo!** well buy it then!

E abbr (= est) E

è vb vedi **essere**

eb'bene cong well (then)

'ebbi ecc vb vedi **avere**

e'braico, -a, -ci, -che ag Hebrew, Hebraic ▷ sm (Ling) Hebrew

e'breo, -a ag Jewish ▷ sm/f Jew/ess

EC abbr (= Eurocity) fast train connecting Western European cities

ecc. av abbr (= eccetera) etc

eccel'lente [ettʃel'lɛnte] ag excellent

ec'centrico, -a, -ci, -che [et'tʃɛntriko] ag eccentric

ecces'sivo, -a [ettʃes'sivo] ag excessive

ec'cesso [et'tʃɛsso] sm excess; **all'~** (gentile, generoso) to excess, excessively; **eccesso di velocità** (Aut) speeding

ec'cetera [et'tʃɛtera] av et cetera, and so on

ec'cetto [et'tʃɛtto] prep except, with the exception of; **~ che** except, other than; **~ che (non)** unless

eccezio'nale [ettʃettsjo'nale] ag exceptional

eccezi'one [ettʃet'tsjone] sf exception; (Dir) objection; **a ~ di** with the exception of, except for; **d'~** exceptional

ecci'tare [ettʃi'tare] vt (curiosità, interesse) to excite, arouse; (folla) to incite; **eccitarsi** vpr to get excited; (sessualmente) to become aroused

'ecco av (per dimostrare): **~ il treno!** here's o here comes the train!; (dav pron): **~mi!** here I am!; **~ne uno!** here's one (of them)!; (dav pp): **~ fatto!** there, that's it done!

ec'come av rather; **ti piace? — ~!** do you like it? — I'll say! o and how! o rather! (BRIT)

e'clisse sf eclipse

'eco (pl(m) **'echi**) sm o f echo

ecogra'fia sf (Med) scan

ecolo'gia [ekolo'dʒia] sf ecology

eco'logico, -a, ci, che [eko'lɔdʒiko] ag ecological

econo'mia sf economy; (scienza) economics sg; (risparmio: azione) saving; **fare ~** to economize, make economies; **eco'nomico, -a, -ci, -che** ag economic; (poco costoso) economical

ecstasy ['ɛkstazi] sf Ecstasy

'edera sf ivy

e'dicola sf newspaper kiosk o stand (US)

edi'ficio [edi'fitʃo] sm building

e'dile ag building cpd

Edim'burgo sf Edinburgh

edi'tore, -'trice ag publishing cpd ▷ sm/f publisher

> Attenzione! In inglese esiste la parola *editor*, che però significa *redattore*.

edizi'one [edit'tsjone] sf edition; (tiratura) printing; **edizione straordinaria** special edition

edu'care vt to educate; (gusto, mente) to train; **~ qn a fare** to train sb to do; **edu'cato, -a** ag polite, well-mannered; **educazi'one** sf education; (familiare) upbringing; (comportamento) (good) manners pl; **educazione fisica** (Ins) physical training o education

> Attenzione! In inglese esiste la parola *educated*, che però significa *istruito*.

educherò ecc [eduke'rɔ] vb vedi **educare**

effemi'nato, -a ag effeminate

efferve'scente [efferveʃ'ʃɛnte] ag effervescent

effet'tivo, -a ag (reale) real, actual; (impiegato, professore) permanent; (Mil) regular ▷ sm (Mil) strength; (di patrimonio ecc) sum total

ef'fetto sm effect; (Comm: cambiale) bill; (fig: impressione) impression; **in effetti** in fact, actually; **effetto serra** greenhouse effect; **effetti personali** personal effects, personal belongings

effi'cace [effi'katʃe] ag effective

effici'ente [effi'tʃɛnte] ag efficient

E'geo [e'dʒɛo] sm **l'~, il mare ~** the Aegean (Sea)

e

E'gitto [e'dʒitto] *sm* **I'~** Egypt

egizi'ano, -a [edʒit'tsjano] *ag, sm/f* Egyptian

'egli ['eʎʎi] *pron* he; **~ stesso** he himself

ego'ismo *sm* selfishness, egoism; **ego'ista, -i, -e** *ag* selfish, egoistic ▷ *sm/f* egoist

Egr. *abbr* = **egregio**

e'gregio, -a, -gi, -gie [e'grɛdʒo] *ag* (*nelle lettere*): **E~ Signore** Dear Sir

E.I. *abbr* = **Esercito Italiano**

elabo'rare *vt* (*progetto*) to work out, elaborate; (*dati*) to process

elasticiz'zato, -a [elastitʃid'dzato] *ag* stretch *cpd*

e'lastico, -a, -ci, -che *ag* elastic; (*fig: andatura*) springy; (: *decisione, vedute*) flexible ▷ *sm* (*di gomma*) rubber band; (*per il cucito*) elastic *no pl*

ele'fante *sm* elephant

ele'gante *ag* elegant

e'leggere [e'lɛddʒere] *vt* to elect

elemen'tare *ag* elementary; **le (scuole) elementari** *sfpl* primary (*BRIT*) o grade (*US*) school

ele'mento *sm* element; (*parte componente*) element, component, part; **elementi** *smpl* (*della scienza ecc*) elements, rudiments

ele'mosina *sf* charity, alms *pl*; **chiedere l'~** to beg

elen'care *vt* to list

elencherò *ecc* [elenke'rɔ] *vb vedi* **elencare**

e'lenco, -chi *sm* list; **elenco telefonico** telephone directory

e'lessi *ecc vb vedi* **eleggere**

eletto'rale *ag* electoral, election *cpd*

elet'tore, -'trice *sm/f* voter, elector

elet'trauto *sm inv* workshop for car electrical repairs; (*tecnico*) car electrician

elettri'cista, -i [elettri'tʃista] *sm* electrician

elettricità [elettritʃi'ta] *sf* electricity

e'lettrico, -a, -ci, -che *ag* electric(al)

elettriz'zante [elettrid'dzante] *ag* (*fig*) electrifying, thrilling

elettriz'zare [elettrid'dzare] *vt* to electrify; **elettrizzarsi** *vpr* to become charged with electricity

e'lettro... *prefisso*; **elettrodo'mestico, -a, -ci, -che** *ag* apparecchi **elettrodomestici** domestic (electrical) appliances; **elet'tronico, -a, -ci, -che** *ag* electronic

elezi'one [elet'tsjone] *sf* election; **elezioni** *sfpl* (*Pol*) election(s)

'elica, -che *sf* propeller

eli'cottero *sm* helicopter

elimi'nare *vt* to eliminate

elisoc'corso *sm* helicopter ambulance

el'metto *sm* helmet

elogi'are [elo'dʒare] *vt* to praise

elo'quente *ag* eloquent

e'ludere *vt* to evade

e'lusi *ecc vb vedi* **eludere**

e-mail [i'mɛil] *sf inv* (*messaggio, sistema*) e-mail ▷ *ag inv* (*indirizzo*) e-mail

emargi'nato, -a [emardʒi'nato] *sm/f* outcast; **emarginazione** [emardʒinat'tsjone] *sf* marginalization

embri'one *sm* embryo

emenda'mento *sm* amendment

emer'genza [emer'dʒɛntsa] *sf* emergency; **in caso di ~** in an emergency

e'mergere [e'mɛrdʒere] *vi* to emerge; (*sommergibile*) to surface; (*fig: distinguersi*) to stand out

e'mersi *ecc vb vedi* **emergere**

e'mettere *vt* (*suono, luce*) to give out, emit; (*onde radio*) to send out; (*assegno, francobollo, ordine*) to issue

emi'crania *sf* migraine

emi'grare *vi* to emigrate

emis'fero *sm* hemisphere; **emisfero australe** southern hemisphere; **emisfero boreale** northern hemisphere

e'misi *ecc vb vedi* **emettere**

emit'tente *ag* (*banca*) issuing; (*Radio*) broadcasting, transmitting ▷ *sf* (*Radio*) transmitter

emorra'gia, -'gie [emorra'dʒia] *sf* haemorrhage

emor'roidi *sfpl* haemorrhoids *pl* (*BRIT*), hemorrhoids *pl* (*US*)

emo'tivo, -a *ag* emotional

emozio'nante [emottsjo'nante] *ag* exciting, thrilling

emozionare [emottsjo'nare] *vt* (*commuovere*) to move; (*agitare*) to make nervous; (*elettrizzare*) to excite; **emozionarsi** *vpr* to be moved; to be nervous; to be excited; **emozionato, -a** [emottsjo'nato] *ag* (*commosso*) moved; (*agitato*) nervous; (*elettrizzato*) excited

emozi'one [emot'tsjone] *sf* emotion; (*agitazione*) excitement

enciclope'dia [entʃiklope'dia] *sf* encyclopaedia

endove'noso, -a *ag* (*Med*) intravenous

'E.N.E.L. ['enel] *sigla m* (= *Ente Nazionale per l'Energia Elettrica*) national electricity company

ener'getico, -a, ci, che [ener'dʒetiko] *ag* (*risorse, crisi*) energy *cpd*; (*sostanza, alimento*) energy-giving

ener'gia, -'gie [ener'dʒia] *sf* (*Fisica*) energy; (*fig*) energy, strength, vigour; **energia eolica** wind power; **energia solare** solar energy, solar power;

e'nergico, -a, -ci, -che ag energetic, vigorous

'enfasi sf emphasis; (peg) bombast, pomposity

en'nesimo, -a ag (Mat, fig) nth; **per l'ennesima volta** for the umpteenth time

e'norme ag enormous, huge

'ente sm (istituzione) body, board, corporation; (Filosofia) being; **enti pubblici** public bodies; **ente di ricerca** research organization

en'trambi, -e pron pl both (of them) ▷ ag pl **~ i ragazzi** both boys, both of the boys

en'trare vi to go (o come) in; **~ in** (luogo) to enter, go (o come) into; (trovar posto, poter stare) to fit into; (essere ammesso a: club ecc) to join, become a member of; **~ in automobile** to get into the car; **far ~ qn** (visitatore ecc) to show sb in; **questo non c'entra** (fig) that's got nothing to do with it; **en'trata** sf entrance, entry; **dov'è l'entrata?** where's the entrance?; **entrate** sfpl (Comm) receipts, takings; (Econ) income sg

'entro prep (temporale) within

entusias'mare vt to excite, fill with enthusiasm; **entusiasmarsi** vpr **entusiasmarsi (per qc/qn)** to become enthusiastic (about sth/sb); **entusi'asmo** sm enthusiasm; **entusi'asta, -i, -e** ag enthusiastic ▷ sm/f enthusiast

epa'tite sf hepatitis

epide'mia sf epidemic

epiles'sia sf epilepsy

epi'lettico, -a, ci, che ag, sm/f epileptic

epi'sodio sm episode

'epoca, -che sf (periodo storico) age, era; (tempo) time; (Geo) age

ep'pure cong and yet, nevertheless

EPT sigla m (= Ente Provinciale per il Turismo) district tourist bureau

equa'tore sm equator

equazi'one [ekwat'tsjone] sf (Mat) equation

e'questre ag equestrian

equi'librio sm balance, equilibrium; **perdere l'equilibrare** to lose one's balance

e'quino, -a ag horse cpd, equine

equipaggia'mento [ekwipaddʒa'mento] sm (operazione: di nave) equipping, fitting out; (: di spedizione, esercito) equipping, kitting out; (attrezzatura) equipment

equipaggi'are [ekwipad'dʒare] vt (di persone) to man; (di mezzi) to equip; **equipaggiarsi** vpr to equip o.s.; **equi'paggio** sm crew

equitazi'one [ekwitat'tsjone] sf (horse-)riding

equiva'lente ag, sm equivalent

e'quivoco, -a, -ci, -che ag equivocal, ambiguous; (sospetto) dubious ▷ sm misunderstanding; **a scanso di equivoci** to avoid any misunderstanding; **giocare sull'~** to equivocate

'equo, -a ag fair, just

'era sf era

'era ecc vb vedi **essere**

'erba sf grass; **in ~** (fig) budding; **erbe aromatiche** herbs; **erba medica** lucerne; **er'baccia, -ce** sf weed

erboriste'ria sf (scienza) study of medicinal herbs; (negozio) herbalist's (shop)

e'rede sm/f heir; **eredità** sf (Dir) inheritance; (Biol) heredity; **lasciare qc in eredità a qn** to leave o bequeath sth to sb; **eredi'tare** vt to inherit; **eredi'tario, -a** ag hereditary

ere'mita, -i sm hermit

er'gastolo sm (Dir: pena) life imprisonment

'erica sf heather

er'metico, -a, -ci, -che ag hermetic

'ernia sf (Med) hernia

'ero vb vedi **essere**

e'roe sm hero

ero'gare vt (somme) to distribute; (gas, servizi) to supply

e'roico, -a, -ci, -che ag heroic

ero'ina sf heroine; (droga) heroin

erosi'one sf erosion

e'rotico, -a, -ci, -che ag erotic

er'rato, -a ag wrong

er'rore sm error, mistake; (morale) error; **per ~** by mistake; **ci dev'essere un ~** there must be some mistake; **errore giudiziario** miscarriage of justice

eruzi'one [erut'tsjone] sf eruption

esacer'bare [ezatʃer'bare] vt to exacerbate

esage'rare [ezadʒe'rare] vt to exaggerate ▷ vi to exaggerate; (eccedere) to go too far

esal'tare vt to exalt; (entusiasmare) to excite, stir

e'same sm examination; (Ins) exam, examination; **fare o dare un ~** to sit o take an exam; **esame di guida** driving test; **esame del sangue** blood test

esami'nare vt to examine

esaspe'rare vt to exasperate, to exacerbate

esatta'mente av exactly; accurately, precisely

esat'tezza [ezat'tettsa] sf exactitude, accuracy, precision

e'satto, -a pp di **esigere** ▷ ag (calcolo, ora) correct, right, exact; (preciso) accurate,

precise; (*puntuale*) punctual
esau'dire *vt* to grant, fulfil
esauri'ente *ag* exhaustive
esauri'mento *sm* exhaustion;
esaurimento nervoso nervous
breakdown
esau'rire *vt* (*stancare*) to exhaust, wear
out; (*provviste, miniera*) to exhaust;
esaurirsi *vpr* to exhaust o.s., wear o.s.
out; (*provviste*) to run out; **esau'rito, -a**
ag exhausted; (*merci*) sold out; **registrare
il tutto esaurito** (*Teatro*) to have a full
house; **e'sausto, -a** *ag* exhausted
'esca (*pl* **'esche**) *sf* bait
'esce ['eʃʃe] *vb vedi* **uscire**
eschi'mese [eski'mese] *ag, sm/f* Eskimo
'esci ['eʃʃi] *vb vedi* **uscire**
escla'mare *vi* to exclaim, cry out
esclama'tivo, -a *ag* **punto ~** exclamation
mark
esclamazi'one *sf* exclamation
es'cludere *vt* to exclude
es'clusi *ecc vb vedi* **escludere**
esclusi'one *sf* exclusion; **a ~ di, fatta
~ per** except (for), apart from; **senza ~
(alcuna)** without exception; **procedere
per ~** to follow a process of elimination;
senza ~ di colpi (*fig*) with no holds barred;
esclusione sociale social exclusion
esclu'siva *sf* (*Dir, Comm*) exclusive *o* sole
rights *pl*
esclusiva'mente *av* exclusively, solely
esclu'sivo, -a *ag* exclusive
es'cluso, -a *pp di* **escludere**
'esco *vb vedi* **uscire**
escogi'tare [eskodʒi'tare] *vt* to devise,
think up
'escono *vb vedi* **uscire**
escursi'one *sf* (*gita*) excursion, trip;
(*: a piedi*) hike, walk; (*Meteor*) range;
escursione termica temperature range
esecuzi'one [ezekut'tsjone] *sf* execution,
carrying out; (*Mus*) performance;
esecuzione capitale execution
esegu'ire *vt* to carry out, execute; (*Mus*) to
perform, execute
e'sempio *sm* example; **per ~** for example,
for instance; **fare un ~** to give an example;
esem'plare *ag* exemplary ▷ *sm* example;
(*copia*) copy
eserci'tare [ezertʃi'tare] *vt* (*professione*)
to practise (BRIT), practice (US); (*allenare:
corpo, mente*) to exercise, train; (*diritto*)
to exercise; (*influenza, pressione*) to exert;
esercitarsi *vpr* to practise; **esercitarsi
alla lotta** to practise fighting
e'sercito [e'zertʃito] *sm* army
eser'cizio [ezer'tʃittsjo] *sm* practice;
exercising; (*fisico: di matematica*) exercise;

(*Econ*) financial year; (*azienda*) business,
concern; **in ~** (*medico ecc*) practising;
esercizio pubblico (*Comm*) commercial
concern
esi'bire *vt* to exhibit, display; (*documenti*)
to produce, present; **esibirsi** *vpr* (*attore*)
to perform; (*fig*) to show off; **esibizi'one**
sf exhibition; (*di documento*) presentation;
(*spettacolo*) show, performance
esi'gente [ezi'dʒɛnte] *ag* demanding
e'sigere [e'zidʒere] *vt* (*pretendere*) to
demand; (*richiedere*) to demand, require;
(*imposte*) to collect
'esile *ag* (*persona*) slender, slim; (*stelo*) thin;
(*voce*) faint
esili'are *vt* to exile; **e'silio** *sm* exile
esis'tenza [ezis'tɛntsa] *sf* existence
e'sistere *vi* to exist
esi'tare *vi* to hesitate
'esito *sm* result, outcome
'esodo *sm* exodus
esone'rare *vt* to exempt
e'sordio *sm* debut
esor'tare *vt* **~ qn a fare** to urge sb to do
e'sotico, -a, -ci, -che *ag* exotic
es'pandere *vt* to expand; (*confini*) to
extend; (*influenza*) to extend, spread;
espandersi *vpr* to expand; **espansi'one**
sf expansion; **espansione di memoria**
(*Inform*) memory upgrade; **espan'sivo, -a**
ag expansive, communicative
espatri'are *vi* to leave one's country
espedi'ente *sm* expedient
es'pellere *vt* to expel
esperi'enza [espe'rjɛntsa] *sf* experience
esperi'mento *sm* experiment
es'perto, -a *ag, sm* expert
espi'rare *vt, vi* to breathe out
es'plicito, -a [es'plitʃito] *ag* explicit
es'plodere *vi* (*anche fig*) to explode ▷ *vt*
to fire
esplo'rare *vt* to explore
esplosi'one *sf* explosion
es'pone *ecc vb vedi* **esporre**
es'pongo, es'poni *ecc vb vedi* **esporre**
es'porre *vt* (*merci*) to display; (*quadro*)
to exhibit, show; (*fatti, idee*) to explain,
set out; (*porre in pericolo, Fot*) to expose;
esporsi *vpr* **esporsi a** (*sole, pericolo*) to
expose o.s. to; (*critiche*) to lay o.s. open to
espor'tare *vt* to export
es'pose *ecc vb vedi* **esporre**
esposizi'one [espozit'tsjone] *sf*
displaying; exhibiting; setting out;
(*anche Fot*) exposure; (*mostra*) exhibition;
(*narrazione*) explanation, exposition
es'posto, -a *pp di* **esporre** ▷ *ag* **~ a nord**
facing north ▷ *sm* (*Amm*) statement,
account; (*: petizione*) petition

espressi'one *sf* expression
espres'sivo, -a *ag* expressive
es'presso, -a *pp di* **esprimere** ▷ *ag*
express ▷ *sm* (*lettera*) express letter;
(*anche:* **treno ~**) express train; (*anche:* **caffè**
~) espresso
es'primere *vt* to express; **esprimersi** *vpr*
to express o.s.
es'pulsi *ecc vb vedi* **espellere**
espulsi'one *sf* expulsion
es'senza [es'sɛntsa] *sf* essence;
essenzi'ale *ag* essential; **l'essenziale** the
main *o* most important thing

PAROLA CHIAVE

'essere *sm* being; **essere umano** human
being
▷ *vb copulativo* **1** (*con attributo, sostantivo*)
to be; **sei giovane/simpatico** you are *o*
you're young/nice; **è medico** he is *o* he's
a doctor
2 (*+ di: appartenere*) to be; **di chi è la**
penna? whose pen is it?; **è di Carla** it is *o*
it's Carla's, it belongs to Carla
3 (*+ di: provenire*) to be; **è di Venezia** he is *o*
he's from Venice
4 (*data, ora*): **è il 15 agosto/lunedì** it is *o*
it's the 15th of August/Monday; **che ora**
è?, che ore sono? what time is it?; **è l'una**
it is *o* it's one o'clock; **sono le due** it is *o* it's
two o'clock
5 (*costare*): **quant'è?** how much is it?; **sono**
10 euro it's 10 euros
▷ *vb aus* **1** (*attivo*): **essere arrivato/**
venuto to have arrived/come; **è già**
partita she has already left
2 (*passivo*) to be; **essere fatto da** to be
made by; **è stata uccisa** she has been
killed
3 (*riflessivo*): **si sono lavati** they washed,
they got washed
4 (*+ da + infinito*): **è da farsi subito** it must
be *o* is to be done immediately
▷ *vi* **1** (*esistere, trovarsi*) to be; **sono a casa**
I'm at home; **essere in piedi/seduto** to be
standing/sitting
2: **esserci**: **c'è** there is; **ci sono** there are;
che c'è? what's the matter?, what is it?; **ci**
sono! (*fig: ho capito*) I get it!; *vedi anche* **ci**
▷ *vb impers*: **è tardi/Pasqua** it's late/
Easter; **è possibile che venga** he may
come; **è così** that's the way it is

'essi, *pron mpl vedi* **esso**
'esso, -a *pron* it; (*riferito a persona: soggetto*)
he/she; (: *complemento*) him/her
est *sm* east
es'tate *sf* summer

esteri'ore *ag* outward, external
es'terno, -a *ag* (*porta, muro*) outer,
outside; (*scala*) outside; (*alunno,*
impressione) external ▷ *sm* outside,
exterior ▷ *sm/f* (*allievo*) day pupil; **all'~**
outside; **per uso ~** for external use only;
esterni *smpl* (*Cinema*) location shots
'estero, -a *ag* foreign ▷ *sm* **all'~** abroad
es'teso, -a *pp di* **estendere** ▷ *ag*
extensive, large; **scrivere per ~** to write
in full
es'tetico, -a, -ci, -che *ag* aesthetic
▷ *sf* (*disciplina*) aesthetics *sg*; (*bellezza*)
attractiveness; **este'tista, -i, -e** *sm/f*
beautician
es'tinguere *vt* to extinguish, put out;
(*debito*) to pay off; **estinguersi** *vpr* to go
out; (*specie*) to become extinct
es'tinsi *ecc vb vedi* **estinguere**
estin'tore *sm* (*fire*) extinguisher
estinzi'one *sf* putting out; (*di specie*)
extinction
estir'pare *vt* (*pianta*) to uproot, pull up;
(*fig: vizio*) to eradicate
es'tivo, -a *ag* summer *cpd*
es'torcere [es'tɔrtʃere] *vt* **~ qc (a qn)** to
extort sth (from sb)
estradizi'one [estradit'tsjone] *sf*
extradition
es'trae, es'traggo *ecc vb vedi* **estrarre**
es'traneo, -a *ag* foreign ▷ *sm/f* stranger;
rimanere ~ a qc to take no part in sth
es'trarre *vt* to extract; (*minerali*) to mine;
(*sorteggiare*) to draw
es'trassi *ecc vb vedi* **estrarre**
estrema'mente *av* extremely
estre'mista, -i, e *sm/f* extremist
estremità *sf inv* extremity, end ▷ *sfpl*
(*Anat*) extremities
es'tremo, -a *ag* extreme; (*ultimo: ora,*
tentativo) final, last ▷ *sm* extreme; (*di*
pazienza, forze) limit, end; **estremi** *smpl*
(*Amm: dati essenziali*) details, particulars;
l'~ Oriente the Far East
estro'verso, -a *ag, sm* extrovert
età *sf inv* age; **all'~ di 8 anni** at the age of
8, at 8 years of age; **ha la mia ~** he (*o* she) is
the same age as me *o* as I am; **raggiungere**
la maggiore ~ to come of age; **essere in ~**
minore to be under age
'etere *sm* ether
eternità *sf* eternity
e'terno, -a *ag* eternal
etero'geneo, -a [etero'dʒɛneo] *ag*
heterogeneous
eterosessu'ale *ag, sm/f* heterosexual
'etica *sf* ethics *sg*; *vedi anche* **etico**
eti'chetta [eti'ketta] *sf* label; (*cerimoniale*):
l'~ etiquette

'etico, -a, -ci, -che *ag* ethical
eti'lometro *sm* Breathalyzer®
etimolo'gia, -'gie [etimolo'dʒia] *sf* etymology
Eti'opia *sf* l'~ Ethiopia
'etnico, -a, -ci, -che *ag* ethnic
e'trusco, -a, -schi, -sche *ag, sm/f* Etruscan
'ettaro *sm* hectare (=10,000 m^2)
'etto *sm abbr* (=*ettogrammo*) 100 grams
'euro *sm inv* (*divisa*) euro
Eu'ropa *sf* l'~ Europe
europarlamen'tare *sm/f* Member of the European Parliament, MEP
euro'peo, -a *ag, sm/f* European
eutana'sia *sf* euthanasia
evacu'are *vt* to evacuate
e'vadere *vi* (*fuggire*): ~ **da** to escape from ▷ *vt* (*sbrigare*) to deal with, dispatch; (*tasse*) to evade
evapo'rare *vi* to evaporate
e'vasi *ecc vb vedi* **evadere**
evasi'one *sf* (*vedi* evadere) escape; dispatch; **evasione fiscale** tax evasion
eva'sivo, -a *ag* evasive
e'vaso, -a *pp di* **evadere** ▷ *sm* escapee
e'vento *sm* event
eventu'ale *ag* possible

> Attenzione! In inglese esiste la parola *eventual*, che però significa *finale*.

eventual'mente *av* if necessary

> Attenzione! In inglese esiste la parola *eventually*, che però significa *alla fine*.

evi'dente *ag* evident, obvious
evidente'mente *av* evidently; (*palesemente*) obviously, evidently
evi'tare *vt* to avoid; ~ **di fare** to avoid doing; ~ **qc a qn** to spare sb sth
evoluzi'one [evolut'tsjone] *sf* evolution
e'volversi *vpr* to evolve
ev'viva *escl* hurrah!; ~ **il re!** long live the king!, hurrah for the king!
ex *prefisso* ex, former
'extra *ag inv* first-rate; top-quality ▷ *sm inv* extra; **extracomuni'tario, -a** *ag* from outside the EC ▷ *sm/f* non-EC citizen
extrater'restre *ag, sm/f* extraterrestrial

fa *vb vedi* **fare** ▷ *sm inv* (*Mus*) F; (: *solfeggiando la scala*) fa ▷ *av* **10 anni fa** 10 years ago
'fabbrica *sf* factory; **fabbri'care** *vt* to build; (*produrre*) to manufacture, make; (*fig*) to fabricate, invent

> Attenzione! In inglese esiste la parola *fabric*, che però significa *stoffa*.

fac'cenda [fat'tʃɛnda] *sf* matter, affair; (*cosa da fare*) task, chore
fac'chino [fak'kino] *sm* porter
'faccia, -ce ['fattʃa] *sf* face; (*di moneta, medaglia*) side; **faccia a faccia** face to face
facci'ata [fat'tʃata] *sf* façade; (*di pagina*) side
'faccio ['fattʃo] *vb vedi* **fare**
fa'cessi [fa'tʃessi] *vb vedi* **fare**
fa'cevo [fa'tʃevo] *vb vedi* **fare**
'facile ['fatʃile] *ag* easy; (*disposto*): ~ **a** inclined to, prone to; (*probabile*): **è ~ che piova** it's likely to rain
facoltà *sf inv* faculty; (*autorità*) power
facolta'tivo, -a *ag* optional; (*fermata d'autobus*) request *cpd*
'faggio ['faddʒo] *sm* beech
fagi'ano [fa'dʒano] *sm* pheasant
fagio'lino [fadʒo'lino] *sm* French (BRIT) o string bean
fagi'olo [fa'dʒɔlo] *sm* bean
'fai *vb vedi* **fare**

'fai·da·'te *sm inv* DIY, do-it-yourself

'falce ['faltʃe] *sf* scythe; **falci'are** *vt* to cut; *(fig)* to mow down

falcia'trice [faltʃa'tritʃe] *sf (per fieno)* reaping machine; *(per erba)* mowing machine

'falco, -chi *sm* hawk

'falda *sf* layer, stratum; *(di cappello)* brim; *(di cappotto)* tails *pl; (di monte)* lower slope; *(di tetto)* pitch

fale'gname [faleɲ'name] *sm* joiner

falli'mento *sm* failure; bankruptcy

fal'lire *vi (non riuscire)*: **~ (in)** to fail (in); *(Dir)* to go bankrupt ▷ *vt (colpo, bersaglio)* to miss

'fallo *sm* error, mistake; *(imperfezione)* defect, flaw; *(Sport)* foul; fault; **senza ~** without fail

falò *sm inv* bonfire

falsifi'care *vt* to forge; *(monete)* to forge, counterfeit

'falso, -a *ag* false; *(errato)* wrong; *(falsificato)* forged; fake; *(: oro, gioielli)* imitation *cpd* ▷ *sm* forgery; **giurare il ~** to commit perjury

'fama *sf* fame; *(reputazione)* reputation, name

'fame *sf* hunger; **aver ~** to be hungry

fa'miglia [fa'miʎʎa] *sf* family

famili'are *ag (della famiglia)* family *cpd; (ben noto)* familiar; *(rapporti, atmosfera)* friendly; *(Ling)* informal, colloquial ▷ *sm/f* relative, relation

fa'moso, -a *ag* famous, well-known

fa'nale *sm (Aut)* light, lamp *(BRIT); (luce stradale, Naut)* light, *(di faro)* beacon

fa'natico, -a, -ci, -che *ag* fanatical; *(del teatro, calcio ecc)*: **~ di** o **per** mad o crazy about ▷ *sm/f* fanatic; *(tifoso)* fan

'fango, -ghi *sm* mud

'fanno *vb vedi* **fare**

fannul'lone, -a *sm/f* idler, loafer

fantasci'enza [fantaʃ'ʃentsa] *sf* science fiction

fanta'sia *sf* fantasy, imagination; *(capriccio)* whim, caprice ▷ *ag inv* **vestito ~** patterned dress

fan'tasma, -i *sm* ghost, phantom

fan'tastico, -a, -ci, -che *ag* fantastic; *(potenza, ingegno)* imaginative

fan'tino *sm* jockey

fara'butto *sm* crook

fard *sm inv* blusher

◯ PAROLA CHIAVE

'fare *sm* **1** *(modo di fare)*: **con fare distratto** absent-mindedly; **ha un fare simpatico** he has a pleasant manner

2: **sul far del giorno/della notte** at daybreak/nightfall

▷ *vt* **1** *(fabbricare, creare)* to make; *(: casa)* to build; *(: assegno)* to make out; **fare un pasto/una promessa/un film** to make a meal/a promise/a film; **fare rumore** to make a noise

2 *(effettuare: lavoro, attività, studi)* to do; *(: sport)* to play; **cosa fa?** *(adesso)* what are you doing?; *(di professione)* what do you do?; **fare psicologia/italiano** *(Ins)* to do psychology/Italian; **fare un viaggio** to go on a trip o journey; **fare una passeggiata** to go for a walk; **fare la spesa** to do the shopping

3 *(funzione)* to be; *(Teatro)* to play, be; **fare il medico** to be a doctor; **fare il malato** *(fingere)* to act the invalid

4 *(suscitare: sentimenti)*: **fare paura a qn** to frighten sb; **(non) fa niente** *(non importa)* it doesn't matter

5 *(ammontare)*: **3 più 3 fa 6** 3 and 3 are o make 6; **fanno 3 euro** that's 3 euros; **Roma fa 2.000.000 di abitanti** Rome has 2,000,000 inhabitants; **che ora fai?** what time do you make it?

6 (+ *infinito*): **far fare qc a qn** *(obbligare)* to make sb do sth; *(permettere)* to let sb do sth; **fammi vedere** let me see; **far partire il motore** to start (up) the engine; **far riparare la macchina/costruire una casa** to get o have the car repaired/a house built

7: **farsi: farsi una gonna** to make o.s. a skirt; **farsi un nome** to make a name for o.s.; **farsi la permanente** to get a perm; **farsi tagliare i capelli** to get one's hair cut; **farsi operare** to have an operation

8 *(fraseologia)*: **farcela** to succeed, manage; **non ce la faccio più** I can't go on; **ce la faremo** we'll make it; **me l'hanno fatta!** *(imbrogliare)* I've been done!; **lo facevo più giovane** I thought he was younger; **fare sì/no con la testa** to nod/shake one's head

▷ *vi* **1** *(agire)* to act, do; **fate come volete** do as you like; **fare presto** to be quick; **fare da** to act as; **non c'è niente da fare** it's no use; **saperci fare con qn/qc** to know how to deal with sb/sth; **faccia pure!** go ahead!

2 *(dire)* to say; **"davvero?" fece** "really?" he said

3: **fare per** *(essere adatto)* to be suitable for; **fare per fare qc** to be about to do sth; **fece per andarsene** he made as if to leave

4: **farsi: si fa così** you do it like this, this is the way it's done; **non si fa così!** *(rimprovero)* that's no way to behave!; **la festa non si fa** the party is off

5: **fare a gara con qn** to compete o vie
with sb; **fare a pugni** to come to blows;
fare in tempo a fare to be in time to do
▷ vb impers **fa bel tempo** the weather
is fine; **fa caldo/freddo** it's hot/cold;
fa notte it's getting dark ▷ vpr **farsi 1**
(diventare) to become; **farsi prete** to
become a priest; **farsi grande/vecchio** to
grow tall/old
2 (spostarsi): **farsi avanti/indietro** to
move forward/back
3 (fam: drogarsi) to be a junkie

far'falla sf butterfly
fa'rina sf flour
farma'cia, -'cie [farma'tʃia] sf pharmacy;
(negozio) chemist's (shop) (BRIT),
pharmacy; **farma'cista, -i, -e** sm/f
chemist (BRIT), pharmacist
'farmaco, -ci o **chi** sm drug, medicine
'faro sm (Naut) lighthouse; (Aer) beacon;
(Aut) headlight
'fascia, -sce ['faʃʃa] sf band, strip; (Med)
bandage; (di sindaco, ufficiale) sash; (parte
di territorio) strip, belt; (di contribuenti ecc)
group, band; **essere in fasce** (anche fig)
to be in one's infancy; **fascia oraria** time
band
fasci'are [faʃʃare] vt to bind; (Med) to
bandage
fa'scicolo [faʃʃikolo] sm (di documenti)
file, dossier; (di rivista) issue, number;
(opuscolo) booklet, pamphlet
'fascino ['faʃʃino] sm charm, fascination
fa'scismo [faʃʃizmo] sm fascism
'fase sf phase; (Tecn) stroke; **fuori ~**
(motore) rough
fas'tidio sm bother, trouble; **dare ~ a
qn** to bother o annoy sb; **sento ~ allo
stomaco** my stomach's upset; **avere
fastidi con la polizia** to have trouble o
bother with the police; **fastidi'oso, -a** ag
annoying, tiresome

Attenzione! In inglese esiste la parola
fastidious, che però significa pignolo.

'fata sf fairy
fa'tale ag fatal; (inevitabile) inevitable; (fig)
irresistible
fa'tica, -che sf hard work, toil; (sforzo)
effort; (di metalli) fatigue; **a ~ with**
difficulty; **fare ~ a fare qc** to have a
job doing sth; **fati'coso, -a** ag tiring,
exhausting; (lavoro) laborious
'fatto, -a pp di **fare** ▷ ag **un uomo ~** a
grown man; **~ a mano/in casa** hand-
/home-made ▷ sm fact; (azione) deed;
(avvenimento) event, occurrence; (di
romanzo, film) action, story; **cogliere qn
sul ~** to catch sb red-handed; **il ~ sta** o **è**

che the fact remains o is that; **in ~ di** as for,
as far as ... is concerned
fat'tore sm (Agr) farm manager; (Mat,
elemento costitutivo) factor; **fattore di
protezione** (di lozione solare) factor; **vorrei
una crema solare con ~ di protezione 15**
I'd like a factor 15 suntan cream
fatto'ria sf farm; farmhouse

Attenzione! In inglese esiste la parola
factory, che però significa fabbrica.

fatto'rino sm errand-boy; (di ufficio) office-
boy; (d'albergo) porter
fat'tura sf (Comm) invoice; (di abito)
tailoring; (malia) spell
fattu'rato sm (Comm) turnover
'fauna sf fauna
'fava sf broad bean
'favola sf (fiaba) fairy tale; (d'intento morale)
fable; (fandonia) yarn; **favo'loso, -a** ag
fabulous; (incredibile) incredible
fa'vore sm favour; **per ~** please; **fare un ~
a qn** to do sb a favour
favo'rire vt to favour; (il commercio,
l'industria, le arti) to promote, encourage;
vuole ~? won't you help yourself?;
favorisca in salotto please come into the
sitting room
fax sm inv fax; **mandare qc via ~** to fax sth
fazzo'letto [fattso'letto] sm
handkerchief; (per la testa) (head)scarf;
fazzoletto di carta tissue
feb'braio sm February
'febbre sf fever; **aver la ~** to have a high
temperature; **febbre da fieno** hay fever
'feci ecc ['fɛtʃi] vb vedi **fare**
fecondazi'one [fekondat'tsjone] sf
fertilization; **fecondazione artificiale**
artificial insemination
fe'condo, -a ag fertile
'fede sf (credenza) belief, faith; (Rel)
faith; (fiducia) faith, trust; (fedeltà)
loyalty; (anello) wedding ring; (attestato)
certificate; **aver ~ in qn** to have faith in sb;
in buona/cattiva ~ in good/bad faith; **"in
~"** (Dir) "in witness whereof"; **fe'dele** ag
fedele (a) faithful (to) ▷ sm/f follower; **i
fedeli** (Rel) the faithful
'federa sf pillowslip, pillowcase
fede'rale ag federal
'fegato sm liver; (fig) guts pl, nerve
'felce ['fɛltʃe] sf fern
fe'lice [fe'litʃe] ag happy; (fortunato) lucky;
felicità sf happiness
felici'tarsi [felitʃi'tarsi] vpr (congratularsi):
~ con qn per qc to congratulate sb on sth
fe'lino, -a ag, sm feline
'felpa sf sweatshirt
'femmina sf (Zool, Tecn) female; (figlia)
girl, daughter; (spesso peg) woman;

femmi'nile *ag* feminine; (*sesso*) female; (*lavoro, giornale, moda*) woman's ▷ *sm* (*Ling*) feminine

'femore *sm* thighbone, femur

fe'nomeno *sm* phenomenon

feri'ale *ag* giorno ~ weekday

'ferie *sfpl* holidays (BRIT), vacation *sg* (US); **andare in ~** to go on holiday *o* vacation

fe'rire *vt* to injure; (*deliberatamente: Mil ecc*) to wound; (*colpire*) to hurt; **ferirsi** *vpr* to hurt o.s., injure o.s; **fe'rita** *sf* injury, wound; **fe'rito, -a** *sm/f* wounded *o* injured man/woman

fer'maglio [fer'maʎʎo] *sm* clasp; (*per documenti*) clip

fer'mare *vt* to stop, halt; (*Polizia*) to detain, hold ▷ *vi* to stop; **fermarsi** *vpr* to stop, halt; **fermarsi a fare qc** to stop to do sth; **può fermarsi qui/all'angolo?** could you stop here/at the corner?

fer'mata *sf* stop; **fermata dell'autobus** bus stop

fer'menti *smpl* ~ **lattici** probiotic bacteria

fer'mezza [fer'mettsa] *sf* (*fig*) firmness, steadfastness

'fermo, -a *ag* still, motionless; (*veicolo*) stationary; (*orologio*) not working; (*saldo: anche fig*) firm; (*voce, mano*) steady ▷ *escl* stop!; keep still! ▷ *sm* (*chiusura*) catch, lock; (*Dir*): **fermo di polizia** police detention

fe'roce [fe'rotʃe] *ag* (*animale*) fierce, ferocious; (*persona*) cruel, fierce; (*fame, dolore*) raging; **le bestie feroci** wild animals

ferra'gosto *sm* (*festa*) feast of the Assumption; (*periodo*) August holidays *pl*

○ **FERRAGOSTO**
●
● **Ferragosto**, August 15th, is a national
● holiday. Marking the Feast of the
● Assumption, its origins are religious
● but in recent years it has simply become
● the most important public holiday of
● the summer season. Most people take
● some extra time off work and head out
● of town to the holiday resorts.

ferra'menta *sfpl* negozio di ~ ironmonger's (BRIT), hardware shop *o* store (US)

'ferro *sm* iron; **una bistecca ai ferri** a grilled steak; **ferro battuto** wrought iron; **ferro da calza** knitting needle; **ferro di cavallo** horseshoe; **ferro da stiro** iron

ferro'via *sf* railway (BRIT), railroad (US); **ferrovi'ario, -a** *ag* railway *cpd* (BRIT), railroad *cpd* (US); **ferrovi'ere** *sm*

railwayman (BRIT), railroad man (US)

'fertile *ag* fertile

'fesso, -a *pp di* **fendere** ▷ *ag* (*fam: sciocco*) crazy, cracked

fes'sura *sf* crack, split; (*per gettone, moneta*) slot

'festa *sf* (*religiosa*) feast; (*pubblica*) holiday; (*compleanno*) birthday; (*onomastico*) name day; (*ricevimento*) celebration, party; **far ~** to have a holiday; to live it up; **far ~ a qn** to give sb a warm welcome

festeggi'are [fested'dʒare] *vt* to celebrate; (*persona*) to have a celebration for

fes'tivo, -a *ag* (*atmosfera*) festive; **giorno ~** holiday

'feto *sm* foetus (BRIT), fetus (US)

'fetta *sf* slice

fettuc'cine [fettut'tʃine] *sfpl* (*Cuc*) ribbon-shaped pasta

FF.SS. *abbr* – **Ferrovie dello Stato**

FI *sigla* = **Firenze** ▷ *abbr* (= **Forza Italia**) *Italian centre-right political party*

fi'aba *sf* fairy tale

fi'acca *sf* weariness; (*svogliatezza*) listlessness

fi'acco, -a, -chi, -che *ag* (*stanco*) tired, weary; (*svogliato*) listless; (*debole*) weak; (*mercato*) slack

fi'accola *sf* torch

fi'ala *sf* phial

fi'amma *sf* flame

fiam'mante *ag* (*colore*) flaming; **nuovo ~** brand new

fiam'mifero *sm* match

fiam'mingo, -a, -ghi, -ghe *ag* Flemish ▷ *sm/f* Fleming ▷ *sm* (*Ling*) Flemish; **i Fiamminghi** the Flemish

fi'anco, -chi *sm* side; (*Mil*) flank; **di ~** sideways, from the side; **a ~ a ~** side by side

fi'asco, -schi *sm* flask; (*fig*) fiasco; **fare ~** to fail

fia'tare *vi* (*fig: parlare*): **senza ~** without saying a word

fi'ato *sm* breath; (*resistenza*) stamina; **avere il ~ grosso** to be out of breath; **prendere ~** to catch one's breath

'fibbia *sf* buckle

'fibra *sf* fibre; (*fig*) constitution

fic'care *vt* to push, thrust, drive; **ficcarsi** *vpr* (*andare a finire*) to get to

ficcherò *ecc* [fikke'rɔ] *vb vedi* **ficcare**

'fico, -chi *sm* (*pianta*) fig tree; (*frutto*) fig; **fico d'India** prickly pear; **fico secco** dried fig

fidanza'mento [fidantsa'mento] *sm* engagement

fidan'zarsi [fidan'tsarsi] *vpr* to get engaged; **fidan'zato, -a** *sm/f* fiancé/

fiancée

fi'darsi *vpr* ~ **di** to trust; **fi'dato, -a** *ag* reliable, trustworthy

fi'ducia [fi'dutʃa] *sf* confidence, trust; **incarico di** ~ position of trust, responsible position; **persona di** ~ reliable person

fie'nile *sm* barn; hayloft

fi'eno *sm* hay

fi'era *sf* fair

fi'ero, -a *ag* proud; (*audace*) bold

'fifa (*fam*) *sf* **aver** ~ to have the jitters

fig. *abbr* (= *figura*) fig.

'figlia ['fiʎʎa] *sf* daughter

figli'astro, -a [fiʎ'ʎastro] *sm/f* stepson/daughter

'figlio ['fiʎʎo] *sm* son; (*senza distinzione di sesso*) child; **figlio di papà** spoilt, wealthy young man; **figlio unico** only child

fi'gura *sf* figure; (*forma, aspetto esterno*) form, shape; (*illustrazione*) picture, illustration; **far** ~ to look smart; **fare una brutta** ~ to make a bad impression

figu'rina *sf* figurine; (*cartoncino*) picture card

'fila *sf* row, line; (*coda*) queue; (*serie*) series, string; **di** ~ in succession; **fare la** ~ to queue; **in** ~ **indiana** in single file

fi'lare *vt* to spin ▷ *vi* (*baco, ragno*) to spin; (*formaggio fuso*) to go stringy; (*discorso*) to hang together; (*fam: amoreggiare*) to go steady; (*muoversi a forte velocità*) to go at full speed; ~ **diritto** (*fig*) to toe the line; ~ **via** to dash off

filas'trocca, -che *sf* nursery rhyme

filate'lia *sf* philately, stamp collecting

fi'letto *sm* (*di vite*) thread; (*di carne*) fillet

fili'ale *ag* filial ▷ *sf* (*di impresa*) branch

film *sm inv* film

'filo *sm* (*anche fig*) thread; (*filato*) yarn; (*metallico*) wire; (*di lama, rasoio*) edge; **per** ~ **e per segno** in detail; **con un** ~ **di voce** in a whisper; **filo d'erba** blade of grass; **filo interdentale** dental floss; **filo di perle** string of pearls; **filo spinato** barbed wire

fi'lone *sm* (*di minerali*) seam, vein; (*pane*) ≈ Vienna loaf; (*fig*) trend

filoso'fia *sf* philosophy; **fi'losofo, -a** *sm/f* philosopher

fil'trare *vt, vi* to filter

'filtro *sm* filter; **filtro dell'olio** (*Aut*) oil filter

fi'nale *ag* final ▷ *sm* (*di opera*) end, ending; (: *Mus*) finale ▷ *sf* (*Sport*) final; **final'mente** *av* finally, at last

fi'nanza [fi'nantsa] *sf* finance; **finanze** *sfpl* (*di individuo, Stato*) finances

finché [fin'ke] *cong* (*per tutto il tempo che*) as long as; (*fino al momento in cui*) until; **aspetta ~ io (non) sia ritornato** wait

until I get back

'fine *ag* (*lamina, carta*) thin; (*capelli, polvere*) fine; (*vista, udito*) keen, sharp; (*persona: raffinata*) refined, distinguished; (*osservazione*) subtle ▷ *sf* end ▷ *sm* aim, purpose; (*esito*) result, outcome; **secondo** ~ ulterior motive; **in** *o* **alla** ~ in the end, finally

fi'nestra *sf* window; **fines'trino** *sm* window; **vorrei un posto vicino al finestrino** I'd like a window seat

'fingere ['findʒere] *vt* to feign; (*supporre*) to imagine, suppose; **fingersi** *vpr* **fingersi ubriaco/pazzo** to pretend to be drunk/mad; ~ **di fare** to pretend to do

fi'nire *vt* to finish ▷ *vi* to finish, end; **quando finisce lo spettacolo?** when does the show finish?; ~ **di fare** (*compiere*) to finish doing; (*smettere*) to stop doing; ~ **in galera** to end up *o* finish up in prison

finlan'dese *ag, sm* (*Ling*) Finnish ▷ *sm/f* Finn

Fin'landia *sf* **la** ~ Finland

'fino, -a *ag* (*capelli, seta*) fine; (*oro*) pure; (*fig: acuto*) shrewd ▷ *av* (*spesso troncato in* **fin**: *pure, anche*) even ▷ *prep* (*spesso troncato in fin*: *tempo*): **fin quando?** till when?; (: *luogo*): **fin qui** as far as here; ~ **a** (*tempo*) until, till; (*luogo*) as far as, (up) to; **fin da domani** from tomorrow onwards; **fin da ieri** since yesterday; **fin dalla nascita** from *o* since birth

fi'nocchio [fi'nɔkkjo] *sm* fennel; (*fam: peg: omosessuale*) queer

fi'nora *av* up till now

'finsi *ecc vb vedi* **fingere**

'finta *sf* pretence, sham; (*Sport*) feint; **far** ~ **(di fare)** to pretend (to do)

'finto, -a *pp di* **fingere** ▷ *ag* false; artificial

finzi'one [fin'tsjone] *sf* pretence, sham

fi'occo, -chi *sm* (*di nastro*) bow; (*di stoffa, lana*) flock; (*di neve*) flake; (*Naut*) jib; **coi fiocchi** (*fig*) first-rate; **fiocchi di avena** oatflakes; **fiocchi di granturco** cornflakes

fi'ocina ['fjɔtʃina] *sf* harpoon

fi'oco, -a, -chi, -che *ag* faint, dim

fi'onda *sf* catapult

fio'raio, -a *sm/f* florist

fi'ore *sm* flower; **fiori** *smpl* (*Carte*) clubs; **a fior d'acqua** on the surface of the water; **avere i nervi a fior di pelle** to be on edge; **fior di latte** cream; **fiori di campo** wild flowers

fioren'tino, -a *ag* Florentine

fio'retto *sm* (*Scherma*) foil

fio'rire *vi* (*rosa*) to flower; (*albero*) to blossom; (*fig*) to flourish

Fi'renze [fi'rɛntse] *sf* Florence

'firma sf signature

Attenzione! In inglese esiste la parola firm, che però significa ditta.

fir'mare vt to sign; **un abito firmato** a designer suit; **dove devo ~?** where do I sign?

fisar'monica, -che sf accordion

fis'cale ag fiscal, tax cpd; **medico ~** doctor employed by Social Security to verify cases of sick leave

fischi'are [fis'kjare] vi to whistle ▷ vt to whistle; (attore) to boo, hiss

fischi'etto [fis'kjetto] sm (strumento) whistle

'fischio ['fiskjo] sm whistle

'fisco sm tax authorities pl, ≈ Inland Revenue (BRIT), ≈ Internal Revenue Service (US)

'fisica sf physics sg

'fisico, -a, -ci, -che ag physical ▷ sm/f physicist ▷ sm physique

fisiotera'pia sf physiotherapy

fisiotera'pista sm/f physiotherapist

fis'sare vt to fix, fasten; (guardare intensamente) to stare at; (data, condizioni) to fix, establish, set; (prenotare) to book; **fissarsi** vpr **fissarsi su** (sguardo, attenzione) to focus on; (fig: idea) to become obsessed with

'fisso, -a ag fixed; (stipendio, impiego) regular ▷ av **guardare ~ qc/qn** to stare at sth/sb

'fitta sf sharp pain; vedi anche **fitto**

fit'tizio, -a ag fictitious, imaginary

'fitto, -a ag thick, dense; (pioggia) heavy ▷ sm depths pl, middle; (affitto, pigione) rent

fi'ume sm river

fiu'tare vt to smell, sniff; (animale) to scent; (fig: inganno) to get wind of, smell, ~ **tabacco/cocaina** to take snuff/cocaine

fla'grante ag **cogliere qn in ~** to catch sb red-handed

fla'nella sf flannel

flash [flaʃ] sm inv (Fot) flash; (giornalistico) newsflash

'flauto sm flute

fles'sibile ag pliable; (fig: che si adatta) flexible

flessibili'tà sf (anche fig) flexibility

flessi'one sf (gen) bending; (Ginnastica: a terra) sit-up; (: in piedi) forward bend; (: sulle gambe) knee-bend; (diminuzione) slight drop, slight fall; (Ling) inflection; **fare una ~** to bend; **una ~ economica** a downward trend in the economy

'flettere vt to bend

'flipper sm inv pinball machine

F.lli abbr (= fratelli) Bros.

'flora sf flora

'florido, -a ag flourishing; (fig) glowing with health

'floscio, -a, -sci, -sce ['floʃʃo] ag (cappello) floppy, soft; (muscoli) flabby

'flotta sf fleet

'fluido, -a ag, sm fluid

flu'oro sm fluorine

'flusso sm flow; (Fisica, Med) flux; **~ e ri~** ebb and flow

fluvi'ale ag river cpd, fluvial

FMI sigla m (= Fondo Monetario Internazionale) IMF

'foca, -che sf (Zool) seal

fo'caccia, -ce [fo'kattʃa] sf kind of pizza; (dolce) bun

'foce ['fotʃe] sf (Geo) mouth

foco'laio sm (Med) centre of infection; (fig) hotbed

foco'lare sm hearth, fireside; (Tecn) furnace

'fodera sf (di vestito) lining; (di libro, poltrona) cover

'fodero sm (di spada) scabbard; (di pugnale) sheath; (di pistola) holster

'foga sf enthusiasm, ardour

'foglia ['fɔʎʎa] sf leaf; **foglia d'argento/ d'oro** silver/gold leaf

'foglio ['fɔʎʎo] sm (di carta) sheet (of paper); (di metallo) sheet; **foglio di calcolo** (Inform) spreadsheet; **foglio rosa** (Aut) provisional licence; **foglio di via** (Dir) expulsion order; **foglio volante** pamphlet

'fogna ['foɲɲa] sf drain, sewer

föhn [føːn] sm inv hair dryer

'folla sf crowd, throng

'folle ag mad, insane; (Tecn) idle; **in ~** (Aut) in neutral

fol'lia sf folly, foolishness; foolish act; (pazzia) madness, lunacy

'folto, -a ag thick

fon sm inv hair dryer

fondamen'tale ag fundamental, basic

fonda'mento sm foundation; **fondamenta** sfpl (Edil) foundations

fon'dare vt to found; (fig: dar base): **~ qc su** to base sth on

fon'dente ag **cioccolato ~** plain o dark chocolate

'fondere vt (neve) to melt; (metallo) to fuse, melt; (fig: colori) to merge, blend; (: imprese, gruppi) to merge ▷ vi to melt; **fondersi** vpr to melt; (fig: partiti, correnti) to unite, merge

'fondo, -a ag deep ▷ sm (di recipiente, pozzo) bottom; (di stanza) back; (quantità di liquido che resta, deposito) dregs pl; (sfondo) background; (unità immobiliare) property, estate; (somma di denaro) fund; (Sport) long-distance race; **fondi** *smpl* (*denaro*) funds; **a notte fonda** at dead of night; **in ~ a** at the bottom of; at the back of; (*strada*) at the end of; **andare a ~** (*nave*) to sink; **conoscere a ~** to know inside out; **dar ~ a** (*fig*: *provviste, soldi*) to use up; **in ~** (*fig*) after all, all things considered; **andare fino in ~ a** (*fig*) to examine thoroughly; **a ~ perduto** (*Comm*) without security; **fondi di magazzino** old *o* unsold stock *sg*; **fondi di caffè** coffee grounds; **fondo comune di investimento** investment trust

fondo'tinta *sm inv* (*cosmetico*) foundation

fo'netica *sf* phonetics *sg*

fon'tana *sf* fountain

'fonte *sf* spring, source; (*fig*) source ▷ *sm*: **fonte battesimale** (*Rel*) font; **fonte energetica** source of energy

fo'raggio [fo'raddʒo] *sm* fodder, forage

fo'rare *vt* to pierce, make a hole in; (*pallone*) to burst; (*biglietto*) to punch; **~ una gomma** to burst a tyre (BRIT) *o* tire (US)

'forbici ['fɔrbitʃi] *sfpl* scissors

'forca, -che *sf* (*Agr*) fork, pitchfork; (*patibolo*) gallows *sg*

for'chetta [for'ketta] *sf* fork

for'cina [for'tʃina] *sf* hairpin

fo'resta *sf* forest

foresti'ero, -a *ag* foreign ▷ *sm/f* foreigner

'forfora *sf* dandruff

'forma *sf* form; (*aspetto esteriore*) form, shape; (*Dir*: *procedura*) procedure; (*per calzature*) last; (*stampo da cucina*) mould

formag'gino [formad'dʒino] *sm* processed cheese

for'maggio [for'maddʒo] *sm* cheese

for'male *ag* formal

for'mare *vt* to form, shape, make; (*numero di telefono*) to dial; (*fig*: *carattere*) to form, mould; **formarsi** *vpr* to form, take shape; **for'mato** *sm* format, size; **formazi'one** *sf* formation; (*fig*: *educazione*) training; **formazione professionale** vocational training

for'mica¹, -che *sf* ant

formica®² ['fɔrmika] *sf* (*materiale*) Formica®

formi'dabile *ag* powerful, formidable; (*straordinario*) remarkable

'formula *sf* formula; **formula di cortesia** courtesy form

formu'lare *vt* to formulate; to express

for'naio *sm* baker

for'nello *sm* (*elettrico, a gas*) ring; (*di pipa*) bowl

for'nire *vt* **~ qn di qc, ~ qc a qn** to provide *o* supply sb with sth, supply sth to sb

'forno *sm* (*di cucina*) oven; (*panetteria*) bakery; (*Tecn*: *per calce ecc*) kiln; (: *per metalli*) furnace; **forno a microonde** microwave oven

'foro *sm* (*buco*) hole; (*Storia*) forum; (*tribunale*) (law) court

'forse *av* perhaps, maybe; (*circa*) about; **essere in ~** to be in doubt

'forte *ag* strong; (*suono*) loud; (*spesa*) considerable, great; (*passione, dolore*) great, deep ▷ *av* strongly; (*velocemente*) fast; (*a voce alta*) loud(ly); (*violentemente*) hard ▷ *sm* (*edificio*) fort; (*specialità*) forte, strong point; **essere ~ in qc** to be good at sth

for'tezza [for'tettsa] *sf* (*morale*) strength; (*luogo fortificato*) fortress

for'tuito, -a *ag* fortuitous, chance

for'tuna *sf* (*destino*) fortune, luck; (*buona sorte*) success, fortune; (*eredità, averi*) fortune; **per ~** luckily, fortunately; **di ~** makeshift, improvised; **atterraggio di ~** emergency landing; **fortu'nato, -a** *ag* lucky, fortunate; (*coronato da successo*) successful

'forza ['fɔrtsa] *sf* strength; (*potere*) power; (*Fisica*) force; **forze** *sfpl* (*fisiche*) strength *sg*; (*Mil*) forces *escl* come on!; **per ~** against one's will; (*naturalmente*) of course; **a viva ~** by force; **a ~ di** by dint of; **~ maggiore** circumstances beyond one's control; **la ~ pubblica** the police *pl*; **forze armate** armed forces; **forze dell'ordine** the forces of law and order; **Forza Italia** *Italian centre-right political party*; **forza di pace** peacekeeping force

for'zare [for'tsare] *vt* to force; **~ qn a fare** to force sb to do

for'zista, -i, e [for'tsista] *ag* of Forza Italia ▷ *sm/f* member (*o* supporter) of Forza Italia

fos'chia [fos'kia] *sf* mist, haze

'fosco, -a, -schi, -sche *ag* dark, gloomy

'fosforo *sm* phosphorous

'fossa *sf* pit; (*di cimitero*) grave; **fossa biologica** septic tank

fos'sato *sm* ditch; (*di fortezza*) moat

fos'setta *sf* dimple

'fossi *ecc vb vedi* **essere**

'fossile *ag, sm* fossil

'fosso *sm* ditch; (*Mil*) trench

'foste *ecc vb vedi* **essere**

'foto *sf* photo; **può farci una ~, per favore?** would you take a picture of us, please? ▷ *prefisso*: **foto ricordo** souvenir photo; **foto tessera** passport(-type) photo; **foto'camera** *sf* **fotocamera digitale** digital camera; **foto'copia** *sf* photocopy; **fotocopi'are** *vt* to photocopy; **fotocopia'trice** [fotokopja'tritʃe] *sf* photocopier; **fotogra'fare** *vt* to photograph; **fotogra'fia** *sf* (*procedimento*) photography; (*immagine*) photograph; **fare una fotografia** to take a photograph; **una fotografia a colori/in bianco e nero** a colour/black and white photograph; **foto'grafico, -a, -ci, che** *ag* photographic; **macchina fotografica** camera; **fo'tografo, -a** *sm/f* photographer; **fotoro'manzo** *sm* romantic picture story

fou'lard [fu'lar] *sm inv* scarf

fra *prep* = **tra**

'fradicio, -a, -ci, -ce ['fraditʃo] *ag* (*molto bagnato*) soaking (wet); **ubriaco ~** blind drunk

'fragile ['fradʒile] *ag* fragile; (*fig: salute*) delicate

'fragola *sf* strawberry

fra'grante *ag* fragrant

frain'tendere *vt* to misunderstand

fram'mento *sm* fragment

'frana *sf* landslide; (*fig: persona*): **essere una ~** to be useless

fran'cese [fran'tʃeze] *ag* French ▷ *sm/f* Frenchman/woman ▷ *sm* (*Ling*) French; **i Francesi** the French

'Francia ['frantʃa] *sf* **la ~** France

'franco, -a, -chi, -che *ag* (*Comm*) free; (*sincero*) frank, open, sincere ▷ *sm* (*moneta*) franc; **farla franca** (*fig*) to get off scot-free; **prezzo ~ fabbrica** ex-works price; **franco di dogana** duty-free

franco'bollo *sm* (postage) stamp

'frangia, -ge ['frandʒa] *sf* fringe

frap'pé *sm* milk shake

'frase *sf* (*Ling*) sentence; (*locuzione, espressione, Mus*) phrase; **frase fatta** set phrase

'frassino *sm* ash (tree)

frastagli'ato, -a [frastaʎ'ʎato] *ag* (*costa*) indented, jagged

frastor'nare *vt* to daze; to befuddle

frastu'ono *sm* hubbub, din

'frate *sm* friar, monk

fratel'lastro *sm* stepbrother; (*con genitore in comune*) half-brother

fra'tello *sm* brother; **fratelli** *smpl* brothers; (*nel senso di fratelli e sorelle*) brothers and sisters

fra'terno, -a *ag* fraternal, brotherly

frat'tempo *sm* **nel ~** in the meantime, meanwhile

frat'tura *sf* fracture; (*fig*) split, break

frazi'one [frat'tsjone] *sf* fraction; (*di comune*) small town

'freccia, -ce ['frettʃa] *sf* arrow; **freccia di direzione** (*Aut*) indicator

fred'dezza [fred'dettsa] *sf* coldness

'freddo, -a *ag, sm* cold; **fa ~** it's cold;

aver ~ to be cold; **a ~** (*fig*) deliberately; **freddo'loso, -a** *ag* sensitive to the cold

fre'gare *vt* to rub; (*fam: truffare*) to take in, cheat; (*: rubare*) to swipe, pinch; **fregarsene** (*fam!*): **chi se ne frega?** who gives a damn (about it)?

fregherò *ecc* [frege'rɔ] *vb vedi* **fregare**

fre'nare *vt* (*veicolo*) to slow down; (*cavallo*) to rein in; (*lacrime*) to restrain, hold back ▷ *vi* to brake; **frenarsi** *vpr* (*fig*) to restrain o.s., control o.s.

'freno *sm* brake; (*morso*) bit; **tenere a ~** to restrain; **freno a disco** disc brake; **freno a mano** handbrake

frequen'tare *vt* (*scuola, corso*) to attend; (*locale, bar*) to go to, frequent; (*persone*) to see (often)

frequen'tato, -a *ag* (*locale*) busy

fre'quente *ag* frequent; **di ~** frequently

fres'chezza [fres'kettsa] *sf* freshness

'fresco, -a, -schi, -sche *ag* fresh; (*temperatura*) cool; (*notizia*) recent, fresh ▷ *sm* **godere il ~** to enjoy the cool air; **stare ~** (*fig*) to be in for it; **mettere al ~** to put in a cool place

'fretta *sf* hurry, haste; **in ~** in a hurry; **in ~ e furia** in a mad rush; **aver ~** to be in a hurry

'friggere ['friddʒere] *vt* to fry ▷ *vi* (*olio ecc*) to sizzle

'frigido, -a ['fridʒido] *ag* (*Med*) frigid

'frigo *sm* fridge

frigo'bar *sm inv* minibar

frigo'rifero, -a *ag* refrigerating ▷ *sm* refrigerator

fringu'ello *sm* chaffinch

'frissi *ecc* *vb vedi* **friggere**

frit'tata *sf* omelette; **fare una ~** (*fig*) to make a mess of things

frit'tella *sf* (*Cuc*) fritter

'fritto, -a *pp di* **friggere** ▷ *ag* fried ▷ *sm* fried food; **fritto misto** mixed fry

frit'tura *sf* (*Cuc*): **frittura di pesce** mixed fried fish

'frivolo, -a *ag* frivolous

frizi'one [frit'tsjone] *sf* friction; (*sulla pelle*) rub, rub-down; (*Aut*) clutch

friz'zante [frid'dzante] *ag* (*anche fig*) sparkling

fro'dare *vt* to defraud, cheat

'frode *sf* fraud; **frode fiscale** tax evasion

'fronda *sf* (leafy) branch; (*di partito politico*) internal opposition, **fronde** *sfpl* (*di albero*) foliage *sg*

fron'tale *ag* frontal; (*scontro*) head-on

'fronte *sf* (*Anat*) forehead; (*di edificio*) front, façade ▷ *sm* (*Mil, Pol, Meteor*) front; **a ~**, **di ~** facing, opposite; **di ~ a** (*posizione*) opposite, facing, in front of; (*a paragone di*) compared with

fronti'era sf border, frontier

'frottola sf fib

fru'gare vi to rummage ▷ vt to search

frugherò ecc [fruge'rɔ] vb vedi **frugare**

frul'lare vt (Cuc) to whisk ▷ vi (uccelli) to flutter; **frul'lato** sm milk shake; fruit drink; **frulla'tore** sm electric mixer

fru'mento sm wheat

fru'scio [fruʃʃio] sm rustle; rustling; (di acque) murmur

'frusta sf whip; (Cuc) whisk

frus'tare vt to whip

frus'trato, -a ag frustrated

'frutta sf fruit; (portata) dessert; **frutta candita** candied fruit; **frutta secca** dried fruit

frut'tare vi to bear dividends, give a return

frut'teto sm orchard

frutti'vendolo, -a sm/f greengrocer (BRIT), produce dealer (US)

'frutto sm fruit; (fig: risultato) result(s); (Econ: interesse) interest; (: reddito) income; **frutti di bosco** berries; **frutti di mare** seafood sg

FS abbr = **Ferrovie dello Stato**

fu vb vedi **essere** ▷ ag inv **il fu Paolo Bianchi** the late Paolo Bianchi

fuci'lare [futʃi'lare] vt to shoot

fu'cile [fu'tʃile] sm rifle, gun; (da caccia) shotgun, gun

'fucsia sf fuchsia

'fuga sf escape, flight; (di gas, liquidi) leak; (Mus) fugue; **fuga di cervelli** brain drain

fug'gire [fud'dʒire] vi to flee, run away; (fig: passar veloce) to fly ▷ vt to avoid

'fui vb vedi **essere**

fu'liggine [fu'liddʒine] sf soot

'fulmine sm thunderbolt; lightning no pl

fu'mare vi to smoke; (emettere vapore) to steam ▷ vt to smoke; **le dà fastidio se fumo?** do you mind if I smoke?; **fuma'tore, -'trice** sm/f smoker

fu'metto sm comic strip; **giornale** sm, **a fumetti** comic

'fummo vb vedi **essere**

'fumo sm smoke; (vapore) steam; (il fumare tabacco) smoking; **fumi** smpl (industriali ecc) fumes; **i fumi dell'alcool** the after-effects of drink; **vendere ~** to deceive, cheat; **fumo passivo** passive smoking

'fune sf rope, cord; (più grossa) cable

'funebre ag (rito) funeral; (aspetto) gloomy, funereal

fune'rale sm funeral

'fungere ['fundʒere] vi **~ da** to act as

'fungo, -ghi sm fungus; (commestibile) mushroom; **fungo velenoso** toadstool

funico'lare sf funicular railway

funi'via sf cable railway

'funsi ecc vb vedi **fungere**

funzio'nare [funtsjo'nare] vi to work, function; (fungere): **~ da** to act as; **come funziona?** how does this work?; **la TV non funziona** the TV isn't working

funzio'nario [funtsjo'narjo] sm official; **funzionario statale** civil servant

funzi'one [fun'tsjone] sf function; (carica) post, position; (Rel) service; **in ~** (meccanismo) in operation; **in ~ di** (come) as; **fare la ~ di qn** (farne le veci) to take sb's place

fu'oco, -chi sm fire; (fornello) ring; (Fot, Fisica) focus; **dare ~ a qc** to set fire to sth; **far ~** (sparare) to fire; **al ~!** fire!; **fuoco d'artificio** firework

fuorché [fwor'ke] cong, prep except

fu'ori av outside; (all'aperto) outdoors, outside; (fuori di casa, Sport) out; (esclamativo) get out! ▷ prep **~ (di)** out of, outside ▷ sm outside; **lasciar ~ qc/qn** to leave sth/sb out; **far ~ qn** (fam) to kill sb, do sb in; **essere ~ di sé** to be beside o.s.; **~ luogo** (inopportuno) out of place, uncalled for; **~ mano** out of the way, remote; **~ pericolo** out of danger; **~ uso** old-fashioned; obsolete; **fuorigi'oco** sm offside; **fuori'strada** sm (Aut) cross-country vehicle

'furbo, -a ag clever, smart; (peg) cunning

fu'rente ag **~ (contro)** furious (with)

fur'fante sm rascal, scoundrel

fur'gone sm van

'furia sf (ira) fury, rage; (fig: impeto) fury, violence; (fretta) rush; **a ~ di** by dint of; **andare su tutte le furie** to get into a towering rage; **furi'bondo, -a** ag furious

furi'oso, -a ag furious

'furono vb vedi **essere**

fur'tivo, -a ag furtive

'furto sm theft; **vorrei denunciare un ~** I'd like to report a theft; **furto con scasso** burglary

'fusa sfpl **fare le ~** to purr

fu'seaux smpl inv leggings

'fusi ecc vb vedi **fondere**

fu'sibile sm (Elettr) fuse

fusi'one sf (di metalli) fusion, melting; (colata) casting; (Comm) merger; (fig) merging

'fuso, -a pp di **fondere** ▷ sm (Filatura) spindle; **fuso orario** time zone

fus'tino sm (di detersivo) tub

'fusto sm stem; (Anat, di albero) trunk; (recipiente) drum, can

fu'turo, -a ag, sm future

'gabbia *sf* cage; (*da imballaggio*) crate; **gabbia dell'ascensore** lift (BRIT) *o* elevator (US) shaft; **gabbia toracica** (*Anat*) rib cage

gabbi'ano *sm* (sea)gull

gabi'netto *sm* (*Med ecc*) consulting room; (*Pol*) ministry; (*WC*) toilet, lavatory; (*Ins: di fisica ecc*) laboratory

'gaffe [gaf] *sf inv* blunder

ga'lante *ag* gallant, courteous; (*avventura*) amorous

ga'lassia *sf* galaxy

ga'lera *sf* (*Naut*) galley; (*prigione*) prison

'galla *sf* **a ~** afloat; **venire a ~** to surface, come to the surface; (*fig: verità*) to come out

galleggi'are [galled'dʒare] *vi* to float

galle'ria *sf* (*traforo*) tunnel; (*Archit, d'arte*) gallery; (*Teatro*) circle; (*strada coperta con negozi*) arcade

'Galles *sm* **il ~** Wales

gal'lina *sf* hen

'gallo *sm* cock

galop'pare *vi* to gallop

ga'loppo *sm* gallop; **al o di ~** at a gallop

'gamba *sf* leg; (*asta: di lettera*) stem; **in ~** (*in buona salute*) well; (*bravo, sveglio*) bright, smart; **prendere qc sotto ~** (*fig*) to treat sth too lightly

gambe'retto *sm* shrimp

'gambero *sm* (*di acqua dolce*) crayfish; (*di mare*) prawn

'gambo *sm* stem; (*di frutta*) stalk

'gamma *sf* (*Mus*) scale; (*di colori, fig*) range

'gancio ['gantʃo] *sm* hook

'gara *sf* competition; (*Sport*) competition; contest; match; (: *corsa*) race; **fare a ~** to compete, vie

ga'rage [ga'raʒ] *sm inv* garage

garan'tire *vt* to guarantee; (*debito*) to stand surety for; (*dare per certo*) to assure

garan'zia [garan'tsia] *sf* guarantee; (*pegno*) security

gar'bato, -a *ag* courteous, polite

gareggi'are [gared'dʒare] *vi* to compete

garga'rismo *sm* gargle; **fare i gargarismi** to gargle

ga'rofano *sm* carnation; **chiodo di ~** clove

'garza ['gardza] *sf* (*per bende*) gauze

gar'zone [gar'dzone] *sm* (*di negozio*) boy

gas *sm inv* gas; **sento odore di ~** I can smell gas; **a tutto ~** at full speed; **dare ~** (*Aut*) to accelerate

ga'solio *sm* diesel (oil)

gas'sato, -a *ag* fizzy

gast'rite *sf* gastritis

gastrono'mia *sf* gastronomy

gat'tino *sm* kitten

'gatto, -a *sm/f* cat, tomcat/she-cat; **gatto delle nevi** (*Aut, Sci*) snowcat; **gatto selvatico** wildcat

'gazza ['gaddza] *sf* magpie

gel [dʒɛl] *sm inv* gel

ge'lare [dʒe'lare] *vt, vi, vb impers* to freeze

gelate'ria [dʒelate'ria] *sf* ice-cream shop

gela'tina [dʒela'tina] *sf* gelatine; **gelatina esplosiva** dynamite; **gelatina di frutta** fruit jelly

ge'lato, -a [dʒe'lato] *ag* frozen ▷ *sm* ice cream

'gelido, -a ['dʒɛlido] *ag* icy, ice-cold

'gelo ['dʒɛlo] *sm* (*temperatura*) intense cold; (*brina*) frost; (*fig*) chill

gelo'sia [dʒelo'sia] *sf* jealousy

ge'loso, -a [dʒe'loso] *ag* jealous

'gelso ['dʒɛlso] *sm* mulberry (tree)

gelso'mino [dʒelso'mino] *sm* jasmine

ge'mello, -a [dʒe'mɛllo] *ag, sm/f* twin; **gemelli** *smpl* (*di camicia*) cufflinks; (*dello zodiaco*): **Gemelli** Gemini *sg*

'gemere ['dʒɛmere] *vi* to moan, groan; (*cigolare*) to creak

'gemma ['dʒɛmma] *sf* (*Bot*) bud; (*pietra preziosa*) gem

gene'rale [dʒene'rale] *ag, sm* general; **in ~** (*per sommi capi*) in general terms; (*di solito*) usually, in general

gene'rare [dʒene'rare] *vt* (*dar vita*) to give birth to; (*produrre*) to produce; (*causare*)

to arouse; (Tecn) to produce, generate;
generazi'one sf generation

'genere ['dʒɛnere] sm kind, type, sort;
(Biol) genus; (merce) article, product;
(Ling) gender; (Arte, Letteratura) genre;
in ~ generally, as a rule; **genere umano**
mankind; **generi alimentari** foodstuffs

ge'nerico, -a, -ci, -che [dʒe'nɛriko] ag
generic; (vago) vague, imprecise

'genero ['dʒɛnero] sm son-in-law

gene'roso, -a [dʒene'roso] ag generous

ge'netica [dʒe'nɛtika] sf genetics sg

ge'netico, -a, -ci, -che [dʒe'nɛtiko] ag
genetic

gen'giva [dʒen'dʒiva] sf (Anat) gum

geni'ale [dʒeni'jale] ag (persona) of genius;
(idea) ingenious, brilliant

'genio ['dʒɛnjo] sm genius; **andare a ~ a
qn** to be to sb's liking, appeal to sb

geni'tore [dʒeni'tore] sm parent, father
o mother; **i miei genitori** my parents, my
father and mother

gen'naio [dʒen'najo] sm January

'Genova ['dʒɛnova] sf Genoa

'gente ['dʒɛnte] sf people pl

gen'tile [dʒen'tile] ag (persona, atto) kind;
(: garbato) courteous, polite; (nelle lettere):
G~ Signore Dear Sir; (: sulla busta): **G~
Signor Fernando Villa** Mr Fernando Villa

genu'ino, -a [dʒenu'ino] ag (prodotto)
natural; (persona, sentimento) genuine,
sincere

geogra'fia [dʒeogra'fia] sf geography

geolo'gia [dʒeolo'dʒia] sf geology

ge'ometra, -i, -e [dʒe'ɔmetra] sm/f
(professionista) surveyor

geome'tria [dʒeome'tria] sf geometry

ge'ranio [dʒe'ranjo] sm geranium

gerar'chia [dʒerar'kia] sf hierarchy

'gergo, -ghi ['dʒɛrgo] sm jargon; slang

geria'tria [dʒerja'tria] sf geriatrics sg

Ger'mania [dʒer'manja] sf **la ~** Germany;
la ~ occidentale/orientale West/East
Germany

'germe ['dʒɛrme] sm germ; (fig) seed

germogli'are [dʒermoʎ'ʎare] vi to sprout;
to germinate

gero'glifico, -ci [dʒero'glifiko] sm
hieroglyphic

ge'rundio [dʒe'rundjo] sm gerund

'gesso ['dʒɛsso] sm chalk; (Scultura, Med,
Edil) plaster; (statua) plaster figure;
(minerale) gypsum

gesti'one [dʒes'tjone] sf management

ges'tire [dʒes'tire] vt to run, manage

'gesto ['dʒɛsto] sm gesture

Gesù [dʒe'zu] sm Jesus

gesu'ita, -i [dʒezu'ita] sm Jesuit

get'tare [dʒet'tare] vt to throw; (anche:

~ via) to throw away o out; (Scultura) to
cast; (Edil) to lay; (acqua) to spout; (grido)
to utter; **gettarsi** vpr **gettarsi in** (fiume)
to flow into; **~ uno sguardo su** to take a
quick look at

'getto ['dʒetto] sm (di gas, liquido, Aer) jet;
a ~ continuo uninterruptedly; **di ~** (fig)
straight off, in one go

get'tone [dʒet'tone] sm token; (per giochi)
counter; (: roulette ecc) chip; **gettone
telefonico** telephone token

ghiacci'aio [gjat'tʃajo] sm glacier

ghiacci'ato, -a ag frozen; (bevanda)
ice-cold

ghi'accio ['gjattʃo] sm ice

ghiacci'olo [gjat'tʃɔlo] sm icicle; (tipo di
gelato) ice lolly (BRIT), Popsicle® (US)

ghi'aia ['gjaja] sf gravel

ghi'anda ['gjanda] sf (Bot) acorn

ghi'andola ['gjandola] sf gland

ghi'otto, -a ['gjotto] ag greedy; (cibo)
delicious, appetizing

ghir'landa [gir'landa] sf garland, wreath

'ghiro ['giro] sm dormouse

'ghisa ['giza] sf cast iron

già [dʒa] av already; (ex, in precedenza)
formerly ▷ escl of course!, yes indeed!

gi'acca, -che ['dʒakka] sf jacket; **giacca
a vento** windcheater (BRIT), windbreaker
(US)

giacché [dʒak'ke] cong since, as

giac'cone [dʒak'kone] sm heavy jacket

gi'ada ['dʒada] sf jade

giagu'aro [dʒa'gwaro] sm jaguar

gi'allo ['dʒallo] ag yellow; (carnagione)
sallow ▷ sm yellow; (anche: **romanzo ~**)
detective novel; (anche: **film ~**) detective
film; **giallo dell'uovo** yolk

Giamaica [dʒa'maika] sf **la ~** Jamaica

Giap'pone [dʒap'pone] sm Japan;
giappo'nese ag, sm/f, sm Japanese inv

giardi'naggio [dʒardi'naddʒo] sm
gardening

giardini'ere, -a [dʒardi'njɛre] sm/f
gardener

giar'dino [dʒar'dino] sm garden; **giardino
d'infanzia** nursery school; **giardino
pubblico** public gardens pl, (public) park;
giardino zoologico zoo

giavel'lotto [dʒavel'lɔtto] sm javelin

gigabyte [dʒiga'bait] sm inv gigabyte

gi'gante, -'essa [dʒi'gante] sm/f giant
▷ ag giant, gigantic; (Comm) giant-size

'giglio ['dʒiʎʎo] sm lily

gilè [dʒi'lɛ] sm inv waistcoat

gin [dʒin] sm inv gin

gine'cologo, -a, -gi, -ghe [dʒine'kɔlogo]
sm/f gynaecologist

gi'nepro [dʒi'nepro] sm juniper

gi'nestra [dʒi'nɛstra] *sf* (Bot) broom

Gi'nevra [dʒi'nevra] *sf* Geneva

gin'nastica *sf* gymnastics *sg*; (esercizio fisico) keep-fit exercises; (Ins) physical education

gi'nocchio [dʒi'nɔkkjo] (pl(m) **gi'nocchi**, o pl(f) **gi'nocchia**) *sm* knee; **stare in ~** to kneel, be on one's knees; **mettersi in ~** to kneel (down)

gio'care [dʒo'kare] *vt* to play; (scommettere) to stake, wager, bet; (ingannare) to take in ▷ *vi* to play; (a roulette ecc) to gamble; (fig) to play a part, be important; **~ a** (gioco, sport) to play; (cavalli) to bet on; **giocarsi la carriera** to put one's career at risk; **gioca'tore, -'trice** *sm/f* player; gambler

gio'cattolo [dʒo'kattolo] *sm* toy

giocherò ecc [dʒoke'rɔ] *vb vedi* **giocare**

gi'oco, -chi ['dʒɔko] *sm* game; (divertimento, Tecn) play; (al casinò) gambling; (Carte) hand; (insieme di pezzi ecc necessari per un gioco) set; **per ~** for fun; **fare il doppio ~ con qn** to double-cross sb; **i Giochi Olimpici** the Olympic Games; **gioco d'azzardo** game of chance; **gioco degli scacchi** chess set

giocoli'ere [dʒoko'ljɛre] *sm* juggler

gi'oia ['dʒɔja] *sf* joy, delight; (pietra preziosa) jewel, precious stone

gioielle'ria [dʒojelle'ria] *sf* jeweller's craft; jeweller's (shop)

gioiel'liere, -a [dʒojel'ljɛre] *sm/f* jeweller

gioi'ello [dʒo'jɛllo] *sm* jewel, piece of jewellery; **i miei gioielli** my jewels o jewellery; **gioielli** *smpl* (anelli, collane ecc) jewellery; **i gioielli della Corona** the crown jewels

Gior'dania [dʒor'danja] *sf* **la ~** Jordan

giorna'laio, -a [dʒorna'lajo] *sm/f* newsagent (BRIT), newsdealer (US)

gior'nale [dʒor'nale] *sm* (news)paper; (diario) journal, diary; (Comm) journal; **giornale di bordo** log; **giornale radio** radio news *sg*

giornali'ero, -a [dʒorna'ljɛro] *ag* daily; (che varia: umore) changeable ▷ *sm* day labourer

giorna'lismo [dʒorna'lizmo] *sm* journalism

giorna'lista, -i, -e [dʒorna'lista] *sm/f* journalist

gior'nata [dʒor'nata] *sf* day; **giornata lavorativa** working day

gi'orno ['dʒorno] *sm* day; (opposto alla notte) day, daytime; (anche: **luce del ~**) daylight; **al ~** per day; **di ~** by day; **al ~ d'oggi** nowadays

gi'ostra ['dʒɔstra] *sf* (per bimbi) merry-go-round; (torneo storico) joust

gi'ovane ['dʒovane] *ag* young; (aspetto) youthful ▷ *sm/f* youth/girl, young man/woman; **i giovani** young people

gio'vare [dʒo'vare] *vi* **~ a** (essere utile) to be useful to; (far bene) to be good for ▷ *vb impers* (essere bene, utile) to be useful; **giovarsi di qc** to make use of sth

giovedì [dʒove'di] *sm inv* Thursday; **di o il ~** on Thursdays

gioventù [dʒoven'tu] *sf* (periodo) youth; (i giovani) young people *pl*, youth

G.I.P. [dʒip] *sigla m inv* (= Giudice per le Indagini Preliminari) judge for preliminary enquiries

gira'dischi [dʒira'diski] *sm inv* record player

gi'raffa [dʒi'raffa] *sf* giraffe

gi'rare [dʒi'rare] *vt* (far ruotare) to turn; (percorrere, visitare) to go round; (Cinema) to shoot; to make; (Comm) to endorse ▷ *vi* to turn; (più veloce) to spin; (andare in giro) to wander, go around; **girarsi** *vpr* to turn; **~ attorno a** to go round; to revolve round; **al prossimo incrocio giri a destra/sinistra** turn right/left at the next junction; **far ~ la testa a qn** to make sb dizzy; (fig) to turn sb's head

girar'rosto [dʒirar'rɔsto] *sm* (Cuc) spit

gira'sole [dʒira'sole] *sm* sunflower

gi'revole [dʒi'revole] *ag* revolving, turning

gi'rino [dʒi'rino] *sm* tadpole

'giro ['dʒiro] *sm* (circuito, cerchio) circle; (di chiave, manovella) turn; (viaggio) tour, excursion; (passeggiata) stroll, walk; (in macchina) drive; (in bicicletta) ride; (Sport: della pista) lap; (di denaro) circulation; (Carte) hand; (Tecn) revolution; **prendere in ~ qn** (fig) to pull sb's leg; **fare un ~** to go for a walk (o a drive o a ride); **andare in ~** to go about, walk around; **a stretto ~ di posta** by return of post; **nel ~ di un mese** in a month's time; **essere nel ~** (fig) to belong to a circle (of friends); **giro d'affari** (Comm) turnover; **giro di parole** circumlocution; **giro di prova** (Aut) test drive; **giro turistico** sightseeing tour; **giro'collo** *sm* **a girocollo** crew-neck *cpd*

gironzo'lare [dʒirondzo'lare] *vi* to stroll about

'gita ['dʒita] *sf* excursion, trip; **fare una ~** to go for a trip, go on an outing

gi'tano, -a [dʒi'tano] *sm/f* gipsy

giù [dʒu] *av* down; (dabbasso) downstairs; **in ~** downwards, down; **~ di lì** (pressappoco) thereabouts; **bambini dai 6 anni in ~** children aged 6 and under; **~ per, cadere ~ per le scale** to fall down the stairs; **essere ~** (fig: di salute) to be run down; (: di spirito) to be depressed

giub'botto [dʒub'bɔtto] *sm* jerkin; **giubbotto antiproiettile** bulletproof vest; **giubbotto salvagente** life jacket

giudi'care [dʒudi'kare] *vt* to judge; (*accusato*) to try; (*lite*) to arbitrate in; ~ **qn/qc bello** to consider sb/sth (to be) beautiful

gi'udice ['dʒuditʃe] *sm* judge; **giudice conciliatore** justice of the peace; **giudice istruttore** examining (BRIT) *o* committing (US) magistrate; **giudice popolare** member of a jury

giu'dizio [dʒu'dittsjo] *sm* judgment; (*opinione*) opinion; (*Dir*) judgment, sentence; (: *processo*) trial; (: *verdetto*) verdict; **aver ~** to be wise *o* prudent; **citare in ~** to summons

gi'ugno ['dʒuɲɲo] *sm* June

gi'ungere ['dʒundʒere] *vi* to arrive ▷ *vt* (*mani ecc*) to join; ~ **a** to arrive at, reach

gi'ungla ['dʒungla] *sf* jungle

gi'unsi *ecc* ['dʒunsi] *vb vedi* **giungere**

giura'mento [dʒura'mento] *sm* oath; **giuramento falso** perjury

giu'rare [dʒu'rare] *vt* to swear ▷ *vi* to swear, take an oath

giu'ria [dʒu'ria] *sf* jury

giu'ridico, -a, -ci, -che [dʒu'ridiko] *ag* legal

giustifi'care [dʒustifi'kare] *vt* to justify; **giustificazi'one** *sf* justification; (*Ins*) (note of) excuse

gius'tizia [dʒus'tittsja] *sf* justice; **giustizi'are** *vt* to execute, put to death

gi'usto, -a ['dʒusto] *ag* (*equo*) fair, just; (*vero*) true, correct; (*adatto*) right, suitable; (*preciso*) exact, correct ▷ *av* (*esattamente*) exactly, precisely; (*per l'appunto, appena*) just; **arrivare ~** to arrive just in time; **ho ~ bisogno di te** you're just the person I need

glaci'ale [gla'tʃale] *ag* glacial

gli [ʎi] (*dav V, s impura, gn, pn, ps, x, z*) *det mpl* the ▷ *pron* (*a lui*) to him; (*in coppia con lo, la, li, le, ne: a lui, a lei, a loro ecc*): **~ele do** I'm giving them to him (*o her o* them); *vedi anche* **il**

glo'bale *ag* overall

'globo *sm* globe

'globulo *sm* (*Anat*): **globulo rosso/bianco** red/white corpuscle

'gloria *sf* glory

gnocchi ['ɲɔkki] *smpl* (*Cuc*) small dumplings made of semolina pasta or potato

'gobba *sf* (*Anat*) hump; (*protuberanza*) bump

'gobbo, -a *ag* hunchbacked; (*ricurvo*) round-shouldered ▷ *sm/f* hunchback

'goccia, -ce ['gɔttʃa] *sf* drop; **goccio'lare** *vi, vt* to drip

go'dere *vi* (*compiacersi*): ~ **(di)** to be delighted (at), rejoice (at); (*trarre vantaggio*): ~ **di** benefit from ▷ *vt* to enjoy; **godersi la vita** to enjoy life; **godersela** to have a good time, enjoy o.s.

godrò *ecc vb vedi* **godere**

'goffo, -a *ag* clumsy, awkward

'gola *sf* (*Anat*) throat; (*golosità*) gluttony, greed; (*di camino*) flue; (*di monte*) gorge; **fare ~** (*anche fig*) to tempt

golf *sm inv* (*Sport*) golf; (*maglia*) cardigan

'golfo *sm* gulf

go'loso, -a *ag* greedy

gomi'tata *sf* **dare una ~ a qn** to elbow sb; **farsi avanti a (forza o furia di) gomitate** to elbow one's way through; **fare a gomitate per qc** to fight to get sth

'gomito *sm* elbow; (*di strada ecc*) sharp bend

go'mitolo *sm* ball

'gomma *sf* rubber; (*per cancellare*) rubber, eraser; (*di veicolo*) tyre (BRIT), tire (US); **gomma americana** *o* **da masticare** chewing gum; **gomma a terra** flat tyre (BRIT) *o* tire (US); **ho una ~ a terra** I've got a flat tyre; **gom'mone** *sm* rubber dinghy

gonfi'are *vt* (*pallone*) to blow up, inflate; (*dilatare, ingrossare*) to swell; (*fig: notizia*) to exaggerate; **gonfiarsi** *vpr* to swell; (*fiume*) to rise; **'gonfio, -a** *ag* swollen; (*stomaco*) bloated; (*vela*) full; **gonfi'ore** *sm* swelling

'gonna *sf* skirt; **gonna pantalone** culottes *pl*

'gorgo, -ghi *sm* whirlpool

gorgogli'are [gorgoʎ'ʎare] *vi* to gurgle

go'rilla *sm inv* gorilla; (*guardia del corpo*) bodyguard

'gotico, -a, ci, che *ag, sm* Gothic

'gotta *sf* gout

gover'nare *vt* (*stato*) to govern, rule; (*pilotare, guidare*) to steer; (*bestiame*) to tend, look after

go'verno *sm* government

GPL *sigla m* (= *Gas di Petrolio Liquefatto*) LPG

GPS *sigla m* (= *Global Positioning System*) GPS

graci'dare [gratʃi'dare] *vi* to croak

'gracile ['gratʃile] *ag* frail, delicate

gradazi'one [gradat'tsjone] *sf* (*sfumatura*) gradation; **gradazione alcolica** alcoholic content, strength

gra'devole *ag* pleasant, agreeable

gradi'nata *sf* flight of steps; (*in teatro, stadio*) tiers *pl*

gra'dino *sm* step; (*Alpinismo*) foothold

gra'dire *vt* (*accettare con piacere*) to accept; (*desiderare*) to wish, like; **gradisce una tazza di tè?** would you like a cup of tea?

'grado *sm* (*Mat, Fisica ecc*) degree; (*stadio*)

degree, level; (*Mil, sociale*) rank; **essere in ~ di fare** to be in a position to do

gradu'ale *ag* gradual

graf'fetta *sf* paper clip

graffi'are *vt* to scratch; **graffiarsi** *vpr* to get scratched; (*con unghie*) to scratch o.s.

'**graffio** *sm* scratch

gra'**fia** *sf* spelling; (*scrittura*) handwriting

'**grafico, -a, -ci, -che** *ag* graphic ▷ *sm* graph; (*persona*) graphic designer

gram'matica, -che *sf* grammar

'**grammo** *sm* gram(me)

'**grana** *sf* (*granello, di minerali, corpi spezzati*) grain; (*fam: seccatura*) trouble; (: *soldi*) cash ▷ *sm inv* Parmesan (cheese)

gra'**naio** *sm* granary, barn

gra'**nata** *sf* (*proiettile*) grenade

Gran Bre'tagna [-bre'taɲɲa] *sf* **la ~** Great Britain

'**granchio** ['grankjo] *sm* crab; (*fig*) blunder; **prendere un ~** (*fig*) to blunder

'**grande** (*qualche volta* **gran** + *C*, **grand'** + *V*) *ag* (*grosso, largo, vasto*) big, large; (*alto*) tall; (*lungo*) long; (*in sensi astratti*) great ▷ *sm/f* (*persona adulta*) adult, grown-up; (*chi ha ingegno e potenza*) great man/woman; **fare le cose in ~** to do things in style; **una gran bella donna** a very beautiful woman; **non è una gran cosa** o **un gran che** it's nothing special; **non ne so gran che** I don't know very much about it

gran'dezza [gran'dettsa] *sf* (*dimensione*) size; magnitude; (*fig*) greatness; **in ~ naturale** life-size(d)

grandi'nare *vb impers* to hail

'**grandine** *sf* hail

gra'**nello** *sm* (*di cereali, uva*) seed; (*di frutta*) pip; (*di sabbia, sale ecc*) grain

gra'**nito** *sm* granite

'**grano** *sm* (*in quasi tutti i sensi*) grain; (*frumento*) wheat; (*di rosario, collana*) bead; **grano di pepe** peppercorn

gran'turco *sm* maize

'**grappa** *sf* rough, strong brandy

'**grappolo** *sm* bunch, cluster

gras'setto *sm* (*Tip*) bold (type)

'**grasso, -a** *ag* fat; (*cibo*) fatty; (*pelle*) greasy; (*terreno*) rich; (*fig: guadagno, annata*) plentiful ▷ *sm* (*di persona, animale*) fat; (*sostanza che unge*) grease

'**grata** *sf* grating

gra'**ticola** *sf* grill

'**gratis** *av* free, for nothing

grati'**tudine** *sf* gratitude

'**grato, -a** *ag* grateful; (*gradito*) pleasant, agreeable

gratta'capo *sm* worry, headache

grattaci'elo [gratta'tʃɛlo] *sm* skyscraper

gratta e vinci ['gratta e 'vintʃi] *sm*

inv (*biglietto*) scratchcard; (*lotteria*) scratchcard lottery

grat'tare *vt* (*pelle*) to scratch; (*raschiare*) to scrape; (*pane, formaggio, carote*) to grate; (*fam: rubare*) to pinch ▷ *vi* (*stridere*) to grate; (*Aut*) to grind; **grattarsi** *vpr* to scratch o.s.; **grattarsi la pancia** (*fig*) to twiddle one's thumbs

grat'tugia, -gie [grat'tudʒa] *sf* grater; **grattugi'are** *vt* to grate; **pane grattugiato** breadcrumbs *pl*

gra'**tuito, -a** *ag* free; (*fig*) gratuitous

'**grave** *ag* (*danno, pericolo, peccato ecc*) grave, serious; (*responsabilità*) heavy, grave; (*contegno*) grave, solemn; (*voce, suono*) deep, low-pitched; (*Ling*): **accento ~** grave accent; **un malato ~** a person who is seriously ill

grave'**mente** *av* (*ammalato, ferito*) seriously

gravi'**danza** [gravi'dantsa] *sf* pregnancy

gravità *sf* seriousness; (*anche Fisica*) gravity

gra'**voso, -a** *ag* heavy, onerous

'**grazia** ['grattsja] *sf* grace; (*favore*) favour; (*Dir*) pardon

'**grazie** ['grattsje] *escl* thank you!; **~ mille!** o **tante!** o **infinite!** thank you very much!; **~ a** thanks to

grazi'**oso, -a** [grat'tsjoso] *ag* charming, delightful; (*gentile*) gracious

'**Grecia** ['grɛtʃa] *sf* **la ~** Greece; '**greco, -a, -ci, -che** *ag, sm/f, sm* Greek

'**gregge** ['greddʒe] (*pl(f)* **-i**) *sm* flock

grembi'ule *sm* apron; (*sopravveste*) overall

'**grembo** *sm* lap; (*ventre della madre*) womb

'**grezzo, -a** ['greddzo] *ag* raw, unrefined; (*diamante*) rough, uncut; (*tessuto*) unbleached

gri'**dare** *vi* (*per chiamare*) to shout, cry (out); (*strillare*) to scream, yell ▷ *vt* to shout (out), yell (out); **~ aiuto** to cry o shout for help

'**grido** (*pl(m)* **-i**, o *pl(f)* **-a**) *sm* shout, cry; scream, yell; (*di animale*) cry; **di ~** famous

'**grigio, -a, -gi, -gie** ['gridʒo] *ag, sm* grey

'**griglia** ['griʎʎa] *sf* (*per arrostire*) grill; (*Elettr*) grid; (*inferriata*) grating; **alla ~** (*Cuc*) grilled

gril'**letto** *sm* trigger

'**grillo** *sm* (*Zool*) cricket; (*fig*) whim

'**grinta** *sf* grim expression; (*Sport*) fighting spirit

gris'**sino** *sm* bread-stick

Groen'landia *sf* **la ~** Greenland

gron'**daia** *sf* gutter

gron'**dare** *vi* to pour; (*essere bagnato*): **~ di** to be dripping with ▷ *vt* to drip with

'**groppa** *sf* (*di animale*) back, rump; (*fam:*

dell'uomo) back, shoulders *pl*

gros'sezza [gros'settsa] *sf* size; thickness

gros'sista, -i, -e *sm/f* (*Comm*) wholesaler

'grosso, -a *ag* big, large; (*di spessore*) thick; (*grossolano: anche fig*) coarse; (*grave, insopportabile*) serious, great; (*tempo, mare*) rough ▷ *sm* **il ~ di** the bulk of; **un pezzo ~** (*fig*) a VIP, a bigwig; **farla grossa** to do something very stupid; **dirle grosse** to tell tall stories; **sbagliarsi di ~** to be completely wrong

'grotta *sf* cave; grotto

grot'tesco, -a, -schi, -sche *ag* grotesque

gro'viglio [gro'viλλo] *sm* tangle; (*fig*) muddle

gru *sf inv* crane

'gruccia, -ce ['gruttʃa] *sf* (*per camminare*) crutch; (*per abiti*) coat-hanger

'grumo *sm* (*di sangue*) clot; (*di farina ecc*) lump

'gruppo *sm* group; **gruppo sanguigno** blood group

GSM *sigla m* (= *Global System for Mobile Communication*) GSM

guada'gnare [gwadaɲ'ɲare] *vt* (*ottenere*) to gain; (*soldi, stipendio*) to earn; (*vincere*) to win; (*raggiungere*) to reach

gua'dagno [gwa'daɲɲo] *sm* earnings *pl*; (*Comm*) profit; (*vantaggio, utile*) advantage, gain; **guadagno lordo/netto** gross/net earnings *pl*

gu'ado *sm* ford; **passare a ~** to ford

gu'ai *escl* ~ **a te** (*o lui ecc*)! woe betide you (*o him ecc*)!

gu'aio *sm* trouble, mishap; (*inconveniente*) trouble, snag

gua'ire *vi* to whine, yelp

gu'ancia, -ce ['gwantʃa] *sf* cheek

guanci'ale [gwan'tʃale] *sm* pillow

gu'anto *sm* glove

guarda'linee *sm inv* (*Sport*) linesman

guar'dare *vt* (*con lo sguardo: osservare*) to look at; (*film, televisione*) to watch; (*custodire*) to look after, take care of ▷ *vi* to look; (*badare*): **~ a** to pay attention to; (*luoghi: esser orientato*): **~ a** to face; **guardarsi** *vpr* to look at o.s.; **guardarsi da** (*astenersi*) to refrain from; (*stare in guardia*) to beware of; **guardarsi dal fare** to take care not to do; **guarda di non sbagliare** try not to make a mistake; **~ a vista qn** to keep a close watch on sb

guarda'roba *sm inv* wardrobe; (*locale*) cloakroom

gu'ardia *sf* (*individuo, corpo*) guard; (*sorveglianza*) watch; **fare la ~ a qc/qn** to guard sth/sb; **stare in ~** (*fig*) to be on one's guard; **di ~** (*medico*) on call; **guardia carceraria** (prison) warder; **guardia del**

corpo bodyguard; **Guardia di finanza** (*corpo*) customs *pl*; (*persona*) customs officer; **guardia medica** emergency doctor service

● **GUARDIA DI FINANZA**
●
● The **Guardia di Finanza** is a military
● body which deals with infringements
● of the laws governing income tax and
● monopolies. It reports to the Ministers
● of Finance, Justice or Agriculture,
● depending on the function it is
● performing.

guardi'ano, -a *sm/f* (*di carcere*) warder; (*di villa ecc*) caretaker; (*di museo*) custodian; (*di zoo*) keeper; **guardiano notturno** night watchman

guarigi'one [gwari'dʒone] *sf* recovery

gua'rire *vt* (*persona, malattia*) to cure; (*ferita*) to heal ▷ *vi* to recover, be cured; to heal (up)

guar'nire *vt* (*ornare: abiti*) to trim; (*Cuc*) to garnish

guasta'feste *sm/f inv* spoilsport

guastarsi *vpr* (*cibo*) to go bad; (*meccanismo*) to break down; (*tempo*) to change for the worse

gu'asto, -a *ag* (*non funzionante*) broken; (: *telefono ecc*) out of order; (*andato a male*) bad, rotten; (: *dente*) decayed, bad; (*fig: corrotto*) depraved ▷ *sm* breakdown; (*avaria*) failure; **guasto al motore** engine failure

gu'erra *sf* war; (*tecnica: atomica, chimica ecc*) warfare; **fare la ~ (a)** to wage war (against); **guerra mondiale** world war; **guerra preventiva** preventive war

'gufo *sm* owl

gu'ida *sf* (*libro*) guidebook; (*persona*) guide; (*comando, direzione*) guidance, direction; (*Aut*) driving; (*tappeto: di tenda, cassetto*) runner; **avete una ~ in italiano?** do you have a guidebook in Italian?; **c'è una ~ che parla italiano?** is there an Italian-speaking guide?; **guida a destra/a sinistra** (*Aut*) right-/left-hand drive; **guida telefonica** telephone directory; **guida turistica** tourist guide

gui'dare *vt* to guide; (*squadra, rivolta*) to lead; (*auto*) to drive; (*aereo, nave*) to pilot; **sai ~?** can you drive?; **guida'tore, -trice** *sm/f* (*conducente*) driver

guin'zaglio [gwin'tsaλλo] *sm* leash, lead

'guscio ['guʃʃo] *sm* shell

gus'tare *vt* (*cibi*) to taste; (: *assaporare con piacere*) to enjoy, savour; (*fig*) to enjoy, appreciate ▷ *vi* **~ a** to please; **non mi**

gusta affatto I don't like it at all
'gusto sm taste; (sapore) flavour;
(godimento) enjoyment; **che gusti avete?**
which flavours do you have?; **al ~ di
fragola** strawberry-flavoured; **mangiare
di ~** to eat heartily; **prenderci ~: ci ha
preso ~** he's acquired a taste for it, he's
got to like it; **gus'toso, -a** ag tasty; (fig)
agreeable

H, h ['akka] sfo m inv (lettera) H, h ▷ abbr
(= ora) hr; (= etto, altezza) h; **H come hotel**
≈ H for Harry (BRIT), H for How (US)
ha, 'hai [a, ai] vb vedi **avere**
ha'cker [hæ'kəʳ] sm inv hacker
hall [hɔl] sf inv hall, foyer
hamburger [am'burger] sm inv (carne)
hamburger; (panino) burger
'handicap ['handikap] sm inv handicap,
handicap'pato, -a ag handicapped ▷ sm/
f handicapped person, disabled person
'hanno ['anno] vb vedi **avere**
hard discount [ard'kaunt] sm inv
discount supermarket
hard disk [ar'disk] sm inv hard disk
hardware ['ardwer] sm inv hardware
hascisch [aʃʃiʃ] sm hashish
Hawaii [a'vai] sfpl **le ~** Hawaii sg
help [ɛlp] sm inv (Inform) help
'herpes ['ɛrpes] sm (Med) herpes sg; **herpes
zoster** shingles sg
'hi-fi ['haifai] sm inv, ag inv hi-fi
ho [ɔ] vb vedi **avere**
'hobby ['hɔbi] sm inv hobby
'hockey ['hɔki] sm hockey; **hockey su
ghiaccio** ice hockey
home page ['houm'peidʒ] sf inv home
page
Hong Kong ['ɔkɔg] sf Hong Kong
'hostess ['houstis] sf inv air hostess (BRIT)

o stewardess
hot dog ['hɔtdɔg] *sm inv* hot dog
ho'tel *sm inv* hotel
humour ['hjuːmə] *sm inv* (*sense of*)
humour
'humus *sm* humus
husky ['aski] *sm inv* (*cane*) husky *m inv*

i *det mpl* the
IC *abbr* (= *Intercity*) Intercity
ICI ['itʃi] *sigla f* (= *Imposta Comunale sugli
Immobili*) ≈ Council Tax
i'cona *sf* (*Rel, Inform, fig*) icon
i'dea *sf* idea; (*opinione*) opinion, view;
(*ideale*) ideal; **dare l'~ di** to seem, look like;
neanche *o* **neppure per ~!** certainly not!;
idea fissa obsession
ide'ale *ag, sm* ideal
ide'are *vt* (*immaginare*) to think up,
conceive; (*progettare*) to plan
i'dentico, -a, -ci, -che *ag* identical
identifi'care *vt* to identify; **identificarsi**
vpr **identificarsi (con)** to identify o.s.
(with)
identità *sf inv* identity
ideolo'gia, -'gie [ideolo'dʒia] *sf* ideology
idio'matico, -a, -ci, -che *ag* idiomatic;
frase idiomatica idiom
idi'ota, -i, -e *ag* idiotic ▷ *sm/f* idiot
'idolo *sm* idol
idoneità *sf* suitability
i'doneo, -a *ag* **~ a** suitable for, fit for; (*Mil*)
fit for; (*qualificato*) qualified for
i'drante *sm* hydrant
idra'tante *ag* moisturizing ▷ *sm*
moisturizer
i'draulico, -a, -ci, -che *ag* hydraulic ▷ *sm*
plumber

idroe'lettrico, -a, -ci, -che *ag* hydroelectric

i'drofilo, -a *ag vedi* **cotone**

i'drogeno [i'drɔdʒeno] *sm* hydrogen

idrovo'lante *sm* seaplane

i'ena *sf* hyena

i'eri *av, sm* yesterday; **il giornale di ~** yesterday's paper; **~ l'altro** the day before yesterday; **~ sera** yesterday evening

igi'ene [i'dʒɛne] *sf* hygiene; **igiene pubblica** public health; **igi'enico, -a, -ci, -he** *ag* hygienic; (*salubre*) healthy

i'gnaro, -a [iɲ'ɲaro] *ag* **~ di** unaware of, ignorant of

i'gnobile [iɲ'ɲobile] *ag* despicable, vile

igno'rante [iɲɲo'rante] *ag* ignorant

igno'rare [iɲɲo'rare] *vt* (*non sapere, conoscere*) to be ignorant o unaware of, not to know; (*fingere di non vedere, sentire*) to ignore

i'gnoto, -a [iɲ'ɲɔto] *ag* unknown

⭕ **PAROLA CHIAVE**

il (*pl(m)* **i**; *diventa* **lo** (*pl* **gli**) *davanti a s impura, gn, pn, ps, x, z;* **l'**a (*pl* **le**)) *det m* **1** the; **il libro/lo studente/l'acqua** the book/the student/the water; **gli scolari** the pupils

2 (*astrazione*): **il coraggio/l'amore/la giovinezza** courage/love/youth

3 (*tempo*): **il mattino/la sera** in the morning/evening; **il venerdì** *ecc* (*abitualmente*) on Fridays *ecc*; (*quel giorno*) on (the) Friday *ecc*; **la settimana prossima** next week

4 (*distributivo*) a, an; **2 euro il chilo/paio** 2 euros a o per kilo/pair

5 (*partitivo*) some, any; **hai messo lo zucchero?** have you added sugar?; **hai comprato il latte?** did you buy (some o any) milk?

6 (*possesso*): **aprire gli occhi** to open one's eyes; **rompersi la gamba** to break one's leg; **avere i capelli neri/il naso rosso** to have dark hair/a red nose

7 (*con nomi propri*): **il Petrarca** Petrarch; **il Presidente Bush** President Bush; **dov'è la Francesca?** where's Francesca?

8 (*con nomi geografici*): **il Tevere** the Tiber; **l'Italia** Italy; **il Regno Unito** the United Kingdom; **l'Everest** Everest

---

ille'gale *ag* illegal

illeg'gibile [illed'dʒibile] *ag* illegible

ille'gittimo, -a [ille'dʒittimo] *ag* illegitimate

il'leso, -a *ag* unhurt, unharmed

illimi'tato, -a *ag* boundless; unlimited

ill.mo *abbr* = **illustrissimo**

il'ludere *vt* to deceive, delude; **illudersi** *vpr* to deceive o.s., delude o.s.

illumi'nare *vt* to light up, illuminate; (*fig*) to enlighten; **illuminarsi** *vpr* to light up; **~ a giorno** to floodlight; **illuminazi'one** *sf* lighting; illumination; floodlighting; (*fig*) flash of inspiration

il'lusi *ecc vb vedi* **illudere**

illusi'one *sf* illusion; **farsi delle illusioni** to delude o.s.; **illusione ottica** optical illusion

il'luso, -a *pp di* **illudere**

illus'trare *vt* to illustrate; **illustrazi'one** *sf* illustration

il'lustre *ag* eminent, renowned; **illus'trissimo, -a** *ag* (*negli indirizzi*) very revered

imbal'laggio [imbal'laddʒo] *sm* packing *no pl*

imbal'lare *vt* to pack; (*Aut*) to race

imbalsa'mare *vt* to embalm

imbambo'lato, -a *ag* (*sguardo*) vacant, blank

imbaraz'zante [imbarat'tsante] *ag* embarrassing, awkward

imbaraz'zare [imbarat'tsare] *vt* (*mettere a disagio*) to embarrass; (*ostacolare movimenti*) to hamper

imbaraz'zato, -a [imbarat'tsato] *ag* embarrassed; **avere lo stomaco ~** to have an upset stomach

imba'razzo [imba'rattso] *sm* (*disagio*) embarrassment; (*perplessità*) puzzlement, bewilderment; **imbarazzo di stomaco** indigestion

imbar'care *vt* (*passeggeri*) to embark; (*merci*) to load; **imbarcarsi** *vpr* **imbarcarsi su** to board; **imbarcarsi per l'America** to sail for America; **imbarcarsi in** (*fig: affare ecc*) to embark on

imbarcazi'one [imbarkat'tsjone] *sf* (small) boat, (small) craft *inv*; **imbarcazione di salvataggio** lifeboat

im'barco, -chi *sm* embarkation; loading; boarding; (*banchina*) landing stage

imbas'tire *vt* (*cucire*) to tack; (*fig: abbozzare*) to sketch, outline

im'battersi *vpr* **~ in** (*incontrare*) to bump o run into

imbat'tibile *ag* unbeatable, invincible

imbavagli'are [imbavaʎ'ʎare] *vt* to gag

imbe'cille [imbe'tʃille] *ag* idiotic ▷ *sm/f* idiot; (*Med*) imbecile

imbian'care *vt* to whiten; (*muro*) to whitewash ▷ *vi* to become o turn white

imbian'chino [imbjan'kino] *sm* (house) painter, painter and decorator

imboc'care *vt* (*bambino*) to feed; (*entrare: strada*) to enter, turn into

imbocca'tura sf mouth; (di strada, porto) entrance; (Mus, del morso) mouthpiece

imbos'cata sf ambush

imbottigli'are [imbottiʎ'ʎare] vt to bottle; (Naut) to blockade; (Mil) to hem in; **imbottigliarsi** vpr to be stuck in a traffic jam

imbot'tire vt to stuff; (giacca) to pad; **imbottirsi** vpr **imbottirsi di** (rimpinzarsi) to stuff o.s. with; **imbot'tito, -a** ag stuffed; (giacca) padded; **panino imbottito** filled roll

imbra'nato, -a ag clumsy, awkward ▷ sm/f clumsy person

imbrogli'are [imbroʎ'ʎare] vt to mix up; (fig: raggirare) to deceive, cheat; (: confondere) to confuse, mix up; **imbrogli'one, -a** sm/f cheat, swindler

imbronci'ato, -a ag sulky

imbu'care vt to post; **dove posso ~ queste cartoline?** where can I post these cards?

imbur'rare vt to butter

im'buto sm funnel

imi'tare vt to imitate; (riprodurre) to copy; (assomigliare) to look like

immagazzi'nare [immagaddzi'nare] vt to store

immagi'nare [immadʒi'nare] vt to imagine; (supporre) to suppose; (inventare) to invent; **s'immagini!** don't mention it!, not at all!; **immaginazi'one** sf imagination; (cosa immaginata) fancy

im'magine [im'madʒine] sf image; (rappresentazione grafica, mentale) picture

imman'cabile ag certain; unfailing

im'mane ag (smisurato) enormous; (spaventoso) terrible

immangi'abile [imman'dʒabile] ag inedible

immatrico'lare vt to register; **immatricolarsi** vpr (Ins) to matriculate, enrol

imma'turo, -a ag (frutto) unripe; (persona) immature; (prematuro) premature

immedesi'marsi vpr ~ **in** to identify with

immediata'mente av immediately, at once

immedi'ato, -a ag immediate

im'menso, -a ag immense

im'mergere [im'mɛrdʒere] vt to immerse, plunge; **immergersi** vpr to plunge; (sommergibile) to dive, submerge; (dedicarsi a): **immergersi in** to immerse o.s. in

immeri'tato, -a ag undeserved

immersi'one sf immersion; (di sommergibile) submersion, dive; (di palombaro) dive

im'mettere vt ~ **(in)** to introduce (into); ~ **dati in un computer** to enter data on a computer

immi'grato, -a sm/f immigrant

immi'nente ag imminent

immischiarsi vpr ~ **in** to interfere o meddle in

im'mobile ag motionless, still; **immobili'are** ag (Dir) property cpd

immon'dizia [immon'dittsja] sf dirt, filth; (spesso al pl: spazzatura, rifiuti) rubbish no pl, refuse no pl

immo'rale ag immoral

immor'tale ag immortal

im'mune ag (esente) exempt; (Med, Dir) immune

immu'tabile ag immutable; unchanging

impacchet'tare [impakket'tare] vt to pack up

impacci'ato, -a ag awkward, clumsy; (imbarazzato) embarrassed

im'pacco, -chi sm (Med) compress

impadro'nirsi vpr ~ **di** to seize, take possession of; (fig: apprendere a fondo) to master

impa'gabile ag priceless

impa'lato, -a ag (fig) stiff as a board

impalca'tura sf scaffolding

impalli'dire vi to turn pale; (fig) to fade

impa'nato, -a ag (Cuc) coated in breadcrumbs

impanta'narsi vpr to sink (in the mud); (fig) to get bogged down

impappi'narsi vpr to stammer, falter

impa'rare vt to learn

impar'tire vt to bestow, give

imparzi'ale [impar'tsjale] ag impartial, unbiased

impas'sibile ag impassive

impas'tare vt (pasta) to knead

impastic'carsi vpr to pop pills

im'pasto sm (l'impastare: di pane) kneading; (: di cemento) mixing; (pasta) dough; (anche fig) mixture

im'patto sm impact

impau'rire vt to scare, frighten ▷ vi (anche: **impaurirsi**) to become scared o frightened

impazi'ente [impat'tsjɛnte] ag impatient

impaz'zata [impat'tsata] sf all'~ (precipitosamente) at breakneck speed

impaz'zire [impat'tsire] vi to go mad; ~ **per qn/qc** to be crazy about sb/sth

impec'cabile ag impeccable

impedi'mento sm obstacle, hindrance

impe'dire vt (vietare): ~ **a qn di fare** to prevent sb from doing; (ostruire) to obstruct; (*impacciare*) to hamper, hinder

impegnarsi *vpr* (*vincolarsi*): **~ a fare** to undertake to do; (*mettersi risolutamente*): **~ in qc** to devote o.s. to sth; **~ con qn** (*accordarsi*) to come to an agreement with sb

impegna'tivo, -a *ag* binding; (*lavoro*) demanding, exacting

impe'gnato, -a *ag* (*occupato*) busy; (*fig: romanzo, autore*) committed, engagé

im'pegno [im'peɲɲo] *sm* (*obbligo*) obligation; (*promessa*) promise, pledge; (*zelo*) diligence, zeal; (*compito, d'autore*) commitment

impel'lente *ag* pressing, urgent

impen'narsi *vpr* (*cavallo*) to rear up; (*Aer*) to nose up; (*fig*) to bridle

impensie'rire *vt* to worry; **impensierirsi** *vpr* to worry

impera'tivo, -a *ag, sm* imperative

impera'tore, -'trice *sm/f* emperor/empress

imperdo'nabile *ag* unforgivable, unpardonable

imper'fetto, -a *ag* imperfect ▷ *sm* (*Ling*) imperfect (tense)

imperi'ale *ag* imperial

imperi'oso, -a *ag* (*persona*) imperious; (*motivo, esigenza*) urgent, pressing

imperme'abile *ag* waterproof ▷ *sm* raincoat

im'pero *sm* empire; (*forza, autorità*) rule, control

imperso'nale *ag* impersonal

imperso'nare *vt* to personify; (*Teatro*) to play, act (the part of)

imperter'rito, -a *ag* fearless, undaunted; impassive

imperti'nente *ag* impertinent

'impeto *sm* (*moto, forza*) force, impetus; (*assalto*) onslaught; (*fig: impulso*) impulse; (: *slancio*) transport; **con ~** energetically; vehemently

impet'tito, -a *ag* stiff, erect

impetu'oso, -a *ag* (*vento*) strong, raging; (*persona*) impetuous

impi'anto *sm* (*installazione*) installation; (*apparecchiature*) plant; (*sistema*) system; **impianto elettrico** wiring; **impianto di risalita** (*Sci*) ski lift; **impianto di riscaldamento** heating system; **impianto sportivo** sports complex

impic'care *vt* to hang; **impiccarsi** *vpr* to hang o.s.

impicciarsi [impit'tʃarsi] *vpr* (*immischiarsi*): **~ (in)** to meddle (in); **impicciati degli affari tuoi!** mind your own business!

impicci'one, -a [impit'tʃone] *sm/f* busybody

impie'gare *vt* (*usare*) to use, employ; (*spendere: denaro, tempo*) to spend; (*investire*) to invest; **impie'gato, -a** *sm/f* employee

impi'ego, -ghi *sm* (*uso*) use; (*occupazione*) employment; (*posto di lavoro*) (regular) job, post; (*Econ*) investment

impieto'sire *vt* to move to pity; **impietosirsi** *vpr* to be moved to pity

impigli'arsi *vpr* to get caught up *o* entangled

impi'grirsi *vpr* to grow lazy

impli'care *vt* to imply; (*coinvolgere*) to involve

im'plicito, -a [im'plitʃito] *ag* implicit

implo'rare *vt* to implore; (*pietà ecc*) to beg for

impolve'rarsi *vpr* to get dusty

im'pone *ecc vb vedi* **imporre**

impo'nente *ag* imposing, impressive

im'pongo *ecc vb vedi* **imporre**

impo'nibile *ag* taxable ▷ *sm* taxable income

impopo'lare *ag* unpopular

im'porre *vt* to impose; (*costringere*) to force, make; (*far valere*) to impose, enforce; **imporsi** *vpr* (*persona*) to assert o.s.; (*cosa: rendersi necessario*) to become necessary; (*aver successo: moda, attore*) to become popular; **~ a qn di fare** to force sb to do, make sb do

impor'tante *ag* important; **impor'tanza** *sf* importance; **dare importanza a qc** to attach importance to sth; **darsi importanza** to give o.s. airs

impor'tare *vt* (*introdurre dall'estero*) to import ▷ *vi* to matter, be important ▷ *vb impers* (*essere necessario*) to be necessary; (*interessare*) to matter; **non importa!** it doesn't matter!; **non me ne importa!** I don't care!

im'porto *sm* (*totale*) amount

importu'nare *vt* to bother

im'posi *ecc vb vedi* **imporre**

imposizi'one [impozit'tsjone] *sf* imposition; order, command; (*onere, imposta*) tax

imposses'sarsi *vpr* **~ di** to seize, take possession of

impos'sibile *ag* impossible; **fare l'~** to do one's utmost, do all one can

im'posta *sf* (*di finestra*) shutter; (*tassa*) tax; **imposta sul reddito** income tax; **imposta sul valore aggiunto** (*BRIT*), sales tax (*US*)

impos'tare *vt* (*imbucare*) to post; (*preparare*) to plan, set out; (*avviare*) to begin, start off; (*voce*) to pitch

impostazi'one [impostat'tsjone] *sf*
(*di lettera*) posting (BRIT), mailing (US);
(*di problema, questione*) formulation,
statement; (*di lavoro*) organization,
planning; (*di attività*) setting up; (*Mus:
di voce*) pitch; **impostazioni** *sfpl* (*di
computer*) settings

impo'tente *ag* weak, powerless; (*anche
Med*) impotent

imprati'cabile *ag* (*strada*) impassable;
(*campo da gioco*) unplayable

impre'care *vi* to curse, swear; **~ contro** to
hurl abuse at

imprecazi'one [imprekat'tsjone] *sf*
abuse, curse

impre'gnare [impreɲ'ɲare] *vt* **~ (di)**
(*imbevere*) to soak *o* impregnate (with);
(*riempire*) to fill (with)

imprendi'tore *sm* (*industriale*)
entrepreneur; (*appaltatore*) contractor;
piccolo ~ small businessman

im'presa *sf* (*iniziativa*) enterprise; (*azione*)
exploit; (*azienda*) firm, concern

impressio'nante *ag* impressive;
upsetting

impressio'nare *vt* to impress; (*turbare*) to
upset; (*Fot*) to expose; **impressionarsi** *vpr*
to be easily upset

impressi'one *sf* impression; (*fig:
sensazione*) sensation, feeling; (*stampa*)
printing; **fare ~** (*colpire*) to impress;
(*turbare*) to frighten, upset; **fare
buona/cattiva ~ a** to make a good/bad
impression on

impreve'dibile *ag* unforeseeable;
(*persona*) unpredictable

impre'visto, -a *ag* unexpected,
unforeseen ▷ *sm* unforeseen event; **salvo
imprevisti** unless anything unexpected
happens

imprigio'nare [impridʒo'nare] *vt* to
imprison

impro'babile *ag* improbable, unlikely

im'pronta *sf* imprint, impression, sign;
(*di piede, mano*) print; (*fig*) mark, stamp;
impronta digitale fingerprint

improvvisa'mente *av* suddenly;
unexpectedly

improvvi'sare *vt* to improvise

improv'viso, -a *ag* (*imprevisto*)
unexpected; (*subitaneo*) sudden; **all'~**
unexpectedly; suddenly

impru'dente *ag* unwise, rash

impu'gnare [impuɲ'ɲare] *vt* to grasp,
grip; (*Dir*) to contest

impul'sivo, -a *ag* impulsive

im'pulso *sm* impulse

impun'tarsi *vpr* to stop dead, refuse to
budge; (*fig*) to be obstinate

impu'tato, -a *sm/f* (*Dir*) accused,
defendant

⊙ **PAROLA CHIAVE**

in (*in + il* = **nel**, *in + lo* = **nello**, *in + l'* = **nell'**, *in
+ la* = **nella**, *in + i* = **nei**, *in + gli* = **negli**, *in + le*
= **nelle**) *prep* **1** (*stato in luogo*) in; **vivere in
Italia/città** to live in Italy/town; **essere in
casa/ufficio** to be at home/the office; **se
fossi in te** if I were you

2 (*moto a luogo*) to; (*: dentro*) into; **andare
in Germania/città** to go to Germany/
town; **andare in ufficio** to go to the office;
entrare in macchina/casa to get into the
car/go into the house

3 (*tempo*) in; **nel 1989** in 1989; **in giugno/
estate** in June/summer

4 (*modo, maniera*) in; **in silenzio** in silence;
in abito da sera in evening dress; **in
guerra** at war; **in vacanza** on holiday;
Maria Bianchi in Rossi Maria Rossi née
Bianchi

5 (*mezzo*) by; **viaggiare in autobus/treno**
to travel by bus/train

6 (*materia*) made of; **in marmo** made of
marble, marble *cpd*; **una collana in oro** a
gold necklace

7 (*misura*) in; **siamo in quattro** there are
four of us; **in tutto** in all

8 (*fine*): **dare in dono** to give as a gift;
spende tutto in alcool he spends all his
money on drink; **in onore di** in honour of

inabi'tabile *ag* uninhabitable

inacces'sibile [inattʃes'sibile] *ag* (*luogo*)
inaccessible; (*persona*) unapproachable

inaccet'tabile [inattʃet'tabile] *ag*
unacceptable

ina'datto, -a *ag* **~ (a)** unsuitable *o* unfit
(for)

inadegu'ato, -a *ag* inadequate

inaffi'dabile *ag* unreliable

inami'dato, -a *ag* starched

inar'care *vt* (*schiena*) to arch; (*sopracciglia*)
to raise

inaspet'tato, -a *ag* unexpected

inas'prire *vt* (*disciplina*) to tighten up,
make harsher; (*carattere*) to embitter;
inasprirsi *vpr* to become harsher; to
become bitter; to become worse

inattac'cabile *ag* (*anche fig*) unassailable;
(*alibi*) cast-iron

inatten'dibile *ag* unreliable

inat'teso, -a *ag* unexpected

inattu'abile *ag* impracticable

inau'dito, -a *ag* unheard of

inaugu'rare *vt* to inaugurate, open;
(*monumento*) to unveil

inaugurazi'one [inaugurat'tsjone] *sf*
inauguration; unveiling

incal'lito, -a *ag* calloused; (*fig*) hardened,
inveterate; (: *insensibile*) hard

incande'scente [inkandeʃʃɛnte] *ag*
incandescent, white-hot

incan'tare *vt* to enchant, bewitch;
incantarsi *vpr* (*rimanere intontito*) to be
spellbound; to be in a daze; (*meccanismo:
bloccarsi*) to jam; **incan'tevole** *ag*
charming, enchanting

in'canto *sm* spell, charm, enchantment;
(*asta*) auction; **come per ~** as if by magic;
mettere all'~ to put up for auction

inca'pace [inka'patʃe] *ag* incapable

incarce'rare [inkartʃe'rare] *vt* to imprison

incari'care *vt* **~ qn di fare** to give sb the
responsibility of doing; **incaricarsi di** to
take care o charge of

in'carico, -chi *sm* task, job

incarta'mento *sm* dossier, file

incar'tare *vt* to wrap (in paper)

incas'sare *vt* (*merce*) to pack (in cases);
(*gemma: incastonare*) to set; (*Econ:
riscuotere*) to collect; (*Pugilato: colpi*) to
take, stand up to; **in'casso** *sm* cashing,
encashment; (*introito*) takings *pl*

incas'trare *vt* to fit in, insert; (*fig:
intrappolare*) to catch; **incastrarsi** *vpr*
(*combaciare*) to fit together; (*restare
bloccato*) to become stuck

incate'nare *vt* to chain up

in'cauto, -a *ag* imprudent, rash

inca'vato, -a *ag* hollow; (*occhi*) sunken

incendi'are [intʃen'djare] *vt* to set fire to;
incendiarsi *vpr* to catch fire, burst into
flames

in'cendio [in'tʃendjo] *sm* fire

inceneri'tore [intʃeneri'tore] *sm*
incinerator

in'censo [in'tʃɛnso] *sm* incense

incensu'rato, -a [intʃensu'rato] *ag* (*Dir*):
essere ~ to have a clean record

incenti'vare [intʃenti'vare] *vt* (*produzione,
vendite*) to boost; (*persona*) to motivate

incen'tivo [intʃen'tivo] *sm* incentive

incepparsi *vpr* to jam

incer'tezza [intʃer'tettsa] *sf* uncertainty

in'certo, -a [in'tʃɛrto] *ag* uncertain;
(*irresoluto*) undecided, hesitating ▷ *sm*
uncertainty

in'cetta [in'tʃetta] *sf* buying up; **fare ~ di
qc** to buy up sth

inchi'esta [in'kjɛsta] *sf* investigation,
inquiry

inchinarsi *vpr* to bend down; (*per riverenza*)
to bow; (: *donna*) to curtsy

inchio'dare [inkjo'dare] *vt* to nail (down);
~ la macchina (*Aut*) to jam on the brakes

inchi'ostro [in'kjɔstro] *sm* ink; **inchiostro
simpatico** invisible ink

inciam'pare [intʃam'pare] *vi* to trip,
stumble

inci'dente [intʃi'dɛnte] *sm* accident;
ho avuto un ~ I've had an accident;
incidente automobilistico *o* **d'auto**
car accident; **incidente diplomatico**
diplomatic incident

in'cidere [in'tʃidere] *vi* **~ su** to bear upon,
affect ▷ *vt* (*tagliare incavando*) to cut into;
(*Arte*) to engrave; to etch; (*canzone*) to
record

in'cinta [in'tʃinta] *ag f* pregnant

incipri'are [intʃi'prjare] *vt* to powder
incipriarsi ▷ *vpr* to powder one's face

in'circa [in'tʃirka] *av* **all'~** more or less,
very nearly

in'cisi *ecc* [in'tʃizi] *vb vedi* **incidere**

incisi'one [intʃi'zjone] *sf* cut; (*disegno*)
engraving; etching; (*registrazione*)
recording; (*Med*) incision

in'ciso, -a [in'tʃizo] *pp di* **incidere** ▷ *sm*
per ~ incidentally, by the way

inci'tare [intʃi'tare] *vt* to incite

inci'vile [intʃi'vile] *ag* uncivilized; (*villano*)
impolite

incl. *abbr* (= *incluso*) encl.

incli'nare *vt* to tilt; **inclinarsi** *vpr* (*barca*)
to list; (*aereo*) to bank

in'cludere *vt* to include; (*accludere*) to
enclose; **in'cluso, -a** *pp di* **includere** ▷ *ag*
included; enclosed

incoe'rente *ag* incoherent;
(*contraddittorio*) inconsistent

in'cognita [in'konnita] *sf* (*Mat, fig*)
unknown quantity

in'cognito, -a [in'konnito] *ag* unknown
▷ *sm* **in ~** incognito

incol'lare *vt* to glue, gum; (*unire con colla*)
to stick together

inco'lore *ag* colourless

incol'pare *vt* **~ qn di** to charge sb with

in'colto, -a *ag* (*terreno*) uncultivated;
(*trascurato: capelli*) neglected; (*persona*)
uneducated

in'colume *ag* safe and sound, unhurt

incom'benza [inkom'bɛntsa] *sf* duty,
task

in'combere *vi* (*sovrastare minacciando*): **~
su** to threaten, hang over

incominci'are [inkomin'tʃare] *vi, vt* to
begin, start

incompe'tente *ag* incompetent

incompi'uto, -a *ag* unfinished,
incomplete

incom'pleto, -a *ag* incomplete

incompren'sibile *ag* incomprehensible

inconce'pibile [inkontʃe'pibile] *ag*

inconceivable

inconcili'abile [inkontʃi'ljabile] *ag*
irreconcilable

inconclu'dente *ag* inconclusive; (*persona*)
ineffectual

incondizio'nato, -a [inkondittsjo'nato]
ag unconditional

inconfon'dibile *ag* unmistakable

inconsa'pevole *ag* ~ **di** unaware of,
ignorant of

in'conscio, -a, -sci, -sce [in'kɔnʃo]
ag unconscious ▷ *sm* (*Psic*): **l'~** the
unconscious

inconsis'tente *ag* insubstantial;
unfounded

inconsu'eto, -a *ag* unusual

incon'trare *vt* to meet; (*difficoltà*) to meet
with; **incontrarsi** *vpr* to meet

in'contro *av* ~ **a** (*verso*) towards ▷ *sm*
meeting; (*Sport*) match; meeting;
incontro di calcio football match

inconveni'ente *sm* drawback, snag

incoraggia'mento [inkoraddʒa'mento]
sm encouragement

incoraggi'are [inkorad'dʒare] *vt* to
encourage

incornici'are [inkorni'tʃare] *vt* to frame

incoro'nare *vt* to crown

in'correre *vi* ~ **in** to meet with, run into

incosci'ente [inkoʃ'ʃɛnte] *ag* (*inconscio*)
unconscious; (*irresponsabile*) reckless,
thoughtless

incre'dibile *ag* incredible, unbelievable

in'credulo, -a *ag* incredulous, disbelieving

incremen'tare *vt* to increase; (*dar sviluppo
a*) to promote

incre'mento *sm* (*sviluppo*) development;
(*aumento numerico*) increase, growth

incresci'oso, -a [inkreʃ'ʃoso] *ag* (*incidente
ecc*) regrettable

incrimi'nare *vt* (*Dir*) to charge

incri'nare *vt* to crack; (*fig: rapporti,
amicizia*) to cause to deteriorate;
incrinarsi *vpr* to crack; to deteriorate

incroci'are [inkro'tʃare] *vt* to cross;
(*incontrare*) to meet ▷ *vi* (*Naut, Aer*) to
cruise; **incrociarsi** *vpr* (*strade*) to cross,
intersect; (*persone, veicoli*) to pass each
other; ~ **le braccia/le gambe** to fold one's
arms/cross one's legs

in'crocio [in'krotʃo] *sm* (*anche Ferr*)
crossing; (*di strade*) crossroads

incuba'trice [inkuba'tritʃe] *sf* incubator

'incubo *sm* nightmare

incu'rabile *ag* incurable

incu'rante *ag* ~ **(di)** heedless (of), careless
(of)

incurio'sire *vt* to make curious;
incuriosirsi *vpr* to become curious

incursi'one *sf* raid

incur'vare *vt* to bend, curve; **incurvarsi**
vpr to bend, curve

incusto'dito, -a *ag* unguarded,
unattended

in'cutere *vt* ~ **timore/rispetto a qn** to
strike fear into sb/command sb's respect

'indaco *sm* indigo

indaffa'rato, -a *ag* busy

inda'gare *vt* to investigate

in'dagine [in'dadʒine] *sf* investigation,
inquiry; (*ricerca*) research, study; **indagine
di mercato** market survey

indebi'tarsi *vpr* to run o get into debt

indebo'lire *vt, vi* (*anche*: **indebolirsi**) to
weaken

inde'cente [inde'tʃɛnte] *ag* indecent

inde'ciso, -a [inde'tʃizo] *ag* indecisive;
(*irresoluto*) undecided

indefi'nito, -a *ag* (*anche Ling*) indefinite;
(*impreciso, non determinato*) undefined

in'degno, -a [in'deɲɲo] *ag* (*atto*)
shameful; (*persona*) unworthy

indemoni'ato, -a *ag* possessed (by the
devil)

in'denne *ag* unhurt, uninjured

indenniz'zare [indennid'dzare] *vt* to
compensate

indetermina'tivo, -a *ag* (*Ling*) indefinite

'India *sf* **l'~** India; **indi'ano, -a** *ag* Indian
▷ *sm/f* (*d'India*) Indian; (*d'America*) Native
American, (American) Indian

indi'care *vt* (*mostrare*) to show, indicate;
(: *col dito*) to point to, point out;
(*consigliare*) to suggest, recommend;
indica'tivo, -a *ag* indicative ▷ *sm*
(*Ling*) indicative (mood); **indicazi'one**
sf indication; (*informazione*) piece of
information

'indice ['inditʃe] *sm* index; (*fig*) sign;
(*dito*) index finger, forefinger; **indice di
gradimento** (*Radio, TV*) popularity rating

indicherò *ecc* [indike'rɔ] *vb vedi* **indicare**

indi'cibile [indi'tʃibile] *ag* inexpressible

indietreggi'are [indietred'dʒare] *vi* to
draw back, retreat

indi'etro *av* back; (*guardare*) behind, back;
(*andare, cadere: anche*: **all'~**) backwards;
rimanere ~ to be left behind; **essere** ~ (*col
lavoro*) to be behind; (*orologio*) to be slow;
rimandare qc ~ to send sth back

indi'feso, -a *ag* (*città ecc*) undefended;
(*persona*) defenceless

indiffe'rente *ag* indifferent

in'digeno, -a [in'didʒeno] *ag* indigenous,
native ▷ *sm/f* native

indigesti'one [indidʒes'tjone] *sf*
indigestion

indi'gesto, -a [indi'dʒɛsto] *ag* indigestible

indi'gnare [indiɲ'ɲare] vt to fill with indignation; **indignarsi** vpr to get indignant

indimenti'cabile ag unforgettable

indipen'dente ag independent

in'dire vt (concorso) to announce; (elezioni) to call

indi'retto, -a ag indirect

indiriz'zare [indirit'tsare] vt (dirigere) to direct; (mandare) to send; (lettera) to address

indi'rizzo [indi'rittso] sm address; (direzione) direction; (avvio) trend, course; **il mio ~ è...** my address is ...

indis'creto, -a ag indiscreet

indis'cusso, -a ag unquestioned

indispen'sabile ag indispensable, essential

indispet'tire vt to irritate, annoy ▷ vi (anche: **indispettirsi**) to get irritated o annoyed

individu'ale ag individual

individu'are vt (dar forma distinta a) to characterize; (determinare) to locate; (riconoscere) to single out

indi'viduo sm individual

indizi'ato, -a ag suspected ▷ sm/f suspect

in'dizio [in'dittsjo] sm (segno) sign, indication; (Polizia) clue; (Dir) piece of evidence

'indole sf nature, character

indolen'zito, -a [indolen'tsito] ag stiff, aching; (intorpidito) numb

indo'lore ag painless

indo'mani sm l'~ the next day, the following day

Indo'nesia sf l'~ Indonesia

indos'sare vt (mettere indosso) to put on; (avere indosso) to have on; **indossa'tore, -'trice** sm/f model

indottri'nare vt to indoctrinate

indovi'nare vt (scoprire) to guess; (immaginare) to imagine, guess; (il futuro) to foretell; **indovi'nello** sm riddle

indubbia'mente av undoubtedly

in'dubbio, -a ag certain, undoubted

in'duco ecc vb vedi **indurre**

indugi'are [indu'dʒare] vi to take one's time, delay

in'dugio [in'dudʒo] sm (ritardo) delay; **senza ~** without delay

indul'gente [indul'dʒente] ag indulgent; (giudice) lenient

indu'mento sm article of clothing, garment

indu'rire vt to harden ▷ vi (anche: **indurirsi**) to harden, become hard

in'durre vt ~ **qn a fare qc** to induce o

persuade sb to do sth; ~ **qn in errore** to mislead sb

in'dussi ecc vb vedi **indurre**

in'dustria sf industry; **industri'ale** ag industrial ▷ sm industrialist

inecce'pibile [inettʃe'pibile] ag unexceptionable

i'nedito, -a ag unpublished

ine'rente ag ~ **a** concerning, regarding

i'nerme ag unarmed; defenceless

inerpi'carsi vpr ~ **(su)** to clamber (up)

i'nerte ag inert; (inattivo) indolent, sluggish

ine'satto, -a ag (impreciso) inexact; (erroneo) incorrect; (Amm: non riscosso) uncollected

inesis'tente ag non-existent

inesperi'enza [inespe'rjɛntsa] sf inexperience

ines'perto, -a ag inexperienced

inevi'tabile ag inevitable

i'nezia [i'nettsja] sf trifle, thing of no importance

infagot'tare vt to bundle up, wrap up; **infagottarsi** vpr to wrap up

infal'libile ag infallible

infa'mante ag defamatory

in'fame ag infamous; (fig: cosa, compito) awful, dreadful

infan'gare vt to cover with mud; (fig: reputazione) to sully; **infangarsi** vpr to get covered in mud; to be sullied

infan'tile ag child cpd; childlike; (adulto, azione) childish; **letteratura ~** children's books pl

in'fanzia [in'fantsja] sf childhood; (bambini) children pl; **prima ~** babyhood infancy

infari'nare vt to cover with (o sprinkle with o dip in) flour; **infari'natura** sf (fig) smattering

in'farto sm (Med) heart attack

infasti'dire vt to annoy, irritate; **infastidirsi** vpr to get annoyed o irritated

infati'cabile ag tireless, untiring

in'fatti cong actually, as a matter of fact

Attenzione! In inglese esiste l'espressione in fact che però vuol dire in effetti.

infatu'arsi vpr ~ **di** to become infatuated with, fall for

infe'dele ag unfaithful

infe'lice [infe'litʃe] ag unhappy; (sfortunato) unlucky, unfortunate; (inopportuno) inopportune, ill-timed; (mal riuscito: lavoro) bad, poor

inferi'ore ag lower; (per intelligenza, qualità) inferior ▷ sm/f inferior; ~ **a** (numero, quantità) less o smaller than;

(*meno buono*) inferior to; **~ alla media** below average; **inferiorità** *sf* inferiority

inferme'ria *sf* infirmary; (*di scuola, nave*) sick bay

infermi'ere, -a *sm/f* nurse

infermità *sf inv* illness; infirmity; **infermità mentale** mental illness; (*Dir*) insanity

in'fermo, -a *ag* (*ammalato*) ill; (*debole*) infirm

infer'nale *ag* infernal; (*proposito, complotto*) diabolical

in'ferno *sm* hell

inferri'ata *sf* grating

infes'tare *vt* to infest

infet'tare *vt* to infect; **infettarsi** *vpr* to become infected; **infezi'one** *sf* infection

infiam'mabile *ag* inflammable

infiam'mare *vt* to set alight; (*fig, Med*) to inflame; **infiammarsi** *vpr* to catch fire; (*Med*) to become inflamed; **infiammazi'one** *sf* (*Med*) inflammation

infie'rire *vi* **~ su** (*fisicamente*) to attack furiously; (*verbalmente*) to rage at

infi'lare *vt* (*ago*) to thread; (*mettere: chiave*) to insert; (*: anello, vestito*) to slip *o* put on; (*strada*) to turn into, take; **infilarsi** *vpr* **infilarsi in** to slip into; (*indossare*) to slip on; **~ l'uscio** to slip in; to slip out

infil'trarsi *vpr* to penetrate, seep through; (*Mil*) to infiltrate

infil'zare [infil'tsare] *vt* (*infilare*) to string together; (*trafiggere*) to pierce

'infimo, -a *ag* lowest

in'fine *av* finally; (*insomma*) in short

infinità *sf* infinity; (*in quantità*): **un'~ di** an infinite number of

infi'nito, -a *ag* infinite; (*Ling*) infinitive ▷ *sm* infinity; (*Ling*) infinitive; **all'~** (*senza fine*) endlessly

infinocchi'are [infinok'kjare] (*fam*) *vt* to hoodwink

infischi'arsi [infis'kjarsi] *vpr* **~ di** not to care about

in'fisso, -a (*pp*) *di* **infiggere** *sm* fixture; (*di porta, finestra*) frame

inflazi'one [inflat'tsjone] *sf* inflation

in'fliggere [in'fliddʒere] *vt* to inflict

in'flissi *ecc vb vedi* **infliggere**

influ'ente *ag* influential; **influ'enza** *sf* influence; (*Med*) influenza, flu

influen'zare [influen'tsare] *vt* to influence, have an influence on

influ'ire *vi* **~ su** to influence

in'flusso *sm* influence

infon'dato, -a *ag* unfounded, groundless

in'fondere *vt* **~ qc in qn** to instill sth in sb

infor'mare *vt* to inform, tell; **informarsi**

vpr **informarsi (di** *o* **su)** to inquire (about)

infor'matica *sf* computer science

informa'tivo, -a *ag* informative

infor'mato, -a *ag* informed; **tenersi ~** to keep o.s. (well-)informed

informa'tore *sm* informer

informazi'one [informat'tsjone] *sf* piece of information; **prendere informazioni sul conto di qn** to get information about sb; **chiedere un'~** to ask for (some) information

in'forme *ag* shapeless

informico'larsi *vpr* to have pins and needles

infortu'nato, -a *ag* injured, hurt ▷ *sm/f* injured person

infor'tunio *sm* accident; **infortunio sul lavoro** industrial accident, accident at work

infra'dito *sm inv* (*calzatura*) flip flop (BRIT), thong (us)

infrazi'one [infrat'tsjone] *sf* **~ a** breaking of, violation of

infredda'tura *sf* slight cold

infreddo'lito, -a *ag* cold, chilled

infu'ori *av* out; **all'~** outwards; **all'~ di** (*eccetto*) except, with the exception of

infuri'arsi *vpr* to fly into a rage

infusi'one *sf* infusion

in'fuso, -a *pp di* **infondere** ▷ *sm* infusion

Ing. *abbr* = **ingegnere**

ingaggi'are [ingad'dʒare] *vt* (*assumere con compenso*) to take on, hire; (*Sport*) to sign on; (*Mil*) to engage

ingan'nare *vt* to deceive; (*fisco*) to cheat; (*eludere*) to dodge, elude; (*fig: tempo*) to while away ▷ *vi* (*apparenza*) to be deceptive; **ingannarsi** *vpr* to be mistaken, be wrong

in'ganno *sm* deceit, deception; (*azione*) trick; (*menzogna, frode*) cheat, swindle; (*illusione*) illusion

inge'gnarsi [indʒeɲ'ɲarsi] *vpr* to do one's best, try hard; **~ per vivere** to live by one's wits

inge'gnere [indʒeɲ'ɲɛre] *sm* engineer; **~ civile/navale** civil/naval engineer; **ingegne'ria** *sf* engineering; **ingegnere genetica** genetic engineering

in'gegno [in'dʒeɲɲo] *sm* (*intelligenza*) intelligence, brains *pl*; (*capacità creativa*) ingenuity; (*disposizione*) talent; **inge'gnoso, -a** *ag* ingenious, clever

ingelo'sire [indʒelo'zire] *vt* to make jealous ▷ *vi* (*anche*: **ingelosirsi**) to become jealous

in'gente [in'dʒɛnte] *ag* huge, enormous

ingenuità [indʒenui'ta] *sf* ingenuousness

in'genuo, -a [in'dʒɛnuo] *ag* naïve
Attenzione! In inglese esiste la parola *ingenious*, che però significa *ingegnoso*.

inge'rire [indʒe'rire] *vt* to ingest

inges'sare [indʒes'sare] *vt* (*Med*) to put in plaster; **ingessa'tura** *sf* plaster

Inghil'terra [ingil'tɛrra] *sf* I'~ England

inghiot'tire [ingjot'tire] *vt* to swallow

ingial'lire [indʒal'lire] *vi* to go yellow

inginocchi'arsi [indʒinok'kjarsi] *vpr* to kneel (down)

ingiù [in'dʒu] *av* down, downwards

ingi'uria [in'dʒurja] *sf* insult; (*fig: danno*) damage

ingius'tizia [indʒus'tittsja] *sf* injustice

ingi'usto, -a [in'dʒusto] *ag* unjust, unfair

in'glese *ag* English ▷ *sm/f* Englishman/woman ▷ *sm* (*Ling*) English; **gli Inglesi** the English; **andarsene** *o* **filare all'~** to take French leave

ingoi'are *vt* to gulp (down); (*fig*) to swallow (up)

ingol'farsi *vpr* to flood

ingom'brante *ag* cumbersome

ingom'brare *vt* (*strada*) to block; (*stanza*) to clutter up

in'gordo, -a *ag* ~ **di** greedy for; (*fig*) greedy *o* avid for

in'gorgo, -ghi *sm* blockage, obstruction; (*anche:* ~ **stradale**) traffic jam

ingoz'zarsi *vpr* ~ (**di**) to stuff o.s. (with)

ingra'naggio [ingra'naddʒo] *sm* (*Tecn*) gear; (*di orologio*) mechanism; **gli ingranaggi della burocrazia** the bureaucratic machinery

ingra'nare *vi* to mesh, engage ▷ *vt* to engage; ~ **la marcia** to get into gear

ingrandi'mento *sm* enlargement; extension

ingran'dire *vt* (*anche Fot*) to enlarge; (*estendere*) to extend; (*Ottica, fig*) to magnify ▷ *vi* (*anche:* **ingrandirsi**) to become larger *o* bigger; (*aumentare*) to grow, increase; (*espandersi*) to expand

ingras'sare *vt* to make fat; (*animali*) to fatten; (*lubrificare*) to oil, lubricate ▷ *vi* (*anche:* **ingrassarsi**) to get fat, put on weight

in'grato, -a *ag* ungrateful; (*lavoro*) thankless, unrewarding

ingredi'ente *sm* ingredient

in'gresso *sm* (*porta*) entrance; (*atrio*) hall; (*l'entrare*) entrance, entry; (*facoltà di entrare*) admission; **ingresso libero** admission free

ingros'sare *vt* to increase; (*folla, livello*) to swell ▷ *vi* (*anche:* **ingrossarsi**) to increase; to swell

in'grosso *av* **all'~** (*Comm*) wholesale; (*all'incirca*) roughly, about

Ingua'ribile *ag* incurable

'inguine *sm* (*Anat*) groin

ini'bire *vt* to forbid, prohibit; (*Psic*) to inhibit; **inibirsi** *vpr* to restrain o.s.

ini'bito, -a *ag* inhibited ▷ *sm/f* inhibited person

iniet'tare *vt* to inject; **iniezi'one** *sf* injection

ininterrotta'mente *av* non-stop, continuously

ininter'rotto, -a *ag* unbroken; uninterrupted

inizi'ale [init'tsjale] *ag*, *sf* initial

inizi'are [init'tsjare] *vi*, *vt* to begin, start; **a che ora inizia il film?** when does the film start?; ~ **qn a** to initiate sb into; (*pittura ecc*) to introduce sb to; ~ **a fare qc** to start doing sth

inizia'tiva [inittsja'tiva] *sf* initiative; **iniziativa privata** private enterprise

i'nizio [i'nittsjo] *sm* beginning; **all'~** at the beginning, at the start; **dare** ~ **a qc** to start sth, get sth going

innaffi'are *ecc* = **annaffiare** *ecc*

innamo'rarsi *vpr* ~ (**di qn**) to fall in love (with sb); **innamo'rato, -a** *ag* (*che nutre amore*): **innamorato (di)** in love (with); (*appassionato*): **innamorato di** very fond of ▷ *sm/f* lover; sweetheart

innanzi'tutto *av* first of all

in'nato, -a *ag* innate

innatu'rale *ag* unnatural

inne'gabile *ag* undeniable

innervo'sire *vt* ~ **qn** to get on sb's nerves; **innervosirsi** *vpr* to get irritated *o* upset

innes'care *vt* to prime

'inno *sm* hymn; **inno nazionale** national anthem

inno'cente [inno'tʃɛnte] *ag* innocent

in'nocuo, -a *ag* innocuous, harmless

innova'tivo, -a *ag* innovative

innume'revole *ag* innumerable

inol'trare *vt* (*Amm*) to pass on, forward

i'noltre *av* besides, moreover

inon'dare *vt* to flood

inoppor'tuno, -a *ag* untimely, ill-timed; inappropriate; (*momento*) inopportune

inorri'dire *vt* to horrify ▷ *vi* to be horrified

inosser'vato, -a *ag* (*non notato*) unobserved; (*non rispettato*) not observed, not kept

inossi'dabile *ag* stainless

INPS *sigla m* (= *Istituto Nazionale Previdenza Sociale*) social security service

inqua'drare *vt* (*foto, immagine*) to frame; (*fig*) to situate, set

inqui'eto, -a *ag* restless; (*preoccupato*) worried, anxious

inqui'lino, -a *sm/f* tenant

inquina'mento *sm* pollution

inqui'nare *vt* to pollute

insabbi'are *vt* (*fig: pratica*) to shelve; **insabbiarsi** *vpr* (*arenarsi: barca*) to run aground; (*fig: pratica*) to be shelved

insac'cati *smpl* (*Cuc*) sausages

insa'lata *sf* salad; **insalata mista** mixed salad; **insalata russa** (*Cuc*) Russian salad (*comprised of cold diced cooked vegetables in mayonnaise*); **insalati'era** *sf* salad bowl

insa'nabile *ag* (*piaga*) which cannot be healed; (*situazione*) irremediable; (*odio*) implacable

insa'puta *sf* **all'~ di qn** without sb knowing

inse'diarsi *vpr* to take up office; (*popolo, colonia*) to settle

in'segna [in'seɲɲa] *sf* sign; (*emblema*) sign, emblem; (*bandiera*) flag, banner

insegna'mento [inseɲɲa'mento] *sm* teaching

inse'gnante [inseɲ'ɲante] *ag* teaching ▷ *sm/f* teacher

inse'gnare [inseɲ'ɲare] *vt, vi* to teach; **~ a qn qc** to teach sb sth; **~ a qn a fare qc** to teach sb (how) to do sth

insegui'mento *sm* pursuit, chase

insegu'ire *vt* to pursue, chase

insena'tura *sf* inlet, creek

insen'sato, -a *ag* senseless, stupid

insen'sibile *ag* (*nervo*) insensible; (*persona*) indifferent

inse'rire *vt* to insert; (*Elettr*) to connect; (*allegare*) to enclose; (*annuncio*) to put in, place; **inserirsi** *vpr* (*fig*): **inserirsi in** to become part of

inservi'ente *sm/f* attendant

inserzi'one [inser'tsjone] *sf* insertion; (*avviso*) advertisement; **fare un'~ sul giornale** to put an advertisement in the paper

insetti'cida, -i [insetti'tʃida] *sm* insecticide

in'setto *sm* insect

insi'curo, -a *ag* insecure

insi'eme *av* together ▷ *prep* **~ a o con** together with ▷ *sm* whole; (*Mat, servizio, assortimento*) set; (*Moda*) ensemble, outfit; **tutti ~** all together; **tutto ~** all together; (*in una volta*) at one go; **nell'~** on the whole; **d'~** (*veduta ecc*) overall

in'signe [in'siɲɲe] *ag* (*persona*) famous, distinguished; (*città, monumento*) notable

insignifi'cante [insiɲɲifi'kante] *ag* insignificant

insinu'are *vt* (*introdurre*): **~ qc in** to slip *o* slide sth into; (*fig*) to insinuate, imply; **insinuarsi** *vpr* **insinuarsi in** to seep into;

(*fig*) to creep into; to worm one's way into

in'sipido, -a *ag* insipid

insis'tente *ag* insistent; persistent

in'sistere *vi* **~ su qc** to insist on sth; **~ in qc/a fare** (*perseverare*) to persist in sth/in doing

insoddis'fatto, -a *ag* dissatisfied

insoffe'rente *ag* intolerant

insolazi'one [insolat'tsjone] *sf* (*Med*) sunstroke

inso'lente *ag* insolent

in'solito, -a *ag* unusual, out of the ordinary

inso'luto, -a *ag* (*non risolto*) unsolved

in'somma *av* (*in conclusione*) in short; (*dunque*) well ▷ *escl* for heaven's sake!

in'sonne *ag* sleepless; **in'sonnia** *sf* insomnia, sleeplessness

insonno'lito, -a *ag* sleepy, drowsy

insoppor'tabile *ag* unbearable

in'sorgere [in'sordʒere] *vi* (*ribellarsi*) to rise up, rebel; (*apparire*) to come up, arise

in'sorsi *ecc vb vedi* **insorgere**

insospet'tire *vt* to make suspicious ▷ *vi* (*anche:* **insospettirsi**) to become suspicious

inspi'rare *vt* to breathe in, inhale

in'stabile *ag* (*carico, indole*) unstable; (*tempo*) unsettled; (*equilibrio*) unsteady

instal'lare *vt* to install

instan'cabile *ag* untiring, indefatigable

instau'rare *vt* to introduce, institute

insuc'cesso [insut'tʃɛsso] *sm* failure, flop

insuffici'ente [insuffi'tʃɛnte] *ag* insufficient; (*compito, allievo*) inadequate; **insuffici'enza** *sf* insufficiency; inadequacy; (*Ins*) fail; **insufficienza di prove** (*Dir*) lack of evidence; **insufficienza renale** renal insufficiency

insu'lina *sf* insulin

in'sulso, -a *ag* (*sciocco*) inane, silly; (*persona*) dull, insipid

insul'tare *vt* to insult, affront

in'sulto *sm* insult, affront

intac'care *vt* (*fare tacche*) to cut into; (*corrodere*) to corrode; (*fig: cominciare ad usare: risparmi*) to break into; (*: ledere*) to damage

intagli'are [intaʎ'ʎare] *vt* to carve

in'tanto *av* (*nel frattempo*) meanwhile, in the meantime; (*per cominciare*) just to begin with; **~ che** while

inta'sare *vt* to choke (up), block (up); (*Aut*) to obstruct, block; **intasarsi** *vpr* to become choked *o* blocked

intas'care *vt* to pocket

in'tatto, -a *ag* intact; (*puro*) unsullied

intavo'lare *vt* to start, enter into

inte'grale *ag* complete; (*pane, farina*)

wholemeal (BRIT), whole-wheat (US); (Mat): **calcolo ~** integral calculus

inte'grante ag **parte ~** integral part

inte'grare vt to complete; (Mat) to integrate; **integrarsi** vpr (persona) to become integrated

integra'tore sm **integratori alimentari** nutritional supplements

integrità sf integrity

'integro, -a ag (intatto, intero) complete, whole; (retto) upright

intelaia'tura sf frame; (fig) structure, framework

intel'letto sm intellect; **intellettu'ale** ag, sm/f intellectual

intelli'gente [intelli'dʒɛnte] ag intelligent

intem'perie sfpl bad weather sg

in'tendere vt (avere intenzione): **~ fare qc** to intend o mean to do sth; (comprendere) to understand; (udire) to hear; (significare) to mean; **intendersi** vpr (conoscere): **intendersi di** to know a lot about, be a connoisseur of; (accordarsi) to get on (well); **intendersela con qn** (avere una relazione amorosa) to have an affair with sb; **intendi'tore, -'trice** sm/f connoisseur, expert

inten'sivo, -a ag intensive

in'tenso, -a ag intense

in'tento, -a ag (teso, assorto): **~ (a)** intent (on), absorbed (in) ▷ sm aim, purpose

intenzio'nale [intentsjo'nale] ag intentional

intenzi'one [inten'tsjone] sf intention; (Dir) intent; **avere ~ di fare qc** to intend to do sth, have the intention of doing sth

interat'tivo, -a ag interactive

intercet'tare [intertʃet'tare] vt to intercept

intercity [ɪntəsɪ'tɪ] sm inv (Ferr) ≈ intercity (train)

inter'detto, -a pp di **interdire** ▷ ag forbidden, prohibited; (sconcertato) dumbfounded ▷ sm (Rel) interdict

interes'sante ag interesting; **essere in stato ~** to be expecting (a baby)

interes'sare vt to interest; (concernere) to concern, be of interest to; (far intervenire): **~ qn a** to draw sb's attention to ▷ vi **~ a** to interest, matter to; **interessarsi** vpr (mostrare interesse): **interessarsi a** to take an interest in, be interested in; (occuparsi): **interessarsi di** to take care of

inte'resse sm (anche Comm) interest

inter'faccia, -ce [inter'fattʃa] sf (Inform) interface

interfe'renza [interfe'rɛntsa] sf interference

interfe'rire vi to interfere

interiezi'one [interjet'tsjone] sf exclamation, interjection

interi'ora sfpl entrails

interi'ore ag interior, inner, inside, internal; (fig) inner

inter'medio, -a ag intermediate

inter'nare vt (arrestare) to intern; (Med) to commit (to a mental institution)

internazio'nale [internattsjo'nale] ag international

'Internet ['internet] sf Internet; **in ~** on the Internet

in'terno, -a ag (di dentro) internal, interior, inner; (: mare) inland; (nazionale) domestic; (allievo) boarding ▷ sm inside, interior; (di paese) interior; (fodera) lining; (di appartamento) flat (number); (Tel) extension ▷ sm/f (Ins) boarder; **interni** smpl (Cinema) interior shots; **all'~** inside; **Ministero degli Interni** Ministry of the Interior, ≈ Home Office (BRIT), Department of the Interior (US)

in'tero, -a ag (integro, intatto) whole, entire; (completo, totale) complete; (numero) whole; (non ridotto: biglietto) full; (latte) full-cream

interpel'lare vt to consult

interpre'tare vt to interpret; **in'terprete** sm/f interpreter; (Teatro) actor/actress, performer; (Mus) performer; **ci potrebbe fare da interprete?** could you act as an interpreter for us?

interregio'nale [interredʒo'nale] sm train that travels between two or more regions of Italy, stopping frequently

interro'gare vt to question; (Ins) to test; **interrogazi'one** sf questioning no pl; (Ins) oral test

inter'rompere vt to interrupt; (studi, trattative) to break off, interrupt; **interrompersi** vpr to break off, stop

interrut'tore sm switch

interruzi'one [interrut'tsjone] sf interruption; break

interur'bana sf trunk o long-distance call

inter'vallo sm interval; (spazio) space, gap

interve'nire vi (partecipare): **~ a** to take part in; (intromettersi: anche Pol) to intervene; (Med: operare) to operate; **inter'vento** sm participation; (intromissione) intervention; (Med) operation; **fare un intervento nel corso di** (dibattito, programma) to take part in

inter'vista sf interview; **intervis'tare** vt to interview

intes'tare vt (lettera) to address; (proprietà): **~ a** to register in the name of;

~ un assegno a qn to make out a cheque to sb

intestato, -a ag (proprietà, casa, conto) in the name of; (assegno) made out to; **carta intestata** headed paper

intes'tino sm (Anat) intestine

intimidazi'one [intimidat'tsjone] sf intimidation

intimi'dire vt to intimidate ▷ vi (intimidirsi) to grow shy

intimità sf intimacy; privacy; (familiarità) familiarity

'intimo, -a ag intimate; (affetti, vita) private; (fig: profondo) inmost ▷ sm (persona) intimate o close friend; (dell'animo) bottom, depths pl; **parti intime** (Anat) private parts

in'tingolo sm sauce; (pietanza) stew

intito'lare vt to give a title to; (dedicare) to dedicate; **intitolarsi** vpr (libro, film) to be called

intolle'rabile ag intolerable

intolle'rante ag intolerant

in'tonaco, -ci o **chi** sm plaster

into'nare vt (canto) to start to sing; (armonizzare) to match; **intonarsi** vpr (colori) to go together; **intonarsi a** (carnagione) to suit; (abito) to go with, match

inton'tito, -a ag stunned, dazed; **~ dal sonno** stupid with sleep

in'toppo sm stumbling block, obstacle

in'torno av around; **~ a** (attorno a) around; (riguardo, circa) about

intossi'care vt to poison; **intossicazi'one** sf poisoning

intralci'are [intral'tʃare] vt to hamper, hold up

intransi'tivo, -a ag, sm intransitive

intrapren'dente ag enterprising, go-ahead

intra'prendere vt to undertake

intrat'tabile ag intractable

intratte'nere vt to entertain; to engage in conversation; **intrattenersi** vpr to linger; **intrattenersi su qc** to dwell on sth

intrave'dere vt to catch a glimpse of; (fig) to foresee

intrecci'are [intret'tʃare] vt (capelli) to plait, braid; (intessere: anche fig) to weave, interweave, intertwine

intri'gante ag scheming ▷ sm/f schemer, intriguer

in'trinseco, -a, -ci, -che ag intrinsic

in'triso, -a ag **~ (di)** soaked (in)

intro'durre vt to introduce; (chiave ecc): **~ qc in** to insert sth into; (persone: far entrare) to show in; **introdursi** vpr (moda, tecniche) to be introduced; **introdursi in** (persona: penetrare) to enter; (: entrare furtivamente) to steal o slip into; **introduzi'one** sf introduction

in'troito sm income, revenue

intro'mettersi vpr to interfere, meddle; (interporsi) to intervene

in'truglio [in'truʎʎo] sm concoction

intrusi'one sf intrusion; interference

in'truso, -a sm/f intruder

intu'ire vt to perceive by intuition; (rendersi conto) to realize; **in'tuito** sm intuition; (perspicacia) perspicacity

inu'mano, -a ag inhuman

inumi'dire vt to dampen, moisten; **inumidirsi** vpr to become damp o wet

i'nutile ag useless; (superfluo) pointless, unnecessary

inutil'mente av unnecessarily; (senza risultato) in vain

inva'dente ag (fig) interfering, nosey

in'vadere vt to invade; (affollare) to swarm into, overrun; (acque) to flood

inva'ghirsi [inva'girsi] vpr **~ di** to take a fancy to

invalidità sf infirmity; disability; (Dir) invalidity

in'valido, -a ag (infermo) infirm, invalid; (al lavoro) disabled; (Dir: nullo) invalid ▷ sm/f invalid; disabled person

in'vano av in vain

invasi'one sf invasion

inva'sore, invadi'trice [invadi'tritʃe] ag invading ▷ sm invader

invecchi'are [invek'kjare] vi (persona) to grow old; (vino, popolazione) to age; (moda) to become dated ▷ vt to age; (far apparire più vecchio) to make look older

in'vece [in'vetʃe] av instead; (al contrario) on the contrary; **~ di** instead of

inve'ire vi **~ contro** to rail against

inven'tare vt to invent; (pericoli, pettegolezzi) to make up, invent

inven'tario sm inventory; (Comm) stocktaking no pl

inven'tore sm inventor

invenzi'one [inven'tsjone] sf invention; (bugia) lie, story

inver'nale ag winter cpd; (simile all'inverno) wintry

in'verno sm winter

invero'simile ag unlikely

inversi'one sf inversion; reversal; **"divieto d'~"** (Aut) "no U-turns"

in'verso, -a ag opposite; (Mat) inverse ▷ sm contrary, opposite; **in senso ~** in the opposite direction; **in ordine ~** in reverse order

inver'tire vt to invert, reverse; **~ la marcia** (Aut) to do a U-turn

investi'gare vt, vi to investigate; **investiga'tore, -'trice** sm/f investigator, detective; **investigatore privato** private investigator

investi'mento sm (Econ) investment

inves'tire vt (denaro) to invest; (veicolo: pedone) to knock down; (: altro veicolo) to crash into; (apostrofare) to assail; (incaricare): ~ **qn di** to invest sb with

invi'are vt to send; **invi'ato, -a** sm/f envoy; (Stampa) correspondent; **inviato speciale** (Pol) special envoy; (di giornale) special correspondent

in'vidia sf envy; **invidi'are** vt invidiare **qn (per qc)** to envy sb for sth; **invidiare qc a qn** to envy sb sth; **invidi'oso, -a** ag envious

in'vio, -'vii sm sending; (insieme di merci) consignment; (tasto) Return (key), Enter (key)

invipe'rito, -a ag furious

invi'sibile ag invisible

invi'tare vt to invite; ~ **qn a fare** to invite sb to do; **invi'tato, -a** sm/f guest; **in'vito** sm invitation

invo'care vt (chiedere: aiuto, pace) to cry out for; (appellarsi: la legge, Dio) to appeal to, invoke

invogli'are [invoʎ'ʎare] vt ~ **qn a fare** to tempt sb to do, induce sb to do

involon'tario, -a ag (errore) unintentional; (gesto) involuntary

invol'tino sm (Cuc) roulade

in'volto sm (pacco) parcel; (fagotto) bundle

in'volucro sm cover, wrapping

inzup'pare [intsup'pare] vt to soak; **inzupparsi** vpr to get soaked

'io pron I ▷ sm inv **l'~** the ego, the self; ~ **stesso(a)** I myself

i'odio sm iodine

l'onio sm **lo ~, il mar ~** the Ionian (Sea)

ipermer'cato sm hypermarket

ipertensi'one sf high blood pressure, hypertension

iper'testo sm hypertext

ip'nosi sf hypnosis; **ipnotiz'zare** vt to hypnotize

ipocri'sia sf hypocrisy

i'pocrita, -i, -e ag hypocritical ▷ sm/f hypocrite

ipo'teca, -che sf mortgage

i'potesi sf inv hypothesis

'ippica sf horseracing

'ippico, -a, -ci, -che ag horse cpd

ippocas'tano sm horse chestnut

ip'podromo sm racecourse

ippo'potamo sm hippopotamus

'ipsilon sf o m inv (lettera) Y, y; (: dell'alfabeto greco) epsilon

IR abbr (= Interregionale) long distance train which stops frequently

ira'cheno, -a [ira'kɛno] ag, sm/f Iraqi

l'ran sm **l'~** Iran

irani'ano, -a ag, sm/f Iranian

l'raq sm **l'~** Iraq

'iride sf (arcobaleno) rainbow; (Anat, Bot) iris

'iris sm inv iris

Ir'landa sf **l'~** Ireland; **l'~ del Nord** Northern Ireland, Ulster; **la Repubblica d'~** Eire, the Republic of Ireland; **irlan'dese** ag Irish ▷ sm/f Irishman/woman; **gli Irlandesi** the Irish

iro'nia sf irony; **i'ronico, -a, -ci, -che** ag ironic(al)

irragio'nevole [irradʒo'nevole] ag irrational; unreasonable

irrazio'nale [irrattsjo'nale] ag irrational

irre'ale ag unreal

irrego'lare ag irregular; (terreno) uneven

irremo'vibile ag (fig) unshakeable, unyielding

irrequi'eto, -a ag restless

irresis'tibile ag irresistible

irrespon'sabile ag irresponsible

irri'gare vt (annaffiare) to irrigate; (fiume ecc) to flow through

irrigi'dire [irridʒi'dire] vt to stiffen; **irrigidirsi** vpr to stiffen

irri'sorio, -a ag derisory

irri'tare vt (mettere di malumore) to irritate, annoy; (Med) to irritate; **irritarsi** vpr (stizzirsi) to become irritated o annoyed; (Med) to become irritated

ir'rompere vi ~ **in** to burst into

irru'ente ag (fig) impetuous, violent

ir'ruppi ecc vb vedi **irrompere**

irruzi'one [irrut'tsjone] sf **fare ~ in** to burst into; (polizia) to raid

is'crissi ecc vb vedi **iscrivere**

is'critto, -a pp di **iscrivere** ▷ sm/f member; **per o in ~** in writing

is'crivere vt to register, enter; (persona): ~ **(a)** to register (in), enrol (in); **iscriversi** vpr **iscriversi (a)** (club, partito) to join; (università) to register o enrol (at); (esame, concorso) to register o enter (for); **iscrizi'one** sf (epigrafe ecc) inscription; (a scuola, società) enrolment, registration; (registrazione) registration

Is'lam sm **l'~** Islam

Is'landa sf **l'~** Iceland

islan'dese ag Icelandic ▷ sm/f Icelander ▷ sm (Ling) Icelandic

'isola sf island; **isola pedonale** (Aut) pedestrian precinct

isola'mento sm isolation; (Tecn) insulation

iso'lante ag insulating ▷ sm insulator

iso'lare *vt* to isolate; (*Tecn*) to insulate;
(: *acusticamente*) to soundproof; **isolarsi**
vpr to isolate o.s.; **iso'lato, -a** *ag* isolated;
insulated ▷ *sm* (*gruppo di edifici*) block
ispet'tore *sm* inspector
ispezio'nare [ispettsjo'nare] *vt* to inspect
'ispido, -a *ag* bristly, shaggy
ispi'rare *vt* to inspire
Isra'ele *sm* I'~ Israel; **israeli'ano, -a** *ag*,
sm/f Israeli
is'sare *vt* to hoist
istan'taneo, -a *ag* instantaneous ▷ *sf*
(*Fot*) snapshot
is'tante *sm* instant, moment; **all'~, sull'~**
instantly, immediately
is'terico, -a, -ci, -che *ag* hysterical
isti'gare *vt* to incite
is'tinto *sm* instinct
istitu'ire *vt* (*fondare*) to institute,
found; (*porre: confronto*) to establish;
(*intraprendere: inchiesta*) to set up
isti'tuto *sm* institute; (*di università*)
department; (*ente, Dir*) institution;
istituto di bellezza beauty salon; **istituto
di credito** bank, banking institution;
istituto di ricerca research institute
istituzi'one [istitut'tsjone] *sf* institution
'istmo *sm* (*Geo*) isthmus
'istrice ['istritʃe] *sm* porcupine
istru'ito, -a *ag* educated
istrut'tore, -'trice *sm/f* instructor ▷ *ag*
giudice ~ *vedi* **giudice**
istruzi'one *sf* education; training;
(*direttiva*) instruction; **istruzioni** *sfpl*
(*norme*) instructions; **istruzioni per l'uso**
instructions for use; **~ obbligatoria** (*Scol*)
compulsory education
I'talia *sf* I'~ Italy
itali'ano, -a *ag* Italian ▷ *sm/f* Italian ▷ *sm*
(*Ling*) Italian; **gli Italiani** the Italians
itine'rario *sm* itinerary
'ittico, -a, -ci, -che *ag* fish *cpd*; fishing *cpd*
Iugos'lavia = **Jugoslavia**
IVA ['iva] *sigla f* (= *imposta sul valore
aggiunto*) VAT

jazz [dʒaz] *sm* jazz
jeans [dʒinz] *smpl* jeans
jeep® [dʒip] *sm inv* jeep
'jogging ['dʒɔgiŋ] *sm* jogging; **fare ~** to
go jogging
'jolly ['dʒɔli] *sm inv* joker
joystick [dʒois'tik] *sm inv* joystick
ju'do [dʒu'dɔ] *sm* judo
Jugos'lavia [jugoz'lavja] *sf* (*Storia*): **la ~**
Yugoslavia; **la ex-~** former Yugoslavia;
jugos'lavo, -a *ag*, *sm/f* (*Storia*)
Yugoslav(ian)

K l

K, k ['kappa] *sf o m inv (lettera)* K, k ▷ *abbr*
  (= *kilo-, chilo-*) k; (*Inform*) K; **K come**
  Kursaal ≈ K for King
kamikaze [kami'kaddze] *sm inv* kamikaze
karaoke [ka'raokɛ] *sm inv* karaoke
karatè *sm* karate
ka'yak [ka'jak] *sm inv* kayak
Kenia ['kenja] *sm* **il ~** Kenya
kg *abbr* (= *chilogrammo*) kg
'killer *sm inv* gunman, hired gun
kitsch [kitʃ] *sm* kitsch
'kiwi ['kiwi] *sm inv* kiwi fruit
km *abbr* (= *chilometro*) km
K.O. [kappa'o] *sm inv* knockout
ko'ala [ko'ala] *sm inv* koala (bear)
koso'varo, -a [koso'varo] *ag, sm/f*
  Kosovan
Ko'sovo *sm* Kosovo
'krapfen *sm inv* (*Cuc*) doughnut
Kuwait [ku'vait] *sm* **il ~** Kuwait

l' *det vedi* **la**; **lo**; **il**
la (*dav V* **l'**) *det f* the ▷ *pron* (*oggetto: persona*)
  her; (: *cosa*) it; (: *forma di cortesia*) you; *vedi*
  anche **il**
là *av* there; **di là** (*da quel luogo*) from there;
  (*in quel luogo*) in there; (*dall'altra parte*)
  over there; **di là di** beyond; **per di là** that
  way; **più in là** further on; (*tempo*) later
  on; **fatti in là** move up, **là dentro/**
  sopra/sotto in/up (*o* on)/under there;
  vedi anche **quello**
'labbro (*pl(f)* **labbra**) (*solo nel senso Anat*)
  sm lip
labi'rinto *sm* labyrinth, maze
labora'torio *sm* (*di ricerca*) laboratory;
  (*di arti, mestieri*) workshop; **laboratorio**
  linguistico language laboratory
labori'oso, -a *ag* (*faticoso*) laborious;
  (*attivo*) hard-working
'lacca, -che *sf* lacquer
'laccio ['lattʃo] *sm* noose; (*legaccio, tirante*)
  lasso; (*di scarpa*) lace; **laccio emostatico**
  tourniquet
lace'rare [latʃe'rare] *vt* to tear to shreds,
  lacerate; **lacerarsi** *vpr* to tear
'lacrima *sf* tear; **in lacrime** in tears;
  lacri'mogeno, -a *ag* gas lacrimogeno
  tear gas
la'cuna *sf* (*fig*) gap
'ladro *sm* thief

laggiù [lad'dʒu] av down there; (di là) over there

la'gnarsi [laɲ'ɲarsi] vpr ~ **(di)** to complain (about)

'lago, -ghi sm lake

la'guna sf lagoon

'laico, -a, -ci, -che ag (apostolato) lay; (vita) secular; (scuola) non-denominational ▷ sm/f layman/woman

'lama sm inv (Zool) llama; (Rel) lama ▷ sf blade

lamentarsi vpr (emettere lamenti) to moan, groan; (rammaricarsi): ~ **(di)** to complain (about)

lamen'tela sf complaining no pl

la'metta sf razor blade

'lamina sf (lastra sottile) thin sheet (o layer o plate); **lamina d'oro** gold leaf; gold foil

'lampada sf lamp; **lampada a gas** gas lamp; **lampada da tavolo** table lamp

lampa'dario sm chandelier

lampa'dina sf light bulb; **lampadina tascabile** pocket torch (BRIT) o flashlight (US)

lam'pante ag (fig: evidente) crystal clear, evident

lampeggi'are [lamped'dʒare] vi (luce, fari) to flash ▷ vb impers **lampeggia** there's lightning; **lampeggia'tore** sm (Aut) indicator

lampi'one sm street light o lamp (BRIT)

'lampo sm (Meteor) flash of lightning; (di luce: fig) flash

lam'pone sm raspberry

'lana sf wool; **pura ~ vergine** pure new wool; **lana d'acciaio** steel wool; **lana di vetro** glass wool

lan'cetta [lan'tʃetta] sf (indice) pointer, needle; (di orologio) hand

lancia ['lantʃa] sf (arma) lance; (: picca) spear; (di pompa antincendio) nozzle; (imbarcazione) launch; **lancia di salvataggio** lifeboat

lanciafi'amme [lantʃa'fjamme] sm inv flamethrower

lanci'are [lan'tʃare] vt to throw, hurl, fling; (Sport) to throw; (far partire: automobile) to get up to full speed; (bombe) to drop; (razzo, prodotto, moda) to launch; **lanciarsi** vpr **lanciarsi contro/su** to throw o hurl o fling o.s. against/on; **lanciarsi in** (fig) to embark on

lanci'nante [lantʃi'nante] ag (dolore) shooting, throbbing; (grido) piercing

'lancio ['lantʃo] sm throwing no pl; throw; dropping no pl; drop; launching no pl; launch; **lancio del disco** (Sport) throwing the discus; **lancio del peso** putting the shot

'languido, -a ag (fiacco) languid, weak; (tenero, malinconico) languishing

lan'terna sf lantern; (faro) lighthouse

'lapide sf (di sepolcro) tombstone; (commemorativa) plaque

'lapsus sm inv slip

'lardo sm bacon fat, lard

lar'ghezza [lar'gettsa] sf width; breadth; looseness; generosity; **larghezza di vedute** broad-mindedness

'largo, -a, -ghi, -ghe ag wide; broad; (maniche) wide; (abito: troppo ampio) loose; (fig) generous ▷ sm width; breadth; (mare aperto): **il ~** the open sea ▷ sf **stare** o **tenersi alla larga (da qn/qc)** to keep one's distance (from sb/sth), keep away (from sb/sth); ~ **due metri** two metres wide; ~ **di spalle** broad-shouldered; **di larghe vedute** broad-minded; **su larga scala** on a large scale; **di manica larga** generous, open-handed; **al ~ di Genova** off the coast of) Genoa; **farsi ~ tra la folla** to push one's way through the crowd

'larice ['laritʃe] sm (Bot) larch

larin'gite [larin'dʒite] sf laryngitis

'larva sf larva; (fig) shadow

la'sagne [la'zaɲɲe] sfpl lasagna sg

lasci'are [laʃʃare] vt to leave; (abbandonare) to leave, abandon, give up; (cessare di tenere) to let go of ▷ vb aus ~ **fare qn** to let sb do; ~ **andare** o **correre** o **perdere** to let things go their own way; ~ **stare qc/qn** to leave sth/sb alone; **lasciarsi** vpr (persone) to part; (coppia) to split up; **lasciarsi andare** to let o.s. go

laser ['lazer] ag, sm inv **(raggio)** ~ laser (beam)

lassa'tivo, -a ag, sm laxative

'lasso sm; **lasso di tempo** interval, lapse of time

lassù av up there

'lastra sf (di pietra) slab; (di metallo, Fot) plate; (di ghiaccio, vetro) sheet; (radiografica) X-ray (plate)

lastri'cato sm paving

late'rale ag lateral, side cpd; (uscita, ingresso ecc) side cpd ▷ sm (Calcio) half-back

la'tino, -a ag, sm Latin

lati'tante sm/f fugitive (from justice)

lati'tudine sf latitude

'lato, -a ag (fig) wide, broad ▷ sm side; (fig) aspect, point of view; **in senso ~** broadly speaking

'latta sf tin (plate); (recipiente) tin, can

lat'tante ag unweaned

'latte sm milk; **latte detergente** cleansing milk o lotion; **latte intero** full-cream milk;

latte a lunga conservazione UHT milk, long-life milk; **latte magro** o **scremato** skimmed milk; **latte in polvere** dried o powdered milk; **latte solare** suntan lotion; **latti'cini** smpl dairy products

lat'tina sf (di birra ecc) can

lat'tuga, -ghe sf lettuce

'laurea sf degree; **laurea in ingegneria** engineering degree; **laurea in lettere** ≈ arts degree

- **LAUREA**
-
- The **laurea** is awarded to students
- who successfully complete their
- degree courses. Traditionally,
- this takes between four and six
- years; a major element of the final
- examinations is the presentation
- and discussion of a dissertation. A
- shorter, more vocational course of
- study, taking from two to three years,
- is also available; at the end of this time
- students receive a diploma called the
- **laurea breve**.

laure'arsi vpr to graduate

laure'ato, -a ag, sm/f graduate

'lauro sm laurel

'lauto, -a ag (pranzo, mancia) lavish

'lava sf lava

la'vabo sm washbasin

la'vaggio [la'vaddʒo] sm washing no pl; **lavaggio del cervello** brainwashing no pl; **lavaggio a secco** dry-cleaning

la'vagna [la'vaɲɲa] sf (Geo) slate; (di scuola) blackboard

la'vanda sf (anche Med) wash; (Bot) lavender; **lavande'ria** sf laundry; **lavanderia automatica** launderette; **lavanderia a secco** dry-cleaner's; **lavan'dino** sm sink

lavapi'atti sm/f dishwasher

la'vare vt to wash; **lavarsi** vpr to wash, have a wash; **~ a secco** to dry-clean; **lavarsi le mani/i denti** to wash one's hands/clean one's teeth

lava'secco sm o f inv dry cleaner's

lavasto'viglie [lavasto'viʎʎe] sm o f inv (macchina) dishwasher

lava'trice [lava'tritʃe] sf washing machine

lavo'rare vi to work; (fig: bar, studio ecc) to do good business ▷ vt to work; **lavorarsi qn** (persuaderlo) to work on sb; **~ a** to work on; **~ a maglia** to knit; **lavora'tivo, -a** ag working; **lavora'tore, -'trice** sm/f worker ▷ ag working

la'voro sm work; (occupazione) job, work no pl; (opera) piece of work, job; (Econ) labour; **che ~ fa?** what do you do?; **lavori forzati** hard labour sg; **lavoro interinale** o **in affitto** temporary work

le det fpl the ▷ pron (oggetto) them; (: a lei, a essa) (to) her; (: forma di cortesia) (to) you; vedi anche **il**

le'ale ag loyal; (sincero) sincere; (onesto) fair

'lecca 'lecca sm inv lollipop

leccapi'edi (peg) sm/f inv toady, bootlicker

lec'care vt to lick; (gatto: latte ecc) to lick o lap up; (fig) to flatter; **leccarsi i baffi** to lick one's lips

leccherò ecc [lekke'rɔ] vb vedi **leccare**

'leccio ['lettʃo] sm holm oak, ilex

leccor'nia sf titbit, delicacy

'lecito, -a ['lɛtʃito] ag permitted, allowed

'lega, -ghe sf league; (di metalli) alloy

le'gaccio [le'gattʃo] sm string, lace

le'gale ag legal ▷ sm lawyer; **legaliz'zare** vt to authenticate; (regolarizzare) to legalize

le'game sm (corda, fig: affettivo) tie, bond; (nesso logico) link, connection

le'gare vt (prigioniero, capelli, cane) to tie (up); (libro) to bind; (Chim) to alloy; (fig: collegare) to bind, join ▷ vi (far lega) to unite; (fig) to get on well

le'genda [le'dʒɛnda] sf (di carta geografica ecc) = **leggenda**

'legge ['leddʒe] sf law

leg'genda [led'dʒɛnda] sf (narrazione) legend; (di carta geografica ecc) key, legend

'leggere ['lɛddʒere] vt, vi to read

legge'rezza [leddʒe'rettsa] sf lightness; thoughtlessness; fickleness

leg'gero, -a [led'dʒɛro] ag light; (agile, snello) nimble, agile, light; (tè, caffè) weak; (fig: non grave, piccolo) slight; (: spensierato) thoughtless; (: incostante) fickle; free and easy; **alla leggera** thoughtlessly

leg'gio, -'gii [led'dʒio] sm lectern; (Mus) music stand

legherò ecc [lege'rɔ] vb vedi **legare**

legisla'tivo, -a [ledʒizla'tivo] ag legislative

legisla'tura [ledʒizla'tura] sf legislature

le'gittimo, -a [le'dʒittimo] ag legitimate; (fig: giustificato, lecito) justified, legitimate; **legittima difesa** (Dir) self-defence

'legna ['leɲɲa] sf firewood

'legno ['leɲɲo] sm wood; (pezzo di legno) piece of wood; **di ~** wooden; **legno compensato** plywood

'lei pron (soggetto) she; (oggetto: per dare rilievo, con preposizione) her; (forma di cortesia: anche: **L~**) you ▷ sm **dare del ~**

a qn to address sb as "lei"; **~ stessa** she herself; you yourself

● **LEI**
●
● **lei** is the third person singular pronoun.
● It is used in Italian to address an adult
● whom you do not know or with whom
● you are on formal terms.

lenta'mente av slowly

'lente sf (Ottica) lens sg; **lenti a contatto** o **corneali** contact lenses; **lenti (a contatto) morbide/rigide** soft/hard contact lenses; **lente d'ingrandimento** magnifying glass; **lenti** sfpl (occhiali) lenses

len'tezza [len'tettsa] sf slowness

len'ticchia [len'tikkja] sf (Bot) lentil

len'tiggine [len'tiddʒine] sf freckle

'lento, -a ag slow; (molle: fune) slack; (non stretto: vite, abito) loose ▷ sm (ballo) slow dance

'lenza ['lɛntsa] sf fishing-line

lenzu'olo [len'tswɔlo] sm sheet

le'one sm lion; (dello zodiaco): **L~** Leo

lepo'rino, -a ag **labbro ~** harelip

'lepre sf hare

'lercio, -a, -ci, -cie ['lɛrtʃo] ag filthy

lesi'one sf (Med) lesion; (Dir) injury, damage; (Edil) crack

les'sare vt (Cuc) to boil

'lessi ecc vb vedi **leggere**

'lessico, -ci sm vocabulary; lexicon

'lesso, -a ag boiled ▷ sm boiled meat

le'tale ag lethal; fatal

leta'maio sm dunghill

le'tame sm manure, dung

le'targo, -ghi sm lethargy; (Zool) hibernation

'lettera sf letter; **lettere** sfpl (letteratura) literature sg; (studi umanistici) arts (subjects); **alla ~** literally; **in lettere** in words, in full

letteral'mente av literally

lette'rario, -a ag literary

lette'rato, -a ag well-read, scholarly

lettera'tura sf literature

let'tiga, -ghe sf (barella) stretcher

let'tino sm cot (BRIT), crib (US); **lettino solare** sunbed

'letto, -a pp di **leggere** ▷ sm bed; **andare a ~** to go to bed; **letto a castello** bunk beds pl; **letto a una piazza** single; **letto a due piazze** o **matrimoniale** double bed

let'tore, -'trice sm/f reader; (Ins) (foreign language) assistant (BRIT), (foreign) teaching assistant (US) ▷ sm (Tecn): **~ ottico** optical character reader; **lettore**

CD CD player; **lettore DVD** DVD player

let'tura sf reading

▮ Attenzione! In inglese esiste la parola *lecture*, che però significa *lezione* oppure *conferenza*.

leuce'mia [leutʃe'mia] sf leukaemia

'leva sf lever; (Mil) conscription; **far ~ su qn** to work on sb; **leva del cambio** (Aut) gear lever

le'vante sm east; (vento) East wind; **il L~** the Levant

le'vare vt (occhi, braccio) to raise; (sollevare, togliere: tassa, divieto) to lift; (indumenti) to take off, remove; (rimuovere) to take away; (: dal di sopra) to take off; (: dal di dentro) to take out

leva'toio, -a ag **ponte ~** drawbridge

lezi'one [let'tsjone] sf lesson; (Univ) lecture; **fare ~** to teach; to lecture; **dare una ~ a qn** to teach sb a lesson; **lezioni private** private lessons

li pron pl (oggetto) them

lì av there; **di** o **da lì** from there; **per di lì** that way; **di lì a pochi giorni** a few days later; **lì per lì** there and then; at first; **essere lì (lì) per fare** to be on the point of doing, be about to do; **lì dentro** in there; **lì sotto** under there; **lì sopra** on there; up there; vedi anche **quello**

liba'nese ag, sm/f Lebanese inv

Li'bano sm **il ~** the Lebanon

'libbra sf (peso) pound

li'beccio [li'bettʃo] sm south-west wind

li'bellula sf dragonfly

libe'rale ag, sm/f liberal

liberaliz'zare [liberalid'dzare] vt to liberalize

libe'rare vt (rendere libero: prigioniero) to release; (: popolo) to free, liberate; (sgombrare: passaggio) to clear; (: stanza) to vacate; (produrre: energia) to release; **liberarsi** vpr **liberarsi di qc/qn** to get rid of sth/sb; **liberazi'one** sf liberation, freeing; release; rescuing

● **LIBERAZIONE**
●
● The **Liberazione** is a national
● holiday which falls on April 25th. It
● commemorates the liberation of Italy at
● the end of the Second World War.

'libero, -a ag free; (strada) clear; (non occupato: posto ecc) vacant; free; not taken; empty; not engaged; **~ di fare qc** free to do sth; **~ da** free from; **è ~ questo posto?** is this seat free?; **~ arbitrio** free will; **~ professionista** self-employed professional person; **~ scambio** free trade;

libertà sf inv freedom; (tempo disponibile) free time ▷ sfpl (licenza) liberties; **in libertà provvisoria/vigilata** released without bail/on probation

'**Libia** sf **la ~** Libya; '**libico, -a, -ci, -che** ag, sm/f Libyan

li'bidine sf lust

li'braio sm bookseller

li'brarsi vpr to hover

libre'ria sf (bottega) bookshop; (mobile) bookcase

Attenzione! In inglese esiste la parola library, che però significa biblioteca.

li'bretto sm booklet; (taccuino) notebook; (Mus) libretto; **libretto degli assegni** cheque book; **libretto di circolazione** (Aut) logbook; **libretto di risparmio** (savings) bank-book, passbook; **libretto universitario** student's report book

'**libro** sm book; **libro di cassa** cash book; **libro mastro** ledger; **libro paga** payroll; **libro di testo** textbook

li'cenza [li'tʃɛntsa] sf (permesso) permission, leave; (di pesca, caccia, circolazione) permit, licence; (Mil) leave; (Ins) school leaving certificate; (libertà) liberty; licence; licentiousness; **andare in ~** (Mil) to go on leave

licenzia'mento [litʃentsja'mento] sm dismissal

licenzi'are [litʃen'tsjare] vt (impiegato) to dismiss; (Comm: per eccesso di personale) to make redundant; (Ins) to award a certificate to; **licenziarsi** vpr (impiegato) to resign, hand in one's notice; (Ins) to obtain one's school-leaving certificate

li'ceo [li'tʃɛo] sm (Ins) secondary (BRIT) o high (US) school (for 14- to 19-year-olds)

'**lido** sm beach, shore

Liechtenstein ['liktənstain] sm **il ~** Liechtenstein

li'eto, -a ag happy, glad; "**molto ~**" (nelle presentazioni) "pleased to meet you"

li'eve ag light; (di poco conto) slight; (sommesso: voce) faint, soft

lievi'tare vi (anche fig) to rise ▷ vt to leaven

li'evito sm yeast; **lievito di birra** brewer's yeast

'**ligio, -a, -gi, -gie** ['lidʒo] ag faithful, loyal

'**lilla** sm inv lilac

'**lillà** sm inv lilac

'**lima** sf file; **lima da unghie** nail file

limacci'oso, -a [limat'tʃoso] ag slimy; muddy

li'mare vt to file (down); (fig) to polish

limi'tare vt to limit, restrict; (circoscrivere) to bound, surround; **limitarsi** vpr **limitarsi nel mangiare** to limit one's eating; **limitarsi a qc/a fare qc** to limit o.s. to sth/to doing sth

'**limite** sm limit; (confine) border, boundary; **limite di velocità** speed limit

limo'nata sf lemonade (BRIT), (lemon) soda (US); lemon squash (BRIT), lemonade (US)

li'mone sm (pianta) lemon tree; (frutto) lemon

'**limpido, -a** ag clear; (acqua) limpid, clear

'**lince** ['lintʃe] sf lynx

linci'are vt to lynch

'**linea** sf line; (di mezzi pubblici di trasporto: itinerario) route; (: servizio) service; **a grandi linee** in outline; **mantenere la ~** to look after one's figure; **aereo di ~** airliner; **nave di ~** liner; **volo di ~** scheduled flight; **linea aerea** airline; **linea di partenza/d'arrivo** (Sport) starting/finishing line; **linea di tiro** line of fire

linea'menti smpl features; (fig) outlines

line'are ag linear; (fig) coherent, logical

line'etta sf (trattino) dash; (d'unione) hyphen

lin'gotto sm ingot, bar

'**lingua** sf (Anat, Cuc) tongue; (idioma) language; **mostrare la ~** to stick out one's tongue; **di ~ italiana** Italian-speaking; **che lingue parla?** what languages do you speak?; **una ~ di terra** a spit of land; **lingua madre** mother tongue

lingu'aggio [lin'gwaddʒo] sm language

lingu'etta sf (di strumento) reed; (di scarpa, Tecn) tongue; (di busta) flap

'**lino** sm (pianta) flax; (tessuto) linen

li'noleum sm inv linoleum, lino

liposuzi'one [liposut'tsjone] sf liposuction

lique'fatto, -a pp di liquefare

liqui'dare vt (società, beni: persona: uccidere) to liquidate; (persona: sbarazzarsene) to get rid of; (conto, problema) to settle; (Comm: merce) to sell off, clear; **liquidazi'one** sf liquidation; settlement; clearance sale

liquidità sf liquidity

'**liquido, -a** ag, sm liquid; **liquido per freni** brake fluid

liqui'rizia [likwi'rittsja] sf liquorice

li'quore sm liqueur

'**lira** sf (Storia: unità monetaria) lira; (Mus) lyre; **lira sterlina** pound sterling

'**lirico, -a, -ci, -che** ag lyric(al); (Mus) lyric; **cantante/teatro ~** opera singer/house

Lis'bona sf Lisbon

'**lisca, -sche** sf (di pesce) fishbone

lisci'are [liʃʃare] vt to smooth; (fig) to flatter

'**liscio, -a, -sci, -sce** ['liʃʃo] ag smooth;

(capelli) straight; (mobile) plain; (bevanda alcolica) neat; (fig) straightforward, simple ▷ av andare ~ to go smoothly; passarla liscia to get away with it

'liso, -a ag worn out, threadbare

'lista sf (elenco) list; lista elettorale electoral roll; lista delle spese shopping list; lista dei vini wine list; lista delle vivande menu

lis'tino sm list; listino dei cambi (foreign) exchange rate; listino dei prezzi price list

'lite sf quarrel, argument; (Dir) lawsuit

liti'gare vi to quarrel; (Dir) to litigate

li'tigio [li'tidʒo] sm quarrel

lito'rale ag coastal, coast cpd ▷ sm coast

'litro sm litre

livel'lare vt to level, make level

li'vello sm level; (fig) level, standard; ad alto ~ (fig) high-level; livello del mare sea level

'livido, -a ag livid; (per percosse) bruised, black and blue; (cielo) leaden ▷ sm bruise

Li'vorno sf Livorno, Leghorn

'lizza ['littsa] sf lists pl; scendere in ~ to enter the lists

lo (dav s impura, gn, pn, ps, x, z; dav V l') det m the ▷ pron (oggetto: persona) him; (: cosa) it; lo sapevo I knew it; lo so I know; sii buono, anche se lui non lo è be good, even if he isn't; vedi anche il

lo'cale ag local ▷ sm room; (luogo pubblico) premises pl; locale notturno nightclub; località sf inv locality

lo'canda sf inn

locomo'tiva sf locomotive

locuzi'one [lokut'tsjone] sf phrase, expression

lo'dare vt to praise

'lode sf praise; (Ins): laurearsi con 110 e ~ ≈ to graduate with a first-class honours degree (BRIT), graduate summa cum laude (US)

'loden sm inv (stoffa) loden; (cappotto) loden overcoat

lo'devole ag praiseworthy

loga'ritmo sm logarithm

'loggia, -ge ['lɔddʒa] sf (Archit) loggia; (circolo massonico) lodge; loggi'one sm (di teatro): il loggione the Gods sg

'logico, -a, -ci, -che ['lɔdʒiko] ag logical

logo'rare vt to wear out; (sciupare) to waste; logorarsi vpr to wear out; (fig) to wear o.s. out

'logoro, -a ag (stoffa) worn out, threadbare; (persona) worn out

Lombar'dia sf la ~ Lombardy

lom'bata sf (taglio di carne) loin

lom'brico, -chi sm earthworm

londi'nese ag London cpd ▷ sm/f Londoner

'Londra sf London

lon'gevo, -a [lon'dʒevo] ag long-lived

longi'tudine [londʒi'tudine] sf longitude

lon'tananza [lonta'nantsa] sf distance; absence

lon'tano, -a ag (distante) distant, faraway; (assente) absent; (vago: sospetto) slight, remote; (tempo: remoto) far-off, distant; (parente) distant, remote ▷ av far; è lontana la casa? is it far to the house?, is the house far from here?; è ~ un chilometro it's a kilometre away o a kilometre from here; più ~ farther; da o di ~ from a distance; ~ da a long way from; è molto ~ da qui? is it far from here?; alla lontana slightly, vaguely

lo'quace [lo'kwatʃe] ag talkative, loquacious; (fig: gesto ecc) eloquent

'lordo, -a ag dirty, filthy; (peso, stipendio) gross

'loro pron pl (oggetto, con preposizione) them; (complemento di termine) to them; (soggetto) they; (forma di cortesia: anche: L~) you; to you; il(la) ~, i(le) ~ det their; (forma di cortesia: anche: L~) your ▷ pron theirs; (forma di cortesia: anche: L~) yours; ~ stessi(e) they themselves; you yourselves

'losco, -a, -schi, -sche ag (fig) shady, suspicious

'lotta sf struggle, fight; (Sport) wrestling; lotta libera all-in wrestling; lot'tare vi to fight, struggle; to wrestle

lotte'ria sf lottery; (di gara ippica) sweepstake

'lotto sm (gioco) (state) lottery; (parte) lot; (Edil) site

● LOTTO
●
● The Lotto is an official lottery run by the
● Italian Finance Ministry. It consists of
● a weekly draw of numbers and is very
● popular.

lozi'one [lot'tsjone] sf lotion

lubrifi'cante sm lubricant

lubrifi'care vt to lubricate

luc'chetto [luk'ketto] sm padlock

lucci'care [luttʃi'kare] vi to sparkle, glitter, twinkle

'luccio ['luttʃo] sm (Zool) pike

'lucciola ['luttʃola] sf (Zool) firefly; glowworm

'luce ['lutʃe] sf light; (finestra) window; alla ~ di by the light of; fare ~ su qc (fig) to shed o throw light on sth; ~ del sole/della luna

sun/moonlight
lucer'nario [lutʃer'narjo] *sm* skylight
lu'certola [lu'tʃertola] *sf* lizard
luci'dare [lutʃi'dare] *vt* to polish
lucida'trice [lutʃida'tritʃe] *sf* floor
polisher
'lucido, -a ['lutʃido] *ag* shining, bright;
(*lucidato*) polished; (*fig*) lucid ▷ *sm* shine,
lustre; (*disegno*) tracing; **lucido per scarpe**
shoe polish
'lucro *sm* profit, gain
'luglio ['luʎʎo] *sm* July
'lugubre *ag* gloomy
'lui *pron* (*soggetto*) he; (*oggetto: per dare
rilievo, con preposizione*) him; **~ stesso** he
himself
lu'maca, -che *sf* slug; (*chiocciola*) snail
lumi'noso, -a *ag* (*che emette luce*)
luminous; (*cielo, colore, stanza*) bright;
(*sorgente*) of light, light *cpd*; (*fig: sorriso*)
bright, radiant
'luna *sf* moon; **luna nuova/piena** new/
full moon; **luna di miele** honeymoon;
siamo in ~ di miele we're on honeymoon
'luna park *sm inv* amusement park,
funfair
lu'nare *ag* lunar, moon *cpd*
lu'nario *sm* almanac; **sbarcare il ~** to
make ends meet
lu'natico, -a, -ci, -che *ag* whimsical,
temperamental
lunedì *sm inv* Monday; **di** *o* **il ~** on
Mondays
lun'ghezza [lun'gettsa] *sf* length;
lunghezza d'onda (*Fisica*) wavelength
'lungo, -a, -ghi, -ghe *ag* long; (*lento:
persona*) slow; (*diluito: caffè, brodo*) weak,
watery, thin ▷ *sm* length ▷ *prep* along; **~
3 metri** 3 metres long; **a ~** for a long time;
a ~ andare in the long run; **di gran lunga**
(*molto*) by far; **andare in ~** *o* **per le lunghe**
to drag on; **saperla lunga** to know what's
what; **in ~ e in largo** far and wide, all
over; **~ il corso dei secoli** throughout the
centuries
lungo'mare *sm* promenade
lu'notto *sm* (*Aut*) rear *o* back window;
lunotto termico heated rear window
lu'ogo, -ghi *sm* place; (*posto: di incidente
ecc*) scene, site; (*punto, passo di libro*)
passage; **in ~ di** instead of; **in primo ~**
in the first place; **aver ~** to take place;
dar ~ a to give rise to; **luogo di nascita**
birthplace; (*Amm*) place of birth; **luogo
di provenienza** place of origin; **luogo
comune** commonplace
'lupo, -a *sm/f* wolf
'luppolo *sm* (*Bot*) hop
'lurido, -a *ag* filthy

lusin'gare *vt* to flatter
Lussem'burgo *sm* (*stato*): **il ~**
Luxembourg ▷ *sf* (*città*) Luxembourg
'lusso *sm* luxury; **di ~** luxury *cpd*;
lussu'oso, -a *ag* luxurious
lus'suria *sf* lust
lus'trino *sm* sequin
'lutto *sm* mourning; **essere in/portare il
~** to be in/wear mourning

m

m. *abbr* = **mese**; **metro**; **miglia**; **monte**

ma *cong* but; **ma insomma!** for goodness sake!; **ma no!** of course not!

'macabro, -a *ag* gruesome, macabre

macché [mak'ke] *escl* not at all!, certainly not!

macche'roni [makke'roni] *smpl* macaroni *sg*

'macchia ['makkja] *sf* stain, spot; (*chiazza di diverso colore*) spot, splash, patch; (*tipo di boscaglia*) scrub; **alla ~** (*fig*) in hiding; **macchi'are** *vt* (*sporcare*) to stain, mark; **macchiarsi** *vpr* (*persona*) to get o.s. dirty; (*stoffa*) to stain; to get stained *o* marked

macchi'ato, -a [mak'kjato] *ag* (*pelle, pelo*) spotted; **~ di** stained with; **caffè ~** coffee with a dash of milk

'macchina ['makkina] *sf* machine; (*motore, locomotiva*) engine; (*automobile*) car; (*fig: meccanismo*) machinery; **andare in ~** (*Aut*) to go by car; (*Stampa*) to go to press; **macchina da cucire** sewing machine; **macchina fotografica** camera; **macchina da presa** cine *o* movie camera; **macchina da scrivere** typewriter; **macchina a vapore** steam engine

macchi'nario [makki'narjo] *sm* machinery

macchi'nista, -i [makki'nista] *sm* (*di treno*) engine-driver; (*di nave*) engineer

Macedonia [matʃe'dɔnja] *sf* **la ~** Macedonia

mace'donia [matʃe'dɔnja] *sf* fruit salad

macel'laio [matʃel'lajo] *sm* butcher

macelle'ria *sf* butcher's (shop)

ma'cerie [ma'tʃɛrje] *sfpl* rubble *sg*, debris *sg*

ma'cigno [ma'tʃiɲɲo] *sm* (*masso*) rock, boulder

maci'nare [matʃi'nare] *vt* to grind; (*carne*) to mince (BRIT), grind (US)

macrobi'otico, -a *ag* macrobiotic ▷ *sf* macrobiotics *sg*

Ma'donna *sf* (*Rel*) Our Lady

mador'nale *ag* enormous, huge

'madre *sf* mother; (*matrice di bolletta*) counterfoil ▷ *ag inv* mother *cpd*; **ragazza ~** unmarried mother; **scena ~** (*Teatro*) principal scene; (*fig*) terrible scene

madre'lingua *sf* mother tongue, native language

madre'perla *sf* mother-of-pearl

ma'drina *sf* godmother

maestà *sf inv* majesty

ma'estra *sf vedi* **maestro**

maes'trale *sm* north-west wind, mistral

ma'estro, -a *sm/f* (*Ins: anche:* **~ di scuola o elementare**) primary (BRIT) *o* grade school (US) teacher; (*esperto*) expert ▷ *sm* (*artigiano, fig: guida*) master; (*Mus*) maestro ▷ *ag* (*principale*) main; (*di grande abilità*) masterly, skilful; **maestra d'asilo** nursery teacher; **~ di cerimonie** master of ceremonies

'mafia *sf* Mafia

'maga *sf* sorceress

ma'gari *escl* (*esprime desiderio*): **~ fosse vero!** if only it were true!; **ti piacerebbe andare in Scozia? — ~!** would you like to go to Scotland? — and how! ▷ *av* (*anche*) even; (*forse*) perhaps

magaz'zino [magad'dzino] *sm* warehouse; **grande ~** department store

Attenzione! In inglese esiste la parola *magazine* che però significa *rivista*.

'maggio ['maddʒo] *sm* May

maggio'rana [maddʒo'rana] *sf* (*Bot*) (sweet) marjoram

maggio'ranza [maddʒo'rantsa] *sf* majority

maggior'domo [maddʒor'dɔmo] *sm* butler

maggi'ore [mad'dʒore] *ag* (*comparativo: più grande*) bigger, larger; taller; greater; (*: più vecchio: sorella, fratello*) older, elder; (*: di grado superiore*) senior; (*: più importante: Mil, Mus*) major; (*superlativo*) biggest, largest; tallest; greatest; oldest, eldest ▷ *sm/f* (*di grado*) superior; (*di età*) elder;

(*Mil*) major; (: *Aer*) squadron leader; **la maggior parte** the majority; **andare per la ~** (*cantante ecc*) to be very popular; **maggio'renne** *ag* of age ▷ *sm/f* person who has come of age

ma'gia [ma'dʒia] *sf* magic; **'magico, -a, -ci, -che** *ag* magic; (*fig*) fascinating, charming, magical

magis'trato [madʒis'trato] *sm* magistrate

'maglia ['maʎʎa] *sf* stitch; (*lavoro ai ferri*) knitting *no pl*; (*tessuto, Sport*) jersey; (*maglione*) jersey, sweater; (*di catena*) link; (*di rete*) mesh; **maglia diritta/rovescia** plain/purl; **magli'etta** *sf* (*canottiera*) vest; (*tipo camicia*) T-shirt

magli'one *sm* sweater, jumper

ma'gnetico, -a, -ci, -che *ag* magnetic

ma'gnifico, -a, -ci, -che [maɲ'ɲifiko] *ag* magnificent, splendid; (*ospite*) generous

ma'gnolia [maɲ'nɔlja] *sf* magnolia

'mago, -ghi *sm* (*stregone*) magician, wizard; (*illusionista*) magician

ma'grezza [ma'grettsa] *sf* thinness

'magro, -a *ag* (*very*) thin, skinny; (*carne*) lean; (*formaggio*) low-fat; (*fig*: *scarso, misero*) meagre, poor; (: *meschino*: *scusa*) poor, lame; **mangiare di ~** not to eat meat

'mai *av* (*nessuna volta*) never; (*talvolta*) ever; **non ... ~** never; **~ più** never again; **non sono ~ stato in Spagna** I've never been to Spain; **come ~?** why (*o* how) on earth?; **chi/dove/quando ~?** whoever/wherever/whenever?

mai'ale *sm* (*Zool*) pig; (*carne*) pork

maio'nese *sf* mayonnaise

'mais *sm inv* maize

mai'uscolo, -a *ag* (*lettera*) capital; (*fig*) enormous, huge

mala'fede *sf* bad faith

malan'dato, -a *ag* (*persona: di salute*) in poor health; (: *di condizioni finanziarie*) badly off; (*trascurato*) shabby

ma'lanno *sm* (*disgrazia*) misfortune; (*malattia*) ailment

mala'pena *sf* **a ~** hardly, scarcely

ma'laria *sf* (*Med*) malaria

ma'lato, -a *ag* ill, sick; (*gamba*) bad; (*pianta*) diseased ▷ *sm/f* sick person; (*in ospedale*) patient; **malat'tia** *sf* (*infettiva ecc*) illness, disease; (*cattiva salute*) illness, sickness; (*di pianta*) disease

mala'vita *sf* underworld

mala'voglia [mala'vɔʎʎa] *sf* **di ~** unwillingly, reluctantly

Mala'ysia *sf* Malaysia

mal'concio, -a, -ci, -ce [mal'kontʃo] *ag* in a sorry state

malcon'tento *sm* discontent

malcos'tume *sm* immorality

mal'destro, -a *ag* (*inabile*) inexpert, inexperienced; (*goffo*) awkward

'male *av* badly ▷ *sm* (*ciò che è ingiusto, disonesto*) evil; (*danno, svantaggio*) harm; (*sventura*) misfortune; (*dolore fisico, morale*) pain, ache; **di ~ in peggio** from bad to worse; **sentirsi ~** to feel ill; **far ~** (*dolere*) to hurt; **far ~ alla salute** to be bad for one's health; **far del ~ a qn** to hurt *o* harm sb; **restare** *o* **rimanere ~** to be sorry; to be disappointed; to be hurt; **andare a ~** to go bad; **come va? — non c'è ~** how are you? — not bad; **avere mal di gola/testa** to have a sore throat/a headache; **avere ~ ai piedi** to have sore feet; **mal d'auto** carsickness; **mal di cuore** heart trouble; **male di dente** toothache; **mal di mare** seasickness

male'detto, -a *pp di* **maledire** ▷ *ag* cursed, damned; (*fig*: *fam*) damned, blasted

male'dire *vt* to curse; **maledizi'one** *sf* curse; **maledizione!** damn it!

maledu'cato, -a *ag* rude, ill-mannered

maleducazi'one [maledukat'tsjone] *sf* rudeness

ma'lefico, -a, -ci, -che *ag* (*influsso, azione*) evil

ma'lessere *sm* indisposition, slight illness; (*fig*) uneasiness

malfa'mato, -a *ag* notorious

malfat'tore, -'trice *sm/f* wrongdoer

mal'fermo, -a *ag* unsteady, shaky; (*salute*) poor, delicate

mal'grado *prep* in spite of, despite ▷ *cong* although; **mio (*o* tuo *ecc*) ~** against my (*o* your *ecc*) will

ma'ligno, -a [ma'liɲɲo] *ag* (*malvagio*) malicious, malignant; (*Med*) malignant

malinco'nia *sf* melancholy, gloom; **malin'conico, -a, -ci, -che** *ag* melancholy

malincu'ore: a ~ *av* reluctantly, unwillingly

malin'teso, -a *ag* misunderstood; (*riguardo, senso del dovere*) mistaken, wrong ▷ *sm* misunderstanding; **c'è stato un ~** there's been a misunderstanding

ma'lizia [ma'littsja] *sf* (*malignità*) malice; (*furbizia*) cunning; (*espediente*) trick; **mali'zioso, -a** *ag* malicious; cunning; (*vivace, birichino*) mischievous

malme'nare *vt* to beat up

ma'locchio [ma'lɔkkjo] *sm* evil eye

ma'lora *sf* **andare in ~** to go to the dogs

ma'lore *sm* (*sudden*) illness

mal'sano, -a *ag* unhealthy

'malta *sf* (*Edil*) mortar

mal'tempo *sm* bad weather

m

'malto *sm* malt

maltrat'tare *vt* to ill-treat

malu'more *sm* bad mood; (*irritabilità*) bad temper; (*discordia*) ill feeling; **di ~** in a bad mood

'malva *sf* (*Bot*) mallow ▷ *ag, sm inv* mauve

mal'vagio, -a, -gi, -gie [mal'vadʒo] *ag* wicked, evil

malvi'vente *sm* criminal

malvolenti'eri *av* unwillingly, reluctantly

'mamma *sf* mummy, mum; **~ mia!** my goodness!

mam'mella *sf* (*Anat*) breast; (*di vacca, capra ecc*) udder

mam'mifero *sm* mammal

ma'nata *sf* (*colpo*) slap; (*quantità*) handful

man'canza [man'kantsa] *sf* lack; (*carenza*) shortage, scarcity; (*fallo*) fault; (*imperfezione*) failing, shortcoming; **per ~ di tempo** through lack of time; **in ~ di meglio** for lack of anything better

man'care *vi* (*essere insufficiente*) to be lacking; (*venir meno*) to fail; (*sbagliare*) to be wrong, make a mistake; (*non esserci*) to be missing, not to be there; (*essere lontano*): **~ (da)** to be away (from) ▷ *vt* to miss; **~ di** to lack; **~ a** (*promessa*) to fail to keep; **tu mi manchi** I miss you; **mancò poco che morisse** he very nearly died; **mancano ancora 10 sterline** we're still £10 short; **manca un quarto alle 6** it's a quarter to 6

mancherò *ecc* [manke'rɔ] *vb vedi* **mancare**

'mancia, -ce ['mantʃa] *sf* tip; **quanto devo lasciare di ~?** how much should I tip?; **~ competente** reward

manci'ata [man'tʃata] *sf* handful

man'cino, -a [man'tʃino] *ag* (*braccio*) left; (*persona*) left-handed; (*fig*) underhand

manda'rancio [manda'rantʃo] *sm* clementine

man'dare *vt* to send; (*far funzionare: macchina*) to drive; (*emettere*) to send out; (*: grido*) to give, utter, let out; **~ a chiamare qn** to send for sb; **~ avanti** (*fig: famiglia*) to provide for; (*: fabbrica*) to run, look after; **~ giù** to send down; (*anche fig*) to swallow; **~ via** to send away; (*licenziare*) to fire

manda'rino *sm* mandarin (orange); (*cinese*) mandarin

man'data *sf* (*quantità*) lot, batch; (*di chiave*) turn; **chiudere a doppia ~** to double-lock

man'dato *sm* (*incarico*) commission; (*Dir: provvedimento*) warrant; (*di deputato ecc*) mandate; (*ordine di pagamento*) postal *o* money order; **mandato d'arresto** warrant for arrest

man'dibola *sf* mandible, jaw

'mandorla *sf* almond; **'mandorlo** *sm* almond tree

'mandria *sf* herd

maneggi'are [maned'dʒare] *vt* (*creta, cera*) to mould, work, fashion; (*arnesi, utensili*) to handle; (*: adoperare*) to use; (*fig: persone, denaro*) to handle, deal with; **ma'neggio** *sm* moulding; handling; use; (*intrigo*) plot, scheme; (*per cavalli*) riding school

ma'nesco, -a, -schi, -sche *ag* free with one's fists

ma'nette *sfpl* handcuffs

manga'nello *sm* club

mangi'are [man'dʒare] *vt* to eat; (*intaccare*) to eat into o away; (*Carte, Scacchi ecc*) to take ▷ *vi* to eat ▷ *sm* eating; (*cibo*) food; (*cucina*) cooking; **possiamo ~ qualcosa?** can we have something to eat?; **mangiarsi le parole** to mumble; **mangiarsi le unghie** to bite one's nails

man'gime [man'dʒime] *sm* fodder

'mango, -ghi *sm* mango

ma'nia *sf* (*Psic*) mania; (*fig*) obsession, craze; **ma'niaco, -a, -ci, -che** *ag* suffering from a mania; **maniaco (di)** obsessed (by), crazy (about)

'manica *sf* sleeve; (*fig: gruppo*) gang, bunch; (*Geo*): **la M~, il Canale della M~** the (English) Channel; **essere di ~ larga/ stretta** to be easy-going/strict; **manica a vento** (*Aer*) wind sock

mani'chino [mani'kino] *sm* (*di sarto, vetrina*) dummy

'manico, -ci *sm* handle; (*Mus*) neck

mani'comio *sm* mental hospital; (*fig*) madhouse

mani'cure *sm o f inv* manicure ▷ *sf inv* manicurist

mani'era *sf* way, manner; (*stile*) style, manner; **maniere** *sfpl* (*comportamento*) manners; **in ~ che** so that; **in ~ da** so as to; **in tutte le maniere** at all costs

manifes'tare *vt* to show, display; (*esprimere*) to express; (*rivelare*) to reveal, disclose ▷ *vi* to demonstrate; **manifestazi'one** *sf* show, display; expression; (*sintomo*) sign, symptom; (*dimostrazione pubblica*) demonstration; (*cerimonia*) event

mani'festo, -a *ag* obvious, evident ▷ *sm* poster, bill; (*scritto ideologico*) manifesto

ma'niglia [ma'niʎʎa] *sf* handle; (*sostegno: negli autobus ecc*) strap

manipo'lare *vt* to manipulate; (*alterare: vino*) to adulterate

man'naro: lupo ~ *sm* werewolf

'mano, -i *sf* hand; (*strato: di vernice ecc*) coat; **di prima ~** (*notizia*) first-hand; **di**

seconda ~ second-hand; **man ~** little by little, gradually; **man ~ che** as; **darsi** o **stringersi la ~** to shake hands; **mettere le mani avanti** (fig) to safeguard o.s.; **restare a mani vuote** to be left empty-handed; **venire alle mani** to come to blows; **a ~** by hand; **mani in alto!** hands up!

mano'dopera sf labour

ma'nometro sm gauge, manometer

mano'mettere vt (alterare) to tamper with; (aprire indebitamente) to break open illegally

ma'nopola sf (dell'armatura) gauntlet; (guanto) mitt; (di impugnatura) hand-grip; (pomello) knob

manos'critto, -a ag handwritten ▷ sm manuscript

mano'vale sm labourer

mano'vella sf handle; (Tecn) crank

ma'novra sf manoeuvre (BRIT), maneuver (US); (Ferr) shunting

man'sarda sf attic

mansi'one sf task, duty, job

mansu'eto, -a ag gentle, docile

man'tello sm cloak; (di neve ecc) blanket, mantle; (Zool) coat

mante'nere vt to maintain; (adempiere: promesse) to keep, abide by; (provvedere a) to support, maintain; **mantenersi** vpr **mantenersi calmo/giovane** to stay calm/young

'Mantova sf Mantua

manu'ale ag manual ▷ sm (testo) manual, handbook

ma'nubrio sm handle; (di bicicletta ecc) handlebars pl; (Sport) dumbbell

manutenzi'one [manuten'tsjone] sf maintenance, upkeep; (d'impianti) maintenance, servicing

'manzo ['mandzo] sm (Zool) steer; (carne) beef

'mappa sf (Geo) map; **mappa'mondo** sm map of the world; (globo girevole) globe

mara'tona sf marathon

'marca, -che sf (Comm: di prodotti) brand; (contrassegno, scontrino) ticket, check; **prodotto di ~** (di buona qualità) high-class product; **marca da bollo** official stamp

mar'care vt (munire di contrassegno) to mark; (a fuoco) to brand; (Sport: gol) to score; (: avversario) to mark; (accentuare) to stress; **~ visita** (Mil) to report sick

marcherò ecc [marke'rɔ] vb vedi **marcare**

mar'chese, -a [mar'keze] sm/f marquis o marquess/marchioness

marchi'are [mar'kjare] vt to brand

'marcia, -ce ['martʃa] sf (anche Mus, Mil) march; (funzionamento) running; (il

camminare) walking; (Aut) gear; **mettere in ~** to start; **mettersi in ~** to get moving; **far ~ indietro** (Aut) to reverse; (fig) to back-pedal

marciapi'ede [martʃa'pjɛde] sm (di strada) pavement (BRIT), sidewalk (US); (Ferr) platform

marci'are [mar'tʃare] vi to march; (andare: treno, macchina) to go; (funzionare) to run, work

'marcio, -a, -ci, -ce ['martʃo] ag (frutta, legno) rotten, bad; (Med) festering; (fig) corrupt, rotten

mar'cire [mar'tʃire] vi (andare a male) to go bad, rot; (suppurare) to fester; (fig) to rot, waste away

'marco, -chi sm (unità monetaria) mark

'mare sm sea; **in ~** at sea; **andare al ~** (in vacanza ecc) to go to the seaside; **il M~ del Nord** the North Sea

ma'rea sf tide; **alta/bassa ~** high/low tide

mareggi'ata [mared'dʒata] sf heavy sea

mare'moto sm seaquake

maresci'allo [mareʃ'ʃallo] sm (Mil) marshal; (: sottufficiale) warrant officer

marga'rina sf margarine

marghe'rita [marge'rita] sf (ox-eye) daisy, marguerite; (di stampante) daisy wheel

'margine ['mardʒine] sm margin; (di bosco, via) edge, border

mariju'ana [mæri'wa:nə] sf marijuana

ma'rina sf navy; (costa) coast; (quadro) seascape; **marina mercantile/militare** navy/merchant navy (BRIT) o marine (US)

mari'naio sm sailor

mari'nare vt (Cuc) to marinate; **~ la scuola** to play truant

ma'rino, -a ag sea cpd, marine

mario'netta sf puppet

ma'rito sm husband

ma'rittimo, -a ag maritime, sea cpd

marmel'lata sf jam; (di agrumi) marmalade

mar'mitta sf (recipiente) pot; (Aut) silencer; **marmitta catalitica** catalytic converter

'marmo sm marble

mar'motta sf (Zool) marmot

maroc'chino, -a [marok'kino] ag, sm/f Moroccan

Ma'rocco sm **il ~** Morocco

mar'rone ag inv brown ▷ sm (Bot) chestnut

> Attenzione! In inglese esiste la parola maroon, che però indica un altro colore, il rosso bordeaux.

mar'supio sm pouch; (per denaro) bum bag; (per neonato) sling

martedì sm inv Tuesday; **di** o **il ~** on

m

Tuesdays; **martedì grasso** Shrove Tuesday
martel'lare vt to hammer ▷ vi (pulsare) to throb; (: cuore) to thump
mar'tello sm hammer; (: di uscio) knocker; **martello pneumatico** pneumatic drill
'martire sm/f martyr
mar'xista, -i, -e ag, sm/f Marxist
marza'pane [martsa'pane] sm marzipan
'marzo ['martso] sm March
mascal'zone [maskal'tsone] sm rascal, scoundrel
mas'cara sm inv mascara
ma'scella [maʃʃella] sf (Anat) jaw
'maschera ['maskera] sf mask; (travestimento) disguise; (: per un ballo ecc) fancy dress; (Teatro, Cinema) usher/usherette; (personaggio del teatro) stock character; **masche'rare** vt to mask; (travestire) to disguise; to dress up; (fig: celare) to hide, conceal; (Mil) to camouflage; **mascherarsi da** to disguise o.s. as; to dress up as; (fig) to masquerade as
mas'chile [mas'kile] ag masculine; (sesso, popolazione) male; (abiti) men's; (per ragazzi: scuola) boys'
mas'chilista, -i, -e ag, sm/f (uomo) (male) chauvinist, sexist; (donna) sexist
'maschio, -a ['maskjo] ag (Biol) male; (virile) manly ▷ sm (anche Zool, Tecn) male; (uomo) man; (ragazzo) boy; (figlio) son
masco'lino, -a ag masculine
'massa sf mass; (di errori ecc): **una ~ di** heaps of, masses of; (di gente) mass, multitude; (Elettr) earth; **in ~** (Comm) in bulk; (tutti insieme) en masse; **adunata in ~** mass meeting; **di ~** (cultura, manifestazione) mass cpd
mas'sacro sm massacre, slaughter; (fig) mess, disaster
massaggi'are [massad'dʒare] vt to massage
mas'saggio [mas'saddʒo] sm massage; **massaggio cardiaco** cardiac massage
mas'saia sf housewife
masse'rizie [masse'rittsje] sfpl (household) furnishings
mas'siccio, -a, -ci, -ce [mas'sittʃo] ag (oro, legno) solid; (palazzo) massive; (corporatura) stout ▷ sm (Geo) massif
'massima sf (sentenza, regola) maxim; (Meteor) maximum temperature; **in linea di ~** generally speaking; vedi **massimo**
massi'male sm maximum
'massimo, -a ag, sm maximum; **al ~** at (the) most
'masso sm rock, boulder
masteriz'zare [masterid'dzare] vt (CD, DVD) to burn

masterizza'tore [masteriddza'tore] sm CD burner o writer
masti'care vt to chew
'mastice ['mastitʃe] sm mastic; (per vetri) putty
mas'tino sm mastiff
ma'tassa sf skein
mate'matica sf mathematics sg
mate'matico, -a, -ci, -che ag mathematical ▷ sm/f mathematician
materas'sino sm mat; **materassino gonfiabile** air bed
mate'rasso sm mattress; **materasso a molle** spring o interior-sprung mattress
ma'teria sf (Fisica) matter; (Tecn, Comm) material, matter no pl; (disciplina) subject; (argomento) subject matter, material; **in ~ di** (per quanto concerne) on the subject of; **materie prime** raw materials
materi'ale ag material; (fig: grossolano) rough, rude ▷ sm material; (insieme di strumenti ecc) equipment no pl, materials pl
maternità sf motherhood, maternity; (reparto) maternity ward
ma'terno, -a ag (amore, cura ecc) maternal, motherly; (nonno) maternal; (lingua, terra) mother cpd
ma'tita sf pencil; **matite colorate** coloured pencils; **matita per gli occhi** eyeliner (pencil)
ma'tricola sf (registro) register; (numero) registration number; (nell'università) freshman, fresher
ma'trigna [ma'triɲɲa] sf stepmother
matrimoni'ale ag matrimonial, marriage cpd
matri'monio sm marriage, matrimony; (durata) marriage, married life; (cerimonia) wedding
mat'tina sf morning
'matto, -a ag mad, crazy; (fig: falso) false, imitation ▷ sm/f madman/woman; **avere una voglia matta di qc** to be dying for sth
mat'tone sm brick; (fig): **questo libro/film è un ~** this book/film is heavy going
matto'nella sf tile
matu'rare vi (anche: maturarsi: frutta, grano) to ripen; (ascesso) to come to a head; (fig: persona, idea, Econ) to mature ▷ vt to ripen, to (make) mature
maturità sf maturity; (di frutta) ripeness, maturity; (Ins) school-leaving examination, ≈ GCE A-levels (BRIT)
ma'turo, -a ag mature; (frutto) ripe, mature
max. abbr (= massimo) max
maxischermo [maxis'kermo] sm giant screen
'mazza ['mattsa] sf (bastone) club;

(*martello*) sledge-hammer; (*Sport: da golf*) club; (: *da baseball, cricket*) bat

maz'zata [mat'tsata] *sf* (*anche fig*) heavy blow

'mazzo ['mattso] *sm* (*di fiori, chiavi ecc*) bunch; (*di carte da gioco*) pack

me *pron* me; **me stesso(a)** myself; **sei bravo quanto me** you are as clever as I (am) o as me

mec'canico, -a, -ci, -che *ag* mechanical ▷ *sm* mechanic; **può mandare un ~?** can you send a mechanic?

mecca'nismo *sm* mechanism

me'daglia [me'daʎʎa] *sf* medal

me'desimo, -a *ag* same; (*in persona*): **io ~** I myself

'media *sf* average; (*Mat*) mean; (*Ins: voto*) end-of-term average; **le medie** *sfpl* = **scuola media**; **in ~** on average; *vedi anche* **medio**

medi'ante *prep* by means of

media'tore, -'trice *sm/f* mediator; (*Comm*) middle man, agent

medi'care *vt* to treat; (*ferita*) to dress

medi'cina [medi'tʃina] *sf* medicine; **medicina legale** forensic medicine

'medico, -a, -ci, -che *ag* medical ▷ *sm* doctor; **chiamate un ~** call a doctor; **medico generico** general practitioner, GP

medie'vale *ag* medieval

'medio, -a *ag* average; (*punto, ceto*) middle; (*altezza, statura*) medium ▷ *sm* (*dito*) middle finger; **licenza media** *leaving certificate awarded at the end of 3 years of secondary education*; **scuola media** *first 3 years of secondary school*

medi'ocre *ag* mediocre, poor

medi'tare *vt* to ponder over, meditate on; (*progettare*) to plan, think out ▷ *vi* to meditate

mediter'raneo, -a *ag* Mediterranean; **il (mare) M~** the Mediterranean (Sea)

me'dusa *sf* (*Zool*) jellyfish

mega'byte *sm inv* (*Comput*) megabyte

me'gafono *sm* megaphone

'meglio ['mɛʎʎo] *av, ag inv* better; (*con senso superlativo*) best ▷ *sm* (*la cosa migliore*) **il ~** the best (thing); **faresti ~ ad andartene** you had better leave; **alla ~** as best one can; **andar di bene in ~** to get better and better; **fare del proprio ~** to do one's best; **per il ~** for the best; **aver la ~ su qn** to get the better of sb

'mela *sf* apple; **mela cotogna** quince

mela'grana *sf* pomegranate

melan'zana [melan'dzana] *sf* aubergine (BRIT), eggplant (US)

melato'nina *sf* melatonin

'melma *sf* mud, mire

'melo *sm* apple tree

melo'dia *sf* melody

me'lone *sm* (musk)melon

'membro *sm* member (*pl(f)* **membra**) (*arto*) limb

memo'randum *sm inv* memorandum

me'moria *sf* memory; **memorie** *sfpl* (*opera autobiografica*) memoirs; **a ~** (*imparare, sapere*) by heart; **a ~ d'uomo** within living memory

mendi'cante *sm/f* beggar

○ **PAROLA CHIAVE**

'meno *av* **1** (*in minore misura*) less; **dovresti mangiare meno** you should eat less, you shouldn't eat so much

2 (*comparativo*): **meno ... di** not as ... as, less ... than; **sono meno alto di te** I'm not as tall as you (are), I'm less tall than you (are); **meno ... che** not as ... as, less ... than; **meno che mai** less than ever; **è meno intelligente che ricco** he's more rich than intelligent; **meno fumo più mangio** the less I smoke the more I eat

3 (*superlativo*) least; **il meno dotato degli studenti** the least gifted of the students; **è quello che compro meno spesso** it's the one I buy least often

4 (*Mat*) minus; **8 meno 5** 8 minus 5, 8 take away 5; **sono le 8 meno un quarto** it's a quarter to 8; **meno 5 gradi** 5 degrees below zero, minus 5 degrees; **1 euro in meno** 1 euro less

5 (*fraseologia*): **quanto meno poteva telefonare** he could at least have phoned; **non so se accettare o meno** I don't know whether to accept or not; **fare a meno di qc/qn** to do without sth/sb; **non potevo fare a meno di ridere** I couldn't help laughing; **meno male!** thank goodness!; **meno male che sei arrivato** it's a good job that you've come

▷ *ag inv* (*tempo, denaro*) less; (*errori, persone*) fewer; **ha fatto meno errori di tutti** he made fewer mistakes than anyone, he made the fewest mistakes of all ▷ *sm inv* **1**: **il meno** (*il minimo*) the least; **parlare del più e del meno** to talk about this and that

2 (*Mat*) minus

▷ *prep* (*eccetto*) except (for), apart from; **a meno che, a meno di** unless; **a meno che non piova** unless it rains; **non posso, a meno di prendere ferie** I can't, unless I take some leave

meno'pausa *sf* menopause

'mensa *sf* (*locale*) canteen; (: *Mil*) mess; (: *nelle università*) refectory

men'sile ag monthly ▷ sm (periodico) monthly (magazine); (stipendio) monthly salary

'mensola sf bracket; (ripiano) shelf; (Archit) corbel

'menta sf mint; (anche: ~ piperita) peppermint; (bibita) peppermint cordial; (caramella) mint, peppermint

men'tale ag mental; **mentalità** sf inv mentality

'mente sf mind; **imparare/sapere qc a ~** to learn/know sth by heart; **avere in ~ qc** to have sth in mind; **passare di ~ a qn** to slip sb's mind

men'tire vi to lie

'mento sm chin

'mentre cong (temporale) while; (avversativo) whereas

menù sm inv menu; **ci può portare il ~?** could we see the menu?; **menù turistico** set menu

menzio'nare [mentsjo'nare] vt to mention

men'zogna [men'tsɔɲɲa] sf lie

mera'viglia [mera'viʎʎa] sf amazement, wonder; (persona, cosa) marvel, wonder; **a ~** perfectly, wonderfully; **meravigli'are** vt to amaze, astonish; **meravigliarsi (di)** to marvel (at); (stupirsi) to be amazed (at), be astonished (at); **meravigli'oso, -a** ag wonderful, marvellous

mer'cante sm merchant; **mercante d'arte** art dealer

merca'tino sm (rionale) local street market; (Econ) unofficial stock market

mer'cato sm market; **mercato dei cambi** exchange market; **mercato nero** black-market

'merce ['mɛrtʃe] sf goods pl, merchandise

mercé [mer'tʃe] sf mercy

merce'ria [mertʃe'ria] sf (articoli) haberdashery (BRIT), notions pl (US); (bottega) haberdasher's shop (BRIT), notions store (US)

mercoledì sm inv Wednesday; **di o il ~** on Wednesdays; **mercoledì delle Ceneri** Ash Wednesday

mer'curio sm mercury

'merda (fam!) sf shit (!)

me'renda sf afternoon snack

meren'dina sf snack

meridi'ana sf (orologio) sundial

meridi'ano, -a ag meridian; midday cpd, noonday ▷ sm meridian

meridio'nale ag southern ▷ sm/f southerner

meridi'one sm south

me'ringa, -ghe sf (Cuc) meringue

meri'tare vt to deserve, merit ▷ vb impers **merita andare** it's worth going

meri'tevole ag worthy

'merito sm merit; (valore) worth; **in ~ a** as regards, with regard to; **dare ~ a qn di** to give sb credit for; **finire a pari ~** to finish joint first (o second ecc); to tie

mer'letto sm lace

'merlo sm (Zool) blackbird; (Archit) battlement

mer'luzzo [mer'luttso] sm (Zool) cod

mes'chino, -a [mes'kino] ag wretched; (scarso) scanty, poor; (persona: gretta) mean; (: limitata) narrow-minded, petty

mesco'lare vt to mix; (vini, colori) to blend; (mettere in disordine) to mix up, muddle up; (carte) to shuffle

'mese sm month

'messa sf (Rel) mass; (il mettere): **messa in moto** starting; **messa in piega** set; **messa a punto** (Tecn) adjustment; (Aut) tuning; (fig) clarification; **messa in scena** = **messinscena**

messag'gero [messad'dʒɛro] sm messenger

messaggino [messad'dʒino] sm (di telefonino) text (message)

mes'saggio [mes'saddʒo] sm message; **posso lasciare un ~?** can I leave a message?; **ci sono messaggi per me?** are there any messages for me?; **messaggio di posta elettronica** e-mail message

messag'gistica [messad'dʒistica] sf ~ **immediata** (Inform) instant messaging; **programma di ~ immediata** instant messenger

mes'sale sm (Rel) missal

messi'cano, -a ag, sm/f Mexican

'Messico sm il ~ Mexico

messin'scena [messin'ʃɛna] sf (Teatro) production

'messo, -a pp di mettere ▷ sm messenger

mesti'ere sm (professione) job; (: manuale) trade; (: artigianale) craft; (fig: abilità nel lavoro) skill, technique; **essere del ~** to know the tricks of the trade

'mestolo sm (Cuc) ladle

mestruazi'one [mestruat'tsjone] sf menstruation

'meta sf destination; (fig) aim, goal

metà sf inv half; (punto di mezzo) middle; **dividere qc a o per ~** to divide sth in half, halve sth; **fare a ~ (di qc con qn)** to go halves (with sb in sth); **a ~ prezzo** at half price; **a ~ strada** halfway

meta'done sm methadone

me'tafora sf metaphor

me'tallico, -a, -ci, -che ag (di metallo) metal cpd; (splendore, rumore ecc) metallic

me'tallo sm metal

metalmec'canico, -a, -ci, -che ag
engineering cpd ▷ sm engineering worker

me'tano sm methane

me'ticcio, -a, -ci, -ce [me'tittʃo] sm/f
half-caste, half-breed

me'todico, -a, -ci, -che ag methodical

'metodo sm method

'metro sm metre; (nastro) tape measure;
(asta) (metre) rule

metropoli'tana sf underground, subway

'mettere vt to put; (abito) to put on;
(: portare) to wear; (installare: telefono) to
put in; (fig: provocare): **~ fame/allegria a
qn** to make sb hungry/happy; (supporre):
mettiamo che ... let's suppose o say
that ...; **mettersi** vpr (persona) to put
o.s.; (oggetto) to go; (disporsi: faccenda) to
turn out; **mettersi a sedere** to sit down;
mettersi a letto to get into bed; (per
malattia) to take to one's bed; **mettersi il
cappello** to put on one's hat; **mettersi a**
(cominciare) to begin to, start to; **mettersi
al lavoro** to set to work, **mettersi con qn**
(in società) to team up with sb; (in coppia)
to start going out with sb; **metterci:
metterci molta cura/molto tempo** to
take a lot of care/a lot of time; **ci ho messo
3 ore per venire** it's taken me 3 hours to
get here; **mettercela tutta** to do one's
best; **~ a tacere qn/qc** to keep sb/sth
quiet; **~ su casa** to set up house; **~ su un
negozio** to start a shop; **~ via** to put away

mezza'notte [meddza'nɔtte] sf midnight

'mezzo, -a ['mɛddzo] ag half; **un ~ litro/
panino** half a litre/roll ▷ av half-; **~ morto**
half-dead ▷ sm (metà) half; (parte centrale:
di strada ecc) middle; (per raggiungere un fine)
means sg; (veicolo) vehicle; (nell'indicare
l'ora): **le nove e ~** half past nine; **~giorno e
~** half past twelve; **mezzi** smpl (possibilità
economiche) means; **di mezza età** middle-
aged; **un soprabito di mezza stagione**
a spring (o autumn) coat; **di ~** middle, in
the middle; **andarci di ~** (patir danno) to
suffer; **levarsi o togliersi di ~** to get out of
the way; **in ~ a** in the middle of; **per o a ~
di** by means of; **mezzi di comunicazione
di massa** mass media pl; **mezzi pubblici**
public transport sg; **mezzi di trasporto**
means of transport

mezzo'giorno [meddzo'dʒorno] sm
midday, noon; **a ~** at 12 (o'clock) o midday o
noon; **il ~ d'Italia** southern Italy

mi (dav lo, la, li, le, ne diventa **me**) pron
(oggetto) me; (complemento di termine)
to me; (riflessivo) myself ▷ sm (Mus) E;
(: solfeggiando la scala) mi

miago'lare vi to miaow, mew

'mica av (fam): **non ... ~** not ... at all; **non**
sono **~ stanco** I'm not a bit tired; **non sarà
~ partito?** he wouldn't have left, would
he?; **~ male** not bad

'miccia, -ce ['mittʃa] sf fuse

micidi'ale [mitʃi'djale] ag fatal;
(dannosissimo) deadly

micro'fibra sf microfibre

mi'crofono sm microphone

micros'copio sm microscope

mi'dollo (pl(f) **midolla**) sm (Anat) marrow;
midollo osseo bone marrow

mi'ele sm honey

'miglia ['miʎʎa] sfpl di **miglio**

migli'aio [miʎ'ʎajo] ((pl)f **migliaia**) sm
thousand; **un ~ (di)** about a thousand; **a
migliaia** by the thousand, in thousands

'miglio ['miʎʎo] sm (Bot) millet (pl(f)
miglia) (unità di misura) mile; **~ marino** o
nautico nautical mile

migliora'mento [miʎʎora'mento] sm
improvement

miglio'rare [miʎʎo'rare] vt, vi to improve

migli'ore [miʎ'ʎore] ag (comparativo)
better; (superlativo) best ▷ sm **il ~** the best
(thing) ▷ sm/f **il(la) ~** the best (person); **il
miglior vino di questa regione** the best
wine in this area

'mignolo ['miɲɲolo] sm (Anat) little finger,
pinkie; (: dito del piede) little toe

Mi'lano sf Milan

miliar'dario, -a sm/f millionaire

mili'ardo sm thousand million, billion (us)

mili'one sm million; **mille euro** one
thousand euros

mili'tante ag, sm/f militant

mili'tare vi (Mil) to be a soldier, serve; (fig:
in un partito) to be a militant ▷ ag military
▷ sm serviceman; **fare il ~** to do one's
military service

'mille (pl **mila**) num a o one thousand; **dieci
mila** ten thousand

mil'lennio sm millennium

millepi'edi sm inv centipede

mil'lesimo, -a ag, sm thousandth

milli'grammo sm milligram(me)

mil'limetro sm millimetre

'milza ['miltsa] sf (Anat) spleen

mimetiz'zare [mimetid'dzare] vt to
camouflage; **mimetizzarsi** vpr to
camouflage o.s.

'mimo sm (attore, componimento) mime

mi'mosa sf mimosa

min. abbr (= minuto, minimo) min.

'mina sf (esplosiva) mine; (di matita) lead

mi'naccia, -ce [mi'nattʃa] sf threat;
minacci'are vt to threaten; **minacciare
qn di morte** to threaten to kill sb;
minacciare di fare qc to threaten to do
sth

mi'nare *vt* (*Mil*) to mine; (*fig*) to undermine

mina'tore *sm* miner

mine'rale *ag, sm* mineral

mine'rario, -a *ag* (*delle miniere*) mining; (*dei minerali*) ore *cpd*

mi'nestra *sf* soup; **minestra in brodo** noodle soup; **minestra di verdure** vegetable soup

minia'tura *sf* miniature

mini'bar *sm inv* minibar

mini'era *sf* mine

mini'gonna *sf* miniskirt

'minimo, -a *ag* minimum, least, slightest; (*piccolissimo*) very small, slight; (*il più basso*) lowest, minimum ▷ *sm* minimum; **al ~** at least; **girare al ~** (*Aut*) to idle

minis'tero *sm* (*Pol, Rel*) ministry; (*governo*) government; **M~ delle Finanze** Ministry of Finance, ≈ Treasury

mi'nistro *sm* (*Pol, Rel*) minister

mino'ranza [mino'rantsa] *sf* minority

mi'nore *ag* (*comparativo*) less; (*più piccolo*) smaller; (*numero*) lower; (*inferiore*) lower, inferior; (*meno importante*) minor; (*più giovane*) younger; (*superlativo*) least; smallest; lowest; youngest ▷ *sm/f* = **minorenne**

mino'renne *ag* under age ▷ *sm/f* minor, person under age

mi'nuscolo, -a *ag* (*scrittura, carattere*) small; (*piccolissimo*) tiny ▷ *sf* small letter

mi'nuto, -a *ag* tiny, minute; (*pioggia*) fine; (*corporatura*) delicate, fine ▷ *sm* (*unità di misura*) minute; **al ~** (*Comm*) retail

'mio (*f* **'mia**, *pl* **mi'ei** or **'mie**) *det* **il ~, la mia** *ecc* my ▷ *pron* **il ~, la mia** *ecc* mine; **i miei** my family; **un ~ amico** a friend of mine

'miope *ag* short-sighted

'mira *sf* (*anche fig*) aim; **prendere la ~** to take aim; **prendere di ~ qn** (*fig*) to pick on sb

mi'racolo *sm* miracle

mi'raggio [mi'raddʒo] *sm* mirage

mi'rare *vi* **~ a** to aim at

mi'rino *sm* (*Tecn*) sight; (*Fot*) viewer, viewfinder

mir'tillo *sm* bilberry (*BRIT*), blueberry (*US*), whortleberry

mi'scela [miʃ'ʃela] *sf* mixture; (*di caffè*) blend

'mischia ['miskja] *sf* scuffle; (*Rugby*) scrum, scrummage

mis'cuglio [mis'kuʎʎo] *sm* mixture, hotchpotch, jumble

'mise *vb vedi* **mettere**

mise'rabile *ag* (*infelice*) miserable, wretched; (*povero*) poverty-stricken; (*di scarso valore*) miserable

mi'seria *sf* extreme poverty; (*infelicità*) misery

miseri'cordia *sf* mercy, pity

'misero, -a *ag* miserable, wretched; (*povero*) poverty-stricken; (*insufficiente*) miserable

'misi *vb vedi* **mettere**

mi'sogino [mi'zɔdʒino] *sm* misogynist

'missile *sm* missile

missio'nario, -a *ag, sm/f* missionary

missi'one *sf* mission

misteri'oso, -a *ag* mysterious

mis'tero *sm* mystery

'misto, -a *ag* mixed; (*scuola*) mixed, coeducational ▷ *sm* mixture

mis'tura *sf* mixture

mi'sura *sf* measure; (*misurazione, dimensione*) measurement; (*taglia*) size; (*provvedimento*) measure, step; (*moderazione*) moderation; (*Mus*) time; (: *divisione*) bar; (*fig: limite*) bounds *pl*, limit; **nella ~ in cui** inasmuch as, insofar as; (**fatto**) **su ~** made to measure

misu'rare *vt* (*ambiente, stoffa*) to measure; (*terreno*) to survey; (*abito*) to try on; (*pesare*) to weigh; (*fig: parole ecc*) to weigh up; (: *spese, cibo*) to limit ▷ *vi* to measure; **misurarsi** *vpr* **misurarsi con qn** to have a confrontation with sb; to compete with sb

'mite *ag* mild

'mitico, -a, ci, che *ag* mythical

'mito *sm* myth; **mitolo'gia, -'gie** *sf* mythology

'mitra *sf* (*Rel*) mitre ▷ *sm inv* (*arma*) sub-machine gun

mit'tente *sm/f* sender

mm *abbr* (= *millimetro*) mm

'mobile *ag* mobile; (*parte di macchina*) moving; (*Dir: bene*) movable, personal ▷ *sm* (*arredamento*) piece of furniture; **mobili** *smpl* (*mobilia*) furniture *sg*

mocas'sino *sm* moccasin

'moda *sf* fashion; **alla ~, di ~** fashionable, in fashion

modalità *sf inv* formality

mo'della *sf* model

mo'dello *sm* model; (*stampo*) mould ▷ *ag inv* model *cpd*

'modem *sm inv* modem

modera'tore, -'trice *sm/f* moderator

mo'derno, -a *ag* modern

mo'desto, -a *ag* modest

'modico, -a, -ci, -che *ag* reasonable, moderate

mo'difica, -che *sf* modification

modifi'care *vt* to modify, alter

'modo *sm* way, manner; (*mezzo*) means, way; (*occasione*) opportunity; (*Ling*) mood; (*Mus*) mode; **modi** *smpl* (*comportamento*) manners; **a suo ~, a ~ suo** in his own way;

ad o **in ogni ~** anyway; **di** o **in ~ che** so that; **in ~ da** so as to; **in tutti i modi** at all costs; (*comunque sia*) anyway; (*in ogni caso*) in any case; **in qualche ~** somehow or other; **per ~ di dire** so to speak; **modo di dire** turn of phrase

'**modulo** sm (*modello*) form; (*Archit, lunare, di comando*) module

'**mogano** sm mahogany

'**mogio, -a, -gi, -gie** ['mɔdʒo] ag down in the dumps, dejected

'**moglie** ['moʎʎe] sf wife

mo'ine sfpl cajolery sg; (*leziosità*) affectation sg

mo'lare sm (*dente*) molar

'**mole** sf mass; (*dimensioni*) size; (*edificio grandioso*) massive structure

moles'tare vt to bother, annoy; **mo'lestia** sf annoyance, bother; **recar molestia a qn** to bother sb; **molestie sessuali** sexual harassment sg

'**molla** sf spring; **molle** sfpl (*per camino*) tongs

mol'lare vt to release, let go; (*Naut*) to ease; (*fig: ceffone*) to give ▷ vi (*cedere*) to give in

'**molle** ag soft; (*muscoli*) flabby

mol'letta sf (*per capelli*) hairgrip; (*per panni stesi*) clothes peg

mol'lica, -che sf crumb, soft part

mol'lusco, -schi sm mollusc

'**molo** sm mole, breakwater; jetty

moltipli'care vt to multiply; **moltiplicarsi** vpr to multiply; to increase in number; **moltiplicazi'one** sf multiplication

PAROLA CHIAVE

'**molto, -a** det (*quantità*) a lot of, much; (*numero*) a lot of, many; **molto pane/carbone** a lot of bread/coal; **molta gente** a lot of people, many people; **molti libri** a lot of books, many books; **non ho molto tempo** I haven't got much time; **per molto (tempo)** for a long time
▷ av **1** a lot, (very) much; **viaggia molto** he travels a lot; **non viaggia molto** he doesn't travel much o a lot
2 (*intensivo: con aggettivi, avverbi*) very; (*: con participio passato*) (very) much; **molto buono** very good; **molto migliore, molto meglio** much o a lot better
▷ pron much, a lot

momentanea'mente av at the moment, at present

momen'taneo, -a ag momentary, fleeting

mo'mento sm moment; **da un ~ all'altro**

at any moment; (*all'improvviso*) suddenly; **al ~ di fare** just as I was (o you were o he was *ecc*) doing; **per il ~** for the time being; **dal ~ che** ever since; (*dato che*) since; **a momenti** (*da un momento all'altro*) any time o moment now; (*quasi*) nearly

'**monaca, -che** sf nun

'**Monaco** sf Monaco; **Monaco (di Baviera)** Munich

'**monaco, -ci** sm monk

monar'chia sf monarchy

monas'tero sm (*di monaci*) monastery; (*di monache*) convent

mon'dano, -a ag (*anche fig*) worldly; (*anche*: **dell'alta società**) society cpd; fashionable

mondi'ale ag (*campionato, popolazione*) world cpd; (*influenza*) world-wide

'**mondo** sm world; (*grande quantità*): **un ~ di** lots of, a host of; **il bel ~** high society

mo'nello, -a sm/f street urchin, (*ragazzo vivace*) scamp, imp

mo'neta sf coin; (*Econ: valuta*) currency; (*denaro spicciolo*) (small) change; **moneta estera** foreign currency; **moneta legale** legal tender

mongol'fiera sf hot-air balloon

'**monitor** sm inv (*Tecn, TV*) monitor

monolo'cale sm studio flat

mono'polio sm monopoly

mo'notono, -a ag monotonous

monovo'lume ag inv, sf inv (**automobile**) ~ people carrier, MPV

mon'sone sm monsoon

monta'carichi [monta'kariki] sm inv hoist, goods lift

mon'taggio [mon'taddʒo] sm (*Tecn*) assembly; (*Cinema*) editing

mon'tagna [mon'taɲɲa] sf mountain; (*zona montuosa*): **la ~** the mountains pl; **andare in ~** to go to the mountains; **montagne russe** roller coaster sg, big dipper sg (BRIT)

monta'naro, -a ag mountain cpd ▷ sm/f mountain dweller

mon'tano, -a ag mountain cpd; alpine

mon'tare vt to go (o come) up; (*cavallo*) to ride; (*apparecchiatura*) to set up, assemble; (*Cuc*) to whip; (*Zool*) to cover; (*incastonare*) to mount, set; (*Cinema*) to edit; (*Fot*) to mount ▷ vi to go (o come) up; (*a cavallo*): ~ **bene/male** to ride well/badly; (*aumentare di livello, volume*) to rise

monta'tura sf assembling no pl; (*di occhiali*) frames pl; (*di gioiello*) mounting, setting; (*fig*): **montatura pubblicitaria** publicity stunt

'**monte** sm mountain; **a ~** upstream; **mandare a ~ qc** to upset sth, cause sth to fail; **il M~ Bianco** Mont Blanc; **monte di pietà** pawnshop; **monte premi** prize

mon'tone sm (Zool) ram; **carne di ~** mutton

montu'oso, -a ag mountainous

monu'mento sm monument

mo'quette [mɔ'kɛt] sf inv fitted carpet

'mora sf (del rovo) blackberry; (del gelso) mulberry; (Dir) delay; (: somma) arrears pl

mo'rale ag moral ▷ sf (scienza) ethics sg, moral philosophy; (complesso di norme) moral standards pl, morality; (condotta) morals pl; (insegnamento morale) moral ▷ sm morale; **essere giù di ~** to be feeling down

'morbido, -a ag soft; (pelle) soft, smooth
Attenzione! In inglese esiste la parola morbid, che però significa morboso.

mor'billo sm (Med) measles sg

'morbo sm disease

mor'boso, -a ag (fig) morbid

'mordere vt to bite; (addentare) to bite into

mori'bondo, -a ag dying, moribund

mo'rire vi to die; (abitudine, civiltà) to die out; **~ di fame** to die of hunger; (fig) to be starving; **~ di noia/paura** to be bored/scared to death; **fa un caldo da ~** it's terribly hot

mormo'rare vi to murmur; (brontolare) to grumble

'moro, -a ag dark(-haired), dark(-complexioned)

'morsa sf (Tecn) vice; (fig: stretta) grip

morsi'care vt to nibble (at), gnaw (at); (insetto) to bite

'morso, -a pp di **mordere** ▷ sm bite; (di insetto) sting; (parte della briglia) bit; **morsi della fame** pangs of hunger

morta'della sf (Cuc) mortadella (type of salted pork meat)

mor'taio sm mortar

mor'tale ag, sm mortal

'morte sf death

'morto, -a pp di **morire** ▷ ag dead ▷ sm/f dead man/woman; **i morti** the dead; **fare il ~** (nell'acqua) to float on one's back; **il Mar M~** the Dead Sea

mo'saico, -ci sm mosaic

'Mosca sf Moscow

'mosca, -sche sf fly; **mosca cieca** blind-man's-buff

mosce'rino [moʃʃe'rino] sm midge, gnat

mos'chea [mos'kɛa] sf mosque

'moscio, -a, -sci, -sce ['mɔʃʃo] ag (fig) lifeless

mos'cone sm (Zool) bluebottle; (barca) pedalo; (: a remi) kind of pedalo with oars

'mossa sf movement; (nel gioco) move

'mossi ecc vb vedi **muovere**

'mosso, -a pp di **muovere** ▷ ag (mare) rough; (capelli) wavy; (Fot) blurred

mos'tarda sf mustard; **mostarda di Cremona** pickled fruit with mustard

'mostra sf exhibition, show; (ostentazione) show; **in ~** on show; **far ~ di** (fingere) to pretend; **far ~ di sé** to show off

mos'trare vt to show; **può mostrarmi dov'è, per favore?** can you show me where it is, please?

'mostro sm monster; **mostru'oso, -a** ag monstrous

mo'tel sm inv motel

moti'vare vt (causare) to cause; (giustificare) to justify, account for

mo'tivo sm (causa) reason, cause; (movente) motive; (letterario) (central) theme; (disegno) motif, design, pattern; (Mus) motif; **per quale ~?** why?, for what reason?

'moto sm (anche Fisica) motion; (movimento, gesto) movement; (esercizio fisico) exercise; (sommossa) rising, revolt; (commozione) feeling, impulse ▷ sf inv (motocicletta) motorbike; **mettere in ~** to set in motion; (Aut) to start up

motoci'clista, -i, -e sm/f motorcyclist

mo'tore, -'trice ag motor; (Tecn) driving ▷ sm engine, motor; **a ~** motor cpd, power-driven; **~ a combustione interna/a reazione** internal combustion/jet engine; **motore di ricerca** (Inform) search engine; **moto'rino** sm moped; **motorino di avviamento** (Aut) starter

motos'cafo sm motorboat

'motto sm (battuta scherzosa) witty remark; (frase emblematica) motto, maxim

'mouse ['maus] sm inv (Inform) mouse

mo'vente sm motive

movi'mento sm movement; (fig) activity, hustle and bustle; (Mus) tempo, movement

mozi'one [mot'tsjone] sf (Pol) motion

mozza'rella [mottsa'rɛlla] sf mozzarella, a moist Neapolitan curd cheese

mozzi'cone [mottsi'kone] sm stub, butt, end; (anche: **~ di sigaretta**) cigarette end

'mucca, -che sf cow; **mucca pazza** mad cow disease

'mucchio ['mukkjo] sm pile, heap; (fig): **un ~ di** lots of, heaps of

'muco, -chi sm mucus

'muffa sf mould, mildew

mug'gire [mud'dʒire] vi (vacca) to low, moo; (toro) to bellow; (fig) to roar

mu'ghetto [mu'getto] sm lily of the valley

mu'lino sm mill; **mulino a vento** windmill

'mulo sm mule

'multa sf fine

multi'etnico, -a, -ci, -che *ag* multiethnic
multirazziale [multirat'tsjale] *ag*
  multiracial
multi'sala *ag inv* multiscreen
multivitami'nico, -a, -ci, -che *ag*
  complesso ~ multivitamin
'mummia *sf* mummy
'mungere ['mundʒere] *vt* (anche fig) to
  milk
munici'pale [munitʃi'pale] *ag* municipal;
  town *cpd*
muni'cipio [muni'tʃipjo] *sm* town
  council, corporation; (edificio) town hall
munizi'oni [munit'tsjoni] *sfpl* (Mil)
  ammunition *sg*
'munsi *ecc vb vedi* **mungere**
mu'oio *ecc vb vedi* **morire**
mu'overe *vt* to move; (ruota, macchina)
  to drive; (sollevare: questione, obiezione) to
  raise, bring up; (: accusa) to make, bring
  forward; **muoversi** *vpr* to move; **muoviti!**
  hurry up!, get a move on!
'mura *sfpl vedi* **muro**
mu'rale *ag* wall *cpd*; mural
mura'tore *sm* mason; bricklayer
'muro *sm* wall
'muschio ['muskjo] *sm* (Zool) musk; (Bot)
  moss
musco'lare *ag* muscular, muscle *cpd*
'muscolo *sm* (Anat) muscle
mu'seo *sm* museum
museru'ola *sf* muzzle
'musica *sf* music; **musica da ballo/
  camera** dance/chamber music; **musi'cale**
  ag musical; **musi'cista, -i, -e** *sm/f*
  musician
'müsli ['mysli] *sm* muesli
'muso *sm* muzzle; (di auto, aereo) nose;
  tenere il ~ to sulk
mussul'mano, -a *ag, sm/f* Muslim,
  Moslem
'muta *sf* (di animali) moulting; (di serpenti)
  sloughing; (per immersioni subacquee) diving
  suit; (gruppo di cani) pack
mu'tande *sfpl* (da uomo) (under)pants
'muto, -a *ag* (Med) dumb; (emozione, dolore,
  Cinema) silent; (Ling) silent, mute; (carta
  geografica) blank; **~ per lo stupore** *ecc*
  speechless with amazement *ecc*
'mutuo, -a *ag* (reciproco) mutual ▷ *sm*
  (Econ) (long term) loan

N *abbr* (= nord) N
n. *abbr* (= numero) no.
'nafta *sf* naphtha; (per motori diesel) diesel
  oil
nafta'lina *sf* (Chim) naphthalene;
  (tarmicida) mothballs *pl*
'naia *sf* (Mil) slang term for national service
na'if [na'if] *ag inv* naïve
'nanna *sf* (linguaggio infantile): **andare a ~**
  to go to beddy-byes
'nano, -a *ag, sm/f* dwarf
napole'tano, -a *ag, sm/f* Neapolitan
'Napoli *sf* Naples
nar'ciso [nar'tʃizo] *sm* narcissus
nar'cotico, -ci *sm* narcotic
na'rice [na'ritʃe] *sf* nostril
nar'rare *vt* to tell the story of, recount;
  narra'tiva *sf* (branca letteraria) fiction
na'sale *ag* nasal
'nascere ['naʃʃere] *vi* (bambino) to be born;
  (pianta) to come o spring up; (fiume) to
  rise, have its source; (sole) to rise; (dente)
  to come through; (fig: derivare, conseguire):
  ~ da to arise from, be born out of; **è nata
  nel 1952** she was born in 1952; **'nascita**
  sf birth
nas'condere *vt* to hide, conceal;
  nascondersi *vpr* to hide; **nascon'diglio**
  sm hiding place; **nascon'dino** *sm*
  (gioco) hide-and-seek; **nas'cosi** *ecc vb*

vedi **nascondere**; **nas'costo, -a** *pp di*
nascondere ▷ *ag* hidden; **di nascosto**
secretly
na'sello *sm* (*Zool*) hake
'naso *sm* nose
'nastro *sm* ribbon; (*magnetico, isolante,*
Sport) tape; **nastro adesivo** adhesive
tape; **nastro trasportatore** conveyor belt
nas'turzio [nas'turtsjo] *sm* nasturtium
na'tale *ag* of one's birth ▷ *sm* (*Rel*): **N~**
Christmas; (*giorno della nascita*) birthday;
nata'lizio, -a *ag* (*del Natale*) Christmas *cpd*
'natica, -che *sf* (*Anat*) buttock
'nato, -a *pp di* nascere ▷ *ag* **un attore ~** a
born actor; **nata Pieri** née Pieri
na'tura *sf* nature; **pagare in ~** to pay in
kind; **natura morta** still life
natu'rale *ag* natural
natural'mente *av* naturally; (*certamente,*
sì) of course
natu'rista, -i, e *ag, sm/f* naturist, nudist
naufra'gare *vi* (*nave*) to be wrecked;
(*persona*) to be shipwrecked; (*fig*) to fall
through; **'naufrago, -ghi** *sm* castaway,
shipwreck victim
'nausea *sf* nausea; **nause'ante** *ag* (*odore*)
nauseating; (*sapore*) disgusting; (*fig*)
sickening
'nautico, -a, -ci, -che *ag* nautical
na'vale *ag* naval
na'vata *sf* (*anche:* ~ **centrale**) nave; (*anche:*
~ **laterale**) aisle
'nave *sf* ship, vessel; **nave cisterna**
tanker; **nave da guerra** warship; **nave**
passeggeri passenger ship
na'vetta *sf* shuttle; (*servizio di*
collegamento) shuttle (service)
navi'cella [navi'tʃɛlla] *sf* (*di aerostato*)
gondola; **navicella spaziale** spaceship
navi'gare *vi* to sail; ~ **in Internet** to surf
the Net; **navigazi'one** *sf* navigation
nazio'nale [nattsjo'nale] *ag* national ▷ *sf*
(*Sport*) national team; **nazionalità** *sf inv*
nationality
nazi'one [nat'tsjone] *sf* nation
naziskin ['naːtsiskin] *sm inv* Nazi
skinhead
NB *abbr* (= *nota bene*) NB

🔵 **PAROLA CHIAVE**

ne *pron* **1** (*di lui, lei, loro*) of him/her/them;
about him/her/them; **ne riconosco la**
voce I recognize his (*o* her) voice
2 (*di questa, quella cosa*) of it; about it; **ne**
voglio ancora I want some more (of it *o*
them); **non parliamone più!** let's not talk
about it any more!
3 (*con valore partitivo*): **hai dei libri? — sì,**

ne ho have you any books? — yes, I have
(some); **hai del pane? — no, non ne ho**
have you any bread? — no, I haven't any;
quanti anni hai? — ne ho 17 how old are
you? — I'm 17
▷ *av* (*moto da luogo: da lì*) from there; **ne**
vengo ora I've just come from there

né *cong* **né … né** neither … nor; **né l'uno**
né l'altro lo vuole neither of them wants
it; **non parla né l'italiano né il tedesco**
he speaks neither Italian nor German, he
doesn't speak either Italian or German;
non piove né nevica it isn't raining or
snowing
ne'anche [ne'anke] *av, cong* not even;
non … ~ not even; **~ se volesse**
potrebbe venire he couldn't come even
if he wanted to; **non l'ho visto — ~ io**
I didn't see him — neither did I *o* I didn't
either; **~ per idea** *o* **sogno!** not on your
life!
'nebbia *sf* fog; (*foschia*) mist
necessaria'mente [netʃessarjamɛnte]
av necessarily
neces'sario, -a [netʃes'sarjo] *ag*
necessary
necessità [netʃessi'ta] *sf inv* necessity;
(*povertà*) need, poverty
necro'logio [nekro'lɔdʒo] *sm* obituary
notice
ne'gare *vt* to deny; (*rifiutare*) to deny,
refuse; **~ di aver fatto/che** to deny
having done/that; **nega'tivo, -a** *ag, sf, sm*
negative
negherò *ecc* [nege'rɔ] *vb vedi* **negare**
negli'gente [negli'dʒɛnte] *ag* negligent,
careless
negozi'ante [negot'tsjante] *sm/f* trader,
dealer; (*bottegaio*) shopkeeper (BRIT),
storekeeper (US)
negozi'are [negot'tsjare] *vt* to negotiate
▷ *vi* **~ in** to trade *o* deal in; **negozi'ato** *sm*
negotiation
ne'gozio [ne'gɔttsjo] *sm* (*locale*) shop
(BRIT), store (US)
'negro, -a *ag, sm/f* Negro
ne'mico, -a, -ci, -che *ag* hostile; (*Mil*)
enemy *cpd* ▷ *sm/f* enemy; **essere ~ di** to be
strongly averse *o* opposed to
nem'meno *av, cong* = **neanche**
'neo *sm* mole; (*fig*) (slight) flaw
'neon *sm* (*Chim*) neon
neo'nato, -a *ag* newborn ▷ *sm/f* newborn
baby
neozelan'dese [neoddzelan'dese] *ag*
New Zealand *cpd* ▷ *sm/f* New Zealander
'Nepal *sm* **il ~** Nepal
nep'pure *av, cong* = **neanche**

'nero, -a *ag* black; (*scuro*) dark ▷ *sm* black;
il Mar N~ the Black Sea
'nervo *sm* (*Anat*) nerve; (*Bot*) vein; **avere
i nervi** to be on edge; **dare sui nervi a
qn** to get on sb's nerves; **ner'voso, -a** *ag*
nervous; (*irritabile*) irritable. ▷ *sm* (*fam*):
far venire il nervoso a qn to get on sb's
nerves
'nespola *sf* (*Bot*) medlar; (*fig*) blow, punch
'nesso *sm* connection, link

PAROLA CHIAVE

nes'suno, -a (*det: dav sm* **nessun** +C, V,
nessuno +s *impura, gn, pn, ps, x, z; dav sf*
nessuna +C, **nessun'** +V) *det* **1** (*non uno*)
no; (, *espressione negativa* +) any; **non c'è
nessun libro** there isn't any book, there
is no book; **nessun altro** no one else,
nobody else; **nessun'altra cosa** nothing
else; **In nessun luogo** nowhere
2 (*qualche*) any; **hai nessuna obiezione?**
do you have any objections?
▷ *pron* **1** (*non uno*) no one, nobody; (,
espressione negativa +) any(one); (: *cosa*)
none; (, *espressione negativa* +) any;
**nessuno è venuto, non è venuto
nessuno** nobody came
2 (*qualcuno*) anyone, anybody; **ha
telefonato nessuno?** did anyone phone?

net'tare *vt* to clean
net'tezza [net'tettsa] *sf* cleanness,
cleanliness; **nettezza urbana** cleansing
department
'netto, -a *ag* (*pulito*) clean; (*chiaro*) clear,
clear cut; (*deciso*) definite; (*Econ*) net
nettur'bino *sm* dustman (BRIT), garbage
collector (US)
neu'trale *ag* neutral
'neutro, -a *ag* neutral; (*Ling*) neuter ▷ *sm*
(*Ling*) neuter
'neve *sf* snow; **nevi'care** *vb impers* to
snow; **nevi'cata** *sf* snowfall
ne'vischio [ne'viskjo] *sm* sleet
ne'voso, -a *ag* snowy; snow-covered
nevral'gia [nevral'dʒia] *sf* neuralgia
nevras'tenico, -a, -ci, -che *ag* (*Med*)
neurasthenic; (*fig*) hot-tempered
ne'vrosi *sf* neurosis
ne'vrotico, -a, ci, che *aq, sm/f* (*anche fig*)
neurotic
'nicchia ['nikkja] *sf* niche; (*naturale*) cavity,
hollow; **nicchia di mercato** (*Comm*) niche
market
nicchi'are [nik'kjare] *vi* to shilly-shally,
hesitate
'nichel ['nikel] *sm* nickel
nico'tina *sf* nicotine

'nido *sm* nest; **a ~ d'ape** (*tessuto ecc*)
honeycomb *cpd*

PAROLA CHIAVE

ni'ente *pron* **1** (*nessuna cosa*) nothing;
niente può fermarlo nothing can stop
him; **niente di niente** absolutely nothing;
nient'altro nothing else; **nient'altro che**
nothing but, just, only; **niente affatto**
not at all, not in the least; **come se niente
fosse** as if nothing had happened; **cose da
niente** trivial matters; **per niente** (*gratis,
invano*) for nothing
2 (*qualcosa*): **hai bisogno di niente?** do
you need anything?
3: **non ... niente** nothing; (*espressione
negativa* +) anything; **non ho visto niente**
I saw nothing, I didn't see anything; **non
ho niente da dire** I have nothing o haven't
anything to say
▷ *sm* nothing; **un bel niente** absolutely
nothing; **basta un niente per farla
piangere** the slightest thing is enough to
make her cry ▷ *av* (*in nessuna misura*): **non
... niente** not ... at all; **non è (per) niente
buono** it isn't good at all

Ni'geria [ni'dʒɛrja] *sf* **la ~** Nigeria
'ninfa *sf* nymph
nin'fea *sf* water lily
ninna-'nanna *sf* lullaby
'ninnolo *sm* (*gingillo*) knick-knack
ni'pote *sm/f* (*di zii*) nephew/niece; (*di
nonni*) grandson/daughter, grandchild
'nitido, -a *ag* clear; (*specchio*) bright
ni'trire *vi* to neigh
ni'trito *sm* (*di cavallo*) neighing *no pl*; neigh;
(*Chim*) nitrite
nitroglice'rina [nitroglitʃe'rina] *sf*
nitroglycerine
no *av* (*risposta*) no; **vieni o no?** are you
coming or not?; **perché no?** why not?;
lo conosciamo? — tu no ma io sì do we
know him? — you don't but I do; **verrai,
no?** you'll come, won't you?
'nobile *ag* noble ▷ *sm/f* noble, nobleman/
woman
'nocca, -che *sf* (*Anat*) knuckle
'noccio *ecc* ['nɔttʃo] *vb vedi* **nuocere**
nocci'ola [not'tʃɔla] *ag inv* (*colore*) hazel,
light brown ▷ *sf* hazelnut
noccio'lina [nottʃo'lina] *sf*; **nocciolina
americana** peanut
'nocciolo ['nɔttʃolo] *sm* (*di frutto*) stone;
(*fig*) heart, core
'noce ['notʃe] *sm* (*albero*) walnut tree ▷ *sf*
(*frutto*) walnut; **noce di cocco** coconut;
noce moscata nutmeg

n

no'cevo *ecc* [no'tʃevo] *vb vedi* **nuocere**

no'civo, -a [no'tʃivo] *ag* harmful, noxious

'nocqui *ecc vb vedi* **nuocere**

'nodo *sm* (*di cravatta, legname, Naut*) knot; (*Aut, Ferr*) junction; (*Med, Astr, Bot*) node; (*fig: legame*) bond, tie; (: *punto centrale*) heart, crux; **avere un ~ alla gola** to have a lump in one's throat

no-'global *sm/f* anti-globalization protester ▷ *ag* (*movimento, manifestante*) .anti-globalization

'noi *pron* (*soggetto*) we; (*oggetto: per dare rilievo, con preposizione*) us; **~ stessi(e)** we ourselves; (*oggetto*) ourselves

'noia *sf* boredom; (*disturbo, impaccio*) bother *no pl*, trouble *no pl*; **avere qn/qc a ~** not to like sb/sth; **mi è venuto a ~** I'm tired of it; **dare ~ a** to annoy; **avere delle noie con qn** to have trouble with sb

noi'oso, -a *ag* boring; (*fastidioso*) annoying, troublesome

> Attenzione! In inglese esiste la parola *noisy*, che però significa *rumoroso*.

noleggi'are [noled'dʒare] *vt* (*prendere a noleggio*) to hire (BRIT), rent; (*dare a noleggio*) to hire out (BRIT), rent (out); (*aereo, nave*) to charter; **vorrei ~ una macchina** I'd like to hire a car; **no'leggio** *sm* hire (BRIT), rental; charter

'nomade *ag* nomadic ▷ *sm/f* nomad

'nome *sm* name; (*Ling*) noun; **in/a ~ di** in the name of; **di o per ~** (*chiamato*) called, named; **conoscere qn di ~** to know sb by name; **nome d'arte** stage name; **nome di battesimo** Christian name; **nome di famiglia** surname

no'mignolo [no'miɲɲolo] *sm* nickname

'nomina *sf* appointment

nomi'nale *ag* nominal; (*Ling*) noun *cpd*

nomi'nare *vt* to name; (*eleggere*) to appoint; (*citare*) to mention

nomina'tivo, -a *ag* (*Ling*) nominative; (*Econ*) registered ▷ *sm* (*Ling: anche:* **caso ~**) nominative (case); (*Amm*) name

non *av* not ▷ *prefisso* non-; *vedi* **affatto; appena** *ecc*

nonché [non'ke] *cong* (*tanto più, tanto meno*) let alone; (*e inoltre*) as well as

noncu'rante *ag* **~ (di)** careless (of), indifferent (to)

'nonno, -a *sm/f* grandfather/mother; (*in senso più familiare*) grandma/grandpa; **i nonni** *smpl* the grandparents

non'nulla *sm inv* **un ~** nothing, a trifle

'nono, -a *ag, sm* ninth

nonos'tante *prep* in spite of, notwithstanding ▷ *cong* although, even though

nontiscordardimé *sm inv* (*Bot*) forget-me-not

nord *sm* North ▷ *ag inv* north; northern; **il Mare del N~** the North Sea; **nor'dest** *sm* north-east; **nor'dovest** *sm* north-west

'norma *sf* (*principio*) norm; (*regola*) regulation, rule; (*consuetudine*) custom, rule; **a ~ di legge** according to law, as laid down by law; **norme per l'uso** instructions for use; **norme di sicurezza** safety regulations

nor'male *ag* normal; standard *cpd*

normal'mente *av* normally

norve'gese [norve'dʒese] *ag, sm/f, sm* Norwegian

Nor'vegia [nor'vedʒa] *sf* **la ~** Norway

nostal'gia [nostal'dʒia] *sf* (*di casa, paese*) homesickness; (*del passato*) nostalgia

nos'trano, -a *ag* local; national; home-produced

'nostro, -a *det* **il (la) ~(-a)** *ecc* our ▷ *pron* **il (la) ~(-a)** *ecc* ours ▷ *sm* **il ~** our money; our belongings; **i nostri** our family; our own people; **è dei nostri** he's one of us

'nota *sf* (*segno*) mark; (*comunicazione scritta, Mus*) note; (*fattura*) bill; (*elenco*) list; **degno di ~** noteworthy, worthy of note

no'taio *sm* notary

no'tare *vt* (*segnare: errori*) to mark; (*registrare*) to note (down), write down; (*rilevare, osservare*) to note, notice; **farsi ~** to get o.s. noticed

no'tevole *ag* (*talento*) notable, remarkable; (*peso*) considerable

no'tifica, -che *sf* notification

no'tizia [no'tittsja] *sf* (*piece of*) news *sg*; (*informazione*) piece of information; **notizi'ario** *sm* (*Radio, TV, Stampa*) news *sg*

'noto, -a *ag* (well-)known

notorietà *sf* fame; notoriety

no'torio, -a *ag* well-known; (*peg*) notorious

not'tambulo, -a *sm/f* night-bird; (*fig*)

not'tata *sf* night

'notte *sf* night; **di ~** at night; (*durante la notte*) in the night, during the night; **notte bianca** sleepless night

not'turno, -a *ag* nocturnal; (*servizio, guardiano*) night *cpd*

no'vanta *num* ninety; **novan'tesimo, -a** *num* ninetieth

'nove *num* nine

nove'cento [nove'tʃento] *num* nine hundred ▷ *sm* **il N~** the twentieth century

no'vella *sf* (*Letteratura*) short story

no'vello, -a *ag* (*piante, patate*) new; (*insalata, verdura*) early; (*sposo*) newly-married

no'vembre *sm* November

novità *sf inv* novelty; (*innovazione*)

innovation; (*cosa originale, insolita*) something new; (*notizia*) (piece of) news *sg*; **le ~ della moda** the latest fashions

nozi'one [not'tsjone] *sf* notion, idea

'nozze ['nɔttse] *sfpl* wedding *sg*, marriage *sg*; **nozze d'argento/d'oro** silver/golden wedding *sg*

'nubile *ag* (*donna*) unmarried, single

'nuca *sf* nape of the neck

nucle'are *ag* nuclear

'nucleo *sm* nucleus; (*gruppo*) team, unit, group; (*Mil, Polizia*) squad; **nucleo familiare** family unit

nu'dista, -i, -e *sm/f* nudist

'nudo, -a *ag* (*persona*) bare, naked, nude; (*membra*) bare, naked; (*montagna*) bare ▷ *sm* (*Arte*) nude

'nulla *pron, av* = **niente** ▷ *sm* = **il nulla** nothing

nullità *sf inv* nullity; (*persona*) nonentity

'nullo, -a *ag* useless, worthless; (*Dir*) null (and void); (*Sport*): **incontro ~** draw

nume'rale *ag, sm* numeral

nume'rare *vt* to number

nu'merico, -a, -ci, -che *ag* numerical

'numero *sm* number; (*romano, arabo*) numeral; (*di spettacolo*) act, turn; **numero civico** house number; **numero di scarpe** shoe size; **numero di telefono** telephone number; **nume'roso, -a** *ag* numerous, many; (*con sostantivo sg*) large

nu'occio *ecc* ['nwɔttʃo] *vb vedi* **nuocere**

nu'ocere ['nwɔtʃere] *vi* **~ a** to harm, damage

nu'ora *sf* daughter-in-law

nuo'tare *vi* to swim; (*galleggiare: oggetti*) to float; **nuota'tore, -'trice** *sm/f* swimmer; **nu'oto** *sm* swimming

nu'ova *sf* (*notizia*) (piece of) news *sg*; *vedi anche* **nuovo**

nuova'mente *av* again

Nu'ova Ze'landa [-dze'landa] *sf* **la ~** New Zealand

nu'ovo, -a *ag* new; **di ~** again; **~ fiammante** *o* **di zecca** brand-new

nutri'ente *ag* nutritious, nourishing

nutri'mento *sm* food, nourishment

nu'trire *vt* to feed; (*fig: sentimenti*) to harbour, nurse; **nutrirsi** *vpr* **nutrirsi di** to feed on, to eat

'nuvola *sf* cloud; **nuvo'loso, -a** *ag* cloudy

nuzi'ale [nut'tsjale] *ag* nuptial; wedding *cpd*

'nylon ['nailən] *sm* nylon

o (*dav V spesso* **od**) *cong* or; **o ... o** either ... or; **o l'uno o l'altro** either (of them)

O *abbr* (= *ovest*) W

'oasi *sf inv* oasis

obbedi'ente *ecc* = **ubbidiente** *ecc*

obbli'gare *vt* (*costringere*): **~ qn a fare** to force *o* oblige sb to do; (*Dir*) to bind; **obbliga'torio, -a** *ag* compulsory, obligatory; **'obbligo, -ghi** *sm* obligation; (*dovere*) duty; **avere l'obbligo di fare** to be obliged to do; **essere d'obbligo** (*discorso, applauso*) to be called for

o'beso, -a *ag* obese

obiet'tare *vt* **~ che** to object that; **~ su qc** to object to sth, raise objections concerning sth

obiet'tivo, -a *ag* objective ▷ *sm* (*Ottica, Fot*) lens *sg*, objective; (*Mil, fig*) objective

obiet'tore *sm* objector; **obiettore di coscienza** conscientious objector

obiezi'one [objet'tsjone] *sf* objection

obi'torio *sm* morgue, mortuary

o'bliquo, -a *ag* oblique; (*inclinato*) slanting; (*fig*) devious, underhand

oblite'rare *vt* (*biglietto*) to stamp; (*francobollo*) to cancel

oblò *sm inv* porthole

'oboe *sm* (*Mus*) oboe

'oca (*pl* **'oche**) *sf* goose

occasi'one *sf* (*caso favorevole*) opportunity;

(*causa, motivo, circostanza*) occasion; (*Comm*) bargain; **d'~** (*a buon prezzo*) bargain *cpd*; (*usato*) secondhand

occhi'aia [ok'kjaja] *sf* **avere le occhiaie** to have shadows under one's eyes

occhi'ali [ok'kjali] *smpl* glasses, spectacles; **occhiali da sole/da vista** sunglasses/(prescription) glasses

occhi'ata [ok'kjata] *sf* look, glance; **dare un'~ a** to have a look at

occhi'ello [ok'kjɛllo] *sm* buttonhole; (*asola*) eyelet

'occhio ['ɔkkjo] *sm* eye; **~!** careful!, watch out!; **a ~ nudo** with the naked eye; **a quattr'occhi** privately, tête-à-tête; **dare all'~ o nell'~ a qn** to catch sb's eye; **fare l'~ a qc** to get used to sth; **tenere d'~ qn** to keep an eye on sb; **vedere di buon/mal ~ qc** to look favourably/unfavourably on sth

occhio'lino [okkjo'lino] *sm* **fare l'~ a qn** to wink at sb

occiden'tale [ottʃiden'tale] *ag* western ▷ *sm/f* Westerner

occi'dente [ottʃi'dɛnte] *sm* west; (*Pol*): **l'O~** the West; **a ~** in the west

occor'rente *ag* necessary ▷ *sm* all that is necessary

occor'renza [okkor'rɛntsa] *sf* necessity, need; **all'~** in case of need

oc'correre *vi* to be needed, be required ▷ *vb impers* **occorre farlo** it must be done; **occorre che tu parta** you must leave, you'll have to leave; **mi occorrono i soldi** I need the money

Attenzione! In inglese esiste il verbo *to occur*, che però significa *succedere*.

oc'culto, -a *ag* hidden, concealed; (*scienze, forze*) occult

occu'pare *vt* to occupy; (*manodopera*) to employ, (*ingombrare*) to occupy, take up; **occuparsi** *vpr* to occupy o.s., keep o.s. busy; (*impiegarsi*) to get a job; **occuparsi di** (*interessarsi*) to take an interest in; (*prendersi cura di*) to look after, take care of; **occu'pato, -a** *ag* (*Mil, Pol*) occupied; (*persona: affaccendato*) busy; (*posto, sedia*) taken; (*toilette, Tel*) engaged; **la linea è occupata** the line's engaged; **è occupato questo posto?** is this seat taken?; **occupazi'one** *sf* occupation; (*impiego, lavoro*) job; (*Econ*) employment

o'ceano [o'tʃɛano] *sm* ocean

'ocra *sf* ochre

'OCSE *sigla f* (= *Organizzazione per la Cooperazione e lo Sviluppo Economico*) OECD (*Organization for Economic Cooperation and Development*)

ocu'lare *ag* ocular, eye *cpd*; **testimone ~** eye witness

ocu'lato, -a *ag* (*attento*) cautious, prudent; (*accorto*) shrewd

ocu'lista, -i, -e *sm/f* eye specialist, oculist

odi'are *vt* to hate, detest

odi'erno, -a *ag* today's, of today; (*attuale*) present

'odio *sm* hatred; **avere in ~ qc/qn** to hate o detest sth/sb; **odi'oso, -a** *ag* hateful, odious

odo'rare *vt* (*annusare*) to smell; (*profumare*) to perfume, scent ▷ *vi* **~ (di)** to smell (of)

o'dore *sm* smell; **odori** *smpl* (*Cuc*) (aromatic) herbs

of'fendere *vt* to offend; (*violare*) to break, violate; (*insultare*) to insult; (*ferire*) to hurt; **offendersi** *vpr* (*con senso reciproco*) to insult one another; (*risentirsi*): **offendersi (di)** to take offence (at), be offended (by)

offe'rente *sm* (*in aste*): **al maggior ~** to the highest bidder

of'ferta *sf* offer; (*donazione, anche Rel*) offering; (*in gara d'appalto*) tender; (*in aste*) bid; (*Econ*) supply; **fare un'~** to make an offer; to tender; to bid; **"offerte d'impiego"** "situations vacant"; **offerta speciale** special offer

of'fesa *sf* insult, affront; (*Mil*) attack; (*Dir*) offence; *vedi anche* **offeso**

of'feso, -a *pp di* **offendere** ▷ *ag* offended; (*fisicamente*) hurt, injured ▷ *sm/f* offended party; **essere ~ con qn** to be annoyed with sb; **parte offesa** (*Dir*) plaintiff

offi'cina [offi'tʃina] *sf* workshop

of'frire *vt* to offer; **offrirsi** *vpr* (*proporsi*) to offer (o.s.), volunteer; (*occasione*) to present itself; (*esporsi*): **offrirsi a** to expose o.s. to; **ti offro da bere** I'll buy you a drink

offus'care *vt* to obscure, darken; (*fig: intelletto*) to dim, cloud; (: *fama*) to obscure, overshadow; **offuscarsi** *vpr* to grow dark; to cloud, grow dim; to be obscured

ogget'tivo, -a [oddʒet'tivo] *ag* objective

og'getto [od'dʒetto] *sm* object; (*materia, argomento*) subject (matter); **oggetti smarriti** lost property *sg*

'oggi ['ɔddʒi] *av, sm* today; **~ a otto** a week today; **oggi'giorno** *av* nowadays

OGM *sigla m* (= *organismo geneticamente modificato*) GMO

'ogni ['oɲɲi] *det* every, each; (*tutti*) all; (*con valore distributivo*) every; **~ uomo è mortale** all men are mortal; **viene ~ due giorni** he comes every two days; **~ cosa** everything; **ad ~ costo** at all costs, at any price; **in ~ luogo** everywhere; **~ tanto** every so often; **~ volta che** every time that

Ognis'santi [oɲɲis'santi] *sm* All Saints' Day

o'gnuno [oɲ'ɲuno] *pron* everyone,

everybody

O'landa sf l'~ Holland; **olan'dese** ag Dutch ▷ sm (Ling) Dutch ▷ sm/f Dutchman/woman; **gli Olandesi** the Dutch

ole'andro sm oleander

oleo'dotto sm oil pipeline

ole'oso, -a ag oily; (che contiene olio) oil-yielding

ol'fatto sm sense of smell

oli'are vt to oil

oli'era sf oil cruet

Olim'piadi sfpl Olympic games; **o'limpico, -a, -ci, -che** ag Olympic

'olio sm oil; **sott'~** (Cuc) in oil; **~ di fegato di merluzzo** cod liver oil; **olio d'oliva** olive oil; **olio di semi** vegetable oil

o'liva sf olive; **o'livo** sm olive tree

'olmo sm elm

OLP sigla f (= Organizzazione per la Liberazione della Palestina) PLO

ol'traggio [ol'traddʒo] sm outrage; offence, insult; **~ a pubblico ufficiale** (Dir) insulting a public official; **oltraggio al pudore** (Dir) indecent behaviour

ol'tranza [ol'trantsa] sf **a ~** to the last, to the bitter end

'oltre av (più in là) further; (di più: aspettare) longer, more ▷ prep (di là da) beyond, over, on the other side of; (più di) more than, over; (in aggiunta a) besides; (eccetto): **~ a** except, apart from; **oltrepas'sare** vt to go beyond, exceed

o'maggio [o'maddʒo] sm (dono) gift; (segno di rispetto) homage, tribute; **omaggi** smpl (complimenti) respects; **rendere ~ a** to pay homage o tribute to; **in ~** (copia, biglietto) complimentary

ombe'lico, -chi sm navel

'ombra sf (zona non assolata, fantasma) shade; (sagoma scura) shadow; **sedere all'~** to sit in the shade; **restare nell'~** (fig) to remain in obscurity

om'brello sm umbrella; **ombrel'lone** sm beach umbrella

om'bretto sm eye shadow

O.M.C. sigla f (= Organizzazione Mondiale del Commercio) WTO

ome'lette [ɔmə'lɛt] sf inv omelet(te)

ome'lia sf (Rel) homily, sermon

omeopa'tia sf homoeopathy

omertà sf conspiracy of silence

o'mettere vt to omit, leave out; **~ di fare** to omit o fail to do

omi'cida, -i, -e [omi'tʃida] ag homicidal, murderous ▷ sm/f murderer/eress

omi'cidio [omi'tʃidjo] sm murder; **omicidio colposo** culpable homicide

o'misi ecc vb vedi **omettere**

omissi'one sf omission; **omissione di soccorso** (Dir) failure to stop and give assistance

omogeneiz'zato [omodʒeneid'dzato] sm baby food

omo'geneo, -a [omo'dʒɛneo] ag homogeneous

o'monimo, -a sm/f namesake ▷ sm (Ling) homonym

omosessu'ale ag, sm/f homosexual

O.M.S. sigla f (= Organizzazione Mondiale della Sanità) WHO

On. abbr (Pol) = **onorevole**

'onda sf wave; **mettere** o **mandare in ~** (Radio, TV) to broadcast; **andare in ~** (Radio, TV) to go on the air; **onde corte/lunghe/medie** short/long/medium wave

'onere sm burden; **oneri fiscali** taxes

onestà sf honesty

o'nesto, -a ag (probo, retto) honest; (giusto) fair; (casto) chaste, virtuous

ONG sigla f inv **Organizzazione Non Governativa** NGO

onnipo'tente ag omnipotent

ono'mastico, -ci sm name-day

ono'rare vt to honour; (far onore a) to do credit to

ono'rario, -a ag honorary ▷ sm fee

o'nore sm honour; **in ~ di** in honour of; **fare gli onori di casa** to play host (o hostess); **fare ~ a** to honour; (pranzo) to do justice to; (famiglia) to be a credit to; **farsi ~** to distinguish o.s.; **ono'revole** ag honourable ▷ sm/f (Pol) ≈ Member of Parliament (BRIT), ≈ Congressman/woman (US)

on'tano sm (Bot) alder

'O.N.U. ['ɔnu] sigla f (= Organizzazione delle Nazioni Unite) UN, UNO

o'paco, -a, -chi, -che ag (vetro) opaque; (metallo) dull, matt

o'pale sm o f opal

'opera sf work; (azione rilevante) action, deed, work; (Mus) work; opus; (: melodramma) opera; (: teatro) opera house; (ente) institution, organization; **opere pubbliche** public works; **opera d'arte** work of art; **opera lirica** (grand) opera

ope'raio, -a ag working-class; workers' ▷ sm/f worker; **classe operaia** working class

ope'rare vt to carry out, make; (Med) to operate on ▷ vi to operate, work; (rimedio) to act, work; (Med) to operate; **operarsi** vpr (Med) to have an operation; **operarsi d'appendicite** to have one's appendix out; **operazi'one** sf operation

ope'retta sf (Mus) operetta, light opera

opini'one *sf* opinion; **opinione pubblica** public opinion

'oppio *sm* opium

op'pongo *ecc vb vedi* **opporre**

op'porre *vt* to oppose; **opporsi** *vpr* **opporsi (a qc)** to oppose (sth); to object (to sth); **~ resistenza/un rifiuto** to offer resistance/refuse

opportu'nista, -i, -e *sm/f* opportunist

opportunità *sf inv* opportunity; *(convenienza)* opportuneness, timeliness

oppor'tuno, -a *ag* timely, opportune

op'posi *ecc vb vedi* **opporre**

opposizi'one [oppozit'tsjone] *sf* opposition; *(Dir)* objection

op'posto, -a *pp di* **opporre** ▷ *ag* opposite; *(opinioni)* conflicting ▷ *sm* opposite, contrary; **all'~** on the contrary

oppressi'one *sf* oppression

oppri'mente *ag (caldo, noia)* oppressive; *(persona)* tiresome; *(deprimente)* depressing

op'primere *vt (premere, gravare)* to weigh down; *(estenuare: caldo)* to suffocate, oppress; *(tiranneggiare: popolo)* to oppress

op'pure *cong* or (else)

op'tare *vi* **~ per** to opt for

o'puscolo *sm* booklet, pamphlet

opzi'one [op'tsjone] *sf* option

'ora *sf (60 minuti)* hour; *(momento)* time; **che ~ è?, che ore sono?** what time is it?; **a che ~ apre il museo/negozio?** what time does the museum/shop open?; **non veder l'~ di fare** to long to do, look forward to doing; **di buon'~** early; **alla buon'~!** at last!; **~ legale** *o* **estiva** summer time *(BRIT)*, daylight saving time *(US)*; **ora di cena** dinner time; **ora locale** local time; **ora di pranzo** lunchtime; **ora di punta** *(Aut)* rush hour

o'racolo *sm* oracle

o'rale *ag, sm* oral

o'rario, -a *ag* hourly; *(fuso, segnale)* time *cpd*; *(velocità)* per hour ▷ *sm* timetable, schedule; *(di ufficio, visite ecc)* hours *pl*, time(s *pl*); **in ~** on time

o'rata *sf (Zool)* sea bream

ora'tore, -'trice *sm/f* speaker; orator

'orbita *sf (Astr, Fisica)* orbit; *(Anat)* (eye-)socket

or'chestra [or'kɛstra] *sf* orchestra

orchi'dea [orki'dɛa] *sf* orchid

or'digno [or'diɲɲo] *sm (esplosivo)* explosive device

ordi'nale *ag, sm* ordinal

ordi'nare *vt (mettere in ordine)* to arrange, organize; *(Comm)* to order; *(prescrivere: medicina)* to prescribe; *(comandare)*: **posso ~ per favore?** can I order now please?; **~ a qn di fare qc** to order *o* command sb to do

sth; *(Rel)* to ordain

ordi'nario, -a *ag (comune)* ordinary; everyday; standard; *(grossolano)* coarse, common ▷ *sm* ordinary; *(Ins: di università)* full professor

ordi'nato, -a *ag* tidy, orderly

ordinazi'one [ordinat'tsjone] *sf (Comm)* order; *(Rel)* ordination; **eseguire qc su ~** to make sth to order

'ordine *sm* order; *(carattere)*: **d'~ pratico** of a practical nature; **all'~** *(Comm: assegno)* to order; **di prim'~** first-class; **fino a nuovo ~** until further notice; **essere in ~** *(documenti)* to be in order; *(stanza, persona)* to be tidy; **mettere in ~** to put in order, tidy (up); **l'~ pubblico** law and order; **ordini (sacri)** *(Rel)* holy orders; **ordine del giorno** *(di seduta)* agenda; *(Mil)* order of the day; **ordine di pagamento** *(Comm)* order for payment

orec'chino [orek'kino] *sm* earring

o'recchio [o'rekkjo] *(pl(f)* **o'recchie)** *sm (Anat)* ear

orecchi'oni [orek'kjoni] *smpl (Med)* mumps *sg*

o'refice [o'refitʃe] *sm* goldsmith; jeweller; **orefice'ria** *sf (arte)* goldsmith's art; *(negozio)* jeweller's (shop)

'orfano, -a *ag* orphan(ed) ▷ *sm/f* orphan; **~ di padre/madre** fatherless/motherless

orga'netto *sm* barrel organ; *(fam: armonica a bocca)* mouth organ; (: *fisarmonica)* accordion

or'ganico, -a, -ci, -che *ag* organic ▷ *sm* personnel, staff

organi'gramma, -i *sm* organization chart

orga'nismo *sm (Biol)* organism; *(corpo umano)* body; *(Amm)* body, organism

organiz'zare [organid'dzare] *vt* to organize; **organizzarsi** *vpr* to get organized; **organizzazi'one** *sf* organization

'organo *sm* organ; *(di congegno)* part; *(portavoce)* spokesman, mouthpiece

'orgia, -ge ['ɔrdʒa] *sf* orgy

or'goglio [or'ɡoʎʎo] *sm* pride; **orgogli'oso, -a** *ag* proud

orien'tale *ag* oriental; eastern; east

orienta'mento *sm* positioning; orientation; direction; **senso di ~** sense of direction; **perdere l'~** to lose one's bearings; **orientamento professionale** careers guidance

orien'tarsi *vpr* to find one's bearings; *(fig: tendere)* to tend, lean; (: *indirizzarsi)*: **~ verso** to take up, go in for

ori'ente *sm* east; **l'O~** the East, the Orient; **a ~** in the east o'rigano sm oregano

origi'nale [oridʒi'nale] ag original; (bizzarro) eccentric ▷ sm original

origi'nario, -a [oridʒi'narjo] ag original; essere ~ di to be a native of; (provenire da) to originate from; to be native to

o'rigine [o'ridʒine] sf origin; all'~ originally; d'~ inglese of English origin; dare ~ a to give rise to

origli'are [oriʎ'ʎare] vi ~ (a) to eavesdrop (on)

o'rina sf urine

ori'nare vi to urinate ▷ vt to pass

orizzon'tale [oriddzon'tale] ag horizontal

oriz'zonte [orid'dzonte] sm horizon

'orlo sm edge, border; (di recipiente) rim, brim; (di vestito ecc) hem

'orma sf (di persona) footprint; (di animale) track; (impronta, traccia) mark, trace

or'mai av by now, by this time; (adesso) now; (quasi) almost, nearly

ormeggi'are [ormed'dʒare] vt (Naut) to moor

or'mone sm hormone

ornamen'tale ag ornamental, decorative

or'nare vt to adorn, decorate; ornarsi vpr ornarsi (di) to deck o.s. (out) (with)

ornitolo'gia [ornitolo'dʒia] sf ornithology

'oro sm gold; d'~, in ~ gold cpd; d'~ (colore, occasione) golden; (persona) marvellous

oro'logio [oro'lɔdʒo] sm clock; (da tasca, da polso) watch; orologio al quarzo quartz watch; orologio da polso wristwatch

o'roscopo sm horoscope

or'rendo, -a ag (spaventoso) horrible, awful; (bruttissimo) hideous

or'ribile ag horrible

or'rore sm horror; avere in ~ qn/qc to loathe o detest sb/sth; mi fanno ~ I loathe o detest them

orsacchi'otto [orsak'kjɔtto] sm teddy bear

'orso sm bear; orso bruno/bianco brown/polar bear

or'taggio [or'taddʒo] sm vegetable

or'tensia sf hydrangea

or'tica, -che sf (stinging) nettle

orti'caria sf nettle rash

'orto sm vegetable garden, kitchen garden; (Agr) market garden (BRIT), truck farm (US); orto botanico botanical garden(s) (pl)

orto'dosso, -a ag orthodox

ortogra'fia sf spelling

orto'pedico, -a, -ci, -che ag orthopaedic ▷ sm orthopaedic specialist

orzai'olo [ordza'jɔlo] sm (Med) stye

'orzo ['ordzo] sm barley

o'sare vt, vi to dare; ~ fare to dare (to) do

oscenità [oʃʃeni'ta] sf inv obscenity

o'sceno, -a [oʃ'ʃeno] ag obscene; (ripugnante) ghastly

oscil'lare [oʃʃil'lare] vi (pendolo) to swing; (dondolare: al vento ecc) to rock; (variare) to fluctuate; (Tecn) to oscillate; (fig): ~ fra to waver o hesitate between

oscu'rare vt to darken, obscure; (fig) to obscure; oscurarsi vpr (cielo) to darken, cloud over; (persona): si oscurò in volto his face clouded over

oscurità sf (vedi ag) darkness; obscurity

os'curo, -a ag dark; (fig) obscure; humble, lowly ▷ sm all'~ in the dark; tenere qn all'~ di qc to keep sb in the dark about sth

ospe'dale sm hospital; dov'è l'~ più vicino? where's the nearest hospital?

ospi'tale ag hospitable

ospi'tare vt to give hospitality to; (albergo) to accommodate

'ospite sm/f (persona che ospita) host/hostess; (persona ospitata) guest

os'pizio [os'pittsjo] sm (per vecchi ecc) home

osser'vare vt to observe, watch; (esaminare) to examine; (notare, rilevare) to notice, observe; (Dir: la legge) to observe, respect; (mantenere: silenzio) to keep, observe; far ~ qc a qn to point sth out to sb; osservazi'one sf observation; (di legge ecc) observance; (considerazione critica) observation, remark; (rimprovero) reproof; in osservazione under observation

ossessio'nare vt to obsess, haunt; (tormentare) to torment, harass

ossessi'one sf obsession

os'sia cong that is, to be precise

'ossido sm oxide; ossido di carbonio carbon monoxide

ossige'nare [ossidʒe'nare] vt to oxygenate; (decolorare) to bleach; acqua ossigenata hydrogen peroxide

os'sigeno sm oxygen

'osso (pl(f) ossa) (nel senso Anat) sm bone; d'~ (bottone ecc) of bone, bone cpd; osso di seppia cuttlebone

ostaco'lare vt to block, obstruct

os'tacolo sm obstacle; (Equitazione) hurdle, jump

os'taggio [os'taddʒo] sm hostage

os'tello sm; ostello della gioventù youth hostel

osten'tare vt to make a show of, flaunt

oste'ria sf inn

os'tetrico, -a, -ci, -che ag obstetric ▷ sm obstetrician

'ostia sf (Rel) host; (per medicinali) wafer

'ostico, -a, -ci, -che ag (fig) harsh; hard, difficult; unpleasant

os'tile ag hostile

osti'narsi *vpr* to insist, dig one's heels in; **~ a fare** to persist (obstinately) in doing; **osti'nato, -a** *ag* (*caparbio*) obstinate; (*tenace*) persistent, determined

'ostrica, -che *sf* oyster

> Attenzione! In inglese esiste la parola *ostrich*, che però significa *struzzo*.

ostru'ire *vt* to obstruct, block

o'tite *sf* ear infection

ot'tanta *num* eighty

ot'tavo, -a *num* eighth

otte'nere *vt* to obtain, get; (*risultato*) to achieve, obtain

'ottica *sf* (*scienza*) optics *sg*; (*Fot: lenti, prismi ecc*) optics *pl*

'ottico, -a, -ci, -che *ag* (*della vista: nervo*) optic; (*dell'ottica*) optical ▷ *sm* optician

ottima'mente *av* excellently, very well

otti'mismo *sm* optimism; **otti'mista, -i, -e** *sm/f* optimist

'ottimo, -a *ag* excellent, very good

'otto *num* eight

ot'tobre *sm* October

otto'cento [otto'tʃɛnto] *num* eight hundred ▷ *sm* **l'O~** the nineteenth century

ot'tone *sm* brass; **gli ottoni** (*Mus*) the brass

ottu'rare *vt* to close (up); (*dente*) to fill; **il lavandino è otturato** the sink is blocked; **otturarsi** *vpr* to become o get blocked up; **otturazi'one** *sf* closing (up); (*dentaria*) filling

ot'tuso, -a *ag* (*Mat, fig*) obtuse; (*suono*) dull

o'vaia *sf* (*Anat*) ovary

o'vale *ag, sm* oval

o'vatta *sf* cotton wool; (*per imbottire*) padding, wadding

'ovest *sm* west

o'vile *sm* pen, enclosure

ovulazi'one [ovulat'tsjone] *sf* ovulation

'ovulo *sm* (*Fisiol*) ovum

o'vunque *av* = **dovunque**

ovvi'are *vi* **~ a** to obviate

'ovvio, -a *ag* obvious

ozi'are [ot'tsjare] *vi* to laze, idle

'ozio ['ɔttsjo] *sm* idleness; (*tempo libero*) leisure; **ore d'~** leisure time; **stare in ~** to be idle

o'zono [o'dzɔno] *sm* ozone

P *abbr* (= *parcheggio*) P; (*Aut*: = *principiante*) L

p. *abbr* (= *pagina*) p.

pac'chetto [pak'ketto] *sm* packet; **pacchetto azionario** (*Comm*) shareholding

'pacco, -chi *sm* parcel; (*involto*) bundle; **pacco postale** parcel

'pace ['patʃe] *sf* peace; **darsi ~** to resign o.s.; **fare la ~ con** to make it up with

pa'cifico, -a, -ci, -che [pa'tʃi:fiko] *ag* (*persona*) peaceable; (*vita*) peaceful; (*fig: indiscusso*) indisputable; (: *ovvio*) obvious, clear ▷ *sm* **il P~, l'Oceano P~** the Pacific (Ocean)

paci'fista, -i, -e [patʃi'fista] *sm/f* pacifist

pa'della *sf* frying pan; (*per infermi*) bedpan

padigli'one [padiʎ'ʎone] *sm* pavilion

'Padova *sf* Padua

'padre *sm* father

pa'drino *sm* godfather

padro'nanza [padro'nantsa] *sf* command, mastery

pa'drone, -a *sm/f* master/mistress; (*proprietario*) owner; (*datore di lavoro*) employer; **essere ~ di sé** to be in control of o.s.; **padrone(a) di casa** master/mistress of the house; (*per gli inquilini*) landlord/lady

pae'saggio [pae'zaddʒo] *sm* landscape

pa'ese *sm* (*nazione*) country, nation; (*terra*) country, land; (*villaggio*) village, (small) town; **i Paesi Bassi** the Netherlands; **paese di provenienza** country of origin

'paga, -ghe *sf* pay, wages *pl*

paga'mento *sm* payment

pa'gare *vt* to pay; (*acquisto*, *fig*: *colpa*) to pay for; (*contraccambiare*) to repay, pay back ▷ *vi* to pay; **quanto l'hai pagato?** how much did you pay for it?; **posso ~ con la carta di credito?** can I pay by credit card?; **~ in contanti** to pay cash

pa'gella [pa'dʒɛlla] *sf* (*Ins*) report card

pagherò [page'rɔ] *sm inv* acknowledgement of a debt, IOU

'pagina ['padʒina] *sf* page; **pagine bianche** phone book, telephone directory; **pagine gialle** Yellow Pages

'paglia ['paʎʎa] *sf* straw

pagli'accio [paʎ'ʎattʃo] *sm* clown

pagli'etta [paʎ'ʎetta] *sf* (*cappello per uomo*) (straw) boater; (*per tegami ecc*) steel wool

pa'gnotta [paɲ'ɲɔtta] *sf* round loaf

'paio (*pl(f)* **'paia**) *sm* pair; **un ~ di** (*alcuni*) a couple of

'Pakistan *sm* **il ~** Pakistan

'pala *sf* shovel; (*di remo, ventilatore, elica*) blade; (*di ruota*) paddle

pa'lato *sm* palate

pa'lazzo [pa'lattso] *sm* (*reggia*) palace; (*edificio*) building; **palazzo di giustizia** courthouse; **palazzo dello sport** sports stadium

'palco, -chi *sm* (*Teatro*) box; (*tavolato*) platform, stand; (*ripiano*) layer

palco'scenico, -ci [palkoʃ'ʃeniko] *sm* (*Teatro*) stage

pa'lese *ag* clear, evident

Pales'tina *sf* **la ~** Palestine

palesti'nese *ag, sm/f* Palestinian

pa'lestra *sf* gymnasium; (*esercizio atletico*) exercise, training; (*fig*) training ground, school

pa'letta *sf* spade; (*per il focolare*) shovel; (*del capostazione*) signalling disc

pa'letto *sm* stake, peg; (*spranga*) bolt

'palio *sm* (*gara*): **il P~** horse race run at Siena; **mettere qc in ~** to offer sth as a prize

'palla *sf* ball; (*pallottola*) bullet; **palla di neve** snowball; **palla ovale** rugby ball; **pallaca'nestro** *sf* basketball; **palla'mano** *sf* handball; **pallanu'oto** *sf* water polo; **palla'volo** *sf* volleyball

palleggi'are [palled'dʒare] *vi* (*Calcio*) to practise with the ball; (*Tennis*) to knock up

pallia'tivo *sm* palliative; (*fig*) stopgap measure

'pallido, -a *ag* pale

pal'lina *sf* (*bilia*) marble

pallon'cino [pallon'tʃino] *sm* balloon; (*lampioncino*) Chinese lantern

pal'lone *sm* (*palla*) ball; (*Calcio*) football; (*aerostato*) balloon; **gioco del ~** football

pal'lottola *sf* pellet; (*proiettile*) bullet

'palma *sf* (*Anat*) = **palmo**; (*Bot, simbolo*) palm; **palma da datteri** date palm

'palmo *sm* (*Anat*) palm; **restare con un ~ di naso** to be badly disappointed

'palo *sm* (*legno appuntito*) stake; (*sostegno*) pole; **fare da ~ il ~** (*fig*) to act as look-out

palom'baro *sm* diver

pal'pare *vt* to feel, finger

'palpebra *sf* eyelid

pa'lude *sf* marsh, swamp

pan'cetta [pan'tʃetta] *sf* (*Cuc*) bacon

pan'china [pan'kina] *sf* garden seat; (*di giardino pubblico*) (park) bench

'pancia, -ce ['pantʃa] *sf* belly, stomach; **mettere o fare ~** to be getting a paunch; **avere mal di ~** to have stomachache o a sore stomach

panci'otto [pan'tʃɔtto] *sm* waistcoat

'pancreas *sm inv* pancreas

'panda *sm inv* panda

'pane *sm* bread; (*pagnotta*) loaf (of bread); (*forma*): **un ~ di burro** a pat of butter; **guadagnarsi il ~** to earn one's living; **pane a cassetta** sliced bread; **pane di Spagna** sponge cake; **pane integrale** wholemeal bread; **pane tostato** toast

panette'ria *sf* (*forno*) bakery; (*negozio*) baker's (shop), bakery

panetti'ere, -a *sm/f* baker

panet'tone *sm* a kind of spiced brioche with sultanas, eaten at Christmas

pangrat'tato *sm* breadcrumbs *pl*

'panico, -a, -ci, -che *ag, sm* panic

pani'ere *sm* basket

pani'ficio [pani'fitʃo] *sm* (*forno*) bakery; (*negozio*) baker's (shop), bakery

pa'nino *sm* roll; **panino caldo** toasted sandwich; **panino imbottito** filled roll;

sandwich

'panna sf (Cuc) cream; (Tecn) = **panne**; **panna da cucina** cooking cream; **panna montata** whipped cream

'panne sf inv **essere in ~** (Aut) to have broken down

pan'nello sm panel; **pannello solare** solar panel

'panno sm cloth; **panni** smpl (abiti) clothes; **mettiti nei miei panni** (fig) put yourself in my shoes

pan'nocchia [pan'nɔkkja] sf (di mais ecc) ear

panno'lino sm (per bambini) nappy (BRIT), diaper (US)

pano'rama, -i sm panorama

panta'loni smpl trousers (BRIT), pants (US), pair sg, of trousers o pants

pan'tano sm bog

pan'tera sf panther

pan'tofola sf slipper

'Papa, -i sm pope

papà sm inv dad(dy)

pa'pavero sm poppy

'pappa sf baby cereal; **pappa reale** royal jelly

pappa'gallo sm parrot; (fig: uomo) Romeo, wolf

pa'rabola sf (Mat) parabola; (Rel) parable

para'bolico, -a, ci, che ag (Mat) parabolic; vedi anche **antenna**

para'brezza [para'breddza] sm inv (Aut) windscreen (BRIT), windshield (US)

paraca'dute sm inv parachute

para'diso sm paradise

parados'sale ag paradoxical

para'fulmine sm lightning conductor

pa'raggi [pa'raddʒi] smpl **nei ~** in the vicinity, in the neighbourhood

parago'nare vt **~ con/a** to compare with/to

para'gone sm comparison; (esempio analogo) analogy, parallel; **reggere al ~** to stand comparison

pa'ragrafo sm paragraph

pa'ralisi sf paralysis

paral'lelo, -a ag parallel ▷ sm (Geo) parallel; (comparazione): **fare un ~ tra** to draw a parallel between

para'lume sm lampshade

pa'rametro sm parameter

para'noia sf paranoia; **para'noico, -a, -ci, -che** ag, sm/f paranoid

para'occhi [para'ɔkki] smpl blinkers

para'petto sm balustrade

pa'rare vt (addobbare) to adorn, deck; (proteggere) to shield, protect; (scansare: colpo) to parry; (Calcio) to save ▷ vi **dove**

vuole andare a ~? what are you driving at?

pa'rata sf (Sport) save; (Mil) review, parade

para'urti sm inv (Aut) bumper

para'vento sm folding screen; **fare da ~ a qn** (fig) to shield sb

par'cella [par'tʃɛlla] sf account, fee (of lawyer etc)

parcheggi'are [parked'dʒare] vt to park; **posso ~ qui?** can I park here?; **parcheggiatore, -trice** [parkeddʒa'tore] sm/f (Aut) parking attendant

par'cheggio sm parking no pl; (luogo) car park; (singolo posto) parking space

par'chimetro [par'kimetro] sm parking meter

'parco, -chi sm park; (spazio per deposito) depot; (complesso di veicoli) fleet

par'cometro sm (pay-and-display) ticket machine

pa'recchio, -a [pa'rekkjo] det quite a lot of; (tempo) quite a lot of, a long

pareggi'are [pared'dʒare] vt to make equal; (terreno) to level, make level; (bilancio, conti) to balance ▷ vi (Sport) to draw; **pa'reggio** sm (Econ) balance; (Sport) draw

pa'rente sm/f relative, relation

> ▮ Attenzione! In inglese esiste la parola **parent**, che però significa **genitore**.

paren'tela sf (vincolo di sangue, fig) relationship

pa'rentesi sf (segno grafico) bracket, parenthesis; (frase incisa) parenthesis; (digressione) parenthesis, digression

pa'rere sm (opinione) opinion; (consiglio) advice, opinion; **a mio ~** in my opinion ▷ vi to seem, appear ▷ vb impers **pare che** it seems o appears that, they say that; **mi pare che** it seems to me that; **mi pare di sì** I think so; **fai come ti pare** do as you like; **che ti pare del mio libro?** what do you think of my book?

pa'rete sf wall

'pari ag inv (uguale) equal, same; (in giochi) equal; drawn, tied; (Mat) even ▷ sm inv (Pol: di Gran Bretagna) peer ▷ sm/f inv peer, equal; **copiato ~ ~** copied word for word; **alla ~** on the same level; **ragazza alla ~** au pair girl; **mettersi alla ~ con** to place o.s. on the same level as; **mettersi in ~ con** to catch up with; **andare di ~ passo con qn** to keep pace with sb

Pa'rigi [pa'ridʒi] sf Paris

pari'gino, -a [pari'dʒino] ag, sm/f Parisian

parità sf parity, equality; (Sport) draw, tie

parlamen'tare ag parliamentary ▷ sm/f ≈ Member of Parliament (BRIT), ≈ Congressman/woman (US) ▷ vi to

negotiate, parley
parla'mento sm parliament

parlan'tina (fam) sf talkativeness; **avere ~** to have the gift of the gab
par'lare vi to speak, talk; (confidare cose segrete) to talk ▷ vt to speak; **~ (a qn) di** to speak o talk (to sb) about; **posso ~ con...?** can I speak to ...?; **parla italiano?** do you speak Italian?, **non parlo inglese** I don't speak English
parmigi'ano [parmi'dʒano] sm (grana) Parmesan (cheese)
pa'rola sf word; (facoltà) speech; **parole** sfpl (chiacchiere) talk sg; **chiedere la ~** to ask permission to speak; **prendere la ~** to take the floor; **parola d'onore** word of honour; **parola d'ordine** (Mil) password; **parole incrociate** crossword (puzzle) sg; **paro'laccia, -ce** sf bad word, swearword
parrò ecc vb vedi **parere**
par'rocchia [par'rɔkkja] sf parish; parish church
par'rucca, -che sf wig
parrucchi'ere, -a [parruk'kjɛre] sm/f hairdresser ▷ sm barber
'parte sf part; (lato) side; (quota spettante a ciascuno) share; (direzione) direction; (Pol) party; faction; (Dir) party, **a ~** ag separate ▷ av separately; **scherzi a ~** joking aside; **a ~ ciò** apart from that; **da ~** (in disparte) to one side, aside; **d'altra ~** on the other hand; **da ~ di** (per conto di) on behalf of; **da ~ mia** as far as I'm concerned, as for me; **da ~ a ~** right through; **da ogni ~** on all sides, everywhere; (moto da luogo) from all sides, **da nessuna ~** nowhere; **da questa ~** (in questa direzione) this way; **prendere ~ a qc** to take part in sth; **mettere da ~** to put aside; **mettere qn a ~ di** to inform sb of
parteci'pare [partetʃi'pare] vi **~ a** to take part in, participate in; (utili ecc) to share in; (spese ecc) to contribute to; (dolore, successo di qn) to share (in)
parteggi'are [parted'dʒare] vi **~ per** to side with, be on the side of
par'tenza [par'tɛntsa] sf departure; (Sport) start; **essere in ~** to be about to leave, be leaving
parti'cipio [parti'tʃipjo] sm participle

partico'lare ag (specifico) particular; (proprio) personal, private; (speciale) special, particular; (caratteristico) distinctive, characteristic; (fuori dal comune) peculiar ▷ sm detail, particular; **in ~** in particular, particularly
par'tire vi to go, leave; (allontanarsi) to go (o drive ecc) away o off; (petardo, colpo) to go off; (fig: avere inizio, Sport) to start; **sono partita da Roma alle 7** I left Rome at 7; **a che ora parte il treno/l'autobus?** what time does the train/bus leave?; **il volo parte da Ciampino** the flight leaves from Ciampino; **a ~ da** from
par'tita sf (Comm) lot, consignment; (Econ: registrazione) entry, item; (Carte, Sport: gioco) game; (: competizione) match, game; **partita di caccia** hunting party; **partita IVA** VAT registration number
par'tito sm (Pol) party; (decisione) decision, resolution; (persona da maritare) match
'parto sm (Med) delivery, (child)birth; labour
'parvi ecc vb vedi **parere**
parzi'ale [par'tsjale] ag (limitato) partial; (non obiettivo) biased, partial
pasco'lare vt, vi to graze
'pascolo sm pasture
'Pasqua sf Easter; **Pas'quetta** sf Easter Monday
pas'sabile ag fairly good, passable
pas'saggio [pas'saddʒo] sm passing no pl, passage; (traversata) crossing no pl, passage; (luogo, prezzo della traversata, brano di libro ecc) passage; (su veicolo altrui) lift (BRIT), ride; (Sport) pass; **di ~** (persona) passing through; **può darmi un ~ fino alla stazione?** can you give me a lift to the station?; **passaggio a livello** level (BRIT) o grade (US) crossing; **passaggio pedonale** pedestrian crossing
passamon'tagna [passamon'taɲɲa] sm inv balaclava
pas'sante sm/f passer-by ▷ sm loop
passa'porto sm passport
pas'sare vi (andare) to go; (veicolo, pedone) to pass (by), go by; (fare una breve sosta: postino ecc) to come, call; (: amico: per fare una visita) to call o drop in; (sole, aria, luce) to get through; (trascorrere: giorni, tempo) to pass, go by; (fig: proposta di legge) to be passed; (: dolore) to pass, go away; (Carte) to pass ▷ vt (attraversare) to cross; (trasmettere: messaggio): **~ qc a qn** to pass sth on to sb; (dare): **~ qc a qn** to pass sth to sb, give sb sth; (trascorrere: tempo) to spend; (superare: esame) to pass; (triturare: verdura) to strain; (approvare) to pass, approve; (oltrepassare, sorpassare: anche fig) to go

beyond, pass; (fig: subire) to go through; **mi passa il sale/l'olio per favore?** could you pass the salt/oil please?; **~ da ... a** to pass from ... to; **~ di padre in figlio** to be handed down o to pass from father to son; **~ per** (anche fig) to go through; **~ per stupido/un genio** to be taken for a fool/a genius; **~ sopra** (anche fig) to pass over; **~ attraverso** (anche fig) to go through; **~ alla storia** to pass into history; **~ a un esame** to go up (to the next class) after an exam; **~ inosservato** to go unnoticed; **~ di moda** to go out of fashion; **le passo il Signor X** (al telefono) here is Mr X; I'm putting you through to Mr X; **lasciar ~ qn/qc** to let sb/sth through; **come te la passi?** how are you getting on o along?

passa'tempo sm pastime, hobby

pas'sato, -a ag past; (sfiorito) faded ▷ sm past; (Ling) past (tense); **passato prossimo/remoto** (Ling) present perfect/past historic; **passato di verdura** (Cuc) vegetable purée

passeg'gero, -a [passed'dʒero] ag passing ▷ sm/f passenger

passeggi'are [passed'dʒare] vi to go for a walk; (in veicolo) to go for a drive; **passeggi'ata** sf walk; drive; (luogo) promenade; **fare una passeggiata** to go for a walk (o drive); **passeg'gino** sm pushchair (BRIT), stroller (US)

passe'rella sf footbridge; (di nave, aereo) gangway; (pedana) catwalk

'passero sm sparrow

passi'one sf passion

pas'sivo, -a ag passive ▷ sm (Ling) passive; (Econ) debit; (: complesso dei debiti) liabilities pl

'passo sm step; (andatura) pace; (rumore) (foot)step; (orma) footprint; (passaggio, fig: brano) passage; (valico) pass; **a ~ d'uomo** at walking pace; **~ (a) ~** step by step; **fare due** o **quattro passi** to go for a walk o a stroll; **di questo ~** at this rate; **"passo carraio"** "vehicle entrance — keep clear"

'pasta sf (Cuc) dough; (: impasto per dolce) pastry; (: anche: **~ alimentare**) pasta; (massa molle di materia) paste; (fig: indole) nature; **paste** sfpl (pasticcini) pastries; **pasta in brodo** noodle soup; **pasta sfoglia** puff pastry o paste (US)

pastasci'utta [pastaʃ'ʃutta] sf pasta

pas'tella sf batter

pas'tello sm pastel

pasticce'ria [pastittʃe'ria] sf (pasticcini) pastries pl, cakes pl; (negozio) cake shop; (arte) confectionery

pasticci'ere, -a [pastit'tʃɛre] sm/f pastrycook; confectioner

pastic'cino [pastit'tʃino] sm petit four

pas'ticcio [pas'tittʃo] sm (Cuc) pie; (lavoro disordinato, imbroglio) mess; **trovarsi nei pasticci** to get into trouble

pas'tiglia [pas'tiʎʎa] sf pastille, lozenge

pas'tina sf small pasta shapes used in soup

'pasto sm meal

pas'tore sm shepherd; (Rel) pastor, minister; (anche: **cane ~**) sheepdog; **pastore tedesco** (Zool) Alsatian, German shepherd

pa'tata sf potato; **patate fritte** chips (BRIT), French fries; **pata'tine** sfpl (potato) crisps; **patatine fritte** chips

pa'tente sf licence; **patente di guida** driving licence (BRIT), driver's license (US); **patente a punti** driving licence with penalty points

Attenzione! In inglese esiste la parola patent, che però significa brevetto.

paternità sf paternity, fatherhood

pa'tetico, -a, -ci, -che ag pathetic; (commovente) moving, touching

pa'tibolo sm gallows sg, scaffold

'patina sf (su rame ecc) patina; (sulla lingua) fur, coating

pa'tire vt, vi to suffer

pa'tito, -a sm/f enthusiast, fan, lover

patolo'gia [patolo'dʒia] sf pathology

'patria sf homeland

pa'trigno [pa'triɲɲo] sm stepfather

patri'monio sm estate, property; (fig) heritage

pa'trono sm (Rel) patron saint; (socio di patronato) patron; (Dir) counsel

patteggi'are [patted'dʒare] vt, vi to negotiate; (Dir) to plea-bargain

patti'naggio [patti'naddʒo] sm skating; **pattinaggio a rotelle/sul ghiaccio** roller-/ice-skating

patti'nare vi to skate; **~ sul ghiaccio** to ice-skate; **pattina'tore, -'trice** sm/f skater; **pattino** sm skate; (di slitta) runner; (Aer) skid; (Tecn) sliding block; **pattini in linea** Rollerblades®; **pattini da ghiaccio/a rotelle** ice/roller skates

'patto sm (accordo) pact, agreement; (condizione) term, condition; **a ~ che** on condition that

pat'tuglia [pat'tuʎʎa] sf (Mil) patrol

pattu'ire vt to reach an agreement on

pattumi'era sf (dust)bin (BRIT), ashcan (US)

pa'ura sf fear; **aver ~ di/di fare/che** to be frightened o afraid of/of doing/that; **far ~ a** to frighten; **per ~ di/che** for fear of/that; **pau'roso, -a** ag (che fa paura) frightening; (che ha paura) fearful, timorous

'pausa sf (sosta) break; (nel parlare, Mus) pause

pavi'mento sm floor

Attenzione! In inglese esiste la parola pavement, che però significa marciapiede.

pa'vone sm peacock

pazien'tare [pattsjen'tare] vi to be patient

pazi'ente [pat'tsjɛnte] ag, sm/f patient; **pazi'enza** sf patience

paz'zesco, -a, -schi, -sche [pat'tsesko] ag mad, crazy

paz'zia [pat'tsia] sf (Med) madness, insanity; (azione) folly; (di azione, decisione) madness, folly

'pazzo, -a ['pattso] ag (Med) mad, insane; (strano) wild, mad ▷ sm/f madman/woman; **~ di** (gioia, amore ecc) mad o crazy with; **~ per qc/qn** mad o crazy about sth/sb

PC [pit'tʃi] sigla m inv (= personal computer) PC; **PC portatile** laptop

pec'care vi to sin; (fig) to err

pec'cato sm sin; **è un ~ che** it's a pity that; **che ~!** what a shame o pity!

peccherò ecc [pekke'rɔ] vb vedi **peccare**

'pece ['petʃe] sf pitch

Pe'chino [pe'kino] sf Beijing

'pecora sf sheep; **peco'rino** sm sheep's milk cheese

pe'daggio [pe'daddʒo] sm toll

pedago'gia [pedago'dʒia] sf pedagogy, educational methods pl

peda'lare vi to pedal; (andare in bicicletta) to cycle

pe'dale sm pedal

pe'dana sf footboard; (Sport: nel salto) springboard; (: nella scherma) piste

pe'dante ag pedantic ▷ sm/f pedant

pe'data sf (impronta) footprint; (colpo) kick; **prendere a pedate qn/qc** to kick sb/sth

pedi'atra, -i, -e sm/f paediatrician

pedi'cure sm/f inv chiropodist

pe'dina sf (della dama) draughtsman (BRIT), draftsman (US); (fig) pawn

pedi'nare vt to shadow, tail

pe'dofilo, -a ag, sm/f paedophile

pedo'nale ag pedestrian

pe'done, -a sm/f pedestrian ▷ sm (Scacchi) pawn

'peggio ['pɛddʒo] av, ag inv worse ▷ sm o f **il** o **la ~** the worst; **alla ~** at worst, if the worst comes to the worst; **peggio'rare** vt to make worse, worsen ▷ vi to grow worse, worsen; **peggi'ore** ag (comparativo) worse; (superlativo) worst ▷ sm/f **il(la) peggiore** the worst (person)

'pegno ['peɲɲo] sm (Dir) security, pledge; (nei giochi di società) forfeit; (fig) pledge, token; **dare in ~ qc** to pawn sth

pe'lare vt (spennare) to pluck; (spellare) to skin; (sbucciare) to peel; (fig) to make pay through the nose

pe'lato, -a ag **pomodori pelati** tinned tomatoes

'pelle sf skin; (di animale) skin, hide; (cuoio) leather; **avere la ~ d'oca** to have goose pimples o goose flesh

pellegri'naggio [pellegri'naddʒo] sm pilgrimage

pelle'rossa (pl **pelli'rosse**) sm/f Red Indian

pelli'cano sm pelican

pel'liccia, -ce [pel'littʃa] sf (mantello di animale) coat, fur; (indumento) fur coat; **pelliccia ecologica** fake fur

pel'licola sf (membrana sottile) film, layer; (Fot, Cinema) film

'pelo sm hair; (pelame) coat, hair; (pelliccia) fur; (di tappeto) pile; (di liquido) surface; **per un ~: per un ~ non ho perduto il treno** I very nearly missed the train; **c'è mancato un ~ che affogasse** he escaped drowning by the skin of his teeth; **pe'loso, -a** ag hairy

'peltro sm pewter

pe'luche [pə'lyʃ] sm plush; **giocattoli di ~** soft toys

pe'luria sf down

'pena sf (Dir) sentence; (punizione) punishment; (sofferenza) sadness no pl, sorrow; (fatica) trouble no pl, effort; (difficoltà) difficulty; **far ~** to be pitiful; **mi fai ~** I feel sorry for you; **prendersi** o **darsi la ~ di fare** to go to the trouble of doing; **pena di morte** death sentence; **pena pecuniaria** fine; **pe'nale** ag penal

pen'dente ag hanging; leaning ▷ sm (ciondolo) pendant; (orecchino) drop earring

'pendere vi (essere appeso): **~ da** to hang from; (essere inclinato) to lean; (fig: incombere): **~ su** to hang over

pen'dio, -'dii sm slope, slant; (luogo in pendenza) slope

'pendola sf pendulum clock

pendo'lare sm/f commuter

pendo'lino sm high-speed train

pene'trante ag piercing, penetrating

pene'trare vi to come o get in ▷ vt to penetrate; **~ in** to enter; (proiettile) to penetrate; (: acqua, aria) to go o come into

penicil'lina [penitʃil'lina] sf penicillin

pe'nisola sf peninsula

penitenzi'ario [peniten'tsjarjo] sm prison

'penna *sf* (*di uccello*) feather; (*per scrivere*) pen; **penne** *sfpl* (*Cuc*) quills (*type of pasta*); **penna a sfera** ballpoint pen; **penna stilografica** fountain pen

penna'rello *sm* felt(-tip) pen

pen'nello *sm* brush; (*per dipingere*) (paint)brush; **a ~** (*perfettamente*) to perfection, perfectly; **pennello per la barba** shaving brush

pe'nombra *sf* half-light, dim light

pen'sare *vi* to think ▷ *vt* to think; (*inventare, escogitare*) to think out; **~ a** to think of; (*amico, vacanze*) to think of o about; (*problema*) to think about; **~ di fare qc** to think of doing sth; **ci penso io** I'll see to o take care of it

pensi'ero *sm* thought; (*modo di pensare, dottrina*) thinking *no pl*; (*preoccupazione*) worry, care, trouble; **stare in ~ per qn** to be worried about sb; **pensie'roso, -a** *ag* thoughtful

'pensile *ag* hanging

pensio'nato, -a *sm/f* pensioner

pensi'one *sf* (*al prestatore di lavoro*) pension; (*vitto e alloggio*) board and lodging; (*albergo*) boarding house; **andare in ~** to retire; **mezza ~** half board; **pensione completa** full board

pen'tirsi *vpr* **~ di** to repent of; (*rammaricarsi*) to regret, be sorry for

'pentola *sf* pot; **pentola a pressione** pressure cooker

pe'nultimo, -a *ag* last but one (BRIT), next to last, penultimate

penzo'lare [pendzo'lare] *vi* to dangle, hang loosely

'pepe *sm* pepper; **pepe in grani/macinato** whole/ground pepper

peperon'cino [peperon'tʃino] *sm* chilli pepper

pepe'rone *sm* pepper, capsicum; (*piccante*) chili

pe'pita *sf* nugget

⊙ PAROLA CHIAVE

per *prep* **1** (*moto attraverso luogo*) through; **i ladri sono passati per la finestra** the thieves got in (*o* out) through the window; **l'ho cercato per tutta la casa** I've searched the whole house *o* all over the house for it

2 (*moto a luogo*) for, to; **partire per la Germania/il mare** to leave for Germany/the sea; **il treno per Roma** the Rome train, the train for *o* to Rome

3 (*stato in luogo*): **seduto/sdraiato per terra** sitting/lying on the ground

4 (*tempo*) for; **per anni/lungo tempo** for years/a long time; **per tutta l'estate** throughout the summer, all summer long; **lo rividi per Natale** I saw him again at Christmas; **lo faccio per lunedì** I'll do it for Monday

5 (*mezzo, maniera*) by; **per lettera/via aerea/ferrovia** by letter/airmail/rail; **prendere qn per un braccio** to take sb by the arm

6 (*causa, scopo*) for; **assente per malattia** absent because of *o* through *o* owing to illness; **ottimo per il mal di gola** excellent for sore throats

7 (*limitazione*) for; **è troppo difficile per lui** it's too difficult for him; **per quel che mi riguarda** as far as I'm concerned; **per poco che sia** however little it may be; **per questa volta ti perdono** I'll forgive you this time

8 (*prezzo, misura*) for; (*distributivo*) a, per; **venduto per 3 milioni** sold for 3 million; **1 euro per persona** 1 euro a *o* per person; **uno per volta** one at a time; **uno per uno** one by one; **5 per cento** 5 per cent; **3 per 4 fa 12** 3 times 4 equals 12; **dividere/moltiplicare 12 per 4** to divide/multiply 12 by 4

9 (*in qualità di*) as; (*al posto di*) for; **avere qn per professore** to have sb as a teacher; **ti ho preso per Mario** I mistook you for Mario, I thought you were Mario; **dare per morto qn** to give sb up for dead

10 (*seguito da vb: finale*): **per fare qc** so as to do sth, in order to do sth; (*: causale*): **per aver fatto qc** for having done sth; (*: consecutivo*): **è abbastanza grande per andarci da solo** he's big enough to go on his own

'pera *sf* pear

per'bene *ag inv* respectable, decent ▷ *av* (*con cura*) properly, well

percentu'ale [pertʃentu'ale] *sf* percentage

perce'pire [pertʃe'pire] *vt* (*sentire*) to perceive; (*ricevere*) to receive

⊙ PAROLA CHIAVE

perché [per'ke] *av* why; **perché no?** why not?; **perché non vuoi andarci?** why don't you want to go?; **spiegami perché l'hai fatto** tell me why you did it

▷ *cong* **1** (*causale*) because; **non posso uscire perché ho da fare** I can't go out because *o* as I've a lot to do

2 (*finale*) in order that, so that; **te lo do perché tu lo legga** I'm giving it to you so (that) you can read it

3 (consecutivo): **è troppo forte perché si possa batterlo** he's too strong to be beaten
▷ sm inv reason; **il perché di** the reason for

perciò [per'tʃɔ] cong so, for this (o that) reason

per'correre vt (luogo) to go all over; (: paese) to travel up and down, go all over; (distanza) to cover

per'corso, -a pp di **percorrere** ▷ sm (tragitto) journey; (tratto) route

percu'otere vt to hit, strike

percussi'one sf percussion; **strumenti a ~** (Mus) percussion instruments

'perdere vt to lose; (lasciarsi sfuggire) to miss; (sprecare: tempo, denaro) to waste ▷ vi to lose; (serbatoio ecc) to leak; **perdersi** vpr (smarrirsi) to get lost; (svanire) to disappear, vanish; **mi sono perso** I'm lost; **ho perso il portafoglio/passaporto** I've lost my wallet/passport; **abbiamo perso il treno** we missed our train; **saper ~** to be a good loser; **lascia ~!** forget it!, never mind!

perdigi'orno [perdi'dʒorno] sm/f inv idler, waster

'perdita sf loss; (spreco) waste; (fuoriuscita) leak; **siamo in ~** (Comm) we are running at a loss; **a ~ d'occhio** as far as the eye can see

perdo'nare vt to pardon, forgive; (scusare) to excuse, pardon

per'dono sm forgiveness; (Dir) pardon

perduta'mente av desperately, passionately

pe'renne ag eternal, perpetual, perennial; (Bot) perennial

perfetta'mente av perfectly; **sai ~ che ...** you know perfectly well that ...

per'fetto, -a ag perfect ▷ sm (Ling) perfect (tense)

perfeziona'mento [perfettsjona'mento] sm **~ (di)** improvement (in), perfection (of); **corso di ~** proficiency course

perfezio'nare [perfettsjo'nare] vt to improve, perfect; **perfezionarsi** vpr to improve

perfezi'one [perfet'tsjone] sf perfection

per'fino av even

perfo'rare vt to perforate, to punch a hole (o holes) in; (banda, schede) to punch; (trivellare) to drill

perga'mena sf parchment

perico'lante ag precarious

pe'ricolo sm danger; **mettere in ~** to endanger, put in danger; **perico'loso, -a** ag dangerous

perife'ria sf (di città) outskirts pl

pe'rifrasi sf circumlocution

pe'rimetro sm perimeter

peri'odico, -a, -ci, -che ag periodic(al); (Mat) recurring ▷ sm periodical

pe'riodo sm period

peripe'zie [peripet'tsie] sfpl ups and downs, vicissitudes

pe'rito, -a ag expert, skilled ▷ sm/f expert; (agronomo, navale) surveyor; **perito chimico** qualified chemist

peri'zoma, -i [peri'dzoma] sm G-string

'perla sf pearl; **per'lina** sf bead

perlus'trare vt to patrol

perma'loso, -a ag touchy

perma'nente ag permanent ▷ sf permanent wave, perm; **perma'nenza** sf permanence; (soggiorno) stay

perme'are vt to permeate

per'messo, -a pp di **permettere** ▷ sm (autorizzazione) permission, leave; (dato a militare, impiegato) leave; (licenza) licence, permit; (Mil: foglio) pass; **~?, è ~?** (posso entrare?) may I come in?; (posso passare?) excuse me; **permesso di lavoro/pesca** work/fishing permit; **permesso di soggiorno** residence permit

per'mettere vt to allow, permit; **~ a qn qc/di fare qc** to allow sb sth/to do sth; **permettersi qc/di fare qc** to allow o.s. sth/to do sth; (avere la possibilità) to afford sth/to do sth

per'misi ecc vb vedi **permettere**

per'nacchia [per'nakkja] (fam) sf **fare una ~** to blow a raspberry

per'nice [per'nitʃe] sf partridge

'perno sm pivot

pernot'tare vi to spend the night, stay overnight

'pero sm pear tree

però cong (ma) but; (tuttavia) however, nevertheless

perpendico'lare ag, sf perpendicular

per'plesso, -a ag perplexed; uncertain, undecided

perqui'sire vt to search; **perquisizi'one** sf (police) search

'perse ecc vb vedi **perdere**

persecuzi'one [persekut'tsjone] sf persecution

persegui'tare vt to persecute

perseve'rante ag persevering

'persi ecc vb vedi **perdere**

persi'ana sf shutter; **persiana avvolgibile** roller shutter

per'sino av = **perfino**

persis'tente ag persistent

'perso, -a pp di **perdere**

per'sona sf person; (qualcuno): **una ~** someone, somebody; (espressione interrogativa +) anyone o anybody

perso'naggio [perso'naddʒo] sm (persona

ragguardevole) personality, figure; (*tipo*) character, individual; (*Letteratura*) character

perso'nale *ag* personal ▷ *sm* staff; personnel; (*figura fisica*) build

personalità *sf inv* personality

perspi'cace [perspi'katʃe] *ag* shrewd, discerning

persu'adere *vt* **~ qn (di qc/a fare)** to persuade sb (of sth/to do)

per'tanto *cong* (*quindi*) so, therefore

'pertica, -che *sf* pole

perti'nente *ag* **~ (a)** relevant (to), pertinent (to)

per'tosse *sf* whooping cough

perturbazi'one [perturbat'tsjone] *sf* disruption; perturbation; **perturbazione atmosferica** atmospheric disturbance

per'vadere *vt* to pervade

per'verso, -a *ag* depraved; perverse

perver'tito, -a *sm/f* pervert

p.es. *abbr* (= *per esempio*) e.g.

pe'sante *ag* heavy; **è troppo ~** it's too heavy

pe'sare *vt* to weigh ▷ *vi* (*avere un peso*) to weigh; (*essere pesante*) to be heavy; (*fig*) to carry weight; **~ su** (*fig*) to lie heavy on; to influence; to hang over; **pesarsi** *vpr* to weigh o.s.; **~ le parole** to weigh one's words; **~ sulla coscienza** to weigh on sb's conscience; **mi pesa ammetterlo** I don't like admitting it; **tutta la responsabilità pesa su di lui** all the responsibility rests on him; **è una situazione che mi pesa** I find the situation difficult; **il suo parere pesa molto** his opinion counts for a lot

'pesca (*pl* **pesche**) (: *frutto*) *sf* peach; (*il pescare*) fishing; **andare a ~** to go fishing; **~ con la lenza** angling; **pesca di beneficenza** (*lotteria*) lucky dip

pes'care *vt* (*pesce*) to fish for; to catch; (*qc nell'acqua*) to fish out; (*fig: trovare*) to get hold of, find; **andare a ~** to go fishing

pesca'tore *sm* fisherman; angler

'pesce ['peʃʃe] *sm* fish *gen inv*; **Pesci** (*dello zodiaco*) Pisces; **pesce d'aprile!** April Fool!; **pesce rosso** goldfish; **pesce spada** swordfish; **pesce'cane** *sm* shark

pesche'reccio [peske'rettʃo] *sm* fishing boat

pesche'ria [peske'ria] *sf* fishmonger's (shop) (BRIT), fish store (US)

pescherò *ecc* [peske'rɔ] *vb vedi* **pescare**

'peso *sm* weight; (*Sport*) shot; **rubare sul ~** to give short weight; **essere di ~ a qn** (*fig*) to be a burden to sb; **peso lordo/netto** gross/net weight; **peso massimo/medio** (*Pugilato*) heavy/middleweight

pessi'mismo *sm* pessimism; **pessi'mista,**

-i, -e *ag* pessimistic ▷ *sm/f* pessimist

'pessimo, -a *ag* very bad, awful

pes'tare *vt* to tread on, trample on; (*sale, pepe*) to grind; (*uva, aglio*) to crush; (*fig: picchiare*): **~ qn** to beat sb up

'peste *sf* plague; (*persona*) nuisance, pest

pes'tello *sm* pestle

'petalo *sm* (*Bot*) petal

pe'tardo *sm* firecracker, banger (BRIT)

petizi'one [petit'tsjone] *sf* petition

petroli'era *sf* (*nave*) oil tanker

pe'trolio *sm* oil, petroleum; (*per lampada, fornello*) paraffin

> Attenzione! In inglese esiste la parola *petrol* che però significa *benzina*.

pettego'lare *vi* to gossip

pettego'lezzo [pettego'leddzo] *sm* gossip *no pl*; **fare pettegolezzi** to gossip

pet'tegolo, -a *ag* gossipy ▷ *sm/f* gossip

petti'nare *vt* to comb (the hair of); **pettinarsi** *vpr* to comb one's hair; **pettina'tura** (*acconciatura*) hairstyle

'pettine *sm* comb; (*Zool*) scallop

petti'rosso *sm* robin

'petto *sm* chest; (*seno*) breast, bust; (*Cuc: di carne bovina*) brisket; (: *di pollo ecc*) breast; **a doppio ~** (*abito*) double-breasted

petu'lante *ag* insolent

'pezza ['pettsa] *sf* piece of cloth; (*toppa*) patch; (*cencio*) rag, cloth

pez'zente [pet'tsɛnte] *sm/f* beggar

'pezzo ['pettso] *sm* (*gen*) piece; (*brandello, frammento*) piece, bit; (*di macchina, arnese ecc*) part; (*Stampa*) article; (*di tempo*): **aspettare un ~** to wait quite a while *o* some time; **in** *o* **a pezzi** in pieces; **andare in pezzi** to break into pieces; **un bel ~ d'uomo** a fine figure of a man; **abito a due pezzi** two-piece suit; **pezzo di cronaca** (*Stampa*) report; **pezzo grosso** (*fig*) bigwig; **pezzo di ricambio** spare part

pi'accio *ecc* ['pjattʃo] *vb vedi* **piacere**

pia'cente [pja'tʃɛnte] *ag* attractive

pia'cere [pja'tʃere] *vi* to please; **una ragazza che piace** a likeable girl; an attractive girl; **~ a: mi piace** I like it; **quei ragazzi non mi piacciono** I don't like those boys; **gli~bbe andare al cinema** he would like to go to the cinema ▷ *sm* pleasure; (*favore*) favour; **"~!"** (*nelle presentazioni*) "pleased to meet you!"; **~ (di conoscerla)** nice to meet you; **con ~** certainly, with pleasure; **per ~!** please; **fare un ~ a qn** to do sb a favour; **pia'cevole** *ag* pleasant, agreeable

pi'acqui *ecc* *vb vedi* **piacere**

pi'aga, -ghe *sf* (*lesione*) sore; (*ferita: anche fig*) wound; (*fig: flagello*) scourge, curse; (: *persona*) pest, nuisance

piagnuco'lare [pjaɲɲuko'lare] vi to whimper

pianeggi'ante [pjaned'dʒante] ag flat, level

piane'rottolo sm landing

pia'neta sm (Astr) planet

pi'angere ['pjandʒere] vi to cry, weep; (occhi) to water ▷ vt to cry, weep; (lamentare) to bewail, lament; **~ la morte di qn** to mourn sb's death

pianifi'care vt to plan

pia'nista, -i, -e sm/f pianist

pi'ano, -a ag (piatto) flat, level; (Mat) plane; (chiaro) clear, plain ▷ av (adagio) slowly; (a bassa voce) softly; (con cautela) slowly, carefully ▷ sm (Mat) plane; (Geo) plain; (livello) level, plane; (di edificio) floor; (programma) plan; (Mus) piano; **a che ~ si trova?** what floor is it on?; **pian ~** very slowly; (poco a poco) little by little; **in primo/secondo ~** in the foreground/background; **di primo ~** (fig) prominent, high-ranking

piano'forte sm piano, pianoforte

piano'terra sm inv ground floor

pi'ansi ecc vb vedi **piangere**

pi'anta sf (Bot) plant; (Anat: anche: **~ del piede**) sole (of the foot); (grafico) plan; (topografica) map; **in ~ stabile** on the permanent staff; **pian'tare** vt to plant; (conficcare) to drive o hammer in; (tenda) to put up, pitch; (fig: lasciare) to leave, desert; **piantarsi** vpr **piantarsi davanti a qn** to plant o.s. in front of sb; **piantala!** (fam) cut it out!

pianter'reno sm = **pianoterra**

pia'nura sf plain

pi'astra sf plate; (di pietra) slab; (di fornello) hotplate; **panino alla ~** ≈ toasted sandwich; **piastra di registrazione** tape deck

pias'trella sf tile

pias'trina sf (Mil) identity disc

piatta'forma sf (anche fig) platform

piat'tino sm saucer

pi'atto, -a ag flat; (fig: scialbo) dull ▷ sm (recipiente, vivanda) dish; (portata) course; (parte piana) flat (part); **piatti** smpl (Mus) cymbals; **piatto fondo** soup dish; **piatto forte** main course; **piatto del giorno** dish of the day, plat du jour; **piatto del giradischi** turntable; **piatto piano** dinner plate

pi'azza ['pjattsa] sf square; (Comm) market; **far ~ pulita** to make a clean sweep; **piazza d'armi** (Mil) parade ground; **piaz'zale** sm (large) square; **piaz'zola** [pjat'tsɔla] sf (Aut) lay-by; (di tenda) pitch

pic'cante ag hot, pungent; (fig) racy; biting

pic'chetto [pik'ketto] sm (Mil, di scioperanti) picket; (di tenda) peg

picchi'are [pik'kjare] vt (persona: colpire) to hit, strike; (: prendere a botte) to beat (up); (battere) to beat; (sbattere) to bang ▷ vi (bussare) to knock; (: con forza) to bang; (colpire) to hit, strike; (sole) to beat down; **picchi'ata** sf (Aer) dive

'picchio ['pikkjo] sm woodpecker

pic'cino, -a [pit'tʃino] ag tiny, very small

picci'one [pit'tʃone] sm pigeon

'picco, -chi sm peak; **a ~** vertically

'piccolo, -a ag small; (oggetto, mano, di età: bambino) small, little; (dav sostantivo: di breve durata: viaggio) short; (fig) mean, petty ▷ sm/f child, little one

pic'cone sm pick(-axe)

pic'cozza [pik'kɔttsa] sf ice-axe

pic'nic sm inv picnic

pi'docchio [pi'dɔkkjo] sm louse

pi'ede sm foot; (di mobile) leg; **in piedi** standing; **a piedi** on foot; **a piedi nudi** barefoot; **su due piedi** (fig) at once; **prendere ~** (fig) to gain ground, catch on; **sul ~ di guerra** (Mil) ready for action; **piede di porco** crowbar

pi'ega, -ghe sf (piegatura, Geo) fold; (di gonna) pleat; (di pantaloni) crease; (grinza) wrinkle, crease; **prendere una brutta ~** (fig) to take a turn for the worse

pie'gare vt to fold; (braccia, gambe, testa) to bend ▷ vi to bend; **piegarsi** vpr to bend; (fig): **piegarsi (a)** to yield (to), submit (to)

pieghe'rò ecc [pjege'rɔ] vb vedi **piegare**

pie'ghevole ag pliable, flexible; (porta) folding

Pie'monte sm **il ~** Piedmont

pi'ena sf (di fiume) flood, spate

pi'eno, -a ag full; (muro, mattone) solid ▷ sm (colmo) height, peak; (carico) full load; **~ di** full of; **in ~ giorno** in broad daylight; **il ~, per favore** (Aut) fill it up, please

piercing ['pirsing] sm piercing; **farsi il ~ all'ombelico** to have one's navel pierced

pietà sf pity; (Rel) piety; **senza ~** pitiless, merciless; **avere ~ di** (compassione) to pity, feel sorry for; (misericordia) to have pity o mercy on

pie'tanza [pje'tantsa] sf dish, course

pie'toso, -a ag (compassionevole) pitying, compassionate; (che desta pietà) pitiful

pi'etra sf stone; **pietra preziosa** precious stone, gem

'piffero sm (Mus) pipe

pigi'ama, -i [pi'dʒama] sm pyjamas pl

pigli'are [piʎ'ʎare] vt to take, grab; (afferrare) to catch

'pigna ['piɲɲa] sf pine cone
pi'gnolo, -a [piɲ'ɲɔlo] ag pernickety
pi'grizia [pi'grittsja] sf laziness
'pigro, -a ag lazy
PIL sigla m (= prodotto interno lordo) GDP
'pila sf (catasta, di ponte) pile; (Elettr) battery; (torcia) torch (BRIT), flashlight
pi'lastro sm pillar
'pile ['pail] sm inv fleece
'pillola sf pill; **prendere la ~** to be on the pill
pi'lone sm (di ponte) pier; (di linea elettrica) pylon
pi'lota, -i, -e sm/f pilot; (Aut) driver
▷ ag inv pilot cpd; **pilota automatico** automatic pilot
pinaco'teca, -che sf art gallery
pi'neta sf pinewood
ping-'pong [piŋ'pɔŋ] sm table tennis
pingu'ino sm (Zool) penguin
'pinna sf (di pesce) fin; (di cetaceo, per nuotare) flipper
'pino sm pine (tree); **pi'nolo** sm pine kernel
'pinza ['pintsa] sf pliers pl; (Med) forceps pl; (Zool) pincer
pinzette [pin'tsette] sfpl tweezers
pi'oggia, -ge ['pjɔddʒa] sf rain; **pioggia acida** acid rain
pi'olo sm peg; (di scala) rung
piom'bare vi to fall heavily; (gettarsi con impeto): **~ su** to fall upon, assail ▷ vt (dente) to fill; **piomba'tura** sf (di dente) filling
piom'bino sm (sigillo) (lead) seal; (del filo a piombo) plummet; (Pesca) sinker
pi'ombo sm (Chim) lead; **a ~** (cadere) straight down; **senza ~** (benzina) unleaded
pioni'ere, -a sm/f pioneer
pi'oppo sm poplar
pi'overe vb impers to rain ▷ vi (fig: scendere dall'alto) to rain down; (lettere, regali) to pour into; **piovig'ginare** vb impers to drizzle; **pio'voso, -a** ag rainy
pi'ovra sf octopus
pi'ovve ecc vb vedi **piovere**
'pipa sf pipe
pipì (fam) sf **fare ~** to have a wee (wee)
pipis'trello sm (Zool) bat
pi'ramide sf pyramid
pi'rata, -i sm pirate; **pirata della strada** hit-and-run driver; **pirata informatica** hacker
Pire'nei smpl **i ~** the Pyrenees
pi'romane sm/f pyromaniac; arsonist
pi'roscafo sm steamer, steamship
pisci'are [piʃʃare] (fam!) vi to piss (!), pee (!)
pi'scina [piʃʃina] sf (swimming) pool; (stabilimento) (swimming) baths pl
pi'sello sm pea

piso'lino sm nap
'pista sf (traccia) track, trail; (di stadio) track; (di pattinaggio) rink; (da sci) run; (Aer) runway; (di circo) ring; **pista da ballo** dance floor
pis'tacchio [pis'takkjo] sm pistachio (tree); pistachio (nut)
pis'tola sf pistol, gun
pis'tone sm piston
pi'tone sm python
pit'tore, -'trice sm/f painter; **pitto'resco, -a, -schi, -sche** ag picturesque
pit'tura sf painting; **pittu'rare** vt to paint

◯ PAROLA CHIAVE

più av **1** (in maggiore quantità) more; **più del solito** more than usual; **in più, di più** more; **ne voglio di più** I want some more; **ci sono 3 persone in o di più** there are 3 more o extra people; **più o meno** more or less; **per di più** (inoltre) what's more, moreover

2 (comparativo) more; (aggettivo corto +) ...er; **più ... di/che** more ... than; **lavoro più di te/Paola** I work harder than you/Paola; **è più intelligente che ricco** he's more intelligent than rich

3 (superlativo) most; (aggettivo corto +) ...est; **il più grande/intelligente** the biggest/most intelligent; **è quello che compro più spesso** that's the one I buy most often; **al più presto** as soon as possible; **al più tardi** at the latest

4 (negazione): **non ... più** no more, no longer; **non ho più soldi** I've got no more money, I don't have any more money; **non lavoro più** I'm no longer working, I don't work any more; **a più non posso** (gridare) at the top of one's voice; (correre) as fast as one can

5 (Mat) plus; **4 più 5 fa 9** 4 plus 5 equals 9; **più 5 gradi** 5 degrees above freezing, plus 5 ▷ prep plus ▷ ag inv **1**: **più ... (di)** more ... (than); **più denaro/tempo** more money/time; **più persone di quante ci aspettassimo** more people than we expected

2 (numerosi, diversi) several; **l'aspettai per più giorni** I waited for it for several days ▷ sm **1** (la maggior parte): **il più è fatto** most of it is done

2 (Mat) plus (sign)

3: **i più** the majority

---

pi'uma sf feather; **piu'mino** sm (eider)down; (per letto) eiderdown; (: tipo *danese*) duvet, continental quilt; (*giacca*) quilted jacket (*with goose-feather padding*); (*per cipria*) powder puff; (*per spolverare*) feather duster

piut'tosto *av* rather; **~ che** (*anziché*) rather than

'pizza ['pittsa] *sf* pizza; **pizze'ria** *sf* place *where pizzas are made, sold or eaten*

pizzi'care [pittsi'kare] *vt* (*stringere*) to nip, pinch; (*pungere*) to sting, to bite; (*Mus*) to pluck ▷ *vi* (*prudere*) to itch, be itchy; (*cibo*) to be hot o spicy

'pizzico, -chi ['pittsiko] *sm* (*pizzicotto*) pinch, nip; (*piccola quantità*) pinch, dash; (*d'insetto*) sting; bite

pizzi'cotto [pittsi'kɔtto] *sm* pinch, nip

'pizzo ['pittso] *sm* (*merletto*) lace; (*barbetta*) goatee beard

plagi'are [pla'dʒare] *vt* (*copiare*) to plagiarize

plaid [plɛd] *sm inv* (*travelling*) rug (*BRIT*), lap robe (*US*)

pla'nare *vi* (*Aer*) to glide

'plasma *sm* plasma

plas'mare *vt* to mould, shape

'plastica, -che *sf* (*arte*) plastic arts *pl*; (*Med*) plastic surgery; (*sostanza*) plastic; **plastica facciale** face lift

'platano *sm* plane tree

pla'tea *sf* (*Teatro*) stalls *pl*

'platino *sm* platinum

plau'sibile *ag* plausible

pleni'lunio *sm* full moon

'plettro *sm* plectrum

pleu'rite *sf* pleurisy

'plico, -chi *sm* (*pacco*) parcel; **in ~ a parte** (*Comm*) under separate cover

plo'tone *sm* (*Mil*) platoon; **plotone d'esecuzione** firing squad

plu'rale *ag, sm* plural

PM *abbr* (*Pol*) = **Pubblico Ministero**; (= *Polizia Militare*) MP (*Military Police*)

pneu'matico, -a, -ci, -che *ag* inflatable; pneumatic ▷ *sm* (*Aut*) tyre (*BRIT*), tire (*US*)

po' *av, sm vedi* **poco**

PAROLA CHIAVE

'poco, -a, -chi, -che *ag* (*quantità*) little, not much; (*numero*) few, not many; **poco pane/denaro/spazio** little o not much bread/money/space; **poche persone/ idee** few o not many people/ideas; **ci vediamo tra poco** (*sottinteso: tempo*) see you soon
▷ *av* **1** (*in piccola quantità*) little, not much; (*numero limitato*) few, not many; **guadagna poco** he doesn't earn much, he earns little

2 (*con ag, av*) (a) little, not very; **sta poco bene** he isn't very well; **è poco più vecchia di lui** she's a little o slightly older than him

3 (*tempo*): **poco dopo/prima** shortly afterwards/before; **il film dura poco** the film doesn't last very long; **ci vediamo molto poco** we don't see each other very often, we hardly ever see each other

4: **un po'** a little, a bit; **è un po' corto** it's a little o a bit short; **arriverà fra un po'** he'll arrive shortly o in a little while

5: **a dir poco** to say the least; **a poco a poco** little by little; **per poco non cadevo** I nearly fell; **è una cosa da poco** it's nothing, it's of no importance; **una persona da poco** a worthless person
▷ *pron* (a) little

po'dere *sm* (*Agr*) farm

'podio *sm* dais, platform; (*Mus*) podium

po'dismo *sm* (*Sport*) track events *pl*

poe'sia *sf* (*arte*) poetry; (*componimento*) poem

po'eta, -'essa *sm/f* poet/poetess

poggi'are [pod'dʒare] *vt* to lean, rest; (*posare*) to lay, place; **poggia'testa** *sm inv* (*Aut*) headrest

'poggio ['pɔddʒo] *sm* hillock, knoll

'poi *av* then; (*alla fine*) finally, at last; **e ~** (*inoltre*) and besides; **questa ~ (è bella)!** (*ironico*) that's a good one!

poiché [poi'ke] *cong* since, as

'poker *sm* poker

po'lacco, -a, -chi, -che *ag* Polish ▷ *sm/f* Pole

po'lare *ag* polar

po'lemica, che *sf* controversy

po'lemico, -a, -ci, -che *ag* polemic(al), controversial

po'lenta *sf* (*Cuc*) sort of thick porridge made with maize flour

'polio(mie'lite) *sf* polio(myelitis)

'polipo *sm* polyp

polisti'rolo *sm* polystyrene

po'litica, -che *sf* politics *sg*; (*linea di condotta*) policy; (*anche*: **politico**); **politica'mente** *av* politically; **politicamente corretto** politically correct

po'litico, -a, -ci, -che *ag* political ▷ *sm/f* politician

poli'zia [polit'tsia] *sf* police; **polizia giudiziaria** ≈ Criminal Investigation Department (*BRIT*), ≈ Federal Bureau of Investigation (*US*); **polizia stradale** traffic police; **polizi'esco, -a, -schi, -sche** *ag* police *cpd*; (*film, romanzo*) detective *cpd*; **polizi'otto** *sm* policeman; **cane poliziotto** police dog; **donna poliziotto**

policewoman; **poliziotto di quartiere** local police officer

'polizza ['pɔlittsa] *sf* (*Comm*) bill; **~ di assicurazione** insurance policy; **polizza di carico** bill of lading

pol'laio *sm* henhouse

'pollice ['pɔllitʃe] *sm* thumb

'polline *sm* pollen

'pollo *sm* chicken

pol'mone *sm* lung; **polmone d'acciaio** (*Med*) iron lung; **polmo'nite** *sf* pneumonia; **polmonite atipica** SARS

'polo *sm* (*Geo, Fisica*) pole; (*gioco*) polo; **polo nord/sud** North/South Pole

Po'lonia *sf* **la ~** Poland

'polpa *sf* flesh, pulp; (*carne*) lean meat

pol'paccio [pol'pattʃo] *sm* (*Anat*) calf

polpas'trello *sm* fingertip

pol'petta *sf* (*Cuc*) meatball

'polpo *sm* octopus

pol'sino *sm* cuff

'polso *sm* (*Anat*) wrist; (*pulsazione*) pulse; (*fig: forza*) drive, vigour

pol'trire *vi* to laze about

pol'trona *sf* armchair; (*Teatro: posto*) seat in the front stalls (*BRIT*) o orchestra (*US*)

'polvere *sf* dust; (*sostanza ridotta minutissima*) powder, dust; **latte in ~** dried o powdered milk; **caffè in ~** instant coffee; **sapone in ~** soap powder; **polvere da sparo/pirica** gunpowder

po'mata *sf* ointment, cream

po'mello *sm* knob

pome'riggio [pome'riddʒo] *sm* afternoon

'pomice ['pɔmitʃe] *sf* pumice

'pomo *sm* (*mela*) apple; (*ornamentale*) knob; (*di sella*) pommel; **pomo d'Adamo** (*Anat*) Adam's apple

pomo'doro *sm* tomato; **pomodori pelati** skinned tomatoes

'pompa *sf* pump; (*sfarzo*) pomp (and ceremony); **pompe funebri** funeral parlour *sg* (*BRIT*), undertaker's *sg*; **pompa di benzina** petrol (*BRIT*) o gas (*US*) pump; (*distributore*) filling o gas (*US*) station; **pom'pare** *vt* to pump; (*trarre*) to pump out; (*gonfiare d'aria*) to pump up

pom'pelmo *sm* grapefruit

pompi'ere *sm* fireman

po'nente *sm* west

pongo, poni *ecc vb vedi* **porre**

'ponte *sm* bridge; (*di nave*) deck; (: *anche:* **~ di comando**) bridge; (*impalcatura*) scaffold; **fare il ~** (*fig*) to take the extra day off (*between 2 public holidays*); **governo ~** interim government; **ponte aereo** airlift; **ponte levatoio** drawbridge; **ponte sospeso** suspension bridge

pon'tefice [pon'tefitʃe] *sm* (*Rel*) pontiff

'popcorn ['pɔpkɔːn] *sm inv* popcorn

popo'lare *ag* popular; (*quartiere, clientela*) working-class ▷ *vt* (*rendere abitato*) to populate; **popolarsi** *vpr* to fill with people, get crowded; **popolazi'one** *sf* population

'popolo *sm* people

'poppa *sf* (*di nave*) stern; (*seno*) breast

porcel'lana [portʃel'lana] *sf* porcelain, china; piece of china

porcel'lino, -a [portʃel'lino] *sm/f* piglet; **porcellino d'India** guinea pig

porche'ria [porke'ria] *sf* filth, muck; (*fig: oscenità*) obscenity; (: *azione disonesta*) dirty trick; (: *cosa mal fatta*) rubbish

por'cile [por'tʃile] *sm* pigsty

por'cino, -a [por'tʃino] *ag* of pigs, pork *cpd* ▷ *sm* (*fungo*) type of edible mushroom

'porco, -ci *sm* pig; (*carne*) pork

porcos'pino *sm* porcupine

'porgere ['pɔrdʒere] *vt* to hand, give; (*tendere*) to hold out

pornogra'fia *sf* pornography; **porno'grafico, -a, -ci, -che** *ag* pornographic

'poro *sm* pore

'porpora *sf* purple

'porre *vt* (*mettere*) to put; (*collocare*) to place; (*posare*) to lay (down), put (down); (*fig: supporre*): **poniamo (il caso) che ...** let's suppose that ...

'porro *sm* (*Bot*) leek; (*Med*) wart

'porsi *ecc vb vedi* **porgere**

'porta *sf* door; (*Sport*) goal; **portaba'gagli** *sm inv* (*facchino*) porter; (*Aut, Ferr*) luggage rack; **porta-CD** [portatʃi'di] *sm inv* (*mobile*) CD rack; (*astuccio*) CD holder; **porta'cenere** *sm inv* ashtray; **portachi'avi** *sm inv* keyring; **porta'erei** *sf inv* (*nave*) aircraft carrier; **portafi'nestra** (*pl* **portefi'nestre**) *sf* French window; **porta'foglio** *sm* wallet; (*Pol, Borsa*) portfolio; **non trovo il portafoglio** I can't find my wallet; **portafor'tuna** *sm inv* lucky charm; mascot

por'tale *sm* (*di chiesa, Inform*) portal

porta'mento *sm* carriage, bearing

portamo'nete *sm inv* purse

por'tante *ag (muro ecc)* supporting, load-bearing

portan'tina *sf* sedan chair; *(per ammalati)* stretcher

portaom'brelli *sm inv* umbrella stand

porta'pacchi [porta'pakki] *sm inv (di moto, bicicletta)* luggage rack

por'tare *vt (sostenere, sorreggere: peso, bambino, pacco)* to carry; *(indossare: abito, occhiali)* to wear; *(: capelli lunghi)* to have; *(avere: nome, titolo)* to have, bear; *(recare):* **~ qc a qn** to take (o bring) sth to sb; *(fig: sentimenti)* to bear

portasiga'rette *sm inv* cigarette case

por'tata *sf (vivanda)* course; *(Aut)* carrying *(o loading)* capacity; *(di arma)* range; *(volume d'acqua)* (rate of) flow; *(fig: limite)* scope, capability; *(: importanza)* impact, import; **alla ~ di tutti** *(conoscenza)* within everybody's capabilities; *(prezzo)* within everybody's means; **a/fuori ~ (di)** within/out of reach (of); **a ~ di mano** within (arm's) reach

por'tatile *ag* portable

por'tato, -a *ag (incline):* **~ a** inclined *o* apt to

portau'ovo *sm inv* eggcup

porta'voce [porta'votʃe] *sm/f inv* spokesman/woman

por'tento *sm* wonder, marvel

porti'era *sf (Aut)* door

porti'ere *sm (portinaio)* concierge, caretaker; *(di hotel)* porter; *(nel calcio)* goalkeeper

porti'naio, -a *sm/f* concierge, caretaker

portine'ria *sf* caretaker's lodge

'porto, -a *pp di* **porgere** ▷ *sm (Naut)* harbour, port ▷ *sm inv* port (wine); **porto d'armi** *(documento)* gun licence

Porto'gallo *sm* **il ~** Portugal; **porto'ghese** *ag, sm/f, sm* Portuguese *inv*

por'tone *sm* main entrance, main door

portu'ale *ag* harbour *cpd,* port *cpd* ▷ *sm* dock worker

porzi'one [por'tsjone] *sf* portion, share; *(di cibo)* portion, helping

'posa *sf (Fot)* exposure; *(atteggiamento, di modello)* pose

po'sare *vt* to put (down), lay (down) ▷ *vi (ponte, edificio, teoria):* **~ su** to rest on; *(Fot: atteggiarsi)* to pose; **posarsi** *vpr (aereo)* to land; *(uccello)* to alight; *(sguardo)* to settle

po'sata *sf* piece of cutlery

pos'critto *sm* postscript

'posi *ecc vb vedi* **porre**

posi'tivo, -a *ag* positive

posizi'one [pozit'tsjone] *sf* position; **prendere ~** *(fig)* to take a stand; **luci di ~** *(Aut)* sidelights

pos'porre *vt* to place after; *(differire)* to postpone, defer

posse'dere *vt* to own, possess; *(qualità, virtù)* to have, possess

posses'sivo, -a *ag* possessive

pos'sesso *sm* ownership *no pl;* possession

posses'sore *sm* owner

pos'sibile *ag* possible ▷ *sm* **fare tutto il ~** to do everything possible; **nei limiti del ~** as far as possible; **al più tardi ~** as late as possible; **possibilità** *sf inv* possibility ▷ *sfpl (mezzi)* means; **aver la possibilità di fare** to be in a position to do; to have the opportunity to do

possi'dente *sm/f* landowner

possi'edo *ecc vb vedi* **possedere**

'posso *ecc vb vedi* **potere**

'posta *sf (servizio)* post, postal service; *(corrispondenza)* post, mail; *(ufficio postale)* post office; *(nei giochi d'azzardo)* stake; **Poste** *sfpl (amministrazione)* post office; **c'è ~ per me?** are there any letters for me?; **ministro delle Poste e Telecomunicazioni** Postmaster General; **posta aerea** airmail; **posta elettronica** E-mail, e-mail, electronic mail; **posta ordinaria** ≈ second-class mail; **posta prioritaria** ≈ first-class post; **pos'tale** *ag* postal, post office *cpd*

posteggi'are [posted'dʒare] *vt, vi* to park; **pos'teggio** *sm* car park (BRIT), parking lot (US); *(di taxi)* rank (BRIT), stand (US)

'poster *sm inv* poster

posteri'ore *ag (dietro)* back; *(dopo)* later ▷ *sm (fam: sedere)* behind

postici'pare [postitʃi'pare] *vt* to defer, postpone

pos'tino *sm* postman (BRIT), mailman (US)

'posto, -a *pp di* **porre** ▷ *sm (sito, posizione)* place; *(impiego)* job; *(spazio libero)* room, space; *(di parcheggio)* space, *(sedile: al teatro, in treno ecc)* seat; *(Mil)* post; **a ~ (in ordine)** in place, tidy; *(fig)* settled; *(: persona)* reliable; **vorrei prenotare due posti** I'd like to book two seats; **al ~ di** in place of; **sul ~** on the spot; **mettere a ~** to tidy (up), put in order; *(faccende)* to straighten out; **posto di blocco** roadblock; **posto di lavoro** job; **posti in piedi** *(in teatro, in autobus)* standing room; **posto di polizia** police station

po'tabile *ag* drinkable; **acqua ~** drinking water

po'tare *vt* to prune

po'tassio *sm* potassium

po'tente *ag (nazione)* strong, powerful; *(veleno, farmaco)* potent, strong; **po'tenza** *sf* power; *(forza)* strength

potenzi'ale [poten'tsjale] *ag, sm* potential

 PAROLA CHIAVE

po'tere *sm* power; **al potere** (*partito ecc*) in power; **potere d'acquisto** purchasing power
▷ *vb aus* **1** (*essere in grado di*) can, be able to; **non ha potuto ripararlo** he couldn't *o* he wasn't able to repair it; **non è potuto venire** he couldn't *o* he wasn't able to come; **spiacente di non poter aiutare** sorry not to be able to help
2 (*avere il permesso*) can, may, be allowed to; **posso entrare?** can *o* may I come in?; **si può sapere dove sei stato?** where on earth have you been?
3 (*eventualità*) may, might, could; **potrebbe essere vero** it might *o* could be true; **può aver avuto un incidente** he may *o* might *o* could have had an accident; **può darsi** perhaps; **può darsi** *o* **essere che non venga** he may *o* might not come
4 (*augurio*): **potessi almeno parlargli!** if only I could speak to him!
5 (*suggerimento*): **potresti almeno scusarti!** you could at least apologize!
▷ *vt* can, be able to; **può molto per noi** he can do a lot for us; **non ne posso più** (*per stanchezza*) I'm exhausted; (*per rabbia*) I can't take any more

potrò *ecc vb vedi* **potere**
'povero, -a *ag* poor; (*disadorno*) plain, bare ▷ *sm/f* poor man/woman; **i poveri** the poor; **~ di** lacking in, having little; **povertà** *sf* poverty
poz'zanghera [pot'tsangera] *sf* puddle
'pozzo ['pottso] *sm* well; (*cava: di carbone*) pit; (*di miniera*) shaft; **pozzo petrolifero** oil well
P.R.A. [pra] *sigla m* (= *Pubblico Registro Automobilistico*) ≈ DVLA
pran'zare [pran'dzare] *vi* to dine, have dinner; (*a* **to lunch, have lunch**
'pranzo ['prandzo] *sm* dinner; (*a mezzogiorno*) lunch
'prassi *sf* usual procedure
'pratica, -che *sf* practice; (*esperienza*) experience; (*conoscenza*) knowledge, familiarity; (*tirocinio*) training, practice; (*Amm: affare*) matter, case; (*: incartamento*) file, dossier; **in ~** (*praticamente*) in practice; **mettere in ~** to put into practice
prati'cabile *ag* (*progetto*) practicable, feasible; (*luogo*) passable, practicable
pratica'mente *av* (*in modo pratico*) in a practical way, practically; (*quasi*) practically, almost

prati'care *vt* to practise; (*Sport: tennis ecc*) to play; (*: nuoto, scherma ecc*) to go in for; (*eseguire: apertura, buco*) to make; **~ uno sconto** to give a discount
'pratico, -a, -ci, -che *ag* practical; **~ di** (*esperto*) experienced *o* skilled in; (*familiare*) familiar with
'prato *sm* meadow; (*di giardino*) lawn
preav'viso *sm* notice; **telefonata con ~** personal *o* person to person call
pre'cario, -a *ag* precarious; (*Ins*) temporary
precauzi'one [prekaut'tsjone] *sf* caution, care; (*misura*) precaution
prece'dente [pretfe'dɛnte] *ag* previous ▷ *sm* precedent; **il discorso/film ~** the previous *o* preceding speech/film; **senza precedenti** unprecedented; **precedenti penali** criminal record *sg*; **prece'denza** *sf* priority, precedence; (*Aut*) right of way
pre'cedere [pre'tfɛdere] *vt* to precede, go (*o come*) before
precipi'tare [pretfipi'tare] *vi* (*cadere*) to fall headlong; (*fig: situazione*) to get out of control ▷ *vt* (*gettare dall'alto in basso*) to hurl, fling; (*fig: affrettare*) to rush; **precipitarsi** *vpr* (*gettarsi*) to hurl *o* fling o.s.; (*: affrettarsi*) to rush; **precipi'toso, -a** *ag* (*caduta, fuga*) headlong; (*fig: avventato*) rash, reckless; (*: affrettato*) hasty, rushed
preci'pizio [pretfi'pittsjo] *sm* precipice; **a ~** (*fig: correre*) headlong
precisa'mente [pretfiza'mente] *av* (*gen*) precisely; (*con esattezza*) exactly
preci'sare [pretfi'zare] *vt* to state, specify; (*spiegare*) to explain (in detail)
precisi'one [pretfi'zjone] *sf* precision; accuracy
pre'ciso, -a [pre'tfizo] *ag* (*esatto*) precise; (*accurato*) accurate, precise; (*deciso: idee*) precise, definite; (*uguale*): **2 vestiti precisi** 2 dresses exactly the same; **sono le 9 precise** it's exactly 9 o'clock
pre'cludere *vt* to block, obstruct
pre'coce [pre'kɔtfe] *ag* early; (*bambino*) precocious; (*vecchiaia*) premature
precon'cetto [prekon'tfetto] *sm* preconceived idea, prejudice
precur'sore *sm* forerunner, precursor
'preda *sf* (*bottino*) booty; (*animale, fig*) prey; **essere ~ di** to fall prey to; **essere in ~ a** to be prey to
'predica, -che *sf* sermon; (*fig*) lecture, talking-to
predi'care *vt, vi* to preach
predi'cato *sm* (*Ling*) predicate
predi'letto, -a *pp di* **prediligere** ▷ *ag, sm/f* favourite

predi'ligere [predi'lidʒere] vt to prefer, have a preference for

pre'dire vt to foretell, predict

predis'porre vt to get ready, prepare; **~ qn a qc** to predispose sb to sth

predizi'one [predit'tsjone] sf prediction

prefazi'one [prefat'tsjone] sf preface, foreword

prefe'renza [prefe'rɛntsa] sf preference

prefe'rire vt to prefer, like better; **~ il caffè al tè** to prefer coffee to tea, like coffee better than tea

pre'figgersi [pre'fiddʒersi] vpr **~ uno scopo** to set o.s. a goal

pre'fisso, -a pp di **prefiggere** ▷ sm (Ling) prefix; (Tel) dialling (BRIT) o dial (US) code; **qual è il ~ telefonico di Londra?** what is the dialling code for London?

pre'gare vi to pray ▷ vt (Rel) to pray to; (implorare) to beg; (chiedere): **~ qn di fare** to ask sb to do; **farsi ~** to need coaxing o persuading

pre'gevole [pre'dʒevole] ag valuable

pregherò ecc [prege'rɔ] vb vedi **pregare**

preghi'era [pre'gjɛra] sf (Rel) prayer; (domanda) request

pregi'ato, -a [pre'dʒato] ag (di valore) valuable; **vino ~** vintage wine

'pregio ['prɛdʒo] sm (stima) esteem, regard; (qualità) (good) quality, merit; (valore) value, worth

pregiudi'care [predʒudi'kare] vt to prejudice, harm, be detrimental to

pregiu'dizio [predʒu'dittsjo] sm (idea errata) prejudice; (danno) harm no pl

'prego escl (a chi ringrazia) don't mention it!; (invitando qn ad accomodarsi) please sit down!; (invitando qn ad andare prima) after you!

pregus'tare vt to look forward to

prele'vare vt (denaro) to withdraw; (campione) to take; (polizia) to take, capture

preli'evo sm (di denaro) withdrawal; (Med): **fare un ~ (di)** to take a sample (of); **prelievo di sangue, fare un ~ di sangue** to take a blood sample

prelimi'nare ag preliminary

'premere vt to press ▷ vi **~ su** to press down on; (fig) to put pressure on; **~ a** (fig: importare) to matter to

pre'mettere vt to put before; (dire prima) to start by saying, state first

premi'are vt to give a prize to; (fig: merito, onestà) to reward

premiazi'one [premjat'tsjone] sf prize giving

'premio sm prize; (ricompensa) reward; (Comm) premium; (Amm: indennità) bonus

pre'misi ecc vb vedi **premettere**

premu'nirsi vpr **~ di** to provide o.s. with; **~ contro** to protect o.s. from, guard o.s. against

pre'mura sf (fretta) haste, hurry; (riguardo) attention, care; **premure** sfpl (attenzioni, cure) care sg; **aver ~** to be in a hurry; **far ~ a qn** to hurry sb; **usare ogni ~ nei riguardi di qn** to be very attentive to sb; **premu'roso, -a** ag thoughtful, considerate

'prendere vt to take; (andare a prendere) to get, fetch; (ottenere) to get; (guadagnare) to get, earn; (catturare: ladro, pesce) to catch; (collaboratore, dipendente) to take on; (passeggero) to pick up; (chiedere: somma, prezzo) to charge, ask; (trattare: persona) to handle ▷ vi (colla, cemento) to set; (pianta) to take; (fuoco: nel camino) to catch; (voltare): **~ a destra** to turn (to the) right; **prendersi** vpr (azzuffarsi): **prendersi a pugni** to come to blows; **dove si prende il traghetto per...** where do we get the ferry to ...; **prendi qualcosa?** (da bere, da mangiare) would you like something to eat (o drink)?; **prendo un caffè** I'll have a coffee; **~ qn/qc per** (scambiare) to take sb/sth for; **~ fuoco** to catch fire; **~ parte a** to take part in; **prendersi cura di qn/qc** to look after sb/sth; **prendersela** (adirarsi) to get annoyed; (preoccuparsi) to get upset, worry

preno'tare vt to book, reserve; **vorrei ~ una camera doppia** I'd like to book a double room; **ho prenotato un tavolo al nome di ...** I booked a table in the name of ...; **prenotazi'one** sf booking, reservation; **ho confermato la prenotazione per fax/e-mail** I confirmed my booking by fax/e-mail

preoccu'pare vt to worry; to preoccupy; **preoccuparsi** vpr **preoccuparsi di qn/qc** to worry about sb/sth; **preoccuparsi per qn** to be anxious for sb; **preoccupazi'one** sf worry, anxiety

prepa'rare vt to prepare; (esame, concorso) to prepare for; **prepararsi** vpr (vestirsi) to get ready; **prepararsi a qc/a fare** to get ready o prepare (o.s.) for sth/to do; **~ da mangiare** to prepare a meal; **prepara'tivi** smpl preparations

preposizi'one [prepozit'tsjone] sf (Ling) preposition

prepo'tente ag (persona) domineering, arrogant; (bisogno, desiderio) overwhelming, pressing ▷ sm/f bully

'presa sf taking no pl; catching no pl; (di città) capture; (indurimento: di cemento) setting; (appiglio, Sport) hold; (di acqua, gas) (supply) point; (piccola quantità: di sale *ecc*) pinch; (*Carte*) trick; **far ~** (*colla*) to set; **far ~ sul pubblico** to catch the public's imagination; **essere alle prese con** (*fig*) to be struggling with; **presa d'aria** air inlet; **presa (di corrente)** (*Elettr*) socket; (: *al muro*) point

pre'sagio [pre'zadʒo] *sm* omen

'presbite *ag* long-sighted

pres'crivere *vt* to prescribe

'prese *ecc vb vedi* **prendere**

presen'tare *vt* to present; (*far conoscere*): **~ qn (a)** to introduce sb (to); (*Amm: inoltrare*) to submit; **presentarsi** *vpr* (*recarsi, farsi vedere*) to present o.s., appear; (*farsi conoscere*) to introduce o.s.; (*occasione*) to arise; **presentarsi come candidato** (*Pol*) to stand as a candidate; **presentarsi bene/male** to have a good/poor appearance

pre'sente *ag* present; (*questo*) this ▷ *sm* present; **i presenti** those present; **aver ~ qc/qn** to remember sth/sb; **presenti** (*persone*) people present; **aver ~ qc/qn** to remember sth/sb; **tenere ~ qn/qc** to keep sth/sb in mind

presenti'mento *sm* premonition

pre'senza [pre'zɛntsa] *sf* presence; (*aspetto esteriore*) appearance; **presenza di spirito** presence of mind

pre'sepio, pre'sepe *sm* crib

preser'vare *vt* to protect; to save; **preserva'tivo** *sm* sheath, condom

'presi *ecc vb vedi* **prendere**

'preside *sm/f* (*Ins*) head (teacher) (*BRIT*), principal (*US*); (*di facoltà universitaria*) dean; **preside di facoltà** (*Univ*) dean of faculty

presi'dente *sm* (*Pol*) president; (*di assemblea, Comm*) chairman; **presidente del consiglio** prime minister

presi'edere *vt* to preside over ▷ *vi* **~ a** to direct, be in charge of

pressap'poco *av* about, roughly

pres'sare *vt* to press

pressi'one *sf* pressure; **far ~ su qn** to put pressure on sb; **pressione sanguigna** blood pressure; **pressione atmosferica** atmospheric pressure

'presso *av* (*vicino*) nearby, close at hand ▷ *prep* (*vicino a*) near; (*accanto a*) beside, next to; (*in casa di*): **~ qn** at sb's home; (*nelle lettere*) care of, c/o; (*alle dipendenze di*): **lavora ~ di noi** he works for o with us ▷ *smpl* **nei pressi di** near, in the vicinity of

pres'tante *ag* good-looking

pres'tare *vt* **~ (qc a qn)** to lend (sb sth o sth to sb); **prestarsi** *vpr* (*offrirsi*): **prestarsi a fare** to offer to do; (*essere adatto*): **prestarsi a** to lend itself to, be suitable for; **mi può ~ dei soldi?** can you

lend me some money?; **~ aiuto** to lend a hand; **~ attenzione** to pay attention; **~ fede a qc/qn** to give credence to sth/sb; **~ orecchio** to listen; **prestazi'one** *sf* (*Tecn, Sport*) performance

prestigia'tore, -'trice [prestidʒa'tore] *sm/f* conjurer

pres'tigio [pres'tidʒo] *sm* (*fama*) prestige; (*illusione*): **gioco di ~** conjuring trick

'prestito *sm* lending *no pl*; loan; **dar in ~** to lend; **prendere in ~** to borrow

'presto *av* (*tra poco*) soon; (*in fretta*) quickly; (*di buon'ora*) early; **a ~** see you soon; **fare ~ a fare qc** to hurry up and do sth; (*non costare fatica*) to have no trouble doing sth; **si fa ~ a criticare** it's easy to criticize

pre'sumere *vt* to presume, assume

pre'sunsi *ecc vb vedi* **presumere**

presuntu'oso, -a *ag* presumptuous

presunzi'one [prezun'tsjone] *sf* presumption

'prete *sm* priest

preten'dente *sm/f* pretender ▷ *sm* (*corteggiatore*) suitor

pre'tendere *vt* (*esigere*) to demand, require; (*sostenere*): **~ che** to claim that; **pretende di aver sempre ragione** he thinks he's always right

> Attenzione! In inglese esiste il verbo *to pretend*, che però significa *far finta*.

pre'tesa *sf* (*esigenza*) claim, demand; (*presunzione, sforzo*) pretentiousness; **senza pretese** unpretentious

pre'testo *sm* pretext, excuse

preva'lere *vi* to prevail

preve'dere *vt* (*indovinare*) to foresee; (*presagire*) to foretell; (*considerare*) to make provision for

preve'nire *vt* (*anticipare*) to forestall; to anticipate; (*evitare*) to avoid, prevent

preven'tivo, -a *ag* preventive ▷ *sm* (*Comm*) estimate

prevenzi'one [preven'tsjone] *sf* prevention; (*preconcetto*) prejudice

previ'dente *ag* showing foresight; prudent; **previ'denza** *sf* foresight; **istituto di previdenza** provident institution; **previdenza sociale** social security (*BRIT*), welfare (*US*)

pre'vidi *ecc vb vedi* **prevedere**

previsi'one *sf* forecast, prediction; **previsioni meteorologiche** weather forecast *sg*; **previsioni del tempo** weather forecast *sg*

pre'visto, -a *pp di* **prevedere** ▷ *sm* **più/ meno del ~** more/less than expected

prezi'oso, -a [pret'tsjoso] *ag* precious; invaluable ▷ *sm* jewel; valuable

prez'zemolo [pret'tsemolo] *sm* parsley

'prezzo ['prɛttso] *sm* price; **prezzo d'acquisto/di vendita** buying/selling price

prigi'one [pri'dʒone] *sf* prison; **prigioni'ero, -a** *ag* captive ▷ *sm/f* prisoner

'prima *sf* (*Teatro*) first night; (*Cinema*) première; (*Aut*) first gear; *vedi anche* **primo** ▷ *av* before; (*in anticipo*) in advance, beforehand; (*per l'addietro*) at one time, formerly; (*più presto*) sooner, earlier; (*in primo luogo*) first ▷ *cong* **~ di fare/che parta** before doing/he leaves; **~ di** before; **~ o poi** sooner or later

pri'mario, -a *ag* primary; (*principale*) chief, leading, primary ▷ *sm* (*Med*) chief physician

prima'tista, -i, e *sm/f* (*Sport*) record holder

pri'mato *sm* supremacy; (*Sport*) record

prima'vera *sf* spring

primi'tivo, -a *ag* primitive; original

pri'mizie [pri'mittsje] *sfpl* early produce *sg*

'primo, -a *ag* first; (*fig*) initial; basic; prime ▷ *sm/f* first (one) ▷ *sm* (*Cuc*) first course; (*in date*): **il ~ luglio** the first of July; **le prime ore del mattino** the early hours of the morning; **ai primi di maggio** at the beginning of May; **viaggiare in prima** to travel first-class; **in ~ luogo** first of all, in the first place; **di prim'ordine** *o* **prima qualità** first-class, first-rate; **in un ~ tempo** at first; **prima donna** leading lady; (*di opera lirica*) prima donna

primordi'ale *ag* primordial

'primula *sf* primrose

princi'pale [printʃi'pale] *ag* main, principal ▷ *sm* manager, boss

principal'mente [printʃipal'mente] *av* mainly, principally

'principe ['printʃipe] *sm* prince; **principe ereditario** crown prince; **princi'pessa** *sf* princess

principi'ante [printʃi'pjante] *sm/f* beginner

prin'cipio [prin'tʃipjo] *sm* (*inizio*) beginning, start; (*origine*) origin, cause; (*concetto, norma*) principle; **al** *o* **in ~** at first; **per ~** on principle; **principi** *smpl* (*concetti fondamentali*) principles; **una questione di ~** a matter of principle

priorità *sf* priority

priori'tario, -a *ag* having priority, of utmost importance

pri'vare *vt* **~ qn di** to deprive sb of; **privarsi di** to go *o* do without

pri'vato, -a *ag* private ▷ *sm/f* private citizen; **in ~** in private

privilegi'are [privile'dʒare] *vt* to grant a privilege to

privilegi'ato, -a [privile'dʒato] *ag* (*individuo, classe*) privileged; (*trattamento, Comm: credito*) preferential; **azioni ~e** preference shares (BRIT), preferred stock (US)

privi'legio [privi'lɛdʒo] *sm* privilege

'privo, -a *ag* **~ di** without, lacking

pro *prep* for, on behalf of ▷ *sm inv* (*utilità*) advantage, benefit; **a che ~?** what's the use?; **il ~ e il contro** the pros and cons

pro'babile *ag* probable, likely; **probabilità** *sf inv* probability

probabil'mente *av* probably

pro'blema, -i *sm* problem

pro'boscide [pro'bɔʃʃide] *sf* (*di elefante*) trunk

pro'cedere [pro'tʃedere] *vi* to proceed; (*comportarsi*) to behave; (*iniziare*): **~ a** to start; **~ contro** (*Dir*) to start legal proceedings against; **proce'dura** *sf* (*Dir*) procedure

proces'sare [protʃes'sare] *vt* (*Dir*) to try

processi'one [protʃes'sjone] *sf* procession

pro'cesso [pro'tʃɛsso] *sm* (*Dir*) trial; proceedings *pl*; (*metodo*) process

pro'cinto [pro'tʃinto] *sm* **in ~ di fare** about to do, on the point of doing

procla'mare *vt* to proclaim

procre'are *vt* to procreate

procu'rare *vt* **~ qc a qn** (*fornire*) to get *o* obtain sth for sb; (*causare: noie ecc*) to bring *o* give sb sth

pro'digio [pro'didʒo] *sm* marvel, wonder; (*persona*) prodigy

pro'dotto, -a *pp di* **produrre** ▷ *sm* product; **prodotti agricoli** farm produce *sg*

pro'duco *ecc vb vedi* **produrre**

pro'durre *vt* to produce

pro'dussi *ecc vb vedi* **produrre**

produzi'one *sf* production; (*rendimento*) output

Prof. *abbr* (= *professore*) Prof.

profa'nare *vt* to desecrate

profes'sare *vt* to profess; (*medicina ecc*) to practise

professio'nale *ag* professional

professi'one *sf* profession; **professio'nista, -i, -e** *sm/f* professional

profes'sore, -'essa *sm/f* (*Ins*) teacher; (: *di università*) lecturer, (: *titolare di cattedra*) professor

pro'filo *sm* profile; (*breve descrizione*) sketch, outline; **di ~** in profile

pro'fitto *sm* advantage, profit, benefit; (*fig: progresso*) progress; (*Comm*) profit

profondità *sf inv* depth

pro'fondo, -a *ag* deep; (*rancore,*

meditazione) profound ▷ *sm* depth(s *pl*),
bottom; **quanto è profonda l'acqua?**
how deep is the water?; **~ 8 metri** 8 metres
deep
°profugo, -a, -ghi, -ghe *sm/f* refugee
profu'mare *vt* to perfume ▷ *vi* to be
fragrant; **profumarsi** *vpr* to put on
perfume *o* scent
profu'mato, -a *ag* (*fiore, aria*) fragrant;
(*fazzoletto, saponetta*) scented; (*pelle*)
sweet-smelling; (*persona*) with perfume on
profume'ria *sf* perfumery; (*negozio*)
perfume shop
pro'fumo *sm* (*prodotto*) perfume, scent;
(*fragranza*) scent, fragrance
proget'tare [prodʒet'tare] *vt* to plan;
(*edificio*) to plan, design; **pro'getto** *sm*
plan; (*idea*) plan, project; **progetto di
legge** bill
pro'gramma, -i *sm* programme; (*TV,
Radio*) programmes *pl*; (*Ins*) syllabus,
curriculum; (*Inform*) program;
program'mare *vt* (*TV, Radio*) to put
on; (*Inform*) to program; (*Econ*) to plan;
programma'tore, -'trice *sm/f* (*Inform*)
computer programmer
progre'dire *vi* to progress, make progress
pro'gresso *sm* progress *no pl*; **fare
progressi** to make progress
proi'bire *vt* to forbid, prohibit
proiet'tare *vt* (*gen, Geom, Cinema*) to
project; (: *presentare*) to show, screen; (*luce,
ombra*) to throw, cast, project; **proi'ettile**
sm projectile, bullet (*o shell ecc*);
proiet'tore *sm* (*Cinema*) projector; (*Aut*)
headlamp; (*Mil*) searchlight; **proiezi'one**
sf (*Cinema*) projection; showing
prolife'rare *vi* (*fig*) to proliferate
pro'lunga, -ghe *sf* (*di cavo ecc*) extension
prolun'gare *vt* (*discorso, attesa*) to
prolong; (*linea, termine*) to extend
prome'moria *sm inv* memorandum
pro'messa *sf* promise
pro'mettere *vt* to promise ▷ *vi* to be *o*
look promising; **~ a qn di fare** to promise
sb that one will do
promi'nente *ag* prominent
pro'misi *ecc vb vedi* **promettere**
promon'torio *sm* promontory, headland
promozi'one [promot'tsjone] *sf*
promotion
promu'overe *vt* to promote
proni'pote *sm/f* (*di nonni*) great-
grandchild, great-grandson/
granddaughter; (*di zii*) great-nephew/
niece
pro'nome *sm* (*Ling*) pronoun
pron'tezza [pron'tettsa] *sf* readiness;
quickness, promptness

°pronto, -a *ag* ready; (*rapido*) fast, quick,
prompt; **quando saranno pronte le mie
foto?** when will my photos be ready?;
~! (*Tel*) hello!; **~ all'ira** quick-tempered;
pronto soccorso (*cure*) first aid; (*reparto*)
A&E (*BRIT*), ER (*US*)
prontu'ario *sm* manual, handbook
pro'nuncia [pro'nuntʃa] *sf* pronunciation
pronunci'are [pronun'tʃare] *vt* (*parola,
sentenza*) to pronounce; (*dire*) to utter;
(*discorso*) to deliver; **come si pronuncia?**
how do you pronounce it?
propa'ganda *sf* propaganda
pro'pendere *vi* **~ per** to favour, lean
towards
propi'nare *vt* to administer
pro'porre *vt* (*suggerire*): **~ qc (a qn)** to
suggest sth (to sb); (*candidato*) to put
forward; (*legge, brindisi*) to propose; **~ di
fare** to suggest *o* propose doing; **proporsi
di fare** to propose *o* intend to do; **proporsi
una meta** to set o.s. a goal
proporzio'nale [proportsjo'nale] *ag*
proportional
proporzi'one [propor'tsjone] *sf*
proportion; **in ~ a** in proportion to;
proporzioni *sfpl* (*dimensioni*) proportions;
di vaste proporzioni huge
pro'posito *sm* (*intenzione*) intention,
aim; (*argomento*) subject, matter; **a ~ di**
regarding, with regard to; **di ~** (*apposta*)
deliberately, on purpose; **a ~** by the way;
capitare a ~ (*cosa, persona*) to turn up at
the right time
proposizi'one [propozit'tsjone] *sf* (*Ling*)
clause; (: *periodo*) sentence
pro'posta *sf* proposal; (*suggerimento*)
suggestion; **proposta di legge** bill
proprietà *sf inv* (*ciò che si possiede*) property
gen no pl, estate; (*caratteristica*) property;
(*correttezza*) correctness; **proprietà
privata** private property; **proprie'tario,
-a** *sm/f* owner; (*di albergo ecc*) proprietor,
owner; (*per l'inquilino*) landlord/lady
°proprio, -a *ag* (*possessivo*) own;
(: *impersonale*) one's; (*esatto*) exact,
correct, proper; (*senso, significato*)
literal; (*Ling: nome*) proper; (*particolare*):
~ di characteristic of, peculiar to ▷ *av*
(*precisamente*) just, exactly; (*davvero*) really;
(*affatto*): **non ... ~** not ... at all; **l'ha visto
con i (suoi) propri occhi** he saw it with
his own eyes
proro'gare *vt* to extend; (*differire*) to
postpone, defer
°prosa *sf* prose
pro'sciogliere [proʃʃoʎʎere] *vt* to release;
(*Dir*) to acquit
prosciu'gare [proʃʃu'gare] *vt* (*terreni*) to

drain, reclaim; **prosciugarsi** *vpr* to dry up
prosci'utto [proʃ'ʃutto] *sm* ham;
  prosciutto cotto/crudo cooked/cured
  ham
prosegui'mento *sm* continuation; **buon**
  ~! all the best!; (*a chi viaggia*) enjoy the rest
  of your journey!
prosegu'ire *vt* to carry on with, continue
  ▷ *vi* to carry on, go on
prospe'rare *vi* to thrive
prospet'tare *vt* (*esporre*) to point out,
  show; **prospettarsi** *vpr* to look, appear
prospet'tiva *sf* (*Arte*) perspective; (*veduta*)
  view; (*fig: previsione, possibilità*) prospect
pros'petto *sm* (*Disegno*) elevation; (*veduta*)
  view, prospect; (*facciata*) façade, front;
  (*tabella*) table; (*sommario*) summary;
  prospetto informativo prospectus
prossimità *sf* nearness, proximity; **in ~ di**
  near (to), close to
'prossimo, -a *ag* (*vicino*): **~ a** near (to),
  close to; (*che viene subito dopo*) next;
  (*parente*) close ▷ *sm* neighbour, fellow man
prostitu'irsi *vpr* to prostitute o.s.
prosti'tuta *sf* prostitute
protago'nista, -i, -e *sm/f* protagonist
pro'teggere [pro'tɛddʒere] *vt* to protect
prote'ina *sf* protein
pro'tendere *vt* to stretch out
pro'testa *sf* protest
protes'tante *ag, sm/f* Protestant
protes'tare *vt, vi* to protest
pro'tetto, -a *pp di* **proteggere**
protezi'one [protet'tsjone] *sf* protection;
  (*patrocinio*) patronage
pro'totipo *sm* prototype
pro'trarre *vt* (*prolungare*) to prolong;
  protrarsi *vpr* to go on, continue
protube'ranza [protube'rantsa] *sf*
  protuberance, bulge
'prova *sf* (*esperimento, cimento*) test,
  trial; (*tentativo*) attempt, try; (*Mat,
  testimonianza, documento ecc.*) proof; (*Dir*)
  evidence *no pl*, proof; (*Ins*) exam, test;
  (*Teatro*) rehearsal; (*di abito*) fitting; **a ~ di** (*in
  testimonianza di*) as proof of; **a ~ di fuoco**
  fireproof; **fino a ~ contraria** until it is
  proved otherwise; **mettere alla ~** to put
  to the test; **giro di ~** test *o* trial run; **prova**
  generale (*Teatro*) dress rehearsal
pro'vare *vt* (*sperimentare*) to test; (*tentare*)
  to try, attempt; (*assaggiare*) to try, taste;
  (*sperimentare in sé*) to experience; (*sentire*)
  to feel; (*cimentare*) to put to the test;
  (*dimostrare*) to prove; (*abito*) to try on; **~ a**
  fare to try *o* attempt to do
proveni'enza [prove'njentsa] *sf* origin,
  source
prove'nire *vi* **~ da** to come from

pro'venti *smpl* revenue *sg*
pro'verbio *sm* proverb
pro'vetta *sf* test tube; **bambino in ~**
  test-tube baby
pro'vider [pro'vaider] *sm inv* (*Inform*)
  service provider
pro'vincia, -ce *o* **cie** [pro'vintʃa] *sf*
  province
pro'vino *sm* (*Cinema*) screen test;
  (*campione*) specimen
provo'cante *ag* (*attraente*) provocative
provo'care *vt* (*causare*) to cause, bring
  about; (*eccitare: riso, pietà*) to arouse;
  (*irritare, sfidare*) to provoke; **provocazi'one**
  sf provocation
provve'dere *vi* (*disporre*): **~ (a)** to provide
  (for); (*prendere un provvedimento*) to take
  steps, act; **provvedi'mento** *sm* measure;
  (*di previdenza*) precaution
provvi'denza [provvi'dɛntsa] *sf* **la ~**
  providence
provvigi'one [provvi'dʒone] *sf* (*Comm*)
  commission
provvi'sorio, -a *ag* temporary
prov'viste *sfpl* supplies
'prua *sf* (*Naut*) bow(s) (*pl*), prow
pru'dente *ag* cautious, prudent;
  (*assennato*) sensible, wise; **pru'denza** *sf*
  prudence, caution; wisdom
'prudere *vi* to itch, be itchy
'prugna ['pruɲɲa] *sf* plum; **prugna secca**
  prune
pru'rito *sm* itchiness *no pl*; itch
P.S. *abbr* (= *postscriptum*) P.S.; (*Polizia*)
  = **Pubblica Sicurezza**
pseu'donimo *sm* pseudonym
psica'nalisi *sf* psychoanalysis
psicana'lista, -i, -e *sm/f* psychoanalyst
'psiche ['psike] *sf* (*Psic*) psyche
psichi'atra, -i, -e [psi'kjatra] *sm/f*
  psychiatrist; **psichi'atrico, -a, -ci, -che** *ag*
  psychiatric
psicolo'gia [psikolo'dʒia] *sf* psychology;
  psico'logico, -a, -ci, -che *ag*
  psychological; **psi'cologo, -a, -gi, -ghe**
  sm/f psychologist
psico'patico, -a, -ci, -che *ag*
  psychopathic ▷ *sm/f* psychopath
pubbli'care *vt* to publish
pubblicazi'one [pubblikat'tsjone] *sf*
  publication
pubblicità [pubblitʃi'ta] *sf* (*diffusione*)
  publicity; (*attività*) advertising; (*annunci nei
  giornali*) advertisements *pl*
'pubblico, -a, -ci, -che *ag* public;
  (*statale: scuola ecc*) state *cpd* ▷ *sm* public;
  (*spettatori*) audience; **in ~** in public; **P~**
  Ministero Public Prosecutor's Office; **la**
  Pubblica Sicurezza the police; **pubblico**

funzionario civil servant

'pube sm (Anat) pubis

pubertà sf puberty

'pudico, -a, -ci, -che ag modest

pu'dore sm modesty

pue'rile ag childish

pugi'lato [pudʒi'lato] sm boxing

'pugile ['pudʒile] sm boxer

pugna'lare [puɲɲa'lare] vt to stab

pu'gnale [puɲ'ɲale] sm dagger

'pugno ['puɲɲo] sm fist; (colpo) punch; (quantità) fistful

'pulce ['pultʃe] sf flea

pul'cino [pul'tʃino] sm chick

pu'lire vt to clean; (lucidare) to polish; **pu'lito, -a** ag (anche fig) clean; (ordinato) neat, tidy; **puli'tura** sf cleaning; **pulitura a secco** dry cleaning; **puli'zia** sf cleaning; cleanness; **fare le pulizie** to do the cleaning o the housework; **pulizia etnica** ethnic cleansing

'pullman sm inv coach

pul'lover sm inv pullover, jumper

pullu'lare vi to swarm, teem

pul'mino sm minibus

'pulpito sm pulpit

pul'sante sm (push-)button

pul'sare vi to pulsate, beat

pul'viscolo sm fine dust; **pulviscolo atmosferico** specks pl of dust

'puma sm inv puma

pun'gente [pun'dʒɛnte] ag prickly; stinging; (anche fig) biting

'pungere ['pundʒere] vt to prick; (insetto, ortica) to sting; (: freddo) to bite

pungigli'one [pundʒiʎ'ʎone] sm sting

pu'nire vt to punish; **punizi'one** sf punishment; (Sport) penalty

'punsi ecc vb vedi **pungere**

'punta sf point; (parte terminale) tip, end; (di monte) peak; (di costa) promontory; (minima parte) touch, trace; **in ~ di piedi** on tip-toe; **ore di ~** peak hours; **uomo di ~** front-rank o leading man

pun'tare vt (piedi a terra, gomiti sul tavolo) to plant; (dirigere: pistola) to point; (scommettere) to bet ▷ vi (mirare): **~ a** to aim at; **~ su** (dirigersi) to head o make for; (fig: contare) to count o rely on

pun'tata sf (gita) short trip; (scommessa) bet; (parte di opera) instalment; **romanzo a puntate** serial

punteggia'tura [puntedddʒa'tura] sf (Ling) punctuation

pun'teggio [pun'teddʒo] sm score

puntel'lare vt to support

pun'tello sm prop, support

pun'tina sf; **puntina da disegno** drawing pin

pun'tino sm dot; **fare qc a ~** to do sth properly

'punto, -a pp di **pungere** ▷ sm (segno, macchiolina) dot; (Ling) full stop; (di indirizzo e-mail) dot; (Mat, momento, di punteggio: fig: argomento) point; (posto) spot; (a scuola) mark; (nel cucire, nella maglia, Med) stitch ▷ av **non ... ~** not at all; **punto cardinale** point of the compass, cardinal point; **punto debole** weak point; **punto esclamativo** exclamation mark; **punto interrogativo** question mark; **punto nero** (comedone) blackhead; **punto di partenza** (anche fig) starting point; **punto di riferimento** landmark; (fig) point of reference; **punto (di) vendita** retail outlet; **punto e virgola** semicolon; **punto di vista** (fig) point of view

puntu'ale ag punctual

pun'tura sf (di ago) prick; (Med) puncture; (: iniezione) injection; (dolore) sharp pain; **puntura d'insetto** sting, bite

> Attenzione! In inglese esiste la parola *puncture*, che si usa per indicare la foratura di una gomma.

punzecchi'are [puntsek'kjare] vt to prick; (fig) to tease

può ecc, **-pu'oi** vb vedi **potere**

pu'pazzo [pu'pattso] sm puppet

pu'pilla sf (Anat) pupil

purché [pur'ke] cong provided that, on condition that

'pure cong (tuttavia) and yet, nevertheless; (anche se) even if ▷ av (anche) too, also; **pur di** (al fine di) just to; **faccia ~!** go ahead!, please do!

purè sm (Cuc) purée; (: di patate) mashed potatoes

pu'rezza [pu'rettsa] sf purity

pur'gante sm (Med) purgative, purge

purga'torio sm purgatory

purifi'care vt to purify; (metallo) to refine

'puro, -a ag pure; (acqua) clear, limpid; (vino) undiluted; **puro'sangue** sm/f inv thoroughbred

pur'troppo av unfortunately

pus sm pus

'pustola sf pimple

puti'ferio sm rumpus, row

putre'fatto, -a pp di **putrefare**

put'tana (fam!) sf whore (!)

puz'zare [put'tsare] vi to stink

'puzzo ['puttso] sm stink, foul smell

'puzzola ['puttsola] sf polecat

puzzo'lente [puttso'lɛnte] ag stinking

pvc [pivi'tʃi] sigla m (= polyvinyl chloride) PVC

q *abbr* (= *quintale*) q.

qua *av* here; **in ~** (*verso questa parte*) this way; **da un anno in ~** for a year now; **da ~ndo in ~?** since when?; **per di ~** (*passare*) this way; **al di ~ di** (*fiume, strada*) on this side of; **~ dentro/fuori** *ecc* in/out here *ecc*; *vedi anche* **questo**

qua'derno *sm* notebook; (*per scuola*) exercise book

qua'drante *sm* quadrant; (*di orologio*) face

qua'drare *vi* (*bilancio*) to balance, tally; (*descrizione*) to correspond ▷ *vt* (*Mat*) to square; **non mi quadra** I don't like it; **qua'drato, -a** *ag* square; (*fig: equilibrato*) level-headed, sensible; (: *peg*) square ▷ *sm* (*Mat*) square; (*Pugilato*) ring; **5 al quadrato** 5 squared

quadri'foglio [kwadri'fɔʎʎo] *sm* four-leaf clover

quadri'mestre *sm* (*periodo*) four-month period; (*Ins*) term

'quadro *sm* (*pittura*) painting, picture; (*quadrato*) square; (*tabella*) table, chart; (*Tecn*) board, panel; (*Teatro*) scene; (*fig: scena, spettacolo*) sight; (: *descrizione*) outline, description; **quadri** *smpl* (*Pol*) party organizers; (*Mil*) cadres; (*Comm*) managerial staff; (*Carte*) diamonds

'quadruplo, -a *ag, sm* quadruple

quaggiù [kwad'dʒu] *av* down here
'quaglia ['kwaʎʎa] *sf* quail

○ **PAROLA CHIAVE**

'qualche ['kwalke] *det* **1** some, a few; (*in interrogative*) any; **ho comprato qualche libro** I've bought some *o* a few books; **qualche volta** sometimes; **hai qualche sigaretta?** have you any cigarettes?
2 (*uno*): **c'è qualche medico?** is there a doctor?; **in qualche modo** somehow
3 (*un certo, parecchio*) some; **un personaggio di qualche rilievo** a figure of some importance
4: **qualche cosa** = **qualcosa**

qual'cosa *pron* something; (*in espressioni interrogative*) anything; **qualcos'altro** something else; anything else; **~ di nuovo** something new; anything new; **~ da mangiare** something to eat; anything to eat; **c'è ~ che non va?** is there something *o* anything wrong?
qual'cuno *pron* (*persona*) someone, somebody; (: *in espressioni interrogative*) anyone, anybody; (*alcuni*) some; **~ è favorevole a noi** some are on our side; **qualcun altro** someone *o* somebody else; anyone *o* anybody else

○ **PAROLA CHIAVE**

'quale (*spesso troncato in* **qual**) *det* **1** (*interrogativo*) what; (: *scegliendo tra due o più cose o persone*) which; **quale uomo/denaro?** what man/money?, which man/money?; **quali sono i tuoi programmi?** what are your plans?; **quale stanza preferisci?** which room do you prefer?
2 (*relativo: come*): **il risultato fu quale ci si aspettava** the result was as expected
3 (*esclamativo*) what; **quale disgrazia!** what bad luck!
▷ *pron* **1** (*interrogativo*) which; **quale dei due scegli?** which of the two do you want?
2 (*relativo*): **il (la) quale** (*persona: soggetto*) who; (: *oggetto, con preposizione*) whom; (*cosa*) which; (*possessivo*) whose; **suo padre, il quale è avvocato, ...** his father, who is a lawyer, ...; **il signore con il quale parlavo** the gentleman to whom I was speaking; **l'albergo al quale ci siamo fermati** the hotel where we stayed *o* which we stayed at; **la signora della quale ammiriamo la bellezza** the lady whose beauty we admire
3 (*relativo: in elenchi*) such as, like; **piante**

quali l'edera plants like o such as ivy; **quale sindaco di questa città** as mayor of this town

qua'lifica, -che sf qualification; (titolo) title

qualifi'cato, -a ag (dotato di qualifica) qualified; (esperto, abile) skilled; **non mi ritengo ~ per questo lavoro** I don't think I'm qualified for this job; **è un medico molto ~** he is a very distinguished doctor

qualificazi'one sf **gara di ~** (Sport) qualifying event

qualità sf inv quality; **in ~ di** in one's capacity as

qua'lora cong in case, if

qual'siasi det inv = **qualunque**

qua'lunque det inv any; (quale che sia) whatever; (discriminativo) whichever; (posposto: mediocre) poor, indifferent; ordinary; **mettiti un vestito ~** put on any old dress; **~ cosa** anything; **~ cosa accada** whatever happens; **a ~ costo** at any cost, whatever the cost; **l'uomo ~** the man in the street; **~ persona** anyone, anybody

'quando cong, av when; **~ sarò ricco** when I'm rich; **da ~** (dacché) since; (interrogativo): **da ~ sei qui?** how long have you been here?; **quand'anche** even if

quantità sf inv quantity; (gran numero): **una ~ di** a great deal of; a lot of; **in grande ~** in large quantities

PAROLA CHIAVE

'quanto, -a det **1** (interrogativo: quantità) how much; (: numero) how many; **quanto pane/denaro?** how much bread/money?; **quanti libri/ragazzi?** how many books/boys?; **quanto tempo?** how long?; **quanti anni hai?** how old are you?

2 (esclamativo): **quante storie!** what a lot of nonsense!; **quanto tempo sprecato!** what a waste of time!

3 (relativo: quantità) as much ... as; (: numero) as many ... as; **ho quanto denaro mi occorre** I have as much money as I need; **prendi quanti libri vuoi** take as many books as you like

▷ pron **1** (interrogativo: quantità) how much; (: numero) how many; (: tempo) how long; **quanto mi dai?** how much will you give me?; **quanti me ne hai portati?** how many did you bring me?; **da quanto sei qui?** how long have you been here?; **quanti ne abbiamo oggi?** what's the date today?

2 (relativo: quantità) as much as; (: numero) as many as; **farò quanto posso** I'll do as much as I can; **possono venire quanti**

sono stati invitati all those who have been invited can come

▷ av **1** (interrogativo: con ag, av) how; (: con vb) how much; **quanto stanco ti sembrava?** how tired did he seem to you?; **quanto corre la tua moto?** how fast can your motorbike go?; **quanto costa?** how much does it cost?; **quant'è?** how much is it?

2 (esclamativo: con ag, av) how; (: con vb) how much; **quanto sono felice!** how happy I am!; **sapessi quanto abbiamo camminato!** if you knew how far we've walked!; **studierò quanto posso** I'll study as much as o all I can; **quanto prima** as soon as possible

3: **in quanto** (in qualità di) as; (perché, per il fatto che) as, since; **(in) quanto a** (per ciò che riguarda) as for, as regards

4: **per quanto** (nonostante, anche se) however; **per quanto si sforzi, non ce la farà** try as he may, he won't manage it; **per quanto sia brava, fa degli errori** however good she may be, she makes mistakes; **per quanto io sappia** as far as I know

qua'ranta num forty

quaran'tena sf quarantine

quaran'tesimo, -a num fortieth

quaran'tina sf **una ~ (di)** about forty

'quarta sf (Aut) fourth (gear); vedi anche **quarto**

quar'tetto sm quartet(te)

quarti'ere sm district, area; (Mil) quarters pl; **quartier generale** headquarters pl

'quarto, -a ag fourth ▷ sm fourth; (quarta parte) quarter; **le 6 e un ~** a quarter past six; **quarti di finale** quarter final; **quarto d'ora** quarter of an hour

'quarzo ['kwartso] sm quartz

'quasi av almost, nearly ▷ cong (anche: **~ che**) as if; **(non) ... ~ mai** hardly ever; **~ ~ me ne andrei** I've half a mind to leave

quassù av up here

quat'tordici [kwat'torditʃi] num fourteen

quat'trini smpl money sg, cash sg

'quattro num four; **in ~ e quattr'otto** in less than no time; **quattro'cento** num four hundred ▷ sm **il Quattrocento** the fifteenth century

PAROLA CHIAVE

'quello, -a (dav sm **quel** + C, **quell'** + V, **quello** + s impura, gn, pn, ps, x, z; pl **quei** + C, **quegli** + V o s impura, gn, pn, ps, x, z; dav sf **quella** + C, **quell'** + V; pl **quelle**) det that; those pl; **quella casa** that house; **quegli**

uomini those men; **voglio quella camicia (lì** o **là)** I want that shirt
▷ pron **1** (*dimostrativo*) that (one), those (ones) pl; (*ciò*) that; **conosci quella?** do you know that woman?; **prendo quello bianco** I'll take the white one; **chi è quello?** who's that?; **prendi quello (lì** o **là)** take that one (there)
2 (*relativo*): **quello(a) che** (*persona*) the one (who); (*cosa*) the one (which), the one (that); **quelli(e) che** (*persone*) those who; (*cose*) those which; **è lui quello che non voleva venire** he's the one who didn't want to come; **ho fatto quello che potevo** I did what I could

'quercia, -ce ['kwɛrtʃa] *sf* oak (tree); (*legno*) oak
que'rela *sf* (*Dir*) (legal) action
que'sito *sm* question, query; problem
questio'nario *sm* questionnaire
questi'one *sf* problem, question; (*controversia*) issue; (*litigio*) quarrel; **in ~** in question; **è ~ di tempo** it's a matter o question of time

---

🔵 **PAROLA CHIAVE**

'questo, -a *det* **1** (*dimostrativo*) this; these pl; **questo libro (qui** o **qua)** this book; **io prendo questo cappotto, tu quello** I'll take this coat, you take that one; **quest'oggi** today; **questa sera** this evening
2 (*enfatico*): **non fatemi più prendere di queste paure** don't frighten me like that again
▷ pron (*dimostrativo*) this (one); these (ones) pl; (*ciò*) this; **prendo questo (qui** o **qua)** I'll take this one; **preferisci questi o quelli?** do you prefer these (ones) or those (ones)?; **questo intendevo io** this is what I meant; **vengono Paolo e Luca: questo da Roma, quello da Palermo** Paolo and Luca are coming: the former from Palermo, the latter from Rome

ques'tura *sf* police headquarters pl
qui *av* here; **da** o **di ~** from here; **di ~ in avanti** from now on; **di ~ a poco/una settimana** in a little while/a week's time; **~ dentro/sopra/vicino** in/up/near here; *vedi anche* **questo**
quie'tanza [kwje'tantsa] *sf* receipt
qui'ete *sf* quiet, quietness; calmness; stillness; peace
qui'eto, -a *ag* quiet; (*notte*) calm, still; (*mare*) calm
'quindi *av* then ▷ *cong* therefore, so

'quindici ['kwinditʃi] *num* fifteen; **~ giorni** a fortnight (BRIT), two weeks
quindi'cina [kwindi'tʃina] *sf* (*serie*): **una ~ (di)** about fifteen; **fra una ~ di giorni** in a fortnight
quinta *sf vedi* **quinto**
quin'tale *sm* quintal (100 kg)
'quinto, -a *num* fifth
quiz [kwidz] *sm inv* (*domanda*) question; (*anche*): **gioco a ~** quiz game
'quota *sf* (*parte*) quota, share; (*Aer*) height, altitude; (*Ippica*) odds pl; **prendere/ perdere ~** (*Aer*) to gain/lose height o altitude; **quota d'iscrizione** enrolment fee; (*a club*) membership fee
quotidi'ano, -a *ag* daily; (*banale*) everyday
▷ *sm* (*giornale*) daily (paper)
quozi'ente [kwot'tsjɛnte] *sm* (*Mat*) quotient; **quoziente d'intelligenza** intelligence quotient, IQ

r

R, r ['ɛrre] *sf o m* (*lettera*) R, r; **R come Roma**
≈ R for Robert (BRIT), R for Roger (US)
'rabbia *sf* (*ira*) anger, rage; (*accanimento*,
furia) fury; (*Med: idrofobia*) rabies *sg*
rab'bino *sm* rabbi
rabbi'oso, -a *ag* angry, furious; (*facile
all'ira*) quick-tempered; (*forze, acqua ecc*)
furious, raging; (*Med*) rabid, mad
rabbo'nire *vt* to calm down
rabbrivi'dire *vi* to shudder, shiver
raccapez'zarsi [rakkapet'tsarsi] *vpr* **non
~** to be at a loss
raccapricci'ante [rakkaprit't∫ante] *ag*
horrifying
raccatta'palle *sm inv* (*Sport*) ballboy
raccat'tare *vt* to pick up
rac'chetta [rak'ketta] *sf* (*per tennis*)
racket; (*per ping-pong*) bat; **racchetta da
neve** snowshoe; **racchetta da sci** ski stick
racchi'udere [rak'kjudere] *vt* to contain
rac'cogliere [rak'kɔʎʎere] *vt* to collect;
(*raccattare*) to pick up; (*frutti, fiori*) to pick,
pluck; (*Agr*) to harvest; (*approvazione, voti*)
to win
rac'colta *sf* collecting *no pl*; collection;
(*Agr*) harvesting *no pl*, gathering *no pl*;
harvest, crop; (*adunata*) gathering;
raccolta differenziata (*dei rifiuti*) *separate
collection of different kinds of household waste*
rac'colto, -a *pp di* **raccogliere** ▷ *ag*
(*persona: pensoso*) thoughtful; (*luogo:
appartato*) secluded, quiet ▷ *sm* (*Agr*) crop,
harvest
raccoman'dabile *ag* (*highly*)
commendable; **è un tipo poco ~** he is not
to be trusted
raccoman'dare *vt* to recommend;
(*affidare*) to entrust; (*esortare*): **~ a qn
di non fare** to tell *o* warn sb not to do;
raccoman'data *sf* (*anche:* **lettera
raccomandata**) recorded-delivery letter
raccon'tare *vt* **~ (a qn)** (*dire*) to tell (sb);
(*narrare*) to relate (to sb), tell (sb) about;
rac'conto *sm* telling *no pl*, relating *no pl*;
(*fatto raccontato*) story, tale; **racconti per
bambini** children's stories
rac'cordo *sm* (*Tecn: giunto*) connection,
joint; (*Aut*): **raccordo anulare** (*Aut*)
ring road (BRIT), beltway (US); **raccordo
autostradale** slip road (BRIT), entrance
(*o exit*) ramp (US); **raccordo ferroviario**
siding; **raccordo stradale** link road
racimo'lare [rat∫imo'lare] *vt* (*fig*) to
scrape together, glean
'rada *sf* (*natural*) harbour
'radar *sm* radar
raddoppi'are *vt, vi* to double
raddriz'zare [raddrit'tsare] *vt* to
straighten; (*fig: correggere*) to put straight,
correct
'radere *vt* (*barba*) to shave off; (*mento*) to
shave; (*fig: rasentare*) to graze; to skim;
radersi *vpr* to shave (o.s.); **~ al suolo** to
raze to the ground
radi'are *vt* to strike off
radia'tore *sm* radiator
radiazi'one [radjat'tsjone] *sf* (*Fisica*)
radiation; (*cancellazione*) striking off
radi'cale *ag* radical ▷ *sm* (*Ling*) root
ra'dicchio [ra'dikkjo] *sm* chicory
ra'dice [ra'dit∫e] *sf* root
'radio *sf inv* radio ▷ *sm* (*Chim*) radium;
radioat'tivo, -a *ag* radioactive;
radio'cronaca, -che *sf* radio
commentary; **radiogra'fia** *sf*
radiography; (*foto*) X-ray photograph
radi'oso, -a *ag* radiant
radios'veglia [radjoz'veʎʎa] *sf* radio
alarm
'rado, -a *ag* (*capelli*) sparse, thin; (*visite*)
infrequent; **di ~** rarely
radu'nare *vt* to gather, assemble;
radunarsi *vpr* to gather, assemble
ra'dura *sf* clearing
raf'fermo, -a *ag* stale
'raffica, -che *sf* (*Meteor*) gust (of wind); (*di
colpi: scarica*) burst of gunfire
raffigu'rare *vt* to represent
raffi'nato, -a *ag* refined

raffor'zare [raffor'tsare] *vt* to reinforce

raffredda'mento *sm* cooling

raffred'dare *vt* to cool; (*fig*) to dampen, have a cooling effect on; **raffreddarsi** *vpr* to grow cool *o* cold; (*prendere un raffreddore*) to catch a cold; (*fig*) to cool (off)

raffred'dato, -a *ag* (*Med*): **essere ~** to have a cold

raffred'dore *sm* (*Med*) cold

raf'fronto *sm* comparison

'rafia *sf* (*fibra*) raffia

rafting ['rafting] *sm* white-water rafting

ra'gazza [ra'gattsa] *sf* girl; (*fam: fidanzato*) girlfriend; **nome da ~** maiden name; **ragazza madre** unmarried mother

ra'gazzo [ra'gattso] *sm* boy; (*fam: fidanzato*) boyfriend; **ragazzi** *smpl* (*figli*) kids; **ciao ragazzi!** (*gruppo*) hi guys!

raggi'ante [rad'dʒante] *ag* radiant, shining

'raggio ['raddʒo] *sm* (*di sole ecc*) ray; (*Mat, distanza*) radius; (*di ruota ecc*) spoke; **raggio d'azione** range; **raggi X** X-rays

raggi'rare [raddʒi'rare] *vt* to take in, trick

raggi'ungere [rad'dʒundʒere] *vt* to reach; (*persona: riprendere*) to catch up (with); (*bersaglio*) to hit; (*fig: meta*) to achieve

raggomito'larsi *vpr* to curl up

raggranel'lare *vt* to scrape together

raggrup'pare *vt* to group (together)

ragiona'mento [radʒona'mento] *sm* reasoning *no pl*; arguing *no pl*; argument

ragio'nare [radʒo'nare] *vi* to reason; **~ di** (*discorrere*) to talk about

ragi'one [ra'dʒone] *sf* reason; (*dimostrazione, prova*) argument, reason; (*diritto*) right; **aver ~** to be right, **aver ~ di qn** to get the better of sb; **dare ~ a qn** to agree with sb; to prove sb right; **perdere la ~** to become insane; (*fig*) to take leave of one's senses; **in ~ di** at the rate of; to the amount of; according to; **a o con ~** rightly, justly; **a ragion veduta** after due consideration; **ragione sociale** (*Comm*) corporate name

ragione'ria [radʒone'ria] *sf* accountancy; accounts department

ragio'nevole [radʒo'nevole] *ag* reasonable

ragioni'ere, -a [radʒo'njɛre] *sm/f* accountant

ragli'are [raʎ'ʎare] *vi* to bray

ragna'tela [raɲɲa'tela] *sf* cobweb, spider's web

'ragno ['raɲɲo] *sm* spider

ragù *sm inv* (*Cuc*) meat sauce; stew

RAI-TV [raiti'vu] *sigla f* = **Radio televisione italiana**

ralle'grare *vt* to cheer up; **rallegrarsi** *vpr* to cheer up; (*provare allegrezza*) to rejoice; **rallegrarsi con qn** to congratulate sb

rallen'tare *vt* to slow down; (*fig*) to lessen, slacken ▷ *vi* to slow down

rallenta'tore *sm* (*Cinema*) slow-motion camera; **al ~** (*anche fig*) in slow motion

raman'zina [raman'dzina] *sf* lecture, telling-off

'rame *sm* (*Chim*) copper

rammari'carsi *vpr* **~ (di)** (*rincrescersi*) to be sorry (about), regret; (*lamentarsi*) to complain (about)

rammen'dare *vt* to mend; (*calza*) to darn

'ramo *sm* branch

ramo'scello [ramoʃ'ʃɛllo] *sm* twig

'rampa *sf* flight (of stairs); **rampa di lancio** launching pad

rampi'cante *ag* (*Bot*) climbing

'rana *sf* frog

'rancido, -a ['rantʃido] *ag* rancid

ran'core *sm* rancour, resentment

ran'dagio, -a, -gi, -gie o ge [ran'dadʒo] *ag* (*gatto, cane*) stray

ran'dello *sm* club, cudgel

'rango, -ghi *sm* (*condizione sociale, Mil, riga*) rank

rannicchi'arsi [rannik'kjarsi] *vpr* to crouch, huddle

rannuvo'larsi *vpr* to cloud over, become overcast

'rapa *sf* (*Bot*) turnip

ra'pace [ra'patʃe] *ag* (*animale*) predatory; (*fig*) rapacious, grasping ▷ *sm* bird of prey

ra'pare *vt* (*capelli*) to crop, cut very short

rapida'mente *av* quickly, rapidly

rapidità *sf* speed

'rapido, -a *ag* fast; (*esame, occhiata*) quick, rapid ▷ *sm* (*Ferr*) express (train)

rapi'mento *sm* kidnapping; (*fig*) rapture

ra'pina *sf* robbery; **rapina in banca** bank robbery; **rapina a mano armata** armed robbery; **rapi'nare** *vt* to rob; **rapina'tore, -'trice** *sm/f* robber

ra'pire *vt* (*cose*) to steal; (*persone*) to kidnap; (*fig*) to enrapture, delight; **rapi'tore, -'trice** *sm/f* kidnapper

rap'porto *sm* (*resoconto*) report; (*legame*) relationship; (*Mat, Tecn*) ratio; **rapporti sessuali** sexual intercourse *sg*

rappre'saglia [rappre'saʎʎa] *sf* reprisal, retaliation

rappresen'tante *sm/f* representative

rappresen'tare *vt* to represent; (*Teatro*) to perform; **rappresentazi'one** *sf* representation; performing *no pl*; (*spettacolo*) performance

rara'mente *av* seldom, rarely

rare'fatto, -a *ag* rarefied

'raro, -a *ag* rare

ra'sare vt (barba ecc) to shave off; (siepi, erba) to trim, cut; **rasarsi** vpr to shave (o.s.)

raschi'are [ras'kjare] vt to scrape; (macchia, fango) to scrape off ▷ vi to clear one's throat

ra'sente prep **~ (a)** close to, very near

'raso, -a pp di **radere** ▷ ag (barba) shaved; (capelli) cropped; (con misure di capacità) level; (pieno: bicchiere) full to the brim ▷ sm (tessuto) satin; **un cucchiaio ~** a level spoonful; **raso terra** close to the ground

ra'soio sm razor; **rasoio elettrico** electric shaver o razor

ras'segna [ras'seɲɲa] sf (Mil) inspection, review; (esame) inspection; (resoconto) review, survey; (pubblicazione letteraria ecc) review; (mostra) exhibition, show; **passare in ~** (Mil, fig) to review

rassegnarsi vpr (accettare): **~ a qc/a fare)** to resign o.s. (to sth/to doing)

rassicu'rare vt to reassure

rasso'dare vt to harden, stiffen; **rassodarsi** vpr to harden, to strengthen

rassomigli'anza [rassomiʎ'ʎantsa] sf resemblance

rassomigli'are [rassomiʎ'ʎare] vi **~ a** to resemble, look like

rastrel'lare vt to rake; (fig: perlustrare) to comb

ras'trello sm rake

'rata sf (quota) instalment; **pagare a rate** to pay by instalments o on hire purchase (BRIT)

ratifi'care vt (Dir) to ratify

'ratto sm (Dir) abduction; (Zool) rat

rattop'pare vt to patch

rattris'tare vt to sadden; **rattristarsi** vpr to become sad

'rauco, -a, -chi, -che ag hoarse

rava'nello sm radish

ravi'oli smpl ravioli sg

ravvi'vare vt to revive; (fig) to brighten up, enliven

razio'nale [rattsjo'nale] ag rational

razio'nare [rattsjo'nare] vt to ration

razi'one [rat'tsjone] sf ration; (porzione) portion, share

'razza ['rattsa] sf race; (Zool) breed; (discendenza, stirpe) stock, race; (sorta) sort, kind

razzi'ale [rat'tsjale] ag racial

raz'zismo [rat'tsizmo] sm racism, racialism

raz'zista, -i, -e [rat'tsista] ag, sm/f racist, racialist

'razzo ['raddzo] sm rocket

R.C. sigla m (= partito della Rifondazione Comunista) left-wing Italian political party

re sm inv king; (Mus) D; (: solfeggiando) re

rea'gire [rea'dʒire] vi to react

re'ale ag real; (di, da re) royal ▷ sm **il ~** reality

realiz'zare [realid'dzare] vt (progetto ecc) to realize, carry out; (sogno, desiderio) to realize, fulfil; (scopo) to achieve; (Comm: titoli ecc) to realize; (Calcio ecc) to score; **realizzarsi** vpr to be realized

real'mente av really, actually

realtà sf inv reality

re'ato sm offence

reat'tore sm (Fisica) reactor; (Aer: aereo) jet; (: motore) jet engine

reazio'nario, -a [reattsjo'narjo] ag (Pol) reactionary

reazi'one [reat'tsjone] sf reaction

'rebus sm inv rebus; (fig) puzzle; enigma

recapi'tare vt to deliver

re'capito sm (indirizzo) address; (consegna) delivery; **recapito a domicilio** home delivery (service); **recapito telefonico** phone number

re'cedere [re'tʃedere] vi to withdraw

recensi'one [retʃen'sjone] sf review

re'cente [re'tʃente] ag recent; **di ~** recently; **recente'mente** av recently

re'cidere [re'tʃidere] vt to cut off, chop off

recin'tare [retʃin'tare] vt to enclose, fence off

re'cinto [re'tʃinto] sm enclosure; (ciò che recinge) fence; surrounding wall

recipi'ente [retʃi'pjɛnte] sm container

re'ciproco, -a, -ci, -che [re'tʃiproko] ag reciprocal

'recita ['rɛtʃita] sf performance

reci'tare [retʃi'tare] vt (poesia, lezione) to recite; (dramma) to perform; (ruolo) to play o act (the part of)

recla'mare vi to complain ▷ vt (richiedere) to demand

re'clamo sm complaint

recli'nabile ag (sedile) reclining

reclusi'one sf (Dir) imprisonment

'recluta sf recruit

re'condito, -a ag secluded; (fig) secret, hidden

'record ag inv record cpd ▷ sm inv record; **in tempo ~, a tempo di ~** in record time; **detenere il ~ di** to hold the record for; **record mondiale** world record

recriminazi'one [rekriminat'tsjone] sf recrimination

recupe'rare vt (rientrare in possesso di) to recover, get back; (tempo perduto) to make up for; (Naut) to salvage; (: naufraghi) to rescue; (delinquente) to rehabilitate; **~ lo svantaggio** (Sport) to close the gap

redargu'ire vt to rebuke

re'dassi ecc vb vedi **redigere**

reddi'tizio, -a [reddi'tittsjo] ag profitable

'reddito sm income; (dello Stato) revenue; (di un capitale) yield

re'digere [re'didʒere] vt to write; (contratto) to draw up

'redini sfpl reins

'reduce ['redutʃe] ag ~ **da** returning from, back from ▷ sm/f survivor

refe'rendum sm inv referendum

referenze [refe'rɛntse] sfpl references

re'ferto sm medical report

rega'lare vt to give (as a present), make a present of

re'galo sm gift, present

re'gata sf regatta

'reggere ['rɛddʒere] vt (tenere) to hold; (sostenere) to support, bear, hold up; (portare) to carry, bear; (resistere) to withstand; (dirigere: impresa) to manage, run; (governare) to rule, govern; (Ling) to take, be followed by ▷ vi (resistere): ~ **a** to stand up to, hold out against; (sopportare): ~ **a** to stand; (durare) to last; (fig: teoria ecc) to hold water; **reggersi** vpr (stare ritto) to stand

'reggia, -ge ['rɛddʒa] sf royal palace

reggi'calze [reddʒi'kaltse] sm inv suspender belt

reggi'mento [reddʒi'mento] sm (Mil) regiment

reggi'seno [reddʒi'seno] sm bra

re'gia, -'gie [re'dʒia] sf (TV, Cinema ecc) direction

re'gime [re'dʒime] sm (Pol) regime; (Dir: aureo, patrimoniale ecc) system; (Med) diet; (Tecn) (engine) speed

re'gina [re'dʒina] sf queen

regio'nale [redʒo'nale] ag regional ▷ sm local train (stopping frequently)

regi'one [re'dʒone] sf region; (territorio) region, district, area

re'gista, -i, -e [re'dʒista] sm/f (TV, Cinema ecc) director

regis'trare [redʒis'trare] vt (Amm) to register; (Comm) to enter; (notare) to note, take note of; (canzone, conversazione: strumento di misura) to record; (mettere a punto) to adjust, regulate; (bagagli) to check in; **registra'tore** sm (strumento) recorder, register; (magnetofono) tape recorder; **registratore di cassa** cash register; **registratore a cassette** cassette recorder

re'gistro [re'dʒistro] sm (libro, Mus, Tech) register; ledger; logbook; (Dir) registry

re'gnare [reɲ'ɲare] vi to reign, rule

'regno ['reɲɲo] sm kingdom; (periodo) reign; (fig) realm; **il R~ Unito** the United Kingdom; **regno animale/vegetale** animal/vegetable kingdom

'regola sf rule; **a ~ d'arte** duly; perfectly; **in ~** in order

rego'labile ag adjustable

regola'mento sm (complesso di norme) regulations pl; (di debito) settlement; **regolamento di conti** (fig) settling of scores

rego'lare ag regular; (in regola: domanda) in order, lawful ▷ vt to regulate, control; (apparecchio) to adjust, regulate; (questione, conto, debito) to settle; **regolarsi** vpr (moderarsi): **regolarsi nel bere/nello spendere** to control one's drinking/spending; (comportarsi) to behave, act

rela'tivo, -a ag relative

relazi'one [relat'tsjone] sf (fra cose, persone) relation(ship); (resoconto) report, account

rele'gare vt to banish; (fig) to relegate

religi'one [reli'dʒone] sf religion

re'liquia sf relic

re'litto sm wreck; (fig) down-and-out

re'mare vi to row

remini'scenze [reminiʃ'ʃentse] sfpl reminiscences

remis'sivo, -a ag submissive, compliant

'remo sm oar

re'moto, -a ag remote

'rendere vt (ridare) to return, give back; (: saluto ecc) to return; (produrre) to yield, bring in; (esprimere, tradurre) to render; ~ **qc possibile** to make sth possible; **rendersi** vpr **rendersi utile** to make o.s. useful; **rendersi conto di qc** to realize sth; ~ **qc possibile** to make sth possible; ~ **grazie a qn** give thanks to sb; ~ **omaggio a qn** to pay homage to sb; ~ **un servizio a qn** to do sb a service; ~ **una testimonianza** to give evidence; **non so se rendo l'idea** I don't know if I'm making myself clear

rendi'mento sm (reddito) yield; (di manodopera, Tecn) efficiency; (capacità di produrre) output; (di studenti) performance

'rendita sf (di individuo) private o unearned income; (Comm) revenue; **rendita annua** annuity

'rene sm kidney

'renna sf reindeer inv

re'parto sm department, section; (Mil) detachment

repel'lente ag repulsive

repen'taglio [repen'taʎʎo] sm **mettere a ~** to jeopardize, risk

repen'tino, -a ag sudden, unexpected

reper'torio sm (Teatro) repertory; (elenco) index, (alphabetical) list

'replica, -che sf repetition; reply, answer;

(*obiezione*) objection; (*Teatro, Cinema*) repeat performance; (*copia*) replica

repli'care *vt* (*ripetere*) to repeat; (*rispondere*) to answer, reply

repressi'one *sf* repression

re'presso, -a *pp di* **reprimere**

re'primere *vt* to suppress, repress

re'pubblica, -che *sf* republic

reputazi'one [reputat'tsjone] *sf* reputation

requi'sire *vt* to requisition

requi'sito *sm* requirement

'resa *sf* (*l'arrendersi*) surrender; (*restituzione, rendimento*) return; **resa dei conti** rendering of accounts; (*fig*) day of reckoning

'resi *ecc vb vedi* **rendere**

resi'dente *ag* resident; **residenzi'ale** *ag* residential

re'siduo, -a *ag* residual, remaining ▷ *sm* remainder; (*Chim*) residue

'resina *sf* resin

resis'tente *ag* (*che resiste*): ~ **a** resistant to; (*forte*) strong; (*duraturo*) long-lasting, durable; ~ **al caldo** heat-resistant;

resis'tenza *sf* resistance; (*di persona: fisica*) stamina, endurance; (: *mentale*) endurance, resistance

● **RESISTENZA**
●
● The **Resistenza** in Italy fought against
● the Nazis and the Fascists during the
● Second World War. Members of the
● **Resistenza** spanned a wide political
● spectrum and played a vital role in the
● Liberation and in the formation of the
● new democratic government at the end
● of the war.

re'sistere *vi* to resist; ~ **a** (*assalto, tentazioni*) to resist; (*dolore: pianta*) to withstand; (*non patir danno*) to be resistant to

reso'conto *sm* report, account

res'pingere [res'pindʒere] *vt* to drive back, repel; (*rifiutare*) to reject; (*Ins: bocciare*) to fail

respi'rare *vi* to breathe; (*fig*) to get one's breath; to breathe again ▷ *vt* to breathe (in), inhale; **respirazi'one** *sf* breathing; **respirazione artificiale** artificial respiration; **res'piro** *sm* breathing *no pl*; (*singolo atto*) breath; (*fig*) respite, rest; **mandare un respiro di sollievo** to give a sigh of relief

respon'sabile *ag* responsible ▷ *sm/f* person responsible; (*capo*) person in charge; ~ **di** responsible for; (*Dir*) liable

for; **responsabilità** *sf inv* responsibility; (*legale*) liability

res'ponso *sm* answer

'ressa *sf* crowd, throng

'ressi *ecc vb vedi* **reggere**

res'tare *vi* (*rimanere*) to remain, stay; (*avanzare*) to be left, remain; ~ **orfano/ cieco** to become o be left an orphan/ become blind; ~ **d'accordo** to agree; **non resta più niente** there's nothing left; **restano pochi giorni** there are only a few days left

restau'rare *vt* to restore

res'tio, -a, -'tii, -'tie *ag* ~ **a** reluctant to

restitu'ire *vt* to return, give back; (*energie, forze*) to restore

'resto *sm* remainder, rest; (*denaro*) change; (*Mat*) remainder; **resti** *smpl* (*di cibo*) leftovers; (*di città*) remains; **del ~** moreover, besides; **tenga pure il ~** keep the change; **resti mortali** (mortal) remains

res'tringere [res'trindʒere] *vt* to reduce; (*vestito*) to take in; (*stoffa*) to shrink; (*fig*) to restrict, limit; **restringersi** *vpr* (*strada*) to narrow; (*stoffa*) to shrink

'rete *sf* net; (*fig*) trap, snare; (*di recinzione*) wire netting; (*Aut, Ferr, di spionaggio ecc*) network; **segnare una** ~ (*Calcio*) to score a goal; **la R~** the Web; **rete ferroviaria** railway network; **rete del letto** (sprung) bed base; **rete stradale** road network; **rete (televisiva)** (*sistema*) network; (*canale*) channel

reti'cente [reti'tʃɛnte] *ag* reticent

retico'lato *sm* grid; (*rete*) wire netting; (*di filo spinato*) barbed wire (fence)

'retina *sf* (*Anat*) retina

re'torico, -a, -ci, -che *ag* rhetorical

retribu'ire *vt* to pay

'retro *sm inv* back ▷ *av* (*dietro*): **vedi** ~ see over(leaf)

retro'cedere [retro'tʃedere] *vi* to withdraw ▷ *vt* (*Calcio*) to relegate; (*Mil*) to degrade

re'trogrado, -a *ag* (*fig*) reactionary, backward-looking

retro'marcia [retro'martʃa] *sf* (*Aut*) reverse; (: *dispositivo*) reverse gear

retro'scena [retroʃʃɛna] *sm inv* (*Teatro*) backstage; **i** ~ (*fig*) the behind-the-scenes activities

retrovi'sore *sm* (*Aut*) (rear-view) mirror

'retta *sf* (*Mat*) straight line; (*di convitto*) charge for bed and board; (*fig: ascolto*): **dar ~ a** to listen to, pay attention to

rettango'lare *ag* rectangular

ret'tangolo, -a *ag* right-angled ▷ *sm* rectangle

ret'tifica, -che sf rectification, correction

'rettile sm reptile

retti'lineo, -a ag rectilinear

'retto, -a pp di **reggere** ▷ ag straight; (Mat): **angolo ~** right angle; (onesto) honest, upright; (giusto, esatto) correct, proper, right

ret'tore sm (Rel) rector; (di università) ≈ chancellor

reuma'tismo sm rheumatism

revisi'one sf auditing no pl; audit; servicing no pl; overhaul; review; revision; **revisione di bozze** proofreading

revi'sore sm; **revisore di bozze** proofreader; **revisore di conti** auditor

revival [ri'vaivəl] sm inv revival

'revoca sf revocation

revo'care vt to revoke

re'volver sm inv revolver

ri'abbia ecc vb vedi **riavere**

riabili'tare vt to rehabilitate

rianimazi'one [rianimat'tsjone] sf (Med) resuscitation; **centro di ~** intensive care unit

ria'prire vt to reopen, open again; **riaprirsi** vpr to reopen, open again

ri'armo sm (Mil) rearmament

rias'sumere vt (riprendere) to resume; (impiegare di nuovo) to re-employ; (sintetizzare) to summarize; **rias'sunto, -a** pp di **riassumere** ▷ sm summary

riattac'care vt (attaccare di nuovo): **~ (a)** (manifesto, francobollo) to stick back (on); (bottone) to sew back (on); (quadro, chiavi) to hang back up (on); **~ (il telefono** o **il ricevitore)** to hang up (the receiver)

ria'vere vt to have again; (avere indietro) to get back; (riacquistare) to recover; **riaversi** vpr to recover

riba'dire vt (fig) to confirm

ri'balta sf flap; (Teatro: proscenio) front of the stage; (fig) limelight; **luci della ~** footlights pl

ribal'tabile ag (sedile) tip-up

ribal'tare vt, vi (anche: **ribaltarsi**) to turn over, tip over

ribas'sare vt to lower, bring down ▷ vi to come down, fall

ri'battere vt to return, hit back; (confutare) to refute; **~ che** to retort that

ribel'larsi vpr **~ (a)** to rebel (against); **ri'belle** ag (soldati) rebel; (ragazzo) rebellious ▷ sm/f rebel

'ribes sm inv currant; **ribes nero** blackcurrant; **ribes rosso** redcurrant

ri'brezzo [ri'breddzo] sm disgust, loathing; **far ~ a** to disgust

ribut'tante ag disgusting, revolting

rica'dere vi to fall again; (scendere a terra: fig: nel peccato ecc) to fall back; (vestiti, capelli ecc) to hang (down); (riversarsi: fatiche, colpe): **~ su** to fall on; **rica'duta** sf (Med) relapse

rica'mare vt to embroider

ricambi'are vt to change again; (contraccambiare) to repay, return; **ri'cambio** sm exchange, return; (Fisiol) metabolism

ri'camo sm embroidery

ricapito'lare vt to recapitulate, sum up

ricari'care vt (arma, macchina fotografica) to reload; (pipa) to refill; (orologio) to rewind; (batteria) to recharge

ricat'tare vt to blackmail; **ri'catto** sm blackmail

rica'vare vt (estrarre) to draw out, extract; (ottenere) to obtain, gain

ric'chezza [rik'kettsa] sf wealth; (fig) richness

'riccio, -a ['rittʃo] ag curly ▷ sm (Zool) hedgehog; **riccio di mare** sea urchin; **'ricciolo** sm curl

'ricco, -a, -chi, -che ag rich; (persona, paese) rich, wealthy ▷ sm/f rich man/woman; **i ricchi** the rich; **~ di** full of; rich in

ri'cerca, -che [ri'tʃerka] sf search; (indagine) investigation, inquiry; (studio): **la ~** research; **una ~** piece of research; **ricerca di mercato** market research

ricer'care [ritʃer'kare] vt (motivi, cause) to look for, try to determine; (successo, piacere) to pursue; (onore, gloria) to seek; **ricer'cato, -a** ag (apprezzato) much sought-after; (affettato) studied, affected ▷ sm/f (Polizia) wanted man/woman

ricerca'tore, -'trice [ritʃerka'tore] sm/f (Ins) researcher

ri'cetta [ri'tʃetta] sf (Med) prescription; (Cuc) recipe; **mi può fare una ~ medica?** could you write me a prescription?

ricettazi'one [ritʃettat'tsjone] sf (Dir) receiving (stolen goods)

ri'cevere [ri'tʃevere] vt to receive; (stipendio, lettera) to get, receive; (accogliere: ospite) to welcome; (vedere: cliente, rappresentante ecc) to see; **ricevi'mento** sm receiving no pl; (festa) reception; **ricevi'tore** sm (Tecn) receiver; **rice'vuta** sf receipt; **posso avere una ricevuta, per favore?** can I have a receipt, please?; **ricevuta fiscale** receipt for tax purposes; **ricevuta di ritorno** (Posta) advice of receipt

richia'mare [rikja'mare] vt (chiamare indietro, ritelefonare) to call back; (ambasciatore, truppe) to recall; (rimproverare) to reprimand; (attirare) to attract, draw; **può ~ più tardi?** can you call back later?; **richiamarsi a** (*riferirsi a*) to refer to

richi'edere [ri'kjɛdere] *vt* to ask again for; (*chiedere indietro*): **~ qc** to ask for sth back; (*chiedere: per sapere*) to ask; (*: per avere*) to ask for; (*Amm: documenti*) to apply for; (*esigere*) to need, require; **richi'esta** *sf* (*domanda*) request; (*Amm*) application, request; (*esigenza*) demand, request; **a richiesta** on request

rici'clare [ritʃi'klare] *vt* to recycle

'ricino ['ritʃino] *sm* **olio di ~** castor oil

ricognizi'one [rikoɲɲit'tsjone] *sf* (*Mil*) reconnaissance; (*Dir*) recognition, acknowledgement

ricominci'are [rikomin'tʃare] *vt, vi* to start again, begin again

ricom'pensa *sf* reward

ricompen'sare *vt* to reward

riconciliarsi *vpr* to be reconciled

ricono'scente [rikonoʃ'ʃɛnte] *ag* grateful

rico'noscere [riko'noʃʃere] *vt* to recognize; (*Dir: figlio, debito*) to acknowledge; (*ammettere: errore*) to admit, acknowledge

rico'perto, -a *pp di* **ricoprire**

ricopi'are *vt* to copy

rico'prire *vt* (*coprire*) to cover; (*occupare: carica*) to hold

ricor'dare *vt* to remember, recall; (*richiamare alla memoria*): **~ qc a qn** to remind sb of sth; **ricordarsi** *vpr* **ricordarsi (di)** to remember; **ricordarsi di qc/di aver fatto** to remember sth/having done

ri'cordo *sm* memory; (*regalo*) keepsake, souvenir; (*di viaggio*) souvenir

ricor'rente *ag* recurrent, recurring; **ricor'renza** *sf* recurrence; (*festività*) anniversary

ri'correre *vi* (*ripetersi*) to recur; **~ a** (*rivolgersi*) to turn to; (*: Dir*) to appeal to; (*servirsi di*) to have recourse to

ricostitu'ente *ag* (*Med*) **cura ~** tonic

ricostru'ire *vt* (*casa*) to rebuild; (*fatti*) to reconstruct

ri'cotta *sf soft white unsalted cheese made from sheep's milk*

ricove'rare *vt* to give shelter to; **~ qn in ospedale** to admit sb to hospital

ri'covero *sm* shelter, refuge; (*Mil*) shelter; (*Med*) admission (to hospital)

ricreazi'one [rikreat'tsjone] *sf* recreation, entertainment; (*Ins*) break

ri'credersi *vpr* to change one's mind

ridacchi'are [ridak'kjare] *vi* to snigger

ri'dare *vt* to return, give back

'ridere *vi* to laugh; (*deridere, beffare*): **~ di** to laugh at, make fun of

ri'dicolo, -a *ag* ridiculous, absurd

ridimensio'nare *vt* to reorganize; (*fig*) to see in the right perspective

ri'dire *vt* to repeat; (*criticare*) to find fault with; to object to; **trova sempre qualcosa da ~** he always manages to find fault

ridon'dante *ag* redundant

ri'dotto, -a *pp di* **ridurre** ▷ *ag* (*biglietto*) reduced; (*formato*) small

ri'duco *ecc vb vedi* **ridurre**

ri'durre *vt* (*anche Chim, Mat*) to reduce; (*prezzo, spese*) to cut, reduce; (*accorciare: opera letteraria*) to abridge; (*: Radio, TV*) to adapt; **ridursi** *vpr* (*diminuirsi*) to be reduced, shrink; **ridursi a** to be reduced to; **ridursi pelle e ossa** to be reduced to skin and bone; **ri'dussi** *ecc vb vedi* **ridurre**; **ridut'tore** *sm* (*Elec*) adaptor; **riduzi'one** *sf* reduction; abridgement; adaptation; **ci sono riduzioni per i bambini/gli studenti?** is there a reduction for children/students?

ri'ebbi *ecc vb vedi* **riavere**

riem'pire *vt* to fill (up); (*modulo*) to fill in o out; **riempirsi** *vpr* to fill (up); **~ qc di** to fill sth (up) with

rien'tranza [rien'trantsa] *sf* recess; indentation

rien'trare *vi* (*entrare di nuovo*) to go (o come) back in; (*tornare*) to return; (*fare una rientranza*) to go in, curve inwards; to be indented; (*riguardare*): **~ in** to be included among, form part of

riepilo'gare *vt* to summarize ▷ *vi* to recapitulate

ri'esco *ecc vb vedi* **riuscire**

ri'fare *vt* to do again; (*ricostruire*) to make again; (*nodo*) to tie again, do up again; (*imitare*) to imitate, copy; **rifarsi** *vpr* (*risarcirsi*): **rifarsi di** to make up for; (*vendicarsi*): **rifarsi di qc su qn** to get one's own back on sb for sth; (*riferirsi*): **rifarsi a** to go back to; to follow; **~ il letto** to make the bed; **rifarsi una vita** to make a new life for o.s.

riferi'mento *sm* reference; **in** o **con ~ a** with reference to

rife'rire *vt* (*riportare*) to report ▷ *vi* to do a report; **riferirsi** *vpr* **riferirsi a** to refer to

rifi'nire *vt* to finish off, put the finishing touches to

rifiu'tare *vt* to refuse; **~ di fare** to refuse to do; **rifi'uto** *sm* refusal; **rifiuti** *smpl* (*spazzatura*) rubbish *sg*, refuse *sg*

riflessi'one *sf* (*Fisica, meditazione*) reflection; (*il pensare*) thought, reflection; (*osservazione*) remark

rifles'sivo, -a *ag* (*persona*) thoughtful, reflective; (*Ling*) reflexive

ri'flesso, -a pp di **riflettere** ▷ sm (di luce, allo specchio) reflection; (Fisiol) reflex; **di o per ~** indirectly

riflessologia [riflessolo'dʒia] sf reflexology

ri'flettere vt to reflect ▷ vi to think; **riflettersi** vpr to be reflected; **~ su** to think over

riflet'tore sm reflector; (proiettore) floodlight; searchlight

ri'flusso sm flowing back; (della marea) ebb; **un'epoca di ~** an era of nostalgia

ri'forma sf reform; **la R~** (Rel) the Reformation

riforma'torio sm (Dir) community home (BRIT), reformatory (US)

riforni'mento sm supplying, providing; restocking; **rifornimenti** smpl (provviste) supplies, provisions

rifor'nire vt (provvedere): **~ di** to supply o provide with; (fornire di nuovo: casa ecc) to restock; **rifornirsi** vpr **rifornirsi di qc** to stock up on sth

rifugi'arsi [rifu'dʒarsi] vpr to take refuge; **rifugi'ato, -a** sm/f refugee

ri'fugio [ri'fudʒo] sm refuge, shelter; (in montagna) shelter; **rifugio antiaereo** air-raid shelter

'riga, -ghe sf line; (striscia) stripe; (di persone, cose) line, row; (regolo) ruler; (scriminatura) parting; **mettersi in ~** to line up; **a righe** (foglio) lined; (vestito) striped

ri'gare vt (foglio) to rule ▷ vi **~ diritto** (fig) to toe the line

rigatti'ere sm junk dealer

righerò ecc [rige'rɔ] vb vedi **rigare**

'rigido, -a ['ridʒido] ag rigid, stiff; (membra ecc: indurite) stiff; (Meteor) harsh, severe; (fig) strict

rigogli'oso, -a [rigoʎ'ʎoso] ag (pianta) luxuriant; (fig: commercio, sviluppo) thriving

ri'gore sm (Meteor) harshness, rigours pl; (fig) severity, strictness; (anche: **calcio di ~**) penalty; **di ~** compulsory; **a rigor di termini** strictly speaking

riguar'dare vt to look at again; (considerare) to regard, consider; (concernere) to regard, concern; **riguardarsi** vpr (aver cura di sé) to look after o.s.

rigu'ardo sm (attenzione) care; (considerazione) regard, respect; **~ a** concerning, with regard to; **non aver riguardi nell'agire/nel parlare** to act/speak freely

rilasci'are [rilaʃ'ʃare] vt (rimettere in libertà) to release; (Amm: documenti) to issue

rilassarsi vpr to relax; (fig: disciplina) to become slack

rile'gare vt (libro) to bind

ri'leggere [ri'lɛddʒere] vt to reread, read again; (rivedere) to read over

ri'lento: a ~ av slowly

rile'vante ag considerable; important

rile'vare vt (ricavare) to find; (notare) to notice; (mettere in evidenza) to point out; (venire a conoscere: notizia) to learn; (raccogliere: dati) to gather, collect; (Topografia) to survey; (Mil) to relieve; (Comm) to take over

rili'evo sm (Arte, Geo) relief; (fig: rilevanza) importance; (Topografia) survey; **dar ~ a** o **mettere in ~ qc** (fig) to bring sth out, highlight sth

rilut'tante ag reluctant

'rima sf rhyme; (verso) verse

riman'dare vt to send again; (restituire, rinviare) to send back, return; (differire): **~ qc (a)** to postpone sth o put sth off (till); (fare riferimento): **~ qn a** to refer sb to; **essere rimandato** (Ins) to have to repeat one's exams

ri'mando sm (rinvio) return; (dilazione) postponement; (riferimento) cross-reference

rima'nente ag remaining ▷ sm rest, remainder; **i rimanenti** (persone) the rest of them, the others

rima'nere vi (restare) to remain, stay; (avanzare) to be left, remain; (restare stupito) to be amazed; (restare, mancare): **rimangono poche settimane a Pasqua** there are only a few weeks left till Easter; **rimane da vedere se** it remains to be seen whether; (diventare): **~ vedovo** to be left a widower; (trovarsi): **~ sorpreso** to be surprised

rimangi'are [riman'dʒare] vt to eat again; **~rsi la parola/una promessa** (fig) to go back on one's word/one's promise

ri'mango ecc vb vedi **rimanere**

rimargi'narsi vpr to heal

rimbal'zare [rimbal'tsare] vi to bounce back, rebound; (proiettile) to ricochet

rimbam'bito, -a ag senile, in one's dotage

rimboc'care (coperta) to tuck in; (maniche, pantaloni) to turn o roll up

rimbom'bare vi to resound

rimbor'sare vt to pay back, repay

rimedi'are vi **~ a** to remedy ▷ vt (fam: procurarsi) to get o scrape together

ri'medio sm (medicina) medicine; (cura, fig) remedy, cure

ri'mettere vt (mettere di nuovo) to put back; (indossare di nuovo): **~ qc** to put sth back on, put sth on again; (affidare) to entrust; (: decisione) to refer; (condonare) to remit; (Comm: merci) to deliver; (: denaro)

r

to remit; (*vomitare*) to bring up; (*perdere: anche:* **rimetterci**) to lose; **rimettersi al bello** (*tempo*) to clear up; **rimettersi in salute** to get better, recover one's health

ri'misi *ecc vb vedi* **rimettere**

'**rimmel**® *sm inv* mascara

rimoder'nare *vt* to modernize

rimorchi'are [rimor'kjare] *vt* to tow; (*fig: ragazza*) to pick up

ri'morchio [ri'mɔrkjo] *sm* tow; (*veicolo*) trailer

ri'morso *sm* remorse

rimozi'one [rimot'tsjone] *sf* removal; (*da un impiego*) dismissal; (*Psic*) repression

rimpatri'are *vi* to return home ▷ *vt* to repatriate

rimpi'angere [rim'pjandʒere] *vt* to regret; (*persona*) to miss; **rimpi'anto, -a** *pp di* **rimpiangere** ▷ *sm* regret

rimpiaz'zare [rimpjat'tsare] *vt* to replace

rimpiccio'lire [rimpittʃo'lire] *vt* to make smaller ▷ *vi* (*anche:* **rimpicciolirsi**) to become smaller

rimpinzarsi [rimpin'tsarsi] *vpr* ~ (**di qc**) to stuff o.s. (with sth)

rimprove'rare *vt* to rebuke, reprimand

rimu'overe *vt* to remove; (*destituire*) to dismiss

Rinasci'mento [rinaʃʃi'mento] *sm* **il** ~ the Renaissance

ri'nascita [ri'naʃʃita] *sf* rebirth, revival

rinca'rare *vt* to increase the price of ▷ *vi* to go up, become more expensive

rinca'sare *vi* to go home

rinchi'udere [rin'kjudere] *vt* to shut (*o* lock) up; **rinchiudersi** *vpr* **rinchiudersi in** to shut o.s. up in; **rinchiudersi in se stesso** to withdraw into o.s.

rin'correre *vt* to chase, run after; **rin'corsa** *sf* short run

rin'crescere [rin'kreʃʃere] *vb impers* **mi rincresce che/di non poter fare** I'm sorry that/I can't do, I regret that/being unable to do

rinfacci'are [rinfat'tʃare] *vt* (*fig*) ~ **qc a qn** to throw sth in sb's face

rinfor'zare [rinfor'tsare] *vt* to reinforce, strengthen ▷ *vi* (*anche:* **rinforzarsi**) to grow stronger

rinfres'care *vt* (*atmosfera, temperatura*) to cool (down); (*abito, pareti*) to freshen up ▷ *vi* (*tempo*) to grow cooler; **rinfrescarsi** *vpr* (*ristorarsi*) to refresh o.s.; (*lavarsi*) to freshen up; **rin'fresco, -schi** *sm* (*festa*) party; **rinfreschi** *smpl* refreshments

rin'fusa *sf* **alla** ~ in confusion, higgledy-piggledy

ringhi'are [rin'gjare] *vi* to growl, snarl

ringhi'era [rin'gjɛra] *sf* railing; (*delle scale*)

banister(s) (*pl*)

ringiova'nire [rindʒova'nire] *vt* (*vestito, acconciatura ecc*): ~ **qn** to make sb look younger; (*persona*) to miss ▷ *vi* (*anche: vacanze ecc*) to rejuvenate ▷ *vi* (*anche:* **ringiovanirsi**) to become (*o* look) younger

ringrazia'mento [ringrattsja'mento] *sm* thanks *pl*

ringrazi'are [ringrat'tsjare] *vt* to thank; ~ **qn di qc** to thank sb for sth

rinne'gare *vt* (*fede*) to renounce; (*figlio*) to disown, repudiate

rinnova'mento *sm* renewal; (*economico*) revival

rinno'vare *vt* to renew; (*ripetere*) to repeat, renew

rinoce'ronte [rinotʃe'ronte] *sm* rhinoceros

rino'mato, -a *ag* renowned, celebrated

rintracci'are [rintrat'tʃare] *vt* to track down

rintro'nare *vi* to boom, roar ▷ *vt* (*assordare*) to deafen; (*stordire*) to stun

rinunci'are [rinun'tʃare] *vi* ~ **a** to give up, renounce; ~ **a fare qc** to give up doing sth

rinvi'are *vt* (*rimandare indietro*) to send back, return; (*differire*): ~ **qc (a)** to postpone sth *o* put sth off (till); to adjourn sth (till); (*fare un rimando*): ~ **qn a** to refer sb to

rin'vio, -'vii *sm* (*rimando*) return; (*differimento*) postponement; (: *di seduta*) adjournment; (: *in un testo*) cross-reference; **rinvio a giudizio** (*Dir*) indictment

riò *ecc vb vedi* **riavere**

ri'one *sm* district, quarter

riordi'nare *vt* (*rimettere in ordine*) to tidy; (*riorganizzare*) to reorganize

riorganiz'zare [riorganid'dzare] *vt* to reorganize

ripa'gare *vt* to repay

ripa'rare *vt* (*proteggere*) to protect, defend; (*correggere: male, torto*) to make up for; (: *errore*) to put right; (*aggiustare*) to repair ▷ *vi* (*mettere rimedio*): ~ **a** to make up for; **ripararsi** *vpr* (*rifugiarsi*) to take refuge *o* shelter; **dove lo posso far ~?** where can I get this repaired?; **riparazi'one** *sf* (*di un torto*) reparation; (*di guasto, scarpe*) repairing *no pl*; repair; (*risarcimento*) compensation

ri'paro *sm* (*protezione*) shelter, protection; (*rimedio*) remedy

ripar'tire *vt* (*dividere*) to divide up; (*distribuire*) to share out ▷ *vi* to set off again; to leave again

ripas'sare *vi* to come (*o* go) back ▷ *vt* (*scritto, lezione*) to go over (again)

ripen'sare *vi* to think; (*cambiare pensiero*)

to change one's mind; (*tornare col pensiero*): ~ **a** to recall

ripercu'otersi *vpr* ~ **su** (*fig*) to have repercussions on

ripercussi'one *sf* (*fig*): **avere una ~ o delle ripercussioni su** to have repercussions on

ripes'care *vt* (*pesce*) to catch again; (*persona, cosa*) to fish out; (*fig: ritrovare*) to dig out

ri'petere *vt* to repeat; (*ripassare*) to go over; **può ~ per favore?** can you repeat that please?; **ripetizi'one** *sf* repetition; (*di lezione*) revision; **ripetizioni** *sfpl* (*Ins*) private tutoring *o* coaching *sg*

ripi'ano *sm* (*di mobile*) shelf

ri'picca *sf* **per ~** out of spite

'ripido, -a *ag* steep

ripie'gare *vt* to refold; (*piegare più volte*) to fold (up) ▷ *vi* (*Mil*) to retreat, fall back; (*fig: accontentarsi*): **~ su** to make do with

ripi'eno, -a *ag* full; (*Cuc*) stuffed ▷ *sm* (*Cuc*) stuffing

ri'pone, ri'pongo *ecc vb vedi* **riporre**

ri'porre *vt* (*porre al suo posto*) to put back, replace; (*mettere via*) to put away; (*fiducia, speranza*): **~ qc in qn** to place *o* put sth in sb

ripor'tare *vt* (*portare indietro*) to bring (*o* take) back; (*riferire*) to report; (*citare*) to quote; (*vittoria*) to gain; (*successo*) to have; (*Mat*) to carry; **riportarsi a** (*anche fig*) to go back to; (*riferirsi a*) to refer to; **~ danni** to suffer damage

ripo'sare *vt, vi* to rest; **riposarsi** *vpr* to rest

ri'posi *ecc vb vedi* **riporre**

ri'poso *sm* rest; (*Mil*): **~!** at ease!; **a ~** (*in pensione*) retired; **giorno di ~** day off

ripos'tiglio [ripos'tiλλo] *sm* lumber-room

ri'prendere *vt* (*prigioniero, fortezza*) to recapture; (*prendere indietro*) to take back; (*ricominciare: lavoro*) to resume; (*andare a prendere*) to fetch, come back for; (*riassumere: impiegati*) to take on again, re-employ; (*rimproverare*) to tell off; (*restringere: abito*) to take in; (*Cinema*) to shoot; **riprendersi** *vpr* to recover; (*correggersi*) to correct o.s.; **ri'presa** *sf* recapture; resumption; (*economica, da malattia, emozione*) recovery; (*Aut*) acceleration *no pl*; (*Teatro, Cinema*) rerun; (*Cinema: presa*) shooting *no pl*; shot; (*Sport*) second half; (*: Pugilato*) round; **a più riprese** on several occasions, several times; **ripresa cinematografica** shot

ripristi'nare *vt* to restore

ripro'durre *vt* to reproduce; **riprodursi** *vpr* (*Biol*) to reproduce; (*riformarsi*) to form again

ripro'vare *vt* (*provare di nuovo: gen*) to try again; (*vestito*) to try on again; (*: sensazione*) to experience again ▷ *vi* (*tentare*): **~ (a fare qc)** to try (to do sth) again; **riproverò più tardi** I'll try again later

ripudi'are *vt* to repudiate; disown

ripu'gnante [ripuɲ'ɲante] *ag* disgusting, repulsive

ri'quadro *sm* square; (*Archit*) panel

ri'saia *sf* paddy field

risa'lire *vi* (*ritornare in su*) to go back up; **~ a** (*ritornare con la mente*) to go back to; (*datare da*) to date back to, go back to

risal'tare *vi* (*fig: distinguersi*) to stand out; (*Archit*) to project, jut out

risa'puto, -a *ag* **è ~ che ...** everyone knows that ..., it is common knowledge that ...

risarci'mento [risartʃi'mento] *sm* **~ (di)** compensation (for); **risarcimento danni** damages

risar'cire [risar'tʃire] *vt* (*cose*) to pay compensation for; (*persona*): **~ qn di qc** to compensate sb for sth

ri'sata *sf* laugh

riscalda'mento *sm* heating; **riscaldamento centrale** central heating

riscal'dare *vt* (*scaldare*) to heat; (*: mani, persona*) to warm; (*minestra*) to reheat; **riscaldarsi** *vpr* to warm up

ris'catto *sm* ransom; redemption

rischia'rare [riskja'rare] *vt* (*illuminare*) to light up; (*colore*) to make lighter; **rischiararsi** *vpr* (*tempo*) to clear up; (*cielo*) to clear; (*fig: volto*) to brighten up; **rischiararsi la voce** to clear one's throat

rischi'are [ris'kjare] *vt* to risk ▷ *vi* **~ di fare qc** to risk *o* run the risk of doing sth

'rischio ['riskjo] *sm* risk; **rischi'oso, -a** *ag* risky, dangerous

riscia'cquare [riʃʃa'kware] *vt* to rinse

riscon'trare *vt* (*rilevare*) to find

ris'cuotere *vt* (*ritirare: somma*) to collect; (*: stipendio*) to draw, collect; (*assegno*) to cash; (*fig: successo ecc*) to win, earn

'rise *ecc vb vedi* **ridere**

risenti'mento *sm* resentment

risen'tire *vt* to hear again; (*provare*) to feel ▷ *vi* **~ di** to feel (*o* show) the effects of; **risentirsi** *vpr* **risentirsi di** *o* **per** to take offence at, resent; **risen'tito, -a** *ag* resentful

ri'serbo *sm* reserve

ri'serva *sf* reserve; (*di caccia, pesca*) preserve; (*restrizione, segreto*) reservation; **di ~** (*provviste ecc*) in reserve

riser'vare *vt* (*tenere in serbo*) to keep, put aside; (*prenotare*) to book, reserve; **ho riservato un tavolo a nome ...** I booked a table in the name of ...; **riser'vato,**

-a *ag* (*prenotato:* fig: *persona*) reserved; (*confidenziale*) confidential

'risi *ecc vb vedi* **ridere**

risi'edere *vi* ~ **a** *o* in to reside in

'risma *sf* (*di carta*) ream; (*fig*) kind, sort

'riso (*pl(f)* **risa**) (*: il ridere*) *sm* **il** ~ laughter; (*pianta*) rice ▷ *pp di* **ridere**

riso'lino *sm* snigger

ri'solsi *ecc vb vedi* **risolvere**

ri'solto, -a *pp di* **risolvere**

riso'luto, -a *ag* determined, resolute

risoluzi'one [risolut'tsjone] *sf* solving *no pl;* (*Mat*) solution; (*decisione, di schermo, immagine*) resolution

ri'solvere *vt* (*difficoltà, controversia*) to resolve; (*problema*) to solve; (*decidere*): ~ **di fare** to resolve to do; **risolversi** *vpr* (*decidersi*): **risolversi a fare** to make up one's mind to do; (*andare a finire*): **risolversi in** to end up, turn out; **risolversi in nulla** to come to nothing

riso'nanza [riso'nantsa] *sf* resonance; **aver vasta** ~ (*fig: fatto ecc*) to be known far and wide

ri'sorgere [ri'sordʒere] *vi* to rise again; **risorgi'mento** *sm* revival; **il Risorgimento** (*Storia*) the Risorgimento

● **RISORGIMENTO**
●
● The **Risorgimento** was the political
● movement which led to the
● proclamation of the Kingdom of Italy
● in 1861, and eventually to unification
● in 1871.

ri'sorsa *sf* expedient, resort; **risorse umane** human resources

ri'sorsi *ecc vb vedi* **risorgere**

ri'sotto *sm* (*Cuc*) risotto

risparmi'are *vt* to save; (*non uccidere*) to spare ▷ *vi* to save; ~ **qc a qn** to spare sb sth

ris'parmio *sm* saving *no pl;* (*denaro*) savings *pl;* **risparmi** *smpl* (*denaro*) savings

rispec'chiare [rispek'kjare] *vt* to reflect

rispet'tabile *ag* respectable

rispet'tare *vt* to respect; **farsi** ~ to command respect

rispet'tivo, -a *ag* respective

ris'petto *sm* respect; **rispetti** *smpl* (*saluti*) respects, regards; ~ **a** (*in paragone a*) compared to; (*in relazione a*) as regards, as for

ris'pondere *vi* to answer, reply; (*freni*) to respond; ~ **a** (*domanda*) to answer, reply to; (*persona*) to answer; (*invito*) to reply to; (*provocazione: veicolo, apparecchio*) to respond to; (*corrispondere a*) to correspond to; (*: speranze, bisogno*) to answer; ~ **di** to

answer for; **ris'posta** *sf* answer, reply; **in risposta a** in reply to

'rissa *sf* brawl

ris'tampa *sf* reprinting *no pl;* reprint

risto'rante *sm* restaurant; **mi può consigliare un buon ~?** can you recommend a good restaurant?

ris'tretto, -a *pp di* **restringere** ▷ *ag* (*racchiuso*) enclosed, hemmed in; (*angusto*) narrow; (*limitato*): ~ **(a)** restricted *o* limited (to); (*Cuc: brodo*) thick; (*: caffè*) extra strong

ristruttu'rare *vt* (*azienda*) to reorganize; (*edificio*) to restore; (*appartamento*) to alter; (*crema, balsamo*) to repair

risucchi'are [risuk'kjare] *vt* to suck in

risul'tare *vi* (*dimostrarsi*) to prove (to be), turn out (to be); (*riuscire*): ~ **vincitore** to emerge as the winner; ~ **da** (*provenire*) to result from, be the result of; **mi risulta che ...** I understand that ...; **non mi risulta** not as far as I know; **risul'tato** *sm* result

risuo'nare *vi* (*rimbombare*) to resound

risurrezi'one [risurret'tsjone] *sf* (*Rel*) resurrection

risusci'tare [risuʃʃi'tare] *vt* to resuscitate, restore to life; (*fig*) to revive, bring back ▷ *vi* to rise (from the dead)

ris'veglio [riz'veʎʎo] *sm* waking up; (*fig*) revival

ris'volto *sm* (*di giacca*) lapel; (*di pantaloni*) turn-up; (*di manica*) cuff; (*di tasca*) flap; (*di libro*) inside flap; (*fig*) implication

ritagli'are [ritaʎ'ʎare] *vt* (*tagliar via*) to cut out

ritar'dare *vi* (*persona, treno*) to be late; (*orologio*) to be slow ▷ *vt* (*rallentare*) to slow down; (*impedire*) to delay, hold up; (*differire*) to postpone, delay

ri'tardo *sm* delay; (*di persona aspettata*) lateness *no pl;* (*fig: mentale*) backwardness; **in** ~ late; **il volo ha due ore di** ~ the flight is two hours late; **scusi il** ~ sorry I'm late

ri'tegno [ri'teɲɲo] *sm* restraint

rite'nere *vt* (*trattenere*) to hold back; (*: somma*) to deduct; (*giudicare*) to consider, believe

ri'tengo, ri'tenni *ecc vb vedi* **ritenere**

riterrò, ritiene *ecc vb vedi* **ritenere**

riti'rare *vt* to withdraw; (*Pol: richiamare*) to recall; (*andare a prendere: pacco ecc*) to collect, pick up; **ritirarsi** *vpr* to withdraw; (*da un'attività*) to retire; (*stoffa*) to shrink; (*marea*) to recede

'ritmo *sm* rhythm; (*fig*) rate; (*: della vita*) pace, tempo

'rito *sm* rite; **di** ~ usual, customary

ritoc'care *vt* (*disegno, fotografia*) to touch up; (*testo*) to alter

ritor'nare *vi* to return, go (*o come*)

back, to get back; (*ripresentarsi*) to recur;
(*ridiventare*). **~ ricco** to become rich
again ▷ vt (*restituire*) to return, give back;
quando ritorniamo? when do we get
back?

ritor'nello *sm* refrain

ri'torno *sm* return; **essere di ~** to be back;
avere un ~ di fiamma (*Aut*) to backfire;
(*fig: persona*) to be back in love again

ri'trarre *vt* (*trarre indietro, via*) to withdraw;
(*distogliere: sguardo*) to turn away;
(*rappresentare*) to portray, depict; (*ricavare*)
to get, obtain

ritrat'tare *vt* (*disdire*) to retract, take back;
(*trattare nuovamente*) to deal with again

ri'tratto, -a *pp di* ritrarre ▷ *sm* portrait

ritro'vare *vt* to find; (*salute*) to regain;
(*persona*) to find; to meet again;
ritrovarsi *vpr* (*essere, capitare*) to find o.s.;
(*raccapezzarsi*) to find one's way; (*con senso
reciproco*) to meet (again)

'ritto, -a *ag* (*in piedi*) standing, on one's
feet; (*levato in alto*) erect, raised; (: *capelli*)
standing on end; (*posto verticalmente*)
upright

ritu'ale *ag, sm* ritual

riuni'one *sf* (*adunanza*) meeting;
(*riconciliazione*) reunion

riu'nire *vt* (*ricongiungere*) to join (together);
(*riconciliare*) to reunite, bring together
(again); **riunirsi** *vpr* (*adunarsi*) to meet;
(*tornare insieme*) to be reunited

riu'scire [riuʃ'ʃire] *vi* (*uscire di nuovo*) to go
out again, go back out; (*aver esito: fatti,
azioni*) to go, turn out; (*aver successo*) to
succeed, be successful; (*essere, apparire*) to
be, prove; (*raggiungere il fine*) to manage,
succeed; **~ a fare qc** to manage to do *o*
succeed in doing *o* be able to do sth

'riva *sf* (*di fiume*) bank; (*di lago, mare*) shore

ri'vale *sm/f* rival; **rivalità** *sf* rivalry

rivalu'tare *vt* (*Econ*) to revalue

rive'dere *vt* to see again; (*ripassare*) to
revise; (*verificare*) to check

rivedrò *ecc vb vedi* rivedere

rive'lare *vt* to reveal; (*divulgare*) to reveal,
disclose; (*dare indizio*) to reveal, show;
rivelarsi *vpr* (*manifestarsi*) to be revealed;
rivelarsi onesto *ecc* to prove to be honest
ecc; **rivelazi'one** *sf* revelation

rivendi'care *vt* to claim, demand

rivendi'tore, -'trice *sm/f* retailer;
rivenditore autorizzato (*Comm*)
authorized dealer

ri'verbero *sm* (*di luce, calore*) reflection; (*di
suono*) reverberation

rivesti'mento *sm* covering; coating

rives'tire *vt* to dress again; (*ricoprire*) to
cover; to coat; (*fig: carica*) to hold

ri'vidi *ecc vb vedi* rivedere

ri'vincita [ri'vintʃita] *sf* (*Sport*) return
match; (*fig*) revenge

ri'vista *sf* review; (*periodico*) magazine,
review; (*Teatro*) revue; variety show

ri'volgere [ri'voldʒere] *vt* (*attenzione,
sguardo*) to turn, direct; (*parole*) to address;
rivolgersi *vpr* to turn round; (*fig: dirigersi
per informazioni*): **rivolgersi a** to go and
see, go and speak to; (: *ufficio*) to enquire at

ri'volsi *ecc vb vedi* rivolgere

ri'volta *sf* revolt, rebellion

rivol'tella *sf* revolver

rivoluzio'nare [rivoluttsjo'nare] *vt* to
revolutionize

rivoluzio'nario, -a [rivoluttsjo'narjo] *ag,
sm/f* revolutionary

rivoluzi'one [rivolut'tsjone] *sf* revolution

riz'zare [rit'tsare] *vt* to raise, erect;
rizzarsi *vpr* to stand up; (*capelli*) to stand
on end

'roba *sf* stuff, things *pl*; (*possessi, beni*)
belongings *pl*, things *pl*, possessions *pl*; **~
da mangiare** things *pl* to eat, food; **~ da
matti** sheer madness *o* lunacy

'robot *sm inv* robot

ro'busto, -a *ag* robust, sturdy; (*solido:
catena*) strong

roc'chetto [rok'ketto] *sm* reel, spool

'roccia, -ce ['rottʃa] *sf* rock; **fare ~** (*Sport*)
to go rock climbing

'roco, -a, chi, che *ag* hoarse

ro'daggio [ro'daddʒo] *sm* running (BRIT)
o breaking (US) in; **in ~** running (BRIT) *o*
breaking (US) in

rodi'tore *sm* (*Zool*) rodent

rodo'dendro *sm* rhododendron

ro'gnone [roɲ'ɲone] *sm* (*Cuc*) kidney

'rogo, -ghi *sm* (*per cadaveri*) (funeral) pyre;
(*supplizio*): **il ~** the stake

rol'lio *sm* roll(ing)

'Roma *sf* Rome

Roma'nia *sf* **la ~** Romania

ro'manico, -a, -ci, -che *ag* Romanesque

ro'mano, -a *ag, sm/f* Roman

ro'mantico, -a, -ci, -che *ag* romantic

romanzi'ere [roman'dzjɛre] *sm* novelist

ro'manzo, -a [ro'mandzo] *ag* (*Ling*)
romance *cpd* ▷ *sm* novel; **romanzo
d'appendice** serial (story); **romanzo
giallo/poliziesco** detective story;
romanzo rosa romantic novel

'rombo *sm* rumble, thunder, roar; (*Mat*)
rhombus; (*Zool*) turbot; brill

'rompere *vt* to break; (*fidanzamento*) to
break off ▷ *vi* to break; **rompersi** *vpr* to
break; **mi rompe le scatole** (*fam*) he (*o*
she) is a pain in the neck; **rompersi un
braccio** to break an arm; **mi si è rotta**

la macchina my car has broken down;
rompis'catole (*fam*) *sm/f inv* pest, pain
in the neck

'**rondine** *sf* (*Zool*) swallow

ron'zare [ron'dzare] *vi* to buzz, hum

ron'zio [ron'dzio] *sm* buzzing

'**rosa** *sf* rose ▷ *ag inv*, *sm* pink; **ro'sato, -a**
ag pink, rosy ▷ *sm* (*vino*) rosé (wine)

rosicchi'are [rosik'kjare] *vt* to gnaw (at);
(*mangiucchiare*) to nibble (at)

rosma'rino *sm* rosemary

roso'lare *vt* (*Cuc*) to brown

roso'lia *sf* (*Med*) German measles *sg*,
rubella

ro'sone *sm* rosette; (*vetrata*) rose window

'**rospo** *sm* (*Zool*) toad

ros'setto *sm* (*per labbra*) lipstick

'**rosso, -a** *ag*, *sm*, *sm/f* red; **il mar R~** the
Red Sea; **rosso d'uovo** egg yolk

rosticce'ria [rostittʃe'ria] *sf* shop selling
roast meat and other cooked food

ro'taia *sf* rut, track; (*Ferr*) rail

ro'tella *sf* small wheel; (*di mobile*) castor

roto'lare *vt*, *vi* to roll; **rotolarsi** *vpr* to roll
(about)

'**rotolo** *sm* roll; **andare a rotoli** (*fig*) to go to
rack and ruin

ro'tondo, -a *ag* round

'**rotta** *sf* (*Aer*, *Naut*) course, route; (*Mil*)
rout; **a ~ di collo** at breakneck speed;
essere in ~ con qn to be on bad terms
with sb

rotta'mare *vt* to scrap

rottamazione [rottama'tsjone] *sf* (*come
incentivo*) *the scrapping of old vehicles in
return for incentives*

rot'tame *sm* fragment, scrap, broken bit;
rottami *smpl* (*di nave, aereo ecc*) wreckage
sg

'**rotto, -a** *pp di* **rompere** ▷ *ag* broken;
(*calzoni*) torn, split; **per il ~ della cuffia** by
the skin of one's teeth

rot'tura *sf* breaking *no pl*; break; breaking
off; (*Med*) fracture, break

rou'lotte [ru'lɔt] *sf* caravan

ro'vente *ag* red-hot

'**rovere** *sm* oak

ro'vescia [ro'veʃʃa] *sf* **alla ~** upside-down;
inside-out; **oggi mi va tutto alla ~**
everything is going wrong (for me) today

rovesci'are [roveʃʃare] *vt* (*versare in
giù*) to pour; (: *accidentalmente*) to spill;
(*capovolgere*) to turn upside down; (*gettare
a terra*) to knock down; (: *fig*: *governo*)
to overthrow; (*piegare all'indietro*: *testa*)
to throw back; **rovesciarsi** *vpr* (*sedia,
macchina*) to overturn; (*barca*) to capsize;
(*liquido*) to spill; (*fig*: *situazione*) to be
reversed

ro'vescio, -sci [ro'veʃʃo] *sm* other side,
wrong side; (*della mano*) back; (*di moneta*)
reverse; (*pioggia*) sudden downpour; (*fig*)
setback; (*Maglia*: anche: **punto ~**) purl
(stitch); (*Tennis*) backhand (stroke); **a ~**
upside-down; inside-out; **capire qc a ~** to
misunderstand sth

ro'vina *sf* ruin; **andare in ~** (*andare a pezzi*)
to collapse; (*fig*) to go to rack and ruin;
rovine *sfpl* (*ruderi*) ruins; **mandare in ~**
to ruin

rovi'nare *vi* to collapse, fall down ▷ *vt*
(*danneggiare*: *fig*) to ruin; **rovinarsi** *vpr*
(*persona*) to ruin o.s.; (*oggetto, vestito*) to
be ruined

rovis'tare *vt* (*casa*) to ransack; (*tasche*) to
rummage in (*o* through)

'**rovo** *sm* (*Bot*) blackberry bush, bramble
bush

'**rozzo, -a** ['roddzo] *ag* rough, coarse

ru'bare *vt* to steal; **~ qc a qn** to steal sth
from sb; **mi hanno rubato il portafoglio**
my wallet has been stolen

rubi'netto *sm* tap, faucet (*us*)

ru'bino *sm* ruby

ru'brica, -che *sf* (*Stampa*) column;
(*quadernetto*) index book; address book;
rubrica d'indirizzi address book; **rubrica
telefonica** list of telephone numbers

'**rudere** *sm* (*rovina*) ruins *pl*

rudimen'tale *ag* rudimentary, basic

rudi'menti *smpl* rudiments; basic
principles; basic knowledge *sg*

ruffi'ano *sm* pimp

'**ruga, -ghe** *sf* wrinkle

'**ruggine** ['ruddʒine] *sf* rust

rug'gire [rud'dʒire] *vi* to roar

rugi'ada [ru'dʒada] *sf* dew

ru'goso, -a *ag* wrinkled

rul'lino *sm* (*Fot*) spool; (: *pellicola*) film;
vorrei un ~ da 36 pose I'd like a 36-
exposure film

'**rullo** *sm* (*di tamburi*) roll; (*arnese cilindrico*,
Tip) roller; **rullo compressore** steam
roller; **rullo di pellicola** roll of film

rum *sm* rum

ru'meno, -a *ag*, *sm/f*, *sm* Romanian

rumi'nare *vt* (*Zool*) to ruminate

ru'more *sm* **un ~** a noise, a sound; **il ~**
noise; **non riesco a dormire a causa del
~** I can't sleep for the noise; **rumo'roso,
-a** *ag* noisy

Attenzione! In inglese esiste la
parola *rumour*, che però significa *voce*
nel senso *diceria*.

ru'olo *sm* (*Teatro*: *fig*) role, part; (*elenco*)
roll, register, list; **di ~** permanent, on the
permanent staff

ru'ota *sf* wheel; **ruota anteriore/**

posteriore front/back wheel; **ruota di scorta** spare wheel

ruo'tare *vt, vi* to rotate

'rupe *sf* cliff

'ruppi *ecc vb vedi* **rompere**

ru'rale *ag* rural, country *cpd*

ru'scello [ruʃʃɛllo] *sm* stream

'ruspa *sf* excavator

rus'sare *vi* to snore

'Russia *sf* **la ~** Russia; **'russo, -a** *ag, sm/f,* *sm* Russian

'rustico, -a, -ci, -che *ag* rustic; (*fig*) rough, unrefined

rut'tare *vi* to belch; **'rutto** *sm* belch

'ruvido, -a *ag* rough, coarse

S. *abbr* (= *sud*) S; (= *santo*) St

sa *vb vedi* **sapere**

'sabato *sm* Saturday; **di** *o* **il ~** on Saturdays

'sabbia *sf* sand; **sabbie mobili** quicksand(s); **sabbi'oso, -a** *ag* sandy

'sacca, -che *sf* bag; (*bisaccia*) haversack; **sacca da viaggio** travelling bag

sacca'rina *sf* saccharin(e)

saccheggi'are [sakked'dʒare] *vt* to sack, plunder

sac'chetto [sak'ketto] *sm* (small) bag, (small) sack, **sacchetto di carta/di plastica** paper/plastic bag

'sacco, -chi *sm* bag; (*per carbone ecc*) sack; (*Anat, Biol*) sac; (*tela*) sacking; (*saccheggio*) sack(ing); (*fig: grande quantità*): **un ~ di** lots of, heaps of; **sacco a pelo** sleeping bag; **sacco per i rifiuti** bin bag

sacer'dote [satʃer'dɔte] *sm* priest

sacrifi'care *vt* to sacrifice; **sacrificarsi** *vpr* to sacrifice o.s.; (*privarsi di qc*) to make sacrifices

sacri'ficio [sakri'fitʃo] *sm* sacrifice

'sacro, -a *ag* sacred

'sadico, -a, -ci, -che *ag* sadistic ▷ *sm/f* sadist

sa'etta *sf* arrow; (*fulmine*) thunderbolt; flash of lightning

sa'fari *sm inv* safari

sag'gezza [sad'dʒettsa] *sf* wisdom

'saggio, -a, -gi, -ge ['saddʒo] *ag* wise ▷ *sm* (*persona*) sage; (*esperimento*) test; (*fig: prova*) proof; (*campione*) sample; (*scritto*) essay

Sagit'tario [sadʒit'tarjo] *sm* Sagittarius

'sagoma *sf* (*profilo*) outline, profile; (*forma*) form, shape; (*Tecn*) template; (*bersaglio*) target; (*fig: persona*) character

'sagra *sf* festival

sagres'tano *sm* sacristan; sexton

sagres'tia *sf* sacristy

Sa'hara [sa'ara] *sm* **il (deserto del) ~** the Sahara (Desert)

'sai *vb vedi* **sapere**

'sala *sf* hall; (*stanza*) room; (*Cinema: Yyy: di proiezione*) cinema; **sala d'aspetto** waiting room; **sala da ballo** ballroom; **sala giochi** amusement arcade; **sala operatoria** operating theatre; **sala da pranzo** dining room; **sala per concerti** concert hall

sa'lame *sm* salami *no pl*, salami sausage

sala'moia *sf* (*Cuc*) brine

sa'lato, -a *ag* (*sapore*) salty; (*Cuc*) salted, salt *cpd*; (*fig: prezzo*) steep, stiff

sal'dare *vt* (*congiungere*) to join, bind; (*parti metalliche*) to solder; (: *con saldatura autogena*) to weld; (*conto*) to settle, pay

'saldo, -a *ag* (*resistente, forte*) strong, firm; (*fermo*) firm, steady, stable; (*fig*) firm, steadfast ▷ *sm* (*svendita*) sale; (*di conto*) settlement; (*Econ*) balance; **saldi** *smpl* (*Comm*) sales; **essere ~ nella propria fede** (*fig*) to stick to one's guns

'sale *sm* salt; (*fig*): **ha poco ~ in zucca** he doesn't have much sense; **sale fino** table salt; **sale grosso** cooking salt

'salgo *ecc vb vedi* **salire**

'salice ['salitʃe] *sm* willow; **salice piangente** weeping willow

sali'ente *ag* (*fig*) salient, main

sali'era *sf* salt cellar

sa'lire *vi* to go (*o come*) up; (*aereo ecc*) to climb, go up; (*passeggero*) to get on; (*sentiero, prezzi, livello*) to go up, rise ▷ *vt* (*scale, gradini*) to go (*o come*) up; **~ su** to climb (up); **~ sul treno/sull'autobus** to board the train/the bus; **~ in macchina** to get into the car; **sa'lita** *sf* climb, ascent; (*erta*) hill, slope; **in salita** *ag, av* uphill

sa'liva *sf* saliva

'salma *sf* corpse

'salmo *sm* psalm

sal'mone *sm* salmon

sa'lone *sm* (*stanza*) sitting room, lounge; (*in albergo*) lounge; (*su nave*) lounge, saloon; (*mostra*) show, exhibition; **salone di bellezza** beauty salon

sa'lotto *sm* lounge, sitting room; (*mobilio*) lounge suite

sal'pare *vi* (*Naut*) to set sail; (*anche*: **~ l'ancora**) to weigh anchor

'salsa *sf* (*Cuc*) sauce; **salsa di pomodoro** tomato sauce

sal'siccia, -ce [sal'sittʃa] *sf* pork sausage

sal'tare *vi* to jump, leap; (*esplodere*) to blow up, explode; (: *valvola*) to blow; (*venir via*) to pop off; (*non aver luogo: corso ecc*) to be cancelled ▷ *vt* to jump (over), leap (over); (*fig: pranzo, capitolo*) to skip, miss (out); (*Cuc*) to sauté; **far ~** to blow up; to burst open; **~ fuori** (*fig: apparire all'improvviso*) to turn up

saltel'lare *vi* to skip; to hop

'salto *sm* jump; (*Sport*) jumping; **fare un ~** to jump, leap; **fare un ~ da qn** to pop over to sb's (place); **salto in alto/lungo** high/long jump; **salto con l'asta** pole vaulting; **salto mortale** somersault

saltu'ario, -a *ag* occasional, irregular

sa'lubre *ag* healthy, salubrious

salume'ria *sf* delicatessen

sa'lumi *smpl* salted pork meats

salu'tare *ag* healthy; (*fig*) salutary, beneficial ▷ *vt* (*incontrandosi*) to greet; (*congedandosi*) to say goodbye to; (*Mil*) to salute

sa'lute *sf* health; **~!** (*a chi starnutisce*) bless you!; (*nei brindisi*) cheers!; **bere alla ~ di qn** to drink (to) sb's health

sa'luto *sm* (*gesto*) wave; (*parola*) greeting; (*Mil*) salute

salvada'naio *sm* money box, piggy bank

salva'gente [salva'dʒɛnte] *sm* (*Naut*) lifebuoy; (*ciambella*) life belt; (*giubbotto*) life jacket; (*stradale*) traffic island

salvaguar'dare *vt* to safeguard

sal'vare *vt* to save; (*trarre da un pericolo*) to rescue; (*proteggere*) to protect; **salvarsi** *vpr* to save o.s.; to escape; **salvaschermo** [salvas'kermo] *sm* (*Inform*) screen saver; **salvaslip** [salva'zlip] *sm inv* panty liner; **salva'taggio** *sm* rescue

'salve (*fam*) *escl* hi!

'salvia *sf* (*Bot*) sage

salvi'etta *sf* napkin; **salvietta umidificata** baby wipe

'salvo, -a *ag* safe, unhurt, unharmed; (*fuori pericolo*) safe, out of danger ▷ *sm* **in ~ safe** ▷ *prep* (*eccetto*) except; **mettere qc in ~** to put sth in a safe place; **~ che** (*a meno che*) unless; (*eccetto che*) except (that); **~ imprevisti** barring accidents

sam'buco *sm* elder (tree)

'sandalo *sm* (*Bot*) sandalwood; (*calzatura*) sandal

'sangue *sm* blood; **farsi cattivo ~** to fret, get in a state; **sangue freddo** (*fig*) sang-froid, calm; **a ~ freddo** in cold blood;

sangui'nare vi to bleed

sanità sf health; (salubrità) healthiness; **Ministero della S~** Department of Health; **sanità mentale** sanity

sani'tario, -a ag health cpd; (condizioni) sanitary ▷ sm (Amm) doctor; **sanitari** smpl (impianti) bathroom o sanitary fittings

'sanno vb vedi **sapere**

'sano, -a ag healthy; (denti, costituzione) healthy, sound; (integro) whole, unbroken; (fig: politica, consigli) sound; **~ di mente** sane; **di sana pianta** completely, entirely; **~ e salvo** safe and sound

'santo, -a ag holy; (fig) saintly; (seguito da nome proprio) saint ▷ sm/f saint; **la Santa Sede** the Holy See

santu'ario sm sanctuary

sanzi'one [san'tsjone] sf sanction; (penale, civile) sanction, penalty

sa'pere vt to know; (essere capace di): **so nuotare** I know how to swim, I can swim ▷ vi: **~ di** (aver sapore) to taste of; (aver odore) to smell of ▷ sm knowledge; **far ~ qc a qn** to inform sb about sth, let sb know sth; **mi sa che non sia vero** I don't think that's true; **non lo so** I don't know; **non so l'inglese** I don't speak English; **sa dove posso...?** do you know where I can ...?

sa'pone sm soap; **sapone da bucato** washing soap

sa'pore sm taste, flavour; **sapo'rito, -a** ag tasty

sappi'amo vb vedi **sapere**

saprò ecc vb vedi **sapere**

sarà ecc vb vedi **essere**

saraci'nesca [saratʃi'neska] sf (serranda) rolling shutter

sar'castico, -a, ci, che ag sarcastic

Sar'degna [sar'deɲɲa] sf **la ~** Sardinia

sar'dina sf sardine

sa'rei ecc vb vedi **essere**

SARS sigla f (Med: = severe acute respiratory syndrome) SARS

'sarta sf vedi **sarto**

'sarto, -a sm/f tailor/dressmaker

'sasso sm stone; (ciottolo) pebble; (masso) rock

sas'sofono sm saxophone

sas'soso, -a ag stony; pebbly

'Satana sm Satan

sa'tellite sm, ag satellite

'satira sf satire

'sauna sf sauna

sazi'are [sat'tsjare] vt to satisfy, satiate; **saziarsi** vpr **saziarsi (di)** to eat one's fill (of); (fig): **saziarsi di** to grow tired o weary of

'sazio, -a ['sattsjo] ag **~ (di)** sated (with), full (of); (fig: stufo) fed up (with), sick (of);

sono ~ I'm full (up)

sba'dato, -a ag careless, inattentive

sbadigli'are [zbadiʎ'ʎare] vi to yawn; **sba'diglio** sm yawn

sbagli'are [zbaʎ'ʎare] vt to make a mistake in, get wrong ▷ vi to make a mistake, be mistaken, be wrong; (operare in modo non giusto) to err; **sbagliarsi** vpr to make a mistake, be mistaken, be wrong; **~ strada/la mira** to take the wrong road/ miss one's aim

sbagli'ato, -a [zbaʎ'ʎato] ag (gen) wrong; (compito) full of mistakes; (conclusione) erroneous

'sbaglio sm mistake, error; (morale) error; **fare uno ~** to make a mistake

sbalor'dire vt to stun, amaze ▷ vi to be stunned, be amazed

sbal'zare [zbal'tsare] vt to throw, hurl ▷ vi (balzare) to bounce; (saltare) to leap, bound

sban'dare vi (Naut) to list; (Aer) to bank; (Aut) to skid

sba'raglio [zba'raʎʎo] sm rout; defeat; **gettarsi allo ~** to risk everything

sbaraz'zarsi [zbarat'tsarsi] vpr **~ di** to get rid of, rid o.s. of

sbar'care vt (passeggeri) to disembark; (merci) to unload ▷ vi to disembark

'sbarra sf bar; (di passaggio a livello) barrier; (Dir): **presentarsi alla ~** to appear before the court

sbar'rare vt (strada ecc) to block, bar; (assegno) to cross; **~ il passo** to bar the way; **~ gli occhi** to open one's eyes wide

'sbattere vt (porta) to slam, bang; (tappeti, ali, Cuc) to beat; (urtare) to knock, hit ▷ vi (porta, finestra) to bang; (agitarsi: ali, vele ecc) to flap; **me ne sbatto!** (fam) I don't give a damn!

sba'vare vi to dribble; (colore) to smear, smudge

'sberla sf slap

sbia'dire vi, vt to fade; **sbia'dito, -a** ag faded; (fig) colourless, dull

sbian'care vt to whiten; (tessuto) to bleach ▷ vi (impallidire) to grow pale o white

sbirci'ata [zbir'tʃata] sf **dare una ~ a qc** to glance at sth, have a look at sth

sbloc'care vt to unblock, free; (freno) to release; (prezzi, affitti) to decontrol; **sbloccarsi** vpr (gen) to become unblocked; (passaggio, strada) to clear, become unblocked

sboc'care vi **~ in** (fiume) to flow into; (strada) to lead into; (persona) to come (out) into; (fig: concludersi) to end (up) in

sboc'cato, -a ag (persona) foul-mouthed; (linguaggio) foul

sbocci'are [zbot'tʃare] vi (fiore) to bloom,

open (out)

sbol'lire vi (fig) to cool down, calm down

'sbornia (fam) sf **prendersi una ~** to get plastered

sbor'sare vt (denaro) to pay out

sbot'tare vi **~ in una risata/per la collera** to burst out laughing/explode with anger

sbotto'nare vt to unbutton, undo

sbrai'tare vi to yell, bawl

sbra'nare vt to tear to pieces

sbricio'lare [zbritʃo'lare] vt to crumble; **sbriciolarsi** vpr to crumble

sbri'gare vt to deal with; **sbrigarsi** vpr to hurry (up)

'sbronza ['zbrontsa] (fam) sf (ubriaco): **prendersi una ~** to get plastered

sbron'zarsi [zbron'tsarsi] vpr (fam) to get sozzled

'sbronzo, -a ['zbrontso] (fam) ag plastered

sbruf'fone, -a sm/f boaster

sbu'care vi to come out, emerge; (improvvisamente) to pop out (o up)

sbucci'are [zbut'tʃare] vt (arancia, patata) to peel; (piselli) to shell; **sbucciarsi un ginocchio** to graze one's knee

sbucherò ecc [zbuke'rɔ] vb vedi **sbucare**

sbuf'fare vi (persona, cavallo) to snort; (ansimare) to puff, pant; (treno) to puff

sca'broso, -a ag (fig: difficile) difficult, thorny; (: imbarazzante) embarrassing; (: sconcio) indecent

scacchi smpl (gioco) chess sg; **a ~** (tessuto) check(ed)

scacchi'era [skak'kjɛra] sf chessboard

scacci'are [skat'tʃare] vt to chase away o out, drive away o out

'scaddi ecc vb vedi **scadere**

sca'dente ag shoddy, of poor quality

sca'denza [ska'dɛntsa] sf (di cambiale, contratto) maturity; (di passaporto) expiry date; **a breve/lunga ~** short-/long-term; **data di ~** expiry date

sca'dere vi (contratto ecc) to expire; (debito) to fall due; (valore, forze, peso) to decline, go down

sca'fandro sm (di palombaro) diving suit; (di astronauta) space-suit

scaf'fale sm shelf; (mobile) set of shelves

'scafo sm (Naut, Aer) hull

scagio'nare [skadʒo'nare] vt to exonerate, free from blame

'scaglia ['skaʎʎa] sf (Zool) scale; (scheggia) chip, flake

scagli'are [skaʎ'ʎare] vt (lanciare: anche fig) to hurl, fling; **scagliarsi** (anche: **vr**): **scagliarsi su** o **contro** to hurl o fling o.s. at; (fig) to rail at

'scala sf (a gradini ecc) staircase, stairs pl;

(a pioli, di corda) ladder; (Mus, Geo, di colori, valori, fig) scale; **scale** sfpl (scalinata) stairs; **su vasta ~/~ ridotta** on a large/small scale; **~ mobile (dei salari)** index-linked pay scale; **scala a libretto** stepladder; **scala mobile** escalator; (Econ) sliding scale

sca'lare vt (Alpinismo, muro) to climb, scale; (debito) to scale down, reduce

scalda'bagno [skalda'baɲɲo] sm water-heater

scal'dare vt to heat; **scaldarsi** vpr to warm up, heat up; (al fuoco, al sole) to warm o.s.; (fig) to get excited

scal'fire vt to scratch

scali'nata sf staircase

sca'lino sm (anche fig) step; (di scala a pioli) rung

'scalo sm (Naut) slipway; (: porto d'approdo) port of call; (Aer) stopover; **fare ~ (a)** (Naut) to call (at); (Aer) to land (at), make a stop (at); **scalo merci** (Ferr) goods (BRIT) o freight yard

scalop'pina sf (Cuc) escalope

scal'pello sm chisel

scal'pore sm noise, row; **far ~** (notizia) to cause a sensation o a stir

'scaltro, -a ag cunning, shrewd

'scalzo, -a ['skaltso] ag barefoot

scambi'are vt to exchange; (confondere): **~ qn/qc per** to take o mistake sb/sth for; **mi hanno scambiato il cappello** they've given me the wrong hat; **scambiarsi** vpr (auguri, confidenze, visite) to exchange; **~ qn/qc per** (confondere) to mistake sth/sb for

'scambio sm exchange; (Ferr) points pl; **fare (uno) ~** to make a swap

scampa'gnata [skampaɲ'ɲata] sf trip to the country

scam'pare vt (salvare) to rescue, save; (evitare: morte, prigione) to escape ▷ vi **~ (a qc)** to survive (sth), escape (sth); **scamparla bella** to have a narrow escape

'scampo sm (salvezza) escape; (Zool) prawn; **cercare ~ nella fuga** to seek safety in flight

'scampolo sm remnant

scanala'tura sf (incavo) channel, groove
scandagli'are [skanda.ʎʎare] vt (Naut) to sound; (fig) to sound out; to probe
scandaliz'zare [skandalid'dzare] vt to shock, scandalize; **scandalizzarsi** vpr to be shocked
'scandalo sm scandal
Scandi'navia sf **la ~** Scandinavia; **scandi'navo, -a** ag, sm/f Scandinavian
scanner ['skanner] sm inv (Inform) scanner
scansafa'tiche [skansafa'tike] sm/f inv idler, loafer
scan'sare vt (rimuovere) to move (aside), shift; (schivare: schiaffo) to dodge; (sfuggire) to avoid; **scansarsi** vpr to move aside
scan'sia sf shelves pl; (per libri) bookcase
'scanso sm **a ~ di** in order to avoid, as a precaution against
scanti'nato sm basement
scapacci'one [skapat'tʃone] sm clout
scapes'trato, -a ag dissolute
'scapola sf shoulder blade
'scapolo sm bachelor
scappa'mento sm (Aut) exhaust
scap'pare vi (fuggire) to escape; (andare via in fretta) to rush off; **lasciarsi ~ un'occasione** to let an opportunity go by; **~ di prigione** to escape from prison; **~ di mano** (oggetto) to slip out of one's hands; **~ di mente a qn** to slip sb's mind; **mi scappò detto** I let it slip; **scappa'toia** sf way out
scara'beo sm beetle
scarabocchi'are [skarabok'kjare] vt to scribble, scrawl; **scara'bocchio** sm scribble, scrawl
scara'faggio [skara'faddʒo] sm cockroach
scaraman'zia [skaraman'tsia] sf **per ~** for luck
scaraven'tare vt to fling, hurl; **scaraventarsi** vpr to fling o.s.
scarce'rare [skartʃe'rare] vt to release (from prison)
scardi'nare vt **~ una porta** to take a door off its hinges
scari'care vt (merci, camion ecc) to unload; (passeggeri) to set down, put off; (arma) to unload; (: sparare, Elettr) to discharge; (corso d'acqua) to empty, pour; (fig: liberare da un peso) to unburden, relieve; (da Internet) to download; **scaricarsi** vpr (orologio) to run o wind down; (batteria, accumulatore) to go flat o dead; (fig: rilassarsi) to unwind; (: sfogarsi) to let off steam
'scarico, -a, -chi, -che ag unloaded; (orologio) run down; (accumulatore) dead, flat ▷ sm (di merci, materiali) unloading; (di immondizie) dumping, tipping (BRIT); (Tecn:

deflusso) draining; (: dispositivo) drain; (Aut) exhaust
scarlat'tina sf scarlet fever
scar'latto, -a ag scarlet
'scarpa sf shoe; **scarpe da ginnastica/ tennis** gym/tennis shoes
scar'pata sf escarpment
scarpi'era sf shoe rack
scar'pone sm boot; **scarponi da montagna** climbing boots; **scarponi da sci** ski-boots
scarseggi'are [skarsed'dʒare] vi to be scarce; **~ di** to be short of, lack
'scarso, -a ag (insufficiente) insufficient, meagre; (povero: annata) poor, lean; (Ins: voto) poor; **~ di** lacking in; **3 chili scarsi** just under 3 kilos, barely 3 kilos
scar'tare vt (pacco) to unwrap; (idea) to reject; (Mil) to declare unfit for military service; (carte da gioco) to discard; (Calcio) to dodge (past) ▷ vi to swerve
'scarto sm (cosa scartata: anche Comm) reject; (di veicolo) swerve; (differenza) gap, difference
scassi'nare vt to break, force
scate'nare vt (fig) to incite, stir up; **scatenarsi** vpr (temporale) to break; (rivolta) to break out; (persona: infuriarsi) to rage
'scatola sf box; (di latta) tin (BRIT), can; **cibi in ~** tinned (BRIT) o canned foods; **scatola cranica** cranium; **scato'lone** sm (big) box
scat'tare vt (fotografia) to take ▷ vi (congegno, molla ecc) to be released; (balzare) to spring up; (Sport) to put on a spurt; (fig: per l'ira) to fly into a rage; **~ in piedi** to spring to one's feet
'scatto sm (dispositivo) release; (: di arma da fuoco) trigger mechanism; (rumore) click; (balzo) jump, start; (Sport) spurt; (fig: di ira ecc) fit; (: di stipendio) increment; **di ~** suddenly
scaval'care vt (ostacolo) to pass (o climb) over; (fig) to get ahead of, overtake
sca'vare vt (terreno) to dig; (legno) to hollow out; (pozzo, galleria) to bore; (città sepolta ecc) to excavate
'scavo sm excavating no pl; excavation
'scegliere ['ʃeʎʎere] vt to choose, select
sce'icco, -chi [ʃe'ikko] sm sheik
'scelgo ecc ['ʃelgo] vb vedi **scegliere**
scel'lino [ʃel'lino] sm shilling
'scelta ['ʃelta] sf choice; selection; **di prima ~** top grade o quality; **frutta o formaggi a ~** choice of fruit or cheese
'scelto, -a ['ʃelto] pp di **scegliere** ▷ ag (gruppo) carefully selected; (frutta, verdura) choice, top quality; (Mil: specializzato) crack cpd, highly skilled

'scemo, -a ['ʃemo] *ag* stupid, silly

'scena ['ʃɛna] *sf* (*gen*) scene; (*palcoscenico*) stage; **le scene** (*fig*: *teatro*) the stage; **fare una ~** to make a scene; **andare in ~** to be staged *o* put on *o* performed; **mettere in ~** to stage

sce'nario [ʃe'narjo] *sm* scenery; (*di film*) scenario

sce'nata [ʃe'nata] *sf* row, scene

'scendere ['ʃendere] *vi* to go (*o come*) down; (*strada, sole*) to go down; (*notte*) to fall; (*passeggero: fermarsi*) to get out, alight; (*fig: temperatura, prezzi*) to go *o* come down, fall, drop ▷ *vt* (*scale, pendio*) to go (*o come*) down; **~ dalle scale** to go (*o come*) down the stairs; **~ dal treno** to get off *o* out of the train; **dove devo ~?** where do I get off?; **~ dalla macchina** to get out of the car; **~ da cavallo** to dismount, get off one's horse

sceneggi'ato [ʃened'dʒato] *sm* television drama

'scettico, -a, -ci, -che ['ʃettiko] *ag* sceptical

'scettro ['ʃettro] *sm* sceptre

'scheda ['skɛda] *sf* (*index*) card; **scheda elettorale** ballot paper; **scheda ricaricabile** (*Tel*) top-up card; **scheda telefonica** phone card; **sche'dario** *sm* file; (*mobile*) filing cabinet

sche'dina [ske'dina] *sf* ≈ pools coupon (*BRIT*)

'scheggia, -ge ['skeddʒa] *sf* splinter, sliver

'scheletro ['skeletro] *sm* skeleton

'schema, -i ['skɛma] *sm* (*diagramma*) diagram, sketch; (*progetto, abbozzo*) outline, plan

'scherma ['skerma] *sf* fencing

scher'maglia [sker'maʎʎa] *sf* (*fig*) skirmish

'schermo ['skermo] *sm* shield, screen; (*Cinema, TV*) screen

scher'nire [sker'nire] *vt* to mock, sneer at

scher'zare [sker'tsare] *vi* to joke

'scherzo ['skertso] *sm* joke; (*tiro*) trick; (*Mus*) scherzo; **è uno ~!** (*una cosa facile*) it's child's play!, it's easy!; **per ~** in jest; for a joke *o* a laugh; **fare un brutto ~ a qn** to play a nasty trick on sb

schiaccia'noci [skjattʃa'notʃi] *sm inv* nutcracker

schiacci'are [skjat'tʃare] *vt* (*dito*) to crush; (*noci*) to crack; **~ un pisolino** to have a nap; **schiacciarsi** *vpr* (*appiattirsi*) to get squashed; (*frantumarsi*) to get crushed

schiaffeggi'are [skjaffed'dʒare] *vt* to slap

schi'affo ['skjaffo] *sm* slap

schiantarsi *vpr* to break (up), shatter

schia'rire [skja'rire] *vt* to lighten, make

lighter; **schiarirsi** *vpr* to grow lighter; (*tornar sereno*) to clear, brighten up; **schiarirsi la voce** to clear one's throat

schiavitù [skjavi'tu] *sf* slavery

schi'avo, -a ['skjavo] *sm/f* slave

schi'ena ['skjɛna] *sf* (*Anat*) back; **schie'nale** *sm* (*di sedia*) back

schi'era ['skjɛra] *sf* (*Mil*) rank; (*gruppo*) group, band

schiera'mento [skjera'mento] *sm* (*Mil, Sport*) formation; (*fig*) alliance

schie'rare [skje'rare] *vt* (*esercito*) to line up, draw up, marshal; **schierarsi** *vpr* to line up; (*fig*): **schierarsi con** *o* **dalla parte di/contro qn** to side with/oppose sb

'schifo ['skifo] *sm* disgust; **fare ~** (*essere fatto male, dare pessimi risultati*) to be awful; **mi fa ~** it makes me sick, it's disgusting; **quel libro è uno ~** that book's rotten; **schi'foso, -a** *ag* disgusting, revolting; (*molto scadente*) rotten, lousy

schioc'care [skjok'kare] *vt* (*frusta*) to crack; (*dita*) to snap; (*lingua*) to click; **~ le labbra** to smack one's lips

schiudersi *vpr* to open

schi'uma ['skjuma] *sf* foam; (*di sapone*) lather; (*di latte*) froth; (*fig: feccia*) scum

schi'vare [ski'vare] *vt* to dodge, avoid

'schivo, -a ['skivo] *ag* (*ritroso*) stand-offish, reserved; (*timido*) shy

schiz'zare [skit'tsare] *vt* (*spruzzare*) to spurt, squirt; (*sporcare*) to splash, spatter; (*fig: abbozzare*) to sketch ▷ *vi* to spurt, squirt; (*saltar fuori*) to dart up (*o off ecc*)

schizzi'noso, -a [skittsi'noso] *ag* fussy, finicky

'schizzo ['skittso] *sm* (*di liquido*) spurt; splash, spatter; (*abbozzo*) sketch

sci [ʃi] *sm* (*attrezzo*) ski; (*attività*) skiing; **sci d'acqua** water-skiing; **sci di fondo** cross-country skiing, ski touring (*us*); **sci nautico** water-skiing

'scia ['ʃia] (*pl* **scie**) *sf* (*di imbarcazione*) wake; (*di profumo*) trail

scià [ʃa] *sm inv* shah

sci'abola ['ʃabola] *sf* sabre

scia'callo [ʃa'kallo] *sm* jackal

sciac'quare [ʃak'kware] *vt* to rinse

scia'gura [ʃa'gura] *sf* disaster, calamity; misfortune

scialac'quare [ʃalak'kware] *vt* to squander

sci'albo, -a ['ʃalbo] *ag* pale, dull; (*fig*) dull, colourless

sci'alle ['ʃalle] *sm* shawl

scia'luppa [ʃa'luppa] *sf*: **scialuppa di salvataggio** lifeboat

sci'ame ['ʃame] *sm* swarm

sci'are [ʃi'are] *vi* to ski

sci'arpa ['ʃarpa] sf scarf; (fascia) sash

scia'tore, -'trice [ʃia'tore] sm/f skier

sci'atto, -a ['ʃatto] ag (persona) slovenly, unkempt

scien'tifico, -a, -ci, -che [ʃen'tifiko] ag scientific

sci'enza ['ʃentsa] sf science; (sapere) knowledge; **scienze** sfpl (Ins) science sg; **scienze naturali** natural sciences; **scienzi'ato, -a** sm/f scientist

'scimmia ['ʃimmja] sf monkey

scimpanzé [ʃimpan'tse] sm inv chimpanzee

scin'tilla [ʃin'tilla] sf spark; **scintil'lare** vi to spark; (acqua, occhi) to sparkle

scioc'chezza [ʃok'kettsa] sf stupidity no pl; stupid o foolish thing; **dire sciocchezze** to talk nonsense

sci'occo, -a, -chi, -che ['ʃokko] ag stupid, foolish

sci'ogliere ['ʃɔʎʎere] vt (nodo) to untie; (capelli) to loosen; (persona, animale) to untie, release; (fig: persona): ~ **da** to release from; (neve) to melt; (nell'acqua: zucchero ecc) to dissolve; (fig: mistero) to solve; (porre fine a: contratto) to cancel; (: società, matrimonio) to dissolve; (: riunione) to bring to an end; **sciogliersi** vpr to loosen, come untied; to melt; to dissolve; (assemblea ecc) to break up; ~ **i muscoli** to limber up; **scioglilingua** [ʃoʎʎi'lingwa] sm inv tongue-twister

sci'olgo ecc ['ʃɔlgo] vb vedi **sciogliere**

sci'olto, -a ['ʃɔlto] pp di **sciogliere** ▷ ag loose; (agile) agile, nimble; supple; (disinvolto) free and easy; **versi sciolti** (Poesia) blank verse

sciope'rare [ʃope'rare] vi to strike, go on strike

sci'opero ['ʃopero] sm strike; **fare ~** to strike; **sciopero bianco** work-to-rule (BRIT), slowdown (US); **sciopero selvaggio** wildcat strike; **sciopero a singhiozzo** on-off strike

scio'via [ʃio'via] sf ski lift

scip'pare [ʃip'pare] vt ~ **qn** to snatch sb's bag; **mi hanno scippato** they snatched my bag

sci'rocco [ʃi'rokko] sm sirocco

sci'roppo [ʃi'roppo] sm syrup

'scisma, -i ['ʃizma] sm (Rel) schism

scissi'one [ʃis'sjone] sf (anche fig) split, division; (Fisica) fission

sciu'pare [ʃu'pare] vt (abito, libro, appetito) to spoil, ruin; (tempo, denaro) to waste

scivo'lare [ʃivo'lare] vi to slide o glide along; (involontariamente) to slip, slide; **'scivolo** sm slide; (Tecn) chute; **scivo'loso, -a** ag slippery

scle'rosi sf sclerosis

scoc'care vt (freccia) to shoot ▷ vi (guizzare) to shoot up; (battere: ora) to strike

scoccherò ecc [skokke'rɔ] vb vedi **scoccare**

scocci'are [skot'tʃare] (fam) vt to bother, annoy; **scocciarsi** vpr to be bothered o annoyed

sco'della sf bowl

scodinzo'lare [skodintso'lare] vi to wag its tail

scogli'era [skoʎ'ʎera] sf reef; cliff

'scoglio ['skɔʎʎo] sm (al mare) rock

scoi'attolo sm squirrel

scola'pasta sm inv colander

scolapi'atti sm inv drainer (for plates)

sco'lare ag **età scolare** school age ▷ vt to drain ▷ vi to drip

scola'resca sf schoolchildren pl, pupils pl

sco'laro, -a sm/f pupil, schoolboy/girl

> Attenzione! In inglese esiste la parola *scholar*, che però significa *studioso*.

sco'lastico, -a, -ci, -che ag school cpd; scholastic

scol'lato, -a ag (vestito) low-cut, low-necked; (donna) wearing a low-cut dress (o blouse ecc)

scolla'tura sf neckline

scolle'gare vt (fili, apparecchi) to disconnect

'scolo sm drainage

scolo'rire vt to fade; to discolour; **scolorirsi** vpr to fade; to become discoloured; (impallidire) to turn pale

scol'pire vt to carve, sculpt

scombusso'lare vt to upset

scom'messa sf bet, wager

scom'mettere vt, vi to bet

scomo'dare vt to trouble, bother; to disturb; **scomodarsi** vpr to put o.s. out; **scomodarsi a fare** to go to the bother o trouble of doing

'scomodo, -a ag uncomfortable; (sistemazione, posto) awkward, inconvenient

scompa'rire vi (sparire) to disappear, vanish; (fig) to be insignificant

scomparti'mento sm compartment; **uno ~ per non-fumatori** a non-smoking compartment

scompigli'are [skompiʎ'ʎare] vt (cassetto, capelli) to mess up, disarrange; (fig: piani) to upset

scomuni'care vt to excommunicate

'sconcio, -a, -ci, -ce ['skontʃo] ag (osceno) indecent, obscene ▷ sm disgrace

scon'figgere [skon'fiddʒere] vt to defeat, overcome

sconfi'nare vi to cross the border; (in proprietà privata) to trespass; (fig): ~ **da** to stray o digress from

scon'fitta sf defeat

scon'forto sm despondency

sconge'lare [skondʒe'lare] vt to defrost

scongiu'rare [skondʒu'rare] vt (implorare) to entreat, beseech, implore; (eludere: pericolo) to ward off, avert; **scongi'uro** sm entreaty; (esorcismo) exorcism; **fare gli scongiuri** to touch wood (BRIT), knock on wood (US)

scon'nesso, -a ag incoherent

sconosci'uto, -a [skonoʃ'ʃuto] ag unknown; new, strange ▷ sm/f stranger; unknown person

sconsigli'are [skonsiʎ'ʎare] vt ~ qc a qn to advise sb against sth; ~ qn dal fare qc to advise sb not to do o against doing sth

sconso'lato, -a ag inconsolable; desolate

scon'tare vt (Comm: detrarre) to deduct; (: debito) to pay off; (: cambiale) to discount; (pena) to serve; (colpa, errori) to pay for, suffer for

scon'tato, -a ag (previsto) foreseen, taken for granted; **dare per ~ che** to take it for granted that

scon'tento, -a ag ~ (di) dissatisfied (with) ▷ sm dissatisfaction

'sconto sm discount; **fare uno ~** to give a discount; **ci sono sconti per studenti?** are there discounts for students?

scon'trarsi vpr (treni ecc) to crash, collide; (venire ad uno scontro, fig) to clash; ~ con to crash into, collide with

scon'trino sm ticket; (di cassa) receipt; **potrei avere lo ~ per favore?** can I have a receipt, please?

'scontro sm clash, encounter; crash, collision

scon'troso, -a ag sullen, surly; (permaloso) touchy

sconveni'ente ag unseemly, improper

scon'volgere [skon'vɔldʒere] vt to throw into confusion, upset; (turbare) to shake, disturb, upset; **scon'volto, -a** pp di **sconvolgere**

scooter ['skuter] sm inv scooter

'scopa sf broom; (Carte) Italian card game; **sco'pare** vt to sweep

sco'perta sf discovery

sco'perto, -a pp di **scoprire** ▷ ag uncovered; (capo) uncovered, bare; (macchina) open; (Mil) exposed, without cover; (conto) overdrawn

'scopo sm aim, purpose; **a che ~?** what for?

scoppi'are vi (spaccarsi) to burst; (esplodere) to explode; (fig) to break out; ~ **in pianto** o **a piangere** to burst out crying;

~ **dalle risa** o **dal ridere** to split one's sides laughing

scoppiet'tare vi to crackle

'scoppio sm explosion; (di tuono, arma ecc) crash, bang; (fig: di risa, ira) fit, outburst; (: di guerra) outbreak; **a ~ ritardato** delayed-action

sco'prire vt to discover; (liberare da ciò che copre) to uncover; (: monumento) to unveil; **scoprirsi** vpr to put on lighter clothes; (fig) to give o.s. away

scoraggi'are [skorad'dʒare] vt to discourage; **scoraggiarsi** vpr to become discouraged, lose heart

scorcia'toia [skortʃa'toja] sf short cut

'scorcio ['skortʃo] sm (Arte) foreshortening; (di secolo, periodo) end, close; **scorcio panoramico** vista

scor'dare vt to forget; **scordarsi** vpr **scordarsi di qc/di fare** to forget sth/to do

'scorgere ['skɔrdʒere] vt to make out, distinguish, see

scorpacci'ata [skorpat'tʃata] sf **fare una ~ (di)** to stuff o.s. (with), eat one's fill (of)

scorpi'one sm scorpion; (dello zodiaco): **S~** Scorpio

'scorrere vt (giornale, lettera) to run o skim through ▷ vi (liquido, fiume) to run, flow; (fune) to run; (cassetto, porta) to slide easily; (tempo) to pass (by)

scor'retto, -a ag incorrect; (sgarbato) impolite; (sconveniente) improper

scor'revole ag (porta) sliding; (fig: stile) fluent, flowing

'scorsi ecc vb vedi **scorgere**

'scorso, -a pp di **scorrere** ▷ ag last

scor'soio, -a ag nodo ~ noose

'scorta sf (di personalità, convoglio) escort; (provvista) supply, stock

scor'tese ag discourteous, rude

'scorza ['skɔrdza] sf (di albero) bark; (di agrumi) peel, skin

sco'sceso, -a [skoʃ'ʃeso] ag steep

'scossa sf jerk, jolt, shake; (Elettr: fig) shock; **scossa di terremoto** earth tremor

'scosso, -a pp di **scuotere** ▷ ag (turbato) shaken, upset

scos'tante ag (fig) off-putting (BRIT), unpleasant

scotch [skɔtʃ] sm inv (whisky) Scotch; (nastro adesivo) Scotch tape®, Sellotape®

scot'tare vt (ustionare) to burn; (: con liquido bollente) to scald ▷ vi to burn; (caffè) to be too hot; **scottarsi** vpr to burn/scald o.s.; (fig) to have one's fingers burnt; **scotta'tura** sf burn; scald

'scotto, -a ag overcooked ▷ sm (fig):

pagare lo ~ (di) to pay the penalty (for)
sco'vare vt to drive out, flush out; (fig) to discover
'Scozia ['skɔttsia] sf **la ~** Scotland; **scoz'zese** ag Scottish ▷ sm/f Scot
scredi'tare vt to discredit
screen saver ['skriːn'seɪvər] sm inv (Inform) screen saver
scre'mato, -a ag skimmed; **parzialmente ~** semi-skimmed
screpo'lato, -a ag (labbra) chapped; (muro) cracked
'screzio ['skrɛttsjo] sm disagreement
scricchio'lare [skrikkjo'lare] vi to creak, squeak
'scrigno ['skriɲɲo] sm casket
scrimina'tura sf parting
'scrissi ecc vb vedi **scrivere**
'scritta sf inscription
'scritto, -a pp di **scrivere** ▷ ag written ▷ sm writing; (lettera) letter, note
scrit'toio sm writing desk
scrit'tore, -'trice sm/f writer
scrit'tura sf writing; (Comm) entry; (contratto) contract; (Rel): **la Sacra S~** the Scriptures pl
scrittu'rare vt (Teatro, Cinema) to sign up, engage; (Comm) to enter
scriva'nia sf desk
'scrivere vt to write; **come si scrive?** how is it spelt?, how do you write it?
scroc'cone, -a sm/f scrounger
'scrofa sf (Zool) sow
scrol'lare vt to shake; **scrollarsi** vpr (anche fig) to give o.s. a shake; (anche: **~ le spalle/il capo**) to shrug one's shoulders/shake one's head
'scrupolo sm scruple; (meticolosità) care, conscientiousness
scrupo'loso, -a ag scrupulous; conscientious
scru'tare vt to scrutinize; (intenzioni, causa) to examine, scrutinize
scu'cire [sku'tʃire] vt (orlo ecc) to unpick, undo; **scucirsi** vpr to come unstitched
scude'ria sf stable
scu'detto sm (Sport) (championship) shield; (distintivo) badge
'scudo sm shield
sculacci'are [skulat'tʃare] vt to spank
scul'tore, -'trice sm/f sculptor
scul'tura sf sculpture
scu'ola sf school; **scuola elementare/materna** primary (BRIT) o grade (US) /nursery school; **scuola guida** driving school; **scuola media** secondary (BRIT) o high (US) school; **scuola dell'obbligo** compulsory education; **scuola tecnica** technical college; **scuole serali** evening classes, night school sg
scu'otere vt to shake
'scure sf axe
'scuro, -a ag dark; (fig: espressione) grim ▷ sm darkness; dark colour; (imposta) (window) shutter; **verde/rosso** ecc **~** dark green/red ecc
'scusa sf apology; (pretesto) excuse; **chiedere ~ a qn (per)** to apologize to sb (for); **chiedo ~** I'm sorry; (disturbando ecc) excuse me
scu'sare vt to excuse; **scusarsi** vpr **scusarsi (di)** to apologize (for); **(mi) scusi** I'm sorry; (per richiamare l'attenzione) excuse me
sde'gnato, -a [zdeɲ'ɲato] ag indignant, angry
'sdegno ['zdeɲɲo] sm scorn, disdain
sdolci'nato, -a [zdoltʃi'nato] ag mawkish, oversentimental
sdrai'arsi vpr to stretch out, lie down
'sdraio sm **sedia a ~** deck chair
sdruccio'levole [zdruttʃo'levole] ag slippery

○ **PAROLA CHIAVE**

se pron vedi **si**
▷ cong **1** (condizionale, ipotetica) if; **se nevica non vengo** I won't come if it snows; **sarei rimasto se me l'avessero chiesto** I would have stayed if they'd asked me; **non puoi fare altro se non telefonare** all you can do is phone; **se mai** if, if ever; **siamo noi se mai che le siamo grati** it is we who should be grateful to you; **se no** (altrimenti) or (else), otherwise
2 (in frasi dubitative, interrogative indirette) if, whether; **non so se scrivere o telefonare** I don't know whether o if I should write or phone

sé pron (gen) oneself; (esso, essa, lui, lei, loro) itself; himself; herself; themselves; **sé stesso(a)** pron oneself; itself; himself; herself
seb'bene cong although, though
sec. abbr (= secolo) c.
'secca sf (del mare) shallows pl; vedi anche **secco**
sec'care vt to dry; (prosciugare) to dry up; (fig: importunare) to annoy, bother ▷ vi to dry; to dry up; **seccarsi** vpr to dry; to dry up; (fig) to grow annoyed
sec'cato, -a ag (fig: infastidito) bothered, annoyed; (: stufo) fed up
secca'tura sf (fig) bother no pl, trouble no pl
seccherò ecc [sekke'rɔ] vb vedi **seccare**

secchi'ello sm bucket; **secchiello del ghiaccio** ice bucket

'secchio ['sekkjo] sm bucket, pail

'secco, -a, -chi, -che ag dry; (fichi, pesce) dried; (foglie, ramo) withered; (magro: persona) thin, skinny; (fig: risposta, modo di fare) curt, abrupt; (: colpo) clean, sharp ▷ sm (siccità) drought; **restarci ~** (fig: morire sul colpo) to drop dead; **mettere in ~** (barca) to beach; **rimanere a ~** (fig) to be left in the lurch

seco'lare ag age-old, centuries-old; (laico, mondano) secular

'secolo sm century; (epoca) age

se'conda sf (Aut) second (gear); **viaggiare in ~** to travel second-class; vedi anche **secondo**; **seconda colazione** lunch

secon'dario, -a ag secondary

se'condo, -a ag second ▷ sm second; (di pranzo) main course ▷ prep according to; (nel modo prescritto) in accordance with; **~ me** in my opinion, to my mind; **di seconda mano** second-hand; **a seconda di** according to; in accordance with; **seconda classe** second-class

'sedano sm celery

seda'tivo, -a ag, sm sedative

'sede sf seat; (di ditta) head office; (di organizzazione) headquarters pl; **sede centrale** head office; **sede sociale** registered office

seden'tario, -a ag sedentary

se'dere vi to sit, be seated

'sedia sf chair; **sedia elettrica** electric chair; **sedia a rotelle** wheelchair

'sedici ['seditʃi] num sixteen

se'dile sm seat; (panchina) bench

sedu'cente [sedu'tʃɛnte] ag seductive; (proposta) very attractive

se'durre vt to seduce

se'duta sf session, sitting; (riunione) meeting; **seduta spiritica** séance; **seduta stante** (fig) immediately

seduzi'one [sedut'tsjone] sf seduction; (fascino) charm, appeal

SEeO abbr (= salvo errori e omissioni) E and OE

'sega, -ghe sf saw

'segale sf rye

se'gare vt to saw; (recidere) to saw off

'seggio ['sɛddʒo] sm seat; **seggio elettorale** polling station

'seggiola ['sɛddʒola] sf chair; **seggio'lone** sm (per bambini) highchair

seggio'via [sɛddʒo'via] sf chairlift

segherò ecc [sege'rɔ] vb vedi **segare**

segna'lare [seɲɲa'lare] vt (manovra ecc) to signal; to indicate; (annunciare) to announce; to report; (fig: far conoscere) to point out; (: persona) to single out

se'gnale [seɲ'ɲale] sm signal; (cartello): **segnale acustico** acoustic o sound signal; **segnale d'allarme** alarm; (Ferr) communication cord; **segnale orario** (Radio) time signal; **segnale stradale** road sign

segna'libro [seɲɲa'libro] sm (anche Inform) bookmark

se'gnare [seɲ'ɲare] vt to mark; (prendere nota) to note; (indicare) to indicate, mark; (Sport: goal) to score

'segno ['seɲɲo] sm sign; (impronta, contrassegno) mark; (limite) limit, bounds pl; (bersaglio) target; **fare ~ di sì/no** to nod (one's head)/shake one's head; **fare ~ a qn di fermarsi** to motion (to) sb to stop; **cogliere o colpire nel ~** (fig) to hit the mark; **segno zodiacale** star sign

segre'tario, -a sm/f secretary; **segretario comunale** town clerk; **Segretario di Stato** Secretary of State

segrete'ria sf (di ditta, scuola) (secretary's) office; (d'organizzazione internazionale) secretariat; (Pol ecc: carica) office of Secretary; **segreteria telefonica** answering service

se'greto, -a ag secret ▷ sm secret; secrecy no pl; **in ~** in secret, secretly

segu'ace [se'gwatʃe] sm/f follower, disciple

segu'ente ag following, next

segu'ire vt to follow; (frequentare: corso) to attend ▷ vi to follow; (continuare: testo) to continue

segui'tare vt to continue, carry on with ▷ vi to continue, carry on

'seguito sm (scorta) suite, retinue; (discepoli) followers pl; (favore) following; (continuazione) continuation; (conseguenza) result; **di ~** at a stretch, on end; **in ~** later on; **in ~ a, a ~ di** following; (a causa di) as a result of, owing to

'sei vb vedi **essere** ▷ num six

sei'cento [sei'tʃɛnto] num six hundred ▷ sm **il S~** the seventeenth century

selci'ato [sel'tʃato] sm cobbled surface

selezio'nare [selettsjo'nare] vt to select

selezi'one [selet'tsjone] sf selection

'sella sf saddle

sel'lino sm saddle

selvag'gina [selvad'dʒina] sf (animali) game

sel'vaggio, -a, -gi, -ge [sel'vaddʒo] ag wild; (tribù) savage, uncivilized; (fig) savage, brutal ▷ sm/f savage

sel'vatico, -a, -ci, -che ag wild

se'maforo sm (Aut) traffic lights pl

sem'brare *vi* to seem ▷ *vb impers* **sembra che** it seems that; **mi sembra che** it seems to me that, I think (that); **~ di essere** to seem to be

'seme *sm* seed; (*sperma*) semen; (*Carte*) suit

se'mestre *sm* half-year, six-month period

semifi'nale *sf* semifinal

semi'freddo *sm* ice-cream cake

semi'nare *vt* to sow

semi'nario *sm* seminar; (*Rel*) seminary

seminter'rato *sm* basement; (*appartamento*) basement flat

'semola *sf*; **semola di grano duro** durum wheat

semo'lino *sm* semolina

'semplice ['semplitʃe] *ag* simple; (*di un solo elemento*) single

'sempre *av* always; (*ancora*) still; **posso ~ tentare** I can always o still try; **da ~** always; **per ~** forever; **una volta per ~** once and for all; **~ che** provided (that); **~ più** more and more; **~ meno** less and less

sempre'verde *ag*, *sm o f* (*Bot*) evergreen

'senape *sf* (*Cuc*) mustard

se'nato *sm* senate; **sena'tore, -'trice** *sm/f* senator

'senno *sm* judgment, (common) sense; **col ~ di poi** with hindsight

'seno *sm* (*Anat*: *petto, mammella*) breast; (: *grembo, fig*) womb; (: *cavità*) sinus

sen'sato, -a *ag* sensible

sensazio'nale [sensattsjo'nale] *ag* sensational

sensazi'one [sensat'tsjone] *sf* feeling, sensation; **avere la ~ che** to have a feeling that; **fare ~** to cause a sensation, create a stir

sen'sibile *ag* sensitive; (*ai sensi*) perceptible; (*rilevante, notevole*) appreciable, noticeable; **~ a** sensitive to

> Attenzione! In inglese esiste la parola *sensible*, che però significa *ragionevole*.

'senso *sm* (*Fisiol, istinto*) sense; (*impressione, sensazione*) feeling, sensation; (*significato*) meaning, sense; (*direzione*) direction; **sensi** *smpl* (*coscienza*) consciousness *sg*; (*sensualità*) senses; **ciò non ha ~** that doesn't make sense; **fare ~ a** (*ripugnare*) to disgust, repel; **in ~ orario/antiorario** clockwise/anticlockwise; **senso di colpa** sense of guilt; **senso comune** common sense; **senso unico** (*strada*) one-way; **senso vietato** (*Aut*) no entry

sensu'ale *ag* sensual; sensuous

sen'tenza [sen'tentsa] *sf* (*Dir*) sentence; (*massima*) maxim

senti'ero *sm* path

sentimen'tale *ag* sentimental; (*vita, avventura*) love *cpd*

senti'mento *sm* feeling

senti'nella *sf* sentry

sen'tire *vt* (*percepire al tatto, fig*) to feel; (*udire*) to hear; (*ascoltare*) to listen to; (*odore*) to smell; (*avvertire con il gusto, assaggiare*) to taste ▷ *vi* **~ di** (*avere sapore*) to taste of; (*avere odore*) to smell of; **sentirsi** *vpr* (*uso reciproco*) to be in touch; **sentirsi bene/male** to feel well/unwell o ill; **non mi sento bene** I don't feel well; **sentirsi di fare qc** (*essere disposto*) to feel like doing sth

sen'tito, -a *ag* (*sincero*) sincere, warm; **per ~ dire** by hearsay

'senza ['sɛntsa] *prep, cong* without; **~ dir nulla** without saying a word; **fare ~ qc** to do without sth; **~ di me** without me; **~ che io lo sapessi** without me o my knowing; **senz'altro** of course, certainly; **~ dubbio** no doubt; **~ scrupoli** unscrupulous; **~ amici** friendless

sepa'rare *vt* to separate; (*dividere*) to divide; (*tenere distinto*) to distinguish; **separarsi** *vpr* (*coniugi*) to separate, part; (*amici*) to part, leave each other; **separarsi da** (*coniuge*) to separate o part from; (*amico, socio*) to part company with; (*oggetto*) to part with; **sepa'rato, -a** *ag* (*letti, conto ecc*) separate; (*coniugi*) separated

seppel'lire *vt* to bury

'seppi *ecc* *vb* *vedi* **sapere**

'seppia *sf* cuttlefish ▷ *ag inv* sepia

se'quenza [se'kwentsa] *sf* sequence

seques'trare *vt* (*Dir*) to impound; (*rapire*) to kidnap; **se'questro** *sm* (*Dir*) impoundment; **sequestro di persona** kidnapping

'sera *sf* evening; **di ~** in the evening; **domani ~** tomorrow evening, tomorrow night; **se'rale** *ag* evening *cpd*; **se'rata** *sf* evening; (*ricevimento*) party

ser'bare *vt* to keep; (*mettere da parte*) to put aside; **~ rancore/odio verso qn** to bear sb a grudge/hate sb

serba'toio *sm* tank; (*cisterna*) cistern

'Serbia *sf* **la ~** Serbia

'serbo *ag* Serbian, Serb ▷ *sm/f* Serbian, Serb ▷ *sm* (*Ling*) Serbian; (*il serbare*): **mettere/tenere o avere in ~ qc** to put/keep sth aside

se'reno, -a *ag* (*tempo, cielo*) clear; (*fig*) serene, calm

ser'gente [ser'dʒɛnte] *sm* (*Mil*) sergeant

'serie *sf inv* (*successione*) series *inv*; (*gruppo, collezione*) set; (*Sport*) division; league; (*Comm*): **modello di ~/fuori ~** standard/

custom-built model; **in ~** in quick succession; (*Comm*) mass *cpd*

serietà *sf* seriousness; reliability

'serio, -a *ag* serious; (*impiegato*) responsible, reliable; (*ditta, cliente*) reliable, dependable; **sul ~** (*davvero*) really, truly; (*seriamente*) seriously, in earnest

ser'pente *sm* snake; **serpente a sonagli** rattlesnake

'serra *sf* greenhouse; hothouse

ser'randa *sf* roller shutter

serra'tura *sf* lock

server ['sɛrver] *sm inv* (*Inform*) server

ser'vire *vt* to serve; (*clienti: al ristorante*) to wait on; (: *al negozio*) to serve, attend to; (*fig: giovare*) to aid, help; (*Carte*) to deal ▷ *vi* (*Tennis*) to serve; (*essere utile*): **~ a qn** to be of use to sb; **~ a qc/a fare** (*utensile ecc*) to be used for sth/for doing; **~ (a qn) da** to serve as (for sb); **servirsi** *vpr* (*usare*): **servirsi di** to use; (*prendere: cibo*): **servirsi (di)** to help o.s. to (to); **serviti pure!** help yourself!; (*essere cliente abituale*): **servirsi da** to be a regular customer at, go to

servizi'evole [servit'tsjevole] *ag* obliging, willing to help

ser'vizio [ser'vittsjo] *sm* service; (*al ristorante: sul conto*) service (charge); (*Stampa, TV, Radio*) report; (*da tè, caffè ecc*) set, service; **servizi** *smpl* (*di casa*) kitchen and bathroom; (*Econ*) services; **essere di ~** to be on duty; **fuori ~** (*telefono ecc*) out of order; **~ compreso** service included; **servizio militare** military service; **servizio di posate** set of cutlery; **servizi segreti** secret service *sg*; **servizio da tè** tea set

ses'santa *num* sixty; **sessan'tesimo, -a** *num* sixtieth

sessi'one *sf* session

'sesso *sm* sex; **sessu'ale** *ag* sexual, sex *cpd*

ses'tante *sm* sextant

'sesto, -a *ag, sm* sixth

'seta *sf* silk

'sete *sf* thirst; **avere ~** to be thirsty

'setola *sf* bristle

'setta *sf* sect

set'tanta *num* seventy; **settan'tesimo, -a** *num* seventieth

set'tare *vt* (*Inform*) to set up

'sette *num* seven

sette'cento [sette'tʃɛnto] *num* seven hundred ▷ *sm* **il S~** the eighteenth century

set'tembre *sm* September

settentrio'nale *ag* northern

settentri'one *sm* north

setti'mana *sf* week; **settima'nale** *ag, sm* weekly

● **SETTIMANA BIANCA**

● **Settimana bianca** is the name given to a week-long winter-sports holiday taken by many Italians some time in the skiing season.

'settimo, -a *ag, sm* seventh

set'tore *sm* sector

severità *sf* severity

se'vero, -a *ag* severe

sevizi'are [sevit'tsjare] *vt* to torture

sezio'nare [settsjo'nare] *vt* to divide into sections; (*Med*) to dissect

sezi'one [set'tsjone] *sf* section

sfacchi'nata [sfakki'nata] *sf* (*fam*) chore, drudgery *no pl*

sfacci'ato, -a [sfat'tʃato] *ag* (*maleducato*) cheeky, impudent; (*vistoso*) gaudy

sfa'mare *vt* to feed; (*cibo*) to fill; **sfamarsi** *vpr* to satisfy one's hunger, fill o.s. up

sfasci'are [sfaʃʃare] *vt* (*ferita*) to unbandage; (*distruggere*) to smash, shatter; **sfasciarsi** *vpr* (*rompersi*) to smash, shatter

sfavo'revole *ag* unfavourable

'sfera *sf* sphere

sfer'rare *vt* (*fig: colpo*) to land, deal; (: *attacco*) to launch

'sfida *sf* challenge

sfi'dare *vt* to challenge; (*fig*) to defy, brave

sfi'ducia [sfi'dutʃa] *sf* distrust, mistrust

sfi'gato, -a (*fam*) *ag* (*sfortunato*) unlucky

sfigu'rare *vt* (*persona*) to disfigure; (*quadro, statua*) to deface ▷ *vi* (*far cattiva figura*) to make a bad impression

sfi'lare *vt* (*ago*) to unthread; (*abito, scarpe*) to slip off ▷ *vi* (*truppe*) to march past; (*atleti*) to parade; **sfilarsi** *vpr* (*perle ecc*) to come unstrung; (*orlo, tessuto*) to fray; (*calza*) to run, ladder; **sfi'lata** *sf* march past; parade; **sfilata di moda** fashion show

'sfinge ['sfindʒe] *sf* sphinx

sfi'nito, -a *ag* exhausted

sfio'rare *vt* to brush (against); (*argomento*) to touch upon

sfio'rire *vi* to wither, fade

sfo'cato, -a *ag* (*Fot*) out of focus

sfoci'are [sfo'tʃare] *vi* **~ in** to flow into; (*fig: malcontento*) to develop into

sfode'rato, -a *ag* (*vestito*) unlined

sfogarsi *vpr* (*sfogare la propria rabbia*) to give vent to one's anger; (*confidarsi*): **~ (con)** to pour out one's feelings (to); **non**

sfogarti su di me! don't take your bad temper out on me!

sfoggi'are [sfod'dʒare] vt, vi to show off

'sfoglia ['sfɔʎʎa] sf sheet of pasta dough; **pasta ~** (Cuc) puff pastry

sfogli'are [sfoʎ'ʎare] vt (libro) to leaf through

'sfogo, -ghi sm (eruzione cutanea) rash; (fig) outburst; **dare ~ a** (fig) to give vent to

sfon'dare vt (porta) to break down; (scarpe) to wear a hole in; (cesto, scatola) to burst, knock the bottom out of; (Mil) to break through ▷ vi (riuscire) to make a name for o.s.

'sfondo sm background

sfor'mato sm (Cuc) type of soufflé

sfor'tuna sf misfortune, ill luck no pl; **avere ~** to be unlucky; **sfortu'nato, -a** ag unlucky; (impresa, film) unsuccessful

sforzarsi vpr **~ di** o **a** o **per fare** to try hard to do

'sforzo ['sfɔrtso] sm effort; (tensione eccessiva, Tecn) strain; **fare uno ~** to make an effort

sfrat'tare vt to evict; **'sfratto** sm eviction

sfrecci'are [sfret'tʃare] vi to shoot o flash past

sfre'gare vt (strofinare) to rub; (graffiare) to scratch; **sfregarsi le mani** to rub one's hands; **~ un fiammifero** to strike a match

sfregi'are [sfre'dʒare] vt to slash, gash; (persona) to disfigure; (quadro) to deface

sfre'nato, -a ag (fig) unrestrained, unbridled

sfron'tato, -a ag shameless

sfrutta'mento sm exploitation

sfrut'tare vt (terreno) to overwork, exhaust; (miniera) to exploit, work; (fig: operai, occasione, potere) to exploit

sfug'gire [sfud'dʒire] vi to escape; **~ a** (custode) to escape (from); (morte) to escape; **~ a qn** (dettaglio, nome) to escape sb; **~ di mano a qn** to slip out of sb's hand (o hands)

sfu'mare vt (colori, contorni) to soften, shade off ▷ vi to shade (off), fade; (fig: svanire) o vanish, disappear; (: speranze) to come to nothing

sfuma'tura sf shading off no pl; (tonalità) shade, tone; (fig) touch, hint

sfuri'ata sf (scatto di collera) fit of anger; (rimprovero) sharp rebuke

sga'bello sm stool

sgabuz'zino [sgabud'dzino] sm lumber room

sgambet'tare vi to kick one's legs about

sgam'betto sm **far lo ~ a qn** to trip sb up; (fig) to oust sb

sganci'are [zgan'tʃare] vt to unhook; (Ferr) to uncouple; (bombe: da aereo) to release, drop; (fig: fam: soldi) to fork out; **sganciarsi** vpr (fig): **sganciarsi (da)** to get away (from)

sganghe'rato, -a ag (porta) off its hinges; (auto) ramshackle; (risata) wild, boisterous

sgar'bato, -a ag rude, impolite

'sgarbo sm **fare uno ~ a qn** to be rude to sb

sgargi'ante [zgar'dʒante] ag gaudy, showy

sgattaio'lare vi to sneak away o off

sge'lare [zdʒe'lare] vi, vt to thaw

sghignaz'zare [zgiɲɲat'tsare] vi to laugh scornfully

sgob'bare (fam) vi (scolaro) to swot; (operaio) to slog

sgombe'rare vt (tavolo, stanza) to clear; (piazza, città) to evacuate ▷ vi to move

'sgombro, -a ~ (di) clear (of), free (from) ▷ sm (Zool) mackerel; (anche: **sgombero**) clearing; vacating; evacuation; (: trasloco) removal

sgonfi'are vt to let down, deflate; **sgonfiarsi** vpr to go down

'sgonfio, -a ag (pneumatico, pallone) flat

'sgorbio sm blot; scribble

sgra'devole ag unpleasant, disagreeable

sgra'dito, -a ag unpleasant, unwelcome

sgra'nare vt (piselli) to shell; **~ gli occhi** to open one's eyes wide

sgranchire [zgran'kire] vt (anche: **sgranchirsi**) to stretch; **~ le gambe** to stretch one's legs

sgranocchi'are [zgranok'kjare] vt to munch

'sgravio sm **~ fiscale** tax relief

sgrazi'ato, -a [zgrat'tsjato] ag clumsy, ungainly

sgri'dare vt to scold

sgual'cire [zgwal'tʃire] vt to crumple (up), crease

sgual'drina (peg) sf slut

sgu'ardo sm (occhiata) look, glance; (espressione) look (in one's eye)

sguaz'zare [zgwat'tsare] vi (nell'acqua) to splash about; (nella melma) to wallow; **~ nell'oro** to be rolling in money

sguinzagli'are [zgwintsaʎ'ʎare] vt to let off the leash; (fig: persona): **~ qn dietro a qn** to set sb on sb

sgusci'are [zguʃ'ʃare] vt to shell ▷ vi (sfuggire di mano) to slip; **~ via** to slip o slink away

'shampoo ['ʃampo] sm inv shampoo

shiatzu [ʃi'atstsu] sm inv shiatsu

shock [ʃɔk] *sm inv* shock

O PAROLA CHIAVE

si (*dav lo, la, li, le, ne diventa* **se**) *pron* **1**
(*riflessivo: maschile*) himself; (: *femminile*)
herself; (: *neutro*) itself; (: *impersonale*)
oneself; (: *pl*) themselves; **lavarsi** to wash
(oneself); **si è tagliato** he has cut himself;
si credono importanti they think a lot of
themselves
2 (*riflessivo: con complemento oggetto*):
lavarsi le mani to wash one's hands; **si
sta lavando i capelli** he (o she) is washing
his (o her) hair
3 (*reciproco*) one another, each other; **si
amano** they love one another o each other
4 (*passivo*): **si ripara facilmente** it is easily
repaired
5 (*impersonale*): **si dice che ...** they o
people say that ...; **si vede che è vecchio**
one o you can see that it's old
6 (*noi*) we; **tra poco si parte** we're leaving
soon

sì *av* yes; **un giorno sì e uno no** every
other day
'sia *cong* ~ ... ~ (o ... o): ~ **che lavori,** ~ **che
non lavori** whether he works or not;
(*tanto ... quanto*): **verranno** ~ **Luigi** ~ **suo
fratello** both Luigi and his brother will be
coming
si'amo *vb vedi* **essere**
si'cario *sm* hired killer
sicché [sik'ke] *cong* (*perciò*) so (that),
therefore; (*e quindi*) (and) so
siccità [sittʃi'ta] *sf* drought
sic'come *cong* since, as
Si'cilia [si'tʃilja] *sf* la ~ Sicily
si'cura *sf* safety catch; (*Aut*) safety lock
sicu'rezza [siku'rettsa] *sf* safety; security;
(*fiducia*) confidence; (*certezza*) certainty; **di
~ safety** *cpd*; **la ~ stradale** road safety
si'curo, -a *ag* safe; (*ben difeso*) secure;
(*fiducioso*) confident; (*certo*) sure, certain;
(*notizia, amico*) reliable; (*esperto*) skilled
▷ *av* (*anche*: **di ~**) certainly; **essere/
mettere al** ~ to be safe/put in a safe place;
~ **di sé** self-confident, sure of o.s.; **sentirsi
~** to feel safe o secure
si'edo *ecc vb vedi* **sedere**
si'epe *sf* hedge
si'ero *sm* (*Med*) serum; **sieronega'tivo,
-a** *ag* HIV-negative; **sieroposi'tivo, -a** *ag*
HIV-positive
si'ete *vb vedi* **essere**
si'filide *sf* syphilis
Sig. *abbr* (= *signore*) Mr
siga'retta *sf* cigarette

'sigaro *sm* cigar
Sigg. *abbr* (= *signori*) Messrs
sigil'lare [sidʒil'lare] *vt* to seal
si'gillo [si'dʒillo] *sm* seal
'sigla *sf* initials *pl*; acronym, abbreviation;
sigla automobilistica abbreviation of
province on vehicle number plate; **sigla
musicale** signature tune
Sig.na *abbr* (= *signorina*) Miss
signifi'care [siɲnifi'kare] *vt* to mean;
signifi'cato *sm* meaning
si'gnora [siɲ'ɲora] *sf* lady; **la ~ X** Mrs X;
buon giorno S~/Signóre/Signorina
good morning; (*deferente*) good morning
Madam/Sir/Madam; (*quando si conosce
il nome*) good morning Mrs/Mr/Miss X;
Gentile S~/Signore/Signorina (*in una
lettera*) Dear Madam/Sir/Madam; **il signor
Rossi e ~** Mr Rossi and his wife; **signore e
signori** ladies and gentlemen
si'gnore [siɲ'ɲore] *sm* gentleman;
(*padrone*) lord, master; (*Rel*): **il S~** the Lord;
il signor X Mr X; **i signori Bianchi** (*coniugi*)
Mr and Mrs Bianchi; *vedi anche* **signora**
signo'rile [siɲɲo'rile] *ag* refined
signo'rina [siɲɲo'rina] *sf* young lady; **la ~
X** Miss X; *vedi anche* **signora**
Sig.ra *abbr* (= *signora*) Mrs
silenzia'tore [silentsja'tore] *sm* silencer
si'lenzio [si'lɛntsjo] *sm* silence; **fare ~** to
be quiet, stop talking; **silenzi'oso, -a** *ag*
silent, quiet
si'licio [si'litʃo] *sm* silicon
sili'cone *sm* silicone
'sillaba *sf* syllable
si'luro *sm* torpedo
simboleggi'are [simboled'dʒare] *vt* to
symbolize
'simbolo *sm* symbol
'simile *ag* (*analogo*) similar; (*di questo tipo*)
un uomo ~ such a man, a man like this;
libri simili such books; **~ a** similar to; **i suoi
simili** one's fellow men; one's peers
simme'tria *sf* symmetry
simpa'tia *sf* (*qualità*) pleasantness;
(*inclinazione*) liking; **avere ~ per qn** to like
sb, have a liking for sb; **sim'patico, -a, -ci,
-che** *ag* (*persona*) nice, pleasant, likeable;
(*casa, albergo ecc*) nice, pleasant

> Attenzione! In inglese esiste la
> parola *sympathetic*, che però significa
> *comprensivo*.

simpatiz'zare [simpatid'dzare] *vi* ~ **con**
to take a liking to
simu'lare *vt* to sham, simulate; (*Tecn*) to
simulate
simul'taneo, -a *ag* simultaneous
sina'goga, -ghe *sf* synagogue
sincerità [sintʃeri'ta] *sf* sincerity

sin'cero, -a [sin'tʃero] *ag* sincere; genuine; heartfelt

sinda'cale *ag* (trade-)union *cpd*

sinda'cato *sm* (*di lavoratori*) (trade) union; (*Amm, Econ, Dir*) syndicate, trust, pool

'sindaco, -ci *sm* mayor

sinfo'nia *sf* (*Mus*) symphony

singhioz'zare [singjot'tsare] *vi* to sob; to hiccup

singhi'ozzo [sin'gjottso] *sm* sob; (*Med*) hiccup, **avere il ~** to have the hiccups; **a ~** (*fig*) by fits and starts

single ['singol] *ag inv, sm/f inv* single

singo'lare *ag* (*insolito*) remarkable, singular; (*Ling*) singular ▷ *sm* (*Ling*) singular; (*Tennis*): **~ maschile/femminile** men's/women's singles

'singolo, -a *ag* single, individual ▷ *sm* (*persona*) individual; (*Tennis*) = **singolare**

si'nistra *sf* (*Pol*) left (wing); **a ~** on the left; (*direzione*) to the left

si'nistro, -a *ag* left, left-hand; (*fig*) sinister ▷ *sm* (*incidente*) accident

si'nonimo *sm* synonym; **~ di** synonymous with

sin'tassi *sf* syntax

'sintesi *sf* synthesis; (*riassunto*) summary, résumé

sin'tetico, -a, -ci, -che *ag* synthetic

sintetiz'zare [sintetid'dzare] *vt* to synthesize; (*riassumere*) to summarize

sinto'matico, -a, -ci, -che *ag* symptomatic

'sintomo *sm* symptom

sintonizzarsi *vpr* **~ su** to tune in to

si'pario *sm* (*Teatro*) curtain

si'rena *sf* (*apparecchio*) siren; (*nella mitologia, fig*) siren, mermaid

'Siria *sf* **la ~** Syria

si'ringa, -ghe *sf* syringe

'sismico, -a, -ci, -che *ag* seismic

sis'tema, -i *sm* system; method, way; **sistema nervoso** nervous system; **sistema operativo** (*Inform*) operating system; **sistema solare** solar system

siste'mare *vt* (*mettere a posto*) to tidy, put in order; (*risolvere: questione*) to sort out, settle; (*procurare un lavoro a*) to find a job for; (*dare un alloggio a*) to settle, find accommodation for; **sistemarsi** *vpr* (*problema*) to be settled; (*persona: trovare alloggio*) to find accommodation (BRIT) o accommodations (US); (: *trovarsi un lavoro*) to get fixed up with a job; **ti sistemo io!** I'll soon sort you out!

siste'matico, -a, -ci, -che *ag* systematic

sistemazi'one [sistemat'tsjone] *sf* arrangement, order; settlement; employment; accommodation (BRIT), accommodations (US)

'sito *sm* **~ Internet** website

situazi'one [situat'tsjone] *sf* situation

ski-lift ['ski:lift] *sm inv* ski tow

slacci'are [zlat'tʃare] *vt* to undo, unfasten

slanci'ato, -a [zlan'tʃato] *ag* slender

'slancio *sm* dash, leap; (*fig*) surge; **di ~** impetuously

'slavo, -a *ag* Slav(onic), Slavic

sle'ale *ag* disloyal; (*concorrenza ecc*) unfair

sle'gare *vt* to untie

slip [zlip] *sm inv* briefs *pl*

'slitta *sf* sledge; (*trainata*) sleigh

slit'tare *vi* to slip, slide; (*Aut*) to skid

s.l.m. *abbr* (= *sul livello del mare*) a.s.l.

slo'gare *vt* (*Med*) to dislocate

sloggi'are [zlod'dʒare] *vt* (*inquilino*) to turn out ▷ *vi* to move out

Slo'vacchia [zlo'vakkja] *sf* Slovakia

slo'vacco, -a, -chi, -che *ag, sm/f* Slovak

Slovenia [zlo'vɛnja] *sf* Slovenia

slo'veno, -a *ag, sm/f* Slovene, Slovenian ▷ *sm* (*Ling*) Slovene

smacchi'are [zmak'kjare] *vt* to remove stains from; **smacchia'tore** *sm* stain remover

'smacco, -chi *sm* humiliating defeat

smagli'ante [zmaʎ'ʎante] *ag* brilliant, dazzling

smaglia'tura [zmaʎʎa'tura] *sf* (*su maglia, calza*) ladder; (*della pelle*) stretch mark

smalizi'ato, -a [zmalit'tsjato] *ag* shrewd, cunning

smalti'mento *sm* (*di rifiuti*) disposal

smal'tire *vt* (*merce*) to sell off; (*rifiuti*) to dispose of; (*cibo*) to digest; (*peso*) to lose; (*rabbia*) to get over; **~ la sbornia** to sober up

'smalto *sm* (*anche: di denti*) enamel; (*per ceramica*) glaze; **smalto per unghie** nail varnish

smantel'lare *vt* to dismantle

smarri'mento *sm* loss; (*fig*) bewilderment; dismay

smar'rire *vt* to lose; (*non riuscire a trovare*) to mislay; **smarrirsi** *vpr* (*perdersi*) to lose one's way, get lost; (: *oggetto*) to go astray

smasche'rare [zmaske'rare] *vt* to unmask

SME *sigla m* (= *Sistema Monetario Europeo*) EMS (European Monetary System)

smen'tire *vt* (*negare*) to deny; (*testimonianza*) to refute; **smentirsi** *vpr* to be inconsistent

sme'raldo *sm* emerald

'smesso, -a *pp di* **smettere**

'smettere *vt* to stop; (*vestiti*) to stop wearing ▷ *vi* to stop, cease; **~ di fare** to stop doing

'smilzo, -a ['zmiltso] *ag* thin, lean

sminu'ire *vt* to diminish, lessen; (*fig*) to belittle

sminuz'zare [zminut'tsare] *vt* to break into small pieces; to crumble

'smisi *ecc vb vedi* **smettere**

smis'tare *vt* (*pacchi ecc*) to sort; (*Ferr*) to shunt

smisu'rato, -a *ag* boundless, immeasurable; (*grandissimo*) immense, enormous

smoking ['sməukɪŋ] *sm inv* dinner jacket

smon'tare *vt* (*mobile, macchina ecc*) to take to pieces, dismantle; (*fig: scoraggiare*) to dishearten ▷ *vi* (*scendere: da cavallo*) to dismount; (: *da treno*) to get off; (*terminare il lavoro*) to stop (work); **smontarsi** *vpr* to lose heart; to lose one's enthusiasm

'smorfia *sf* grimace; (*atteggiamento lezioso*) simpering; **fare smorfie** to make faces; to simper

'smorto, -a *ag* (*viso*) pale, wan; (*colore*) dull

smor'zare [zmor'tsare] *vt* (*suoni*) to deaden; (*colori*) to tone down; (*luce*) to dim; (*sete*) to quench; (*entusiasmo*) to dampen; **smorzarsi** *vpr* (*suono, luce*) to fade; (*entusiasmo*) to dampen

SMS *sigla m inv* (= *short message service*) text (message)

smu'overe *vt* to move, shift; (*fig: commuovere*) to move; (: *dall'inerzia*) to rouse, stir

snatu'rato, -a *ag* inhuman, heartless

'snello, -a *ag* (*agile*) agile; (*svelto*) slender, slim

sner'vante *ag* (*attesa, lavoro*) exasperating

snob'bare *vt* to snub

sno'dare *vt* (*rendere agile, mobile*) to loosen; **snodarsi** *vpr* to come loose; (*articolarsi*) to bend; (*strada, fiume*) to wind

sno'dato, -a *ag* (*articolazione, persona*) flexible; (*fune ecc*) undone

so *vb vedi* **sapere**

sobbar'carsi *vpr* ~ **a** to take on, undertake

'sobrio, -a *ag* sober

socchi'udere [sok'kjudere] *vt* (*porta*) to leave ajar; (*occhi*) to half-close; **socchi'uso, -a** *pp di* **socchiudere**

soc'correre *vt* to help, assist

soccorri'tore, -'trice *sm/f* rescuer

soc'corso, -a *pp di* **soccorrere** ▷ *sm* help, aid, assistance; **soccorso stradale** breakdown service

soci'ale [so't∫ale] *ag* social; (*di associazione*) club *cpd*, association *cpd*

socia'lismo [sot∫a'lizmo] *sm* socialism; **socia'lista, -i, -e** *ag, sm/f* socialist

società [sot∫e'ta] *sf inv* society; (*sportiva*) club; (*Comm*) company; ~ **a responsabilità limitata** *type of limited liability company*; **società per azioni** limited (BRIT) o incorporated (US) company

soci'evole [so't∫evole] *ag* sociable

'socio ['sɔt∫o] *sm* (*Dir, Comm*) partner; (*membro di associazione*) member

'soda *sf* (*Chim*) soda; (*bibita*) soda (water)

soddisfa'cente [soddisfa't∫ɛnte] *ag* satisfactory

soddis'fare *vt, vi* ~ **a** to satisfy; (*impegno*) to fulfil; (*debito*) to pay off; (*richiesta*) to meet, comply with; **soddis'fatto, -a** *pp di* **soddisfare** ▷ *ag* satisfied; **soddisfatto di** happy o satisfied with; pleased with; **soddisfazi'one** *sf* satisfaction

'sodo, -a *ag* firm, hard; (*uovo*) hard-boiled ▷ *av* (*picchiare, lavorare*) hard; (*dormire*) soundly

sofà *sm inv* sofa

soffe'renza [soffe'rɛntsa] *sf* suffering

sof'ferto, -a *pp di* **soffrire**

soffi'are *vt* to blow; (*notizia, segreto*) to whisper ▷ *vi* to blow; (*sbuffare*) to puff (and blow); **soffiarsi il naso** to blow one's nose; ~ **qc a qn** (*fig*) to pinch o steal sth/sb from sb; ~ **via qc** to blow sth away

soffi'ata *sf* (*fam*) tip-off; **fare una ~ alla polizia** to tip off the police

'soffice ['sɔffit∫e] *ag* soft

'soffio *sm* (*di vento*) breath; **soffio al cuore** heart murmur

sof'fitta *sf* attic

sof'fitto *sm* ceiling

soffo'cante *ag* suffocating, stifling

soffo'care *vi* (*anche:* **soffocarsi**) to suffocate, choke ▷ *vt* to suffocate, choke; (*fig*) to stifle, suppress

sof'frire *vt* to suffer, endure; (*sopportare*) to bear, stand ▷ *vi* to suffer; to be in pain; ~ **(di)** (*Med*) to suffer from sth

sof'fritto, -a *pp di* **soffriggere** ▷ *sm* (*Cuc*) fried mixture of herbs, bacon and onions

sofisti'cato, -a *ag* sophisticated; (*vino*) adulterated

'software ['sɔftwɛə] *sm* ~ **applicativo** applications package

sogget'tivo, -a [soddʒet'tivo] *ag* subjective

sog'getto, -a [sod'dʒetto] *ag* ~ **a** (*sottomesso*) subject to; (*esposto: a variazioni, danni ecc*) subject o liable to ▷ *sm* subject

soggezi'one [soddʒet'tsjone] *sf* subjection; (*timidezza*) awe; **avere ~ di qn** to stand in awe of sb; to be ill at ease in sb's presence

soggi'orno *sm* (*invernale, marino*) stay; (*stanza*) living room

'soglia ['sɔλλa] *sf* doorstep; (*anche fig*)

threshold
'sogliola ['sɔʎʎola] sf (Zool) sole
so'gnare [soɲˈɲare] vt, vi to dream; **~ a occhi aperti** to daydream
'sogno ['soɲɲo] sm dream
'soia sf (Bot) soya
sol sm (Mus) G; (: solfeggiando) so(h)
so'laio sm (soffitta) attic
sola'mente av only, just
so'lare ag solar, sun cpd
'solco, -chi sm (scavo, flg: ruga) furrow; (incavo) rut, track; (di disco) groove
sol'dato sm soldier; **soldato semplice** private
soldi smpl (denaro) money sg; **non ho ~** I haven't got any money
'sole sm sun; (luce) sun(light); (tempo assolato) sun(shine); **prendere il ~** to sunbathe
soleggi'ato, -a [soledˈdʒato] ag sunny
so'lenne ag solemn
soli'dale ag **essere ~ (con)** to be in agreement (with)
solidarietà sf solidarity
'solido, -a ag solid; (forte, robusto) sturdy, solid; (fig: ditta) sound, solid ▷ sm (Mat) solid
so'lista, -i, -e ag solo ▷ sm/f soloist
solita'mente av usually, as a rule
soli'tario, -a ag (senza compagnia) solitary, lonely; (solo, isolato) solitary, lone; (deserto) lonely ▷ sm (gioiello, gioco) solitaire
'solito, -a ag usual; **essere ~ fare** to be in the habit of doing; **di ~** usually; **più tardi del ~** later than usual; **come al ~** as usual
soli'tudine sf solitude
sol'letico sm tickling; **soffrire il ~** to be ticklish
solleva'mento sm raising; lifting; revolt; **sollevamento pesi** (Sport) weight-lifting
solle'vare vt to lift, raise; (fig: persona: alleggerire): **~ (da)** to relieve (of); (: dar conforto) to comfort, relieve; (: questione) to raise; (: far insorgere) to stir (to revolt); **sollevarsi** vpr to rise; (fig: riprendersi) to recover; (: ribellarsi) to rise up
solli'evo sm relief; (conforto) comfort
'solo, -a ag alone; (in senso spirituale: isolato) lonely; (unico): **un ~ libro** only one book, a single book; (con ag numerale): **veniamo noi tre soli** just o only the three of us are coming ▷ av (soltanto) only, just; **non ~ ... ma anche** not only ... but also; **fare qc da ~** to do sth (all) by oneself
sol'tanto av only
so'lubile ag (sostanza) soluble
soluzi'one [solutˈtsjone] sf solution
sol'vente ag, sm solvent
so'maro sm ass, donkey

somigli'anza [somiʎˈʎantsa] sf resemblance
somigli'are [somiʎˈʎare] vi **~ a** to be like, resemble; (nell'aspetto fisico) to look like; **somigliarsi** vpr to be (o look) alike
'somma sf (Mat) sum; (di denaro) sum (of money)
som'mare vt to add up; (aggiungere) to add; **tutto sommato** all things considered
som'mario, -a ag (racconto, indagine) brief; (giustizia) summary ▷ sm summary
sommer'gibile [sommerˈdʒibile] sm submarine
som'merso, -a pp di **sommergere**
sommità sf inv summit, top; (fig) height
som'mossa sf uprising
'sonda sf (Med, Meteor, Aer) probe; (Mineralogia) drill ▷ ag inv **pallone** m **~** weather balloon
son'daggio [sonˈdaddʒo] sm sounding; probe; boring, drilling; (indagine) survey; **sondaggio d'opinioni** opinion poll
son'dare vt (Naut) to sound; (atmosfera, piaga) to probe; (Mineralogia) to bore, drill; (fig: opinione ecc) to survey, poll
so'netto sm sonnet
son'nambulo, -a sm/f sleepwalker
sonnel'lino sm nap
son'nifero sm sleeping drug (o pill)
'sonno sm sleep; **prendere ~** to fall asleep; **aver ~** to be sleepy
'sono vb vedi **essere**
so'noro, -a ag (ambiente) resonant; (voce) sonorous, ringing; (onde, film) sound cpd
sontu'oso, -a ag sumptuous; lavish
sop'palco, -chi sm mezzanine
soppor'tare vt (subire: perdita, spese) to bear, sustain; (soffrire: dolore) to bear, endure; (cosa: freddo) to withstand; (persona: freddo, vino) to take; (tollerare) to put up with, tolerate

> Attenzione! In inglese esiste il verbo to support, che però non significa sopportare.

sop'primere vt (carica, privilegi, testimone) to do away with; (pubblicazione) to suppress; (parola, frase) to delete
'sopra prep (gen) on; (al di sopra di, più in alto di) above; over; (riguardo a) on, about ▷ av on top; (attaccato, scritto) on it; (al di sopra) above; (al piano superiore) upstairs; **donne ~ i 30 anni** women over 30 (years of age); **abito di ~** I live upstairs; **dormirci ~** (fig) to sleep on it
so'prabito sm overcoat
soprac'ciglio [soprat'tʃiʎʎo] (pl(f) **soprac'ciglia**) sm eyebrow
sopraf'fare vt to overcome, overwhelm
sopral'luogo, -ghi sm (di esperti)

inspection; (di polizia) on-the-spot investigation

sopram'mobile sm ornament

soprannatu'rale ag supernatural

sopran'nome sm nickname

so'prano, -a sm/f (persona) soprano ▷ sm (voce) soprano

soprappensi'ero av lost in thought

sopras'salto sm di ~ with a start; suddenly

soprasse'dere vi ~ a to delay, put off

soprat'tutto av (anzitutto) above all; (specialmente) especially

sopravvalu'tare vt to overestimate

soprav'vento sm avere/prendere il ~ su to have/get the upper hand over

sopravvis'suto, -a pp di **sopravvivere**

soprav'vivere vi to survive; (continuare a vivere): ~ (in) to live on (in); ~ a (incidente ecc) to survive; (persona) to outlive

so'pruso sm abuse of power; **subire un ~** to be abused

soq'quadro sm mettere a ~ to turn upside-down

sor'betto sm sorbet, water ice

sor'dina sf in ~ softly; (fig) on the sly

'sordo, -a ag deaf; (rumore) muffled; (dolore) dull; (odio, rancore) veiled ▷ sm/f deaf person; **sordo'muto, -a** ag deaf-and-dumb ▷ sm/f deaf-mute

so'rella sf sister; **sorel'lastra** sf stepsister; (con genitore in comune) half-sister

sor'gente [sor'dʒɛnte] sf (d'acqua) spring; (di fiume, Fisica, fig) source

'sorgere ['sordʒere] vi to rise; (scaturire) to spring, rise; (fig: difficoltà) to arise

sorni'one, -a ag sly

sorpas'sare vt (Aut) to overtake; (fig) to surpass; (: eccedere) to exceed, go beyond; ~ **in altezza** to be higher than; (persona) to be taller than

sorpren'dente ag surprising

sor'prendere vt (cogliere: in flagrante ecc) to catch; (stupire) to surprise; **sorprendersi** vpr **sorprendersi (di)** to be surprised (at); **sor'presa** sf surprise; **fare una sorpresa a qn** to give sb a surprise; **sor'preso, -a** pp di **sorprendere**

sor'reggere [sor'redʒere] vt to support, hold up; (fig) to sustain; **sorreggersi** vpr (tenersi ritto) to stay upright

sor'ridere vi to smile; **sor'riso, -a** pp di **sorridere** ▷ sm smile

'sorsi ecc vb vedi **sorgere**

'sorso sm sip

'sorta sf sort, kind; **di ~** whatever, of any kind, at all

'sorte sf (fato) fate, destiny; (evento fortuito) chance; **tirare a ~** to draw lots

sor'teggio [sor'teddʒo] sm draw

sorvegli'ante [sorveʎ'ʎante] sm/f (di carcere) guard, warder (BRIT); (di fabbrica ecc) supervisor

sorvegli'anza [sorveʎ'ʎantsa] sf watch; supervision; (Polizia, Mil) surveillance

sorvegli'are [sorveʎ'ʎare] vt (bambino, bagagli, prigioniero) to watch, keep an eye on; (malato) to watch over; (territorio, casa) to watch o keep watch over; (lavori) to supervise

sorvo'lare vt (territorio) to fly over ▷ vi ~ **su** (fig) to skim over

S.O.S. sigla m mayday, SOS

'sosia sm inv double

sos'pendere vt (appendere) to hang (up); (interrompere, privare di una carica) to suspend; (rimandare) to defer; (appendere) to hang

sospet'tare vt to suspect ▷ vi ~ **di** to suspect; (diffidare) to be suspicious of

sos'petto, -a ag suspicious ▷ sm suspicion; **sospet'toso, -a** ag suspicious

sospi'rare vi to sigh ▷ vt to long for, yearn for; **sos'piro** sm sigh

'sosta sf (fermata) stop, halt; (pausa) pause, break; **senza ~** non-stop, without a break

sostan'tivo sm noun, substantive

sos'tanza [sos'tantsa] sf substance; **sostanze** sfpl (ricchezze) wealth sg, possessions; **in ~** in short, to sum up

sos'tare vi (fermarsi) to stop (for a while), stay; (fare una pausa) to take a break

sos'tegno [sos'teɲɲo] sm support

soste'nere vt to support; (prendere su di sé) to take on, bear; (resistere) to withstand, stand up to; (affermare): ~ **che** to maintain that; **sostenersi** vpr to hold o.s. up, support o.s.; (fig) to keep up one's strength; ~ **gli esami** to sit exams

sostenta'mento sm maintenance, support

sostitu'ire vt (mettere al posto di): ~ **qn/qc a** to substitute sb/sth for; (prendere il posto di: persona) to substitute for; (: cosa) to take the place of

sosti'tuto, -a sm/f substitute

sostituzi'one [sostitut'tsjone] sf substitution; **in ~ di** as a substitute for, in place of

sotta'ceti [sotta'tʃeti] smpl pickles

sot'tana sf (sottoveste) underskirt; (gonna) skirt; (Rel) soutane, cassock

sotter'fugio [sotter'fudʒo] sm subterfuge

sotter'raneo, -a ag underground ▷ sm cellar

sotter'rare vt to bury

sot'tile ag thin; (figura, caviglia) thin, slim,

slender; (*fine: polvere, capelli*) fine; (*fig: leggero*) light; (*: vista*) sharp, keen; (*: olfatto*) fine, discriminating; (*: mente*) subtle; shrewd ▷ *sm* **non andare per il ~** not to mince matters

sottin'teso, -a *pp di* **sottintendere** ▷ *sm* allusion; **parlare senza sottintesi** to speak plainly

'**sotto** *prep* (*gen*) under; (*più in basso di*) below ▷ *av* underneath, beneath; below; (**al piano**) **di ~** downstairs; **~ forma di** in the form of; **~ il monte** at the foot of the mountain; **siamo ~ Natale** it's nearly Christmas; **~ la pioggia/il sole** in the rain/ sun(shine); **~ terra** underground; **chiuso ~ vuoto** vacuum-packed

sotto'fondo *sm* background; **sottofondo musicale** background music

sottoline'are *vt* to underline; (*fig*) to emphasize, stress

sottoma'rino, -a *ag* (*flora*) submarine; (*cavo, navigazione*) underwater ▷ *sm* (*Naut*) submarine

sottopas'saggio [sottopas'saddʒo] *sm* (*Aut*) underpass; (*pedonale*) subway, underpass

sotto'porre *vt* (*costringere*) to subject; (*fig: presentare*) to submit; **sottoporsi** *vpr* to submit; **sottoporsi a** (*subire*) to undergo

sottos'critto, -a *pp di* **sottoscrivere**

sotto'sopra *av* upside-down

sotto'terra *av* underground

sotto'titolo *sm* subtitle

sottovalu'tare *vt* to underestimate

sotto'veste *sf* underskirt

sotto'voce [sotto'votʃe] *av* in a low voice

sottovu'oto *av* confezionare **~** to vacuum-pack ▷ *ag* **confezione** *f* **~** vacuum packed

sot'trarre *vt* (*Mat*) to subtract, take away; **~ qn/qc a** (*togliere*) to remove sb/sth from; (*salvare*) to save o rescue sb/sth from; **~ qc a qn** (*rubare*) to steal sth from sb; **sottrarsi** *vpr* **sottrarsi a** (*sfuggire*) to escape; (*evitare*) to avoid; **sottrazi'one** *sf* subtraction; removal

souve'nir [suv(ə)'nir] *sm inv* souvenir

sovi'etico, -a, -ci, -che *ag* Soviet ▷ *sm/f* Soviet citizen

sovrac'carico, -a, chi, che *ag* **~ (di)** overloaded (with) ▷ *sm* excess load; **~ di lavoro** extra work

sovraffol'lato, -a *ag* overcrowded

sovrannatu'rale *ag* = **soprannatu'rale**

so'vrano, -a *ag* sovereign; (*fig: sommo*) supreme ▷ *sm/f* sovereign, monarch

sovrap'porre *vt* to place on top of, put on top of

sovvenzi'one [sovven'tsjone] *sf* subsidy,

grant

'**sozzo, -a** ['sottso] *ag* filthy, dirty

S.P.A. *abbr* = **società per azioni**

spac'care *vt* to split, break; (*legna*) to chop; **spaccarsi** *vpr* to split, break; **spacca'tura** *sf* split

spaccherò *ecc* [spakke'rɔ] *vb vedi* **spaccare**

spacci'are [spat'tʃare] *vt* (*vendere*) to sell (off); (*mettere in circolazione*) to circulate; (*droga*) to peddle, push; **spacciarsi** *vpr* **spacciarsi per** (*farsi credere*) to pass o.s. off as, pretend to be; **spaccia'tore, -'trice** *sm/f* (*di droga*) pusher; (*di denaro falso*) dealer; '**spaccio** *sm* (*di merce rubata, droga*): **spaccio (di)** trafficking (in); **spaccio (di)** passing (of); (*vendita*) sale; (*bottega*) shop

'**spacco, -chi** *sm* (*fenditura*) split, crack; (*strappo*) tear; (*di gonna*) slit

spac'cone *sm/f* boaster, braggart

'**spada** *sf* sword

spae'sato, -a *ag* disorientated, lost

spa'ghetti [spa'getti] *smpl* (*Cuc*) spaghetti *sg*

'**Spagna** ['spaɲɲa] *sf* **la ~** Spain; **spa'gnolo, -a** *ag* Spanish ▷ *sm/f* Spaniard ▷ *sm* (*Ling*) Spanish; **gli Spagnoli** the Spanish

'**spago, -ghi** *sm* string, twine

spai'ato, -a *ag* (*calza, guanto*) odd

spalan'care *vt* to open wide; **spalancarsi** *vpr* to open wide

spa'lare *vt* to shovel

'**spalla** *sf* shoulder; (*fig: Teatro*) stooge; **spalle** *sfpl* (*dorso*) back

spalli'era *sf* (*di sedia ecc*) back; (*di letto: da capo*) head(board); (*: da piedi*) foot(board); (*Ginnastica*) wall bars *pl*

spal'lina *sf* (*bretella*) strap; (*imbottitura*) shoulder pad

spal'mare *vt* to spread

'**spalti** *smpl* (*di stadio*) terracing

'**spandere** *vt* to spread; (*versare*) to pour (out)

spa'rare *vt* to fire ▷ *vi* (*far fuoco*) to fire; (*tirare*) to shoot; **spara'toria** *sf* exchange of shots

sparecchi'are [sparek'kjare] *vt* **~ (la tavola)** to clear the table

spa'reggio [spa'reddʒo] *sm* (*Sport*) play-off

'**spargere** ['spardʒere] *vt* (*spargagliare*) to scatter; (*versare: vino*) to spill; (*: lacrime, sangue*) to shed; (*diffondere*) to spread; (*emanare*) to give off (o out); **spargersi** *vpr* to spread

spa'rire *vi* to disappear, vanish

spar'lare *vi* **~ di** to run down, speak ill of

'**sparo** *sm* shot

spar'tire vt (eredità, bottino) to share out; (avversari) to separate

spar'tito sm (Mus) score

sparti'traffico sm inv (Aut) central reservation (BRIT), median (strip) (US)

sparvi'ero sm (Zool) sparrowhawk

spasi'mante sm suitor

spassio'nato, -a ag dispassionate, impartial

'spasso sm (divertimento) amusement, enjoyment; **andare a ~** to go out for a walk; **essere a ~** (fig) to be out of work; **mandare qn a ~** (fig) to give sb the sack

'spatola sf spatula; (di muratore) trowel

spa'valdo, -a ag arrogant, bold

spaventa'passeri sm inv scarecrow

spaven'tare vt to frighten, scare; **spaventarsi** vpr to be frightened, be scared; to get a fright; **spa'vento** sm fear, fright; **far spavento a qn** to give sb a fright; **spaven'toso, -a** ag frightening, terrible; (fig: fam) tremendous, fantastic

spazientirsi [spattsjen'tirsi] vpr to lose one's patience

'spazio ['spattsjo] sm space; **spazio aereo** airspace; **spazi'oso, -a** ag spacious

spazzaca'mino [spattsaka'mino] sm chimney sweep

spazza'neve [spattsa'neve] sm inv snowplough

spaz'zare [spat'tsare] vt to sweep; (foglie ecc) to sweep up; (cacciare) to sweep away; **spazza'tura** sf sweepings pl; (immondizia) rubbish; **spaz'zino** sm street sweeper

'spazzola ['spattsola] sf brush; **spazzola da capelli** hairbrush; **spazzola per abiti** clothesbrush; **spazzo'lare** vt to brush; **spazzo'lino** sm (small) brush; **spazzolino da denti** toothbrush

specchi'arsi [spek'kjarsi] vpr to look at o.s. in a mirror; (riflettersi) to be mirrored, be reflected

specchi'etto [spek'kjetto] sm (tabella) table, chart; **specchietto da borsetta** pocket mirror; **specchietto retrovisore** (Aut) rear-view mirror

'specchio ['spekkjo] sm mirror

speci'ale [spe'tʃale] ag special; **specia'lista, -i, -e** sm/f specialist; **specialità** sf inv speciality; (branca di studio) special field, speciality; **vorrei assaggiare una specialità del posto** I'd like to try a local speciality; **special'mente** av especially, particularly

'specie ['spetʃe] sf inv (Biol, Bot, Zool) species inv; (tipo) kind, sort ▷ av especially, particularly; **una ~ di** a kind of; **fare ~ a qn** to surprise sb; **la ~ umana** mankind

specifi'care [spetʃifi'kare] vt to specify, state

spe'cifico, -a, -ci, -che [spe'tʃifiko] ag specific

specu'lare vi **~ su** (Comm) to speculate in; (sfruttare) to exploit; (meditare) to speculate on; **speculazi'one** sf speculation

spe'dire vt to send

'spegnere ['spɛɲɲere] vt (fuoco, sigaretta) to put out, extinguish; (apparecchio elettrico) to turn o switch off; (gas) to turn off; (fig: suoni, passioni) to stifle; (debito) to extinguish; **spegnersi** vpr to go out; to go off; (morire) to pass away; **puoi ~ la luce?** could you switch off the light?; **non riesco a ~ il riscaldamento** I can't turn the heating off

spellarsi vpr to peel

'spendere vt to spend

'spengo ecc vb vedi **spegnere**

'spensi ecc vb vedi **spegnere**

spensie'rato, -a ag carefree

'spento, -a pp di **spegnere** ▷ ag (suono) muffled; (colore) dull; (sigaretta) out; (civiltà, vulcano) extinct

spe'ranza [spe'rantsa] sf hope

spe'rare vt to hope for ▷ vi **~ in** to trust in; **~ che/di fare** to hope that/to do; **lo spero, spero di sì** I hope so

sper'duto, -a ag (isolato) out-of-the-way; (persona: smarrita, a disagio) lost

sperimen'tale ag experimental

sperimen'tare vt to experiment with, test; (fig) to test, put to the test

'sperma, -i sm sperm

spe'rone sm spur

sperpe'rare vt to squander

'spesa sf (somma di denaro) expense; (costo) cost; (acquisto) purchase; (fam: acquisto del cibo quotidiano) shopping; **spese postali** postage sg; **spese di viaggio** travelling expenses

'spesso, -a ag (fitto) thick; (frequente) frequent ▷ av often; **spesse volte** frequently, often

spes'sore sm thickness

Spett. abbr vedi **spettabile**

spet'tabile (abbr: **Spett.**: in lettere) ag **~ Ditta X** Messrs X and Co.

spet'tacolo sm (rappresentazione) performance, show; (vista, scena) sight; **dare ~ di sé** to make an exhibition o a spectacle of o.s.

spet'tare vi **~ a** (decisione) to be up to; (stipendio) to be due to; **spetta a te decidere** it's up to you to decide

spetta'tore, -'trice sm/f (Cinema, Teatro) member of the audience; (di avvenimento) onlooker, witness

spettego'lare vi to gossip

spetti'nato, -a *ag* dishevelled

'spettro *sm* (*fantasma*) spectre; (*Fisica*) spectrum

'spezie ['spɛttsje] *sfpl* (*Cuc*) spices

spez'zare [spet'tsare] *vt* (*rompere*) to break; (*fig: interrompere*) to break up; **spezzarsi** *vpr* to break

spezza'tino [spettsa'tino] *sm* (*Cuc*) stew

spezzet'tare [spettset'tare] *vt* to break up (*o chop*) into small pieces

'spia *sf* spy; (*confidente della polizia*) informer; (*Elettr*) indicating light; warning light; (*fessura*) peep-hole; (*fig: sintomo*) sign, indication

spia'cente [spja'tʃɛnte] *ag* sorry; **essere ~ di qc/di fare qc** to be sorry about sth/for doing sth

spia'cevole [spja'tʃevole] *ag* unpleasant

spi'aggia, -ge ['spjaddʒa] *sf* beach; **spiaggia libera** public beach

spia'nare *vt* (*terreno*) to level, make level; (*edificio*) to raze to the ground; (*pasta*) to roll out; (*rendere liscio*) to smooth (out)

spi'are *vt* to spy on

spi'azzo ['spjattso] *sm* open space; (*radura*) clearing

'spicchio ['spikkjo] *sm* (*di agrumi*) segment; (*di aglio*) clove; (*parte*) piece, slice

spicci'arsi *vpr* to hurry up

spiccioli *smpl* (*small*) change; **mi dispiace, non ho ~** sorry, I don't have any change

'spicco, -chi *sm* **di ~** outstanding; (*tema*) main, principal; **fare ~** to stand out

spie'dino *sm* (*utensile*) skewer; (*pietanza*) kebab

spi'edo *sm* (*Cuc*) spit

spie'gare *vt* (*far capire*) to explain; (*tovaglia*) to unfold; (*vele*) to unfurl; **spiegarsi** *vpr* to explain o.s., make o.s. clear; **~ qc a qn** to explain sth to sb; **spiegazi'one** *sf* explanation

spiegherò *ecc* [spjege'rɔ] *vb vedi* **spiegare**

spie'tato, -a *ag* ruthless, pitiless

spiffe'rare (*fam*) *vt* to blurt out, blab

'spiffero *sm* draught (BRIT); draft (US)

'spiga, -ghe *sf* (*Bot*) ear

spigli'ato, -a [spiʎ'ʎato] *ag* self-possessed, self-confident

'spigolo *sm* corner; (*Mat*) edge

'spilla *sf* brooch; (*da cravatta, cappello*) pin; **~ di sicurezza** *o* **da balia** safety pin

'spillo *sm* pin; **spillo da balia** *o* **di sicurezza** safety pin

spi'lorcio, -a, -ci, -ce [spi'lortʃo] *ag* mean, stingy

'spina *sf* (*Bot*) thorn; (*Zool*) spine, prickle; (*di pesce*) bone; (*Elettr*) plug; (*di botte*) bunghole; **birra alla ~** draught beer; **spina dorsale** (*Anat*) backbone

spinaci [spi'natʃi] *smpl* spinach *sg*

spi'nello *sm* (*Droga: gergo*) joint

'spingere ['spindʒere] *vt* to push; (*condurre: anche fig*) to drive; (*stimolare*): **~ qn a fare** to urge o press sb to do

spi'noso, -a *ag* thorny, prickly

'spinsi *ecc vb vedi* **spingere**

'spinta *sf* (*urto*) push; (*Fisica*) thrust; (*fig: stimolo*) incentive, spur; (*: appoggio*) string-pulling *no pl*; **dare una ~ a qn** (*fig*) to pull strings for sb

'spinto, -a *pp di* **spingere**

spio'naggio [spio'naddʒo] *sm* espionage, spying

spion'cino [spion'tʃino] *sm* peephole

spi'raglio [spi'raʎʎo] *sm* (*fessura*) chink, narrow opening; (*raggio di luce, fig*) glimmer, gleam

spi'rale *sf* spiral; (*contraccettivo*) coil; **a ~** spiral(-shaped)

spiri'tato, -a *ag* possessed; (*fig: persona, espressione*) wild

spiri'tismo *sm* spiritualism

'spirito *sm* (*Rel, Chim, disposizione d'animo, di legge ecc, fantasma*) spirit; (*pensieri, intelletto*) mind; (*arguzia*) wit; (*umorismo*) humour, wit; **lo S~ Santo** the Holy Spirit *o* Ghost

spirito'saggine [spirito'saddʒine] *sf* witticism; (*peg*) wisecrack

spiri'toso, -a *ag* witty

spiritu'ale *ag* spiritual

'splendere *vi* to shine

'splendido, -a *ag* splendid; (*splendente*) shining; (*sfarzoso*) magnificent, splendid

splen'dore *sm* splendour; (*luce intensa*) brilliance, brightness

spogli'are [spoʎ'ʎare] *vt* (*svestire*) to undress; (*privare, fig: depredare*): **~ qn di qc** to deprive sb of sth; (*togliere ornamenti: anche fig*): **~ qn/qc di** to strip sb/sth of; **spogliarsi** *vpr* to undress, strip; **spogliarsi di** (*ricchezze ecc*) to deprive o.s. of, give up; (*pregiudizi*) to rid o.s. of; **spoglia'rello** [spoʎʎa'rɛllo] *sm* striptease; **spoglia'toio** *sm* dressing room; (*di scuola ecc*) cloakroom; (*Sport*) changing room

'spola *sf* (*bobina di filo*) cop; **fare la ~ (fra)** to go to and fro o shuttle (between)

spolve'rare *vt* (*anche Cuc*) to dust; (*con spazzola*) to brush; (*con battipanni*) to beat; (*fig*) to polish off ▷ *vi* to dust

spon'taneo, -a *ag* spontaneous; (*persona*) unaffected, natural

spor'care *vt* to dirty, make dirty; (*fig*) to sully, soil; **sporcarsi** *vpr* to get dirty

spor'cizia [spor'tʃittsja] *sf* (*stato*) dirtiness; (*sudiciume*) dirt, filth; (*cosa* *sporca*) dirt *no pl*, something dirty

'sporco, -a, -chi, -che *ag* dirty, filthy

spor'genza [spor'dʒɛntsa] *sf* projection

'sporgere ['spɔrdʒere] *vt* to put out, stretch out ▷ *vi* (*venire in fuori*) to stick out; **sporgersi** *vpr* to lean out; **~ querela contro qn** (*Dir*) to take legal action against sb

'sporsi *ecc vb vedi* **sporgere**

sport *sm inv* sport

spor'tello *sm* (*di treno, auto ecc*) door; (*di banca, ufficio*) window, counter; **sportello automatico** (*Banca*) cash dispenser, automated telling machine

spor'tivo, -a *ag* (*gara, giornale, centro*) sports *cpd*; (*persona*) sporty; (*abito*) casual; (*spirito, atteggiamento*) sporting

'sposa *sf* bride; (*moglie*) wife

sposa'lizio [spoza'littsjo] *sm* wedding

spo'sare *vt* to marry; (*fig: idea, fede*) to espouse; **sposarsi** *vpr* to get married, marry; **sposarsi con qn** to marry sb, get married to sb; **spo'sato, -a** *ag* married

'sposo *sm* (bride)groom; (*marito*) husband

spos'sato, -a *ag* exhausted, weary

spos'tare *vt* to move, shift; (*cambiare: orario*) to change; **spostarsi** *vpr* to move; **può ~ la macchina, per favore?** can you move your car please?

'spranga, -ghe *sf* (*sbarra*) bar

spre'care *vt* to waste

spre'gevole [spre'dʒevole] *ag* contemptible, despicable

'spremere *vt* to squeeze

spremia'grumi *sm inv* lemon squeezer

spre'muta *sf* fresh juice; **spremuta d'arancia** fresh orange juice

sprez'zante [spret'tsante] *ag* scornful, contemptuous

sprofon'dare *vi* to sink; (*casa*) to collapse; (*suolo*) to give way, subside

spro'nare *vt* to spur (on)

sproporzio'nato, -a [sproportsjo'nato] *ag* disproportionate, out of all proportion

sproporzi'one [spropor'tsjone] *sf* disproportion

spro'posito *sm* blunder; **a ~** at the wrong time; (*rispondere, parlare*) irrelevantly

sprovve'duto, -a *ag* inexperienced, naïve

sprov'visto, -a *ag* (*mancante*): **~ di** lacking in, without; **alla sprovvista** unawares

spruz'zare [sprut'tsare] *vt* (*a nèbulizzazione*) to spray; (*aspergere*) to sprinkle; (*inzaccherare*) to splash

'spugna ['spuɲɲa] *sf* (*Zool*) sponge; (*tessuto*) towelling

'spuma *sf* (*schiuma*) foam; (*bibita*) fizzy drink

spu'mante *sm* sparkling wine

spun'tare *vt* (*coltello*) to break the point of; (*capelli*) to trim ▷ *vi* (*uscire: germogli*) to sprout; (*: capelli*) to begin to grow; (*: denti*) to come through; (*apparire*) to appear (suddenly)

spun'tino *sm* snack

'spunto *sm* (*Teatro, Mus*) cue; (*fig*) starting point; **dare lo ~ a** (*fig*) to give rise to

spu'tare *vt* to spit out; (*fig*) to belch (out) ▷ *vi* to spit

'squadra *sf* (*strumento*) (set) square; (*gruppo*) team, squad; (*di operai*) gang, squad; (*Mil*) squad; (*: Aer, Naut*) squadron; (*Sport*) team; **lavoro a squadre** teamwork

squagli'arsi [skwaʎ'ʎarsi] *vpr* to melt; (*fig*) to sneak off

squa'lifica *sf* disqualification

squalifi'care *vt* to disqualify

'squallido, -a *ag* wretched, bleak

'squalo *sm* shark

'squama *sf* scale

squarcia'gola [skwartʃa'gola]: **a ~** *av* at the top of one's voice

squattri'nato, -a *ag* penniless

squili'brato, -a *ag* (*Psic*) unbalanced

squil'lante *ag* shrill, sharp

squil'lare *vi* (*campanello, telefono*) to ring (out); (*tromba*) to blare; **'squillo** *sm* ring, ringing *no pl*; blare; **ragazza** *f* **squillo** *inv* call girl

squi'sito, -a *ag* exquisite; (*cibo*) delicious; (*persona*) delightful

squit'tire *vi* (*uccello*) to squawk; (*topo*) to squeak

sradi'care *vt* to uproot; (*fig*) to eradicate

srego'lato, -a *ag* (*senza ordine: vita*) disorderly; (*smodato*) immoderate; (*dissoluto*) dissolute

S.r.l. *abbr* = **società a responsabilità limitata**

sroto'lare *vt*, **sroto'larsi** ▷ *vpr* to unroll

SS *sigla* = **strada statale**

S.S.N. *abbr* (= *Servizio Sanitario Nazionale*) ≈ NHS

sta *ecc vb vedi* **stare**

'stabile *ag* stable, steady; (*tempo: non variabile*) settled; (*Teatro: compagnia*) resident ▷ *sm* (*edificio*) building

stabili'mento *sm* (*edificio*) establishment; (*fabbrica*) plant, factory

stabi'lire *vt* to establish; (*fissare: prezzi, data*) to fix; (*decidere*) to decide; **stabilirsi** *vpr* (*prendere dimora*) to settle

stac'care *vt* (*levare*) to detach, remove; (*separare: anche fig*) to separate, divide; (*strappare*) to tear off (o out); (*scandire: parole*) to pronounce clearly; (*Sport*) to leave behind; **staccarsi** *vpr* (*bottone ecc*) to come off; (*scostarsi*): **staccarsi (da)**

to move away (from); (fig: separarsi):
staccarsi da to leave; **non ~ gli occhi da
qn** not to take one's eyes off sb
'**stadio** sm (Sport) stadium; (periodo, fase)
phase, stage
'**staffa** sf (di sella, Tecn) stirrup; **perdere le
staffe** (fig) to fly off the handle
staf'**fetta** sf (messo) dispatch rider; (Sport)
relay race
stagio'**nale** [stadʒo'nale] ag seasonal
stagio'**nato, -a** [stadʒo'nato] ag (vedi vb)
seasoned; matured; (scherzoso: attempato)
getting on in years
stagi'**one** [sta'dʒone] sf season; **alta/
bassa ~** high/low season
sta'**gista, -i, -e** [sta'd[gh]ista] sm/f
trainee, intern (us)
'**stagno, -a** ['staɲɲo] ag watertight; (a
tenuta d'aria) airtight ▷ sm (acquitrino)
pond; (Chim) tin
sta'**gnola** [staɲ'ɲɔla] sf tinfoil
'**stalla** sf (per bovini) cowshed; (per cavalli)
stable
stal'**lone** sm stallion
stamat'**tina** av this morning
stam'**becco, -chi** sm ibex
'**stampa** sf (Tip, Fot: tecnica) printing;
(impressione, copia fotografica) print;
(insieme di quotidiani, giornalisti ecc) press
stam'**pante** sf (Inform) printer
stam'**pare** vt to print; (pubblicare) to
publish; (coniare) to strike, coin; (imprimere:
anche fig) to impress
stampa'**tello** sm block letters pl
stam'**pella** sf crutch
'**stampo** sm mould; (fig: indole) type, kind,
sort
sta'**nare** vt to drive out
stan'**care** vt to tire, make tired; (annoiare)
to bore; (infastidire) to annoy; **stancarsi**
vpr to get tired, tire o.s. out; **stancarsi (di)**
to grow weary (of), grow tired (of)
stan'**chezza** [stan'kettsa] sf tiredness,
fatigue
'**stanco, -a, -chi, -che** ag tired; **~ di** tired
of, fed up with
stan'**ghetta** [stan'getta] sf (di occhiali) leg;
(Mus, di scrittura) bar
'**stanno** vb vedi **stare**
sta'**notte** av tonight; (notte passata) last
night
'**stante** prep **a sé ~** (appartamento, casa)
independent, separate
stan'**tio, -a, -'tii, -'tie** ag stale; (burro)
rancid; (fig) old
stan'**tuffo** sm piston
'**stanza** ['stantsa] sf room; (Poesia) stanza;
stanza da bagno bathroom; **stanza da
letto** bedroom

stap'**pare** vt to uncork; to uncap
'**stare** vi (restare in un luogo) to stay, remain;
(abitare) to stay, live; (essere situato) to be,
be situated; (anche: **~ in piedi**) to be, stand;
(essere, trovarsi) to be; (dipendere): **se stesse
in me** if it were up to me, if it depended on
me; (seguito da gerundio): **sta studiando**
he's studying; **starci** (esserci spazio): **nel
baule non ci sta più niente** there's no
more room in the boot; (accettare) to
accept; **ci stai?** is that okay with you?; **~
a** (attenersi a) to follow, stick to; (seguito
dall'infinito): **stiamo a discutere** we're
talking; (toccare a): **sta a te giocare** it's
your turn to play; **~ per fare qc** to be about
to do sth; **come sta?** how are you?; **io sto
bene/male** I'm very well/not very well; **~
a qn** (abiti ecc) to fit sb; **queste scarpe mi
stanno strette** these shoes are tight for
me; **il rosso ti sta bene** red suits you
starnu'**tire** vi to sneeze; **star'nuto** sm
sneeze
sta'**sera** av this evening, tonight
sta'**tale** ag state cpd; government cpd
▷ sm/f state employee, local authority
employee; (nell'amministrazione) ≈ civil
servant; **strada statale** ≈ trunk (Brit) o
main road
sta'**tista, -i** sm statesman
sta'**tistica** sf statistics sg
'**stato, -a** pp di **essere; stare** ▷ sm
(condizione) state, condition; (Pol) state;
(Dir) status; **essere in ~ d'accusa** (Dir)
to be committed for trial; **~ d'assedio/
d'emergenza** state of siege/emergency;
~ civile (Amm) marital status; **gli Stati
Uniti (d'America)** the United States (of
America); **stato d'animo** mood; **stato
maggiore** (Mil) staff
'**statua** sf statue
statuni'**tense** ag United States cpd, of the
United States
sta'**tura** sf (Anat) height, stature; (fig)
stature
sta'**tuto** sm (Dir) statute; constitution
sta'**volta** av this time
stazio'**nario, -a** [stattsjo'narjo] ag
stationary; (fig) unchanged
stazi'**one** [stat'tsjone] sf station;
(balneare, termale) resort; **stazione degli
autobus** bus station; **stazione balneare**
seaside resort; **stazione ferroviaria**
railway (Brit) o railroad (us) station;
stazione invernale winter sports resort;
stazione di polizia police station (in small
town); **stazione di servizio** service o petrol
(Brit) o filling station
'**stecca, -che** sf stick; (di ombrello) rib; (di
sigarette) carton; (Med) splint; (stonatura):

fare una ~ to sing (o play) a wrong note
stec'cato sm fence
'**stella** sf star; **stella alpina** (Bot)
edelweiss; **stella cadente** shooting star;
stella di mare (Zool) starfish
'**stelo** sm stem; (asta) rod; **lampada a ~**
standard lamp
'**stemma, -i** sm coat of arms
'**stemmo** vb vedi **stare**
stempi'ato, -a ag with a receding hairline
'**stendere** vt (braccia, gambe) to stretch
(out); (tovaglia) to spread (out); (bucato)
to hang out; (mettere a giacere) to lay
(down); (spalmare: colore) to spread;
(mettere per iscritto) to draw up; **stendersi**
vpr (coricarsi) to stretch out, lie down;
(estendersi) to extend, stretch
stenogra'fia sf shorthand
sten'tare vi **~ a fare** to find it hard to do,
have difficulty doing
'**stento** sm (fatica) difficulty; **stenti** smpl
(privazioni) hardship sg, privation sg; **a ~**
with difficulty, barely
'**sterco** sm dung
stereo ['stɛreo] ag inv stereo ▷ sm inv
(impianto) stereo
'**sterile** ag sterile; (terra) barren; (fig) futile,
fruitless
steriliz'zare [sterilid'dzare] vt to sterilize
ster'lina sf pound (sterling)
stermi'nare vt to exterminate, wipe out
stermi'nato, -a ag immense; endless
ster'minio sm extermination, destruction
'**sterno** sm (Anat) breastbone
ste'roide sm steroid
ster'zare [ster'tsare] vt, vi (Aut) to steer;
'**sterzo** sm steering; (volante) steering
wheel
'**stessi** ecc vb vedi **stare**
'**stesso, -a** ag same; (rafforzativo: in
persona, proprio): **il re ~** the king himself o in
person ▷ pron **lo(la) ~(a)** the same (one); **i
suoi stessi avversari lo ammirano** even
his enemies admire him; **fa lo ~** it doesn't
matter; **per me è lo ~** it's all the same to
me, it doesn't matter to me; vedi **io; tu** ecc
ste'sura sf drafting no pl, drawing up no
pl; draft
'**stetti** ecc vb vedi **stare**
'**stia** ecc vb vedi **stare**
sti'lare vt to draw up, draft
'**stile** sm style; **stile libero** freestyle;
sti'lista, -i sm designer
stilo'grafica, -che sf (anche: **penna ~**)
fountain pen
'**stima** sf esteem; valuation; assessment,
estimate
sti'mare vt (persona) to esteem, hold in
high regard; (terreno, casa ecc) to value;

(stabilire in misura approssimativa) to
estimate, assess; (ritenere): **~ che** to
consider that; **stimarsi fortunato** to
consider o.s. (to be) lucky
stimo'lare vt to stimulate; (incitare): **~ qn
(a fare)** to spur sb on (to do)
'**stimolo** sm (anche fig) stimulus
'**stingere** ['stindʒere] vt, vi (anche:
stingersi) to fade; '**stinto, -a** pp di
stingere
sti'pare vt to cram, pack; **stiparsi** vpr
(accalcarsi) to crowd, throng
sti'pendio sm salary
'**stipite** sm (di porta, finestra) jamb
stipu'lare vt (redigere) to draw up
sti'rare vt (abito) to iron; (distendere) to
stretch; (strappare: muscolo) to strain;
stirarsi vpr to stretch (o.s.)
stiti'chezza [stiti'kettsa] sf constipation
'**stitico, -a, -ci, -che** ag constipated
'**stiva** sf (di nave) hold
sti'vale sm boot
'**stizza** ['stittsa] sf anger, vexation
'**stoffa** sf material, fabric; (fig): **aver la ~ di**
to have the makings of
'**stomaco, -chi** sm stomach; **dare di ~** to
vomit, be sick
sto'nato, -a ag (persona) off-key;
(strumento) off-key, out of tune
stop sm inv (Tel) stop; (Aut: cartello) stop
sign; (: fanalino d'arresto) brake-light
'**storcere** ['stɔrtʃere] vt to twist; **storcersi**
vpr to writhe, twist; **~ il naso** (fig) to turn
up one's nose; **storcersi la caviglia** to
twist one's ankle
stor'dire vt (intontire) to stun, daze;
stor'dito, -a ag stunned
'**storia** sf (scienza, avvenimenti) history;
(racconto, bugia) story; (faccenda, questione)
business no pl; (pretesto) excuse, pretext;
storie sfpl (smancerie) fuss sg; '**storico, -a,
-ci, -che** ag historic(al) ▷ sm historian
stori'one sm (Zool) sturgeon
'**stormo** sm (di uccelli) flock
'**storpio, -a** ag crippled, maimed
'**storsi** ecc vb vedi **storcere**
'**storta** sf (distorsione) sprain, twist
'**storto, -a** pp di **storcere** ▷ ag (chiodo)
twisted, bent; (gamba, quadro) crooked
sto'viglie [sto'viʎʎe] sfpl dishes pl,
crockery
stra'bico, -a, -ci, -che ag squint-eyed;
(occhi) squint
strac'chino [strak'kino] sm type of soft
cheese
stracci'are [strat'tʃare] vt to tear;
stracciarsi vpr to tear
'**straccio, -a, -ci, -ce** ['strattʃo] ag **carta
straccia** waste paper ▷ sm rag; (per pulire)

cloth, duster; **stracci** *smpl* (*peg*: *indumenti*) rags; **si è ridotto a uno ~** he's worn himself out; **non ha uno ~ di lavoro** he's not got a job of any sort

'**strada** *sf* road; (*di città*) street; (*cammino, via, fig*) way; **che ~ devo prendere per andare a …?** which road do I take for …?; **farsi ~** (*fig*) to do well for o.s.; **essere fuori ~** (*fig*) to be on the wrong track; **~ facendo** on the way; **strada senza uscita** dead end; **stra'dale** *ag* road *cpd*

strafalci'one [strafal'tʃone] *sm* blunder, howler

stra'fare *vi* to overdo it

strafot'tente *ag* **è ~** he doesn't give a damn, he couldn't care less

'**strage** ['stradʒe] *sf* massacre, slaughter

stralu'nato, -a *ag* (*occhi*) rolling; (*persona*) beside o.s., very upset

'**strambo, -a** *ag* strange, queer

strampa'lato, -a *ag* odd, eccentric

stra'nezza [stra'nettsa] *sf* strangeness

strango'lare *vt* to strangle

strani'ero, -a *ag* foreign ▷ *sm/f* foreigner
> Attenzione! In inglese esiste la parola *stranger*, che però significa *sconosciuto* oppure *estraneo*.

'**strano, -a** *ag* strange, odd

straordi'nario, -a *ag* extraordinary; (*treno ecc*) special ▷ *sm* (*lavoro*) overtime

strapi'ombo *sm* overhanging rock; **a ~** overhanging

strap'pare *vt* (*gen*) to tear, rip; (*pagina ecc*) to tear off, tear out; (*sradicare*) to pull up; (*togliere*): **~ qc a qn** to snatch sth from sb; (*fig*) to wrest sth from sb; **strapparsi** *vpr* (*lacerarsi*) to rip, tear; (*rompersi*) to break; **strapparsi un muscolo** to tear a muscle; '**strappo** *sm* pull, tug; tear, rip; **fare uno strappo alla regola** to make an exception to the rule; **strappo muscolare** torn muscle

strari'pare *vi* to overflow

'**strascico, -chi** ['straʃʃiko] *sm* (*di abito*) train; (*conseguenza*) after-effect

strata'gemma, -i [strata'dʒemma] *sm* stratagem

strate'gia, -'gie [strate'dʒia] *sf* strategy; **stra'tegico, -a, -ci, -che** *ag* strategic

'**strato** *sm* layer; (*rivestimento*) coat, coating; (*Geo, fig*) stratum; (*Meteor*) stratus; **strato d'ozono** ozone layer

strat'tone *sm* tug, jerk; **dare uno ~ a qc** to tug o jerk sth, give sth a tug o jerk

strava'gante *ag* odd, eccentric

stra'volto, -a *pp di* **stravolgere**

'**strazio** *sm* torture; (*fig*: *cosa fatta male*): **essere uno ~** to be appalling

'**strega, -ghe** *sf* witch

stre'gare *vt* to bewitch

stre'gone *sm* (*mago*) wizard; (*di tribù*) witch doctor

strepi'toso, -a *ag* clamorous, deafening; (*fig*: *successo*) resounding

stres'sante *ag* stressful

stres'sato, -a *ag* under stress

stretch [strɛtʃ] *ag inv* stretch

'**stretta** *sf* (*di mano*) grasp; (*finanziaria*) squeeze; (*fig*: *dolore, turbamento*) pang; **una ~ di mano** a handshake; **essere alle strette** to have one's back to the wall; *vedi anche* **stretto**

stretta'mente *av* tightly; (*rigorosamente*) strictly

'**stretto, -a** *pp di* **stringere** ▷ *ag* (*corridoio, limiti*) narrow; (*gonna, scarpe, nodo, curva*) tight; (*intimo*: *parente, amico*) close; (*rigoroso*: *osservanza*) strict; (*preciso*: *significato*) precise, exact ▷ *sm* (*braccio di mare*) strait; **a denti stretti** with clenched teeth; **lo ~ necessario** the bare minimum; **stret'toia** *sf* bottleneck; (*fig*) tricky situation

stri'ato, -a *ag* streaked

'**stridulo, -a** *ag* shrill

stril'lare *vt, vi* to scream, shriek; '**strillo** *sm* scream, shriek

strimin'zito, -a [strimin'tsito] *ag* (*misero*) shabby; (*molto magro*) skinny

strimpel'lare *vt* (*Mus*) to strum

'**stringa, -ghe** *sf* lace

strin'gato, -a *ag* (*fig*) concise

'**stringere** ['strindʒere] *vt* (*avvicinare due cose*) to press (together), squeeze (together); (*tenere stretto*) to hold tight, clasp, clutch; (*pugno, mascella, denti*) to clench; (*labbra*) to compress; (*avvitare*) to tighten; (*abito*) to take in; (*scarpe*) to pinch, be tight for; (*fig*: *concludere*: *patto*) to make; (: *accelerare*: *passo, tempo*) to quicken ▷ *vi* (*essere stretto*) to be tight; (*tempo*: *incalzare*) to be pressing

'**strinsi** *ecc vb vedi* **stringere**

'**striscia, -sce** ['striʃʃa] *sf* (*di carta, tessuto ecc*) strip; (*riga*) stripe; **strisce (pedonali)** zebra crossing *sg*

strisci'are [striʃʃare] *vt* (*piedi*) to drag; (*muro, macchina*) to graze ▷ *vi* to crawl, creep

'**striscio** ['striʃʃo] *sm* graze; (*Med*) smear; **colpire di ~** to graze

strisci'one [striʃʃone] *sm* banner

strito'lare *vt* to grind

striz'zare [strit'tsare] *vt* (*panni*) to wring (out); **~ l'occhio** to wink

'**strofa** *sf* strophe

strofi'naccio [strofi'nattʃo] *sm* duster, cloth; (*per piatti*) dishcloth; (*per pavimenti*) floorcloth

strofi'nare vt to rub

stron'care vt to break off; (fig: ribellione) to suppress, put down; (: film, libro) to tear to pieces

'stronzo ['strontso] sm (sterco) turd; (fig fam!: persona) shit (!)

stroz'zare [strot'tsare] vt (soffocare) to choke, strangle

struccarsi vpr to remove one's make-up

strumen'tale ag (Mus) instrumental

strumentaliz'zare [strumentalid'dzare] vt to exploit, use to one's own ends

stru'mento sm (arnese, fig) instrument, tool; (Mus) instrument; ~ **a corda** o **ad arco/a fiato** stringed/wind instrument

'strutto sm lard

strut'tura sf structure

'struzzo ['struttso] sm ostrich

stuc'care vt (muro) to plaster; (vetro) to putty; (decorare con stucchi) to stucco

'stucco, -chi sm plaster; (da vetri) putty; (ornamentale) stucco; **rimanere di ~** (fig) to be dumbfounded

stu'dente, -'essa sm/f student; (scolaro) pupil, schoolboy/girl

studi'are vt to study

'studio sm studying; (ricerca, saggio, stanza) study; (di professionista) office; (di artista, Cinema, TV, Radio) studio; **studi** smpl (Ins) studies; **studio medico** doctor's surgery (BRIT) o office (US)

studi'oso, -a ag studious, hard-working ▷ sm/f scholar

'stufa sf stove; **stufa elettrica** electric fire o heater

stu'fare vt (Cuc) to stew; (fig: fam) to bore; **stufarsi** vpr (fam): **stufarsi (di)** (fig) to get fed up (with); **'stufo, -a** (fam) ag **essere stufo di** to be fed up with, be sick and tired of

stu'oia sf mat

stupefa'cente [stupefa'tʃɛnte] ag stunning, astounding ▷ sm drug, narcotic

stupe'fatto, -a pp di **stupefare**

stu'pendo, -a ag marvellous, wonderful

stupi'daggine [stupi'daddʒine] sf stupid thing (to do o say)

stupidità sf stupidity

'stupido, -a ag stupid

stu'pire vt to amaze, stun ▷ vi **stupirsi**; ~ **(di)** to be amazed (at), be stunned (by)

stu'pore sm amazement, astonishment

stu'prare vt to rape

'stupro sm rape

stu'rare vt (lavandino) to clear

stuzzica'denti [stuttsika'dɛnti] sm toothpick

stuzzi'care [stuttsi'kare] vt (ferita ecc)

to poke (at), prod (at); (fig) to tease; (: appetito) to whet; (: curiosità) to stimulate; ~ **i denti** to pick one's teeth

🔵 **PAROLA CHIAVE**

su (su +il = **sul**, su +lo = **sullo**, su +l' = **sull'**, su +la = **sulla**, su +i = **sui**, su +gli = **sugli**, su +le = **sulle**) prep **1** (gen) on; (moto) on(to); (in cima a) on (top of); **mettilo sul tavolo** put it on the table; **un paesino sul mare** a village by the sea

2 (argomento) about, on; **un libro su Cesare** a book on o about Caesar

3 (circa) about; **costerà sui 3 milioni** it will cost about 3 million; **una ragazza sui 17 anni** a girl of about 17 (years of age)

4: **su misura** made to measure; **su richiesta** on request; **3 casi su dieci** 3 cases out of 10

▷ av **1** (in alto, verso l'alto) up; **vieni su** come on up; **guarda su** look up; **su le mani!** hands up!; **in su** (verso l'alto) up(wards); (in poi) onwards; **dai 20 anni in su** from the age of 20 onwards

2 (addosso) on; **cos'hai su?** what have you got on?

▷ escl come on!; **su coraggio!** come on, cheer up!

su'bacqueo, -a ag underwater ▷ sm skin-diver

sub'buglio [sub'buʎʎo] sm confusion, turmoil

'subdolo, -a ag underhand, sneaky

suben'trare vi ~ **a qn in qc** to take over sth from sb

su'bire vt to suffer, endure

'subito av immediately, at once, straight away

subodo'rare vt (insidia ecc) to smell, suspect

subordi'nato, -a ag subordinate; (dipendente): ~ **a** dependent on, subject to

suc'cedere [sut'tʃedere] vi (prendere il posto di qn): ~ **a** to succeed; (venire dopo): ~ **a** to follow; (accadere) to happen; **cos'è successo?** what happened?; **succes'sivo, -a** ag successive; **suc'cesso, -a** pp di **succedere** ▷ sm (esito) outcome; (buona riuscita) success; **di successo** (libro, personaggio) successful

succhi'are [suk'kjare] vt to suck (up); **succhi'otto** sm (per bambino) dummy

succhi'otto [suk'kjɔtto] sm dummy (BRIT), pacifier (US), comforter (US)

suc'cinto, -a [sut'tʃinto] ag (discorso) succinct; (abito) brief

'succo, -chi sm juice; (fig) essence, gist;

succo di frutta/pomodoro fruit/tomato juice

succur'sale sf branch (office)

sud sm south ▷ ag inv south; (lato) south, southern

Su'dafrica sm **il ~** South Africa; **sudafri'cano, -a** ag, sm/f South African

Suda'merica sm **il ~** South America

su'dare vi to perspire, sweat; **~ freddo** to come out in a cold sweat

su'dato, -a ag (persona, mani) sweaty; (fig: denaro) hard-earned ▷ sf (anche fig) sweat; **una vittoria sudata** a hard-won victory; **ho fatto una bella sudata per finirlo in tempo** it was a real sweat to get it finished in time

suddi'videre vt to subdivide

su'dest sm south-east

'sudicio, -a, -ci, -ce ['suditʃo] ag dirty, filthy

su'dore sm perspiration, sweat

su'dovest sm south-west

suffici'ente [suffi'tʃɛnte] ag enough, sufficient; (borioso) self-important; (Ins) satisfactory; **suffici'enza** sf self-importance; pass mark; **a sufficienza** enough; **ne ho avuto a sufficienza!** I've had enough of this!

suf'fisso sm (Ling) suffix

suggeri'mento [suddʒeri'mento] sm suggestion; (consiglio) piece of advice, advice no pl

sugge'rire [suddʒe'rire] vt (risposta) to tell; (consigliare) to advise; (proporre) to suggest; (Teatro) to prompt

suggestio'nare [suddʒestjo'nare] vt to influence

sugges'tivo, -a [suddʒes'tivo] ag (paesaggio) evocative; (teoria) interesting, attractive

'sughero ['sugero] sm cork

'sugo, -ghi sm (succo) juice; (di carne) gravy; (condimento) sauce; (fig) gist, essence

sui'cida, -i, -e [sui'tʃida] ag suicidal ▷ sm/f suicide

suici'darsi [suitʃi'darsi] vpr to commit suicide

sui'cidio [sui'tʃidjo] sm suicide

su'ino, -a ag **carne suina** pork ▷ sm pig

sul'tano, -a sm/f sultan/sultana

'suo (f **sua**, pl **'sue, su'oi**) det **il ~, la sua** ecc (di lui) his; (di lei) her; (di esso) its; (con valore indefinito) one's, his/her; (anche: **S~**: forma di cortesia) your ▷ pron **il ~, la sua** ecc his; hers; yours; **i ~i** his (o her o one's o your) family

su'ocero, -a ['swɔtʃero] sm/f father/mother-in-law

su'ola sf (di scarpa) sole

su'olo sm (terreno) ground; (terra) soil

suo'nare vt (Mus) to play; (campana) to ring; (ore) to strike; (clacson, allarme) to sound ▷ vi to play; (telefono, campana) to ring; (ore) to strike; (clacson, fig: parole) to sound

suone'ria sf alarm

su'ono sm sound

su'ora sf (Rel) sister

'super sf (anche: **benzina ~**) ≈ four-star (petrol) (BRIT), premium (US)

supe'rare vt (oltrepassare: limite) to exceed, surpass; (percorrere) to cover; (attraversare: fiume) to cross; (sorpassare: veicolo) to overtake; (fig: essere più bravo di) to surpass, outdo; (: difficoltà) to overcome; (: esame) to get through; **~ qn in altezza/peso** to be taller/heavier than sb; **ha superato la cinquantina** he's over fifty (years of age)

su'perbia sf pride; **su'perbo, -a** ag proud; (fig) magnificent, superb

superfici'ale [superfi'tʃale] ag superficial

super'ficie, -ci [super'fitʃe] sf surface

su'perfluo, -a ag superfluous

superi'ore ag (piano, arto, classi) upper; (più elevato: temperatura, livello): **~ (a)** higher (than); (migliore): **~ (a)** superior (to)

superla'tivo, -a ag, sm superlative

supermer'cato sm supermarket

su'perstite ag surviving ▷ sm/f survivor

superstizi'one [superstit'tsjone] sf superstition; **superstizi'oso, -a** ag superstitious

super'strada sf ≈ (toll-free) motorway

su'pino, -a ag supine

supplemen'tare ag extra; (treno) relief cpd; (entrate) additional

supple'mento sm supplement

sup'plente sm/f temporary member of staff, supply (o substitute) teacher

'supplica, -che sf (preghiera) plea; (domanda scritta) petition, request

suppli'care vt to implore, beseech

sup'plizio [sup'plittsjo] sm torture

sup'pongo, sup'poni ecc vb vedi **supporre**

sup'porre vt to suppose

sup'porto sm (sostegno) support

sup'posta sf (Med) suppository

su'premo, -a ag supreme

surge'lare [surdʒe'lare] vt to (deep-)freeze

surge'lato, -a [surdʒe'lato] ag (deep-)frozen ▷ smpl **i surgelati** frozen food sg

sur'plus sm inv (Econ) surplus

surriscal'dare vt to overheat

suscet'tibile [suʃʃet'tibile] ag (sensibile) touchy, sensitive

susci'tare [suʃʃi'tare] vt to provoke,

arouse

su'sina *sf* plum

susseguirsi *vpr* to follow one another

sus'sidio *sm* subsidy; **sussidi didattici** teaching aids

sussul'tare *vi* to shudder

sussur'rare *vt, vi* to whisper, murmur; **sus'surro** *sm* whisper, murmur

svagarsi *vpr* to amuse o.s.; to enjoy o.s.

'svago, -ghi *sm* (*riposo*) relaxation; (*ricreazione*) amusement; (*passatempo*) pastime

svaligi'are [zvali'dʒare] *vt* to rob, burgle (BRIT), burglarize (US)

svalutarsi *vpr* (*Econ*) to be devalued

svalutazi'one *sf* devaluation

sva'nire *vi* to disappear, vanish

svantaggi'ato, -a [zvantad'dʒato] *ag* at a disadvantage

svan'taggio [zvan'taddʒo] *sm* disadvantage; (*inconveniente*) drawback, disadvantage

svari'ato, -a *ag* varied; various

'svastica *sf* swastika

sve'dese *ag* Swedish ▷ *sm/f* Swede ▷ *sm* (*Ling*) Swedish

'sveglia ['zveʎʎa] *sf* waking up; (*orologio*) alarm (clock); **sveglia telefonica** alarm call

svegli'are [zveʎ'ʎare] *vt* to wake up; (*fig*) to awaken, arouse; **svegliarsi** *vpr* to wake up; (*fig*) to be revived, reawaken; **vorrei essere svegliato alle 7, per favore** could I have an alarm call at 7 am, please?

'sveglio, -a ['zveʎʎo] *ag* awake; (*fig*) quick-witted

sve'lare *vt* to reveal

'svelto, -a *ag* (*passo*) quick; (*mente*) quick, alert; **alla svelta** quickly

'svendere *vt* to sell off, clear

'svendita *sf* (*Comm*) (clearance) sale

'svengo *ecc vb vedi* **svenire**

sveni'mento *sm* fainting fit, faint

sve'nire *vi* to faint

sven'tare *vt* to foil, thwart

sven'tato, -a *ag* (*distratto*) scatterbrained; (*imprudente*) rash

svento'lare *vt, vi* to wave, flutter

sven'tura *sf* misfortune

sverrò *ecc vb vedi* **svenire**

sves'tire *vt* to undress; **svestirsi** *vpr* to get undressed

'Svezia ['zvɛttsja] *sf* **la ~** Sweden

svi'are *vt* to divert; (*fig*) to lead astray

svi'gnarsela [zviɲ'ɲarsela] *vpr* to slip away, sneak off

svilup'pare *vt* to develop; **svilupparsi** *vpr* to develop; **può ~ questo rullino?** can you develop this film?

svi'luppo *sm* development

'svincolo *sm* (*stradale*) motorway (BRIT) *o* expressway (US) intersection

'svista *sf* oversight

svi'tare *vt* to unscrew

'Svizzera ['zvittsera] *sf* **la ~** Switzerland

'svizzero, -a ['zvittsero] *ag, sm/f* Swiss

svogli'ato, -a [zvoʎ'ʎato] *ag* listless; (*pigro*) lazy

'svolgere ['zvɔldʒere] *vt* to unwind; (*srotolare*) to unroll; (*fig: argomento*) to develop; (: *piano, programma*) to carry out; **svolgersi** *vpr* to unwind; to unroll; (*fig: aver luogo*) to take place; (: *procedere*) to go on

'svolsi *ecc vb vedi* **svolgere**

'svolta *sf* (*atto*) turning *no pl*; (*curva*) turn, bend; (*fig*) turning-point

svol'tare *vi* to turn

svuo'tare *vt* to empty (out)

T, t [ti] *sf o m inv* (*lettera*) T, t; **T come Taranto** ≈ T for Tommy

t *abbr* = **tonnellata**

tabacche'ria [tabakke'ria] *sf* tobacconist's (shop)

ta'bacco, -chi *sm* tobacco

ta'bella *sf* (*tavola*) table; (*elenco*) list

tabel'lone *sm* (*pubblicitario*) billboard; (*con orario*) timetable board

TAC *sigla f* (*Med:* = *Tomografia Assiale Computerizzata*) CAT

tac'chino [tak'kino] *sm* turkey

'tacco, -chi *sm* heel; **tacchi a spillo** stiletto heels

taccu'ino *sm* notebook

ta'cere [ta'tʃere] *vi* to be silent o quiet; (*smettere di parlare*) to fall silent ▷ *vt* to keep to oneself, say nothing about; **far ~ qn** to make sb be quiet; (*fig*) to silence sb

ta'chimetro [ta'kimetro] *sm* speedometer

'tacqui *ecc vb vedi* **tacere**

ta'fano *sm* horsefly

'taglia ['taʎʎa] *sf* (*statura*) height; (*misura*) size; (*riscatto*) ransom; (*ricompensa*) reward; **taglia forte** (*di abito*) large size

taglia'carte [taʎʎa'karte] *sm inv* paperknife

tagli'ando [taʎ'ʎando] *sm* coupon

tagli'are [taʎ'ʎare] *vt* to cut; (*recidere, interrompere*) to cut off; (*intersecare*) to cut across, intersect; (*carne*) to carve; (*vini*) to blend ▷ *vi* to cut; (*prendere una scorciatoia*) to take a short-cut; **tagliarsi** *vpr* to cut o.s.; **mi sono tagliato** I've cut myself; **~ corto** (*fig*) to cut short; **~ la corda** (*fig*) to sneak off; **~ i ponti (con)** (*fig*) to break off relations (with); **~ la strada a qn** to cut across sb; **mi sono tagliato** I've cut myself

taglia'telle [taʎʎa'telle] *sfpl* tagliatelle *pl*

taglia'unghie [taʎʎa'ungje] *sm inv* nail clippers *pl*

tagli'ente [taʎ'ʎɛnte] *ag* sharp

'taglio ['taʎʎo] *sm* cutting *no pl*; cut; (*parte tagliente*) cutting edge; (*di abito*) cut, style; (*di stoffa: lunghezza*) length; (*di vini*) blending; **di ~** on edge, edgeways; **banconote di piccolo/grosso ~** notes of small/large denomination; **taglio cesareo** Caesarean section

tailan'dese *ag, sm/f, sm* Thai

Tai'landia *sf* **la ~** Thailand

'talco *sm* talcum powder

⬤ **PAROLA CHIAVE**

'tale *det* **1** (*simile, così grande*) such; **un(a) tale ...** such (a) ...; **non accetto tali discorsi** I won't allow such talk; **è di una tale arroganza** he is so arrogant; **fa una tale confusione!** he makes such a mess! **2** (*persona o cosa indeterminata*) such-and-such; **il giorno tale all'ora tale** on such-and-such a day at such-and-such a time; **la tal persona** that person; **ha telefonato una tale Giovanna** somebody called Giovanna phoned

3 (*nelle similitudini*): **tale ... tale** like ... like; **tale padre tale figlio** like father, like son; **hai il vestito tale quale il mio** your dress is just o exactly like mine

▷ *pron* (*indefinito: persona*): **un(a) tale** someone; **quel (o quella) tale** that person, that man (o woman); **il tal dei tali** what's-his-name

tale'bano *sm* Taliban

ta'lento *sm* talent

talis'mano *sm* talisman

tallon'cino [tallon'tʃino] *sm* counterfoil
tal'lone *sm* heel
tal'mente *av* so
'talpa *sf* (*Zool*) mole
tal'volta *av* sometimes, at times
tambu'rello *sm* tambourine
tam'buro *sm* drum
Ta'migi [ta'midʒi] *sm* **il ~** the Thames
tampo'nare *vt* (*otturare*) to plug; (*urtare: macchina*) to crash o ram into
tam'pone *sm* (*Med*) wad, pad; (*per timbri*) ink-pad; (*respingente*) buffer; **tampone assorbente** tampon
'tana *sf* lair, den
'tanga *sm inv* G-string
tan'gente [tan'dʒɛnte] *ag* (*Mat*): **~ a** tangential to ▷ *sf* tangent; (*quota*) share
tangenzi'ale [tandʒen'tsjale] *sf* (*Aut*) bypass
'tanica *sf* (*contenitore*) jerry can

⊙ **PAROLA CHIAVE**

'tanto, -a *det* **1** (*molto: quantità*) a lot of, much; (*: numero*) a lot of, many; (*così tanto: quantità*) so much, such a lot of; (*: numero*) so many, such a lot of; **tante volte** so many times, so often; **tanti auguri!** all the best!; **tante grazie** many thanks; **tanto tempo** so long, such a long time; **ogni tanti chilometri** every so many kilometres
2: **tanto ... quanto** (*quantità*) as much ... as; (*numero*) as many ... as; **ho tanta pazienza quanta ne hai tu** I have as much patience as you have o as you; **ha tanti amici quanti nemici** he has as many friends as he has enemies
3 (*rafforzativo*) such; **ho aspettato per tanto tempo** I waited so long o for such a long time
▷ *pron* **1** (*molto*) much, a lot; (*così tanto*) so much, such a lot; **tanti, e** many, a lot; so many, such a lot; **credevo ce ne fosse tanto** I thought there was (such) a lot, I thought there was plenty
2: **tanto quanto** (*denaro*) as much as; (*cioccolatini*) as many as; **ne ho tanto quanto basta** I have as much as I need; **due volte tanto** twice as much
3 (*indeterminato*) so much; **tanto per l'affitto, tanto per il gas** so much for the rent, so much for the gas; **costa un tanto al metro** it costs so much per metre; **di tanto in tanto, ogni tanto** every so often; **tanto vale che ...** I (*o* we *ecc*) may as well ...; **tanto meglio!** so much the better!; **tanto peggio per lui!** so much the worse for him!

▷ *av* **1** (*molto*) very; **vengo tanto volentieri** I'd be very glad to come; **non ci vuole tanto a capirlo** it doesn't take much to understand it
2 (*così tanto: con ag, av*) so; (*: con vb*) so much, such a lot; **è tanto bella!** she's so beautiful!; **non urlare tanto** don't shout so much; **sto tanto meglio adesso** I'm so much better now; **tanto ... che** so ... (that); **tanto ... da** so ... as
3: **tanto ... quanto** as ... as; **conosco tanto Carlo quanto suo padre** I know both Carlo and his father; **non è poi tanto complicato quanto sembri** it's not as difficult as it seems; **tanto più insisti, tanto più non mollerà** the more you insist, the more stubborn he'll be; **quanto più ... tanto meno** the more ... the less
4 (*solamente*) just; **tanto per cambiare/scherzare** just for a change/a joke; **una volta tanto** for once
5 (*a lungo*) (for) long
▷ *cong* after all

'tappa *sf* (*luogo di sosta, fermata*) stop, halt; (*parte di un percorso*) stage, leg; (*Sport*) lap; **a tappe** in stages
tap'pare *vt* to plug, stop up; (*bottiglia*) to cork; **tapparsi** *vpr* **tapparsi in casa** to shut o.s. up at home; **tapparsi la bocca** to shut up; **tapparsi le orecchie** to turn a deaf ear
tappa'rella *sf* rolling shutter
tappe'tino *sm* (*per auto*) car mat; **tappetino antiscivolo** (*da bagno*) non-slip mat
tap'peto *sm* carpet; (*anche*: **tappetino**) rug; (*Sport*): **andare al ~** to go down for the count; **mettere sul ~** (*fig*) to bring up for discussion
tappez'zare [tappet'tsare] *vt* (*con carta*) to paper; (*rivestire*): **~ qc (di)** to cover sth (with); **tappez'ria** *sf* (*tessuto*) tapestry; (*carta da parati*) wallpaper; (*arte*) upholstery; **far da tappezzeria** (*fig*) to be a wallflower
'tappo *sm* stopper; (*in sughero*) cork
tar'dare *vi* to be late ▷ *vt* to delay; **~ a fare** to delay doing
'tardi *av* late; **più ~** later (on); **al più ~** at the latest; **sul ~** (*verso sera*) late in the day; **far ~** to be late; (*restare alzato*) to stay up late; **è troppo ~** it's too late
'targa, -ghe *sf* plate; (*Aut*) number (*BRIT*) o license (*US*) plate; **tar'ghetta** *sf* (*su bagaglio*) name tag; (*su porta*) nameplate
ta'riffa *sf* (*gen*) rate, tariff; (*di trasporti*) fare; (*elenco*) price list; tariff
'tarlo *sm* woodworm

'**tarma** sf moth
tarocchi smpl (gioco) tarot sg
tarta'ruga, -ghe sf tortoise; (di mare) turtle; (materiale) tortoiseshell
tar'tina sf canapé
tar'tufo sm (Bot) truffle
'**tasca, -sche** sf pocket; **tas'cabile** ag (libro) pocket cpd
'**tassa** sf (imposta) tax; (doganale) duty; (per iscrizione: a scuola ecc) fee; **tassa di circolazione** road tax; **tassa di soggiorno** tourist tax
tas'sare vt to tax; to levy a duty on
tas'sello sm plug; wedge
tassì sm inv = **taxi**; **tas'sista, -i, -e** sm/f taxi driver
'**tasso** sm (di natalità, d'interesse ecc) rate; (Bot) yew; (Zool) badger; **tasso di cambio/d'interesse** rate of exchange/interest
tas'tare vt to feel; ~ **il terreno** (fig) to see how the land lies
tasti'era sf keyboard
'**tasto** sm key; (tatto) touch, feel
tas'toni av **procedere (a) ~** to grope one's way forward
'**tatto** sm (senso) touch; (fig) tact; **duro al ~** hard to the touch; **aver ~** to be tactful, have tact
tatu'aggio [tatu'addʒo] sm tattooing; (disegno) tattoo
tatu'are vt to tattoo
'**tavola** sf table; (asse) plank, board; (lastra) tablet; (quadro) panel (painting); (illustrazione) plate; **tavola calda** snack bar; **tavola rotonda** (fig) round table; **tavola a vela** windsurfer
tavo'letta sf tablet, bar; **a ~** (Aut) flat out
tavo'lino sm small table; (scrivania) desk
'**tavolo** sm table; **un ~ per 4 per favore** a table for 4, please
'**taxi** sm inv taxi; **può chiamarmi un ~ per favore?** can you call me a taxi, please?
'**tazza** ['tattsa] sf cup; **una ~ di caffè/tè** a cup of coffee/tea; **tazza da tè/caffè** tea/coffee cup
TBC abbr f (= tubercolosi) TB
te pron (soggetto: in forme comparative, oggetto) you
tè sm inv tea; (trattenimento) tea party
tea'trale ag theatrical
te'atro sm theatre
techno ['tɛkno] ag inv (musica) techno
'**tecnica, -che** sf technique; (tecnologia) technology
'**tecnico, -a, -ci, -che** ag technical ▷ sm/f technician
tecnolo'gia [teknolo'dʒia] sf technology
te'desco, -a, -schi, -sche ag, sm/f, sm German

te'game sm (Cuc) pan
'**tegola** sf tile
tei'era sf teapot
tel. abbr (= telefono) tel.
'**tela** sf (tessuto) cloth; (per vele, quadri) canvas; (dipinto) canvas, painting; **di ~** (calzoni) cotton cpd; (scarpe, borsa) canvas cpd; **tela cerata** oilcloth
te'laio sm (apparecchio) loom; (struttura) frame
tele'camera sf television camera
tele'co'mando sm remote control
tele'cronaca sf television report
telefo'nare vi to telephone, ring; to make a phone call ▷ vt to telephone; ~ **a** to phone up, ring up, call up
telefo'nata sf (telephone) call; ~ **a carico del destinatario** reverse charge (BRIT) o collect (US) call
tele'fonico, -a, -ci, -che ag (tele)phone cpd
telefon'ino sm mobile phone
te'lefono sm telephone; **telefono a gettoni** ≈ pay phone
telegior'nale [teledʒor'nale] sm television news (programme)
tele'gramma, -i sm telegram
telela'voro sm teleworking
Tele'pass® sm inv automatic payment card for use on Italian motorways
telepa'tia sf telepathy
teles'copio sm telescope
teleselezi'one [teleselet'tsjone] sf direct dialling
telespetta'tore, -'trice sm/f (television) viewer
tele'vendita sf teleshopping
televisi'one sf television
televi'sore sm television set
'**tema, -i** sm theme; (Ins) essay, composition
te'mere vt to fear, be afraid of; (essere sensibile a: freddo, calore) to be sensitive to ▷ vi to be afraid; (essere preoccupato): ~ **per** to worry about, fear for; ~ **di/che** to be afraid of/that
temperama'tite sm inv pencil sharpener
tempera'mento sm temperament
tempera'tura sf temperature
tempe'rino sm penknife
tem'pesta sf storm; **tempesta di sabbia/neve** sand/snowstorm
'**tempia** sf (Anat) temple
'**tempio** sm (edificio) temple
'**tempo** sm (Meteor) weather; (cronologico) time; (epoca) time, times pl; (di film, gioco: parte) part; (Mus) time; (: battuta) beat; (Ling) tense; **che ~ fa?** what's the weather like?; **un ~** once; ~ **fa** some time ago; **al ~**

stesso *o* **a un ~** at the same time; **per ~** early; **ha fatto il suo ~** it has had its day; **primo/secondo ~** (*Teatro*) first/second part; (*Sport*) first/second half; **in ~ utile** in due time *o* course; **a ~ pieno** full-time; **tempo libero** free time

tempo'rale *ag* temporal ▷ *sm* (*Meteor*) (thunder)storm

tempo'raneo, -a *ag* temporary

te'nace [te'natʃe] *ag* strong, tough; (*fig*) tenacious

te'naglie [te'naʎʎe] *sfpl* pincers *pl*

'tenda *sf* (*riparo*) awning; (*di finestra*) curtain; (*per campeggio ecc*) tent

ten'denza [ten'dɛntsa] *sf* tendency; (*orientamento*) trend; **avere ~ a** *o* **per qc** to have a bent for sth

'tendere *vt* (*allungare al massimo*) to stretch, draw tight; (*porgere: mano*) to hold out; (*fig: trappola*) to lay, set ▷ *vi* **~ a qc/a fare** to tend towards sth/to do; **~ l'orecchio** to prick up one's ears; **il tempo tende al caldo** the weather is getting hot; **un blu che tende al verde** a greenish blue

'tendine *sm* tendon, sinew

ten'done *sm* (*da circo*) tent

'tenebre *sfpl* darkness *sg*

te'nente *sm* lieutenant

te'nere *vt* to hold; (*conservare, mantenere*) to keep; (*ritenere, considerare*) to consider; (*spazio: occupare*) to take up, occupy; (*seguire: strada*) to keep to ▷ *vi* to hold; (*colori*) to be fast; (*dare importanza*): **~ a** to care about; **~ a fare** to want to do, be keen to do; **tenersi** *vpr* (*stare in una determinata posizione*) to stand; (*stimarsi*) to consider o.s.; (*aggrapparsi*): **tenersi a** to hold on to; (*attenersi*): **tenersi a** to stick to; **~ una conferenza** to give a lecture; **~ conto di qc** to take sth into consideration; **~ presente qc** to bear sth in mind

'tenero, -a *ag* tender; (*pietra, cera, colore*) soft; (*fig*) tender, loving

'tengo *ecc vb vedi* **tenere**

'tenni *ecc vb vedi* **tenere**

'tennis *sm* tennis

ten'nista, -i, e *sm/f* tennis player

te'nore *sm* (*tono*) tone; (*Mus*) tenor; **tenore di vita** (*livello*) standard of living

tensi'one *sf* tension

ten'tare *vt* (*indurre*) to tempt; (*provare*): **~ qc/di fare** to attempt *o* try sth/to do; **tenta'tivo** *sm* attempt; **tentazi'one** *sf* temptation

tenten'nare *vi* to shake, be unsteady; (*fig*) to hesitate, waver

ten'toni *av* **andare a ~** (*anche fig*) to grope one's way

'tenue *ag* (*sottile*) fine; (*colore*) soft; (*fig*)

slender, slight

te'nuta *sf* (*capacità*) capacity; (*divisa*) uniform; (*abito*) dress; (*Agr*) estate; **a ~ d'aria** airtight; **tenuta di strada** roadholding power

teolo'gia [teolo'dʒia] *sf* theology

teo'ria *sf* theory

te'pore *sm* warmth

tep'pista, -i *sm* hooligan

tera'pia *sf* therapy; **terapia intensiva** intensive care

tergicris'tallo [terdʒikris'tallo] *sm* windscreen (*BRIT*) *o* windshield (*US*) wiper

tergiver'sare [terdʒiver'sare] *vi* to shilly-shally

ter'male *ag* thermal; **stazione** *sf* **~ spa**

'terme *sfpl* thermal baths

termi'nale *ag, sm* terminal

termi'nare *vt* to end; (*lavoro*) to finish ▷ *vi* to end

'termine *sm* term; (*fine, estremità*) end; (*di territorio*) boundary, limit; (*Comm*) forward contract; **a breve/lungo ~** short-/long-term; **parlare senza mezzi termini** to talk frankly, not to mince one's words

ter'mometro *sm* thermometer

'termos *sm inv* = **thermos®**

termosi'fone *sm* radiator

ter'mostato *sm* thermostat

'terra *sf* (*gen, Elettr*) earth; (*sostanza*) soil, earth; (*opposto al mare*) land *no pl*; (*regione, paese*) land; (*argilla*) clay; **terre** *sfpl* (*possedimento*) lands, land *sg*; **a** *o* **per ~** (*stato*) on the ground (*o floor*); (*moto*) to the ground, down; **mettere a ~** (*Elettr*) to earth

terra'cotta *sf* terracotta; **vasellame** *sm* **di ~** earthenware

terra'ferma *sf* dry land, terra firma; (*continente*) mainland

ter'razza [ter'rattsa] *sf* terrace

ter'razzo [ter'rattso] *sm* = **terrazza**

terre'moto *sm* earthquake

ter'reno, -a *ag* (*vita, beni*) earthly ▷ *sm* (*suolo, fig*) ground; (*Comm*) land *no pl*, plot (of land); site; (*Sport, Mil*) field

ter'restre *ag* (*superficie*) of the earth, earth's; (*di terra: battaglia, animale*) land *cpd*; (*Rel*) earthly, worldly

ter'ribile *ag* terrible, dreadful

terrifi'cante *ag* terrifying

ter'rina *sf* tureen

territori'ale *ag* territorial

terri'torio *sm* territory

ter'rore *sm* terror; **terro'rismo** *sm* terrorism; **terro'rista, -i, -e** *sm/f* terrorist

terroriz'zare [terrorid'dzare] *vt* to terrorize

terza ['tɛrtsa] *sf* (*Scol: elementare*) ≈ third year at primary school; (: *media*) ≈ second year at secondary school; (: *superiore*) ≈ fifth year at secondary school; (*Aut*) third gear

ter'zino [ter'tsino] *sm* (*Calcio*) fullback, back

'terzo, -a ['tɛrtso] *ag* third ▷ *sm* (*frazione*) third; (*Dir*) third party; **terza pagina** (*Stampa*) Aɪ ʟs page; **terzi** *smpl* (*altri*) others, other people

'teschio ['tɛskjo] *sm* skull

'tesi[1] *sf* thesis; **tesi di laurea** degree thesis

'tesi *ecc*[2] *vb vedi* **tendere**

'teso, -a *pp di* **tendere** ▷ *ag* (*tirato*) taut, tight; (*fig*) tense

te'soro *sm* treasure; **il Ministero del T~** the Treasury

'tessera *sf* (*documento*) card

tes'suto *sm* fabric, material; (*Biol*) tissue

test ['tɛst] *sm inv* test

'testa *sf* head; (*di cose: estremità, parte anteriore*) head, front; **di ~** (*vettura ecc*) front; **tenere ~ a qn** (*nemico ecc*) to stand up to sb; **fare di ~ propria** to go one's own way; **in ~** (*Sport*) in the lead; **~ o croce?** heads or tails?; **avere la ~ dura** to be stubborn; **testa d'aglio** bulb of garlic; **testa di serie** (*Tennis*) seed, seeded player

testa'mento *sm* (*atto*) will; **l'Antico/il Nuovo T~** (*Rel*) the Old/New Testament

tes'tardo, -a *ag* stubborn, pig-headed

tes'tata *sf* (*parte anteriore*) head; (*intestazione*) heading

tes'ticolo *sm* testicle

testi'mone *sm/f* (*Dir*) witness; **testimone oculare** eye witness

testimoni'are *vt* to testify; (*fig*) to bear witness to, testify to ▷ *vi* to give evidence, testify

'testo *sm* text; **fare ~** (*opera, autore*) to be authoritative; **questo libro non fa ~** this book is not essential reading

tes'tuggine [tes'tudd3ine] *sf* tortoise; (*di mare*) turtle

'tetano *sm* (*Med*) tetanus

'tetto *sm* roof; **tet'toia** *sf* roofing; canopy

tettuccio [tet'tuttʃo] *sm* **~ apribile** (*Aut*) sunroof

'Tevere *sm* **il ~** the Tiber

TG, Tg *abbr* = **telegiornale**

'thermos® ['tɛrmos] *sm inv* vacuum *o* Thermos® flask

ti *pron* (*dav lo, la, li, le, ne diventa* **te**) ▷ *pron* (*oggetto*) you; (*complemento di termine*) (to) you; (*riflessivo*) yourself

'Tibet *sm* **il ~** Tibet

'tibia *sf* tibia, shinbone

tic *sm inv* tic, (nervous) twitch; (*fig*) mannerism

ticchet'tio [tikket'tio] *sm* (*di macchina da scrivere*) clatter; (*di orologio*) ticking; (*della pioggia*) patter

'ticket *sm inv* (*su farmaci*) prescription charge

ti'ene *ecc vb vedi* **tenere**

ti'epido, -a *ag* lukewarm, tepid

'tifo *sm* (*Med*) typhus; (*fig*): **fare il ~ per** to be a fan of

ti'fone *sm* typhoon

ti'foso, -a *sm/f* (*Sport ecc*) fan

tigì [ti'dʒi] *sm inv* TV news

'tiglio ['tiʎʎo] *sm* lime (tree), linden (tree)

'tigre *sf* tiger

tim'brare *vt* to stamp; (*annullare: francobolli*) to postmark; **~ il cartellino** to clock in

'timbro *sm* stamp; (*Mus*) timbre, tone

'timido, -a *ag* shy; timid

'timo *sm* thyme

ti'mone *sm* (*Naut*) rudder

ti'more *sm* (*paura*) fear; (*rispetto*) awe

'timpano *sm* (*Anat*) eardrum; (*Mus*)

'tingere ['tindʒere] *vt* to dye

'tinsi *ecc vb vedi* **tingere**

'tinta *sf* (*materia colorante*) dye; (*colore*) colour, shade

tintin'nare *vi* to tinkle

tinto'ria *sf* (*lavasecco*) dry cleaner's (shop)

tin'tura *sf* (*operazione*) dyeing; (*colorante*) dye; **tintura di iodio** tincture of iodine

'tipico, -a, -ci, -che *ag* typical

'tipo *sm* type; (*genere*) kind, type; (*fam*) chap, fellow; **che ~ di...?** what kind of ...?

tipogra'fia *sf* typography; (*procedimento*) letterpress (printing); (*officina*) printing house

TIR *sigla m* (= *Transports Internationaux Routiers*) International Heavy Goods Vehicle

ti'rare *vt* (*gen*) to pull; (*estrarre*): **~ qc da** to take *o* pull sth out of; to get sth out of; to extract sth from; (*chiudere: tenda ecc*) to draw, pull; (*tracciare, disegnare*) to draw, trace; (*lanciare: sasso, palla*) to throw; (*stampare*) to print; (*pistola, freccia*) to fire ▷ *vi* (*pipa, camino*) to draw; (*vento*) to blow; (*abito*) to be tight; (*fare fuoco*) to fire; (*fare del tiro, Calcio*) to shoot; **~ avanti** *vi* to struggle on ▷ *vt* to keep going; **~ fuori** (*estrarre*) to take out, pull out; **~ giù** (*abbassare*) to bring down, to lower; (*da scaffale ecc.*) to take down; **~ su** to pull up; (*capelli*) to put up; (*fig: bambino*) to bring up; **tirarsi** *vpr* **tirarsi indietro** to draw back; (*fig*) to back out; **~ a indovinare** to take a guess; **~ sul prezzo** to bargain; **tirar dritto** to keep right on going; **tirati su!** (*fig*) cheer up!; **~ via** (*togliere*) to take off

tira'tura sf (azione) printing; (di libro) (print) run; (di giornale) circulation

'tirchio, -a ['tirkjo] ag mean, stingy

'tiro sm shooting no pl, firing no pl; (colpo, sparo) shot; (di palla: lancio) throwing no pl; throw; (fig) trick; **cavallo da ~** draught (BRIT) o draft (US) horse; **tiro a segno** target shooting; (luogo) shooting range; **tiro con l'arco** archery

tiro'cinio [tiro'tʃinjo] sm apprenticeship; (professionale) training

ti'roide sf thyroid (gland)

Tir'reno sm **il (mar) ~** the Tyrrhenian Sea

ti'sana sf herb tea

tito'lare sm/f incumbent; (proprietario) owner; (Calcio) regular player

'titolo sm title; (di giornale) headline; (diploma) qualification; (Comm) security; (: azione) share; **a che ~?** for what reason?; **a ~ di amicizia** out of friendship; **a ~ di premio** as a prize; **titolo di credito** share; **titoli di stato** government securities; **titoli di testa** (Cinema) credits

titu'bante ag hesitant, irresolute

toast [toust] sm inv toasted sandwich (generally with ham and cheese)

toc'cante ag touching

toc'care vt to touch; (tastare) to feel; (fig: riguardare) to concern; (: commuovere) to touch, move; (: pungere) to hurt, wound; (: far cenno a: argomento) to touch on, mention ▷ vi **~ a** (accadere) to happen to; (spettare) to be up to; **~ (il fondo)** (in acqua) to touch the bottom; **tocca a te difenderci** it's up to you to defend us; **a chi tocca?** whose turn is it?; **mi toccò pagare** I had to pay

toccherò ecc [tokke'rɔ] vb vedi **toccare**

'togliere ['tɔʎʎere] vt (rimuovere) to take away (o off), remove; (riprendere, non concedere più) to take away, remove; (Mat) to take away, subtract; **~ qc a qn** to take sth (away) from sb; **ciò non toglie che** nevertheless, be that as it may; **togliersi il cappello** to take off one's hat

toi'lette [twa'lɛt] sf inv toilet; (mobile) dressing table; **dov'è la ~?** where's the toilet?

'Tokyo sf Tokyo

'tolgo ecc vb vedi **togliere**

tolle'rare vt to tolerate

'tolsi ecc vb vedi **togliere**

'tomba sf tomb

tom'bino sm manhole cover

'tombola sf (gioco) tombola; (ruzzolone) tumble

'tondo, -a ag round

'tonfo sm splash; (rumore sordo) thud; (caduta): **fare un ~** to take a tumble

tonifi'care vt (muscoli, pelle) to tone up; (irrobustire) to invigorate, brace

tonnel'lata sf ton

'tonno sm tuna (fish)

'tono sm (gen) tone; (Mus: di pezzo) key; (di colore) shade, tone

ton'silla sf tonsil

'tonto, -a ag dull, stupid

to'pazio [to'pattsjo] sm topaz

'topo sm mouse

'toppa sf (serratura) keyhole; (pezza) patch

to'race [to'ratʃe] sm chest

'torba sf peat

'torcere ['tɔrtʃere] vt to twist; **torcersi** vpr to twist, writhe

'torcia, -ce ['tɔrtʃa] sf torch; **torcia elettrica** torch (BRIT), flashlight (US)

torci'collo [tortʃi'kɔllo] sm stiff neck

'tordo sm thrush

To'rino sf Turin

tor'menta sf snowstorm

tormen'tare vt to torment; **tormentarsi** vpr to fret, worry o.s.

tor'nado sm tornado

tor'nante sm hairpin bend

tor'nare vi to return, go (o come) back; (ridiventare: anche fig) to become (again); (riuscire giusto, esatto: conto) to work out; (risultare) to turn out (to be), prove (to be); **~ utile** to prove o turn out (to be) useful; **~ a casa** to go (o come) home; **torno a casa martedì** I'm going home on Tuesday

tor'neo sm tournament

'tornio sm lathe

'toro sm bull; (dello zodiaco): **T~** Taurus

'torre sf tower; (Scacchi) rook, castle; **torre di controllo** (Aer) control tower

tor'rente sm torrent

torri'one sm keep

tor'rone sm nougat

'torsi ecc vb vedi **torcere**

torsi'one sf twisting; torsion

'torso sm torso, trunk; (Arte) torso

'torsolo sm (di cavolo ecc) stump; (di frutta) core

'torta sf cake

tortel'lini smpl (Cuc) tortellini

'torto, -a pp di **torcere** ▷ ag (ritorto) twisted; (storto) twisted, crooked ▷ sm (ingiustizia) wrong; (colpa) fault; **a ~** wrongly; **aver ~** to be wrong

tor'tora sf turtle dove

tor'tura sf torture; **tortu'rare** vt to torture

to'sare vt (pecora) to shear; (siepe) to clip

Tos'cana sf **la ~** Tuscany

'tosse sf cough; **ho la ~** I've got a cough

'tossico, -a, -ci, -che ag toxic

tossicodipen'dente sm/f drug addict

tos'sire vi to cough

tosta'pane sm inv toaster

to'tale ag, sm total

toto'calcio [toto'kaltʃo] sm gambling pool betting on football results, ≈ (football) pools pl (BRIT)

to'vaglia [to'vaʎʎa] sf tablecloth; **tovagli'olo** sm napkin

tra prep (di due persone, cose) between; (di più persone, cose) among(st); (tempo: entro) within, in; ~ **5 giorni** in 5 days' time; **sia detto ~ noi ...** between you and me ...; **litigano ~ (di) loro** they're fighting amongst themselves; ~ **breve** soon; ~ **sé e sé** (parlare ecc) to oneself

traboc'care vi to overflow

traboc'chetto [trabok'ketto] sm (fig) trap

'traccia, -ce ['trattʃa] sf (segno, striscia) trail, track; (orma) tracks pl; (residuo, testimonianza) trace, sign; (abbozzo) outline

tracci'are [trat'tʃare] vt to trace, mark (out); (disegnare) to draw; (fig: abbozzare) to outline

tra'chea [tra'kɛa] sf windpipe, trachea

tra'colla sf shoulder strap; **borsa a ~** shoulder bag

tradi'mento sm betrayal; (Dir, Mil) treason

tra'dire vt to betray; (coniuge) to be unfaithful to; (doveri: mancare) to fail in; (rivelare) to give away, reveal; **tradirsi** vpr to give o.s. away

tradizio'nale [tradittsjo'nale] ag traditional

tradizi'one [tradit'tsjone] sf tradition

tra'durre vt to translate; (spiegare) to render, convey; **me lo può ~?** can you translate this for me?; **traduzi'one** sf translation

'trae vb vedi **trarre**

traffi'cante sm/f dealer; (peg) trafficker

traffi'care vi (commerciare): ~ **(in)** to trade (in), deal (in); (affaccendarsi) to busy o.s. ▷ vt (peg) to traffic in

'traffico, -ci sm traffic; (commercio) trade, traffic; **traffico di armi/droga** arms/drug trafficking

tra'gedia [tra'dʒɛdja] sf tragedy

'traggo ecc vb vedi **trarre**

tra'ghetto [tra'getto] sm ferry(boat)

'tragico, -a, -ci, -che ['tradʒiko] ag tragic

tra'gitto [tra'dʒitto] sm (passaggio) crossing; (viaggio) journey

tragu'ardo sm (Sport) finishing line; (fig) goal, aim

'trai ecc vb vedi **trarre**

traiet'toria sf trajectory

trai'nare vt to drag, haul; (rimorchiare) to tow

tralasci'are [tralaʃ'ʃare] vt (studi) to neglect; (dettagli) to leave out, omit

tra'liccio [tra'littʃo] sm (Elettr) pylon

tram sm inv tram

'trama sf (filo) weft, woof; (fig: argomento, maneggio) plot

traman'dare vt to pass on, hand down

tram'busto sm turmoil

tramez'zino [tramed'dzino] sm sandwich

'tramite prep through

tramon'tare vi to set, go down; **tra'monto** sm setting; (del sole) sunset

trampo'lino sm (per tuffi) springboard, diving board; (per lo sci) ski-jump

tra'nello sm trap

'tranne prep except (for), but (for); ~ **che** unless

tranquil'lante sm (Med) tranquillizer

tranquillità sf calm, stillness; quietness; peace of mind

tranquilliz'zare [trankwillid'dzare] vt to reassure

> Attenzione! In inglese esiste il verbo to tranquillize, che però significa "calmare con un tranquillante".

tran'quillo, -a ag calm, quiet; (bambino, scolaro) quiet; (sereno) with one's mind at rest; **sta' ~** don't worry

transazi'one [transat'tsjone] sf compromise; (Dir) settlement; (Comm) transaction, deal

tran'senna sf barrier

transgenico, -a, -ci, -che [trans'dʒɛniko] ag genetically modified

tran'sigere [tran'sidʒere] vi (venire a patti) to compromise, come to an agreement

transi'tabile ag passable

transi'tare vi to pass

transi'tivo, -a ag transitive

'transito sm transit; **di ~** (merci) in transit; (stazione) transit cpd; **"divieto di ~"** "no entry"

'trapano sm (utensile) drill; (Med) trepan

trape'lare vi to leak, drip; (fig) to leak out

tra'pezio [tra'pɛttsjo] sm (Mat) trapezium; (attrezzo ginnico) trapeze

trapian'tare vt to transplant; **trapi'anto** sm transplanting; (Med) transplant; **trapianto cardiaco** heart transplant

'trappola sf trap

tra'punta sf quilt

'trarre vt to draw, pull; (portare) to take; (prendere, tirare fuori) to take (out), draw; (derivare) to obtain; ~ **origine da qc** to have its origins o originate in sth

trasa'lire vi to start, jump

trasan'dato, -a ag shabby

trasci'nare [traʃʃi'nare] vt to drag; **trascinarsi** vpr to drag o.s. along; (fig) to drag on

tras'correre vt (tempo) to spend, pass ▷ vi to pass

tras'crivere vt to transcribe

trascu'rare vt to neglect; (non considerare) to disregard

trasferi'mento sm transfer; (trasloco) removal, move; **trasferimento di chiamata** (Tel) call forwarding

trasfe'rire vt to transfer; **trasferirsi** vpr to move; **tras'ferta** sf transfer; (indennità) travelling expenses pl; (Sport) away game

trasfor'mare vt to transform, change; **trasformarsi** vpr to be transformed; **trasformarsi in qc** to turn into sth; **trasforma'tore** sm (Elec) transformer

trasfusi'one sf (Med) transfusion

trasgre'dire vt to disobey, contravene

traslo'care vt to move, transfer; **tras'loco, -chi** sm removal

tras'mettere vt (passare): **~ qc a qn** to pass sth on to sb; (mandare) to send; (Tecn, Tel, Med) to transmit; (TV, Radio) to broadcast; **trasmissi'one** sf (gen, Fisica, Tecn) transmission; (passaggio) transmission, passing on; (TV, Radio) broadcast

traspa'rente ag transparent

traspor'tare vt to carry, move; (merce) to transport, convey; **lasciarsi ~ (da qc)** (fig) to let o.s. be carried away (by sth); **tras'porto** sm transport

'trassi ecc vb vedi **trarre**

trasver'sale ag transverse, cross(-); running at right angles

'tratta sf (Econ) draft; (di persone): **la ~ delle bianche** the white slave trade

tratta'mento sm treatment; (servizio) service

trat'tare vt (gen) to treat; (commerciare) to deal in; (svolgere: argomento) to discuss, deal with; (negoziare) to negotiate ▷ vi **~ di** to deal with; **~ con** (persona) to deal with; **si tratta di ...** it's about ...

tratte'nere vt (far rimanere: persona) to detain; (intrattenere: ospiti) to entertain; (tenere, frenare, reprimere) to hold back, keep back; (astenersi dal consegnare) to hold, keep; (detrarre: somma) to deduct; **trattenersi** vpr (astenersi) to restrain o.s., stop o.s.; (soffermarsi) to stay, remain

trat'tino sm dash; (in parole composte) hyphen

'tratto, -a pp di **trarre** ▷ sm (di penna, matita) stroke; (parte) part, piece; (di strada) stretch; (di mare, cielo) expanse; (di tempo) period (of time)

trat'tore sm tractor

tratto'ria sf restaurant

'trauma, -i sm trauma

tra'vaglio [tra'vaʎʎo] sm (angoscia) pain, suffering; (Med) pains pl

trava'sare vt to decant

tra'versa sf (trave) crosspiece; (via) side street; (Ferr) sleeper (BRIT), (railroad) tie (US); (Calcio) crossbar

traver'sata sf crossing; (Aer) flight, trip; **quanto dura la ~?** how long does the crossing take?

traver'sie sfpl mishaps, misfortunes

tra'verso, -a ag oblique; **di ~** ag askew ▷ av sideways; **andare di ~** (cibo) to go down the wrong way; **guardare di ~** to look askance at

travesti'mento sm disguise

travestirsi vpr to disguise o.s.

tra'volgere [tra'vɔldʒere] vt to sweep away, carry away; (fig) to overwhelm

tre num three

'treccia, -ce ['trettʃa] sf plait, braid

tre'cento [tre'tʃɛnto] num three hundred ▷ sm **il T~** the fourteenth century

'tredici ['treditʃi] num thirteen

'tregua sf truce; (fig) respite

tre'mare vi **~ di** (freddo ecc) to shiver o tremble with; (paura, rabbia) to shake o tremble with

tre'mendo, -a ag terrible, awful

> Attenzione! In inglese esiste la parola *tremendous*, che però significa *enorme* oppure *fantastico, strepitoso*.

'tremito sm trembling no pl; shaking no pl; shivering no pl

'treno sm train; **è questo il ~ per...?** is this the train for ...?; **treno di gomme** set of tyres (BRIT) o tires (US); **treno merci** goods (BRIT) o freight'train; **treno viaggiatori** passenger train

● There are various types of train in
● Italy. For short journeys there are
● the "Regionali" (R), which generally
● operate within a particular region,
● and the "Interregionali" (IR), which
● operate beyond regional boundaries.
● Medium- and long-distance passenger
● journeys are carried out by "Intercity" (I)
● and "Eurocity" (EC) trains. The "Eurostar"
● service (ES) offers fast connections
● between the major Italian cities. Night
● services are operated by "Intercity
● Notte" (ICN), "Euronight" (EN) and by
● "Espressi" (EXP).

'trenta num thirty; **tren'tesimo, -a** num thirtieth; **tren'tina** sf **una trentina (di)** thirty or so, about thirty '**trepidante** *ag* anxious

tri'**angolo** *sm* triangle

tri**bù** *sf inv* tribe

tri'**buna** *sf* (*podio*) platform; (*in aule ecc*) gallery; (*di stadio*) stand

tribu'**nale** *sm* court

tri'**ciclo** [tri'tʃiklo] *sm* tricycle

tri'**foglio** [tri'fɔʎʎo] *sm* clover

'**triglia** ['triʎʎa] *sf* red mullet

tri'**mestre** *sm* period of three months; (*Ins*) term, quarter (*us*); (*Comm*) quarter

trin'**cea** [trin'tʃea] *sf* trench

trion'**fare** *vi* to triumph, win; ~ **su** to triumph over, overcome; **tri'onfo** *sm* triumph

tripli'**care** *vt* to triple

'**triplo, -a** *ag* triple; treble ▷ *sm* **il ~ (di)** three times as much (as); **la spesa è tripla** it costs three times as much

'**trippa** *sf* (*Cuc*) tripe

'**triste** *ag* sad; (*luogo*) dreary, gloomy

tri'**tare** *vt* to mince, grind (*us*)

trivi'**ale** *ag* vulgar, low

tro'**feo** *sm* trophy

'**tromba** *sf* (*Mus*) trumpet; (*Aut*) horn; **tromba d'aria** whirlwind; **tromba delle scale** stairwell

trom'**bone** *sm* trombone

trom'**bosi** *sf* thrombosis

tron'**care** *vt* to cut off; (*spezzare*) to break off

'**tronco, -a, -chi, -che** *ag* cut off; broken off; (*Ling*) truncated; (*fig*) cut short ▷ *sm* (*Bot, Anat*) trunk; (*fig: tratto*) section; **licenziare qn in ~** to fire sb on the spot

'**trono** *sm* throne

tropi'**cale** *ag* tropical

PAROLA CHIAVE

'**troppo, -a** *det* (*in eccesso: quantità*) too much; (*: numero*) too many; **c'era troppa gente** there were too many people; **fa troppo caldo** it's too hot
▷ *pron* (*in eccesso: quantità*) too much; (*: numero*) too many; **ne hai messo troppo** you've put in too much; **meglio troppi che pochi** better too many than too few
▷ *av* (*eccessivamente: con ag, av*) too; (*: con vb*) too much; **troppo amaro/tardi** too bitter/late; **lavora troppo** he works too much; **costa troppo** it costs too much; **di troppo** too much; too many; **qualche tazza di troppo** a few cups too many; **2 euro di troppo** 2 euros too much; **essere di troppo** to be in the way

'**trota** *sf* trout

'**trottola** *sf* spinning top

tro'**vare** *vt* to find; (*giudicare*): **trovo che** I find o think that; **trovarsi** *vpr* (*reciproco: incontrarsi*) to meet; (*essere, stare*) to be; (*arrivare, capitare*) to find o.s.; **~ qn colpevole** to find sb guilty; **trovarsi bene** (*in un luogo, con qn*) to get on well

truc'**care** *vt* (*falsare*) to fake; (*attore ecc*) to make up; (*travestire*) to disguise; (*Sport*) to fix; (*Aut*) to soup up; **truccarsi** *vpr* to make up (one's face)

'**trucco, -chi** *sm* trick; (*cosmesi*) make-up

'**truffa** *sf* fraud, swindle; **truf'fare** *vt* to swindle, cheat

truffa'**tore, -'trice** *sm/f* swindler, cheat

'**truppa** *sf* troop

tu *pron* you; **tu stesso(a)** you yourself; **dare del tu a qn** to address sb as "tu"

'**tubo** *sm* tube; pipe; **tubo digerente** (*Anat*) alimentary canal, digestive tract; **tubo di scappamento** (*Aut*) exhaust pipe

tuffarsi *vpr* to plunge, dive

'**tuffo** *sm* dive; (*breve bagno*) dip

tuli'**pano** *sm* tulip

tu'**more** *sm* (*Med*) tumour

Tuni'**sia** *sf* **la ~** Tunisia

'**tuo** (*f* '**tua**, *pl* **tu'oi, 'tue**) *det* **il ~, la tua** *ecc* your ▷ *pron* **il ~, la tua** *ecc* yours

tuo'**nare** *vi* to thunder; **tuona** it is thundering, there's some thunder

tu'**ono** *sm* thunder

tu'**orlo** *sm* yolk

tur'**bante** *sm* turban

tur'**bare** *vt* to disturb, trouble

tur'**bato, -a** *ag* upset; (*preoccupato, ansioso*) anxious

turbo'**lenza** [turbo'lɛntsa] *sf* turbulence

tur'**chese** [tur'kese] *sf* turquoise

Tur'**chia** [tur'kia] *sf* **la ~** Turkey

'**turco, -a, -chi, -che** *ag* Turkish ▷ *sm/f* Turk/Turkish woman ▷ *sm* (*Ling*) Turkish; **parlare ~** (*fig*) to talk double-dutch

tu'**rismo** *sm* tourism; tourist industry; **tu'rista, -i, -e** *sm/f* tourist; **turismo sessuale** sex tourism; **tu'ristico, -a, -ci, -che** *ag* tourist *cpd*

'**turno** *sm* turn; (*di lavoro*) shift; **di ~** (*soldato, medico, custode*) on duty; **a ~** (*rispondere*) in turn; (*lavorare*) in shifts; **fare a ~ a fare qc** to take turns to do sth; **è il suo ~** it's your (*o* his *ecc* turn)

'**turpe** *ag* filthy, vile

'**tuta** *sf* overalls *pl*; (*Sport*) tracksuit

tu'**tela** *sf* (*Dir: di minore*) guardianship; (*: protezione*) protection; (*difesa*) defence

t

tutta'via *cong* nevertheless, yet

○ **PAROLA CHIAVE**

'tutto, -a *det* **1** (*intero*) all; **tutto il latte**
all the milk; **tutta la notte** all night, the
whole night; **tutto il libro** the whole book;
tutta una bottiglia a whole bottle
2 (*pl, collettivo*) all; every; **tutti i libri** all the
books; **tutte le notti** every night; **tutti i
venerdì** every Friday; **tutti gli uomini** all
the men; (*collettivo*) all men; **tutto l'anno**
all year long; **tutti e due** both *o* each of us
(*o* them *o* you); **tutti e cinque** all five of us
(*o* them *o* you)
3 (*completamente*): **era tutta sporca**
she was all dirty; **tremava tutto** he was
trembling all over; **è tutta sua madre**
she's just *o* exactly like her mother
4: **a tutt'oggi** so far, up till now; **a tutta
velocità** at full *o* top speed
▷ *pron* **1** (*ogni cosa*) everything, all;
(*qualsiasi cosa*) anything; **ha mangiato
tutto** he's eaten everything; **tutto
considerato** all things considered; **in
tutto: 5 euro in tutto** 5 euros in all; **in
tutto eravamo 50** there were 50 of us
in all
2: **tutti, e** (*ognuno*) all, everybody;
vengono tutti they are all coming,
everybody's coming; **tutti quanti** all and
sundry
▷ *av* (*completamente*) entirely, quite; **è
tutto il contrario** it's quite *o* exactly the
opposite; **tutt'al più: saranno stati
tutt'al più una cinquantina** there were
about fifty of them at (the very) most;
tutt'al più possiamo prendere un treno
if the worst comes to the worst we can
take a train; **tutt'altro** on the contrary;
è tutt'altro che felice he's anything but
happy; **tutt'a un tratto** suddenly ▷ *sm* **il
tutto** the whole lot, all of it

tut'tora *av* still
TV [ti'vu] *sf inv* (= *televisione*) TV ▷ *sigla*
= **Treviso**

ubbidi'ente *ag* obedient
ubbi'dire *vi* to obey; **~ a** to obey; (*veicolo,
macchina*) to respond to
ubria'care *vt* **~ qn** to get sb drunk; (*alcool*)
to make sb drunk; (*fig*) to make sb's head
spin *o* reel; **ubriacarsi** *vpr* to get drunk;
ubriacarsi di (*fig*) to become intoxicated
with
ubri'aco, -a, -chi, -che *ag, sm/f* drunk
uc'cello [ut'tʃɛllo] *sm* bird
uc'cidere [ut'tʃidere] *vt* to kill; **uccidersi**
vpr (*suicidarsi*) to kill o.s.; (*perdere la vita*) to
be killed
u'dito *sm* (sense of) hearing
UE *sigla f* (= *Unione Europea*) EU
UEM *sigla f* (= *Unione economica e monetaria*)
EMU
'uffa *escl* tut!
uffici'ale [uffi'tʃale] *ag* official ▷ *sm* (*Amm*)
official, officer; (*Mil*) officer; **~ di stato
civile** registrar
uf'ficio [uf'fitʃo] *sm* (*gen*) office; (*dovere*)
duty; (*mansione*) task, function, job;
(*agenzia*) agency, bureau; (*Rel*) service; **d'~
ag** office *cpd*; official ▷ *av* officially; **ufficio
di collocamento** employment office;
ufficio informazioni information bureau;
ufficio oggetti smarriti lost property
office (BRIT), lost and found (US); **ufficio
(del) personale** personnel department;

ufficio postale post office
uffici'oso, -a [uffi'tʃoso] *ag* unofficial
uguagli'anza [ugwaʎ'ʎantsa] *sf* equality
uguagli'are [ugwaʎ'ʎare] *vt* to make
equal; (*essere uguale*) to equal, be equal to;
(*livellare*) to level; **uguagliarsi a** *o* **con qn**
(*paragonarsi*) to compare o.s. to sb
ugu'ale *ag* (*identico*) identical, the
same; (*uniforme*) level, even ▷ *av* **costano**
~ they cost the same; **sono bravi ~** they're
equally good
UIL *sigla f* (= *Unione Italiana del Lavoro*) trade
union federation
'ulcera ['ultʃera] *sf* ulcer
U'livo *sm* **l'~** centre-left Italian political
grouping
u'livo = **olivo**
ulteri'ore *ag* further
ulti'mamente *av* lately, of late
ulti'mare *vt* to finish, complete
'ultimo, -a *ag* (*finale*) last; (*estremo*)
farthest, utmost; (*recente: notizia, moda*)
latest; (*fig: sommo, fondamentale*) ultimate
▷ *sm/f* last (one); **fino all'~** to the last,
until the end; **da ~, in ~** in the end; **abitare**
all'~ piano to live on the top floor; **per ~**
(*entrare, arrivare*) last
ulu'lare *vi* to howl
umanità *sf* humanity
u'mano, -a *ag* human; (*comprensivo*)
humane
umidità *sf* dampness; humidity
'umido, -a *ag* damp; (*mano, occhi*) moist;
(*clima*) humid ▷ *sm* dampness, damp;
carne in ~ stew
'umile *ag* humble
umili'are *vt* to humiliate; **umiliarsi** *vpr* to
humble o.s.
u'more *sm* (*disposizione d'animo*) mood;
(*carattere*) temper; **di buon/cattivo ~** in a
good/bad mood
umo'rismo *sm* humour; **avere il senso**
dell'~ to have a sense of humour;
umo'ristico, -a, -ci, -che *ag* humorous,
funny
u'nanime *ag* unanimous
unci'netto [untʃi'netto] *sm* crochet hook
un'cino [un'tʃino] *sm* hook
undi'cenne [undi'tʃɛnne] *ag, sm/f* eleven-
year-old
undi'cesimo, -a [undi'tʃezimo] *num*
eleventh
'undici ['unditʃi] *num* eleven
'ungere ['undʒere] *vt* to grease, oil; (*Rel*) to
anoint; (*fig*) to flatter, butter up
unghe'rese [unge'rese] *ag, sm/f, sm*
Hungarian
Unghe'ria [unge'ria] *sf* **l'~** Hungary
'unghia ['ungja] *sf* (*Anat*) nail; (*di animale*)

claw; (*di rapace*) talon; (*di cavallo*) hoof
ungu'ento *sm* ointment
'unico, -a, -ci, -che *ag* (*solo*) only;
(*ineguagliabile*) unique; (*singolo: binario*)
single; **figlio(a) ~(a)** only son/daughter,
only child
unifi'care *vt* to unite, unify; (*sistemi*) to
standardize; **unificazi'one** *sf* uniting;
unification; standardization
uni'forme *ag* uniform; (*superficie*) even ▷ *sf*
(*divisa*) uniform
uni'one *sf* union; (*fig: concordia*) unity,
harmony; **Unione europea** European
Union; **ex Unione Sovietica** former
Soviet Union
u'nire *vt* to unite; (*congiungere*) to join,
connect; (: *ingredienti, colori*) to combine;
(*in matrimonio*) to unite, join together;
unirsi *vpr* to unite; (*in matrimonio*) to be
joined together; **~ qc a** to unite sth with;
to join *o* connect sth with; to combine sth
with; **unirsi a** (*gruppo, società*) to join
unità *sf inv* (*unione, concordia*) unity; (*Mat,*
Mil, Comm, di misura) unit; **unità di misura**
unit of measurement
u'nito, -a *ag* (*paese*) united; (*amici, famiglia*)
close; **in tinta unita** plain, self-coloured
univer'sale *ag* universal; general
università *sf inv* university
uni'verso *sm* universe

⬤ **PAROLA CHIAVE**

'uno, -a (*dav sm* **un** + C, V, **uno** + *s impura, gn,*
pn, ps, x, z; dav sf **un'** + V, **una** + C) *art indef* **1**
a; (*dav vocale*) an; **un bambino** a child; **una**
strada a street; **uno zingaro** a gypsy
2 (*intensivo*): **ho avuto una paura!** I got
such a fright!
▷ *pron* **1** one; **prendine uno** take one (of
them); **l'uno o l'altro** either (of them);
l'uno e l'altro both (of them); **aiutarsi**
l'un l'altro to help one another *o* each
other; **sono entrati l'uno dopo l'altro**
they came in one after the other
2 (*un tale*) someone, somebody
3 (*con valore impersonale*) one, you; **se uno**
vuole if one wants, if you want
▷ *num* one; **una mela e due pere** one
apple and two pears; **uno più uno fa due**
one plus one equals two, one and one are
two ▷ *sf* **è l'una** it's one (o'clock)

'unsi *ecc vb vedi* **ungere**
'unto, -a *pp di* **ungere** ▷ *ag* greasy, oily
▷ *sm* grease
u'omo (*pl* **u'omini**) *sm* man; **da ~** (*abito,*
scarpe) men's, for men; **uomo d'affari**
businessman; **uomo di paglia** stooge;

uomo politico politician; **uomo rana** frogman

u'ovo (pl(f) **u'ova**) sm egg; **uovo affogato/alla coque** poached/boiled egg; **uovo bazzotto/sodo** soft-/hard-boiled egg; **uovo di Pasqua** Easter egg; **uovo in camicia** poached egg; **uova strapazzate/al tegame** scrambled/fried eggs

ura'gano sm hurricane

urba'nistica sf town planning

ur'bano, -a ag urban, city cpd; town cpd; (Tel: chiamata) local; (fig) urbane

ur'gente [ur'dʒɛnte] ag urgent; **ur'genza** sf urgency; **in caso d'urgenza** in (case of) an emergency; **d'urgenza** ag emergency ▷ av urgently, as a matter of urgency

ur'lare vi (persona) to scream, yell; (animale, vento) to howl ▷ vt to scream, yell

'urlo (pl(m) **'urli**, pl(f) **'urla**) sm scream, yell; howl

urrà escl hurrah!

U.R.S.S. abbr f **l'U.R.S.S.** the USSR

ur'tare vt to bump into, knock against; (fig: irritare) to annoy ▷ vi ~ **contro** o **in** to bump into, knock against, crash into; (fig: imbattersi) to come up against; **urtarsi** vpr (reciproco: scontrarsi) to collide; (: fig) to clash; (irritarsi) to get annoyed

'U.S.A. ['uza] smpl **gli U.S.A.** the USA

u'sanza [u'zantsa] sf custom; (moda) fashion

u'sare vt to use, employ ▷ vi (servirsi): ~ **di** to use; (: diritto) to exercise; (essere di moda) to be fashionable; (essere solito): ~ **fare** to be in the habit of doing, be accustomed to doing ▷ vb impers **qui usa così** it's the custom round here; **u'sato, -a** ag used; (consumato) worn; (di seconda mano) used, second-hand ▷ sm second-hand goods pl

u'scire [uʃʃire] vi (gen) to come out; (partire, andare a passeggio, a uno spettacolo ecc) to go out; (essere sorteggiato: numero) to come up; ~ **da** (gen) to leave; (posto) to go (o come) out of, leave; (solco, vasca ecc) to come out of; (muro) to stick out of; (competenza ecc) to be outside; (infanzia, adolescenza) to leave behind; (famiglia nobile ecc) to come from; ~ **da** o **di casa** to go out; (fig) to leave home; ~ **in automobile** to go out in the car, go for a drive; ~ **di strada** (Aut) to go off o leave the road

u'scita [uʃʃita] sf (passaggio, varco) exit, way out; (per divertimento) outing; (Econ: somma) expenditure; (Teatro) entrance; (fig: battuta) witty remark; **dov'è l'~?** where's the exit?; **uscita di sicurezza** emergency exit

usi'gnolo [uziɲ'ɲɔlo] sm nightingale

'uso sm (utilizzazione) use; (esercizio) practice; (abitudine) custom; **a ~ di** for (the use of); **d'~** (corrente) in use; **fuori ~** out of use; **uso esterno; per ~ esterno** for external use only

usti'one sf burn

usu'ale ag common, everyday

u'sura sf usury; (logoramento) wear (and tear)

uten'sile sm tool, implement; **utensili da cucina** kitchen utensils

u'tente sm/f user

'utero sm uterus

'utile ag useful ▷ sm (vantaggio) advantage, benefit; (Econ: profitto) profit

utiliz'zare [utilid'dzare] vt to use, make use of, utilize

'uva sf grapes pl; **uva passa** raisins pl; **uva spina** gooseberry

UVA abbr (= ultravioletto prossimo) UVA

UVB abbr (= ultravioletto remoto) UVB

V

v. _abbr_ (= _vedi_) v

va, va' _vb vedi_ **andare**

va'cante _ag_ vacant

va'canza [va'kantsa] _sf_ (_riposo, ferie_) holiday(s) _pl_ (BRIT), vacation (US); (_giorno di permesso_) day off, holiday; **vacanze** _sfpl_ (_periodo di ferie_) holidays (BRIT), vacation _sg_ (US) _o_ vacation; **essere/andare in ~** to be/go on holiday _o_ vacation; **sono qui in ~** I'm on holiday here; **vacanze estive** summer holiday(s) _o_ vacation; **vacanze natalizie** Christmas holidays _o_ vacation

Attenzione! In inglese esiste la parola _vacancy_ che però indica un posto vacante o una camera disponibile.

'vacca, -che _sf_ cow

vacci'nare [vattʃi'nare] _vt_ to vaccinate

vac'cino [vat'tʃino] _sm_ (Med) vaccine

vacil'lare [vatʃil'lare] _vi_ to sway, wobble; (_luce_) to flicker; (_fig: memoria, coraggio_) to be failing, falter

'vacuo, -a _ag_ (_fig_) empty, vacuous

'vado _ecc vb vedi_ **andare**

vaga'bondo, -a _sm/f_ tramp, vagrant

va'gare _vi_ to wander

vagherò _ecc_ [vage'rɔ] _vb vedi_ **vagare**

va'gina [va'dʒina] _sf_ vagina

'vaglia ['vaʎʎa] _sm inv_ money order; **vaglia postale** postal order

vagli'are [vaʎ'ʎare] _vt_ to sift; (_fig_) to weigh up

'vago, -a, -ghi, -ghe _ag_ vague

va'gone _sm_ (Ferr: per passeggeri) coach; (: per merci) truck, wagon; **vagone letto** sleeper, sleeping car; **vagone ristorante** dining _o_ restaurant car

'vai _vb vedi_ **andare**

vai'olo _sm_ smallpox

va'langa, -ghe _sf_ avalanche

va'lere _vi_ (_avere forza, potenza_) to have influence; (_essere valido_) to be valid; (_avere vigore, autorità_) to hold, apply; (_essere capace: poeta, studente_) to be good, be able ▷ _vt_ (_prezzo, sforzo_) to be worth; (_corrispondere_) to correspond to; (_procurare_): **~ qc a qn** to earn sb sth; **valersi di** to make use of, take advantage of; **far ~** (_autorità ecc_) to assert; **vale a dire** that is to say; **~ la pena** to be worth the effort _o_ worth it

'valgo _ecc vb vedi_ **valere**

vali'care _vt_ to cross

'valico, -chi _sm_ (_passo_) pass

'valido, -a _ag_ valid; (_rimedio_) effective; (_aiuto_) real; (_persona_) worthwhile

vali'getta [vali'dʒetta] _sf_ briefcase; **valigetta ventiquattrore** overnight bag _o_ case

va'ligia, -gie _o_ **ge** [va'lidʒa] _sf_ (suit)case; **fare le valigie** to pack (up)

'valle _sf_ valley; **a ~** (_di fiume_) downstream; **scendere a ~** to go downhill

va'lore _sm_ (_gen_) value; (_merito_) merit, worth; (_coraggio_) valour, courage; (Comm: titolo) security; **valori** _smpl_ (_oggetti preziosi_) valuables

valoriz'zare [valorid'dzare] _vt_ (_terreno_) to develop; (_fig_) to make the most of

va'luta _sf_ currency, money; (Banca): **~ 15 gennaio** interest to run from January 15th

valu'tare _vt_ (_casa, gioiello, fig_) to value; (_stabilire: peso, entrate, fig_) to estimate

'valvola _sf_ (Tecn, Anat) valve; (Elettr) fuse

'valzer ['valtser] _sm inv_ waltz

vam'pata _sf_ (_di fiamma_) blaze; (_di calore_) blast; (: _al viso_) flush

vam'piro _sm_ vampire

vanda'lismo _sm_ vandalism

'vandalo _sm_ vandal

vaneggi'are [vaned'dʒare] _vi_ to rave

'vanga, -ghe _sf_ spade

van'gelo [van'dʒɛlo] _sm_ gospel

va'niglia [va'niʎʎa] _sf_ vanilla

vanità _sf_ vanity; (_di promessa_) emptiness; (_di sforzo_) futility; **vani'toso, -a** _ag_ vain, conceited

'vanno _vb vedi_ **andare**

'vano, -a _ag_ vain ▷ _sm_ (_spazio_) space; (_apertura_) opening; (_stanza_) room

van'taggio [van'taddʒo] *sm* advantage;
essere/portarsi in ~ (*Sport*) to be
in/take the lead; **vantaggi'oso, -a** *ag*
advantageous; favourable

vantarsi *vpr* **~ (di/di aver fatto)** to boast
o brag (about/about having done)

'vanvera *sf* **a ~** haphazardly; **parlare a ~**
to talk nonsense

va'pore *sm* vapour; (*anche: ~ acqueo*)
steam; (*nave*) steamer; **a ~** (*turbina ecc*)
steam *cpd*; **al ~** (*Cuc*) steamed

va'rare *vt* (*Naut, fig*) to launch; (*Dir*) to pass

var'care *vt* to cross

'varco, -chi *sm* passage; **aprirsi un ~ tra
la folla** to push one's way through the
crowd

vare'china [vare'kina] *sf* bleach

vari'abile *ag* variable; (*tempo, umore*)
changeable, variable ▷ *sf* (*Mat*) variable

vari'cella [vari'tʃɛlla] *sf* chickenpox

vari'coso, -a *ag* varicose

varietà *sf inv* variety ▷ *sm inv* variety show

'vario, -a *ag* varied; (*parecchi: col sostantivo
al pl*) various; (*mutevole: umore*) changeable

'varo *sm* (*Naut: fig*) launch; (*di leggi*) passing

varrò *ecc vb vedi* **valere**

Var'savia *sf* Warsaw

va'saio *sm* potter

'vasca, -sche *sf* basin; **vasca da bagno**
bathtub, bath

vas'chetta [vas'ketta] *sf* (*per gelato*) tub;
(*per sviluppare fotografie*) dish

vase'lina *sf* Vaseline®

'vaso *sm* (*recipiente*) pot; (: *barattolo*) jar;
(: *decorativo*) vase; (*Anat*) vessel; **vaso da
fiori** vase; (*per piante*) flowerpot

vas'soio *sm* tray

'vasto, -a *ag* vast, immense

Vati'cano *sm* **il ~** the Vatican

ve *pron, av vedi* **vi**

vecchi'aia [vek'kjaja] *sf* old age

'vecchio, -a ['vɛkkjo] *ag* old ▷ *sm/f* old
man/woman; **i vecchii** the old

ve'dere *vt, vi* to see; **vedersi** *vpr* to meet,
see one another; **avere a che ~ con** to
have something to do with; **far ~ qc a qn**
to show sb sth; **farsi ~** to show o.s.; (*farsi
vivo*) to show one's face; **vedi di non farlo**
make sure *o* see you don't do it; **non (ci) si
vede** (*è buio ecc*) you can't see a thing; **non
lo posso ~** (*fig*) I can't stand him

ve'detta *sf* (*sentinella, posto*) look-out;
(*Naut*) patrol boat

'vedovo, -a *sm/f* widower/widow

vedrò *ecc vb vedi* **vedere**

ve'duta *sf* view; **vedute** *sfpl* (*fig: opinioni*)
views; **di larghe** *o* **ampie vedute** broad-
minded; **di vedute limitate** narrow-
minded

vege'tale [vedʒe'tale] *ag, sm* vegetable

vegetari'ano, -a [vedʒeta'rjano] *ag, sm/f*
vegetarian; **avete piatti vegetariani?** do
you have any vegetarian dishes?

vegetazi'one [vedʒetat'tsjone] *sf*
vegetation

'vegeto, -a ['vɛdʒeto] *ag* (*pianta*) thriving;
(*persona*) strong, vigorous

'veglia ['veʎʎa] *sf* wakefulness;
(*sorveglianza*) watch; (*trattenimento*)
evening gathering; **fare la ~ a un malato**
to watch over a sick person

vegli'one [veʎ'ʎone] *sm* ball, dance;
veglione di Capodanno New Year's Eve
party

ve'icolo *sm* vehicle

'vela *sf* (*Naut: tela*) sail; (*Sport*) sailing

ve'leno *sm* poison; **vele'noso, -a** *ag*
poisonous

veli'ero *sm* sailing ship

vel'luto *sm* velvet; **velluto a coste** cord

'velo *sm* veil; (*tessuto*) voile

ve'loce [ve'lotʃe] *ag* fast, quick ▷ *av*
fast, quickly; **velocità** *sf* speed; **a forte
velocità** at high speed; **velocità di
crociera** cruising speed

'vena *sf* (*gen*) vein; (*filone*) vein, seam; (*fig:
ispirazione*) inspiration; (: *umore*) mood;
essere in ~ di qc to be in the mood for sth

ve'nale *ag* (*prezzo, valore*) market *cpd*; (*fig*)
venal; mercenary

ven'demmia *sf* (*raccolta*) grape harvest;
(*quantità d'uva*) grape crop, grapes *pl*; (*vino
ottenuto*) vintage

'vendere *vt* to sell; **"vendesi"** "for sale"

ven'detta *sf* revenge

vendicarsi *vpr* **~ (di)** to avenge o.s. (for);
(*per rancore*) to take one's revenge (for); **~
su qn** to revenge o.s. on sb

'vendita *sf* sale; **la ~** (*attività*) selling;
(*smercio*) sales *pl*; **in ~** on sale; **vendita
all'asta** sale by auction; **vendita per
telefono** telesales *sg*

vene'rare *vt* to venerate

venerdì *sm inv* Friday; **di** *o* **il ~** on Fridays;
V~ Santo Good Friday

ve'nereo, -a *ag* venereal

Ve'nezia [ve'nɛttsja] *sf* Venice

'vengo *ecc vb vedi* **venire**

veni'ale *ag* venial

ve'nire *vi* to come; (*riuscire: dolce,
fotografia*) to turn out; (*come ausiliare:
essere*): **viene ammirato da tutti** he is
admired by everyone; **~ da** to come from;
quanto viene? how much does it cost?;
far ~ (*mandare a chiamare*) to send for; **~ giù**
to come down; **~ meno** (*svenire*) to faint;
~ meno a qc not to fulfil sth; **~ su** to come
up; **~ a trovare qn** to come and see sb; **~**

via to come away

'venni *ecc vb vedi* **venire**

ven'taglio [ven'taʎʎo] *sm* fan

ven'tata *sf* gust (of wind)

ven'tenne *ag* **una ragazza ~** a twenty-year-old girl, a girl of twenty

ven'tesimo, -a *num* twentieth

'venti *num* twenty

venti'lare *vt* (*stanza*) to air, ventilate; (*fig: idea, proposta*) to air; **ventila'tore** *sm* ventilator, fan

ven'tina *sf* **una ~ (di)** around twenty, twenty or so

'vento *sm* wind

'ventola *sf* (*Aut, Tecn*) fan

ven'tosa *sf* (*Zool*) sucker; (*di gomma*) suction pad

ven'toso, -a *ag* windy

'ventre *sm* stomach

'vera *sf* wedding ring

vera'mente *av* really

ve'randa *sf* veranda(h)

ver'bale *ag* verbal ▷ *sm* (*di riunione*) minutes *pl*

'verbo *sm* (*Ling*) verb; (*parola*) word; (*Rel*): **il V~** the Word

'verde *ag, sm* green; **essere al ~** to be broke; **verde bottiglia/oliva** bottle/olive green

ver'detto *sm* verdict

ver'dura *sf* vegetables *pl*

'vergine ['verdʒine] *sf* virgin; (*dello zodiaco*): **V~** Virgo ▷ *ag* virgin; (*ragazza*): **essere ~** to be a virgin

ver'gogna [ver'goɲɲa] *sf* shame; (*timidezza*) shyness, embarrassment; **vergo'gnarsi** *vpr* **vergognarsi (di)** to be o feel ashamed (of); to be shy (about), be embarrassed (about); **vergo'gnoso, -a** *ag* ashamed; (*timido*) shy, embarrassed; (*causa di vergogna: azione*) shameful

ve'rifica, -che *sf* checking *no pl*, check

verifi'care *vt* (*controllare*) to check; (*confermare*) to confirm, bear out

verità *sf inv* truth

'verme *sm* worm

ver'miglio [ver'miʎʎo] *sm* vermilion, scarlet

ver'nice [ver'nitʃe] *sf* (*colorazione*) paint; (*trasparente*) varnish; (*pelle*) patent leather; **"~ fresca"** "wet paint"; **vernici'are** *vt* to paint; to varnish

'vero, -a *ag* (*veridico: fatti, testimonianza*) true; (*autentico*) real ▷ *sm* (*verità*) truth; (*realtà*) (real) life; **un ~ e proprio delinquente** a real criminal, an out-and-out criminal

vero'simile *ag* likely, probable

verrò *ecc vb vedi* **venire**

ver'ruca, -che *sf* wart

versa'mento *sm* (*pagamento*) payment; (*deposito di denaro*) deposit

ver'sante *sm* slopes *pl*, side

ver'sare *vt* (*fare uscire: vino, farina*) to pour (out); (*spargere: lacrime, sangue*) to shed; (*rovesciare*) to spill; (*Econ*) to pay; (: *depositare*) to deposit, pay in

versa'tile *ag* versatile

versi'one *sf* version; (*traduzione*) translation

'verso *sm* (*di poesia*) verse, line; (*di animale, uccello*) cry; (*direzione*) direction; (*modo*) way; (*di foglio di carta*) verso; (*di moneta*) reverse; **versi** *smpl* (*poesia*) verse *sg*; **non c'è ~ di persuaderlo** there's no way of persuading him, he can't be persuaded *prep* (*in direzione di*) toward(s); (*nei pressi di*) near, around (about); (*in senso temporale*) about, around; (*nei confronti di*) for; **~ di me** towards me; **~ sera** towards evening

'vertebra *sf* vertebra

verte'brale *ag* vertebral; **colonna ~** spinal column, spine

verti'cale *ag, sf* vertical

'vertice ['vertitʃe] *sm* summit, top; (*Mat*) vertex; **conferenza al ~** (*Pol*) summit conference

ver'tigine [ver'tidʒine] *sf* dizziness *no pl*; dizzy spell; (*Med*) vertigo; **avere le vertigini** to feel dizzy

ve'scica, -che [veʃʃika] *sf* (*Anat*) bladder; (*Med*) blister

'vescovo *sm* bishop

'vespa *sf* wasp

ves'taglia [ves'taʎʎa] *sf* dressing gown

ves'tire *vt* (*bambino, malato*) to dress; (*avere indosso*) to have on, wear; **vestirsi** *vpr* to dress, get dressed; **ves'tito, -a** *ag* dressed ▷ *sm* garment; (*da donna*) dress; (*da uomo*) suit; **vestiti** *smpl* (*indumenti*) clothes; **vestito di bianco** dressed in white

veteri'nario, -a *ag* veterinary ▷ *sm* veterinary surgeon (BRIT), veterinarian (US), vet

'veto *sm inv* veto

ve'traio *sm* glassmaker; glazier

ve'trata *sf* glass door (o window); (*di chiesa*) stained glass window

ve'trato, -a *ag* (*porta, finestra*) glazed; (*che contiene vetro*) glass *cpd* ▷ *sf* glass door (o window); (*di chiesa*) stained glass window; **carta vetrata** sandpaper

ve'trina *sf* (*di negozio*) (shop) window; (*armadio*) display cabinet; **vetri'nista, -i, -e** *sm/f* window dresser

'vetro *sm* glass; (*per finestra, porta*) pane (of glass)

'vetta *sf* peak, summit, top

V

vet'tura *sf (carrozza)* carriage; *(Ferr)* carriage *(BRIT)*, car *(US)*; *(auto)* car *(BRIT)*, automobile *(US)*

vezzeggia'tivo [vettseddʒa'tivo] *sm (Ling)* term of endearment

vi *(dav lo, la, li, le, ne diventa ve)* *pron (oggetto)* you; *(complemento di termine)* (to) you; *(riflessivo)* yourselves; *(reciproco)* each other ▷ *av (li)* there; *(qui)* here; *(per questo/quel luogo)* through here/there; **vi è/sono** there is/are

'via *sf (gen)* way; *(strada)* street; *(sentiero, pista)* path, track; *(Amm: procedimento)* channels *pl* ▷ *prep (passando per)* via, by way of ▷ *av* away ▷ *escl (suvvia)* come on!; *(Sport)* go! ▷ *sm (Sport)* starting signal; **in ~ di guarigione** on the road to recovery; **per ~ di** *(a causa di)* because of, on account of; **in o per ~** on the way; **per ~ aerea** by air; *(lettere)* by airmail; **andare/essere ~** to go/be away; **~ ~ che** *(a mano a mano)* as; **dare il ~** *(Sport)* to give the starting signal; **dare il ~ a** *(fig)* to start; **in ~ provvisoria** provisionally; **Via lattea** *(Astr)* Milky Way; **via di mezzo** middle course; **via d'uscita** *(fig)* way out

via'dotto *sm* viaduct

viaggi'are [viad'dʒare] *vi* to travel; **viaggia'tore, -'trice** *ag* travelling ▷ *sm* traveller; *(passeggero)* passenger

vi'aggio [vi'addʒo] *sm* travel(ling); *(tragitto)* journey, trip; **buon ~!** have a good trip!; **com'è andato il ~?** how was your journey?; **il ~ dura due ore** the journey takes two hours; **viaggio di nozze** honeymoon; **siamo in ~ di nozze** we're on honeymoon

vi'ale *sm* avenue

via'vai *sm* coming and going, bustle

vi'brare *vi* to vibrate

'vice ['vitʃe] *sm/f* deputy

vi'cenda [vi'tʃenda] *sf* event; **a ~** in turn

vice'versa [vitʃe'versa] *av* vice versa; **da Roma a Pisa e ~** from Rome to Pisa and back

vici'nanza [vitʃi'nantsa] *sf* nearness, closeness

vi'cino, -a [vi'tʃino] *ag (gen)* near; *(nello spazio)* near, nearby; *(accanto)* next; *(nel tempo)* near, close at hand ▷ *sm/f* neighbour ▷ *av* near, close; **da ~** *(guardare)* close up; *(esaminare, seguire)* closely; *(conoscere)* well, intimately; **~ a** near (to), close to; *(accanto a)* beside; **c'è una banca qui ~?** is there a bank nearby?; **~ di casa** neighbour

'vicolo *sm* alley; **vicolo cieco** blind alley

'video *sm inv (TV: schermo)* screen; **video'camera** *sf* camcorder;

videocas'setta *sf* videocassette; **videoclip** [video'klip] *sm inv* videoclip; **videogi'oco, -chi** [video'dʒɔko] *sm* video game; **videoregistra'tore** *sm* video (recorder); **videote'lefono** *sm* videophone

'vidi *ecc vb vedi* **vedere**

vie'tare *vt* to forbid; *(Amm)* to prohibit; **~ a qn di fare** to forbid sb to do; to prohibit sb from doing; **"vietato fumare/l'ingresso"** "no smoking/admittance"

vie'tato, -a *ag (vedi vb)* forbidden; prohibited; banned; **"~ fumare/l'ingresso"** "no smoking/admittance"; **~ ai minori di 14/18 anni** prohibited to children under 14/18; **"senso ~"** *(Aut)* "no entry"; **"sosta vietata"** *(Aut)* "no parking"

Viet'nam *sm* **il ~** Vietnam; **vietna'mita, -i, -e** *ag, sm/f, sm* Vietnamese *inv*

vi'gente [vi'dʒente] *ag* in force

'vigile ['vidʒile] *ag* watchful ▷ *sm (anche:* **~ urbano)** policeman *(in towns)*; **vigile del fuoco** fireman

vi'gilia [vi'dʒilja] *sf (giorno antecedente)* eve; **la ~ di Natale** Christmas Eve

vigli'acco, -a, -chi, -che [viʎ'ʎakko] *ag* cowardly ▷ *sm/f* coward

vi'gneto [viɲ'ɲeto] *sm* vineyard

vi'gnetta [viɲ'ɲetta] *sf* cartoon

vi'gore *sm* vigour; *(Dir)*: **essere/entrare in ~** to be in/come into force

'vile *ag (spregevole)* low, mean, base; *(codardo)* cowardly

'villa *sf* villa

vil'laggio [vil'laddʒo] *sm* village; **villaggio turistico** holiday village

vil'lano, -a *ag* rude, ill-mannered

villeggia'tura [villeddʒa'tura] *sf* holiday(s) *pl (BRIT)*, vacation *(US)*

vil'letta *sf*, **vil'lino** ▷ *sm* small house (with a garden), cottage

'vimini *smpl* **di ~** wicker

'vincere ['vintʃere] *vt (in guerra, al gioco, a una gara)* to defeat, beat; *(premio, guerra, partita)* to win; *(fig)* to overcome, conquer ▷ *vi* to win; **~ qn in bellezza** to be better-looking than sb; **vinci'tore** *sm* winner; *(Mil)* victor

vi'nicolo, -a *ag* wine *cpd*

'vino *sm* wine; **vino bianco/rosato/rosso** white/rosé/red wine; **vino da pasto** table wine

'vinsi *ecc vb vedi* **vincere**

vi'ola *sf (Bot)* violet; *(Mus)* viola ▷ *ag, sm inv (colore)* purple

vio'lare *vt (chiesa)* to desecrate, violate; *(giuramento, legge)* to violate

violen'tare *vt* to use violence on; *(donna)* to rape

vio'lento, -a *ag* violent; **vio'lenza** *sf* violence; **violenza carnale** rape

vio'letta *sf* (*Bot*) violet

vio'letto, -a *ag*, *sm* (*colore*) violet

violi'nista, -i, -e *sm/f* violinist

vio'lino *sm* violin

violon'cello [violon'tʃɛllo] *sm* cello

vi'ottolo *sm* path, track

vip [vip] *sigla m* (= *very important person*) VIP

'vipera *sf* viper, adder

vi'rare *vi* (*Naut*, *Aer*) to turn; (*Fot*) to tone; **~ di bordo** (*Naut*) to tack

'virgola *sf* (*Ling*) comma; (*Mat*) point; **virgo'lette** *sfpl* inverted commas, quotation marks

vi'rile *ag* (*proprio dell'uomo*) masculine; (*non puerile, da uomo*) manly, virile

virtù *sf inv* virtue; **in o per ~ di** by virtue of, by

virtu'ale *ag* virtual

'virus *sm inv* (*anche Inform*) virus

'viscere *sfpl* (*di animale*) entrails *pl*; (*fig*) bowels *pl*

'vischio ['viskjo] *sm* (*Bot*) mistletoe; (*pania*) birdlime

'viscido, -a ['viʃʃido] *ag* slimy

vi'sibile *ag* visible

visibilità *sf* visibility

visi'era *sf* (*di elmo*) visor; (*di berretto*) peak

visi'one *sf* vision; **prendere ~ di qc** to examine sth, look sth over; **prima/seconda ~** (*Cinema*) first/second showing

'visita *sf* visit; (*Med*) visit, call; (: *esame*) examination; **visita guidata** guided tour; **a che ora comincia la ~ guidata?** what time does the guided tour start?; **visita medica** medical examination; **visi'tare** *vt* to visit; (*Med*) to visit, call on; (: *esaminare*) to examine; **visita'tore, -'trice** *sm/f* visitor

vi'sivo, -a *ag* visual

'viso *sm* face

vi'sone *sm* mink

'vispo, -a *ag* quick, lively

'vissi *ecc* *vb vedi* **vivere**

'vista *sf* (*facoltà*) (eye)sight; (*fatto di vedere*): **la ~ di** the sight of; (*veduta*) view; **sparare a ~** to shoot on sight; **in ~** in sight; **perdere qn di ~** to lose sight of sb; (*fig*) to lose touch with sb; **a ~ d'occhio** as far as the eye can see; (*fig*) before one's very eyes; **far ~ di fare** to pretend to do

'visto, -a *pp di* **vedere** ▷ *sm* visa; **~ che** seeing (that)

vis'toso, -a *ag* gaudy, garish; (*ingente*) considerable

visu'ale *ag* visual

'vita *sf* life; (*Anat*) waist; **a ~ for** life

vi'tale *ag* vital

vita'mina *sf* vitamin

'vite *sf* (*Bot*) vine; (*Tecn*) screw

vi'tello *sm* (*Zool*) calf; (*carne*) veal; (*pelle*) calfskin

'vittima *sf* victim

'vitto *sm* food; (*in un albergo ecc*) board; **vitto e alloggio** board and lodging

vit'toria *sf* victory

'viva *escl* **~ il re!** long live the king!

vi'vace [vi'vatʃe] *ag* (*vivo, animato*) lively; (: *mente*) lively, sharp; (*colore*) bright

vi'vaio *sm* (*di pesci*) hatchery; (*Agr*) nursery

vivavoce [viva'votʃe] *sm inv* (*dispositivo*) loudspeaker; **mettere il ~** to switch on the loudspeaker

vi'vente *ag* living, alive; **i viventi** the living

'vivere *vi* to live ▷ *vt* to live; (*passare: brutto momento*) to live through, go through; (*sentire: gioie, pene di qn*) to share ▷ *sm* life; (*anche: modo di ~*) way of life; **viveri** *smpl* (*cibo*) food *sg*, provisions; **~ di** to live on

'vivido, -a *ag* (*colore*) vivid, bright

vivisezi'one [viviset'tsjone] *sf* vivisection

'vivo, -a *ag* (*vivente*) alive, living; (: *animale*) live; (*fig*) lively; (: *colore*) bright, brilliant; **i vivi** the living; **~ e vegeto** hale and hearty; **farsi ~** to show one's face; to be heard from; **ritrarre dal ~** to paint from life; **pungere qn nel ~** (*fig*) to cut sb to the quick

vivrò *ecc* *vb vedi* **vivere**

vizi'are [vit'tsjare] *vt* (*bambino*) to spoil; (*corrompere moralmente*) to corrupt; **vizi'ato, -a** *ag* spoilt; (*aria, acqua*) polluted

'vizio ['vittsjo] *sm* (*morale*) vice; (*cattiva abitudine*) bad habit; (*imperfezione*) flaw, defect; (*errore*) fault, mistake

V.le *abbr* = **viale**

vocabo'lario *sm* (*dizionario*) dictionary; (*lessico*) vocabulary

vo'cabolo *sm* word

vo'cale *ag* vocal ▷ *sf* vowel

vocazi'one [vokat'tsjone] *sf* vocation; (*fig*) natural bent

'voce ['votʃe] *sf* voice; (*diceria*) rumour; (*di un elenco, in bilancio*) item; **aver ~ in capitolo** (*fig*) to have a say in the matter

'voga *sf* (*Naut*) rowing; (*usanza*): **essere in ~** to be in fashion *o* in vogue

vo'gare *vi* to row

vogherò *ecc* [voge'rɔ] *vb vedi* **vogare**

'voglia ['vɔʎʎa] *sf* desire, wish; (*macchia*) birthmark; **aver ~ di qc/di fare** to feel like sth/like doing; (*più forte*) to want sth/to do

'voglio *ecc* ['vɔʎʎo] *vb vedi* **volere**

'voi *pron* you; **voi'altri** *pron* you

vo'lante *ag* flying ▷ *sm* (steering) wheel

volan'tino *sm* leaflet

vo'lare *vi* (*uccello, aereo, fig*) to fly; (*cappello*) to blow away o off, fly away o off; **~ via** to fly away o off

vo'latile *ag* (*Chim*) volatile ▷ *sm* (*Zool*) bird

volente'roso, -a *ag* willing

volenti'eri *av* willingly; "**~**" "with pleasure", "I'd be glad to"

○ **PAROLA CHIAVE**

vo'lere *sm* will, wish(es); **contro il volere di** against the wishes of; **per volere di qn** in obedience to sb's will o wishes ▷ *vt* **1** (*esigere, desiderare*) to want; **voler fare/che qn faccia** to want to do/sb to do; **volete del caffè?** would you like o do you want some coffee?; **vorrei questo/fare** I would o I'd like this/to do; **come vuoi** as you like; **senza volere** (*inavvertitamente*) without meaning to, unintentionally

2 (*consentire*): **vogliate attendere, per piacere** please wait; **vogliamo andare?** shall we go?; **vuole essere così gentile da ...?** would you be so kind as to ...?; **non ha voluto ricevermi** he wouldn't see me

3: **volerci** (*essere necessario: materiale, attenzione*) to need; (: *tempo*) to take; **quanta farina ci vuole per questa torta?** how much flour do you need for this cake?; **ci vuole un'ora per arrivare a Venezia** it takes an hour to get to Venice

4: **voler bene a qn** (*amore*) to love sb; (*affetto*) to be fond of sb, like sb very much; **voler male a qn** to dislike sb; **volerne a qn** to bear sb a grudge; **voler dire** to mean

vol'gare *ag* vulgar

voli'era *sf* aviary

voli'tivo, -a *ag* strong-willed

'volli *ecc vb vedi* **volere**

'volo *sm* flight; **al ~: colpire qc al ~** to hit sth as it flies past; **capire al ~** to understand straight away; **volo charter** charter flight; **volo di linea** scheduled flight

volontà *sf* will; **a ~** (*mangiare, bere*) as much as one likes; **buona/cattiva ~** goodwill/lack of goodwill

volon'tario, -a *ag* voluntary ▷ *sm* (*Mil*) volunteer

'volpe *sf* fox

'volta *sf* (*momento, circostanza*) time; (*turno, giro*) turn; (*curva*) turn, bend; (*Archit*) vault; (*direzione*): **partire alla ~ di** to set off for; **a mia** (*o* **tua** *ecc*) **~** in turn; **una ~** once; **una ~ sola** only once; **due volte** twice; **una cosa per ~** one thing at a time; **una ~ per tutte** once and for all; **a volte** at times, sometimes; **una ~ che** (*temporale*) once;

(*causale*) since; **3 volte 4** 3 times 4

volta'faccia [volta'fattʃa] *sm inv* (*fig*) volte-face

vol'taggio [vol'taddʒo] *sm* (*Elettr*) voltage

vol'tare *vt* to turn; (*girare: moneta*) to turn over; (*rigirare*) to turn round ▷ *vi* to turn; **voltarsi** *vpr* to turn; to turn over; to turn round

voltas'tomaco *sm* nausea; (*fig*) disgust

'volto, -a *pp di* **volgere** ▷ *sm* face

vo'lubile *ag* changeable, fickle

vo'lume *sm* volume

vomi'tare *vt, vi* to vomit; **'vomito** *sm* vomiting *no pl*; vomit

'vongola *sf* clam

vo'race [vo'ratʃe] *ag* voracious, greedy

vo'ragine [vo'radʒine] *sf* abyss, chasm

vorrò *ecc vb vedi* **volere**

'vortice ['vɔrtitʃe] *sm* whirlwind; whirlpool; (*fig*) whirl

'vostro, -a *det* **il(la) ~(a)** *ecc* your ▷ *pron* **il(la) ~(a)** *ecc* yours

vo'tante *sm/f* voter

vo'tare *vi* to vote ▷ *vt* (*sottoporre a votazione*) to take a vote on; (*approvare*) to vote for; (*Rel*): **~ qc a** to dedicate sth to

'voto *sm* (*Pol*) vote; (*Ins*) mark; (*Rel*) vow; (: *offerta*) votive offering; **aver voti belli/brutti** (*Ins*) to get good/bad marks

vs. *abbr* (*Comm*) = **vostro**

vul'cano *sm* volcano

vulne'rabile *ag* vulnerable

vu'oi, vu'ole *vb vedi* **volere**

vuo'tare *vt* to empty; **vuotarsi** *vpr* to empty

vu'oto, -a *ag* empty; (*fig: privo*): **~ di** (*senso ecc*) devoid of ▷ *sm* empty space, gap; (*spazio in bianco*) blank; (*Fisica*) vacuum; (*fig: mancanza*) gap, void; **a mani vuote** empty-handed; **vuoto d'aria** air pocket; **vuoto a rendere** returnable bottle

W X

'wafer ['vafer] *sm inv* (*Cuc, Elettr*) wafer
'water ['wɔːtəʳ] *sm inv* toilet
watt [vat] *sm inv* watt
W.C. *sm inv* WC
web [uɛb] *sm* **il ~** the Web; **cercare nel ~**
to search the Web ▷ *ag inv* **pagina ~** web
page
'weekend ['wiːkend] *sm inv* weekend
'western ['western] *ag* (*Cinema*) cowboy
cpd ▷ *sm inv* western, cowboy film;
western all'italiana spaghetti western
'whisky ['wiski] *sm inv* whisky
'windsurf ['windsəːf] *sm inv* (*tavola*)
windsurfer; (*sport*) windsurfing
'würstel ['vyrstəl] *sm inv* frankfurter

xe'nofobo, -a [kse'nɔfobo] *ag* xenophobic
▷ *sm/f* xenophobe
xi'lofono [ksi'lɔfono] *sm* xylophone

yacht [jɔt] *sm inv* yacht
'yoga ['jɔga] *ag inv, sm* yoga (*cpd*)
yogurt ['jɔgurt] *sm inv* yog(h)urt

zabai'one [dzaba'jone] *sm dessert made of egg yolks, sugar and marsala*
zaf'fata [tsaffata] *sf* (*tanfo*) stench
zaffe'rano [dzaffe'rano] *sm* saffron
zaf'firo [dzaf'firo] *sm* sapphire
'zaino ['dzaino] *sm* rucksack
'zampa ['tsampa] *sf* (*di animale: gamba*) leg; (: *piede*) paw; **a quattro zampe** on all fours
zampil'lare [tsampil'lare] *vi* to gush, spurt
zan'zara [dzan'dzara] *sf* mosquito; **zanzari'era** *sf* mosquito net
'zappa ['tsappa] *sf* hoe
'zapping ['tsapiŋ] *sm* (*TV*) channel-hopping
zar, za'rina [tsar, tsa'rina] *sm/f* tsar/tsarina
'zattera ['dzattera] *sf* raft
'zebra ['dzebra] *sf* zebra; **zebre** *sfpl* (*Aut*) zebra crossing *sg* (*BRIT*), crosswalk *sg* (*US*)
'zecca, -che ['tsekka] *sf* (*Zool*) tick; (*officina di monete*) mint
'zelo ['dzelo] *sm* zeal
'zenzero ['dzendzero] *sm* ginger
'zeppa ['tseppa] *sf* wedge
'zeppo, -a ['tseppo] *ag* ~ **di** crammed *o* packed with
zer'bino [dzer'bino] *sm* doormat
'zero ['dzɛro] *sm* zero, nought; **vincere per**

tre a ~ (*Sport*) to win three-nil

'zia ['tsia] *sf* aunt

zibel'lino [dzibel'lino] *sm* sable

'zigomo ['dzigomo] *sm* cheekbone

zig'zag [dzig'dzag] *sm inv* zigzag; **andare a ~** to zigzag

Zimbabwe [tsim'babwe] *sm* **lo ~** Zimbabwe

'zinco ['dzinko] *sm* zinc

'zingaro, -a ['dzingaro] *sm/f* gipsy

'zio ['tsio] (*pl* **'zii**) *sm* uncle

zip'pare *vt* (*Inform: file*) to zip

zi'tella [dzi'tɛlla] *sf* spinster; (*peg*) old maid

'zitto, -a ['tsitto] *ag* quiet, silent; **sta' ~!** be quiet!

'zoccolo ['tsɔkkolo] *sm* (*calzatura*) clog; (*di cavallo ecc*) hoof; (*basamento*) base; plinth

zodia'cale [dzodia'kale] *ag* zodiac *cpd*; **segno ~** sign of the zodiac

zo'diaco [dzo'diako] *sm* zodiac

'zolfo ['tsolfo] *sm* sulphur

'zolla ['dzɔlla] *sf* clod (of earth)

zol'letta [dzol'letta] *sf* sugar lump

'zona ['dzɔna] *sf* zone, area; **zona di depressione** (*Meteor*) trough of low pressure; **zona disco** (*Aut*) ≈ meter zone; **zona industriale** industrial estate; **zona pedonale** pedestrian precinct; **zona verde** (*di abitato*) green area

'zonzo ['dzondzo]: **a ~** *av*, **andare a ~** to wander about, stroll about

zoo ['dzɔo] *sm inv* zoo

zoolo'gia [dzoolo'dʒia] *sf* zoology

zoppi'care [tsoppi'kare] *vi* to limp; to be shaky, rickety

'zoppo, -a ['tsɔppo] *ag* lame; (*fig: mobile*) shaky, rickety

Z.T.L. *sigla f* (= *Zona a Traffico Limitato*) controlled traffic zone

'zucca, -che ['tsukka] *sf* (*Bot*) marrow; pumpkin

zucche'rare [tsukke'rare] *vt* to put sugar in; **zucche'rato, -a** *ag* sweet, sweetened

zuccheri'era [tsukke'rjɛra] *sf* sugar bowl

'zucchero ['tsukkero] *sm* sugar; **zucchero di canna** cane sugar; **zucchero filato** candy floss, cotton candy (*US*)

zuc'china [tsuk'kina] *sf* courgette (*BRIT*), zucchini (*US*)

'zuffa ['tsuffa] *sf* brawl

'zuppa ['tsuppa] *sf* soup; (*fig*) mixture, muddle; **zuppa inglese** (*Cuc*) *dessert made with sponge cake, custard and chocolate*, ≈ trifle (*BRIT*)

'zuppo, -a ['tsuppo] *ag* **~ (di)** drenched (with), soaked (with)

z

A [eɪ] *n* (*Mus*) la *m*

○ **KEYWORD**

a [ə] (*before vowel or silent h* **an**) *indef art* **1** un (uno + *s impure*, *gn*, *pn*, *ps*, *x*, *z*), una *f* (un' + *vowel*); **a book** un libro; **a mirror** uno specchio; **an apple** una mela; **she's a doctor** è medico
2 (*instead of the number "one"*) un(o), *f* una; **a year ago** un anno fa; **a hundred/thousand** *etc* **pounds** cento/mille *etc* sterline
3 (*in expressing ratios, prices etc*) a, per; **3 a day/week** 3 al giorno/alla settimana; **10 km an hour** 10 km all'ora; **£5 a person** 5 sterline a persona *or* per persona

A.A. *n abbr* (= *Alcoholics Anonymous*) AA, (*BRIT*: = *Automobile Association*) ≈ A.C.I. *m*
A.A.A. (*US*) *n abbr* (= *American Automobile Association*) ≈ A.C.I. *m*
aback [ə'bæk] *adv* **to be taken ~** essere sbalordito(-a)
abandon [ə'bændən] *vt* abbandonare ▷ *n* **with ~** sfrenatamente, spensieratamente
abattoir ['æbətwɑːʳ] (*BRIT*) *n* mattatoio
abbey ['æbɪ] *n* abbazia, badia
abbreviation [əbriːvɪ'eɪʃən] *n* abbreviazione *f*

abdomen ['æbdəmən] *n* addome *m*
abduct [æb'dʌkt] *vt* rapire
abide [ə'baɪd] *vt* **I can't ~ it/him** non lo posso soffrire *or* sopportare; **abide by** *vt fus* conformarsi a
ability [ə'bɪlɪtɪ] *n* abilità *f inv*
able ['eɪbl] *adj* capace; **to be ~ to do sth** essere capace di fare qc, poter fare qc
abnormal [æb'nɔːməl] *adj* anormale
aboard [ə'bɔːd] *adv* a bordo ▷ *prep* a bordo di
abolish [ə'bɔlɪʃ] *vt* abolire
abolition [æbəu'lɪʃən] *n* abolizione *f*
abort [ə'bɔːt] *vt* abortire; **abortion** [ə'bɔːʃən] *n* aborto; **to have an abortion** abortire

○ **KEYWORD**

about [ə'baut] *adv* **1** (*approximately*) circa, quasi; **about a hundred/thousand** *etc* un centinaio/migliaio *etc*, circa cento/mille *etc*; **it takes about 10 hours** ci vogliono circa 10 ore; **at about 2 o'clock** verso le 2; **I've just about finished** ho quasi finito
2 (*referring to place*) qua e là, in giro; **to leave things lying about** lasciare delle cose in giro; **to run about** correre qua e là; **to walk about** camminare
3: **to be about to do sth** stare per fare qc ▷ *prep* **1** (*relating to*) su, di; **a book about London** un libro su Londra; **what is it about?** di che si tratta?; (*book, film etc*) di cosa tratta?; **we talked about it** ne abbiamo parlato; **what** *or* **how about doing this?** che ne dici di fare questo?
2 (*referring to place*): **to walk about the town** camminare per la città; **her clothes were scattered about the room** i suoi vestiti erano sparsi *or* in giro per tutta la stanza

above [ə'bʌv] *adv*, *prep* sopra; **mentioned ~** suddetto; **~ all** soprattutto
abroad [ə'brɔːd] *adv* all'estero
abrupt [ə'brʌpt] *adj* (*sudden*) improvviso(-a); (*gruff, blunt*) brusco(-a)
abscess ['æbsɪs] *n* ascesso
absence ['æbsəns] *n* assenza
absent ['æbsənt] *adj* assente; **absent-minded** *adj* distratto(-a)
absolute ['æbsəluːt] *adj* assoluto(-a); **absolutely** [-'luːtlɪ] *adv* assolutamente
absorb [əb'zɔːb] *vt* assorbire; **to be ~ed in a book** essere immerso in un libro; **absorbent cotton** [əb'zɔːbənt-] (*US*) *n* cotone *m* idrofilo; **absorbing** *adj* avvincente, molto interessante
abstain [əb'steɪn] *vi* **to ~ (from)**

astenersi (da)

abstract ['æbstrækt] adj astratto(-a)

absurd [əb'sə:d] adj assurdo(-a)

abundance [ə'bʌndəns] n abbondanza

abundant [ə'bʌndənt] adj abbondante

abuse [n ə'bju:s, vb ə'bju:z] n abuso; (insults) ingiurie fpl ▷ vt abusare di; **abusive** adj ingiurioso(-a)

abysmal [ə'bɪzməl] adj spaventoso(-a)

academic [ækə'dɛmɪk] adj accademico(-a); (pej: issue) puramente formale ▷ n universitario(-a); **academic year** n anno accademico

academy [ə'kædəmɪ] n (learned body) accademia; (school) scuola privata; **academy of music** n conservatorio

accelerate [æk'sɛləreɪt] vt, vi accelerare; **acceleration** n accelerazione f; **accelerator** n acceleratore m

accent ['æksɛnt] n accento

accept [ək'sɛpt] vt accettare; **acceptable** adj accettabile; **acceptance** n accettazione f

access ['æksɛs] n accesso; **accessible** [æk'sɛsəbl] adj accessibile

accessory [æk'sɛsərɪ] n accessorio; (Law): **~ to** complice m/f di

accident ['æksɪdənt] n incidente m; (chance) caso; **I've had an ~** ho avuto un incidente; **by ~** per caso; **accidental** [-'dɛntl] adj accidentale; **accidentally** [-'dɛntəlɪ] adv per caso; **Accident and Emergency Department** n (BRIT) pronto soccorso; **accident insurance** n assicurazione f contro gli infortuni

acclaim [ə'kleɪm] n acclamazione f

accommodate [ə'kɔmədeɪt] vt alloggiare; (oblige, help) favorire

accommodation [əkɔmə'deɪʃən] (US **accommodations**) n alloggio

accompaniment [ə'kʌmpənɪmənt] n accompagnamento

accompany [ə'kʌmpənɪ] vt accompagnare

accomplice [ə'kʌmplɪs] n complice m/f

accomplish [ə'kʌmplɪʃ] vt compiere; (goal) raggiungere; **accomplishment** n compimento; realizzazione f

accord [ə'kɔ:d] n accordo ▷ vt accordare; **of his own ~** di propria iniziativa; **accordance**: **in accordance with** in conformità con; **according**: **according to** prep secondo; **accordingly** adv in conformità

account [ə'kaunt] n (Comm) conto; (report) descrizione f; **~s** npl (Comm) conti mpl; **of no ~** di nessuna importanza; **on ~** in acconto; **on no ~** per nessun motivo; **on ~ of** a causa di; **to take into ~, take ~ of** tener conto di; **account for** vt fus spiegare; giustificare; **accountable** adj accountable (to) responsabile (verso); **accountant** [ə'kauntənt] n ragioniere(-a); **account number** n numero di conto

accumulate [ə'kju:mjuleɪt] vt accumulare ▷ vi accumularsi

accuracy ['ækjurəsɪ] n precisione f

accurate ['ækjurɪt] adj preciso(-a); **accurately** adv precisamente

accusation [ækju'zeɪʃən] n accusa

accuse [ə'kju:z] vt accusare; **accused** n accusato(-a)

accustomed [ə'kʌstəmd] adj **~ to** abituato(-a) a

ace [eɪs] n asso

ache [eɪk] n male m, dolore m ▷ vi (be sore) far male, dolere; **my head ~s** mi fa male la testa

achieve [ə'tʃi:v] vt (aim) raggiungere; (victory, success) ottenere; **achievement** n compimento; successo

acid ['æsɪd] adj acido(-a) ▷ n acido

acknowledge [ək'nɔlɪdʒ] vt (letter: also: **~ receipt of**) confermare la ricevuta di; (fact) riconoscere; **acknowledgement** n conferma; riconoscimento

acne ['æknɪ] n acne f

acorn ['eɪkɔ:n] n ghianda

acoustic [ə'ku:stɪk] adj acustico(-a)

acquaintance [ə'kweɪntəns] n conoscenza; (person) conoscente m/f

acquire [ə'kwaɪə'] vt acquistare; **acquisition** [ækwɪ'zɪʃən] n acquisto

acquit [ə'kwɪt] vt assolvere; **to ~ o.s. well** comportarsi bene

acre ['eɪkə'] n acro, ≈ 4047 m²

acronym ['ækrənɪm] n acronimo

across [ə'krɔs] prep (on the other side) dall'altra parte di; (crosswise) attraverso ▷ adv dall'altra parte; in larghezza; **to run/ swim ~** attraversare di corsa/a nuoto; **~ from** di fronte a

acrylic [ə'krɪlɪk] adj acrilico(-a)

act [ækt] n atto; (in music-hall etc) numero; (Law) decreto ▷ vi agire; (Theatre) recitare; (pretend) fingere ▷ vt (part) recitare; **to ~ as** agire da; **act up** (inf) vi (person) comportarsi male; (knee, back, injury) fare male; (machine) non funzionare; **acting** adj che fa le funzioni di ▷ n (of actor) recitazione f; (activity): **to do some acting** fare del teatro (or del cinema)

action ['ækʃən] n azione f; (Mil) combattimento; (Law) processo; **out of ~** fuori combattimento; fuori servizio; **to take ~** agire; **action replay** n (TV) replay m inv

activate ['æktɪveɪt] vt (*mechanism*) attivare

active ['æktɪv] adj attivo(-a); **actively** adv (*participate*) attivamente; (*discourage, dislike*) vivamente

activist ['æktɪvɪst] n attivista m/f

activity [æk'tɪvɪtɪ] n attività f inv; **activity holiday** n vacanza organizzata con attività ricreative per ragazzi

actor ['æktə'] n attore m

actress ['æktrɪs] n attrice f

actual ['æktjuəl] adj reale, effettivo(-a)

▮ Be careful not to translate *actual* by the Italian word *attuale*.

actually ['æktjuəlɪ] adv veramente; (*even*) addirittura

▮ Be careful not to translate *actually* by the Italian word *attualmente*.

acupuncture ['ækjupʌŋktʃə'] n agopuntura

acute [ə'kju:t] adj acuto(-a); (*mind, person*) perspicace

ad [æd] n abbr = **advertisement**

A.D. adv abbr (= *Anno Domini*) d.C.

adamant ['ædəmənt] adj irremovibile

adapt [ə'dæpt] vt adattare ▷ vi **to ~ (to)** adattarsi (a); **adapter, adaptor** n (*Elec*) adattatore m

add [æd] vt aggiungere ▷ vi **to ~ to** (*increase*) aumentare; **add up** vt (*figures*) addizionare ▷ vi (*fig*): **it doesn't ~ up** non ha senso; **add up to** vt fus (*Math*) ammontare a; (*fig: mean*) significare; **it doesn't ~ up to much** non è un granché

addict ['ædɪkt] n tossicomane m/f; (*fig*) fanatico(-a); **addicted** [ə'dɪktɪd] adj **to be addicted to** (*drink etc*) essere dedito(-a) a; (*fig: football etc*) essere tifoso(-a) di; **addiction** [ə'dɪkʃən] n (*Med*) tossicodipendenza; **addictive** [ə'dɪktɪv] adj che dà assuefazione

addition [ə'dɪʃən] n addizione f; (*thing added*) aggiunta; **in ~** inoltre; **in ~ to** oltre; **additional** adj supplementare

additive ['ædɪtɪv] n additivo

address [ə'drɛs] n indirizzo; (*talk*) discorso ▷ vt indirizzare; (*speak to*) fare un discorso a; (*issue*) affrontare; **my ~ is ...** Il mio indirizzo è...; **address book** n rubrica

adequate ['ædɪkwɪt] adj adeguato(-a), sufficiente

adhere [əd'hɪə'] vi **to ~ to** aderire a; (*fig: rule, decision*) seguire

adhesive [əd'hi:zɪv] n adesivo; **adhesive tape** n (BRIT: *for parcels etc*) nastro adesivo; (US Med) cerotto adesivo

adjacent [ə'dʒeɪsənt] adj adiacente; **~ to** accanto a

adjective ['ædʒɛktɪv] n aggettivo

adjoining [ə'dʒɔɪnɪŋ] adj accanto inv, adiacente

adjourn [ə'dʒə:n] vt rimandare ▷ vi essere aggiornato(-a)

adjust [ə'dʒʌst] vt aggiustare; (*change*) rettificare ▷ vi **to ~ (to)** adattarsi (a); **adjustable** adj regolabile; **adjustment** n (*Psych*) adattamento; (*of machine*) regolazione f; (*of prices, wages*) modifica

administer [əd'mɪnɪstə'] vt amministrare; (*justice, drug*) somministrare; **administration** [ədmɪnɪs'treɪʃən] n amministrazione f; **administrative** [əd'mɪnɪstrətɪv] adj amministrativo(-a)

administrator [əd'mɪnɪstreɪtə'] n amministratore(-trice)

admiral ['ædmərəl] n ammiraglio

admiration [ædmə'reɪʃən] n ammirazione f

admire [əd'maɪə'] vt ammirare; **admirer** n ammiratore(-trice)

admission [əd'mɪʃən] n ammissione f; (*to exhibition, nightclub etc*) ingresso; (*confession*) confessione f

admit [əd'mɪt] vt ammettere; far entrare; (*agree*) riconoscere; **admit to** vt fus riconoscere; **admittance** n ingresso; **admittedly** adv bisogna pur riconoscere (che)

adolescent [ædəu'lɛsnt] adj, n adolescente m/f

adopt [ə'dɔpt] vt adottare; **adopted** adj adottivo(-a); **adoption** [ə'dɔpʃən] n adozione f

adore [ə'dɔ:'] vt adorare

adorn [ə'dɔ:n] vt ornare

Adriatic [eɪdrɪ'ætɪk] n **the ~ (Sea)** il mare Adriatico, l'Adriatico

adrift [ə'drɪft] adv alla deriva

adult ['ædʌlt] adj adulto(-a); (*work, education*) per adulti ▷ n adulto(-a); **adult education** n scuola per adulti

adultery [ə'dʌltərɪ] n adulterio

advance [əd'vɑ:ns] n avanzamento; (*money*) anticipo ▷ adj (*booking etc*) in anticipo ▷ vt (*money*) anticipare ▷ vi avanzare; **in ~** in anticipo; **do I need to book in ~?** occorre che prenoti in anticipo?; **advanced** adj avanzato(-a); (*Scol: studies*) superiore

advantage [əd'vɑ:ntɪdʒ] n (*also Tennis*) vantaggio; **to take ~ of** approfittarsi di

advent ['ædvənt] n avvento; (*Rel*): **A~** Avvento

adventure [əd'vɛntʃə'] n avventura; **adventurous** [əd'vɛntʃərəs] adj avventuroso(-a)

adverb ['ædvə:b] n avverbio

adversary ['ædvəsərɪ] n avversario(-a)
adverse ['ædvə:s] adj avverso(-a)
advert ['ædvə:t] (BRIT) n abbr
= **advertisement**
advertise ['ædvətaɪz] vi, vt fare pubblicità
or réclame (a); fare un'inserzione (per
vendere); **to ~ for** (staff) mettere un
annuncio sul giornale per trovare;
advertisement [əd'və:tɪsmənt] n
(Comm) réclame f inv, pubblicità f inv; (in
classified ads) inserzione f; **advertiser** n
azienda che reclamizza un prodotto; (in
newspaper) inserzionista m/f; **advertising**
['ædvətaɪzɪŋ] n pubblicità
advice [əd'vaɪs] n consigli mpl; **piece of ~**
consiglio; **to take legal ~** consultare un
avvocato
advisable [əd'vaɪzəbl] adj consigliabile
advise [əd'vaɪz] vt consigliare; **to ~ sb of**
sth informare qn di qc; **to ~ sb against**
sth/doing sth sconsigliare qc a qn/a qn
di fare qc; **adviser** n consigliere(-a); (in
business) consulente m/f, consigliere(-a);
advisory [-ərɪ] adj consultivo(-a)
advocate [n 'ædvəkət, vb 'ædvəkeɪt]
n (upholder) sostenitore(-trice); (Law)
avvocato (difensore) ▷ vt propugnare
Aegean [ɪ'dʒi:ən] n **the ~ (Sea)** il mar
Egeo, l'Egeo
aerial ['ɛərɪəl] n antenna ▷ adj aereo(-a)
aerobics [ɛə'rəubɪks] n aerobica
aeroplane ['ɛərəpleɪn] (BRIT) n aeroplano
aerosol ['ɛərəsɔl] (BRIT) n aerosol m inv
affair [ə'fɛəʳ] n affare m; (also: **love ~**)
relazione f amorosa; **~s** (business) affari
affect [ə'fɛkt] vt toccare; (influence)
influire su, incidere su; (feign) fingere;
affected adj affettato(-a); **affection**
[ə'fɛkʃən] n affezione f; **affectionate** adj
affettuoso(-a)
afflict [ə'flɪkt] vt affliggere
affluent ['æfluənt] adj ricco(-a); **the ~**
society la società del benessere
afford [ə'fɔ:d] vt permettersi; (provide)
fornire; **affordable** adj (che ha un prezzo)
abbordabile
Afghanistan [æf'gænɪstɑ:n] n Afganistan
m
afraid [ə'freɪd] adj impaurito(-a); **to be ~**
of or **to/that** aver paura di/che; **I am ~**
so/not ho paura di sì/no
Africa ['æfrɪkə] n Africa; **African** adj, n
africano(-a); **African-American** adj, n
afroamericano(-a)
after ['ɑ:ftəʳ] prep, adv dopo ▷ conj dopo
che; **what/who are you ~?** che/chi
cerca?; **~ he left/having done** dopo
che se ne fu andato/dopo aver fatto; **to**
name sb ~ sb dare a qn il nome di qn; **it's**

twenty ~ eight (US) sono le otto e venti;
to ask ~ sb chiedere di qn; **~ all** dopo
tutto; **~ you!** dopo di lei!; **after-effects**
npl conseguenze fpl; (of illness) postumi
mpl; **aftermath** n conseguenze fpl; **in**
the aftermath of nel periodo dopo;
afternoon n pomeriggio; **after-shave**
(lotion) ['ɑ:ftəʃeɪv-] n dopobarba m inv;
aftersun (lotion/cream) n doposole m
inv; **afterwards** (US **afterward**) adv dopo
again [ə'gɛn] adv di nuovo; **to begin/see ~**
ricominciare/rivedere; **not ... ~** non ... più;
~ and ~ ripetutamente
against [ə'gɛnst] prep contro
age [eɪdʒ] n età f inv ▷ vt, vi invecchiare;
it's been ~s since sono secoli che; **he is**
20 years of ~ ha 20 anni; **to come of ~**
diventare maggiorenne; **~d 10** di 10 anni;
the ~d ['eɪdʒɪd] gli anziani; **age group** n
generazione f; **age limit** n limite m d'età
agency ['eɪdʒənsɪ] n agenzia
agenda [ə'dʒɛndə] n ordine m del giorno
agent ['eɪdʒənt] n agente m
aggravate ['ægrəveɪt] vt aggravare;
(person) irritare
aggression [ə'grɛʃən] n aggressione f
aggressive [ə'grɛsɪv] adj aggressivo(-a)
agile ['ædʒaɪl] adj agile
agitated ['ædʒɪteɪtɪd] adj agitato(-a),
turbato(-a)
AGM n abbr = **annual general meeting**
ago [ə'gəu] adv **2 days ~** 2 giorni fa; **not**
long ~ poco tempo fa; **how long ~?**
quanto tempo fa?
agony ['ægənɪ] n dolore m atroce; **to be in**
~ avere dolori atroci
agree [ə'gri:] vt (price) pattuire ▷ vi **to**
~ (with) essere d'accordo (con); (Ling)
concordare (con); **to ~ to sth/to do sth**
accettare qc/di fare qc; **to ~ that** (admit)
ammettere che; **to ~ on sth** accordarsi su
qc; **garlic doesn't ~ with me** l'aglio non
mi va; **agreeable** adj gradevole; (willing)
disposto(-a); **agreed** adj (time, place)
stabilito(-a); **agreement** n accordo; **in**
agreement d'accordo
agricultural [ægrɪ'kʌltʃərəl] adj
agricolo(-a)
agriculture ['ægrɪkʌltʃəʳ] n agricoltura
ahead [ə'hɛd] adv avanti; davanti; **~ of**
davanti a; (fig: schedule etc) in anticipo su;
~ of time in anticipo; **go right** or **straight**
~ tira diritto
aid [eɪd] n aiuto ▷ vt aiutare; **in ~ of** a
favore di
aide [eɪd] n (person) aiutante m/f
AIDS [eɪdz] n abbr (= acquired immune
deficiency syndrome) AIDS f
ailing ['eɪlɪŋ] adj sofferente; (fig: economy,

industry etc) in difficoltà
ailment ['eɪlmənt] *n* indisposizione *f*
aim [eɪm] *vt* **to ~ sth at** (*such as gun*) mirare qc a, puntare qc a; (*camera*) rivolgere qc a; (*missile*) lanciare qc contro ▷ *vi* (*also:* **to take ~**) prendere la mira ▷ *n* mira; **to ~ at** mirare; **to ~ to do** aver l'intenzione di fare
ain't [eɪnt] (*inf*) = **am not; aren't; isn't**
air [ɛəʳ] *n* aria ▷ *vt* (*room*) arieggiare; (*clothes*) far prendere aria a; (*grievances, ideas*) esprimere pubblicamente ▷ *cpd* (*currents*) d'aria; (*attack*) aereo(-a); **to throw sth into the ~** lanciare qc in aria; **by ~** (*travel*) in aereo; **on the ~** (*Radio, TV*) in onda; **airbag** *n* airbag *m inv*; **airbed** (*BRIT*) *n* materassino; **airborne** ['ɛəbɔːn] *adj* (*plane*) in volo; (*troops*) aerotrasportato(-a); **as soon as the plane was airborne** appena l'aereo ebbe decollato; **air-conditioned** *adj* con or ad aria condizionata; **air conditioning** *n* condizionamento d'aria; **aircraft** *n inv* apparecchio; **airfield** *n* campo d'aviazione; **Air Force** *n* aviazione *f* militare; **air hostess** (*BRIT*) *n* hostess *f inv*; **airing cupboard** ['ɛərɪŋ-] *n* armadio riscaldato per asciugare panni.; **airlift** *n* ponte *m* aereo; **airline** *n* linea aerea; **airliner** *n* aereo di linea; **airmail** *n* **by airmail** per via aerea; **airplane** (*US*) *n* aeroplano; **airport** *n* aeroporto; **air raid** *n* incursione *f* aerea; **airsick** *adj* **to be airsick** soffrire di mal d'aria; **airspace** *n* spazio aereo; **airstrip** *n* pista d'atterraggio; **air terminal** *n* air-terminal *m inv*; **airtight** *adj* ermetico(-a); **air-traffic controller** *n* controllore *m* del traffico aereo; **airy** *adj* arioso(-a); (*manners*) noncurante
aisle [aɪl] *n* (*of church*) navata laterale; navata centrale; (*of plane*) corridoio; **aisle seat** *n* (*on plane*) posto sul corridoio
ajar [ə'dʒɑːʳ] *adj* socchiuso(-a)
à la carte [ɑːlɑː'kɑːt] *adv* alla carta
alarm [ə'lɑːm] *n* allarme *m* ▷ *vt* allarmare; **alarm call** *n* (*in hotel etc*) sveglia; **I have an alarm call at 7 am, please?** vorrei essere svegliato alle 7, per favore; **alarm clock** *n* sveglia; **alarmed** *adj* (*person*) allarmato(-a); (*house, car etc*) dotato(-a) di allarme; **alarming** *adj* allarmante, preoccupante
Albania [æl'beɪnɪə] *n* Albania
albeit [ɔːl'biːɪt] *conj* sebbene + *sub*, benché + *sub*
album ['ælbəm] *n* album *m inv*
alcohol ['ælkəhɔl] *n* alcool *m*; **alcohol-free** *adj* analcolico(-a); **alcoholic** [-'hɔlɪk] *adj* alcolico(-a) ▷ *n* alcolizzato(-a)

alcove ['ælkəuv] *n* alcova
ale [eɪl] *n* birra
alert [ə'ləːt] *adj* vigile ▷ *n* allarme *m* ▷ *vt* avvertire; mettere in guardia; **on the ~** all'erta
algebra ['ældʒɪbrə] *n* algebra
Algeria [æl'dʒɪərɪə] *n* Algeria
alias ['eɪlɪəs] *adv* alias ▷ *n* pseudonimo, falso nome *m*
alibi ['ælɪbaɪ] *n* alibi *m inv*
alien ['eɪlɪən] *n* straniero(-a); (*extraterrestrial*) alieno(-a) ▷ *adj* **~ (to)** estraneo(-a) (a); **alienate** *vt* alienare
alight [ə'laɪt] *adj* acceso(-a) ▷ *vi* scendere; (*bird*) posarsi
align [ə'laɪn] *vt* allineare
alike [ə'laɪk] *adj* simile ▷ *adv* sia ... sia; **to look ~** assomigliarsi
alive [ə'laɪv] *adj* vivo(-a); (*lively*) vivace

KEYWORD

all [ɔːl] *adj* tutto(-a); **all day** tutto il giorno; **all night** tutta la notte; **all men** tutti gli uomini; **all five came** sono venuti tutti e cinque; **all the books** tutti i libri; **all the food** tutto il cibo; **all the time** sempre; tutto il tempo; **all his life** tutta la vita ▷ *pron* **1** tutto(-a); **I ate it all, I ate all of it** l'ho mangiato tutto; **all of us went** tutti noi siamo andati; **all of the boys went** tutti i ragazzi sono andati

2 (*in phrases*): **above all** soprattutto; **after all** dopotutto; **at all: not at all** (*in answer to question*) niente affatto; (*in answer to thanks*) prego!, di niente!, s'immagini!; **I'm not at all tired** non sono affatto stanco(-a); **anything at all will do** andrà bene qualsiasi cosa; **all in all** tutto sommato
▷ *adv* **all alone** tutto(-a) solo(-a); **it's not as hard as all that** non è poi così difficile; **the more/the better** tanto più/meglio; **all but** quasi; **the score is two all** il punteggio è di due a due

Allah ['ælə] *n* Allah *m*
allegation [ælɪ'geɪʃən] *n* asserzione *f*
alleged [ə'lɛdʒd] *adj* presunto(-a); **allegedly** [ə'lɛdʒɪdlɪ] *adv* secondo quanto si asserisce
allegiance [ə'liːdʒəns] *n* fedeltà
allergic [ə'ləːdʒɪk] *adj* **~ to** allergico(-a) a; **I'm ~ to penicillin** sono allergico alla penicillina
allergy ['ælədʒɪ] *n* allergia
alleviate [ə'liːvɪeɪt] *vt* sollevare
alley ['ælɪ] *n* vicolo
alliance [ə'laɪəns] *n* alleanza

allied ['ælaɪd] *adj* alleato(-a)
alligator ['ælɪɡeɪtə'] *n* alligatore *m*
all-in ['ɔːlɪn] *adj* (BRIT: *also adv: charge*) tutto compreso
allocate ['æləkeɪt] *vt* assegnare
allot [ə'lɔt] *vt* assegnare
all-out ['ɔːlaut] *adj* (*effort etc*) totale ▷ *adv* **to go all out for** mettercela tutta per
allow [ə'lau] *vt* (*practice, behaviour*) permettere; (*sum to spend etc*) accordare; (*sum, time estimated*) dare; (*concede*): **to ~ that** ammettere che; **to ~ sb to do** permettere a qn di fare; **he is ~ed to** lo può fare; **allow for** *vt fus* tener conto di; **allowance** *n* (*money received*) assegno; indennità *f inv*; (*Tax*) detrazione *f* di imposta; **to make allowances for** tener conto di
all right *adv* (*feel, work*) bene; (*as answer*) va bene
ally ['ælaɪ] *n* alleato
almighty [ɔːl'maɪtɪ] *adj* onnipotente; (*row etc*) colossale
almond ['ɑːmənd] *n* mandorla
almost ['ɔːlməust] *adv* quasi
alone [ə'ləun] *adj, adv* solo(-a); **to leave sb ~** lasciare qn in pace; **to leave sth ~** lasciare stare qc; **let ~ ...** figuriamoci poi ..., tanto meno ...
along [ə'lɔŋ] *prep* lungo ▷ *adv* **is he coming ~?** viene con noi?; **he was limping ~** veniva zoppicando; **~ with** insieme con; **all ~** (*all the time*) sempre, fin dall'inizio; **alongside** *prep* accanto a; lungo ▷ *adv* accanto
aloof [ə'luːf] *adj* distaccato(-a) ▷ *adv* **to stand ~** tenersi a distanza *or* in disparte
aloud [ə'laud] *adv* ad alta voce
alphabet ['ælfəbet] *n* alfabeto
Alps [ælps] *npl* **the ~** le Alpi
already [ɔːl'redɪ] *adv* già
alright ['ɔːl'raɪt] (BRIT) *adv* = **all right**
also ['ɔːlsəu] *adv* anche
altar ['ɔltə'] *n* altare *m*
alter ['ɔltə'] *vt, vi* alterare; **alteration** [ɔltə'reɪʃən] *n* modificazione *f*, alterazione *f*; **alterations** (*Sewing, Archit*) modifiche *fpl*; **timetable subject to alteration** orario soggetto a variazioni
alternate [*adj* ɔl'təːnɪt, *vb* 'ɔltə:neɪt] *adj* alterno(-a); (US: *plan etc*) alternativo(-a) ▷ *vi* **to ~ (with)** alternarsi (a); **on ~ days** ogni due giorni
alternative [ɔl'təːnətɪv] *adj* alternativo(-a) ▷ *n* (*choice*) alternativa; **alternatively** *adv* **alternatively one could ...** come alternativa si potrebbe ...
although [ɔːl'ðəu] *conj* benché + *sub*, sebbene + *sub*

altitude ['æltɪtjuːd] *n* altitudine *f*
altogether [ɔːltə'ɡeðə'] *adv* del tutto, completamente; (*on the whole*) tutto considerato; (*in all*) in tutto
aluminium [ælju'mɪnɪəm] (BRIT), **aluminum** [ə'luːmɪnəm] (US) *n* alluminio
always ['ɔːlweɪz] *adv* sempre
Alzheimer's (disease) ['æltshaɪməz-] *n* (malattia di) Alzheimer
am [æm] *vb see* **be**
amalgamate [ə'mælɡəmeɪt] *vt* amalgamare ▷ *vi* amalgamarsi
amass [ə'mæs] *vt* ammassare
amateur ['æmətə'] *n* dilettante *m/f* ▷ *adj* (*Sport*) dilettante
amaze [ə'meɪz] *vt* stupire; **amazed** *adj* sbalordito(-a); **to be amazed (at)** essere sbalordito (da); **amazement** *n* stupore *m*; **amazing** *adj* sorprendente, sbalorditivo(-a)
Amazon ['æməzən] *n* (*Mythology*) Amazzone *f*; (*river*): **the ~** il Rio delle Amazzoni ▷ *cpd* (*basin, jungle*) amazzonico(-a)
ambassador [æm'bæsədə'] *n* ambasciatore(-trice)
amber ['æmbə'] *n* ambra; **at ~** (BRIT Aut) giallo
ambiguous [æm'bɪɡjuəs] *adj* ambiguo(-a)
ambition [æm'bɪʃən] *n* ambizione *f*; **ambitious** [æm'bɪʃəs] *adj* ambizioso(-a)
ambulance ['æmbjuləns] *n* ambulanza; **call an ~!** chiamate un'ambulanza!
ambush ['æmbuʃ] *n* imboscata
amen ['ɑː'mɛn] *excl* così sia, amen
amend [ə'mɛnd] *vt* (*law*) emendare; (*text*) correggere; **to make ~s** fare ammenda; **amendment** *n* emendamento; correzione *f*
amenities [ə'miːnɪtɪz] *npl* attrezzature *fpl* ricreative e culturali
America [ə'mɛrɪkə] *n* America; **American** *adj, n* americano(-a); **American football** *n* (BRIT) football *m* americano
amicable ['æmɪkəbl] *adj* amichevole
amid(st) [ə'mɪd(st)] *prep* in mezzo a
ammunition [æmju'nɪʃən] *n* munizioni *fpl*
amnesty ['æmnɪstɪ] *n* amnistia; **to grant an ~ to** concedere l'amnistia a, amnistiare
among(st) [ə'mʌŋ(st)] *prep* fra, tra, in mezzo a
amount [ə'maunt] *n* somma; ammontare *m*; quantità *f inv* ▷ *vi* **to ~ to** (*total*) ammontare a; (*be same as*) essere come
amp(ère) ['æmp(ɛə')] *n* ampère *m inv*
ample ['æmpl] *adj* ampio(-a); spazioso(-a); (*enough*): **this is ~** questo è più che sufficiente

amplifier ['æmplɪfaɪə'] n amplificatore m
amputate ['æmpjuteɪt] vt amputare
Amtrak ['æmtræk] (US) n società ferroviaria americana
amuse [ə'mju:z] vt divertire; **amusement** n divertimento; **amusement arcade** n sala giochi; **amusement park** n luna park m inv
amusing [ə'mju:zɪŋ] adj divertente
an [æn] indef art see **a**
anaemia [ə'ni:mɪə] (US **anemia**) n anemia
anaemic [ə'ni:mɪk] (US **anemic**) adj anemico(-a)
anaesthetic [ænɪs'θetɪk] (US **anesthetic**) adj anestetico(-a) ▷ n anestetico
analog(ue) ['ænəlɒg] adj (watch, computer) analogico(-a)
analogy [ə'nælədʒɪ] n analogia; **to draw an ~ between** fare un'analogia tra
analyse ['ænəlaɪz] (US **analyze**) vt analizzare; **analysis** [ə'næləsɪs] (pl **analyses**) n analisi f inv; **analyst** ['ænəlɪst] n (Pol etc) analista m/f; (US) (psic)analista m/f
analyze ['ænəlaɪz] (US) vt = **analyse**
anarchy ['ænəkɪ] n anarchia
anatomy [ə'nætəmɪ] n anatomia
ancestor ['ænsɪstə'] n antenato(-a)
anchor ['æŋkə'] n ancora ▷ vi (also: **to drop ~**) gettare l'ancora ▷ vt ancorare; **to weigh ~** salpare or levare l'ancora
anchovy ['æntʃəvɪ] n acciuga
ancient ['eɪnʃənt] adj antico(-a); (person, car) vecchissimo(-a)
and [ænd] conj e; (often ed before vowel): **~ so on** e così via; **try ~ come** cerca di venire; **he talked ~ talked** non la finiva di parlare; **better ~ better** sempre meglio
Andes ['ændi:z] npl **the ~** le Ande
anemia etc [ə'ni:mɪə] (US) = **anaemia** etc
anesthetic [ænɪs'θetɪk] (US) adj, n = **anaesthetic**
angel ['eɪndʒəl] n angelo
anger ['æŋgə'] n rabbia
angina [æn'dʒaɪnə] n angina pectoris
angle ['æŋgl] n angolo; **from their ~** dal loro punto di vista
angler ['æŋglə'] n pescatore m con la lenza
Anglican ['æŋglɪkən] adj, n anglicano(-a)
angling ['æŋglɪŋ] n pesca con la lenza
angrily ['æŋgrɪlɪ] adv con rabbia
angry ['æŋgrɪ] adj arrabbiato(-a), furioso(-a); (wound) infiammato(-a); **to be ~ with sb/at sth** essere in collera con qn/per qc; **to get ~** arrabbiarsi; **to make sb ~** fare arrabbiare qn
anguish ['æŋgwɪʃ] n angoscia
animal ['ænɪməl] adj animale ▷ n animale m

animated ['ænɪmeɪtɪd] adj animato(-a)
animation [ænɪ'meɪʃən] n animazione f
aniseed ['ænɪsi:d] n semi mpl di anice
ankle ['æŋkl] n caviglia
annex [n 'æneks, vb ə'neks] n (BRIT: also: **~e**) (edificio) annesso ▷ vt annettere
anniversary [ænɪ'və:sərɪ] n anniversario
announce [ə'nauns] vt annunciare; **announcement** n annuncio; (letter, card) partecipazione f; **announcer** n (Radio, TV: between programmes) annunciatore(-trice); (: in a programme) presentatore(-trice)
annoy [ə'nɔɪ] vt dare fastidio a; **don't get ~ed!** non irritarti!; **annoying** adj noioso(-a)
annual ['ænjuəl] adj annuale ▷ n (Bot) pianta annua; (book) annuario; **annually** adv annualmente
annum ['ænəm] n see **per**
anonymous [ə'nɒnɪməs] adj anonimo(-a)
anorak ['ænəræk] n giacca a vento
anorexia [ænə'reksɪə] n (Med: also: **~ nervosa**) anoressia
anorexic [ænə'reksɪk] adj, n anoressico(-a)
another [ə'nʌðə'] adj **~ book** (one more) un altro libro, ancora un libro; (a different one) un altro libro ▷ pron un altro(un'altra), ancora uno(-a); see also **one**
answer ['ɑ:nsə'] n risposta; soluzione f ▷ vi rispondere ▷ vt (reply to) rispondere a; (problem) risolvere; (prayer) esaudire; **in ~ to your letter** in risposta alla sua lettera; **to ~ the phone** rispondere (al telefono); **to ~ the bell** rispondere al campanello; **to ~ the door** aprire la porta; **answer back** vi ribattere; **answerphone** n (esp BRIT) segreteria telefonica
ant [ænt] n formica
Antarctic [ænt'ɑ:ktɪk] n **the ~** l'Antartide f
antelope ['æntɪləup] n antilope f
antenatal ['æntɪ'neɪtl] adj prenatale
antenna [æn'tenə, -ni:] (pl **antennae**) n antenna
anthem ['ænθəm] n **national ~** inno nazionale
anthology [æn'θɒlədʒɪ] n antologia
anthrax ['ænθræks] n antrace m
anthropology [ænθrə'pɒlədʒɪ] n antropologia
anti ['æntɪ] prefix anti; **antibiotic** ['æntɪbaɪ'ɒtɪk] n antibiotico; **antibody** ['æntɪbɒdɪ] n anticorpo
anticipate [æn'tɪsɪpeɪt] vt prevedere; pregustare; (wishes, request) prevenire; **anticipation** [æntɪsɪ'peɪʃən] n anticipazione f; (expectation) aspettativa fpl
anticlimax ['æntɪ'klaɪmæks] n **it was an ~** fu una completa delusione

anticlockwise ['ænti'klɔkwaiz] adj, adv in senso antiorario

antics ['æntiks] npl buffonerie fpl

anti: **antidote** ['æntidəut] n antidoto; **antifreeze** ['ænti'fri:z] n anticongelante m; **anti-globalization** [æntiglaubəlai'zeiʃən] n antiglobalizzazione f; **antihistamine** [ænti'histəmin] n antistaminico; **antiperspirant** ['ænti'pə:spərənt] adj antitraspirante

antique [æn'ti:k] n antichità f inv ▷ adj antico(-a); **antique shop** n negozio d'antichità

antiseptic [ænti'sɛptik] n antisettico

antisocial ['ænti'səuʃəl] adj asociale

antlers ['æntləz] npl palchi mpl

anxiety [æŋ'zaiəti] n ansia; (keenness): ~ **to do** smania di fare

anxious ['æŋkʃəs] adj ansioso(-a), inquieto(-a); (worrying) angosciante; (keen): ~ **to do/that** impaziente di fare/che + sub

KEYWORD

any ['ɛni] adj **1** (in questions etc): **have you any butter?** hai del burro?, hai un po' di burro?; **have you any children?** hai bambini?; **if there are any tickets left** se ci sono ancora (dei) biglietti, se c'è ancora qualche biglietto
2 (with negative): **I haven't any money/ books** non ho soldi/libri
3 (no matter which) qualsiasi, qualunque; **choose any book you like** scegli un libro qualsiasi
4 (in phrases): **in any case** in ogni caso; **any day now** da un giorno all'altro; **at any moment** in qualsiasi momento, da un momento all'altro; **at any rate** ad ogni modo
▷ pron **1** (in questions, with negative): **have you got any?** ne hai?; **can any of you sing?** qualcuno di voi sa cantare?; **I haven't any (of them)** non ne ho
2 (no matter which one(s)): **take any of those books (you like)** prendi uno qualsiasi di quei libri
▷ adv **1** (in questions etc): **do you want any more soup/sandwiches?** vuoi ancora un po' di minestra/degli altri panini?; **are you feeling any better?** ti senti meglio?
2 (with negative): **I can't hear him any more** non lo sento più; **don't wait any longer** non aspettare più

any: **anybody** ['ɛnibɔdi] pron (in questions etc) qualcuno, nessuno; (with negative)
nessuno; (no matter who) chiunque; **can you see anybody?** vedi qualcuno or nessuno?; **if anybody should phone ...** se telefona qualcuno ...; **I can't see anybody** non vedo nessuno; **anybody could do it** chiunque potrebbe farlo; **anyhow** ['ɛnihau] adv (at any rate) ad ogni modo, comunque; (haphazard): **do it anyhow you like** fallo come ti pare; **I shall go anyhow** ci andrò lo stesso or comunque; **she leaves things just anyhow** lascia tutto come capita; **anyone** ['ɛniwʌn] pron = **anybody**; **anything** ['ɛniθiŋ] pron (in question etc) qualcosa, niente; (with negative) niente; (no matter what): **you can say anything you like** puoi dire quello che ti pare; **can you see anything?** vedi niente or qualcosa?; **if anything happens to me ...** se mi dovesse succedere qualcosa ...; **I can't see anything** non vedo niente; **anything will do** va bene qualsiasi cosa or tutto; **anytime** adv in qualunque momento; quando vuole; **anyway** ['ɛniwei] adv (at any rate) ad ogni modo, comunque; (besides) ad ogni modo; **anywhere** ['ɛniwɛə'] adv (in questions etc) da qualche parte; (with negative) da nessuna parte; (no matter where) da qualsiasi or qualunque parte, dovunque; **can you see him anywhere?** lo vedi da qualche parte?; **I can't see him anywhere** non lo vedo da nessuna parte; **anywhere in the world** dovunque nel mondo

apart [ə'pɑ:t] adv (to one side) a parte; (separately) separatamente; **with one's legs ~** con le gambe divaricate; **10 miles ~** a 10 miglia di distanza (l'uno dall'altro); **to take ~** smontare; **~ from** a parte, eccetto

apartment [ə'pɑ:tmənt] (us) n appartamento; (room) locale m; **apartment building** (us) n stabile m, caseggiato

apathy ['æpəθi] n apatia

ape [eip] n scimmia ▷ vt scimmiottare

aperitif [ə'pɛriti:f] n aperitivo

aperture ['æpətʃjuə'] n apertura

APEX n abbr (= advance purchase excursion) APEX m inv

apologize [ə'pɔlədʒaiz] vi **to ~ (for sth to sb)** scusarsi (di qc a qn), chiedere scusa (a qn per qc)

apology [ə'pɔlədʒi] n scuse fpl

apostrophe [ə'pɔstrəfi] n (sign) apostrofo

appal [ə'pɔ:l] vt scioccare; **appalling** adj spaventoso(-a)

apparatus [æpə'reitəs] n apparato; (in gymnasium) attrezzatura

apparent [ə'pærənt] adj evidente; **apparently** adv evidentemente

appeal [ə'pi:l] vi (Law) appellarsi alla legge ▷ n (Law) appello; (request) richiesta; (charm) attrattiva; **to ~ for** chiedere (con insistenza); **to ~ to** (person) appellarsi a; (thing) piacere a; **it doesn't ~ to me** mi dice poco; **appealing** adj (nice) attraente

appear [ə'pɪəʳ] vi apparire; (Law) comparire; (publication) essere pubblicato(-a); (seem) sembrare; **it would ~ that** sembra che; **appearance** n apparizione f; apparenza; (look, aspect) aspetto

appendicitis [əpendɪ'saɪtɪs] n appendicite f

appendix [ə'pendɪks] (pl **appendices**) n appendice f

appetite ['æpɪtaɪt] n appetito

appetizer ['æpɪtaɪzəʳ] n stuzzichino

applaud [ə'plɔ:d] vt, vi applaudire

applause [ə'plɔ:z] n applauso

apple ['æpl] n mela; **apple pie** n torta di mele

appliance [ə'plaɪəns] n apparecchio

applicable [ə'plɪkəbl] adj applicabile; **to be ~ to** essere valido per; **the law is ~ from January** la legge entrerà in vigore in gennaio

applicant ['æplɪkənt] n candidato(-a)

application [æplɪ'keɪʃən] n applicazione f; (for a job, a grant etc) domanda; **application form** n modulo per la domanda

apply [ə'plaɪ] vt **to ~ (to)** (paint, ointment) dare (a); (theory, technique) applicare (a) ▷ vi **to ~ to** (ask) rivolgersi a; (be suitable for, relevant to) riguardare, riferirsi a; **to ~ (for)** (permit, grant, job) fare domanda (per); **to ~ o.s. to** dedicarsi a

appoint [ə'pɔɪnt] vt nominare; **appointment** n nomina; (arrangement to meet) appuntamento; **I have an appointment (with) ...** ho un appuntamento (con) ...; **I'd like to make an appointment (with)** vorrei prendere un appuntamento (con)

appraisal [ə'preɪzl] n valutazione f

appreciate [ə'pri:ʃɪeɪt] vt (like) apprezzare; (be grateful for) essere riconoscente di; (be aware of) rendersi conto di ▷ vi (Finance) aumentare; **I'd ~ your help** ti sono grato per l'aiuto; **appreciation** [əpri:ʃɪ'eɪʃən] n apprezzamento; (Finance) aumento del valore

apprehension [æprɪ'henʃən] n (fear) inquietudine f

apprehensive [æprɪ'hensɪv] adj apprensivo(-a)

apprentice [ə'prentɪs] n apprendista m/f

approach [ə'prəʊtʃ] vi avvicinarsi ▷ vt (come near) avvicinarsi a; (ask, apply to) rivolgersi a; (subject, passer-by) avvicinare ▷ n approccio; accesso; (to problem) modo di affrontare

appropriate [adj ə'prəʊprɪɪt, vb ə'prəʊprɪeɪt] adj appropriato(-a), adatto(-a) ▷ vt (take) appropriarsi

approval [ə'pru:vəl] n approvazione f; **on ~** (Comm) in prova, in esame

approve [ə'pru:v] vt, vi approvare; **approve of** vt fus approvare

approximate [ə'prɔksɪmɪt] adj approssimativo(-a); **approximately** adv circa

Apr. abbr (= April) apr.

apricot ['eɪprɪkɔt] n albicocca

April ['eɪprəl] n aprile m; **~ fool!** pesce d'aprile!; **April Fools' Day** n vedi nota nel riquadro

- **APRIL FOOLS' DAY**
-
- **April Fool's Day** è il primo aprile, il
- giorno degli scherzi e delle burle. Il nome
- deriva dal fatto che, se una persona
- cade nella trappola che gli è stata tesa,
- fa la figura del "fool", cioè dello sciocco.
- Tradizionalmente, gli scherzi vengono
- fatti entro mezzogiorno.

apron ['eɪprən] n grembiule m

apt [æpt] adj (suitable) adatto(-a); (able) capace; (likely): **to be ~ to do** avere tendenza a fare

aquarium [ə'kweərɪəm] n acquario

Aquarius [ə'kweərɪəs] n Acquario

Arab ['ærəb] adj, n arabo(-a)

Arabia [ə'reɪbɪə] n Arabia; **Arabian** [ə'reɪbɪən] adj arabo(-a); **Arabic** ['ærəbɪk] adj arabico(-a), arabo(-a) ▷ n arabo; **Arabic numerals** n numeri mpl arabi, numerazione f araba

arbitrary ['ɑ:bɪtrərɪ] adj arbitrario(-a)

arbitration [ɑ:bɪ'treɪʃən] n (Law) arbitrato; (Industry) arbitraggio

arc [ɑ:k] n arco

arcade [ɑ:'keɪd] n portico; (passage with shops) galleria

arch [ɑ:tʃ] n arco; (of foot) arco plantare ▷ vt inarcare

archaeology [ɑ:kɪ'ɔlədʒɪ] (us **archeology**) n archeologia

archbishop [ɑ:tʃ'bɪʃəp] n arcivescovo

archeology etc [ɑ:kɪ'ɔlədʒɪ] (us) = **archaeology** etc

architect ['ɑ:kɪtekt] n architetto; **architectural** [ɑ:kɪ'tektʃərəl] adj architettonico(-a); **architecture** ['ɑ:kɪtektʃəʳ] n architettura

archive ['ɑːkaɪv] n (often pl: also Comput) archivio

Arctic ['ɑːktɪk] adj artico(-a) ▷ n **the ~** l'Artico

are [ɑːʳ] vb see **be**

area ['ɛərɪə] n (Geom) area; (zone) zona; (: smaller) settore m; **area code** (US) n (Tel) prefisso

arena [əˈriːnə] n arena

aren't [ɑːnt] = **are not**

Argentina [ɑːdʒənˈtiːnə] n Argentina; **Argentinian** [-ˈtɪnɪən] adj, n argentino(-a)

arguably ['ɑːɡjuəblɪ] adv **it is ~ ...** si può sostenere che sia ...

argue ['ɑːɡjuː] vi (quarrel) litigare; (reason) ragionare; **to ~ that** sostenere che

argument ['ɑːɡjumənt] n (reasons) argomento; (quarrel) lite f

Aries ['ɛərɪz] n Ariete m

arise [əˈraɪz] (pt **arose**, pp **arisen**) vi (opportunity, problem) presentarsi

arithmetic [əˈrɪθmətɪk] n aritmetica

arm [ɑːm] n braccio ▷ vt armare; **~s** npl (weapons) armi fpl; **~ in ~** a braccetto; **armchair** n poltrona

armed [ɑːmd] adj armato(-a); **armed robbery** n rapina a mano armata

armour ['ɑːməʳ] (US **armor**) n armatura; (Mil: tanks) mezzi mpl blindati

armpit ['ɑːmpɪt] n ascella

armrest ['ɑːmrɛst] n bracciolo

army ['ɑːmɪ] n esercito

A road n strada statale

aroma [əˈrəumə] n aroma; **aromatherapy** n aromaterapia

arose [əˈrəuz] pt of **arise**

around [əˈraund] adv attorno, intorno ▷ prep intorno a; (fig: about): **~ £5/3 o'clock** circa 5 sterline/le 3; **is he ~?** è in giro?

arouse [əˈrauz] vt (sleeper) svegliare; (curiosity, passions) suscitare

arrange [əˈreɪndʒ] vt sistemare; (programme) preparare; **to ~ to do sth** mettersi d'accordo per fare qc; **arrangement** n sistemazione f; (agreement) accordo; **arrangements** npl (plans) progetti mpl, piani mpl

array [əˈreɪ] n **~ of** fila di

arrears [əˈrɪəz] npl arretrati mpl; **to be in ~ with one's rent** essere in arretrato con l'affitto

arrest [əˈrɛst] vt arrestare; (sb's attention) attirare ▷ n arresto; **under ~** in arresto

arrival [əˈraɪvəl] n arrivo; (person) arrivato(-a); **a new ~** un nuovo venuto; (baby) un neonato

arrive [əˈraɪv] vi arrivare; **what time does the train from Rome ~?** a che ora arriva il treno da Roma?; **arrive at** vt fus arrivare a

arrogance ['ærəɡəns] n arroganza

arrogant ['ærəɡənt] adj arrogante

arrow ['ærəu] n freccia

arse [ɑːs] (infl) n culo (!)

arson ['ɑːsn] n incendio doloso

art [ɑːt] n arte f; (craft) mestiere m; **art college** n scuola di belle arti

artery ['ɑːtərɪ] n arteria

art gallery n galleria d'arte

arthritis [ɑːˈθraɪtɪs] n artrite f

artichoke ['ɑːtɪtʃəuk] n carciofo; **Jerusalem ~** topinambur m inv

article ['ɑːtɪkl] n articolo

articulate [adj ɑːˈtɪkjulɪt, vb ɑːˈtɪkjuleɪt] adj (person) che si esprime forbitamente; (speech) articolato(-a) ▷ vi articolare

artificial [ɑːtɪˈfɪʃəl] adj artificiale

artist ['ɑːtɪst] n artista m/f; **artistic** [ɑːˈtɪstɪk] adj artistico(-a)

art school n scuola d'arte

○ **KEYWORD**

as [æz] conj **1** (referring to time) mentre; **as the years went by** col passare degli anni; **he came in as I was leaving** arrivò mentre stavo uscendo; **as from tomorrow** da domani

2 (in comparisons): **as big as** grande come; **twice as big as** due volte più grande di; **as much/many as** tanto quanto/tanti quanti; **as soon as possible** prima possibile

3 (since, because) dal momento che, siccome

4 (referring to manner, way) come; **do as you wish** fa' come vuoi; **as she said** come ha detto lei

5 (concerning): **as for** or **to that** per quanto riguarda or quanto a quello

6: **as if** or **as though** come se; **he looked as if he was ill** sembrava stare male; see also **long**; **such**; **well**

▷ prep **he works as a driver** fa l'autista; **as chairman of the company he ...** come presidente della compagnia lui ...; **he gave me it as a present** me lo ha regalato

a.s.a.p. abbr = **as soon as possible**

asbestos [æzˈbɛstəs] n asbesto, amianto

ascent [əˈsɛnt] n salita

ash [æʃ] n (dust) cenere f; (wood, tree) frassino

ashamed [əˈʃeɪmd] adj vergognoso(-a); **to be ~ of** vergognarsi di

ashore [əˈʃɔːʳ] adv a terra

ashtray ['æʃtreɪ] n portacenere m

Ash Wednesday n mercoledì m inv delle

Ceneri
Asia ['eɪʃə] n Asia; **Asian** adj, n asiatico(-a)
aside [ə'saɪd] adv da parte ▷ n a parte m
ask [ɑːsk] vt (question) domandare; (invite)
invitare; **to ~ sb sth/sb to do sth** chiedere
qc a qn/a qn di fare qc; **to ~ sb about sth**
chiedere a qn di qc; **to ~ (sb) a question**
fare una domanda (a qn); **to ~ sb out to**
dinner invitare qn a mangiare fuori; **ask**
for vt fus chiedere; (trouble etc) cercare
asleep [ə'sliːp] adj addormentato(-a); **to**
be ~ dormire; **to fall ~** addormentarsi
asparagus [əs'pærəgəs] n asparagi mpl
aspect ['æspɛkt] n aspetto
aspirations [æspə'reɪʃənz] npl aspirazioni
fpl
aspire [əs'paɪəʳ] vi **to ~ to** aspirare a
aspirin ['æsprɪn] n aspirina
ass [æs] n asino; (inf) scemo(-a); (US: inf!)
culo (!)
assassin [ə'sæsɪn] n assassino;
assassinate [ə'sæsɪneɪt] vt assassinare
assault [ə'sɔːlt] n (Mil) assalto; (gen: attack)
aggressione f ▷ vt assaltare; aggredire;
(sexually) violentare
assemble [ə'sɛmbl] vt riunire; (Tech)
montare ▷ vi riunirsi
assembly [ə'sɛmblɪ] n (meeting)
assemblea; (construction) montaggio
assert [ə'səːt] vt asserire; (insist on) far
valere; **assertion** [ə'səːʃən] n asserzione f
assess [ə'sɛs] vt valutare; **assessment** n
valutazione f
asset ['æsɛt] n vantaggio; **~s** npl (Finance:
of individual) beni mpl; (: of company) attivo
assign [ə'saɪn] vt **to ~ (to)** (task) assegnare
(a); (resources) riservare (a); (cause, meaning)
attribuire (a); **to ~ a date to sth** fissare la
data di qc; **assignment** n compito
assist [ə'sɪst] vt assistere, aiutare;
assistance n assistenza, aiuto; **assistant**
n assistente m/f; (BRIT: also: **shop**
assistant) commesso(-a)
associate [adj, n ə'səʊʃɪɪt, vb ə'səʊʃɪeɪt] adj
associato(-a); (member) aggiunto(-a) ▷ n
collega m/f ▷ vt associare ▷ vi **to ~ with**
sb frequentare qn
association [əsəʊsɪ'eɪʃən] n associazione
f
assorted [ə'sɔːtɪd] adj assortito(-a)
assortment [ə'sɔːtmənt] n assortimento
assume [ə'sjuːm] vt supporre;
(responsibilities etc) assumere; (attitude,
name) prendere
assumption [ə'sʌmpʃən] n supposizione
f, ipotesi f inv; (of power) assunzione f
assurance [ə'ʃuərəns] n assicurazione f;
(self-confidence) fiducia in se stesso
assure [ə'ʃuəʳ] vt assicurare

asterisk ['æstərɪsk] n asterisco
asthma ['æsmə] n asma
astonish [ə'stɒnɪʃ] vt stupire; **astonished**
adj stupito(-a), sorpreso(-a); **to be**
astonished (at) essere stupito(-a)
(da); **astonishing** adj sorprendente,
stupefacente; **I find it astonishing that**
... mi stupisce che ...; **astonishment** n
stupore m
astound [ə'staund] vt sbalordire
astray [ə'streɪ] adv **to go ~** smarrirsi; **to**
lead ~ portare sulla cattiva strada
astrology [əs'trɒlədʒɪ] n astrologia
astronaut ['æstrənɔːt] n astronauta m/f
astronomer [əs'trɒnəməʳ] n
astronomo(-a)
astronomical [æstrə'nɒmɪkl] adj
astronomico(-a)
astronomy [əs'trɒnəmɪ] n astronomia
astute [əs'tjuːt] adj astuto(-a)
asylum [ə'saɪləm] n (politico) asilo; (per
malati) manicomio

○ **KEYWORD**

at [æt] prep **1** (referring to position, direction)
a; **at the top** in cima; **at the desk** al
banco, alla scrivania; **at home/school**
a casa/scuola; **at the baker's** dal
panettiere; **to look at sth** guardare qc; **to**
throw sth at sb lanciare qc a qn
2 (referring to time) a; **at 4 o'clock** alle 4; **at**
night di notte; **at Christmas** a Natale; **at**
times a volte
3 (referring to rates, speed etc) a; **at £1 a kilo**
a 1 sterlina al chilo; **two at a time** due alla
volta, due per volta; **at 50 km/h** a 50 km/h
4 (referring to manner): **at a stroke** d'un
solo colpo; **at peace** in pace
5 (referring to activity): **to be at work** essere
al lavoro; **to play at cowboys** giocare ai
cowboy; **to be good at sth/doing sth**
essere bravo in qc/fare qc
6 (referring to cause): **shocked/surprised/**
annoyed at sth colpito da/sorpreso
da/arrabbiato per qc; **I went at his**
suggestion ci sono andato dietro suo
consiglio

ate [eɪt] pt of **eat**
atheist ['eɪθɪɪst] n ateo(-a)
Athens ['æθɪnz] n Atene f
athlete ['æθliːt] n atleta m/f
athletic [æθ'lɛtɪk] adj atletico(-a);
athletics n atletica
Atlantic [ət'læntɪk] adj atlantico(-a)
▷ n **the ~ (Ocean)** l'Atlantico, l'Oceano
Atlantico
atlas ['ætləs] n atlante m

A.T.M. n abbr (= automated telling machine)
cassa automatica prelievi, sportello
automatico

atmosphere ['ætməsfɪəʳ] n atmosfera

atom ['ætəm] n atomo; **atomic** [ə'tɒmɪk]
adj atomico(-a); **atom(ic) bomb** n bomba
atomica

A to Z® n (map) stradario

atrocity [ə'trɒsɪtɪ] n atrocità f inv

attach [ə'tætʃ] vt attaccare; (document,
letter) allegare; (importance etc) attribuire;
to be ~ed to sb/sth (to like) essere
affezionato(-a) a qn/qc; **attachment**
[ə'tætʃmənt] n (tool) accessorio; (love):
attachment (to) affetto (per)

attack [ə'tæk] vt attaccare; (person)
aggredire; (task etc) iniziare; (problem)
affrontare ▷ n attacco; **heart ~** infarto;
attacker n aggressore m

attain [ə'teɪn] vt (also: **to ~ to**) arrivare a,
raggiungere

attempt [ə'tɛmpt] n tentativo ▷ vt
tentare; **to make an ~ on sb's life**
attentare alla vita di qn

attend [ə'tɛnd] vt frequentare; (meeting,
talk) andare a; (patient) assistere; **attend
to** vt fus (needs, affairs etc) prendersi cura
di; (customer) occuparsi di; **attendance**
n (being present) presenza; (people present)
gente f presente; **attendant** n custode m/
f; persona di servizio ▷ adj concomitante
▌ Be careful not to translate **attend** by
the Italian word **attendere**.

attention [ə'tɛnʃən] n attenzione f ▷ excl
(Mil) attenti!; **for the ~ of** (Admin) per
l'attenzione di

attic ['ætɪk] n soffitta

attitude ['ætɪtjuːd] n atteggiamento;
posa

attorney [ə'təːnɪ] n (lawyer) avvocato;
(having proxy) mandatario; **Attorney
General** n (BRIT) Procuratore m Generale;
(US) Ministro della Giustizia

attract [ə'trækt] vt attirare; **attraction**
[ə'trækʃən] n (gen pl: pleasant things)
attrattiva; (Physics, fig: towards sth)
attrazione f; **attractive** adj attraente

attribute [n 'ætrɪbjuːt, vb ə'trɪbjuːt] n
attributo ▷ vt **to ~ sth to** attribuire qc a

aubergine ['əubəʒiːn] n melanzana

auburn ['ɔːbən] adj tizianesco(-a)

auction ['ɔːkʃən] n (also: **sale by ~**) asta
▷ vt (also: **to sell by ~**) vendere all'asta;
(also: **to put up for ~**) mettere all'asta

audible ['ɔːdɪbl] adj udibile

audience ['ɔːdɪəns] n (people) pubblico;
spettatori mpl; ascoltatori mpl; (interview)
udienza

audit ['ɔːdɪt] vt rivedere, verificare

audition [ɔː'dɪʃən] n audizione f

auditor ['ɔːdɪtəʳ] n revisore m

auditorium [ɔːdɪ'tɔːrɪəm] n sala,
auditorio

Aug. abbr (= August) ago., ag.

August ['ɔːgəst] n agosto

aunt [ɑːnt] n zia; **auntie** n zietta; **aunty**
n zietta

au pair ['əu'pɛəʳ] n (also: **~ girl**) (ragazza f)
alla pari inv

aura ['ɔːrə] n aura

austerity [ɒs'tɛrɪtɪ] n austerità f inv

Australia [ɒs'treɪlɪə] n Australia;
Australian adj, n australiano(-a).

Austria ['ɒstrɪə] n Austria; **Austrian** adj, n
austriaco(-a)

authentic [ɔː'θɛntɪk] adj autentico(-a)

author ['ɔːθəʳ] n autore(-trice)

authority [ɔː'θɔrɪtɪ] n autorità f inv;
(permission) autorizzazione f; **the
authorities** npl (government etc) le
autorità

authorize ['ɔːθəraɪz] vt autorizzare

auto ['ɔːtəu] (US) n auto f inv;
autobiography [ɔːtəbaɪ'ɒgrəfɪ] n
autobiografia; **autograph** ['ɔːtəgrɑːf] n
autografo ▷ vt firmare; **automatic** [ɔː
tə'mætɪk] adj automatico(-a) ▷ n (gun)
arma automatica; (washing machine)
lavatrice f automatica; (car) automobile f
con cambio automatico; **automatically**
adv automaticamente; **automobile** ['ɔːtə
məbiːl] (US) n automobile f; **autonomous**
[ɔː'tɒnəməs] adj autonomo(-a);
autonomy [ɔː'tɒnəmɪ] n autonomia

autumn ['ɔːtəm] n autunno

auxiliary [ɔːg'zɪlɪərɪ] adj ausiliario(-a) ▷ n
ausiliare m/f

avail [ə'veɪl] vt **to ~ o.s. of** servirsi di;
approfittarsi di ▷ n **to no ~** inutilmente

availability [əveɪlə'bɪlɪtɪ] n disponibilità

available [ə'veɪləbl] adj disponibile

avalanche ['ævəlɑːnʃ] n valanga

Ave. abbr = **avenue**

avenue ['ævənjuː] n viale m; (fig) strada,
via

average ['ævərɪdʒ] n media ▷ adj
medio(-a) ▷ vt (a certain figure) fare di or in
media; **on ~** in media

avert [ə'vəːt] vt evitare, prevenire; (one's
eyes) distogliere

avid ['ævɪd] adj (supporter etc) accanito(-a)

avocado [ævə'kɑːdəu] n (BRIT: also: **~
pear**) avocado m inv

avoid [ə'vɔɪd] vt evitare

await [ə'weɪt] vt aspettare

awake [ə'weɪk] (pt awoke, pp awoken,
awaked) adj sveglio(-a) ▷ vt svegliare ▷ vi
svegliarsi

award [ə'wɔːd] *n* premio; (*Law*) risarcimento ▷ *vt* assegnare; (*Law: damages*) accordare

aware [ə'wɛər] *adj* **~ of** (*conscious*) conscio(-a) di; (*informed*) informato(-a) di; **to become ~ of** accorgersi di; **awareness** *n* consapevolezza

away [ə'weɪ] *adj, adv* via; lontano(-a); **two kilometres ~** a due chilometri di distanza; **two hours ~ by car** a due ore di distanza in macchina; **the holiday was two weeks ~** mancavano due settimane alle vacanze; **he's ~ for a week** è andato via per una settimana; **to take ~** togliere; **he was working/pedalling** *etc* **~** (*la particella indica la continuità e l'energia dell'azione*) lavorava/pedalava *etc* più che poteva; **to fade/wither** *etc* **~** (*la particella rinforza l'idea della diminuzione*)

awe [ɔː] *n* timore *m*; **awesome** *adj* imponente

awful ['ɔːfəl] *adj* terribile; **an ~ lot of** un mucchio di; **awfully** *adv* (*very*) terribilmente

awkward ['ɔːkwəd] *adj* (*clumsy*) goffo(-a); (*inconvenient*) scomodo(-a); (*embarrassing*) imbarazzante

awoke [ə'wəuk] *pt of* **awake**

awoken [ə'wəukn] *pp of* **awake**

axe [æks] (*US* **ax**) *n* scure *f* ▷ *vt* (*project etc*) abolire; (*jobs*) sopprimere

axle ['æksl] *n* (*also:* **~-tree**) asse *m*

ay(e) [aɪ] *excl* (*yes*) sì

azalea [ə'zeɪlɪə] *n* azalea

B [biː] *n* (*Mus*) si *m*

B.A. *n abbr* = **Bachelor of Arts**

baby ['beɪbɪ] *n* bambino(-a); **baby carriage** (*US*) *n* carrozzina; **baby-sit** *vi* fare il (*or* la) baby-sitter; **baby-sitter** *n* baby-sitter *m/f inv*; **baby wipe** *n* salvietta umidificata

bachelor ['bætʃələr] *n* scapolo; **B~ of Arts/ Science** ≈ laureato(-a) in lettere/scienze

back [bæk] *n* (*of person, horse*) dorso, schiena; (*as opposed to front*) dietro; (*of hand*) dorso; (*of train*) coda; (*of chair*) schienale *m*; (*of page*) rovescio; (*of book*) retro; (*Football*) difensore *m* ▷ *vt* (*candidate*) appoggiare; (*horse: at races*) puntare su; (*car*) guidare a marcia indietro ▷ *vi* indietreggiare; (*car etc*) fare marcia indietro ▷ *cpd* posteriore, di dietro; (*Aut: seat, wheels*) posteriore ▷ *adv* (*not forward*) indietro; (*returned*): **he's ~** è tornato; **he ran ~** tornò indietro di corsa; (*restitution*): **throw the ball ~** ritira la palla; **can I have it ~?** posso riaverlo?; (*again*): **he called ~** ha richiamato; **back down** *vi* fare marcia indietro; **back out** *vi* (*of promise*) tirarsi indietro; **back up** *vt* (*support*) appoggiare, sostenere; (*Comput*) fare una copia di riserva di; **backache** *n* mal *m* di schiena; **backbencher** (*BRIT*) *n* membro del Parlamento senza potere amministrativo;

backbone n spina dorsale; **back door** n porta sul retro; **backfire** vi (Aut) dar ritorni di fiamma; (plans) fallire; **backgammon** n tavola reale; **background** n sfondo; (of events) background m inv; (basic knowledge) base f; (experience) esperienza; **family background** ambiente m familiare; **backing** n (fig) appoggio; **backlog** n **backlog of work** lavoro arretrato; **backpack** n zaino; **backpacker** n chi viaggia con zaino e sacco a pelo; **backslash** n backslash m inv, barra obliqua inversa; **backstage** adv nel retroscena; **backstroke** n nuoto sul dorso; **backup** adj (train, plane) supplementare; (Comput) di riserva ▷ n (support) appoggio, sostegno; (also: **backup file**) file m inv di riserva; **backward** adj (movement) indietro inv; (person) tardivo(-a); (country) arretrato(-a); **backwards** adv indietro; (fall, walk) all'indietro; **backyard** n cortile m dietro la casa

bacon ['beɪkən] n pancetta

bacteria [bæk'tɪərɪə] npl batteri mpl

bad [bæd] adj cattivo(-a); (accident, injury) brutto(-a); (meat, food) andato(-a) a male; **his ~ leg** la sua gamba malata; **to go ~** andare a male

badge [bædʒ] n insegna; (of policeman) stemma m

badger ['bædʒə'] n tasso

badly ['bædlɪ] adv (work, dress etc) male; **~ wounded** gravemente ferito; **he needs it ~** ne ha un gran bisogno

bad-mannered [bæd'mænəd] adj maleducato(-a), sgarbato(-a)

badminton ['bædmɪntən] n badminton m

bad-tempered ['bæd'tɛmpəd] adj irritabile; di malumore

bag [bæg] n sacco; (handbag etc) borsa; **~s of** (inf: lots of) un sacco di; **baggage** n bagagli mpl; **baggage allowance** n franchigia f bagaglio inv; **baggage reclaim** n ritiro m bagaglio inv; **baggy** adj largo(-a), sformato(-a); **bagpipes** npl cornamusa

bail [beɪl] n cauzione f ▷ vt (prisoner: also: **grant ~ to**) concedere la libertà provvisoria su cauzione a; (boat: also: **~ out**) aggottare; **on ~** in libertà provvisoria su cauzione

bait [beɪt] n esca ▷ vt (hook) innescare; (trap) munire di esca; (fig) tormentare

bake [beɪk] vt cuocere al forno ▷ vi cuocersi al forno; **baked beans** [-bi:nz] npl fagioli mpl in salsa di pomodoro; **baked potato** n patata cotta al forno con la buccia; **baker** n fornaio(-a), panettiere(-a); **bakery** n panetteria;

baking n cottura (al forno); **baking powder** n lievito in polvere

balance ['bæləns] n equilibrio; (Comm: sum) bilancio; (remainder) resto; (scales) bilancia ▷ vt tenere in equilibrio; (budget) far quadrare; (account) pareggiare; (compensate) contrappesare; **~ of trade/ payments** bilancia commerciale/dei pagamenti; **balanced** adj (personality, diet) equilibrato(-a); **balance sheet** n bilancio

balcony ['bælkənɪ] n balcone m; (in theatre) balconata; **do you have a room with a ~?** avete una camera con balcone?

bald [bɔːld] adj calvo(-a); (tyre) liscio(-a)

Balearics [bælɪ'ærɪks] npl **the ~** le Baleari fpl

ball [bɔːl] n palla; (football) pallone m; (for golf) pallina; (of wool, string) gomitolo; (dance) ballo; **to play ~** (fig) stare al gioco

ballerina [bælə'riːnə] n ballerina

ballet ['bæleɪ] n balletto; **ballet dancer** n ballerino(-a) classico(-a)

balloon [bə'luːn] n pallone m

ballot ['bælət] n scrutinio

ballpoint (pen) ['bɔːlpɔɪnt(-)] n penna a sfera

ballroom ['bɔːlrum] n sala da ballo

Baltic ['bɔːltɪk] adj, n **the ~ Sea** il (mar) Baltico

bamboo [bæm'buː] n bambù m

ban [bæn] n interdizione f ▷ vt interdire

banana [bə'nɑːnə] n banana

band [bænd] n banda; (at a dance) orchestra; (Mil) fanfara

bandage ['bændɪdʒ] n benda, fascia

Band-Aid® ['bændeɪd] (us) n cerotto

B. & B. n abbr = **bed and breakfast**

bandit ['bændɪt] n bandito

bang [bæŋ] n (of door) lo sbattere; (of gun, blow) colpo ▷ vt battere (violentemente); (door) sbattere ▷ vi scoppiare; sbattere

Bangladesh [bɑːŋglə'dɛʃ] n Bangladesh m

bangle ['bæŋgl] n braccialetto

bangs [bæŋz] (us) npl (fringe) frangia, frangetta

banish ['bænɪʃ] vt bandire

banister(s) ['bænɪstə(z)] n(pl) ringhiera

banjo ['bændʒəu] (pl **banjoes** or **banjos**) n banjo m inv

bank [bæŋk] n banca, banco; (of river, lake) riva, sponda; (of earth) banco ▷ vi (Aviat) inclinarsi in virata; **bank on** vt fus contare su; **bank account** n conto in banca; **bank balance** n saldo; **a healthy bank balance** un solido conto in banca; **bank card** n carta f assegni inv; **bank charges** npl (BRIT) spese fpl bancarie; **banker** n banchiere m; **bank holiday** (BRIT) n giorno di festa; vedi nota nel riquadro; **banking**

n attività bancaria; professione *f* di banchiere; **bank manager** *n* direttore *m* di banca; **banknote** *n* banconota

● **BANK HOLIDAY**
●
● Una **bank holiday**, in Gran Bretagna,
● è una giornata in cui banche e molti
● negozi sono chiusi. Generalmente le
● **bank holidays** cadono di lunedì e molti
● ne approfittano per fare una breve
● vacanza fuori città.

bankrupt ['bæŋkrʌpt] *adj* fallito(-a); **to go ~** fallire; **bankruptcy** *n* fallimento
bank statement *n* estratto conto
banner ['bænə'] *n* striscione *m*
bannister(s) ['bænɪstə(z)] *n(pl) see* **banister(s)**
banquet ['bæŋkwɪt] *n* banchetto
baptism ['bæptɪzəm] *n* battesimo
baptize [bæp'taɪz] *vt* battezzare
bar [bɑː'] *n* (*place*) bar *m inv*; (*counter*) banco; (*rod*) barra; (*of window etc*) sbarra; (*of chocolate*) tavoletta; (*Mus*) battuta *f*; (*fig*) ostacolo; restrizione *f*; (*Law*) l'Ordine *m* degli avvocati; **behind ~s** (*prisoner*) dietro le sbarre; **~ none** senza eccezione ▷ *vt* (*road, window*) sbarrare; (*person*) escludere; (*activity*) interdire; **~ of soap** saponetta; **the B~** (*Law*) l'Ordine *m* degli avvocati; **behind ~s** (*prisoner*) dietro le sbarre; **~ none** senza eccezione
barbaric [bɑː'bærɪk] *adj* barbarico(-a)
barbecue ['bɑːbɪkjuː] *n* barbecue *m inv*
barbed wire ['bɑːbd-] *n* filo spinato
barber ['bɑːbə'] *n* barbiere *m*; **barber's (shop)** (*US* **barber (shop)**) *n* barbiere *m*
bar code *n* (*on goods*) codice *m* a barre
bare [beə'] *adj* nudo(-a) ▷ *vt* scoprire, denudare; (*teeth*) mostrare; **the ~ necessities** lo stretto necessario; **barefoot** *adj, adv* scalzo(-a); **barely** *adv* appena
bargain ['bɑːgɪn] *n* (*transaction*) contratto; (*good buy*) affare *m* ▷ *vi* trattare; **into the ~** per giunta; **bargain for** *vt fus* **he got more than he ~ed for** gli è andata peggio di quel che si aspettasse
barge [bɑːdʒ] *n* chiatta; **barge in** *vi* (*walk in*) piombare dentro; (*interrupt talk*) intromettersi a sproposito
bark [bɑːk] *n* (*of tree*) corteccia; (*of dog*) abbaio ▷ *vi* abbaiare
barley ['bɑːlɪ] *n* orzo
barmaid ['bɑːmeɪd] *n* cameriera al banco
barman ['bɑːmən] (*irreg*) *n* barista *m*
barn [bɑːn] *n* granaio
barometer [bə'rɒmɪtə'] *n* barometro
baron ['bærən] *n* barone *m*; **baroness** *n* baronessa

barracks ['bærəks] *npl* caserma
barrage ['bærɑːʒ] *n* (*Mil, dam*) sbarramento; (*fig*) fiume *m*
barrel ['bærəl] *n* barile *m*; (*of gun*) canna
barren ['bærən] *adj* sterile; (*soil*) arido(-a)
barrette [bə'rɛt] (*US*) *n* fermaglio per capelli
barricade [bærɪ'keɪd] *n* barricata
barrier ['bærɪə'] *n* barriera
barring ['bɑːrɪŋ] *prep* salvo
barrister ['bærɪstə'] (*BRIT*) *n* avvocato(-essa) (*con diritto di parlare davanti a tutte le corti*)
barrow ['bærəu] *n* (*cart*) carriola
bartender ['bɑːtɛndə'] (*US*) *n* barista *m*
base [beɪs] *n* base *f* ▷ *vt* **to ~ sth on** basare qc su ▷ *adj* vile
baseball ['beɪsbɔːl] *n* baseball *m*; **baseball cap** *n* berretto da baseball
basement ['beɪsmənt] *n* seminterrato; (*of shop*) interrato
bases[1] ['beɪsiːz] *npl of* **basis**
bases[2] ['beɪsiz] *npl of* **base**
bash [bæʃ] (*inf*) *vt* picchiare
basic ['beɪsɪk] *adj* rudimentale; essenziale; **basically** [-lɪ] *adv* fondamentalmente; sostanzialmente; **basics** *npl* **the basics** l'essenziale *m*
basil ['bæzl] *n* basilico
basin ['beɪsn] *n* (*vessel: also Geo*) bacino; (*also:* **wash~**) lavabo
basis ['beɪsɪs] (*pl* **bases**) *n* base *f*; **on a part-time ~** part-time; **on a trial ~** in prova
basket ['bɑːskɪt] *n* cesta; (*smaller*) cestino; (*with handle*) paniere *m*; **basketball** *n* pallacanestro *f*
bass [beɪs] *n* (*Mus*) basso
bastard ['bɑːstəd] *n* bastardo(-a); (*inf!*) stronzo (*!*)
bat [bæt] *n* pipistrello; (*for baseball etc*) mazza; (*BRIT: for table tennis*) racchetta ▷ *vt* **he didn't ~ an eyelid** non battè ciglio
batch [bætʃ] *n* (*of bread*) infornata; (*of papers*) cumulo
bath [bɑːθ] *n* bagno; (*bathtub*) vasca da bagno ▷ *vt* far fare il bagno a; **to have a ~** fare un bagno; *see also* **baths**
bathe [beɪð] *vi* fare il bagno ▷ *vt* (*wound*) lavare
bathing ['beɪðɪŋ] *n* bagni *mpl*; **bathing costume** (*US* **bathing suit**) *n* costume *m* da bagno
bath: **bathrobe** ['bɑːθrəub] *n* accappatoio; **bathroom** ['bɑːθrum] *n* stanza da bagno; **baths** [bɑːðz] *npl* bagni *mpl* pubblici; **bath towel** *n* asciugamano da bagno; **bathtub** *n* (*vasca da*) bagno
baton ['bætən] *n* (*Mus*) bacchetta;

(*Athletics*) testimone *m*; (*club*) manganello
batter ['bætə'] *vt* battere ▷ *n* pastetta;
battered *adj* (*hat*) sformato(-a); (*pan*)
ammaccato(-a)
battery ['bætərɪ] *n* batteria; (*of torch*) pila;
battery farming *n* allevamento in batteria
battle ['bætl] *n* battaglia ▷ *vi* battagliare,
lottare; **battlefield** *n* campo di battaglia
bay [beɪ] *n* (*of sea*) baia; **to hold sb at ~**
tenere qn a bada
bazaar [bə'zɑ:'] *n* bazar *m inv*; vendita di
beneficenza
BBC *n abbr* (= British Broadcasting
Corporation) rete nazionale di radiotelevisione
in Gran Bretagna

- **BBC**
-
-
- La **BBC** è l'azienda statale che fornisce
- il servizio radiofonico e televisivo in
- Gran Bretagna. Ha due reti televisive
- terrestri (BBC1 e BBC2), e cinque
- stazioni radiofoniche nazionali. Oggi
- la BBC ha anche diverse stazioni
- digitali radiofoniche e televisive. Da
- molti anni fornisce inoltre un servizio
- di intrattenimento e informazione
- internazionale, il "BBC World Service",
- trasmesso in tutto il mondo.

B.C. *adv abbr* (= before Christ) a.C.

◯ **KEYWORD**

be [bi:] (*pt* **was, were**, *pp* **been**) *aux vb* **1**
(with present participle: forming continuous
tenses): **what are you doing?** che fa?, che
sta facendo?; **they're coming tomorrow**
vengono domani; **I've been waiting for
her for hours** sono ore che l'aspetto
2 (with pp: forming passives) essere; **to be
killed** essere *or* venire ucciso(-a); **the box
had been opened** la scatola era stata
aperta; **the thief was nowhere to be
seen** il ladro non si trovava da nessuna
parte
3 (in tag questions): **it was fun, wasn't it?** è
stato divertente, no?; **he's good-looking,
isn't he?** è un bell'uomo, vero?; **she's
back, is she?** così è tornata, eh?
4 (+ to + infinitive): **the house is
to be sold** abbiamo *or* hanno *etc*
intenzione di vendere casa; **you're to
be congratulated for all your work**
dovremo farvi i complimenti per tutto il
vostro lavoro; **he's not to open it** non
deve aprirlo
▷ *vb + complement* **1** (*gen*) essere; **I'm
English** sono inglese; **I'm tired** sono

stanco(-a); **I'm hot/cold** ho caldo/freddo;
he's a doctor è medico; **2 and 2 are 4** 2
più 2 fa 4; **be careful!** sta attento(-a)!; **be
good** sii buono(-a)
2 (*of health*) stare; **how are you?** come
sta?; **he's very ill** sta molto male
3 (*of age*): **how old are you?** quanti anni
hai?; **I'm sixteen (years old)** ho sedici
anni
4 (*cost*) costare; **how much was the
meal?** quant'era *or* quanto costava il
pranzo?; **that'll be £5, please** (fa) 5
sterline, per favore
▷ *vi* **1** (*exist, occur etc*) essere, esistere; **the
best singer that ever was** il migliore
cantante mai esistito *or* di tutti tempi; **be
that as it may** comunque sia, sia come
sia; **so be it** sia pure, e sia
2 (*referring to place*) essere, trovarsi; **I won't
be here tomorrow** non ci sarò domani;
Edinburgh is in Scotland Edimburgo si
trova in Scozia
3 (*referring to movement*): **where have you
been?** dov'è stato?; **I've been to China**
sono stato in Cina
▷ *impers vb* **1** (*referring to time, distance*)
essere; **it's 5 o'clock** sono le 5; **it's the
28th of April** è il 28 aprile; **it's 10 km to
the village** di qui al paese sono 10 km
2 (*referring to the weather*) fare; **it's too
hot/cold** fa troppo caldo/freddo; **it's
windy** c'è vento
3 (*emphatic*): **it's me** sono io; **it was Maria
who paid the bill** è stata Maria che ha
pagato il conto

beach [bi:tʃ] *n* spiaggia ▷ *vt* tirare in secco
beacon ['bi:kən] *n* (*lighthouse*) faro;
(*marker*) segnale *m*
bead [bi:d] *n* perlina; **~s** *npl* (*necklace*)
collana
beak [bi:k] *n* becco
beam [bi:m] *n* trave *f*; (*of light*) raggio ▷ *vi*
brillare
bean [bi:n] *n* fagiolo; (*of coffee*) chicco;
runner ~ fagiolino; **beansprouts** *npl*
germogli *mpl* di soia
bear [bɛə'] (*pt* **bore**, *pp* **borne**) *n* orso ▷ *vt*
portare; (*endure*) sopportare; (*produce*)
generare ▷ *vi* **to ~ right/left** piegare a
destra/sinistra
beard [bɪəd] *n* barba
bearer ['bɛərə'] *n* portatore *m*
bearing ['bɛərɪŋ] *n* portamento;
(*connection*) rapporto
beast [bi:st] *n* bestia
beat [bi:t] (*pt* **beat**, *pp* **beaten**) *n* colpo;
(*of heart*) battito; (*Mus*) tempo; battuta;
(*of policeman*) giro ▷ *vt* battere; (*eggs,*

cream) sbattere ▷ *vi* battere; **off the ~en track** fuori mano; **~ it!** (*inf*) fila!, fuori dai piedi!; **beat up** *vt* (*person*) picchiare; (*eggs*) sbattere; **beating** *n* bastonata

beautiful ['bju:tiful] *adj* bello(-a); **beautifully** *adv* splendidamente

beauty ['bju:tɪ] *n* bellezza; **beauty parlour** [-'pɑ:lə*r*] (*us* **beauty parlor**) *n* salone *m* di bellezza; **beauty salon** *n* istituto di bellezza; **beauty spot** (*BRIT*) *n* (*Tourism*) luogo pittoresco

beaver ['bi:və*r*] *n* castoro

became [bɪ'keɪm] *pt of* **become**

because [bɪ'kɔz] *conj* perché; **~ of** a causa di

beckon ['bɛkən] *vt* (*also:* **~ to**) chiamare con un cenno

become [bɪ'kʌm] (*irreg: like* **come**) *vt* diventare; **to ~ fat/thin** ingrassarsi/dimagrire

bed [bɛd] *n* letto; (*of flowers*) aiuola; (*of coal, clay*) strato; **single/double ~** letto a una piazza/a due piazze *or* matrimoniale; **bed and breakfast** *n* (*place*) ≈ pensione *f* familiare; (*terms*) camera con colazione; *vedi nota nel riquadro*; **bedclothes** ['bɛdkləʊðz] *npl* biancheria e coperte *fpl* da letto; **bedding** *n* coperte e lenzuola *fpl*; **bed linen** *n* biancheria da letto; **bedroom** *n* camera da letto; **bedside** *n* **at sb's bedside** al capezzale di qn; **bedside lamp** *n* lampada da comodino; **bedside table** *n* comodino; **bedsit(ter)** (*BRIT*) *n* monolocale *m*; **bedspread** *n* copriletto; **bedtime** *n* **it's bedtime** è ora di andare a letto

● **BED AND BREAKFAST**
●
● I **bed and breakfasts**, anche **B & Bs**,
● sono piccole pensioni a conduzione
● familiare, più economiche rispetto agli
● alberghi, dove al mattino viene servita
● la tradizionale colazione all'inglese.

bee [bi:] *n* ape *f*

beech [bi:tʃ] *n* faggio

beef [bi:f] *n* manzo; **roast ~** arrosto di manzo; **beefburger** *n* hamburger *m inv*; **Beefeater** *n* guardia della Torre di Londra

been [bi:n] *pp of* **be**

beer [bɪə*r*] *n* birra; **beer garden** *n* (*BRIT*) giardino (*di pub*)

beet [bi:t] (*us*) *n* (*also:* **red ~**) barbabietola rossa

beetle ['bi:tl] *n* scarafaggio; coleottero

beetroot ['bi:tru:t] (*BRIT*) *n* barbabietola

before [bɪ'fɔ:*r*] *prep* (*in time*) prima di; (*in space*) davanti a ▷ *conj* prima che + *sub*;

prima di ▷ *adv* prima; **~ going** prima di andare; **~ she goes** prima che vada; **the week ~** la settimana prima; **I've seen it ~** l'ho già visto; **I've never seen it ~** è la prima volta che lo vedo; **beforehand** *adv* in anticipo

beg [bɛg] *vi* chiedere l'elemosina ▷ *vt* (*also:* **~ for**) chiedere in elemosina; (*favour*) chiedere; **to ~ sb to do** pregare qn di fare

began [bɪ'gæn] *pt of* **begin**

beggar ['bɛgə*r*] *n* mendicante *m/f*

begin [bɪ'gɪn] (*pt* **began**, *pp* **begun**) *vt*, *vi* cominciare; **to ~ doing** *or* **to do sth** incominciare *or* iniziare a fare qc; **beginner** *n* principiante *m/f*; **beginning** *n* inizio, principio

begun [bɪ'gʌn] *pp of* **begin**

behalf [bɪ'hɑ:f] *n* **on ~ of** per conto di; a nome di

behave [bɪ'heɪv] *vi* comportarsi; (*well: also:* **~ o.s.**) comportarsi bene; **behaviour** [bɪ'heɪvjə*r*] (*us* **behavior**) *n* comportamento, condotta

behind [bɪ'haɪnd] *prep* dietro; (*followed by pronoun*) dietro di; (*less advanced than*) indietro con ▷ *adv* dietro; (*leave, stay*) indietro ▷ *n* didietro; **to be ~ (schedule)** essere in ritardo rispetto al programma; **~ the scenes** (*fig*) dietro le quinte

beige [beɪʒ] *adj* beige *inv*

Beijing ['beɪ'dʒɪŋ] *n* Pechino *f*

being ['bi:ɪŋ] *n* essere *m*

belated [bɪ'leɪtɪd] *adj* tardo(-a)

belch [bɛltʃ] *vi* ruttare ▷ *vt* (*gen:* **belch out**: *smoke etc*) eruttare

Belgian ['bɛldʒən] *adj, n* belga *m/f*

Belgium ['bɛldʒəm] *n* Belgio

belief [bɪ'li:f] *n* (*opinion*) opinione *f*, convinzione *f*; (*trust, faith*) fede *f*

believe [bɪ'li:v] *vt, vi* credere; **to ~ in** (*God*) credere in; (*ghosts*) credere a; (*method*) avere fiducia in; **believer** *n* (*Rel*) credente *m/f*; (*in idea, activity*): **to be a believer in** credere in

bell [bɛl] *n* campana; (*small, on door, electric*) campanello

bellboy ['bɛlbɔɪ], (*us* **bellhop**) ['bɛlhɔp] *n* ragazzo d'albergo, fattorino d'albergo

bellow ['bɛləu] *vi* muggire

bell pepper (*esp us*) *n* peperone *m*

belly ['bɛlɪ] *n* pancia; **belly button** *n* ombelico

belong [bɪ'lɔŋ] *vi* **to ~ to** appartenere a; (*club etc*) essere socio di; **this book ~s here** questo libro va qui; **belongings** *npl* cose *fpl*, roba

beloved [bɪ'lʌvɪd] *adj* adorato(-a)

below [bɪ'ləu] *prep* sotto, al di sotto di ▷ *adv* sotto, di sotto; giù; **see ~** vedi sotto *or* oltre

belt [bɛlt] *n* cintura; (*Tech*) cinghia ▷ *vt*
(*thrash*) picchiare ▷ *vi* (*inf*) filarsela;
beltway (*us*) *n* (*Aut*: *ring road*)
circonvallazione *f*; (: *motorway*) autostrada

bemused [bɪ'mjuːzd] *adj* perplesso(-a),
stupito(-a)

bench [bɛntʃ] *n* panca; (*in workshop, Pol*)
banco; **the B~** (*Law*) la Corte

bend [bɛnd] (*pt, pp* **bent**) *vt* curvare; (*leg,
arm*) piegare ▷ *vi* curvarsi; piegarsi ▷ *n*
(*BRIT: in road*) curva; (*in pipe, river*) gomito;
bend down *vi* chinarsi; **bend over** *vi*
piegarsi

beneath [bɪ'niːθ] *prep* sotto, al di sotto di;
(*unworthy of*) indegno(-a) di ▷ *adv* sotto,
di sotto

beneficial [bɛnɪ'fɪʃəl] *adj* che fa bene;
vantaggioso(-a)

benefit ['bɛnɪfɪt] *n* beneficio, vantaggio;
(*allowance of money*) indennità *f* inv ▷ *vt*
far bene a ▷ *vi* **he'll ~ from it** ne trarrà
beneficio *or* profitto

benign [bɪ'naɪn] *adj* (*person, smile*)
benevolo(-a); (*Med*) benigno(-a)

bent [bɛnt] *pt, pp of* **bend** ▷ *n* inclinazione
f ▷ *adj* (*inf: dishonest*) losco(-a); **to be ~ on**
essere deciso(-a) a

bereaved [bɪ'riːvd] *n* **the ~** i familiari in
lutto

beret ['bɛreɪ] *n* berretto

Berlin [bəː'lɪn] *n* Berlino *f*

Bermuda [bəː'mjuːdə] *n* le Bermude

berry ['bɛrɪ] *n* bacca

berth [bəːθ] *n* (*bed*) cuccetta; (*for ship*)
ormeggio ▷ *vi* (*in harbour*) entrare in porto;
(*at anchor*) gettare l'ancora

beside [bɪ'saɪd] *prep* accanto a; **to be ~
o.s.** (**with anger**) essere fuori di sé (dalla
rabbia); **that's ~ the point** non c'entra;
besides [bɪ'saɪdz] *adv* inoltre, per di più
▷ *prep* oltre a; a parte

best [bɛst] *adj* migliore ▷ *adv* meglio; **the
~ part of** (*quantity*) la maggior parte di; **at
~** tutt'al più; **to make the ~ of sth** cavare
il meglio possibile da qc; **to do one's ~**
fare del proprio meglio; **to the ~ of my
knowledge** per quel che ne so; **to the ~ of
my ability** al massimo delle mie capacità;
best-before date *n* scadenza; **best
man** (*irreg*) *n* testimone *m* dello sposo;
bestseller *n* bestseller *m* inv

bet [bɛt] (*pt, pp* **bet** *or* **betted**) *n*
scommessa ▷ *vt, vi* scommettere; **to ~ sb
sth** scommettere qc con qn

betray [bɪ'treɪ] *vt* tradire

better ['bɛtəʳ] *adj* migliore ▷ *adv* meglio
▷ *vt* migliorare ▷ *n* **to get the ~ of** avere la
meglio su; **you had ~ do it** è meglio che lo

faccia; **he thought ~ of it** cambiò idea; **to
get ~** migliorare

betting ['bɛtɪŋ] *n* scommesse *fpl*; **betting
shop** (*BRIT*) *n* ufficio dell'allibratore

between [bɪ'twiːn] *prep* tra ▷ *adv* in
mezzo, nel mezzo

beverage ['bɛvərɪdʒ] *n* bevanda

beware [bɪ'wɛəʳ] *vt, vi* **to ~ (of)** stare
attento(-a) (a); **"~ of the dog"** "attenti
al cane"

bewildered [bɪ'wɪldəd] *adj*
sconcertato(-a), confuso(-a)

beyond [bɪ'jɔnd] *prep* (*in space*) oltre;
(*exceeding*) al di sopra di ▷ *adv* di là; **~
doubt** senza dubbio; **~ repair** irreparabile

bias ['baɪəs] *n* (*prejudice*) pregiudizio;
(*preference*) preferenza; **bias(s)ed** *adj*
parziale

bib [bɪb] *n* bavaglino

Bible ['baɪbl] *n* Bibbia

bicarbonate of soda [baɪ'kɑːbənɪt-] *n*
bicarbonato (di sodio)

biceps ['baɪsɛps] *n* bicipite *m*

bicycle ['baɪsɪkl] *n* bicicletta; **bicycle
pump** *n* pompa della bicicletta

bid [bɪd] (*pt* **bade** *or* **bid**, *pp* **bidden** *or* **bid**)
n offerta; (*attempt*) tentativo ▷ *vi* fare
un'offerta ▷ *vt* fare un'offerta di; **to ~ sb
good day** dire buon giorno a qn; **bidder** *n*
the highest bidder il maggior offerente

bidet ['biːdeɪ] *n* bidè *m* inv

big [bɪg] *adj* grande; grosso(-a); **Big
Apple** *n* vedi nota nel riquadro; **bigheaded**
['bɪg'hɛdɪd] *adj* presuntuoso(-a); **big toe**
n alluce *m*

● **BIG APPLE**
●
● Tutti sanno che **The Big Apple**, la
● Grande Mela, è New York ("apple"
● in gergo significa grande città), ma
● sicuramente i soprannomi di altre città
● americane non sono così conosciuti.
● Chicago è soprannominata "the Windy
● City" perché è ventosa, New Orleans
● si chiama "the Big Easy" per il modo di
● vivere tranquillo e rilassato dei suoi
● abitanti, e l'industria automobilistica
● ha fatto sì che Detroit fosse
● soprannominata "Motown".

bike [baɪk] *n* bici *f* inv; **bike lane** *n* pista
ciclabile

bikini [bɪ'kiːnɪ] *n* bikini *m* inv

bilateral [baɪ'lætərl] *adj* bilaterale

bilingual [baɪ'lɪŋgwəl] *adj* bilingue

bill [bɪl] *n* conto; (*Pol*) atto; (*us*: *banknote*)
banconota; (*of bird*) becco; (*of show*)
locandina; **can I have the ~, please** il

conto, per favore; **put it on my ~** lo metta
sul mio conto; **"post no ~s"** "divieto di
affissione"; **to fit** or **fill the ~** (fig) fare al
caso; **billboard** n tabellone m; **billfold**
['bɪlfəʊld] (US) n portafoglio
billiards ['bɪljədz] n biliardo
billion ['bɪljən] num (BRIT) bilione m; (US)
miliardo
bin [bɪn] n (for coal, rubbish) bidone m; (for
bread) cassetta; (dustbin) pattumiera; (litter
bin) cestino
bind [baɪnd] (pt, pp **bound**) vt legare;
(oblige) obbligare ▷ n (inf) scocciatura
binge [bɪndʒ] (inf) n **to go on a ~** fare
baldoria
bingo ['bɪŋgəʊ] n gioco simile alla tombola
binoculars [bɪ'nɔkjuləz] npl binocolo
bio... [baɪə'...] prefix; **biochemistry**
n biochimica; **biodegradable** adj
biodegradabile; **biography** [baɪ'ɔgrəfɪ]
n biografia; **biological** adj biologico(-a);
biology [baɪ'ɔlədʒɪ] n biologia
birch [bəːtʃ] n betulla
bird [bəːd] n uccello; (BRIT: inf: girl)
bambola; **bird of prey** n (uccello) rapace
m; **birdwatching** n birdwatching m
Biro® ['baɪrəʊ] n biro® f inv
birth [bəːθ] n nascita; **to give ~ to**
partorire; **birth certificate** n certificato
di nascita; **birth control** n controllo
delle nascite; contraccezione f; **birthday**
n compleanno ▷ cpd di compleanno;
birthmark n voglia; **birthplace** n luogo
di nascita
biscuit ['bɪskɪt] (BRIT) n biscotto
bishop ['bɪʃəp] n vescovo
bistro ['biːstrəʊ] n bistrò m inv
bit [bɪt] pt of **bite** ▷ n pezzo; (Comput) bit
m inv; (of horse) morso; **a ~ of** un po' di; **a ~
mad** un po' matto; **~ by ~** a poco a poco
bitch [bɪtʃ] n (dog) cagna; (inf!) vacca
bite [baɪt] (pt, pp **bit, bitten**) vt, vi mordere;
(insect) pungere ▷ n morso; (insect bite)
puntura; (mouthful) boccone m; **let's have
a ~ to eat** mangiamo un boccone; **to ~
one's nails** mangiarsi le unghie
bitten ['bɪtn] pp of **bite**
bitter ['bɪtə'] adj amaro(-a); (wind, criticism)
pungente ▷ n (BRIT: beer) birra amara
bizarre [bɪ'zɑː'] adj bizzarro(-a)
black [blæk] adj nero(-a) ▷ n nero;
(person): **B~** negro(-a) ▷ vt (BRIT Industry)
boicottare; **to give sb a ~ eye** fare un
occhio nero a qn; (bank account)
in attivo; **black out** vi (faint) svenire;
blackberry n mora; **blackbird** n merlo;
blackboard n lavagna; **black coffee** n
caffè m inv nero; **blackcurrant** n ribes
m inv; **black ice** n strato trasparente

di ghiaccio; **blackmail** n ricatto ▷ vt
ricattare; **black market** n mercato nero;
blackout n oscuramento; (TV, Radio)
interruzione f delle trasmissioni; (fainting)
svenimento; **black pepper** n pepe m nero;
black pudding n sanguinaccio; **Black
Sea** n **the Black Sea** il Mar Nero
bladder ['blædə'] n vescica
blade [bleɪd] n lama; (of oar) pala; **~ of
grass** filo d'erba
blame [bleɪm] n colpa ▷ vt **to ~ sb/sth for
sth** dare la colpa di qc a qn/qc; **who's to ~?**
chi è colpevole?
bland [blænd] adj mite; (taste) blando(-a)
blank [blæŋk] adj bianco(-a); (look)
distratto(-a) ▷ n spazio vuoto; (cartridge)
cartuccia a salve
blanket ['blæŋkɪt] n coperta
blast [blɑːst] n (of wind) raffica; (of bomb
etc) esplosione f ▷ vt far saltare
blatant ['bleɪtənt] adj flagrante
blaze [bleɪz] n (fire) incendio; (fig)
vampata; splendore m ▷ vi (fire) ardere,
fiammeggiare; (guns) sparare senza sosta;
(fig: eyes) ardere ▷ vt **to ~ a trail** (fig)
tracciare una via nuova; **in a ~ of publicity**
circondato da grande pubblicità
blazer ['bleɪzə'] n blazer m inv
bleach [bliːtʃ] n (also: **household ~**)
varechina ▷ vt (material) candeggiare;
bleachers (US) npl (Sport) posti mpl di
gradinata
bleak [bliːk] adj tetro(-a)
bled [blɛd] pt, pp of **bleed**
bleed [bliːd] (pt, pp **bled**) vi sanguinare;
my nose is ~ing mi viene fuori sangue
dal naso
blemish ['blɛmɪʃ] n macchia
blend [blɛnd] n miscela ▷ vt mescolare
▷ vi (colours etc: also: **~ in**) armonizzare;
blender n (Culin) frullatore m
bless [blɛs] (pt, pp **blessed** or **blest**) vt
benedire; **~ you!** (after sneeze) salute!;
blessing n benedizione f; fortuna
blew [bluː] pt of **blow**
blight [blaɪt] vt (hopes etc) deludere; (life)
rovinare
blind [blaɪnd] adj cieco(-a) ▷ n (for window)
avvolgibile m; (Venetian blind) veneziana
▷ vt accecare; **the ~** npl i ciechi; **blind
alley** n vicolo cieco; **blindfold** n benda
▷ adj, adv bendato(-a) ▷ vt bendare gli
occhi a
blink [blɪŋk] vi battere gli occhi; (light)
lampeggiare
bliss [blɪs] n estasi f
blister ['blɪstə'] n (on skin) vescica; (on
paintwork) bolla ▷ vi (paint) coprirsi di bolle
blizzard ['blɪzəd] n bufera di neve

bloated ['bləutɪd] *adj* gonfio(-a)

blob [blɔb] *n* (*drop*) goccia; (*stain, spot*) macchia

block [blɔk] *n* blocco; (*in pipes*) ingombro; (*toy*) cubo; (*of buildings*) isolato ▷ *vt* bloccare; **the sink is ~ed** il lavandino è otturato; **block up** *vt* bloccare; (*pipe*) ingorgare, intasare; **blockade** [-'keɪd] *n* blocco; **blockage** *n* ostacolo; **blockbuster** *n* (*film, book*) grande successo; **block capitals** *npl* stampatello; **block letters** *npl* stampatello

bloke [bləuk] (BRIT: *inf*) *n* tizio

blond(e) [blɔnd] *adj, n* biondo(-a)

blood [blʌd] *n* sangue *m*; **blood donor** *n* donatore(-trice) di sangue; **blood group** *n* gruppo sanguigno; **blood poisoning** *n* setticemia; **blood pressure** *n* pressione *f* sanguigna; **bloodshed** *n* spargimento di sangue; **bloodshot** *adj* **bloodshot eyes** occhi iniettati di sangue; **bloodstream** *n* flusso del sangue; **blood test** *n* analisi *f inv* del sangue; **blood transfusion** *n* trasfusione *f* di sangue; **blood type** *n* gruppo sanguigno; **blood vessel** *n* vaso sanguigno; **bloody** *adj* (*fight*) sanguinoso(-a); (*nose*) sanguinante; (BRIT: *inf!*): **this bloody ...** questo maledetto ...; **bloody awful/good** (*inf!*) veramente terribile/forte

bloom [blu:m] *n* fiore *m* ▷ *vi* (*tree*) essere in fiore; (*flower*) aprirsi

blossom ['blɔsəm] *n* fiore *m*; (*with pl sense*) fiori *mpl* ▷ *vi* essere in fiore

blot [blɔt] *n* macchia ▷ *vt* macchiare

blouse [blauz] *n* (*feminine garment*) camicetta

blow [bləu] (*pt* **blew**, *pp* **blown**) *n* colpo ▷ *vi* soffiare ▷ *vt* (*fuse*) far saltare; (*wind*) spingere; (*instrument*) suonare; **to ~ one's nose** soffiarsi il naso; **to ~ a whistle** fischiare; **blow away** *vt* portare via; **blow out** *vi* scoppiare; **blow up** *vi* saltare in aria ▷ *vt* far saltare in aria; (*tyre*) gonfiare; (*Phot*) ingrandire; **blow-dry** *n* messa in piega a fôhn

blown [bləun] *pp of* **blow**

blue [blu:] *adj* azzurro(-a); (*depressed*) giù *inv*; **~ film/joke** film/barzelletta pornografico(-a); **out of the ~** (*fig*) all'improvviso; **bluebell** *n* giacinto dei boschi; **blueberry** *n* mirtillo; **blue cheese** *n* formaggio tipo gorgonzola; **blues** *npl* **the blues** (*Mus*) il blues; **to have the blues** (*inf: feeling*) essere a terra; **bluetit** *n* cinciarella

bluff [blʌf] *vi* bluffare ▷ *n* bluff *m inv* ▷ *adj* (*person*) brusco(-a); **to call sb's ~** mettere alla prova il bluff di qn

blunder ['blʌndə'] *n* abbaglio ▷ *vi* prendere un abbaglio

blunt [blʌnt] *adj* smussato(-a); spuntato(-a); (*person*) brusco(-a)

blur [blə:'] *n* forma indistinta ▷ *vt* offuscare; **blurred** *adj* (*photo*) mosso(-a); (*TV*) sfuocato(-a)

blush [blʌʃ] *vi* arrossire ▷ *n* rossore *m*; **blusher** *n* fard *m inv*

board [bɔːd] *n* tavola; (*on wall*) tabellone *m*; (*committee*) consiglio, comitato; (*in firm*) consiglio d'amministrazione; (*Naut, Aviat*): **on ~** a bordo ▷ *vt* (*ship*) salire a bordo di; (*train*) salire su; **full ~** (BRIT) pensione completa; **half ~** (BRIT) mezza pensione; **~ and lodging** vitto e alloggio; **which goes by the ~** (*fig*) che viene abbandonato; **board game** *n* gioco da tavolo; **boarding card** *n* = **boarding pass**; **boarding pass** *n* (*Aviat, Naut*) carta d'imbarco; **boarding school** *n* collegio; **board room** *n* sala del consiglio

boast [bəust] *vi* **to ~ (about** *or* **of)** vantarsi (di)

boat [bəut] *n* nave *f*; (*small*) barca

bob [bɔb] *vi* (*boat, cork on water: also*: **~ up and down**) andare su e giù

bobby pin ['bɔbɪ-] (US) *n* fermaglio per capelli

body ['bɔdɪ] *n* corpo; (*of car*) carrozzeria; (*of plane*) fusoliera; (*fig: group*) gruppo; (: *organization*) organizzazione *f*; (: *quantity*) quantità *f inv*; **body-building** *n* culturismo; **bodyguard** *n* guardia del corpo; **bodywork** *n* carrozzeria

bog [bɔg] *n* palude *f* ▷ *vt* **to get ~ged down** (*fig*) impantanarsi

bogus ['bəugəs] *adj* falso(-a); finto(-a)

boil [bɔɪl] *vt, vi* bollire ▷ *n* (*Med*) foruncolo; **to come to the** (BRIT) *or* **a** (US) **~** raggiungere l'ebollizione; **boil over** *vi* traboccare (bollendo); **boiled egg** *n* uovo alla coque; **boiled potatoes** *npl* patate *fpl* bollite *or* lesse; **boiler** *n* caldaia; **boiling** *adj* bollente; **I'm boiling (hot)** (*inf*) sto morendo di caldo; **boiling point** *n* punto di ebollizione

bold [bəuld] *adj* audace; (*child*) impudente; (*colour*) deciso(-a)

Bolivia [bə'lɪvɪə] *n* Bolivia

Bolivian [bə'lɪvɪən] *adj, n* boliviano(-a)

bollard ['bɔləd] (BRIT) *n* (*Aut*) colonnina luminosa

bolt [bəult] *n* chiavistello; (*with nut*) bullone *m* ▷ *adv* **~ upright** diritto(-a) come un fuso ▷ *vt* serrare; (*also*: **~ together**) imbullonare; (*food*) mangiare in fretta ▷ *vi* scappare via

bomb [bɔm] *n* bomba ▷ *vt* bombardare;

bombard [bɔmˈbɑːd] vt bombardare;
bomber n (Aviat) bombardiere m; **bomb
scare** n stato di allarme (per sospetta
presenza di una bomba)
bond [bɔnd] n legame m; (binding promise,
Finance) obbligazione f; (Comm): **in ~** in
attesa di sdoganamento
bone [bəun] n osso; (of fish) spina, lisca ▷ vt
disossare; togliere le spine a
bonfire [ˈbɔnfaɪəʳ] n falò m inv
bonnet [ˈbɔnɪt] n cuffia; (BRIT: of car)
cofano
bonus [ˈbəunəs] n premio; (fig) sovrappiù
m inv
boo [buː] excl ba! ▷ vt fischiare
book [buk] n libro; (of stamps etc)
blocchetto ▷ vt (ticket, seat, room)
prenotare; (driver) multare; (football
player) ammonire; **~s** npl (Comm) conti
mpl; **I'd like to ~ a double room** vorrei
prenotare una camera doppia; **I ~ed a
table in the name of ...** ho prenotato un
tavolo al nome di...; **book in** vi (BRIT: at
hotel) prendere una càmera; **book up** vt
riservare, prenotare; **the hotel is ~ed up**
l'albergo è al completo; **all seats are ~ed
up** è tutto esaurito; **bookcase** n scaffale
m; **booking** n (BRIT) prenotazione f; **I
confirmed my booking by fax/e-mail**
ho confermato la mia prenotazione
tramite fax/e-mail; **booking office** (BRIT)
n (Rail) biglietteria; (Theatre) botteghino;
book-keeping n contabilità; **booklet**
n libricino; **bookmaker** n allibratore m;
bookmark (also Comput) n segnalibro
▷ vt (Comput) mettere un segnalibro a;
(Internet Explorer) aggiungere a "Preferiti";
bookseller n libraio; **bookshelf** n
mensola (per libri); **bookshop, bookstore**
n libreria
boom [buːm] n (noise) rimbombo; (in prices
etc) boom m inv ▷ vi rimbombare; andare
a gonfie vele
boost [buːst] n spinta ▷ vt spingere
boot [buːt] n stivale m; (for hiking) scarpone
m da montagna; (for football etc) scarpa;
(BRIT: of car) portabagagli m inv ▷ vt
(Comput) inizializzare; **to ~** (in addition) per
giunta, in più
booth [buːð] n cabina; (at fair) baraccone
m
booze [buːz] (inf) n alcool m
border [ˈbɔːdəʳ] n orlo; margine m; (of
a country) frontiera; (for flowers) aiuola
(laterale) ▷ vt (road) costeggiare; (another
country: also: **~ on**) confinare con; **the B~s**
la zona di confine tra l'Inghilterra e la Scozia;
borderline n (fig): **on the borderline**
incerto(-a)

bore [bɔːʳ] pt of **bear** ▷ vt (hole etc)
scavare; (person) annoiare ▷ n (person)
seccatore(-trice); (of gun) calibro; **bored**
adj annoiato(-a); **to be bored** annoiarsi;
he's bored to tears or **to death** or **stiff** è
annoiato a morte; **boredom** n noia
boring [ˈbɔːrɪŋ] adj noioso(-a)
born [bɔːn] adj **to be ~** nascere; **I was ~ in
1960** sono nato nel 1960
borne [bɔːn] pp of **bear**
borough [ˈbʌrə] n comune m
borrow [ˈbɔrəu] vt **to ~ sth (from sb)**
prendere in prestito qc (da qn)
Bosnia(-Herzegovina) [ˈbɔznɪəˈhɜːzəˈgə
uviːnə)] n Bosnia-Erzegovina; **Bosnian**
[ˈbɔznɪən] n, adj bosniaco(-a) m/f
bosom [ˈbuzəm] n petto; (fig) seno
boss [bɔs] n capo ▷ vt comandare; **bossy**
adj prepotente
both [bəuθ] adj entrambi(-e), tutt'e due
▷ pron: **~ of them** entrambi(-e); **~ of us
went, we ~ went** ci siamo andati tutt'e
due ▷ adv **they sell ~ meat and poultry**
vendono insieme la carne ed il pollame
bother [ˈbɔðəʳ] vt (worry) preoccupare;
(annoy) infastidire ▷ vi (also: **~ o.s.**)
preoccuparsi ▷ n **it is a ~ to have to do** è
una seccatura dover fare; **it was no ~** non
c'era problema; **to ~ doing sth** darsi la
pena di fare qc
bottle [ˈbɔtl] n bottiglia; (baby's) biberon
m inv ▷ vt imbottigliare; **bottle bank** n
contenitore m per la raccolta del vetro;
bottle-opener n apribottiglie m inv
bottom [ˈbɔtəm] n fondo; (buttocks) sedere
m ▷ adj più basso(-a); ultimo(-a); **at the ~
of** in fondo a
bought [bɔːt] pt, pp of **buy**
boulder [ˈbəuldəʳ] n masso (tondeggiante)
bounce [bauns] vi (ball) rimbalzare;
(cheque) essere restituito(-a) ▷ vt far
rimbalzare ▷ n (rebound) rimbalzo;
bouncer (inf) n buttafuori m inv
bound [baund] pt, pp of **bind** ▷ n (gen pl)
limite m; (leap) salto ▷ vi saltare ▷ vt (limit)
delimitare ▷ adj: **~ by law** obbligato(-a) per
legge; **to be ~ to do sth** (obliged) essere
costretto(-a) a fare qc; **he's ~ to fail** (likely)
fallirà di certo; **~ for** diretto(-a) a; **out of ~s**
il cui accesso è vietato
boundary [ˈbaundrɪ] n confine m
bouquet [ˈbukeɪ] n bouquet m inv
bourbon [ˈbuəbən] (US) n (also: **~ whiskey**)
bourbon m inv
bout [baut] n periodo; (of malaria etc)
attacco; (Boxing etc) incontro
boutique [buːˈtiːk] n boutique f inv
bow¹ [bəu] n nodo; (weapon) arco; (Mus)
archetto

bow² [bau] n (with body) inchino; (Naut: also: ~s) prua ▷ vi inchinarsi; (yield): **to ~ to** or **before** sottomettersi a

bowels ['bauəlz] npl intestini mpl; (fig) viscere fpl

bowl [bəul] n (for eating) scodella; (for washing) bacino; (ball) boccia ▷ vi (Cricket) servire (la palla); **bowler** ['bəulər] n (Cricket, Baseball) lanciatore m; (BRIT: also: **bowler hat**) bombetta; **bowling** ['bə ulɪŋ] n (game) gioco delle bocce; **bowling alley** n pista da bowling; **bowling green** n campo di bocce; **bowls** [bəulz] n gioco delle bocce

bow tie n cravatta a farfalla

box [bɔks] n scatola; (also: **cardboard ~**) cartone m; (Theatre) palco ▷ vt inscatolare ▷ vi fare del pugilato; **boxer** n (person) pugile m; **boxer shorts** ['bɔksəfɔ:ts] pl n boxer; **a pair of boxer shorts** un paio di boxer; **boxing** n (Sport) pugilato; **Boxing Day** (BRIT) n ≈ Santo Stefano; vedi nota nel riquadro; **boxing gloves** npl guantoni mpl da pugile; **boxing ring** n ring m inv; **box office** n biglietteria

● **BOXING DAY**
●
● Il **Boxing Day** è un giorno di festa e
● cade in genere il 26 dicembre. Prende
● il nome dalla tradizionale usanza di
● donare pacchi regalo natalizi, chiamati
● "Christmas boxes", a fornitori e
● dipendenti.

boy [bɔɪ] n ragazzo

boycott ['bɔɪkɔt] n boicottaggio ▷ vt boicottare

boyfriend ['bɔɪfrɛnd] n ragazzo

bra [brɑ:] n reggipetto, reggiseno

brace [breɪs] n (on teeth) apparecchio correttore; (tool) trapano ▷ vt rinforzare, sostenere; **~s** (BRIT) npl (Dress) bretelle fpl; **to ~ o.s.** (also fig) tenersi forte

bracelet ['breɪslɪt] n braccialetto

bracket ['brækɪt] n (Tech) mensola; (group) gruppo; (Typ) parentesi f inv ▷ vt mettere fra parentesi

brag [bræg] vi vantarsi

braid [breɪd] n (trimming) passamano; (of hair) treccia

brain [breɪn] n cervello; **~s** npl (intelligence) cervella fpl; **he's got ~s** è intelligente

braise [breɪz] vt brasare

brake [breɪk] n (on vehicle) freno ▷ vi frenare; **brake light** n (fanalino dello) stop m inv

bran [bræn] n crusca

branch [brɑ:ntʃ] n ramo; (Comm)

succursale f; **branch off** vi diramarsi; **branch out** vi (fig) intraprendere una nuova attività

brand [brænd] n marca; (fig) tipo ▷ vt (cattle) marcare (a ferro rovente); **brand name** n marca; **brand-new** adj nuovo(-a) di zecca

brandy ['brændɪ] n brandy m inv

brash [bræʃ] adj sfacciato(-a)

brass [brɑ:s] n ottone m; **the ~** (Mus) gli ottoni; **brass band** n fanfara

brat [bræt] (pej) n marmocchio, monello(-a)

brave [breɪv] adj coraggioso(-a) ▷ vt affrontare; **bravery** n coraggio

brawl [brɔ:l] n rissa

Brazil [brə'zɪl] n Brasile m; **Brazilian** adj, n brasiliano(-a)

breach [bri:tʃ] vt aprire una breccia in ▷ n (gap) breccia, varco; (breaking): **~ of contract** rottura di contratto; **~ of the peace** violazione f dell'ordine pubblico

bread [brɛd] n pane m; **breadbin** n cassetta f portapane inv; **breadbox** (US) n cassetta f portapane inv; **breadcrumbs** npl briciole fpl; (Culin) pangrattato

breadth [brɛtθ] n larghezza; (fig: of knowledge etc) ampiezza

break [breɪk] (pt **broke**, pp **broken**) vt rompere; (law) violare; (record) battere ▷ vi rompersi; (storm) scoppiare; (weather) cambiare; (dawn) spuntare; (news) saltare fuori ▷ n (gap) breccia; (fracture) rottura; (rest, also Scol) intervallo; (: short) pausa; (chance) possibilità f inv; **to ~ one's leg** etc rompersi la gamba ecc; **to ~ the news to sb** comunicare per primo la notizia a qn; **to ~ even** coprire le spese; **to ~ free** or **loose** spezzare i legami; **to ~ open** (door etc) sfondare; **break down** vt (figures, data) analizzare ▷ vi (person) avere un esaurimento (nervoso); (Aut) guastarsi; **my car has broken down** mi si è rotta la macchina; **break in** vt (horse etc) domare ▷ vi (burglar) fare irruzione; (interrupt) interrompere; **break into** vt fus (house) fare irruzione in; **break off** vi (speaker) interrompersi; (branch) troncarsi; **break out** vi evadere; (war, fight) scoppiare; **to ~ out in spots** coprirsi di macchie; **break up** vi (ship) sfondarsi; (meeting) sciogliersi; (crowd) disperdersi; (marriage) andare a pezzi; (Scol) chiudere ▷ vt fare a pezzi, spaccare; (fight etc) interrompere, far cessare; **breakdown** n (Aut) guasto; (in communications) interruzione f; (of marriage) rottura; (Med: also: **nervous breakdown**) esaurimento nervoso; (of statistics) resoconto; **breakdown truck,**

breakdown van n carro m attrezzi inv
breakfast ['brɛkfəst] n colazione f; **what time is ~?** a che ora è servita la colazione?
break: **break-in** n irruzione f;
breakthrough n (fig) passo avanti
breast [brɛst] n (of woman) seno; (chest, Culin) petto; **breast-feed** (irreg: like **feed**) vt, vi allattare (al seno); **breast-stroke** n nuoto a rana
breath [brɛθ] n respiro; **out of ~** senza fiato
Breathalyser® ['brɛθəlaɪzə'] (BRIT) n alcoltest m inv
breathe [bri:ð] vt, vi respirare; **breathe in** vt respirare ▷ vi respirare; **breathe out** vt, vi espirare; **breathing** n respiro, respirazione f
breath: **breathless** ['brɛθlɪs] adj senza fiato; **breathtaking** ['brɛθteɪkɪŋ] adj mozzafiato inv; **breath test** n = prova del palloncino
bred [brɛd] pt, pp of **breed**
breed [bri:d] (pt, pp **bred**) vt allevare ▷ vi riprodursi ▷ n razza; (type, class) varietà f inv
breeze [bri:z] n brezza
breezy ['bri:zɪ] adj allegro(-a), ventilato(-a)
brew [bru:] vt (tea) fare un infuso di; (beer) fare ▷ vi (storm, fig: trouble etc) prepararsi; **brewery** n fabbrica di birra
bribe [braɪb] n bustarella ▷ vt comprare; **bribery** n corruzione f
bric-a-brac ['brɪkəbræk] n bric-a-brac m
brick [brɪk] n mattone m; **bricklayer** n muratore m
bride [braɪd] n sposa; **bridegroom** n sposo; **bridesmaid** n damigella d'onore
bridge [brɪdʒ] n ponte m; (Naut) ponte di comando; (of nose) dorso; (Cards) bridge m inv ▷ vt (fig: gap) colmare
bridle ['braɪdl] n briglia
brief [bri:f] adj breve ▷ n (Law) comparsa; (gen) istruzioni fpl ▷ vt mettere al corrente; **~s** npl (underwear) mutande fpl; **briefcase** n cartella; **briefing** n briefing m inv; **briefly** adv (glance) di sfuggita; (explain, say) brevemente
brigadier [brɪgə'dɪə'] n generale m di brigata
bright [braɪt] adj luminoso(-a); (clever) sveglio(-a); (lively) vivace
brilliant ['brɪljənt] adj brillante; (light, smile) radioso(-a); (inf) splendido(-a)
brim [brɪm] n orlo
brine [braɪn] n (Culin) salamoia
bring [brɪŋ] (pt, pp **brought**) vt portare; **bring about** vt causare; **bring back** vt riportare; **bring down** vt portare giù; abbattere; **bring in** vt (person)

fare entrare; (object) portare; (Pal: bill) presentare; (: legislation) introdurre; (Law: verdict) emettere; (produce: income) rendere; **bring on** vt (illness, attack) causare, provocare; (player, substitute) far scendere in campo; **bring out** vt tirar fuori; (meaning) mettere in evidenza; (book, album) far uscire; **bring up** vt (carry up) portare su; (child) allevare; (question) introdurre; (food: vomit) rimettere, rigurgitare
brink [brɪŋk] n orlo
brisk [brɪsk] adj (manner) spiccio(-a); (trade) vivace; (pace) svelto(-a)
bristle ['brɪsl] n setola ▷ vi rizzarsi; **bristling with** irto(-a) di
Brit [brɪt] n abbr (inf: = British person) britannico(-a)
Britain ['brɪtən] n (also: **Great ~**) Gran Bretagna
British ['brɪtɪʃ] adj britannico(-a); **British Isles** npl Isole Britanniche
Briton ['brɪtən] n britannico(-a)
brittle ['brɪtl] adj fragile
broad [brɔ:d] adj largo(-a); (distinction) generale; (accent) spiccato(-a); **in ~ daylight** in pieno giorno; **broadband** adj (Comput) a banda larga ▷ n banda larga; **broad bean** n fava; **broadcast** (pt, pp **broadcast**) n trasmissione f ▷ vt trasmettere per radio (or per televisione) ▷ vi fare una trasmissione; **broaden** vt allargare ▷ vi allargarsi; **broadly** adv (fig) in generale; **broad-minded** adj di mente aperta
broccoli ['brɔkəlɪ] n broccoli mpl
brochure ['brəʊʃjʊə'] n dépliant m inv
broil [brɔɪl] vt cuocere a fuoco vivo
broiler ['brɔɪlə'] (US) n (grill) griglia
broke [brəʊk] pt of **break** ▷ adj (inf) squattrinato(-a)
broken ['brəʊkn] pp of **break** ▷ adj rotto(-a); **a ~ leg** una gamba rotta; **in ~ English** in un inglese stentato
broker ['brəʊkə'] n agente m
bronchitis [brɔŋ'kaɪtɪs] n bronchite f
bronze [brɔnz] n bronzo
brooch [brəʊtʃ] n spilla
brood [bru:d] n covata ▷ vi (person) rimuginare
broom [brʊm] n scopa; (Bot) ginestra
Bros. abbr (= Brothers) F.lli
broth [brɔθ] n brodo
brothel ['brɔθl] n bordello
brother ['brʌðə'] n fratello; **brother-in-law** n cognato
brought [brɔ:t] pt, pp of **bring**
brow [braʊ] n fronte f; (rare, gen: eyebrow) sopracciglio; (of hill) cima

brown [braun] *adj* bruno(-a), marrone; (*tanned*) abbronzato(-a) ▷ *n* (*colour*) color *m* bruno *or* marrone ▷ *vt* (*Culin*) rosolare; **brown bread** *n* pane *m* integrale, pane nero

Brownie ['brauni] *n* giovane esploratrice *f*

brown rice *n* riso greggio

brown sugar *n* zucchero greggio

browse [brauz] *vi* (*among books*) curiosare fra i libri; **to ~ through a book** sfogliare un libro; **browser** *n* (*Comput*) browser *m inv*

bruise [bru:z] *n* (*on person*) livido ▷ *vt* farsi un livido a

brunette [bru:'nɛt] *n* bruna

brush [brʌʃ] *n* spazzola; (*for painting, shaving*) pennello; (*quarrel*) schermaglia ▷ *vt* spazzolare; (*also*: **~ against**) sfiorare

Brussels ['brʌslz] *n* Bruxelles *f*

Brussels sprout [spraut] *n* cavolo di Bruxelles

brutal ['bru:tl] *adj* brutale

B.Sc. *n abbr* (*Univ*) = **Bachelor of Science**

BSE *n abbr* (= *bovine spongiform encephalopathy*) encefalite *f* bovina spongiforme

bubble ['bʌbl] *n* bolla ▷ *vi* ribollire; (*sparkle: fig*) essere effervescente; **bubble bath** *n* bagnoschiuma *m inv*; **bubble gum** *n* gomma americana

buck [bʌk] *n* maschio (*di camoscio, caprone, coniglio ecc*); (*us: inf*) dollaro ▷ *vi* sgroppare; **to pass the ~ to sb** scaricare (su di qn) la propria responsabilità

bucket ['bʌkɪt] *n* secchio

buckle ['bʌkl] *n* fibbia ▷ *vt* allacciare ▷ *vi* (*wheel etc*) piegarsi

bud [bʌd] *n* gemma; (*of flower*) bocciolo ▷ *vi* germogliare; (*flower*) sbocciare

Buddhism ['budɪzəm] *n* buddismo

Buddhist ['budɪst] *adj, n* buddista (*m/f*)

buddy ['bʌdɪ] (*us*) *n* compagno

budge [bʌdʒ] *vt* scostare; (*fig*) smuovere ▷ *vi* spostarsi; smuoversi

budgerigar ['bʌdʒərɪgɑ:ʳ] *n* pappagallino

budget ['bʌdʒɪt] *n* bilancio preventivo ▷ *vi* **to ~ for sth** fare il bilancio per qc

budgie ['bʌdʒɪ] *n* = **budgerigar**

buff [bʌf] *adj* color camoscio ▷ *n* (*inf: enthusiast*) appassionato(-a)

buffalo ['bʌfələu] (*pl* **buffalo** *or* **buffaloes**) *n* bufalo; (*us*) bisonte *m*

buffer ['bʌfəʳ] *n* respingente *m*; (*Comput*) memoria tampone, buffer *m inv*

buffet¹ ['bʌfɪt] *vt* sferzare

buffet² ['bufeɪ] *n* (*food*, BRIT: *bar*) buffet *m inv*; **buffet car** *n* (*Rail*) ≈ servizio ristoro

bug [bʌg] *n* (*esp us: insect*) insetto; (*Comput, fig: germ*) virus *m inv*; (*spy device*) microfono spia ▷ *vt* mettere sotto controllo; (*inf: annoy*) scocciare

buggy ['bʌgɪ] *n* (*baby buggy*) passeggino

build [bɪld] (*pt, pp* **built**) *n* (*of person*) corporatura ▷ *vt* costruire; **build up** *vt* accumulare; aumentare; **builder** *n* costruttore *m*; **building** *n* costruzione *f*; edificio; (*industry*) edilizia; **building site** *n* cantiere *m* di costruzione; **building society** (BRIT) *n* società *f* inv immobiliare

built [bɪlt] *pt, pp of* **build**; **built-in** *adj* (*cupboard*) a muro; (*device*) incorporato(-a); **built-up** *adj* **built-up area** abitato

bulb [bʌlb] *n* (*Bot*) bulbo; (*Elec*) lampadina

Bulgaria [bʌl'gɛərɪə] *n* Bulgaria; **Bulgarian** *adj* bulgaro(-a) ▷ *n* bulgaro(-a); (*Ling*) bulgaro

bulge [bʌldʒ] *n* rigonfiamento ▷ *vi* essere protuberante *or* rigonfio(-a); **to be bulging with** essere pieno(-a) *or* zeppo(-a) di

bulimia [bə'lɪmɪə] *n* bulimia

bulimic [bju:'lɪmɪk] *adj, n* bulimico(-a)

bulk [bʌlk] *n* massa, volume *m*; **in ~** a pacchi *or* cassette *etc*; (*Comm*) all'ingrosso; **the ~ of** il grosso di; **bulky** *adj* grosso(-a), voluminoso(-a)

bull [bul] *n* toro; (*male elephant, whale*) maschio

bulldozer ['buldəuzəʳ] *n* bulldozer *m inv*

bullet ['bulɪt] *n* pallottola

bulletin ['bulɪtɪn] *n* bollettino; **bulletin board** *n* (*Comput*) bulletin board *m inv*

bullfight ['bulfaɪt] *n* corrida; **bullfighter** *n* torero; **bullfighting** *n* tauromachia

bully ['bulɪ] *n* prepotente *m* ▷ *vt* angariare; (*frighten*) intimidire

bum [bʌm] (*inf*) *n* (*backside*) culo; (*tramp*) vagabondo(-a)

bumblebee ['bʌmblbi:] *n* bombo

bump [bʌmp] *n* (*in car*) piccolo tamponamento; (*jolt*) scossa; (*on road etc*) protuberanza; (*on head*) bernoccolo ▷ *vt* battere; **bump into** *vt fus* scontrarsi con; (*person*) imbattersi in; **bumper** *n* paraurti *m inv* ▷ *adj* **bumper harvest** raccolto eccezionale; **bumpy** ['bʌmpɪ] *adj* (*road*) dissestato(-a)

bun [bʌn] *n* focaccia; (*of hair*) crocchia

bunch [bʌntʃ] *n* (*of flowers, keys*) mazzo; (*of bananas*) casco; (*of people*) gruppo; **~ of grapes** grappolo d'uva; **~es** *npl* (*in hair*) codine *fpl*

bundle ['bʌndl] *n* fascio ▷ *vt* (*also*: **~ up**) legare in un fascio; (*put*) **to ~ sth/sb into** spingere qc/qn in

bungalow ['bʌngələu] *n* bungalow *m inv*

bungee jumping ['bʌndʒiː'dʒʌmpɪŋ] n salto nel vuoto da ponti, grattacieli etc con un cavo fissato alla caviglia

bunion ['bʌnjən] n callo (al piede)

bunk [bʌŋk] n cuccetta; **bunk beds** npl letti mpl a castello

bunker ['bʌŋkəʳ] n (coal store) ripostiglio per il carbone; (Mil, Golf) bunker m inv

bunny ['bʌnɪ] n (also: **~ rabbit**) coniglietto

buoy [bɔɪ] n boa; **buoyant** adj galleggiante; (fig) vivace

burden ['bəːdn] n carico, fardello ▷ vt **to ~ sb with** caricare qn di

bureau [bjuəˈrəu] (pl bureaux) n (BRIT: writing desk) scrivania; (US: chest of drawers) cassettone m; (office) ufficio, agenzia

bureaucracy [bjuəˈrɔkrəsɪ] n burocrazia

bureaucrat ['bjuərəkræt] n burocrate m/f

bureau de change [-dəˈʃãʒ] (pl bureaux de change) n cambiavalute m inv

bureaux [bjuəˈrəuz] npl of **bureau**

burger ['bəːgəʳ] n hamburger m inv

burglar ['bəːgləʳ] n scassinatore m; **burglar alarm** n campanello antifurto; **burglary** n furto con scasso

burial ['berɪəl] n sepoltura

burn [bəːn] (pt, pp burned or burnt) vt, vi bruciare ▷ n bruciatura, scottatura; **burn down** vt distruggere col fuoco; **burn out** vt (writer etc): **to ~ o.s. out** esaurirsi; **burning** adj in fiamme; (sand) che scotta; (ambition) bruciante

Burns Night n vedi nota nel riquadro

● **BURNS NIGHT**
●
● **Burns Night** è la festa celebrata il 25
● gennaio per commemorare il poeta
● scozzese Robert Burns (1759-1796). Gli
● scozzesi festeggiano questa data con
● una cena, la "Burns supper", a base di
● "haggis", piatto tradizionale scozzese,
● e whisky.

burnt [bəːnt] pt, pp of **burn**

burp [bəːp] (inf) n rutto ▷ vi ruttare

burrow ['bʌrəu] n tana ▷ vt scavare

burst [bəːst] (pt, pp burst) vt far scoppiare ▷ vi esplodere; (tyre) scoppiare ▷ n scoppio; (also: **~ pipe**) rottura nel tubo, perdita; **a ~ of speed** uno scatto di velocità; **to ~ into flames/tears** scoppiare in fiamme/lacrime; **to ~ out laughing** scoppiare a ridere; **to be ~ing with** scoppiare di; **burst into** vt fus (room etc) irrompere in

bury ['berɪ] vt seppellire

bus [bʌs] (pl buses) n autobus m inv; **bus conductor** n autista m/f (dell'autobus)

bush [buʃ] n cespuglio; (scrub land) macchia; **to beat about the ~** menare il cane per l'aia

business ['bɪznɪs] n (matter) affare m; (trading) affari mpl; (firm) azienda; (job, duty) lavoro; **to be away on ~** essere andato via per affari; **it's none of my ~** questo non mi riguarda; **he means ~** non scherza; **business class** n (Aer) business class f; **businesslike** adj serio(-a), efficiente; **businessman** (irreg) n uomo d'affari; **business trip** n viaggio d'affari; **businesswoman** (irreg) n donna d'affari

busker ['bʌskəʳ] (BRIT) n suonatore(-trice) ambulante

bus: bus pass n tessera dell'autobus; **bus shelter** n pensilina (alla fermata dell'autobus); **bus station** n stazione f delle corriere, autostazione f; **bus-stop** n fermata d'autobus

bust [bʌst] n busto; (Anat) seno ▷ adj (inf: broken) rotto(-a); **to go ~** fallire

bustling ['bʌslɪŋ] adj movimentato(-a)

busy ['bɪzɪ] adj occupato(-a); (shop, street) molto frequentato(-a) ▷ vt **to ~ o.s.** darsi da fare; **busy signal** (US) n (Tel) segnale m di occupato

○ **KEYWORD**

but [bʌt] conj ma; **I'd love to come, but I'm busy** vorrei tanto venire, ma ho da fare ▷ prep (apart from, except) eccetto, tranne, meno; **he was nothing but trouble** non dava altro che guai; **no-one but him can do it** nessuno può farlo tranne lui; **but for you/your help** se non fosse per te/per il tuo aiuto; **anything but that** tutto ma non questo ▷ adv (just, only) solo, soltanto; **she's but a child** è solo una bambina; **had I but known** se solo avessi saputo; **I can but try** tentar non nuoce; **all but finished** quasi finito

butcher ['butʃəʳ] n macellaio ▷ vt macellare; **butcher's (shop)** n macelleria

butler ['bʌtləʳ] n maggiordomo

butt [bʌt] n (cask) grossa botte f; (of gun) calcio; (of cigarette) mozzicone m; (BRIT: fig: target) oggetto ▷ vt cozzare

butter ['bʌtəʳ] n burro ▷ vt imburrare; **buttercup** n ranuncolo

butterfly ['bʌtəflaɪ] n farfalla; (Swimming: also: **~ stroke**) (nuoto a) farfalla

buttocks ['bʌtəks] npl natiche fpl

button ['bʌtn] n bottone m; (US: badge)

distintivo ▷ vt (also: **~ up**) abbottonare ▷ vi abbottonarsi

buy [baɪ] (pt, pp **bought**) vt comprare ▷ n acquisto; **where can I ~ some postcards?** dove posso comprare delle cartoline?; **to ~ sb sth/sth from sb** comprare qc per qn/qc da qn; **to ~ sb a drink** offrire da bere a qn; **buy out** vt (business) rilevare; **buy up** vt accaparrare; **buyer** n compratore(-trice)

buzz [bʌz] n ronzio; (inf: phone call) colpo di telefono ▷ vi ronzare; **buzzer** ['bʌzəʳ] n cicalino

🔵 **KEYWORD**

by [baɪ] prep 1 (referring to cause, agent) da; **killed by lightning** ucciso da un fulmine; **surrounded by a fence** circondato da uno steccato; **a painting by Picasso** un quadro di Picasso

2 (referring to method, manner, means): **by bus/car/train** in autobus/macchina/treno, con l'autobus/la macchina/il treno; **to pay by cheque** pagare con (un) assegno; **by moonlight** al chiaro di luna; **by saving hard, he …** risparmiando molto, lui …

3 (via, through) per; **we came by Dover** siamo venuti via Dover

4 (close to, past) accanto a; **the house by the river** la casa sul fiume; **a holiday by the sea** una vacanza al mare; **she sat by his bed** si sedette accanto al suo letto; **she rushed by me** mi è passata accanto correndo; **I go by the post office every day** passo davanti all'ufficio postale ogni giorno

5 (not later than) per, entro; **by 4 o'clock** per or entro le 4; **by this time tomorrow** domani a quest'ora; **by the time I got here it was too late** quando sono arrivato era ormai troppo tardi

6 (during): **by day/night** di giorno/notte

7 (amount) a; **by the kilo/metre** a chili/metri; **paid by the hour** pagato all'ora; **one by one** uno per uno; **little by little** a poco a poco

8 (Math, measure): **to divide/multiply by 3** dividere/moltiplicare per 3; **it's broader by a metre** è un metro più largo, è più largo di un metro

9 (according to) per; **to play by the rules** attenersi alle regole; **it's all right by me** per me va bene

10: **(all) by oneself** etc (tutto(-a)) solo(-a); **he did it (all) by himself** lo ha fatto (tutto) da solo

11: **by the way** a proposito; **this wasn't**

my idea by the way tra l'altro l'idea non è stata mia
▷ adv 1 see **go**; **pass** etc
2: **by and by** (in past) poco dopo; (in future) fra breve; **by and large** nel complesso

bye(-bye) ['baɪ('baɪ)] excl ciao!, arrivederci!
by-election ['baɪɪlɛkʃən] (BRIT) n elezione f straordinaria
bypass ['baɪpɑːs] n circonvallazione f; (Med) by-pass m inv ▷ vt fare una deviazione intorno a
byte [baɪt] n (Comput) byte m inv, bicarattere m

C [siː] n (Mus) do

cab [kæb] n taxi m inv; (of train, truck) cabina

cabaret ['kæbəreɪ] n cabaret m inv

cabbage ['kæbɪdʒ] n cavolo

cabin ['kæbɪn] n capanna; (on ship) cabina; **cabin crew** n equipaggio

cabinet ['kæbɪnɪt] n (Pol) consiglio dei ministri; (furniture) armadietto; (also: **display ~**) vetrinetta; **cabinet minister** n ministro (membro del Consiglio)

cable ['keɪbl] n cavo; fune f; (Tel) cablogramma m ▷ vt telegrafare; **cable car** n funivia; **cable television** n televisione f via cavo

cactus ['kæktəs] (pl **cacti**) n cactus m inv

café ['kæfeɪ] n caffè m inv

cafeteria [kæfɪ'tɪərɪə] n self-service m inv

caffein(e) ['kæfiːn] n caffeina

cage [keɪdʒ] n gabbia

cagoule [kə'guːl] n K-way® m inv

cake [keɪk] n (large) torta; (small) pasticcino; **cake of soap** n saponetta

calcium ['kælsɪəm] n calcio

calculate ['kælkjuleɪt] vt calcolare; **calculation** [-'leɪʃən] n calcolo; **calculator** n calcolatrice f

calendar ['kæləndə'] n calendario

calf [kɑːf] (pl **calves**) n (of cow) vitello; (of other animals) piccolo; (also: **~skin**) (pelle f di) vitello; (Anat) polpaccio

calibre ['kælɪbə'] (US **caliber**) n calibro

call [kɔːl] vt (gen: also Tel) chiamare; (meeting) indire ▷ vi chiamare; (visit: also: **~ in**, **~ round**) passare ▷ n (shout) grido, urlo; (Tel) telefonata; **to be ~ed** (person, object) chiamarsi; **can you ~ back later?** può richiamare più tardi?; **can I make a ~ from here?** posso telefonare da qui?; **to be on ~** essere a disposizione; **call back** vi (return) ritornare; (Tel) ritelefonare, richiamare; **call for** vt fus richiedere; (fetch) passare a prendere; **call in** vt (doctor, expert, police) chiamare, far venire; **call off** vt disdire; **call on** vt fus (visit) passare da; (appeal to) chiedere a; **call out** vi (in pain) urlare; (to person) chiamare; **call up** vt (Mil) richiamare; (Tel) telefonare a; **callbox** (BRIT) n cabina telefonica; **call centre** (US **call center**) n centro informazioni telefoniche; **caller** n persona che chiama, visitatore(-trice)

callous ['kæləs] adj indurito(-a), insensibile

calm [kɑːm] adj calmo(-a) ▷ n calma ▷ vt calmare; **calm down** vi calmarsi ▷ vt calmare; **calmly** adv con calma

Calor gas® ['kælə'-] n butano

calorie ['kælərɪ] n caloria

calves [kɑːvz] npl of **calf**

camcorder ['kæmkɔːdə'] n camcorder f inv

came [keɪm] pt of **come**

camel ['kæməl] n cammello

camera ['kæmərə] n macchina fotografica; (Cinema, TV) cinepresa; **in ~** a porte chiuse; **cameraman** (irreg) n cameraman m inv

camouflage ['kæməflɑːʒ] n (Mil, Zool) mimetizzazione f ▷ vt mimetizzare

camp [kæmp] n campeggio; (Mil) campo ▷ vi accamparsi ▷ adj effeminato(-a)

campaign [kæm'peɪn] n (Mil, Pol etc) campagna ▷ vi (also fig) fare una campagna; **campaigner** n **campaigner for** fautore(-trice) di; **campaigner against** oppositore(-trice) di

camp: **campbed** n (BRIT) brandina; **camper** ['kæmpə'] n campeggiatore(-trice); (vehicle) camper m inv; **campground** (US) n campeggio; **camping** ['kæmpɪŋ] n campeggio; **to go camping** andare in campeggio; **campsite** ['kæmpsaɪt] n campeggio

campus ['kæmpəs] n campus m inv

can¹ [kæn] n (of milk) scatola; (of oil) bidone m; (of water) tanica; (tin) scatola ▷ vt mettere in scatola

🔵 **KEYWORD**

can² [kæn] (negative **cannot, can't**, conditional and pt **could**) aux vb **1** (be able to) potere; **I can't go any further** non posso andare oltre; **you can do it if you try** sei in grado di farlo — basta provarci; **I'll help you all I can** ti aiuterò come potrò; **I can't see you** non ti vedo **2** (know how to) sapere, essere capace di; **I can swim** so nuotare; **can you speak French?** parla francese? **3** (may) potere; **could I have a word with you?** posso parlarle un momento? **4** (expressing disbelief, puzzlement etc): **it can't be true!** non può essere vero!; **what can he want?** cosa può mai volere? **5** (expressing possibility, suggestion etc): **he could be in the library** può darsi che sia in biblioteca; **she could have been delayed** può aver avuto un contrattempo

Canada ['kænədə] n Canada m; **Canadian** [kə'neɪdɪən] adj, n canadese m/f
canal [kə'næl] n canale m
canary [kə'nɛərɪ] n canarino
Canary Islands, Canaries [kə'nɛərɪz] npl **the ~** le (isole) Canarie
cancel ['kænsəl] vt annullare; (train) sopprimere; (cross out) cancellare; **I want to ~ my booking** vorrei disdire la mia prenotazione; **cancellation** [-'leɪʃən] n annullamento; soppressione f; cancellazione f; (Tourism) prenotazione f annullata
cancer ['kænsər] n cancro .
Cancer ['kænsər] n (sign) Cancro
candidate ['kændɪdeɪt] n candidato(-a)
candle ['kændl] n candela; (in church) cero; **candlestick** n bugia; (bigger, ornate) candeliere m
candy ['kændɪ] n zucchero candito; (US) caramella; caramelle fpl; **candy bar** (US) n lungo biscotto, in genere ricoperto di cioccolata; **candyfloss** ['kændɪflɒs] n (BRIT) zucchero filato
cane [keɪn] n canna; (for furniture) bambù m; (stick) verga ▷ vt (BRIT Scol) punire a colpi di verga
canister ['kænɪstər] n scatola metallica
cannabis ['kænəbɪs] n canapa indiana
canned ['kænd] adj (food) in scatola
cannon ['kænən] n (pl **cannon** or **cannons**) n (gun) cannone m
cannot ['kænɒt] = **can not**

canoe [kə'nu:] n canoa; **canoeing** n canottaggio
canon ['kænən] n (clergyman) canonico; (standard) canone m
can-opener ['kænəupnər] n apriscatole m inv
can't [kænt] = **can not**
canteen [kæn'ti:n] n mensa; (BRIT: of cutlery) portaposate m inv

> ⬛ Be careful not to translate **canteen** by the Italian word **cantina**.

canter ['kæntər] vi andare al piccolo galoppo
canvas ['kænvəs] n tela
canvass ['kænvəs] vi (Pol): **to ~ for** raccogliere voti per ▷ vt fare un sondaggio di
canyon ['kænjən] n canyon m inv
cap [kæp] n (hat) berretto; (of pen) coperchio; (of bottle, toy gun) tappo; (contraceptive) diaframma m ▷ vt (outdo) superare; (limit) fissare un tetto (a)
capability [keɪpə'bɪlɪtɪ] n capacità f inv, abilità f inv
capable ['keɪpəbl] adj capace
capacity [kə'pæsɪtɪ] n capacità f inv; (of lift etc) capienza
cape [keɪp] n (garment) cappa; (Geo) capo
caper ['keɪpər] n (Culin) cappero; (prank) scherzetto
capital ['kæpɪtl] n (also: **~ city**) capitale f; (money) capitale m; (also: **~ letter**) (lettera) maiuscola; **capitalism** n capitalismo; **capitalist** adj, n capitalista m/f; **capital punishment** n pena capitale
Capitol ['kæpɪtl] n **the ~** il Campidoglio
Capricorn ['kæprɪkɔːn] n Capricorno
capsize [kæp'saɪz] vt capovolgere ▷ vi capovolgersi
capsule ['kæpsjuːl] n capsula
captain ['kæptɪn] n capitano
caption ['kæpʃən] n leggenda
captivity [kæp'tɪvɪtɪ] n cattività
capture ['kæptʃər] vt catturare; (Comput) registrare ▷ n cattura; (data) registrazione f di rilevazione f di dati
car [kɑːr] n (Aut) macchina, automobile f; (Rail) vagone m
carafe [kə'ræf] n caraffa
caramel ['kærəməl] n caramello
carat ['kærət] n carato; **18 ~ gold** oro a 18 carati
caravan ['kærəvæn] n (BRIT) roulotte f inv; (of camels) carovana; **caravan site** (BRIT) n campeggio per roulotte
carbohydrate [kɑːbəu'haɪdreɪt] n carboidrato
carbon ['kɑːbən] n carbonio; **carbon dioxide** [-daɪ'ɒksaɪd] n diossido di

carbonio; **carbon monoxide** [-mɔ'nɔksaɪd] n monossido di carbonio

car boot sale n vedi nota nel riquadro

● **CAR BOOT SALE**
●
● Il **car boot sale** è un mercatino
● dell'usato molto popolare in Gran
● Bretagna. Normalmente ha luogo in
● un parcheggio o in un grande spiazzo,
● e la merce viene in genere esposta nei
● bagagliai, in inglese appunto "boots",
● aperti delle macchine.

carburettor [kɑːbju'rɛtəʳ] (US **carburetor**) n carburatore m

card [kɑːd] n carta; (visiting card etc) biglietto; (Christmas card etc) cartolina; **cardboard** n cartone m; **card game** n gioco di carte

cardigan ['kɑːdɪgən] n cardigan m inv

cardinal ['kɑːdɪnl] adj cardinale ▷ n cardinale m

cardphone ['kɑːdfəun] n telefono a scheda

care [kɛəʳ] n cura, attenzione f; (worry) preoccupazione f ▷ vi **to ~ about** curarsi di; (thing, idea) interessarsi di; **~ of** presso; **in sb's ~** alle cure di qn; **to take ~ (to do)** fare attenzione (a fare); **to take ~ of** curarsi di; (bill, problem) occuparsi di; **I don't ~** non me ne importa; **I couldn't ~ less** non m'interessa affatto; **care for** vt fus aver cura di; (like) volere bene a

career [kə'rɪəʳ] n carriera ▷ vi (also: **~ along**) andare di (gran) carriera

care: **carefree** ['kɛəfriː] adj sgombro(-a) di preoccupazioni; **careful** ['kɛəful] adj attento(-a); (cautious) cauto(-a); **(be) careful!** attenzione!; **carefully** adv con cura; cautamente; **caregiver** (US) n (professional) badante m/f; (unpaid) persona che si prende cura di un parente malato o anziano; **careless** ['kɛəlɪs] adj negligente; (heedless) spensierato(-a); **carelessness** n negligenza; mancanza di tatto; **carer** ['kɛərəʳ] n assistente m/f (di persone malata o handicappata); **caretaker** ['kɛəteɪkəʳ] n custode m

car-ferry ['kɑːfɛrɪ] n traghetto

cargo ['kɑːgəu] (pl **cargoes**) n carico

car hire n autonoleggio

Caribbean [kærɪ'biːən] adj **the ~ Sea** il Mar dei Caraibi

caring ['kɛərɪŋ] adj (person) premuroso(-a); (society, organization) umanitario(-a)

carnation [kɑː'neɪʃən] n garofano

carnival ['kɑːnɪvəl] n (public celebration) carnevale m; (US: funfair) luna park m inv

carol ['kærəl] n **Christmas ~** canto di Natale

carousel [kærə'sɛl] (US) n giostra

car park (BRIT) n parcheggio

carpenter ['kɑːpɪntəʳ] n carpentiere m

carpet ['kɑːpɪt] n tappeto ▷ vt coprire con tappeto

car rental (US) n autonoleggio

carriage ['kærɪdʒ] n vettura; (of goods) trasporto; **carriageway** (BRIT) n (part of road) carreggiata

carrier ['kærɪəʳ] n (of disease) portatore(-trice); (Comm) impresa di trasporti; **carrier bag** (BRIT) n sacchetto

carrot ['kærət] n carota

carry ['kærɪ] vt (person) portare; (: vehicle) trasportare; (involve: responsibilities etc) comportare; (Med) essere portatore(-trice) di ▷ vi (sound) farsi sentire; **to be** or **get carried away** (fig) entusiasmarsi; **carry on** vi **to ~ on with sth/doing** continuare qc/a fare ▷ vt mandare avanti; **carry out** vt (orders) eseguire; (investigation) svolgere

cart [kɑːt] n carro ▷ vt (inf) trascinare

carton ['kɑːtən] n (box) scatola di cartone; (of yogurt) cartone m; (of cigarettes) stecca

cartoon [kɑː'tuːn] n (Press) disegno umoristico; (comic strip) fumetto; (Cinema) disegno animato

cartridge ['kɑːtrɪdʒ] n (for gun, pen) cartuccia; (music tape) cassetta

carve [kɑːv] vt (meat) trinciare; (wood, stone) intagliare; **carving** n (in wood etc) scultura

car wash n lavaggio auto

case [keɪs] n caso; (Law) causa, processo; (box) scatola; (BRIT: also: **suit~**) valigia; **in ~ of** in caso di; **in ~ he** caso mai lui; **in any ~** in ogni caso; **just in ~** in caso di bisogno

cash [kæʃ] n denaro; (coins, notes) denaro liquido ▷ vt incassare; **I haven't got any ~** non ho contanti; **to pay (in) ~** pagare in contanti; **~ on delivery** pagamento alla consegna; **cashback** n (discount) sconto; (at supermarket etc) anticipo di contanti ottenuto presso la cassa di un negozio tramite una carta di debito; **cash card** (BRIT) n tesserino di prelievo; **cash desk** (BRIT) n cassa; **cash dispenser** (BRIT) n sportello automatico

cashew [kæ'ʃuː] n (also: **~ nut**) anacardio

cashier [kæ'ʃɪəʳ] n cassiere(-a)

cashmere ['kæʃmɪəʳ] n cachemire m

cash point n sportello bancario automatico, Bancomat® m inv

cash register n registratore m di cassa

casino [kə'siːnəu] n casinò m inv

casket ['kɑːskɪt] n cofanetto; (US: coffin) bara

casserole ['kæsərəul] n casseruola; (food):
chicken ~ pollo in casseruola

cassette [kæ'sɛt] n cassetta; **cassette
player** n riproduttore m a cassette

cast [kɑːst] (pt, pp **cast**) vt (throw) gettare;
(metal) gettare, fondere; (Theatre): **to ~
sb as Hamlet** scegliere qn per la parte
di Amleto ▷ n (Theatre) cast m inv; (also:
plaster ~) ingessatura; **to ~ one's vote**
votare, dare il voto; **cast off** vi (Naut)
salpare; (Knitting) calare

castanets [kæstə'nɛts] npl castagnette fpl

caster sugar ['kɑːstə'-] (BRIT) n zucchero
semolato

cast-iron ['kɑːstaɪən] adj (lit) di ghisa; (fig:
case) di ferro

castle ['kɑːsl] n castello

casual ['kæʒjul] adj (chance) casuale,
fortuito(-a); (: work etc) avventizio(-a);
(unconcerned) noncurante, indifferente; **~
wear** casual m

casualty ['kæʒjultɪ] n ferito(-a); (dead)
morto(-a), vittima; (Med: department)
pronto soccorso

cat [kæt] n gatto

catalogue ['kætəlɔg] (US **catalog**) n
catalogo ▷ vt catalogare

catalytic converter [kætəlɪtɪk-] n
marmitta catalitica, catalizzatore m

cataract ['kætərækt] n (also Med)
cateratta

catarrh [kə'tɑː'] n catarro

catastrophe [kə'tæstrəfɪ] n catastrofe f

catch [kætʃ] (pt, pp **caught**) vt prendere;
(ball) afferrare; (surprise: person)
sorprendere; (attention) attirare; (comment,
whisper) cogliere; (person) raggiungere
▷ vi (fire) prendere ▷ n (fish etc caught)
retata; (of ball) presa; (trick) inganno;
(Tech) gancio; (game) catch m inv; **to ~ fire**
prendere fuoco; **to ~ sight of** scorgere;
catch up vi mettersi in pari ▷ vt (also: **~
up with**) raggiungere; **catching** ['kætʃɪŋ]
adj (Med) contagioso(-a)

category ['kætɪgərɪ] n categoria

cater ['keɪtə'] vi **~ for** (BRIT: needs)
provvedere a; (: readers, consumers)
incontrare i gusti di; (Comm: provide food)
provvedere alla ristorazione di

caterpillar ['kætəpɪlə'] n bruco

cathedral [kə'θiːdrəl] n cattedrale f,
duomo

Catholic ['kæθəlɪk] adj, n (Rel) cattolico(-a)

Catseye® [kæts'aɪ] (BRIT) n (Aut)
catarifrangente m

cattle ['kætl] npl bestiame m, bestie fpl

catwalk ['kætwɔːk] n passerella

caught [kɔːt] pt, pp of **catch**

cauliflower ['kɔlɪflauə'] n cavolfiore m

cause [kɔːz] n causa ▷ vt causare

caution ['kɔːʃən] n prudenza; (warning)
avvertimento ▷ vt avvertire; ammonire;
cautious ['kɔːʃəs] adj cauto(-a), prudente

cave [keɪv] n caverna, grotta; **cave in** vi
(roof etc) crollare

caviar(e) ['kævɪɑː'] n caviale m

cavity ['kævɪtɪ] n cavità f inv

cc abbr = **cubic centimetres**; **carbon copy**

CCTV n abbr (= closed-circuit television)
televisione f a circuito chiuso

CD abbr (disc) CD m inv; (player) lettore m CD
inv; **CD player** n lettore m CD; **CD-ROM**
[-rɔm] n abbr CD-ROM m inv

cease [siːs] vt, vi cessare; **ceasefire** n
cessate il fuoco m inv

cedar ['siːdə'] n cedro

ceilidh ['keɪlɪ] n festa con musiche e danze
popolari scozzesi o irlandesi

ceiling ['siːlɪŋ] n soffitto; (on wages etc)
tetto

celebrate ['sɛlɪbreɪt] vt, vi celebrare;
celebration [-'breɪʃən] n celebrazione f

celebrity [sɪ'lɛbrɪtɪ] n celebrità f inv

celery ['sɛlərɪ] n sedano

cell [sɛl] n cella; (of revolutionaries, Biol)
cellula; (Elec) elemento (di batteria)

cellar ['sɛlə'] n sottosuolo; cantina

cello ['tʃɛləu] n violoncello

Cellophane® ['sɛləfeɪn] n cellophane® m

cellphone ['sɛləfeɪn] n cellulare m

Celsius ['sɛlsɪəs] adj Celsius inv

Celtic ['kɛltɪk, 'sɛltɪk] adj celtico(-a)

cement [sə'mɛnt] n cemento

cemetery ['sɛmɪtrɪ] n cimitero

censor ['sɛnsə'] n censore m ▷ vt
censurare; **censorship** n censura

census ['sɛnsəs] n censimento

cent [sɛnt] n (US: coin) centesimo (= 1.100
di un dollaro); (unit of euro) centesimo; see
also **per**

centenary [sɛn'tiːnərɪ] n centenario

centennial [sɛn'tɛnɪəl] (US) n centenario

center ['sɛntə'] (US) n, vt = **centre**

centi... [sɛntɪ] prefix: **centigrade**
['sɛntɪgreɪd] adj centigrado(-a);
centimetre ['sɛntɪmiːtə'] (US
centimeter) n centimetro; **centipede**
['sɛntɪpiːd] n centopiedi m inv

central ['sɛntrəl] adj centrale; **Central
America** n America centrale; **central
heating** n riscaldamento centrale;
central reservation n (BRIT Aut)
banchina f spartitraffico inv

centre ['sɛntə'] (US **center**) n centro
▷ vt centrare; **centre-forward** n (Sport)
centroavanti m inv; **centre-half** n (Sport)
centromediano

century ['sɛntjurɪ] n secolo; **twentieth ~**

ventesimo secolo

CEO n abbr = **chief executive officer**

ceramic [sɪ'ræmɪk] adj ceramico(-a)

cereal ['siːrɪəl] n cereale m

ceremony ['sɛrɪmənɪ] n cerimonia; **to stand on ~** fare complimenti

certain ['səːtən] adj certo(-a); **to make ~ of** assicurarsi di; **for ~** per certo, di sicuro; **certainly** adv certamente, certo; **certainty** n certezza

certificate [sə'tɪfɪkɪt] n certificato; diploma m

certify ['səːtɪfaɪ] vt certificare; (award diploma to) conferire un diploma a; (declare insane) dichiarare pazzo(-a)

cf. abbr (= compare) cfr.

CFC n (= chlorofluorocarbon) CFC m inv

chain [tʃeɪn] n catena ▷ vt (also: ~ **up**) incatenare; **chain-smoke** vi fumare una sigaretta dopo l'altra

chair [tʃeəʳ] n sedia; (armchair) poltrona; (of university) cattedra; (of meeting) presidenza ▷ vt (meeting) presiedere; **chairlift** n seggiovia; **chairman** (irreg) n presidente m; **chairperson** n presidente(-essa); **chairwoman** (irreg) n presidentessa

chalet ['ʃæleɪ] n chalet m inv

chalk [tʃɔːk] n gesso; **chalkboard** (US) n lavagna

challenge ['tʃælɪndʒ] n sfida ▷ vt sfidare; (statement, right) mettere in dubbio; **to ~ sb to do** sfidare qn a fare; **challenging** adj (task) impegnativo(-a); (look) di sfida

chamber ['tʃeɪmbəʳ] n camera; **chambermaid** n cameriera

champagne [ʃæm'peɪn] n champagne m inv

champion ['tʃæmpɪən] n campione(-essa); **championship** n campionato

chance [tʃɑːns] n caso; (opportunity) occasione f; (likelihood) possibilità f inv ▷ vt **to ~ it** rischiare, provarci ▷ adj fortuito(-a); **to take a ~** rischiare; **by ~** per caso

chancellor ['tʃɑːnsələʳ] n cancelliere m; **Chancellor of the Exchequer** [-ɪks'tʃɛkəʳ] (BRIT) n Cancelliere dello Scacchiere

chandelier [ʃændə'lɪəʳ] n lampadario

change [tʃeɪndʒ] vt cambiare; (transform): **to ~ sb into** trasformare qn in ▷ vi cambiare; (change one's clothes) cambiarsi; (be transformed): **to ~ into** trasformarsi in ▷ n cambiamento; (of clothes) cambio; (money returned) resto; (coins) spiccioli; **where can I ~ some money?** dove posso cambiare dei soldi?; **to ~ one's mind** cambiare idea; **keep the ~!** tenga pure il resto!; **sorry, I don't have any ~** mi dispiace, non ho spiccioli; **for a ~** tanto per

cambiare; **change over** vi (from sth to sth) passare; (players etc) scambiarsi (di posto o di campo) ▷ vt cambiare; **changeable** adj (weather) variabile; **change machine** n distributore automatico di monete; **changing room** n (BRIT: in shop) camerino; (: Sport) spogliatoio

channel ['tʃænl] n canale m; (of river, sea) alveo ▷ vt canalizzare; **Channel Tunnel** n **the Channel Tunnel** il tunnel sotto la Manica

chant [tʃɑːnt] n canto; salmodia ▷ vt cantare; salmodiare

chaos ['keɪɔs] n caos m

chaotic [keɪ'ɔtɪk] adj caotico(-a)

chap [tʃæp] (BRIT: inf) n (man) tipo

chapel ['tʃæpəl] n cappella

chapped [tʃæpt] adj (skin, lips) screpolato(-a)

chapter ['tʃæptəʳ] n capitolo

character ['kærɪktəʳ] n carattere m; (in novel, film) personaggio; **characteristic** [-'rɪstɪk] adj caratteristico(-a) ▷ n caratteristica; **characterize** ['kærɪktəraɪz] vt caratterizzare; (describe): **to characterize (as)** descrivere (come)

charcoal ['tʃɑːkəul] n carbone m di legna

charge [tʃɑːdʒ] n accusa; (cost) prezzo; (responsibility) responsabilità ▷ vt (gun, battery, Mil: enemy) caricare; (customer) fare pagare a; (sum) fare pagare; (Law): **to ~ sb (with)** accusare qn (di) ▷ vi (gen with: up, along etc) lanciarsi; **charge card** n carta f clienti inv; **charger** n (also: **battery charger**) caricabatterie m inv; (old: warhorse) destriero

charismatic [kærɪz'mætɪk] adj carismatico(-a)

charity ['tʃærɪtɪ] n carità; (organization) opera pia; **charity shop** n (BRIT) negozi che vendono articoli di seconda mano e devolvono il ricavato in beneficenza

charm [tʃɑːm] n fascino; (on bracelet) ciondolo ▷ vt affascinare, incantare; **charming** adj affascinante

chart [tʃɑːt] n tabella; grafico; (map) carta nautica ▷ vt fare una carta nautica di; **~s** npl (Mus) hit parade f

charter ['tʃɑːtəʳ] vt (plane) noleggiare ▷ n (document) carta; **chartered accountant** ['tʃɑːtəd-] (BRIT) n ragioniere(-a) professionista; **charter flight** n volo m charter inv

chase [tʃeɪs] vt inseguire; (also: ~ **away**) cacciare ▷ n caccia

chat [tʃæt] vi (also: **have a ~**) chiacchierare ▷ n chiacchierata; **chat up** vt (BRIT inf: girl) abbordare; **chat room** n (Internet) chat room f inv; **chat show** (BRIT) n talk

show m inv
chatter ['tʃætəʳ] vi (person) ciarlare; (bird)
cinguettare; (teeth) battere ▷ n ciarle fpl;
cinguettio
chauffeur ['ʃəufəʳ] n autista m
chauvinist ['ʃəuvɪnɪst] n (male
chauvinist) maschilista m; (nationalist)
sciovinista m/f
cheap [tʃiːp] adj economico(-a); (joke)
grossolano(-a); (poor quality) di cattiva
qualità ▷ adv a buon mercato; **can you
recommend a ~ hotel/restaurant,
please?** potrebbe indicarmi un albergo/
ristorante non troppo caro?; **cheap day
return** n biglietto ridotto di andata e ritorno
valido in giornata; **cheaply** adv a buon
prezzo, a buon mercato
cheat [tʃiːt] vi imbrogliare; (at school)
copiare ▷ vt ingannare ▷ n imbroglione
m; **to ~ sb out of sth** defraudare qn di qc;
cheat on vt fus (husband, wife) tradire
Chechnya [tʃɪtʃˈnjɑː] n Cecenia
check [tʃɛk] vt verificare; (passport, ticket)
controllare; (halt) fermare; (restrain)
contenere ▷ n verifica; (passport, ticket)
freno; (us: bill) conto; (pattern: gen pl)
quadretti mpl; (us) = **cheque** ▷ adj
(pattern, cloth) a quadretti; **check in** vi (in
hotel) registrare; (at airport) presentarsi
all'accettazione ▷ vt (luggage) depositare;
check off vt segnare; **check out** vi (in
hotel) saldare il conto; **check up** vi **to ~
up (on sth)** investigare (qc); **to ~ up on
sb** informarsi sul conto di qn; **checkbook**
(us) n = **chequebook; checked** adj a
quadretti; **checkers** (us) n dama; **check-
in** n (also: **check-in desk**: at airport)
check-in m inv, accettazione f (bagagli
inv); **checking account** (us) n conto
corrente; **checklist** n lista di controllo;
checkmate n scaccomatto; **checkout**
n (in supermarket) cassa; **checkpoint**
n posto di blocco; **checkroom** (us) n
deposito m bagagli inv; **checkup** n (Med)
controllo medico
cheddar ['tʃɛdəʳ] n formaggio duro di latte di
mucca di colore bianco o arancione
cheek [tʃiːk] n guancia; (impudence) faccia
tosta; **cheekbone** n zigomo; **cheeky** adj
sfacciato(-a)
cheer [tʃɪəʳ] vt applaudire; (gladden)
rallegrare ▷ vi applaudire ▷ n grido (di
incoraggiamento); **cheer up** vi rallegrarsi,
farsi animo ▷ vt rallegrare; **cheerful** adj
allegro(-a)
cheerio ['tʃɪərɪˈəu] (BRIT) excl ciao!
cheerleader ['tʃɪəliːdəʳ] n cheerleader
f inv
cheese [tʃiːz] n formaggio; **cheeseburger**

n cheeseburger m inv; **cheesecake** n
specie di torta di ricotta, a volte con frutta
chef [ʃɛf] n capocuoco
chemical ['kɛmɪkəl] adj chimico(-a) ▷ n
prodotto chimico
chemist ['kɛmɪst] n (BRIT: pharmacist)
farmacista m/f; (scientist) chimico(-a);
chemistry n chimica; **chemist's (shop)**
(BRIT) n farmacia
cheque [tʃɛk] (us **check**) n assegno;
chequebook n libretto degli assegni;
cheque card n carta f assegni inv
cherry ['tʃɛrɪ] n ciliegia; (also: **~ tree**)
ciliegio
chess [tʃɛs] n scacchi mpl
chest [tʃɛst] n petto; (box) cassa
chestnut ['tʃɛsnʌt] n castagna; (also: **~
tree**) castagno
chest of drawers n cassettone m
chew [tʃuː] vt masticare; **chewing gum** n
chewing gum m
chic [ʃiːk] adj elegante
chick [tʃɪk] n pulcino; (inf) pollastrella
chicken ['tʃɪkɪn] n pollo; (inf: coward)
coniglio; **chicken out** (inf) vi avere fifa;
chickenpox n varicella
chickpea ['tʃɪkpiː] n cece m
chief [tʃiːf] n capo ▷ adj principale;
chief executive (officer) n direttore
m generale; **chiefly** adv per lo più,
soprattutto
child [tʃaɪld] (pl **children**) n bambino(-a);
child abuse n molestie fpl a minori; **child
benefit** n (BRIT) ≈ assegni mpl familiari;
childbirth n parto; **child-care** n il
badare ai bambini; **childhood** n infanzia;
childish adj puerile; **child minder**
[-'maɪndəʳ] (BRIT) n bambinaia; **children**
['tʃɪldrən] npl of **child**
Chile ['tʃɪlɪ] n Cile m
Chilean ['tʃɪlɪən] adj, n cileno(-a)
chill [tʃɪl] n freddo; (Med) infreddatura ▷ vt
raffreddare; **chill out** (esp us) vi (inf) darsi
una calmata
chil(l)i ['tʃɪlɪ] n peperoncino
chilly ['tʃɪlɪ] adj freddo(-a), fresco(-a); **to
feel ~** sentirsi infreddolito(-a)
chimney ['tʃɪmnɪ] n camino
chimpanzee [tʃɪmpænˈziː] n scimpanzé
m inv
chin [tʃɪn] n mento
China ['tʃaɪnə] n Cina
china ['tʃaɪnə] n porcellana
Chinese [tʃaɪˈniːz] adj cinese ▷ n inv cinese
m/f; (Ling) cinese m
chip [tʃɪp] n (gen pl: Culin) patatina fritta;
(: us: also: **potato ~**) patatina; (of wood,
glass, stone) scheggia; (also: **micro~**) chip
m inv ▷ vt (cup, plate) scheggiare; **chip**

shop n (BRIT) vedi nota nel riquadro

⬤ **CHIP SHOP**
⬤
⬤ I **chip shops**, anche chiamati "fish
⬤ and chip shops", sono friggitorie che
⬤ vendono principalmente filetti di pesce
⬤ impanati e patatine fritte.

chiropodist [kɪˈrɔpədɪst] (BRIT) n pedicure
m/f inv
chisel [ˈtʃɪzl] n cesello
chives [tʃaɪvz] npl erba cipollina
chlorine [ˈklɔːriːn] n cloro
choc-ice [ˈtʃɔkaɪs] n (BRIT) gelato ricoperto
al cioccolato
chocolate [ˈtʃɔklɪt] ▷ n (substance)
cioccolato, cioccolata; (drink) cioccolata;
(a sweet) cioccolatino
choice [tʃɔɪs] n scelta ▷ adj scelto(-a)
choir [ˈkwaɪəʳ] n coro
choke [tʃəuk] vi soffocare ▷ vt soffocare;
(block): **to be ~d with** essere intasato(-a) di
▷ n (Aut) valvola dell'aria
cholesterol [kəˈlɛstərɔl] n colesterolo
choose [tʃuːz] (pt **chose,**, pp **chosen**)
vt scegliere; **to ~ to do** decidere di fare;
preferire fare
chop [tʃɔp] vt (wood) spaccare; (Culin:
also: **~ up**) tritare ▷ n (Culin) costoletta;
chop down vt (tree) abbattere; **chop off**
vt tagliare; **chopsticks** [ˈtʃɔpstɪks] npl
bastoncini mpl cinesi
chord [kɔːd] n (Mus) accordo
chore [tʃɔːʳ] n faccenda; **household ~s**
faccende fpl domestiche
chorus [ˈkɔːrəs] n coro; (repeated part of
song: also fig) ritornello
chose [tʃəuz] pt of **choose**
chosen [ˈtʃəuzn] pp of **choose**
Christ [kraɪst] n Cristo
christen [ˈkrɪsn] vt battezzare;
christening n battesimo
Christian [ˈkrɪstɪən] adj, n cristiano(-a);
Christianity [-ˈænɪtɪ] n cristianesimo;
Christian name n nome m (di battesimo)
Christmas [ˈkrɪsməs] n Natale m; **Merry
~!** Buon Natale!; **Christmas card** n
cartolina di Natale; **Christmas carol**
n canto natalizio; **Christmas Day** n il
giorno di Natale; **Christmas Eve** n la
vigilia di Natale; **Christmas pudding** n
(esp BRIT) specie di budino con frutta secca,
spezie e brandy; **Christmas tree** n albero
di Natale
chrome [krəum] n cromo
chronic [ˈkrɔnɪk] adj cronico(-a)
chrysanthemum [krɪˈsænθəməm] n
crisantemo

chubby [ˈtʃʌbɪ] adj paffuto(-a)
chuck [tʃʌk] (inf) vt buttare, gettare; (BRIT:
also: **~ up**) piantare; **chuck out** vt buttar
fuori
chuckle [ˈtʃʌkl] vi ridere sommessamente
chum [tʃʌm] n compagno(-a)
chunk [tʃʌŋk] n pezzo
church [tʃəːtʃ] n chiesa; **churchyard** n
sagrato
churn [tʃəːn] n (for butter) zangola; (for milk)
bidone m
chute [ʃuːt] n (also: **rubbish ~**) canale m di
scarico; (BRIT: children's slide) scivolo
chutney [ˈtʃʌtnɪ] n salsa piccante (di frutta,
zucchero e spezie)
CIA (US) n abbr (= Central Intelligence Agency)
CIA f
CID (BRIT) n abbr (= Criminal Investigation
Department) ≈ polizia giudiziaria
cider [ˈsaɪdəʳ] n sidro
cigar [sɪˈgɑːʳ] n sigaro
cigarette [sɪgəˈrɛt] n sigaretta; **cigarette
lighter** n accendino
cinema [ˈsɪnəmə] n cinema m inv
cinnamon [ˈsɪnəmən] n cannella
circle [ˈsəːkl] n cerchio; (of friends etc)
circolo; (in cinema) galleria ▷ vi girare in
circolo ▷ vt (surround) circondare; (move
round) girare intorno a
circuit [ˈsəːkɪt] n circuito
circular [ˈsəːkjuləʳ] adj circolare ▷ n
circolare f
circulate [ˈsəːkjuleɪt] vi circolare ▷ vt
far circolare; **circulation** [-ˈleɪʃən] n
circolazione f; (of newspaper) tiratura
circumstances [ˈsəːkəmstənsɪz] npl
circostanze fpl; (financial condition)
condizioni fpl finanziarie
circus [ˈsəːkəs] n circo
cite [saɪt] vt citare
citizen [ˈsɪtɪzn] n (of country) cittadino(-a);
(of town) abitante m/f; **citizenship** n
cittadinanza
citrus fruits [ˈsɪtrəs-] npl agrumi mpl
city [ˈsɪtɪ] n città f inv; **the C~** la Città di
Londra (centro commerciale); **city centre**
n centro della città; **city technology
college** n (BRIT) istituto tecnico superiore
(finanziato dall'industria)
civic [ˈsɪvɪk] adj civico(-a)
civil [ˈsɪvɪl] adj civile; **civilian** [sɪˈvɪlɪən]
adj, n borghese m/f
civilization [sɪvɪlaɪˈzeɪʃən] n civiltà f inv
civilized [ˈsɪvɪlaɪzd] adj civilizzato(-a); (fig)
cortese
civil: **civil law** n codice m, civile; (study)
diritto civile; **civil rights** npl diritti mpl
civili; **civil servant** n impiegato(-a)
statale; **Civil Service** n amministrazione f

statale; **civil war** n guerra civile

CJD abbr (= Creutzfeld Jacob disease) malattia di Creutzfeldt-Jacob

claim [kleɪm] vt (assert): **to ~ (that)/to be** sostenere (che)/di essere; (credit, rights etc) rivendicare; (damages) richiedere ▷ vi (for insurance) fare una domanda d'indennizzo ▷ n pretesa; rivendicazione f; richiesta; **claim form** n (gen) modulo di richiesta; (for expenses) modulo di rimborso spese

clam [klæm] n vongola

clamp [klæmp] n pinza; morsa ▷ vt stringere con una morsa; (Aut: wheel) applicare i ceppi bloccaruote a

clan [klæn] n clan m inv

clap [klæp] vi applaudire

claret ['klærət] n vino di Bordeaux

clarify ['klærɪfaɪ] vt chiarificare, chiarire

clarinet [klærɪ'nɛt] n clarinetto

clarity ['klærɪtɪ] n clarità

clash [klæʃ] n frastuono; (fig) scontro ▷ vi scontrarsi; cozzare

clasp [klɑːsp] n (hold) stretta; (of necklace, bag) fermaglio, fibbia ▷ vt stringere

class [klɑːs] n classe f ▷ vt classificare

classic ['klæsɪk] adj classico(-a) ▷ n classico; **classical** adj classico(-a)

classification [klæsɪfɪ'keɪʃən] n classificazione f

classify ['klæsɪfaɪ] vt classificare

classmate ['klɑːsmeɪt] n compagno(-a) di classe

classroom ['klɑːsrum] n aula

classy ['klɑːsɪ] adj (inf) chic inv, elegante

clatter ['klætər] n tintinnio; scalpitio ▷ vi tintinnare; scalpitare

clause [klɔːz] n clausola; (Ling) proposizione f

claustrophobic [klɔːstrə'fəubɪk] adj claustrofobico(-a)

claw [klɔː] n (of bird of prey) artiglio; (of lobster) pinza

clay [kleɪ] n argilla

clean [kliːn] adj pulito(-a); (clear, smooth) liscio(-a) ▷ vt pulire; **clean up** vt (also fig) ripulire; **cleaner** n (person) donna delle pulizie; **cleaner's** n (also: **dry cleaner's**) tintoria; **cleaning** n pulizia

cleanser ['klɛnzər] n detergente m

clear [klɪər] adj chiaro(-a); (glass etc) trasparente; (road, way) libero(-a); (conscience) pulito(-a) ▷ vt sgombrare; liberare; (table) sparecchiare; (cheque) fare la compensazione di; (Law: suspect) discolpare; (obstacle) superare ▷ vi (weather) rasserenarsi; (fog) andarsene ▷ adv **~ of** distante da; **clear away** vt (things, clothes etc) mettere a posto; **to ~ away the dishes** sparecchiare la tavola;

clear up vt mettere in ordine; (mystery) risolvere; **clearance** n (removal) sgombro; (permission) autorizzazione f, permesso; **clear-cut** adj ben delineato(-a), distinto(-a); **clearing** n radura; **clearly** adv chiaramente; **clearway** (BRIT) n strada con divieto di sosta

clench [klɛntʃ] vt stringere

clergy ['klɜːdʒɪ] n clero

clerk [klɑːk, (US) klɑːrk] n (BRIT) impiegato(-a); (US) commesso(-a)

clever ['klɛvər] adj (mentally) intelligente; (deft, skilful) abile; (device, arrangement) ingegnoso(-a)

cliché ['kliːʃeɪ] n cliché m inv

click [klɪk] vi scattare ▷ vt (heels etc) battere; (tongue) far schioccare

client ['klaɪənt] n cliente m/f

cliff [klɪf] n scogliera scoscesa, rupe f

climate ['klaɪmɪt] n clima m

climax ['klaɪmæks] n culmine m; (sexual) orgasmo

climb [klaɪm] vi salire; (clamber) arrampicarsi ▷ vt salire; (Climbing) scalare ▷ n salita; arrampicata; scalata; **climb down** vi scendere; (BRIT fig) far marcia indietro; **climber** n rocciatore(-trice); alpinista m/f; **climbing** n alpinismo

clinch [klɪntʃ] vt (deal) concludere

cling [klɪŋ] (pt, pp clung) vi **to ~ (to)** aggrapparsi (a); (of clothes) aderire strettamente (a)

Clingfilm® ['klɪŋfɪlm] n pellicola trasparente (per alimenti)

clinic ['klɪnɪk] n clinica

clip [klɪp] n (for hair) forcina; (also: **paper ~**) graffetta; (TV, Cinema) sequenza ▷ vt attaccare insieme; (hair, nails) tagliare; (hedge) tosare; **clipping** n (from newspaper) ritaglio

cloak [kləuk] n mantello ▷ vt avvolgere; **cloakroom** n (for coats etc) guardaroba m inv; (BRIT: W.C.) gabinetti mpl

clock [klɔk] n orologio; **clock in** or **on** vi timbrare il cartellino (all'entrata); **clock off** or **out** vi timbrare il cartellino (all'uscita); **clockwise** adv in senso orario; **clockwork** n movimento or meccanismo a orologeria ▷ adj a molla

clog [klɔg] n zoccolo ▷ vt intasare ▷ vi (also: **~ up**) intasarsi, bloccarsi

clone [kləun] n clone m

close¹ [kləus] adj **~ (to)** vicino(-a) (a); (watch, link, relative) stretto(-a); (examination) attento(-a); (contest) combattuto(-a); (weather) afoso(-a) ▷ adv vicino, dappresso; **~ to** vicino a; **~ by, ~ at hand** a portata di mano; **a ~ friend** un amico intimo; **to have a ~ shave** (fig) scamparla bella

close² [kləuz] vt chiudere ▷ vi (shop etc) chiudere; (lid, door etc) chiudersi; (end) finire ▷ n (end) fine f; **what time do you ~?** a che ora chiude?; **close down** vi cessare (definitivamente); **closed** adj chiuso(-a)

closely ['kləuslı] adv (examine, watch) da vicino; (related) strettamente

closet ['klɔzɪt] n (cupboard) armadio

close-up ['kləusʌp] n primo piano

closing time n orario di chiusura

closure ['kləuʒəʳ] n chiusura

clot [klɔt] n (also: **blood ~**) coagulo; (inf: idiot) scemo(-a) ▷ vi coagularsi

cloth [klɔθ] n (material) tessuto, stoffa; (rag) strofinaccio

clothes [kləuðz] npl abltl mpl, vestiti mpl; **clothes line** n corda (per stendere il bucato); **clothes peg** (us **clothes pin**) n molletta

clothing ['kləuðɪŋ] n = **clothes**

cloud [klaud] n nuvola; **cloud over** vi rannuvolarsi; (fig) offuscarsi; **cloudy** adj nuvoloso(-a); (liquid) torbido(-a)

clove [kləuv] n chiodo di garofano; **clove of garlic** n spicchio d'aglio

clown [klaun] n pagliaccio ▷ vi (also: **~ about, ~ around**) fare il pagliaccio

club [klʌb] n (society) club m inv, circolo; (weapon, Golf) mazza ▷ vt bastonare ▷ vi **to ~ together** associarsi; **~s** npl (Cards) fiori mpl; **club class** n (Aviat) classe f club inv

clue [klu:] n indizio; (in crosswords) definizione f; **I haven't a ~** non ho la minima idea

clump [klʌmp] n (of flowers, trees) gruppo; (of grass) ciuffo

clumsy ['klʌmzı] adj goffo(-a)

clung [klʌŋ] pt, pp of **cling**

cluster ['klʌstəʳ] n gruppo ▷ vi raggrupparsi

clutch [klʌtʃ] n (grip, grasp) presa, stretta; (Aut) frizione f ▷ vt afferrare, stringere forte

cm abbr (= centimetre) cm

Co. abbr = **county; company**

c/o abbr (= care of) presso

coach [kəutʃ] n (bus) pullman m inv; (horse-drawn, of train) carrozza; (Sport) allenatore(-trice); (tutor) chi dà ripetizioni ▷ vt allenare; dare ripetizioni a; **coach station** (BRIT) n stazione f delle corriere; **coach trip** n viaggio in pullman

coal [kəul] n carbone m

coalition [kəuə'lıʃən] n coalizione f

coarse [kɔ:s] adj (salt, sand etc) grosso(-a); (cloth, person) rozzo(-a)

coast [kəust] n costa ▷ vi (with cycle etc) scendere a ruota libera; **coastal** adj costiero(-a); **coastguard** n guardia costiera; **coastline** n linea costiera

coat [kəut] n cappotto; (of animal) pelo; (of paint) mano f ▷ vt coprire; **coat hanger** n attaccapanni m inv; **coating** n rivestimento

coax [kəuks] vt indurre (con moine)

cob [kɔb] n see **corn**

cobbled ['kɔbld] adj **~ street** strada pavimentata a ciottoli

cobweb ['kɔbwɛb] n ragnatela

cocaine [kə'keın] n cocaina

cock [kɔk] n (rooster) gallo; (male bird) maschio ▷ vt (gun) armare; **cockerel** n galletto

cockney ['kɔknı] n cockney m/f inv (abitante dei quartieri popolari dell'East End di Londra)

cockpit ['kɔkpıt] n abitacolo

cockroach ['kɔkrəutʃ] n blatta

cocktail ['kɔkteıl] n cocktail m inv

cocoa ['kəukəu] n cacao

coconut ['kəukənʌt] n noce f di cocco

cod [kɔd] n merluzzo

C.O.D. abbr = **cash on delivery**

code [kəud] n codice m

coeducational ['kəuɛdju'keıʃənl] adj misto(-a)

coffee ['kɔfı] n caffè m inv; **coffee bar** (BRIT) n caffè m inv; **coffee bean** n grano or chicco di caffè; **coffee break** n pausa per il caffè; **coffee maker** n bollitore m per il caffè; **coffeepot** n caffettiera; **coffee shop** n ≈ caffè m inv; **coffee table** n tavolino

coffin ['kɔfın] n bara

cog [kɔg] n dente m

cognac ['kɔnjæk] n cognac m inv

coherent [kəu'hıərənt] adj coerente

coil [kɔıl] n rotolo; (Elec) bobina; (contraceptive) spirale f ▷ vt avvolgere

coin [kɔın] n moneta ▷ vt (word) coniare

coincide [kəuın'saıd] vi coincidere; **coincidence** [kəu'ınsıdəns] n combinazione f

Coke® [kəuk] n coca

coke [kəuk] n coke m

colander ['kɔləndəʳ] n colino

cold [kəuld] adj freddo(-a) ▷ n freddo; (Med) raffreddore m; **it's ~** fa freddo; **to be ~** (person) aver freddo; (object) essere freddo(-a); **to catch ~** prendere freddo; **to catch a ~** prendere un raffreddore; **in ~ blood** a sangue freddo; **cold sore** n erpete m

coleslaw ['kəulslɔ:] n insalata di cavolo bianco

colic ['kɔlık] n colica

collaborate [kəˈlæbəreɪt] vi collaborare
collapse [kəˈlæps] vi crollare ▷ n crollo;
(Med) collasso
collar [ˈkɔlər] n (of coat, shirt) colletto; (of
dog, cat) collare m; **collarbone** n clavicola
colleague [ˈkɔliːg] n collega m/f
collect [kəˈlɛkt] vt (gen) raccogliere; (as
a hobby) fare collezione di; (BRIT: call and
pick up) prendere; (money owed, pension)
riscuotere; (donations, subscriptions) fare
una colletta di ▷ vi adunarsi, riunirsi;
ammucchiarsi; **to call ~** (US Tel) fare
una chiamata a carico del destinatario;
collection [kəˈlɛkʃən] n raccolta;
collezione f; (for money) colletta; **collective**
adj collettivo(-a) ▷ n collettivo; **collector**
[kəˈlɛktər] n collezionista m/f
college [ˈkɔlɪdʒ] n college m inv; (of
technology etc) istituto superiore
collide [kəˈlaɪd] vi **to ~ with** scontrarsi
(con)
collision [kəˈlɪʒən] n collisione f, scontro
cologne [kəˈləʊn] n (also: **eau de ~**) acqua
di colonia
Colombia [kəˈlɔmbɪə] n Colombia;
Colombian adj, n colombiano(-a)
colon [ˈkəʊlən] n (sign) due punti mpl;
(Med) colon m inv
colonel [ˈkɜːnl] n colonnello
colonial [kəˈləʊnɪəl] adj coloniale
colony [ˈkɔlənɪ] n colonia
colour etc [ˈkʌlər] (US **color**) n colore
m ▷ vt colorare; (tint, dye) tingere; (fig:
affect) influenzare ▷ vi (blush) arrossire;
colour in vt colorare; **colour-blind** adj
daltonico(-a); **coloured** adj (photo) a
colori; (person) di colore; **colour film** n
(for camera) pellicola a colori; **colourful**
adj pieno(-a) di colore, a vivaci colori;
(personality) colorato(-a); **colouring** n
(substance) colorante m; (complexion)
colorito; **colour television** n televisione
f a colori
column [ˈkɔləm] n colonna
coma [ˈkəʊmə] n coma m inv
comb [kəʊm] n pettine m ▷ vt (hair)
pettinare; (area) battere a tappeto
combat [ˈkɔmbæt] n combattimento ▷ vt
combattere, lottare contro
combination [kɔmbɪˈneɪʃən] n
combinazione f
combine [vb kəmˈbaɪn, n ˈkɔmbaɪn] vt
to ~ (with) combinare (con); (one quality
with another) unire (a) ▷ vi unirsi; (Chem)
combinarsi ▷ n (Econ) associazione f
come [kʌm] (pt **came**, pp **come**) vi venire;
arrivare; **to ~ to** (decision etc) raggiungere;
I've ~ to like him ha cominciato a
piacermi; **to ~ undone** slacciarsi; **to ~**
loose allentarsi; **come across** vt fus
trovare per caso; **come along** vi (pupil,
work) fare progressi; **~ along!** avanti!,
andiamo!, forza!; **come back** vi ritornare;
come down vi scendere; (prices) calare;
(buildings) essere demolito(-a); **come from**
vt fus venire da; provenire da; **come in** vi
entrare; **come off** vi (button) staccarsi;
(stain) andar via; (attempt) riuscire; **come
on** vi (pupil, work, project) fare progressi;
(lights) accendersi; (electricity) entrare in
funzione; **~ on!** avanti!, andiamo!, forza!;
come out vi uscire; (stain) andare via;
come round vi (after faint, operation)
riprendere conoscenza, rinvenire; **come
to** vi rinvenire; **come up** vi (sun) salire;
(problem) sorgere; (event) essere in arrivo;
(in conversation) saltar fuori; **come up with**
vt fus **he came up with an idea** venne
fuori con un'idea
comeback [ˈkʌmbæk] n (Theatre etc)
ritorno
comedian [kəˈmiːdɪən] n comico
comedy [ˈkɔmɪdɪ] n commedia
comet [ˈkɔmɪt] n cometa
comfort [ˈkʌmfət] n comodità f inv,
benessere m; (relief) consolazione f,
conforto ▷ vt consolare, confortare;
comfortable adj comodo(-a); (financially)
agiato(-a); **comfort station** (US) n
gabinetti mpl
comic [ˈkɔmɪk] adj (also: **~al**) comico(-a)
▷ n comico; (BRIT: magazine) giornaletto;
comic book (US) n giornalino (a fumetti);
comic strip n fumetto
comma [ˈkɔmə] n virgola
command [kəˈmɑːnd] n ordine m,
comando; (Mil: authority) comando;
(mastery) padronanza ▷ vt comandare;
to ~ sb to do ordinare a qn di fare;
commander n capo; (Mil) comandante m
commemorate [kəˈmɛməreɪt] vt
commemorare
commence [kəˈmɛns] vt, vi cominciare;
commencement (US) n (Univ) cerimonia
di consegna dei diplomi
commend [kəˈmɛnd] vt lodare;
raccomandare
comment [ˈkɔmɛnt] n commento ▷ vi **to
~ (on)** fare commenti (su); **commentary**
[ˈkɔməntərɪ] n commentario; (Sport)
radiocronaca; telecronaca; **commentator**
[ˈkɔmənteɪtər] n commentatore(-trice);
radiocronista m/f; telecronista m/f
commerce [ˈkɔmɜːs] n commercio
commercial [kəˈmɜːʃəl] adj commerciale
▷ n (TV, Radio: advertisement) pubblicità
f inv; **commercial break** n intervallo
pubblicitario

commission [kəˈmɪʃən] n commissione f ▷ vt (work of art) commissionare; **out of ~** (Naut) in disarmo; **commissioner** n (Police) questore m

commit [kəˈmɪt] vt (act) commettere; (to sb's care) affidare; **to ~ o.s. to do** impegnarsi (a fare); **to ~ suicide** suicidarsi; **commitment** n impegno; promessa

committee [kəˈmɪtɪ] n comitato

commodity [kəˈmɔdɪtɪ] n prodotto, articolo

common [ˈkɔmən] adj comune; (pej) volgare; (usual) normale ▷ n terreno comune; **the C~s** (BRIT) ▷ npl la Camera dei Comuni; **in ~** in comune; **commonly** adv comunemente, usualmente; **commonplace** adj banale, ordinario(-a); **Commons** npl (BRIT Pol): **the (House of) Commons** la Camera dei Comuni; **common sense** n buon senso; **Commonwealth** n **the Commonwealth** il Commonwealth

● **COMMONWEALTH**
●
● Il **Commonwealth** è un'associazione
● di stati sovrani indipendenti e di
● alcuni territori annessi che facevano
● parte dell'antico Impero Britannico.
● Nel 1931 questi assunsero il nome
● di "Commonwealth of Nations",
● denominazione successivamente
● semplificata in "Commonwealth".
● Attualmente gli stati del
● "Commonwealth" riconoscono ancora il
● proprio capo di stato.

communal [ˈkɔmjuːnl] adj (for common use) pubblico(-a)

commune [n ˈkɔmjuːn, vb kəˈmjuːn] n (group) comune f ▷ vi **to ~ with** mettersi in comunione con

communicate [kəˈmjuːnɪkeɪt] vt comunicare, trasmettere ▷ vi **to ~ with** comunicare (con)

communication [kəmjuːnɪˈkeɪʃən] n comunicazione f

communion [kəˈmjuːnɪən] n (also: **Holy C~**) comunione f

communism [ˈkɔmjunɪzəm] n comunismo; **communist** adj, n comunista m/f

community [kəˈmjuːnɪtɪ] n comunità f inv; **community centre** (US **community center**) n circolo ricreativo; **community service** n (BRIT) ≈ lavoro sostitutivo

commute [kəˈmjuːt] vi fare il pendolare ▷ vt (Law) commutare; **commuter** n pendolare m/f

compact [adj kəmˈpækt, n ˈkɔmpækt] adj compatto(-a) ▷ n (also: **powder ~**) portacipria m inv; **compact disc** n compact disc m inv; **compact disc player** n lettore m CD inv

companion [kəmˈpænɪən] n compagno(-a)

company [ˈkʌmpənɪ] n (also Comm, Mil, Theatre) compagnia; **to keep sb ~** tenere compagnia a qn; **company car** n macchina (di proprietà) della ditta; **company director** n amministratore m, consigliere m di amministrazione

comparable [ˈkɔmpərəbl] adj simile

comparative [kəmˈpærətɪv] adj relativo(-a); (adjective etc) comparativo(-a); **comparatively** adv relativamente

compare [kəmˈpɛəʳ] vt **to ~ sth/sb with/to** confrontare qc/qn con/a ▷ vi **to ~ (with)** reggere il confronto (con); **comparison** [-ˈpærɪsn] n confronto; **in comparison (with)** in confronto (a)

compartment [kəmˈpɑːtmənt] n compartimento; (Rail) scompartimento; **a non-smoking ~** uno scompartimento per non-fumatori

compass [ˈkʌmpəs] n bussola; **~es** npl (Math) compasso

compassion [kəmˈpæʃən] n compassione f

compatible [kəmˈpætɪbl] adj compatibile

compel [kəmˈpɛl] vt costringere, obbligare; **compelling** adj (fig: argument) irresistibile

compensate [ˈkɔmpənseɪt] vt risarcire ▷ vi **to ~ for** compensare; **compensation** [-ˈseɪʃən] n compensazione f; (money) risarcimento

compete [kəmˈpiːt] vi (take part) concorrere; (vie): **to ~ with** fare concorrenza (a)

competent [ˈkɔmpɪtənt] adj competente

competition [kɔmpɪˈtɪʃən] n gara; concorso; (Econ) concorrenza

competitive [kəmˈpɛtɪtɪv] adj (Econ) concorrenziale; (sport) agonistico(-a); (person) che ha spirito di competizione; che ha spirito agonistico

competitor [kəmˈpɛtɪtəʳ] n concorrente m/f

complacent [kəmˈpleɪsnt] adj compiaciuto(-a) di sé

complain [kəmˈpleɪn] vi lagnarsi, lamentarsi; **complaint** n lamento; (in shop etc) reclamo; (Med) malattia

complement [n ˈkɔmplɪmənt, vb ˈkɔmplɪmɛnt] n complemento; (especially of ship's crew etc) effettivo ▷ vt (enhance) accompagnarsi bene a; **complementary**

[kɔmplɪ'mɛntərɪ] adj complementare
complete [kəm'pliːt] adj completo(-a)
▷ vt completare; (a form) riempire;
completely adv completamente;
completion n completamento
complex ['kɔmplɛks] adj complesso(-a)
▷ n (Psych, of buildings etc) complesso
complexion [kəm'plɛkʃən] n (of face)
carnagione f
compliance [kəm'plaɪəns] n
acquiescenza; **in ~ with** (orders, wishes etc)
in conformità con
complicate ['kɔmplɪkeɪt] vt complicare;
complicated adj complicato(-a);
complication [-'keɪʃən] n complicazione f
compliment [n 'kɔmplɪmənt, vb
'kɔmplɪmɛnt] n complimento ▷ vt fare
un complimento a; **complimentary**
[-'mɛntərɪ] adj complimentoso(-a),
elogiativo(-a); (free) in omaggio
comply [kəm'plaɪ] vi **to ~ with** assentire
a; conformarsi a
component [kəm'pəunənt] adj
componente ▷ n componente m
compose [kəm'pəuz] vt (form) **to be ~d
of** essere composto di; (music, poem etc)
comporre; **to ~ o.s.** ricomporsi; **composer**
n (Mus) compositore(-trice); **composition**
[kɔmpə'zɪʃən] n composizione f
composure [kəm'pəuʒəʳ] n calma
compound ['kɔmpaund] n (Chem, Ling)
composto; (enclosure) recinto ▷ adj
composto(-a)
comprehension [kɔmprɪ'hɛnʃən] n
comprensione f
comprehensive [kɔmprɪ'hɛnsɪv] adj
completo(-a); **comprehensive (school)**
(BRIT) n scuola secondaria aperta a tutti

> Be careful not to translate
> *comprehensive* by the Italian word
> *comprensivo*.

compress [vb kəm'prɛs, n 'kɔmprɛs] vt
comprimere ▷ n (Med) compressa
comprise [kəm'praɪz] vt (also: **be ~d**)
comprendere
compromise ['kɔmprəmaɪz] n
compromesso ▷ vt compromettere ▷ vi
venire a un compromesso
compulsive [kəm'pʌlsɪv] adj (liar, gambler)
che non riesce a controllarsi; (viewing,
reading) cui non si può fare a meno
compulsory [kəm'pʌlsərɪ] adj
obbligatorio(-a)
computer [kəm'pjuːtəʳ] n computer
m inv, elaboratore m elettronico;
computer game n gioco per computer;
computer-generated adj realizzato(-a)
al computer; **computerize** vt
computerizzare; **computer programmer**

n programmatore(-trice); **computer
programming** n programmazione
f di computer; **computer science** n
informatica; **computer studies** npl
informatica; **computing** n informatica
con [kɔn] (inf) vt truffare ▷ n truffa
conceal [kən'siːl] vt nascondere
concede [kən'siːd] vt ammettere
conceited [kən'siːtɪd] adj
presuntuoso(-a), vanitoso(-a)
conceive [kən'siːv] vt concepire ▷ vi
concepire un bambino
concentrate ['kɔnsəntreɪt] vi
concentrarsi ▷ vt concentrare
concentration [kɔnsən'treɪʃən] n
concentrazione f
concept ['kɔnsɛpt] n concetto
concern [kən'səːn] n affare m; (Comm)
azienda, ditta; (anxiety) preoccupazione
f ▷ vt riguardare; **to be ~ed (about)**
preoccuparsi (di); **concerning** prep
riguardo a, circa
concert ['kɔnsət] n concerto; **concert
hall** n sala da concerti
concerto [kən'tʃəːtəu] n concerto
concession [kən'sɛʃən] n concessione f
concise [kən'saɪs] adj conciso(-a)
conclude [kən'kluːd] vt concludere;
conclusion [-'kluːʒən] n conclusione f
concrete ['kɔnkriːt] n calcestruzzo ▷ adj
concreto(-a), di calcestruzzo
concussion [kən'kʌʃən] n commozione
f cerebrale
condemn [kən'dɛm] vt condannare;
(building) dichiarare pericoloso(-a)
condensation [kɔndɛn'seɪʃən] n
condensazione f
condense [kən'dɛns] vi condensarsi ▷ vt
condensare
condition [kən'dɪʃən] n condizione f;
(Med) malattia ▷ vt condizionare; **on ~
that** a condizione che + sub, a condizione
di; **conditional** adj condizionale; **to
be conditional upon** dipendere da;
conditioner n (for hair) balsamo; (for
fabrics) ammorbidente m
condo ['kɔndəu] (US) n abbr (inf)
= **condominium**
condom ['kɔndəm] n preservativo
condominium [kɔndə'mɪnɪəm] (US) n
condominio
condone [kən'dəun] vt condonare
conduct [n 'kɔndʌkt, vb kən'dʌkt]
n condotta ▷ vt condurre; (manage)
dirigere; amministrare; (Mus) dirigere;
to ~ o.s. comportarsi; **conducted tour**
[kən'dʌktɪd-] n gita accompagnata;
conductor n (of orchestra) direttore m
d'orchestra; (on bus) bigliettaio; (US: on

train) controllore *m*; (*Elec*) conduttore *m*

cone [kəun] *n* cono; (*Bot*) pigna, (*traffic cone*) birillo

confectionery [kən'fɛkʃənrɪ] *n* dolciumi *mpl*

confer [kən'fəː'] *vt* **to ~ sth on** conferire qc a ▷ *vi* conferire

conference ['kɔnfərns] *n* congresso

confess [kən'fɛs] *vt* confessare, ammettere ▷ *vi* confessare; **confession** [kən'fɛʃən] *n* confessione *f*

confide [kən'faɪd] *vi* **to ~ in** confidarsi con

confidence ['kɔnfɪdns] *n* confidenza; (*trust*) fiducia; (*self-assurance*) sicurezza di sé; **in ~** (*speak, write*) in confidenza, confidenzialmente; **confident** *adj* sicuro(-a), sicuro(-a) di sé, **confidential** [kɔnfɪ'dɛnʃəl] *adj* riservato(-a), confidenziale

confine [kən'faɪn] *vt* limitare; (*shut up*) rinchiudere; **confined** *adj* (*space*) ristretto(-a)

confirm [kən'fəːm] *vt* confermare; **confirmation** [kɔnfə'meɪʃən] *n* conferma; (*Rel*) cresima

confiscate ['kɔnfɪskeɪt] *vt* confiscare

conflict [*n* 'kɔnflɪkt, *vb* kən'flɪkt] *n* conflitto ▷ *vi* essere in conflitto

conform [kən'fɔːm] *vi* **to ~ to** conformarsi (a)

confront [kən'frʌnt] *vt* (*enemy, danger*) affrontare; **confrontation** [kɔnfrən'teɪʃən] *n* scontro

confuse [kən'fjuːz] *vt* (*one thing with another*) confondere; **confused** *adj* confuso(-a); **confusing** *adj* che fa confondere; **confusion** [-'fjuːʒən] *n* confusione *f*

congestion [kən'dʒɛstʃən] *n* congestione *f*

congratulate [kən'grætjuleɪt] *vt* **to ~ sb (on)** congratularsi con qn (per *or* di); **congratulations** [-'leɪʃənz] *npl* auguri *mpl*; (*on success*) complimenti *mpl*, congratulazioni *fpl*

congregation [kɔŋgrɪ'geɪʃən] *n* congregazione *f*

congress ['kɔŋgrɛs] *n* congresso; **congressman** (*irreg*: *US*) *n* membro del Congresso; **congresswoman** (*irreg*: *US*) *n* (donna) membro del Congresso

conifer ['kɔnɪfə'] *n* conifero

conjugate ['kɔndʒugeɪt] *vt* coniugare

conjugation [kɔndʒə'geɪʃən] *n* coniugazione *f*

conjunction [kən'dʒʌŋkʃən] *n* congiunzione *f*

conjure ['kʌndʒə'] *vi* fare giochi di prestigio

connect [kə'nɛkt] *vt* connettere, collegare; (*Elec, Tel*) collegare; (*fig*) associare ▷ *vi* (*train*): **to ~ with** essere in coincidenza con; **to be ~ed with** (*associated*) aver rapporti con; **connecting flight** *n* volo in coincidenza; **connection** [-ʃən] ▷ *n* relazione *f*, rapporto; (*Elec*) connessione *f*; (*train, plane*) coincidenza; (*Tel*) collegamento

conquer ['kɔŋkə'] *vt* conquistare; (*feelings*) vincere

conquest ['kɔŋkwɛst] *n* conquista

cons [kɔnz] *npl see* **convenience**; **pro**

conscience ['kɔnʃəns] *n* coscienza

conscientious [kɔnʃɪ'ɛnʃəs] *adj* coscienzioso(-a)

conscious ['kɔnʃəs] *adj* consapevole; (*Med*) cosciente; **consciousness** *n* consapevolezza; coscienza

consecutive [kən'sɛkjutɪv] *adj* consecutivo(-a); **on 3 ~ occasions** 3 volte di fila

consensus [kən'sɛnsəs] *n* consenso; **the ~ of opinion** l'opinione *f* unanime *or* comune

consent [kən'sɛnt] *n* consenso ▷ *vi* **to ~ (to)** acconsentire (a)

consequence ['kɔnsɪkwəns] *n* conseguenza, risultato; importanza

consequently ['kɔnsɪkwəntlɪ] *adv* di conseguenza, dunque

conservation [kɔnsə'veɪʃən] *n* conservazione *f*

conservative [kən'səːvətɪv] *adj* conservatore(-trice); (*cautious*) cauto(-a); **Conservative** (*BRIT*) *adj*, *n* (*Pol*) conservatore(-trice)

conservatory [kən'səːvətrɪ] *n* (*greenhouse*) serra; (*Mus*) conservatorio

consider [kən'sɪdə'] *vt* considerare; (*take into account*) tener conto di; **to ~ doing sth** considerare la possibilità di fare qc; **considerable** [kən'sɪdərəbl] *adj* considerevole, notevole; **considerably** *adv* notevolmente, decisamente; **considerate** [kən'sɪdərɪt] *adj* premuroso(-a); **consideration** [kənsɪdə'reɪʃən] *n* considerazione *f*; **considering** [kən'sɪdərɪŋ] *prep* in considerazione di

consignment [kən'saɪnmənt] *n* (*of goods*) consegna; spedizione *f*

consist [kən'sɪst] *vi* **to ~ of** constare di, essere composto(-a) di

consistency [kən'sɪstənsɪ] *n* consistenza; (*fig*) coerenza

consistent [kən'sɪstənt] *adj* coerente

consolation [kɔnsə'leɪʃən] *n* consolazione *f*

console¹ [kən'səul] *vt* consolare

console² ['kɔnsəul] n quadro di comando
consonant ['kɔnsənənt] n consonante f
conspicuous [kən'spɪkjuəs] adj
cospicuo(-a)
conspiracy [kən'spɪrəsɪ] n congiura,
cospirazione f
constable ['kʌnstəbl] (BRIT) n ≈ poliziotto,
agente m di polizia; **chief ~** ≈ questore m
constant ['kɔnstənt] adj costante,
continuo(-a); **constantly** adv
costantemente; continuamente
constipated ['kɔnstɪpeɪtɪd] adj
stitico(-a); **constipation** [kɔnstɪ'peɪʃən]
n stitichezza
constituency [kən'stɪtjuənsɪ] n collegio
elettorale
constitute ['kɔnstɪtjuːt] vt costituire
constitution [kɔnstɪ'tjuːʃən] n
costituzione f
constraint [kən'streɪnt] n costrizione f
construct [kən'strʌkt] vt costruire;
construction [-ʃən] n costruzione f;
constructive adj costruttivo(-a)
consul ['kɔnsl] n console m; **consulate**
['kɔnsjulɪt] n consolato
consult [kən'sʌlt] vt consultare;
consultant n (Med) consulente m medico;
(other specialist) consulente; **consultation**
[-'teɪʃən] n (Med) consulto; (discussion)
consultazione f; **consulting room** [kə
n'sʌltɪŋ-] (BRIT) n ambulatorio
consume [kən'sjuːm] vt consumare;
consumer n consumatore(-trice)
consumption [kən'sʌmpʃən] n consumo
cont. abbr = **continued**
contact ['kɔntækt] n contatto; (person)
conoscenza ▷ vt mettersi in contatto con;
contact lenses npl lenti fpl a contatto
contagious [kən'teɪdʒəs] adj (also fig)
contagioso(-a)
contain [kən'teɪn] vt contenere; **to ~ o.s.**
contenersi; **container** n recipiente m; (for
shipping etc) container m inv
contaminate [kən'tæmɪneɪt] vt
contaminare
cont'd abbr = **continued**
contemplate ['kɔntəmpleɪt] vt
contemplare; (consider) pensare a (or di)
contemporary [kən'tempərərɪ] adj, n
contemporaneo(-a)
contempt [kən'tempt] n disprezzo; **~ of
court** (Law) oltraggio alla Corte
contend [kən'tend] vt **to ~ that** sostenere
che ▷ vi **to ~ with** lottare contro
content¹ ['kɔntent] n contenuto; **~s** npl
(of box, case etc) contenuto; **(table of) ~s**
indice m
content² [kən'tent] adj contento(-a),
soddisfatto(-a) ▷ vt contentare,

soddisfare; **contented** adj contento(-a),
soddisfatto(-a)
contest [n 'kɔntest, vb kən'test] n
lotta; (competition) gara, concorso ▷ vt
contestare; impugnare; (compete for)
essere in lizza per; **contestant** [kə
n'testənt] n concorrente m/f; (in fight)
avversario(-a)
context ['kɔntekst] n contesto
continent ['kɔntɪnənt] n continente
m; **the C~** (BRIT) l'Europa continentale;
continental [-'nentl] adj continentale;
continental breakfast n colazione f
all'europea (senza piatti caldi); **continental
quilt** (BRIT) n piumino
continual [kən'tɪnjuəl] adj continuo(-a);
continually adv di continuo
continue [kən'tɪnjuː] vi continuare ▷ vt
continuare; (start again) riprendere
continuity [kɔntɪ'njuːɪtɪ] n continuità;
(TV, Cinema) (ordine m della) sceneggiatura
continuous [kən'tɪnjuəs] adj
continuo(-a), ininterrotto(-a); **continuous
assessment** n (BRIT) valutazione f
continua; **continuously** adv (repeatedly)
continuamente; (uninterruptedly)
ininterrottamente
contour ['kɔntuə'] n contorno, profilo;
(also: **~ line**) curva di livello
contraception [kɔntrə'sepʃən] n
contraccezione f
contraceptive [kɔntrə'septɪv] adj
contraccettivo(-a) ▷ n contraccettivo
contract [n 'kɔntrækt, vb kən'trækt] n
contratto ▷ vi (become smaller) contrarsi;
(Comm) **to ~ to do sth** fare un contratto
per fare qc ▷ vt (illness) contrarre;
contractor n imprenditore m
contradict [kɔntrə'dɪkt] vt contraddire;
contradiction [kɔntrə'dɪkʃən] n
contraddizione f; **to be in contradiction
with** discordare con
contrary¹ ['kɔntrərɪ] adj contrario(-a);
(unfavourable) avverso(-a), contrario(-a)
▷ n contrario; **on the ~** al contrario;
unless you hear to the ~ salvo
contrordine
contrary² [kən'treərɪ] adj (perverse)
bisbetico(-a)
contrast [n 'kɔntrɑːst, vb kən'trɑːst] n
contrasto ▷ vt mettere in contrasto; **in ~
to** contrariamente a
contribute [kən'trɪbjuːt] vi contribuire
▷ vt **to ~ £10/an article to** dare
10 sterline/un articolo a; **to ~ to**
contribuire a; (newspaper) scrivere
per; **contribution** [kɔntrɪ'bjuːʃən] n
contributo; **contributor** n (to newspaper)
collaboratore(-trice)

control [kən'trəul] vt controllare; (firm, operation etc) dirigere ▷ n controllo; **~s** npl (of vehicle etc) comandi mpl; (governmental) controlli mpl; **under ~** sotto controllo; **to be in ~ of** avere il controllo di; **to go out of ~** (car) non rispondere ai comandi; (situation) sfuggire di mano; **control tower** n (Aviat) torre f di controllo

controversial [kɒntrə'vəːʃl] adj controverso(-a), polemico(-a)

controversy ['kɒntrəvəːsɪ] n controversia, polemica

convenience [kən'viːnɪəns] n comodità f inv; **at your ~** a suo comodo; **all modern ~s** (BRIT), **all mod cons** tutte le comodità moderne

convenient [kən'viːnɪənt] adj comodo(-a)

Be careful not to translate convenient by the Italian word conveniente.

convent ['kɒnvənt] n convento

convention [kən'vɛnʃən] n convenzione f; (meeting) convegno; **conventional** adj convenzionale

conversation [kɒnvə'seɪʃən] n conversazione f

conversely [kɒn'vəːslɪ] adv al contrario, per contro

conversion [kən'vəːʃən] n conversione f; (BRIT: of house) trasformazione f, rimodernamento

convert [vb kən'vəːt, n 'kɒnvəːt] vt (Comm, Rel) convertire; (alter) trasformare ▷ n convertito(-a); **convertible** n macchina decappottabile

convey [kən'veɪ] vt trasportare; (thanks) comunicare; (idea) dare; **conveyor belt** [kən'veɪər-] n nastro trasportatore

convict [vb kən'vɪkt, n 'kɒnvɪkt] vt dichiarare colpevole ▷ n carcerato(-a); **conviction** [-ʃən] n condanna; (belief) convinzione f

convince [kən'vɪns] vt convincere, persuadere; **convinced** adj **convinced of/that** convinto(-a) di/che; **convincing** adj convincente

convoy ['kɒnvɔɪ] n convoglio

cook [kuk] vt cucinare, cuocere ▷ vi cuocere; (person) cucinare ▷ n cuoco(-a); **cook book** n libro di cucina; **cooker** n fornello, cucina; **cookery** n cucina; **cookery book** (BRIT) n = **cook book**; **cookie** (US) n biscotto; **cooking** n cucina

cool [kuːl] adj fresco(-a); (not afraid, calm) calmo(-a); (unfriendly) freddo(-a) ▷ vt raffreddare; (room) rinfrescare ▷ vi (water) raffreddarsi; (air) rinfrescarsi; **cool down** vi raffreddarsi; (fig: person, situation) calmarsi; **cool off** vi (become calmer) calmarsi; (lose enthusiasm) perdere interesse

cop [kɒp] (inf) n sbirro

cope [kəup] vi **to ~ with** (problems) far fronte a

copper ['kɒpər] n rame m; (inf: policeman) sbirro

copy ['kɒpɪ] n copia ▷ vt copiare; **copyright** n diritto d'autore

coral ['kɒrəl] n corallo

cord [kɔːd] n corda; (Elec) filo; **~s** npl (trousers) calzoni mpl (di velluto) a coste; **cordless** adj senza cavo

corduroy ['kɔːdərɔɪ] n fustagno

core [kɔːr] n (of fruit) torsolo; (of organization etc) cuore m ▷ vt estrarre il torsolo da

coriander [kɒrɪ'ændər] n coriandolo

cork [kɔːk] n sughero; (of bottle) tappo; **corkscrew** n cavatappi m inv

corn [kɔːn] n (BRIT: wheat) grano; (US: maize) granturco; (on foot) callo; **~ on the cob** (Culin) pannocchia cotta

corned beef ['kɔːnd-] n carne f di manzo in scatola

corner ['kɔːnər] n angolo; (Aut) curva ▷ vt intrappolare; mettere con le spalle al muro; (Comm: market) accaparrare ▷ vi prendere una curva

corner shop (BRIT) piccolo negozio di generi alimentari

cornflakes ['kɔːnfleɪks] npl fiocchi mpl di granturco

cornflour ['kɔːnflauər] (BRIT) n farina finissima di granturco

cornstarch ['kɔːnstɑːtʃ] (US) n = **cornflour**

Cornwall ['kɔːnwəl] n Cornovaglia

coronary ['kɒrənərɪ] n **~ (thrombosis)** trombosi f coronaria

coronation [kɒrə'neɪʃən] n incoronazione f

coroner ['kɒrənər] n magistrato incaricato di indagare la causa di morte in circostanze sospette

corporal ['kɔːpərl] n caporalmaggiore m ▷ adj **~ punishment** pena corporale

corporate ['kɔːpərɪt] adj costituito(-a) (in corporazione), comune

corporation [kɔːpə'reɪʃən] n (of town) consiglio comunale; (Comm) ente m

corps [kɔː, pl kɔːz] n inv corpo

corpse [kɔːps] n cadavere m

correct [kə'rɛkt] adj (accurate) corretto(-a), esatto(-a); (proper) corretto(-a) ▷ vt correggere; **correction** [-ʃən] n correzione f

correspond [kɒrɪs'pɒnd] vi corrispondere; **correspondence** n corrispondenza; **correspondent** n corrispondente m/f; **corresponding** adj corrispondente

corridor [ˈkɔrɪdɔːʳ] n corridoio
corrode [kəˈrəud] vt corrodere ▷ vi
corrodersi
corrupt [kəˈrʌpt] adj corrotto(-a); (Comput)
alterato(-a) ▷ vt corrompere; **corruption**
n corruzione f
Corsica [ˈkɔːsɪkə] n Corsica
cosmetic [kɔzˈmɛtɪk] n cosmetico ▷ adj
(fig: measure etc) superficiale; **cosmetic
surgery** n chirurgia plastica
cosmopolitan [kɔzməˈpɔlɪtn] adj
cosmopolita
cost [kɔst] (pt, pp cost) n costo ▷ vt
costare; (find out the cost of) stabilire il
prezzo di; **~s** npl (Comm, Law) spese fpl;
how much does it ~? quanto costa?; **at all
~s** a ogni costo
co-star [ˈkəustɑːʳ] n attore/trice della stessa
importanza del protagonista
Costa Rica [ˈkɔstəˈriːkə] n Costa Rica
costly [ˈkɔstlɪ] adj costoso(-a), caro(-a)
cost of living adj **~ allowance** indennità f
inv di contingenza
costume [ˈkɔstjuːm] n costume m; (lady's
suit) tailleur m inv; (BRIT: also: **swimming
~**) costume m da bagno
cosy [ˈkəuzɪ] (US **cozy**) adj intimo(-a); **I'm
very ~ here** sto proprio bene qui
cot [kɔt] n (BRIT: child's) lettino; (US:
campbed) brandina
cottage [ˈkɔtɪdʒ] n cottage m inv; **cottage
cheese** n fiocchi mpl di latte magro
cotton [ˈkɔtn] n cotone m; **cotton on** vi
(inf): **to ~ on (to sth)** afferrare (qc); **cotton
bud** n (BRIT) cotton fioc® m inv; **cotton
candy** (US) n zucchero filato; **cotton wool**
(BRIT) n cotone idrofilo
couch [kautʃ] n sofà m inv
cough [kɔf] vi tossire ▷ n tosse f; **I've got
a ~** ho la tosse; **cough mixture, cough
syrup** n sciroppo per la tosse
could [kud] pt di **can²**
couldn't = could not
council [ˈkaunsl] n consiglio; **city or
town ~** consiglio comunale; **council
estate** (BRIT) n quartiere m di case
popolari; **council house** (BRIT) n casa
popolare; **councillor** (US **councilor**) n
consigliere(-a); **council tax** n (BRIT) tassa
comunale sulla proprietà
counsel [ˈkaunsl] n avvocato;
consultazione f ▷ vt consigliare;
counselling (US **counseling**) n (Psych)
assistenza psicologica; **counsellor**
(US **counselor**) n consigliere(-a); (US)
avvocato
count [kaunt] vt, vi contare ▷ n (of votes etc)
conteggio; (of pollen etc) livello; (nobleman)
conte m; **count in** (inf) vt includere; **~ me**

in ci sto anch'io; **count on** vt fus contare
su; **countdown** n conto alla rovescia
counter [ˈkauntəʳ] n banco ▷ vt opporsi
a ▷ adv **~ to** contro; in opposizione a;
counter clockwise
[-ˈklɔkwaɪz] (US) adv in senso antiorario
counterfeit [ˈkauntəfɪt] n contraffazione
f, falso ▷ vt contraffare, falsificare ▷ adj
falso(-a)
counterpart [ˈkauntəpɑːt] n (of document
etc) copia; (of person) corrispondente m/f
countess [ˈkauntɪs] n contessa
countless [ˈkauntlɪs] adj innumerevole
country [ˈkʌntrɪ] n paese m; (native land)
patria; (as opposed to town) campagna;
(region) regione f; **country and western
(music)** n musica country e western,
country m; **country house** n villa in
campagna; **countryside** n campagna
county [ˈkauntɪ] n contea
coup [kuː] (pl coups) n colpo; (also: **~
d'état**) colpo di Stato
couple [ˈkʌpl] n coppia; **a ~ of** un paio di
coupon [ˈkuːpɔn] n buono; (detachable
form) coupon m inv
courage [ˈkʌrɪdʒ] n coraggio; **courageous**
adj coraggioso(-a)
courgette [kuəˈʒɛt] (BRIT) n zucchina
courier [ˈkurɪəʳ] n corriere m; (for tourists)
guida
course [kɔːs] n corso; (of ship) rotta; (for
golf) campo; (part of meal) piatto; **of ~**
senz'altro, naturalmente; **~ of action**
modo d'agire; **a ~ of treatment** (Med)
una cura
court [kɔːt] n corte f; (Tennis) campo ▷ vt
(woman) fare la corte a; **to take to ~** citare
in tribunale
courtesy [ˈkəːtəsɪ] n cortesia; **(by) ~ of**
per gentile concessione di; **courtesy bus,
courtesy coach** n autobus m inv gratuito
(di hotel, aeroporto)
court: **court-house** (US) n palazzo di
giustizia; **courtroom** n tribunale m;
courtyard n cortile m
cousin [ˈkʌzn] n cugino(-a); **first ~** cugino
di primo grado
cover [ˈkʌvəʳ] vt coprire; (book, table)
rivestire; (include) comprendere; (Press)
fare un servizio su ▷ n (of pan) coperchio;
(over furniture) fodera; (of bed) copriletto;
(of book) copertina; (shelter) riparo; (Comm,
Insurance, of spy) copertura; **~s** npl (on
bed) lenzuola fpl e coperte fpl; **to take ~**
(shelter) ripararsi; **under ~** al riparo; **under
~ of darkness** protetto dall'oscurità;
under separate ~ (Comm) a parte, in
plico separato; **cover up** vi **to ~ up for
sb** coprire qn; **coverage** n (Press, Radio,

TV): **to give full coverage to sth** fare un ampio servizio su qc; **cover charge** n coperto; **cover-up** n occultamento (di informazioni)

cow [kau] n vacca ▷ vt (*person*) intimidire

coward ['kauəd] n vigliacco(-a); **cowardly** adj vigliacco(-a)

cowboy ['kaubɔɪ] n cow-boy m inv

cozy ['kəuzɪ] (*US*) adj = **cosy**

crab [kræb] n granchio

crack [kræk] n fessura, crepa; incrinatura; (*noise*) schiocco; (: *of gun*) scoppio; (*drug*) crack m inv ▷ vt spaccare; incrinare; (*whip*) schioccare; (*nut*) schiacciare; (*problem*) risolvere; (*code*) decifrare ▷ adj (*troops*) fuori classe; **to ~ a joke** fare una battuta; **crack down on** vt fus porre freno a; **cracked** adj (*inf*) matto(-a); **cracker** n cracker m inv ▷ vt; petardo

crackle ['krækl] vi crepitare

cradle ['kreɪdl] n culla

craft [krɑːft] n mestiere m; (*cunning*) astuzia; (*boat*) naviglio; **craftsman** (*irreg*) n artigiano; **craftsmanship** n abilità

cram [kræm] vt (*fill*): **to ~ sth with** riempire qc di; (*put*): **to ~ sth into** stipare qc in ▷ vi (*for exams*) prepararsi (in gran fretta)

cramp [kræmp] n crampo; **I've got ~ in my leg** ho un crampo alla gamba; **cramped** adj ristretto(-a)

cranberry ['krænbərɪ] n mirtillo

crane [kreɪn] n gru f inv

crap [kræp] n (*inf!*) fesserie fpl; **to have a ~** cacare (!)

crash [kræʃ] n fragore m; (*of car*) incidente m; (*of plane*) caduta; (*of business etc*) crollo ▷ vt fracassare ▷ vi (*plane*) fracassarsi; (*car*) avere un incidente; (*two cars*) scontrarsi; (*business etc*) fallire, andare in rovina; **crash course** n corso intensivo; **crash helmet** n casco

crate [kreɪt] n cassa

crave [kreɪv] vt, vi **to ~ (for)** desiderare ardentemente

crawl [krɔːl] vi strisciare carponi; (*vehicle*) avanzare lentamente ▷ n (*Swimming*) crawl m

crayfish ['kreɪfɪʃ] n inv (*freshwater*) gambero (d'acqua dolce); (*saltwater*) gambero

crayon ['kreɪən] n matita colorata

craze [kreɪz] n mania

crazy ['kreɪzɪ] adj matto(-a); (*inf: keen*): **~ about sb** pazzo(-a) di qn; **~ about sth** matto(-a) per qc

creak [kriːk] vi cigolare, scricchiolare

cream [kriːm] n crema; (*fresh*) panna ▷ adj (*colour*) color crema inv; **cream cheese** n formaggio fresco; **creamy** adj cremoso(-a)

crease [kriːs] n grinza; (*deliberate*) piega ▷ vt sgualcire ▷ vi sgualcirsi

create [kriː'eɪt] vt creare; **creation** [-ʃən] n creazione f; **creative** adj creativo(-a); **creator** n creatore(-trice)

creature ['kriːtʃə*] n creatura

crèche [krɛʃ] n asilo infantile

credentials [krɪ'dɛnʃlz] npl credenziali fpl

credibility [krɛdɪ'bɪlɪtɪ] n credibilità

credible ['krɛdɪbl] adj credibile; (*witness, source*) attendibile

credit ['krɛdɪt] n credito; onore m ▷ vt (*Comm*) accreditare; (*believe: also:* **give ~ to**) credere, prestar fede a; **~s** npl (*Cinema*) titoli mpl; **to ~ sb with** (*fig*) attribuire a qn; **to be in ~** (*person*) essere creditore(-trice); (*bank account*) essere coperto(-a); **credit card** n carta di credito; **do you take credit cards?** accettate carte di credito?

creek [kriːk] n insenatura; (*US*) piccolo fiume m

creep [kriːp] (*pt, pp* **crept**) vi avanzare furtivamente (*or pian piano*)

cremate [krɪ'meɪt] vt cremare

crematorium [krɛmə'tɔːrɪəm] (*pl* **crematoria**) n forno crematorio

crept [krɛpt] pt, pp of **creep**

crescent ['krɛsnt] n (*shape*) mezzaluna; (*street*) strada semicircolare

cress [krɛs] n crescione m

crest [krɛst] n cresta; (*of coat of arms*) cimiero

crew [kruː] n equipaggio; **crew-neck** n girocollo

crib [krɪb] n culla ▷ vt (*inf*) copiare

cricket ['krɪkɪt] n (*insect*) grillo; (*game*) cricket m; **cricketer** n giocatore m di cricket

crime [kraɪm] n crimine m; **criminal** ['krɪmɪnl] adj, n criminale m/f

crimson ['krɪmzn] adj color cremisi inv

cringe [krɪndʒ] vi acquattarsi; (*in embarrassment*) sentirsi sprofondare

cripple ['krɪpl] n zoppo(-a) ▷ vt azzoppare

crisis ['kraɪsɪs] (*pl* **crises**) n crisi f inv

crisp [krɪsp] adj croccante; (*fig*) frizzante; vivace; deciso(-a); **crispy** adj croccante

criterion [kraɪ'tɪərɪən] (*pl* **criteria**) n criterio

critic ['krɪtɪk] n critico; **critical** adj critico(-a); **criticism** ['krɪtɪsɪzm] n critica; **criticize** ['krɪtɪsaɪz] vt criticare

Croat ['krəuæt] adj, n = **Croatian**

Croatia [krəu'eɪʃə] n Croazia; **Croatian** adj croato(-a) ▷ n croato(-a); (*Ling*) croato

crockery ['krɔkərɪ] n vasellame m

crocodile ['krɔkədaɪl] n coccodrillo

crocus ['krəukəs] n croco
croissant ['krwas] n brioche f inv, croissant m inv
crook [kruk] n truffatore m; (of shepherd) bastone m; **crooked** ['krukɪd] adj curvo(-a), storto(-a); (action) disonesto(-a)
crop [krɔp] n (produce) coltivazione f; (amount produced) raccolto; (riding crop) frustino ▷ vt (hair) rapare; **crop up** vi presentarsi
cross [krɔs] n croce f; (Biol) incrocio ▷ vt (street etc) attraversare; (arms, legs, Biol) incrociare; (cheque) sbarrare ▷ adj di cattivo umore; **cross off** vt cancellare (tirando una riga con la penna); **cross out** vt cancellare; **cross over** vi attraversare; **cross-Channel ferry** ['krɔs'tʃænl-] n traghetto che attraversa la Manica; **crosscountry (race)** n cross-country m inv; **crossing** n incrocio; (sea passage) traversata; (also: **pedestrian crossing**) passaggio pedonale; **how long does the crossing take?** quanto dura la traversata?; **crossing guard** (us) n dipendente comunale che aiuta i bambini ad attraversare la strada; **crossroads** n incrocio; **crosswalk** (us) n strisce fpl pedonali, passaggio pedonale; **crossword** n cruciverba m inv
crotch [krɔtʃ] n (Anat) inforcatura; (of garment) pattina
crouch [krautʃ] vi acquattarsi; rannicchiarsi
crouton ['kru:tɔn] n crostino
crow [krəu] n (bird) cornacchia; (of cock) canto del gallo ▷ vi (cock) cantare
crowd [kraud] n folla ▷ vt affollare, stipare ▷ vi **to ~ round/in** affollarsi intorno a/in; **crowded** adj affollato(-a); **crowded with** stipato(-a) di
crown [kraun] n corona; (of head) calotta cranica; (of hat) cocuzzolo; (of hill) cima ▷ vt incoronare; (fig: career) coronare; **crown jewels** npl gioielli mpl della Corona
crucial ['kru:ʃl] adj cruciale, decisivo(-a)
crucifix ['kru:sɪfɪks] n crocifisso
crude [kru:d] adj (materials) greggio(-a), non raffinato(-a); (fig: basic) crudo(-a), primitivo(-a); (: vulgar) rozzo(-a), grossolano(-a); **crude (oil)** n (petrolio) greggio
cruel ['kruəl] adj crudele; **cruelty** n crudeltà f inv
cruise [kru:z] n crociera ▷ vi andare a velocità di crociera; (taxi) circolare
crumb [krʌm] n briciola
crumble ['krʌmbl] vt sbriciolare ▷ vi sbriciolarsi; (plaster etc) sgretolarsi; (land, earth) franare; (building, fig) crollare
crumpet ['krʌmpɪt] n specie di frittella

crumple ['krʌmpl] vt raggrinzare, spiegazzare
crunch [krʌntʃ] vt sgranocchiare; (underfoot) scricchiolare ▷ n (fig) punto or momento cruciale; **crunchy** adj croccante
crush [krʌʃ] n folla; (love): **to have a ~ on sb** avere una cotta per qn; (drink): **lemon ~** spremuta di limone ▷ vt schiacciare; (crumple) sgualcire
crust [krʌst] n crosta; **crusty** adj (bread) croccante; (person) brontolone(-a); (remark) brusco(-a)
crutch [krʌtʃ] n gruccia
cry [kraɪ] vi piangere; (shout) urlare ▷ n urlo, grido; **cry out** vi, vt gridare
crystal ['krɪstl] n cristallo
cub [kʌb] n cucciolo; (also: **~ scout**) lupetto
Cuba ['kju:bə] n Cuba
Cuban ['kju:bən] adj, n cubano(-a)
cube [kju:b] n cubo ▷ vt (Math) elevare al cubo; **cubic** adj cubico(-a); (metre, foot) cubo(-a)
cubicle ['kju:bɪkl] n scompartimento separato; cabina
cuckoo ['kuku:] n cucù m inv
cucumber ['kju:kʌmbər] n cetriolo
cuddle ['kʌdl] vt abbracciare, coccolare ▷ vi abbracciarsi
cue [kju:] n (snooker cue) stecca; (Theatre etc) segnale m
cuff [kʌf] n (BRIT: of shirt, coat etc) polsino; (us: of trousers) risvolto; **off the ~** improvvisando; **cufflinks** npl gemelli mpl
cuisine [kwɪ'zi:n] n cucina
cul-de-sac ['kʌldəsæk] n vicolo cieco
cull [kʌl] vt (ideas etc) scegliere ▷ n (of animals) abbattimento selettivo
culminate ['kʌlmɪneɪt] vi **to ~ in** culminare con
culprit ['kʌlprɪt] n colpevole m/f
cult [kʌlt] n culto
cultivate ['kʌltɪveɪt] vt (also fig) coltivare
cultural ['kʌltʃərəl] adj culturale
culture ['kʌltʃər] n (also fig) cultura
cumin ['kʌmɪn] n (spice) cumino
cunning ['kʌnɪŋ] n astuzia, furberia ▷ adj astuto(-a), furbo(-a)
cup [kʌp] n tazza; (prize, of bra) coppa
cupboard ['kʌbəd] n armadio
cup final n (BRIT Football) finale f di coppa
curator [kjuə'reɪtər] n direttore m (di museo ecc)
curb [kə:b] vt tenere a freno ▷ n freno; (us) bordo del marciapiede
curdle ['kə:dl] vi cagliare
cure [kjuə'] vt guarire; (Culin) trattare; affumicare; essiccare ▷ n rimedio
curfew ['kə:fju:] n coprifuoco
curiosity [kjuərɪ'ɔsɪtɪ] n curiosità

curious ['kjʊərɪəs] *adj* curioso(-a)
curl [kə:l] *n* riccio ▷ *vt* ondulare; (*tightly*) arricciare ▷ *vi* arricciarsi; **curl up** *vi* rannicchiarsi; **curler** *n* bigodino; **curly** ['kə:lɪ] *adj* ricciuto(-a)
currant ['kʌrnt] *n* (*dried*) sultanina; (*bush, fruit*) ribes *m inv*
currency ['kʌrnsɪ] *n* moneta; **to gain ~** (*fig*) acquistare larga diffusione
current ['kʌrnt] *adj* corrente ▷ *n* corrente *f*; **current account** (*BRIT*) *n* conto corrente; **current affairs** *npl* attualità *fpl*; **currently** *adv* attualmente
curriculum [kə'rɪkjʊləm] (*pl* **curriculums** *or* **curricula**) *n* curriculum *m inv*; **curriculum vitae** [-'vi:taɪ] *n* curriculum vitae *m inv*
curry ['kʌrɪ] *n* curry *m inv* ▷ *vt* **to ~ favour with** cercare di attirarsi i favori di; **curry powder** *n* curry *m*
curse [kə:s] *vt* maledire ▷ *vi* bestemmiare ▷ *n* maledizione *f*; bestemmia
cursor ['kə:sə'] *n* (*Comput*) cursore *m*
curt [kə:t] *adj* secco(-a)
curtain ['kə:tn] *n* tenda; (*Theatre*) sipario
curve [kə:v] *n* curva ▷ *vi* curvarsi; **curved** *adj* curvo(-a)
cushion ['kuʃən] *n* cuscino ▷ *vt* (*shock*) fare da cuscinetto a
custard ['kʌstəd] *n* (*for pouring*) crema
custody ['kʌstədɪ] *n* (*of child*) tutela; **to take into ~** (*suspect*) mettere in detenzione preventiva
custom ['kʌstəm] *n* costume *m*, consuetudine *f*; (*Comm*) clientela
customer ['kʌstəmə'] *n* cliente *m/f*
customized ['kʌstəmaɪzd] *adj* (*car etc*) fuoriserie *inv*
customs ['kʌstəmz] *npl* dogana; **customs officer** *n* doganiere *m*
cut [kʌt] (*pt, pp* **cut**) *vt* tagliare; (*shape, make*) intagliare; (*reduce*) ridurre ▷ *vi* tagliare ▷ *n* taglio; (*in salary etc*) riduzione *f*; **I've ~ myself** mi sono tagliato; **to ~ a tooth** mettere un dente; **cut back** *vt* (*plants*) tagliare; (*production, expenditure*) ridurre; **cut down** *vt* (*tree etc*) abbattere ▷ *vt fus* (*also:* **~ down on**) ridurre; **cut off** *vt* tagliare; (*fig*) isolare; **cut out** *vt* tagliare fuori; eliminare; ritagliare; **cut up** *vt* tagliare a pezzi; **cutback** *n* riduzione *f*
cute [kju:t] *adj* (*sweet*) carino(-a)
cutlery ['kʌtlərɪ] *n* posate *fpl*
cutlet ['kʌtlɪt] *n* costoletta; (*nut etc cutlet*) cotoletta vegetariana
cut: **cut-price** (*BRIT*) *adj* a prezzo ridotto; **cut-rate** (*US*) *adj* = **cut-price**; **cutting** ['kʌtɪŋ] *adj* tagliente ▷ *n* (*from newspaper*) ritaglio (di giornale); (*from plant*) talea

CV *n abbr* = **curriculum vitae**
cwt *abbr* = **hundredweight(s)**
cybercafé ['saɪbəkaefeɪ] *n* cybercaffè *m inv*
cyberspace ['saɪbəspeɪs] *n* ciberspazio
cycle ['saɪkl] *n* ciclo; (*bicycle*) bicicletta ▷ *vi* andare in bicicletta; **cycle hire** *n* noleggio *m* biciclette *inv*; **cycle lane** *n* pista ciclabile; **cycle path** *n* pista ciclabile; **cycling** ['saɪklɪŋ] *n* ciclismo; **cyclist** ['saɪklɪst] *n* ciclista *m/f*
cyclone ['saɪkləun] *n* ciclone *m*
cylinder ['sɪlɪndə'] *n* cilindro
cymbal ['sɪmbl] *n* piatto
cynical ['sɪnɪkl] *adj* cinico(-a)
Cypriot ['sɪprɪət] *adj, n* cipriota (*m/f*)
Cyprus ['saɪprəs] *n* Cipro
cyst [sɪst] *n* cisti *f inv*; **cystitis** [sɪs'taɪtɪs] *n* cistite *f*
czar [zɑ:'] *n* zar *m inv*
Czech [tʃɛk] *adj* ceco(-a) ▷ *n* ceco(-a); (*Ling*) ceco; **Czech Republic** *n* **the Czech Republic** la Repubblica Ceca

D [di:] n (Mus) re m

dab [dæb] vt (eyes, wound) tamponare; (paint, cream) applicare (con leggeri colpetti)

dad, daddy [dæd, 'dædɪ] n babbo, papà m inv

daffodil ['dæfədɪl] n trombone m, giunchiglia

daft [dɑːft] adj sciocco(-a)

dagger ['dægəʳ] n pugnale m

daily ['deɪlɪ] adj quotidiano(-a), giornaliero(-a) ▷ n quotidiano ▷ adv tutti i giorni

dairy ['dɛərɪ] n (BRIT: shop) latteria; (on farm) caseificio ▷ adj caseario(-a); **dairy produce** npl latticini mpl

daisy ['deɪzɪ] n margherita

dam [dæm] n diga ▷ vt sbarrare; costruire dighe su

damage ['dæmɪdʒ] n danno, danni mpl; (fig) danno ▷ vt danneggiare; **~s** npl (Law) danni

damn [dæm] vt condannare; (curse) maledire ▷ n (inf): **I don't give a ~** non me ne frega niente ▷ adj (inf: also: **~ed**): **this ~ ...** questo maledetto ...; **~ it!** accidenti!

damp [dæmp] adj umido(-a) ▷ n umidità, umido ▷ vt (also: **~en**: cloth, rag) inumidire, bagnare; (: enthusiasm etc) spegnere

dance [dɑːns] n danza, ballo; (ball) ballo ▷ vi ballare; **dance floor** n pista da ballo; **dancer** n danzatore(-trice); (professional) ballerino(-a); **dancing** ['dɑːnsɪŋ] n danza, ballo

dandelion ['dændɪlaɪən] n dente m di leone

dandruff ['dændrəf] n forfora

Dane [deɪn] n danese m/f

danger ['deɪndʒəʳ] n pericolo; **there is a ~ of fire** c'è pericolo di incendio; **in ~** in pericolo; **he was in ~ of falling** rischiava di cadere; **dangerous** adj pericoloso(-a)

dangle ['dæŋgl] vt dondolare; (fig) far balenare ▷ vi pendolare

Danish ['deɪnɪʃ] adj danese ▷ n (Ling) danese m

dare [dɛəʳ] vt **to ~ sb to do** sfidare qn a fare ▷ vi **to ~ to do sth** osare fare qc; **I ~ say** (I suppose) immagino (che); **daring** adj audace, ardito(-a) ▷ n audacia

dark [dɑːk] adj (night, room) buio(-a), scuro(-a); (colour, complexion) scuro(-a); (fig) cupo(-a), tetro(-a), nero(-a) ▷ n **in the ~** al buio; **in the ~ about** (fig) all'oscuro di; **after ~** a notte fatta; **darken** vt (colour) scurire ▷ vi (sky, room) oscurarsi; **darkness** n oscurità, buio; **darkroom** n camera oscura

darling ['dɑːlɪŋ] adj caro(-a) ▷ n tesoro

dart [dɑːt] n freccetta; (Sewing) pince f inv ▷ vi **to ~ towards** precipitarsi verso; **to ~ away/along** sfrecciare via/lungo; **dartboard** n bersaglio (per freccette); **darts** n tiro al bersaglio (con freccette)

dash [dæʃ] n (sign) lineetta; (small quantity) punta ▷ vt (missile) gettare; (hopes) infrangere ▷ vi **to ~ towards** precipitarsi verso

dashboard ['dæʃbɔːd] n (Aut) cruscotto

data ['deɪtə] npl dati mpl; **database** n base f di dati, data base m inv; **data processing** n elaborazione f (elettronica) dei dati

date [deɪt] n data; appuntamento; (fruit) dattero ▷ vt datare; (person) uscire con; **what's the ~ today?** quanti ne abbiamo oggi?; **~ of birth** data di nascita; **to ~** (until now) fino a oggi; **dated** adj passato(-a) di moda

daughter ['dɔːtəʳ] n figlia; **daughter-in-law** n nuora

daunting ['dɔːntɪŋ] adj non invidiabile

dawn [dɔːn] n alba ▷ vi (day) spuntare; (fig): **it ~ed on him that ...** gli è venuto in mente che ...

day [deɪ] n giorno; (as duration) giornata; (period of time, age) tempo, epoca; **the ~ before** il giorno avanti or prima; **the ~ after, the following ~** il giorno dopo

or seguente; **the ~ after tomorrow**
dopodomani; **the ~ before yester~**
l'altroieri; **by ~** di giorno; **day-care
centre** n scuola materna; **daydream** vi
sognare a occhi aperti; **daylight** n luce f
del giorno; **day return** (BRIT) n biglietto
giornaliero di andata e ritorno; **daytime** n
giorno; **day-to-day** adj (life, organization)
quotidiano(-a); **day trip** n gita (di un
giorno)

dazed [deɪzd] adj stordito(-a)

dazzle ['dæzl] vt abbagliare; **dazzling** adj
(light) abbagliante; (colour) violento(-a);
(smile) smagliante

DC abbr (= direct current) c.c.

dead [dɛd] adj morto(-a); (numb)
intirizzito(-a); (telephone) muto(-a);
(battery) scarico(-a) ▷ adv assolutamente,
perfettamente ▷ npl (be about:) **the ~** i morti; **he
was shot ~** fu colpito a morte; **~ tired**
stanco(-a) morto(-a); **to stop ~** fermarsi di
colpo; **dead end** n vicolo cieco; **deadline**
n scadenza; **deadly** adj mortale; (weapon,
poison) micidiale; **Dead Sea** n **the Dead
Sea** il mar Morto

deaf [dɛf] adj sordo(-a); **deafen** vt
assordare; **deafening** adj fragoroso(-a),
assordante

deal [diːl] n (pt, pp dealt) n accordo; (business
deal) affare m ▷ vt (blow, cards) dare; **a
great ~ (of)** molto(-a); **deal with** vt
fus (Comm) fare affari con, trattare con;
(handle) occuparsi di; (be about: book etc)
trattare di; **dealer** n commerciante
m/f; **dealings** npl (Comm) relazioni fpl;
(relations) rapporti mpl

dealt [dɛlt] pt, pp of **deal**

dean [diːn] n (Rel) decano; (Scol) preside m
di facoltà (or di collegio)

dear [dɪə[^r]] adj caro(-a) ▷ n **my ~** caro mio/
cara mia ▷ excl **~ me!** Dio mio!; **D~ Sir/
Madam** (in letter) Egregio Signore/Egregia
Signora; **D~ Mr/Mrs X** Gentile Signor/
Signora X; **dearly** adv (love) moltissimo;
(pay) a caro prezzo

death [dɛθ] n morte f; (Admin) decesso;
death penalty n pena di morte; **death
sentence** n condanna a morte

debate [dɪ'beɪt] n dibattito ▷ vt dibattere;
discutere

debit ['dɛbɪt] n debito ▷ vt **to ~ a sum
to sb** or **to sb's account** addebitare una
somma a qn; **debit card** n carta di debito

debris ['dɛbriː] n detriti mpl

debt [dɛt] n debito; **to be in ~** essere
indebitato(-a)

debut ['deɪbjuː] n debutto

Dec. abbr (= December) dic.

decade ['dɛkeɪd] n decennio

decaffeinated [dɪ'kæfɪneɪtɪd] adj
decaffeinato(-a)

decay [dɪ'keɪ] n decadimento; (also: **tooth
~**) carie f ▷ vi (rot) imputridire

deceased [dɪ'siːst] n defunto(-a)

deceit [dɪ'siːt] n inganno; **deceive** [dɪ'siːv]
vt ingannare

December [dɪ'sɛmbə[^r]] n dicembre m

decency ['diːsənsɪ] n decenza

decent ['diːsənt] adj decente; (respectable)
per bene; (kind) gentile

deception [dɪ'sɛpʃən] n inganno

deceptive [dɪ'sɛptɪv] adj ingannevole

decide [dɪ'saɪd] vt (person) far prendere una
decisione a; (question, argument) risolvere,
decidere ▷ vi decidere, decidersi; **to ~ to
do/that** decidere di fare/che; **to ~ on**
decidere per

decimal ['dɛsɪməl] adj decimale ▷ n
decimale m

decision [dɪ'sɪʒən] n decisione f

decisive [dɪ'saɪsɪv] adj decisivo(-a);
(person) deciso(-a)

deck [dɛk] n (Naut) ponte m; (of bus): **top ~**
imperiale m; (record deck) piatto; (of cards)
mazzo; **deckchair** n sedia a sdraio

declaration [dɛklə'reɪʃən] n
dichiarazione f

declare [dɪ'klɛə[^r]] vt dichiarare

decline [dɪ'klaɪn] n (decay) declino;
(lessening) ribasso ▷ vt declinare; rifiutare
▷ vi declinare; diminuire

decorate ['dɛkəreɪt] vt (adorn, give a medal
to) decorare; (paint and paper) tinteggiare e
tappezzare; **decoration** [-'reɪʃən] n (medal
etc, adornment) decorazione f; **decorator** n
decoratore m

decrease [n 'diːkriːs, vb diː'kriːs] n
diminuzione f ▷ vt, vi diminuire

decree [dɪ'kriː] n decreto

dedicate ['dɛdɪkeɪt] vt consacrare;
(book etc) dedicare; **dedicated**
adj coscienzioso(-a); (Comput)
specializzato(-a), dedicato(-a); **dedication**
[dɛdɪ'keɪʃən] n (devotion) dedizione f; (in
book etc) dedica

deduce [dɪ'djuːs] vt dedurre

deduct [dɪ'dʌkt] vt **to ~ sth from**
dedurre qc (da); **deduction** [dɪ'dʌkʃən] n
deduzione f

deed [diːd] n azione f, atto; (Law) atto

deem [diːm] vt (formal) giudicare,
ritenere; **to ~ it wise to do** ritenere
prudente fare

deep [diːp] adj profondo(-a); **4 metres ~**
profondo(-a) 4 metri ▷ adv **spectators
stood 20 ~** c'erano 20 file di spettatori;
how ~ is the water? quanto è profonda
l'acqua?; **deep-fry** vt friggere in olio

abbondante; **deeply** adv profondamente

deer [dɪəʳ] n inv **the ~** i cervidi; **(red) ~** cervo; **(fallow) ~** daino; **roe ~** capriolo

default [dɪˈfɔːlt] n (Comput: also: **~ value**) default m inv; **by ~** (Sport) per abbandono

defeat [dɪˈfiːt] n sconfitta ▷ vt (team, opponents) sconfiggere

defect [n ˈdiːfɛkt, vb dɪˈfɛkt] n difetto ▷ vi **to ~ to the enemy** passare al nemico; **defective** [dɪˈfɛktɪv] adj difettoso(-a)

defence [dɪˈfɛns] (us defense) n difesa

defend [dɪˈfɛnd] vt difendere; **defendant** n imputato(-a); **defender** n difensore(-a)

defense [dɪˈfɛns] (us) n = **defence**

defensive [dɪˈfɛnsɪv] adj difensivo(-a) ▷ n **on the ~** sulla difensiva

defer [dɪˈfəːʳ] vt (postpone) differire, rinviare

defiance [dɪˈfaɪəns] n sfida; **in ~ of** a dispetto di; **defiant** [dɪˈfaɪənt] adj (attitude) di sfida; (person) ribelle

deficiency [dɪˈfɪʃənsɪ] n deficienza; carenza; **deficient** adj deficiente; insufficiente; **to be deficient in** mancare di

deficit [ˈdɛfɪsɪt] n deficit m inv

define [dɪˈfaɪn] vt definire

definite [ˈdɛfɪnɪt] adj (fixed) definito(-a), preciso(-a); (clear, obvious) ben definito(-a), esatto(-a); (Ling) determinativo(-a); **he was ~ about it** ne era sicuro; **definitely** adv indubbiamente

definition [dɛfɪˈnɪʃən] n definizione f

deflate [diːˈfleɪt] vt sgonfiare

deflect [dɪˈflɛkt] vt deflettere, deviare

defraud [dɪˈfrɔːd] vt defraudare

defrost [diːˈfrɔst] vt (fridge) disgelare

defuse [diːˈfjuːz] vt disinnescare; (fig) distendere

defy [dɪˈfaɪ] vt sfidare; (efforts etc) resistere a; **it defies description** supera ogni descrizione

degree [dɪˈgriː] n grado; (Scol) laurea (universitaria); **a first ~ in maths** una laurea in matematica; **by ~s** (gradually) gradualmente, a poco a poco; **to some ~** fino a un certo punto, in certa misura

dehydrated [diːhaɪˈdreɪtɪd] adj disidratato(-a); (milk, eggs) in polvere

de-icer [diːˈaɪsəʳ] n sbrinatore m

delay [dɪˈleɪ] vt ritardare ▷ vi **to ~ (in doing sth)** ritardare (a fare qc) ▷ n ritardo; **to be ~ed** subire un ritardo; (person) essere trattenuto(-a)

delegate [n ˈdɛlɪgɪt, vb ˈdɛlɪgeɪt] n delegato(-a) ▷ vt delegare

delete [dɪˈliːt] vt cancellare

deli [ˈdɛlɪ] n = **delicatessen**

deliberate [adj dɪˈlɪbərɪt, vb dɪˈlɪbə
reɪt] adj (intentional) intenzionale; (slow) misurato(-a) ▷ vi deliberare, riflettere; **deliberately** adv (on purpose) deliberatamente

delicacy [ˈdɛlɪkəsɪ] n delicatezza

delicate [ˈdɛlɪkɪt] adj delicato(-a)

delicatessen [dɛlɪkəˈtɛsn] n ≈ salumeria

delicious [dɪˈlɪʃəs] adj delizioso(-a), squisito(-a)

delight [dɪˈlaɪt] n delizia, gran piacere m ▷ vt dilettare; **to take (a) ~ in** dilettarsi in; **delighted** adj **delighted (at** or **with)** contentissimo(-a) (di), felice (di); **delighted to do** felice di fare; **delightful** adj delizioso(-a), incantevole

delinquent [dɪˈlɪŋkwənt] adj, n delinquente m/f

deliver [dɪˈlɪvəʳ] vt (mail) distribuire; (goods) consegnare; (speech) pronunciare; (Med) far partorire; **delivery** n distribuzione f; consegna; (of speaker) dizione f; (Med) parto

delusion [dɪˈluːʒən] n illusione f

de luxe [dəˈlʌks] adj di lusso

delve [dɛlv] vi **to ~ into** frugare in; (subject) far ricerche in

demand [dɪˈmɑːnd] vt richiedere; (rights) rivendicare ▷ n domanda; (claim) rivendicazione f; **in ~** ricercato(-a), richiesto(-a); **on ~** a richiesta; **demanding** adj (boss) esigente; (work) impegnativo(-a)

demise [dɪˈmaɪz] n decesso

demo [ˈdɛməu] (inf) n abbr (= demonstration) manifestazione f

democracy [dɪˈmɔkrəsɪ] n democrazia; **democrat** [ˈdɛməkræt] n democratico(-a); **democratic** [dɛməˈkrætɪk] adj democratico(-a)

demolish [dɪˈmɔlɪʃ] vt demolire

demolition [dɛməˈlɪʃən] n demolizione f

demon [ˈdiːmən] n (also fig) demonio ▷ cpd **a ~ squash player** un mago dello squash; **a ~ driver** un guidatore folle

demonstrate [ˈdɛmənstreɪt] vt dimostrare, provare ▷ vi dimostrare, manifestare; **demonstration** [-ˈstreɪʃə
n] n dimostrazione f; (Pol) dimostrazione, manifestazione f; **demonstrator** n (Pol) dimostrante m/f; (Comm) dimostratore(-trice)

demote [dɪˈməut] vt far retrocedere

den [dɛn] n tana, covo; (room) buco

denial [dɪˈnaɪəl] n diniego; rifiuto

denim [ˈdɛnɪm] n tessuto di cotone ritorto; **~s** npl (jeans) blue jeans mpl

Denmark [ˈdɛnmɑːk] n Danimarca

denomination [dɪnɔmɪˈneɪʃən] n (money) valore m; (Rel) confessione f

denounce [dɪ'nauns] vt denunciare
dense [dɛns] adj fitto(-a); (smoke)
denso(-a); (inf: person) ottuso(-a), duro(-a)
density ['dɛnsɪtɪ] n densità f inv
dent [dɛnt] n ammaccatura ▷ vt (also:
make a ~ in) ammaccare
dental ['dɛntl] adj dentale; **dental floss**
[-flɔs] n filo interdentale; **dental surgery**
n ambulatorio del dentista
dentist ['dɛntɪst] n dentista m/f
dentures ['dɛntʃəz] npl dentiera
deny [dɪ'naɪ] vt negare; (refuse) rifiutare
deodorant [diː'əudərənt] n deodorante m
depart [dɪ'paːt] vi partire; **to ~ from** (fig)
deviare da
department [dɪ'paːtmənt] n (Comm)
reparto; (Scol) sezione f, dipartimento;
(Pol) ministero; **department store** n
grande magazzino
departure [dɪ'paːtʃə'] n partenza; (fig): **~
from** deviazione f da; **a new ~** una svolta
(decisiva); **departure lounge** n (at airport)
sala d'attesa
depend [dɪ'pɛnd] vi **to ~ on** dipendere
da; (rely on) contare su; **it ~s** dipende;
~ing on the result ... a seconda del
risultato ...; **dependant** n persona a
carico; **dependent** adj **to be dependent
on** dipendere da; (child, relative) essere a
carico di ▷ n = **dependant**
depict [dɪ'pɪkt] vt (in picture) dipingere; (in
words) descrivere
deport [dɪ'pɔːt] vt deportare; espellere
deposit [dɪ'pɔzɪt] n (Comm, Geo) deposito;
(of ore, oil) giacimento; (Chem) sedimento;
(part payment) acconto; (for hired goods
etc) cauzione f ▷ vt depositare; dare in
acconto; mettere or lasciare in deposito;
deposit account n conto vincolato
depot ['dɛpəu] n deposito; (US) stazione f
ferroviaria
depreciate [dɪ'priːʃɪeɪt] vi svalutarsi
depress [dɪ'prɛs] vt deprimere; (price,
wages) abbassare; (press down) premere;
depressed adj (person) depresso(-a),
abbattuto(-a); (price) in ribasso; (industry)
in crisi; **depressing** adj deprimente;
depression [dɪ'prɛʃən] n depressione f
deprive [dɪ'praɪv] vt **to ~ sb of** privare qn
di; **deprived** adj disgraziato(-a)
dept. abbr = **department**
depth [dɛpθ] n profondità f inv; **in the ~s of**
nel profondo di; nel cuore di; **out of one's
~** (in water) dove non si tocca; (fig) a disagio
deputy ['dɛpjutɪ] adj **~ head** (BRIT Scol)
vicepreside m/f ▷ n (assistant) vice m/f inv;
(US: also: **~ sheriff**) vice-sceriffo
derail [dɪ'reɪl] vt **to be ~ed** deragliare
derelict ['dɛrɪlɪkt] adj abbandonato(-a)

derive [dɪ'raɪv] vt **to ~ sth from** derivare
qc da; trarre qc da ▷ vi **to ~ from** derivare
da
descend [dɪ'sɛnd] vt, vi discendere,
scendere; **to ~ from** discendere da; **to ~ to**
(lying, begging) abbassarsi a; **descendant**
n discendente m/f; **descent** [dɪ'sɛnt] n
discesa; (origin) discendenza, famiglia
describe [dɪs'kraɪb] vt descrivere;
description [-'krɪpʃən] n descrizione f;
(sort) genere m, specie f
desert [n 'dɛzət, vb dɪ'zəːt] n deserto ▷ vt
lasciare, abbandonare ▷ vi (Mil) disertare;
deserted [dɪ'zəːtɪd] adj deserto(-a)
deserve [dɪ'zəːv] vt meritare
design [dɪ'zaɪn] n (art, sketch) disegno;
(layout, shape) linea; (pattern) fantasia;
(intention) intenzione f ▷ vt disegnare;
progettare
designate [vb 'dɛzɪgneɪt, adj 'dɛzɪgnɪt]
designare ▷ adj designato(-a)
designer [dɪ'zaɪnə'] n (Art, Tech)
disegnatore(-trice); (of fashion) modellista
m/f
desirable [dɪ'zaɪərəbl] adj desiderabile; **it
is ~ that** è opportuno che + sub
desire [dɪ'zaɪə'] n desiderio, voglia ▷ vt
desiderare, volere
desk [dɛsk] n (in office) scrivania; (for pupil)
banco; (BRIT: in shop, restaurant) cassa; (in
hotel) ricevimento; (at airport) accettazione
f; **desk-top publishing** n desktop
publishing m
despair [dɪs'pɛə'] n disperazione f ▷ vi **to ~
of** disperare di
despatch [dɪs'pætʃ] n, vt = **dispatch**
desperate ['dɛspərɪt] adj disperato(-a);
(fugitive) capace di tutto; **to be ~ for
sth/to do** volere disperatamente qc/fare;
desperately adv disperatamente;
(very) terribilmente, estremamente;
desperation [dɛspə'reɪʃən] n
disperazione f
despise [dɪs'paɪz] vt disprezzare, sdegnare
despite [dɪs'paɪt] prep malgrado, a
dispetto di, nonostante
dessert [dɪ'zəːt] n dolce m; frutta;
dessertspoon n cucchiaio da dolci
destination [dɛstɪ'neɪʃən] n destinazione
f
destined ['dɛstɪnd] adj **to be ~ to do/for**
essere destinato(-a) a fare/per
destiny ['dɛstɪnɪ] n destino
destroy [dɪs'trɔɪ] vt distruggere
destruction [dɪs'trʌkʃən] n distruzione f
destructive [dɪs'trʌktɪv] adj
distruttivo(-a)
detach [dɪ'tætʃ] vt staccare, distaccare;
detached adj (attitude) distante;

d

detached house n villa
detail ['di:teɪl] n particolare m, dettaglio
▷ vt dettagliare, particolareggiare;
in ~ nei particolari; **detailed** adj
particolareggiato(-a)
detain [dɪ'teɪn] vt trattenere; (in captivity)
detenere
detect [dɪ'tɛkt] vt scoprire, scorgere; (Med,
Police, Radar etc) individuare; **detection**
[dɪ'tɛkʃən] n scoperta; individuazione
f; **detective** n investigatore(-trice);
detective story n giallo
detention [dɪ'tɛnʃən] n detenzione f; (Scol)
permanenza forzata per punizione
deter [dɪ'tə:ʳ] vt dissuadere
detergent [dɪ'tə:dʒənt] n detersivo
deteriorate [dɪ'tɪərɪəreɪt] vi deteriorarsi
determination [dɪtə:mɪ'neɪʃən] n
determinazione f
determine [dɪ'tə:mɪn] vt determinare;
determined adj (person) risoluto(-a),
deciso(-a); **determined to do** deciso(-a)
a fare
deterrent [dɪ'tɛrənt] n deterrente m; **to
act as a ~** fungere da deterrente
detest [dɪ'tɛst] vt detestare
detour ['di:tuəʳ] n deviazione f
detract [dɪ'trækt] vi **to ~ from** detrarre da
detrimental [dɛtrɪ'mɛntl] adj **~ to**
dannoso(-a) a, nocivo(-a) a
devastating ['dɛvəsteɪtɪŋ] adj
devastatore(-trice), sconvolgente
develop [dɪ'vɛləp] vt sviluppare; (habit)
prendere (gradualmente) ▷ vi svilupparsi;
(facts, symptoms: appear) manifestarsi,
rivelarsi; **can you ~ this film?** può
sviluppare questo rullino?; **developing
country** n paese m in via di sviluppo;
development n sviluppo
device [dɪ'vaɪs] n (apparatus) congegno
devil ['dɛvl] n diavolo; demonio
devious ['di:vɪəs] adj (person) subdolo(-a)
devise [dɪ'vaɪz] vt escogitare, concepire
devote [dɪ'vəut] vt **to ~ sth to** dedicare qc
a; **devoted** adj devoto(-a); **to be devoted
to sb** essere molto affezionato(-a) a qn;
devotion [dɪ'vəuʃən] n devozione f,
attaccamento; (Rel) atto di devozione,
preghiera
devour [dɪ'vauəʳ] vt divorare
devout [dɪ'vaut] adj pio(-a), devoto(-a)
dew [dju:] n rugiada
diabetes [daɪə'bi:ti:z] n diabete m
diabetic [daɪə'bɛtɪk] adj, n diabetico(-a)
diagnose [daɪəg'nəuz] vt diagnosticare
diagnosis [daɪəg'nəusɪs] (pl **diagnoses**) n
diagnosi f inv
diagonal [daɪ'ægənl] adj diagonale ▷ n
diagonale f

diagram ['daɪəgræm] n diagramma m
dial ['daɪəl] n quadrante m; (on radio)
lancetta; (on telephone) disco combinatore
▷ vt (number) fare
dialect ['daɪəlɛkt] n dialetto
dialling code, (us **area code**) n prefisso;
what's the ~ for Paris? qual è il prefisso
telefonico di Parigi?
dialling tone ['daɪəlɪŋ-] (us **dial tone**) n
segnale m di linea libera
dialogue ['daɪəlɔg] (us **dialog**) n dialogo
diameter [daɪ'æmɪtəʳ] n diametro
diamond ['daɪəmənd] n diamante m;
(shape) rombo; **~s** npl (Cards) quadri mpl
diaper ['daɪəpəʳ] (us) n pannolino
diarrhoea [daɪə'ri:ə] (us **diarrhea**) n
diarrea
diary ['daɪərɪ] n (daily account) diario; (book)
agenda
dice [daɪs] n inv dado ▷ vt (Culin) tagliare
a dadini
dictate [dɪk'teɪt] vt dettare; **dictation**
[dɪk'teɪʃən] n dettatura; (Scol) dettato
dictator [dɪk'teɪtəʳ] n dittatore m
dictionary ['dɪkʃənrɪ] n dizionario
did [dɪd] pt of **do**
didn't [dɪdnt] = **did not**
die [daɪ] vi morire; **to be dying for sth/to
do sth** morire dalla voglia di qc/di fare
qc; **die down** vi abbassarsi; **die out** vi
estinguersi
diesel ['di:zəl] n (vehicle) diesel m inv
diet ['daɪət] n alimentazione f; (restricted
food) dieta ▷ vi (also: **be on a ~**) stare a
dieta
differ ['dɪfəʳ] vi **to ~ from sth** differire
da qc, essere diverso(-a) da qc; **to ~
from sb over sth** essere in disaccordo
con qn su qc; **difference** n differenza;
(disagreement) screzio; **different** adj
diverso(-a); **differentiate** [-'rɛnʃɪeɪt] vi
to differentiate between discriminare
or fare differenza fra; **differently** adv
diversamente
difficult ['dɪfɪkəlt] adj difficile; **difficulty** n
difficoltà f inv
dig [dɪg] (pt, pp **dug**) vt (hole) scavare;
(garden) vangare ▷ n (prod) gomitata;
(archaeological) scavo; (fig) frecciata; **dig
up** vt (tree etc) sradicare; (information)
scavare fuori
digest [vb daɪ'dʒɛst, n 'daɪdʒɛst] vt digerire
▷ n compendio; **digestion** [dɪ'dʒɛstʃən] n
digestione f
digit ['dɪdʒɪt] n cifra; (finger) dito; **digital**
adj digitale; **digital camera** n macchina
fotografica digitale; **digital TV** n
televisione f digitale
dignified ['dɪgnɪfaɪd] adj dignitoso(-a)

dignity ['dɪgnɪtɪ] n dignità
digs [dɪgz] (BRIT: inf) npl camera ammobiliata
dilemma [daɪ'lɛmə] n dilemma m
dill [dɪl] n aneto
dilute [daɪ'luːt] vt diluire; (with water) annacquare
dim [dɪm] adj (light) debole; (shape etc) vago(-a); (room) in penombra; (inf: person) tonto(-a) ▷ vt (light) abbassare
dime [daɪm] (US) n = 10 cents
dimension [daɪ'mɛnʃən] n dimensione f
diminish [dɪ'mɪnɪʃ] vt, vi diminuire
din [dɪn] n chiasso, fracasso
dine [daɪn] vi pranzare; **diner** n (person) cliente m/f; (US: place) tavola calda
dinghy ['dɪŋgɪ] n battello pneumatico; (also: **rubber ~**) gommone m
dingy ['dɪndʒɪ] adj grigio(-a)
dining car ['daɪnɪŋ-] (BRIT) n vagone m ristorante
dining room n sala da pranzo
dining table n tavolo da pranzo
dinner ['dɪnər] n (lunch) pranzo; (evening meal) cena; (public) banchetto; **dinner jacket** n smoking m inv; **dinner party** n cena; **dinner time** n ora di pranzo (or cena)
dinosaur ['daɪnəsɔːr] n dinosauro
dip [dɪp] n discesa; (in sea) bagno; (Culin) salsetta ▷ vt immergere; bagnare; (BRIT Aut: lights) abbassare ▷ vi abbassarsi
diploma [dɪ'pləumə] n diploma m
diplomacy [dɪ'pləuməsɪ] n diplomazia
diplomat ['dɪpləmæt] n diplomatico; **diplomatic** [dɪplə'mætɪk] adj diplomatico(-a)
dipstick ['dɪpstɪk] n (Aut) indicatore m di livello dell'olio
dire [daɪər] adj terribile; estremo(-a)
direct [daɪ'rɛkt] adj diretto(-a) ▷ vt dirigere; (order): **to ~ sb to do sth** dare direttive a qn di fare qc ▷ adv direttamente; **can you ~ me to ...?** mi può indicare la strada per ...?; **direct debit** n (Banking) addebito effettuato per ordine di un cliente di banca
direction [dɪ'rɛkʃən] n direzione f; **~s** npl (advice) chiarimenti mpl; **sense of ~** senso dell'orientamento; **~s for use** istruzioni fpl
directly [dɪ'rɛktlɪ] adv (in straight line) direttamente; (at once) subito
director [dɪ'rɛktər] n direttore(-trice), amministratore(-trice); (Theatre, Cinema) regista m/f
directory [dɪ'rɛktərɪ] n elenco; **directory enquiries** (US **directory assistance**) n informazioni fpl elenco abbonati inv
dirt [dəːt] n sporcizia; immondizia; (earth)

terra; **dirty** adj sporco(-a) ▷ vt sporcare
disability [dɪsə'bɪlɪtɪ] n invalidità f inv; (Law) incapacità f inv
disabled [dɪs'eɪbld] adj invalido(-a); (mentally) ritardato(-a) ▷ npl **the ~** gli invalidi
disadvantage [dɪsəd'vɑːntɪdʒ] n svantaggio
disagree [dɪsə'griː] vi (differ) discordare; (be against, think otherwise): **to ~ (with)** essere in disaccordo (con), dissentire (da); **disagreeable** adj sgradevole; (person) antipatico(-a); **disagreement** n disaccordo; (argument) dissapore m
disappear [dɪsə'pɪər] vi scomparire; **disappearance** n scomparsa
disappoint [dɪsə'pɔɪnt] vt deludere; **disappointed** adj deluso(-a); **disappointing** adj deludente; **disappointment** n delusione f
disapproval [dɪsə'pruːvəl] n disapprovazione f
disapprove [dɪsə'pruːv] vi **to ~ of** disapprovare
disarm [dɪs'ɑːm] vt disarmare; **disarmament** n disarmo
disaster [dɪ'zɑːstər] n disastro; **disastrous** [dɪ'zɑːstrəs] adj disastroso(-a)
disbelief ['dɪsbə'liːf] n incredulità
disc [dɪsk] n disco; (Comput) = **disk**
discard [dɪs'kɑːd] vt (old things) scartare; (fig) abbandonare
discharge [vb dɪs'tʃɑːdʒ, n 'dɪstʃɑːdʒ] vt (duties) compiere; (Elec, waste etc) scaricare; (Med) emettere; (patient) dimettere; (employee) licenziare; (soldier) congedare; (defendant) liberare ▷ n (Elec) scarica; (Med) emissione f; (dismissal) licenziamento; congedo; liberazione f
discipline ['dɪsɪplɪn] n disciplina ▷ vt disciplinare; (punish) punire
disc jockey n disc jockey m inv
disclose [dɪs'kləuz] vt rivelare, svelare
disco ['dɪskəu] n abbr discoteca
discoloured [dɪs'kʌləd] (US **discolored**) adj scolorito(-a), ingiallito(-a)
discomfort [dɪs'kʌmfət] n disagio; (lack of comfort) scomodità f inv
disconnect [dɪskə'nɛkt] vt sconnettere, staccare; (Elec, Radio) staccare; (gas, water) chiudere
discontent [dɪskən'tɛnt] n scontentezza
discontinue [dɪskən'tɪnjuː] vt smettere, cessare; **"~d"** (Comm) "fuori produzione"
discount [n 'dɪskaunt, vb dɪs'kaunt] n sconto ▷ vt scontare; (idea) non badare a; **are there ~s for students?** ci sono sconti

per studenti?

discourage [dɪsˈkʌrɪdʒ] vt scoraggiare

discover [dɪsˈkʌvəʳ] vt scoprire; **discovery** n scoperta

discredit [dɪsˈkrɛdɪt] vt screditare; mettere in dubbio

discreet [dɪˈskriːt] adj discreto(-a)

discrepancy [dɪˈskrɛpənsɪ] n discrepanza

discretion [dɪˈskrɛʃən] n discrezione f; **use your own ~** giudichi lei

discriminate [dɪˈskrɪmɪneɪt] vi **to ~ between** distinguere tra; **to ~ against** discriminare contro; **discrimination** [-ˈneɪʃən] n discriminazione f; (judgment) discernimento

discuss [dɪˈskʌs] vt discutere; (debate) dibattere; **discussion** [dɪˈskʌʃən] n discussione f

disease [dɪˈziːz] n malattia

disembark [dɪsɪmˈbɑːk] vt, vi sbarcare

disgrace [dɪsˈgreɪs] n vergogna; (disfavour) disgrazia ▷ vt disonorare, far cadere in disgrazia; **disgraceful** adj scandaloso(-a), vergognoso(-a)

disgruntled [dɪsˈgrʌntld] adj scontento(-a), di cattivo umore

disguise [dɪsˈgaɪz] n travestimento ▷ vt **to ~ (as)** travestire (da); **in ~** travestito(-a)

disgust [dɪsˈgʌst] n disgusto, nausea ▷ vt disgustare, far schifo a; **disgusted** [dɪsˈgʌstɪd] adj indignato(-a); **disgusting** [dɪsˈgʌstɪŋ] adj disgustoso(-a), ripugnante

dish [dɪʃ] n piatto; **to do** or **wash the ~es** fare i piatti; **dishcloth** n strofinaccio

dishonest [dɪsˈɒnɪst] adj disonesto(-a)

dishtowel [ˈdɪʃtauəl] (us) n strofinaccio dei piatti

dishwasher [ˈdɪʃwɔʃəʳ] n lavastoviglie f inv

disillusion [dɪsɪˈluːʒən] vt disilludere, disingannare

disinfectant [dɪsɪnˈfɛktənt] n disinfettante m

disintegrate [dɪsˈɪntɪgreɪt] vi disintegrarsi

disk [dɪsk] n (Comput) disco; **single-/ double-sided ~** disco a facciata singola/ doppia; **disk drive** n lettore m; **diskette** (us) n = **disk**

dislike [dɪsˈlaɪk] n antipatia, avversione f; (gen pl) cosa che non piace ▷ vt **he ~s it** non gli piace

dislocate [ˈdɪsləkeɪt] vt slogare

disloyal [dɪsˈlɔɪəl] adj sleale

dismal [ˈdɪzml] adj triste, cupo(-a)

dismantle [dɪsˈmæntl] vt (machine) smontare

dismay [dɪsˈmeɪ] n costernazione f ▷ vt sgomentare

dismiss [dɪsˈmɪs] vt congedare; (employee) licenziare; (idea) scacciare; (Law) respingere; **dismissal** n congedo; licenziamento

disobedient [dɪsəˈbiːdɪənt] adj disubbidiente

disobey [dɪsəˈbeɪ] vt disubbidire a

disorder [dɪsˈɔːdəʳ] n disordine m; (rioting) tumulto; (Med) disturbo

disorganized [dɪsˈɔːgənaɪzd] adj (person, life) disorganizzato(-a); (system, meeting) male organizzato(-a)

disown [dɪsˈəun] vt rinnegare

dispatch [dɪsˈpætʃ] vt spedire, inviare ▷ n spedizione f, invio; (Mil, Press) dispaccio

dispel [dɪsˈpɛl] vt dissipare, scacciare

dispense [dɪsˈpɛns] vt distribuire, amministrare; **dispense with** vt fus fare a meno di; **dispenser** n (container) distributore m

disperse [dɪsˈpəːs] vt disperdere; (knowledge) disseminare ▷ vi disperdersi

display [dɪsˈpleɪ] n esposizione f; (of feeling etc) manifestazione f; (screen) schermo ▷ vt mostrare; (goods) esporre; (pej) ostentare

displease [dɪsˈpliːz] vt dispiacere a, scontentare; **~d with** scontento di

disposable [dɪsˈpəuzəbl] adj (pack etc) a perdere; (income) disponibile

disposal [dɪsˈpəuzl] n eliminazione f; (of property) cessione f; **at one's ~** alla sua disposizione

dispose [dɪsˈpəuz] vi **~ of** sbarazzarsi di; **disposition** [-ˈzɪʃən] n disposizione f; (temperament) carattere m

disproportionate [dɪsprəˈpɔːʃənət] adj sproporzionato(-a)

dispute [dɪsˈpjuːt] n disputa; (also: **industrial ~**) controversia (sindacale) ▷ vt contestare; (matter) discutere; (victory) disputare

disqualify [dɪsˈkwɔlɪfaɪ] vt (Sport) squalificare; **to ~ sb from sth/from doing** rendere qn incapace a qc/a fare; squalificare qn da qc/da fare; **to ~ sb from driving** ritirare la patente a qn

disregard [dɪsrɪˈgɑːd] vt non far caso a, non badare a

disrupt [dɪsˈrʌpt] vt disturbare; creare scompiglio in; **disruption** [dɪsˈrʌpʃən] n disordine m; interruzione f

dissatisfaction [dɪssætɪsˈfækʃən] n scontentezza, insoddisfazione f

dissatisfied [dɪsˈsætɪsfaɪd] adj **~ (with)** scontento or insoddisfatto(a) (di)

dissect [dɪˈsɛkt] vt sezionare

dissent [dɪ'sɛnt] n dissenso
dissertation [dɪsə'teɪʃən] n tesi f inv,
  dissertazione f
dissolve [dɪ'zɔlv] vt dissolvere, sciogliere;
  (Pol, marriage etc) sciogliere ▷ vi dissolversi,
  sciogliersi
distance ['dɪstns] n distanza; **in the ~** in
  lontananza
distant ['dɪstnt] adj lontano(-a), distante;
  (manner) riservato(-a), freddo(-a)
distil [dɪs'tɪl] (US **distill**) vt distillare;
  distillery n distilleria
distinct [dɪs'tɪŋkt] adj distinto(-a);
  as ~ from a differenza di; **distinction**
  [dɪs'tɪŋkʃən] n distinzione f; (in exam) lode
  f; **distinctive** adj distintivo(-a)
distinguish [dɪs'tɪŋgwɪʃ] vt distinguere;
  discernere; **distinguished** adj (eminent)
  eminente
distort [dɪs'tɔːt] vt distorcere; (Tech)
  deformare
distract [dɪs'trækt] vt distrarre;
  distracted adj distratto(-a); **distraction**
  [dɪs'trækʃən] n distrazione f
distraught [dɪs'trɔːt] adj stravolto(-a)
distress [dɪs'trɛs] n angoscia ▷ vt
  affliggere; **distressing** adj doloroso(-a)
distribute [dɪs'trɪbjuːt] vt distribuire;
  distribution [-'bjuːʃən] n distribuzione f;
  distributor n distributore m
district ['dɪstrɪkt] n (of country) regione f;
  (of town) quartiere m; (Admin) distretto;
  district attorney (US) n ≈ sostituto
  procuratore m della Repubblica
distrust [dɪs'trʌst] n diffidenza, sfiducia
  ▷ vt non aver fiducia in
disturb [dɪs'təːb] vt disturbare;
  disturbance n disturbo; (political etc)
  disordini mpl; **disturbed** adj (worried,
  upset) turbato(-a); **emotionally
  disturbed** con turbe emotive; **disturbing**
  adj sconvolgente
ditch [dɪtʃ] n fossa ▷ vt (inf) piantare in
  asso
ditto ['dɪtəu] adv idem
dive [daɪv] n tuffo; (of submarine)
  immersione f ▷ vi tuffarsi; immergersi;
  diver n tuffatore(-trice), palombaro
diverse [daɪ'vəːs] adj vario(-a)
diversion [daɪ'vəːʃən] n (BRIT Aut)
  deviazione f; (distraction) divertimento
diversity [daɪ'vəːsɪtɪ] n diversità f inv,
  varietà f inv
divert [daɪ'vəːt] vt deviare
divide [dɪ'vaɪd] vt dividere; (separate)
  separare ▷ vi dividersi; **divided highway**
  (US) n strada a doppia carreggiata
divine [dɪ'vaɪn] adj divino(-a)
diving ['daɪvɪŋ] n tuffo; **diving board** n

trampolino
division [dɪ'vɪʒən] n divisione f;
  separazione f; (esp Football) serie f
divorce [dɪ'vɔːs] n divorzio ▷ vt divorziare
  da; (dissociate) separare; **divorced**
  adj divorziato(-a); **divorcee** [-'siː] n
  divorziato(-a)
D.I.Y. (BRIT) n abbr = **do-it-yourself**
dizzy ['dɪzɪ] adj **to feel ~** avere il capogiro
DJ n abbr = **disc jockey**
DNA n abbr (= deoxyribonucleic acid) DNA m;
  DNA test n test m inv del DNA

O **KEYWORD**

do [duː] (pt **did**, pp **done**) n (inf: party etc)
  festa; **it was rather a grand do** è stato
  un ricevimento piuttosto importante
  ▷ vb **1** (in negative constructions: non
  tradotto): **I don't understand** non
  capisco
  2 (to form questions: non tradotto): **didn't
  you know?** non lo sapevi?; **why didn't
  you come?** perché non sei venuto?
  3 (for emphasis, in polite expressions): **she
  does seem rather late** sembra essere
  piuttosto in ritardo; **do sit down** si
  accomodi la prego, prego si sieda; **do
  take care!** mi raccomando, sta attento!
  4 (used to avoid repeating vb): **she swims
  better than I do** lei nuota meglio di me;
  do you agree? — yes, I do/no, I don't sei
  d'accordo? — sì/no; **she lives in Glasgow
  — so do I** lei vive a Glasgow — anch'io; **he
  asked me to help him and I did** mi ha
  chiesto di aiutarlo ed io l'ho fatto
  5 (in question tags): **you like him, don't
  you?** ti piace, vero?; **I don't know him,
  do I?** non lo conosco, vero?
  ▷ vt (gen, carry out, perform etc) fare; **what
  are you doing tonight?** che fa stasera?;
  to do the cooking cucinare; **to do the
  washing-up** fare i piatti; **to do one's
  teeth** lavarsi i denti; **to do one's hair/
  nails** farsi i capelli/le unghie; **the car was
  doing 100** la macchina faceva i 100 all'ora
  ▷ vi **1** (act, behave) fare; **do as I do** faccia
  come me, faccia come faccio io
  2 (get on, fare) andare; **he's doing well/
  badly at school** va bene/male a scuola;
  how do you do? piacere!
  3 (suit) andare bene; **this room will do**
  questa stanza va bene
  4 (be sufficient) bastare; **will £10 do?**
  basteranno 10 sterline?; **that'll do** basta
  così; **that'll do!** (in annoyance) ora basta!;
  to make do (with) arrangiarsi (con)
  do away with vt fus (kill) far fuori;
  (abolish) abolire

do up vt (laces) allacciare; (dress, buttons) abbottonare; (renovate: room, house) rimettere a nuovo, rifare

do with vt fus (need) aver bisogno di; (be connected): **what has it got to do with you?** e tu che c'entri?; **I won't have anything to do with it** non voglio avere niente a che farci; **it has to do with money** si tratta di soldi

do without vi fare senza ▷ vt fus fare a meno di

dock [dɔk] n (Naut) bacino; (Law) banco degli imputati ▷ vi entrare in bacino; (Space) agganciarsi; **~s** npl (Naut) dock m inv

doctor ['dɔktə'] n medico(-a); (Ph.D. etc) dottore(-essa) ▷ vt (drink etc) adulterare; **call a ~!** chiamate un dottore!; **Doctor of Philosophy** n dottorato di ricerca; (person) titolare m/f di un dottorato di ricerca

document ['dɔkjumənt] n documento; **documentary** [-'mɛntərɪ] adj (evidence) documentato(-a) ▷ n documentario; **documentation** [dɔkjumən'teɪʃən] n documentazione f

dodge [dɔdʒ] n trucco; schivata ▷ vt schivare, eludere

dodgy ['dɔdʒɪ] adj (inf: uncertain) rischioso(-a); (untrustworthy) sospetto(-a)

does [dʌz] vb see **do**

doesn't ['dʌznt] = **does not**

dog [dɔg] n cane m ▷ vt (follow closely) pedinare; (fig: memory etc) perseguitare; **doggy bag** n sacchetto per gli avanzi (da portare a casa)

do-it-yourself ['du:ɪtjɔː'sɛlf] n il far da sé

dole [dəul] (BRIT) n sussidio di disoccupazione; **to be on the ~** vivere del sussidio

doll [dɔl] n bambola

dollar ['dɔlə'] n dollaro

dolphin ['dɔlfɪn] n delfino

dome [dəum] n cupola

domestic [də'mɛstɪk] adj (duty, happiness, animal) domestico(-a); (policy, affairs, flights) nazionale; **domestic appliance** n elettrodomestico

dominant ['dɔmɪnənt] adj dominante

dominate ['dɔmɪneɪt] vt dominare

domino ['dɔmɪnəu] (pl **dominoes**) n domino; **dominoes** n (game) gioco del domino

donate [də'neɪt] vt donare; **donation** [də'neɪʃən] n donazione f

done [dʌn] pp of **do**

donkey ['dɔŋkɪ] n asino

donor ['dəunə'] n donatore(-trice); **donor card** n tessera di donatore di organi

don't [dəunt] = **do not**

donut ['dəunʌt] (US) n = **doughnut**

doodle ['du:dl] vi scarabocchiare

doom [du:m] n destino; rovina ▷ vt **to be ~ed (to failure)** essere predestinato(-a) (a fallire)

door [dɔː'] n porta; **doorbell** n campanello; **door handle** n maniglia; **doorknob** ['dɔːnɔb] n pomello, maniglia; **doorstep** n gradino della porta; **doorway** n porta

dope [dəup] n (inf: drugs) roba ▷ vt (horse etc) drogare

dormitory ['dɔːmɪtrɪ] n dormitorio; (US) casa dello studente

DOS [dɔs] n abbr (= disk operating system) DOS m

dosage ['dəusɪdʒ] n posologia

dose [dəus] n dose f; (bout) attacco

dot [dɔt] n punto; macchiolina ▷ vt **~ted with** punteggiato(-a) di; **on the ~** in punto; **dotted line** ['dɔtɪd-] n linea punteggiata

double ['dʌbl] adj doppio(-a) ▷ adv (twice): **to cost ~ sth** costare il doppio (di qc) ▷ n sosia m inv ▷ vt raddoppiare; (fold) piegare doppio or in due ▷ vi raddoppiarsi; **at the ~** (BRIT), **on the ~** a passo di corsa; **double back** vi (person) tornare sui propri passi; **double bass** n contrabbasso; **double bed** n letto matrimoniale; **double-check** vt, vi ricontrollare; **double-click** vt (Comput) fare doppio click; **double-cross** vt fare il doppio gioco con; **doubledecker** n autobus m inv a due piani; **double glazing** (BRIT) n doppi vetri mpl; **double room** n camera matrimoniale; **doubles** n (Tennis) doppio; **double yellow lines** npl (BRIT: Aut) linea gialla doppia continua che segnala il divieto di sosta

doubt [daut] n dubbio ▷ vt dubitare di; **to ~ that** dubitare che + sub; **doubtful** adj dubbioso(-a), incerto(-a); (person) equivoco(-a); **doubtless** adv indubbiamente

dough [dəu] n pasta, impasto; **doughnut** (US **donut**) n bombolone m

dove [dʌv] n colombo(-a)

down [daun] n piume fpl ▷ adv giù, di sotto ▷ prep giù per ▷ vt (inf: drink) scolarsi; **~ with X!** abbasso X!; **down-and-out** n barbone m; **downfall** n caduta; rovina; **downhill** adv **to go downhill** andare in discesa; (fig) lasciarsi andare; andare a rotoli

Downing Street ['daunɪŋ-] *n* **lo ~**
residenza del primo ministro inglese

● **DOWNING STREET**
●
● Al numero 10 di **Downing Street**, nel
● quartiere di Westminster a Londra, si
● trova la residenza del primo ministro
● inglese, al numero 11 quella del
● **Chancellor of the Exchequer**.

down: **download** *vt* (*Comput*) scaricare;
downright *adj* franco(-a); (*refusal*)
assoluto(-a)
Down's syndrome *n* sindrome *f* di Down
down: **downstairs** *adv* di sotto; al
piano inferiore; **down-to-earth** *adj*
pratico(-a); **downtown** *adv* in città; **down
under** *adv* (*Australia etc*) agli antipodi;
downward ['daunwəd] *adj*, *adv* in giù, in
discesa; **downwards** ['daunwədz] *adv*
= **downward**
doz. *abbr* = **dozen**
doze [dəuz] *vi* sonnecchiare
dozen ['dʌzn] *n* dozzina; **a ~ books** una
dozzina di libri; **~s of** decine *fpl* di
Dr. *abbr* (= *doctor*) dott.; (*in street names*)
= **drive**
drab [dræb] *adj* tetro(-a), grigio(-a)
draft [drɑːft] *n* abbozzo; (*Pol*) bozza;
(*Comm*) tratta; (*US*: *call-up*) leva ▷ *vt*
abbozzare; *see also* **draught**
drag [dræg] *vt* trascinare; (*river*) dragare
▷ *vi* trascinarsi ▷ *n* (*inf*) noioso(-a); noia,
fatica; (*women's clothing*): **in ~** travestito
(da donna)
dragon ['drægən] *n* drago
dragonfly ['drægənflaɪ] *n* libellula
drain [dreɪn] *n* (*for sewage*) fogna; (*on
resources*) salasso ▷ *vt* (*land*, *marshes*)
prosciugare; (*vegetables*) scolare ▷ *vi*
(*water*) defluire (via); **drainage** *n*
prosciugamento; fognatura; **drainpipe** *n*
tubo di scarico
drama ['drɑːmə] *n* (*art*) dramma
m, teatro; (*play*) commedia; (*event*)
dramma; **dramatic** [drə'mætɪk] *adj*
drammatico(-a)
drank [dræŋk] *pt of* **drink**
drape [dreɪp] *vt* drappeggiare; **~s** (*US*) *npl*
(*curtains*) tende *fpl*
drastic ['dræstɪk] *adj* drastico(-a)
draught [drɑːft] (*US* **draft**) *n* corrente *f*
d'aria; (*Naut*) pescaggio; **on ~** (*beer*) alla
spina; **draught beer** *n* birra alla spina;
draughts (*BRIT*) *n* (gioco della) dama
draw [drɔː] (*pt* **drew**, *pp* **drawn**) *vt* tirare;
(*take out*) estrarre; (*attract*) attirare;
(*picture*) disegnare; (*line*, *circle*) tracciare;

(*money*) ritirare ▷ *vi* (*Sport*) pareggiare
▷ *n* pareggio; (*in lottery*) estrazione *f*; **to ~
near** avvicinarsi; **draw out** *vi* (*lengthen*)
allungarsi ▷ *vt* (*money*) ritirare; **draw
up** *vi* (*stop*) arrestarsi, fermarsi ▷ *vt*
(*chair*) avvicinare; (*document*) compilare;
drawback *n* svantaggio, inconveniente *m*
drawer [drɔːʳ] *n* cassetto
drawing ['drɔːɪŋ] *n* disegno; **drawing pin**
(*BRIT*) *n* puntina da disegno; **drawing
room** *n* salotto
drawn [drɔːn] *pp of* **draw**
dread [drɛd] *n* terrore *m* ▷ *vt* tremare
all'idea di; **dreadful** *adj* terribile
dream [driːm] (*pt*, *pp* **dreamed** *or* **dreamt**)
n sogno ▷ *vt*, *vi* sognare; **dreamer** *n*
sognatore(-trice)
dreamt [drɛmt] *pt*, *pp of* **dream**
dreary ['drɪərɪ] *adj* tetro(-a);
monotono(-a)
drench [drɛntʃ] *vt* inzuppare
dress [drɛs] *n* vestito; (*no pl*: *clothing*)
abbigliamento ▷ *vt* vestire; (*wound*)
fasciare ▷ *vi* vestirsi; **to get ~ed** vestirsi;
dress up *vi* vestirsi a festa; (*in fancy dress*)
vestirsi in costume; **dress circle** (*BRIT*) *n*
prima galleria; **dresser** (*BRIT*: *cupboard*)
credenza; (*US*) cassettone *m*; **dressing** *n*
(*Med*) benda; (*Culin*) condimento; **dressing
gown** (*BRIT*) *n* vestaglia; **dressing
room** *n* (*Theatre*) camerino; (*Sport*)
spogliatoio; **dressing table** *n* toilette *f*
inv; **dressmaker** *n* sarta
drew [druː] *pt of* **draw**
dribble ['drɪbl] *vi* (*baby*) sbavare ▷ *vt* (*ball*)
dribblare
dried [draɪd] *adj* (*fruit*, *beans*) secco(-a);
(*eggs*, *milk*) in polvere
drier ['draɪəʳ] *n* = **dryer**
drift [drɪft] *n* (*of current etc*) direzione
f; forza; (*of snow*) cumulo; turbine *m*;
(*general meaning*) senso ▷ *vi* (*boat*) essere
trasportato(-a) dalla corrente; (*sand*, *snow*)
ammucchiarsi
drill [drɪl] *n* trapano; (*Mil*) esercitazione *f*
▷ *vt* trapanare; (*troops*) addestrare ▷ *vi* (*for
oil*) fare trivellazioni
drink [drɪŋk] (*pt* **drank**, *pp* **drunk**)
n bevanda, bibita; (*alcoholic drink*)
bicchierino; (*sip*) sorso ▷ *vt*, *vi* bere; **to
have a ~** bere qualcosa; **would you
like a ~?** vuoi qualcosa da bere?; **a ~ of
water** un po' d'acqua; **drink-driving** *n*
guida in stato di ebbrezza; **drinker** *n*
bevitore(-trice); **drinking water** *n* acqua
potabile
drip [drɪp] *n* goccia; gocciolamento;
(*Med*) fleboclisi *f inv* ▷ *vi* gocciolare; (*tap*)
sgocciolare

d

drive [draɪv] (*pt* **drove**, *pp* **driven**) *n* passeggiata *or* giro in macchina; (*also*: ~**way**) viale *m* d'accesso; (*energy*) energia; (*campaign*) campagna; (*also*: **disk ~**) lettore *m* ▷ *vt* guidare; (*nail*) piantare; (*push*) cacciare, spingere; (*Tech: motor*) azionare; far funzionare ▷ *vi* (*Aut: at controls*) guidare; (: *travel*) andare in macchina; **left-/right-hand ~** guida a sinistra/destra; **to ~ sb mad** far impazzire qn; **drive out** *vt* (*force out*) cacciare, mandare via; **drive-in** (*esp US*) *adj, n* drive-in (*m inv*)

driven ['drɪvn] *pp of* **drive**

driver ['draɪvə'] *n* conducente *m/f*; (*of taxi*) tassista *m*; (*chauffeur: of bus*) autista *m/f*; **driver's license** (*US*) *n* patente *f* di guida

driveway ['draɪvweɪ] *n* viale *m* d'accesso

driving ['draɪvɪŋ] *n* guida; **driving instructor** *n* istruttore(-trice) di scuola guida; **driving lesson** *n* lezione *f* di guida; **driving licence** (*BRIT*) *n* patente *f* di guida; **driving test** *n* esame *m* di guida

drizzle ['drɪzl] *n* pioggerella

droop [dru:p] *vi* (*flower*) appassire; (*head, shoulders*) chinarsi

drop [drɔp] *n* (*of water*) goccia; (*lessening*) diminuzione *f*; (*fall*) caduta ▷ *vt* lasciare cadere; (*voice, eyes, price*) abbassare; (*set down from car*) far scendere; (*name from list*) lasciare fuori ▷ *vi* cascare; (*wind*) abbassarsi; **drop in** *vi* (*inf: visit*): **to ~ in (on)** fare un salto (da), passare (da); **drop off** *vi* (*sleep*) addormentarsi ▷ *vt* (*passenger*) far scendere; **drop out** *vi* (*withdraw*) ritirarsi; (*student etc*) smettere di studiare

drought [draut] *n* siccità *f inv*

drove [drəuv] *pt of* **drive**

drown [draun] *vt* affogare; (*fig: noise*) soffocare ▷ *vi* affogare

drowsy ['drauzɪ] *adj* sonnolento(-a), assonnato(-a)

drug [drʌg] *n* farmaco; (*narcotic*) droga ▷ *vt* drogare; **to be on ~s** drogarsi; (*Med*) prendere medicinali; **hard/soft ~s** droghe pesanti/leggere; **drug addict** *n* tossicomane *m/f*; **drug dealer** *n* trafficante *m/f* di droga; **druggist** (*US*) *n* persona che gestisce un drugstore; **drugstore** (*US*) *n* drugstore *m inv*

drum [drʌm] *n* tamburo; (*for oil, petrol*) fusto ▷ *vi* tamburellare; **~s** *npl* (*set of drums*) batteria; **drummer** *n* batterista *m/f*

drunk [drʌŋk] *pp of* **drink** ▷ *adj* ubriaco(-a); ebbro(-a) ▷ *n* (*also*: ~**ard**) ubriacone(-a); **drunken** *adj* ubriaco(-a); da ubriaco

dry [draɪ] *adj* secco(-a); (*day, clothes*) asciutto(-a) ▷ *vt* seccare; (*clothes, hair, hands*) asciugare ▷ *vi* asciugarsi; **dry off** *vi* asciugarsi ▷ *vt* asciugare; **dry up** *vi* seccarsi; **dry-cleaner's** *n* lavasecco *m inv*; **dry-cleaning** *n* pulitura a secco; **dryer** *n* (*for hair*) föhn *m inv*, asciugacapelli *m inv*; (*for clothes*) asciugabiancheria; (*US: spin-dryer*) centrifuga

DSS *n abbr* (= *Department of Social Security*) ministero della Previdenza sociale

DTP *n abbr* (= *desk-top publishing*) desktop publishing *m inv*

dual ['djuəl] *adj* doppio(-a); **dual carriageway** (*BRIT*) *n* strada a doppia carreggiata

dubious ['dju:bɪəs] *adj* dubbio(-a)

Dublin ['dʌblɪn] *n* Dublino *f*

duck [dʌk] *n* anatra ▷ *vi* abbassare la testa

due [dju:] *adj* dovuto(-a); (*expected*) atteso(-a); (*fitting*) giusto(-a) ▷ *n* dovuto ▷ *adv* ~ **north** diritto verso nord

duel ['djuəl] *n* duello

duet [dju:'ɛt] *n* duetto

dug [dʌg] *pt, pp of* **dig**

duke [dju:k] *n* duca *m*

dull [dʌl] *adj* (*light*) debole; (*boring*) noioso(-a); (*slow-witted*) ottuso(-a); (*sound, pain*) sordo(-a); (*weather, day*) fosco(-a), scuro(-a) ▷ *vt* (*pain, grief*) attutire; (*mind, senses*) intorpidire

dumb [dʌm] *adj* muto(-a); (*pej*) stupido(-a)

dummy ['dʌmɪ] *n* (*tailor's model*) manichino; (*Tech, Comm*) riproduzione *f*; (*BRIT: for baby*) tettarella ▷ *adj* falso(-a), finto(-a)

dump [dʌmp] *n* (*also*: **rubbish ~**) discarica di rifiuti; (*inf: place*) buco ▷ *vt* (*put down*) scaricare; mettere giù; (*get rid of*) buttar via

dumpling ['dʌmplɪŋ] *n* specie di gnocco

dune [dju:n] *n* duna

dungarees [dʌŋɡə'ri:z] *npl* tuta

dungeon ['dʌndʒən] *n* prigione *f* sotterranea

duplex ['dju:plɛks] (*US*) *n* (*house*) casa con muro divisorio in comune con un'altra; (*apartment*) appartamento su due piani

duplicate [*n* 'dju:plɪkət, *vb* 'dju:plɪkeɪt] *n* doppio ▷ *vt* duplicare; **in ~** in doppia copia

durable ['djuərəbl] *adj* durevole; (*clothes, metal*) resistente

duration [djuə'reɪʃən] *n* durata

during ['djuərɪŋ] *prep* durante, nel corso di

dusk [dʌsk] *n* crepuscolo

dust [dʌst] *n* polvere *f* ▷ *vt* (*furniture*) spolverare; (*cake etc*): **to ~ with** cospargere con; **dustbin** (*BRIT*) *n* pattumiera; **duster** *n* straccio per la polvere; **dustman** (*irreg: BRIT*) *n* netturbino; **dustpan** *n* pattumiera; **dusty** *adj* polveroso(-a)

Dutch [dʌtʃ] *adj* olandese ▷ *n* (*Ling*) olandese *m*; **the ~** *npl* gli Olandesi; **to go ~** (*inf*) fare alla romana; **Dutchman, Dutchwoman** (*irreg*) *n* olandese *m/f*

duty ['djuːtɪ] *n* dovere *m*; (*tax*) dazio, tassa; **on ~** di servizio; **off ~** libero(-a), fuori servizio; **duty-free** *adj* esente da dazio

duvet ['duːveɪ] (*BRIT*) *n* piumino, piumone *m*

DVD *n abbr* (= *digital versatile or video disk*) DVD *m inv*; **DVD player** *n* lettore *m* DVD

dwarf [dwɔːf] *n* nano(-a) ▷ *vt* far apparire piccolo

dwell [dwɛl] (*pt, pp* **dwelt**) *vi* dimorare; **dwell on** *vt fus* indugiare su

dwelt [dwɛlt] *pt, pp of* **dwell**

dwindle ['dwɪndl] *vi* diminuire

dye [daɪ] *n* tinta ▷ *vt* tingere

dying ['daɪɪŋ] *adj* morente, moribondo(-a)

dynamic [daɪ'næmɪk] *adj* dinamico(-a)

dynamite ['daɪnəmaɪt] *n* dinamite *f*

dyslexia [dɪs'lɛksɪə] *n* dislessia

dyslexic [dɪs'lɛksɪk] *adj, n* dislessico(-a)

E [iː] *n* (*Mus*) mi *m*

E111 *n abbr* (*also*: **form ~**) E111 (*modulo CEE per rimborso spese mediche*)

each [iːtʃ] *adj* ogni, ciascuno(-a) ▷ *pron* ciascuno(-a), ognuno(-a); **~ one** ognuno(-a); **~ other** si *or* ci *etc*; **they hate ~ other** si odiano (l'un l'altro); **you are jealous of ~ other** siete gelosi l'uno dell'altro; **they have 2 books ~** hanno 2 libri ciascuno

eager ['iːgəʳ] *adj* impaziente, desideroso(-a); ardente; **to be ~ for** essere desideroso di, aver gran voglia di

eagle ['iːgl] *n* aquila

ear [ɪəʳ] *n* orecchio; (*of corn*) pannocchia; **earache** *n* mal *m* d'orecchi; **eardrum** *n* timpano

earl [əːl] (*BRIT*) *n* conte *m*

earlier ['əːlɪəʳ] *adj* precedente ▷ *adv* prima

early ['əːlɪ] *adv* presto, di buon'ora; (*ahead of time*) in anticipo ▷ *adj* (*near the beginning*) primo(-a); (*sooner than expected*) prematuro(-a); (*quick: reply*) veloce; **at an ~ hour** di buon'ora; **to have an ~ night** andare a letto presto; **in the ~** *or* **~ in the spring/19th century** all'inizio della primavera/dell'Ottocento; **early retirement** *n* ritiro anticipato

earmark ['ɪəmɑːk] *vt* **to ~ sth for** destinare qc a

earn [əːn] vt guadagnare; (rest, reward) meritare

earnest ['əːnɪst] adj serio(-a); **in ~** sul serio

earnings ['əːnɪŋz] npl guadagni mpl; (salary) stipendio

ear: **earphones** ['ɪəfəunz] npl cuffia; **earplugs** npl tappi mpl per le orecchie; **earring** ['ɪərɪŋ] n orecchino

earth [əːθ] n terra ▷ vt (BRIT Elec) mettere a terra; **earthquake** n terremoto

ease [iːz] n agio, comodo ▷ vt (soothe) calmare; (loosen) allentare; **to ~ sth out/in** tirare fuori/infilare qc con delicatezza; facilitare l'uscita/l'entrata di qc; **at ~** a proprio agio; (Mil) a riposo

easily ['iːzɪlɪ] adv facilmente

east [iːst] n est m ▷ adj dell'est ▷ adv a oriente; **the E~** l'Oriente m; (Pol) l'Est; **eastbound** ['iːstbaund] adj (traffic) diretto(-a) a est; (carriageway) che porta a est

Easter ['iːstər] n Pasqua; **Easter egg** n uovo di Pasqua

eastern ['iːstən] adj orientale, d'oriente; dell'est

Easter Sunday n domenica di Pasqua

easy ['iːzɪ] adj facile; (manner) disinvolto(-a) ▷ adv **to take it** or **things ~** prendersela con calma; **easy-going** adj accomodante

eat [iːt] (pt **ate**, pp **eaten**) vt, vi mangiare; **can we have something to ~?** possiamo mangiare qualcosa?; **eat out** vi mangiare fuori

eavesdrop ['iːvzdrɔp] vi **to ~ (on a conversation)** origliare (una conversazione)

e-book ['iːbuk] n libro elettronico

e-business ['iːbɪznɪs] n (company) azienda che opera in Internet; (commerce) commercio elettronico

EC n abbr (= European Community) CE f

eccentric [ɪk'sɛntrɪk] adj, n eccentrico(-a)

echo ['ɛkəu] (pl **echoes**) n eco m or f ▷ vt ripetere; fare eco a ▷ vi echeggiare; dare un eco

eclipse [ɪ'klɪps] n eclissi f inv

eco-friendly [iːkəu'frɛndlɪ] adj ecologico(-a)

ecological [iːkə'lɔdʒɪkəl] adj ecologico(-a)

ecology [ɪ'kɔlədʒɪ] n ecologia

e-commerce [iːkɔməːs] n commercio elettronico

economic [iːkə'nɔmɪk] adj economico(-a); **economical** adj economico(-a); (person) economo(-a); **economics** n economia ▷ npl lato finanziario

economist [ɪ'kɔnəmɪst] n economista m/f

economize [ɪ'kɔnəmaɪz] vi risparmiare, fare economia

economy [ɪ'kɔnəmɪ] n economia; **economy class** n (Aviat) classe f turistica; **economy class syndrome** n sindrome f della classe economica

ecstasy ['ɛkstəsɪ] n estasi f inv; **ecstatic** [ɛks'tætɪk] adj estatico(-a), in estasi

eczema ['ɛksɪmə] n eczema m

edge [ɛdʒ] n margine m; (of table, plate, cup) orlo; (of knife etc) taglio ▷ vt bordare; **on ~** (fig) = **edgy**; **to edge away from** sgattaiolare da

edgy ['ɛdʒɪ] adj nervoso(-a)

edible ['ɛdɪbl] adj commestibile; (meal) mangiabile

Edinburgh ['ɛdɪnbərə] n Edimburgo f

edit ['ɛdɪt] vt curare; **edition** [ɪ'dɪfən] n edizione f; **editor** n (in newspaper) redattore(-trice), redattore(-trice) capo; (of sb's work) curatore(-trice); **editorial** [-'tɔːrɪəl] adj redazionale, editoriale ▷ n editoriale m

> Be careful not to translate **editor** by the Italian word **editore**.

educate ['ɛdjukeɪt] vt istruire; educare; **educated** adj istruito(-a)

education [ɛdju'keɪʃən] n educazione f; (schooling) istruzione f; **educational** adj pedagogico(-a); scolastico(-a); istruttivo(-a)

eel [iːl] n anguilla

eerie ['ɪərɪ] adj che fa accapponare la pelle

effect [ɪ'fɛkt] n effetto ▷ vt effettuare; **to take ~** (law) entrare in vigore; (drug) fare effetto; **in ~** effettivamente; **~s** npl (Theat) effetti mpl scenici; (property) effetti mpl; **effective** adj efficace; (actual) effettivo(-a); **effectively** adv efficacemente; effettivamente

efficiency [ɪ'fɪfənsɪ] n efficienza; rendimento effettivo

efficient [ɪ'fɪfənt] adj efficiente; **efficiently** adv efficientemente; efficacemente

effort ['ɛfət] n sforzo; **effortless** adj senza sforzo, facile

e.g. adv abbr (= exempli gratia) per esempio, p.es.

egg [ɛg] n uovo; **hard-boiled/soft-boiled ~** uovo sodo/alla coque; **eggcup** n portauovo m inv; **eggplant** (esp US) n melanzana; **eggshell** n guscio d'uovo; **egg white** n albume m, bianco d'uovo; **egg yolk** n tuorlo, rosso (d'uovo)

ego ['iːgəu] n ego m inv

Egypt ['iːdʒɪpt] n Egitto; **Egyptian** [ɪ'dʒɪpfən] adj, n egiziano(-a)

eight [eɪt] num otto; **eighteen** num diciotto; **eighteenth** num diciottesimo(-a); **eighth** [eɪtθ] num ottavo(-a); **eightieth** ['eɪtɪɪθ] *num* ottantesimo(-a); **eighty** *num* ottanta

Eire ['eərə] *n* Repubblica d'Irlanda

either ['aɪðəʳ] *adj* l'uno(-a) o l'altro(-a); *(both, each)* ciascuno(-a) ▷ *pron* **~ (of them)** (o) l'uno(-a) o l'altro(-a) ▷ *adv* neanche ▷ *conj* **~ good or bad** o buono o cattivo; **on ~ side** su ciascun lato; **I don't like ~** non mi piace né l'uno né l'altro; **no, I don't ~** no, neanch'io

eject [ɪ'dʒɛkt] *vt* espellere; lanciare

elaborate [*adj* ɪ'læbərɪt, *vb* ɪ'læbəreɪt] *adj* elaborato(-a), minuzioso(-a) ▷ *vt* elaborare ▷ *vi* fornire i particolari

elastic [ɪ'læstɪk] *adj* elastico(-a) ▷ *n* elastico; **elastic band** (BRIT) *n* elastico

elbow ['ɛlbəu] *n* gomito

elder ['ɛldəʳ] *adj* maggiore, più vecchio(-a) ▷ *n* (*tree*) sambuco; **one's ~s** i più anziani; **elderly** *adj* anziano(-a) ▷ *npl* **the elderly** gli anziani

eldest ['ɛldɪst] *adj*, *n* **the ~ (child)** il(la) maggiore (dei bambini)

elect [ɪ'lɛkt] *vt* eleggere ▷ *adj* **the president ~** il presidente designato; **to ~ to do** decidere di fare; **election** [ɪ'lɛkʃən] *n* elezione *f*; **electoral** [ɪ'lɛktərəl] *adj* elettorale; **electorate** *n* elettorato

electric [ɪ'lɛktrɪk] *adj* elettrico(-a); **electrical** *adj* elettrico(-a); **electric blanket** *n* coperta elettrica; **electric fire** *n* stufa elettrica; **electrician** [ɪlɛk'trɪʃən] *n* elettricista *m*; **electricity** [ɪlɛk'trɪsɪtɪ] *n* elettricità; **electric shock** *n* scossa (elettrica); **electrify** [ɪ'lɛktrɪfaɪ] *vt* (*Rail*) elettrificare; (*audience*) elettrizzare

electronic [ɪlɛk'trɔnɪk] *adj* elettronico(-a); **electronic mail** *n* posta elettronica; **electronics** *n* elettronica

elegance ['ɛlɪɡəns] *n* eleganza

elegant ['ɛlɪɡənt] *adj* elegante

element ['ɛlɪmənt] *n* elemento; (*of heater, kettle etc*) resistenza

elementary [ɛlɪ'mɛntərɪ] *adj* elementare; **elementary school** (US) *n* scuola elementare

elephant ['ɛlɪfənt] *n* elefante(-essa)

elevate ['ɛlɪveɪt] *vt* elevare

elevator ['ɛlɪveɪtəʳ] *n* elevatore *m*; (US: lift) ascensore *m*

eleven [ɪ'lɛvn] *num* undici; **eleventh** *adj* undicesimo(-a)

eligible ['ɛlɪdʒəbl] *adj* eleggibile; (*for membership*) che ha i requisiti

eliminate [ɪ'lɪmɪneɪt] *vt* eliminare

elm [ɛlm] *n* olmo

eloquent ['ɛləkwənt] *adj* eloquente

else [ɛls] *adv* altro; **something ~** qualcos'altro; **somewhere ~** altrove;

everywhere ~ in qualsiasi altro luogo; **nobody ~** nessun altro; **where ~?** in quale altro luogo?; **little ~** poco altro; **elsewhere** *adv* altrove

elusive [ɪ'luːsɪv] *adj* elusivo(-a)

e-mail *n abbr* (= *electronic mail*) posta elettronica ▷ *vt* mandare un messaggio di posta elettronica a; **e-mail address** *n* indirizzo di posta elettronica

embankment [ɪm'hæŋkmənt] *n* (*of road, railway*) terrapieno

embargo [ɪm'baːɡəu] *n* (*pl* **embargoes**) (*Comm, Naut*) embargo ▷ *vt* mettere l'embargo su; **to put an ~ on sth** mettere l'embargo su qc

embark [ɪm'baːk] *vi* **to ~ (on)** imbarcarsi (su) ▷ *vt* imbarcare; **to ~ on** (*fig*) imbarcarsi in

embarrass [ɪm'bærəs] *vt* imbarazzare; **embarrassed** *adj* imbarazzato(-a); **embarrassing** *adj* imbarazzante; **embarrassment** *n* imbarazzo

embassy ['ɛmbəsɪ] *n* ambasciata

embrace [ɪm'breɪs] *vt* abbracciare ▷ *vi* abbracciarsi ▷ *n* abbraccio

embroider [ɪm'brɔɪdəʳ] *vt* ricamare; **embroidery** *n* ricamo

embryo ['ɛmbrɪəu] *n* embrione *m*

emerald ['ɛmərəld] *n* smeraldo

emerge [ɪ'məːdʒ] *vi* emergere

emergency [ɪ'məːdʒənsɪ] *n* emergenza; **in an ~** in caso di emergenza; **emergency brake** (US) *n* freno a mano; **emergency exit** *n* uscita di sicurezza; **emergency landing** *n* atterraggio forzato; **emergency room** (US: *Med*) *n* pronto soccorso; **emergency services** *npl* (*fire, police, ambulance*) servizi *mpl* di pronto intervento

emigrate ['ɛmɪɡreɪt] *vi* emigrare; **emigration** [ɛmɪ'ɡreɪʃən] *n* emigrazione *f*

eminent ['ɛmɪnənt] *adj* eminente

emissions [ɪ'mɪʃənz] *npl* emissioni *fpl*

emit [ɪ'mɪt] *vt* emettere

emotion [ɪ'məuʃən] *n* emozione *f*; **emotional** *adj* (*person*) emotivo(-a); (*scene*) commovente; (*tone, speech*) carico(-a) d'emozione

emperor ['ɛmpərəʳ] *n* imperatore *m*

emphasis ['ɛmfəsɪs] (*pl* **-ases**) *n* enfasi *f inv*; importanza

emphasize ['ɛmfəsaɪz] *vt* (*word, point*) sottolineare; (*feature*) mettere in evidenza

empire ['ɛmpaɪəʳ] *n* impero

employ [ɪm'plɔɪ] *vt* impiegare; **employee** [-'iː] *n* impiegato(-a); **employer** *n* principale *m/f*, datore *m* di lavoro; **employment** *n* impiego; **employment agency** *n* agenzia di collocamento

empower [ɪm'pauəʳ] vt **to ~ sb to do** concedere autorità a qn di fare

empress ['ɛmprɪs] n imperatrice f

emptiness ['ɛmptɪnɪs] n vuoto

empty ['ɛmptɪ] adj vuoto(-a); (threat, promise) vano(-a) ▷ vt vuotare ▷ vi vuotarsi; (liquid) scaricarsi; **empty-handed** adj a mani vuote

EMU n abbr (= economic and monetary union) unione f economica e monetaria

emulsion [ɪ'mʌlʃən] n emulsione f

enable [ɪ'neɪbl] vt **to ~ sb to do** permettere a qn di fare

enamel [ɪ'næməl] n smalto; (also: ~ **paint**) vernice f a smalto

enchanting [ɪn'tʃɑːntɪŋ] adj incantevole, affascinante

encl. abbr (= enclosed) all.

enclose [ɪn'kləuz] vt (land) circondare, recingere; (letter etc) **to ~ (with)** allegare (con); **please find ~d** trovi qui accluso

enclosure [ɪn'kləuʒəʳ] n recinto

encore [ɔŋ'kɔːʳ] excl bis ▷ n bis m inv

encounter [ɪn'kauntəʳ] n incontro ▷ vt incontrare

encourage [ɪn'kʌrɪdʒ] vt incoraggiare; **encouragement** n incoraggiamento

encouraging [ɪn'kʌrɪdʒɪŋ] adj incoraggiante

encyclop(a)edia [ɛnsaɪkləu'piːdɪə] n enciclopedia

end [ɛnd] n fine f; (aim) fine m; (of table) bordo estremo; (of pointed object) punta ▷ vt finire; (also: **bring to an ~, put an ~ to**) mettere fine a ▷ vi finire; **in the ~** alla fine; **on ~** (object) ritto(-a); **to stand on ~** (hair) rizzarsi; **for hours on ~** per ore ed ore; **end up** vi **to ~ up in** finire in

endanger [ɪn'deɪndʒəʳ] vt mettere in pericolo

endearing [ɪn'dɪərɪŋ] adj accattivante

endeavour [ɪn'dɛvəʳ] (us **endeavor**) n sforzo, tentativo ▷ vi **to ~ to do** cercare or sforzarsi di fare

ending ['ɛndɪŋ] n fine f, conclusione f; (Ling) desinenza

endless ['ɛndlɪs] adj senza fine

endorse [ɪn'dɔːs] vt (cheque) girare; (approve) approvare, appoggiare; **endorsement** n approvazione f; (on driving licence) contravvenzione registrata sulla patente

endurance [ɪn'djuərəns] n resistenza; pazienza

endure [ɪn'djuəʳ] vt sopportare, resistere a ▷ vi durare

enemy ['ɛnəmɪ] adj, n nemico(-a)

energetic [ɛnə'dʒɛtɪk] adj energico(-a), attivo(-a)

energy ['ɛnədʒɪ] n energia

enforce [ɪn'fɔːs] vt (Law) applicare, far osservare

engaged [ɪn'geɪdʒd] adj (BRIT: busy, in use) occupato(-a); (betrothed) fidanzato(-a); **the line's ~** la linea è occupata; **to get ~** fidanzarsi; **engaged tone** (BRIT) n (Tel) segnale m di occupato

engagement [ɪn'geɪdʒmənt] n impegno, obbligo; appuntamento; (to marry) fidanzamento; **engagement ring** n anello di fidanzamento

engaging [ɪn'geɪdʒɪŋ] adj attraente

engine ['ɛndʒɪn] n (Aut) motore m; (Rail) locomotiva

engineer [ɛndʒɪ'nɪəʳ] n ingegnere m; (BRIT: for repairs) tecnico; (on ship: us: Rail) macchinista m; **engineering** n ingegneria

England ['ɪŋglənd] n Inghilterra

English ['ɪŋglɪʃ] adj inglese ▷ n (Ling) inglese m; **the ~** npl gli Inglesi; **English Channel** n the English Channel la Manica; **Englishman** (irreg) n inglese m; **Englishwoman** (irreg) n inglese f

engrave [ɪn'greɪv] vt incidere

engraving [ɪn'greɪvɪŋ] n incisione f

enhance [ɪn'hɑːns] vt accrescere

enjoy [ɪn'dʒɔɪ] vt godere; (have: success, fortune) avere; **to ~ o.s.** godersela, divertirsi; **enjoyable** adj piacevole; **enjoyment** n piacere m, godimento

enlarge [ɪn'lɑːdʒ] vt ingrandire ▷ vi **to ~ on** (subject) dilungarsi su; **enlargement** n (Phot) ingrandimento

enlist [ɪn'lɪst] vt arruolare; (support) procurare ▷ vi arruolarsi

enormous [ɪ'nɔːməs] adj enorme

enough [ɪ'nʌf] adj, n **~ time/books** assai tempo/libri; **have you got ~?** ne ha abbastanza or a sufficienza? ▷ adv **big ~** abbastanza grande; **he has not worked ~** non ha lavorato abbastanza; **~!** basta!; **that's ~, thanks** basta così, grazie; **I've had ~ of him** ne ho abbastanza di lui; **... which, funnily** or **oddly ~** ... che, strano a dirsi

enquire [ɪn'kwaɪəʳ] vt, vi (esp BRIT) = **inquire**

enquiry [ɪn'kwaɪərɪ] n (esp BRIT) = **inquiry**

enrage [ɪn'reɪdʒ] vt fare arrabbiare

enrich [ɪn'rɪtʃ] vt arricchire

enrol [ɪn'rəul] (us **enroll**) vt iscrivere ▷ vi iscriversi; **enrolment** (us **enrollment**) n iscrizione f

en route [ɔn'ruːt] adv **~ for/from/to** in viaggio per/da/a

en suite [ɔn'swiːt] adj **room with ~**

bathroom camera con bagno
ensure [ɪnˈʃuəʳ] vt assicurare; garantire
entail [ɪnˈteɪl] vt comportare
enter [ˈɛntəʳ] vt entrare in; (army) arruolarsi in; (competition) partecipare a; (sb for a competition) iscrivere; (write down) registrare; (Comput) inserire ▷ vi entrare
enterprise [ˈɛntəpraɪz] n (undertaking, company) impresa; (spirit) iniziativa; **free ~** liberalismo economico; **private ~** iniziativa privata; **enterprising** [ˈɛntəpraɪzɪŋ] adj intraprendente
entertain [ɛntəˈteɪn] vt divertire; (invite) ricevere; (idea, plan) nutrire; **entertainer** n comico(-a); **entertaining** adj divertente; **entertainment** n (amusement) divertimento; (show) spettacolo
enthusiasm [ɪnˈθuːzɪæzəm] n entusiasmo
enthusiast [ɪnˈθuːzɪæst] n entusiasta m/f; **enthusiastic** [-ˈæstɪk] adj entusiasta, entusiastico(-a); **to be enthusiastic about sth/sb** essere appassionato(-a) di qc/entusiasta di qn
entire [ɪnˈtaɪəʳ] adj intero(-a); **entirely** adv completamente, interamente
entitle [ɪnˈtaɪtl] vt (give right): **to ~ sb to sth/to do** dare diritto a qn a qc/a fare; **entitled** adj (book) che si intitola; **to be entitled to do** avere il diritto di fare
entrance [n ˈɛntrns, vb ɪnˈtrɑːns] n entrata, ingresso; (of person) entrata ▷ vt incantare, rapire; **where's the ~?** dov'è l'entrata?; **to gain ~ to** (university etc) essere ammesso a; **entrance examination** n esame m di ammissione; **entrance fee** n tassa d'iscrizione; (to museum etc) prezzo d'ingresso; **entrance ramp** (US) n (Aut) rampa di accesso; **entrant** [ˈɛntrnt] n partecipante m/f; concorrente m/f
entrepreneur [ɔntrəprəˈnəː] n imprenditore m
entrust [ɪnˈtrʌst] vt **to ~ sth to** affidare qc a
entry [ˈɛntrɪ] n entrata; (way in) entrata, ingresso; (item: on list) iscrizione f; (in dictionary) voce f; **no ~** vietato l'ingresso; (Aut) divieto di accesso; **entry phone** n citofono
envelope [ˈɛnvələup] n busta
envious [ˈɛnvɪəs] adj invidioso(-a)
environment [ɪnˈvaɪrnmənt] n ambiente m; **environmental** [-ˈmɛntl] adj ecologico(-a); ambientale; **environmentally** [ɪnvaɪərənˈmɛntəlɪ] adv **environmentally sound/friendly** che rispetta l'ambiente
envisage [ɪnˈvɪzɪdʒ] vt immaginare;

prevedere
envoy [ˈɛnvɔɪ] n inviato(-a)
envy [ˈɛnvɪ] n invidia ▷ vt invidiare; **to ~ sb sth** invidiare qn per qc
epic [ˈɛpɪk] n poema m epico ▷ adj epico(-a)
epidemic [ɛpɪˈdɛmɪk] n epidemia
epilepsy [ˈɛpɪlɛpsɪ] n epilessia
epileptic [ɛpɪˈlɛptɪk] adj, n epilettico(-a); **epileptic fit** n attacco epilettico
episode [ˈɛpɪsəud] n episodio
equal [ˈiːkwl] adj uguale ▷ n pari m/f inv ▷ vt uguagliare; **~ to** (task) all'altezza di; **equality** [iːˈkwɔlɪtɪ] n uguaglianza; **equalize** vi pareggiare; **equally** adv ugualmente
equation [ɪˈkweɪʃən] n (Math) equazione f
equator [ɪˈkweɪtəʳ] n equatore m
equip [ɪˈkwɪp] vt equipaggiare, attrezzare; **to ~ sb/sth with** fornire qn/qc di; **to be well ~ped** (office etc) essere ben attrezzato(-a); **he is well ~ped for the job** ha i requisiti necessari per quel lavoro; **equipment** n attrezzatura; (electrical etc) apparecchiatura
equivalent [ɪˈkwɪvəlnt] adj equivalente ▷ n equivalente m; **to be ~ to** equivalere a
ER abbr (BRIT) = **Elizabeth Regina** (US: Med) = **emergency room**
era [ˈɪərə] n era, età f inv
erase [ɪˈreɪz] vt cancellare; **eraser** n gomma
erect [ɪˈrɛkt] adj eretto(-a) ▷ vt costruire; (assemble) montare; **erection** [ɪˈrɛkʃən] n costruzione f; montaggio; (Physiol) erezione f
ERM n (= Exchange Rate Mechanism) ERM m
erode [ɪˈrəud] vt erodere; (metal) corrodere
erosion [ɪˈrəuʒən] n erosione f
erotic [ɪˈrɔtɪk] adj erotico(-a)
errand [ˈɛrnd] n commissione f
erratic [ɪˈrætɪk] adj imprevedibile; (person, mood) incostante
error [ˈɛrəʳ] n errore m
erupt [ɪˈrʌpt] vi (volcano) mettersi (or essere) in eruzione; (war, crisis) scoppiare; **eruption** [ɪˈrʌpʃən] n eruzione f; scoppio
escalate [ˈɛskəleɪt] vi intensificarsi
escalator [ˈɛskəleɪtəʳ] n scala mobile
escape [ɪˈskeɪp] n evasione f; fuga; (of gas etc) fuga, fuoriuscita ▷ vi fuggire; (from jail) evadere, scappare; (leak) uscire ▷ vt sfuggire a; **to ~ from** (place) fuggire da; (person) sfuggire a
escort [n ˈɛskɔːt, vb ɪˈskɔːt] n scorta; (male companion) cavaliere m ▷ vt scortare; accompagnare
especially [ɪˈspɛʃlɪ] adv specialmente;

soprattutto; espressamente
espionage ['ɛspɪənɑ:ʒ] n spionaggio
essay ['ɛseɪ] n (Scol) composizione f;
(Literature) saggio
essence ['ɛsns] n essenza
essential [ɪ'sɛnʃl] adj essenziale ▷ n
elemento essenziale; **essentially** adv
essenzialmente; **essentials** npl **the
essentials** l'essenziale msg
establish [ɪ'stæblɪʃ] vt stabilire; (business)
mettere su; (one's power etc) affermare;
establishment n stabilimento; **the
Establishment** là classe dirigente,
l'establishment m
estate [ɪ'steɪt] n proprietà f inv; beni
mpl, patrimonio; (BRIT: also: **housing ~**)
complesso edilizio; **estate agent** (BRIT) n
agente m immobiliare; **estate car** (BRIT) n
giardiniera
estimate [n 'ɛstɪmət, vb 'ɛstɪmeɪt] n
stima; (Comm) preventivo ▷ vt stimare,
valutare
etc abbr (= et cetera) etc., ecc.
eternal [ɪ'tə:nl] adj eterno(-a)
eternity [ɪ'tə:nɪtɪ] n eternità
ethical ['ɛθɪkl] adj etico(-a), morale;
ethics ['ɛθɪks] n etica ▷ npl morale f
Ethiopia [i:θɪ'əupɪə] n Etiopia
ethnic ['ɛθnɪk] adj etnico(-a); **ethnic
minority** n minoranza etnica
etiquette ['ɛtɪkɛt] n etichetta
EU n abbr (= European Union) UE f
euro ['juərəu] n (currency) euro m inv
Europe ['juərəp] n Europa; **European**
[-'pi:ən] adj, n europeo(-a); **European
Community** n Comunità Europea;
European Union n Unione f europea
Eurostar® ['juərəustɑ:ʳ] n Eurostar®
m inv
evacuate [ɪ'vækjueɪt] vt evacuare
evade [ɪ'veɪd] vt (tax) evadere; (duties etc)
sottrarsi a; (person) schivare
evaluate [ɪ'væljueɪt] vt valutare
evaporate [ɪ'væpəreɪt] vi evaporare
eve [i:v] n **on the ~ of** alla vigilia di
even ['i:vn] adj regolare; (number) pari
inv ▷ adv anche, perfino; **~ if, ~ though**
anche se; **~ more** ancora di più; **~ so** ciò
nonostante; **not ~** nemmeno; **to get ~
with sb** dare la pari a qn
evening ['i:vnɪŋ] n sera; (as duration,
event) serata; **in the ~** la sera; **evening
class** n corso serale; **evening dress**
n (woman's) abito da sera; **in evening
dress** (man) in abito scuro; (woman) in
abito lungo
event [ɪ'vɛnt] n avvenimento; (Sport)
gara; **in the ~ of** in caso di; **eventful** adj
denso(-a) di eventi

eventual [ɪ'vɛntʃuəl] adj finale

Be careful not to translate **eventual**
by the Italian word **eventuale**.

eventually [ɪ'vɛntʃuəlɪ] adv alla fine

Be careful not to translate **eventually**
by the Italian word **eventualmente**.

ever ['ɛvəʳ] adv mai; (at all times) sempre;
the best ~ il migliore che ci sia mai stato;
have you ~ seen it? l'ha mai visto?; **~
since** adv da allora ▷ conj sin da quando;
~ so pretty così bello(-a); **evergreen** n
sempreverde m
every ['ɛvrɪ] adj ogni; **~ day** tutti i
giorni, ogni giorno; **~ other/third day**
ogni due/tre giorni; **~ other car** una
macchina su due; **~ now and then** ogni
tanto, di quando in quando; **everybody**
pron = **everyone**; **everyday** adj
quotidiano(-a); di ogni giorno; **everyone**
pron ognuno, tutti pl; **everything** pron
tutto, ogni cosa; **everywhere** adv (gen)
dappertutto; (wherever) ovunque
evict [ɪ'vɪkt] vt sfrattare
evidence ['ɛvɪdns] n (proof) prova; (of
witness) testimonianza; (sign): **to show ~
of** dare segni di; **to give ~** deporre
evident ['ɛvɪdnt] adj evidente; **evidently**
adv evidentemente
evil ['i:vl] adj cattivo(-a), maligno(-a) ▷ n
male m
evoke [ɪ'vəuk] vt evocare
evolution [i:və'lu:ʃən] n evoluzione f
evolve [ɪ'vɔlv] vt elaborare ▷ vi
svilupparsi, evolversi
ewe [ju:] n pecora
ex- [inf) [ɛks] n **my ex** il (la) mio(-a) ex
ex- [ɛks] prefix ex
exact [ɪg'zækt] adj esatto(-a) ▷ vt **to ~ sth
(from)** estorcere qc (da); esigere qc (da);
exactly adv esattamente
exaggerate [ɪg'zædʒəreɪt] vt, vi esagerare;
exaggeration [-'reɪʃən] n esagerazione f
exam [ɪg'zæm] n abbr (Scol)
= **examination**
examination [ɪgzæmɪ'neɪʃən] n (Scol)
esame m; (Med) controllo
examine [ɪg'zæmɪn] vt esaminare;
examiner n esaminatore(-trice)
example [ɪg'zɑ:mpl] n esempio; **for ~** ad
or per esempio
exasperated [ɪg'zɑ:spəreɪtɪd] adj
esasperato(-a)
excavate ['ɛkskəveɪt] vt scavare
exceed [ɪk'si:d] vt superare; (one's powers,
time limit) oltrepassare; **exceedingly** adv
eccessivamente
excel [ɪk'sɛl] vi eccellere ▷ vt sorpassare;
to ~ o.s (BRIT) superare se stesso
excellence ['ɛksələns] n eccellenza

excellent ['ɛksələnt] *adj* eccellente

except [ɪk'sɛpt] *prep* (*also*: **~ for, ~ing**) salvo, all'infuori di, eccetto ▷ *vt* escludere; **~ if/when** salvo se/quando; **~ that** salvo che; **exception** [ɪk'sɛpʃən] *n* eccezione *f*; **to take exception to** trovare a ridire su; **exceptional** [ɪk'sɛpʃənl] *adj* eccezionale; **exceptionally** [ɪk'sɛpʃənəlɪ] *adv* eccezionalmente

excerpt ['ɛksə:pt] *n* estratto

excess [ɪk'sɛs] *n* eccesso; **excess baggage** *n* bagaglio in eccedenza; **excessive** *adj* eccessivo(-a)

exchange [ɪks'tʃeɪndʒ] *n* scambio; (*also*: **telephone ~**) centralino ▷ *vt* **to ~ (for)** scambiare (con); **could I ~ this, please?** posso cambiarlo, per favore?; **exchange rate** *n* tasso di cambio

excite [ɪk'saɪt] *vt* eccitare; **to get ~d** eccitarsi; **excited** *adj* **to get excited** essere elettrizzato(-a); **excitement** *n* eccitazione *f*; agitazione *f*; **exciting** *adj* avventuroso(-a); (*film, book*) appassionante

exclaim [ɪk'skleɪm] *vi* esclamare; **exclamation** [ɛksklə'meɪʃən] *n* esclamazione *f*; **exclamation mark** (*us* **exclamation point**) *n* punto esclamativo

exclude [ɪk'sklu:d] *vt* escludere

excluding [ɪk'sklu:dɪŋ] *prep* **~ VAT** IVA esclusa

exclusion [ɪk'sklu:ʒən] *n* esclusione *f*; **to the ~ of** escludendo

exclusive [ɪk'sklu:sɪv] *adj* esclusivo(-a); **~ of VAT** I.V.A. esclusa; **exclusively** *adv* esclusivamente

excruciating [ɪk'skru:ʃieɪtɪŋ] *adj* straziante, atroce

excursion [ɪk'skə:ʃən] *n* escursione *f*, gita

excuse [*n* ɪk'skju:s, *vb* ɪk'skju:z] *n* scusa ▷ *vt* scusare; **to ~ sb from** (*activity*) dispensare qn da; **~ me!** mi scusi!, **now, if you will ~ me ...** ora, mi scusi ma ...

ex-directory ['ɛksdɪ'rɛktərɪ] (*BRIT*) *adj* (*Tel*): **to be ~** non essere sull'elenco

execute ['ɛksɪkju:t] *vt* (*prisoner*) giustiziare; (*plan etc*) eseguire; **execution** [ɛksɪ'kju:ʃən] *n* esecuzione *f*

executive [ɪg'zɛkjutɪv] *n* (*Comm*) dirigente *m*; (*Pol*) esecutivo ▷ *adj* esecutivo(-a)

exempt [ɪg'zɛmpt] *adj* esentato(-a) ▷ *vt* **to ~ sb from** esentare qn da

exercise ['ɛksəsaɪz] *n* (*keep fit*) moto; (*Scol, Mil etc*) esercizio ▷ *vt* esercitare; (*patience*) usare; (*dog*) portar fuori ▷ *vi* (*also*: **take ~**) fare del moto; **exercise book** *n* quaderno

exert [ɪg'zə:t] *vt* esercitare; **to ~ o.s.** sforzarsi; **exertion** [-ʃən] *n* sforzo

exhale [ɛks'heɪl] *vt, vi* espirare

exhaust [ɪg'zɔ:st] *n* (*also*: **~ fumes**) scappamento; (*also*: **~ pipe**) tubo di scappamento ▷ *vt* esaurire; **exhausted** *adj* esaurito(-a); **exhaustion** [ɪg'zɔ:stʃən] *n* esaurimento; **nervous exhaustion** sovraffaticamento mentale

exhibit [ɪg'zɪbɪt] *n* (*Art*) oggetto esposto; (*Law*) documento *or* oggetto esibito ▷ *vt* esporre; (*courage, skill*) dimostrare; **exhibition** [ɛksɪ'bɪʃən] *n* mostra, esposizione *f*

exhilarating [ɪg'zɪləreɪtɪŋ] *adj* esilarante; stimolante

exile ['ɛksaɪl] *n* esilio; (*person*) esiliato(-a) ▷ *vt* esiliare

exist [ɪg'zɪst] *vi* esistere; **existence** *n* esistenza; **existing** *adj* esistente

exit ['ɛksɪt] *n* uscita ▷ *vi* (*Theatre, Comput*) uscire; **where's the ~?** dov'è l'uscita?; **exit ramp** (*us*) *n* (*Aut*) rampa di uscita

exotic [ɪg'zɔtɪk] *adj* esotico(-a)

expand [ɪk'spænd] *vt* espandere; estendere; allargare ▷ *vi* (*business, gas*) espandersi; (*metal*) dilatarsi

expansion [ɪk'spænʃən] *n* (*gen*) espansione *f*; (*of town, economy*) sviluppo; (*of metal*) dilatazione *f*

expect [ɪk'spɛkt] *vt* (*anticipate*) prevedere, aspettarsi, prevedere *or* aspettarsi che + *sub*; (*require*) richiedere, esigere; (*suppose*) supporre; (*await, also baby*) aspettare ▷ *vi* **to be ~ing** essere in stato interessante; **to ~ sb to do** aspettarsi che qn faccia; **expectation** [ɛkspɛk'teɪʃən] *n* aspettativa; speranza

expedition [ɛkspə'dɪʃən] *n* spedizione *f*

expel [ɪk'spɛl] *vt* espellere

expenditure [ɪk'spɛndɪtʃə'] *n* spesa

expense [ɪk'spɛns] *n* spesa; (*high cost*) costo; **~s** *npl* (*Comm*) spese *fpl*, indennità *fpl*; **at the ~ of** a spese di; **expense account** *n* conto *m* spese *inv*

expensive [ɪk'spɛnsɪv] *adj* caro(-a), costoso(-a); **it's too ~** è troppo caro

experience [ɪk'spɪərɪəns] *n* esperienza ▷ *vt* (*pleasure*) provare; (*hardship*) soffrire; **experienced** *adj* esperto(-a)

experiment [*n* ɪk'spɛrɪmənt, *vb* ɪk'spɛrɪmɛnt] *n* esperimento, esperienza ▷ *vi* **to ~ (with/on)** fare esperimenti (con/su); **experimental** [ɪkspɛrɪ'mɛntl] *adj* sperimentale; **at the experimental stage** in via di sperimentazione

expert ['ɛkspə:t] *adj, n* esperto(-a); **expertise** [-'ti:z] *n* competenza

expire [ɪk'spaɪə'] *vi* (*period of time, licence*) scadere; **expiry** *n* scadenza; **expiry date** *n* (*of medicine, food item*) data di scadenza

explain [ɪk'spleɪn] *vt* spiegare;

explanation [ɛksplə'neɪʃən] n spiegazione f

explicit [ɪk'splɪsɪt] adj esplicito(-a)

explode [ɪk'spləʊd] vi esplodere

exploit [n 'eksplɔɪt, vb ɪk'splɔɪt] n impresa ▷ vt sfruttare; **exploitation** [-'teɪʃən] n sfruttamento

explore [ɪk'splɔːʳ] vt esplorare; (possibilities) esaminare; **explorer** n esploratore(-trice)

explosion [ɪk'spləʊʒən] n esplosione f; **explosive** [ɪk'spləʊsɪv] adj esplosivo(-a) ▷ n esplosivo

export [vb ɛk'spɔːt, n 'ɛkspɔːt] vt esportare ▷ n esportazione f; articolo di esportazione ▷ cpd d'esportazione; **exporter** n esportatore m

expose [ɪk'spəʊz] vt esporre; (unmask) smascherare; **exposed** adj (position) esposto(-a); **exposure** [ɪk'spəʊʒəʳ] n esposizione f; (Phot) posa; (Med) assideramento

express [ɪk'sprɛs] adj (definite) chiaro(-a), espresso(-a); (BRIT: letter etc) espresso inv ▷ n (train) espresso ▷ vt esprimere; **expression** [ɪk'sprɛʃən] n espressione f; **expressway** n (US) (urban motorway) autostrada che attraversa la città

exquisite [ɛk'skwɪzɪt] adj squisito(-a)

extend [ɪk'stɛnd] vt (visit) protrarre; (road, deadline) prolungare; (building) ampliare; (offer) offrire, porgere ▷ vi (land, period) estendersi; **extension** [ɪk'stɛnʃən] n (of road, term) prolungamento; (of contract, deadline) proroga; (building) annesso; (to wire, table) prolunga; (telephone) interno; (: in private house) apparecchio supplementare; **extension lead** n prolunga

extensive [ɪk'stɛnsɪv] adj esteso(-a), ampio(-a); (damage) su larga scala; (coverage, discussion) esauriente; (use) grande

extent [ɪk'stɛnt] n estensione f; **to some ~** fino a un certo punto; **to such an ~ that ...** a un tal punto che ...; **to what ~?** fino a che punto?; **to the ~ of ...** fino al punto di ...

exterior [ɛk'stɪərɪəʳ] adj esteriore, esterno(-a) ▷ n esteriore m, esterno; aspetto (esteriore)

external [ɛk'stəːnl] adj esterno(-a), esteriore

extinct [ɪk'stɪŋkt] adj estinto(-a); **extinction** [ɪk'stɪŋkʃən] n estinzione f

extinguish [ɪk'stɪŋgwɪʃ] vt estinguere

extra ['ɛkstrə] adj extra inv, supplementare ▷ adv (in addition) di più ▷ n extra m inv; (surcharge) supplemento; (Cinema, Theatre) comparsa

extract [vb ɪk'strækt, n 'ɛkstrækt] vt estrarre; (money, promise) strappare ▷ n estratto; (passage) brano

extradite ['ɛkstrədaɪt] vt estradare

extraordinary [ɪk'strɔːdnrɪ] adj straordinario(-a)

extravagance [ɪk'strævəgəns] n sperpero; stravaganza

extravagant [ɪk'strævəgənt] adj (lavish) prodigo(-a); (wasteful) dispendioso(-a)

  Be careful not to translate **extravagant** by the Italian word **stravagante**.

extreme [ɪk'striːm] adj estremo(-a) ▷ n estremo; **extremely** adv estremamente

extremist [ɪk'striːmɪst] adj, n estremista (m/f)

extrovert ['ɛkstrəvəːt] n estroverso(-a)

eye [aɪ] n occhio; (of needle) cruna ▷ vt osservare; **to keep an ~ on** tenere d'occhio; **eyeball** n globo dell'occhio; **eyebrow** n sopracciglio; **eyedrops** npl gocce fpl oculari, collirio; **eyelash** n ciglio; **eyelid** n palpebra; **eyeliner** n eye-liner m inv; **eyeshadow** n ombretto; **eyesight** n vista; **eye witness** n testimone m/f oculare

F [εf] n (*Mus*) fa m

fabric ['fæbrɪk] n stoffa, tessuto

fabulous ['fæbjuləs] adj favoloso(-a); (*super*) favoloso(-a), fantastico(-a)

face [feɪs] n faccia, viso, volto; (*expression*) faccia; (*of clock*) quadrante m; (*of building*) facciata ▷ vt essere di fronte a; (*facts, situation*) affrontare; **~ down** a faccia in giù; **to make** *or* **pull a ~** fare una smorfia; **in the ~ of** (*difficulties etc*) di fronte a; **on the ~ of it** a prima vista; **~ to ~** faccia a faccia; **face up to** vt fus affrontare, far fronte a; **face cloth** (*BRIT*) n guanto di spugna; **face pack** n (*BRIT*) maschera di bellezza

facial ['feɪʃəl] adj del viso

facilitate [fə'sɪlɪteɪt] vt facilitare

facilities [fə'sɪlɪtɪz] npl attrezzature fpl; **credit ~** facilitazioni fpl di credito

fact [fækt] n fatto; **in ~** in effetti

faction ['fækʃən] n fazione f

factor ['fæktəʳ] n fattore m; **I'd like a ~ 15 suntan lotion** vorrei una crema solare con fattore di protezione 15

factory ['fæktərɪ] n fabbrica, stabilimento
　Be careful not to translate *factory* by the Italian word *fattoria*.

factual ['fæktjuəl] adj che si attiene ai fatti

faculty ['fækəltɪ] n facoltà f inv; (*us*) corpo insegnante

fad [fæd] n mania; capriccio

fade [feɪd] vi sbiadire, sbiadirsi; (*light, sound, hope*) attenuarsi, affievolirsi; (*flower*) appassire; **fade away** vi (*sound*) affievolirsi

fag [fæg] (*BRIT: inf*) n (*cigarette*) cicca

Fahrenheit ['fɑːrənhaɪt] n Fahrenheit m inv

fail [feɪl] vt (*exam*) non superare; (*candidate*) bocciare; (*courage, memory*) mancare a ▷ vi fallire; (*student*) essere respinto(-a); (*eyesight, health, light*) venire a mancare; **to ~ to do sth** (*neglect*) mancare di fare qc; (*be unable*) non riuscire a fare qc; **without ~** senza fallo; certamente; **failing** n difetto ▷ prep in mancanza di; **failure** ['feɪljəʳ] n fallimento; (*person*) fallito(-a); (*mechanical etc*) guasto

faint [feɪnt] adj debole; (*recollection*) vago(-a); (*mark*) indistinto(-a) ▷ n (*Med*) svenimento ▷ vi svenire; **to feel ~** sentirsi svenire; **faintest** adj **I haven't the faintest idea** non ho la più pallida idea; **faintly** adv debolmente; vagamente

fair [fɛəʳ] adj (*person, decision*) giusto(-a), equo(-a); (*quite large, quite good*) discreto(-a); (*hair etc*) biondo(-a); (*skin, complexion*) chiaro(-a); (*weather*) bello(-a), clemente ▷ adv (*play*) lealmente ▷ n fiera; (*BRIT: funfair*) luna park m inv; **fairground** n luna park m inv; **fair-haired** [fɛə'hɛəd] adj (*person*) biondo(-a); **fairly** adv equamente; (*quite*) abbastanza; **fairway** n (*Golf*) fairway m inv

fairy ['fɛərɪ] n fata; **fairy tale** n fiaba

faith [feɪθ] n fede f; (*trust*) fiducia; (*sect*) religione f, fede f; **faithful** adj fedele; **faithfully** adv fedelmente; **yours faithfully** (*BRIT: in letters*) distinti saluti

fake [feɪk] n imitazione f; (*picture*) falso; (*person*) impostore(-a) ▷ adj falso(-a) ▷ vt (*accounts*) falsificare; (*illness*) fingere; (*painting*) contraffare

falcon ['fɔːlkən] n falco, falcone m

fall [fɔːl] (*pt* fell, *pp* fallen) n caduta; (*in temperature*) abbassamento; (*in price*) ribasso; (*us: autumn*) autunno ▷ vi cadere; (*temperature, price, night*) scendere; **~s** npl (*waterfall*) cascate fpl; **to ~ flat** (*on one's face*) cadere bocconi; (*joke*) fare cilecca; (*plan*) fallire; **fall apart** vi cadere a pezzi; **fall down** vi (*person*) cadere; (*building*) crollare; **fall for** vt fus (*person*) prendere una cotta per; **to ~ for a trick** (*or a story etc*) cascarci; **fall off** vi cadere; (*diminish*) diminuire, abbassarsi; **fall out** vi (*hair, teeth*) cadere; (*friends etc*) litigare; **fall over** vi cadere; **fall through** vi (*plan, project*) fallire

fallen ['fɔːlən] *pp of* **fall**
fallout ['fɔːlaut] *n* fall-out *m*
false [fɔːls] *adj* falso(-a); **under ~
pretences** con l'inganno; **false alarm**
n falso allarme *m*; **false teeth** (*BRIT*) *npl*
denti *mpl* finti
fame [feɪm] *n* fama, celebrità
familiar [fə'mɪlɪə'] *adj* familiare; (*close*)
intimo(-a); **to be ~ with** (*subject*)
conoscere; **familiarize** [fə'mɪlɪəraɪz] *vt*
to familiarize o.s. with familiarizzare con
family ['fæmɪlɪ] *n* famiglia; **family doctor**
n medico di famiglia; **family planning** *n*
pianificazione *f* familiare
famine ['fæmɪn] *n* carestia
famous ['feɪməs] *adj* famoso(-a)
fan [fæn] *n* (*folding*) ventaglio; (*Elec*)
ventilatore *m*; (*person*) ammiratore(-trice),
tifoso(-a) ▷ *vt* far vento a; (*fire, quarrel*)
alimentare
fanatic [fə'nætɪk] *n* fanatico(-a)
fan belt *n* cinghia del ventilatore
fan club *n* fan club *m inv*
fancy ['fænsɪ] *n* immaginazione *f*,
fantasia; (*whim*) capriccio ▷ *adj* (*hat*)
stravagante; (*hotel, food*) speciale ▷ *vt* (*feel
like, want*) aver voglia di; (*imagine, think*)
immaginare; **to take a ~ to** incapricciarsi
di; **he fancies her** (*inf*) gli piace; **fancy
dress** *n* costume *m* (per maschera)
fan heater *n* (*BRIT*) stufa ad aria calda
fantasize ['fæntəsaɪz] *vi* fantasticare,
sognare
fantastic [fæn'tæstɪk] *adj* fantastico(-a)
fantasy ['fæntəsɪ] *n* fantasia,
immaginazione *f*; fantasticheria; chimera
fanzine ['fænziːn] *n* rivista specialistica
(*per appassionati*)
FAQs *abbr* (= *frequently asked questions*)
FAQ *fpl*
far [fɑː'] *adj* lontano(-a) ▷ *adv* lontano;
(*much, greatly*) molto; **is it ~ from here?**
è molto lontano da qui?; **how ~?** quanto
lontano?; (*referring to activity etc*) fino a
dove?; **how ~ is the town centre?** quanto
dista il centro da qui?; **~ away, ~ off**
lontano, distante; **~ better** assai migliore;
~ from lontano da; **by ~** di gran lunga; **go
as ~ as the farm** vada fino alla fattoria; **as
~ as I know** per quel che so
farce [fɑːs] *n* farsa
fare [fɛə'] *n* (*on trains, buses*) tariffa; (*in taxi*)
prezzo della corsa; (*food*) vitto, cibo; **half ~**
metà tariffa; **full ~** tariffa intera
Far East *n* **the ~** l'Estremo Oriente *m*
farewell [fɛə'wɛl] *excl, n* addio
farm [fɑːm] *n* fattoria, podere *m* ▷ *vt*
coltivare; **farmer** *n* coltivatore(-trice),
agricoltore(-trice); **farmhouse** *n* fattoria;

farming *n* (*gen*) agricoltura; (*of crops*)
coltivazione *f*; (*of animals*) allevamento;
farmyard *n* aia
far-reaching [fɑː'riːtʃɪŋ] *adj* di vasta
portata
fart [fɑːt] (*inf!*) *vi* scoreggiare (*!*)
farther ['fɑːðə'] *adv* più lontano ▷ *adj* più
lontano(-a)
farthest ['fɑːðɪst] *superl of* **far**
fascinate ['fæsɪneɪt] *vt* affascinare;
fascinated *adj* affascinato(-a);
fascinating *adj* affascinante;
fascination [-'neɪʃən] *n* fascino
fascist ['fæʃɪst] *adj, n* fascista (*m/f*)
fashion ['fæʃən] *n* moda; (*manner*)
maniera, modo ▷ *vt* foggiare, formare; **in
~** alla moda; **out of ~** passato(-a) di moda;
fashionable *adj* alla moda, di moda;
fashion show *n* sfilata di moda
fast [fɑːst] *adj* rapido(-a), svelto(-a),
veloce; (*clock*): **to be ~** andare avanti; (*dye,
colour*) solido(-a) ▷ *adv* rapidamente;
(*stuck, held*) saldamente ▷ *n* digiuno ▷ *vi*
digiunare; **~ asleep** profondamente
addormentato
fasten ['fɑːsn] *vt* chiudere, fissare; (*coat*)
abbottonare, allacciare ▷ *vi* chiudersi,
fissarsi; abbottonarsi, allacciarsi
fast food *n* fast food *m*
fat [fæt] *adj* grasso(-a); (*book, profit etc*)
grosso(-a) ▷ *n* grasso
fatal ['feɪtl] *adj* fatale; mortale;
disastroso(-a); **fatality** [fə'tælɪtɪ] *n* (*road
death etc*) morto(-a), vittima; **fatally** *adv*
a morte
fate [feɪt] *n* destino; (*of person*) sorte *f*
father ['fɑːðə'] *n* padre *m*; **Father
Christmas** *n* Babbo Natale; **father-in-
law** *n* suocero
fatigue [fə'tiːg] *n* stanchezza
fattening ['fætnɪŋ] *adj* (*food*) che fa
ingrassare
fatty ['fætɪ] *adj* (*food*) grasso(-a) ▷ *n* (*inf*)
ciccione(-a)
faucet ['fɔːsɪt] (*US*) *n* rubinetto
fault [fɔːlt] *n* colpa; (*Tennis*) fallo; (*defect*)
difetto; (*Geo*) faglia ▷ *vt* criticare; **it's my ~**
è colpa mia; **to find ~ with** trovare da ridire
su; **at ~** in fallo; **faulty** *adj* difettoso(-a)
fauna ['fɔːnə] *n* fauna
favour *etc* ['feɪvə'] (*US* **favor**) *n* favore *m*
▷ *vt* (*proposition*) favorire, essere favorevole
a; (*pupil etc*) favorire; (*team, horse*) dare per
vincente; **to do sb a ~** fare un favore or
una cortesia a qn; **to find ~ with** (*person*)
entrare nelle buone grazie di; (: *suggestion*)
avere l'approvazione di; **in ~ of** in favore
di; **favourable** *adj* favorevole; **favourite**
[-rɪt] *adj, n* favorito(-a)

fawn [fɔːn] n daino ▷ adj (also: ~-
coloured) marrone chiaro inv ▷ vi **to ~
(up)on** adulare servilmente
fax [fæks] n (document) facsimile m inv,
telecopia; (machine) telecopiatrice f ▷ vt
telecopiare, trasmettere in facsimile
FBI (US) n abbr (= Federal Bureau of
Investigation) F.B.I. f
fear [fɪəʳ] n paura, timore m ▷ vt aver paura
di, temere; **for ~ of** per paura di; **fearful**
adj pauroso(-a); (sight, noise) terribile,
spaventoso(-a); **fearless** adj intrepido(-a),
senza paura
feasible ['fiːzəbl] adj possibile, realizzabile
feast [fiːst] n festa, banchetto; (Rel: also: ~
day) festa ▷ vi banchettare
feat [fiːt] n impresa, fatto insigne
feather ['fɛðəʳ] n penna
feature ['fiːtʃəʳ] n caratteristica; (Press,
TV) articolo ▷ vt (film) avere come
protagonista ▷ vi figurare; **~s** npl (of face)
fisionomia; **feature film** n film m inv
principale
Feb. [fɛb] abbr (= February) feb
February ['fɛbruərɪ] n febbraio
fed [fɛd] pt, pp of **feed**
federal ['fɛdərəl] adj federale
federation [fɛdə'reɪʃən] n federazione f
fed up adj **to be ~** essere stufo(-a)
fee [fiː] n pagamento; (of doctor, lawyer)
onorario; (for examination) tassa d'esame;
school ~s tasse fpl scolastiche
feeble ['fiːbl] adj debole
feed [fiːd] (pt, pp **fed**) n (of baby) pappa;
(of animal) mangime m; (on printer)
meccanismo di alimentazione ▷ vt
nutrire; (baby) allattare; (horse etc) dare
da mangiare a; (fire, machine) alimentare;
(data, information): **to ~ into** inserire in;
feedback n feed-back m
feel [fiːl] (pt, pp **felt**) n consistenza; (sense of
touch) tatto ▷ vt toccare; palpare; tastare;
(cold, pain, anger) sentire; (think, believe): **to
~ (that)** pensare che; **to ~ hungry/cold**
aver fame/freddo; **to ~ lonely/better**
sentirsi solo/meglio; **I don't ~ well** non mi
sento bene; **it ~s soft** è morbido al tatto;
to ~ like (want) aver voglia di; **to ~ about**
or **around for** cercare a tastoni; **feeling** n
sensazione f; (emotion) sentimento
feet [fiːt] npl of **foot**
fell [fɛl] pt of **fall** ▷ vt (tree) abbattere
fellow ['fɛləu] n individuo, tipo;
compagno; (of learned society) membro cpd;
fellow citizen n concittadino(-a); **fellow
countryman** (irreg) n compatriota m;
fellow men npl simili mpl; **fellowship** n
associazione f; compagnia; specie di borsa
di studio universitaria

felony ['fɛlənɪ] n reato, crimine m
felt [fɛlt] pt, pp of **feel** ▷ n feltro
female ['fiːmeɪl] n (Zool) femmina; (pej:
woman) donna, femmina ▷ adj (Biol, Elec)
femmina inv; (sex, character) femminile;
(vote etc) di donne
feminine ['fɛmɪnɪn] adj femminile
feminist ['fɛmɪnɪst] n femminista m/f
fence [fɛns] n recinto ▷ vt (also: ~ **in**)
recingere ▷ vi (Sport) tirare di scherma;
fencing n (Sport) scherma
fend [fɛnd] vi **to ~ for o.s.** arrangiarsi;
fend off vt (attack, questions) respingere,
difendersi da
fender ['fɛndəʳ] n parafuoco; (on boat)
parabordo; (US) parafango; paraurti m inv
fennel ['fɛnl] n finocchio
ferment [vb fə'mɛnt, n 'fəːmɛnt] vi
fermentare ▷ n (fig) agitazione f,
eccitazione f
fern [fəːn] n felce f
ferocious [fə'rəuʃəs] adj feroce
ferret ['fɛrɪt] n furetto
ferry ['fɛrɪ] n (small) traghetto; (large:
also: ~**boat**) nave f traghetto inv ▷ vt
traghettare
fertile ['fəːtaɪl] adj fertile; (Biol)
fecondo(-a); **fertilize** ['fəːtɪlaɪz] vt
fertilizzare; fecondare; **fertilizer**
['fəːtɪlaɪzə] n fertilizzante m
festival ['fɛstɪvəl] n (Rel) festa; (Art, Mus)
festival m inv
festive ['fɛstɪv] adj di festa; **the ~ season**
(BRIT: Christmas) il periodo delle feste
fetch [fɛtʃ] vt andare a prendere; (sell for)
essere venduto(-a) per
fête [feɪt] n festa
fetus ['fiːtəs] (US) n = **foetus**
feud [fjuːd] n contesa, lotta
fever ['fiːvəʳ] n febbre f; **feverish** adj
febbrile
few [fjuː] adj pochi(-e); **a ~** adj qualche
inv ▷ pron alcuni(-e); **fewer** adj meno inv,
meno numerosi(-e); **fewest** adj il minor
numero di
fiancé [fɪ'ãːnseɪ] n fidanzato; **fiancée** n
fidanzata
fiasco [fɪ'æskəu] n fiasco
fib [fɪb] n piccola bugia
fibre ['faɪbəʳ] (US **fiber**) n fibra;
Fibreglass® ['faɪbəglɑːs] (US **fiberglass**)
n fibra di vetro
fickle ['fɪkl] adj incostante, capriccioso(-a)
fiction ['fɪkʃən] n narrativa, romanzi
mpl; (sth made up) finzione f; **fictional** adj
immaginario(-a)
fiddle ['fɪdl] n (Mus) violino; (cheating)
imbroglio; truffa ▷ vt (BRIT: accounts)
falsificare, falsare; **fiddle with** vt fus

gingillarsi con

fidelity [fɪˈdɛlɪtɪ] n fedeltà; (accuracy) esattezza

field [fiːld] n campo; **field marshal** n feldmaresciallo

fierce [fɪəs] adj (animal, person, fighting) feroce; (loyalty) assoluto(-a); (wind) furioso(-a); (heat) intenso(-a)

fifteen [fɪfˈtiːn] num quindici; **fifteenth** num quindicesimo(-a)

fifth [fɪfθ] num quinto(-a)

fiftieth [ˈfɪftɪɪθ] num cinquantesimo(-a)

fifty [ˈfɪftɪ] num cinquanta; **fifty-fifty** adj **a fifty-fifty chance** una possibilità su due ▷ adv fifty-fifty, metà per ciascuno

fig [fɪg] n fico

fight [faɪt] (pt, pp **fought**) n zuffa, rissa; (Mil) battaglia, combattimento; (against cancer etc) lotta ▷ vt (person) azzuffarsi con; (enemy: also Mil) combattere; (cancer, alcoholism, emotion) lottare contro, combattere; (election) partecipare a ▷ vi combattere; **fight back** vi difendersi; (Sport, after illness) riprendersi ▷ vt (tears) ricacciare; **fight off** vt (attack, attacker) respingere; (disease, sleep, urge) lottare contro; **fighting** n combattimento

figure [ˈfɪgər] n figura; (number, cipher) cifra ▷ vt (think: esp US) pensare ▷ vi (appear) figurare; **figure out** vt riuscire a capire; calcolare

file [faɪl] n (tool) lima; (dossier) incartamento; (folder) cartellina; (Comput) archivio; (row) fila ▷ vt (nails, wood) limare; (papers) archiviare; (Law: claim) presentare; passare agli atti; **filing cabinet** [ˈfaɪlɪŋ-] n casellario

Filipino [fɪlɪˈpiːnəu] n filippino(-a); (Ling) tagal m

fill [fɪl] vt riempire; (job) coprire ▷ n **to eat one's ~** mangiare a sazietà; **fill in** vt (hole) riempire; (form) compilare; **fill out** vt (form, receipt) riempire; **fill up** vt riempire; **~ it up, please** (Aut) il pieno, per favore

fillet [ˈfɪlɪt] n filetto; **fillet steak** n bistecca di filetto

filling [ˈfɪlɪŋ] n (Culin) impasto, ripieno; (for tooth) otturazione f; **filling station** n stazione f di rifornimento

film [fɪlm] n (Cinema) film m inv; (Phot) pellicola, rullino; (of powder, liquid) sottile strato ▷ vt, vi girare; **I'd like a 36-exposure ~** vorrei un rullino da 36 pose; **film star** n divo(-a) dello schermo

filter [ˈfɪltər] n filtro ▷ vt filtrare; **filter lane** (BRIT) n (Aut) corsia di svincolo

filth [fɪlθ] n sporcizia; **filthy** adj lordo(-a), sozzo(-a); (language) osceno(-a)

fin [fɪn] n (of fish) pinna

final [ˈfaɪnl] adj finale, ultimo(-a); definitivo(-a) ▷ n (Sport) finale f; **~s** npl (Scol) esami mpl finali; **finale** [fɪˈnɑːlɪ] n finale m; **finalist** [ˈfaɪnəlɪst] n (Sport) finalista m/f; **finalize** [ˈfaɪnəlaɪz] vt mettere a punto; **finally** [ˈfaɪnəlɪ] adv (lastly) alla fine; (eventually) finalmente

finance [faɪˈnæns] n finanza; (capital) capitale m ▷ vt finanziare; **~s** npl (funds) finanze fpl; **financial** [faɪˈnænʃəl] adj finanziario(-a); **financial year** n anno finanziario, esercizio finanziario

find [faɪnd] (pt, pp **found**) vt trovare; (lost object) ritrovare ▷ n trovata, scoperta; **to ~ sb guilty** (Law) giudicare qn colpevole; **find out** vt (truth, secret) scoprire; (person) cogliere in fallo; **to ~ out about** informarsi su; (by chance) scoprire; **findings** npl (Law) sentenza, conclusioni fpl; (of report) conclusioni

fine [faɪn] adj bello(-a); ottimo(-a); (thin, subtle) fine ▷ adv (well) molto bene ▷ n (Law) multa ▷ vt (Law) multare; **to be ~** (person) stare bene; (weather) far bello; **fine arts** npl belle arti fpl

finger [ˈfɪŋgər] n dito ▷ vt toccare, tastare; **little/index ~** mignolo/(dito) indice m; **fingernail** n unghia; **fingerprint** n impronta digitale; **fingertip** n punta del dito

finish [ˈfɪnɪʃ] n fine f; (polish etc) finitura ▷ vt, vi finire; **when does the show ~?** quando finisce lo spettacolo?; **to ~ doing sth** finire di fare qc; **to ~ third** arrivare terzo(-a); **finish off** vt compiere; (kill) uccidere; **finish up** vi, vt finire

Finland [ˈfɪnlənd] n Finlandia; **Finn** [fɪn] n finlandese m/f; **Finnish** adj finlandese ▷ n (Ling) finlandese m

fir [fəː] n abete m

fire [faɪər] n fuoco; (destructive) incendio; (gas fire, electric fire) stufa ▷ vt (gun) far fuoco con; (arrow) sparare; (fig) infiammare; (inf: dismiss) licenziare ▷ vi sparare, far fuoco; **~!** al fuoco!; **on ~** in fiamme; **fire alarm** n allarme m d'incendio; **firearm** n arma da fuoco; **fire brigade** [-brɪˈgeɪd] (US **fire department**) n (corpo dei) pompieri mpl; **fire engine** n autopompa; **fire escape** n scala di sicurezza; **fire exit** n uscita di sicurezza; **fire extinguisher** [-ɪkˈstɪŋgwɪʃər] n estintore m; **fireman** (irreg) n pompiere m; **fireplace** n focolare m; **fire station** n caserma dei pompieri; **firetruck** (US) n = **fire engine**; **firewall** n (Internet) firewall m inv; **firewood** n legna; **fireworks** npl fuochi mpl d'artificio

firm [fəːm] adj fermo(-a) ▷ n ditta,

azienda; **firmly** *adv* fermamente
first [fɜːst] *adj* primo(-a) ▷ *adv* (*before others*) il primo, la prima; (*before other things*) per primo; (*when listing reasons etc*) per prima cosa ▷ *n* (*person: in race*) primo(-a); (*BRIT Scol*) laurea con lode; (*Aut*) prima; **at ~** dapprima, all'inizio; **~ of all** prima di tutto; **first aid** *n* pronto soccorso; **first-aid kit** *n* cassetta pronto soccorso; **first-class** *adj* di prima classe; **first-hand** *adj* di prima mano; **first lady** (*US*) *n* moglie *f* del presidente; **firstly** *adv* in primo luogo; **first name** *n* prenome *m*; **first-rate** *adj* di prima qualità, ottimo(-a)
fiscal ['fɪskəl] *adj* fiscale; **fiscal year** *n* anno fiscale
fish [fɪʃ] *n inv* pesce *m* ▷ *vt* (*river, area*) pescare in ▷ *vi* pescare; **to go ~ing** andare a pesca; **fish and chip shop** *n see* **chip shop**; **fisherman** (*irreg*) *n* pescatore *m*; **fish fingers** (*BRIT*) *npl* bastoncini *mpl* di pesce (surgelati); **fishing** *n* pesca; **fishing boat** *n* barca da pesca; **fishing line** *n* lenza; **fishmonger** *n* pescivendolo; **fishmonger's (shop)** *n* pescheria; **fish sticks** (*US*) *npl* = **fish fingers**; **fishy** (*inf*) *adj* (*tale, story*) sospetto(-a)
fist [fɪst] *n* pugno
fit [fɪt] *adj* (*Med, Sport*) in forma; (*proper*) adatto(-a), appropriato(-a); conveniente ▷ *vt* (*clothes*) stare bene a; (*put in, attach*) mettere; installare; (*equip*) fornire, equipaggiare ▷ *vi* (*clothes*) stare bene; (*parts*) andare bene, adattarsi; (*in space, gap*) entrare ▷ *n* (*Med*) accesso, attacco; **~ to** in grado di; **~ for** adatto(-a) a, degno(-a) di; **a ~ of anger** un accesso d'ira; **this dress is a good ~** questo vestito sta bene; **by ~s and starts** a sbalzi; **fit in** *vi* accordarsi; adattarsi; **fitness** *n* (*Med*) forma fisica; **fitted** *adj* **fitted cupboards** armadi *mpl* a muro; **fitted carpet** moquette *f inv*; **fitted kitchen** (*BRIT*) cucina componibile; **fitting** *adj* appropriato(-a) ▷ *n* (*of dress*) prova; (*of piece of equipment*) montaggio, aggiustaggio; **fitting room** *n* camerino; **fittings** *npl* (*in building*) impianti *mpl*
five [faɪv] *num* cinque; **fiver** (*inf*) *n* (*BRIT*) biglietto da cinque sterline; (*US*) biglietto da cinque dollari
fix [fɪks] *vt* fissare; (*mend*) riparare; (*meal, drink*) preparare ▷ *n* **to be in a ~** essere nei guai; **fix up** *vt* (*meeting*) fissare; **to ~ sb up with sth** procurare qc a qn; **fixed** [fɪkst] *adj* (*prices etc*) fisso(-a); **fixture** ['fɪkstʃər] *n* impianto (fisso); (*Sport*) incontro (del calendario sportivo)
fizzy ['fɪzɪ] *adj* frizzante; gassato(-a)
flag [flæg] *n* bandiera; (*also*: **~stone**) pietra da lastricare ▷ *vi* stancarsi; affievolirsi; **flagpole** ['flægpəʊl] *n* albero
flair [fleər] *n* (*for business etc*) fiuto; (*for languages etc*) facilità; (*style*) stile *m*
flak [flæk] *n* (*Mil*) fuoco d'artiglieria; (*inf: criticism*) critiche *fpl*
flake [fleɪk] *n* (*of rust, paint*) scaglia; (*of snow, soap powder*) fiocco ▷ *vi* (*also*: **~ off**) sfaldarsi
flamboyant [flæm'bɔɪənt] *adj* sgargiante
flame [fleɪm] *n* fiamma
flamingo [flə'mɪŋgəʊ] *n* fenicottero, fiammingo
flammable ['flæməbl] *adj* infiammabile
flan [flæn] (*BRIT*) *n* flan *m inv*
flank [flæŋk] *n* fianco ▷ *vt* fiancheggiare
flannel ['flænl] *n* (*BRIT: also*: **face ~**) guanto di spugna; (*fabric*) flanella
flap [flæp] *n* (*of pocket*) patta; (*of envelope*) lembo ▷ *vt* (*wings*) battere ▷ *vi* (*sail, flag*) sbattere; (*inf: also*: **be in a ~**) essere in agitazione
flare [fleər] *n* razzo; (*in skirt etc*) svasatura; **~s** (*trousers*) pantaloni *mpl* a zampa d'elefante; **flare up** *vi* andare in fiamme; (*fig: person*) infiammarsi di rabbia; (: *revolt*) scoppiare
flash [flæʃ] *n* vampata; (*also*: **news ~**) notizia *f* lampo *inv*; (*Phot*) flash *m inv* ▷ *vt* accendere e spegnere; (*send: message*) trasmettere; (: *look, smile*) lanciare ▷ *vi* brillare; (*light on ambulance, eyes etc*) lampeggiare; **in a ~** in un lampo; **to ~ one's headlights** lampeggiare; **he ~ed by** *or* **past** ci passò davanti come un lampo; **flashback** *n* flashback *m inv*; **flashbulb** *n* cubo *m* flash *inv*; **flashlight** *n* lampadina tascabile
flask [flɑːsk] *n* fiasco; (*also*: **vacuum ~**) Thermos® *m inv*
flat [flæt] *adj* piatto(-a); (*tyre*) sgonfio(-a), a terra; (*battery*) scarico(-a); (*beer*) svampito(-a); (*denial*) netto(-a); (*Mus*) bemolle *inv*; (: *voice*) stonato(-a); (*rate, fee*) unico(-a) ▷ *n* (*BRIT: rooms*) appartamento; (*Aut*) pneumatico sgonfio; (*Mus*) bemolle *m*; **to work ~ out** lavorare a più non posso; **flatten** *vt* (*also*: **flatten out**) appiattire; (*building, city*) spianare
flatter ['flætər] *vt* lusingare; **flattering** *adj* lusinghiero(-a); (*dress*) che dona
flaunt [flɔːnt] *vt* fare mostra di
flavour *etc* ['fleɪvər] (*US* **flavor**) *n* gusto ▷ *vt* insaporire, aggiungere sapore a; **what ~s do you have?** che gusti avete?; **strawberry-~ed** al gusto di fragola; **flavouring** *n* essenza (artificiale)
flaw [flɔː] *n* difetto; **flawless** *adj* senza difetti

flea [fliː] *n* pulce *f*; **flea market** *n* mercato delle pulci

flee [fliː] (*pt, pp* **fled**) *vt* fuggire da ▷ *vi* fuggire, scappare

fleece [fliːs] *n* vello ▷ *vt* (*inf*) pelare

fleet [fliːt] *n* flotta; (*of lorries etc*) convoglio; parco

fleeting ['fliːtɪŋ] *adj* fugace, fuggitivo(-a); (*visit*) volante

Flemish ['flɛmɪʃ] *adj* fiammingo(-a)

flesh [flɛʃ] *n* carne *f*; (*of fruit*) polpa

flew [fluː] *pt of* **fly**

flex [flɛks] *n* filo (flessibile) ▷ *vt* flettere; (*muscles*) contrarre; **flexibility** *n* flessibilità; **flexible** *adj* flessibile; **flexitime** ['flɛksɪtaɪm] *n* orario flessibile

flick [flɪk] *n* colpetto; scarto ▷ *vt* dare un colpetto a; **flick through** *vt fus* sfogliare

flicker ['flɪkər] *vi* tremolare

flies [flaɪz] *npl of* **fly**

flight [flaɪt] *n* volo; (*escape*) fuga; (*also*: ~ **of steps**) scalinata; **flight attendant** (*us*) *n* steward *m inv*, hostess *f inv*

flimsy ['flɪmzɪ] *adj* (*shoes, clothes*) leggero(-a); (*building*) poco solido(-a); (*excuse*) che non regge

flinch [flɪntʃ] *vi* ritirarsi; **to ~ from** tirarsi indietro di fronte a

fling [flɪŋ] (*pt, pp* **flung**) *vt* lanciare, gettare

flint [flɪnt] *n* selce *f*; (*in lighter*) pietrina

flip [flɪp] *vt* (*switch*) far scattare; (*coin*) lanciare in aria

flip-flops ['flɪpflɔps] *npl* (*esp BRIT: sandals*) infradito *mpl*

flipper ['flɪpər] *n* pinna

flirt [fləːt] *vi* flirtare ▷ *n* civetta

float [fləut] *n* galleggiante *m*; (*in procession*) carro; (*money*) somma ▷ *vi* galleggiare

flock [flɔk] *n* (*of sheep, Rel*) gregge *m*; (*of birds*) stormo ▷ *vi* **to ~ to** accorrere in massa a

flood [flʌd] *n* alluvione *m*; (*of letters etc*) marea ▷ *vt* allagare; (*people*) invadere ▷ *vi* (*place*) allagarsi; (*people*): **to ~ into** riversarsi in; **flooding** *n* inondazione *f*; **floodlight** *n* riflettore *m* ▷ *vt* illuminare a giorno

floor [flɔːʳ] *n* pavimento; (*storey*) piano; (*of sea, valley*) fondo ▷ *vt* (*blow*) atterrare; (: *question*) ridurre al silenzio; **which ~ is it on?** a che piano si trova?; **ground ~** (*BRIT*), **first ~** (*US*) pianterreno; **first ~** (*BRIT*), **second ~** (*US*) primo piano; **floorboard** *n* tavellone *m* di legno; **flooring** *n* (*floor*) pavimento; (*material*) materiale *m* per pavimentazioni; **floor show** *n* spettacolo di varietà

flop [flɔp] *n* fiasco ▷ *vi* far fiasco; (*fall*) lasciarsi cadere; **floppy** ['flɔpɪ] *adj* floscio(-a), molle

floral ['flɔːrl] *adj* floreale

Florence ['flɔrəns] *n* Firenze *f*

Florentine ['flɔrəntaɪn] *adj* fiorentino(-a)

florist ['flɔrɪst] *n* fioraio(-a); **florist's (shop)** *n* fioraio(-a)

flotation [fləu'teɪʃən] *n* (*Comm*) lancio

flour ['flauəʳ] *n* farina

flourish ['flʌrɪʃ] *vi* fiorire ▷ *n* (*bold gesture*): **with a ~** con ostentazione

flow [fləu] *n* flusso; circolazione *f* ▷ *vi* fluire; (*traffic, blood in veins*) circolare; (*hair*) scendere

flower ['flauəʳ] *n* fiore *m* ▷ *vi* fiorire; **flower bed** *n* aiuola; **flowerpot** *n* vaso da fiori

flown [fləun] *pp of* **fly**

fl. oz. *abbr* = **fluid ounce**

flu [fluː] *n* influenza

fluctuate ['flʌktjueɪt] *vi* fluttuare, oscillare

fluent ['fluːənt] *adj* (*speech*) facile, sciolto(-a); corrente; **he speaks ~ Italian, he's ~ in Italian** parla l'italiano correntemente

fluff [flʌf] *n* lanugine *f*; **fluffy** *adj* lanuginoso(-a); (*toy*) di peluche

fluid ['fluːɪd] *adj* fluido(-a) ▷ *n* fluido; **fluid ounce** *n* (*BRIT*) = 0.028 l; 0.05 pints

fluke [fluːk] *n* (*inf*) colpo di fortuna

flung [flʌŋ] *pt, pp of* **fling**

fluorescent [fluə'rɛsnt] *adj* fluorescente

fluoride ['fluəraɪd] *n* fluoruro

flurry ['flʌrɪ] *n* (*of snow*) tempesta; **a ~ of activity** uno scoppio di attività

flush [flʌʃ] *n* rossore *m*; (*fig: of youth, beauty etc*) rigoglio, pieno vigore ▷ *vt* ripulire con un getto d'acqua ▷ *vi* arrossire ▷ *adj* **~ with** a livello di, pari a; **to ~ the toilet** tirare l'acqua

flute [fluːt] *n* flauto

flutter ['flʌtəʳ] *n* agitazione *f*; (*of wings*) battito ▷ *vi* (*bird*) battere le ali

fly [flaɪ] (*pt* **flew**, *pp* **flown**) *n* (*insect*) mosca; (*on trousers: also*: **flies**) chiusura ▷ *vt* pilotare; (*passengers, cargo*) trasportare (in aereo); (*distances*) percorrere ▷ *vi* volare; (*passengers*) andare in aereo; (*escape*) fuggire; (*flag*) sventolare; **fly away** *vi* volar via; **fly-drive** *n* **fly-drive holiday** fly and drive *m inv*; **flying** *n* (*activity*) aviazione *f*; (*action*) volo ▷ *adj* **flying visit** visita volante; **with flying colours** con risultati brillanti; **flying saucer** *n* disco volante; **flyover** (*BRIT*) *n* (*bridge*) cavalcavia *m inv*

FM *abbr* (= *frequency modulation*) FM

foal [fəul] *n* puledro

foam [fəum] *n* schiuma; (*also*: **~ rubber**)

gommapiuma® ▷ vi schiumare; (*soapy water*) fare la schiuma

focus ['fəukəs] (*pl* **focuses**) *n* fuoco; (*of interest*) centro ▷ vt (*field glasses etc*) mettere a fuoco ▷ vi to **~ on** (*with camera*) mettere a fuoco; (*person*) fissare lo sguardo su; **in ~** a fuoco; **out of ~** sfocato(-a)

foetus ['fiːtəs] (*us* **fetus**) *n* feto

fog [fɔg] *n* nebbia; **foggy** *adj* **it's foggy** c'è nebbia; **fog lamp** (*us* **fog light**) *n* (*Aut*) faro *m* antinebbia *inv*

foil [fɔɪl] vt confondere, frustrare ▷ *n* lamina di metallo; (*kitchen foil*) foglio di alluminio; (*Fencing*) fioretto; **to act as a ~ to** (*fig*) far risaltare

fold [fəuld] *n* (*bend, crease*) piega; (*Agr*) ovile *m*; (*fig*) gregge *m* ▷ vt piegare; (*arms*) incrociare; **fold up** vi (*map, bed, table*) piegarsi; (*business*) crollare ▷ vt (*map etc*) piegare, ripiegare; **folder** *n* (*for papers*) cartella; cartellina; **folding** *adj* (*chair, bed*) pieghevole

foliage ['fəuliːdʒ] *n* fogliame *m*

folk [fəuk] *npl* gente *f* ▷ *adj* popolare; **~s** *npl* (*family*) famiglia; **folklore** ['fəuklɔːʳ] *n* folclore *m*; **folk music** *n* musica folk *inv*; **folk song** *n* canto popolare

follow ['fɔləu] vt seguire ▷ vi seguire; (*result*) conseguire, risultare; **to ~ suit** fare lo stesso; **follow up** vt (*letter, offer*) fare seguito a; (*case*) seguire; **follower** *n* seguace *m/f*, discepolo(-a); **following** *adj* seguente ▷ *n* seguito, discepoli *mpl*; **follow-up** *n* seguito

fond [fɔnd] *adj* (*memory, look*) tenero(-a), affettuoso(-a); **to be ~ of sb** volere bene a qn; **he's ~ of walking** gli piace fare camminate

food [fuːd] *n* cibo; **food mixer** *n* frullatore *m*; **food poisoning** *n* intossicazione *f*; **food processor** [-'prəusɛsə] *n* tritatutto *m inv* elettrico; **food stamp** (*us*) *n* buono alimentare dato agli indigenti

fool [fuːl] *n* sciocco(-a); (*Culin*) frullato ▷ vt ingannare ▷ vi (*gen: fool around*) fare lo sciocco; **fool about**, **fool around** vi (*waste time*) perdere tempo; **foolish** *adj* scemo(-a), stupido(-a), imprudente; **foolproof** *adj* (*plan etc*) sicurissimo(-a)

foot [fut] (*pl* **feet**) *n* piede *m*; (*measure*) piede (= 304 mm; 12 inches); (*of animal*) zampa ▷ vt (*bill*) pagare; **on ~** a piedi; **footage** *n* (*Cinema: length*) ≈ metraggio; (: *material*) sequenza; **foot-and-mouth (disease)** [futənd'mauθ-] *n* afta epizootica; **football** *n* pallone *m*; (*sport:* BRIT) calcio; (: *us*) football *m* americano; **footballer** *n* (BRIT) = **football player**; **football match** *n* (BRIT) partita di calcio;

football player *n* (BRIT: *also*: **footballer**) calciatore *m*, (*us*) giocatore *m* di football americano; **footbridge** *n* passerella; **foothills** *npl* contrafforti *fpl*; **foothold** *n* punto d'appoggio; **footing** *n* (*fig*) posizione *f*; **to lose one's footing** mettere un piede in fallo; **footnote** *n* nota (a piè di pagina); **footpath** *n* sentiero; (*in street*) marciapiede *m*; **footprint** *n* orma, impronta; **footstep** *n* passo; (*footprint*) orma, impronta; **footwear** *n* calzatura

Ⓞ KEYWORD

for [fɔːʳ] *prep* **1** (*indicating destination, intention, purpose*) per; **the train for London** il treno per Londra; **he went for the paper** è andato a prendere il giornale; **it's time for lunch** è ora di pranzo; **what's it for?** a che serve?; **what for?** (*why*) perché?

2 (*on behalf of, representing*) per; **to work for sb/sth** lavorare per qn/qc; **I'll ask him for you** glielo chiederò a nome tuo; **G for George** G come George

3 (*because of*) per, a causa di; **for this reason** per questo motivo

4 (*with regard to*) per; **it's cold for July** è freddo per luglio; **for everyone who voted yes, 50 voted no** per ogni voto a favore ce n'erano 50 contro

5 (*in exchange for*) per; **I sold it for £5** l'ho venduto per 5 sterline

6 (*in favour of*) per, a favore di; **are you for or against us?** è con noi o contro di noi?; **I'm all for it** sono completamente a favore

7 (*referring to distance, time*) per; **there are roadworks for 5 km** ci sono lavori in corso per 5 km; **he was away for 2 years** è stato via per 2 anni; **she will be away for a month** starà via un mese; **it hasn't rained for 3 weeks** non piove da 3 settimane; **can you do it for tomorrow?** può farlo per domani?

8 (*with infinitive clauses*): **it is not for me to decide** non sta a me decidere; **it would be best for you to leave** sarebbe meglio che lei se ne andasse; **there is still time for you to do it** ha ancora tempo per farlo; **for this to be possible …** perché ciò sia possibile …

9 (*in spite of*) nonostante; **for all his complaints, he's very fond of her** nonostante tutte le sue lamentele, le vuole molto bene

▷ *conj* (*since, as: rather formal*) dal momento che, poiché

forbid [fə'bɪd] (*pt* **forbad(e)**, *pp* **forbidden**)

vt vietare, interdire; **to ~ sb to do sth** proibire a qn di fare qc; **forbidden** *pt of* **forbid** ▷ *adj* (*food*) proibito(-a); (*area, territory*) vietato(-a); (*word, subject*) tabù *inv*
force [fɔːs] *n* forza ▷ *vt* forzare; **forced** *adj* forzato(-a); **forceful** *adj* forte, vigoroso(-a)
ford [fɔːd] *n* guado
fore [fɔːʳ] *n* **to come to the ~** mettersi in evidenza; **forearm** [ˈfɔːrɑːm] *n* avambraccio; **forecast** [ˈfɔːkɑːst] (*irreg: like* **cast**) *n* previsione *f* ▷ *vt* prevedere; **forecourt** [ˈfɔːkɔːt] *n* (*of garage*) corte *f* esterna; **forefinger** [ˈfɔːfɪŋgəʳ] *n* (*dito*) indice *m*; **forefront** [ˈfɔːfrʌnt] *n* **in the forefront of** all'avanguardia in; **foreground** [ˈfɔːgraund] *n* primo piano; **forehead** [ˈfɔrɪd] *n* fronte *f*
foreign [ˈfɔrɪn] *adj* straniero(-a); (*trade*) estero(-a); (*object, matter*) estraneo(-a); **foreign currency** *n* valuta estera; **foreigner** *n* straniero(-a); **foreign exchange** *n* cambio con l'estero; (*currency*) valuta estera; **Foreign Office** (*BRIT*) *n* Ministero degli Esteri; **Foreign Secretary** (*BRIT*) *n* ministro degli Affari esteri
fore: **foreman** [ˈfɔːmən] (*irreg*) *n* caposquadra *m*; **foremost** [ˈfɔːməust] *adj* principale; più in vista ▷ *adv* **first and foremost** innanzitutto; **forename** *n* nome *m* di battesimo
forensic [fəˈrɛnsɪk] *adj* **~ medicine** medicina legale
foresee [fɔːˈsiː] (*irreg: like* **see**) *vt* prevedere; **foreseeable** *adj* prevedibile
forest [ˈfɔrɪst] *n* foresta; **forestry** [ˈfɔrɪstrɪ] *n* silvicoltura
forever [fəˈrɛvəʳ] *adv* per sempre; (*endlessly*) sempre, di continuo
foreword [ˈfɔːwəːd] *n* prefazione *f*
forfeit [ˈfɔːfɪt] *vt* perdere; (*one's happiness, health*) giocarsi
forgave [fəˈgeɪv] *pt of* **forgive**
forge [fɔːdʒ] *n* fucina ▷ *vt* (*signature, money*) contraffare, falsificare; (*wrought iron*) fucinare, foggiare; **forger** *n* contraffattore *m*; **forgery** *n* falso; (*activity*) contraffazione *f*
forget [fəˈgɛt] (*pt* **forgot**, *pp* **forgotten**) *vt, vi* dimenticare; **I've forgotten my key/passport** ho dimenticato la chiave/il passaporto; **forgetful** *adj* di corta memoria; **forgetful of** dimentico(-a) di
forgive [fəˈgɪv] (*pt* **forgave**, *pp* **forgiven**) *vt* perdonare; **to ~ sb for sth** perdonare qc a qn
forgot [fəˈgɔt] *pt of* **forget**

forgotten [fəˈgɔtn] *pp of* **forget**
fork [fɔːk] *n* (*for eating*) forchetta; (*for gardening*) forca; (*of roads, rivers, railways*) biforcazione *f* ▷ *vi* (*road etc*) biforcarsi
forlorn [fəˈlɔːn] *adj* (*person*) sconsolato(-a); (*place*) abbandonato(-a); (*attempt*) disperato(-a); (*hope*) vano(-a)
form [fɔːm] *n* forma; (*Scol*) classe *f*; (*questionnaire*) scheda ▷ *vt* formare; **in top ~** in gran forma
formal [ˈfɔːml] *adj* formale; (*gardens*) simmetrico(-a), regolare; **formality** [fɔːˈmælɪtɪ] *n* formalità *f inv*
format [ˈfɔːmæt] *n* formato ▷ *vt* (*Comput*) formattare
formation [fɔːˈmeɪʃən] *n* formazione *f*
former [ˈfɔːməʳ] *adj* vecchio(-a); (*before n*) ex *inv* (*before n*); **the ~ ... the latter** quello ... questo; **formerly** *adv* in passato
formidable [ˈfɔːmɪdəbl] *adj* formidabile
formula [ˈfɔːmjulə] *n* formula
fort [fɔːt] *n* forte *m*
forthcoming [fɔːθˈkʌmɪŋ] *adj* (*event*) prossimo(-a); (*help*) disponibile; (*character*) aperto(-a), comunicativo(-a)
fortieth [ˈfɔːtɪɪθ] *num* quarantesimo(-a)
fortify [ˈfɔːtɪfaɪ] *vt* (*city*) fortificare; (*person*) armare
fortnight [ˈfɔːtnaɪt] (*BRIT*) *n* quindici giorni *mpl*, due settimane *fpl*; **fortnightly** *adj* bimensile ▷ *adv* ogni quindici giorni
fortress [ˈfɔːtrɪs] *n* fortezza, rocca
fortunate [ˈfɔːtʃənɪt] *adj* fortunato(-a); **it is ~ that** è una fortuna che; **fortunately** *adv* fortunatamente
fortune [ˈfɔːtʃən] *n* fortuna; **fortune-teller** *n* indovino(-a)
forty [ˈfɔːtɪ] *num* quaranta
forum [ˈfɔːrəm] *n* foro
forward [ˈfɔːwəd] *adj* (*ahead of schedule*) in anticipo; (*movement, position*) in avanti; (*not shy*) aperto(-a), diretto(-a) ▷ *n* (*Sport*) avanti *m inv* ▷ *vt* (*letter*) inoltrare; (*parcel, goods*) spedire; (*career, plans*) promuovere, appoggiare; **to move ~** avanzare; **forwarding address** *n* nuovo recapito cui spedire la posta; **forward(s)** *adv* avanti; **forward slash** *n* barra obliqua
fossil [ˈfɔsl] *adj* fossile ▷ *n* fossile *m*
foster [ˈfɔstəʳ] *vt* incoraggiare, nutrire; (*child*) avere in affidamento; **foster child** *n* bambino(-a) preso(-a) in affidamento; **foster mother** *n* madre *f* affidataria
fought [fɔːt] *pt, pp of* **fight**
foul [faul] *adj* (*smell, food, temper etc*) cattivo(-a); (*weather*) brutto(-a); (*language*) osceno(-a) ▷ *n* (*Sport*) fallo ▷ *vt* sporcare; **foul play** *n* (*Law*): **the police suspect foul play** la polizia sospetta un atto

criminale
found [faund] *pt, pp of* **find** ▷ *vt*
(*establish*) fondare; **foundation** [-'deɪʃə
n] *n* (*act*) fondazione *f*; (*base*) base *f*;
(*also:* **foundation cream**) fondo tinta;
foundations *npl* (*of building*) fondamenta
fpl
founder ['faundə^r] *n* fondatore(-trice) ▷ *vi*
affondare
fountain ['fauntɪn] *n* fontana; **fountain
pen** *n* penna stilografica
four [fɔ:^r] *num* quattro; **on all ~s** a
carponi; **four-letter word** ['fɔ:lɛtə-] *n*
parolaccia; **four-poster** *n* (*also:* **four-
poster bed**) letto a quattro colonne;
fourteen *num* quattordici; **fourteenth**
num quattordicesimo(-a); **fourth** *num*
quarto(-a); **four-wheel drive** ['fɔ:wi:l-] *n*
(*Aut*) **with four-wheel drive** con quattro
ruote motrici
fowl [faul] *n* pollame *m*; volatile *m*
fox [fɔks] *n* volpe *f* ▷ *vt* confondere
foyer ['fɔɪeɪ] *n* atrio; (*Theatre*) ridotto
fraction ['frækʃən] *n* frazione *f*
fracture ['fræktʃə^r] *n* frattura
fragile ['frædʒaɪl] *adj* fragile
fragment ['frægmənt] *n* frammento
fragrance ['freɪgrəns] *n* fragranza,
profumo
frail [freɪl] *adj* debole, delicato(-a)
frame [freɪm] *n* (*of building*) armatura;
(*of human, animal*) ossatura, corpo; (*of
picture*) cornice *f*; (*of door, window*) telaio;
(*of spectacles: also:* **~s**) montatura ▷ *vt*
(*picture*) incorniciare; **framework** *n*
struttura
France [frɑ:ns] *n* Francia
franchise ['fræntʃaɪz] *n* (*Pol*) diritto di
voto; (*Comm*) concessione *f*
frank [fræŋk] *adj* franco(-a), aperto(-a)
▷ *vt* (*letter*) affrancare; **frankly** *adv*
francamente, sinceramente
frantic ['fræntɪk] *adj* frenetico(-a)
fraud [frɔ:d] *n* truffa; (*Law*) frode *f*; (*person*)
impostore(-a)
fraught [frɔ:t] *adj* **~ with** pieno(-a) di,
intriso(-a) da
fray [freɪ] *vt* logorare ▷ *vi* logorarsi
freak [fri:k] *n* fenomeno, mostro
freckle ['frɛkl] *n* lentiggine *f*
free [fri:] *adj* libero(-a); (*gratis*) gratuito(-a)
▷ *vt* (*prisoner, jammed person*) liberare;
(*jammed object*) districare; **is this seat ~?**
è libero questo posto?; **~ of charge, for
~** gratuitamente; **freedom** ['fri:dəm]
n libertà; **Freefone®** *n* numero verde;
free gift *n* regalo, omaggio; **free kick** *n*
calcio libero; **freelance** *adj* indipendente;
freely *adv* liberamente; (*liberally*)

liberalmente; **Freepost®** *n* affrancatura
a carico del destinatario; **free-range** *adj*
(*hen*) ruspante; (*eggs*) di gallina ruspante;
freeway (*us*) *n* superstrada; **free will** *n*
libero arbitrio; **of one's own free will** di
spontanea volontà
freeze [fri:z] (*pt* **froze**, *pp* **frozen**) *vi* gelare
▷ *vt* gelare; (*food*) congelare; (*prices,
salaries*) bloccare ▷ *n* gelo; blocco; **freezer**
n congelatore *m*; **freezing** ['fri:zɪŋ] *adj*
(*wind, weather*) gelido(-a); **freezing point**
n punto di congelamento; **3 degrees
below freezing point** 3 gradi sotto zero
freight [freɪt] *n* (*goods*) merce *f*, merci
fpl; (*money charged*) spese *fpl* di trasporto;
freight train (*us*) *n* treno *m* merci *inv*
French [frɛntʃ] *adj* francese ▷ *n* (*Ling*)
francese *m*; **the ~** *npl* i Francesi; **French
bean** *n* fagiolino; **French bread** *n*
baguette *f inv*; **French dressing** *n* (*Culin*)
condimento per insalata, **French fried
potatoes** (*us* **French fries**) *npl* patate
fpl fritte; **Frenchman** (*irreg*) *n* francese
m; **French stick** *n* baguette *f inv*; **French
window** *n* portafinestra; **Frenchwoman**
(*irreg*) *n* francese *f*
frenzy ['frɛnzɪ] *n* frenesia
frequency ['fri:kwənsɪ] *n* frequenza
frequent [*adj* 'fri:kwənt, *vb* frɪ'kwɛnt] *adj*
frequente ▷ *vt* frequentare; **frequently**
adv frequentemente, spesso
fresh [frɛʃ] *adj* fresco(-a); (*new*) nuovo(-a);
(*cheeky*) sfacciato(-a); **freshen** *vi*
(*wind, air*) rinfrescare; **freshen up** *vi*
rinfrescarsi; **fresher** (*BRIT: inf*) *n* (*Scol*)
matricola; **freshly** *adv* di recente, di
fresco; **freshman** (*irreg: us*) *n* = **fresher**;
freshwater *adj* (*fish*) d'acqua dolce
fret [frɛt] *vi* agitarsi, affliggersi
Fri. *abbr* (= *Friday*) ven.
friction ['frɪkʃən] *n* frizione *f*, attrito
Friday ['fraɪdɪ] *n* venerdì *m inv*
fridge [frɪdʒ] (*BRIT*) *n* frigo, frigorifero
fried [fraɪd] *pt, pp of* **fry** ▷ *adj* fritto(-a)
friend [frɛnd] *n* amico(-a); **friendly** *adj*
amichevole; **friendship** *n* amicizia
fries [fraɪz] (*esp us*) *npl* patate *fpl* fritte
frigate ['frɪgɪt] *n* (*Naut: modern*) fregata
fright [fraɪt] *n* paura, spavento; **to take ~**
spaventarsi; **frighten** *vt* spaventare, far
paura a; **frightened** *adj* spaventato(-a);
frightening *adj* spaventoso(-a),
pauroso(-a); **frightful** *adj* orribile
frill [frɪl] *n* balza
fringe [frɪndʒ] *n* (*decoration: BRIT: of hair*)
frangia; (*edge: of forest etc*) margine *m*
Frisbee® ['frɪzbɪ] *n* frisbee® *m inv*
fritter ['frɪtə^r] *n* frittella
frivolous ['frɪvələs] *adj* frivolo(-a)

fro [frəu] *see* **to**

frock [frɔk] *n* vestito

frog [frɔg] *n* rana; **frogman** (*irreg*) *n* uomo *m* rana *inv*

○ **KEYWORD**

from [frɔm] *prep* **1** (*indicating starting place, origin etc*) da; **where do you come from?**, **where are you from?** da dove viene?, di dov'è?; **from London to Glasgow** da Londra a Glasgow; **a letter from my sister** una lettera da mia sorella; **tell him from me that ...** gli dica da parte mia che ...

2 (*indicating time*) da; **from one o'clock to** *or* **until** *or* **till two** dall'una alle due; **from January (on)** da gennaio, a partire da gennaio

3 (*indicating distance*) da; **the hotel is 1 km from the beach** l'albergo è a 1 km dalla spiaggia

4 (*indicating price, number etc*) da; **prices range from £10 to £50** i prezzi vanno dalle 10 alle 50 sterline

5 (*indicating difference*) da; **he can't tell red from green** non sa distinguere il rosso dal verde

6 (*because of, on the basis of*): **from what he says** da quanto dice lui; **weak from hunger** debole per la fame

front [frʌnt] *n* (*of house, dress*) davanti *m inv*; (*of train*) testa; (*of book*) copertina; (*promenade: also*: **sea ~**) lungomare *m*; (*Mil, Pol, Meteor*) fronte *m*; (*fig: appearances*) fronte *f* ▷ *adj* primo(-a); anteriore, davanti *inv*; **in ~ of** davanti a; **front door** *n* porta d'entrata; (*of car*) sportello anteriore; **frontier** ['frʌntiər] *n* frontiera; **front page** *n* prima pagina; **front-wheel drive** ['frʌntwi:l-] *n* trasmissione *f* anteriore

frost [frɔst] *n* gelo; (*also*: **hoar~**) brina; **frostbite** *n* congelamento; **frosting** (*US*) *n* (*on cake*) glassa; **frosty** *adj* (*weather, look*) gelido(-a)

froth ['frɔθ] *n* spuma; schiuma

frown [fraun] *vi* accigliarsi

froze [frəuz] *pt of* **freeze**

frozen ['frəuzn] *pp of* **freeze**

fruit [fru:t] *n inv* (*also fig*) frutto; (*collectively*) frutta; **fruit juice** *n* succo di frutta; **fruit machine** (*BRIT*) *n* macchina *f* mangiasoldi *inv*; **fruit salad** *n* macedonia

frustrate [frʌs'treɪt] *vt* frustrare; **frustrated** *adj* frustrato(-a)

fry [fraɪ] (*pt*, *pp* **fried**) *vt* friggere; *see also* **small**; **frying pan** *n* padella

ft. *abbr* = **foot**; **feet**

fudge [fʌdʒ] *n* (*Culin*) specie di caramella a base di latte, burro e zucchero

fuel [fjuəl] *n* (*for heating*) combustibile *m*; (*for propelling*) carburante *m*; **fuel tank** *n* deposito *m* nafta *inv*; (*on vehicle*) serbatoio (della benzina)

fulfil [ful'fɪl] *vt* (*function*) compiere; (*order*) eseguire; (*wish, desire*) soddisfare, appagare

full [ful] *adj* pieno(-a); (*details, skirt*) ampio(-a) ▷ *adv* **to know ~ well that** sapere benissimo che; **I'm ~ (up)** sono sazio; **a ~ two hours** due ore intere; **at ~ speed** a tutta velocità; **in ~** per intero; **full-length** *adj* (*film*) a lungometraggio; (*coat, novel*) lungo(-a); (*portrait*) in piedi; **full moon** *n* luna piena; **full-scale** *adj* (*attack, war*) su larga scala; (*model*) in grandezza naturale; **full stop** *n* punto; **full-time** *adj, adv* (*work*) a tempo pieno; **fully** *adv* interamente, pienamente, completamente; (*at least*) almeno

fumble ['fʌmbl] *vi* **to ~ with sth** armeggiare con qc

fume [fju:m] *vi* essere furioso(-a); **fumes** *npl* esalazioni *fpl*, vapori *mpl*

fun [fʌn] *n* divertimento, spasso; **to have ~** divertirsi; **for ~** per scherzo; **to make ~ of** prendersi gioco di

function ['fʌŋkʃən] *n* funzione *f*; cerimonia, ricevimento ▷ *vi* funzionare

fund [fʌnd] *n* fondo, cassa; (*source*) fondo; (*store*) riserva; **~s** *npl* (*money*) fondi *mpl*

fundamental [fʌndə'mɛntl] *adj* fondamentale

funeral ['fju:nərəl] *n* funerale *m*; **funeral director** *n* impresario di pompe funebri; **funeral parlour** [-'pɑ:lər] *n* impresa di pompe funebri

funfair ['fʌnfɛər] *n* luna park *m inv*

fungus ['fʌŋgəs] (*pl* **fungi**) *n* fungo; (*mould*) muffa

funnel ['fʌnl] *n* imbuto; (*of ship*) ciminiera

funny ['fʌnɪ] *adj* divertente, buffo(-a); (*strange*) strano(-a), bizzarro(-a)

fur [fə:r] *n* pelo; pelliccia; (*BRIT: in kettle etc*) deposito calcare; **fur coat** *n* pelliccia

furious ['fjuərɪəs] *adj* furioso(-a); (*effort*) accanito(-a)

furnish ['fə:nɪʃ] *vt* ammobiliare; (*supply*) fornire; **furnishings** *npl* mobili *mpl*, mobilia

furniture ['fə:nɪtʃər] *n* mobili *mpl*; **piece of ~** mobile *m*

furry ['fə:rɪ] *adj* (*animal*) peloso(-a)

further ['fə:ðər] *adj* supplementare, altro(-a); nuovo(-a); più lontano(-a) ▷ *adv* più lontano; (*more*) di più; (*moreover*) inoltre ▷ *vt* favorire, promuovere; **further**

education $n \approx$ corsi *mpl* di formazione;
college of further education istituto
statale con corsi specializzati (di formazione
professionale, aggiornamento professionale
ecc); **furthermore** [fə:ðə'mɔ:ʳ] *adv* inoltre,
per di più

furthest ['fə:ðɪst] *superl of* **far**

fury ['fjuərɪ] *n* furore *m*

fuse [fju:z] (*US* **fuze**) *n* fusibile *m*; (*for bomb
etc*) miccia, spoletta ▷ *vt* fondere ▷ *vi*
fondersi; **to ~ the lights** (*BRIT Elec*) far
saltare i fusibili; **fuse box** *n* cassetta dei
fusibili

fusion ['fju:ʒən] *n* fusione *f*

fuss [fʌs] *n* agitazione *f*; (*complaining*) storie
fpl; **to make a ~** fare delle storie; **fussy** *adj*
(*person*) puntiglioso(-a), esigente; che fa le
storie; (*dress*) carico(-a) di fronzoli; (*style*)
elaborato(-a)

future ['fju:tʃəʳ] *adj* futuro(-a) ▷ *n* futuro,
avvenire *m*; (*Ling*) futuro; **in ~** in futuro, **~s**
npl (*Comm*) operazioni *fpl* a termine

fuze [fju:z] (*US*) = **fuse**

fuzzy ['fʌzɪ] *adj* (*Phot*) indistinto(-a),
sfocato(-a); (*hair*) crespo(-a)

G [dʒi:] *n* (*Mus*) sol *m*

g. *abbr* (= *gram, gravity*) g.

gadget ['gædʒɪt] *n* aggeggio

Gaelic ['geɪlɪk] *adj* gaelico(-a) ▷ *n* (*Ling*)
gaelico

gag [gæg] *n* bavaglio; (*joke*) facezia,
scherzo ▷ *vt* imbavagliare

gain [geɪn] *n* guadagno, profitto ▷ *vt*
guadagnare ▷ *vi* (*clock, watch*) andare
avanti; (*benefit*): **to ~ (from)** trarre
beneficio (da); **to ~ 3lbs (in weight)**
aumentare di 3 libbre; **to ~ on sb** (*in race
etc*) guadagnare su qn

gal. *abbr* = **gallon**

gala ['gɑ:lə] *n* gala; **swimming ~**
manifestazione *f* di nuoto

galaxy ['gæləksɪ] *n* galassia

gale [geɪl] *n* vento forte; burrasca

gall bladder ['gɔ:l-] *n* cistifellea

gallery ['gælərɪ] *n* galleria

gallon ['gælən] *n* gallone *m* (= *8 pints; BRIT*
= 4.543*l*; *US* = 3.785*l*)

gallop ['gæləp] *n* galoppo ▷ *vi* galoppare

gallstone ['gɔ:lstəun] *n* calcolo biliare

gamble ['gæmbl] *n* azzardo, rischio
calcolato ▷ *vt, vi* giocare; **to ~ on** (*fig*)
giocare su; **gambler** *n* giocatore(-trice)
d'azzardo; **gambling** *n* gioco d'azzardo

game [geɪm] *n* gioco; (*event*) partita;
(*Tennis*) game *m inv*; (*Culin, Hunting*)

selvaggina ▷ *adj* (*ready*): **to be ~ (for sth/ to do)** essere pronto(-a) (a qc/a fare); **big ~** selvaggina grossa; **~s** *npl* (*Scol*) attività *fpl* sportive; **big ~** selvaggina grossa; **games console** [geɪmz-] *n* console *f inv* dei videogame; **game show** ['geɪmʃəu] *n* gioco a premi

gammon ['gæmən] *n* (*bacon*) quarto di maiale; (*ham*) prosciutto affumicato

gang [gæŋ] *n* banda, squadra ▷ *vi* **to ~ up on sb** far combutta contro qn

gangster ['gæŋstər] *n* gangster *m inv*

gap [gæp] *n* (*space*) buco; (*in time*) intervallo; (*difference*): **~ (between)** divario (tra)

gape [geɪp] *vi* (*person*) restare a bocca aperta; (*shirt, hole*) essere spalancato(-a)

gap year *n* (*Scol*) anno di pausa durante il quale gli studenti viaggiano o lavorano

garage ['gærɑːʒ] *n* garage *m inv*; **garage sale** *n* vendita di oggetti usati nel garage di un privato

garbage ['gɑːbɪdʒ] (*US*) *n* immondizie *fpl*, rifiuti *mpl*; (*inf*) sciocchezze *fpl*; **garbage can** (*US*) *n* bidone *m* della spazzatura; **garbage collector** (*US*) *n* spazzino(-a)

garden ['gɑːdn] *n* giardino; **~s** *npl* (*public park*) giardini pubblici; **garden centre** *n* vivaio; **gardener** *n* giardiniere(-a); **gardening** *n* giardinaggio

garlic ['gɑːlɪk] *n* aglio

garment ['gɑːmənt] *n* indumento

garnish ['gɑːnɪʃ] *vt* (*food*) guarnire

garrison ['gærɪsn] *n* guarnigione *f*

gas [gæs] *n* gas *m inv*; (*us: gasoline*) benzina ▷ *vt* asfissiare con il gas; **I can smell ~** sento odore di gas; **gas cooker** (*BRIT*) *n* cucina a gas; **gas cylinder** *n* bombola del gas; **gas fire** (*BRIT*) *n* radiatore *m* a gas

gasket ['gæskɪt] *n* (*Aut*) guarnizione *f*

gasoline ['gæsəliːn] (*US*) *n* benzina

gasp [gɑːsp] *n* respiro affannoso, ansito ▷ *vi* ansare, ansimare; (*in surprise*) restare senza fiato

gas: **gas pedal** (*esp US*) *n* pedale *m* dell'acceleratore; **gas station** (*US*) *n* distributore *m* di benzina; **gas tank** (*US*) *n* (*Aut*) serbatoio (di benzina)

gate [geɪt] *n* cancello; (*at airport*) uscita

gateau ['gætəu, -z] (*pl* **gateaux**) *n* torta

gatecrash ['geɪtkræʃ] (*BRIT*) *vt* partecipare senza invito a

gateway ['geɪtweɪ] *n* porta

gather ['gæðər] *vt* (*flowers, fruit*) cogliere; (*pick up*) raccogliere; (*assemble*) radunare; raccogliere; (*understand*) capire; (*Sewing*) increspare ▷ *vi* (*assemble*) radunarsi; **to ~ speed** acquistare velocità; **gathering** *n* adunanza

gauge [geɪdʒ] *n* (*instrument*) indicatore *m* ▷ *vt* misurare; (*fig*) valutare

gave [geɪv] *pt of* **give**

gay [geɪ] *adj* (*homosexual*) omosessuale; (*cheerful*) gaio(-a), allegro(-a); (*colour*) vivace, vivo(-a)

gaze [geɪz] *n* sguardo fisso ▷ *vi* **to ~ at** guardare fisso

GB *abbr* = **Great Britain**

GCSE (*BRIT*) *n abbr* General Certificate of Secondary Education

gear [gɪər] *n* attrezzi *mpl*, equipaggiamento; (*Tech*) ingranaggio; (*Aut*) marcia ▷ *vt* (*fig: adapt*): **to ~ sth to** adattare qc a; **in top** *or* (*US*) **high/low ~** in quarta (*or* quinta)/seconda; **in ~** in marcia; **gear up** *vi* **to ~ up (to do)** prepararsi (a fare); **gear box** *n* scatola del cambio; **gear lever** *n* leva del cambio; **gear shift** (*US*), **gear stick** (*BRIT*) *n* = **gear lever**

geese [giːs] *npl of* **goose**

gel [dʒɛl] *n* gel *m inv*

gem [dʒɛm] *n* gemma

Gemini ['dʒɛmɪnaɪ] *n* Gemelli *mpl*

gender ['dʒɛndər] *n* genere *m*

gene [dʒiːn] *n* (*Biol*) gene *m*

general ['dʒɛnərl] *n* generale *m* ▷ *adj* generale; **in ~** in genere; **general anaesthetic** (*US* **general anesthetic**) *n* anestesia totale; **general election** *n* elezioni *fpl* generali; **generalize** *vi* generalizzare; **generally** *adv* generalmente; **general practitioner** *n* medico generico; **general store** *n* emporio

generate ['dʒɛnəreɪt] *vt* generare

generation [dʒɛnə'reɪʃən] *n* generazione *f*

generator ['dʒɛnəreɪtər] *n* generatore *m*

generosity [dʒɛnə'rɔsɪtɪ] *n* generosità

generous ['dʒɛnərəs] *adj* generoso(-a); (*copious*) abbondante

genetic [dʒɪ'nɛtɪk] *adj* genetico(-a); **~ engineering** ingegneria genetica; **genetically modified** *adj* geneticamente modificato(-a), transgenico(-a); **genetics** *n* genetica

Geneva [dʒɪ'niːvə] *n* Ginevra

genitals ['dʒɛnɪtlz] *npl* genitali *mpl*

genius ['dʒiːnɪəs] *n* genio

Genoa ['dʒɛnəuə] *n* Genova

gent [dʒɛnt] *n abbr* = **gentleman**

gentle ['dʒɛntl] *adj* delicato(-a); (*person*) dolce

Be careful not to translate *gentle* by the Italian word *gentile*.

gentleman ['dʒɛntlmən] (*irreg*) *n* signore *m*; (*well-bred man*) gentiluomo

gently ['dʒɛntlɪ] *adv* delicatamente

gents [dʒɛnts] n W.C. m (per signori)
genuine ['dʒɛnjuɪn] adj autentico(-a);
sincero(-a); **genuinely** adv genuinamente
geographic(al) [dʒɪə'græfɪk(l)] adj
geografico(-a)
geography [dʒɪ'ɔgrəfɪ] n geografia
geology [dʒɪ'ɔlədʒɪ] n geologia
geometry [dʒɪ'ɔmətrɪ] n geometria
geranium [dʒɪ'reɪnjəm] n geranio
geriatric [dʒɛrɪ'ætrɪk] adj geriatrico(-a)
germ [dʒəːm] n (Med) microbo; (Biol, fig)
germe m
German ['dʒəːmən] adj tedesco(-a) ▷ n
tedesco(-a); (Ling) tedesco; **German
measles** (BRIT) n rosolia
Germany ['dʒəːmənɪ] n Germania
gesture ['dʒɛstjəʳ] n gesto

○ **KEYWORD**

get [gɛt] (pt, pp **got**, (US) pp **gotten**) vi **1**
(become, be) diventare, farsi; **to get old**
invecchiare; **to get tired** stancarsi; **to get
drunk** ubriacarsi; **to get killed** venire or
rimanere ucciso(-a); **when do I get paid?**
quando mi pagate?; **it's getting late** si sta
facendo tardi
2 (go): **to get to/from** andare a/da; **to get
home** arrivare or tornare a casa; **how did
you get here?** come sei venuto?
3 (begin) mettersi a, cominciare a; **to get
to know sb** incominciare a conoscere qn;
let's get going or **started** muoviamoci
4 (modal aux vb): **you've got to do it** devi
farlo
▷ vt **1**: **to get sth done** (do) fare qc; (have
done) far fare qc; **to get one's hair cut** farsi
tagliare i capelli; **to get sb to do sth** far
fare qc a qn
2 (obtain: money, permission, results)
ottenere; (find: job, flat) trovare; (fetch:
person, doctor) chiamare; (: object)
prendere; **to get sth for sb** prendere
or procurare qc a qn; **get me Mr Jones,
please** (Tel) mi passi il signor Jones, per
favore; **can I get you a drink?** le posso
offrire da bere?
3 (receive: present, letter, prize) ricevere;
(acquire: reputation) farsi; **how much did
you get for the painting?** quanto le
hanno dato per il quadro?
4 (catch) prendere; (hit: target etc) colpire;
to get sb by the arm/throat afferrare
qn per un braccio/alla gola; **get him!**
prendetelo!
5 (take, move) portare; **to get sth to sb** far
avere qc a qn; **do you think we'll get it
through the door?** pensi che riusciremo a
farlo passare per la porta?

6 (catch, take: plane, bus etc) prendere;
where do we get the ferry to …? dove si
prende il traghetto per …?
7 (understand) afferrare; (hear) sentire; **I've
got it!** ci sono arrivato!, ci sono!; **I'm sorry,
I didn't get your name** scusi, non ho
capito (or sentito) il suo nome
8 (have, possess): **to have got** avere; **how
many have you got?** quanti ne ha?
get along vi (agree) andare d'accordo;
(depart) andarsene; (manage) = **get by**
get at vt fus (attack) prendersela con;
(reach) raggiungere, arrivare a
get away vi partire, andarsene; (escape)
scappare
get away with vt fus cavarsela; farla
franca
get back vi (return) ritornare, tornare ▷ vt
riottenere, riavere; **when do we get back?**
quando ritorniamo?
get by vi (pass) passare; (manage) farcela
get down vi, vt fus scendere ▷ vt far
scendere; (depress) buttare giù
get down to vt fus (work) mettersi a (fare)
get in vi entrare; (train) arrivare; (arrive
home) ritornare, tornare
get into vt fus entrare in; **to get into a
rage** incavolarsi
get off vi (from train etc) scendere; (depart:
person, car) andare via; (escape) cavarsela
▷ vt (remove: clothes, stain) levare ▷ vt fus
(train, bus) scendere da; **where do I get
off?** dove devo scendere?
get on vi (at exam etc) andare; (agree): **to
get on (with)** andare d'accordo (con) ▷ vt
fus montare in; (horse) montare su
get out vi uscire; (of vehicle) scendere ▷ vt
tirar fuori, far uscire
get out of vt fus uscire da; (duty etc)
evitare
get over vt fus (illness) riaversi da
get round vt fus aggirare; (fig: person)
rigirare
get through vi (Tel) avere la linea
get through to vt fus (Tel) parlare a
get together vi riunirsi ▷ vt raccogliere;
(people) adunare
get up vi (rise) alzarsi ▷ vt fus salire su per
get up to vt fus (reach) raggiungere; (prank
etc) fare

getaway ['gɛtəweɪ] n fuga
Ghana ['gɑːnə] n Ghana m
ghastly ['gɑːstlɪ] adj orribile, orrendo(-a);
(pale) spettrale
ghetto ['gɛtəu] n ghetto
ghost [gəust] n fantasma m, spettro
giant ['dʒaɪənt] n gigante m ▷ adj
gigantesco(-a), enorme

g

gift [gɪft] n regalo; (*donation, ability*) dono; **gifted** adj dotato(-a); **gift shop** (US **gift store**) n negozio di souvenir

gift token, gift voucher n buono m omaggio *inv*

gig [gɪg] n (*inf: of musician*) serata

gigabyte [gi:gəbaɪt] n gigabyte m *inv*

gigantic [dʒaɪˈgæntɪk] adj gigantesco(-a)

giggle [ˈgɪgl] vi ridere scioccamente

gills [gɪlz] npl (*of fish*) branchie fpl

gilt [gɪlt] n doratura ▷ adj dorato(-a)

gimmick [ˈgɪmɪk] n trucco

gin [dʒɪn] n (*liquor*) gin m *inv*

ginger [ˈdʒɪndʒəʳ] n zenzero

gipsy [ˈdʒɪpsɪ] n zingaro(-a)

giraffe [dʒɪˈrɑːf] n giraffa

girl [gəːl] n ragazza; (*young unmarried woman*) signorina; (*daughter*) figlia, figliola; **girlfriend** n (*of girl*) amica; (*of boy*) ragazza; **Girl Scout** (US) n Giovane Esploratrice f

gist [dʒɪst] n succo

give [gɪv] (*pt* **gave**, *pp* **given**) vt dare ▷ vi cedere; **to ~ sb sth, ~ sth to sb** dare qc a qn; **I'll ~ you £5 for it** te lo pago £5 sterline; **to ~ a cry/sigh** emettere un grido/sospiro; **to ~ a speech** fare un discorso; **give away** vt dare via; (*disclose*) rivelare; (*bride*) condurre all'altare; **give back** vt rendere; **give in** vi cedere ▷ vt consegnare; **give out** vt distribuire; annunciare; **give up** vi rinunciare ▷ vt rinunciare a; **to ~ up smoking** smettere di fumare; **to ~ o.s. up** arrendersi

given [ˈgɪvn] pp *of* **give** ▷ adj (*fixed: time, amount*) dato(-a), determinato(-a) ▷ conj **~ (that)** ... dato che ...; **~ the circumstances** ... date le circostanze ...

glacier [ˈglæsɪəʳ] n ghiacciaio

glad [glæd] adj lieto(-a), contento(-a); **gladly** [ˈglædlɪ] adv volentieri

glamorous [ˈglæmərəs] adj affascinante, seducente

glamour [ˈglæməʳ] (US **glamor**) n fascino

glance [glɑːns] n occhiata, sguardo ▷ vi **to ~ at** dare un'occhiata a; **to ~ off** (*bullet*) rimbalzare su

gland [glænd] n ghiandola

glare [glɛəʳ] n (*of anger*) sguardo furioso; (*of light*) riverbero, luce f abbagliante; (*of publicity*) chiasso ▷ vi abbagliare; **to ~ at** guardare male; **glaring** adj (*mistake*) madornale

glass [glɑːs] n (*substance*) vetro; (*tumbler*) bicchiere m; **~es** npl (*spectacles*) occhiali mpl

glaze [gleɪz] vt (*door*) fornire di vetri; (*pottery*) smaltare ▷ n smalto

gleam [gliːm] vi luccicare

glen [glɛn] n valletta

glide [glaɪd] vi scivolare; (*Aviat, birds*) planare; **glider** n (*Aviat*) aliante m

glimmer [ˈglɪməʳ] n barlume m

glimpse [glɪmps] n impressione f fugace ▷ vt vedere al volo

glint [glɪnt] vi luccicare

glisten [ˈglɪsn] vi luccicare

glitter [ˈglɪtəʳ] vi scintillare

global [ˈgləubl] adj globale; **global warming** n effetto m serra *inv*

globe [gləub] n globo, sfera

gloom [gluːm] n oscurità, buio; (*sadness*) tristezza, malinconia; **gloomy** adj scuro(-a), fosco(-a), triste

glorious [ˈglɔːrɪəs] adj glorioso(-a), magnifico(-a)

glory [ˈglɔːrɪ] n gloria; splendore m

gloss [glɔs] n (*shine*) lucentezza; (*also: ~ paint*) vernice f a olio

glossary [ˈglɔsərɪ] n glossario

glossy [ˈglɔsɪ] adj lucente

glove [glʌv] n guanto; **glove compartment** n (*Aut*) vano portaoggetti

glow [gləu] vi ardere; (*face*) essere luminoso(-a)

glucose [ˈgluːkəus] n glucosio

glue [gluː] n colla ▷ vt incollare

GM adj abbr (= *genetically modified*) geneticamente modificato(-a)

gm abbr = **gram**

GMO n abbr (= *genetically modified organism*) OGM m *inv*

GMT abbr (= *Greenwich Mean Time*) T.M.G.

gnaw [nɔː] vt rodere

go [gəu] (*pt* **went**, *pp* **gone**) (*pl* **goes**) vi andare; (*depart*) partire, andarsene; (*work*) funzionare; (*time*) passare; (*break etc*) rompersi; (*be sold*): **to go for £10** essere venduto per 10 sterline; (*fit, suit*): **to go with** andare bene con; (*become*): **to go pale** diventare pallido(-a); **to go mouldy** ammuffire ▷ n **to have a go (at)** provare; **to be on the go** essere in moto; **whose go is it?** a chi tocca?; **he's going to do** sta per fare; **to go for a walk** andare a fare una passeggiata; **to go dancing/ shopping** andare a ballare/fare la spesa; **just then the bell went** proprio allora suonò il campanello; **how did it go?** com'è andato?; **to go round the back/by the shop** passare da dietro/davanti al negozio; **go ahead** vi andare avanti; **go away** vi partire, andarsene; **go back** vi tornare, ritornare; **go by** vi (*years, time*) scorrere ▷ vt fus attenersi a, seguire (alla lettera); prestar fede a; **go down** vi scendere; (*ship*) affondare; (*sun*) tramontare ▷ vt fus scendere; **go for** vt fus (*fetch*) andare a prendere; (*like*) andar matto(-a) per; (*attack*) attaccare; saltare addosso a; **go in** *vi* entrare; **go into** *vt fus* entrare in; (*investigate*) indagare, esaminare; (*embark on*) lanciarsi in; **go off** *vi* partire, andar via; (*food*) guastarsi; (*explode*) esplodere, scoppiare; (*event*) passare ▷ *vt fus* **I've ~ne off chocolate** la cioccolata non mi piace più; **the gun went off** il fucile si scaricò; **go on** *vi* continuare; (*happen*) succedere; **to ~ on doing** continuare a fare; **go out** *vi* uscire; (*couple*) **they went out for 3 years** sono stati insieme per 3 anni; (*fire, light*) spegnersi; **go over** *vi* (*ship*) ribaltarsi ▷ *vt fus* (*check*) esaminare; **go past** *vi* passare ▷ *vt fus* passare davanti a; **go round** *vi* (*circulate: news, rumour*) circolare; (*revolve*) girare; (*visit*): **to ~ round (to sb's)** passare (da qn); (*make a detour*): **to ~ round (by)** passare (per); (*suffice*) bastare (per tutti); **go through** *vt fus* (*town etc*) attraversare; (*files, papers*) passare in rassegna; (*examine: list etc*) leggere da cima a fondo; **go up** *vi* salire; **go with** *vt fus* (*accompany*) accompagnare; **go without** *vt fus* fare a meno di

go-ahead ['gəuəhɛd] *adj* intraprendente ▷ *n* via *m*

goal [gəul] *n* (*Sport*) gol *m*, rete *f*; (*: place*) porta; (*fig: aim*) fine *m*, scopo; **goalkeeper** *n* portiere *m*; **goal-post** *n* palo (della porta)

goat [gəut] *n* capra

gobble ['gɔbl] *vt* (*also: ~ **down**, ~ **up***) ingoiare

god [gɔd] *n* dio; **G~** Dio; **godchild** *n* figlioccio(-a); **goddaughter** *n* figlioccia; **goddess** *n* dea; **godfather** *n* padrino; **godmother** *n* madrina; **godson** *n* figlioccio

goggles ['gɔglz] *npl* occhiali *mpl* (di protezione)

going ['gəuɪŋ] *n* (*conditions*) andare *m*, stato del terreno ▷ *adj* **the ~ rate** la tariffa in vigore

gold [gəuld] *n* oro ▷ *adj* d'oro; **golden** *adj* (*made of gold*) d'oro; (*gold in colour*) dorato(-a); **goldfish** *n* pesce *m* dorato *or* rosso; **goldmine** *n* (*also fig*) miniera d'oro; **gold-plated** *adj* placcato(-a) oro *inv*

golf [gɔlf] *n* golf *m*; **golf ball** *n* (*for game*) pallina da golf; (*on typewriter*) pallina; **golf club** *n* circolo di golf; (*stick*) bastone *m or* mazza da golf; **golf course** *n* campo di golf; **golfer** *n* giocatore(-trice) di golf

gone [gɔn] *pp of* **go** ▷ *adj* partito(-a)

gong [gɔŋ] *n* gong *m inv*

good [gud] *adj* buono(-a); (*kind*) buono(-a), gentile; (*child*) bravo(-a) ▷ *n* bene *m*; **~s**

npl (*Comm etc*) beni *mpl*; merci *fpl*; **~!** bene!, ottimo!; **to be ~ at** essere bravo(-a) in; **to be ~ for** andare bene per; **it's ~ for you** fa bene; **would you be ~ enough to ...?** avrebbe la gentilezza di ...?; **a ~ deal (of)** molto(-a), una buona quantità (di); **a ~ many** molti(-e); **to make ~** (*loss, damage*) compensare; **it's no ~ complaining** brontolare non serve a niente; **for ~** per sempre, definitivamente; **~ morning!** buon giorno!; **~ afternoon/evening!** buona sera!; **~ night!** buona notte!;

goodbye *excl* arrivederci!; **Good Friday** *n* Venerdì Santo; **good-looking** *adj* bello(-a); **good-natured** *adj* affabile; **goodness** *n* (*of person*) bontà; **for goodness sake!** per amor di Dio!; **goodness gracious!** santo cielo!, mamma mia!; **goods train** (*BRIT*) *n* treno *m* merci *inv*; **goodwill** *n* amicizia, benevolenza

goose [gu:s] (*pl* **geese**) *n* oca

gooseberry ['guzbərɪ] *n* uva spina; **to play ~** (*BRIT*) tenere la candela

goose bumps, goose pimples *npl* pelle f d'oca

gorge [gɔ:dʒ] *n* gola ▷ *vt* **to ~ o.s. (on)** ingozzarsi (di)

gorgeous ['gɔ:dʒəs] *adj* magnifico(-a)

gorilla [gə'rɪlə] *n* gorilla *m inv*

gosh (*inf*) [gɔʃ] *excl* perdinci!

gospel ['gɔspl] *n* vangelo

gossip ['gɔsɪp] *n* chiacchiere *fpl*; pettegolezzi *mpl*; (*person*) pettegolo(-a) ▷ *vi* chiacchierare; **gossip column** *n* cronaca mondana

got [gɔt] *pt, pp of* **get**

gotten ['gɔtn] (*US*) *pp of* **get**

gourmet ['guəmeɪ] *n* buongustaio(-a)

govern ['gʌvən] *vt* governare; **government** ['gʌvnmənt] *n* governo; **governor** ['gʌvənəʳ] *n* (*of state, bank*) governatore *m*; (*of school, hospital*) amministratore *m*; (*BRIT: of prison*) direttore(-trice)

gown [gaun] *n* vestito lungo; (*of teacher, BRIT: of judge*) toga

G.P. *n abbr* = **general practitioner**

grab [græb] *vt* afferrare, arraffare; (*property, power*) impadronirsi di ▷ *vi* **to ~ at** cercare di afferrare

grace [greɪs] *n* grazia ▷ *vt* onorare; **5 days' ~** dilazione *f* di 5 giorni; **graceful** *adj* elegante, aggraziato(-a); **gracious** ['greɪʃəs] *adj* grazioso(-a), misericordioso(-a)

grade [greɪd] *n* (*Comm*) qualità *f inv*; classe *f*; categoria; (*in hierarchy*) grado; (*Scol: mark*) voto; (*US: school class*) classe ▷ *vt* classificare; ordinare; graduare; **grade crossing** (*US*) *n* passaggio a livello; **grade**

school (us) n scuola elementare

gradient ['greɪdɪənt] n pendenza, inclinazione f

gradual ['grædjuəl] adj graduale; **gradually** adv man mano, a poco a poco

graduate [n 'grædjuɪt, vb 'grædjueɪt] n (of university) laureato(-a); (us: of high school) diplomato(-a) ▷ vi laurearsi; diplomarsi; **graduation** [-'eɪʃən] n (ceremony) consegna delle lauree (or dei diplomi)

graffiti [grə'fi:tɪ] npl graffiti mpl

graft [grɑ:ft] n (Agr, Med) innesto; (bribery) corruzione f; (BRIT: hard work): **it's hard ~** è un lavoraccio ▷ vt innestare

grain [greɪn] n grano; (of sand) granello; (of wood) venatura

gram [græm] n grammo

grammar ['græmə*] n grammatica; **grammar school** (BRIT) n ≈ liceo

gramme [græm] n = **gram**

gran (inf) [græn] n (BRIT) nonna

grand [grænd] adj grande, magnifico(-a); grandioso(-a); **grandad** (inf) n = **granddad**; **grandchild** (pl -**children**) n nipote m; **granddad** (inf) n nonno; **granddaughter** n nipote f; **grandfather** n nonno; **grandma** (inf) n nonna; **grandmother** n nonna; **grandpa** (inf) n = **granddad**; **grandparents** npl nonni mpl; **grand piano** n pianoforte m a coda; **Grand Prix** ['grã:'pri:] n (Aut) Gran Premio, Grand Prix m inv; **grandson** n nipote m

granite ['grænɪt] n granito

granny ['grænɪ] (inf) n nonna

grant [grɑ:nt] vt accordare; (a request) accogliere; (admit) ammettere, concedere ▷ n (Scol) borsa; (Admin) sussidio, sovvenzione f; **to take sth for ~ed** dare qc per scontato; **to take sb for ~ed** dare per scontata la presenza di qn

grape [greɪp] n chicco d'uva, acino

grapefruit ['greɪpfru:t] n pompelmo

graph [grɑ:f] n grafico; **graphic** adj grafico(-a); (vivid) vivido(-a); **graphics** n grafica ▷ npl illustrazioni fpl

grasp [grɑ:sp] vt afferrare ▷ n (grip) presa; (fig) potere m; comprensione f

grass [grɑ:s] n erba; **grasshopper** n cavalletta

grate [greɪt] n graticola (del focolare) ▷ vi cigolare, stridere ▷ vt (Culin) grattugiare

grateful ['greɪtful] adj grato(-a), riconoscente

grater ['greɪtə*] n grattugia

gratitude ['grætɪtju:d] n gratitudine f

grave [greɪv] n tomba ▷ adj grave, serio(-a)

gravel ['grævl] n ghiaia

gravestone ['greɪvstəun] n pietra tombale

graveyard ['greɪvjɑ:d] n cimitero

gravity ['grævɪtɪ] n (Physics) gravità; pesantezza; (seriousness) gravità, serietà

gravy ['greɪvɪ] n intingolo della carne; salsa

gray [greɪ] adj = **grey**

graze [greɪz] vi pascolare, pascere ▷ vt (touch lightly) sfiorare; (scrape) escoriare ▷ n (Med) escoriazione f

grease [gri:s] n (fat) grasso; (lubricant) lubrificante m ▷ vt ingrassare; lubrificare; **greasy** adj grasso(-a), untuoso(-a)

great [greɪt] adj grande; (inf) magnifico(-a), meraviglioso(-a); **Great Britain** n Gran Bretagna; **great-grandfather** n bisnonno; **great-grandmother** n bisnonna; **greatly** adv molto

Greece [gri:s] n Grecia

greed [gri:d] n (also: ~iness) avarizia; (for food) golosità, ghiottoneria; **greedy** adj avido(-a); goloso(-a), ghiotto(-a)

Greek [gri:k] adj greco(-a) ▷ n greco(-a); (Ling) greco

green [gri:n] adj verde; (inexperienced) inesperto(-a), ingenuo(-a) ▷ n verde m; (stretch of grass) prato; (on golf course) green m inv; **~s** npl (vegetables) verdura; **green card** (BRIT Aut) carta verde; (us Admin) permesso di soggiorno e di lavoro; **greengage** ['gri:ngeɪdʒ] n susina Regina Claudia; **greengrocer** (BRIT) n fruttivendolo(-a), erbivendolo(-a); **greenhouse** n serra; **greenhouse effect** n effetto serra

Greenland ['gri:nlənd] n Groenlandia

green salad n insalata verde

greet [gri:t] vt salutare; **greeting** n saluto; **greeting(s) card** n cartolina d'auguri

grew [gru:] pt of **grow**

grey [greɪ] (us **gray**) adj grigio(-a); **grey-haired** adj dai capelli grigi; **greyhound** n levriere m

grid [grɪd] n grata; (Elec) rete f; **gridlock** ['grɪdlɒk] n (traffic jam) paralisi f inv del traffico; **gridlocked** adj paralizzato(-a) dal traffico; (talks etc) in fase di stallo

grief [gri:f] n dolore m

grievance ['gri:vəns] n lagnanza

grieve [gri:v] vi addolorarsi; rattristarsi ▷ vt addolorare; **to ~ for sb** (dead person) piangere qn

grill [grɪl] n (on cooker) griglia; (also: **mixed ~**) grigliata mista ▷ vt (BRIT) cuocere ai ferri; (inf: question) interrogare senza sosta

grille [grɪl] n grata; (Aut) griglia

grim [grɪm] adj sinistro(-a), brutto(-a)

grime [graɪm] n sudiciume m

grin [grɪn] n sorriso smagliante ▷ vi fare un gran sorriso

grind [graɪnd] (pt, pp **ground**) vt macinare; (make sharp) arrotare ▷ n (work) sgobbata

grip [grɪp] n impugnatura; presa; (holdall) borsa da viaggio f ▷ vt (object) afferrare; (attention) catturare; **to come to ~s with** affrontare; cercare di risolvere; **gripping** ['grɪpɪŋ] adj avvincente

grit [grɪt] n ghiaia; (courage) fegato ▷ vt (road) coprire di sabbia; **to ~ one's teeth** stringere i denti

grits [grɪts] (US) npl macinato grosso (di avena etc)

groan [grəun] n gemito ▷ vi gemere

grocer ['grəusəʳ] n negoziante m di generi alimentari; **groceries** npl provviste fpl; **grocer's (shop)** n negozio di (generi) alimentari

grocery ['grəusəri] n (shop) (negozio di) alimentari

groin [grɔɪn] n inguine m

groom [gru:m] n palafreniere m; (also: **bride~**) sposo ▷ vt (horse) strigliare; (fig): **to ~ sb for** avviare qn a; **well-~ed** (person) curato(-a)

groove [gru:v] n scanalatura, solco

grope [grəup] vi **to ~ for** cercare a tastoni

gross [grəus] adj grossolano(-a); (Comm) lordo(-a); **grossly** adv (greatly) molto

grotesque [grəu'tɛsk] adj grottesco(-a)

ground [graund] pt, pp of **grind** ▷ n suolo, terra; (land) terreno; (Sport) campo; (reason: gen pl) ragione f; (US: also: **~ wire**) terra ▷ vt (plane) tenere a terra; (US Elec) mettere la presa a terra a; **~s** npl (of coffee etc) fondi mpl; (gardens etc) terreno, giardini mpl; **on/to the ~** per/a terra; **to gain/lose ~** guadagnare/perdere terreno; **ground floor** n pianterreno; **groundsheet** (BRIT) n telone m impermeabile; **groundwork** n preparazione f

group [gru:p] n gruppo ▷ vt (also: **~ together**) raggruppare ▷ vi (also: **~ together**) raggrupparsi

grouse [graus] n inv (bird) tetraone m ▷ vi (complain) brontolare

grovel ['grɔvl] vi (fig): **to ~ (before)** strisciare (di fronte a)

grow [grəu] (pt **grew**,, pp **grown**) vi crescere; (increase) aumentare; (develop) svilupparsi; (become): **to ~ rich/weak** arricchirsi/indebolirsi ▷ vt coltivare, far crescere; **grow on** vt fus **that painting is ~ing on me** quel quadro più lo guardo più mi piace; **grow up** vi farsi grande, crescere

growl [graul] vi ringhiare

grown [grəun] pp of **grow**; **grown-up** n

adulto(-a), grande m/f

growth [grəuθ] n crescita, sviluppo; (what has grown) crescita; (Med) escrescenza, tumore m

grub [grʌb] n larva; (inf: food) roba (da mangiare)

grubby ['grʌbɪ] adj sporco(-a)

grudge [grʌdʒ] n rancore m ▷ vt **to ~ sb sth** dare qc a qn di malavoglia; invidiare qc a qn; **to bear sb a ~ (for)** serbar rancore a qn (per)

gruelling ['gruəlɪŋ] (US **grueling**) adj estenuante

gruesome ['gru:səm] adj orribile

grumble ['grʌmbl] vi brontolare, lagnarsi

grumpy ['grʌmpɪ] adj scorbutico(-a)

grunt [grʌnt] vi grugnire

guarantee [gærən'ti:] n garanzia ▷ vt garantire

guard [gɑ:d] n guardia; (one man) guardia, sentinella; (BRIT Rail) capotreno; (on machine) schermo protettivo; (also: **fire~**) parafuoco ▷ vt fare la guardia a; (protect): **to ~ (against)** proteggere (da); **to be on one's ~** stare in guardia; **guardian** n custode m; (of minor) tutore(-trice)

guerrilla [gə'rɪlə] n guerrigliero

guess [gɛs] vi indovinare ▷ vt indovinare; (US) credere, pensare ▷ n **to take** or **have a ~** provare a indovinare

guest [gɛst] n ospite m/f; (in hotel) cliente m/f; **guest house** n pensione f; **guest room** n camera degli ospiti

guidance ['gaɪdəns] n guida, direzione f

guide [gaɪd] n (person, book etc) guida; (BRIT: also: **girl ~**) giovane esploratrice f ▷ vt guidare; **is there an English-speaking ~?** c'è una guida che parla inglese?; **guidebook** n guida; **do you have a guidebook in English?** avete una guida in inglese?; **guide dog** n cane m guida.inv; **guided tour** n visita guidata; **what time does the guided tour start?** a che ora comincia la visita guidata?; **guidelines** npl (fig) indicazioni fpl, linee fpl direttive

guild [gɪld] n arte f, corporazione f; associazione f

guilt [gɪlt] n colpevolezza; **guilty** adj colpevole

guinea pig ['gɪnɪ-] n cavia

guitar [gɪ'tɑ:ʳ] n chitarra, **guitarist** n chitarrista m/f

gulf [gʌlf] n golfo; (abyss) abisso

gull [gʌl] n gabbiano

gulp [gʌlp] vi deglutire; (from emotion) avere il nodo in gola ▷ vt (also: **~ down**) tracannare, inghiottire

gum [gʌm] n (Anat) gengiva; (glue) colla;

(*also:* **~drop**) caramella gommosa; (*also:* **chewing ~**) chewing-gum *m inv* ▷ *vt* **to ~ (together)** incollare

gun [gʌn] *n* fucile *m*; (*small*) pistola, rivoltella; (*rifle*) carabina; (*shotgun*) fucile da caccia; (*cannon*) cannone *m*; **gunfire** *n* spari *mpl*; **gunman** (*irreg*) *n* bandito armato; **gunpoint** *n* **at gunpoint** sotto minaccia di fucile; **gunpowder** *n* polvere *f* da sparo; **gunshot** *n* sparo

gush [gʌʃ] *vi* sgorgare; (*fig*) abbandonarsi ad effusioni

gust [gʌst] *n* (*of wind*) raffica; (*of smoke*) buffata

gut [gʌt] *n* intestino, budello; **~s** *npl* (*Anat*) interiora *fpl*; (*courage*) fegato

gutter ['gʌtəʳ] *n* (*of roof*) grondaia; (*in street*) cunetta

guy [gaɪ] *n* (*inf: man*) tipo, elemento; (*also:* **~rope**) cavo *or* corda di fissaggio; (*figure*) effigie di Guy Fawkes

Guy Fawkes Night [-'fɔːks-] *n* (BRIT) vedi nota nel riquadro

gym [dʒɪm] *n* (*also:* **~nasium**) palestra; (*also:* **~nastics**) ginnastica; **gymnasium** [dʒɪm'neɪzɪəm] *n* palestra; **gymnast** ['dʒɪmnæst] *n* ginnasta *m/f*; **gymnastics** [-'næstɪks] *n, npl* ginnastica; **gym shoes** *npl* scarpe *fpl* da ginnastica

gynaecologist [gaɪnɪ'kɔlədʒɪst] (us **gynecologist**) *n* ginecologo(-a)

gypsy ['dʒɪpsɪ] *n* = **gipsy**

haberdashery ['hæbə'dæʃərɪ] (BRIT) *n* merceria

habit ['hæbɪt] *n* abitudine *f*; (*costume*) abito; (*Rel*) tonaca

habitat ['hæbɪtæt] *n* habitat *m inv*

hack [hæk] *vt* tagliare, fare a pezzi ▷ *n* (*pej: writer*) scribacchino(-a); **hacker** ['hækəʳ] *n* (*Comput*) pirata *m* informatico

had [hæd] *pt, pp of* **have**

haddock ['hædək] (*pl* **haddock** *or* **haddocks**) *n* eglefino

hadn't ['hædnt] = **had not**

haemorrhage ['hɛmərɪdʒ] (us **hemorrhage**) *n* emorragia

haemorrhoids ['hɛmərɔɪdz] (us **hemorrhoids**) *npl* emorroidi *fpl*

haggle ['hægl] *vi* mercanteggiare

Hague [heɪg] *n* **The ~** L'Aia

hail [heɪl] *n* grandine *f*; (*of criticism etc*) pioggia ▷ *vt* (*call*) chiamare; (*flag down: taxi*) fermare; (*greet*) salutare ▷ *vi* grandinare; **hailstone** *n* chicco di grandine

hair [hɛəʳ] *n* capelli *mpl*; (*single hair: on head*) capello; (*: on body*) pelo; **to do one's ~** pettinarsi; **hairband** ['hɛə bænd] *n* (*elastic*) fascia per i capelli; (*rigid*) cerchietto; **hairbrush** *n* spazzola per capelli; **haircut** *n* taglio di capelli; **hairdo** ['hɛəduː] *n* acconciatura, pettinatura;

hairdresser n parrucchiere(-a);
hairdresser's n parrucchiere(-a); **hair
dryer** n asciugacapelli m inv; **hair gel** n
gel m inv per capelli; **hair spray** n lacca
per capelli; **hairstyle** n pettinatura,
acconciatura; **hairy** adj irsuto(-a),
peloso(-a); (inf: frightening) spaventoso(-a)

hake [heɪk] (pl **hake** or **hakes**) n nasello

half [hɑːf] (pl **halves**) n mezzo, metà
f inv ▷ adj mezzo(-a) ▷ adv a mezzo, a
metà; **~ an hour** mezz'ora; **~ a dozen**
mezza dozzina; **~ a pound** mezza libbra;
two and a ~ due e mezzo; **a week and
a ~** una settimana e mezza; **~ (of it)** la
metà; **~ (of)** la metà di; **to cut sth in ~**
tagliare qc in due; **~ asleep** mezzo(-a)
addormentato(-a); **half board** (BRIT)
n mezza pensione; **half-brother** n
fratellastro; **half day** n mezza giornata;
half fare n tariffa a metà prezzo; **half-
hearted** adj tiepido(-a); **half-hour** n
mezz'ora; **half-price** adj, adv a metà
prezzo; **half term** (BRIT) n (Scol) vacanza
a or di metà trimestre; **half-time** n (Sport)
intervallo; **halfway** adv a metà strada

hall [hɔːl] n sala, salone m; (entrance way)
entrata

hallmark ['hɔːlmɑːk] n marchio di
garanzia; (fig) caratteristica

hallo [hə'ləu] excl = **hello**

hall of residence (BRIT) n casa dello
studente

Halloween [hæləu'iːn] n vigilia
d'Ognissanti

● **HALLOWEEN**

Negli Stati Uniti e in Gran Bretagna il
31 ottobre si festeggia **Halloween**, la
notte delle streghe e dei fantasmi. I
bambini, travestiti da fantasmi, streghe
o mostri, bussano alle porte e ricevono
dolci e piccoli doni

hallucination [həluːsɪ'neɪʃən] n
allucinazione f

hallway ['hɔːlweɪ] n corridoio; (entrance)
Ingresso

halo ['heɪləu] n (of saint etc) aureola

halt [hɔːlt] n fermata ▷ vt fermare ▷ vi
fermarsi

halve [hɑːv] vt (apple etc) dividere a metà;
(expense) ridurre di metà

halves [hɑːvz] npl of **half**

ham [hæm] n prosciutto

hamburger ['hæmbəːgəʳ] n hamburger
m inv

hamlet ['hæmlɪt] n paesetto

hammer ['hæməʳ] n martello ▷ vt

martellare ▷ vi **to ~ on** or **at the door**
picchiare alla porta

hammock ['hæmək] n amaca

hamper ['hæmpəʳ] vt impedire ▷ n cesta

hamster ['hæmstəʳ] n criceto

hamstring ['hæmstrɪŋ] n (Anat) tendine
m del ginocchio

hand [hænd] n mano f; (of clock) lancetta;
(handwriting) scrittura; (at cards) mano;
(: game) partita; (worker) operaio(-a) ▷ vt
dare, passare; **to give sb a ~** dare una
mano a qn; **at ~** a portata di mano; **in
~** a disposizione; (work) in corso; **on ~**
(person) disponibile; (services) pronto(-a)
a intervenire; **to ~** (information etc) a
portata di mano; **on the one ~ ..., on
the other ~** da un lato ..., dall'altro;
hand down vt passare giù; (tradition,
heirloom) tramandare; (US: sentence, verdict)
emettere; **hand in** vt consegnare; **hand
out** vt distribuire; **hand over** vt passare;
cedere; **handbag** n borsetta; **hand
baggage** n bagaglio a mano; **handbook**
n manuale m; **handbrake** n freno a mano;
handcuffs npl manette fpl; **handful** n
manciata, pugno

handicap ['hændɪkæp] n handicap m inv
▷ vt handicappare; **to be physically ~ped**
essere handicappato(-a); **to be mentally
~ped** essere un(a) handicappato(-a)
mentale

handkerchief ['hæŋkətʃɪf] n fazzoletto

handle ['hændl] n (of door etc) maniglia; (of
cup etc) ansa; (of knife etc) impugnatura; (of
saucepan) manico; (for winding) manovella
▷ vt toccare, maneggiare; (deal with)
occuparsi di; (treat: people) trattare; **"~
with care"** "fragile"; **to fly off the ~** (fig)
perdere le staffe, uscire dai gangheri;
handlebar(s) n(pl) manubrio

hand: hand luggage n bagagli mpl a
mano; **handmade** adj fatto(-a) a mano;
handout n (money, food) elemosina;
(leaflet) volantino; (at lecture) prospetto

handsome ['hænsəm] adj bello(-a); (profit,
fortune) considerevole

handwriting ['hændraɪtɪŋ] n scrittura

handy ['hændɪ] adj (person) bravo(-a);
(close at hand) a portata di mano;
(convenient) comodo(-a)

hang [hæŋ] (pt, pp **hung**) vt appendere;
(criminal: pt, pp **hanged**) impiccare ▷ vi
(painting) essere appeso(-a); (hair)
scendere; (drapery) cadere; **to get the
~ of sth** (inf) capire come qc funziona;
hang about or **around** vi bighellonare,
ciondolare; **hang down** vi ricadere;
hang on vi (wait) aspettare; **hang out**
vt (washing) stendere (fuori); (inf: live)

stare ▷ *vi* penzolare, pendere; **hang round** *vi* = **hang around**; **hang up** *vi* (*Tel*) riattaccare ▷ *vt* appendere

hanger ['hæŋə'] *n* gruccia

hang-gliding ['-glaɪdɪŋ] *n* volo col deltaplano

hangover ['hæŋəʊvə'] *n* (*after drinking*) postumi *mpl* di sbornia

hankie ['hæŋkɪ] *n abbr* = **handkerchief**

happen ['hæpən] *vi* accadere, succedere; (*chance*): **to ~ to do sth** fare qc per caso; **what ~ed?** cos'è successo?; **as it ~s** guarda caso

happily ['hæpɪlɪ] *adv* felicemente; fortunatamente

happiness ['hæpɪnɪs] *n* felicità, contentezza

happy ['hæpɪ] *adj* felice, contento(-a); **~ with** (*arrangements etc*) soddisfatto(-a) di; **to be ~ to do** (*willing*) fare volentieri; **~ birthday!** buon compleanno!

harass ['hærəs] *vt* molestare; **harassment** *n* molestia

harbour ['hɑːbə'] (*US* **harbor**) *n* porto ▷ *vt* (*hope, fear*) nutrire; (*criminal*) dare rifugio a

hard [hɑːd] *adj* duro(-a) ▷ *adv* (*work*) sodo; (*think, try*) bene; **to look ~ at** guardare fissamente; esaminare attentamente; **no ~ feelings!** senza rancore!; **to be ~ of hearing** essere duro(-a) d'orecchio; **to be ~ done by** essere trattato(-a) ingiustamente; **hardback** *n* libro rilegato; **hardboard** *n* legno precompresso; **hard disk** *n* (*Comput*) disco rigido; **harden** *vt*, *vi* indurire

hardly ['hɑːdlɪ] *adv* (*scarcely*) appena; **it's ~ the case** non è proprio il caso; **~ anyone/anywhere** quasi nessuno/da nessuna parte; **~ ever** quasi mai

hard: **hardship** ['hɑːdʃɪp] *n* avversità *f inv*; privazioni *fpl*; **hard shoulder** (*BRIT*) *n* (*Aut*) corsia d'emergenza; **hard-up** (*inf*) *adj* al verde; **hardware** ['hɑːdwɛə'] *n* ferramenta *fpl*; (*Comput*) hardware *m*; (*Mil*) armamenti *mpl*; **hardware shop** (*US* **hardware store**) *n* (negozio di) ferramenta *fpl*; **hard-working** [-'wəːkɪŋ] *adj* lavoratore(-trice)

hardy ['hɑːdɪ] *adj* robusto(-a); (*plant*) resistente al gelo

hare [hɛə'] *n* lepre *f*

harm [hɑːm] *n* male *m*; (*wrong*) danno ▷ *vt* (*person*) fare male a; (*thing*) danneggiare; **out of ~'s way** al sicuro; **harmful** *adj* dannoso(-a); **harmless** *adj* innocuo(-a), inoffensivo(-a)

harmony ['hɑːmənɪ] *n* armonia

harness ['hɑːnɪs] *n* (*for horse*) bardatura, finimenti *mpl*; (*for child*) briglie *fpl*; (*safety harness*) imbracatura ▷ *vt* (*horse*) bardare; (*resources*) sfruttare

harp [hɑːp] *n* arpa ▷ *vi* **to ~ on about** insistere tediosamente su

harsh [hɑːʃ] *adj* (*life, winter*) duro(-a); (*judge, criticism*) severo(-a); (*sound*) rauco(-a); (*light*) violento(-a)

harvest ['hɑːvɪst] *n* raccolto; (*of grapes*) vendemmia ▷ *vt* fare il raccolto di, raccogliere; vendemmiare

has [hæz] *vb see* **have**

hasn't ['hæznt] = **has not**

hassle ['hæsl] (*inf*) *n* sacco di problemi

haste [heɪst] *n* fretta; precipitazione *f*; **hasten** ['heɪsn] *vt* affrettare ▷ *vi* **to hasten (to)** affrettarsi (a); **hastily** *adv* in fretta; precipitosamente; **hasty** *adj* affrettato(-a), precipitoso(-a)

hat [hæt] *n* cappello

hatch [hætʃ] *n* (*Naut: also:* **~way**) boccaporto; (*also:* **service ~**) portello di servizio ▷ *vi* (*bird*) uscire dal guscio; (*egg*) schiudersi

hatchback ['hætʃbæk] *n* (*Aut*) tre (*or* cinque) porte *f inv*

hate [heɪt] *vt* odiare, detestare ▷ *n* odio; **hatred** ['heɪtrɪd] *n* odio

haul [hɔːl] *vt* trascinare, tirare ▷ *n* (*of fish*) pescata; (*of stolen goods etc*) bottino

haunt [hɔːnt] *vt* (*fear*) pervadere; (*person*) frequentare ▷ *n* rifugio; **this house is ~ed** questa casa è abitata da un fantasma; **haunted** *adj* (*castle etc*) abitato(-a) dai fantasmi *or* dagli spiriti; (*look*) ossessionato(-a), tormentato(-a)

⭕ **KEYWORD**

have [hæv] (*pt, pp* **had**) *aux vb* **1** (*gen*) avere; essere; **to have arrived/gone** essere arrivato(-a)/andato(-a); **to have eaten/slept** avere mangiato/dormito; **he has been kind/promoted** è stato gentile/promosso; **having finished** *or* **when he had finished, he left** dopo aver finito, se n'è andato

2 (*in tag questions*): **you've done it, haven't you?** l'ha fatto, (non è) vero?; **he hasn't done it, has he?** non l'ha fatto, vero?

3 (*in short answers and questions*): **you've made a mistake — no I haven't/so I have** ha fatto un errore — ma no, niente affatto/sì, è vero; **we haven't paid — yes we have!** non abbiamo pagato — ma sì che abbiamo pagato!; **I've been there before, have you?** ci sono già stato, e lei? ▷ *modal aux vb* (*be obliged*): **to have (got) to do sth** dover fare qc; **I haven't got**

or **I don't have to wear glasses** non ho bisogno di portare gli occhiali
▷ *vt* **1** (*possess, obtain*) avere; **he has (got) blue eyes/dark hair** ha gli occhi azzurri/i capelli scuri; **do you have** *or* **have you got a car/phone?** ha la macchina/il telefono?; **may I have your address?** potrebbe darmi il suo indirizzo?; **you can have it for £5** te lo lascio per 5 sterline
2 (+ *noun: take, hold etc*): **to have breakfast/a swim/a bath** fare colazione/una nuotata/un bagno; **to have lunch** pranzare; **to have dinner** cenare; **to have a drink** bere qualcosa; **to have a cigarette** fumare una sigaretta
3: **to have sth done** far fare qc; **to have one's hair cut** farsi tagliare i capelli; **to have sb do sth** far fare qc a qn
4 (*experience, suffer*) avere; **to have a cold/flu** avere il raffreddore/l'influenza; **she had her bag stolen** le hanno rubato la borsa
5 (*inf: dupe*): **you've been had!** ci sei cascato!
have out *vt* **to have it out with sb** (*settle a problem etc*) mettere le cose in chiaro con qn

haven ['heɪvn] *n* porto; (*fig*) rifugio
haven't ['hævnt] = **have not**
havoc ['hævək] *n* caos *m*
Hawaii [hə'waɪ:] *n* le Hawaii
hawk [hɔ:k] *n* falco
hawthorn ['hɔ:θɔ:n] *n* biancospino
hay [heɪ] *n* fieno; **hay fever** *n* febbre *f* da fieno; **haystack** *n* pagliaio
hazard ['hæzəd] *n* azzardo, ventura; pericolo, rischio ▷ *vt* (*guess etc*) azzardare; **hazardous** *adj* pericoloso(-a); **hazard warning lights** *npl* (*Aut*) luci *fpl* di emergenza
haze [heɪz] *n* foschia
hazel ['heɪzl] *n* (*tree*) nocciolo ▷ *adj* (*eyes*) (*color*) nocciola *inv*; **hazelnut** ['heɪzlnʌt] *n* nocciola
hazy ['heɪzɪ] *adj* fosco(-a); (*idea*) vago(-a)
he [hi:] *pron* lui, egli; **it is he who ...** è lui che ...
head [hɛd] *n* testa; (*leader*) capo; (*of school*) preside *m/f* ▷ *vt* (*list*) essere in testa a; (*group*) essere a capo di; **~s or tails** testa (o croce), pari (o dispari); **~ first** a capofitto, di testa; **~ over heels in love** pazzamente innamorato(-a); **to ~ the ball** colpire una palla di testa; **head for** *vt fus* dirigersi verso; **head off** *vt* (*threat, danger*) sventare; **headache** *n* mal *m* di testa; **heading** *n* titolo; intestazione *f*; **headlamp** (BRIT) *n*

= **headlight**; **headlight** *n* fanale *m*; **headline** *n* titolo; **head office** *n* sede *f* (centrale); **headphones** *npl* cuffia; **headquarters** *npl* ufficio centrale; (*Mil*) quartiere *m* generale; **headroom** *n* (*in car*) altezza dell'abitacolo; (*under bridge*) altezza limite; **headscarf** *n* foulard *m inv*; **headset** *n* = **headphones**; **headteacher** *n* (*of primary school*) direttore(-trice); (*of secondary school*) preside; **head waiter** *n* capocameriere *m*
heal [hi:l] *vt, vi* guarire
health [hɛlθ] *n* salute *f*; **health care** *n* assistenza sanitaria; **health centre** (BRIT) *n* poliambulatorio; **health food** *n* cibo macrobiotico; **Health Service** (BRIT) *n* **the Health Service** ≈ il Servizio Sanitario Statale; **healthy** *adj* (*person*) sano(-a), in buona salute; (*climate*) salubre; (*appetite, economy etc*) sano(-a)
heap [hi:p] *n* mucchio ▷ *vt* (*stones, sand*): **to ~ (up)** ammucchiare; (*plate, sink*): **to ~ sth with** riempire qc di; **~s of** (*inf*) un mucchio di
hear [hɪə^r] (*pt, pp* **heard**) *vt* sentire; (*news*) ascoltare ▷ *vi* sentire; **to ~ about** avere notizie di; sentire parlare di; **to ~ from sb** ricevere notizie da qn
hearing ['hɪərɪŋ] *n* (*sense*) udito; (*of witnesses*) audizione *f*; (*of a case*) udienza; **hearing aid** *n* apparecchio acustico
hearse [hə:s] *n* carro funebre
heart [hɑ:t] *n* cuore *m*; **~s** *npl* (*Cards*) cuori *mpl*; **to lose ~** scoraggiarsi; **to take ~** farsi coraggio; **at ~** in fondo; **by ~** (*learn, know*) a memoria; **heart attack** *n* attacco di cuore; **heartbeat** *n* battito del cuore; **heartbroken** *adj* **to be heartbroken** avere il cuore spezzato; **heartburn** *n* bruciore *m* di stomaco; **heart disease** *n* malattia di cuore
hearth [hɑ:θ] *n* focolare *m*
heartless ['hɑ:tlɪs] *adj* senza cuore
hearty ['hɑ:tɪ] *adj* caloroso(-a); robusto(-a), sano(-a); vigoroso(-a)
heat [hi:t] *n* calore *m*; (*fig*) ardore *m*; fuoco; (*Sport: also*: **qualifying ~**) prova eliminatoria ▷ *vt* scaldare; **heat up** *vi* (*liquids*) scaldarsi; (*room*) riscaldarsi ▷ *vt* riscaldare; **heated** *adj* riscaldato(-a); (*argument*) acceso(-a); **heater** *n* radiatore *m*; (*stove*) stufa
heather ['hɛðə^r] *n* erica
heating ['hi:tɪŋ] *n* riscaldamento
heatwave ['hi:tweɪv] *n* ondata di caldo
heaven ['hɛvn] *n* paradiso, cielo; **heavenly** *adj* divino(-a), celeste
heavily ['hɛvɪlɪ] *adv* pesantemente; (*drink, smoke*) molto

heavy ['hɛvɪ] *adj* pesante; (*sea*) grosso(-a); (*rain, blow*) forte; (*weather*) afoso(-a); (*drinker, smoker*) gran (*before noun*); **it's too ~** è troppo pesante

Hebrew ['hi:bru:] *adj* ebreo(-a) ▷ *n* (*Ling*) ebraico

hectare ['hɛktɑːʳ] *n* (BRIT) ettaro

hectic ['hɛktɪk] *adj* movimentato(-a)

he'd [hi:d] = **he would**; **he had**

hedge [hɛdʒ] *n* siepe *f* ▷ *vi* essere elusivo(-a); **to ~ one's bets** (*fig*) coprirsi dai rischi

hedgehog ['hɛdʒhɔg] *n* riccio

heed [hi:d] *vt* (*also:* **take ~ of**) badare a, far conto di

heel [hi:l] *n* (*Anat*) calcagno; (*of shoe*) tacco ▷ *vt* (*shoe*) rifare i tacchi a

hefty ['hɛftɪ] *adj* (*person*) robusto(-a); (*parcel*) pesante; (*profit*) grosso(-a)

height [haɪt] *n* altezza; (*high ground*) altura; (*fig: of glory*) apice *m*; (*: of stupidity*) colmo; **heighten** *vt* (*fig*) accrescere

heir [ɛəʳ] *n* erede *m*; **heiress** *n* erede *f*

held [hɛld] *pt, pp of* **hold**

helicopter ['hɛlɪkɔptəʳ] *n* elicottero

hell [hɛl] *n* inferno; **~!** (*inf*) porca miseria!, accidenti!

he'll [hi:l] = **he will**; **he shall**

hello [hə'ləu] *excl* buon giorno!; ciao! (*to sb one addresses as "tu"*); (*surprise*) ma guarda!

helmet ['hɛlmɪt] *n* casco

help [hɛlp] *n* aiuto; (*charwoman*) donna di servizio ▷ *vt* aiutare; **~!** aiuto!; **can you ~ me?** può aiutarmi?; **~ yourself (to bread)** si serva (del pane); **he can't ~ it** non ci può far niente; **help out** *vi* aiutare ▷ *vt* **to ~ sb out** aiutare qn; **helper** *n* aiutante *m/f*, assistente *m/f*; **helpful** *adj* di grande aiuto; (*useful*) utile; **helping** *n* porzione *f*; **helpless** *adj* impotente; debole; **helpline** *n* ≈ telefono amico; (*Comm*) servizio *m* informazioni *inv* (*a pagamento*)

hem [hɛm] *n* orlo ▷ *vt* fare l'orlo a

hemisphere ['hɛmɪsfɪəʳ] *n* emisfero

hemorrhage ['hɛmərɪdʒ] (US) *n* = **haemorrhage**

hemorrhoids ['hɛmərɔɪdz] (US) *npl* = **haemorrhoids**

hen [hɛn] *n* gallina; (*female bird*) femmina

hence [hɛns] *adv* (*therefore*) dunque; **2 years ~** di qui a 2 anni

hen night *n* (*inf*) addio al nubilato

hepatitis [hɛpə'taɪtɪs] *n* epatite *f*

her [həːʳ] *pron* (*direct*) la, l' + *vowel*; (*indirect*) le; (*stressed, after prep*) lei ▷ *adj* il (la) suo(-a), i (le) suoi (sue); *see also* **me**; **my**

herb [həːb] *n* erba; **herbal** *adj* di erbe; **herbal tea** *n* tisana

herd [həːd] *n* mandria

here [hɪəʳ] *adv* qui, qua ▷ *excl* ehi!; **~!** (*at roll call*) presente!; **~ is/are** ecco; **~ he/she is** eccolo/eccola

hereditary [hɪ'rɛdɪtrɪ] *adj* ereditario(-a)

heritage ['hɛrɪtɪdʒ] *n* eredità; (*fig*) retaggio

hernia ['həːnɪə] *n* ernia

hero ['hɪərəu] (*pl* **heroes**) *n* eroe *m*; **heroic** [hɪ'rəuɪk] *adj* eroico(-a)

heroin ['hɛrəuɪn] *n* eroina

heroine ['hɛrəuɪn] *n* eroina

heron ['hɛrən] *n* airone *m*

herring ['hɛrɪŋ] *n* aringa

hers [həːz] *pron* il (la) suo(-a), i (le) suoi (sue); *see also* **mine¹**

herself [həː'sɛlf] *pron* (*reflexive*) si; (*emphatic*) lei stessa; (*after prep*) se stessa, sé; *see also* **oneself**

he's [hi:z] = **he is**; **he has**

hesitant ['hɛzɪtənt] *adj* esitante, indeciso(-a)

hesitate ['hɛzɪteɪt] *vi* **to ~ (about/to do)** esitare (su/a fare); **hesitation** [-'teɪʃən] *n* esitazione *f*

heterosexual ['hɛtərəu'sɛksjuəl] *adj, n* eterosessuale *m/f*

hexagon ['hɛksəgən] *n* esagono

hey [heɪ] *excl* ehi!

heyday ['heɪdeɪ] *n* **the ~ of** i bei giorni di, l'età d'oro di

HGV *n abbr* = **heavy goods vehicle**

hi [haɪ] *excl* ciao!

hibernate ['haɪbəneɪt] *vi* ibernare

hiccough ['hɪkʌp] *vi* singhiozzare

hiccup ['hɪkʌp] = **hiccough**

hid [hɪd] *pt of* **hide**

hidden ['hɪdn] *pp of* **hide**

hide [haɪd] (*pt* **hid**, *pp* **hidden**) *n* (*skin*) pelle *f* ▷ *vt* **to ~ sth** nascondere qc (a qn) ▷ *vi* **to ~ (from sb)** nascondersi (da qn)

hideous ['hɪdɪəs] *adj* laido(-a); orribile

hiding ['haɪdɪŋ] *n* (*beating*) bastonata; **to be in ~** (*concealed*) tenersi nascosto(-a)

hi-fi ['haɪfaɪ] *n* stereo ▷ *adj* ad alta fedeltà, hi-fi *inv*

high [haɪ] *adj* alto(-a); (*speed, respect, number*) grande; (*wind*) forte; (*voice*) acuto(-a) ▷ *adv* alto, in alto; **20m ~** alto(-a) 20m; **highchair** *n* seggiolone *m*; **high-class** *adj* (*neighbourhood*) elegante; (*hotel*) di prim'ordine; (*person*) di gran classe; (*food*) raffinato(-a); **higher education** *n* studi *mpl* superiori; **high heels** *npl* (*heels*) tacchi *mpl* alti; (*shoes*) scarpe *fpl* con i tacchi alti; **high jump** *n* (*Sport*) salto in alto; **highlands** *npl* zona montuosa; **the Highlands** le Highlands scozzesi; **highlight** *n* (*fig: of event*) momento culminante; (*in hair*) colpo di sole ▷ *vt* mettere in evidenza; **highlights** npl (in hair) colpi mpl di sole; **highlighter** n (pen) evidenziatore m; **highly** adv molto; **to speak highly of** parlare molto bene di; **highness** n **Her Highness** Sua Altezza; **high-rise** n (also: **high-rise block, high-rise building**) palazzone m; **high school** n scuola secondaria; (US) istituto superiore d'istruzione; **high season** (BRIT) n alta stagione; **high street** (BRIT) n strada principale; **high-tech** (inf) adj high-tech inv; **highway** ['haɪweɪ] n strada maestra; **Highway Code** (BRIT) n codice m della strada

hijack ['haɪdʒæk] vt dirottare; **hijacker** n dirottatore(-trice)

hike [haɪk] vi fare un'escursione a piedi ▷ n escursione f a piedi; **hiker** n escursionista m/f; **hiking** n escursioni fpl a piedi

hilarious [hɪ'lɛərɪəs] adj (behaviour, event) spassosissimo(-a)

hill [hɪl] n collina, colle m; (fairly high) montagna; (on road) salita; **hillside** n fianco della collina; **hill walking** n escursioni fpl in collina; **hilly** adj collinoso(-a); montagnoso(-a)

him [hɪm] pron (direct) lo, l' + vowel; (indirect) gli; (stressed, after prep) lui; see also **me**; **himself** pron (reflexive) si; (emphatic) lui stesso; (after prep) se stesso, sé; see also **oneself**

hind [haɪnd] adj posteriore ▷ n cerva

hinder ['hɪndə'] vt ostacolare

hindsight ['haɪndsaɪt] n **with ~** con il senno di poi

Hindu ['hɪnduː] n indù m/f inv; **Hinduism** n (Rel) induismo

hinge [hɪndʒ] n cardine m ▷ vi (fig): **to ~ on** dipendere da

hint [hɪnt] n (suggestion) allusione f; (advice) consiglio; (sign) accenno ▷ vt **to ~ that** lasciar capire che ▷ vi **to ~ at** alludere a

hip [hɪp] n anca, fianco

hippie ['hɪpɪ] n hippy m/f inv

hippo ['hɪpəʊ] (pl **hippos**) n ippopotamo

hippopotamus [hɪpə'pɒtəməs] (pl **hippopotamuses** or **hippopotami**) n ippopotamo

hippy ['hɪpɪ] n = **hippie**

hire ['haɪə'] vt (BRIT: car, equipment) noleggiare; (worker) assumere, dare lavoro a ▷ n nolo, noleggio; **for ~** da nolo; (taxi) libero(-a); **I'd like to ~ a car** vorrei noleggiare una macchina; **hire(d) car** (BRIT) n macchina a nolo; **hire purchase** (BRIT) n acquisto (or vendita) rateale

his [hɪz] adj, pron il (la) suo (sua), i (le) suoi (sue); see also **my**; **mine¹**

Hispanic [hɪs'pænɪk] adj ispanico(-a)

hiss [hɪs] vi fischiare; (cat, snake) sibilare

historian [hɪ'stɔːrɪən] n storico(-a)

historic(al) [hɪ'stɒrɪk(l)] adj storico(-a)

history ['hɪstərɪ] n storia

hit [hɪt] (pt, pp **hit**) vt colpire, picchiare; (knock against) battere; (reach: target) raggiungere; (collide with: car) urtare contro; (fig: affect) colpire; (find: problem etc) incontrare ▷ n colpo; (success, song) successo; **to ~ it off with sb** andare molto d'accordo con qn; **hit back** vi **to ~ back at sb** restituire il colpo a qn

hitch [hɪtʃ] vt (fasten) attaccare; (also: **~ up**) tirare su ▷ n (difficulty) intoppo, difficoltà f inv; **to ~ a lift** fare l'autostop; **hitch-hike** vi fare l'autostop; **hitch-hiker** n autostoppista m/f; **hitch-hiking** n autostop m

hi-tech ['haɪ'tɛk] adj high-tech inv

hitman ['hɪtmæn] (irreg) n (inf) sicario

HIV abbr **~-negative/-positive** adj sieronegativo(-a)/sieropositivo(-a)

hive [haɪv] n alveare m

hoard [hɔːd] n (of food) provviste fpl; (of money) gruzzolo ▷ vt ammassare

hoarse [hɔːs] adj rauco(-a)

hoax [həʊks] n scherzo; falso allarme

hob [hɒb] n piastra (con fornelli)

hobble ['hɒbl] vi zoppicare

hobby ['hɒbɪ] n hobby m inv, passatempo

hobo ['həʊbəʊ] (US) n vagabondo

hockey ['hɒkɪ] n hockey m; **hockey stick** n bastone m da hockey

hog [hɒg] n maiale m ▷ vt (fig) arraffare; **to go the whole ~** farlo fino in fondo

Hogmanay [hɒgmə'neɪ] n (Scottish) ≈ San Silvestro

hoist [hɔɪst] n paranco ▷ vt issare

hold [həʊld] (pt, pp **held**) vt tenere; (contain) contenere; (keep back) trattenere; (believe) mantenere; considerare; (possess) avere, possedere; detenere ▷ vi (withstand pressure) tenere; (be valid) essere valido(-a) ▷ n presa; (control): **to have a ~ over** avere controllo su; (Naut) stiva; **~ the line!** (Tel) resti in linea!; **to ~ one's own** (fig) difendersi bene; **to catch** or **get (a) ~ of** afferrare; **hold back** vt trattenere; (secret) tenere celato(-a); **hold on** vi tener fermo; (wait) aspettare; **~ on!** (Tel) resti in linea!; **hold out** vt offrire ▷ vi (resist) resistere; **hold up** vt (raise) alzare; (support) sostenere; (delay) ritardare; (rob) assaltare; **holdall** (BRIT) n borsone m; **holder** n (container) contenitore m; (of ticket, title) possessore/posseditrice; (of office etc) incaricato(-a); (of record) detentore(-trice)

hole [həʊl] n buco, buca

holiday ['hɒlədɪ] n vacanza; (day off) giorno di vacanza; (public) giorno festivo; **on ~** in vacanza; **I'm on ~ here** sono qui in vacanza; **holiday camp** (BRIT) n (also: **holiday centre**) ≈ villaggio (di vacanze); **holiday job** n (BRIT) ≈ lavoro estivo; **holiday-maker** (BRIT) n villeggiante m/f; **holiday resort** n luogo di villeggiatura

Holland ['hɒlənd] n Olanda

hollow ['hɒləu] adj cavo(-a); (container, claim) vuoto(-a); (laugh, sound) cupo(-a) ▷ n cavità f inv; (in land) valletta, depressione f ▷ vt **to ~ out** scavare

holly ['hɒlɪ] n agrifoglio

Hollywood ['hɒlɪwud] n Hollywood f

holocaust ['hɒləkɔ:st] n olocausto

holy ['həulɪ] adj santo(-a); (bread, ground) benedetto(-a), consacrato(-a)

home [həum] n casa; (country) patria; (institution) casa, ricovero ▷ cpd familiare; (cooking etc) casalingo(-a); (Econ, Pol) nazionale, interno(-a); (Sport) di casa ▷ adv a casa; in patria; (right in: nail etc) fino in fondo; **at ~** a casa, (in situation) a proprio agio; **to go** or **come ~** tornare a casa (or in patria); **make yourself at ~** si metta a suo agio; **home address** n indirizzo di casa; **homeland** n patria; **homeless** adj senza tetto; spatriato(-a); **homely** adj semplice, alla buona; accogliente; **home-made** adj casalingo(-a); **home match** n partita in casa; **Home Office** (BRIT) n ministero degli Interni; **home owner** n proprietario(-a) di casa; **home page** n (Comput) home page f inv; **Home Secretary** (BRIT) n ministro degli Interni; **homesick** adj **to be homesick** avere la nostalgia; **home town** n città f inv natale; **homework** n compiti mpl (per casa)

homicide ['hɒmɪsaɪd] (US) n omicidio

homoeopathic [həumɪə'pæθɪk] (US **homeopathic**) adj omeopatico(-a)

homoeopathy [həumɪ'ɔpəθɪ] (US **homeopathy**) n omeopatia

homosexual [hɒməu'sɛksjuəl] adj, n omosessuale m/f

honest ['ɒnɪst] adj onesto(-a); sincero(-a); **honestly** adv onestamente; sinceramente; **honesty** n onestà

honey ['hʌnɪ] n miele m; **honeymoon** n luna di miele, viaggio di nozze; **we're on honeymoon** siamo in luna di miele; **honeysuckle** n (Bot) caprifoglio

Hong Kong ['hɒŋ'kɒŋ] n Hong Kong f

honorary ['ɒnərərɪ] adj onorario(-a); (duty, title) onorifico(-a)

honour ['ɒnə*] (US **honor**) vt onorare ▷ n onore m; **honourable** (US **honorable**) adj onorevole; **honours degree** n (Scol) laurea specializzata

hood [hud] n cappuccio; (on cooker) cappa; (BRIT Aut) capote f; (US Aut) cofano

hoof [hu:f] (pl **hooves**) n zoccolo

hook [huk] n gancio; (for fishing) amo ▷ vt uncinare; (dress) agganciare

hooligan ['hu:lɪgən] n giovinastro, teppista m

hoop [hu:p] n cerchio

hooray [hu:'reɪ] excl = **hurray**

hoot [hu:t] vi (Aut) suonare il clacson; (siren) ululare; (owl) gufare

Hoover® ['hu:və*] (BRIT) n aspirapolvere m inv ▷ vt **hoover** pulire con l'aspirapolvere

hooves [hu:vz] npl of **hoof**

hop [hɒp] vi saltellare, saltare; (on one foot) saltare su una gamba

hope [həup] vt **to ~ that/to do** sperare che/di fare ▷ vi sperare ▷ n speranza; **I ~ so/not** spero di sì/no; **hopeful** adj (person) pieno(-a) di speranza; (situation) promettente; **hopefully** adv con speranza; **hopefully he will recover** speriamo che si riprenda; **hopeless** adj senza speranza, disperato(-a); (useless) inutile

hops [hɒps] npl luppoli mpl

horizon [hə'raɪzn] n orizzonte m; **horizontal** [hɒrɪ'zɒntl] adj orizzontale

hormone ['hɔ:məun] n ormone m

horn [hɔ:n] n (Zool, Mus) corno; (Aut) clacson m inv

horoscope ['hɒrəskəup] n oroscopo

horrendous [hə'rɛndəs] adj orrendo(-a)

horrible ['hɒrɪbl] adj orribile, tremendo(-a)

horrid ['hɒrɪd] adj orrido(-a); (person) odioso(-a)

horrific [hɒ'rɪfɪk] adj (accident) spaventoso(-a); (film) orripilante

horrifying ['hɒrɪfaɪɪŋ] adj terrificante

horror ['hɒrə*] n orrore m; **horror film** n film m inv dell'orrore

hors d'œuvre [ɔ:'də:vrə] n antipasto

horse [hɔ:s] n cavallo; **horseback: on horseback** adj, adv a cavallo; **horse chestnut** n ippocastano; **horsepower** n cavallo (vapore); **horse-racing** n ippica; **horseradish** n rafano; **horse riding** n (BRIT) equitazione f

hose [həuz] n (also: **~pipe**) tubo; (also: **garden ~**) tubo per annaffiare

hospital ['hɒspɪtl] n ospedale m; **where's the nearest ~?** dov'è l'ospedale più vicino?

hospitality [hɒspɪ'tælɪtɪ] n ospitalità

host [həust] n ospite m; (Rel) ostia; (large number): **a ~ of** una schiera di

hostage ['hɒstɪdʒ] n ostaggio(-a)

hostel ['hɒstl] n ostello; (also: **youth ~**) ostello della gioventù

hostess ['həustɪs] n ospite f; (BRIT: air hostess) hostess f inv

hostile ['hɒstaɪl] adj ostile

hostility [hɒ'stɪlɪtɪ] n ostilità f inv

hot [hɒt] adj caldo(-a); (as opposed to only warm) molto caldo(-a); (spicy) piccante; (fig) accanito(-a); ardente; violento(-a), focoso(-a); **to be ~** (person) aver caldo; (object) essere caldo(-a); (weather) far caldo; **hot dog** n hot dog m inv

hotel [həu'tɛl] n albergo

hot-water bottle [hɒt'wɔːtə-] n borsa dell'acqua calda

hound [haund] vt perseguitare ▷ n segugio

hour ['auə^r] n ora; **hourly** adj all'ora

house [n haus, pl 'hauzɪz] [vb hauz] n (also: firm) casa; (Pol) camera; (Theatre) sala; pubblico; spettacolo; (dynasty) casata ▷ vt (person) ospitare, alloggiare; **on the ~** (fig) offerto(-a) dalla casa; **household** n famiglia; casa; **householder** n padrone(-a) di casa; (head of house) capofamiglia m/f; **housekeeper** n governante f; **housekeeping** n (work) governo della casa; (money) soldi mpl per le spese di casa; **housewife** (irreg) n massaia, casalinga; **house wine** n vino della casa; **housework** n faccende fpl domestiche

housing ['hauzɪŋ] n alloggio; **housing development** (BRIT), **housing estate** n zona residenziale con case popolari e/o private

hover ['hɒvə^r] vi (bird) librarsi; **hovercraft** n hovercraft m inv

how [hau] adv come; **~ are you?** come sta?; **~ do you do?** piacere!; **~ far is it to the river?** quanto è lontano il fiume?; **~ long have you been here?** da quando è qui?; **~ lovely!/awful!** che bello!/orrore!; **~ many?** quanti(-e)?; **~ much?** quanto(-a)?; **~ much milk?** quanto latte?; **~ many people?** quante persone?; **~ old are you?** quanti anni ha?

however [hau'ɛvə^r] adv in qualsiasi modo or maniera che; (+ adjective) per quanto + sub; (in questions) come ▷ conj comunque, però

howl [haul] vi ululare; (baby, person) urlare

H.P. abbr = **hire purchase**; **horsepower**

h.p. n abbr = H.P

HQ n, abbr = **headquarters**

hr(s) abbr (= hour(s)) h

HTML abbr (= hypertext markup language) HTML m inv

hubcap ['hʌbkæp] n coprimozzo

huddle ['hʌdl] vi **to ~ together** rannicchiarsi l'uno contro l'altro

huff [hʌf] n **in a ~** stizzito(-a)

hug [hʌg] vt abbracciare; (shore, kerb) stringere

huge [hjuːdʒ] adj enorme, immenso(-a)

hull [hʌl] n (of ship) scafo

hum [hʌm] vt (tune) canticchiare ▷ vi canticchiare; (insect, plane, tool) ronzare

human ['hjuːmən] (irreg) adj umano(-a) ▷ n essere m umano

humane [hjuː'meɪn] adj umanitario(-a)

humanitarian [hjuːmænɪ'tɛərɪən] adj umanitario(-a)

humanity [hjuː'mænɪtɪ] n umanità

human rights npl diritti mpl dell'uomo

humble ['hʌmbl] adj umile, modesto(-a) ▷ vt umiliare

humid ['hjuːmɪd] adj umido(-a); **humidity** [hjuː'mɪdɪtɪ] n umidità

humiliate [hjuː'mɪlɪeɪt] vt umiliare; **humiliating** adj umiliante; **humiliation** [-'eɪʃən] n umiliazione f

hummus ['hʊməs] n purè di ceci

humorous ['hjuːmərəs] adj umoristico(-a); (person) buffo(-a)

humour ['hjuːmə^r] (US humor) n umore m ▷ vt accontentare

hump [hʌmp] n gobba

hunch [hʌntʃ] n (premonition) intuizione f

hundred ['hʌndrəd] num cento; **~s of** centinaia fpl di; **hundredth** [-ɪdθ] num centesimo(-a)

hung [hʌŋ] pt, pp of **hang**

Hungarian [hʌŋ'gɛərɪən] adj ungherese ▷ n ungherese m/f; (Ling) ungherese m

Hungary ['hʌŋgərɪ] n Ungheria

hunger ['hʌŋgə^r] n fame f ▷ vi **to ~ for** desiderare ardentemente

hungry ['hʌŋgrɪ] adj affamato(-a); **to be ~** aver fame

hunt [hʌnt] vt (seek) cercare, (Sport) cacciare ▷ vi **to ~ (for)** andare a caccia (di) ▷ n caccia; **hunter** n cacciatore m; **hunting** n caccia

hurdle ['həːdl] n (Sport, fig) ostacolo

hurl [həːl] vt lanciare con violenza

hurrah [hu'rɑː] excl = **hurray**

hurray [hu'reɪ] excl urra!, evviva!

hurricane ['hʌrɪkən] n uragano

hurry ['hʌrɪ] n fretta ▷ vi (also: ~ up) affrettarsi ▷ vt (also: ~ up: person) affrettare; (work) far in fretta; **to be in a ~** aver fretta; **hurry up** vi sbrigarsi

hurt [həːt] (pt, pp hurt) vt (cause pain to) far male a; (injure, fig) ferire ▷ vi far male

husband ['hʌzbənd] n marito

hush [hʌʃ] n silenzio, calma ▷ vt zittire

husky ['hʌskɪ] adj roco(-a) ▷ n cane m eschimese

hut [hʌt] n rifugio; (shed) ripostiglio

hyacinth ['haɪəsɪnθ] n giacinto

hydrangea [haɪ'dreɪnʒə] n ortensia
hydrofoil ['haɪdrəufɔɪl] n aliscafo
hydrogen ['haɪdrədʒən] n idrogeno
hygiene ['haɪdʒi:n] n igiene f; **hygienic** [haɪ'dʒi:nɪk] adj igienico(-a)
hymn [hɪm] n inno; cantica
hype [haɪp] (inf) n campagna pubblicitaria
hyphen ['haɪfn] n trattino
hypnotize ['hɪpnətaɪz] vt ipnotizzare
hypocrite ['hɪpəkrɪt] n ipocrita m/f
hypocritical [hɪpə'krɪtɪkl] adj ipocrita
hypothesis [haɪ'pɔθɪsɪs] (pl **hypotheses**) n ipotesi f inv
hysterical [hɪ'stɛrɪkl] adj isterico(-a)
hysterics [hɪ'stɛrɪks] npl accesso di isteria; (laughter) attacco di riso

I [aɪ] pron io
ice [aɪs] n ghiaccio; (on road) gelo; (ice cream) gelato ▷ vt (cake) glassare ▷ vi (also: ~ **over**) ghiacciare; (also: ~ **up**) gelare; **iceberg** n iceberg m inv; **ice cream** n gelato; **ice cube** n cubetto di ghiaccio; **ice hockey** n hockey m su ghiaccio
Iceland ['aɪslənd] n Islanda; **Icelander** n islandese m/f; **Icelandic** [aɪs'lændɪk] adj islandese ▷ n (Ling) islandese m
ice: **ice lolly** (BRIT) n ghiacciolo; **ice rink** n pista di pattinaggio; **ice skating** n pattinaggio sul ghiaccio
icing ['aɪsɪŋ] n (Culin) glassa; **icing sugar** (BRIT) n zucchero a velo
icon ['aɪkɔn] n icona
icy ['aɪsɪ] adj ghiacciato(-a); (weather, temperature) gelido(-a)
I'd [aɪd] = **I would**; **I had**
ID card n = **identity card**
idea [aɪ'dɪə] n idea
ideal [aɪ'dɪəl] adj ideale ▷ n ideale m; **ideally** [aɪ'dɪəlɪ] adv perfettamente, assolutamente; **ideally the book should have ...** l'ideale sarebbe che il libro avesse ...
identical [aɪ'dɛntɪkl] adj identico(-a)
identification [aɪdɛntɪfɪ'keɪʃən] n identificazione f; (means of) ~ carta

d'identità

identify [aɪˈdɛntɪfaɪ] *vt* identificare

identity [aɪˈdɛntɪtɪ] *n* identità *f inv*;
identity card *n* carta d'identità

ideology [aɪdɪˈɔlədʒɪ] *n* ideologia

idiom [ˈɪdɪəm] *n* idioma *m*; (*phrase*)
espressione *f* idiomatica

idiot [ˈɪdɪət] *n* idiota *m/f*

idle [ˈaɪdl] *adj* inattivo(-a); (*lazy*) pigro(-a),
ozioso(-a); (*unemployed*) disoccupato(-a);
(*question, pleasures*) ozioso(-a) ▷ *vi* (*engine*)
girare al minimo

idol [ˈaɪdl] *n* idolo

idyllic [ɪˈdɪlɪk] *adj* idillico(-a)

i.e. *adv abbr* (= *that is*) cioè

if [ɪf] *conj* se; **if I were you ...** se fossi in te
..., io al tuo posto ...; **if so** se è così; **if not** se
no; **if only** se solo *or* soltanto

ignite [ɪgˈnaɪt] *vt* accendere ▷ *vi*
accendersi

ignition [ɪgˈnɪʃən] *n* (*Aut*) accensione *f*; **to
switch on/off the ~** accendere/spegnere
il motore

ignorance [ˈɪgnərəns] *n* ignoranza; **to
keep sb in ~ of sth** tenere qn all'oscuro
di qc

ignorant [ˈɪgnərənt] *adj* ignorante; **to be
~ of** (*subject*) essere ignorante in; (*events*)
essere ignaro(-a) di

ignore [ɪgˈnɔːʳ] *vt* non tener conto di;
(*person, fact*) ignorare

I'll [aɪl] = **I will; I shall**

ill [ɪl] *adj* (*sick*) malato(-a); (*bad*) cattivo(-a)
▷ *n* male *m* ▷ *adv* **to speak** *etc* **~ of sb**
parlare *etc* male di qn; **to take** *or* **be taken
~** ammalarsi

illegal [ɪˈliːgl] *adj* illegale

illegible [ɪˈlɛdʒɪbl] *adj* illeggibile

illegitimate [ɪlɪˈdʒɪtɪmət] *adj*
illegittimo(-a)

ill health *n* problemi *mpl* di salute

illiterate [ɪˈlɪtərət] *adj* analfabeta,
illetterato(-a); (*letter*) scorretto(-a)

illness [ˈɪlnɪs] *n* malattia

illuminate [ɪˈluːmɪneɪt] *vt* illuminare

illusion [ɪˈluːʒən] *n* illusione *f*

illustrate [ˈɪləstreɪt] *vt* illustrare

illustration [ɪləˈstreɪʃən] *n* illustrazione *f*

I'm [aɪm] = **I am**

image [ˈɪmɪdʒ] *n* immagine *f*; (*public face*)
immagine (pubblica)

imaginary [ɪˈmædʒɪnərɪ] *adj*
immaginario(-a)

imagination [ɪmædʒɪˈneɪʃən] *n*
immaginazione *f*, fantasia

imaginative [ɪˈmædʒɪnətɪv] *adj*
immaginoso(-a)

imagine [ɪˈmædʒɪn] *vt* immaginare

imbalance [ɪmˈbæləns] *n* squilibrio

imitate [ˈɪmɪteɪt] *vt* imitare; **imitation**
[-ˈteɪʃən] *n* imitazione *f*

immaculate [ɪˈmækjulət] *adj*
immacolato(-a); (*dress, appearance*)
impeccabile

immature [ɪməˈtjuəʳ] *adj* immaturo(-a)

immediate [ɪˈmiːdɪət] *adj* immediato(-a);
immediately *adv* (*at once*) subito,
immediatamente; **immediately next to**
proprio accanto a

immense [ɪˈmɛns] *adj* immenso(-a);
enorme; **immensely** *adv*
immensamente

immerse [ɪˈməːs] *vt* immergere

immigrant [ˈɪmɪgrənt] *n* immigrante *m/f*;
immigrato(-a); **immigration** [ɪmɪˈgreɪʃə
n] *n* immigrazione *f*

imminent [ˈɪmɪnənt] *adj* imminente

immoral [ɪˈmɔrl] *adj* immorale

immortal [ɪˈmɔːtl] *adj*, *n* immortale *m/f*

immune [ɪˈmjuːn] *adj* **~ (to)** immune
(da); **immune system** *n* sistema *m*
immunitario

immunize [ˈɪmjunaɪz] *vt* immunizzare

impact [ˈɪmpækt] *n* impatto

impair [ɪmˈpɛəʳ] *vt* danneggiare

impartial [ɪmˈpɑːʃl] *adj* imparziale

impatience [ɪmˈpeɪʃəns] *n* impazienza

impatient [ɪmˈpeɪʃənt] *adj* impaziente; **to
get** *or* **grow ~** perdere la pazienza

impeccable [ɪmˈpɛkəbl] *adj* impeccabile

impending [ɪmˈpɛndɪŋ] *adj* imminente

imperative [ɪmˈpɛrətɪv] *adj*
imperativo(-a); necessario(-a), urgente;
(*voice*) imperioso(-a)

imperfect [ɪmˈpəːfɪkt] *adj* imperfetto(-a);
(*goods etc*) difettoso(-a) ▷ *n* (*Ling: also:* **~
tense**) imperfetto

imperial [ɪmˈpɪərɪəl] *adj* imperiale;
(*measure*) legale

impersonal [ɪmˈpəːsənl] *adj*
impersonale

impersonate [ɪmˈpəːsəneɪt] *vt*
impersonare; (*Theatre*) fare la mimica di

impetus [ˈɪmpətəs] *n* impeto

implant [ɪmˈplɑːnt] *vt* (*Med*) innestare;
(*fig: idea, principle*) inculcare

implement [*n* ˈɪmplɪmənt, *vb* ˈɪmplɪmɛnt]
n attrezzo; (*for cooking*) utensile *m* ▷ *vt*
effettuare

implicate [ˈɪmplɪkeɪt] *vt* implicare

implication [ɪmplɪˈkeɪʃən] *n* implicazione
f; **by ~** implicitamente

implicit [ɪmˈplɪsɪt] *adj* implicito(-a);
(*complete*) completo(-a)

imply [ɪmˈplaɪ] *vt* insinuare; suggerire

impolite [ɪmpəˈlaɪt] *adj* scortese

import [*vb* ɪmˈpɔːt, *n* ˈɪmpɔːt] *vt* importare
▷ *n* (*Comm*) importazione *f*

importance [ɪm'pɔːtns] *n* importanza
important [ɪm'pɔːtnt] *adj* importante;
it's not ~ non ha importanza
importer [ɪm'pɔːtə'] *n*
importatore(-trice)
impose [ɪm'pəuz] *vt* imporre ▷ *vi* **to ~
on sb** sfruttare la bontà di qn; **imposing**
[ɪm'pəuzɪŋ] *adj* imponente
impossible [ɪm'pɔsɪbl] *adj* impossibile
impotent ['ɪmpətnt] *adj* impotente
impoverished [ɪm'pɔvərɪʃt] *adj*
impoverito(-a)
impractical [ɪm'præktɪkl] *adj* non
pratico(-a)
impress [ɪm'prɛs] *vt* impressionare; (*mark*)
imprimere, stampare; **to ~ sth on sb** far
capire qc a qn
impression [ɪm'prɛʃən] *n* impressione
f; **to be under the ~ that** avere
l'impressione che
impressive [ɪm'prɛsɪv] *adj* notevole
imprison [ɪm'prɪzn] *vt* imprigionare;
imprisonment *n* imprigionamento
improbable [ɪm'prɔbəbl] *adj* improbabile;
(*excuse*) inverosimile
improper [ɪm'prɔpə'] *adj* scorretto(-a);
(*unsuitable*) inadatto(-a), improprio(-a);
sconveniente, indecente
improve [ɪm'pruːv] *vt* migliorare ▷ *vi*
migliorare; (*pupil etc*) fare progressi;
improvement *n* miglioramento;
progresso
improvise ['ɪmprəvaɪz] *vt*, *vi* improvvisare
impulse ['ɪmpʌls] *n* impulso; **on ~**
d'impulso, impulsivamente; **impulsive**
[ɪm'pʌlsɪv] *adj* impulsivo(-a)

O KEYWORD

in [ɪn] *prep* **1** (*indicating place, position*) in;
in the house/garden in casa/giardino;
in the box nella scatola; **in the fridge**
nel frigorifero; **I have it in my hand** ce
l'ho in mano; **in town/the country** in
città/campagna; **in school** a scuola; **in
here/there** qui/lì dentro
2 (*with place names: of town, region,
country*): **in London** a Londra; **in England**
in Inghilterra; **in the United States** negli
Stati Uniti; **in Yorkshire** nello Yorkshire
3 (*indicating time: during, in the space of*) in;
in spring/summer in primavera/estate;
in 1988 nel 1988; **in May** in *or* a maggio; **I'll
see you in July** ci vediamo a luglio; **in the
afternoon** nel pomeriggio; **at 4 o'clock
in the afternoon** alle 4 del pomeriggio;
I did it in 3 hours/days l'ho fatto in 3
ore/giorni; **I'll see you in 2 weeks** *or* **in 2
weeks' time** ci vediamo tra 2 settimane

4 (*indicating manner etc*) a; **in a loud/soft
voice** a voce alta/bassa; **in pencil** a
matita; **in English/French** in inglese/
francese; **the boy in the blue shirt** il
ragazzo con la camicia blu
5 (*indicating circumstances*): **in the sun**
al sole; **in the shade** all'ombra; **in the
rain** sotto la pioggia; **a rise in prices** un
aumento dei prezzi
6 (*indicating mood, state*): **in tears** in
lacrime; **in anger** per la rabbia; **in
despair** disperato(-a); **in good condition**
in buono stato, in buone condizioni; **to
live in luxury** vivere nel lusso
7 (*with ratios, numbers*): **1 in 10** 1 su 10;
20 pence in the pound 20 pence per
sterlina; **they lined up in twos** si misero
in fila a due a due
8 (*referring to people, works*) in; **the
disease is common in children** la
malattia è comune nei bambini; **in (the
works of) Dickens** in Dickens
9 (*indicating profession etc*) in; **to be in
teaching** fare l'insegnante, insegnare; **to
be in publishing** essere nell'editoria
10 (*after superlative*) di; **the best in the
class** il migliore della classe
11 (*with present participle*): **in saying this**
dicendo questo, nel dire questo
▷ *adv* **to be in** (*person: at home, work*)
esserci; (*train, ship, plane*) essere
arrivato(-a); (*in fashion*) essere di moda; **to
ask sb in** invitare qn ad entrare; **to run/
limp** *etc* **in** entrare di corsa/zoppicando
etc
▷ *n* **the ins and outs of the problem**
tutti i particolari del problema

inability [ɪnə'bɪlɪtɪ] *n* **~ (to do)** incapacità
(di fare)
inaccurate [ɪn'ækjurət] *adj* inesatto(-a),
impreciso(-a)
inadequate [ɪn'ædɪkwət] *adj*
insufficiente
inadvertently [ɪnəd'vəːtntlɪ] *adv* senza
volerlo
inappropriate [ɪnə'prəuprɪət] *adj*
non adatto(-a); (*word, expression*)
improprio(-a)
inaugurate [ɪ'nɔːgjureɪt] *vt* inaugurare;
(*president, official*) insediare
Inc. (*us*) *abbr* (= *incorporated*) S.A.
incapable [ɪn'keɪpəbl] *adj* incapace
incense [*n* 'ɪnsɛns, *vb* ɪn'sɛns] *n* incenso
▷ *vt* (*anger*) infuriare
incentive [ɪn'sɛntɪv] *n* incentivo
inch [ɪntʃ] *n* pollice *m* (*25 mm, 12 in a foot*);
within an ~ of a un pelo da; **he didn't give
an ~** non ha ceduto di un millimetro

incidence ['ɪnsɪdns] n (of crime, disease)
incidenza

incident ['ɪnsɪdnt] n incidente m; (in book)
episodio

incidentally [ɪnsɪ'dɛntəlɪ] adv (by the way)
a proposito

inclination [ɪnklɪ'neɪʃən] n inclinazione f

incline [n 'ɪnklaɪn, vb ɪn'klaɪn] n
pendenza, pendio ▷ vt inclinare ▷ vi
(surface) essere inclinato(-a); **to be ~d to
do** tendere a fare; essere propenso(-a) a
fare

include [ɪn'kluːd] vt includere,
comprendere; **is service ~d?** il servizio è
compreso?; **including** prep compreso(-a),
incluso(-a); **inclusion** [ɪn'kluːʒən] n
inclusione f; **inclusive** [ɪn'kluːsɪv] adj
incluso(-a), compreso(-a); **inclusive of
tax** etc tasse etc comprese

income ['ɪnkʌm] n reddito; **income
support** n (BRIT) sussidio di indigenza
or povertà; **income tax** n imposta sul
reddito

incoming ['ɪnkʌmɪŋ] adj (flight, mail) in
arrivo; (government) subentrante; (tide)
montante

incompatible [ɪnkəm'pætɪbl] adj
incompatibile

incompetence [ɪn'kɒmpɪtns] n
incompetenza, incapacità

incompetent [ɪn'kɒmpɪtnt] adj
incompetente, incapace

incomplete [ɪnkəm'pliːt] adj
incompleto(-a)

inconsistent [ɪnkən'sɪstənt] adj
incoerente; **~ with** non coerente con

inconvenience [ɪnkən'viːnjəns] n
inconveniente m; (trouble) disturbo ▷ vt
disturbare

inconvenient [ɪnkən'viːnjənt] adj
scomodo(-a)

incorporate [ɪn'kɔːpəreɪt] vt incorporare;
(contain) contenere

incorrect [ɪnkə'rɛkt] adj scorretto(-a);
(statement) inesatto(-a)

increase [n 'ɪnkriːs, vb ɪn'kriːs] n aumento
▷ vi, vt aumentare; **increasingly** adv
sempre più

incredible [ɪn'krɛdɪbl] adj incredibile;
incredibly adv incredibilmente

incur [ɪn'kəːr] vt (expenses) incorrere;
(anger, risk) esporsi a; (debt) contrarre;
(loss) subire

indecent [ɪn'diːsnt] adj indecente

indeed [ɪn'diːd] adv infatti; veramente;
yes ~! certamente!

indefinitely [ɪn'dɛfɪnɪtlɪ] adv (wait)
indefinitamente

independence [ɪndɪ'pɛndns] n

indipendenza; **Independence Day** (US) n
vedi nota nel riquadro

● **INDEPENDENCE DAY**
●
● Negli Stati Uniti il 4 luglio si festeggia
● **l'Independence Day**, giorno in
● cui, nel 1776, 13 colonie britanniche
● proclamarono la propria indipendenza
● dalla Gran Bretagna ed entrarono
● ufficialmente a far parte degli Stati Uniti
● d'America.

independent [ɪndɪ'pɛndnt] adj
indipendente; **independent school** n
(BRIT) istituto scolastico indipendente che si
autofinanzia

index ['ɪndɛks] (pl **indexes**) n (in book)
indice m; (: in library etc) catalogo; (pl
indices: ratio, sign) indice m

India ['ɪndɪə] n India; **Indian** adj, n
indiano(-a)

indicate ['ɪndɪkeɪt] vt indicare; **indication**
[-'keɪʃən] n indicazione f, segno;
indicative [ɪn'dɪkətɪv] adj **indicative of**
indicativo(-a) di; **indicator** ['ɪndɪkeɪtər] n
indicatore m; (Aut) freccia

indices ['ɪndɪsiːz] npl of **index**

indict [ɪn'daɪt] vt accusare; **indictment**
[ɪn'daɪtmənt] n accusa

indifference [ɪn'dɪfrəns] n indifferenza

indifferent [ɪn'dɪfrənt] adj indifferente;
(poor) mediocre

indigenous [ɪn'dɪdʒɪnəs] adj indigeno(-a)

indigestion [ɪndɪ'dʒɛstʃən] n
indigestione f

indignant [ɪn'dɪgnənt] adj **~ (at sth/with
sb)** indignato(-a) (per qc/contro qn)

indirect [ɪndɪ'rɛkt] adj indiretto(-a)

indispensable [ɪndɪ'spɛnsəbl] adj
indispensabile

individual [ɪndɪ'vɪdjuəl] n individuo
▷ adj individuale; (characteristic)
particolare, originale; **individually** adv
singolarmente, uno(-a) per uno(-a)

Indonesia [ɪndə'niːzɪə] n Indonesia

indoor ['ɪndɔːr] adj da interno; (plant)
d'appartamento; (swimming pool)
coperto(-a); (sport, games) fatto(-a) al
coperto; **indoors** [ɪn'dɔːz] adv all'interno

induce [ɪn'djuːs] vt persuadere; (bring
about, Med) provocare

indulge [ɪn'dʌldʒ] vt (whim) compiacere,
soddisfare; (child) viziare ▷ vi **to ~ in
sth** concedersi qc; abbandonarsi a qc;
indulgent adj indulgente

industrial [ɪn'dʌstrɪəl] adj industriale;
(injury) sul lavoro; **industrial estate**
(BRIT) n zona industriale; **industrialist**

[ɪnˈdʌstrɪəlɪst] n industriale m; **industrial park** (US) n = **industrial estate**

industry [ˈɪndəstrɪ] n industria; (diligence) operosità

inefficient [ɪnɪˈfɪʃənt] adj inefficiente

inequality [ɪnɪˈkwɔlɪtɪ] n ineguaglianza

inevitable [ɪnˈɛvɪtəbl] adj inevitabile; **inevitably** adv inevitabilmente

inexpensive [ɪnɪkˈspɛnsɪv] adj poco costoso(-a)

inexperienced [ɪnɪksˈpɪərɪənst] adj inesperto(-a), senza esperienza

inexplicable [ɪnɪkˈsplɪkəbl] adj inesplicabile

infamous [ˈɪnfəməs] adj infame

infant [ˈɪnfənt] n bambino(-a)

infantry [ˈɪnfəntrɪ] n fanteria

infant school n (BRIT) scuola elementare (per bambini dall'età di 5 a 7 anni)

infect [ɪnˈfɛkt] vt infettare; **infection** [ɪnˈfɛkʃən] n infezione f; **infectious** [ɪnˈfɛkʃəs] adj (disease) infettivo(-a), contagioso(-a); (person: fig: enthusiasm) contagioso(-a)

infer [ɪnˈfəːʳ] vt inferire, dedurre

inferior [ɪnˈfɪərɪəʳ] adj inferiore; (goods) di qualità scadente ▷ n inferiore m/f; (in rank) subalterno(-a)

infertile [ɪnˈfəːtaɪl] adj sterile

infertility [ɪnfəːˈtɪlɪtɪ] n sterilità

infested [ɪnˈfɛstɪd] adj ~ (with) infestato(-a) (di)

infinite [ˈɪnfɪnɪt] adj infinito(-a); **infinitely** adv infinitamente

infirmary [ɪnˈfəːmərɪ] n ospedale m; (in school, factory) infermeria

inflamed [ɪnˈfleɪmd] adj infiammato(-a)

inflammation [ɪnfləˈmeɪʃən] n infiammazione f

inflatable [ɪnˈfleɪtəbl] adj gonfiabile

inflate [ɪnˈfleɪt] vt (tyre, balloon) gonfiare; (fig) esagerare; gonfiare; **inflation** [ɪnˈfleɪʃən] n (Econ) inflazione f

inflexible [ɪnˈflɛksɪbl] adj inflessibile, rigido(-a)

inflict [ɪnˈflɪkt] vt **to ~ on** infliggere a

influence [ˈɪnfluəns] n influenza ▷ vt influenzare; **under the ~ of alcohol** sotto l'effetto dell'alcool; **influential** [ɪnfluˈɛnʃl] adj influente

influx [ˈɪnflʌks] n afflusso

info (inf) [ˈɪnfəu] n = **information**

inform [ɪnˈfɔːm] vt **to ~ sb (of)** informare qn (di) ▷ vi **to ~ on sb** denunciare qn

informal [ɪnˈfɔːml] adj informale; (announcement, invitation) non ufficiale

information [ɪnfəˈmeɪʃən] n informazioni fpl; particolari mpl; **a piece of ~** un'informazione; **information office** n

ufficio m informazioni inv; **information technology** n informatica

informative [ɪnˈfɔːmətɪv] adj istruttivo(-a)

infra-red [ɪnfrəˈrɛd] adj infrarosso(-a)

infrastructure [ˈɪnfrəstrʌktʃəʳ] n infrastruttura

infrequent [ɪnˈfriːkwənt] adj infrequente, raro(-a)

infuriate [ɪnˈfjuərɪeɪt] vt rendere furioso(-a)

infuriating [ɪnˈfjuərɪeɪtɪŋ] adj molto irritante

ingenious [ɪnˈdʒiːnjəs] adj ingegnoso(-a)

ingredient [ɪnˈgriːdɪənt] n ingrediente m; elemento

inhabit [ɪnˈhæbɪt] vt abitare; **inhabitant** [ɪnˈhæbɪtnt] n abitante m/f

inhale [ɪnˈheɪl] vt inalare ▷ vi (in smoking) aspirare; **inhaler** n inalatore m

inherent [ɪnˈhɪərənt] adj ~ (in or to) inerente (a)

inherit [ɪnˈhɛrɪt] vt ereditare; **inheritance** n eredità

inhibit [ɪnˈhɪbɪt] vt (Psych) inibire; **inhibition** [-ˈbɪʃən] n inibizione f

initial [ɪˈnɪʃl] adj iniziale ▷ n iniziale f ▷ vt siglare; **~s** npl (of name) iniziali fpl; (as signature) sigla; **initially** adv inizialmente, all'inizio

initiate [ɪˈnɪʃɪeɪt] vt (start) avviare; intraprendere; iniziare; (person) iniziare; **to ~ sb into a secret** mettere qn a parte di un segreto; **to ~ proceedings against sb** (Law) intentare causa contro qn

initiative [ɪˈnɪʃətɪv] n iniziativa

inject [ɪnˈdʒɛkt] vt (liquid) iniettare; (patient): **to ~ sb with sth** fare a qn un'iniezione di qc; (funds) immettere; **injection** [ɪnˈdʒɛkʃən] n iniezione f, puntura

injure [ˈɪndʒəʳ] vt ferire; (damage: reputation etc) nuocere a; **injured** adj ferito(-a); **injury** [ˈɪndʒərɪ] n ferita

injustice [ɪnˈdʒʌstɪs] n ingiustizia

ink [ɪŋk] n inchiostro; **ink-jet printer** [ˈɪŋkdʒɛt-] n stampante a getto d'inchiostro

inland [adj ˈɪnlənd, adv ɪnˈlænd] adj interno(-a) ▷ adv all'interno; **Inland Revenue** (BRIT) n Fisco

in-laws [ˈɪnlɔːz] npl suoceri mpl; famiglia del marito (or della moglie)

inmate [ˈɪnmeɪt] n (in prison) carcerato(-a); (in asylum) ricoverato(-a)

inn [ɪn] n locanda

inner [ˈɪnəʳ] adj interno(-a), interiore; **inner-city** n centro di una zona urbana

inning [ˈɪnɪŋ] n (US: Baseball) ripresa; **~s**

(*Cricket*) turno di battuta
innocence ['ɪnəsns] *n* innocenza
innocent ['ɪnəsnt] *adj* innocente
innovation [ˌɪnəu'veɪʃən] *n* innovazione *f*
innovative ['ɪnəu'veɪtɪv] *adj*
  innovativo(-a)
in-patient ['ɪnpeɪʃənt] *n* ricoverato(-a)
input ['ɪnput] *n* input *m*
inquest ['ɪnkwɛst] *n* inchiesta
inquire [ɪn'kwaɪər] *vi* informarsi ▷ *vt*
  domandare, informarsi su; **inquiry** *n*
  domanda; (*Law*) indagine *f*, investigazione
  f; **"inquiries"** "informazioni"
ins. *abbr* = **inches**
insane [ɪn'seɪn] *adj* matto(-a), pazzo(-a);
  (*Med*) alienato(-a)
insanity [ɪn'sænɪtɪ] *n* follia; (*Med*)
  alienazione *f* mentale
insect ['ɪnsɛkt] *n* insetto; **insect repellent**
  n insettifugo
insecure [ˌɪnsɪ'kjuər] *adj* malsicuro(-a);
  (*person*) insicuro(-a)
insecurity [ˌɪnsɪ'kjuərɪtɪ] *n* mancanza di
  sicurezza
insensitive [ɪn'sɛnsɪtɪv] *adj* insensibile
insert [ɪn'səːt] *vt* inserire, introdurre
inside ['ɪn'saɪd] *n* interno, parte *f* interiore
  ▷ *adj* interno(-a), interiore ▷ *adv* dentro,
  all'interno ▷ *prep* dentro, all'interno di; (*of
  time*): **~ 10 minutes** entro 10 minuti; **inside
  lane** *n* (*Aut*) corsia di marcia; **inside out**
  adv (*turn*) a rovescio; (*know*) in fondo
insight ['ɪnsaɪt] *n* acume *m*, perspicacia;
  (*glimpse, idea*) percezione *f*
insignificant [ˌɪnsɪg'nɪfɪknt] *adj*
  insignificante
insincere [ˌɪnsɪn'sɪər] *adj* insincero(-a)
insist [ɪn'sɪst] *vi* insistere; **to ~ on doing**
  insistere per fare; **to ~ that** insistere
  perché + *sub*; (*claim*) sostenere che;
  insistent *adj* insistente
insomnia [ɪn'sɔmnɪə] *n* insonnia
inspect [ɪn'spɛkt] *vt* ispezionare; (*BRIT:
  ticket*) controllare; **inspection** [ɪn'spɛkʃə
  n] *n* ispezione *f*; controllo; **inspector** *n*
  ispettore(-trice); (*BRIT: on buses, trains*)
  controllore *m*
inspiration [ˌɪnspə'reɪʃən] *n* ispirazione *f*;
  inspire [ɪn'spaɪər] *vt* ispirare; **inspiring**
  adj stimolante
instability [ˌɪnstə'bɪlɪtɪ] *n* instabilità
install [ɪn'stɔːl] (*us* **instal**) *vt* installare;
  installation [ˌɪnstə'leɪʃən] *n* installazione
  f
instalment [ɪn'stɔːlmənt] (*us*
  installment) *n* rata; (*of TV serial etc*)
  puntata; **in ~s** (*pay*) a rate; (*receive*) una
  parte per volta; (: *publication*) a fascicoli
instance ['ɪnstəns] *n* esempio, caso; **for ~**

per *or* ad esempio; **in the first ~** in primo
  luogo
instant ['ɪnstənt] *n* istante *m*, attimo ▷ *adj*
  immediato(-a); urgente; (*coffee, food*) in
  polvere; **instantly** *adv* immediatamente,
  subito
instead [ɪn'stɛd] *adv* invece; **~ of** invece di
instinct ['ɪnstɪŋkt] *n* istinto; **instinctive**
  adj istintivo(-a)
institute ['ɪnstɪtjuːt] *n* istituto ▷ *vt*
  istituire, stabilire; (*inquiry*) avviare;
  (*proceedings*) iniziare
institution [ˌɪnstɪ'tjuːʃən] *n* istituzione *f*;
  (*educational institution, mental institution*)
  istituto
instruct [ɪn'strʌkt] *vt* **to ~ sb in sth**
  insegnare qc a qn; **to ~ sb to do** dare
  ordini a qn di fare; **instruction** [ɪn'strʌkʃə
  n] *n* istruzione *f*; **instructions (for
  use)** istruzioni per l'uso; **instructor** *n*
  istruttore(-trice); (*for skiing*) maestro(-a)
instrument ['ɪnstrəmənt] *n* strumento;
  instrumental [-'mɛntl] *adj* (*Mus*)
  strumentale; **to be instrumental in**
  essere d'aiuto in
insufficient [ˌɪnsə'fɪʃənt] *adj* insufficiente
insulate ['ɪnsjuleɪt] *vt* isolare; **insulation**
  [-'leɪʃən] *n* isolamento
insulin ['ɪnsjulɪn] *n* insulina
insult [*n* 'ɪnsʌlt, *vb* ɪn'sʌlt] *n* insulto,
  affronto ▷ *vt* insultare; **insulting** *adj*
  offensivo(-a), ingiurioso(-a)
insurance [ɪn'ʃuərəns] *n* assicurazione
  f; **fire/life ~** assicurazione contro gli
  incendi/sulla vita; **insurance company** *n*
  società di assicurazioni; **insurance policy**
  n polizza d'assicurazione
insure [ɪn'ʃuər] *vt* assicurare
intact [ɪn'tækt] *adj* intatto(-a)
intake ['ɪnteɪk] *n* (*Tech*) immissione *f*; (*of
  food*) consumo; (*BRIT: of pupils etc*) afflusso
integral ['ɪntɪgrəl] *adj* integrale; (*part*)
  integrante
integrate ['ɪntɪgreɪt] *vt* integrare ▷ *vi*
  integrarsi
integrity [ɪn'tɛgrɪtɪ] *n* integrità
intellect ['ɪntəlɛkt] *n* intelletto;
  intellectual [-'lɛktjuəl] *adj, n*
  intellettuale *m/f*
intelligence [ɪn'tɛlɪdʒəns] *n* intelligenza;
  (*Mil etc*) informazioni *fpl*
intelligent [ɪn'tɛlɪdʒənt] *adj* intelligente
intend [ɪn'tɛnd] *vt* (*gift etc*): **to ~ sth for**
  destinare qc a; **to ~ to do** aver l'intenzione
  di fare
intense [ɪn'tɛns] *adj* intenso(-a); (*person*)
  di forti sentimenti
intensify [ɪn'tɛnsɪfaɪ] *vt* intensificare
intensity [ɪn'tɛnsɪtɪ] *n* intensità

intensive [ɪnˈtɛnsɪv] *adj* intensivo(-a);
intensive care *n* terapia intensiva;
intensive care unit (ICU) *n* reparto
terapia intensiva
intent [ɪnˈtɛnt] *n* intenzione *f* ▷ *adj* ~ **(on)**
intento(-a) (a), immerso(-a) (in); **to all ~s
and purposes** a tutti gli effetti; **to be ~ on
doing sth** essere deciso a fare qc
intention [ɪnˈtɛnʃən] *n* intenzione
f; **intentional** *adj* intenzionale,
deliberato(-a)
interact [ɪntərˈækt] *vi* interagire;
interaction [ɪntərˈækʃən] *n* azione *f*
reciproca, interazione *f*; **interactive** *adj*
(*Comput*) interattivo(-a)
intercept [ɪntəˈsɛpt] *vt* intercettare;
(*person*) fermare
interchange [ˈɪntətʃeɪndʒ] *n* (*exchange*)
scambio; (*on motorway*) incrocio
pluridirezionale
intercourse [ˈɪntəkɔːs] *n* rapporti *mpl*
interest [ˈɪntrɪst] *n* interesse *m*; (*Comm:
stake, share*) interessi *mpl* ▷ *vt* interessare;
interested *adj* interessato(-a); **to be
interested in** interessarsi di; **interesting**
adj interessante; **interest rate** *n* tasso di
interesse
interface [ˈɪntəfeɪs] *n* (*Comput*) interfaccia
interfere [ɪntəˈfɪəʳ] *vi* **to ~ in** (*quarrel,
other people's business*) immischiarsi in;
to ~ with (*object*) toccare; (*plans, duty*)
interferire con; **interference** [ɪntəˈfɪərə
ns] *n* interferenza
interim [ˈɪntərɪm] *adj* provvisorio(-a) ▷ *n*
in the ~ nel frattempo
interior [ɪnˈtɪərɪəʳ] *n* interno; (*of
country*) entroterra ▷ *adj* interno(-a);
(*minister*) degli Interni; **interior design** *n*
architettura d'interni
intermediate [ɪntəˈmiːdɪət] *adj*
intermedio(-a)
intermission [ɪntəˈmɪʃən] *n* pausa;
(*Theatre, Cinema*) intermissione *f*, intervallo
intern [*vb* ɪnˈtəːn, *n* ˈɪntəːn] *vt* internare
▷ *n* (*US*) medico interno
internal [ɪnˈtəːnl] *adj* interno(-a); **Internal
Revenue Service** (*US*) *n* Fisco
international [ɪntəˈnæʃənl] *adj*
internazionale ▷ *n* (*BRIT Sport*) incontro
internazionale
Internet [ˈɪntənɛt] *n* **the ~** Internet *f*;
Internet café *n* cybercaffè *m inv*; **Internet
Service Provider** *n* Provider *m inv*;
Internet user *n* utente *m/f* Internet
interpret [ɪnˈtəːprɪt] *vt* interpretare
▷ *vi* fare da interprete; **interpretation**
[ɪntəːprɪˈteɪʃən] *n* interpretazione *f*;
interpreter *n* interprete *m/f*; **could you
act as an interpreter for us?** ci potrebbe

fare da interprete?
interrogate [ɪnˈtɛrəʊgeɪt] *vt* interrogare;
interrogation [-ˈgeɪʃən] *n* interrogazione
f; (*of suspect etc*) interrogatorio
interrogative [ɪntəˈrɔgətɪv] *adj*
interrogativo(-a) ▷ *n* (*Ling*) interrogativo
interrupt [ɪntəˈrʌpt] *vt, vi* interrompere;
interruption [-ˈrʌpʃən] *n* interruzione *f*
intersection [ɪntəˈsɛkʃən] *n* intersezione
f; (*of roads*) incrocio
interstate [ˈɪntəsteɪt] (*US*) *n* fra stati
interval [ˈɪntəvl] *n* intervallo; **at ~s** a
intervalli
intervene [ɪntəˈviːn] *vi* (*time*) intercorrere;
(*event, person*) intervenire
interview [ˈɪntəvjuː] *n* (*Radio, TV
etc*) intervista; (*for job*) colloquio ▷ *vt*
intervistare; avere un colloquio con;
interviewer *n* intervistatore(-trice)
intimate [*adj* ˈɪntɪmət, *vb* ˈɪntɪmeɪt] *adj*
intimo(-a); (*knowledge*) profondo(-a) ▷ *vt*
lasciar capire
intimidate [ɪnˈtɪmɪdeɪt] *vt* intimidire,
intimorire
intimidating [ɪnˈtɪmɪdeɪtɪŋ] *adj* (*sight*)
spaventoso(-a); (*appearance, figure*)
minaccioso(-a)
into [ˈɪntuː] *prep* dentro, in; **come ~ the
house** entra in casa; **he worked late ~ the
night** lavorò fino a tarda notte; **~ Italian**
in italiano
intolerant [ɪnˈtɔlərnt] *adj* **~ of**
intollerante di
intranet [ˈɪntrənɛt] *n* intranet *f*
intransitive [ɪnˈtrænsɪtɪv] *adj*
intransitivo(-a)
intricate [ˈɪntrɪkət] *adj* intricato(-a),
complicato(-a)
intrigue [ɪnˈtriːg] *n* intrigo ▷ *vt*
affascinare; **intriguing** *adj* affascinante
introduce [ɪntrəˈdjuːs] *vt* introdurre;
to ~ sb (to sb) presentare qn (a qn); **to
~ sb to** (*pastime, technique*) iniziare qn a;
introduction [-ˈdʌkʃən] *n* introduzione
f; (*of person*) presentazione *f*; (*to new
experience*) iniziazione *f*; **introductory** *adj*
introduttivo(-a)
intrude [ɪnˈtruːd] *vi* (*person*): **to ~ (on)**
intromettersi (in); **intruder** *n* intruso(-a)
intuition [ɪntjuːˈɪʃən] *n* intuizione *f*
inundate [ˈɪnʌndeɪt] *vt* **to ~ with**
inondare di
invade [ɪnˈveɪd] *vt* invadere
invalid [*n* ˈɪnvəlɪd, *adj* ɪnˈvælɪd] *n*
malato(-a); (*with disability*) invalido(-a)
▷ *adj* (*not valid*) invalido(-a), non valido(-a)
invaluable [ɪnˈvæljuəbl] *adj* prezioso(-a);
inestimabile
invariably [ɪnˈvɛərɪəblɪ] *adv*

invariabilmente; sempre

invasion [ɪn'veɪʒən] n invasione f

invent [ɪn'vɛnt] vt inventare; **invention** [ɪn'vɛnʃən] n invenzione f; **inventor** n inventore m

inventory ['ɪnvəntrɪ] n inventario

inverted commas [ɪn'və:tɪd-] (BRIT) npl virgolette fpl

invest [ɪn'vɛst] vt investire ▷ vi **to ~ (in)** investire (in)

investigate [ɪn'vɛstɪgeɪt] vt investigare, indagare; (crime) fare indagini su; **investigation** [-'geɪʃən] n investigazione f; (of crime) indagine f

investigator [ɪn'vɛstɪgeɪtəʳ] n investigatore(-trice); **a private ~** un investigatore privato, un detective

investment [ɪn'vɛstmənt] n investimento

investor [ɪn'vɛstəʳ] n investitore(-trice); azionista m/f

invisible [ɪn'vɪzɪbl] adj invisibile

invitation [ɪnvɪ'teɪʃən] n invito

invite [ɪn'vaɪt] vt invitare; (opinions etc) sollecitare; **inviting** adj invitante, attraente

invoice ['ɪnvɔɪs] n fattura ▷ vt fatturare

involve [ɪn'vɔlv] vt (entail) richiedere, comportare; (associate): **to ~ sb (in)** implicare qn (in); coinvolgere qn (in); **involved** adj involuto(-a), complesso(-a); **to be involved in** essere coinvolto(-a) in; **involvement** n implicazione f; coinvolgimento

inward ['ɪnwəd] adj (movement) verso l'interno; (thought, feeling) interiore, intimo(-a); **inward(s)** adv verso l'interno

IQ n abbr (= intelligence quotient) quoziente m d'intelligenza

IRA n abbr (= Irish Republican Army) IRA f

Iran [ɪ'rɑ:n] n Iran m; **Iranian** adj, n iraniano(-a)

Iraq [ɪ'rɑ:k] n Iraq m; **Iraqi** adj, n iracheno(-a)

Ireland ['aɪələnd] n Irlanda

iris ['aɪrɪs] (pl irises) n iride f; (Bot) giaggiolo, iride

Irish ['aɪrɪʃ] adj irlandese ▷ npl **the ~** gli Irlandesi; **Irishman** (irreg) n irlandese m; **Irish Sea** n Mar m d'Irlanda; **Irishwoman** (irreg) n irlandese f

iron ['aɪən] n ferro; (for clothes) ferro da stiro ▷ adj di or in ferro ▷ vt (clothes) stirare

ironic(al) [aɪ'rɔnɪk(l)] adj ironico(-a); **ironically** adv ironicamente

ironing ['aɪənɪŋ] n (act) stirare m; (clothes) roba da stirare; **ironing board** n asse f da stiro

irony ['aɪrənɪ] n ironia

irrational [ɪ'ræʃənl] adj irrazionale

irregular [ɪ'rɛgjuləʳ] adj irregolare

irrelevant [ɪ'rɛləvənt] adj non pertinente

irresistible [ɪrɪ'zɪstɪbl] adj irresistibile

irresponsible [ɪrɪ'spɔnsɪbl] adj irresponsabile

irrigation [ɪrɪ'geɪʃən] n irrigazione f

irritable ['ɪrɪtəbl] adj irritabile

irritate ['ɪrɪteɪt] vt irritare; **irritating** adj (person, sound etc) irritante; **irritation** [-'teɪʃən] n irritazione f

IRS (US) n abbr = **Internal Revenue Service**

is [ɪz] vb see **be**

ISDN n abbr (= Integrated Services Digital Network) I.S.D.N. f

Islam ['ɪzlɑ:m] n Islam m; **Islamic** [ɪz'læmɪk] adj islamico(-a)

island ['aɪlənd] n isola; **islander** n isolano(-a)

isle [aɪl] n isola

isn't ['ɪznt] = **is not**

isolated ['aɪsəleɪtɪd] adj isolato(-a)

isolation [aɪsə'leɪʃən] n isolamento

ISP n abbr (= Internet Service Provider) provider m inv

Israel ['ɪzreɪl] n Israele m; **Israeli** [ɪz'reɪlɪ] adj, n israeliano(-a)

issue ['ɪʃju:] n questione f, problema m; (of banknotes etc) emissione f; (of newspaper etc) numero ▷ vt (statement) rilasciare; (rations, equipment) distribuire; (book) pubblicare; (banknotes, cheques, stamps) emettere; **at ~** in gioco, in discussione; **to take ~ with sb (over sth)** prendere posizione contro qn (riguardo a qc); **to make an ~ of sth** fare un problema di qc

KEYWORD

it [ɪt] pron **1** (specific: subject) esso(-a); (: direct object) lo (la), l'; (: indirect object) gli (le); **where's my book? — it's on the table** dov'è il mio libro? — è sulla tavola; **I can't find it** non lo (or la) trovo; **give it to me** dammelo (or dammela); **about/from/ of it** ne; **I spoke to him about it** gliene ho parlato; **what did you learn from it?** quale insegnamento ne hai tratto?; **I'm proud of it** ne sono fiero; **did you go to it?** ci sei andato?; **put the book in it** mettici il libro

2 (impers): **it's raining** piove; **it's Friday tomorrow** domani è venerdì; **it's 6 o'clock** sono le 6; **who is it? — it's me** chi è? — sono io

IT n abbr see **information technology**

Italian [ɪ'tæljən] adj italiano(-a) ▷ n

italiano(-a); (*Ling*) italiano; **the ~s** gli
Italiani; **what's the ~ (word) for ...?** come
si dice in italiano ...?
italics [ɪ'tælɪks] *npl* corsivo
Italy ['ɪtəlɪ] *n* Italia
itch [ɪtʃ] *n* prurito ▷ *vi* (*person*) avere il
prurito; (*part of body*) prudere; **to ~ to do
sth** aver una gran voglia di fare qc; **itchy**
adj che prude; **to be itchy = to itch**
it'd ['ɪtd] = **it would; it had**
item ['aɪtəm] *n* articolo; (*on agenda*) punto;
(*also:* **news ~**) notizia
itinerary [aɪ'tɪnərərɪ] *n* itinerario
it'll ['ɪtl] = **it will; it shall**
its [ɪts] *adj* il (la) suo(-a), i (le) suoi (sue)
it's [ɪts] = **it is; it has**
itself [ɪt'sɛlf] *pron* (*emphatic*) esso(-a)
stesso(-a); (*reflexive*) si
ITV (*BRIT*) *n abbr* (= *Independent Television*)
rete televisiva in concorrenza con la BBC
I've [aɪv] = **I have**
ivory ['aɪvərɪ] *n* avorio
ivy ['aɪvɪ] *n* edera

J

jab [dʒæb] *vt* dare colpetti a ▷ *n* (*Med:
inf*) puntura; **to ~ sth into** affondare *or*
piantare qc dentro
jack [dʒæk] *n* (*Aut*) cricco; (*Cards*) fante *m*
jacket ['dʒækɪt] *n* giacca; (*of book*)
copertura; **jacket potato** *n* patata cotta al
forno con la buccia
jackpot ['dʒækpɔt] *n* primo premio (in
denaro)
Jacuzzi® [dʒə'kuːzɪ] *n* vasca per
idromassaggio Jacuzzi®
jagged ['dʒægɪd] *adj* seghettato(-a); (*cliffs
etc*) frastagliato(-a)
jail [dʒeɪl] *n* prigione *f* ▷ *vt* mandare in
prigione; **jail sentence** *n* condanna al
carcere
jam [dʒæm] *n* marmellata; (*also:* **traffic
~**) ingorgo; (*inf*) pasticcio ▷ *vt* (*passage
etc*) ingombrare, ostacolare; (*mechanism,
drawer etc*) bloccare; (*Radio*) disturbare con
interferenze ▷ *vi* incepparsi; **to ~ sth into**
forzare qc dentro; infilare qc a forza dentro
Jamaica [dʒə'meɪkə] *n* Giamaica
jammed [dʒæmd] *adj* (*door*) bloccato(-a);
(*rifle, printer*) inceppato(-a)
Jan. *abbr* (= *January*) gen., genn.
janitor ['dʒænɪtər] *n* (*caretaker*) portiere *m*;
(: *Scol*) bidello
January ['dʒænjuərɪ] *n* gennaio
Japan [dʒə'pæn] *n* Giappone *m*; **Japanese**

[dʒæpə'ni:z] *adj* giapponese ▷ *n inv* giapponese *m/f*; (*Ling*) giapponese *m*

jar [dʒɑːʳ] *n* (*glass*) barattolo, vasetto ▷ *vi* (*sound*) stridere; (*colours etc*) stonare

jargon ['dʒɑːgən] *n* gergo

javelin ['dʒævlɪn] *n* giavellotto

jaw [dʒɔː] *n* mascella

jazz [dʒæz] *n* jazz *m*

jealous ['dʒeləs] *adj* geloso(-a); **jealousy** *n* gelosia

jeans [dʒiːnz] *npl* (blue-)jeans *mpl*

Jello® ['dʒeləu] (*us*) *n* gelatina di frutta

jelly ['dʒelɪ] *n* gelatina; **jellyfish** *n* medusa

jeopardize ['dʒepədaɪz] *vt* mettere in pericolo

jerk [dʒəːk] *n* sobbalzo, scossa; sussulto; (*inf: idiot*) tonto(-a) ▷ *vt* dare una scossa a ▷ *vi* (*vehicles*) sobbalzare

Jersey ['dʒəːzɪ] *n* Jersey *m*

jersey ['dʒəːzɪ] *n* maglia; (*fabric*) jersey *m*

Jesus ['dʒiːzəs] *n* Gesù *m*

jet [dʒet] *n* (*of gas, liquid*) getto; (*Aviat*) aviogetto; **jet lag** *n* (problemi *mpl* dovuti allo) sbalzo dei fusi orari; **jet-ski** *vi* acquascooter *m inv*

jetty ['dʒetɪ] *n* molo

Jew [dʒuː] *n* ebreo

jewel ['dʒuːəl] *n* gioiello; **jeweller** (*us* **jeweler**) *n* orefice *m*, gioielliere(-a); **jeweller's (shop)** (*us* **jewelry store**) *n* oreficeria, gioielleria; **jewellery** (*us* **jewelry**) *n* gioielli *mpl*

Jewish ['dʒuːɪʃ] *adj* ebreo(-a), ebraico(-a)

jigsaw ['dʒɪgsɔː] *n* (*also:* ~ **puzzle**) puzzle *m inv*

job [dʒɔb] *n* lavoro; (*employment*) impiego, posto; **it's not my** ~ (*duty*) non è compito mio; **it's a good** ~ **that ...** meno male che ...; **just the** ~! proprio quello che ci vuole; **job centre** (*BRIT*) *n* ufficio di collocamento; **jobless** *adj* senza lavoro, disoccupato(-a)

jockey ['dʒɔkɪ] *n* fantino, jockey *m inv* ▷ *vi* **to** ~ **for position** manovrare per una posizione di vantaggio

jog [dʒɔg] *vt* urtare ▷ *vi* (*Sport*) fare footing, fare jogging; **to** ~ **sb's memory** rinfrescare la memoria a qn; **to** ~ **along** trottare; (*fig*) andare avanti piano piano; **jogging** *n* footing *m*, jogging *m*

join [dʒɔɪn] *vt* unire, congiungere; (*become member of*) iscriversi a; (*meet*) raggiungere; riunirsi a ▷ *vi* (*roads, rivers*) confluire ▷ *n* giuntura; **join in** *vi* partecipare ▷ *vt fus* unirsi a; **join up** *vi* incontrarsi; (*Mil*) arruolarsi

joiner ['dʒɔɪnəʳ] (*BRIT*) *n* falegname *m*

joint [dʒɔɪnt] *n* (*Tech*) giuntura; giunto; (*Anat*) articolazione *f*, giuntura; (*BRIT Culin*) arrosto; (*inf: place*) locale *m*; (: *of cannabis*) spinello ▷ *adj* comune; **joint account** *n* (*at bank etc*) conto in partecipazione, conto comune; **jointly** *adv* in comune, insieme

joke [dʒəuk] *n* scherzo; (*funny story*) barzelletta; (*also:* **practical** ~) beffa ▷ *vi* scherzare; **to play a** ~ **on sb** fare uno scherzo a qn; **joker** *n* (*Cards*) matta, jolly *m inv*

jolly ['dʒɔlɪ] *adj* allegro(-a), gioioso(-a) ▷ *adv* (*BRIT: inf*) veramente, proprio

jolt [dʒəult] *n* scossa, sobbalzo ▷ *vt* urtare

Jordan ['dʒɔːdən] *n* (*country*) Giordania; (*river*) Giordano

journal ['dʒəːnl] *n* giornale *m*; rivista; diario; **journalism** *n* giornalismo; **journalist** *n* giornalista *m/f*

journey ['dʒəːnɪ] *n* viaggio; (*distance covered*) tragitto; **how was your** ~? com'è andato il viaggio?; **the** ~ **takes two hours** il viaggio dura due ore

joy [dʒɔɪ] *n* gioia; **joyrider** *n* chi ruba un'auto per farvi un giro; **joy stick** *n* (*Aviat*) barra di comando; (*Comput*) joystick *m inv*

Jr *abbr* = **junior**

judge [dʒʌdʒ] *n* giudice *m/f* ▷ *vt* giudicare

judo ['dʒuːdəu] *n* judo

jug [dʒʌg] *n* brocca, bricco

juggle ['dʒʌgl] *vi* fare giochi di destrezza; **juggler** *n* giocoliere(-a)

juice [dʒuːs] *n* succo; **juicy** ['dʒuːsɪ] *adj* succoso(-a)

Jul. *abbr* (= *July*) lug., lu.

July [dʒuː'laɪ] *n* luglio

jumble ['dʒʌmbl] *n* miscuglio ▷ *vt* (*also:* ~ **up**) mischiare; **jumble sale** (*BRIT*) *n* vendita di beneficenza

● **JUMBLE SALE**
●
● Una **jumble sale** è un mercatino di
● oggetti di seconda mano organizzato
● in chiese, scuole o in circoli ricreativi,
● i cui proventi vengono devoluti in
● beneficenza.

jumbo ['dʒʌmbəu] *adj* ~ **jet** jumbo-jet *m inv*; ~ **size** formato gigante

jump [dʒʌmp] *vi* saltare, balzare; (*start*) sobbalzare; (*increase*) rincarare ▷ *vt* saltare ▷ *n* salto, balzo; sobbalzo

jumper ['dʒʌmpəʳ] *n* (*BRIT: pullover*) maglione *m*, pullover *m inv*; (*us: dress*) scamiciato

jumper cables (*us*) *npl* = **jump leads**

jump leads (*BRIT*) *npl* cavi *mpl* per batteria

Jun. *abbr* = **junior**

junction ['dʒʌŋkʃən] *n* (*BRIT: of roads*) incrocio; (*of rails*) nodo ferroviario

June [dʒuːn] *n* giugno

jungle ['dʒʌŋgl] *n* giungla

junior ['dʒuːnɪə'] *adj, n* **he's ~ to me by 2 years, he's my ~ by 2 years** è più giovane di me (di 2 anni); **he's ~ to me** (*seniority*) è al di sotto di me, ho più anzianità di lui; **junior high school** (*US*) *n* scuola media (*da 12 a 15 anni*); **junior school** (*BRIT*) *n* scuola elementare (*da 8 a 11 anni*)

junk [dʒʌŋk] *n* cianfrusaglie *fpl*; (*cheap goods*) robaccia; **junk food** *n* porcherie *fpl*

junkie ['dʒʌŋkɪ] (*inf*) *n* drogato(-a)

junk mail *n* stampe *fpl* pubblicitarie

Jupiter ['dʒuːpɪtə'] *n* (*planet*) Giove *m*

jurisdiction [dʒuərɪs'dɪkʃən] *n* giurisdizione *f*; **it falls** *or* **comes within/outside our ~** è/non è di nostra competenza

jury ['dʒuərɪ] *n* giuria

just [dʒʌst] *adj* giusto(-a) ▷ *adv* **he's ~ done it/left** lo ha appena fatto/è appena partito; **~ right** proprio giusto; **~ 2 o'clock** le 2 precise; **she's ~ as clever as you** è in gamba proprio quanto te; **it's ~ as well that …** meno male che …; **~ as I arrived** proprio mentre arrivavo; **it was ~ before/enough/here** era poco prima/appena assai/proprio qui; **it's ~ me** sono solo io; **~ missed/caught** appena perso/preso; **~ listen to this!** senta un po' questo!

justice ['dʒʌstɪs] *n* giustizia

justification [dʒʌstɪfɪ'keɪʃən] *n* giustificazione *f*; (*Typ*) giustezza

justify ['dʒʌstɪfaɪ] *vt* giustificare

jut [dʒʌt] *vi* (*also*: **~ out**) sporgersi

juvenile ['dʒuːvənaɪl] *adj* giovane, giovanile; (*court*) dei minorenni; (*books*) per ragazzi ▷ *n* giovane *m/f*, minorenne *m/f*

K *abbr* (= *one thousand*) mille; (= *kilobyte*) K

kangaroo [kæŋgə'ruː] *n* canguro

karaoke [kɑːrə'əʊkɪ] *n* karaoke *m inv*

karate [kə'rɑːtɪ] *n* karatè *m*

kebab [kə'bæb] *n* spiedino

keel [kiːl] *n* chiglia; **on an even ~** (*fig*) in uno stato normale

keen [kiːn] *adj* (*interest, desire*) vivo(-a); (*eye, intelligence*) acuto(-a); (*competition*) serrato(-a); (*edge*) affilato(-a); (*eager*) entusiasta; **to be ~ to do** *or* **on doing sth** avere una gran voglia di fare qc; **to be ~ on sth** essere appassionato(-a) di qc; **to be ~ on sb** avere un debole per qn

keep [kiːp] (*pt, pp* kept) *vt* tenere; (*hold back*) trattenere; (*feed: one's family etc*) mantenere, sostentare; (*a promise*) mantenere; (*chickens, bees, pigs etc*) allevare ▷ *vi* (*food*) mantenersi; (*remain: in a certain state or place*) restare ▷ *n* (*of castle*) maschio; (*food etc*): **enough for his ~** abbastanza per vitto e alloggio; (*inf*): **for ~s** per sempre; **to ~ doing sth** continuare a fare qc; fare qc di continuo; **to ~ sb from doing** impedire a qn di fare; **to ~ sb busy/a place tidy** tenere qn occupato(-a)/un luogo in ordine; **to ~ sth to o.s.** tenere qc per sé; **to ~ sth (back) from sb** celare qc a qn; **to ~ time** (*clock*) andar bene; **keep away** *vt* **to ~ sth/sb away from sb**

tenere qc/qn lontano da qn ▷ vi **to ~ away (from)** stare lontano (da); **keep back** vt (*crowds, tears, money*) trattenere ▷ vi tenersi indietro; **keep off** vt (*dog, person*) tenere lontano da ▷ vi stare alla larga; **~ your hands off!** non toccare!, giù le mani!; **"~ off the grass"** "non calpestare l'erba"; **keep on** vi **to ~ on doing** continuare a fare; **to ~ on (about sth)** continuare a insistere (su qc); **keep out** vt tener fuori; **"~ out"** "vietato l'accesso"; **keep up** vt continuare, mantenere ▷ vi **to ~ up with** tener dietro a, andare di pari passo con; (*work etc*) farcela a seguire; **keeper** n custode m/f, guardiano(-a); **keeping** n (*care*) custodia; **in keeping with** in armonia con; in accordo con

kennel ['kɛnl] n canile m; **~s** npl canile m; **to put a dog in ~s** mettere un cane al canile

Kenya ['kɛnjə] n Kenia m

kept [kɛpt] pt, pp of **keep**

kerb [kə:b] (*BRIT*) n orlo del marciapiede

kerosene ['kɛrəsiːn] n cherosene m

ketchup ['kɛtʃəp] n ketchup m inv

kettle ['kɛtl] n bollitore m

key [kiː] n (*gen, Mus*) chiave f; (*of piano, typewriter*) tasto ▷ adj chiave inv ▷ vt (*also: ~ in*) digitare; **can I have my ~?** posso avere la mia chiave?; **keyboard** n tastiera; **keyhole** n buco della serratura; **keyring** n portachiavi m inv

kg abbr (= *kilogram*) Kg

khaki ['kɑːkɪ] adj cachi ▷ n cachi m

kick [kɪk] vt calciare, dare calci a; (*inf: habit etc*) liberarsi di ▷ vi (*horse*) tirar calci ▷ n calcio; (*thrill*): **he does it for ~s** lo fa giusto per il piacere di farlo; **kick off** vi (*Sport*) dare il primo calcio; **kick-off** n (*Sport*) calcio d'inizio

kid [kɪd] n (*inf: child*) ragazzino(-a); (*animal, leather*) capretto ▷ vi (*inf*) scherzare

kidnap ['kɪdnæp] vt rapire, sequestrare; **kidnapping** n sequestro (di persona)

kidney ['kɪdnɪ] n (*Anat*) rene m; (*Culin*) rognone m; **kidney bean** n fagiolo borlotto

kill [kɪl] vt uccidere, ammazzare ▷ n uccisione f; **killer** n uccisore m, killer m inv; assassino(-a); **killing** n assassinio; **to make a killing** (*inf*) fare un bel colpo

kiln [kɪln] n forno

kilo ['kiːləu] n chilo; **kilobyte** n (*Comput*) kilobyte m inv; **kilogram(me)** ['kɪlə ugræm] n chilogrammo; **kilometre** ['kɪlə miːtə'] (*us* **kilometer**) n chilometro; **kilowatt** ['kɪləuwɔt] n chilowatt m inv

kilt [kɪlt] n gonnellino scozzese

kin [kɪn] n see **next**; **kith**

kind [kaɪnd] adj gentile, buono(-a) ▷ n sorta, specie f; (*species*) genere m; **what ~ of ...?** che tipo di ...?; **to be two of a ~** essere molto simili; **in ~** (*Comm*) in natura

kindergarten ['kɪndəgɑːtn] n giardino d'infanzia

kindly ['kaɪndlɪ] adj pieno(-a) di bontà, benevolo(-a) ▷ adv con bontà, gentilmente; **will you ~ ...** vuole ... per favore

kindness ['kaɪndnɪs] n bontà, gentilezza

king [kɪŋ] n re m inv; **kingdom** n regno, reame m; **kingfisher** n martin m inv pescatore; **king-size(d) bed** n letto king-size

kiosk ['kiːɔsk] n edicola, chiosco; (*BRIT Tel*) cabina (telefonica)

kipper ['kɪpə'] n aringa affumicata

kiss [kɪs] n bacio ▷ vt baciare; **to ~ (each other)** baciarsi; **kiss of life** n respirazione f bocca a bocca

kit [kɪt] n equipaggiamento, corredo; (*set of tools etc*) attrezzi mpl; (*for assembly*) scatola di montaggio

kitchen ['kɪtʃɪn] n cucina

kite [kaɪt] n (*toy*) aquilone m

kitten ['kɪtn] n gattino(-a), micino(-a)

kiwi ['kiːwiː] n (*also: ~ fruit*) kiwi m inv

km abbr (= *kilometre*) km

km/h abbr (= *kilometres per hour*) km/h

knack [næk] n **to have the ~ of** avere l'abilità di

knee [niː] n ginocchio; **kneecap** n rotula

kneel [niːl] (*pt, pp* **knelt**) vi (*also: ~ down*) inginocchiarsi

knelt [nɛlt] pt, pp of **kneel**

knew [njuː] pt of **know**

knickers ['nɪkəz] (*BRIT*) npl mutandine fpl

knife [naɪf] (*pl* **knives**) n coltello ▷ vt accoltellare, dare una coltellata a

knight [naɪt] n cavaliere m; (*Chess*) cavallo

knit [nɪt] vt fare a maglia ▷ vi lavorare a maglia; (*broken bones*) saldarsi; **to ~ one's brows** aggrottare le sopracciglia; **knitting** n lavoro a maglia; **knitting needle** n ferro (da calza); **knitwear** n maglieria

knives [naɪvz] npl of **knife**

knob [nɔb] n bottone m, manopola

knock [nɔk] vt colpire; urtare; (*fig: inf*) criticare ▷ vi (*at door etc*): **to ~ at/on** bussare a ▷ n bussata; colpo, botta; **knock down** vt abbattere; **knock off** vi (*inf: finish*) smettere (di lavorare) ▷ vt (*from price*) far abbassare; (*inf: steal*) sgraffignare; **knock out** vt stendere; (*Boxing*) mettere K.O.; (*defeat*) battere; **knock over** vt (*person*) investire; (*object*) far cadere; **knockout** n (*Boxing*) knock out m inv ▷ cpd a eliminazione

knot [nɔt] *n* nodo ▷ *vt* annodare
know [nəu] (*pt* **knew**, *pp* **known**) *vt* sapere; (*person, author, place*) conoscere; **I don't ~** non lo so; **do you ~ where I can …?** sa dove posso …?; **to ~ how to do** sapere fare; **to ~ about** *or* **of sth/sb** conoscere qc/qn; **know-all** *n* sapientone(-a); **know-how** *n* tecnica; pratica; **knowing** *adj* (*look etc*) d'intesa; **knowingly** *adv* (*purposely*) consapevolmente; (*smile, look*) con aria d'intesa; **know-it-all** (*US*) *n* = **know-all**
knowledge ['nɔlɪdʒ] *n* consapevolezza; (*learning*) conoscenza, sapere *m*; **knowledgeable** *adj* ben informato(-a)
known [nəun] *pp of* **know**
knuckle ['nʌkl] *n* nocca
koala [kəu'ɑːlə] *n* (*also:* **~ bear**) koala *m inv*
Koran [kɔ'rɑːn] *n* Corano
Korea [kə'rɪə] *n* Corea; **Korean** *adj, n* coreano(-a)
kosher ['kəuʃəʳ] *adj* kasher *inv*
Kosovar, Kosovan ['kɔsəvaʳ, 'kɔsəvən] *adj* kosovaro(-a)
Kosovo ['kusəvəu] *n* Kosovo
Kremlin ['krɛmlɪn] *n* **the ~** il Cremlino
Kuwait [ku'weɪt] *n* Kuwait *m*

L (*BRIT*) *abbr* = **learner driver**
l. *abbr* (= *litre*) l
lab [læb] *n abbr* (= *laboratory*) laboratorio
label ['leɪbl] *n* etichetta, cartellino; (*brand: of record*) casa ▷ *vt* etichettare
labor *etc* ['leɪbəʳ] (*US*) = **labour** *etc*
laboratory [lə'bɔrətərɪ] *n* laboratorio
Labor Day (*US*) *n* festa del lavoro

> ● **LABOR DAY**
> ●
> ● Negli Stati Uniti e nel Canada il **Labor**
> ● **Day**, la festa del lavoro, cade il primo
> ● lunedì di settembre, contrariamente a
> ● quanto accade nella maggior parte dei
> ● paesi europei dove tale celebrazione ha
> ● luogo il primo maggio.

labor union (*US*) *n* sindacato
labour ['leɪbəʳ] (*US* **labor**) *n* (*task*) lavoro; (*workmen*) manodopera; (*Med*): **to be in ~** avere le doglie ▷ *vi* **to ~ (at)** lavorare duro (a); **L~, the L~ party** (*BRIT*) il partito laburista, i laburisti; **hard ~** lavori *mpl* forzati; **labourer** *n* manovale *m*; **farm labourer** lavoratore *m* agricolo
lace [leɪs] *n* merletto, pizzo; (*of shoe etc*) laccio ▷ *vt* (*shoe: also:* **~ up**) allacciare
lack [læk] *n* mancanza ▷ *vt* mancare di; **through** *or* **for ~ of** per mancanza di; **to be**

~ing mancare; **to be ~ing in** mancare di

lacquer ['lækəʳ] *n* lacca

lacy ['leɪsɪ] *adj (like lace)* che sembra un pizzo

lad [læd] *n* ragazzo, giovanotto

ladder ['lædəʳ] *n* scala; (BRIT: *in tights*) smagliatura

ladle ['leɪdl] *n* mestolo

lady ['leɪdɪ] *n* signora; dama; **L~ Smith** lady Smith; **the ladies' (room)** i gabinetti per signore; **ladybird** (US **ladybug**) *n* coccinella

lag [læg] *n (of time)* lasso, intervallo ▷ *vi (also: ~ behind)* trascinarsi ▷ *vt (pipes)* rivestire di materiale isolante

lager ['lɑːgəʳ] *n* lager *m inv*

lagoon [lə'guːn] *n* laguna

laid [leɪd] *pt, pp of* **lay; laid back** *(inf) adj* rilassato(-a), tranquillo(-a)

lain [leɪn] *pp of* **lie**

lake [leɪk] *n* lago

lamb [læm] *n* agnello

lame [leɪm] *adj* zoppo(-a); *(excuse etc)* zoppicante

lament [lə'mɛnt] *n* lamento ▷ *vt* lamentare, piangere

lamp [læmp] *n* lampada; **lamppost** ['læmppəʊst] (BRIT) *n* lampione *m*; **lampshade** ['læmpʃeɪd] *n* paralume *m*

land [lænd] *n (as opposed to sea)* terra (ferma); *(country)* paese *m*; *(soil)* terreno; suolo; *(estate)* terreni *mpl*, terre *fpl* ▷ *vi (from ship)* sbarcare; *(Aviat)* atterrare; *(fig: fall)* cadere ▷ *vt (passengers)* sbarcare; *(goods)* scaricare; **to ~ sb with sth** affibbiare qc a qn; **landing** *n* atterraggio; *(of staircase)* pianerottolo; **landing card** *n* carta di sbarco; **landlady** *n* padrona *or* proprietaria di casa; **landlord** *n* padrone *m or* proprietario di casa; *(of pub etc)* padrone *m*; **landmark** *n* punto di riferimento; *(fig)* pietra miliare; **landowner** *n* proprietario(-a) terriero(-a); **landscape** *n* paesaggio; **landslide** *n (Geo)* frana; *(fig: Pol)* valanga

lane [leɪn] *n* stradina; *(Aut, in race)* corsia; **"get in ~"** "immettersi in corsia"

language ['læŋgwɪdʒ] *n* lingua; *(way one speaks)* linguaggio; **what ~s do you speak?** che lingue parla?; **bad ~** linguaggio volgare; **language laboratory** *n* laboratorio linguistico

lantern ['læntn] *n* lanterna

lap [læp] *n (of track)* giro; *(of body):* **in** *or* **on one's ~** in grembo ▷ *vt (also: ~ up)* papparsi, leccare ▷ *vi (waves)* sciabordare

lapel [lə'pɛl] *n* risvolto

lapse [læps] *n* lapsus *m inv*; *(longer)* caduta ▷ *vi (law)* cadere; *(membership, contract)* scadere; **to ~ into bad habits** pigliare cattive abitudini; **~ of time** spazio di tempo

laptop (computer) ['læptɔp-] *n* laptop *m inv*

lard [lɑːd] *n* lardo

larder ['lɑːdəʳ] *n* dispensa

large [lɑːdʒ] *adj* grande; *(person, animal)* grosso(-a); **at ~** *(free)* in libertà; *(generally)* in generale; nell'insieme; **largely** *adv* in gran parte; **large-scale** *adj (map, drawing etc)* in grande scala; *(reforms, business activities)* su vasta scala

lark [lɑːk] *n (bird)* allodola; *(joke)* scherzo, gioco

laryngitis [lærɪn'dʒaɪtɪs] *n* laringite *f*

lasagne [lə'zænjə] *n* lasagne *fpl*

laser ['leɪzəʳ] *n* laser *m*; **laser printer** *n* stampante *f* laser *inv*

lash [læʃ] *n* frustata; *(also:* **eye~***)* ciglio ▷ *vt* frustare; *(tie):* **to ~ to/together** legare a insieme; **lash out** *vi* **to ~ out (at** *or* **against sb)** attaccare violentemente (qn)

lass [læs] *n* ragazza

last [lɑːst] *adj* ultimo(-a); *(week, month, year)* scorso(-a), passato(-a) ▷ *adv* per ultimo ▷ *vi* durare; **~ week** la settimana scorsa; **~ night** ieri sera, la notte scorsa; **at ~** finalmente, alla fine; **~ but one** penultimo(-a); **lastly** *adv* infine, per finire; **last-minute** *adj* fatto(-a) *(or* preso(-a) *etc)* all'ultimo momento

latch [lætʃ] *n* chiavistello; **latch onto** *vt fus (cling to: person)* attaccarsi a, appiccicarsi a; *(: idea)* afferrare, capire

late [leɪt] *adj (not on time)* in ritardo; *(far on in day etc)* tardi *inv*; tardo(-a); *(former)* ex; *(dead)* defunto(-a) ▷ *adv* tardi; *(behind time, schedule)* in ritardo; **sorry I'm ~** scusi il ritardo; **the flight is two hours ~** il volo ha due ore di ritardo; **it's too ~** è troppo tardi; **of ~** di recente; **in the ~ afternoon** nel tardo pomeriggio; **in ~ May** verso la fine di maggio; **latecomer** *n* ritardatario(-a); **lately** *adv* recentemente; **later** ['leɪtəʳ] *adj (date etc)* posteriore; *(version etc)* successivo(-a) ▷ *adv* più tardi; **later on** più avanti; **latest** ['leɪtɪst] *adj* ultimo(-a), più recente; **at the latest** al più tardi

lather ['lɑːðəʳ] *n* schiuma di sapone ▷ *vt* insaponare

Latin ['lætɪn] *n* latino ▷ *adj* latino(-a); **Latin America** *n* America Latina; **Latin American** *adj* sudamericano(-a)

latitude ['lætɪtjuːd] *n* latitudine *f*; *(fig)* libertà d'azione

latter ['lætəʳ] *adj* secondo(-a), più recente ▷ *n* **the ~** quest'ultimo, il secondo

laugh [lɑːf] *n* risata ▷ *vi* ridere; **laugh at**

vt fus (*misfortune etc*) ridere di; **laughter** *n* riso; risate *fpl*

launch [lɔːntʃ] *n* (*of rocket, Comm*) lancio; (*of new ship*) varo; (*also:* **motor ~**) lancia ▷ *vt* (*rocket, Comm*) lanciare; (*ship, plan*) varare; **launch into** *vt fus* lanciarsi in

launder [ˈlɔːndəʳ] *vt* lavare e stirare

Launderette® [lɔːnˈdrɛt] (*BRIT*) *n* lavanderia (automatica)

Laundromat® [ˈlɔːndrəmæt] (*US*) *n* lavanderia automatica

laundry [ˈlɔːndrɪ] *n* lavanderia; (*clothes*) biancheria; (: *dirty*) panni *mpl* da lavare

lava [ˈlɑːvə] *n* lava

lavatory [ˈlævətərɪ] *n* gabinetto

lavender [ˈlævəndəʳ] *n* lavanda

lavish [ˈlævɪʃ] *adj* copioso(-a), abbondante; (*giving freely*): **~ with** prodigo(-a) di, largo(-a) in ▷ *vt* **to ~ sth on sb** colmare qn di qc

law [lɔː] *n* legge *f*; **civil/criminal ~** diritto civile/penale; **lawful** *adj* legale, lecito(-a); **lawless** *adj* che non conosce nessuna legge

lawn [lɔːn] *n* tappeto erboso; **lawnmower** *n* tosaerba *m or f inv*

lawsuit [ˈlɔːsuːt] *n* processo, causa

lawyer [ˈlɔːjəʳ] *n* (*for sales, wills etc*) ≈ notaio; (*partner, in court*) ≈ avvocato(-essa)

lax [læks] *adj* rilassato(-a), negligente

laxative [ˈlæksətɪv] *n* lassativo

lay [leɪ] (*pt, pp* **laid**) *pt of* **lie** ▷ *adj* laico(-a); (*not expert*) profano(-a) ▷ *vt* posare, mettere; (*eggs*) fare; (*trap*) tendere; (*plans*) fare, elaborare; **to ~ the table** apparecchiare la tavola; **lay down** *vt* mettere giù; (*rules etc*) formulare, fissare; **to ~ down the law** dettar legge; **to ~ down one's life** dare la propria vita; **lay off** *vt* (*workers*) licenziare; **lay on** *vt* (*provide*) fornire; **lay out** *vt* (*display*) presentare, disporre; **lay-by** (*BRIT*) *n* piazzola (di sosta)

layer [ˈleɪəʳ] *n* strato

layman [ˈleɪmən] (*irreg*) *n* laico; profano

layout [ˈleɪaut] *n* lay-out *m inv*, disposizione *f*; (*Press*) impaginazione *f*

lazy [ˈleɪzɪ] *adj* pigro(-a)

lb. *abbr* = **pound** (*weight*)

lead¹ [liːd] (*pt, pp* **led**) *n* (*front position*) posizione *f* di testa; (*distance, time ahead*) vantaggio; (*clue*) indizio; (*Elec*) filo (elettrico); (*for dog*) guinzaglio; (*Theatre*) parte *f* principale ▷ *vt* guidare, condurre; (*induce*) indurre; (*be leader of*) essere a capo di ▷ *vi* condurre; (*Sport*) essere in testa; **in the ~** in testa; **to ~ the way** fare strada; **lead up to** *vt fus* portare a

lead² [lɛd] *n* (*metal*) piombo; (*in pencil*) mina

leader [ˈliːdəʳ] *n* capo; leader *m inv*; (*in newspaper*) articolo di fondo; (*Sport*) chi è in testa; **leadership** *n* direzione *f*; capacità di comando

lead-free [ˈlɛdfriː] *adj* senza piombo

leading [ˈliːdɪŋ] *adj* primo(-a), principale

lead singer *n* cantante alla testa di un gruppo

leaf [liːf] (*pl* **leaves**) *n* foglia ▷ *vi* **to ~ through sth** sfogliare qc; **to turn over a new ~** cambiar vita

leaflet [ˈliːflɪt] *n* dépliant *m inv*; (*Pol, Rel*) volantino

league [liːg] *n* lega; (*Football*) campionato; **to be in ~ with** essere in lega con

leak [liːk] *n* (*out*) fuga; (*in*) infiltrazione *f*; (*security leak*) fuga d'informazioni ▷ *vi* (*roof, bucket*) perdere; (*liquid*) uscire; (*shoes*) lasciar passare l'acqua ▷ *vt* (*information*) divulgare

lean [liːn] (*pt, pp* **leaned** *or* **leant**) *adj* magro(-a) ▷ *vt* **to ~ sth on sth** appoggiare qc su qc ▷ *vi* (*slope*) pendere; (*rest*): **to ~ against** appoggiarsi contro; essere appoggiato(-a) a; **to ~ on** appoggiarsi a; **lean forward** *vi* sporgersi in avanti; **lean over** *vi* inclinarsi; **leaning** *n* leaning (towards) propensione *f* (per)

leant [lɛnt] *pt, pp of* **lean**

leap [liːp] (*pt, pp* **leaped** *or* **leapt**) *n* salto, balzo ▷ *vi* saltare, balzare

leapt [lɛpt] *pt, pp of* **leap**

leap year *n* anno bisestile

learn [ləːn] (*pt, pp* **learned** *or* **learnt**) *vt, vi* imparare; **to ~ about sth** (*hear, read*) apprendere qc; **to ~ to do sth** imparare a fare qc; **learner** *n* principiante *m/f*; apprendista *m/f*; (*BRIT: also:* **learner driver**) guidatore(-trice) *m/f* principiante; **learning** *n* erudizione *f*, sapienza

learnt [ləːnt] *pt, pp of* **learn**

lease [liːs] *n* contratto d'affitto ▷ *vt* affittare

leash [liːʃ] *n* guinzaglio

least [liːst] *adj* **the ~** (+ *noun*) il (la) più piccolo(-a), il (la) minimo(-a); (*smallest amount of*) il (la) meno ▷ *adv* (+ *verb*) meno; **the ~** (+ *adjective*): **the ~ beautiful girl** la ragazza meno bella; **the ~ possible effort** il minimo sforzo possibile; **I have the ~ money** ho meno denaro di tutti; **at ~** almeno; **not in the ~** affatto, per nulla

leather [ˈlɛðəʳ] *n* cuoio

leave [liːv] (*pt, pp* **left**) *vt* lasciare; (*go away from*) partire da ▷ *vi* partire, andarsene; (*bus, train*) partire ▷ *n* (*time off*) congedo; (*Mil, consent*) licenza; **what time does the train/bus ~?** a che ora parte il treno/

l'autobus?; **to be left** rimanere; **there's some milk left over** c'è rimasto del latte; **on ~** in congedo; **leave behind** vt (person, object) lasciare; (: forget) dimenticare; **leave out** vt omettere, tralasciare

leaves [li:vz] npl of **leaf**

Lebanon ['lɛbənən] n Libano

lecture ['lɛktʃəʳ] n conferenza; (Scol) lezione f ▷ vi fare conferenze; fare lezioni ▷ vt (scold): **to ~ sb on** or **about sth** rimproverare qn or fare una rimanzina a qn per qc; **to give a ~ on** tenere una conferenza su; **lecture hall** n aula magna; **lecturer** ['lɛktʃərəʳ] (BRIT) n (at university) professore(-essa), docente m/f; **lecture theatre** n = **lecture hall**

led [lɛd] pt, pp of **lead**

ledge [lɛdʒ] n (of window) davanzale m; (on wall etc) sporgenza; (of mountain) cornice f, cengia

leek [li:k] n porro

left [lɛft] pt, pp of **leave** ▷ adj sinistro(-a) ▷ adv a sinistra ▷ n sinistra; **on the ~, to the ~** a sinistra; **the L~** (Pol) la sinistra; **left-hand** adj **the left-hand side** il lato sinistro; **left-hand drive** adj guida a sinistra; **left-handed** adj mancino(-a); **left-luggage locker** n armadietto per deposito bagagli; **left-luggage (office)** (BRIT) n deposito m bagagli inv; **left-overs** npl avanzi mpl, resti mpl; **left-wing** adj (Pol) di sinistra

leg [lɛg] n gamba; (of animal) zampa; (of furniture) piede m; (Culin: of chicken) coscia; (of journey) tappa; **1st/2nd ~** (Sport) partita di andata/ritorno

legacy ['lɛgəsɪ] n eredità f inv

legal ['li:gl] adj legale; **legal holiday** (US) n giorno festivo, festa nazionale; **legalize** vt legalizzare; **legally** adv legalmente; **legally binding** legalmente vincolante

legend ['lɛdʒənd] n leggenda; **legendary** ['lɛdʒəndərɪ] adj leggendario(-a)

leggings ['lɛgɪŋz] npl ghette fpl

legible ['lɛdʒəbl] adj leggibile

legislation [lɛdʒɪs'leɪʃən] n legislazione f

legislative ['lɛdʒɪslətɪv] adj legislativo(-a)

legitimate [lɪ'dʒɪtɪmət] adj legittimo(-a)

leisure ['lɛʒəʳ] n agio, tempo libero; ricreazioni fpl; **at ~** con comodo; **leisure centre** n centro di ricreazione; **leisurely** adj tranquillo(-a), fatto(-a) con comodo or senza fretta

lemon ['lɛmən] n limone m; **lemonade** [-'neɪd] n limonata; **lemon tea** n tè m inv al limone

lend [lɛnd] (pt, pp **lent**) vt **to ~ sth (to sb)** prestare qc (a qn); **could you ~ me some money?** mi può prestare dei soldi?

length [lɛŋθ] n lunghezza; (distance) distanza; (section: of road, pipe etc) pezzo, tratto; (of time) periodo; **at ~** (at last) finalmente, alla fine; (lengthily) a lungo; **lengthen** vt allungare, prolungare ▷ vi allungarsi; **lengthways** adv per il lungo; **lengthy** adj molto lungo(-a)

lens [lɛnz] n lente f; (of camera) obiettivo

Lent [lɛnt] n Quaresima

lent [lɛnt] pt, pp of **lend**

lentil ['lɛntl] n lenticchia

Leo ['li:əu] n Leone m

leopard ['lɛpəd] n leopardo

leotard ['li:əta:d] n calzamaglia

leprosy ['lɛprəsɪ] n lebbra

lesbian ['lɛzbɪən] n lesbica

less [lɛs] adj, pron, adv meno ▷ prep **~ tax/10% discount** meno tasse/il 10% di sconto; **~ than ever** meno che mai; **~ than half** meno della metà; **~ and ~** sempre meno; **the ~ he works ...** meno lavora ...; **lessen** ['lɛsn] vi diminuire, attenuarsi ▷ vt diminuire, ridurre; **lesser** ['lɛsəʳ] adj minore, più piccolo(-a); **to a lesser extent** in grado or misura minore

lesson ['lɛsn] n lezione f; **to teach sb a ~** dare una lezione a qn

let [lɛt] (pt, pp **let**) vt lasciare; (BRIT: lease) dare in affitto; **to ~ sb do sth** lasciar fare qc a qn, lasciare che qn faccia qc; **to ~ sb know sth** far sapere qc a qn; **~'s go** andiamo; **~ him come** lo lasci venire; **"to ~"** "affittasi"; **let down** vt (lower) abbassare; (dress) allungare; (hair) sciogliere; (tyre) sgonfiare; (disappoint) deludere; **let in** vt lasciare entrare; (visitor etc) far entrare; **let off** vt (allow to go) lasciare andare; (firework etc) far partire; **let out** vt lasciare uscire; (scream) emettere

lethal ['li:θl] adj letale, mortale

letter ['lɛtəʳ] n lettera; **letterbox** (BRIT) n buca delle lettere

lettuce ['lɛtɪs] n lattuga, insalata

leukaemia [lu:'ki:mɪə] (US **leukemia**) n leucemia

level ['lɛvl] adj piatto(-a), piano(-a); orizzontale ▷ adv **to draw ~ with** mettersi alla pari di ▷ n livello ▷ vt livellare, spianare; **to be ~ with** essere alla pari di; **level crossing** (BRIT) n passaggio a livello

lever ['li:vəʳ] n leva; **leverage** n **leverage (on** or **with)** forza (su); (fig) ascendente m (su)

levy ['lɛvɪ] n tassa, imposta ▷ vt imporre

liability [laɪə'bɪlətɪ] n responsabilità f inv; (handicap) peso

liable ['laɪəbl] adj (subject): **~ to**

soggetto(-a) a; passibile di; (*responsible*): ~ **for** responsabile (di); (*likely*): ~ **to do** propenso(-a) a fare

liaise [liː'eɪz] *vi* **to ~ (with)** mantenere i contatti (con)

liar ['laɪəʳ] *n* bugiardo(-a)

liberal ['lɪbərl] *adj* liberale; (*generous*): **to be ~ with** distribuire liberalmente; **Liberal Democrat** *n* liberaldemocratico(-a)

liberate ['lɪbəreɪt] *vt* liberare

liberation [lɪbə'reɪʃən] *n* liberazione *f*

liberty ['lɪbətɪ] *n* libertà *f inv*; **at ~** (*criminal*) in libertà; **at ~ to do** libero(-a) di fare

Libra ['liːbrə] *n* Bilancia

librarian [laɪ'brɛərɪən] *n* bibliotecario(-a)

library ['laɪbrərɪ] *n* biblioteca

Libya ['lɪbɪə] *n* Libia

lice [laɪs] *npl of* **louse**

licence ['laɪsns] (*us* **license**) *n* autorizzazione *f*, permesso; (*Comm*) licenza; (*Radio, TV*) canone *m*, abbonamento; (*also*: **driving ~**: *us: also*: **driver's license**) patente *f* di guida; (*excessive freedom*) licenza

license ['laɪsns] *n* (*us*) = **licence** ▷ *vt* dare una licenza a; **licensed** *adj* (*for alcohol*) che ha la licenza di vendere bibite alcoliche; **license plate** (*esp us*) *n* (*Aut*) targa (automobilistica); **licensing hours** (*brit*) *npl* orario d'apertura (*di un pub*)

lick [lɪk] *vt* leccare; (*inf: defeat*) stracciare; **to ~ one's lips** (*fig*) leccarsi i baffi

lid [lɪd] *n* coperchio; (*eyelid*) palpebra

lie [laɪ] (*pt* **lay**, *pp* **lain**) *vi* (*rest*) giacere, star disteso(-a); (*of object: be situated*) trovarsi, essere; (*tell lies: pt, pp* **lied**) mentire, dire bugie ▷ *n* bugia, menzogna; **to ~ low** (*fig*) latitare; **lie about or around** *vi* (*things*) essere in giro; (*person*) bighellonare; **lie down** *vi* stendersi, sdraiarsi

Liechtenstein ['lɪktənstaɪn] *n* Liechtenstein *m*

lie-in ['laɪɪn] (*brit*) *n* **to have a ~** rimanere a letto

lieutenant [lɛf'tɛnənt, (*us*) luː'tɛnənt] *n* tenente *m*

life [laɪf] (*pl* **lives**) *n* vita ▷ *cpd* di vita; della vita; a vita; **to come to ~** rianimarsi; **life assurance** (*brit*) *n* = **life insurance**; **lifeboat** *n* scialuppa di salvataggio; **lifeguard** *n* bagnino; **life insurance** *n* assicurazione *f* sulla vita; **life jacket** *n* giubbotto di salvataggio; **lifelike** *adj* verosimile; rassomigliante; **life preserver** [-prɪ'zə:vəʳ] (*us*) *n* salvagente *m*; giubbotto di salvataggio; **life sentence** *n* ergastolo; **lifestyle** *n* stile *m* di vita; **lifetime** *n* **in his lifetime** durante

la sua vita; **once in a lifetime** una volta nella vita

lift [lɪft] *vt* sollevare; (*ban, rule*) levare ▷ *vi* (*fog*) alzarsi ▷ *n* (*brit: elevator*) ascensore *m*; **to give sb a ~** (*brit*) dare un passaggio a qn; **can you give me a ~ to the station?** può darmi un passaggio fino alla stazione?; **lift up** *vt* sollevare, alzare; **lift-off** *n* decollo

light [laɪt] (*pt, pp* **lighted** *or* **lit**) *n* luce *f*, lume *m*; (*daylight*) luce *f*, giorno; (*lamp*) lampada; (*Aut: rear light*) luce *f* di posizione; (: *headlamp*) fanale *m*; (*for cigarette etc*): **have you got a ~?** ha da accendere?; ~**s** *npl* (*Aut: traffic lights*) semaforo *m* (*candle, cigarette, fire*) accendere; (*room*): **to be lit by** essere illuminato(-a) da *adj* (*room, colour*) chiaro(-a); (*not heavy, also fig*) leggero(-a); **to come to ~** venire alla luce, emergere; **light up** *vi* illuminarsi ▷ *vt* illuminare; **light bulb** *n* lampadina; **lighten** *vt* (*make less heavy*) alleggerire; **lighter** *n* (*also*: **cigarette lighter**) accendino; **light-hearted** *adj* gioioso(-a), gaio(-a); **lighthouse** *n* faro; **lighting** *n* illuminazione *f*; **lightly** *adv* leggermente; **to get off lightly** cavarsela a buon mercato

lightning ['laɪtnɪŋ] *n* lampo, fulmine *m*

lightweight ['laɪtweɪt] *adj* (*suit*) leggero(-a) ▷ *n* (*Boxing*) peso leggero

like [laɪk] *vt* (*person*) volere bene a; (*activity, object, food*): **I ~ swimming/ that book/chocolate** mi piace nuotare/quel libro/il cioccolato ▷ *prep* come ▷ *adj* simile, uguale ▷ *n* **the ~** uno(-a) uguale; **his ~s and dis~s** i suoi gusti; **I would ~, I'd ~** mi piacerebbe, vorrei; **would you ~ a coffee?** gradirebbe un caffè?; **to be/look ~ sb/sth** somigliare a qn/qc; **what does it look/taste ~?** che aspetto/gusto ha?; **what does it sound ~?** come fa?; **that's just ~ him** è proprio da lui; **do it ~ this** fallo così; **it is nothing ~ ...** non è affatto come ...; **likeable** *adj* simpatico(-a)

likelihood ['laɪklɪhud] *n* probabilità

likely ['laɪklɪ] *adj* probabile; plausibile; **he's ~ to leave** probabilmente partirà, è probabile che parta; **not ~!** neanche per sogno!

likewise ['laɪkwaɪz] *adv* similmente, nello stesso modo

liking ['laɪkɪŋ] *n* ~ **(for)** debole *m* (per); **to be to sb's ~** piacere a qn

lilac ['laɪlək] *n* lilla *m inv*

Lilo® ['laɪləu] *n* materassino gonfiabile

lily ['lɪlɪ] *n* giglio

limb [lɪm] *n* arto

limbo ['lɪmbəu] *n* **to be in ~** (*fig*) essere lasciato(-a) nel dimenticatoio

lime [laɪm] *n* (*tree*) tiglio; (*fruit*) limetta; (*Geo*) calce *f*

limelight ['laɪmlaɪt] *n* **in the ~** (*fig*) alla ribalta, in vista

limestone ['laɪmstəun] *n* pietra calcarea; (*Geo*) calcare *m*

limit ['lɪmɪt] *n* limite *m* ⊳ *vt* limitare; **limited** *adj* limitato(-a), ristretto(-a); **to be limited to** limitarsi a

limousine ['lɪməziːn] *n* limousine *f inv*

limp [lɪmp] *n* **to have a ~** zoppicare ⊳ *vi* zoppicare ⊳ *adj* floscio(-a), flaccido(-a)

line [laɪn] *n* linea; (*rope*) corda; (*for fishing*) lenza; (*wire*) filo; (*of poem*) verso; (*row, series*) fila, riga; coda; (*on face*) ruga ⊳ *vt* (*clothes*): **to ~ (with)** foderare (di); (*box*): **to ~ (with)** rivestire or foderare (di); (*trees, crowd*) fiancheggiare; **~ of business** settore *m* or ramo d'attività; **in ~ with** in linea con; **line up** *vi* allinearsi, mettersi in fila ⊳ *vt* mettere in fila; (*event, celebration*) preparare

linear ['lɪnɪər] *adj* lineare

linen ['lɪnɪn] *n* biancheria, panni *mpl*; (*cloth*) tela di lino

liner ['laɪnər] *n* nave *f* di linea; (*for bin*) sacchetto

line-up ['laɪnʌp] *n* allineamento, fila; (*Sport*) formazione *f* di gioco

linger ['lɪŋgər] *vi* attardarsi; indugiare; (*smell, tradition*) persistere

lingerie ['lænʒəriː] *n* biancheria intima femminile

linguist ['lɪŋgwɪst] *n* linguista *m/f*; poliglotta *m/f*; **linguistic** *adj* linguistico(-a)

lining ['laɪnɪŋ] *n* fodera

link [lɪŋk] *n* (*of a chain*) anello; (*relationship*) legame *m*; (*connection*) collegamento ⊳ *vt* collegare, unire, congiungere; (*associate*): **to ~ with** or **to** collegare a; **~s** *npl* (*Golf*) pista or terreno da golf; **link up** *vt* collegare, unire ⊳ *vi* riunirsi; associarsi

lion ['laɪən] *n* leone *m*; **lioness** *n* leonessa

lip [lɪp] *n* labbro; (*of cup etc*) orlo; **lip-read** *vi* leggere sulle labbra; **lip salve** [-sælv] *n* burro di cacao; **lipstick** *n* rossetto

liqueur [lɪ'kjuər] *n* liquore *m*

liquid ['lɪkwɪd] *n* liquido ⊳ *adj* liquido(-a); **liquidizer** *n* frullatore *m* (a brocca)

liquor ['lɪkər] *n* alcool *m*; **liquor store** (*US*) *n* negozio di liquori

Lisbon ['lɪzbən] *n* Lisbona

lisp [lɪsp] *n* pronuncia blesa della "s"

list [lɪst] *n* lista, elenco ⊳ *vt* (*write down*) mettere in lista; fare una lista di; (*enumerate*) elencare

listen ['lɪsn] *vi* ascoltare; **to ~ to** ascoltare; **listener** *n* ascoltatore(-trice)

lit [lɪt] *pt, pp of* **light**

liter ['liːtər] (*US*) *n* = **litre**

literacy ['lɪtərəsɪ] *n* il sapere leggere e scrivere

literal ['lɪtərl] *adj* letterale; **literally** *adv* alla lettera, letteralmente

literary ['lɪtərərɪ] *adj* letterario(-a)

literate ['lɪtərət] *adj* che sa leggere e scrivere

literature ['lɪtərɪtʃər] *n* letteratura; (*brochures etc*) materiale *m*

litre ['liːtər] (*US* **liter**) *n* litro

litter ['lɪtər] *n* (*rubbish*) rifiuti *mpl*; (*young animals*) figliata; **litter bin** (*BRIT*) *n* cestino per rifiuti; **littered** *adj* **littered with** coperto(-a) di

little ['lɪtl] *adj* (*small*) piccolo(-a); (*not much*) poco(-a) ⊳ *adv* poco; **a ~** un po' (di), **a ~ bit** un pochino; **~ by ~** a poco a poco; **little finger** *n* mignolo

live¹ [lɪv] *vi* vivere; (*reside*) vivere, abitare; **where do you ~?** dove abita?; **live together** *vi* vivere insieme, convivere; **live up to** *vt fus* tener fede a, non venir meno a

live² [laɪv] *adj* (*animal*) vivo(-a); (*wire*) sotto tensione; (*bullet, missile*) inesploso(-a); (*broadcast*) diretto(-a); (*performance*) dal vivo

livelihood ['laɪvlɪhud] *n* mezzi *mpl* di sostentamento

lively ['laɪvlɪ] *adj* vivace, vivo(-a)

liven up ['laɪvnʌp] *vt* (*discussion, evening*) animare ⊳ *vi* ravvivarsi

liver ['lɪvər] *n* fegato

lives [laɪvz] *npl of* **life**

livestock ['laɪvstɔk] *n* bestiame *m*

living ['lɪvɪŋ] *adj* vivo(-a), vivente ⊳ *n* **to earn** or **make a ~** guadagnarsi la vita; **living room** *n* soggiorno

lizard ['lɪzəd] *n* lucertola

load [ləud] *n* (*weight*) peso; (*thing carried*) carico ⊳ *vt* (*also*: **~ up**): **to ~ (with)** (*lorry, ship*) caricare (di); (*gun, camera, Comput*) caricare (con); **a ~ of, ~s of** (*fig*) un sacco di; **loaded** *adj* (*vehicle*): **loaded (with)** carico(-a) (di); (*question*) capzioso(-a); (*inf: rich*) carico(-a) di soldi

loaf [ləuf] (*pl* **loaves**) *n* pane *m*, pagnotta

loan [ləun] *n* prestito ⊳ *vt* dare in prestito; **on ~** in prestito

loathe [ləuð] *vt* detestare, aborrire

loaves [ləuvz] *npl of* **loaf**

lobby ['lɔbɪ] *n* atrio, vestibolo; (*Pol: pressure group*) gruppo di pressione ⊳ *vt* fare pressione su

lobster ['lɔbstəʳ] n aragosta
local ['ləukl] adj locale ▷ n (BRIT: pub)
≈ bar m inv all'angolo; **the ~s** npl (local
inhabitants) la gente della zona; **local
anaesthetic** n anestesia locale; **local
authority** n ente m locale; **local
government** n amministrazione f locale;
locally ['ləukəlɪ] adv da queste parti; nel
vicinato
locate [ləu'keɪt] vt (find) trovare; (situate)
collocare; situare
location [ləu'keɪʃən] n posizione f; **on ~**
(Cinema) all'esterno
loch [lɔx] n lago
lock [lɔk] n (of door, box) serratura; (of
canal) chiusa; (of hair) ciocca, riccio ▷ vt
(with key) chiudere a chiave ▷ vi (door etc)
chiudersi; (wheels) bloccarsi, incepparsi;
lock in vt chiudere dentro (a chiave);
lock out vt chiudere fuori; **lock up** vt
(criminal, mental patient) rinchiudere;
(house) chiudere (a chiave) ▷ vi chiudere
tutto (a chiave)
locker ['lɔkəʳ] n armadietto; **locker-room**
(US) n (Sport) spogliatoio
locksmith ['lɔksmɪθ] n magnano
locomotive [ləukə'məutɪv] n
locomotiva
lodge [lɔdʒ] n casetta, portineria; (hunting
lodge) casino di caccia ▷ vi (person): **to
~ (with)** essere a pensione (presso or
da); (bullet etc) conficcarsi ▷ vt (appeal
etc) presentare, fare; **to ~ a complaint**
presentare un reclamo; **lodger** n
affittuario(-a); (with room and meals)
pensionante m/f
lodging ['lɔdʒɪŋ] n alloggio; see also
board
loft [lɔft] n solaio, soffitta
log [lɔg] n (of wood) ceppo; (also: ~book:
Naut, Aviat) diario di bordo; (Aut) libretto
di circolazione ▷ vt registrare; **log in** vi
(Comput) aprire una sessione (con codice
di riconoscimento); **log off** vi (Comput)
terminare una sessione
logic ['lɔdʒɪk] n logica; **logical** adj
logico(-a)
logo ['ləugəu] n logo m inv
lollipop ['lɔlɪpɔp] n lecca lecca m inv
lolly ['lɔlɪ] (inf) n lecca lecca m inv; (also: **ice
~**) ghiacciolo; (money) grana
London ['lʌndən] n Londra; **Londoner** n
londinese m/f
lone [ləun] adj solitario(-a)
loneliness ['ləunlɪnɪs] n solitudine f,
isolamento
lonely ['ləunlɪ] adj solo(-a); solitario(-a),
isolato(-a)
long [lɔŋ] adj lungo(-a) ▷ adv a lungo,

per molto tempo ▷ vi **to ~ for sth/to do**
desiderare qc/di fare, non veder l'ora di
aver qc/di fare; **so** or **as ~ as** (while) finché;
(provided that) sempre che + sub; **don't be
~!** fai presto!; **how ~ is this river/course?**
quanto è lungo questo fiume/corso?;
6 metres ~ lungo 6 metri; **6 months ~**
che dura 6 mesi, di 6 mesi; **all night ~**
tutta la notte; **he no ~er comes** non
viene più; **~ before** molto tempo prima;
before ~ (+ future) presto, fra poco; (+ past)
poco tempo dopo; **at ~ last** finalmente;
long-distance adj (race) di fondo; (call)
interurbano(-a); **long-haul** ['lɔŋhɔ:l] adj
(flight) a lunga percorrenza inv; **longing** n
desiderio, voglia, brama
longitude ['lɔŋgɪtju:d] n longitudine f
long: long jump n salto in lungo; **long-
life** adj (milk) a lunga conservazione;
(batteries) di lunga durata; **long-sighted**
adj presbite; **long-standing** adj di
vecchia data; **long-term** adj a lungo
termine
loo [lu:] (BRIT: inf) n W.C. m inv, cesso
look [luk] vi guardare; (seem) sembrare,
parere; (building etc): **to ~ south/on
to the sea** dare a sud/sul mare ▷ n
sguardo; (appearance) aspetto, aria;
~s npl (good looks) bellezza; **look after**
vt fus occuparsi di, prendere cura di;
(keep an eye on) guardare, badare a; **look
around** vi guardarsi intorno; **look at** vt
fus guardare; **look back** vi **to ~ back on**
(event etc) ripensare a; **look down on** vt
fus (fig) guardare dall'alto, disprezzare;
look for vt fus cercare; **we're ~ing for a
hotel/restaurant** stiamo cercando un
albergo/ristorante; **look forward to** vt fus
non veder l'ora di; (in letters): **we ~ forward
to hearing from you** in attesa di una
vostra gentile risposta; **look into** vt fus
esaminare; **look out** vi (beware): **to ~ out
(for)** stare in guardia (per); **look out for** vt
fus cercare; **look round** vi (turn) girarsi,
voltarsi; (in shop) dare un'occhiata; **look
through** vt fus (papers, book) scorrere;
(telescope) guardare attraverso; **look up**
vi alzare gli occhi; (improve) migliorare
▷ vt (word) cercare; (friend) andare a
trovare; **look up to** vt fus avere rispetto
per; **lookout** n posto d'osservazione;
guardia; **to be on the lookout (for)** stare
in guardia (per)
loom [lu:m] n telaio ▷ vi (also: **~ up**)
apparire minaccioso(-a); (event) essere
imminente
loony ['lu:nɪ] (inf) n pazzo(-a)
loop [lu:p] n cappio ▷ vt **to ~ sth round
sth** passare qc intorno a qc; **loophole** n

via d'uscita; scappatoia

loose [luːs] *adj* (*knot*) sciolto(-a); (*screw*) allentato(-a); (*stone*) cadente; (*clothes*) ampio(-a), largo(-a); (*animal*) in libertà; scappato(-a); (*life, morals*) dissoluto(-a) ▷ *n* **to be on the ~** essere in libertà; **loosely** *adv* senza stringere; approssimativamente; **loosen** *vt* sciogliere; (*belt etc*) allentare

loot [luːt] *n* bottino ▷ *vt* saccheggiare

lop-sided [ˈlɔpˈsaɪdɪd] *adj* non equilibrato(-a), asimmetrico(-a)

lord [lɔːd] *n* signore *m*; **L~ Smith** lord Smith; **the L~** il Signore; **good L~!** buon Dio!; **the (House of) L~s** (BRIT) la Camera dei Lord

lorry [ˈlɔrɪ] (BRIT) *n* camion *m inv*; **lorry driver** (BRIT) *n* camionista *m*

lose [luːz] (*pt, pp* **lost**) *vt* perdere ▷ *vi* perdere; **I've lost my wallet/passport** ho perso il portafoglio/passaporto; **to ~ (time)** (*clock*) ritardare; **lose out** *vi* rimetterci; **loser** *n* perdente *m/f*

loss [lɔs] *n* perdita; **to be at a ~** essere perplesso(-a)

lost [lɔst] *pt, pp of* **lose** ▷ *adj* perduto(-a); **I'm ~** mi sono perso; **lost property** (US **lost and found**) *n* oggetti *mpl* smarriti

lot [lɔt] *n* (*at auctions*) lotto; (*destiny*) destino, sorte *f*; **the ~** tutto(-a) quanto(-a); tutti(-e) quanti(-e); **a ~** molto; **a ~ of** una gran quantità di, un sacco di; **~s of** molto(-a); **to draw ~s (for sth)** tirare a sorte (per qc)

lotion [ˈləʊʃən] *n* lozione *f*

lottery [ˈlɔtərɪ] *n* lotteria

loud [laud] *adj* forte, alto(-a); (*gaudy*) vistoso(-a), sgargiante ▷ *adv* (*speak etc*) forte; **out ~** (*read etc*) ad alta voce; **loudly** *adv* fortemente, ad alta voce; **loudspeaker** *n* altoparlante *m*

lounge [laundʒ] *n* salotto, soggiorno; (*at airport, station*) sala d'attesa; (BRIT: *also:* **~ bar**) bar *m inv* con servizio a tavolino ▷ *vi* oziare

louse [laus] (*pl* **lice**) *n* pidocchio

lousy [ˈlauzɪ] (*inf*) *adj* orrendo(-a), schifoso(-a); **to feel ~** stare da cani

love [lʌv] *n* amore *m* ▷ *vt* amare; voler bene a; **to ~ to do: I ~ to do** mi piace fare; **to be/fall in ~ with** essere innamorato(-a)/innamorarsi di; **to make ~** fare l'amore; **"15 ~"** (*Tennis*) "15 a zero"; **love affair** *n* relazione *f*; **love life** *n* vita sentimentale

lovely [ˈlʌvlɪ] *adj* bello(-a); (*delicious: smell, meal*) buono(-a)

lover [ˈlʌvəʳ] *n* amante *m/f*; (*person in love*) innamorato(-a); (*amateur*): **a ~ of** un(-un') amante di; un(-un') appassionato(-a) di

loving [ˈlʌvɪŋ] *adj* affettuoso(-a)

low [ləʊ] *adj* basso(-a) ▷ *adv* in basso ▷ *n* (*Meteor*) depressione *f*; **to be ~ on** (*supplies etc*) avere scarsità di; **to feel ~** sentirsi giù; **low-alcohol** *adj* a basso contenuto alcolico; **low-calorie** *adj* a basso contenuto calorico

lower [ˈləʊəʳ] *adj* (*bottom: of 2 things*) più basso; (*less important*) meno importante ▷ *vt* calare; (*prices, eyes, voice*) abbassare

low-fat [ˈləʊˈfæt] *adj* magro(-a)

loyal [ˈlɔɪəl] *adj* fedele, leale; **loyalty** *n* fedeltà, lealtà; **loyalty card** *n* carta che offre sconti a clienti abituali

L.P. *n abbr* = **long-playing record**

L-plates [ˈɛlpleɪts] (BRIT) *npl* contrassegno P principiante

Lt *abbr* (= *lieutenant*) Ten.

Ltd *abbr* (= *limited*) ≈ S.r.l.

luck [lʌk] *n* fortuna, sorte *f*; **bad ~** sfortuna, mala sorte; **good ~!** buona fortuna!; **luckily** *adv* fortunatamente, per fortuna; **lucky** *adj* fortunato(-a); (*number etc*) che porta fortuna

lucrative [ˈluːkrətɪv] *adj* lucrativo(-a), lucroso(-a), profittevole

ludicrous [ˈluːdɪkrəs] *adj* ridicolo(-a)

luggage [ˈlʌgɪdʒ] *n* bagagli *mpl*; **our ~ hasn't arrived** i nostri bagagli non sono arrivati; **luggage rack** *n* portabagagli *m inv*

lukewarm [ˈluːkwɔːm] *adj* tiepido(-a)

lull [lʌl] *n* intervallo di calma ▷ *vt* **to ~ sb to sleep** cullare qn finché si addormenta

lullaby [ˈlʌləbaɪ] *n* ninnananna

lumber [ˈlʌmbəʳ] *n* (*wood*) legname *m*; (*junk*) roba vecchia

luminous [ˈluːmɪnəs] *adj* luminoso(-a)

lump [lʌmp] *n* pezzo; (*in sauce*) grumo; (*swelling*) gonfiore *m*; (*also:* **sugar ~**) zolletta ▷ *vt* (*also:* **~ together**) riunire, mettere insieme; **lump sum** *n* somma globale; **lumpy** *adj* (*sauce*) pieno(-a) di grumi; (*bed*) bitorzoluto(-a)

lunatic [ˈluːnətɪk] *adj* pazzo(-a), matto(-a)

lunch [lʌntʃ] *n* pranzo, colazione *f*; **lunch break** *n* intervallo del pranzo; **lunch time** *n* ora di pranzo

lung [lʌŋ] *n* polmone *m*

lure [ljuəʳ] *n* richiamo; lusinga ▷ *vt* attirare (con l'inganno)

lurk [ləːk] *vi* stare in agguato

lush [lʌʃ] *adj* lussureggiante

lust [lʌst] *n* lussuria; cupidigia; desiderio; (*fig*): **~ for** sete *f* di

Luxembourg [ˈlʌksəmbəːg] *n* (*state*) Lussemburgo *m*; (*city*) Lussemburgo *f*

luxurious [lʌg'zjuərɪəs] *adj* sontuoso(-a), di lusso
luxury ['lʌkʃərɪ] *n* lusso ▷ *cpd* di lusso
   Be careful not to translate *luxury* by the Italian word *lussuria*.
Lycra® ['laɪkrə] *n* lycra® *f inv*
lying ['laɪɪŋ] *n* bugie *fpl*, menzogne *fpl* ▷ *adj* bugiardo(-a)
lyrics ['lɪrɪks] *npl* (*of song*) parole *fpl*

m. *abbr* = **metre; mile; million**
M.A. *abbr* = **Master of Arts**
ma (*inf*) [mɑː] *n* mamma
mac [mæk] (BRIT) *n* impermeabile *m*
macaroni [mækə'rəunɪ] *n* maccheroni *mpl*
Macedonia [mæsɪ'dəunɪə] *n* Macedonia; **Macedonian** [mæsɪ'dəunɪən] *adj* macedone ▷ *n* macedone *m/f*; (*Ling*) macedone *m*
machine [mə'ʃiːn] *n* macchina ▷ *vt* (*Tech*) lavorare a macchina; (*dress etc*) cucire a macchina; **machine gun** *n* mitragliatrice *f*; **machinery** *n* macchinario, macchine *fpl*; (*fig*) macchina; **machine washable** *adj* lavabile in lavatrice
macho ['mætʃəu] *adj* macho *inv*
mackerel ['mækrl] *n inv* sgombro
mackintosh ['mækɪntɔʃ] (BRIT) *n* impermeabile *m*
mad [mæd] *adj* matto(-a), pazzo(-a); (*foolish*) sciocco(-a); (*angry*) furioso(-a); **to be ~ about** (*keen*) andare pazzo(-a) per
Madagascar [mædə'gæskəʳ] *n* Madagascar *m*
madam ['mædəm] *n* signora
mad cow disease *n* encefalite *f* bovina spongiforme
made [meɪd] *pt, pp of* **make**; **made-to-measure** (BRIT) *adj* fatto(-a) su

misura; **made-up** ['meɪdʌp] *adj* (*story*) inventato(-a)

madly ['mædlɪ] *adv* follemente

madman ['mædmən] (*irreg*) *n* pazzo, alienato

madness ['mædnɪs] *n* pazzia

Madrid [mə'drɪd] *n* Madrid *f*

Mafia ['mæfɪə] *n* mafia *f*

mag [mæg] *n abbr* (BRIT *inf*) = **magazine** (*Press*)

magazine [mægə'ziːn] *n* (*Press*) rivista; (*Radio, TV*) rubrica

> Be careful not to translate *magazine* by the Italian word *magazzino*.

maggot ['mægət] *n* baco, verme *m*

magic ['mædʒɪk] *n* magia ▷ *adj* magico(-a); **magical** *adj* magico(-a); **magician** [mə'dʒɪʃən] *n* mago(-a)

magistrate ['mædʒɪstreɪt] *n* magistrato; giudice *m/f*

magnet ['mægnɪt] *n* magnete *m*, calamita; **magnetic** [-'nɛtɪk] *adj* magnetico(-a)

magnificent [mæg'nɪfɪsnt] *adj* magnifico(-a)

magnify ['mægnɪfaɪ] *vt* ingrandire; **magnifying glass** *n* lente *f* d'ingrandimento

magpie ['mægpaɪ] *n* gazza

mahogany [mə'hɔgənɪ] *n* mogano

maid [meɪd] *n* domestica; (*in hotel*) cameriera

maiden name ['meɪdn-] *n* nome *m* da nubile *or* da ragazza

mail [meɪl] *n* posta ▷ *vt* spedire (per posta); **mailbox** (US) *n* cassetta delle lettere; **mailing list** *n* elenco d'indirizzi; **mailman** (*irreg*: US) *n* portalettere *m* inv, postino; **mail-order** *n* vendita (*or* acquisto) per corrispondenza

main [meɪn] *adj* principale ▷ *n* (*pipe*) conduttura principale; **main course** *n* (*Culin*) piatto principale, piatto forte; **mainland** *n* continente *m*; **mainly** *adv* principalmente, soprattutto; **main road** *n* strada principale; **mainstream** *n* (*fig*) corrente *f* principale; **main street** *n* strada principale

maintain [meɪn'teɪn] *vt* mantenere; (*affirm*) sostenere; **maintenance** ['meɪntənəns] *n* manutenzione *f*; (*alimony*) alimenti *mpl*

maisonette [meɪzə'nɛt] *n* (BRIT) appartamento a due piani

maize [meɪz] *n* granturco, mais *m*

majesty ['mædʒɪstɪ] *n* maestà *f inv*

major ['meɪdʒə*] *n* (*Mil*) maggiore *m* ▷ *adj* (*greater, Mus*) maggiore; (*in importance*) principale, importante

Majorca [mə'jɔːkə] *n* Maiorca

majority [mə'dʒɔrɪtɪ] *n* maggioranza

make [meɪk] (*pt, pp* **made**) *vt* fare; (*manufacture*) fare, fabbricare; (*cause to be*): **to ~ sb sad** *etc* rendere qn triste *etc*; (*force*): **to ~ sb do sth** costringere qn a fare qc, far fare qc a qn; (*equal*): **2 and 2 ~ 4** 2 più 2 fa 4 ▷ *n* fabbricazione *f*; (*brand*) marca; **to ~ a fool of sb** far fare a qn la figura dello scemo; **to ~ a profit** realizzare un profitto; **to ~ a loss** subire una perdita; **to ~ it** (*arrive*) arrivare; (*achieve sth*) farcela; **what time do you ~ it?** che ora fai?; **to ~ do with** arrangiarsi con; **make off** *vi* svignarsela; **make out** *vt* (*write out*) scrivere; (: *cheque*) emettere; (*understand*) capire; (*see*) distinguere; (: *numbers*) decifrare; **make up** *vt* (*constitute*) formare; (*invent*) inventare; (*parcel*) fare ▷ *vi* conciliarsi; (*with cosmetics*) truccarsi; **make up for** *vt fus* compensare; ricuperare; **makeover** ['meɪkəʊvə*] *n* (*change of image*) cambiamento di immagine; (*of room, house*) trasformazione *f*; **maker** *n* (*of programme etc*) creatore(-trice); (*manufacturer*) fabbricante *m*; **makeshift** *adj* improvvisato(-a); **make-up** *n* trucco

making ['meɪkɪŋ] *n* (*fig*): **in the ~** in formazione; **to have the ~s of** (*actor, athlete etc*) avere la stoffa di

malaria [mə'lɛərɪə] *n* malaria

Malaysia [mə'leɪzɪə] *n* Malaysia

male [meɪl] *n* (*Biol*) maschio ▷ *adj* maschile; maschio(-a)

malicious [mə'lɪʃəs] *adj* malevolo(-a); (*Law*) doloso(-a)

malignant [mə'lɪgnənt] *adj* (*Med*) maligno(-a)

mall [mɔːl] *n* (*also*: **shopping ~**) centro commerciale

mallet ['mælɪt] *n* maglio

malnutrition [mælnjuː'trɪʃən] *n* denutrizione *f*

malpractice [mæl'præktɪs] *n* prevaricazione *f*; negligenza

malt [mɔːlt] *n* malto

Malta ['mɔːltə] *n* Malta; **Maltese** [mɔːl'tiːz] *adj, n* (*pl inv*) maltese (*m/f*), (*Ling*) maltese *m*

mammal ['mæml] *n* mammifero

mammoth ['mæməθ] *adj* enorme, gigantesco(-a)

man [mæn] (*pl* **men**) *n* uomo ▷ *vt* fornire d'uomini; stare a; **an old ~** un vecchio; **~ and wife** marito e moglie

manage ['mænɪdʒ] *vi* farcela ▷ *vt* (*be in charge of*) occuparsi di; gestire; **to ~ to do sth** riuscire a far qc; **manageable** *adj* maneggevole; fattibile; **management** *n*

amministrazione f, direzione f; **manager**
n direttore m; (of shop, restaurant)
gerente m; (of artist, Sport) manager m
inv; **manageress** [-ə'rɛs] n direttrice
f; gerente f; **managerial** [-ə'dʒɪərɪəl]
adj dirigenziale; **managing director** n
amministratore m delegato
mandarin ['mændərɪn] n (person, fruit)
mandarino
mandate ['mændeɪt] n mandato
mandatory ['mændətərɪ] adj
obbligatorio(-a), ingiuntivo(-a)
mane [meɪn] n criniera
mangetout ['mɔnʒ'tu:] n pisello dolce,
taccola
mango ['mæŋgəu] (pl **mangoes**) n mango
man: **manhole** ['mænhəul] n botola
stradale; **manhood** ['mænhud] n età
virile; virilità
mania ['meɪnɪə] n mania; **maniac**
['meɪnɪæk] n maniaco(-a)
manic ['mænɪk] adj (behaviour, activity)
maniacale
manicure ['mænɪkjuəʳ] n manicure f inv
manifest ['mænɪfɛst] vt manifestare ▷ adj
manifesto(-a), palese
manifesto [mænɪ'fɛstəu] n manifesto
manipulate [mə'nɪpjuleɪt] vt manipolare
man: **mankind** [mæn'kaɪnd] n umanità,
genere m umano; **manly** ['mænlɪ] adj
virile; coraggioso(-a); **man-made** adj
sintetico(-a); artificiale
manner ['mænəʳ] n maniera, modo;
(behaviour) modo di fare; (type, sort):
all ~ of things ogni genere di cosa;
~s npl (conduct) maniere fpl; **bad ~s**
maleducazione f
manoeuvre [mə'nu:vəʳ] (US **maneuver**)
vt manovrare ▷ vi far manovre ▷ n
manovra
manpower ['mænpauəʳ] n manodopera
mansion ['mænʃən] n casa signorile
manslaughter ['mænslɔ:təʳ] n omicidio
preterintenzionale
mantelpiece ['mæntlpi:s] n mensola del
caminetto
manual ['mænjuəl] adj manuale ▷ n
manuale m
manufacture [mænju'fæktʃə
ʳ] vt fabbricare ▷ n fabbricazione
f, manifattura; **manufacturer** n
fabbricante m
manure [mə'njuəʳ] n concime m
manuscript ['mænjuskrɪpt] n
manoscritto
many ['mɛnɪ] adj molti(-e) ▷ pron
molti(-e); **a great ~** moltissimi(-e), un gran
numero (di); **~ a time** molte volte
map [mæp] n carta (geografica); (of city)

cartina; **can you show it to me on the ~?**
può indicarmelo sulla cartina?
maple ['meɪpl] n acero
mar [mɑ:ʳ] vt sciupare
Mar. abbr (= March) mar.
marathon ['mærəθən] n maratona
marble ['mɑ:bl] n marmo; (toy) pallina,
bilia
March [mɑ:tʃ] n marzo
march [mɑ:tʃ] vi marciare; sfilare ▷ n
marcia
mare [mɛəʳ] n giumenta
margarine [mɑ:dʒə'ri:n] n margarina
margin ['mɑ:dʒɪn] n margine m; **marginal**
adj marginale; **marginal seat** (Pol)
seggio elettorale ottenuto con una stretta
maggioranza; **marginally** adv (bigger,
better) lievemente, di poco; (different) un po'
marigold ['mærɪgəuld] n calendola
marijuana [mærɪ'wɑ:nə] n marijuana
marina [mə'ri:nə] n marina
marinade n [mærɪ'neɪd] marinata ▷ vt
['mærɪneɪd] = **marinate**
marinate ['mærɪneɪt] vt marinare
marine [mə'ri:n] adj (animal, plant)
marino(-a); (forces, engineering)
marittimo(-a) ▷ n (BRIT) fante m di marina;
(US) marine m inv
marital ['mærɪtl] adj maritale, coniugale;
marital status n stato civile
maritime ['mærɪtaɪm] adj marittimo(-a)
marjoram ['mɑ:dʒərəm] n maggiorana
mark [mɑ:k] n segno; (stain) macchia; (of
skid etc) traccia; (BRIT Scol) voto; (Sport)
bersaglio; (currency) marco ▷ vt segnare;
(stain) macchiare; (indicate) indicare; (BRIT
Scol) dare un voto a; correggere; **to ~ time**
segnare il passo; **marked** adj spiccato(-a),
chiaro(-a); **marker** n (sign) segno;
(bookmark) segnalibro
market ['mɑ:kɪt] n mercato ▷ vt (Comm)
mettere in vendita; **marketing** n
marketing m; **marketplace** n (piazza del)
mercato; (world of trade) piazza, mercato;
market research n indagine f o ricerca
di mercato
marmalade ['mɑ:məleɪd] n marmellata
d'arance
maroon [mə'ru:n] vt (also fig): **to be ~ed
(in or at)** essere abbandonato(-a) (in) ▷ adj
bordeaux inv
marquee [mɑ:'ki:] n padiglione m
marriage ['mærɪdʒ] n matrimonio;
marriage certificate n certificato di
matrimonio
married ['mærɪd] adj sposato(-a); (life,
love) coniugale, matrimoniale
marrow ['mærəu] n midollo; (vegetable)
zucca

marry ['mærɪ] vt sposare, sposarsi con; (vicar, priest etc) dare in matrimonio ▷ vi (also: **get married**) sposarsi

Mars [mɑːz] n (planet) Marte m

marsh [mɑːʃ] n palude f

marshal ['mɑːʃl] n maresciallo; (us: fire) capo; (: police) capitano ▷ vt (thoughts, support) ordinare; (soldiers) adunare

martyr ['mɑːtəʳ] n martire m/f

marvel ['mɑːvl] n meraviglia ▷ vi **to ~ (at)** meravigliarsi (di); **marvellous** (us **marvelous**) adj meraviglioso(-a)

Marxism ['mɑːksɪzəm] n marxismo

Marxist ['mɑːksɪst] adj, n marxista m/f

marzipan ['mɑːzɪpæn] n marzapane m

mascara [mæs'kɑːrə] n mascara m

mascot ['mæskət] n mascotte f inv

masculine ['mæskjulɪn] adj maschile; (woman) mascolino(-a)

mash [mæʃ] vt passare, schiacciare; **mashed potatoes** npl purè m di patate

mask [mɑːsk] n maschera ▷ vt mascherare

mason ['meɪsn] n (also: **stone~**) scalpellino; (also: **free~**) massone m; **masonry** n muratura

mass [mæs] n moltitudine f, massa; (Physics) massa; (Rel) messa ▷ cpd di massa ▷ vi ammassarsi; **the ~es** npl (ordinary people) le masse; **~es of** (inf) una montagna di

massacre ['mæsəkəʳ] n massacro

massage ['mæsɑːʒ] n massaggio

massive ['mæsɪv] adj enorme, massiccio(-a)

mass media npl mass media mpl

mass-produce ['mæsprə'djuːs] vt produrre in serie

mast [mɑːst] n albero

master ['mɑːstəʳ] n padrone m; (Art etc, teacher: in primary school) maestro; (: in secondary school) professore m; (title for boys): **M~ X** Signorino X ▷ vt domare; (learn) imparare a fondo; (understand) conoscere a fondo; **mastermind** n mente f superiore ▷ vt essere il cervello di; **Master of Arts/Science** n Master m inv in lettere/scienze; **masterpiece** n capolavoro

masturbate ['mæstəbeɪt] vi masturbare

mat [mæt] n stuoia; (also: **door~**) stoino, zerbino; (also: **table ~**) sottopiatto ▷ adj = **matt**

match [mætʃ] n fiammifero; (game) partita, incontro; (fig) uguale m/f; matrimonio; partito ▷ vt intonare; (go well with) andare benissimo con; (equal) uguagliare; (correspond to) corrispondere a; (pair: also: **~ up**) accoppiare ▷ vi combaciare; **to be a good ~** andare bene; **matchbox** n scatola per fiammiferi; **matching** adj ben assortito(-a)

mate [meɪt] n compagno(-a) di lavoro; (inf: friend) amico(-a); (animal) compagno(-a); (in merchant navy) secondo ▷ vi accoppiarsi

material [mə'tɪərɪəl] n (substance) materiale m, materia; (cloth) stoffa ▷ adj materiale; **~s** npl (equipment) materiali mpl

materialize [mə'tɪərɪəlaɪz] vi materializzarsi, realizzarsi

maternal [mə'təːnl] adj materno(-a)

maternity [mə'təːnɪtɪ] n maternità; **maternity hospital** n ≈ clinica ostetrica; **maternity leave** n congedo di maternità

math [mæθ] (us) n = **maths**

mathematical [mæθə'mætɪkl] adj matematico(-a)

mathematician [mæθəmə'tɪʃən] n matematico(-a)

mathematics [mæθə'mætɪks] n matematica

maths [mæθs] (us **math**) n matematica

matinée ['mætɪneɪ] n matinée f inv

matron ['meɪtrən] n (in hospital) capoinfermiera; (in school) infermiera

matt [mæt] adj opaco(-a)

matter ['mætəʳ] n questione f; (Physics) materia, sostanza; (content) contenuto; (Med: pus) pus m ▷ vi importare; **it doesn't ~** non importa; (I don't mind) non fa niente; **what's the ~?** che cosa c'è?; **no ~ what** qualsiasi cosa accada; **as a ~ of course** come cosa naturale; **as a ~ of fact** in verità; **~s** npl (affairs) questioni

mattress ['mætrɪs] n materasso

mature [mə'tjuəʳ] adj maturo(-a); (cheese) stagionato(-a) ▷ vi maturare; stagionare; **mature student** n studente universitario che ha più di 25 anni; **maturity** n maturità

maul [mɔːl] vt lacerare

mauve [məuv] adj malva inv

max abbr = **maximum**

maximize ['mæksɪmaɪz] vt (profits etc) massimizzare; (chances) aumentare al massimo

maximum ['mæksɪməm] (pl **maxima**) adj massimo(-a) ▷ n massimo

May [meɪ] n maggio

may [meɪ] (conditional **might**) vi (indicating possibility): **he ~ come** può darsi che venga; (be allowed to): **~ I smoke?** posso fumare?; (wishes): **~ God bless you!** Dio la benedica!; **you ~ as well go** tanto vale che tu te ne vada

maybe ['meɪbiː] adv forse, può darsi; **~ he'll ...** può darsi che lui ... + sub, forse lui ...

May Day n il primo maggio

mayhem ['meɪhɛm] n cagnara

mayonnaise [meɪəˈneɪz] n maionese f
mayor [mɛəʳ] n sindaco; **mayoress** n
sindaco (donna); moglie f del sindaco
maze [meɪz] n labirinto, dedalo
MD n abbr (= Doctor of Medicine) titolo di
studio; (Comm) see **managing director**
me [mi:] pron mi, m' + vowel or silent "h";
(stressed, after prep) me; **he heard me** mi ha
or m'ha sentito; **give me a book** dammi (or
mi dia) un libro; **it's me** sono io; **with me**
con me; **without me** senza di me
meadow [ˈmɛdəu] n prato
meagre [ˈmiːgəʳ] (us **meager**) adj
magro(-a)
meal [mi:l] n pasto; (flour) farina;
mealtime n l'ora di mangiare
mean [mi:n] (pt, pp **meant**) adj (with
money) avaro(-a), gretto(-a); (unkind)
meschino(-a), maligno(-a); (shabby)
misero(-a); (average) medio(-a) ▷ vt
(signify) significare, voler dire; (intend):
to ~ to do aver l'intenzione di fare ▷ n
mezzo; (Math) media; **~s** npl (way, money)
mezzi mpl; **by ~s of** per mezzo di; **by all
~s** ma certo, prego; **to be ~t for** essere
destinato(-a) a; **do you ~ it?** dice sul serio?;
what do you ~? che cosa vuol dire?
meaning [ˈmiːnɪŋ] n significato, senso;
meaningful adj significativo(-a);
meaningless adj senza senso
meant [mɛnt] pt, pp of **mean**
meantime [ˈmiːntaɪm] adv (also: **in the ~**)
nel frattempo
meanwhile [ˈmiːnwaɪl] adv nel frattempo
measles [ˈmiːzlz] n morbillo
measure [ˈmɛʒəʳ] vt, vi misurare ▷ n
misura; (also: **tape ~**) metro
measurement [ˈmɛʒəmənt] n (act)
misurazione f; (measure) misura; **chest/
hip ~** giro petto/fianchi; **to take sb's ~s**
prendere le misure di qn
meat [mi:t] n carne f; **I don't eat ~** non
mangio carne; **cold ~** affettato; **meatball**
n polpetta di carne
Mecca [ˈmɛkə] n (also fig) la Mecca
mechanic [mɪˈkænɪk] n meccanico;
can you send a ~? può mandare
un meccanico?; **mechanical** adj
meccanico(-a)
mechanism [ˈmɛkənɪzəm] n meccanismo
medal [ˈmɛdl] n medaglia; **medallist**
(us **medalist**) n (Sport): **to be a gold
medallist** essere medaglia d'oro
meddle [ˈmɛdl] vi **to ~ in** immischiarsi in,
mettere le mani in; **to ~ with** toccare
media [ˈmiːdɪə] npl media mpl
mediaeval [mɛdɪˈiːvl] adj = **medieval**
mediate [ˈmiːdɪeɪt] vi fare da
mediatore(-trice)

medical [ˈmɛdɪkl] adj medico(-a) ▷ n visita
medica; **medical certificate** n certificato
medico
medicated [ˈmɛdɪkeɪtɪd] adj medicato(-a)
medication [mɛdɪˈkeɪʃən] n medicinali
mpl, farmaci mpl
medicine [ˈmɛdsɪn] n medicina
medieval [mɛdɪˈiːvl] adj medievale
mediocre [miːdɪˈəukəʳ] adj mediocre
meditate [ˈmɛdɪteɪt] vi **to ~ (on)** meditare
(su)
meditation [mɛdɪˈteɪʃən] n meditazione f
Mediterranean [mɛdɪtəˈreɪnɪən] adj
mediterraneo(-a); **the ~ (Sea)** il (mare)
Mediterraneo
medium [ˈmiːdɪəm] (pl **media**) adj
medio(-a) ▷ n (means) mezzo; (pl **mediums**:
person) medium m inv; **medium-sized** adj
(tin etc) di grandezza media; (clothes) di
taglia media; **medium wave** n onde fpl
medie
meek [mi:k] adj dolce, umile
meet [mi:t] (pt, pp **met**) vt incontrare; (for
the first time) fare la conoscenza di; (go and
fetch) andare a prendere; (fig) affrontare;
soddisfare; raggiungere ▷ vi incontrarsi;
(in session) riunirsi; (join: objects) unirsi;
nice to ~ you piacere (di conoscerla);
meet up vi **to ~ up with sb** incontrare
qn; **meet with** vt fus incontrare; **meeting**
n incontro; (session: of club etc) riunione f;
(interview) intervista; **she's at a meeting**
(Comm) è in riunione; **meeting place** n
luogo d'incontro
megabyte [ˈmɛgəbaɪt] n (Comput)
megabyte m inv
megaphone [ˈmɛgəfəun] n megafono
melancholy [ˈmɛlənkəlɪ] n malinconia
▷ adj malinconico(-a)
melody [ˈmɛlədɪ] n melodia
melon [ˈmɛlən] n melone m
melt [mɛlt] vi (gen) sciogliersi, struggersi;
(metals) fondersi ▷ vt sciogliere, struggere;
fondere
member [ˈmɛmbəʳ] n membro; **Member
of Congress** (us) n membro del
Congresso; **Member of Parliament** (BRIT)
n deputato(-a); **Member of the European
Parliament** (BRIT) n eurodeputato(-a);
Member of the Scottish Parliament
(BRIT) n deputato(-a) del Parlamento
scozzese; **membership** n iscrizione
f, (numero d')iscritti mpl, membri mpl;
membership card n tessera (di iscrizione)
memento [məˈmɛntəu] n ricordo,
souvenir m inv
memo [ˈmɛməu] n appunto; (Comm etc)
comunicazione f di servizio
memorable [ˈmɛmərəbl] adj memorabile

memorandum [mɛmə'rændəm] (pl **memoranda**) n appunto; (Comm etc) comunicazione f di servizio

memorial [mɪ'mɔːrɪəl] n monumento commemorativo ▷ adj commemorativo(-a)

memorize ['mɛmərɑɪz] vt memorizzare

memory ['mɛmərɪ] n (also Comput) memoria; (recollection) ricordo

men [mɛn] npl of **man**

menace ['mɛnəs] n minaccia ▷ vt minacciare

mend [mɛnd] vt aggiustare, riparare; (darn) rammendare ▷ n **on the ~** in via di guarigione

meningitis [mɛnɪn'dʒɑɪtɪs] n meningite f

menopause ['mɛnəupɔːz] n menopausa

men's room n **the men's room** (esp US) la toilette degli uomini

menstruation [mɛnstru'eɪʃən] n mestruazione f

menswear ['mɛnzwɛəʳ] n abbigliamento maschile

mental ['mɛntl] adj mentale; **mental hospital** n ospedale m psichiatrico; **mentality** [mɛn'tælɪtɪ] n mentalità f inv; **mentally** adv **to be mentally handicapped** essere minorato psichico

menthol ['mɛnθɒl] n mentolo

mention ['mɛnʃən] n menzione f ▷ vt menzionare, far menzione di; **don't ~ it!** non c'è di che!, prego!

menu ['mɛnjuː] n (set menu, Comput) menù m inv; (printed) carta; **could we see the ~?** ci può portare il menù?

MEP n abbr = **Member of the European Parliament**

mercenary ['məːsɪnərɪ] adj venale ▷ n mercenario

merchandise ['məːtʃəndɑɪz] n merci fpl

merchant ['məːtʃənt] n mercante m, commerciante m; **merchant navy** (US **merchant marine**) n marina mercantile

merciless ['məːsɪlɪs] adj spietato(-a)

mercury ['məːkjurɪ] n mercurio

mercy ['məːsɪ] n pietà; (Rel) misericordia; **at the ~ of** alla mercé di

mere [mɪəʳ] adj semplice; **by a ~ chance** per mero caso; **merely** adv semplicemente, non ... che

merge [məːdʒ] vt unire ▷ vi fondersi, unirsi; (Comm) fondersi; **merger** n (Comm) fusione f

meringue [mə'ræŋ] n meringa

merit ['mɛrɪt] n merito, valore m ▷ vt meritare

mermaid ['məːmeɪd] n sirena

merry ['mɛrɪ] adj gaio(-a), allegro(-a); **M~ Christmas!** Buon Natale!; **merry-go-round** n carosello

mesh [mɛʃ] n maglia; rete f

mess [mɛs] n confusione f, disordine m; (fig) pasticcio; (dirt) sporcizia; (Mil) mensa; **mess about** or **around** (inf) vi trastullarsi; **mess with** (inf) vt fus (challenge, confront) litigare con; (drugs, drinks) abusare di; **mess up** vt sporcare; fare un pasticcio di; rovinare

message ['mɛsɪdʒ] n messaggio; **can I leave a ~?** posso lasciare un messaggio?; **are there any ~s for me?** ci sono messaggi per me?

messenger ['mɛsɪndʒəʳ] n messaggero(-a)

Messrs ['mɛsəz] abbr (on letters) Spett.

messy ['mɛsɪ] adj sporco(-a), disordinato(-a)

met [mɛt] pt, pp of **meet**

metabolism [mɛ'tæbəlɪzəm] n metabolismo

metal ['mɛtl] n metallo; **metallic** [-'tælɪk] adj metallico(-a)

metaphor ['mɛtəfəʳ] n metafora

meteor ['miːtɪəʳ] n meteora; **meteorite** ['miːtɪərɑɪt] n meteorite m

meteorology [miːtɪə'rɔlədʒɪ] n meteorologia

meter ['miːtəʳ] n (instrument) contatore m; (parking meter) parchimetro; (US: unit) = **metre**

method ['mɛθəd] n metodo; **methodical** [mɪ'θɒdɪkl] adj metodico(-a)

meths [mɛθs] (BRIT) n alcool m denaturato

meticulous [mɛ'tɪkjuləs] adj meticoloso(-a)

metre ['miːtəʳ] (US **meter**) n metro

metric ['mɛtrɪk] adj metrico(-a)

metro ['mɛtrəu] n metro m inv

metropolitan [mɛtrə'pɔlɪtən] adj metropolitano(-a)

Mexican ['mɛksɪkən] adj, n messicano(-a)

Mexico ['mɛksɪkəu] n Messico

mg abbr (= milligram) mg

mice [mɑɪs] npl of **mouse**

micro... ['mɑɪkrəu] prefix micro...; **microchip** n microcircuito integrato; **microphone** n microfono; **microscope** n microscopio; **microwave** n (also: **microwave oven**) forno a microonde

mid [mɪd] adj ~ **May** metà maggio; ~ **afternoon** metà pomeriggio; **in ~ air** a mezz'aria; **midday** n mezzogiorno

middle ['mɪdl] n mezzo; centro; (waist) vita ▷ adj di mezzo; **in the ~ of the night** nel bel mezzo della notte; **middle-aged** adj di mezza età; **Middle Ages** npl **the Middle Ages** il Medioevo; **middle-class** adj ≈ borghese; **Middle East** n Medio

m

Oriente *m*; **middle name** *n* secondo nome
m; **middle school** *n* (*US*) scuola media per
ragazzi dagli 11 ai 14 anni; (*BRIT*) scuola media
per ragazzi dagli 8 o 9 ai 12 o 13 anni
midge [mɪdʒ] *n* moscerino
midget ['mɪdʒɪt] *n* nano(-a)
midnight ['mɪdnaɪt] *n* mezzanotte *f*
midst [mɪdst] *n* **in the ~ of** in mezzo a
midsummer [mɪd'sʌməʳ] *n* mezza or
piena estate *f*
midway [mɪd'weɪ] *adj, adv* **~ (between)** a
mezza strada (fra); **~ (through)** a metà (di)
midweek [mɪd'wiːk] *adv* a metà
settimana
midwife ['mɪdwaɪf] (*pl* **midwives**) *n*
levatrice *f*
midwinter [mɪd'wɪntəʳ] *n* pieno inverno
might [maɪt] *vb see* **may** ▷ *n* potere *m*,
forza; **mighty** *adj* forte, potente
migraine ['miːgreɪn] *n* emicrania
migrant ['maɪgrənt] *adj* (*bird*)
migratore(-trice); (*worker*) emigrato(-a)
migrate [maɪ'greɪt] *vi* (*bird*) migrare;
(*person*) emigrare
migration [maɪ'greɪʃən] *n* migrazione *f*
mike [maɪk] *n abbr* (= *microphone*)
microfono
Milan [mɪ'læn] *n* Milano *f*
mild [maɪld] *adj* mite; (*person, voice*) dolce;
(*flavour*) delicato(-a); (*illness*) leggero(-a);
(*interest*) blando(-a) ▷ *n* (*beer*) birra
leggera; **mildly** ['maɪldlɪ] *adv* mitemente;
dolcemente; delicatamente; leggermente;
blandamente; **to put it mildly** a dire poco
mile [maɪl] *n* miglio *m*; **mileage** *n* distanza
in miglia, ≈ chilometraggio; **mileometer**
[maɪ'lɔmɪtəʳ] *n* ≈ contachilometri *m inv*;
milestone ['maɪlstəun] *n* pietra miliare
military ['mɪlɪtərɪ] *adj* militare
militia [mɪ'lɪʃə] *n* milizia
milk [mɪlk] *n* latte *m* ▷ *vt* (*cow*) mungere;
(*fig*) sfruttare; **milk chocolate** *n*
cioccolato al latte; **milkman** (*irreg*) *n*
lattaio; **milky** *adj* lattiginoso(-a); (*colour*)
latteo(-a)
mill [mɪl] *n* mulino; (*small: for coffee, pepper
etc*) macinino; (*factory*) fabbrica; (*spinning
mill*) filatura ▷ *vt* macinare ▷ *vi* (*also: ~
about*) brulicare
millennium [mɪ'lɛnɪəm] (*pl* **millenniums**
or **millennia**) *n* millennio
milli... ['mɪlɪ] *prefix*: **milligram(me)** *n*
milligrammo; **millilitre** ['mɪlɪliːtəʳ] (*US*
milliliter) *n* millilitro; **millimetre** (*US*
millimeter) *n* millimetro
million ['mɪljən] *num* milione *m*;
millionaire *n* milionario, ≈ miliardario;
millionth *num* milionesimo(-a)
milometer [maɪ'lɔmɪtəʳ] *n* = **mileometer**

mime [maɪm] *n* mimo ▷ *vt, vi* mimare
mimic ['mɪmɪk] *n* imitatore(-trice) ▷ *vt*
fare la mimica di
min. *abbr* = **minute(s)**; **minimum**
mince [mɪns] *vt* tritare, macinare ▷ *n*
(*BRIT Culin*) carne *f* tritata or macinata;
mincemeat *n* frutta secca tritata per uso in
pasticceria; (*US*) carne *f* tritata or macinata;
mince pie *n* specie di torta con frutta secca
mind [maɪnd] *n* mente *f* ▷ *vt* (*attend to, look
after*) badare a, occuparsi di; (*be careful*) fare
attenzione a, stare attento(-a) a; (*object
to*): **I don't ~ the noise** il rumore non mi
dà alcun fastidio; **I don't ~** non m'importa;
do you ~ if ...? le dispiace se...?; **it is on
my ~** mi preoccupa; **to my ~** secondo me,
a mio parere; **to be out of one's ~** essere
uscito(-a) di mente; **to keep** *or* **bear sth in
~** non dimenticare qc; **to make up one's
~** decidersi; **~ you, ...** sì, però va detto che
...; **never ~** non importa, non fa niente;
(*don't worry*) non preoccuparti; **"~ the
step"** "attenzione allo scalino"; **mindless**
adj idiota
mine¹ [maɪn] *pron* il (la) mio(-a); (*pl*) i (le)
miei (mei); **that book is ~** quel libro è mio;
yours is red, ~ is green il tuo è rosso, il
mio è verde; **a friend of ~** un mio amico
mine² [maɪn] *n* miniera; (*explosive*) mina
▷ *vt* (*coal*) estrarre; (*ship, beach*) minare;
minefield *n* (*also fig*) campo minato;
miner ['maɪnəʳ] *n* minatore *m*
mineral ['mɪnərəl] *adj* minerale ▷ *n*
minerale *m*; **mineral water** *n* acqua
minerale
mingle ['mɪŋgl] *vi* **to ~ with** mescolarsi a,
mischiarsi con
miniature ['mɪnətʃəʳ] *adj* in miniatura ▷ *n*
miniatura
minibar ['mɪnɪbɑːʳ] *n* minibar *m inv*
minibus ['mɪnɪbʌs] *n* minibus *m inv*
minicab ['mɪnɪkæb] *n* (*BRIT*) ≈ taxi *m inv*
minimal ['mɪnɪml] *adj* minimo(-a)
minimize ['mɪnɪmaɪz] *vt* minimizzare
minimum ['mɪnɪməm] (*pl* **minima**) *n*
minimo ▷ *adj* minimo(-a)
mining ['maɪnɪŋ] *n* industria mineraria
miniskirt ['mɪnɪskəːt] *n* minigonna
minister ['mɪnɪstəʳ] *n* (*BRIT Pol*) ministro;
(*Rel*) pastore *m*
ministry ['mɪnɪstrɪ] *n* ministero
minor ['maɪnəʳ] *adj* minore, di poca
importanza; (*Mus*) minore ▷ *n* (*Law*)
minorenne *m/f*
Minorca [mɪ'nɔːkə] *n* Minorca
minority [maɪ'nɔrɪtɪ] *n* minoranza
mint [mɪnt] *n* (*plant*) menta; (*sweet*)
pasticca di menta ▷ *vt* (*coins*) battere;
the (Royal) M~ (*BRIT*), **the (US) M~** (*US*)

la Zecca; **in ~ condition** come nuovo(-a)
di zecca
minus ['maɪnəs] n (also: **~ sign**) segno
meno ▷ prep meno
minute [adj maɪ'njuːt, n 'mɪnɪt] adj
minuscolo(-a); (detail) minuzioso(-a) ▷ n
minuto; **~s** npl (of meeting) verbale m
miracle ['mɪrəkl] n miracolo
miraculous [mɪ'rækjʊləs] adj
miracoloso(-a)
mirage ['mɪrɑːʒ] n miraggio
mirror ['mɪrər] n specchio; (in car)
specchietto
misbehave [mɪsbɪ'heɪv] vi comportarsi
male
misc. abbr = **miscellaneous**; **miscarriage**
['mɪskærɪdʒ] n (Med) aborto spontaneo;
miscarriage of justice errore m
giudiziario
miscellaneous [mɪsɪ'leɪnɪəs] adj (items)
vario(-a); (selection) misto(-a)
mischief ['mɪstʃɪf] n (naughtiness)
birichineria; (maliciousness) malizia;
mischievous adj birichino(-a)
misconception ['mɪskən'sɛpʃən] n idea
sbagliata
misconduct [mɪs'kɒndʌkt] n cattiva
condotta; **professional ~** reato
professionale
miser ['maɪzər] n avaro
miserable ['mɪzərəbl] adj infelice;
(wretched) miserabile; (weather)
deprimente; (offer, failure) misero(-a)
misery ['mɪzərɪ] n (unhappiness) tristezza;
(wretchedness) miseria
misfortune [mɪs'fɔːtʃən] n sfortuna
misgiving [mɪs'gɪvɪŋ] n apprensione f; **to
have ~s about** avere dei dubbi per quanto
riguarda
misguided [mɪs'gaɪdɪd] adj sbagliato(-a),
poco giudizioso(-a)
mishap ['mɪshæp] n disgrazia
misinterpret [mɪsɪn'təːprɪt] vt
interpretare male
misjudge [mɪs'dʒʌdʒ] vt giudicare male
mislay [mɪs'leɪ] (irreg) vt smarrire
mislead [mɪs'liːd] (irreg) vt sviare;
misleading adj ingannevole
misplace [mɪs'pleɪs] vt smarrire
misprint ['mɪsprɪnt] n errore m di stampa
misrepresent [mɪsrɛprɪ'zɛnt] vt travisare
Miss [mɪs] n Signorina
miss [mɪs] vt (fail to get) perdere; (fail to
hit) mancare; (regret the absence
of): **I ~ him** sento la sua mancanza ▷ vi
mancare ▷ n (shot) colpo mancato; **we
~ed our train** abbiamo perso il treno;
miss out (BRIT) vt omettere; **miss out on**

vt fus (fun, party) perdersi; (chance, bargain)
lasciarsi sfuggire
missile ['mɪsaɪl] n (Mil) missile m; (object
thrown) proiettile m
missing ['mɪsɪŋ] adj perso(-a),
smarrito(-a); (person) scomparso(-a); (:
after disaster, Mil) disperso(-a); (removed)
mancante; **to be ~** mancare
mission ['mɪʃən] n missione f; **missionary**
n missionario(-a)
misspell [mɪs'spɛl] vt (irreg: like **spell**)
sbagliare l'ortografia di
mist [mɪst] n nebbia, foschia ▷ vi (also: **~
over, ~ up**) annebbiarsi; (: BRIT: windows)
appannarsi
mistake [mɪs'teɪk] (irreg: like **take**) n
sbaglio, errore m ▷ vt sbagliarsi di;
fraintendere; **to make a ~** fare uno
sbaglio, sbagliare; **there must be some
~** ci dev'essere un errore; **by ~** per sbaglio;
to ~ for prendere per; **mistaken** pp of
mistake ▷ adj (idea etc) sbagliato(-a); **to
be mistaken** sbagliarsi
mister ['mɪstər] (inf) n signore m; see **Mr**
mistletoe ['mɪsltəu] n vischio
mistook [mɪs'tuk] pt of **mistake**
mistress ['mɪstrɪs] n padrona; (lover)
amante f; (BRIT Scol) insegnante f
mistrust [mɪs'trʌst] vt diffidare di
misty ['mɪstɪ] adj nebbioso(-a),
brumoso(-a)
misunderstand [mɪsʌndə'stænd]
(irreg) vt, vi capire male, fraintendere;
misunderstanding n malinteso,
equivoco; **there's been a
misunderstanding** c'è stato un malinteso
misunderstood [mɪsʌndə'stud] pt, pp of
misunderstand
misuse [n mɪs'juːs, vb mɪs'juːz] n cattivo
uso; (of power) abuso ▷ vt far cattivo uso
di; abusare di
mitt(en) ['mɪt(n)] n mezzo guanto;
manopola
mix [mɪks] vt mescolare ▷ vi (people): **to ~
with** avere a che fare con ▷ n mescolanza;
preparato; **mix up** vt mescolare; (confuse)
confondere; **mixed** adj misto(-a); **mixed
grill** n (BRIT) misto alla griglia; **mixed
salad** n insalata mista; **mixed-up** adj
(confused) confuso(-a); **mixer** n (for food:
electric) frullatore m; (: hand) frullino;
(person): **he is a good mixer** è molto
socievole; **mixture** n mescolanza; (blend:
of tobacco etc) miscela; (Med) sciroppo;
mix-up n confusione f
ml abbr (= millilitre(s)) ml
mm abbr (= millimetre) mm
moan [məun] n gemito ▷ vi (inf: complain):
to ~ (about) lamentarsi (di)

moat [məut] *n* fossato

mob [mɔb] *n* calca ▷ *vt* accalcarsi intorno a

mobile ['məubaɪl] *adj* mobile ▷ *n* (*decoration*) mobile *m*; **mobile home** *n* grande roulotte *f inv* (utilizzata come domicilio); **mobile phone** *n* telefono portatile, telefonino

mobility [məu'bɪlɪtɪ] *n* mobilità; (*of applicant*) disponibilità a viaggiare

mobilize ['məubɪlaɪz] *vt* mobilitare ▷ *vi* mobilitarsi

mock [mɔk] *vt* deridere, burlarsi di ▷ *adj* falso(-a); **~s** *npl* (BRIT: Scol: inf) simulazione *f* degli esami; **mockery** *n* derisione *f*; **to make a mockery of** burlarsi di; (*exam*) rendere una farsa

mod cons ['mɔd'kɔnz] *npl abbr* (BRIT) = **modern conveniences**; *see* **convenience**

mode [məud] *n* modo

model ['mɔdl] *n* modello; (*person: for fashion*) indossatore(-trice); (: *for artist*) modello(-a) ▷ *adj* (*small-scale: railway etc*) in miniatura; (*child, factory*) modello *inv* ▷ *vt* modellare ▷ *vi* fare l'indossatore (*or* l'indossatrice); **to ~ clothes** presentare degli abiti

modem ['məudɛm] *n* modem *m inv*

moderate [*adj* 'mɔdərət, *vb* 'mɔdəreɪt] *adj* moderato(-a) ▷ *vi* moderarsi, placarsi ▷ *vt* moderare

moderation [mɔdə'reɪʃən] *n* moderazione *f*, misura; **in ~** in quantità moderata, con moderazione

modern ['mɔdən] *adj* moderno(-a); **mod cons** comodità *fpl* moderne; **modernize** *vt* modernizzare; **modern languages** *npl* lingue *fpl* moderne

modest ['mɔdɪst] *adj* modesto(-a); **modesty** *n* modestia

modification [mɔdɪfɪ'keɪʃən] *n* modificazione *f*; **to make ~s** fare *or* apportare delle modifiche

modify ['mɔdɪfaɪ] *vt* modificare

module ['mɔdju:l] *n* modulo

mohair ['məuhɛər] *n* mohair *m*

Mohammed [məu'hæmɪd] *n* Maometto

moist [mɔɪst] *adj* umido(-a); **moisture** ['mɔɪstʃər] *n* umidità; (*on glass*) goccioline *fpl* di vapore; **moisturizer** ['mɔɪstʃəraɪzər] *n* idratante *f*

mold *etc* [məuld] (US) *n*, *vt* = **mould**

mole [məul] *n* (*animal, fig*) talpa; (*spot*) neo

molecule ['mɔlɪkju:l] *n* molecola

molest [məu'lɛst] *vt* molestare

molten ['məultən] *adj* fuso(-a)

mom [mɔm] (US) *n* = **mum**

moment ['məumənt] *n* momento, istante *m*; **at that ~** in quel momento; **at the ~** al momento, in questo momento; **momentarily** ['məuməntərɪlɪ] *adv* per un momento; (US: *very soon*) da un momento all'altro; **momentary** *adj* momentaneo(-a), passeggero(-a); **momentous** [-'mɛntəs] *adj* di grande importanza

momentum [məu'mɛntəm] *n* (*Physics*) momento; (*fig*) impeto; **to gather ~** aumentare di velocità

mommy ['mɔmɪ] (US) *n* = **mummy**

Mon. *abbr* (= *Monday*) lun.

Monaco ['mɔnəkəu] *n* Principato di Monaco

monarch ['mɔnək] *n* monarca *m*; **monarchy** *n* monarchia

monastery ['mɔnəstərɪ] *n* monastero

Monday ['mʌndɪ] *n* lunedì *m inv*

monetary ['mʌnɪtərɪ] *adj* monetario(-a)

money ['mʌnɪ] *n* denaro, soldi *mpl*; **I haven't got any ~** non ho soldi; **money belt** *n* marsupio (*per soldi*); **money order** *n* vaglia *m inv*

mongrel ['mʌŋgrəl] *n* (*dog*) cane *m* bastardo

monitor ['mɔnɪtər] *n* (*TV, Comput*) monitor *m inv* ▷ *vt* controllare

monk [mʌŋk] *n* monaco

monkey ['mʌŋkɪ] *n* scimmia

monologue ['mɔnəlɔg] *n* monologo

monopoly [mə'nɔpəlɪ] *n* monopolio

monosodium glutamate [mɔnə'səudɪə m'glu:təmeɪt] *n* glutammato di sodio

monotonous [mə'nɔtənəs] *adj* monotono(-a)

monsoon [mɔn'su:n] *n* monsone *m*

monster ['mɔnstər] *n* mostro

month [mʌnθ] *n* mese *m*; **monthly** *adj* mensile ▷ *adv* al mese; ogni mese

monument ['mɔnjumənt] *n* monumento

mood [mu:d] *n* umore *m*; **to be in a good/ bad ~** essere di buon/cattivo umore; **moody** *adj* (*variable*) capriccioso(-a), lunatico(-a); (*sullen*) imbronciato(-a)

moon [mu:n] *n* luna; **moonlight** *n* chiaro di luna

moor [muər] *n* brughiera ▷ *vt* (*ship*) ormeggiare ▷ *vi* ormeggiarsi

moose [mu:s] *n inv* alce *m*

mop [mɔp] *n* lavapavimenti *m inv*; (*also:* **~ of hair**) zazzera ▷ *vt* lavare con lo straccio; (*face*) asciugare; **mop up** *vt* asciugare con uno straccio

mope [məup] *vi* fare il broncio

moped ['məupɛd] *n* (BRIT) ciclomotore *m*

moral ['mɔrl] *adj* morale ▷ *n* morale *f*; **~s** *npl* (*principles*) moralità

morale [mɔ'rɑ:l] *n* morale *m*

morality [mə'rælɪtɪ] *n* moralità
morbid ['mɔːbɪd] *adj* morboso(-a)

🔵 **KEYWORD**

more [mɔːʳ] *adj* 1 (*greater in number etc*)
più; **more people/letters than we
expected** più persone/lettere di quante
ne aspettavamo; **I have more wine/
money than you** ho più vino/soldi di te;
I have more wine than beer ho più vino
che birra
2 (*additional*) altro(-a), ancora; **do you
want (some) more tea?** vuole dell'altro
tè?, vuole ancora del tè?; **I have no** *or* **I
don't have any more money** non ho
più soldi
▷ *pron* 1 (*greater amount*) più; **more than 10**
più di 10; **it cost more than we expected**
ha costato più di quanto ci aspettavamo
2 (*further or additional amount*) ancora;
is there any more? ce n'è ancora?;
there's no more non ce n'è più; **a little
more** ancora un po'; **many/much more**
molti(-e)/molto(-a) di più
▷ *adv* **more dangerous/easily (than)**
più pericoloso/facilmente (di); **more and
more** sempre di più; **more and more
difficult** sempre più difficile; **more or less**
più o meno; **more than ever** più che mai

moreover [mɔː'rəuvəʳ] *adv* inoltre, di più
morgue [mɔːg] *n* obitorio
morning ['mɔːnɪŋ] *n* mattina, mattino;
(*duration*) mattinata ▷ *cpd* del mattino;
in the ~ la mattina; **7 o'clock in the ~** le 7
di *or* della mattina; **morning sickness** *n*
nausee *fpl* mattutine
Moroccan [mə'rɔkən] *adj, n*
marocchino(-a)
Morocco [mə'rɔkəu] *n* Marocco
moron ['mɔːrɔn] (*inf*) *n* deficiente *m/f*
morphine ['mɔːfiːn] *n* morfina
morris dancing *n* vedi nota nel riquadro

⬤ **MORRIS DANCING**
⬤
⬤ Il **morris dancing** è una danza
⬤ folcloristica inglese tradizionalmente
⬤ riservata agli uomini. Vestiti di bianco
⬤ e con dei campanelli attaccati alle
⬤ caviglie, i ballerini eseguono una danza
⬤ tenendo in mano dei fazzoletti bianchi
⬤ e lunghi bastoni. Questa danza è molto
⬤ popolare nelle feste paesane.

Morse [mɔːs] *n* (*also*: **~ code**) alfabeto
Morse
mortal ['mɔːtl] *adj* mortale ▷ *n* mortale *m*

mortar ['mɔːtəʳ] *n* (*Constr*) malta; (*dish*)
mortaio
mortgage ['mɔːgɪdʒ] *n* ipoteca; (*loan*)
prestito ipotecario ▷ *vt* ipotecare
mortician [mɔː'tɪʃən] (*us*) *n* impresario di
pompe funebri
mortified ['mɔːtɪfaɪd] *adj* umiliato(-a)
mortuary ['mɔːtjuərɪ] *n* camera
mortuaria; obitorio
mosaic [məu'zeɪɪk] *n* mosaico
Moscow ['mɔskəu] *n* Mosca
Moslem ['mɔzləm] *adj, n* = **Muslim**
mosque [mɔsk] *n* moschea
mosquito [mɔs'kiːtəu] (*pl* **mosquitoes**)
n zanzara
moss [mɔs] *n* muschio
most [məust] *adj* (*almost all*) la maggior
parte di; (*largest, greatest*): **who has (the)
~ money?** chi ha più soldi di tutti? ▷ *pron*
la maggior parte ▷ *adv* più; (*work, sleep
etc*) di più; (*very*) molto, estremamente;
the ~ (*also*: **+ adjective**) il(-la) più; **~ of** la
maggior parte di; **~ of them** quasi tutti; **I
saw (the) ~** ho visto più io; **at the (very)
~** al massimo; **to make the ~ of** trarre il
massimo vantaggio da; **a ~ interesting
book** un libro estremamente interessante;
mostly *adv* per lo più
MOT (*brit*) *n abbr* = **Ministry of
Transport; the ~ (test)** *revisione annuale
obbligatoria degli autoveicoli*
motel [məu'tɛl] *n* motel *m inv*
moth [mɔθ] *n* farfalla notturna; tarma
mother ['mʌðəʳ] *n* madre *f* ▷ *vt* (*care
for*) fare da madre a; **motherhood** *n*
maternità; **mother-in-law** *n* suocera;
mother-of-pearl [mʌðərəv'pəːl] *n*
madreperla; **Mother's Day** *n* la festa della
mamma; **mother-to-be** [mʌðətə'biː]
n futura mamma; **mother tongue** *n*
madrelingua
motif [məu'tiːf] *n* motivo
motion ['məuʃən] *n* movimento, moto;
(*gesture*) gesto; (*at meeting*) mozione *f* ▷ *vt,
vi* **to ~ (to) sb to do** fare cenno a qn di
fare; **motionless** *adj* immobile; **motion
picture** *n* film *m inv*
motivate ['məutɪveɪt] *vt* (*act, decision*)
dare origine a, motivare; (*person*) spingere
motivation [məutɪ'veɪʃən] *n* motivazione
f
motive ['məutɪv] *n* motivo
motor ['məutəʳ] *n* motore *m*;
(*brit: inf: vehicle*) macchina ▷ *cpd*
automobilistico(-a); **motorbike** *n* moto *f
inv*; **motorboat** *n* motoscafo; **motorcar**
(*brit*) *n* automobile *f*; **motorcycle**
n motocicletta; **motorcyclist** *n*
motociclista *m/f*; **motoring** (*brit*) *n*

turismo automobilistico; **motorist** n
automobilista m/f; **motor racing** (BRIT)
n corse fpl automobilistiche; **motorway**
(BRIT) n autostrada
motto ['mɔtəu] (pl **mottoes**) n motto
mould [məuld] (US **mold**) n forma,
stampo; (mildew) muffa ▷ vt formare;
(fig) foggiare; **mouldy** adj ammuffito(-a);
(smell) di muffa
mound [maund] n rialzo, collinetta; (heap)
mucchio
mount [maunt] n (Geo) monte m ▷ vt
montare; (horse) montare a ▷ vi (increase)
aumentare; **mount up** vi (build up)
accumularsi
mountain ['mauntɪn] n montagna
▷ cpd di montagna; **mountain bike** n
mountain bike f inv; **mountaineer** [-'nɪə
'] n alpinista m/f; **mountaineering** [-'nɪə
rɪŋ] n alpinismo; **mountainous** adj
montagnoso(-a); **mountain range** n
catena montuosa
mourn [mɔːn] vt piangere, lamentare ▷ vi
to ~ (for sb) piangere (la morte di qn);
mourner n parente m/f o amico(-a) del
defunto; **mourning** n lutto; **in mourning**
in lutto
mouse [maus] (pl **mice**) n topo; (Comput)
mouse m inv; **mouse mat, mouse pad** n
(Comput) tappetino del mouse
moussaka [mu'sɑːkə] n moussaka
mousse [muːs] n mousse f inv
moustache [məs'tɑːʃ] (US **mustache**) n
baffi mpl
mouth [mauθ, pl mauðz] n bocca; (of river)
bocca, foce f; (opening) orifizio; **mouthful**
n boccata; **mouth organ** n armonica;
mouthpiece n (Mus) imboccatura,
bocchino; (spokesman) portavoce m/f inv;
mouthwash n collutorio
move [muːv] n (movement) movimento; (in
game) mossa; (: turn to play) turno; (change:
of house) trasloco; (: of job) cambiamento
▷ vt muovere; (change position of) spostare;
(emotionally) commuovere; (Pol: resolution
etc) proporre ▷ vi (gen) muoversi,
spostarsi; (also: ~ **house**) cambiar casa,
traslocare; **to get a ~ on** affrettarsi,
sbrigarsi; **can you ~ your car, please?**
può spostare la macchina, per favore?;
to ~ sb to do sth indurre or spingere qn
a fare qc; **to ~ towards** andare verso;
move back vi (return) ritornare; **move
in** vi (to a house) entrare (in una nuova
casa); (police etc) intervenire; **move off** vi
partire; **move on** vi riprendere la strada;
move out vi (of house) sgombrare; **move
over** vi spostarsi; **move up** vi avanzare;
movement ['muːvmənt] n (gen)

movimento; (gesture) gesto; (of stars, water,
physical) moto
movie ['muːvɪ] n film m inv; **the ~s** il
cinema; **movie theater** (US) n cinema
m inv
moving ['muːvɪŋ] adj mobile; (causing
emotion) commovente
mow [məu] (pt **mowed**, pp **mowed** or
mown) vt (grass) tagliare; (corn) mietere;
mower n (also: **lawnmower**) tagliaerba
m inv
Mozambique [məuzəm'biːk] n
Mozambico
MP n abbr = **Member of Parliament**
MP3 n abbr M3; **MP3 player** n lettore m
MP3
mpg n abbr = **miles per gallon** (30 mpg
= 9.4 l. per 100 km)
m.p.h. n abbr = **miles per hour** (60 m.p.h
= 96 km/h)
Mr ['mɪstə'] (US **Mr.**) n **Mr X** Signor X, Sig. X
Mrs ['mɪsɪz] (US **Mrs.**) n **Mrs X** Signora X,
Sig.ra X
Ms [mɪz] (US **Ms.**) n = **Miss or Mrs**; **Ms X**
≈ Signora X, ≈ Sig.ra X

● **Ms**
●
● In inglese si usa **Ms** al posto di "Mrs"
● (Signora) o "Miss" (Signorina) per evitare
● la distinzione tradizionale tra le donne
● sposate e quelle nubili.

MSP n abbr = **Member of the Scottish
Parliament**
Mt abbr (Geo: = mount) M.

O KEYWORD

much [mʌtʃ] adj, pron molto(-a); **he's done
so much work** ha lavorato così tanto; **I
have as much money as you** ho tanti
soldi quanti ne hai tu; **how much is it?**
quant'è?; **it costs too much** costa troppo;
as much as you want quanto vuoi
▷ adv **1** (greatly) molto; **thank you very
very much** molte grazie; **he's very much
the gentleman** è il vero gentiluomo;
I read as much as I can leggo quanto
posso; **as much as you** tanto quanto te
2 (by far) molto; **it's much the biggest
company in Europe** è di gran lunga la più
grossa società in Europa
3 (almost) grossomodo, praticamente;
they're much the same sono
praticamente uguali

muck [mʌk] n (dirt) sporcizia; **muck up**
(inf) vt (ruin) rovinare; **mucky** adj (dirty)

sporco(-a), lordo(-a)

mucus ['mju:kəs] n muco

mud [mʌd] n fango

muddle ['mʌdl] n confusione f, disordine m; pasticcio ▷ vt (also: ~ **up**) confondere

muddy ['mʌdɪ] adj fangoso(-a)

mudguard ['mʌdgɑ:d] n parafango

muesli ['mju:zlɪ] n muesli m

muffin ['mʌfɪn] n specie di pasticcino soffice da tè

muffled ['mʌfld] adj smorzato(-a), attutito(-a)

muffler ['mʌfləʳ] (us) n (Aut) marmitta; (: on motorbike) silenziatore m

mug [mʌg] n (cup) tazzone m; (for beer) boccale m; (inf: face) muso; (: fool) scemo(-a) ▷ vt (assault) assalire; **mugger** ['mʌgəʳ] n aggressore m; **mugging** n assalto

muggy ['mʌgɪ] adj afoso(-a)

mule [mju:l] n mulo

multicoloured ['mʌltɪkʌləd] (us **multicolored**) adj multicolore, variopinto(-a)

multimedia ['mʌltɪ'mi:dɪə] adj multimedia inv

multinational [mʌltɪ'næʃənl] adj, n multinazionale (f)

multiple ['mʌltɪpl] adj multiplo(-a), molteplice ▷ n multiplo; **multiple choice (test)** n esercizi mpl a scelta multipla; **multiple sclerosis** [-sklɪ'rəusɪs] n sclerosi f a placche

multiplex cinema ['mʌltɪpleks-] n cinema m inv multisala inv

multiplication [mʌltɪplɪ'keɪʃən] n moltiplicazione f

multiply ['mʌltɪplaɪ] vt moltiplicare ▷ vi moltiplicarsi

multistorey ['mʌltɪ'stɔ:rɪ] (BRIT) adj (building, car park) a più piani

mum [mʌm] (BRIT: inf) n mamma ▷ adj **to keep ~** non aprire bocca

mumble ['mʌmbl] vt, vi borbottare

mummy ['mʌmɪ] n (BRIT: mother) mamma; (embalmed) mummia

mumps [mʌmps] n orecchioni mpl

munch [mʌntʃ] vt, vi sgranocchiare

municipal [mju:'nɪsɪpl] adj municipale

mural ['mjuərl] n dipinto murale

murder ['mə:dəʳ] n assassinio, omicidio ▷ vt assassinare; **murderer** n omicida m, assassino

murky ['mə:kɪ] adj tenebroso(-a)

murmur ['mə:məʳ] n mormorio ▷ vt, vi mormorare

muscle ['mʌsl] n muscolo; (fig) forza; **muscular** ['mʌskjuləʳ] adj muscolare; (person, arm) muscoloso(-a)

museum [mju:'zɪəm] n museo

mushroom ['mʌʃrum] n fungo ▷ vi crescere in fretta

music ['mju:zɪk] n musica; **musical** adj musicale; (person) portato(-a) per la musica ▷ n (show) commedia musicale; **musical instrument** n strumento musicale; **musician** [-'zɪʃən] n musicista m/f

Muslim ['mʌzlɪm] adj, n musulmano(-a)

muslin ['mʌzlɪn] n mussola

mussel ['mʌsl] n cozza

must [mʌst] aux vb (obligation): **I ~ do it** devo farlo; (probability): **he ~ be there by now** dovrebbe essere arrivato ormai; **I ~ have made a mistake** devo essermi sbagliato ▷ n **it's a ~** è d'obbligo

mustache ['mʌstæʃ] (us) n = **moustache**

mustard ['mʌstəd] n senape f, mostarda

mustn't ['mʌsnt] = **must not**

mute [mju:t] adj, n muto(-a)

mutilate ['mju:tɪleɪt] vt mutilare

mutiny ['mju:tɪnɪ] n ammutinamento

mutter ['mʌtəʳ] vt, vi borbottare, brontolare

mutton ['mʌtn] n carne f di montone

mutual ['mju:tʃuəl] adj mutuo(-a), reciproco(-a)

muzzle ['mʌzl] n muso; (protective device) museruola; (of gun) bocca ▷ vt mettere la museruola a

my [maɪ] adj il (la) mio(-a); (pl) i (le) miei (mie); **my house** la mia casa; **my books** i miei libri; **my brother** mio fratello; **I've washed my hair/cut my finger** mi sono lavato i capelli/tagliato il dito

myself [maɪ'self] pron (reflexive) mi; (emphatic) io stesso(-a); (after prep) me; see also **oneself**

mysterious [mɪs'tɪərɪəs] adj misterioso(-a)

mystery ['mɪstərɪ] n mistero

mystical ['mɪstɪkəl] adj mistico(-a)

mystify ['mɪstɪfaɪ] vt mistificare; (puzzle) confondere

myth [mɪθ] n mito; **mythology** [mɪ'θɔlədʒɪ] n mitologia

m

n

n/a _abbr_ = **not applicable**
nag [næg] _vt_ tormentare ▷ _vi_ brontolare in continuazione
nail [neɪl] _n_ (_human_) unghia; (_metal_) chiodo ▷ _vt_ inchiodare; **to ~ sb down to (doing) sth** costringere qn a (fare) qc; **nailbrush** _n_ spazzolino da or per unghie; **nailfile** _n_ lima da or per unghie; **nail polish** _n_ smalto da or per unghie; **nail polish remover** _n_ acetone _m_, solvente _m_; **nail scissors** _npl_ forbici _fpl_ da or per unghie; **nail varnish** (_BRIT_) _n_ = **nail polish**
naïve [naɪ'iːv] _adj_ ingenuo(-a)
naked ['neɪkɪd] _adj_ nudo(-a)
name [neɪm] _n_ nome _m_; (_reputation_) nome, reputazione _f_ ▷ _vt_ (_baby etc_) chiamare; (_plant, illness_) nominare; (_person, object_) identificare; (_price, date_) fissare; **what's your ~?** come si chiama?; **by ~** di nome; **she knows them all by ~** li conosce tutti per nome; **namely** _adv_ cioè
nanny ['nænɪ] _n_ bambinaia
nap [næp] _n_ (_sleep_) pisolino; (_of cloth_) peluria; **to be caught ~ping** essere preso alla sprovvista
napkin ['næpkɪn] _n_ (_also:_ **table ~**) tovagliolo
nappy ['næpɪ] (_BRIT_) _n_ pannolino
narcotics [nɑː'kɔtɪkz] _npl_ (_drugs_) narcotici, stupefacenti _mpl_

narrative ['nærətɪv] _n_ narrativa
narrator [nə'reɪtəʳ] _n_ narratore(-trice)
narrow ['nærəu] _adj_ stretto(-a); (_fig_) limitato(-a), ristretto(-a) ▷ _vi_ restringersi; **to have a ~ escape** farcela per un pelo; **narrow down** _vt_ (_search, investigation, possibilities_) restringere; (_list_) ridurre; **narrowly** _adv_ per un pelo; (_time_) per poco; **narrow-minded** _adj_ meschino(-a)
nasal ['neɪzl] _adj_ nasale
nasty ['nɑːstɪ] _adj_ (_person, remark: unpleasant_) cattivo(-a); (: _rude_) villano(-a); (_smell, wound, situation_) brutto(-a)
nation ['neɪʃən] _n_ nazione _f_
national ['næʃənl] _adj_ nazionale ▷ _n_ cittadino(-a); **national anthem** _n_ inno nazionale; **national dress** _n_ costume _m_ nazionale; **National Health Service** (_BRIT_) _n_ servizio nazionale di assistenza sanitaria, ≈ S.S.N. _m_; **National Insurance** (_BRIT_) _n_ ≈ Previdenza Sociale; **nationalist** _adj, n_ nazionalista (_m/f_); **nationality** [-'nælɪtɪ] _n_ nazionalità _f inv_; **nationalize** _vt_ nazionalizzare; **national park** _n_ parco nazionale; **National Trust** _n_ sovrintendenza ai beni culturali e ambientali

● **NATIONAL TRUST**
●
● Fondato nel 1895, il **National Trust** è
● un'organizzazione che si occupa della
● tutela e della salvaguardia di luoghi
● di interesse storico o ambientale nel
● Regno Unito.

nationwide ['neɪʃənwaɪd] _adj_ diffuso(-a) in tutto il paese ▷ _adv_ in tutto il paese
native ['neɪtɪv] _n_ abitante _m/f_ del paese ▷ _adj_ indigeno(-a); (_country_) natio(-a); (_ability_) innato(-a); **a ~ of Russia** un nativo della Russia; **a ~ speaker of French** una persona di madrelingua francese; **Native American** _n_ discendente di tribù dell'America settentrionale
NATO ['neɪtəu] _n abbr_ (= _North Atlantic Treaty Organization_) N.A.T.O. _f_
natural ['nætʃrəl] _adj_ naturale; (_ability_) innato(-a); (_manner_) semplice; **natural gas** _n_ gas _m_ metano; **natural history** _n_ storia naturale; **naturally** _adv_ naturalmente; (_by nature: gifted_) di natura; **natural resources** _npl_ risorse _fpl_ naturali
nature ['neɪtʃəʳ] _n_ natura; (_character_) natura, indole _f_; **by ~** di natura; **nature reserve** _n_ (_BRIT_) parco naturale
naughty ['nɔːtɪ] _adj_ (_child_) birichino(-a), cattivello(-a); (_story, film_) spinto(-a)
nausea ['nɔːsɪə] _n_ (_Med_) nausea; (_fig: disgust_) schifo

naval ['neɪvl] *adj* navale

navel ['neɪvl] *n* ombelico

navigate ['nævɪgeɪt] *vt* percorrere navigando ▷ *vi* navigare; (*Aut*) fare da navigatore; **navigation** [-'geɪʃən] *n* navigazione *f*

navy ['neɪvɪ] *n* marina

Nazi ['nɑːtsɪ] *n* nazista *m/f*

NB *abbr* (= *nota bene*) N.B.

near [nɪə^r] *adj* vicino(-a); (*relation*) prossimo(-a) ▷ *adv* vicino ▷ *prep* (*also:* **~ to**) vicino a, presso; (: *time*) verso ▷ *vt* avvicinarsi a; **nearby** [nɪə'baɪ] *adj* vicino(-a) ▷ *adv* vicino; **is there a bank nearby?** c'è una banca qui vicino?; **nearly** *adv* quasi; **I nearly fell** per poco non sono caduto; **near-sighted** [nɪə'saɪtɪd] *adj* miope

neat [niːt] *adj* (*person, room*) ordinato(-a); (*work*) pulito(-a); (*solution, plan*) ben indovinato(-a), azzeccato(-a); (*spirits*) liscio(-a); **neatly** *adv* con ordine; (*skilfully*) abilmente

necessarily ['nɛsɪsrɪlɪ] *adv* necessariamente

necessary ['nɛsɪsrɪ] *adj* necessario(-a)

necessity [nɪ'sɛsɪtɪ] *n* necessità *f inv*

neck [nɛk] *n* collo; (*of garment*) colletto ▷ *vi* (*inf*) pomiciare, sbaciucchiarsi; **~ and ~** testa a testa; **necklace** ['nɛklɪs] *n* collana; **necktie** ['nɛktaɪ] *n* cravatta

nectarine ['nɛktərɪn] *n* nocepesca

need [niːd] *n* bisogno ▷ *vt* aver bisogno di; **do you ~ anything?** ha bisogno di qualcosa?; **to ~ to do** dover fare; aver bisogno di fare; **you don't ~ to go** non devi andare, non c'è bisogno che tu vada

needle ['niːdl] *n* ago; (*on record player*) puntina ▷ *vt* punzecchiare

needless ['niːdlɪs] *adj* inutile

needlework ['niːdlwəːk] *n* cucito

needn't ['niːdnt] = **need not**

needy ['niːdɪ] *adj* bisognoso(-a)

negative ['nɛgətɪv] *n* (*Ling*) negazione *f*; (*Phot*) negativo ▷ *adj* negativo(-a)

neglect [nɪ'glɛkt] *vt* trascurare ▷ *n* (*of person, duty*) negligenza; (*of child, house etc*) scarsa cura; **state of ~** stato di abbandono

negotiate [nɪ'gəuʃɪeɪt] *vi* **to ~ (with)** negoziare (con) ▷ *vt* (*Comm*) negoziare; (*obstacle*) superare; **negotiations** [nɪgəuʃɪ'eɪʃənz] *pl n* trattative *fpl*, negoziati *mpl*

negotiator [nɪ'gəuʃɪeɪtə^r] *n* negoziatore(-trice)

neighbour ['neɪbə^r] (*US* **neighbor**) *n* vicino(-a); **neighbourhood** *n* vicinato; **neighbouring** *adj* vicino(-a)

neither ['naɪðə^r] *adj, pron* né l'uno(-a) né l'altro(-a), nessuno(-a) dei (delle) due ▷ *conj* neanche, nemmeno, neppure ▷ *adv* **~ good nor bad** né buono né cattivo; **I didn't move and ~ did Claude** io non mi mossi e nemmeno Claude; **..., ~ did I refuse** ..., ma non ho nemmeno rifiutato

neon ['niːɔn] *n* neon *m*

Nepal [nɪ'pɔːl] *n* Nepal *m*

nephew ['nɛvjuː] *n* nipote *m*

nerve [nəːv] *n* nervo; (*fig*) coraggio; (*impudence*) faccia tosta; **~s** (*nervousness*) nervoso; **a fit of ~s** una crisi di nervi

nervous ['nəːvəs] *adj* nervoso(-a); (*anxious*) agitato(-a), in apprensione; **nervous breakdown** *n* esaurimento nervoso

nest [nɛst] *n* nido ▷ *vi* fare il nido, nidificare

net [nɛt] *n* rete *f* ▷ *adj* netto(-a) ▷ *vt* (*fish etc*) prendere con la rete; (*profit*) ricavare un utile netto di; **the N~** (*Internet*) Internet *f*; **netball** *n* specie di pallacanestro

Netherlands ['nɛðələndz] *npl* **the ~** í Paesi Bassi

nett [nɛt] *adj* = **net**

nettle ['nɛtl] *n* ortica

network ['nɛtwəːk] *n* rete *f*

neurotic [njuə'rɔtɪk] *adj, n* nevrotico(-a)

neuter ['njuːtə^r] *adj* neutro(-a) ▷ *vt* (*cat etc*) castrare

neutral ['njuːtrəl] *adj* neutro(-a); (*person, nation*) neutrale ▷ *n* (*Aut*): **in ~** in folle

never ['nɛvə^r] *adv* (non...) mai; **I've ~ been to Spain** non sono mai stato in Spagna; **~ again** mai più; **I'll ~ go there again** non ci vado più; **~ in my life** mai in vita mia; *see also* **mind**; **never-ending** *adj* interminabile; **nevertheless** [nɛvəðə'lɛs] *adv* tuttavia, ciò nonostante, ciò nondimeno

new [njuː] *adj* nuovo(-a); (*brand new*) nuovo(-a) di zecca; **New Age** *n* New Age *f inv*; **newborn** *adj* neonato(-a); **newcomer** ['njuːkʌmə^r] *n* nuovo(-a) venuto(-a); **newly** *adv* di recente

news [njuːz] *n* notizie *fpl*; (*Radio*) giornale *m* radio; (*TV*) telegiornale *m*; **a piece of ~** una notizia; **news agency** *n* agenzia di stampa; **newsagent** (*BRIT*) *n* giornalaio; **newscaster** *n* (*Radio, TV*) annunciatore(-trice); **news dealer** (*US*) *n* = **newsagent**; **newsletter** *n* bollettino; **newspaper** *n* giornale *m*; **newsreader** *n* = **newscaster**

newt [njuːt] *n* tritone *m*

New Year *n* Anno Nuovo; **New Year's Day** *n* il Capodanno; **New Year's Eve** *n* la vigilia di Capodanno

New York [-'jɔːk] n New York f
New Zealand [-'ziːlənd] n Nuova Zelanda;
New Zealander n neozelandese m/f
next [nɛkst] adj prossimo(-a) ▷ adv
accanto; (in time) dopo; **the ~ day** il giorno
dopo, l'indomani; **~ time** la prossima
volta; **~ year** l'anno prossimo; **when do
we meet ~?** quando ci rincontriamo?; **~
to** accanto a; **~ to nothing** quasi niente;
~ please! (avanti) il prossimo!; **next door**
adv, adj accanto inv; **next-of-kin** n parente
m/f prossimo(-a)
NHS n abbr = **National Health Service**
nibble ['nɪbl] vt mordicchiare
nice [naɪs] adj (holiday, trip) piacevole; (flat,
picture) bello(-a); (person) simpatico(-a),
gentile; **nicely** adv bene
niche [niːʃ] n (Archit) nicchia
nick [nɪk] n taglietto; tacca ▷ vt (inf)
rubare; **in the ~ of time** appena in tempo
nickel ['nɪkl] n nichel m; (us) moneta da
cinque centesimi di dollaro
nickname ['nɪkneɪm] n
soprannome m
nicotine ['nɪkətiːn] n nicotina
niece [niːs] n nipote f
Nigeria [naɪ'dʒɪərɪə] n Nigeria
night [naɪt] n notte f; (evening) sera; **at
~** la sera; **by ~** di notte; **the ~ before
last** l'altro ieri notte (or sera); **night
club** n locale m notturno; **nightdress**
n camicia da notte; **nightie** ['naɪtɪ] n
= **nightdress**; **nightlife** ['naɪtlaɪf] n vita
notturna; **nightly** ['naɪtlɪ] adj di ogni
notte or sera; (by night) notturno(-a)
▷ adv ogni notte or sera; **nightmare**
['naɪtmɛəʳ] n incubo
night: **night school** n scuola serale; **night
shift** n turno di notte; **night-time** n
notte f
nil [nɪl] n nulla m; (BRIT Sport) zero
nine [naɪn] num nove; **nineteen** num
diciannove; **nineteenth** [naɪn'tiːnθ] num
diciannovesimo(-a); **ninetieth** ['naɪntɪɪθ]
num novantesimo(-a); **ninety** num
novanta; **ninth** [naɪnθ] num nono(-a)
nip [nɪp] vt pizzicare; (bite) mordere
nipple ['nɪpl] n (Anat) capezzolo
nitrogen ['naɪtrədʒən] n azoto

⬤ **KEYWORD**

no [nəu] (pl **noes**) adv (opposite of "yes") no;
are you coming? — no (I'm not) viene?
— no (non vengo); **would you like some
more? — no thank you** ne vuole ancora
un po'? — no, grazie
▷ adj (not any) nessuno(-a); **I have no
money/time/books** non ho soldi/

tempo/libri; **no student would have
done it** nessuno studente lo avrebbe
fatto; **"no parking"** "divieto di sosta"; **"no
smoking"** "vietato fumare"
▷ n no m inv

nobility [nəu'bɪlɪtɪ] n nobiltà
noble ['nəubl] adj nobile
nobody ['nəubədɪ] pron nessuno
nod [nɔd] vi accennare col capo, fare un
cenno; (in agreement) annuire con un cenno
del capo; (sleep) sonnecchiare ▷ vt **to ~
one's head** fare di sì col capo ▷ n cenno;
nod off vi assopirsi
noise [nɔɪz] n rumore m; (din, racket)
chiasso; **I can't sleep for the ~** non riesco
a dormire a causa del rumore; **noisy**
adj (street, car) rumoroso(-a); (person)
chiassoso(-a)
nominal ['nɔmɪnl] adj nominale; (rent)
simbolico(-a)
nominate ['nɔmɪneɪt] vt (propose)
proporre come candidato; (elect)
nominare; **nomination** [nɔmɪ'neɪʃə
n] n nomina; candidatura; **nominee**
[nɔmɪ'niː] n persona nominata,
candidato(-a)
none [nʌn] pron (not one thing) niente;
(not one person) nessuno(-a); **~ of you**
nessuno(-a) di voi; **I've ~ left** non ne ho
più; **he's ~ the worse for it** non ne ha
risentito
nonetheless [nʌnðə'lɛs] adv
nondimeno
non-fiction [nɔn'fɪkʃən] n saggistica
nonsense ['nɔnsəns] n sciocchezze fpl
non: **non-smoker** n non fumatore(-trice);
non-smoking adj (person) che non fuma;
(area, section) per non fumatori; **non-stick**
adj antiaderente, antiadesivo(-a)
noodles ['nuːdlz] npl taglierini mpl
noon [nuːn] n mezzogiorno
no-one ['nəuwʌn] pron = **nobody**
nor [nɔːʳ] conj = **neither** ▷ adv see **neither**
norm [nɔːm] n norma
normal ['nɔːml] adj normale; **normally**
adv normalmente
north [nɔːθ] n nord m, settentrione m
▷ adj nord inv, del nord, settentrionale
▷ adv verso nord; **North America** n
America del Nord; **North American**
adj, n nordamericano(-a); **northbound**
['nɔːθbaund] adj (traffic) diretto(-a)
a nord; (carriageway) nord inv; **north-
east** n nord-est m; **northeastern** adj
nordorientale; **northern** ['nɔːðən] adj del
nord, settentrionale; **Northern Ireland**
n Irlanda del Nord; **North Korea** n Corea
del Nord; **North Pole** n Polo Nord; **North**

Sea *n* Mare *m* del Nord; **north-west** *n* nord-ovest *m*; **northwestern** *adj* nordoccidentale

Norway ['nɔːweɪ] *n* Norvegia; **Norwegian** [nɔː'wiːdʒən] *adj* norvegese ▷ *n* norvegese *m/f*; (*Ling*) norvegese *m*

nose [nəuz] *n* naso; (*of animal*) muso ▷ *vi* **to ~ about** aggirarsi; **nosebleed** *n* emorragia nasale; **nosey** (*inf*) *adj* = **nosy**

nostalgia [nɔs'tældʒɪə] *n* nostalgia

nostalgic [nɔs'tældʒɪk] *adj* nostalgico(-a)

nostril ['nɔstrɪl] *n* narice *f*; (*of horse*) frogia

nosy ['nəuzɪ] (*inf*) *adj* curioso(-a)

not [nɔt] *adv* non; **he is ~** *or* **isn't here** non è qui, non c'è; **you must ~** *or* **you mustn't do that** non devi fare quello; **it's too late, isn't it** *or* **is it ~?** è troppo tardi, vero?; **~ that I don't like him** non che (lui) non mi piaccia; **~ yet/now** non ancora/ora; *see also* **all; only**

notable ['nəutəbl] *adj* notevole; **notably** ['nəutəblɪ] *adv* (*markedly*) notevolmente; (*particularly*) in particolare

notch [nɔtʃ] *n* tacca; (*in saw*) dente *m*

note [nəut] *n* nota; (*letter, banknote*) biglietto ▷ *vt* (*also:* **~ down**) prendere nota di; **to take ~s** prendere appunti; **notebook** *n* taccuino; **noted** ['nəutɪd] *adj* celebre; **notepad** *n* bloc-notes *m inv*; **notepaper** *n* carta da lettere

nothing ['nʌθɪŋ] *n* nulla *m*, niente *m*; (*zero*) zero; **he does ~** non fa niente; **~ new/much** *etc* niente di nuovo/speciale *etc*; **for ~** per niente

notice ['nəutɪs] *n* avviso; (*of leaving*) preavviso ▷ *vt* notare, accorgersi di; **to take ~ of** fare attenzione a; **to bring sth to sb's ~** far notare qc a qn; **at short ~** con un breve preavviso; **until further ~** fino a nuovo avviso; **to hand in one's ~** licenziarsi; **noticeable** *adj* evidente

notify ['nəutɪfaɪ] *vt* **to ~ sth to sb** far sapere qc a qn; **to ~ sb of sth** avvisare qn di qc

notion ['nəuʃən] *n* idea; (*concept*) nozione *f*; **~s** *npl* (*US: haberdashery*) merceria

notorious [nəu'tɔːrɪəs] *adj* famigerato(-a)

notwithstanding [nɔtwɪθ'stændɪŋ] *adv* nondimeno ▷ *prep* nonostante, malgrado

nought [nɔːt] *n* zero

noun [naun] *n* nome *m*, sostantivo

nourish ['nʌrɪʃ] *vt* nutrire; **nourishment** *n* nutrimento

Nov. *abbr* (= *November*) nov.

novel ['nɔvl] *n* romanzo ▷ *adj* nuovo(-a); **novelist** *n* romanziere(-a); **novelty** *n*

novità *f inv*

November [nəu'vɛmbər] *n* novembre *m*

novice ['nɔvɪs] *n* principiante *m/f*; (*Rel*) novizio(-a)

now [nau] *adv* ora, adesso ▷ *conj* **~ (that)** adesso che, ora che; **by ~** ormai; **just ~** proprio ora; **right ~** subito, immediatamente; **~ and then, ~ and again** ogni tanto; **from ~ on** da ora in poi; **nowadays** ['nauədeɪz] *adv* oggidì

nowhere ['nəuwɛər] *adv* in nessun luogo, da nessuna parte

nozzle ['nɔzl] *n* (*of hose etc*) boccaglio; (*of fire extinguisher*) lancia

nr *abbr* (*BRIT*) = **near**

nuclear ['njuːklɪər] *adj* nucleare

nucleus ['njuːklɪəs] (*pl* **nuclei**) *n* nucleo

nude [njuːd] *adj* nudo(-a) ▷ *n* (*Art*) nudo; **in the ~** tutto(-a) nudo(-a)

nudge [nʌdʒ] *vt* dare una gomitata a

nudist ['njuːdɪst] *n* nudista *m/f*

nudity ['njuːdɪtɪ] *n* nudità

nuisance ['njuːsns] *n* **it's a ~** è una seccatura; **he's a ~** è uno scocciatore

numb [nʌm] *adj* **~ (with)** intorpidito(-a) (da); (*with fear*) impietrito(-a) (da); **~ with cold** intirizzito(-a) (dal freddo)

number ['nʌmbər] *n* numero ▷ *vt* numerare; (*include*) contare; **a ~ of** un certo numero di; **to be ~ed among** venire annoverato(-a) tra; **they were 10 in ~** erano in tutto 10; **number plate** (*BRIT*) *n* (*Aut*) targa; **Number Ten** *n* (*BRIT*: = 10 *Downing Street*) residenza del Primo Ministro del Regno Unito

numerical [njuː'mɛrɪkl] *adj* numerico(-a)

numerous ['njuːmərəs] *adj* numeroso(-a)

nun [nʌn] *n* suora, monaca

nurse [nəːs] *n* infermiere(-a); (*also:* **~maid**) bambinaia ▷ *vt* (*patient, cold*) curare; (*baby*: *BRIT*) cullare; (: *US*) allattare, dare il latte a

nursery ['nəːsərɪ] *n* (*room*) camera dei bambini; (*institution*) asilo; (*for plants*) vivaio; **nursery rhyme** *n* filastrocca; **nursery school** *n* scuola materna; **nursery slope** (*BRIT*) *n* (*Ski*) pista per principianti

nursing ['nəːsɪŋ] *n* (*profession*) professione *f* di infermiere (*or* di infermiera); (*care*) cura; **nursing home** *n* casa di cura

nurture ['nəːtʃər] *vt* allevare; nutrire

nut [nʌt] *n* (*of metal*) dado; (*fruit*) noce *f*

nutmeg ['nʌtmɛg] *n* noce *f* moscata

nutrient ['njuːtrɪənt] *adj* nutriente ▷ *n* sostanza nutritiva

n

nutrition [njuːˈtrɪʃən] *n* nutrizione *f*
nutritious [njuːˈtrɪʃəs] *adj* nutriente
nuts [nʌts] (*inf*) *adj* matto(-a)
NVQ *n abbr* (*BRIT*) = **National Vocational Qualification**
nylon [ˈnaɪlɔn] *n* nailon *m* ▷ *adj* di nailon

oak [əuk] *n* quercia ▷ *adj* di quercia
O.A.P. (*BRIT*) *n, abbr* = **old age pensioner**
oar [ɔːʳ] *n* remo
oasis [əuˈeɪsɪs] (*pl* **oases**) *n* oasi *f inv*
oath [əuθ] *n* giuramento; (*swear word*) bestemmia
oatmeal [ˈəutmiːl] *n* farina d'avena
oats [əuts] *npl* avena
obedience [əˈbiːdɪəns] *n* ubbidienza
obedient [əˈbiːdɪənt] *adj* ubbidiente
obese [əuˈbiːs] *adj* obeso(-a)
obesity [əuˈbiːsɪtɪ] *n* obesità
obey [əˈbeɪ] *vt* ubbidire a; (*instructions, regulations*) osservare
obituary [əˈbɪtjuərɪ] *n* necrologia
object [*n* ˈɔbdʒɪkt, *vb* əbˈdʒɛkt] *n* oggetto; (*purpose*) scopo, intento; (*Ling*) complemento oggetto ▷ *vi* **to ~ to** (*attitude*) disapprovare; (*proposal*) protestare contro, sollevare delle obiezioni contro; **expense is no ~** non si bada a spese; **to ~ that** obiettare che; **objection** [əbˈdʒɛkʃən] *n* obiezione *f*; **objective** *n* obiettivo
obligation [ɔblɪˈɡeɪʃən] *n* obbligo, dovere *m*; **without ~** senza impegno
obligatory [əˈblɪɡətərɪ] *adj* obbligatorio(-a)
oblige [əˈblaɪdʒ] *vt* (*force*): **to ~ sb to do** costringere qn a fare; (*do a favour*) fare una

cortesia a; **to be ~d to** sb for sth essere grato a qn per qc

oblique [ə'bli:k] *adj* obliquo(-a); (*allusion*) indiretto(-a)

obliterate [ə'blɪtəreɪt] *vt* cancellare

oblivious [ə'blɪvɪəs] *adj* ~ **of** incurante di; inconscio(-a) di

oblong ['ɔblɔŋ] *adj* oblungo(-a) ▷ *n* rettangolo

obnoxious [əb'nɔkʃəs] *adj* odioso(-a); (*smell*) disgustoso(-a), ripugnante

oboe ['əubəu] *n* oboe *m*

obscene [əb'si:n] *adj* osceno(-a)

obscure [əb'skjuəʳ] *adj* oscuro(-a) ▷ *vt* oscurare; (*hide: sun*) nascondere

observant [əb'zə:vnt] *adj* attento(-a)

■ Be careful not to translate *observant* by the Italian word *osservante*.

observation [ɔbzə'veɪʃən] *n* osservazione *f*; (*by police etc*) sorveglianza

observatory [əb'zə:vətrɪ] *n* osservatorio

observe [əb'zə:v] *vt* osservare; (*remark*) fare osservare; **observer** *n* osservatore(-trice)

obsess [əb'sɛs] *vt* ossessionare; **obsession** [əb'sɛʃən] *n* ossessione *f*; **obsessive** *adj* ossessivo(-a)

obsolete ['ɔbsəli:t] *adj* obsoleto(-a)

obstacle ['ɔbstəkl] *n* ostacolo

obstinate ['ɔbstɪnɪt] *adj* ostinato(-a)

obstruct [əb'strʌkt] *vt* (*block*) ostruire, ostacolare; (*halt*) fermare; (*hinder*) impedire; **obstruction** [əb'strʌkʃən] *n* ostruzione *f*; ostacolo

obtain [əb'teɪn] *vt* ottenere

obvious ['ɔbvɪəs] *adj* ovvio(-a), evidente; **obviously** *adv* ovviamente; certo

occasion [ə'keɪʒən] *n* occasione *f*; (*event*) avvenimento; **occasional** *adj* occasionale; **occasionally** *adv* ogni tanto

occult [ɔ'kʌlt] *adj* occulto(-a) ▷ *n* **the ~** l'occulto

occupant ['ɔkjupənt] *n* occupante *m/f*; (*of boat, car etc*) persona a bordo

occupation [ɔkju'peɪʃən] *n* occupazione *f*; (*job*) mestiere *m*, professione *f*

occupy ['ɔkjupaɪ] *vt* occupare; **to ~ o.s. in doing** occuparsi a fare

occur [ə'kə:ʳ] *vi* succedere, capitare; **to ~ to sb** venire in mente a qn; **occurrence** *n* caso, fatto; presenza

■ Be careful not to translate *occur* by the Italian word *occorrere*.

ocean ['əuʃən] *n* oceano

o'clock [ə'klɔk] *adv* **it is 5 o'clock** sono le 5

Oct. *abbr* (= *October*) ott.

October [ɔk'təubəʳ] *n* ottobre *m*

octopus ['ɔktəpəs] *n* polpo, piovra

odd [ɔd] *adj* (*strange*) strano(-a), bizzarro(-a); (*number*) dispari *inv*; (*not of a set*) spaiato(-a); **60-~** 60 e oltre; **at ~ times** di tanto in tanto; **the ~ one out** l'eccezione *f*; **oddly** *adv* stranamente; **odds** *npl* (*in betting*) quota

odometer [ɔ'dɔmɪtəʳ] *n* odometro

odour ['əudəʳ] (*us* **odor**) *n* odore *m*; (*unpleasant*) cattivo odore

⊙ **KEYWORD**

of [ɔv, əv] *prep* **1** (*gen*) di; **a boy of 10** un ragazzo di 10 anni; **a friend of ours** un nostro amico; **that was kind of you** è stato molto gentile da parte sua

2 (*expressing quantity, amount, dates etc*) di; **a kilo of flour** un chilo di farina; **how much of this do you need?** quanto gliene serve?; **there were 3 of them** (*people*) erano in 3; (*objects*) ce n'erano 3; **3 of us went** 3 di noi sono andati; **the 5th of July** il 5 luglio

3 (*from, out of*) di, in; *of* **made of wood** (fatto) di *or* in legno

⊙ **KEYWORD**

off [ɔf] *adv* **1** (*distance, time*): **it's a long way off** è lontano; **the game is 3 days off** la partita è tra 3 giorni

2 (*departure, removal*) via; **to go off to Paris** andarsene a Parigi; **I must be off** devo andare via; **to take off one's coat** togliersi il cappotto; **the button came off** il bottone è venuto via *or* si è staccato; **10% off** con lo sconto del 10%

3 (*not at work*): **to have a day off** avere un giorno libero; **to be off sick** essere assente per malattia

▷ *adj* (*engine*) spento(-a); (*tap*) chiuso(-a); (*cancelled*) sospeso(-a); (*BRIT: food*) andato(-a) a male; **on the off chance** nel caso; **to have an off day** non essere in forma

▷ *prep* **1** (*motion, removal etc*) da; (*distant from*) a poca distanza da; **a street off the square** una strada che parte dalla piazza

2: **to be off meat** non mangiare più la carne

offence [ə'fɛns] (*us* **offense**) *n* (*Law*) contravvenzione *f*; (: *more serious*) reato; **to take ~ at** offendersi per

offend [ə'fɛnd] *vt* (*person*) offendere; **offender** *n* delinquente *m/f*; (*against regulations*) contravventore(-trice)

offense [ə'fɛns] (*us*) *n* = **offence**

offensive [əˈfɛnsɪv] adj offensivo(-a); (smell etc) sgradevole, ripugnante ▷ n (Mil) offensiva

offer [ˈɔfəʳ] n offerta, proposta ▷ vt offrire; **"on ~"** (Comm) "in offerta speciale"

offhand [ɔfˈhænd] adj disinvolto(-a), noncurante ▷ adv su due piedi

office [ˈɔfɪs] n (place) ufficio; (position) carica; **doctor's ~** (US) studio; **to take ~** entrare in carica; **office block** (US **office building**) n complesso di uffici; **office hours** npl orario d'ufficio; (US Med) orario di visite

officer [ˈɔfɪsəʳ] n (Mil etc) ufficiale m; (also: **police ~**) agente m di polizia; (of organization) funzionario

office worker n impiegato(-a) d'ufficio

official [əˈfɪʃl] adj (authorized) ufficiale ▷ n ufficiale m; (civil servant) impiegato(-a) statale; funzionario

off: **off-licence** (BRIT) n (shop) spaccio di bevande alcoliche; **off-line** adj, adv (Comput) off-line inv, fuori linea; (: switched off) spento(-a); **off-peak** adj (ticket, heating etc) a tariffa ridotta; (time) non di punta; **off-putting** (BRIT) adj sgradevole, antipatico(-a); **off-season** adj, adv fuori stagione; **offset** [ˈɔfsɛt] (irreg) vt (counteract) controbilanciare, compensare; **offshore** [ɔfˈʃɔːʳ] adj (breeze) di terra; (island) vicino alla costa; (fishing) costiero(-a); **offside** [ˈɔfsaɪd] adj (Sport) fuori gioco; (Aut: in Britain) destro(-a); (: in Italy etc) sinistro(-a); **offspring** [ˈɔfsprɪŋ] n inv prole f, discendenza

often [ˈɔfn] adv spesso; **how ~ do you go?** quanto spesso ci vai?

oh [əu] excl oh!

oil [ɔɪl] n olio; (petroleum) petrolio; (for central heating) nafta ▷ vt (machine) lubrificare; **oil filter** n (Aut) filtro dell'olio; **oil painting** n quadro a olio; **oil refinery** n raffineria di petrolio; **oil rig** n derrick m inv; (at sea) piattaforma per trivellazioni subacquee; **oil slick** n chiazza d'olio; **oil tanker** n (ship) petroliera; (truck) autocisterna per petrolio; **oil well** n pozzo petrolifero; **oily** adj unto(-a), oleoso(-a); (food) grasso(-a)

ointment [ˈɔɪntmənt] n unguento

O.K. [ˈəuˈkeɪ] excl d'accordo! ▷ adj non male inv ▷ vt approvare; **is it O.K.?, are you O.K.?** tutto bene?

old [əuld] adj vecchio(-a); (ancient) antico(-a), vecchio(-a); (person) vecchio(-a), anziano(-a); **how ~ are you?** quanti anni ha?; **he's 10 years ~** ha 10 anni; **~er brother** fratello maggiore; **old age** n

vecchiaia; **old-age pension** [ˈəuldeɪdʒ-] n (BRIT) pensione f di vecchiaia; **old-age pensioner** (BRIT) n pensionato(-a); **old-fashioned** adj antiquato(-a), fuori moda; (person) all'antica; **old people's home** n ricovero per anziani

olive [ˈɔlɪv] n (fruit) oliva; (tree) olivo ▷ adj (also: **~-green**) verde oliva inv; **olive oil** n olio d'oliva

Olympic [əuˈlɪmpɪk] adj olimpico(-a); **the ~ Games, the ~s** i giochi olimpici, le Olimpiadi

omelet(te) [ˈɔmlɪt] n omelette f inv

omen [ˈəumən] n presagio, augurio

ominous [ˈɔmɪnəs] adj minaccioso(-a); (event) di malaugurio

omit [əuˈmɪt] vt omettere

◯ KEYWORD

on [ɔn] prep **1** (indicating position) su; **on the wall** sulla parete; **on the left** a or sulla sinistra

2 (indicating means, method, condition etc): **on foot** a piedi; **on the train/plane** in treno/aereo; **on the telephone** al telefono; **on the radio/television** alla radio/televisione; **to be on drugs** drogarsi; **on holiday** in vacanza

3 (of time): **on Friday** venerdì; **on Fridays** il or di venerdì; **on June 20th** il 20 giugno; **on Friday, June 20th** venerdì, 20 giugno; **a week on Friday** venerdì a otto; **on his arrival** al suo arrivo; **on seeing this** vedendo ciò

4 (about, concerning) su, di; **information on train services** informazioni sui collegamenti ferroviari; **a book on Goldoni/physics** un libro su Goldoni/di or sulla fisica

▷ adv **1** (referring to dress, covering): **to have one's coat on** avere indosso il cappotto; **to put one's coat on** mettersi il cappotto; **what's she got on?** cosa indossa?; **she put her boots/gloves/hat on** si mise gli stivali/i guanti/il cappello; **screw the lid on tightly** avvita bene il coperchio

2 (further, continuously): **to walk on, go on** etc continuare, proseguire etc; **to read on** continuare a leggere; **on and off** ogni tanto

▷ adj **1** (in operation: machine, TV, light) acceso(-a); (: tap) aperto(-a); (: brake) inserito(-a); **is the meeting still on?** (in progress) la riunione è ancora in corso?; (not cancelled) è confermato l'incontro?; **there's a good film on at the cinema** danno un buon film al cinema

2 (*inf*): **that's not on!** (*not acceptable*) non si fa così!; (*not possible*) non se ne parla neanche!

once [wʌns] *adv* una volta ▷ *conj* non appena, quando; **~ he had left/it was done** dopo che se n'era andato/fu fatto; **at ~** subito; (*simultaneously*) a un tempo; **~ a week** una volta per settimana; **~ more** ancora una volta; **~ and for all** una volta per sempre; **~ upon a time** c'era una volta

oncoming [ˈɒnkʌmɪŋ] *adj* (*traffic*) che viene in senso opposto

○ KEYWORD

one [wʌn] *num* uno(-a); **one hundred and fifty** centocinquanta, **one day** un giorno ▷ *adj* **1** (*sole*) unico(-a); **the one book which** l'unico libro che; **the one man who** l'unico che

2 (*same*) stesso(-a); **they came in the one car** sono venuti nella stessa macchina ▷ *pron* **1** this one questo(-a); **that one** quello(-a); **I've already got one/a red one** ne ho già uno/uno rosso; **one by one** uno per uno

2: one another l'un l'altro; **to look at one another** guardarsi; **to help one another** aiutarsi l'un l'altro *or* a vicenda

3 (*impersonal*) si; **one never knows** non si sa mai; **to cut one's finger** tagliarsi un dito; **one needs to eat** bisogna mangiare

one: **one-off** (*BRIT: inf*) *n* fatto eccezionale

oneself [wʌnˈsɛlf] *pron* (*reflexive*) si; (*after prep*) se stesso(-a), sé; **to do sth (by) ~** fare qc da sé; **to hurt ~** farsi male; **to keep sth for ~** tenere qc per sé; **to talk to ~** parlare da solo

one: **one-shot** [wʌnˈʃɒt] (*US*) *n* = **one-off**; **one-sided** *adj* (*argument*) unilaterale; **one-to-one** *adj* (*relationship*) univoco(-a); **one-way** *adj* (*street, traffic*) a senso unico

ongoing [ˈɒngəuɪŋ] *adj* in corso; in attuazione

onion [ˈʌnjən] *n* cipolla

on-line [ˈɒnlaɪn] *adj, adv* (*Comput*) on-line *inv*

onlooker [ˈɒnlukəʳ] *n* spettatore(-trice)

only [ˈəunlɪ] *adv* solo, soltanto ▷ *adj* solo(-a), unico(-a) ▷ *conj* solo che, ma; **an ~ child** un figlio unico; **not ~ ... but also** non solo ... ma anche

on-screen [ɒnˈskriːn] *adj* sullo schermo *inv*

onset [ˈɒnsɛt] *n* inizio

onto [ˈɒntu] *prep* = **on to**

quella volta in poi

oops [ups] *excl* ops! (*esprime rincrescimento per un piccolo contrattempo*); **~-a-daisy!** oplà!

ooze [uːz] *vi* stillare

opaque [əuˈpeɪk] *adj* opaco(-a)

open [ˈəupn] *adj* aperto(-a); (*road*) libero(-a); (*meeting*) pubblico(-a) ▷ *vt* aprire ▷ *vi* (*eyes, door, debate*) aprirsi; (*flower*) sbocciare; (*shop, bank, museum*) aprire; (*book etc: commence*) cominciare; **is it ~ to the public?** è aperto al pubblico?; **in the ~ (air)** all'aperto; **what time do you ~?** a che ora aprite?; **open up** *vt* aprire; (*blocked road*) sgombrare ▷ *vi* (*shop, business*) aprire; **open-air** *adj* all'aperto; **opening** *adj* (*speech*) di apertura ▷ *n* apertura; (*opportunity*) occasione *f*, opportunità *f inv*; sbocco; **opening hours** *npl* orario d'apertura; **open learning** *n* sistema educativo secondo il quale lo studente ha maggior controllo e gestione delle modalità di apprendimento; **openly** *adv* apertamente; **open-minded** *adj* che ha la mente aperta; **open-necked** *adj* col collo slacciato; **open-plan** *adj* senza pareti divisorie; **Open University** *n* (*BRIT*) vedi nota nel riquadro

● **OPEN UNIVERSITY**

● La **Open University**, fondata in Gran
● Bretagna nel 1969, organizza corsi
● di laurea per corrispondenza o via
● Internet. Alcune lezioni possono venir
● seguite per radio o alla televisione e
● vengono organizzati regolari corsi
● estivi.

opera [ˈɒpərə] *n* opera; **opera house** *n* opera; **opera singer** *n* cantante *m/f* d'opera *or* lirico(-a)

operate [ˈɒpəreɪt] *vt* (*machine*) azionare, far funzionare; (*system*) usare ▷ *vi* funzionare; (*drug*) essere efficace; **to ~ on sb (for)** (*Med*) operare qn (di)

operating room (*US*) *n* = **operating theatre**

operating theatre *n* (*Med*) sala operatoria

operation [ɒpəˈreɪʃən] *n* operazione *f*; **to be in ~** (*machine*) essere in azione *or* funzionamento; (*system*) essere in vigore; **to have an ~** (*Med*) subire un'operazione; **operational** *adj* in funzione; d'esercizio

operative [ˈɒpərətɪv] *adj* (*measure*) operativo(-a)

operator [ˈɒpəreɪtəʳ] *n* (*of machine*) operatore(-trice); (*Tel*) centralinista *m/f*

opinion [ə'pɪnɪən] n opinione f, parere m;
in my ~ secondo me, a mio avviso; **opinion
poll** n sondaggio di opinioni

opponent [ə'pəunənt] n avversario(-a)

opportunity [ɔpə'tju:nɪtɪ] n opportunità
f inv, occasione f; **to take the ~ of doing**
cogliere l'occasione per fare

oppose [ə'pəuz] vt opporsi a; **~d to**
contrario(-a) a; **as ~d to** in contrasto con

opposite ['ɔpəzɪt] adj opposto(-a); (house
etc) di fronte ▷ adv di fronte, dirimpetto
▷ prep di fronte a ▷ n **the ~** il contrario,
l'opposto; **the ~ sex** l'altro sesso

opposition [ɔpə'zɪʃən] n opposizione f

oppress [ə'prɛs] vt opprimere

opt [ɔpt] vi **to ~ for** optare per; **to ~ to do**
scegliere di fare; **opt out** vi **to ~ out of**
ritirarsi da

optician [ɔp'tɪʃən] n ottico

optimism ['ɔptɪmɪzəm] n ottimismo

optimist ['ɔptɪmɪst] n ottimista m/f;
optimistic [-'mɪstɪk] adj ottimistico(-a)

optimum ['ɔptɪməm] adj ottimale

option ['ɔpʃən] n scelta; (Scol) materia
facoltativa; (Comm) opzione f; **optional**
adj facoltativo(-a); (Comm) a scelta

or [ɔː'] conj o, oppure; (with negative): **he
hasn't seen or heard anything** non
ha visto né sentito niente; **or else** se no,
altrimenti; oppure

oral ['ɔːrəl] adj orale ▷ n esame m orale

orange ['ɔrɪndʒ] n (fruit) arancia ▷ adj
arancione; **orange juice** n succo
d'arancia; **orange squash** n succo
d'arancia (da diluire con l'acqua)

orbit ['ɔːbɪt] n orbita ▷ vt orbitare intorno
a

orchard ['ɔːtʃəd] n frutteto

orchestra ['ɔːkɪstrə] n orchestra; (US:
seating) platea

orchid ['ɔːkɪd] n orchidea

ordeal [ɔː'diːl] n prova, travaglio

order ['ɔːdə'] n ordine m; (Comm)
ordinazione f ▷ vt ordinare; **can I ~ now,
please?** posso ordinare, per favore?; **in
~** in ordine; (of document) in regola; **in
(working) ~** funzionante; **in ~ to do** per
fare; **in ~ that** affinché + sub; **on ~** (Comm)
in ordinazione; **out of ~** non in ordine; (not
working) guasto; **to ~ sb to do** ordinare
a qn di fare; **order form** n modulo
d'ordinazione; **orderly** n (Mil) attendente
m; (Med) inserviente m ▷ adj (room) in
ordine; (mind) metodico(-a); (person)
ordinato(-a), metodico(-a)

ordinary ['ɔːdnrɪ] adj normale, comune;
(pej) mediocre; **out of the ~** diverso dal
solito, fuori dell'ordinario

ore [ɔː'] n minerale m grezzo

oregano [ɔrɪ'gɑːnəu] n origano

organ ['ɔːgən] n organo; **organic**
[ɔː'gænɪk] adj organico(-a); (of food)
biologico(-a); **organism** n organismo

organization [ɔːgənaɪ'zeɪʃən] n
organizzazione f

organize ['ɔːgənaɪz] vt organizzare; **to
get ~d** organizzarsi; **organized** ['ɔːgə
naɪzd] adj organizzato(-a); **organizer** n
organizzatore(-trice)

orgasm ['ɔːgæzəm] n orgasmo

orgy ['ɔːdʒɪ] n orgia

oriental [ɔːrɪ'ɛntl] adj, n orientale m/f

orientation [ɔːrɪen'teɪʃən] n
orientamento

origin ['ɔrɪdʒɪn] n origine f

original [ə'rɪdʒɪnl] adj originale; (earliest)
originario(-a) ▷ n originale m; **originally**
adv (at first) all'inizio

originate [ə'rɪdʒɪneɪt] vi **to ~ from** essere
originario(-a) di; (suggestion) provenire da;
to ~ in avere origine in

Orkneys ['ɔːknɪz] npl **the ~** (also: **the
Orkney Islands**) le Orcadi

ornament ['ɔːnəmənt] n ornamento;
(trinket) ninnolo; **ornamental** [-'mɛntl]
adj ornamentale

ornate [ɔː'neɪt] adj molto ornato(-a)

orphan ['ɔːfn] n orfano(-a)

orthodox ['ɔːθədɔks] adj ortodosso(-a)

orthopaedic [ɔːθə'piːdɪk] (US **orthopedic**)
adj ortopedico(-a)

osteopath ['ɔstɪəpæθ] n specialista m/f di
osteopatia

ostrich ['ɔstrɪtʃ] n struzzo

other ['ʌðə'] adj altro(-a) ▷ pron **the ~
(one)** l'altro(-a); **~s** (other people) altri mpl;
~ than altro che; a parte; **otherwise** adv,
conj altrimenti

otter ['ɔtə'] n lontra

ouch [autʃ] excl ohi!, ahi!

ought [ɔːt] (pt ought) aux vb **I ~ to do
it** dovrei farlo; **this ~ to have been
corrected** questo avrebbe dovuto essere
corretto; **he ~ to win** dovrebbe vincere

ounce [auns] n oncia (= 28.35 g, 16 in a
pound)

our ['auə'] adj il (la) nostro(-a); (pl) i (le)
nostri(-e); see also **my**; **ours** pron il (la)
nostro(-a); (pl) i (le) nostri(-e); see also
mine; **ourselves** pron pl (reflexive) ci; (after
preposition) noi; (emphatic) noi stessi(-e);
see also **oneself**

oust [aust] vt cacciare, espellere

out [aut] adv (gen) fuori; **~ here/there**
qui/là fuori; **to speak ~ loud** parlare
forte; **to have a night ~** uscire una sera;
the boat was 10 km ~ la barca era a 10
km dalla costa; **3 days ~ from Plym~h** a 3

giorni da Plymouth; **~ of** (*outside*) fuori di; (*because of*) per; **~ of 10** su 10; **~ of petrol** senza benzina; **outback** ['autbæk] *n* (*in Australia*) interno, entroterra; **outbound** *adj* **outbound (for** *or* **from)** in partenza (per *or* da); **outbreak** ['autbreɪk] *n* scoppio; epidemia; **outburst** ['autbɜːst] *n* scoppio; **outcast** ['autkɑːst] *n* esule *m/f*; (*socially*) paria *m inv*; **outcome** ['autkʌm] *n* esito, risultato; **outcry** ['autkraɪ] *n* protesta, clamore *m*; **outdated** [aut'deɪtɪd] *adj* (*custom, clothes*) fuori moda; (*idea*) sorpassato(-a); **outdoor** [aut'dɔːʳ] *adj* all'aperto; **outdoors** *adv* fuori; all'aria aperta

outer ['autəʳ] *adj* esteriore; **outer space** *n* spazio cosmico

outfit ['autfɪt] *n* (*clothes*) completo; (: *for sport*) tenuta

out: **outgoing** ['autgəuɪŋ] *adj* (*character*) socievole; **outgoings** (BRIT) *npl* (*expenses*) spese *fpl*, uscite *fpl*; **outhouse** ['authaus] *n* costruzione *f* annessa

outing ['autɪŋ] *n* gita; escursione *f*

out: **outlaw** ['autlɔː] *n* fuorilegge *m/f* ▷ *vt* bandire; **outlay** ['autleɪ] *n* spese *fpl*; (*investment*) sborsa, spesa; **outlet** ['autlɛt] *n* (*for liquid etc*) sbocco, scarico; (*us Elec*) presa di corrente; (*also*: **retail outlet**) punto di vendita; **outline** ['autlaɪn] *n* contorno, profilo; (*summary*) abbozzo, grandi linee *fpl* ▷ *vt* (*fig*) descrivere a grandi linee; **outlook** ['autluk] *n* prospettiva, vista; **outnumber** [aut'nʌmbəʳ] *vt* superare in numero; **out-of-date** *adj* (*passport*) scaduto(-a); (*clothes*) fuori moda *inv*; **out-of-doors** [autəv'dɔːz] *adv* all'aperto; **out-of-the-way** *adj* (*place*) fuori mano *inv*; **out-of-town** [autəv'taun] *adj* (*shopping centre etc*) fuori città; **outpatient** ['autpeɪʃənt] *n* paziente *m/f* esterno(-a); **outpost** ['autpəust] *n* avamposto; **output** ['autput] *n* produzione *f*; (*Comput*) output *m inv*

outrage ['autreɪdʒ] *n* oltraggio; scandalo ▷ *vt* oltraggiare; **outrageous** [-'reɪdʒəs] *adj* oltraggioso(-a), scandaloso(-a)

outright [*adv* aut'raɪt, *adj* 'autraɪt] *adv* completamente; schiettamente; apertamente; sul colpo ▷ *adj* completo(-a), schietto(-a) e netto(-a)

outset ['autsɛt] *n* inizio

outside [aut'saɪd] *n* esterno, esteriore *m* ▷ *adj* esterno(-a), esteriore ▷ *adv* fuori, all'esterno ▷ *prep* fuori di, all'esterno di; **at the ~** (*fig*) al massimo; **outside lane** *n* (*Aut*) corsia di sorpasso; **outside line** *n* (*Tel*) linea esterna; **outsider** *n* (*in race etc*) outsider *m inv*; (*stranger*) estraneo(-a)

out: **outsize** ['autsaɪz] *adj* (*clothes*) per taglie forti; **outskirts** ['autskəːts] *npl* sobborghi *mpl*; **outspoken** [aut'spəukən] *adj* molto franco(-a); **outstanding** [aut'stændɪŋ] *adj* eccezionale, di rilievo; (*unfinished*) non completo(-a); non evaso(-a); non regolato(-a)

outward ['autwəd] *adj* (*sign, appearances*) esteriore; (*journey*) d'andata; **outwards** ['autwədz] *adv* (*esp* BRIT) = **outward**

outweigh [aut'weɪ] *vt* avere maggior peso di

oval ['əuvl] *adj* ovale ▷ *n* ovale *m*

ovary ['əuvərɪ] *n* ovaia

oven ['ʌvn] *n* forno; **oven glove** *n* guanto da forno; **ovenproof** *adj* da forno; **oven-ready** *adj* pronto(-a) da infornare

over ['əuvəʳ] *adv* al di sopra ▷ *adj* (*or adv*) (*finished*) finito(-a), terminato(-a); (*too*) troppo; (*remaining*) che avanza ▷ *prep* su; sopra; (*above*) al di sopra di; (*on the other side of*) di là di; (*more than*) più di; (*during*) durante; **~ here** qui; **~ there** là; **all ~** (*everywhere*) dappertutto; (*finished*) tutto(-a) finito(-a); **~ and ~ (again)** più e più volte; **~ and above** oltre (a); **to ask sb ~** invitare qn (a passare)

overall [*adj, n* 'əuvərɔːl, *adv* əuvər'ɔːl] *adj* totale ▷ *n* (BRIT) grembiule *m* ▷ *adv* nell'insieme, complessivamente; **~s** *npl* (*worker's overalls*) tuta (da lavoro)

overboard ['əuvəbɔːd] *adv* (*Naut*) fuori bordo, in mare

overcame [əuvə'keɪm] *pt of* **overcome**

overcast ['əuvəkɑːst] *adj* (*sky*) coperto(-a)

overcharge [əuvə'tʃɑːdʒ] *vt* **to ~ sb for sth** far pagare troppo caro a qn per qc

overcoat ['əuvəkəut] *n* soprabito, cappotto

overcome [əuvə'kʌm] (*irreg*) *vt* superare; sopraffare

over: **overcrowded** [əuvə'kraudɪd] *adj* sovraffollato(-a); **overdo** [əuvə'duː] (*irreg*) *vt* esagerare; (*overcook*) cuocere troppo; **overdone** [əuvə'dʌn] *adj* troppo cotto(-a); **overdose** ['əuvədəus] *n* dose *f* eccessiva; **overdraft** ['əuvədrɑːft] *n* scoperto (di conto); **overdrawn** [əuvə'drɔːn] *adj* (*account*) scoperto(-a); **overdue** [əuvə'djuː] *adj* in ritardo; **overestimate** [əuvər'estɪmeɪt] *vt* sopravvalutare

overflow [*vb* əuvə'fləu, *n* 'əuvəfləu] *vi* traboccare ▷ *n* (*also*: **~ pipe**) troppopieno

overgrown [əuvə'grəun] *adj* (*garden*) ricoperto(-a) di vegetazione

overhaul [*vb* əuvə'hɔːl, *n* 'əuvəhɔːl] *vt* revisionare ▷ *n* revisione *f*

overhead [*adv* əuvə'hɛd, *adj, n* 'əuvəhɛd] *adv* di sopra ▷ *adj* aereo(-a); (*lighting*)

verticale ▷ *n* (*us*) = **overheads**;
overhead projector *n* lavagna luminosa;
overheads *npl* spese *fpl* generali

over: **overhear** [əʊvə'hɪəʳ] (*irreg*) *vt* sentire
(per caso); **overheat** [əʊvə'hi:t] *vi* (*engine*)
surriscaldare; **overland** *adj*, *adv* per via di
terra; **overlap** [əʊvə'læp] *vi* sovrapporsi;
overleaf [əʊvə'li:f] *adv* a tergo; **overload**
[əʊvə'ləʊd] *vt* sovraccaricare; **overlook**
[əʊvə'lʊk] *vt* (*have view of*) dare su; (*miss*)
trascurare; (*forgive*) passare sopra a

overnight [əʊvə'naɪt] *adv* (*happen*)
durante la notte; (*fig*) tutto ad un tratto
▷ *adj* di notte; **he stayed there ~** ci ha
passato la notte; **overnight bag** *n* borsa
da viaggio

overpass [ˈəʊvəpɑːs] *n* cavalcavia *m inv*
overpower [əʊvə'paʊəʳ] *vt* sopraffare;
overpowering *adj* irresistibile; (*heat,
stench*) soffocante

over: **overreact** [əʊvəri:'ækt] *vi* reagire
in modo esagerato; **overrule** [əʊvə'ru:l]
vt (*decision*) annullare; (*claim*) respingere;
overrun [əʊvə'rʌn] (*irreg: like* **run**) *vt*
(*country*) invadere; (*time limit*) superare

overseas [əʊvə'si:z] *adv* oltremare;
(*abroad*) all'estero ▷ *adj* (*trade*) estero(-a);
(*visitor*) straniero(-a)

oversee [əʊvə'si:] *vt irreg* sorvegliare
overshadow [əʊvə'ʃædəʊ] *vt* far ombra
su; (*fig*) eclissare

oversight [ˈəʊvəsaɪt] *n* omissione *f*, svista
oversleep [əʊvə'sli:p] (*irreg*) *vt* dormire
troppo a lungo

overspend [əʊvə'spɛnd] *vi irreg* spendere
troppo; **we have overspent by 5000
dollars** abbiamo speso 5000 dollari di
troppo

overt [əʊ'və:t] *adj* palese
overtake [əʊvə'teɪk] (*irreg*) *vt* sorpassare
over: **overthrow** [əʊvə'θrəʊ] (*irreg*) *vt*
(*government*) rovesciare; **overtime** [ˈəʊvə
taɪm] *n* (*lavoro*) straordinario

overtook [əʊvə'tʊk] *pt of* **overtake**
over: **overturn** [əʊvə'tə:n] *vt* rovesciare
▷ *vi* rovesciarsi; **overweight** [əʊvə'weɪt]
adj (*person*) troppo grasso(-a); **overwhelm**
[əʊvə'wɛlm] *vt* sopraffare; sommergere;
schiacciare; **overwhelming** *adj* (*victory,
defeat*) schiacciante; (*heat, desire*)
intenso(-a)

ow [aʊ] *excl* ahi!
owe [əʊ] *vt* **to ~ sb sth, to ~ sth to sb**
dovere qc a qn; **how much do I ~ you?**
quanto le devo?; **owing to** *prep* a causa di
owl [aʊl] *n* gufo
own [əʊn] *vt* possedere ▷ *adj* proprio(-a);
a room of my ~ la mia propria camera; **to
get one's ~ back** vendicarsi; **on one's ~**

tutto(-a) solo(-a); **own up** *vi* confessare;
owner *n* proprietario(-a); **ownership** *n*
possesso

ox [ɔks] (*pl* **oxen**) *n* bue *m*
Oxbridge [ˈɔksbrɪdʒ] *n* le università di
Oxford e/o Cambridge

oxen [ˈɔksn] *npl of* **ox**
oxygen [ˈɔksɪdʒən] *n* ossigeno
oyster [ˈɔɪstəʳ] *n* ostrica
oz. *abbr* = **ounce(s)**
ozone [ˈəʊzəʊn] *n* ozono; **ozone friendly**
adj che non danneggia l'ozono; **ozone
layer** *n* fascia d'ozono

p

p [piː] *abbr* = **penny; pence**

P.A. *n abbr* = **personal assistant; public address system**

p.a. *abbr* = **per annum**

pace [peɪs] *n* passo; (*speed*) passo; velocità ▷ *vi* **to ~ up and down** camminare su e giù; **to keep ~ with** camminare di pari passo a; (*events*) tenersi al corrente di; **pacemaker** *n* (*Med*) segnapasso; (*Sport: also:* **pace setter**) battistrada *m inv*

Pacific [pəˈsɪfɪk] *n* **the ~ (Ocean)** il Pacifico, l'Oceano Pacifico

pacifier [ˈpæsɪfaɪəʳ] (*US*) *n* (*dummy*) succhiotto, ciuccio (*col*)

pack [pæk] *n* pacco; (*US: of cigarettes*) pacchetto; (*backpack*) zaino; (*of hounds*) muta; (*of thieves etc*) banda; (*of cards*) mazzo ▷ *vt* (*in suitcase etc*) mettere; (*box*) riempire; (*cram*) stipare, pigiare; **to ~ (one's bags)** fare la valigia; **to ~ sb off** spedire via qn; **~ it in!** (*inf*) dacci un taglio!; **pack in** (*BRIT inf*) *vi* (*watch, car*) guastarsi ▷ *vt* mollare, piantare; **~ it in!** piantala!; **pack up** *vi* (*BRIT inf: machine*) guastarsi; (*: person*) far fagotto ▷ *vt* (*belongings, clothes*) mettere in una valigia; (*goods, presents*) imballare

package [ˈpækɪdʒ] *n* pacco; balla; (*also:* **~ deal**) pacchetto; forfait *m inv*; **package holiday** *n* vacanza organizzata; **package**

tour *n* viaggio organizzato

packaging [ˈpækɪdʒɪŋ] *n* confezione *f*, imballo

packed [pækt] *adj* (*crowded*) affollato(-a); **packed lunch** *n* pranzo al sacco

packet [ˈpækɪt] *n* pacchetto

packing [ˈpækɪŋ] *n* imballaggio

pact [pækt] *n* patto, accordo; trattato

pad [pæd] *n* blocco; (*to prevent friction*) cuscinetto; (*inf: flat*) appartamentino ▷ *vt* imbottire; **padded** *adj* imbottito(-a)

paddle [ˈpædl] *n* (*oar*) pagaia; (*US: for table tennis*) racchetta da ping-pong ▷ *vi* sguazzare ▷ *vt* **to ~ a canoe** *etc* vogare con la pagaia; **paddling pool** (*BRIT*) *n* piscina per bambini

paddock [ˈpædək] *n* prato recintato; (*at racecourse*) paddock *m inv*

padlock [ˈpædlɔk] *n* lucchetto

paedophile [ˈpiːdəufaɪl] (*US* **pedophile**) *adj, n* pedofilo(-a)

page [peɪdʒ] *n* pagina; (*also:* **~ boy**) paggio ▷ *vt* (*in hotel etc*) (far) chiamare

pager [ˈpeɪdʒəʳ] *n* (*Tel*) cercapersone *m inv*

paid [peɪd] *pt, pp of* **pay** ▷ *adj* (*work, official*) rimunerato(-a); **to put ~ to** (*BRIT*) mettere fine a

pain [peɪn] *n* dolore *m*; **to be in ~** soffrire, aver male; **to take ~s to do** mettercela tutta per fare; **painful** *adj* doloroso(-a), che fa male; difficile, penoso(-a); **painkiller** *n* analgico, antidolorifico; **painstaking** [ˈpeɪnzteɪkɪŋ] *adj* (*person*) sollecito(-a); (*work*) accurato(-a)

paint [peɪnt] *n* vernice *f*, colore *m* ▷ *vt* dipingere; (*walls, door etc*) verniciare; **to ~ the door blue** verniciare la porta di azzurro; **paintbrush** *n* pennello; **painter** *n* (*artist*) pittore *m*; (*decorator*) imbianchino; **painting** *n* pittura; verniciatura; (*picture*) dipinto, quadro

pair [pɛəʳ] *n* (*of shoes, gloves etc*) paio; (*of people*) coppia; duo *m inv*; **a ~ of scissors/trousers** un paio di forbici/pantaloni

pajamas [pɪˈdʒɑːməz] (*US*) *npl* pigiama *m*

Pakistan [pɑːkɪˈstɑːn] *n* Pakistan *m*; **Pakistani** *adj, n* pakistano(-a)

pal [pæl] (*inf*) *n* amico(-a), compagno(-a)

palace [ˈpæləs] *n* palazzo

pale [peɪl] *adj* pallido(-a) ▷ *n* **to be beyond the ~** aver oltrepassato ogni limite

Palestine [ˈpælɪstaɪn] *n* Palestina; **Palestinian** [-ˈtɪnɪən] *adj, n* palestinese *m/f*

palm [pɑːm] *n* (*Anat*) palma, palmo; (*also:* **~ tree**) palma ▷ *vt* **to ~ sth off on sb** (*inf*) rifilare qc a qn

pamper [ˈpæmpəʳ] *vt* viziare, coccolare

pamphlet [ˈpæmflət] *n* dépliant *m inv*

pan [pæn] n (also: **sauce~**) casseruola; (also: **frying ~**) padella

pancake ['pænkeik] n frittella

panda ['pændə] n panda m inv

pane [pein] n vetro

panel ['pænl] n (of wood, cloth etc) pannello; (Radio, TV) giuria

panhandler ['pænhændlər] (US) n (inf) accattone(-a)

panic ['pænik] n panico ▷ vi perdere il sangue freddo

panorama [pænə'rɑ:mə] n panorama m

pansy ['pænzi] n (Bot) viola del pensiero, pensée f inv; (inf: pej) femminuccia

pant [pænt] vi ansare

panther ['pænθər] n pantera

panties ['pæntiz] npl slip m, mutandine fpl

pantomime ['pæntəmaim] (BRIT) n pantomima

● **PANTOMIME**
●
● In Gran Bretagna la **pantomime** è una
● sorta di libera interpretazione delle
● favole più conosciute, che vengono
● messe in scena a teatro durante il
● periodo natalizio. È uno spettacolo
● per tutta la famiglia che prevede la
● partecipazione del pubblico.

pants [pænts] npl mutande fpl, slip m; (US: trousers) pantaloni mpl

paper ['peipər] n carta; (also: **wall~**) carta da parati, tappezzeria; (also: **news~**) giornale m; (study, article) saggio; (exam) prova scritta ▷ adj di carta ▷ vt tappezzare; **~s** npl (also: **identity ~s**) carte fpl, documenti mpl; **paperback** n tascabile m; edizione f economica; **paper bag** n sacchetto di carta; **paper clip** n graffetta, clip f inv; **paper shop** n (BRIT) giornalaio (negozio); **paperwork** n lavoro amministrativo

paprika ['pæprikə] n paprica

par [pɑ:r] n parità, pari f; (Golf) norma; **on a ~ with** alla pari con

paracetamol [pærə'si:təmɔl] (BRIT) n paracetamolo

parachute ['pærəʃu:t] n paracadute m inv

parade [pə'reid] n parata ▷ vt (fig) fare sfoggio di ▷ vi sfilare in parata

paradise ['pærədais] n paradiso

paradox ['pærədɔks] n paradosso

paraffin ['pærəfin] (BRIT) n **~ (oil)** paraffina

paragraph ['pærəgrɑ:f] n paragrafo

parallel ['pærəlɛl] adj parallelo(-a); (fig) analogo(-a) ▷ n (line) parallela; (fig, Geo) parallelo

paralysed ['pærəlaizd] adj paralizzato(-a)

paralysis [pə'rælisis] n paralisi f inv

paramedic [pærə'mɛdik] n paramedico

paranoid ['pærənɔid] adj paranoico(-a)

parasite ['pærəsait] n parassita m

parcel ['pɑ:sl] n pacco, pacchetto ▷ vt (also: **~ up**) impaccare

pardon ['pɑ:dn] n perdono; grazia ▷ vt perdonare; (Law) graziare; **~ me!** mi scusi!; **I beg your ~!** scusi!; **I beg your ~?** (BRIT), **~ me?** (US) prego?

parent ['pɛərənt] n genitore m; **~s** npl (mother and father) genitori mpl; **parental** [pə'rɛntl] adj dei genitori.

▌ Be careful not to translate **parent** by the Italian word **parente**.

Paris ['pæris] n Parigi f

parish ['pæriʃ] n parrocchia; (BRIT: civil) ≈ municipio

Parisian [pə'riziən] adj, n parigino(-a)

park [pɑ:k] n parco ▷ vt, vi parcheggiare; **can I ~ here?** posso parcheggiare qui?

parking ['pɑ:kiŋ] n parcheggio; **"no ~"** "sosta vietata"; **parking lot** (US) n posteggio, parcheggio; **parking meter** n parchimetro; **parking ticket** n multa per sosta vietata

parkway ['pɑ:kwei] (US) n viale m

parliament ['pɑ:ləmənt] n parlamento; **parliamentary** [pɑ:lə'mɛntəri] adj parlamentare

Parmesan [pɑ:mi'zæn] n (also: **~ cheese**) parmigiano

parole [pə'rəul] n **on ~** in libertà per buona condotta

parrot ['pærət] n pappagallo

parsley ['pɑ:sli] n prezzemolo

parsnip ['pɑ:snip] n pastinaca

parson ['pɑ:sn] n prete m; (Church of England) parroco

part [pɑ:t] n parte f; (of machine) pezzo; (US: in hair) scriminatura ▷ adj in parte ▷ adv = **partly** ▷ vt separare ▷ vi (people) separarsi; **to take ~ in** prendere parte a; **for my ~** per parte mia; **to take sth in good ~** prendere bene qc; **to take sb's ~** parteggiare per or prendere le parti di qn; **for the most ~** in generale; nella maggior parte dei casi; **part with** vt fus separarsi da; rinunciare a

partial ['pɑ:ʃl] adj parziale; **to be ~ to** avere un debole per

participant [pɑ:'tisipənt] n **~ (in)** partecipante m/f(a)

participate [pɑ:'tisipeit] vi **to ~ (in)** prendere parte a (a), partecipare (a)

particle ['pɑ:tikl] n particella

particular [pə'tikjulər] adj particolare;

speciale; (*fussy*) difficile; meticoloso(-a);
in ~ in particolare, particolarmente;
particularly *adv* particolarmente; in
particolare; **particulars** *npl* particolari
mpl, dettagli *mpl*; (*information*)
informazioni *fpl*

parting ['pɑːtɪŋ] *n* separazione *f*; (BRIT: *in
hair*) scriminatura ▷ *adj* d'addio

partition [pɑːˈtɪʃən] *n* (*Pol*) partizione *f*;
(*wall*) tramezzo

partly ['pɑːtlɪ] *adv* parzialmente; in parte

partner ['pɑːtnəʳ] *n* (*Comm*) socio(-a);
(*wife, husband etc, Sport*) compagno(-a);
(*at dance*) cavaliere/dama; **partnership** *n*
associazione *f*; (*Comm*) società *f inv*

part of speech *n* parte *f* del discorso

partridge ['pɑːtrɪdʒ] *n* pernice *f*

part-time ['pɑːt'taɪm] *adj, adv* a orario
ridotto

party ['pɑːtɪ] *n* (*Pol*) partito; (*group*)
gruppo; (*Law*) parte *f*; (*celebration*)
ricevimento; serata; festa ▷ *cpd* (*Pol*) del
partito, di partito

pass [pɑːs] *vt* (*gen*) passare; (*place*) passare
davanti a; (*exam*) passare, superare;
(*candidate*) promuovere; (*overtake, surpass*)
sorpassare, superare; (*approve*) approvare
▷ *vi* passare ▷ *n* (*permit*) lasciapassare
m inv; permesso; (*in mountains*) passo,
gola; (*Sport*) passaggio; (*Scol*): **to get a ~**
prendere la sufficienza; **could you ~ the
salt/oil, please?** mi passa il sale/l'olio,
per favore?; **to ~ sth through a hole** *etc*
far passare qc attraverso un buco *etc*; **to
make a ~ at sb** (*inf*) fare delle proposte *or*
delle avances a qn; **pass away** *vi* morire;
pass by *vi* passare ▷ *vt* trascurare; **pass
on** *vt* passare; **pass out** *vi* svenire; **pass
over** *vi* (*die*) spirare ▷ *vt* lasciare da parte;
pass up *vt* (*opportunity*) lasciarsi sfuggire,
perdere; **passable** *adj* (*road*) praticabile;
(*work*) accettabile

passage ['pæsɪdʒ] *n* (*gen*) passaggio; (*also:*
~way) corridoio; (*in book*) brano, passo; (*by
boat*) traversata

passenger ['pæsɪndʒəʳ] *n* passeggero(-a)

passer-by [pɑːsəˈbaɪ] *n* passante *m/f*

passing place *n* (*Aut*) piazzola di sosta

passion ['pæʃən] *n* passione *f*; amore
m; **passionate** *adj* appassionato(-a);
passion fruit *n* frutto della passione

passive ['pæsɪv] *adj* (*also Ling*) passivo(-a)

passport ['pɑːspɔːt] *n* passaporto;
passport control *n* controllo *m*
passaporti *inv*; **passport office** *n* ufficio
m, passaporti *inv*

password ['pɑːswəːd] *n* parola d'ordine

past [pɑːst] *prep* (*further than*) oltre, di là di;
dopo; (*later than*) dopo ▷ *adj* passato(-a);

(*president etc*) ex *inv* ▷ *n* passato; **he's ~
forty** ha più di quarant'anni; **ten ~ eight** le
otto e dieci; **for the ~ few days** da qualche
giorno; in questi ultimi giorni; **to run ~**
passare di corsa

pasta ['pæstə] *n* pasta

paste [peɪst] *n* (*glue*) colla; (*Culin*) pâté *m
inv*; pasta ▷ *vt* collare

pastel ['pæstl] *adj* pastello *inv*

pasteurized ['pæstəraɪzd] *adj*
pastorizzato(-a)

pastime ['pɑːstaɪm] *n* passatempo

pastor ['pɑːstəʳ] *n* pastore *m*

past participle [-'pɑːtɪsɪpl] *n* (*Ling*)
participio passato

pastry ['peɪstrɪ] *n* pasta

pasture ['pɑːstʃəʳ] *n* pascolo

pasty¹ ['pæstɪ] *n* pasticcio di carne

pasty² ['peɪstɪ] *adj* (*face etc*) smorto(-a)

pat [pæt] *vt* accarezzare, dare un colpetto
(affettuoso) a

patch [pætʃ] *n* (*of material, on tyre*) toppa;
(*eye patch*) benda; (*spot*) macchia ▷ *vt*
(*clothes*) rattoppare; **(to go through) a
bad ~** (attraversare) un brutto periodo;
patchy *adj* irregolare

pâté ['pæteɪ] *n* pâté *m inv*

patent ['peɪtnt] *n* brevetto ▷ *vt* brevettare
▷ *adj* patente, manifesto(-a)

paternal [pəˈtəːnl] *adj* paterno(-a)

paternity leave [pəˈtəːnɪtɪ-] *n* congedo
di paternità

path [pɑːθ] *n* sentiero, viottolo; viale
m; (*fig*) via, strada; (*of planet, missile*)
traiettoria

pathetic [pəˈθɛtɪk] *adj* (*pitiful*)
patetico(-a); (*very bad*) penoso(-a)

pathway ['pɑːθweɪ] *n* sentiero

patience ['peɪʃns] *n* pazienza; (BRIT *Cards*)
solitario

patient ['peɪʃnt] *n* paziente *m/f*,
malato(-a) ▷ *adj* paziente

patio ['pætɪəu] *n* terrazza

patriotic [pætrɪˈɒtɪk] *adj* patriottico(-a)

patrol [pəˈtrəul] *n* pattuglia ▷ *vt*
pattugliare; **patrol car** *n* autoradio *f inv*
(della polizia)

patron ['peɪtrən] *n* (*in shop*) cliente *m/f*; (*of
charity*) benefattore(-trice); **~ of the arts**
mecenate *m/f*

patronizing ['pætrənaɪzɪŋ] *adj*
condiscendente

pattern ['pætən] *n* modello; (*design*)
disegno, motivo; **patterned** *adj* a disegni,
a motivi; (*material*) fantasia *inv*

pause [pɔːz] *n* pausa ▷ *vi* fare una pausa,
arrestarsi

pave [peɪv] *vt* pavimentare; **to ~ the way
for** aprire la via a

p

pavement ['peɪvmənt] (BRIT) n
marciapiede m

▪ Be careful not to translate *pavement*
by the Italian word *pavimento*.

pavilion [pə'vɪlɪən] n (Sport) edificio
annesso a campo sportivo
paving ['peɪvɪŋ] n pavimentazione f
paw [pɔ:] n zampa
pawn [pɔ:n] n (Chess) pedone m; (fig)
pedina ▷ vt dare in pegno; **pawn broker** n
prestatore m su pegno
pay [peɪ] (pt, pp **paid**) n stipendio; paga
▷ vt pagare ▷ vi (be profitable) rendere;
can I ~ by credit card? posso pagare
con la carta di credito?; **to ~ attention
(to)** fare attenzione (a); **to ~ sb a visit**
far visita a qn; **to ~ one's respects to sb**
porgere i propri rispetti a qn; **pay back** vt
rimborsare; **pay for** vt fus pagare; **pay
in** vt versare; **pay off** vt (debt) saldare;
(person) pagare; (employee) pagare e
licenziare ▷ vi (scheme, decision) dare
dei frutti; **pay out** vt (money) sborsare,
tirar fuori; (rope) far allentare; **pay up** vt
saldare; **payable** adj pagabile; **pay day**
n giorno di paga; **pay envelope** (US) n
= **pay packet**; **payment** n pagamento;
versamento; saldo; **payout** n pagamento;
(in competition) premio; **pay packet** (BRIT)
n busta f paga inv; **pay phone** n cabina
telefonica; **payroll** n ruolo (organico); **pay
slip** n foglio m paga inv; **pay television** n
televisione f a pagamento, pay-tv f inv
PC n abbr = **personal computer** ▷ adv abbr
= **politically correct**
p.c. abbr = **per cent**
PDA n abbr (= personal digital assistant) PDA
m inv
PE n abbr (= physical education) ed. fisica
pea [pi:] n pisello
peace [pi:s] n pace f; **peaceful** adj
pacifico(-a), calmo(-a)
peach [pi:tʃ] n pesca
peacock ['pi:kɔk] n pavone m
peak [pi:k] n (of mountain) cima, vetta;
(mountain itself) picco; (of cap) visiera; (fig)
apice m, culmine m; **peak hours** npl ore
fpl di punta
peanut ['pi:nʌt] n arachide f, nocciolina
americana; **peanut butter** n burro di
arachidi
pear [pɛə'] n pera
pearl [pə:l] n perla
peasant ['pɛznt] n contadino(-a)
peat [pi:t] n torba
pebble ['pɛbl] n ciottolo
peck [pɛk] vt (also: **~ at**) beccare ▷ n colpo
di becco; (kiss) bacetto; **peckish** (BRIT: inf)
adj **I feel peckish** ho un languorino

peculiar [pɪ'kju:lɪə'] adj strano(-a),
bizzarro(-a); peculiare; **~ to** peculiare di
pedal ['pɛdl] n pedale m ▷ vi pedalare
pedalo ['pɛdələu] n pedalò m inv
pedestal ['pɛdəstl] n piedestallo
pedestrian [pɪ'dɛstrɪən] n pedone(-a)
▷ adj pedonale; (fig) prosaico(-a),
pedestre; **pedestrian crossing** (BRIT) n
passaggio pedonale; **pedestrianized**
adj **a pedestrianized street** una zona
pedonalizzata; **pedestrian precinct**
(BRIT), **pedestrian zone** (US) n zona
pedonale
pedigree ['pɛdɪgri:] n (of animal) pedigree
m inv; (fig) background m inv ▷ cpd (animal)
di razza
pedophile ['pi:dəufaɪl] (US) n
= **paedophile**
pee [pi:] (inf) vi pisciare
peek [pi:k] vi guardare furtivamente
peel [pi:l] n buccia; (of orange, lemon) scorza
▷ vt sbucciare ▷ vi (paint etc) staccarsi
peep [pi:p] n (BRIT: look) sguardo furtivo,
sbirciata; (sound) pigolio ▷ vi (BRIT)
guardare furtivamente
peer [pɪə'] vi **to ~ at** scrutare ▷ n (noble)
pari m inv; (equal) pari m/f inv, uguale m/f;
(contemporary) contemporaneo(-a)
peg [pɛg] n caviglia; (for coat etc)
attaccapanni m inv; (BRIT: also: **clothes ~**)
molletta
pelican ['pɛlɪkən] n pellicano; **pelican
crossing** (BRIT) n (Aut) attraversamento
pedonale con semaforo a controllo manuale
pelt [pɛlt] vt **to ~ sb (with)** bombardare qn
(con) ▷ vi (rain) piovere a dirotto; (inf: run)
filare ▷ n pelle f
pelvis ['pɛlvɪs] n pelvi f inv, bacino
pen [pɛn] n penna; (for sheep) recinto
penalty ['pɛnltɪ] n penalità f inv;
sanzione f penale; (fine) ammenda; (Sport)
penalizzazione f
pence [pɛns] npl of **penny**
pencil ['pɛnsl] n matita; **pencil in**
vt scrivere a matita; **pencil case** n
astuccio per matite; **pencil sharpener** n
temperamatite m inv
pendant ['pɛndnt] n pendaglio
pending ['pɛndɪŋ] prep in attesa di ▷ adj
in sospeso
penetrate ['pɛnɪtreɪt] vt penetrare
penfriend ['pɛnfrɛnd] (BRIT) n
corrispondente m/f
penguin ['pɛŋgwɪn] n pinguino
penicillin [pɛnɪ'sɪlɪn] n penicillina
peninsula [pə'nɪnsjulə] n penisola
penis ['pi:nɪs] n pene m
penitentiary [pɛnɪ'tɛnʃərɪ] (US) n carcere
m

penknife ['pɛnnaɪf] n temperino
penniless ['pɛnɪlɪs] adj senza un soldo
penny ['pɛnɪ] (pl **pennies** or **pence**) (BRIT)
n penny m; (US) centesimo
penpal ['pɛnpæl] n corrispondente m/f
pension ['pɛnʃən] n pensione f; **pensioner**
(BRIT) n pensionato(-a)
pentagon ['pɛntəgən] n pentagono; **the**
P~ (US Pol) il Pentagono
penthouse ['pɛnthaus] n appartamento
(di lusso) nell'attico
penultimate [pɪ'nʌltɪmət] adj
penultimo(-a)
people ['piːpl] npl gente f; persone fpl;
(citizens) popolo ▷ n (nation, race) popolo;
4/several ~ came 4/parecchie persone
sono venute; **~ say that ...** si dice che ...
pepper ['pɛpəʳ] n pepe m; (vegetable)
peperone m ▷ vt (fig): **to ~ with** spruzzare
di; **peppermint** n (sweet) pasticca di
menta
per [pəːʳ] prep per; a; **~ hour** all'ora; **~ kilo**
etc il chilo etc; **~ day** al giorno
perceive [pə'siːv] vt percepire; (notice)
accorgersi di
per cent adv per cento
percentage [pə'sɛntɪdʒ] n percentuale f
perception [pə'sɛpʃən] n percezione f;
sensibilità; perspicacia
perch [pəːtʃ] n (fish) pesce m persico; (for
bird) sostegno, ramo ▷ vi appollaiarsi
percussion [pə'kʌʃən] n percussione f;
(Mus) strumenti mpl a percussione
perfect [adj, n 'pəːfɪkt, vb pə'fɛkt] adj
perfetto(-a) ▷ n (also: **~ tense**) perfetto,
passato prossimo ▷ vt perfezionare;
mettere a punto; **perfection** [pə'fɛkʃə
n] n perfezione f; **perfectly** adv
perfettamente, alla perfezione
perform [pə'fɔːm] vt (carry out) eseguire,
fare; (symphony etc) suonare; (play, ballet)
dare; (opera) fare ▷ vi suonare; recitare;
performance n esecuzione f; (at theatre
etc) rappresentazione f, spettacolo; (of
an artist) interpretazione f; (of player etc)
performance f; (of car, engine) prestazione f;
performer n artista m/f
perfume ['pəːfjuːm] n profumo
perhaps [pə'hæps] adv forse
perimeter [pə'rɪmɪtəʳ] n perimetro
period ['pɪərɪəd] n periodo; (History) epoca;
(Scol) lezione f; (full stop) punto; (Med)
mestruazioni fpl ▷ adj (costume, furniture)
d'epoca; **periodical** [-'ɔdɪkl] n periodico;
periodically adv periodicamente
perish ['pɛrɪʃ] vi perire, morire; (decay)
deteriorarsi
perjury ['pəːdʒərɪ] n spergiuro
perk [pəːk] (inf) n vantaggio

perm [pəːm] n (for hair) permanente f
permanent ['pəːmənənt] adj
permanente; **permanently** adv
definitivamente
permission [pə'mɪʃən] n permesso
permit [n 'pəːmɪt, vb pə'mɪt] n permesso
▷ vt permettere; **to ~ sb to do** permettere
a qn di fare
perplex [pə'plɛks] vt lasciare perplesso(-a)
persecute ['pəːsɪkjuːt] vt perseguitare
persecution [pəːsɪ'kjuːʃən] n
persecuzione f
persevere [pəːsɪ'vɪəʳ] vi perseverare
Persian ['pəːʃən] adj persiano(-a) ▷ n (Ling)
persiano; **the (~) Gulf** n il Golfo Persico
persist [pə'sɪst] vi **to ~ (in doing)**
persistere (nel fare); ostinarsi (a fare);
persistent adj persistente; ostinato(-a)
person ['pəːsn] n persona; **in ~** di or in
persona, personalmente; **personal**
adj personale; individuale; **personal**
assistant n segretaria personale;
personal computer n personal computer
m inv; **personality** [-'nælɪtɪ] n personalità
f inv; **personally** adv personalmente; **to**
take sth personally prendere qc come
una critica personale; **personal organizer**
n (Filofax®) Fulltime®; (electronic)
agenda elettronica; **personal stereo** n
Walkman® m inv
personnel [pəːsə'nɛl] n personale m
perspective [pə'spɛktɪv] n prospettiva
perspiration [pəːspɪ'reɪʃən] n
traspirazione f, sudore m
persuade [pə'sweɪd] vt **to ~ sb to do sth**
persuadere qn a fare qc
persuasion [pə'sweɪʒən] n persuasione f;
(creed) convinzione f, credo
persuasive [pə'sweɪsɪv] adj persuasivo(-a)
perverse [pə'vəːs] adj perverso(-a)
pervert [n 'pəːvəːt, vb pə'vəːt] n
pervertito(-a) ▷ vt pervertire
pessimism ['pɛsɪmɪzəm] n pessimismo
pessimist ['pɛsɪmɪst] n pessimista
m/f; **pessimistic** [-'mɪstɪk] adj
pessimistico(-a)
pest [pɛst] n animale m (or insetto)
pestifero; (fig) peste f
pester ['pɛstəʳ] vt tormentare, molestare
pesticide ['pɛstɪsaɪd] n pesticida m
pet [pɛt] n animale m domestico ▷ cpd
favorito(-a) ▷ vt accarezzare; **teacher's ~**
favorito(-a) del maestro
petal ['pɛtl] n petalo
petite [pə'tiːt] adj piccolo(-a) e
aggraziato(-a)
petition [pə'tɪʃən] n petizione f
petrified ['pɛtrɪfaɪd] adj (fig) morto(-a)
di paura

P

petrol ['pεtrəl] (BRIT) n benzina; **two/four-star ~** = benzina normale/super; **I've run out of ~** sono rimasto senza benzina

> Be careful not to translate *petrol* by the Italian word *petrolio*.

petroleum [pə'trəʊlɪəm] n petrolio
petrol: **petrol pump** (BRIT) n (in car, at garage) pompa di benzina; **petrol station** (BRIT) n stazione f di rifornimento; **petrol tank** (BRIT) n serbatoio della benzina
petticoat ['pεtɪkəʊt] n sottana
petty ['pεtɪ] adj (mean) meschino(-a); (unimportant) insignificante
pew [pju:] n panca (di chiesa)
pewter ['pju:təʳ] n peltro
phantom ['fæntəm] n fantasma m
pharmacist ['fɑːməsɪst] n farmacista m/f
pharmacy ['fɑːməsɪ] n farmacia
phase [feɪz] n fase f, periodo; **phase in** vt introdurre gradualmente; **phase out** vt (machinery) eliminare gradualmente; (product) ritirare gradualmente; (job, subsidy) abolire gradualmente
Ph.D. n abbr = **Doctor of Philosophy**
peasant ['fεznt] n fagiano
phenomena [fə'nɔmɪnə] npl of **phenomenon**
phenomenal [fɪ'nɔmɪnl] adj fenomenale
phenomenon [fə'nɔmɪnən] (pl **phenomena**) n fenomeno
Philippines ['fɪlɪpi:nz] npl **the ~** le Filippine
philosopher [fɪ'lɔsəfəʳ] n filosofo(-a)
philosophical [fɪlə'sɔfɪkl] adj filosofico(-a)
philosophy [fɪ'lɔsəfɪ] n filosofia
phlegm [flεm] n flemma
phobia ['fəʊbjə] n fobia
phone [fəʊn] n telefono ▷ vt telefonare; **to be on the ~** avere il telefono; (be calling) essere al telefono; **phone back** vt, vi richiamare; **phone up** vt telefonare a ▷ vi telefonare; **phone book** n guida del telefono, elenco telefonico; **phone booth** n = **phone box**; **phone box** n cabina telefonica; **phone call** n telefonata; **phonecard** n scheda telefonica; **phone number** n numero di telefono
phonetics [fə'nεtɪks] n fonetica
phoney ['fəʊnɪ] adj falso(-a), fasullo(-a)
photo ['fəʊtəʊ] n foto f inv
photo... ['fəʊtəʊ] prefix: **photo album** n (new) album m inv per fotografie; (containing photos) album m inv delle fotografie; **photocopier** n fotocopiatrice f; **photocopy** n fotocopia ▷ vt fotocopiare
photograph ['fəʊtəgræf] n fotografia ▷ vt fotografare; **photographer** [fə'tɔgrəfəʳ] n fotografo; **photography** [fə'tɔgrəfɪ] n fotografia
phrase [freɪz] n espressione f; (Ling) locuzione f; (Mus) frase f ▷ vt esprimere; **phrase book** n vocabolarietto
physical ['fɪzɪkl] adj fisico(-a); **physical education** n educazione f fisica; **physically** adv fisicamente
physician [fɪ'zɪʃən] n medico
physicist ['fɪzɪsɪst] n fisico
physics ['fɪzɪks] n fisica
physiotherapist [fɪzɪəʊ'θεrəpɪst] n fisioterapista m/f
physiotherapy [fɪzɪəʊ'θεrəpɪ] n fisioterapia
physique [fɪ'zi:k] n fisico; costituzione f
pianist ['pi:ənɪst] n pianista m/f
piano [pɪ'ænəʊ] n pianoforte m
pick [pɪk] n (tool: also: **~-axe**) piccone m ▷ vt scegliere; (gather) cogliere; (remove) togliere; (lock) far scattare; **take your ~** scelga; **the ~ of** il fior fiore di; **to ~ one's nose** mettersi le dita nel naso; **to ~ one's teeth** pulirsi i denti con lo stuzzicadenti; **to ~ a quarrel** attaccar briga; **pick on** vt fus (person) avercela con; **pick out** vt scegliere; (distinguish) distinguere; **pick up** vi (improve) migliorarsi ▷ vt raccogliere; (Police, Radio) prendere; (collect) passare a prendere; (Aut: give lift to) far salire; (person: for sexual encounter) rimorchiare; (learn) imparare; **to ~ up speed** acquistare velocità; **to ~ o.s. up** rialzarsi
pickle ['pɪkl] n (also: **~s**: as condiment) sottaceti mpl; (fig: mess) pasticcio ▷ vt mettere sottaceto; mettere in salamoia
pickpocket ['pɪkpɔkɪt] n borsaiolo
pick-up ['pɪkʌp] n (BRIT: on record player) pick-up m inv; (small truck: also: **~ truck, ~ van**) camioncino
picnic ['pɪknɪk] n picnic m inv; **picnic area** n area per il picnic
picture ['pɪktʃəʳ] n quadro; (painting) pittura; (photograph) foto(grafia); (drawing) disegno; (film) film m inv ▷ vt raffigurarsi; **~s** (BRIT) npl (cinema): **the ~s** il cinema; **would you take a ~ of us, please?** può farci una foto, per favore?; **picture frame** n cornice m inv; **picture messaging** n picture messaging m, invio di messaggini con disegni
picturesque [pɪktʃə'rεsk] adj pittoresco(-a)
pie [paɪ] n torta; (of meat) pasticcio
piece [pi:s] n pezzo; (of land) appezzamento; (item): **a ~ of furniture/advice** un mobile/consiglio ▷ vt **to ~ together** mettere insieme; **to take to ~s** smontare

pie chart n grafico a torta

pier [pɪəʳ] n molo; (of bridge etc) pila

pierce [pɪəs] vt forare; (with arrow etc) trafiggere; **pierced** adj **I've got pierced ears** ho i buchi per gli orecchini

pig [pɪg] n maiale m, porco

pigeon ['pɪdʒən] n piccione m

piggy bank ['pɪgɪ-] n salvadanaro

pigsty ['pɪgstaɪ] n porcile m

pigtail ['pɪgteɪl] n treccina

pike [paɪk] n (fish) luccio

pilchard ['pɪltʃəd] n specie di sardina

pile [paɪl] n (pillar, of books) pila; (heap) mucchio; (of carpet) pelo; **to ~ into** (car) stiparsi or ammucchiarsi in; **pile up** vt ammucchiare ▷ vi ammucchiarsi; **piles** [paɪlz] npl emorroidi fpl; **pile-up** ['paɪlʌp] n (Aut) tamponamento a catena

pilgrimage ['pɪlgrɪmɪdʒ] n pellegrinaggio

pill [pɪl] n pillola; **the ~** la pillola

pillar ['pɪləʳ] n colonna

pillow ['pɪləu] n guanciale m; **pillowcase** n federa

pilot ['paɪlət] n pilota m/f ▷ cpd (scheme etc) pilota inv ▷ vt pilotare; **pilot light** n fiamma pilota

pimple ['pɪmpl] n foruncolo

pin [pɪn] n spillo; (Tech) perno ▷ vt attaccare con uno spillo; **~s and needles** formicolio; **to ~ sb down** (fig) obbligare qn a pronunziarsi; **to ~ sth on sb** (fig) addossare la colpa di qc a qn

PIN n abbr (= personal identification number) codice m segreto

pinafore ['pɪnəfɔːʳ] n (also: **~ dress**) grembiule m (senza maniche)

pinch [pɪntʃ] n pizzicotto, pizzico ▷ vt pizzicare; (inf: steal) grattare; **at a ~** in caso di bisogno

pine [paɪn] n (also: **~ tree**) pino ▷ vi **to ~ for** struggersi dal desiderio di

pineapple ['paɪnæpl] n ananas m inv

ping [pɪŋ] n (noise) tintinnio; **ping-pong®** n ping-pong m

pink [pɪŋk] adj rosa inv ▷ n (colour) rosa m inv; (Bot) garofano

pinpoint ['pɪnpɔɪnt] vt indicare con precisione

pint [paɪnt] n pinta (BRIT = 0.57l; US = 0.47l); (BRIT: inf) ≈ birra da mezzo

pioneer [paɪə'nɪəʳ] n pioniere(-a)

pious ['paɪəs] adj pio(-a)

pip [pɪp] n (seed) seme m; (BRIT: time signal on radio) segnale m orario

pipe [paɪp] n tubo; (for smoking) pipa ▷ vt portare per mezzo di tubazione; **pipeline** n conduttura; (for oil) oleodotto; **piper** n piffero; suonatore(-trice) di cornamusa

pirate ['paɪərət] n pirata m ▷ vt riprodurre

abusivamente

Pisces ['paɪsiːz] n Pesci mpl

piss [pɪs] (inf) vi pisciare; **pissed** (inf) adj (drunk) ubriaco(-a) fradicio(-a)

pistol ['pɪstl] n pistola

piston ['pɪstən] n pistone m

pit [pɪt] n buca, fossa; (also: **coal ~**) miniera; (quarry) cava ▷ vt **to ~ sb against sb** opporre qn a qn

pitch [pɪtʃ] n (BRIT Sport) campo; (Mus) tono; (tar) pece f; (fig) grado, punto ▷ vt (throw) lanciare ▷ vi (fall) cascare; **to ~ a tent** piantare una tenda; **pitch-black** adj nero(-a) come la pece

pitfall ['pɪtfɔːl] n trappola

pith [pɪθ] n (of plant) midollo; (of orange) parte f interna della scorza; (fig) essenza, succo; vigore m

pitiful ['pɪtɪful] adj (touching) pietoso(-a)

pity ['pɪtɪ] n pietà ▷ vt aver pietà di; **what a ~!** che peccato!

pizza ['piːtsə] n pizza

placard ['plækɑːd] n affisso

place [pleɪs] n posto, luogo; (proper position, rank, seat) posto; (house) casa, alloggio; (home): **at/to his ~** a casa sua ▷ vt (object) posare, mettere; (identify) riconoscere; individuare; **to take ~** aver luogo; succedere; **to change ~s with sb** scambiare il posto con qn; **out of ~** (not suitable) inopportuno(-a); **in the first ~** in primo luogo; **to ~ an order** dare un'ordinazione; **to be ~d** (in race, exam) classificarsi; **place mat** n sottopiatto; (in linen etc) tovaglietta; **placement** n collocamento; (job) lavoro

placid ['plæsɪd] adj placido(-a), calmo(-a)

plague [pleɪg] n peste f ▷ vt tormentare

plaice [pleɪs] n inv pianuzza

plain [pleɪn] adj (clear) chiaro(-a), palese; (simple) semplice; (frank) franco(-a), aperto(-a); (not handsome) bruttino(-a); (without seasoning etc) scondito(-a); naturale; (in one colour) tinta unita inv ▷ adv francamente, chiaramente ▷ n pianura; **plain chocolate** n cioccolato fondente; **plainly** adv chiaramente; (frankly) francamente

plaintiff ['pleɪntɪf] n attore(-trice)

plait [plæt] n treccia

plan [plæn] n pianta; (scheme) progetto, piano ▷ vt (think in advance) progettare; (prepare) organizzare ▷ vi far piani or progetti; **to ~ to do** progettare di fare

plane [pleɪn] n (Aviat) aereo; (tree) platano; (tool) pialla; (Art, Math etc) piano ▷ adj piano(-a), piatto(-a) ▷ vt (with tool) piallare

planet ['plænɪt] n pianeta m

plank [plæŋk] n tavola, asse f

P

planning ['plænɪŋ] n progettazione f;
family ~ pianificazione f delle nascite
plant [plɑ:nt] n pianta; (machinery)
impianto; (factory) fabbrica ▷ vt piantare;
(bomb) mettere
plantation [plæn'teɪʃən] n piantagione f
plaque [plæk] n placca
plaster ['plɑ:stə'] n intonaco; (also: ~
of Paris) gesso; (BRIT: also: sticking ~)
cerotto ▷ vt intonacare; ingessare; (cover):
to ~ with coprire di; **plaster cast** n (Med)
ingessatura, gesso; (model, statue) modello
in gesso
plastic ['plæstɪk] n plastica ▷ adj (made
of plastic) di or in plastica; **plastic bag** n
sacchetto di plastica; **plastic surgery** n
chirurgia plastica
plate [pleɪt] n (dish) piatto; (in book) tavola;
(dental plate) dentiera; **gold/silver ~**
vasellame m d'oro/d'argento
plateau ['plætəʊ] (pl plateaus or
plateaux) n altipiano
platform ['plætfɔ:m] n (stage, at meeting)
palco; (Rail) marciapiede m; (BRIT: of bus)
piattaforma; **which ~ does the train for
… go from?** da che binario parte il
… per Roma?
platinum ['plætɪnəm] n platino
platoon [plə'tu:n] n plotone m
platter ['plætə'] n piatto
plausible ['plɔ:zɪbl] adj plausibile,
credibile; (person) convincente
play [pleɪ] n gioco; (Theatre) commedia
▷ vt (game) giocare a; (team, opponent)
giocare contro; (instrument, piece of music)
suonare; (record, tape) ascoltare; (role,
part) interpretare ▷ vi giocare; suonare;
recitare; **to ~ safe** giocare sul sicuro;
play back vt riascoltare, risentire;
play up vi (cause trouble) fare i capricci;
player n giocatore(-trice); (Theatre)
attore(-trice); (Mus) musicista m/f;
playful adj giocoso(-a); **playground** n
(in school) cortile m per la ricreazione; (in
park) parco m giochi inv; **playgroup** n
giardino d'infanzia; **playing card** n carta
da gioco; **playing field** n campo sportivo;
playschool n = playgroup; **playtime**
n (Scol) ricreazione f; **playwright** n
drammaturgo(-a)
plc abbr (= public limited company) società
per azioni a responsabilità limitata quotata
in borsa
plea [pli:] n (request) preghiera, domanda;
(Law) (argomento di) difesa
plead [pli:d] vt patrocinare; (give as excuse)
addurre a pretesto ▷ vi (fall) perorare la
causa; (beg): **to ~ with sb** implorare qn
pleasant ['plɛznt] adj piacevole, gradevole

please [pli:z] excl per piacere!, per favore!;
(acceptance): **yes, ~** sì, grázie ▷ vt piacere
a ▷ vi piacere; (think fit): **do as you ~**
faccia come le pare; **~ yourself!** come ti
(or le) pare!; **pleased** adj pleased (with)
contento(-a) (di); **pleased to meet you!**
piacere!
pleasure ['plɛʒə'] n piacere m; **"it's a ~"**
"prego"
pleat [pli:t] n piega
pledge [plɛdʒ] n pegno; (promise)
promessa ▷ vt impegnare; promettere
plentiful ['plɛntɪful] adj abbondante,
copioso(-a)
plenty ['plɛntɪ] n **~ of** tanto(-a), molto(-a);
un'abbondanza di
pliers ['plaɪəz] npl pinza
plight [plaɪt] n situazione f critica
plod [plɒd] vi camminare a stento; (fig)
sgobbare
plonk [plɒŋk] (inf) n (BRIT: wine) vino da
poco ▷ vt **to ~ sth down** buttare giù qc
bruscamente
plot [plɒt] n congiura, cospirazione f; (of
story, play) trama; (of land) lotto ▷ vt (mark
out) fare la pianta di; rilevare; (: diagram etc)
tracciare; (conspire) congiurare, cospirare
▷ vi congiurare
plough [plaʊ] (US plow) n aratro ▷ vt
(earth) arare; **to ~ money into** (company
etc) investire danaro in; **ploughman's
lunch** ['plaʊmənz-] (BRIT) n pasto a base di
pane, formaggio e birra
plow [plaʊ] (US) = plough
ploy [plɔɪ] n stratagemma m
pluck [plʌk] vt (fruit) cogliere; (musical
instrument) pizzicare; (bird) spennare;
(hairs) togliere ▷ n coraggio, fegato; **to ~
up courage** farsi coraggio
plug [plʌg] n tappo; (Elec) spina; (Aut: also:
spark(ing) ~) candela ▷ vt (hole) tappare;
(inf: advertise) spingere; **plug in** vt (Elec)
attaccare a una presa; **plughole** n (BRIT)
scarico
plum [plʌm] n (fruit) susina
plumber ['plʌmə'] n idraulico
plumbing ['plʌmɪŋ] n (trade) lavoro di
idraulico; (piping) tubature fpl
plummet ['plʌmɪt] vi **to ~ (down)** cadere
a piombo
plump [plʌmp] adj grassoccio(-a) ▷ vi **to ~
for** (inf: choose) decidersi per
plunge [plʌndʒ] n tuffo; (fig) caduta ▷ vt
immergere ▷ vi (fall) cadere, precipitare;
(dive) tuffarsi; **to take the ~** saltare il fosso
plural ['pluərl] adj plurale ▷ n plurale m
plus [plʌs] n (also: ~ sign) segno più ▷ prep
più; **ten/twenty ~** più di dieci/venti
ply [plaɪ] vt (a trade) esercitare ▷ vi (ship)

fare il servizio ▷ n (of wool, rope) capo; **to ~ sb with drink** dare di bere continuamente a qn; **plywood** n legno compensato

P.M. n abbr = **prime minister**

p.m. adv abbr (= post meridiem) del pomeriggio

PMS n abbr (= premenstrual syndrome) sindrome f premestruale

PMT n abbr (= premenstrual tension) sindrome f premestruale

pneumatic drill [njuː'mætɪk-] n martello pneumatico

pneumonia [njuː'məʊnɪə] n polmonite f

poach [pəʊtʃ] vt (cook: egg) affogare; (: fish) cuocere in bianco; (steal) cacciare (or pescare) di frodo ▷ vi fare il bracconiere; **poached** adj (egg) affogato(-a)

P.O. Box n abbr = **Post Office Box**

pocket ['pɒkɪt] n tasca ▷ vt intascare; **to be out of ~** (BRIT) rimetterci; **pocketbook** (US) n (wallet) portafoglio; **pocket money** n paghetta, settimana

pod [pɒd] n guscio

podiatrist [pɒ'diːətrɪst] (US) n callista m/f, pedicure m/f

podium ['pəʊdɪəm] n podio

poem ['pəʊɪm] n poesia

poet ['pəʊɪt] n poeta/essa; **poetic** [-'ɛtɪk] adj poetico(-a); **poetry** n poesia

poignant ['pɔɪnjənt] adj struggente

point [pɔɪnt] n (gen) punto; (tip: of needle etc) punta; (in time) punto, momento; (Scol) voto; (main idea, important part) nocciolo; (Elec) presa (di corrente); (also: **decimal ~**): **2 ~ 3 (2.3)** 2 virgola 3 (2,3) ▷ vt (show) indicare; (gun etc): **to ~ sth at** puntare qc contro ▷ vi **to ~ at** mostrare a dito; **~s** npl (Aut) puntine fpl; (Rail) scambio; **to be on the ~ of doing sth** essere sul punto di or stare per fare qc; **to make a ~** fare un'osservazione; **to get/miss the ~** capire/non capire; **to come to the ~** venire al fatto; **there's no ~ in doing** è inutile (fare); **point out** vt far notare; **point-blank** adv (also: **at point-blank range**) a bruciapelo; (fig) categoricamente; **pointed** adj (shape) aguzzo(-a), appuntito(-a); (remark) specifico(-a); **pointer** n (needle) lancetta; (fig) indicazione f, consiglio; **pointless** adj inutile, vano(-a); **point of view** n punto di vista

poison ['pɔɪzn] n veleno ▷ vt avvelenare; **poisonous** adj velenoso(-a)

poke [pəʊk] vt (fire) attizzare; (jab with finger, stick etc) punzecchiare; (put): **to ~ sth in(to)** spingere qc dentro; **poke about** or **around** vi frugare; **poke out** vi (stick out) sporger fuori

poker ['pəʊkəʳ] n attizzatoio; (Cards) poker m

Poland ['pəʊlənd] n Polonia

polar ['pəʊləʳ] adj polare; **polar bear** n orso bianco

Pole [pəʊl] n polacco(-a)

pole [pəʊl] n (of wood) palo; (Elec, Geo) polo; **pole bean** (US) n (runner bean) fagiolino; **pole vault** n salto con l'asta

police [pə'liːs] n polizia ▷ vt mantenere l'ordine in; **police car** n macchina della polizia; **police constable** (BRIT) n agente m di polizia; **police force** n corpo di polizia, polizia; **policeman** (irreg) n poliziotto, agente m di polizia; **police officer** n = **police constable**; **police station** n posto di polizia; **policewoman** (irreg) n donna f poliziotto inv

policy ['pɒlɪsɪ] n politica; (also: **insurance ~**) polizza (d'assicurazione)

polio ['pəʊlɪəʊ] n polio f

Polish ['pəʊlɪʃ] adj polacco(-a) ▷ n (Ling) polacco

polish ['pɒlɪʃ] n (for shoes) lucido; (for floor) cera; (for nails) smalto; (shine) lucentezza, lustro; (fig: refinement) raffinatezza ▷ vt lucidare; (fig: improve) raffinare; **polish off** vt (food) mangiarsi; **polished** adj (fig) raffinato(-a)

polite [pə'laɪt] adj cortese; **politeness** n cortesia

political [pə'lɪtɪkl] adj politico(-a); **politically** adv politicamente; **politically correct** politicamente corretto(-a)

politician [pɒlɪ'tɪʃən] n politico

politics ['pɒlɪtɪks] n politica ▷ npl (views, policies) idee fpl politiche

poll [pəʊl] n scrutinio; (votes cast) voti mpl; (also: **opinion ~**) sondaggio (d'opinioni) ▷ vt ottenere

pollen ['pɒlən] n polline m

polling station ['pəʊlɪŋ-] (BRIT) n sezione f elettorale

pollute [pə'luːt] vt inquinare

pollution [pə'luːʃən] n inquinamento

polo ['pəʊləʊ] n polo; **polo-neck** n collo alto; (also: **polo-neck sweater**) dolcevita ▷ adj a collo alto; **polo shirt** n polo f inv

polyester [pɒlɪ'ɛstəʳ] n poliestere m

polystyrene [pɒlɪ'staɪriːn] n polistirolo

polythene ['pɒlɪθiːn] n politene m; **polythene bag** n sacco di plastica

pomegranate ['pɒmɪɡrænɪt] n melagrana

pompous ['pɒmpəs] adj pomposo(-a)

pond [pɒnd] n pozza; stagno

ponder ['pɒndəʳ] vt ponderare, riflettere su

pony ['pəʊnɪ] n pony m inv; **ponytail** n coda di cavallo; **pony trekking**

[-trɛkɪŋ] (BRIT) n escursione f a cavallo

poodle ['puːdl] n barboncino, barbone m

pool [puːl] n (puddle) pozza; (pond) stagno; (also: **swimming ~**) piscina; (fig: of light) cerchio; (billiards) specie di biliardo a buca ▷ vt mettere in comune; **~s** npl (football pools) ≈ totocalcio; **typing ~** servizio comune di dattilografia

poor [puə^r] adj povero(-a); (mediocre) mediocre, cattivo(-a) ▷ npl **the ~** i poveri; **~ in** povero(-a) di; **poorly** adv poveramente; male ▷ adj indisposto(-a), malato(-a)

pop [pɔp] n (noise) schiocco; (Mus) musica pop; (drink) bibita gasata; (US: inf: father) babbo ▷ vt (put) mettere (in fretta) ▷ vi scoppiare; (cork) schioccare; **pop in** vi passare; **pop out** vi fare un salto fuori; **popcorn** n pop-corn m

poplar ['pɔplə^r] n pioppo

popper ['pɔpə^r] n bottone m a pressione

poppy ['pɔpɪ] n papavero

Popsicle® ['pɔpsɪkl] (US) n (ice lolly) ghiacciolo

pop star n pop star f inv

popular ['pɔpjulə^r] adj popolare; (fashionable) in voga; **popularity** [-'lærɪtɪ] n popolarità

population [pɔpju'leɪʃən] n popolazione f

porcelain ['pɔːslɪn] n porcellana

porch [pɔːtʃ] n veranda

pore [pɔː^r] n poro ▷ vi **to ~ over** essere immerso(-a) in

pork [pɔːk] n carne f di maiale; **pork chop** n braciola or costoletta di maiale; **pork pie** n (BRIT: Culin) pasticcio di maiale in crosta

porn [pɔːn] (inf) n pornografia ▷ adj porno inv; **pornographic** [pɔːnə'ɡræfɪk] adj pornografico(-a); **pornography** [pɔː'nɔɡrəfɪ] n pornografia

porridge ['pɔrɪdʒ] n porridge m

port [pɔːt] n (gen, wine) porto; (Naut: left side) babordo

portable ['pɔːtəbl] adj portatile

porter ['pɔːtə^r] n (for luggage) facchino, portabagagli m inv; (doorkeeper) portiere m, portinaio

portfolio [pɔːt'fəuliəu] n (case) cartella; (Pol, Finance) portafoglio; (of artist) raccolta dei propri lavori

portion ['pɔːʃən] n porzione f

port of call n (porto di) scalo

portrait ['pɔːtreɪt] n ritratto

portray [pɔː'treɪ] vt fare il ritratto di; (character on stage) rappresentare; (in writing) ritrarre

Portugal ['pɔːtjuɡl] n Portogallo

Portuguese [pɔːtju'ɡiːz] adj portoghese ▷ n inv portoghese m/f; (Ling) portoghese m

pose [pəuz] n posa ▷ vi posare; (pretend): **to ~ as** atteggiarsi a, posare a ▷ vt porre

posh [pɔʃ] (inf) adj elegante; (family) per bene

position [pə'zɪʃən] n posizione f; (job) posto ▷ vt sistemare

positive ['pɔzɪtɪv] adj positivo(-a); (certain) sicuro(-a), certo(-a); (definite) preciso(-a), definitivo(-a); **positively** adv (affirmatively, enthusiastically) positivamente; (decisively) decisamente; (really) assolutamente

possess [pə'zɛs] vt possedere; **possession** [pə'zɛʃən] n possesso; **possessions** npl (belongings) beni mpl; **possessive** adj possessivo(-a)

possibility [pɔsɪ'bɪlɪtɪ] n possibilità f inv

possible ['pɔsɪbl] adj possibile; **as big as ~** il più grande possibile; **possibly** ['pɔsɪblɪ] adv (perhaps) forse; **if you possibly can** se le è possibile; **I cannot possibly come** proprio non posso venire

post [pəust] n (BRIT) posta; (: collection) levata; (job, situation) posto; (Mil) postazione f; (pole) palo ▷ vt (BRIT: send by post) imbucare; (: appoint): **to ~ to** assegnare a; **where can I ~ these cards?** dove posso imbucare queste cartoline?; **postage** n affrancatura; **postal** adj postale; **postal order** n vaglia m inv postale; **postbox** (BRIT) n cassetta postale; **postcard** n cartolina; **postcode** n (BRIT) codice m (di avviamento) postale

poster ['pəustə^r] n manifesto, affisso

postgraduate ['pəust'ɡrædjuət] n laureato/a che continua gli studi

postman ['pəustmən] (irreg) n postino

postmark ['pəustmɑːk] n bollo or timbro postale

post-mortem [-'mɔːtəm] n autopsia

post office n (building) ufficio postale; (organization): **the Post Office** ≈ le Poste e Telecomunicazioni

postpone [pəs'pəun] vt rinviare

posture ['pɔstʃə^r] n portamento; (pose) posa, atteggiamento

postwoman ['pəustwumən] (BRIT: irreg) n postina

pot [pɔt] n (for cooking) pentola; casseruola; (teapot) teiera; (coffeepot) caffettiera; (for plants, jam) vaso; (inf: marijuana) erba ▷ vt (plant) piantare in vaso; **a ~ of tea for two** tè per due; **to go to ~** (inf: work, performance) andare in malora

potato [pə'teɪtəu] (pl **potatoes**) n patata; **potato peeler** n sbucciapatate m inv

potent ['pəutnt] adj potente, forte

potential [pə'tɛnʃl] adj potenziale ▷ n possibilità fpl

pothole ['pɔthəul] n (in road) buca; (BRIT:

underground) caverna
pot plant _n_ pianta in vaso
potter ['pɒtə'] _n_ vasaio ▷ _vi_ **to ~ around,
~ about** (_BRIT_) lavoracchiare; **pottery**
_n_ ceramiche _fpl_; (_factory_) fabbrica di
ceramiche
potty ['pɒtɪ] _adj_ (_inf: mad_) tocco(-a) ▷ _n_
(_child's_) vasino
pouch [pautʃ] _n_ borsa; (_Zool_) marsupio
poultry ['pəʊltrɪ] _n_ pollame _m_
pounce [pauns] _vi_ **to ~ (on)** piombare (su)
pound [paund] _n_ (_weight_) libbra; (_money_)
(lira) sterlina ▷ _vt_ (_beat_) battere; (_crush_)
pestare, polverizzare ▷ _vi_ (_beat_) battere,
martellare; **pound sterling** _n_ sterlina
(inglese)
pour [pɔ:'] _vt_ versare ▷ _vi_ riversarsi; (_rain_)
piovere a dirotto; **pour in** _vi_ affluire in
gran quantità; **pour out** _vi_ (_people_) uscire
a fiumi ▷ _vt_ vuotare; versare; (_fig_) sfogare;
pouring _adj_ **pouring rain** pioggia
torrenziale
pout [paut] _vi_ sporgere le labbra; fare il
broncio
poverty ['pɒvətɪ] _n_ povertà, miseria
powder ['paudə'] _n_ polvere _f_ ▷ _vt_ **to ~
one's face** incipriarsi il viso; **powdered
milk** _n_ latte _m_ in polvere
power ['pauə'] _n_ (_strength_) potenza, forza;
(_ability, Pol: of party, leader_) potere _m_; (_Elec_)
corrente _f_; **to be in ~** (_Pol etc_) essere al
potere; **power cut** (_BRIT_) _n_ interruzione
_f_ or mancanza di corrente; **power
failure** _n_ interruzione _f_ della corrente
elettrica; **powerful** _adj_ potente, forte;
powerless _adj_ impotente; **powerless to
do** impossibilitato(-a) a fare; **power point**
(_BRIT_) _n_ presa di corrente; **power station**
_n_ centrale _f_ elettrica
p.p. _abbr_ = **per procurationem**; **p.p. J.
Smith** per J. Smith; (= _pages_) p.p.
PR _abbr_ = **public relations**
practical ['præktɪkl] _adj_ pratico(-a);
practical joke _n_ beffa; **practically** _adv_
praticamente
practice ['præktɪs] _n_ pratica; (_of profession_)
esercizio; (_at football etc_) allenamento;
(_business_) gabinetto; clientela ▷ _vt, vi_ (_US_)
= **practise**; **in ~** (_in reality_) in pratica; **out of
~** fuori esercizio
practise ['præktɪs] (_US_ **practice**) _vt_ (_work
at: piano, one's backhand etc_) esercitarsi a;
(_train for: skiing, running etc_) allenarsi a; (_a
sport, religion_) praticare; (_method_) usare;
(_profession_) esercitare ▷ _vi_ esercitarsi;
(_train_) allenarsi; (_lawyer, doctor_) esercitare;
practising _adj_ (_Christian etc_) praticante;
(_lawyer_) che esercita la professione
practitioner [præk'tɪʃənə'] _n_

professionista _m/f_
pragmatic [præg'mætɪk] _adj_
pragmatico(-a)
prairie ['prɛərɪ] _n_ prateria
praise [preɪz] _n_ elogio, lode _f_ ▷ _vt_ elogiare,
lodare
pram [præm] (_BRIT_) _n_ carrozzina
prank [præŋk] _n_ burla
prawn [prɔ:n] _n_ gamberetto; **prawn
cocktail** _n_ cocktail _m inv_ di gamberetti
pray [preɪ] _vi_ pregare; **prayer** [prɛə'] _n_
preghiera
preach [pri:tʃ] _vt, vi_ predicare; **preacher** _n_
predicatore(-trice); (_US: minister_) pastore _m_
precarious [prɪ'kɛərɪəs] _adj_ precario(-a)
precaution [prɪ'kɔ:ʃən] _n_ precauzione _f_
precede [prɪ'si:d] _vt_ precedere; **precedent**
['prɛsɪdənt] _n_ precedente _m_; **preceding**
[prɪ'si:dɪŋ] _adj_ precedente
precinct ['pri:sɪŋkt] (_US_) _n_ circoscrizione _f_
precious ['prɛʃəs] _adj_ prezioso(-a)
precise [prɪ'saɪs] _adj_ preciso(-a); **precisely**
adv precisamente
precision [prɪ'sɪʒən] _n_ precisione _f_
predator ['prɛdətə'] _n_ predatore _m_
predecessor ['pri:dɪsɛsə'] _n_
predecessore(-a)
predicament [prɪ'dɪkəmənt] _n_ situazione
_f_ difficile
predict [prɪ'dɪkt] _vt_ predire; **predictable**
adj prevedibile; **prediction** [prɪ'dɪkʃən] _n_
predizione _f_
predominantly [prɪ'dɒmɪnəntlɪ] _adv_ in
maggior parte; soprattutto
preface ['prɛfəs] _n_ prefazione _f_
prefect ['pri:fɛkt] _n_ (_BRIT: in school_)
studente(-essa) con funzioni disciplinari;
(_French etc, Admin_) prefetto
prefer [prɪ'fə:'] _vt_ preferire; **to ~ doing** or
to do preferire fare; **preferable** ['prɛfrəbl]
adj preferibile; **preferably** ['prɛfrəblɪ] _adv_
preferibilmente; **preference** ['prɛfrəns] _n_
preferenza
prefix ['pri:fɪks] _n_ prefisso
pregnancy ['prɛgnənsɪ] _n_ gravidanza
pregnant ['prɛgnənt] _adj_ incinta _ag_
prehistoric ['pri:hɪs'tɒrɪk] _adj_
preistorico(-a)
prejudice ['prɛdʒudɪs] _n_ pregiudizio;
(_harm_) torto, danno; **prejudiced** _adj_
prejudiced (against) prevenuto(-a)
(contro); **prejudiced (in favour of)** ben
disposto(-a) (verso)
preliminary [prɪ'lɪmɪnərɪ] _adj_ preliminare
prelude ['prɛlju:d] _n_ preludio
premature ['prɛmətʃuə'] _adj_
prematuro(-a)
premier ['prɛmɪə'] _adj_ primo(-a) ▷ _n_ (_Pol_)
primo ministro

première [ˈprɛmɪɛəʳ] n prima
Premier League n = serie A
premises [ˈprɛmɪsɪz] npl locale m; **on the ~** sul posto; **business ~** locali commerciali
premium [ˈpriːmɪəm] n premio; **to be at a ~** essere ricercatissimo
premonition [prɛməˈnɪʃən] n premonizione f
preoccupied [priːˈɔkjupaɪd] adj preoccupato(-a)
repaid [priːˈpeɪd] adj pagato(-a) in anticipo
reparation [prɛpəˈreɪʃən] n reparazione f; **~s** npl (for trip, war) reparativi mpl
reparatory school [prɪˈpærətərɪ-] n uola elementare privata
pare [prɪˈpɛəʳ] vt preparare ▷ vi **to ~** prepararsi a; **~d to** pronto(-a) a
position [prɛpəˈzɪʃən] n preposizione f
school n = **preparatory school**
equisite [priːˈrɛkwɪzɪt] n requisito spensabile
school [ˈpriːˌskuːl] adj (age) colastico(-a); (child) in età colastica
prescribe [prɪˈskraɪb] vt (Med) prescrivere
prescription [prɪˈskrɪpʃən] n prescrizione f; (Med) ricetta; **could you write me a ~?** mi può fare una ricetta medica?
presence [ˈprɛzns] n presenza; **~ of mind** presenza di spirito
present [adj, n ˈprɛznt, vb prɪˈzɛnt] adj presente; (wife, residence, job) attuale ▷ n (actuality): **the ~** il presente; (gift) regalo ▷ vt presentare; (give): **to ~ sb with sth** offrire qc a qn; **to give sb a ~** fare un regalo a qn; **at ~** al momento; **presentable** [prɪˈzɛntəbl] adj presentabile; **presentation** [-ˈteɪʃən] n presentazione f; (ceremony) consegna ufficiale; **present-day** adj attuale, d'oggigiorno; **presenter** n (Radio, TV) presentatore(-trice); **presently** adv (soon) fra poco, presto; (at present) al momento; **present participle** n participio presente
preservation [prɛzəˈveɪʃən] n preservazione f, conservazione f
preservative [prɪˈzəːvətɪv] n conservante m
preserve [prɪˈzəːv] vt (keep safe) preservare, proteggere; (maintain) conservare; (food) mettere in conserva ▷ n (often pl: jam) marmellata; (: fruit) frutta sciroppata
preside [prɪˈzaɪd] vi **to ~ (over)** presiedere (a)
president [ˈprɛzɪdənt] n presidente m; **presidential** [-ˈdɛnʃl] adj presidenziale

press [prɛs] n (newspapers etc): **the P~** la stampa; (tool, machine) pressa; (for wine) torchio ▷ vt (push) premere, pigiare; (squeeze) spremere; (: hand) stringere; (clothes: iron) stirare; (pursue) incalzare; (insist): **to ~ sth on sb** far accettare qc da qn ▷ vi premere; accalcare; **we are ~ed for time** ci manca il tempo; **to ~ for sth** insistere per avere qc; **press conference** n conferenza f stampa inv; **pressing** adj urgente; **press stud** (BRIT) n bottone m a pressione; **press-up** (BRIT) n flessione f sulle braccia
pressure [ˈprɛʃəʳ] n pressione f; **to put ~ on sb (to do)** mettere qn sotto pressione (affinché faccia); **pressure cooker** n pentola a pressione; **pressure group** n gruppo di pressione
prestige [prɛsˈtiːʒ] n prestigio
prestigious [prɛsˈtɪdʒəs] adj prestigioso(-a)
presumably [prɪˈzjuːməblɪ] adv presumibilmente
presume [prɪˈzjuːm] vt supporre
pretence [prɪˈtɛns] (us **pretense**) n (claim) pretesa; **to make a ~ of doing** far finta di fare; **under false ~s** con l'inganno
pretend [prɪˈtɛnd] vt (feign) fingere ▷ vi far finta; **to ~ to do** far finta di fare
pretense [prɪˈtɛns] (us) n = **pretence**
pretentious [prɪˈtɛnʃəs] adj pretenzioso(-a)
pretext [ˈpriːtɛkst] n pretesto
pretty [ˈprɪtɪ] adj grazioso(-a), carino(-a) ▷ adv abbastanza, assai
prevail [prɪˈveɪl] vi (win, be usual) prevalere; (persuade): **to ~ (up)on sb to do** persuadere qn a fare; **prevailing** adj dominante
prevalent [ˈprɛvələnt] adj (belief) predominante; (customs) diffuso(-a); (fashion) corrente; (disease) comune
prevent [prɪˈvɛnt] vt **to ~ sb from doing** impedire a qn di fare; **to ~ sth from happening** impedire che qc succeda; **prevention** [-ˈvɛnʃən] n prevenzione f; **preventive** adj preventivo(-a)
preview [ˈpriːvjuː] n (of film) anteprima
previous [ˈpriːvɪəs] adj precedente; anteriore; **previously** adv prima
prey [preɪ] n preda ▷ vi **to ~ on** far preda di; **it was ~ing on his mind** lo stava ossessionando
price [praɪs] n prezzo ▷ vt (goods) fissare il prezzo di; valutare; **priceless** adj inapprezzabile; **price list** n listino (dei) prezzi
prick [prɪk] n puntura ▷ vt pungere; **to ~ up one's ears** drizzare gli orecchi

prickly ['prɪklɪ] *adj* spinoso(-a)
pride [praɪd] *n* orgoglio; superbia ▷ *vt* **to ~ o.s. on** essere orgoglioso(-a) di, vantarsi di
priest [priːst] *n* prete *m*, sacerdote *m*
primarily ['praɪmərɪlɪ] *adv* principalmente, essenzialmente
primary ['praɪmərɪ] *adj* primario(-a); (*first in importance*) primo(-a) ▷ *n* (*us: election*) primarie *fpl*; **primary school** (BRIT) *n* scuola elementare
prime [praɪm] *adj* primario(-a), fondamentale; (*excellent*) di prima qualità ▷ *vt* (*wood*) preparare; (*fig*) mettere al corrente ▷ *n* **in the ~ of life** nel fiore della vita; **Prime Minister** *n* primo ministro
primitive ['prɪmɪtɪv] *adj* primitivo(-a)
primrose ['prɪmrəuz] *n* primavera
prince [prɪns] *n* principe *m*
princess [prɪn'sɛs] *n* principessa
principal ['prɪnsɪpl] *adj* principale ▷ *n* (*headmaster*) preside *m*; **principally** *adv* principalmente
principle ['prɪnsɪpl] *n* principio; **in ~** in linea di principio; **on ~** per principio
print [prɪnt] *n* (*mark*) impronta; (*letters*) caratteri *mpl*; (*fabric*) tessuto stampato; (*Art, Phot*) stampa ▷ *vt* imprimere; (*publish*) stampare, pubblicare; (*write in capitals*) scrivere in stampatello; **out of ~** esaurito(-a); **print out** *vt* (*Comput*) stampare; **printer** *n* tipografo; (*machine*) stampante *f*; **printout** *n* tabulato
prior ['praɪə'] *adj* precedente; (*claim etc*) più importante; **~ to doing** prima di fare
priority [praɪ'ɔrɪtɪ] *n* priorità *f inv*; precedenza
prison ['prɪzn] *n* prigione *f* ▷ *cpd* (*system*) carcerario(-a); (*conditions, food*) nelle or delle prigioni; **prisoner** *n* prigioniero(-a); **prisoner-of-war** *n* prigioniero(-a) di guerra
pristine ['prɪstiːn] *adj* immacolato(-a)
privacy ['prɪvəsɪ] *n* solitudine *f*, intimità
private ['praɪvɪt] *adj* privato(-a); personale ▷ *n* soldato semplice; **"~"** (*on envelope*) "riservata", (*on door*) "privato"; **in ~** in privato; **privately** *adv* in privato; (*within oneself*) dentro di sé; **private property** *n* proprietà privata; **private school** *n* scuola privata
privatize ['praɪvɪtaɪz] *vt* privatizzare
privilege ['prɪvɪlɪdʒ] *n* privilegio
prize [praɪz] *n* premio ▷ *adj* (*example, idiot*) perfetto(-a); (*bull, novel*) premiato(-a) ▷ *vt* apprezzare, pregiare; **prize-giving** *n* premiazione *f*; **prizewinner** *n* premiato(-a)
pro [prəu] *n* (*Sport*) professionista *m/f* ▷ *prep* pro; **the ~s and cons** il pro e il

contro
probability [prɔbə'bɪlɪtɪ] *n* probabilità *f inv*; **in all ~** con tutta probabilità
probable ['prɔbəbl] *adj* probabile
probably ['prɔbəblɪ] *adv* probabilmente
probation [prə'beɪʃən] *n* **on ~** (*employee*) in prova; (*Law*) in libertà vigilata
probe [prəub] *n* (*Med, Space*) sonda; (*enquiry*) indagine *f*, investigazione *f* ▷ *vt* sondare, esplorare; indagare
problem ['prɔbləm] *n* problema *m*
procedure [prə'siːdʒə'] *n* (*Admin, Law*) procedura; (*method*) metodo, procedimento
proceed [prə'siːd] *vi* (*go forward*) avanzare, andare avanti; (*go about it*) procedere; (*continue*): **to ~ (with)** continuare; **to ~ to** andare a; passare a; **to ~ to do** mettersi a fare; **proceedings** *npl* misure *fpl*; (*Law*) procedimento; (*meeting*) riunione *f*; (*records*) rendiconti *mpl*; atti *mpl*; **proceeds** ['prəusiːdz] *npl* profitto, incasso
process ['prəusɛs] *n* processo; (*method*) metodo, sistema *m* ▷ *vt* trattare; (*information*) elaborare
procession [prə'sɛʃən] *n* processione *f*, corteo; **funeral ~** corteo funebre
proclaim [prə'kleɪm] *vt* proclamare, dichiarare
prod [prɔd] *vt* dare un colpetto a; pungolare ▷ *n* colpetto
produce [*n* 'prɔdjuːs, *vb* prə'djuːs] *n* (*Agr*) prodotto, prodotti *mpl* ▷ *vt* produrre; (*show*) esibire, mostrare; (*cause*) cagionare, causare; **producer** *n* (*Theatre*) regista *m/f*; (*Agr, Cinema*) produttore *m*
product ['prɔdʌkt] *n* prodotto; **production** [prə'dʌkʃən] *n* produzione *f*; **productive** [prə'dʌktɪv] *adj* produttivo(-a); **productivity** [prɔdʌk'tɪvɪtɪ] *n* produttività
Prof. *abbr* (= *professor*) Prof.
profession [prə'fɛʃən] *n* professione *f*; **professional** *n* professionista *m/f* ▷ *adj* professionale; (*work*) da professionista
professor [prə'fɛsə'] *n* professore *m* (*titolare di una cattedra*); (*us*) professore(-essa)
profile ['prəufaɪl] *n* profilo
profit ['prɔfɪt] *n* profitto; beneficio ▷ *vi* **to ~ (by** or **from)** approfittare (di); **profitable** *adj* redditizio(-a)
profound [prə'faund] *adj* profondo(-a)
programme ['prəugræm] (*us* **program**) *n* programma *m* ▷ *vt* programmare; **programmer** (*us* **programer**) *n* programmatore(-trice); **programming** (*us* **programing**) *n* programmazione *f*
progress [*n* 'prəugrɛs, *vb* prə'grɛs] *n*

progresso ▷ *vi* avanzare, procedere;
in ~ in corso; **to make ~** far progressi;
progressive [-'grɛsɪv] *adj* progressivo(-a);
(*person*) progressista
prohibit [prə'hɪbɪt] *vt* proibire, vietare
project [*n* 'prɔdʒɛkt, *vb* prə'dʒɛkt] *n* (*plan*)
piano; (*venture*) progetto; (*Scol*) studio
▷ *vt* proiettare ▷ *vi* (*stick out*) sporgere;
projection [prə'dʒɛkʃən] *n* proiezione
f; sporgenza; **projector** [prə'dʒɛktə^r] *n*
proiettore *m*
prolific [prə'lɪfɪk] *adj* (*artist etc*)
fecondo(-a)
prolong [prə'lɔŋ] *vt* prolungare
prom [prɔm] *n abbr* = **promenade**; (*US:
ball*) ballo studentesco

● **PROM**
●
● In Gran Bretagna i **Proms**, o
● "promenade concerts", sono concerti di
● musica classica, i più noti dei quali sono
● eseguiti nella prestigiosa **Royal Albert
● Hall** a Londra. Si chiamano così perché
● un tempo il pubblico seguiva i concerti
● in piedi, passeggiando (in inglese
● "promenade" voleva dire, appunto,
● passeggiata). Negli Stati Uniti, invece,
● con **prom**, si intende l'annuale ballo
● studentesco di un'università o di una
● scuola secondaria.

promenade [prɔmə'nɑːd] *n* (*by sea*)
lungomare *m*
prominent ['prɔmɪnənt] *adj*
(*standing out*) prominente; (*important*)
importante
promiscuous [prə'mɪskjuəs] *adj* (*sexually*)
di facili costumi
promise ['prɔmɪs] *n* promessa ▷ *vt*,
vi promettere; **to ~ sb sth, ~ sth to sb**
promettere qc a qn; **to ~ (sb) that/to
do sth** promettere (a qn) che/di fare qc;
promising *adj* promettente
promote [prə'məut] *vt* promuovere;
(*venture, event*) organizzare; **promotion**
[-'məuʃən] *n* promozione *f*
prompt [prɔmpt] *adj* rapido(-a),
svelto(-a); puntuale; (*reply*) sollecito(-a)
▷ *adv* (*punctually*) in punto ▷ *n* (*Comput*)
prompt *m* ▷ *vt* incitare; provocare;
(*Theatre*) suggerire a; **to ~ sb to do** incitare
qn a fare; **promptly** *adv* prontamente;
puntualmente
prone [prəun] *adj* (*lying*) prono(-a); **~ to**
propenso(-a) a, incline a
prong [prɔŋ] *n* rebbio, punta
pronoun ['prəunaun] *n* pronome *m*
pronounce [prə'nauns] *vt* pronunciare;

how do you ~ it? come si pronuncia?
pronunciation [prənʌnsɪ'eɪʃən] *n*
pronuncia
proof [pruːf] *n* prova; (*of book*) bozza; (*Phot*)
provino ▷ *adj* **~ against** a prova di
prop [prɔp] *n* sostegno, appoggio ▷ *vt*
(*also:* **~ up**) sostenere, appoggiare; (*lean*):
to ~ sth against appoggiare qc contro
or a; **~s** oggetti *m inv* di scena; **prop up** *vt*
sostenere, appoggiare
propaganda [prɔpə'gændə] *n*
propaganda
propeller [prə'pɛlə^r] *n* elica
proper ['prɔpə^r] *adj* (*suited, right*)
adatto(-a), appropriato(-a); (*seemly*)
decente; (*authentic*) vero(-a); (*inf: real:
noun*) + vero(-a) e proprio(-a); **properly**
['prɔpəlɪ] *adv* (*eat, study*) bene; (*behave*)
come si deve; **proper noun** *n* nome *m*
proprio
property ['prɔpətɪ] *n* (*things owned*) beni
mpl; (*land, building*) proprietà *f inv*; (*Chem
etc: quality*) proprietà
prophecy ['prɔfɪsɪ] *n* profezia
prophet ['prɔfɪt] *n* profeta *m*
proportion [prə'pɔːʃən] *n* proporzione *f*;
(*share*) parte *f*; **~s** *npl* (*size*) proporzioni *fpl*;
proportional *adj* proporzionale
proposal [prə'pəuzl] *n* proposta; (*plan*)
progetto; (*of marriage*) proposta di
matrimonio
propose [prə'pəuz] *vt* proporre, suggerire
▷ *vi* fare una proposta di matrimonio; **to
~ to do** proporsi di fare, aver l'intenzione
di fare
proposition [prɔpə'zɪʃən] *n* proposizione
f; (*offer*) proposta
proprietor [prə'praɪətə^r] *n*
proprietario(-a)
prose [prəuz] *n* prosa
prosecute ['prɔsɪkjuːt] *vt* processare;
prosecution [-'kjuːʃən] *n* processo;
(*accusing side*) accusa; **prosecutor** *n* (*also:*
public prosecutor) ≈ procuratore *m* della
Repubblica
prospect [*n* 'prɔspɛkt, *vb* prə'spɛkt] *n*
prospettiva; (*hope*) speranza ▷ *vi* **to ~ for**
cercare; **~s** *npl* (*for work etc*) prospettive
fpl; **prospective** [-'spɛktɪv] *adj* possibile;
futuro(-a)
prospectus [prə'spɛktəs] *n* prospetto,
programma *m*
prosper ['prɔspə^r] *vi* prosperare;
prosperity [prɔ'spɛrɪtɪ] *n* prosperità;
prosperous *adj* prospero(-a)
prostitute ['prɔstɪtjuːt] *n* prostituta;
male ~ uomo che si prostituisce
protect [prə'tɛkt] *vt* proteggere,
salvaguardare; **protection** *n* protezione *f*;

protective adj protettivo(-a)
protein ['prəuti:n] n proteina
protest [n 'prəutɛst, vb prə'tɛst] n protesta
▷ vt, vi protestare
Protestant ['prɔtɪstənt] adj, n protestante
m/f
protester [prə'tɛstə^r] n dimostrante m/f
protractor [prə'træktə^r] n (Geom)
goniometro
proud [praud] adj fiero(-a), orgoglioso(-a);
(pej) superbo(-a)
prove [pru:v] vt provare, dimostrare ▷ vi
to ~ (to be) correct etc risultare vero(-a)
etc; **to ~ o.s.** mostrare le proprie capacità
proverb ['prɔvə:b] n proverbio
provide [prə'vaɪd] vt fornire, provvedere;
to ~ sb with sth fornire or provvedere qn di
qc; **provide for** vt fus provvedere a; (future
event) prevedere; **provided** conj **provided
(that)** purché + sub, a condizione che +
sub; **providing** [prə'vaɪdɪŋ] conj purché
+sub, a condizione che +sub
province ['prɔvɪns] n provincia;
provincial [prə'vɪnʃəl] adj provinciale
provision [prə'vɪʒən] n (supply) riserva;
(supplying) provvista, rifornimento;
(stipulation) condizione f; **~s** npl
(food) provviste fpl; **provisional** adj
provvisorio(-a)
provocative [prə'vɔkətɪv] adj (aggressive)
provocatorio(-a); (thought-provoking)
stimolante; (seductive) provocante
provoke [prə'vəuk] vt provocare; incitare
prowl [praul] vi (also: ~ about, ~ around)
aggirarsi ▷ n **to be on the ~** aggirarsi
proximity [prɔk'sɪmɪtɪ] n prossimità
proxy ['prɔksɪ] n **by ~** per procura
prudent ['pru:dnt] adj prudente
prune [pru:n] n prugna secca ▷ vt potare
pry [praɪ] vi **to ~ into** ficcare il naso in
PS abbr (= postscript) P.S.
pseudonym ['sju:dənɪm] n pseudonimo
psychiatric [saɪkɪ'ætrɪk] adj
psichiatrico(-a)
psychiatrist [saɪ'kaɪətrɪst] n psichiatra
m/f
psychic ['saɪkɪk] adj (also: ~al) psichico(-a);
(person) dotato(-a) di qualità telepatiche
psychoanalysis [saɪkəuə'næləsɪs, -si:z]
(pl -ses) n psicanalisi f inv
psychological [saɪkə'lɔdʒɪkl] adj
psicologico(-a)
psychologist [saɪ'kɔlədʒɪst] n
psicologo(-a)
psychology [saɪ'kɔlədʒɪ] n psicologia
psychotherapy [saɪkəu'θɛrəpɪ] n
psicoterapia
pt abbr (= pint; point) pt.
PTO abbr (= please turn over) v.r.

pub [pʌb] n abbr (= public house) pub m inv
puberty ['pju:bətɪ] n pubertà
public ['pʌblɪk] adj pubblico(-a) ▷ n
pubblico, **in ~** in pubblico
publication [pʌblɪ'keɪʃən] n
pubblicazione f
public: public company n società f inv
per azioni (costituita tramite pubblica
sottoscrizione); **public convenience** (BRIT)
n gabinetti mpl; **public holiday** n giorno
festivo, festa nazionale; **public house**
(BRIT) n pub m inv
publicity [pʌb'lɪsɪtɪ] n pubblicità
publicize ['pʌblɪsaɪz] vt rendere
pubblico(-a)
public: public limited company n
≈ società per azioni a responsabilità
limitata (quotata in Borsa); **publicly**
['pʌblɪklɪ] adv pubblicamente; **public
opinion** n opinione f pubblica; **public
relations** n pubbliche relazioni fpl; **public
school** n (BRIT) scuola privata; (US) scuola
statale; **public transport** n mezzi mpl
pubblici
publish ['pʌblɪʃ] vt pubblicare; **publisher** n
editore m; **publishing** n (industry) editoria;
(of a book) pubblicazione f
pub lunch n pranzo semplice ed economico
servito nei pub
pudding ['pudɪŋ] n budino; (BRIT:
dessert) dolce m; **black ~,** (US) **blood ~**
sanguinaccio
puddle ['pʌdl] n pozza, pozzanghera
Puerto Rico ['pwə:təu'ri:kəu] n Portorico
puff [pʌf] n sbuffo ▷ vt **to ~ one's pipe**
tirare sboccate di fumo ▷ vi (pant) ansare;
puff pastry n pasta sfoglia
pull [pul] n (tug): **to give sth a ~** tirare su
qc ▷ vt tirare; (muscle) strappare; (trigger)
premere ▷ vi tirare; **to ~ to pieces** fare
a pezzi; **to ~ one's punches** (Boxing)
risparmiare l'avversario; **to ~ one's
weight** dare il proprio contributo; **to ~
o.s. together** ricomporsi, riprendersi;
to ~ sb's leg prendere in giro qn; **pull
apart** vt (break) fare a pezzi; **pull away** vi
(move off: vehicle) muoversi, partire; (boat)
staccarsi dal molo, salpare; (draw back:
person) indietreggiare; **pull back** vt (lever
etc) tirare indietro; (curtains) aprire ▷ vi
(from confrontation etc) tirarsi indietro, (Mil:
withdraw) ritirarsi; **pull down** vt (house)
demolire; (tree) abbattere; **pull in** vi (Aut:
at the kerb) accostarsi; (Rail) entrare in
stazione; **pull off** vt (clothes) togliere;
(deal etc) portare a compimento; **pull out**
vi partire; (Aut: come out of line) spostarsi
sulla mezzeria ▷ vt staccare; far uscire;
(withdraw) ritirare; **pull over** vi (Aut)

p

accostare; **pull up** vi (stop) fermarsi ▷ vt
(raise) sollevare; (uproot) sradicare
pulley ['pulɪ] n puleggia, carrucola
pullover ['puləuvəᵊ] n pullover m inv
pulp [pʌlp] n (of fruit) polpa
pulpit ['pulpɪt] n pulpito
pulse [pʌls] n polso; (Bot) legume m; ~s npl
(Culin) legumi mpl
puma ['pju:mə] n puma m inv
pump [pʌmp] n pompa; (shoe) scarpetta
▷ vt pompare; **pump up** vt gonfiare
pumpkin ['pʌmpkɪn] n zucca
pun [pʌn] n gioco di parole
punch [pʌntʃ] n (blow) pugno; (tool)
punzone m; (drink) ponce m ▷ vt (hit): **to ~
sb/sth** dare un pugno a qn/qc; **punch-up**
(BRIT: inf) n rissa
punctual ['pʌŋktjuəl] adj puntuale
punctuation [pʌŋktju'eɪʃən] n
interpunzione f, punteggiatura
puncture ['pʌŋktʃəᵊ] n foratura ▷ vt forare

> Be careful not to translate **puncture**
> by the Italian word **puntura**.

punish ['pʌnɪʃ] vt punire; **punishment** n
punizione f
punk [pʌŋk] n (also: ~ rocker) punk m/f inv;
(also: ~ rock) musica punk, punk rock m;
(US: inf: hoodlum) teppista m
pup [pʌp] n cucciolo(-a)
pupil ['pju:pl] n allievo(-a); (Anat) pupilla
puppet ['pʌpɪt] n burattino
puppy ['pʌpɪ] n cucciolo(-a), cagnolino(-a)
purchase ['pə:tʃɪs] n acquisto, compera
▷ vt comprare
pure [pjuəᵊ] adj puro(-a); **purely** ['pjuəlɪ]
adv puramente
purify ['pjuərɪfaɪ] vt purificare
purity ['pjuərɪtɪ] n purezza
purple ['pə:pl] adj di porpora; viola inv
purpose ['pə:pəs] n intenzione f, scopo;
on ~ apposta
purr [pə:ᵊ] vi fare le fusa
purse [pə:s] n (BRIT) borsellino; (US)
borsetta ▷ vt contrarre
pursue [pə'sju:] vt inseguire; (fig: activity
etc) continuare con; (: aim etc) perseguire
pursuit [pə'sju:t] n inseguimento; (fig)
ricerca; (pastime) passatempo
pus [pʌs] n pus m
push [puʃ] n spinta; (effort) grande
sforzo; (drive) energia ▷ vt spingere;
(button) premere; (thrust): **to ~ sth (into)**
ficcare qc (in); (fig) fare pubblicità a ▷ vi
spingere; premere; **to ~ for** (fig) insistere
per; **push in** vi introdursi a forza; **push
off** (inf) vi filare; **push on** vi (continue)
continuare; **push over** vt far cadere; **push
through** vi farsi largo spingendo ▷ vt
(measure) far approvare; **pushchair** (BRIT)

n passeggino; **pusher** n (drug pusher)
spacciatore(-trice); **push-up** (US) n (press-
up) flessione f sulle braccia
pussy(-cat) ['pusɪ(-)] (inf) n micio
put [put] (pt, pp put) vt mettere, porre;
(say) dire, esprimere; (a question) fare;
(estimate) stimare; **put away** vt (return)
mettere a posto; **put back** vt (replace)
rimettere (a posto); (postpone) rinviare;
(delay) ritardare; **put by** vt (money)
mettere da parte; **put down** vt (parcel
etc) posare, mettere giù; (pay) versare;
(in writing) mettere per iscritto; (revolt,
animal) sopprimere; (attribute) attribuire;
put forward vt (ideas) avanzare,
proporre; **put in** vt (application, complaint)
presentare; (time, effort) mettere; **put
off** vt (postpone) rimandare, rinviare;
(discourage) dissuadere; **put on** vt (clothes,
lipstick etc) mettere; (light etc) accendere;
(play etc) mettere in scena; (food, meal)
mettere su; (brake) mettere; **to ~ on
weight** ingrassare; **to ~ on airs** darsi
delle arie; **put out** vt mettere fuori; (one's
hand) porgere; (light etc) spegnere; (person:
inconvenience) scomodare; **put through**
vt (Tel: call) passare; (: person) mettere in
comunicazione; (plan) far approvare; **put
up** vt (raise) sollevare, alzare; (: umbrella)
aprire; (: tent) montare; (pin up) affiggere;
(hang) appendere; (build) costruire, erigere;
(increase) aumentare; (accommodate)
alloggiare; **put aside** vt (lay down: book
etc) mettere da una parte, posare; (save)
mettere da parte; (in shop) tenere da
parte; **put together** vt mettere insieme,
riunire; (assemble: furniture) montare; (:
meal) improvvisare; **put up with** vt fus
sopportare
putt [pʌt] n colpo leggero; **putting green**
n green m inv; campo da putting
puzzle ['pʌzl] n enigma m, mistero;
(jigsaw) puzzle m; (also: **crossword ~**)
parole fpl incrociate, cruciverba m inv ▷ vt
confondere, rendere perplesso(-a) ▷ vi
scervellarsi; **puzzled** adj perplesso(-a);
puzzling adj (question) poco chiaro(-a);
(attitude, set of instructions) incomprensibile
pyjamas [pɪ'dʒɑ:məz] (BRIT) npl pigiama m
pylon ['paɪlən] n pilone m
pyramid ['pɪrəmɪd] n piramide f
Pyrenees [pɪrɪ'ni:z] npl **the ~** i Pirenei

quack [kwæk] *n* (*of duck*) qua qua *m inv*; (*pej: doctor*) dottoruccio(-a)

quadruple [kwɔ'drupl] *vt* quadruplicare ▷ *vi* quadruplicarsi

quail [kweɪl] *n* (*Zool*) quaglia ▷ *vi* (*person*): **to ~ at** *or* **before** perdersi d'animo davanti a

quaint [kweɪnt] *adj* bizzarro(-a); (*old-fashioned*) antiquato(-a); grazioso(-a), pittoresco(-a)

quake [kweɪk] *vi* tremare ▷ *n abbr* = **earthquake**

qualification [kwɔlɪfɪ'keɪʃən] *n* (*degree etc*) qualifica, titolo; (*ability*) competenza, qualificazione *f*; (*limitation*) riserva, restrizione *f*

qualified ['kwɔlɪfaɪd] *adj* qualificato(-a); (*able*). **~ to** competente in, qualificato(-a) a; (*limited*) condizionato(-a)

qualify ['kwɔlɪfaɪ] *vt* abilitare; (*limit: statement*) modificare, precisare ▷ *vi* **to ~ (as)** qualificarsi (come); **to ~ (for)** acquistare i requisiti necessari (per); (*Sport*) qualificarsi (per *or* a)

quality ['kwɔlɪtɪ] *n* qualità *f inv*

qualm [kwɑːm] *n* dubbio; scrupolo

quantify ['kwɔntɪfaɪ] *vt* quantificare

quantity ['kwɔntɪtɪ] *n* quantità *f inv*

quarantine ['kwɔrntiːn] *n* quarantena

quarrel ['kwɔrl] *n* lite *f*, disputa ▷ *vi* litigare

quarry ['kwɔrɪ] *n* (*for stone*) cava; (*animal*) preda

quart [kwɔːt] *n* ≈ litro

quarter ['kwɔːtəʳ] *n* quarto; (*US: coin*) quarto di dollaro; (*of year*) trimestre *m*; (*district*) quartiere *m* ▷ *vt* dividere in quattro; (*Mil*) alloggiare; **~s** *npl* (*living quarters*) alloggio; (*Mil*) alloggi *mpl*, quadrato; **a ~ of an hour** un quarto d'ora; **quarter final** *n* quarto di finale; **quarterly** *adj* trimestrale ▷ *adv* trimestralmente

quartet(te) [kwɔː'tɛt] *n* quartetto

quartz [kwɔːts] *n* quarzo

quay [kiː] *n* (*also: ~side*) banchina

queasy ['kwiːzɪ] *adj* (*stomach*) delicato(-a); **to feel ~** aver la nausea

queen [kwiːn] *n* (*gen*) regina; (*Cards etc*) regina, donna

queer [kwɪəʳ] *adj* strano(-a), curioso(-a) ▷ *n* (*inf*) finocchio

quench [kwɛntʃ] *vt* **to ~ one's thirst** dissetarsi

query ['kwɪərɪ] *n* domanda, questione *f* ▷ *vt* mettere in questione

quest [kwɛst] *n* cerca, ricerca

question ['kwɛstʃən] *n* domanda, questione *f* ▷ *vt* (*person*) interrogare; (*plan, idea*) mettere in questione *or* in dubbio; **it's a ~ of doing** si tratta di fare; **beyond ~** fuori di dubbio; **out of the ~** fuori discussione, impossibile; **questionable** *adj* discutibile; **question mark** *n* punto interrogativo; **questionnaire** [kwɛstʃə'nɛəʳ] *n* questionario

queue [kjuː] (BRIT) *n* coda, fila ▷ *vi* fare la coda

quiche [kiːʃ] *n* torta salata a base di uova, formaggio, prosciutto o altro

quick [kwɪk] *adj* rapido(-a), veloce; (*reply*) pronto(-a); (*mind*) pronto(-a), acuto(-a) ▷ *n* **cut to the ~** (*fig*) toccato(-a) sul vivo; **be ~!** fa presto!; **quickly** *adv* rapidamente, velocemente

quid [kwɪd] (BRIT: *inf*) *n inv* sterlina

quiet ['kwaɪət] *adj* tranquillo(-a), quieto(-a); (*ceremony*) semplice ▷ *n* tranquillità, calma ▷ *vt, vi* (*US*) = **quieten**; **keep ~!** sta zitto!; **quieten** (*also:* **quieten down**) *vi* calmarsi, chetarsi ▷ *vt* calmare, chetare; **quietly** *adv* tranquillamente, calmamente; sommessamente

quilt [kwɪlt] *n* trapunta; (*continental quilt*) piumino

quirky ['kwəːkɪ] *adj* stravagante

quit [kwɪt] (*pt, pp* **quit** *or* **quitted**) *vt* mollare; (*premises*) lasciare, partire da ▷ *vi* (*give up*) mollare; (*resign*) dimettersi

quite [kwaɪt] *adv* (*rather*) assai; (*entirely*) completamente, del tutto; **I ~ understand** capisco perfettamente; **that's not ~ big enough** non è proprio sufficiente; **~ a few of them** non pochi di loro; **~ (so)!** esatto!

quits [kwɪts] *adj* **~ (with)** pari (con); **let's call it ~** adesso siamo pari

quiver ['kwɪvəʳ] *vi* tremare, fremere

quiz [kwɪz] *n* (*game*) quiz *m inv*; indovinello ▷ *vt* interrogare

quota ['kwəʊtə] *n* quota

quotation [kwəʊ'teɪʃən] *n* citazione *f*; (*of shares etc*) quotazione *f*; (*estimate*) preventivo; **quotation marks** *npl* virgolette *fpl*

quote [kwəʊt] *n* citazione *f* ▷ *vt* (*sentence*) citare; (*price*) dare, fissare; (*shares*) quotare ▷ *vi* **to ~ from** citare; **~s** *npl* = **quotation marks**

rabbi ['ræbaɪ] *n* rabbino

rabbit ['ræbɪt] *n* coniglio

rabies ['reɪbiːz] *n* rabbia

RAC (*BRIT*) *n abbr* = **Royal Automobile Club**

rac(c)oon [rə'kuːn] *n* procione *m*

race [reɪs] *n* razza; (*competition, rush*) corsa ▷ *vt* (*horse*) far correre ▷ *vi* correre; (*engine*) imballarsi; **race car** (*US*) *n* = **racing car**; **racecourse** *n* campo di corse, ippodromo; **racehorse** *n* cavallo da corsa; **racetrack** *n* pista

racial ['reɪʃl] *adj* razziale

racing ['reɪsɪŋ] *n* corsa; **racing car** (*BRIT*) *n* macchina da corsa; **racing driver** (*BRIT*) *n* corridore *m* automobilista

racism ['reɪsɪzəm] *n* razzismo; **racist** *adj, n* razzista *m/f*

rack [ræk] *n* rastrelliera; (*also*: **luggage ~**) rete *f*, portabagagli *m inv*; (*also*: **roof ~**) portabagagli; (*dish rack*) scolapiatti *m inv* ▷ *vt* **~ed by** torturato(-a) da; **to ~ one's brains** scervellarsi

racket ['rækɪt] *n* (*for tennis*) racchetta; (*noise*) fracasso; baccano; (*swindle*) imbroglio, truffa; (*organized crime*) racket *m inv*

racquet ['rækɪt] *n* racchetta

radar ['reɪdɑːʳ] *n* radar *m*

radiation [reɪdɪ'eɪʃən] *n* irradiamento;

(*radioactive*) radiazione *f*
radiator ['reɪdɪeɪtə'] *n* radiatore *m*
radical ['rædɪkl] *adj* radicale
radio ['reɪdɪəʊ] *n* radio *f inv*; **on the ~** alla
radio; **radioactive** [reɪdɪəʊ'æktɪv] *adj*
radioattivo(-a); **radio station** *n* stazione
f radio *inv*
radish ['rædɪʃ] *n* ravanello
RAF *n abbr* = **Royal Air Force**
raffle ['ræfl] *n* lotteria
raft [rɑːft] *n* zattera; (*also*: **life ~**) zattera di
salvataggio
rag [ræg] *n* straccio, cencio; (*pej*: *newspaper*)
giornalaccio, bandiera; (*for charity*)
iniziativa studentesca a scopo benefico; **~s** *npl*
(*torn clothes*) stracci *mpl*, brandelli *mpl*
rage [reɪdʒ] *n* (*fury*) collera, furia ▷ *vi*
(*person*) andare su tutte le furie; (*storm*)
infuriare; **it's all the ~** fa furore
ragged ['rægɪd] *adj* (*edge*) irregolare;
(*clothes*) logoro(-a); (*appearance*) pezzente
raid [reɪd] *n* (*Mil*) incursione *f*; (*criminal*)
rapina; (*by police*) irruzione *f* ▷ *vt* fare
un'incursione in; rapinare; fare irruzione in
rail [reɪl] *n* (*on stair*) ringhiera; (*on bridge*,
balcony) parapetto; (*of ship*) battagliola;
railcard *n* (*BRIT*) tessera di riduzione
ferroviaria; **railing(s)** *n(pl)* ringhiere *fpl*;
railroad (*US*) *n* = **railway**; **railway** (*BRIT*:
irreg) *n* ferrovia; **railway line** (*BRIT*) *n*
linea ferroviaria; **railway station** (*BRIT*) *n*
stazione *f* ferroviaria
rain [reɪn] *n* pioggia ▷ *vi* piovere; **in the ~**
sotto la pioggia; **it's ~ing** piove; **rainbow**
n arcobaleno; **raincoat** *n* impermeabile
m; **raindrop** *n* goccia di pioggia; **rainfall**
n pioggia; (*measurement*) piovosità;
rainforest *n* foresta pluviale; **rainy** *adj*
piovoso(-a)
raise [reɪz] *n* aumento ▷ *vt* (*lift*) alzare;
sollevare; (*increase*) aumentare; (*a protest*,
doubt, *question*) sollevare; (*cattle*, *family*)
allevare; (*crop*) coltivare; (*army*, *funds*)
raccogliere; (*loan*) ottenere; **to ~ one's**
voice alzare la voce
raisin ['reɪzn] *n* uva secca
rake [reɪk] *n* (*tool*) rastrello ▷ *vt* (*garden*)
rastrellare
rally ['rælɪ] *n* (*Pol etc*) riunione *f*; (*Aut*)
rally *m inv*; (*Tennis*) scambio ▷ *vt* riunire,
radunare ▷ *vi* (*sick person*, *Stock Exchange*)
riprendersi
RAM [ræm] *n abbr* (= *random access memory*)
memoria ad accesso casuale
ram [ræm] *n* montone *m*, ariete *m* ▷ *vt*
conficcare; (*crash into*) cozzare, sbattere
contro; percuotere; speronare
Ramadan [ræmə'dæn] *n*
Ramadan *m inv*

ramble ['ræmbl] *n* escursione *f* ▷ *vi*
(*pej*: *also*: **~ on**) divagare; **rambler** *n*
escursionista *m/f*; (*Bot*) rosa rampicante;
rambling *adj* (*speech*) sconnesso(-a);
(*house*) tutto(-a) a nicchie e corridoi; (*Bot*)
rampicante
ramp [ræmp] *n* rampa; **on/off ~** (*US Aut*)
raccordo di entrata/uscita
rampage [ræm'peɪdʒ] *n* **to go on the ~**
scatenarsi in modo violento
ran [ræn] *pt of* **run**
ranch [rɑːntʃ] *n* ranch *m inv*
random ['rændəm] *adj* fatto(-a) *or*
detto(-a) per caso; (*Comput*, *Math*) casuale
▷ *n* **at ~** a casaccio
rang [ræŋ] *pt of* **ring**
range [reɪndʒ] *n* (*of mountains*) catena;
(*of missile*, *voice*) portata; (*of proposals*,
products) gamma; (*Mil*: *also*: **shooting ~**)
campo di tiro; (*also*: **kitchen ~**) fornello,
cucina economica ▷ *vt* disporre ▷ *vi* **to**
~ over coprire; **to ~ from ... to** andare
da ... a
ranger ['reɪndʒə'] *n* guardia forestale
rank [ræŋk] *n* fila; (*status*, *Mil*) grado;
(*BRIT*: *also*: **taxi ~**) posteggio di taxi ▷ *vi*
to ~ among essere tra ▷ *adj* puzzolente;
vero(-a) e proprio(-a); **the ~ and file** (*fig*) la
gran massa
ransom ['rænsəm] *n* riscatto; **to hold sb**
to ~ (*fig*) esercitare pressione su qn
rant [rænt] *vi* vociare
rap [ræp] *vt* bussare a; picchiare su ▷ *n*
(*music*) rap *m inv*
rape [reɪp] *n* violenza carnale, stupro; (*Bot*)
ravizzone *m* ▷ *vt* violentare
rapid ['ræpɪd] *adj* rapido(-a); **rapidly** *adv*
rapidamente; **rapids** *npl* (*Geo*) rapida
rapist ['reɪpɪst] *n* violentatore *m*
rapport [ræ'pɔː'] *n* rapporto
rare [reə'] *adj* raro(-a); (*Culin*: *steak*) al
sangue; **rarely** ['reəlɪ] *adv* raramente
rash [ræʃ] *adj* imprudente, sconsiderato(-a)
▷ *n* (*Med*) eruzione *f*; (*of events etc*) scoppio
rasher ['ræʃə'] *n* fetta sottile (di lardo *or*
prosciutto)
raspberry ['rɑːzbərɪ] *n* lampone *m*
rat [ræt] *n* ratto
rate [reɪt] *n* (*proportion*) tasso, percentuale
f; (*speed*) velocità *f inv*; (*price*) tariffa ▷ *vt*
giudicare; stimare; **~s** *npl* (*BRIT*: *property*
tax) imposte *fpl* comunali; (*fees*) tariffe *fpl*;
to ~ sb/sth as valutare qn/qc come
rather ['rɑːðə'] *adv* piuttosto; **it's ~**
expensive è piuttosto caro; (*too*) è un po'
caro; **there's ~ a lot** ce n'è parecchio; **I**
would *or* **I'd ~ go** preferirei andare
rating ['reɪtɪŋ] *n* (*assessment*) valutazione *f*;
(*score*) punteggio di merito; **~s** *npl* (*Radio*,

_TV)_ indice _m_ di ascolto
ratio ['reɪʃɪəu] _n_ proporzione _f_, rapporto
ration ['ræʃən] _n (gen pl)_ razioni _fpl_ ▷ _vt_
  razionare; **~s** _npl_ razioni _fpl_
rational ['ræʃənl] _adj_ razionale,
  ragionevole; _(solution, reasoning)_
  logico(-a)
rattle ['rætl] _n_ tintinnio; _(louder)_ strepito;
  (for baby) sonaglino ▷ _vi_ risuonare,
  tintinnare; fare un rumore di ferraglia ▷ _vt_
  scuotere (con strepito)
rave [reɪv] _vi (in anger)_ infuriarsi; _(with_
  enthusiasm) andare in estasi; _(Med)_ delirare
  ▷ _n (BRIT: inf: party)_ rave _m inv_
raven ['reɪvən] _n_ corvo
ravine [rə'viːn] _n_ burrone _m_
raw [rɔ:] _adj (uncooked)_ crudo(-a); _(not_
  processed) greggio(-a); _(sore)_ vivo(-a);
  (inexperienced) inesperto(-a); _(weather, day)_
  gelido(-a)
ray [reɪ] _n_ raggio; **a ~ of hope** un barlume
  di speranza
razor ['reɪzə'] _n_ rasoio; **razor blade** _n_ lama
  di rasoio
Rd _abbr_ = **road**
re [ri:] _prep_ con riferimento a
RE _n abbr (BRIT Mil: = Royal Engineers)_ ≈ G.
  M. _(Genio Militare)_; _(BRIT)_ = **religious**
  education
reach [ri:tʃ] _n_ portata; _(of river etc)_ tratto
  ▷ _vt_ raggiungere; arrivare a ▷ _vi_ stendersi;
  out of/within ~ fuori/a portata di mano;
  within ~ of the shops/station vicino ai
  negozi/alla stazione; **reach out** _vt (hand)_
  allungare ▷ _vi_ **to ~ out for** stendere la
  mano per prendere
react [ri:'ækt] _vi_ reagire; **reaction** [-'ækʃə
  n] _n_ reazione _f_; **reactor** [ri:'æktə'] _n_
  reattore _m_
read [ri:d, _pt, pp_ rɛd] _(pt, pp_ **read**) _vi_ leggere
  ▷ _vt_ leggere; _(understand)_ intendere,
  interpretare; _(study)_ studiare; **read**
  out _vt_ leggere ad alta voce; **reader** _n_
  lettore(-trice); _(BRIT: at university)_ professore
  con funzioni preminenti di ricerca
readily ['rɛdɪlɪ] _adv_ volentieri; _(easily)_
  facilmente; _(quickly)_ prontamente
reading ['ri:dɪŋ] _n_ lettura; _(understanding)_
  interpretazione _f_; _(on instrument)_
  indicazione _f_
ready ['rɛdɪ] _adj_ pronto(-a); _(willing)_
  pronto(-a), disposto(-a); _(available)_
  disponibile ▷ _n_ **at the ~** _(Mil)_ pronto a
  sparare; **when will my photos be ~?**
  quando saranno pronte le mie foto?; **to**
  get ~ _vi_ prepararsi ▷ _vt_ preparare; **ready-**
  made _adj_ prefabbricato(-a); _(clothes)_
  confezionato(-a)
real [rɪəl] _adj_ reale; vero(-a); **in ~ terms**

in realtà; **real ale** _n_ birra ad effervescenza
  naturale; **real estate** _n_ beni _mpl_ immobili;
  realistic [-'lɪstɪk] _adj_ realistico(-a);
  reality [ri:'ælɪtɪ] _n_ realtà _f_
realization [rɪəlaɪ'zeɪʃən] _n_ presa di
  coscienza; realizzazione _f_
realize ['rɪəlaɪz] _vt (understand)_ rendersi
  conto di
really ['rɪəlɪ] _adv_ veramente, davvero; **~!**
  (indicating annoyance) oh, insomma!
realm [rɛlm] _n_ reame _m_, regno
Realtor® ['rɪəltɔ:'] _(US)_ _n_ agente _m_
  immobiliare
reappear [ri:ə'pɪə'] _vi_ ricomparire,
  riapparire
rear [rɪə'] _adj_ di dietro; _(Aut: wheel etc)_
  posteriore ▷ _n_ didietro, parte _f_ posteriore
  ▷ _vt (cattle, family)_ allevare ▷ _vi (also:_ **~ up**:
  animal) impennarsi
rearrange [ri:ə'reɪndʒ] _vt_ riordinare
rear: rear-view mirror ['rɪəvju:-] _n (Aut)_
  specchio retrovisore; **rear-wheel drive** _n_
  trazione _fpl_ posteriore
reason ['ri:zn] _n_ ragione _f_; _(cause, motive)_
  ragione, motivo ▷ _vi_ **to ~ with sb** far
  ragionare qn; **it stands to ~ that** è
  ovvio che; **reasonable** _adj_ ragionevole;
  (not bad) accettabile; **reasonably**
  adv ragionevolmente; **reasoning** _n_
  ragionamento
reassurance [ri:ə'ʃuərəns] _n_
  rassicurazione _f_
reassure [ri:ə'ʃuə'] _vt_ rassicurare; **to ~ sb**
  of rassicurare qn di _or_ su
rebate ['ri:beɪt] _n (on tax etc)_ sgravio
rebel [_n_ 'rɛbl, _vb_ rɪ'bɛl] _n_ ribelle _m/f_
  ▷ _vi_ ribellarsi; **rebellion** _n_ ribellione _f_;
  rebellious _adj_ ribelle
rebuild [ri:'bɪld] _vt irreg_ ricostruire
recall [rɪ'kɔ:l] _vt_ richiamare; _(remember)_
  ricordare, richiamare alla mente ▷ _n_
  richiamo
rec'd _abbr_ = **received**
receipt [rɪ'si:t] _n (document)_ ricevuta; _(act_
  of receiving) ricevimento; **~s** _npl (Comm)_
  introiti _mpl_; **can I have a ~, please?** posso
  avere una ricevuta, per favore?
receive [rɪ'si:v] _vt_ ricevere; _(guest)_
  ricevere, accogliere; **receiver** [rɪ'si:
  və'] _n (Tel)_ ricevitore _m_; _(Radio, TV)_
  apparecchio ricevente; _(of stolen goods)_
  ricettatore(-trice); _(Comm)_ curatore _m_
  fallimentare
recent ['ri:snt] _adj_ recente; **recently** _adv_
  recentemente
reception [rɪ'sɛpʃən] _n_ ricevimento;
  (welcome) accoglienza; _(TV etc)_ ricezione
  _f_; **reception desk** _n (in hotel)_ reception _f_
  inv; _(in hospital, at doctor's)_ accettazione _f_;

(in offices etc) portineria; **receptionist** n
receptionist m/f inv
recession [rɪ'sɛʃən] n recessione f
recharge [riː'tʃɑːdʒ] vt (battery) ricaricare
recipe ['rɛsɪpɪ] n ricetta
recipient [rɪ'sɪpɪənt] n beneficiario(-a); (of
letter) destinatario(-a)
recital [rɪ'saɪtl] n recital m inv
recite [rɪ'saɪt] vt (poem) recitare
reckless ['rɛkləs] adj (driver etc)
spericolato(-a); (spending) folle
reckon ['rɛkən] vt (count) calcolare; (think):
I ~ that … penso che …
reclaim [rɪ'kleɪm] vt (demand back)
richiedere, reclamare; (land) bonificare;
(materials) recuperare
recline [rɪ'klaɪn] vi stare sdraiato(-a)
recognition [rɛkəg'nɪʃən] n
riconoscimento; **transformed beyond ~**
irriconoscibile
recognize ['rɛkəgnaɪz] vt **to ~ (by/as)**
riconoscere (a or da/come)
recollection [rɛkə'lɛkʃən] n ricordo
recommend [rɛkə'mɛnd] vt
raccomandare; (advise) consigliare;
can you ~ a good restaurant? mi
può consigliare un buon ristorante?;
recommendation [rɛkəmən'deɪʃən] n
raccomandazione f; consiglio
reconcile ['rɛkənsaɪl] vt (two people)
riconciliare; (two facts) conciliare,
quadrare; **to ~ o.s. to** rassegnarsi a
reconsider [riː.kən'sɪdəʳ] vt riconsiderare
reconstruct [riː.kən'strʌkt] vt ricostruire
record [n 'rɛkɔːd, vb rɪ'kɔːd] n ricordo,
documento; (of meeting etc) nota, verbale
m; (register) registro, (file) pratica, dossier
m inv; (Comput) record m inv; (also: **criminal
~**) fedina penale sporca; (Mus: disc) disco;
(Sport) record m inv, primato ▷ vt (set
down) prendere nota di, registrare; (Mus:
song etc) registrare; **in ~ time** a tempo di
record; **off the ~** adj ufficioso(-a) ▷ adv
ufficiosamente; **recorded delivery** (BRIT)
n (Post): **recorded delivery letter** etc
lettera etc raccomandata; **recorder** n
(Mus) flauto diritto; **recording** n (Mus)
registrazione f; **record player** n giradischi
m inv
recount [rɪ'kaunt] vt raccontare, narrare
recover [rɪ'kʌvəʳ] vt ricuperare ▷ vi **to ~
(from)** riprendersi (da); **recovery** [rɪ'kʌvərɪ]
n ricupero; ristabilimento; ripresa

> Be careful not to translate *recover* by
> the Italian word *ricoverare*.

recreate [riː.krɪ'eɪt] vt ricreare
recreation [rɛkrɪ'eɪʃən] n ricreazione f;
svago; **recreational drug** [rɛkrɪ'eɪʃənl-] n
sostanza stupefacente usata a scopo ricreativo;

recreational vehicle (us) n camper m inv
recruit [rɪ'kruːt] n recluta; (in company)
nuovo(-a) assunto(-a) ▷ vt reclutare;
recruitment n reclutamento
rectangle ['rɛktæŋgl] n rettangolo;
rectangular [-'tæŋgjuləʳ] adj
rettangolare
rectify ['rɛktɪfaɪ] vt (error) rettificare;
(omission) riparare
rector ['rɛktəʳ] n (Rel) parroco (anglicano)
recur [rɪ'kəːʳ] vi riaccadere; (symptoms)
ripresentarsi; **recurring** adj (Math)
periodico(-a)
recyclable [riː'saɪkləbl] adj riciclabile
recycle [riː'saɪkl] vt riciclare
recycling [riː'saɪklɪŋ] n riciclaggio
red [rɛd] n rosso; (Pol: pej) rosso(-a) ▷ adj
rosso(-a); **in the ~** (account) scoperto;
(business) in deficit; **Red Cross** n Croce f
Rossa; **redcurrant** n ribes m inv
redeem [rɪ'diːm] vt (debt) riscattare; (sth in
pawn) ritirare; (fig, also Rel) redimere
red: red-haired [-'hɛəd] adj dai capelli
rossi; **redhead** ['rɛdhɛd] n rosso(-a);
red-hot adj arroventato(-a); **red light** n
to go through a red light (Aut) passare
col rosso; **red-light district** ['rɛdlaɪt-] n
quartiere m a luci rosse; **red meat** n carne
f rossa
reduce [rɪ'djuːs] vt ridurre; (lower)
ridurre, abbassare; **"~ speed now"** (Aut)
"rallentare"; **at a ~d price** scontato(-a);
reduced adj (decreased) ridotto(-a); **at
a reduced price** a prezzo ribassato or
ridotto; **"greatly reduced prices"** "grandi
ribassi"; **reduction** [rɪ'dʌkʃən] n riduzione
f; (of price) ribasso; (discount) sconto;
**is there a reduction for children/
students?** ci sono riduzioni per i bambini/
gli studenti?
redundancy [rɪ'dʌndənsɪ] n
licenziamento
redundant [rɪ'dʌndnt] adj (worker)
licenziato(-a); (detail, object) superfluo(-a);
to be made ~ essere licenziato (per
eccesso di personale)
reed [riːd] n (Bot) canna; (Mus: of clarinet
etc) ancia
reef [riːf] n (at sea) scogliera
reel [riːl] n bobina, rocchetto; (Fishing)
mulinello; (Cinema) rotolo; (dance) danza
veloce scozzese ▷ vi (sway) barcollare
ref [rɛf] (inf) n abbr (= referee) arbitro
refectory [rɪ'fɛktərɪ] n refettorio
refer [rɪ'fəːʳ] vt **to ~ sth to** (dispute,
decision) deferire qc a; **to ~ sb to** (inquirer,
Med: patient) indirizzare qn a; (reader: to
text) rimandare qn a ▷ vi **~ to** (allude to)
accennare a; (consult) rivolgersi a

r

referee [rɛfə'riː] n arbitro; (BRIT: for job application) referenza ▷ vt arbitrare

reference ['rɛfrəns] n riferimento; (mention) menzione f, allusione f; (for job application) referenza; **with ~ to** (Comm: in letter) in or con riferimento a; **reference number** n numero di riferimento

refill [vb riː'fɪl, n 'riːfɪl] vt riempire di nuovo; (pen, lighter etc) ricaricare ▷ n (for pen etc) ricambio

refine [rɪ'faɪn] vt raffinare; **refined** adj (person, taste) raffinato(-a); **refinery** n raffineria

reflect [rɪ'flɛkt] vt (light, image) riflettere; (fig) rispecchiare ▷ vi (think) riflettere, considerare; **it ~s badly/well on him** si ripercuote su di lui in senso negativo/positivo; **reflection** [-'flɛkʃən] n riflessione f, (image) riflesso; (criticism): **reflection on** giudizio su; attacco a; **on reflection** pensandoci sopra

reflex ['riːflɛks] adj riflesso(-a) ▷ n riflesso

reform [rɪ'fɔːm] n (of sinner etc) correzione f; (of law etc) riforma ▷ vt correggere; riformare

refrain [rɪ'freɪn] vi **to ~ from doing** trattenersi dal fare ▷ n ritornello

refresh [rɪ'frɛʃ] vt rinfrescare; (food, sleep) ristorare; **refreshing** adj (drink) rinfrescante; (sleep) riposante, ristoratore(-trice); **refreshments** npl rinfreschi mpl

refrigerator [rɪ'frɪdʒəreɪtə'] n frigorifero

refuel [riː'fjuəl] vi far rifornimento (di carburante)

refuge ['rɛfjuːdʒ] n rifugio; **to take ~ in** rifugiarsi in; **refugee** [rɛfju'dʒiː] n rifugiato(-a), profugo(-a)

refund [n 'riːfʌnd, vb rɪ'fʌnd] n rimborso ▷ vt rimborsare

refurbish [riː'fəːbɪʃ] vt rimettere a nuovo

refusal [rɪ'fjuːzəl] n rifiuto; **to have first ~ on** avere il diritto d'opzione su

refuse [n 'rɛfjuːs, vb rɪ'fjuːz] n rifiuti mpl ▷ vt, vi rifiutare; **to ~ to do** rifiutare di fare

regain [rɪ'geɪn] vt riguadagnare; riacquistare, ricuperare

regard [rɪ'gɑːd] n riguardo, stima ▷ vt considerare, stimare; **to give one's ~s to** porgere i suoi saluti a; **"with kindest ~s"** "cordiali saluti"; **regarding** prep riguardo a, per quanto riguarda; **regardless** adv lo stesso; **regardless of** a dispetto di, nonostante

regenerate [rɪ'dʒɛnəreɪt] vt rigenerare

reggae ['rɛgeɪ] n reggae m

regiment ['rɛdʒɪmənt] n reggimento

region ['riːdʒən] n regione f; **in the ~ of** (fig) all'incirca di; **regional** adj regionale

register ['rɛdʒɪstə'] n registro; (also: **electoral ~**) lista elettorale ▷ vt registrare; (vehicle) immatricolare; (letter) assicurare; (instrument) segnare ▷ vi iscriversi; (at hotel) firmare il registro; (make impression) entrare in testa; **registered** (BRIT) adj (letter) assicurato(-a)

registrar ['rɛdʒɪstrɑː'] n ufficiale m di stato civile; segretario

registration [rɛdʒɪs'treɪʃən] n (act) registrazione f; iscrizione f; (Aut: also: **~ number**) numero di targa

registry office (BRIT) n anagrafe f; **to get married in a ~** ≈ sposarsi in municipio

regret [rɪ'grɛt] n rimpianto, rincrescimento ▷ vt rimpiangere; **regrettable** adj deplorevole

regular ['rɛgjulə'] adj regolare; (usual) abituale, normale; (soldier) dell'esercito regolare ▷ n (client etc) cliente m/f abituale; **regularly** adv regolarmente

regulate ['rɛgjuleɪt] vt regolare; **regulation** [-'leɪʃən] n regolazione f; (rule) regola, regolamento

rehabilitation ['riːhəbɪlɪ'teɪʃən] n (of offender) riabilitazione f; (of disabled) riadattamento

rehearsal [rɪ'həːsəl] n prova

rehearse [rɪ'həːs] vt provare

reign [reɪn] n regno ▷ vi regnare

reimburse [riːɪm'bəːs] vt rimborsare

rein [reɪn] n (for horse) briglia

reincarnation [riːɪnkɑː'neɪʃən] n reincarnazione f

reindeer ['reɪndɪə'] n inv renna

reinforce [riːɪn'fɔːs] vt rinforzare; **reinforcements** npl (Mil) rinforzi mpl

reinstate [riːɪn'steɪt] vt reintegrare

reject [n 'riːdʒɛkt, vb rɪ'dʒɛkt] n (Comm) scarto ▷ vt rifiutare, respingere; (Comm: goods) scartare; **rejection** [rɪ'dʒɛkʃən] n rifiuto

rejoice [rɪ'dʒɔɪs] vi **to ~ (at or over)** provare diletto in

relate [rɪ'leɪt] vt (tell) raccontare; (connect) collegare ▷ vi **to ~ to** (connect) riferirsi a; (get on with) stabilire un rapporto con; **relating to** che riguarda, rispetto a; **related** adj **related (to)** imparentato(-a) (con); collegato(-a) or connesso(-a) (a)

relation [rɪ'leɪʃən] n (person) parente m/f; (link) rapporto, relazione f; **~s** npl (relatives) parenti mpl; **relationship** n rapporto; (personal ties) rapporti mpl, relazioni fpl; (also: **family relationship**) legami mpl di parentela

relative ['rɛlətɪv] n parente m/f ▷ adj relativo(-a); (respective) rispettivo(-a); **relatively** adv relativamente; (fairly, *rather*) abbastanza

relax [rɪ'læks] *vi* rilasciarsi; (*person: unwind*) rilassarsi ▷ *vt* rilasciare; (*mind, person*) rilassare; **relaxation** [riː'læk'seɪʃən] *n* rilasciamento; rilassamento; (*entertainment*) ricreazione *f*, svago; **relaxed** *adj* rilassato(-a); **relaxing** *adj* rilassante

relay ['riːleɪ] *n* (*Sport*) corsa a staffetta ▷ *vt* (*message*) trasmettere

release [rɪ'liːs] *n* (*from prison*) rilascio; (*from obligation*) liberazione *f*; (*of gas etc*) emissione *f*; (*of film etc*) distribuzione *f*; (*record*) disco; (*device*) disinnesto ▷ *vt* (*prisoner*) rilasciare; (*from obligation, wreckage etc*) liberare; (*book, film*) fare uscire; (*news*) rendere pubblico(-a); (*gas etc*) emettere; (*Tech: catch, spring etc*) disinnestare

relegate ['relǝgeɪt] *vt* relegare; (BRIT Sport): **to be ~d** essere retrocesso(-a)

relent [rɪ'lent] *vi* cedere; **relentless** *adj* implacabile

relevant ['relǝvǝnt] *adj* pertinente; (*chapter*) in questione; **~ to** pertinente a

▮ Be careful not to translate *relevant* by the Italian word *rilevante*.

reliable [rɪ'laɪǝbl] *adj* (*person, firm*) fidato(-a), che dà affidamento; (*method*) sicuro(-a); (*machine*) affidabile

relic ['relɪk] *n* (*Rel*) reliquia; (*of the past*) resto

relief [rɪ'liːf] *n* (*from pain, anxiety*) sollievo; (*help, supplies*) soccorsi *mpl*; (*Art, Geo*) rilievo

relieve [rɪ'liːv] *vt* (*pain, patient*) sollevare; (*bring help*) soccorrere; (*take over from: gen*) sostituire; (: *guard*) rilevare; **to ~ sb of sth** (*load*) alleggerire qn di qc; **to ~ o.s.** fare i propri bisogni; **relieved** *adj* sollevato(-a); **to be relieved that ...** essere sollevato(-a) (dal fatto) che ...; **I'm relieved to hear it** mi hai tolto un peso con questa notizia

religion [rɪ'lɪdʒǝn] *n* religione *f*

religious [rɪ'lɪdʒǝs] *adj* religioso(-a); **religious education** *n* religione *f*

relish ['relɪʃ] *n* (*Culin*) condimento; (*enjoyment*) gran piacere *m* ▷ *vt* (*food etc*) godere; **to ~ doing** adorare fare

relocate ['riːlǝu'keɪt] *vt* trasferire ▷ *vi* trasferirsi

reluctance [rɪ'lʌktǝns] *n* riluttanza

reluctant [rɪ'lʌktǝnt] *adj* riluttante, mal disposto(-a); **reluctantly** *adv* di mala voglia, a malincuore

rely [rɪ'laɪ]: **to ~ on** *vt fus* contare su; (*be dependent*) dipendere da

remain [rɪ'meɪn] *vi* restare, rimanere; **remainder** *n* resto; (*Comm*) rimanenza; **remaining** *adj* che rimane; **remains** *npl*

resti *mpl*

remand [rɪ'mɑːnd] *n* **on ~** in detenzione preventiva ▷ *vt* **to ~ in custody** rinviare in carcere; trattenere a disposizione della legge

remark [rɪ'mɑːk] *n* osservazione *f* ▷ *vt* osservare, dire; **remarkable** *adj* notevole; eccezionale

remarry [riː'mærɪ] *vi* risposarsi

remedy ['remǝdɪ] *n* **~ (for)** rimedio (per) ▷ *vt* rimediare a

remember [rɪ'membǝ'] *vt* ricordare, ricordarsi di; **~ me to him** salutalo da parte mia; **Remembrance Day** [rɪ'membrǝns-] *n* 11 novembre, *giorno della commemorazione dei caduti in guerra*

● **REMEMBRANCE DAY**
●
● In Gran Bretagna, il **Remembrance**
● **Day** è un giorno di commemorazione
● dei caduti in guerra. Si celebra ogni anno
● la domenica più vicina all'11 novembre,
● anniversario della firma dell'armistizio
● con la Germania nel 1918.

remind [rɪ'maɪnd] *vt* **to ~ sb of sth** ricordare qc a qn; **to ~ sb to do** ricordare a qn di fare; **reminder** *n* richiamo; (*note etc*) promemoria *m inv*

reminiscent [remɪ'nɪsnt] *adj* **~ of** che fa pensare a, che richiama

remnant ['remnǝnt] *n* resto, avanzo

remorse [rɪ'mɔːs] *n* rimorso

remote [rɪ'mǝut] *adj* remoto(-a), lontano(-a); (*person*) distaccato(-a); **remote control** *n* telecomando; **remotely** *adv* remotamente; (*slightly*) vagamente

removal [rɪ'muːvǝl] *n* (*taking away*) rimozione *f*; soppressione *f*; (BRIT: *from house*) trasloco; (*from office: dismissal*) destituzione *f*; (*Med*) ablazione *f*; **removal man** (*irreg*) *n* (BRIT) addetto ai traslochi; **removal van** (BRIT) *n* furgone *m* per traslochi

remove [rɪ'muːv] *vt* togliere, rimuovere; (*employee*) destituire; (*stain*) far sparire; (*doubt, abuse*) sopprimere, eliminare

Renaissance [rɪ'neɪsɑːns] *n* **the ~** il Rinascimento

rename [riː'neɪm] *vt* ribattezzare

render ['rendǝ'] *vt* rendere

rendezvous ['rɒndɪvuː] *n* appuntamento; (*place*) luogo d'incontro; (*meeting*) incontro

renew [rɪ'njuː] *vt* rinnovare; (*negotiations*) riprendere

renovate ['renǝveɪt] *vt* rinnovare; (*art work*) restaurare

r

renowned [rɪ'naund] *adj* rinomato(-a)
rent [rɛnt] *n* affitto ▷ *vt* (*take for rent*)
prendere in affitto; (*also:* **~ out**) dare in
affitto; **rental** *n* (*for television, car*) fitto
reorganize [ri:'ɔ:gənaɪz] *vt* riorganizzare
rep [rɛp] *n abbr* (*Comm:* = *representative*)
rappresentante *m/f*; (*Theatre:* = *repertory*)
teatro di repertorio
repair [rɪ'pɛəʳ] *n* riparazione *f* ▷ *vt*
riparare; **in good/bad ~** in buone/cattive
condizioni; **where can I get this ~ed?**
dove lo posso far riparare?; **repair kit** *n*
corredo per riparazioni
repay [ri:'peɪ] (*irreg*) *vt* (*money, creditor*)
rimborsare, ripagare; (*sb's efforts*)
ricompensare; (*favour*) ricambiare;
repayment *n* pagamento; rimborso
repeat [rɪ'pi:t] *n* (*Radio, TV*) replica ▷ *vt*
ripetere; (*pattern*) riprodurre; (*promise,
attack, also Comm: order*) rinnovare
▷ *vi* ripetere; **can you ~ that, please?**
può ripetere, per favore?; **repeatedly**
adv ripetutamente, spesso; **repeat
prescription** *n* (BRIT) ricetta ripetibile
repellent [rɪ'pɛlənt] *adj* repellente ▷ *n*
insect ~ prodotto *m* anti-insetti *inv*
repercussions [ri:pə'kʌʃənz] *npl*
ripercussioni *fpl*
repetition [rɛpɪ'tɪʃən] *n* ripetizione *f*
repetitive [rɪ'pɛtɪtɪv] *adj* (*movement*) che
si ripete; (*work*) monotono(-a); (*speech*)
pieno(-a) di ripetizioni
replace [rɪ'pleɪs] *vt* (*put back*) rimettere
a posto; (*take the place of*) sostituire;
replacement *n* rimessa; sostituzione *f*;
(*person*) sostituto(-a)
replay ['ri:pleɪ] *n* (*of match*) partita
ripetuta; (*of tape, film*) replay *m inv*
replica ['rɛplɪkə] *n* replica, copia
reply [rɪ'plaɪ] *n* risposta ▷ *vi* rispondere
report [rɪ'pɔ:t] *n* rapporto; (*Press etc*)
cronaca; (BRIT: *also:* **school ~**) pagella; (*of
gun*) sparo ▷ *vt* riportare; (*Press etc*) fare
una cronaca su; (*bring to notice: occurrence*)
segnalare; (: *person*) denunciare ▷ *vi* (*make
a report*) fare un rapporto (*or* una cronaca);
(*present o.s.*): **to ~ (to sb)** presentarsi (a
qn); **I'd like to ~ a theft** vorrei denunciare
un furto; **report card** (US, Scottish) *n*
pagella; **reportedly** *adv* stando a quanto
si dice; **he reportedly told them to
...** avrebbe detto loro di ...; **reporter** *n*
reporter *m inv*
represent [rɛprɪ'zɛnt] *vt*
rappresentare; **representation** [-'teɪʃə
n] *n* rappresentazione *f*; (*petition*)
rappresentanza; **representative** *n*
rappresentante *m/f*; (US Pol) deputato(-a)
▷ *adj* rappresentativo(-a)

repress [rɪ'prɛs] *vt* reprimere; **repression**
[-'prɛʃən] *n* repressione *f*
reprimand ['rɛprɪmɑ:nd] *n* rimprovero
▷ *vt* rimproverare
reproduce [ri:prə'dju:s] *vt* riprodurre ▷ *vi*
riprodursi; **reproduction** [-'dʌkʃən] *n*
riproduzione *f*
reptile ['rɛptaɪl] *n* rettile *m*
republic [rɪ'pʌblɪk] *n* repubblica;
republican *adj*, *n* repubblicano(-a)
reputable ['rɛpjutəbl] *adj* di buona
reputazione; (*occupation*) rispettabile
reputation [rɛpju'teɪʃən] *n* reputazione *f*
request [rɪ'kwɛst] *n* domanda; (*formal*)
richiesta ▷ *vt* **to ~ (of** *or* **from sb)** chiedere
(a qn); **request stop** (BRIT) *n* (*for bus*)
fermata facoltativa *or* a richiesta
require [rɪ'kwaɪəʳ] *vt* (*need: person*) aver
bisogno di; (: *thing, situation*) richiedere;
(*want*) volere; esigere; (*order*): **to ~ sb to do
sth** ordinare a qn di fare qc; **requirement**
n esigenza; bisogno; requisito
resat [ri:'sæt] *pt, pp of* **resit**
rescue ['rɛskju:] *n* salvataggio; (*help*)
soccorso ▷ *vt* salvare
research [rɪ'sə:tʃ] *n* ricerca, ricerche *fpl*
▷ *vt* fare ricerche su
resemblance [rɪ'zɛmbləns] *n* somiglianza
resemble [rɪ'zɛmbl] *vt* assomigliare a
resent [rɪ'zɛnt] *vt* risentirsi di; **resentful**
adj pieno(-a) di risentimento; **resentment**
n risentimento
reservation [rɛzə'veɪʃən] *n* (*booking*)
prenotazione *f*; (*doubt*) dubbio; (*protected
area*) riserva; (BRIT: *on road: also:* **central ~**)
spartitraffico *m inv*; **reservation desk** (US)
n (*in hotel*) reception *f inv*
reserve [rɪ'zə:v] *n* riserva ▷ *vt* (*seats etc*)
prenotare; **reserved** *adj* (*shy*) riservato(-a)
reservoir ['rɛzəvwɑ:ʳ] *n* serbatoio
residence ['rɛzɪdəns] *n* residenza;
residence permit (BRIT) *n* permesso di
soggiorno
resident ['rɛzɪdənt] *n* residente *m/f*; (*in
hotel*) cliente *m/f* fisso(-a) ▷ *adj* residente;
(*doctor*) fisso(-a); (*course, college*) a tempo
pieno con pernottamento; **residential** [-
'dɛnʃəl] *adj* di residenza; (*area*) residenziale
residue ['rɛzɪdju:] *n* resto; (*Chem, Physics*)
residuo
resign [rɪ'zaɪn] *vt* (*one's post*) dimettersi da
▷ *vi* dimettersi; **to ~ o.s. to** rassegnarsi a;
resignation [rɛzɪg'neɪʃən] *n* dimissioni
fpl; rassegnazione *f*
resin ['rɛzɪn] *n* resina
resist [rɪ'zɪst] *vt* resistere a; **resistance** *n*
resistenza
resit ['ri:sɪt] (BRIT) (*pt, pp* **resat**) *vt* (*exam*)
ripresentarsi a; (*subject*) ridare l'esame di

▷ *n* **he's got his French ~ on Friday** deve ridare l'esame di francese venerdì

resolution [rɛzə'luːʃən] *n* risoluzione *f*

resolve [rɪ'zɔlv] *n* risoluzione *f* ▷ *vi* (*decide*): **to ~ to do** decidere di fare ▷ *vt* (*problem*) risolvere

resort [rɪ'zɔːt] *n* (*town*) stazione *f*; (*recourse*) ricorso ▷ *vi* **to ~ to** aver ricorso a; **in the last ~** come ultima risorsa

resource [rɪ'sɔːs] *n* risorsa; **resourceful** *adj* pieno(-a) di risorse, intraprendente

respect [rɪs'pɛkt] *n* rispetto ▷ *vt* rispettare; **respectable** *adj* rispettabile; **respectful** *adj* rispettoso(-a); **respective** [rɪs'pɛktɪv] *adj* rispettivo(-a); **respectively** *adv* rispettivamente

respite ['rɛspaɪt] *n* respiro, tregua

respond [rɪs'pɔnd] *vi* rispondere; **response** [rɪs'pɔns] *n* risposta

responsibility [rɪspɔnsɪ'bɪlɪtɪ] *n* responsabilità *f inv*

responsible [rɪs'pɔnsɪbl] *adj* (*trustworthy*) fidato(-a); (*job*) di (grande) responsabilità; **~ (for)** responsabile (di); **responsibly** *adv* responsabilmente

responsive [rɪs'pɔnsɪv] *adj* che reagisce

rest [rɛst] *n* riposo; (*stop*) sosta, pausa; (*Mus*) pausa; (*object: to support sth*) appoggio, sostegno; (*remainder*) resto, avanzi *mpl* ▷ *vi* riposarsi; (*remain*) rimanere, restare; (*be supported*): **to ~ on** appoggiarsi su ▷ *vt* (*far*) riposare; (*lean*): **to ~ sth on/against** appoggiare qc su/ contro; **the ~ of them** gli altri; **it ~s with him to decide** sta a lui decidere

restaurant ['rɛstərɔn] *n* ristorante *m*; **restaurant car** (*BRIT*) *n* vagone *m* ristorante

restless ['rɛstlɪs] *adj* agitato(-a), irrequieto(-a)

restoration [rɛstə'reɪʃən] *n* restauro; restituzione *f*

restore [rɪ'stɔː*ʳ*] *vt* (*building, to power*) restaurare; (*sth stolen*) restituire; (*peace, health*) ristorare

restrain [rɪs'treɪn] *vt* (*feeling, growth*) contenere, frenare; (*person*): **to ~ (from doing)** trattenere (dal fare); **restraint** *n* (*restriction*) limitazione *f*; (*moderation*) ritegno; (*of style*) contenutezza

restrict [rɪs'trɪkt] *vt* restringere, limitare; **restriction** [-kʃən] *n* **restriction (on)** restrizione *f* (di), limitazione *f*

rest room (*US*) *n* toletta

restructure [riː'strʌktʃəʳ] *vt* ristrutturare

result [rɪ'zʌlt] *n* risultato ▷ *vi* **to ~ in** avere per risultato; **as a ~ of** in or di conseguenza a, in seguito a

resume [rɪ'zjuːm] *vt, vi* (*work, journey*) riprendere

résumé ['reɪzjumeɪ] *n* riassunto; (*US*) curriculum *m inv* vitae

resuscitate [rɪ'sʌsɪteɪt] *vt* (*Med*) risuscitare

retail ['riːteɪl] *adj, adv* al minuto ▷ *vt* vendere al minuto; **retailer** *n* commerciante *m/f* al minuto, dettagliante *m/f*

retain [rɪ'teɪn] *vt* (*keep*) tenere, serbare

retaliation [rɪtælɪ'eɪʃən] *n* rappresaglie *fpl*

retarded [rɪ'tɑːdɪd] *adj* ritardato(-a)

retire [rɪ'taɪəʳ] *vi* (*give up work*) andare in pensione; (*withdraw*) ritirarsi, andarsene; (*go to bed*) andare a letto, ritirarsi; **retired** *adj* (*person*) pensionato(-a); **retirement** *n* pensione *f*; (*act*) pensionamento

retort [rɪ'tɔːt] *vi* rimbeccare

retreat [rɪ'triːt] *n* ritirata; (*place*) rifugio ▷ *vi* battere in ritirata

retrieve [rɪ'triːv] *vt* (*sth lost*) ricuperare, ritrovare; (*situation, honour*) salvare; (*error, loss*) rimediare a

retrospect ['rɛtrəspɛkt] *n* **in ~** guardando indietro; **retrospective** [-'spɛktɪv] *adj* retrospettivo(-a); (*law*) retroattivo(-a)

return [rɪ'təːn] *n* (*going or coming back*) ritorno; (*of sth stolen etc*) restituzione *f*; (*Finance: from land, shares*) profitto, reddito ▷ *cpd* (*journey, match*) di ritorno; (*BRIT: ticket*) di andata e ritorno ▷ *vi* tornare, ritornare ▷ *vt* rendere, restituire; (*bring back*) riportare; (*send back*) mandare indietro; (*put back*) rimettere; (*Pol: candidate*) eleggere; **~s** *npl* (*Comm*) incassi *mpl*; profitti *mpl*; **in ~ (for)** in cambio (di); **by ~ of post** a stretto giro di posta; **many happy ~s (of the day)!** cento di questi giorni!; **return ticket** *n* (*esp BRIT*) biglietto di andata e ritorno

reunion [riː'juːnɪən] *n* riunione *f*

reunite [riːjuː'naɪt] *vt* riunire

revamp ['riː'væmp] *vt* (*firm*) riorganizzare

reveal [rɪ'viːl] *vt* (*make known*) rivelare, svelare; (*display*) rivelare, mostrare; **revealing** *adj* rivelatore(-trice); (*dress*) scollato(-a)

revel ['rɛvl] *vi* **to ~ in sth/in doing** dilettarsi di qc/a fare

revelation [rɛvə'leɪʃən] *n* rivelazione *f*

revenge [rɪ'vɛndʒ] *n* vendetta ▷ *vt* vendicare; **to take ~ on** vendicarsi di

revenue ['rɛvənjuː] *n* reddito

Reverend ['rɛvərənd] *adj* (*in titles*) reverendo(-a)

reversal [rɪ'vəːsl] *n* capovolgimento

reverse [rɪ'vəːs] *n* contrario, opposto; (*back, defeat*) rovescio; (*Aut: also:* **~ gear**) marcia indietro ▷ *adj* (*order, direction*) contrario(-a), opposto(-a) ▷ vt (turn) invertire, rivoltare; (change) capovolgere, rovesciare; (Law: judgment) cassare; (car) fare marcia indietro con ▷ vi (BRIT Aut, person etc) fare marcia indietro; **reverse-charge call** [rɪ'vəːstʃɑːdʒ-] (BRIT) n (Tel) telefonata con addebito al ricevente; **reversing lights** (BRIT) npl (Aut) luci fpl per la retromarcia

revert [rɪ'vəːt] vi **to ~ to** tornare a

review [rɪ'vjuː] n rivista; (of book, film) recensione f; (of situation) esame m ▷ vt passare in rivista; fare la recensione di; fare il punto di

revise [rɪ'vaɪz] vt (manuscript) rivedere, correggere; (opinion) emendare, modificare; (study: subject, notes) ripassare; **revision** [rɪ'vɪʒən] n revisione f; ripasso

revival [rɪ'vaɪvəl] n ripresa; ristabilimento; (of faith) risveglio

revive [rɪ'vaɪv] vt (person) rianimare; (custom) far rivivere; (hope, courage, economy) ravvivare; (play, fashion) riesumare ▷ vi (person) rianimarsi; (hope) ravvivarsi; (activity) riprendersi

revolt [rɪ'vəult] n rivolta, ribellione f ▷ vi rivoltarsi, ribellarsi ▷ vt (far) rivoltare; **revolting** adj ripugnante

revolution [rɛvə'luːʃən] n rivoluzione f; (of wheel etc) rivoluzione, giro; **revolutionary** adj, n rivoluzionario(-a)

revolve [rɪ'vɔlv] vi girare

revolver [rɪ'vɔlvər] n rivoltella

reward [rɪ'wɔːd] n ricompensa, premio ▷ vt **to ~ (for)** ricompensare (per); **rewarding** adj (fig) gratificante

rewind [riː'waɪnd] (irreg) vt (watch) ricaricare; (ribbon etc) riavvolgere

rewrite [riː'raɪt] vt irreg riscrivere

rheumatism ['ruːmətɪzəm] n reumatismo

rhinoceros [raɪ'nɔsərəs] n rinoceronte m

rhubarb ['ruːbɑːb] n rabarbaro

rhyme [raɪm] n rima; (verse) poesia

rhythm ['rɪðm] n ritmo

rib [rɪb] n (Anat) costola ▷ vt (tease) punzecchiare

ribbon ['rɪbən] n nastro; **in ~s** (torn) a brandelli

rice [raɪs] n riso; **rice pudding** n budino di riso

rich [rɪtʃ] adj ricco(-a); (clothes) sontuoso(-a); (abundant): **~ in** ricco(-a) di

rid [rɪd] (pt, pp **rid**) vt **to ~ sb of** sbarazzare or liberare qn di; **to get ~ of** sbarazzarsi di

riddle ['rɪdl] n (puzzle) indovinello ▷ vt **to be ~d with** (holes) essere crivellato(-a) di; (doubts) essere pieno(-a) di

ride [raɪd] (pt **rode**, pp **ridden**) n (on horse)

cavalcata; (outing) passeggiata; (distance covered) cavalcata; corsa ▷ vi (as sport) cavalcare; (go somewhere: on horse, bicycle) andare (a cavallo or in bicicletta etc); (journey: on bicycle, motorcycle, bus) andare, viaggiare ▷ vt (a horse) montare, cavalcare; **to take sb for a ~** (fig) prendere in giro qn; fregare qn; **to ~ a horse/bicycle/camel** montare a cavallo/in bicicletta/in groppa a un cammello; **rider** n cavalcatore(-trice); (in race) fantino; (on bicycle) ciclista m/f; (on motorcycle) motociclista m/f

ridge [rɪdʒ] n (of hill) cresta; (of roof) colmo; (on object) riga (in rilievo)

ridicule ['rɪdɪkjuːl] n ridicolo; scherno ▷ vt mettere in ridicolo; **ridiculous** [rɪ'dɪkjuləs] adj ridicolo(-a)

riding ['raɪdɪŋ] n equitazione f; **riding school** n scuola d'equitazione

rife [raɪf] adj diffuso(-a); **to be ~ with** abbondare di

rifle ['raɪfl] n carabina ▷ vt vuotare

rift [rɪft] n fessura, crepatura; (fig: disagreement) incrinatura, disaccordo

rig [rɪg] n (also: **oil ~**: on land) derrick m inv; (: at sea) piattaforma di trivellazione ▷ vt (election etc) truccare

right [raɪt] adj giusto(-a); (suitable) appropriato(-a); (not left) destro(-a) ▷ n giusto; (title, claim) diritto; (not left) destra ▷ adv (answer) correttamente; (not on the left) a destra ▷ vt raddrizzare; (fig) riparare ▷ excl bene!; **to be ~** (person) aver ragione; (answer) essere giusto(-a) or corretto(-a); **by ~s** di diritto; **on the ~** a destra; **to be in the ~** aver ragione, essere nel giusto; **~ now** proprio adesso; subito; **~ away** subito; **right angle** n angolo retto; **rightful** adj (heir) legittimo(-a); **right-hand** adj **right-hand drive** guida a destra; **the right-hand side** il lato destro; **right-handed** adj (person) che adopera la mano destra; **rightly** adv bene, correttamente; (with reason) a ragione; **right of way** n diritto di passaggio; (Aut) precedenza; **right-wing** adj (Pol) di destra

rigid ['rɪdʒɪd] adj rigido(-a); (principle) rigoroso(-a)

rigorous ['rɪgərəs] adj rigoroso(-a)

rim [rɪm] n orlo; (of spectacles) montatura; (of wheel) cerchione m

rind [raɪnd] n (of bacon) cotenna; (of lemon etc) scorza

ring [rɪŋ] (pt **rang**, pp **rung**) n anello; (of people, objects) cerchio; (of spies) giro; (of smoke etc) spirale m; (arena) pista, arena; (for boxing) ring m inv; (sound of bell) scampanio ▷ vi (person, bell, telephone) suonare; (also: **~ out**: voice, words) risuonare; (*Tel*) telefonare; (*ears*) fischiare ▷ *vt* (*BRIT Tel*) telefonare a; (: *bell, doorbell*) suonare; **to give sb a ~** (*BRIT Tel*) dare un colpo di telefono a qn; **ring back** *vt, vi* (*Tel*) richiamare; **ring off** (*BRIT*) *vi* (*Tel*) mettere giù, riattaccare; **ring up** (*BRIT*) *vt* (*Tel*) telefonare a; **ringing tone** (*BRIT*) *n* (*Tel*) segnale *m* di libero; **ringleader** *n* (*of gang*) capobanda *m*; **ring road** (*BRIT*) *n* raccordo anulare

ring tone *n* suoneria

rink [rɪŋk] *n* (*also:* **ice ~**) pista di pattinaggio

rinse [rɪns] *n* risciacquatura; (*hair tint*) cachet *m inv* ▷ *vt* sciacquare

riot ['raɪət] *n* sommossa, tumulto; (*of colours*) orgia ▷ *vi* tumultuare; **to run ~** creare disordine

rip [rɪp] *n* strappo ▷ *vt* strappare ▷ *vi* strapparsi; **rip off** *vt* (*inf: cheat*) fregare; **rip up** *vt* stracciare

ripe [raɪp] *adj* (*fruit, grain*) maturo(-a); (*cheese*) stagionato(-a)

rip-off ['rɪpɔf] *n* (*inf*): **it's a ~!** è un furto!

ripple ['rɪpl] *n* increspamento, ondulazione *f*; mormorio ▷ *vi* incresparsi

rise [raɪz] (*pt* **rose**, *pp* **risen**) *n* (*slope*) salita, pendio; (*hill*) altura; (*increase: in wages*: *BRIT*) aumento; (: *in prices, temperature*) rialzo, aumento; (*fig: to power etc*) ascesa ▷ *vi* alzarsi, levarsi; (*prices*) aumentare; (*waters, river*) crescere; (*sun, wind, person: from chair, bed*) levarsi; (*also:* **~ up**: *building*) ergersi; (: *rebel*) insorgere; ribellarsi; (*in rank*) salire; **to give ~ to** provocare, dare origine a; **to ~ to the occasion** essere all'altezza; **risen** ['rɪzn] *pp of* **rise**; **rising** *adj* (*increasing: number*) sempre crescente; (: *prices*) in aumento; (*tide*) montante; (*sun, moon*) nascente, che sorge

risk [rɪsk] *n* rischio; pericolo ▷ *vt* rischiare; **to take** *or* **run the ~ of doing** correre il rischio di fare; **at ~** in pericolo; **at one's own ~** a proprio rischio e pericolo; **risky** *adj* rischioso(-a)

rite [raɪt] *n* rito; **last ~s** l'estrema unzione

ritual ['rɪtjuəl] *adj* rituale ▷ *n* rituale *m*

rival ['raɪvl] *n* rivale *m/f*; (*in business*) concorrente *m/f* ▷ *adj* rivale; che fa concorrenza ▷ *vt* essere in concorrenza con; **to ~ sb/sth in** competere con qn/qc in; **rivalry** *n* rivalità; concorrenza

river ['rɪvə'] *n* fiume *m* ▷ *cpd* (*port, traffic*) fluviale; **up/down ~** a monte/valle; **riverbank** *n* argine *m*

rivet ['rɪvɪt] *n* ribattino, rivetto ▷ *vt* (*fig*) concentrare, fissare

Riviera [rɪvɪ'ɛərə] *n* **the (French) ~** la Costa Azzurra; **the Italian ~** la Riviera

road [rəud] *n* strada; (*small*) cammino; (*in town*) via ▷ *cpd* stradale; **major/ minor ~** strada con/senza diritto di precedenza; **which ~ do I take for ...?** che strada devo prendere per andare a...?; **roadblock** *n* blocco stradale; **road map** *n* carta stradale; **road rage** *n* comportamento aggressivo al volante; **road safety** *n* sicurezza sulle strade; **roadside** *n* margine *m* della strada; **roadsign** *n* cartello stradale; **road tax** *n* (*BRIT*) tassa di circolazione; **roadworks** *npl* lavori *mpl* stradali

roam [rəum] *vi* errare, vagabondare

roar [rɔː'] *n* ruggito; (*of crowd*) tumulto; (*of thunder, storm*) muggito; (*of laughter*) scoppio ▷ *vi* ruggire; tumultuare; muggire; **to ~ with laughter** scoppiare dalle risa; **to do a ~ing trade** fare affari d'oro

roast [rəust] *n* arrosto ▷ *vt* arrostire; (*coffee*) tostare, torrefare; **roast beef** *n* arrosto di manzo

rob [rɔb] *vt* (*person*) rubare; (*bank*) svaligiare; **to ~ sb of sth** derubare qn di qc; (*fig: deprive*) privare qn di qc; **robber** *n* ladro; (*armed*) rapinatore *m*; **robbery** *n* furto; rapina

robe [rəub] *n* (*for ceremony etc*) abito; (*also:* **bath ~**) accappatoio; (*US: also:* **lap ~**) coperta

robin ['rɔbɪn] *n* pettirosso

robot ['rəubɔt] *n* robot *m inv*

robust [rəu'bʌst] *adj* robusto(-a); (*economy*) solido(-a)

rock [rɔk] *n* (*substance*) roccia; (*boulder*) masso, roccia; (*in sea*) scoglio; (*US: pebble*) ciottolo; (*BRIT: sweet*) zucchero candito ▷ *vt* (*swing gently: cradle*) dondolare; (: *child*) cullare; (*shake*) scrollare, far tremare ▷ *vi* dondolarsi; scrollarsi, tremare; **on the ~s** (*drink*) col ghiaccio; (*marriage etc*) in crisi; **rock and roll** *n* rock and roll *m*; **rock climbing** *n* roccia

rocket ['rɔkɪt] *n* razzo

rocking chair *n* sedia a dondolo

rocky ['rɔkɪ] *adj* (*hill*) roccioso(-a); (*path*) sassoso(-a); (*marriage etc*) instabile

rod [rɔd] *n* (*metallic, Tech*) asta; (*wooden*) bacchetta; (*also:* **fishing ~**) canna da pesca

rode [rəud] *pt of* **ride**

rodent ['rəudnt] *n* roditore *m*

rogue [rəug] *n* mascalzone *m*

role [rəul] *n* ruolo; **role-model** *n* modello (di comportamento)

roll [rəul] *n* rotolo; (*of banknotes*) mazzo; (*also:* **bread ~**) panino; (*register*) lista; (*sound: of drums etc*) rullo ▷ *vt* rotolare; (*also:* **~ up**: *string*) aggomitolare; (: *sleeves*) rimboccare; (*cigarettes*) arrotolare; (*eyes*) roteare; (*also:* ~ **out**: *pastry*) stendere; (*lawn, road etc*) spianare ▷ *vi* rotolare; (*wheel*) girare; (*drum*) rullare; (*vehicle: also:* ~ **along**; (*ship*) rollare; **roll over** *vi* rivoltarsi; **roll up** (*inf*) *vi* (*arrive*) arrivare ▷ *vt* (*carpet*) arrotolare; **roller** *n* rullo; (*wheel*) rotella; (*for hair*) bigodino; **Rollerblades®** *npl* pattini *mpl* in linea; **roller coaster** [-ˈkəustəʳ] *n* montagne *fpl* russe; **roller skates** *npl* pattini *mpl* a rotelle; **roller-skating** *n* pattinaggio a rotelle; **to go roller-skating** andare a pattinare (*con i pattini a rotelle*); **rolling pin** *n* matterello

ROM [rɔm] *n abbr* (= *read only memory*) memoria di sola lettura

Roman [ˈrəumən] *adj, n* romano(-a); **Roman Catholic** *adj, n* cattolico(-a)

romance [rəˈmæns] *n* storia (*or* avventura *or* film *m inv*) romantico(-a); (*charm*) poesia; (*love affair*) idillio

Romania [rəuˈmeɪnɪə] *n* Romania

Romanian [rəuˈmeɪnɪən] *adj* romeno(-a) ▷ *n* romeno; (*Ling*) romeno

Roman numeral *n* numero romano

romantic [rəˈmæntɪk] *adj* romantico(-a); sentimentale

Rome [rəum] *n* Roma

roof [ru:f] *n* tetto; (*of tunnel, cave*) volta ▷ *vt* coprire (con un tetto); ~ **of the mouth** palato; **roof rack** *n* (*Aut*) portabagagli *m inv*

rook [ruk] *n* (*bird*) corvo nero; (*Chess*) torre *f*

room [ru:m] *n* (*in house*) stanza; (*bedroom, in hotel*) camera; (*in school etc*) sala; (*space*) posto, spazio; **roommate** *n* compagno(-a) di stanza; **room service** *n* servizio da camera; **roomy** *adj* spazioso(-a); (*garment*) ampio(-a)

rooster [ˈru:stəʳ] *n* gallo

root [ru:t] *n* radice *f* ▷ *vi* (*plant, belief*) attecchire

rope [rəup] *n* corda, fune *f*; (*Naut*) cavo ▷ *vt* (*box*) legare; (*climbers*) legare in cordata; (*area: also:* ~ **off**) isolare cingendo con cordoni; **to know the ~s** (*fig*) conoscere i trucchi del mestiere

rose [rəuz] *pt of* **rise** ▷ *n* rosa; (*also:* ~ **bush**) rosaio; (*on watering can*) rosetta

rosé [ˈrəuzeɪ] *n* vino rosato

rosemary [ˈrəuzmərɪ] *n* rosmarino

rosy [ˈrəuzɪ] *adj* roseo(-a)

rot [rɔt] *n* (*decay*) putrefazione *f*; (*inf: nonsense*) stupidaggini *fpl* ▷ *vt, vi* imputridire, marcire

rota [ˈrəutə] *n* tabella dei turni

rotate [rəuˈteɪt] *vt* (*revolve*) far girare; (*change round: jobs*) fare a turno ▷ *vi*

(*revolve*) girare

rotten [ˈrɔtn] *adj* (*decayed*) putrido(-a), marcio(-a); (*dishonest*) corrotto(-a); (*inf: bad*) brutto(-a); (: *action*) vigliacco(-a); **to feel ~** (*ill*) sentirsi da cani

rough [rʌf] *adj* (*skin, surface*) ruvido(-a); (*terrain, road*) accidentato(-a); (*voice*) rauco(-a); (*person, manner: coarse*) rozzo(-a), aspro(-a); (: *violent*) brutale; (*district*) malfamato(-a); (*weather*) cattivo(-a); (*sea*) mosso(-a); (*plan*) abbozzato(-a); (*guess*) approssimativo(-a) ▷ *n* (*Golf*) macchia; **to ~ it** far vita dura; **to sleep ~** (BRIT) dormire all'addiaccio; **roughly** *adv* (*handle*) rudemente, brutalmente; (*make*) grossolanamente; (*speak*) bruscamente; (*approximately*) approssimativamente

roulette [ru:ˈlɛt] *n* roulette *f*

round [raund] *adj* rotondo(-a); (*figures*) tondo(-a) ▷ *n* (BRIT: *of toast*) fetta; (*duty: of policeman, milkman etc*) giro; (: *of doctor*) visite *fpl*; (*game: of cards, golf, in competition*) partita; (*of ammunition*) cartuccia; (*Boxing*) round *m inv*; (*of talks*) serie *f inv* ▷ *vt* (*corner*) girare; (*bend*) prendere ▷ *prep* intorno a ▷ *adv* **all ~** tutt'attorno; **to go the long way ~** fare il giro più lungo; **all the year ~** tutto l'anno; **it's just ~ the corner** (*also fig*) è dietro l'angolo; ~ **the clock** ininterrottamente; **to go ~ to sb's house** andare da qn; **go ~ the back** passi dietro; **enough to go ~** abbastanza per tutti; ~ **of applause** applausi *mpl*; ~ **of drinks** giro di bibite; ~ **of sandwiches** sandwich *m inv*; **round off** *vt* (*speech etc*) finire; **round up** *vt* radunare; (*criminals*) fare una retata di; (*prices*) arrotondare; **roundabout** *n* (BRIT *Aut*) rotatoria; (: *at fair*) giostra ▷ *adj* (*route, means*) indiretto(-a); **round trip** *n* (viaggio di) andata e ritorno; **roundup** *n* raduno; (*of criminals*) retata

rouse [rauz] *vt* (*wake up*) svegliare; (*stir up*) destare; provocare; risvegliare

route [ru:t] *n* itinerario; (*of bus*) percorso

routine [ru:ˈti:n] *adj* (*work*) corrente, abituale; (*procedure*) solito(-a) ▷ *n* (*pej*) routine *f*, tran tran *m*; (*Theatre*) numero

row¹ [rəu] *n* (*line*) riga, fila; (*Knitting*) ferro; (*behind one another: of cars, people*) fila; (*in boat*) remata ▷ *vi* (*in boat*) remare; (*as sport*) vogare ▷ *vt* (*boat*) manovrare a remi; **in a ~** (*fig*) di fila

row² [rau] *n* (*racket*) baccano, chiasso; (*dispute*) lite *f*; (*scolding*) sgridata ▷ *vi* (*argue*) litigare

rowboat [ˈrəubəut] (US) *n* barca a remi

rowing [ˈrəuɪŋ] *n* canottaggio; **rowing boat** (BRIT) *n* barca a remi

royal ['rɔɪəl] *adj* reale; **royalty** ['rɔɪə lti] *n* (*royal persons*) (membri *mpl* della) famiglia reale; (*payment: to author*) diritti *mpl* d'autore

rpm *abbr* (= *revolutions per minute*) giri/min.

R.S.V.P. *abbr* (= *répondez s'il vous plaît*) R.S.V.P.

Rt. Hon. (BRIT) *abbr* (= *Right Honourable*) ≈ Onorevole

rub [rʌb] *n* **to give sth a ~** strofinare qc; (*sore place*) massaggiare qc ▷ *vt* strofinare; massaggiare; (*hands: also: ~ together*) sfregarsi; **to ~ sb up** (BRIT) *or* **~ sb the wrong way** (US) lisciare qn contro pelo; **rub in** *vt* (*ointment*) far penetrare (massaggiando *or* frizionando); **rub off** *vi* andare via; **rub out** *vt* cancellare

rubber ['rʌbə'] *n* gomma; **rubber band** *n* elastico; **rubber gloves** *npl* guanti *mpl* di gomma

rubbish ['rʌbɪʃ] *n* (*from household*) immondizie *fpl*, rifiuti *mpl*; (*fig, pej*) cose *fpl* senza valore; robaccia; sciocchezze *fpl*; **rubbish bin** (BRIT) *n* pattumiera; **rubbish dump** (*in town*) immondezzaio

rubble ['rʌbl] *n* macerie *fpl*; (*smaller*) pietrisco

ruby ['ruːbɪ] *n* rubino

rucksack ['rʌksæk] *n* zaino

rudder ['rʌdə'] *n* timone *m*

rude [ruːd] *adj* (*impolite: person*) scortese, rozzo(-a); (: *word, manners*) grossolano(-a), rozzo(-a); (*shocking*) indecente

ruffle ['rʌfl] *vt* (*hair*) scompigliare; (*clothes, water*) increspare; (*fig: person*) turbare

rug [rʌg] *n* tappeto; (BRIT: *for knees*) coperta

rugby ['rʌgbɪ] *n* (*also: ~ football*) rugby *m*

rugged ['rʌgɪd] *adj* (*landscape*) aspro(-a); (*features, determination*) duro(-a); (*character*) brusco(-a)

ruin ['ruːɪn] *n* rovina ▷ *vt* rovinare; **~s** *npl* (*of building, castle etc*) rovine *fpl*, ruderi *mpl*

rule [ruːl] *n* regola; (*regulation*) regolamento, regola; (*government*) governo; (*ruler*) riga ▷ *vt* (*country*) governare; (*person*) dominare ▷ *vi* regnare; decidere; (*Law*) dichiarare; **as a ~** normalmente; **rule out** *vt* escludere; **ruler** *n* (*sovereign*) sovrano(-a); (*for measuring*) regolo, riga; **ruling** *adj* (*party*) al potere; (*class*) dirigente ▷ *n* (*Law*) decisione *f*

rum [rʌm] *n* rum *m*

Rumania *etc* [ruːˈmeɪnɪə] *n* = **Romania** *etc*

rumble ['rʌmbl] *n* rimbombo; brontolio ▷ *vi* rimbombare; (*stomach, pipe*) brontolare

rumour ['ruːmə'] (US **rumor**) *n* voce *f* ▷ *vt* it is **~ed that** corre voce che

> Be careful not to translate *rumour* by the Italian word *rumore*.

rump steak [rʌmp-] *n* bistecca di girello

run [rʌn] (*pt* **ran**, *pp* **run**) *n* corsa; (*outing*) gita (in macchina); (*distance travelled*) percorso, tragitto; (*Ski*) pista; (*Cricket, Baseball*) meta; (*series*) serie *f*; (*Theatre*) periodo di rappresentazione; (*in tights, stockings*) smagliatura ▷ *vt* (*distance*) correre; (*operate: business*) gestire, dirigere; (: *competition, course*) organizzare; (: *hotel*) gestire; (: *house*) governare; (*Comput*) eseguire; (*water, bath*) far scorrere; (*force through: rope, pipe*) **to ~ sth through** far passare qc attraverso; (*pass: hand, finger*) **to ~ sth over** passare qc su; (*Press: feature*) presentare ▷ *vi* correre; (*flee*) scappare; (*pass: road etc*) passare; (*work: machine, factory*) funzionare, andare; (*bus, train: operate*) far servizio; (: *travel*) circolare; (*continue: play, contract*) durare; (*slide: drawer; flow: river, bath*) scorrere; (*colours, washing*) stemperarsi; (*in election*) presentarsi candidato; (*nose*) colare; **there was a ~ on ...** c'era una corsa a ...; **in the long ~** a lungo andare; **on the ~** in fuga; **to ~ a race** partecipare ad una gara; **I'll ~ you to the station** la porto alla stazione; **to ~ a risk** correre un rischio; **run after** *vt fus* (*to catch up*) rincorrere; (*chase*) correre dietro a; **run away** *vi* fuggire; **run down** *vt* (*production*) ridurre gradualmente; (*factory*) rallentare l'attività di; (*Aut*) investire; (*criticize*) criticare; **to be ~ down** (*person: tired*) essere esausto(-a); **run into** *vt fus* (*meet: person*) incontrare per caso; (: *trouble*) incontrare, trovare; (*collide with*) andare a sbattere contro; **run off** *vi* fuggire ▷ *vt* (*water*) far scolare; (*copies*) fare; **run out** *vi* (*person*) uscire di corsa; (*liquid*) colare, (*lease*) scadere; (*money*) esaurirsi; **run out of** *vt fus* rimanere a corto di; **run over** *vt* (*Aut*) investire, mettere sotto ▷ *vt fus* (*revise*) rivedere; **run through** *vt fus* (*instructions*) dare una scorsa a; (*rehearse: play*) riprovare, ripetere; **run up** *vt* (*debt*) lasciar accumulare; **to ~ up against** (*difficulties*) incontrare; **runaway** *adj* (*person*) fuggiasco(-a); (*horse*) in libertà; (*truck*) fuori controllo

rung [rʌŋ] *pp of* **ring** ▷ *n* (*of ladder*) piolo

runner ['rʌnə'] *n* (*in race*) corridore *m*; (: *horse*) partente *m/f*; (*on sledge*) pattino; (*for drawer etc*) guida; **runner bean** (BRIT) *n* fagiolo rampicante; **runner-up** *n* secondo(-a) arrivato(-a)

running ['rʌnɪŋ] *n* corsa; direzione *f*; organizzazione *f*; funzionamento

▷ *adj* (*water*) corrente; (*commentary*) simultaneo(-a); **to be in/out of the ~ for sth** essere/non essere più in lizza per qc; **6 days ~** 6 giorni di seguito

runny ['rʌnɪ] *adj* che cola

run-up ['rʌnʌp] *n* **~ to** (*election etc*) periodo che precede

runway ['rʌnweɪ] *n* (*Aviat*) pista (di decollo)

rupture ['rʌptʃəʳ] *n* (*Med*) ernia

rural ['ruərəl] *adj* rurale

rush [rʌʃ] *n* corsa precipitosa; (*hurry*) furia, fretta; (*sudden demand*): **~ for** corsa a; (*current*) flusso; (*of emotion*) impeto; (*Bot*) giunco ▷ *vt* mandare *or* spedire velocemente; (*attack: town etc*) prendere d'assalto ▷ *vi* precipitarsi; **rush hour** *n* ora di punta

Russia ['rʌʃə] *n* Russia; **Russian** *adj* russo(-a) ▷ *n* russo(-a); (*Ling*) russo

rust [rʌst] *n* ruggine *f* ▷ *vi* arrugginirsi

rusty ['rʌstɪ] *adj* arrugginito(-a)

ruthless ['ru:θlɪs] *adj* spietato(-a)

RV *abbr* (= *revised version*) versione riveduta della Bibbia ▷ *n abbr* (*US*) *see* **recreational vehicle**

rye [raɪ] *n* segale *f*

Sabbath ['sæbəθ] *n* (*Jewish*) sabato; (*Christian*) domenica

sabotage ['sæbətɑːʒ] *n* sabotaggio ▷ *vt* sabotare

saccharin(e) ['sækərɪn] *n* saccarina

sachet ['sæʃeɪ] *n* bustina

sack [sæk] *n* (*bag*) sacco ▷ *vt* (*dismiss*) licenziare, mandare a spasso; (*plunder*) saccheggiare; **to get the ~** essere mandato a spasso

sacred ['seɪkrɪd] *adj* sacro(-a)

sacrifice ['sækrɪfaɪs] *n* sacrificio ▷ *vt* sacrificare

sad [sæd] *adj* triste

saddle ['sædl] *n* sella ▷ *vt* (*horse*) sellare; **to be ~d with sth** (*inf*) avere qc sulle spalle

sadistic [sə'dɪstɪk] *adj* sadico(-a)

sadly ['sædlɪ] *adv* tristemente; (*regrettably*) sfortunatamente; **~ lacking in** penosamente privo di

sadness ['sædnɪs] *n* tristezza

s.a.e. *n abbr* (= *stamped addressed envelope*) busta affrancata e con indirizzo

safari [sə'fɑːrɪ] *n* safari *m inv*

safe [seɪf] *adj* sicuro(-a); (*out of danger*) salvo(-a), al sicuro; (*cautious*) prudente ▷ *n* cassaforte *f*; **~ from** al sicuro da; **~ and sound** sano(-a) e salvo(-a); **(just) to be on the ~ side** per non correre rischi; **could you put this in the ~, please?** lo potrebbe mettere nella cassaforte, per favore?; **safely** adv sicuramente; sano(-a) e salvo(-a); prudentemente; **safe sex** n sesso sicuro

safety ['seɪftɪ] n sicurezza; **safety belt** n cintura di sicurezza; **safety pin** n spilla di sicurezza

saffron ['sæfrən] n zafferano

sag [sæg] vi incurvarsi; afflosciarsi

sage [seɪdʒ] n (herb) salvia; (man) saggio

Sagittarius [sædʒɪ'teərɪəs] n Sagittario

Sahara [sə'hɑ:rə] n **the ~ (Desert)** il (deserto del) Sahara

said [sɛd] pt, pp of **say**

sail [seɪl] n (on boat) vela; (trip): **to go for a ~** fare un giro in barca a vela ▷ vt (boat) condurre, governare ▷ vi (travel: ship) navigare; (: passenger) viaggiare per mare; (set off) salpare; (sport) fare della vela; **they ~ed into Genoa** entrarono nel porto di Genova; **sailboat** (US) n barca a vela; **sailing** n (sport) vela; **to go sailing** fare della vela; **sailing boat** n barca a vela; **sailor** n marinaio

saint [seɪnt] n santo(-a)

sake [seɪk] n **for the ~ of** per, per amore di

salad ['sæləd] n insalata; **salad cream** (BRIT) n (tipo di) maionese f; **salad dressing** n condimento per insalata

salami [sə'lɑ:mɪ] n salame m

salary ['sælərɪ] n stipendio

sale [seɪl] n vendita; (at reduced prices) svendita, liquidazione f; (auction) vendita all'asta; **"for ~"** "in vendita"; **on ~** in vendita; **on ~ or return** da vendere o rimandare; **~s** npl (total amount sold) vendite fpl; **sales assistant** (US **sales clerk**) n commesso(-a); **salesman/ woman** (irreg) n commesso(-a); (representative) rappresentante m/f; **salesperson** (irreg) n (in shop) commesso; (representative) rappresentante m/f di commercio; **sales rep** n rappresentante m/f di commercio

saline ['seɪlaɪn] adj salino(-a)

saliva [sə'laɪvə] n saliva

salmon ['sæmən] n inv salmone m

salon ['sælɔn] n (hairdressing salon) parrucchiere(-a); (beauty salon) salone m di bellezza

saloon [sə'lu:n] n (US) saloon m inv, bar m inv; (BRIT: Aut) berlina; (ship's lounge) salone m

salt [sɔlt] n sale m ▷ vt salare; **saltwater** adj di mare; **salty** adj salato(-a)

salute [sə'lu:t] n saluto ▷ vt salutare

salvage ['sælvɪdʒ] n (saving) salvataggio; (things saved) beni mpl salvati or recuperati ▷ vt salvare, mettere in salvo

Salvation Army [sæl'veɪʃən-] n Esercito della Salvezza

same [seɪm] adj stesso(-a), medesimo(-a) ▷ pron **the ~** lo (la) stesso(-a), gli (le) stessi(-e); **the ~ book as** lo stesso libro di (o che); **at the ~ time** allo stesso tempo; **all** or **just the ~** tuttavia; **to do the ~ as sb** fare come qn; **the ~ to you!** altrettanto a te!

sample ['sɑ:mpl] n campione m ▷ vt (food) assaggiare; (wine) degustare

sanction ['sæŋkʃən] n sanzione f ▷ vt sancire, sanzionare; **~s** npl (Pol) sanzioni fpl

sanctuary ['sæŋktjuərɪ] n (holy place) santuario; (refuge) rifugio; (for wildlife) riserva

sand [sænd] n sabbia ▷ vt (also: **~ down**) cartavetrare

sandal ['sændl] n sandalo

sand: **sandbox** ['sændbɔks] (US) n = **sandpit**; **sandcastle** ['sændkɑ:sl] n castello di sabbia; **sand dune** n duna di sabbia; **sandpaper** ['sændpeɪpəʳ] n carta vetrata; **sandpit** ['sændpɪt] n (for children) buca di sabbia; **sands** npl spiaggia; **sandstone** ['sændstəun] n arenaria

sandwich ['sændwɪtʃ] n tramezzino, panino, sandwich m inv ▷ vt **~ed between** incastrato(-a) fra; **cheese/ham ~** sandwich al formaggio/prosciutto

sandy ['sændɪ] adj sabbioso(-a); (colour) color sabbia inv, biondo(-a) rossiccio(-a)

sane [seɪn] adj (person) sano(-a) di mente; (outlook) sensato(-a)

sang [sæŋ] pt of **sing**

sanitary towel ['sænɪtərɪ-] (US **sanitary napkin**) n assorbente m (igienico)

sanity ['sænɪtɪ] n sanità mentale; (common sense) buon senso

sank [sæŋk] pt of **sink**

Santa Claus [sæntə'klɔ:z] n Babbo Natale

sap [sæp] n (of plants) linfa ▷ vt (strength) fiaccare

sapphire ['sæfaɪəʳ] n zaffiro

sarcasm ['sɑ:kæzm] n sarcasmo

sarcastic [sɑ:'kæstɪk] adj sarcastico(-a); **to be ~** fare del sarcasmo

sardine [sɑ:'di:n] n sardina

Sardinia [sɑ:'dɪnɪə] n Sardegna

SASE (US) n abbr (= self-addressed stamped envelope) busta affrancata e con indirizzo

sat [sæt] pt, pp of **sit**

Sat. abbr (= Saturday) sab.

satchel ['sætʃl] n cartella

satellite ['sætəlaɪt] adj satellite ▷ n satellite m; **satellite dish** n antenna parabolica; **satellite television** n televisione f via satellite

satin ['sætɪn] n raso ▷ adj di raso
satire ['sætaɪəʳ] n satira
satisfaction [sætɪs'fækʃən] n
soddisfazione f
satisfactory [sætɪs'fæktərɪ] adj
soddisfacente
satisfied ['sætɪsfaɪd] adj (customer)
soddisfatto(-a); **to be ~ (with sth)** essere
soddisfatto(-a) (di qc)
satisfy ['sætɪsfaɪ] vt soddisfare; (convince)
convincere
Saturday ['sætədɪ] n sabato
sauce [sɔːs] n salsa; (containing meat, fish)
sugo; **saucepan** n casseruola
saucer ['sɔːsəʳ] n sottocoppa m, piattino
Saudi Arabia ['saudɪ-] n Arabia Saudita
sauna ['sɔːnə] n sauna
sausage ['sɔsɪdʒ] n salsiccia; **sausage roll**
n rotolo di pasta sfoglia ripieno di salsiccia
sautéed ['səuteɪd] adj saltato(-a)
savage ['sævɪdʒ] adj (cruel, fierce)
selvaggio(-a), feroce; (primitive)
primitivo(-a) ▷ n selvaggio(-a) ▷ vt
attaccare selvaggiamente
save [seɪv] vt (person, belongings, Comput)
salvare; (money) risparmiare, mettere
da parte; (time) risparmiare; (food)
conservare; (avoid: trouble) evitare; (Sport)
parare ▷ vi (also: ~ up) economizzare ▷ n
(Sport) parata ▷ prep salvo, a eccezione di
savings ['seɪvɪŋz] npl (money) risparmi mpl;
savings account n libretto di risparmio;
savings and loan association (us) n
≈ società di credito immobiliare
savoury ['seɪvərɪ] (us **savory**) adj (dish: not
sweet) salato(-a)
saw [sɔː] (pt **sawed**, pp **sawed** or **sawn**) pt
of **see** ▷ n (tool) sega ▷ vt segare; **sawdust**
n segatura
sawn [sɔːn] pp of **saw**
saxophone ['sæksəfəun] n sassofono
say [seɪ] (pt, pp **said**) n **to have one's ~**
fare sentire il proprio parere; **to have**
a or **some ~** avere voce in capitolo ▷ vt
dire; **could you ~ that again?** potrebbe
ripeterlo?; **that goes without ~ing** va da
sé; **saying** n proverbio, detto
scab [skæb] n crosta; (pej) crumiro(-a)
scaffolding ['skæfəldɪŋ] n impalcatura
scald [skɔːld] n scottatura ▷ vt scottare
scale [skeɪl] n scala; (of fish) squama ▷ vt
(mountain) scalare; **~s** npl (for weighing)
bilancia; **on a large ~** su vasta scala; **~ of**
charges tariffa
scallion ['skæljən] n cipolla; (us: shallot)
scalogna; (: leek) porro
scallop ['skɔləp] n (Zool) pettine m;
(Sewing) smerlo
scalp [skælp] n cuoio capelluto ▷ vt

scotennare
scalpel ['skælpl] n bisturi m inv
scam [skæm] n (inf) truffa
scampi ['skæmpɪ] npl scampi mpl
scan [skæn] vt scrutare; (glance at
quickly) scorrere, dare un'occhiata a; (TV)
analizzare; (Radar) esplorare ▷ n (Med)
ecografia
scandal ['skændl] n scandalo, (gossip)
pettegolezzi mpl
Scandinavia [skændɪ'neɪvɪə] n
Scandinavia; **Scandinavian** adj, n
scandinavo(-a)
scanner ['skænəʳ] n (Radar, Med) scanner
m inv
scapegoat ['skeɪpgəut] n capro espiatorio
scar [skɑː] n cicatrice f ▷ vt sfregiare
scarce [skɛəs] adj scarso(-a); (copy, edition)
raro(-a); **to make o.s. ~** (inf) squagliarsela;
scarcely adv appena
scare [skɛəʳ] n spavento; panico ▷ vt
spaventare, atterrire; **there was a bomb ~**
at the bank hanno evacuato la banca per
paura di un attentato dinamitardo; **to ~ sb**
stiff spaventare a morte qn; **scarecrow** n
spaventapasseri m inv; **scared** adj **to be**
scared aver paura
scarf [skɑːf] (pl **scarves** or **scarfs**) n (long)
sciarpa; (square) fazzoletto da testa,
foulard m inv
scarlet ['skɑːlɪt] adj scarlatto(-a)
scarves [skɑːvz] npl of **scarf**
scary ['skɛərɪ] adj che spaventa
scatter ['skætəʳ] vt spargere; (crowd)
disperdere ▷ vi disperdersi
scenario [sɪ'nɑːrɪəu] n (Theatre, Cinema)
copione m; (fig) situazione f
scene [siːn] n (Theatre, fig etc) scena;
(of crime, accident) scena, luogo; (sight,
view) vista, veduta; **scenery** n (Theatre)
scenario; (landscape) panorama m; **scenic**
adj scenico(-a); panoramico(-a)
scent [sɛnt] n profumo; (sense of smell)
olfatto, odorato; (fig: track) pista
sceptical ['skɛptɪkəl] (us **skeptical**) adj
scettico(-a)
schedule ['ʃɛdjuːl, (us) 'skɛdjuːl] n
programma m, piano; (of trains) orario; (of
prices etc) lista, tabella ▷ vt fissare; **on ~** in
orario; **to be ahead of/behind ~** essere in
anticipo/ritardo sul previsto; **scheduled**
flight n volo di linea
scheme [skiːm] n piano, progetto;
(method) sistema m; (dishonest plan, plot)
intrigo, trama; (arrangement) disposizione
f, sistemazione f; (pension scheme etc)
programma m ▷ vi fare progetti; (intrigue)
complottare
schizophrenic [skɪtsə'frɛnɪk] adj, n

schizofrenico(-a)

scholar ['skɔləʳ] n (expert) studioso(-a); **scholarship** n erudizione f; (grant) borsa di studio

school [sku:l] n (primary, secondary) scuola; (university: US) università f inv ▷ cpd scolare, scolastico(-a) ▷ vt (animal) addestrare; **schoolbook** n libro scolastico; **schoolboy** n scolaro; **school children** npl scolari mpl; **schoolgirl** n scolara; **schooling** n istruzione f; **schoolteacher** n insegnante m/f, docente m/f; (primary) maestro(-a)

science ['saɪəns] n scienza; **science fiction** n fantascienza; **scientific** [-'tɪfɪk] adj scientifico(-a); **scientist** n scienziato(-a)

sci-fi ['saɪfaɪ] n abbr (inf) = **science fiction**

scissors ['sɪzəz] npl forbici fpl

scold [skəʊld] vt rimproverare

scone [skɔn] n focaccina da tè

scoop [sku:p] n mestolo; (for ice cream) cucchiaio dosatore; (Press) colpo giornalistico, notizia (in) esclusiva

scooter ['sku:təʳ] n (motor cycle) motoretta, scooter m inv; (toy) monopattino

scope [skəʊp] n (capacity: of plan, undertaking) portata; (: of person) capacità fpl; (opportunity) possibilità fpl

scorching ['skɔ:tʃɪŋ] adj cocente, scottante

score [skɔ:ʳ] n punti mpl, punteggio; (Mus) partitura, spartito; (twenty) venti ▷ vt (goal, point) segnare, fare; (success) ottenere ▷ vi segnare; (Football) fare un goal; (keep score) segnare i punti; **~s of** (very many) un sacco di; **on that ~** a questo riguardo; **to ~ 6 out of 10** prendere 6 su 10; **score out** vt cancellare con un segno; **scoreboard** n tabellone m segnapunti; **scorer** n marcatore(trice); (keeping score) segnapunti m inv

scorn [skɔ:n] n disprezzo ▷ vt disprezzare

Scorpio ['skɔ:pɪəʊ] n Scorpione m

scorpion ['skɔ:pɪən] n scorpione m

Scot [skɔt] n scozzese m/f

Scotch tape® n scotch® m

Scotland ['skɔtlənd] n Scozia

Scots [skɔts] adj scozzese; **Scotsman** (irreg) n scozzese m; **Scotswoman** (irreg) n scozzese f; **Scottish** ['skɔtɪʃ] adj scozzese; **Scottish Parliament** n Parlamento scozzese

scout [skaut] n (Mil) esploratore m; (also: **boy ~**) giovane esploratore, scout m inv

scowl [skaul] vi accigliarsi, aggrottare le sopracciglia; **to ~ at** guardare torvo

scramble ['skræmbl] n arrampicata ▷ vi inerpicarsi; **to ~ out** etc uscire etc in fretta; **to ~ for** azzuffarsi per; **scrambled eggs** npl uova fpl strapazzate

scrap [skræp] n pezzo, pezzetto; (fight) zuffa; (also: **~ iron**) rottami mpl di ferro, ferraglia ▷ vt demolire; (fig) scartare ▷ vi **to ~ (with sb)** fare a botte (con qn); **~s** npl (waste) scarti mpl; **scrapbook** n album m inv di ritagli

scrape [skreɪp] vt, vi raschiare, grattare ▷ n **to get into a ~** cacciarsi in un guaio

scrap paper n cartaccia

scratch [skrætʃ] n graffio ▷ cpd **~ team** squadra raccogliticcia ▷ vt graffiare, rigare ▷ vi grattare; (paint, car) graffiare; **to start from ~** cominciare or partire da zero; **to be up to ~** essere all'altezza; **scratch card** n (BRIT) cartolina f gratta e vinci

scream [skri:m] n grido, urlo ▷ vi urlare, gridare

screen [skri:n] n schermo; (fig) muro, cortina, velo ▷ vt schermare, fare schermo a; (from the wind etc) riparare; (film) proiettare; (book) adattare per lo schermo; (candidates etc) selezionare; **screening** n (Med) dépistage m inv; **screenplay** n sceneggiatura; **screen saver** n (Comput) screen saver m inv

screw [skru:] n vite f ▷ vt avvitare; **screw up** vt (paper etc) spiegazzare; (inf: ruin) rovinare; **to ~ up one's eyes** strizzare gli occhi; **screwdriver** n cacciavite m

scribble ['skrɪbl] n scarabocchio ▷ vt scribacchiare in fretta ▷ vi scarabocchiare

script [skrɪpt] n (Cinema etc) copione m; (in exam) elaborato or compito d'esame

scroll [skrəʊl] n rotolo di carta

scrub [skrʌb] n (land) boscaglia ▷ vt pulire strofinando; (reject) annullare

scruffy ['skrʌfɪ] adj sciatto(-a)

scrum(mage) ['skrʌm(ɪdʒ)] n mischia

scrutiny ['skru:tɪnɪ] n esame m accurato

scuba diving ['sku:bə-] n immersioni fpl subacquee

sculptor ['skʌlptəʳ] n scultore m

sculpture ['skʌlptʃəʳ] n scultura

scum [skʌm] n schiuma; (pej: people) feccia

scurry ['skʌrɪ] vi sgambare, affrettarsi

sea [si:] n mare m ▷ cpd marino(-a), del mare; (bird, fish) di mare; (route, transport) marittimo(-a); **by ~** (travel) per mare; **on the ~** (boat) in mare; (town) di mare; **to be all at ~** (fig) non sapere che pesci pigliare; **out to ~** al largo; **(out) at ~** in mare; **seafood** n frutti mpl di mare; **sea front** n lungomare m; **seagull** n gabbiano

seal [si:l] n (animal) foca; (stamp) sigillo;

(*impression*) impronta del sigillo ▷ *vt* sigillare; **seal off** *vt* (*close*) sigillare; (*forbid entry to*) bloccare l'accesso a

sea level *n* livello del mare

seam [siːm] *n* cucitura; (*of coal*) filone *m*

search [səːtʃ] *n* ricerca; (*Law: at sb's home*) perquisizione *f* ▷ *vt* frugare ▷ *vi* **to ~ for** ricercare; **in ~ of** alla ricerca di; **search engine** *n* (*Comput*) motore *m* di ricerca; **search party** *n* squadra di soccorso

sea: seashore ['siːʃɔːʳ] *n* spiaggia; **seasick** ['siːsɪk] *adj* che soffre il mal di mare; **seaside** ['siːsaɪd] *n* spiaggia; **seaside resort** *n* stazione *f* balneare

season ['siːzn] *n* stagione *f* ▷ *vt* condire, insaporire; **seasonal** *adj* stagionale; **seasoning** *n* condimento; **season ticket** *n* abbonamento

seat [siːt] *n* sedile *m*; (*in bus, train: place*) posto; (*Parliament*) seggio; (*buttocks*) didietro; (*of trousers*) fondo ▷ *vt* far sedere; (*have room for*) avere or essere fornito(-a) di posti a sedere per; **I'd like to book two ~s** vorrei prenotare due posti; **to be ~ed** essere seduto(-a); **seat belt** *n* cintura di sicurezza; **seating** *n* posti *mpl* a sedere

sea: sea water *n* acqua di mare; **seaweed** ['siːwiːd] *n* alghe *fpl*

sec. *abbr* = **second(s)**

secluded [sɪ'kluːdɪd] *adj* isolato(-a), appartato(-a)

second ['sɛkənd] *num* secondo(-a) ▷ *adv* (*in race etc*) al secondo posto ▷ *n* (*unit of time*) secondo; (*Aut: also: ~ gear*) seconda; (*Comm: imperfect*) scarto; (*BRIT: Scol: degree*) laurea con punteggio discreto ▷ *vt* (*motion*) appoggiare; **secondary** *adj* secondario(-a); **secondary school** *n* scuola secondaria; **second-class** *adj* di seconda classe ▷ *adv* in seconda classe; **secondhand** *adj* di seconda mano, usato(-a); **secondly** *adv* in secondo luogo; **second-rate** *adj* scadente; **second thoughts** *npl* ripensamenti *mpl*; **on second thoughts** (*BRIT*) *or* **thought** (*US*) ripensandoci bene

secrecy ['siːkrəsɪ] *n* segretezza

secret ['siːkrɪt] *adj* segreto(-a) ▷ *n* segreto; **in ~** in segreto

secretary ['sɛkrətrɪ] *n* segretario(-a); **S~ of State (for)** (*BRIT: Pol*) ministro (di)

secretive ['siːkrətɪv] *adj* riservato(-a)

secret service *n* servizi *mpl* segreti

sect [sɛkt] *n* setta

section ['sɛkʃən] *n* sezione *f*

sector ['sɛktəʳ] *n* settore *m*

secular ['sɛkjuləʳ] *adj* secolare

secure [sɪ'kjuəʳ] *adj* sicuro(-a); (*firmly fixed*)

assicurato(-a), ben fermato(-a); (*in safe place*) al sicuro ▷ *vt* (*fix*) fissare, assicurare; (*get*) ottenere, assicurarsi; **securities** *npl* (*Stock Exchange*) titoli *mpl*

security [sɪ'kjuərɪtɪ] *n* sicurezza; (*for loan*) garanzia; **security guard** *n* guardia giurata

sedan [sə'dæn] (*US*) *n* (*Aut*) berlina

sedate [sɪ'deɪt] *adj* posato(-a), calmo(-a) ▷ *vt* calmare

sedative ['sɛdɪtɪv] *n* sedativo, calmante *m*

seduce [sɪ'djuːs] *vt* sedurre; **seductive** [-'dʌktɪv] *adj* seducente

see [siː] (*pt* **saw**, *pp* **seen**) *vt* vedere; (*accompany*): **to ~ sb to the door** accompagnare qn alla porta ▷ *vi* vedere; (*understand*) capire ▷ *n* sede *f* vescovile; **to ~ that** (*ensure*) badare che + *sub*, fare in modo che + *sub*; **~ you soon!** a presto!; **see off** *vt* salutare alla partenza; **see out** *vt* (*take to the door*) accompagnare alla porta; **see through** *vt* portare a termine ▷ *vt fus* non lasciarsi ingannare da; **see to** *vt fus* occuparsi di

seed [siːd] *n* seme *m*; (*fig*) germe *m*; (*Tennis etc*) testa di serie; **to go to ~** fare seme; (*fig*) scadere

seeing ['siːɪŋ] *conj* **~ (that)** visto che

seek [siːk] (*pt*, *pp* **sought**) *vt* cercare

seem [siːm] *vi* sembrare, parere; **there ~s to be ...** sembra che ci sia ...; **seemingly** *adv* apparentemente

seen [siːn] *pp of* **see**

seesaw ['siːsɔː] *n* altalena a bilico

segment ['sɛgmənt] *n* segmento

segregate ['sɛgrɪgeɪt] *vt* segregare, isolare

seize [siːz] *vt* (*grasp*) afferrare; (*take possession of*) impadronirsi di; (*Law*) sequestrare

seizure ['siːʒəʳ] *n* (*Med*) attacco; (*Law*) confisca, sequestro

seldom ['sɛldəm] *adv* raramente

select [sɪ'lɛkt] *adj* scelto(-a) ▷ *vt* scegliere, selezionare; **selection** [-'lɛkʃən] *n* selezione *f*, scelta; **selective** *adj* selettivo(-a)

self [sɛlf] *n* **the ~** l'io *m* ▷ *prefix* auto-...; **self-assured** *adj* sicuro(-a) di sé; **self-catering** (*BRIT*) *adj* in cui ci si cucina da sé; **self-centred** (*US* **self-centered**) *adj* egocentrico(-a); **self-confidence** *n* sicurezza di sé; **self-confident** *adj* sicuro(-a) di sé; **self-conscious** *adj* timido(-a); **self-contained** (*BRIT*) *adj* (*flat*) indipendente; **self-control** *n* autocontrollo; **self-defence** (*US* **self-defense**) *n* autodifesa; (*Law*) legittima difesa; **self-drive** *adj* (*BRIT: rented car*) senza autista; **self-employed** *adj* che lavora in proprio; **self-esteem** *n* amor proprio *m*; **self-indulgent** *adj* indulgente verso se stesso(-a); **self-interest** *n* interesse *m* personale; **selfish** *adj* egoista; **self-pity** *n* autocommiserazione *f*; **self-raising** (*US* **self-rising**) *adj* **self-raising flour** miscela di farina e lievito; **self-respect** *n* rispetto di sé, amor proprio; **self-service** *n* autoservizio, self-service *m*

sell [sɛl] (*pt, pp* **sold**) *vt* vendere ▷ *vi* vendersi; **to ~ at** *or* **for 1000 euros** essere in vendita a 1000 euro; **sell off** *vt* svendere, liquidare; **sell out** *vi* **to ~ out (of sth)** esaurire (qc); **the tickets are all sold out** i biglietti sono esauriti; **sell-by date** ['sɛlbaɪ-] *n* data di scadenza; **seller** *n* venditore(-trice)

Sellotape® ['sɛləuteɪp] (*BRIT*) *n* nastro adesivo, scotch® *m*

selves [sɛlvz] *npl of* **self**

semester [sɪ'mɛstər] (*US*) *n* semestre *m*

semi... ['sɛmɪ] *prefix* semi...; **semicircle** *n* semicerchio; **semidetached (house)** [sɛmɪdɪ'tætʃt-] (*BRIT*) *n* casa gemella; **semi-final** *n* semifinale *f*

seminar ['sɛmɪnɑːr] *n* seminario

semi-skimmed ['sɛmɪ'skɪmd] *adj* (*milk*) parzialmente scremato(-a)

senate ['sɛnɪt] *n* senato; **senator** *n* senatore(-trice)

send [sɛnd] (*pt, pp* **sent**) *vt* mandare; **send back** *vt* rimandare; **send for** *vt fus* mandare a chiamare, far venire; **send in** *vt* (*report, application, resignation*) presentare; **send off** *vt* (*goods*) spedire; (*BRIT: Sport: player*) espellere; **send on** *vt* (*BRIT: letter*) inoltrare; (*luggage etc: in advance*) spedire in anticipo; **send out** *vt* (*invitation*) diramare; **send up** *vt* (*person, price*) far salire; (*BRIT: parody*) mettere in ridicolo; **sender** *n* mittente *m/f*; **send-off** *n* **to give sb a good send-off** festeggiare la partenza di qn

senile ['siːnaɪl] *adj* senile

senior ['siːnɪər] *adj* (*older*) più vecchio(-a); (*of higher rank*) di grado più elevato; **senior citizen** *n* persona anziana; **senior high school** (*US*) *n* ≈ liceo

sensation [sɛn'seɪʃən] *n* sensazione *f*; **sensational** *adj* sensazionale; (*marvellous*) eccezionale

sense [sɛns] *n* senso; (*feeling*) sensazione *f*, senso; (*meaning*) senso, significato; (*wisdom*) buonsenso ▷ *vt* sentire, percepire; **it makes ~** ha senso; **senseless** *adj* sciocco(-a); (*unconscious*) privo(-a) di sensi; **sense of humour** (*BRIT*) *n* senso dell'umorismo

sensible ['sɛnsɪbl] *adj* sensato(-a), ragionevole

▮ Be careful not to translate **sensible** by the Italian word **sensibile**.

sensitive ['sɛnsɪtɪv] *adj* sensibile; (*skin, question*) delicato(-a)

sensual ['sɛnsjuəl] *adj* sensuale

sensuous ['sɛnsjuəs] *adj* sensuale

sent [sɛnt] *pt, pp of* **send**

sentence ['sɛntns] *n* (*Ling*) frase *f*; (*Law: judgment*) sentenza; (: *punishment*) condanna ▷ *vt* **to ~ sb to death/to 5 years** condannare qn a morte/a 5 anni

sentiment ['sɛntɪmənt] *n* sentimento; (*opinion*) opinione *f*; **sentimental** [-'mɛntl] *adj* sentimentale

Sep. *abbr* (= *September*) Sett.

separate [*adj* 'sɛprɪt, *vb* 'sɛpəreɪt] *adj* separato(-a) ▷ *vt* separare ▷ *vi* separarsi; **separately** *adv* separatamente; **separates** *npl* (*clothes*) coordinati *mpl*; **separation** [-'reɪʃən] *n* separazione *f*

September [sɛp'tɛmbər] *n* settembre *m*

septic ['sɛptɪk] *adj* settico(-a); (*wound*) infettato(-a); **septic tank** *n* fossa settica

sequel ['siːkwl] *n* conseguenza; (*of story*) seguito; (*of film*) sequenza

sequence ['siːkwəns] *n* (*series*) serie *f*; (*order*) ordine *m*

sequin ['siːkwɪn] *n* lustrino, paillette *f inv*

Serb [səːb] *adj, n* = **Serbian**

Serbia ['səːbɪə] *n* Serbia

Serbian ['səːbɪən] *adj* serbo(-a) ▷ *n* serbo(-a); (*Ling*) serbo

sergeant ['sɑːdʒənt] *n* sergente *m*; (*Police*) brigadiere *m*

serial ['sɪərɪəl] *n* (*Press*) romanzo a puntate; (*Radio, TV*) trasmissione *f* a puntate, serial *m inv*; **serial killer** *n* serial-killer *m/f inv*; **serial number** *n* numero di serie

series ['sɪəriːz] *n inv* serie *f inv*; (*Publishing*) collana

serious ['sɪərɪəs] *adj* serio(-a), grave; **seriously** *adv* seriamente

sermon ['səːmən] *n* sermone *m*

servant ['səːvənt] *n* domestico(-a)

serve [səːv] *vt* (*employer etc*) servire, essere a servizio di; (*purpose*) servire a; (*customer, food, meal*) servire; (*apprenticeship*) fare, (*prison term*) scontare ▷ *vi* (*also Tennis*) servire; (*be useful*): **to ~ as/for/to do** servire da/per/per fare ▷ *n* (*Tennis*) servizio; **it ~s him right** se gli sta, se l'è meritata; **server** *n* (*Comput*) server *m inv*

service ['səːvɪs] *n* servizio; (*Aut: maintenance*) assistenza, revisione *f* ▷ *vt* (*car, washing machine*) revisionare; **to be of ~ to sb** essere d'aiuto a qn; **~ included/**

not included servizio compreso/escluso;
~s (BRIT: *on motorway*) stazione *f* di
servizio; (*Mil*): **the S~s** le Forze Armate;
service area *n* (*on motorway*) area di
servizio; **service charge** (BRIT) *n* servizio;
serviceman (*irreg*) *n* militare *m*; **service
station** *n* stazione *f* di servizio

serviette [sə'vɪ'ɛt] (BRIT) *n* tovagliolo

session ['sɛʃən] *n* (*sitting*) seduta, sessione
f; (*Scol*) anno scolastico (*or* accademico)

set [sɛt] (*pt*, *pp* **set**) *n* serie *f* inv; (*of cutlery
etc*) servizio; (*Radio*, *TV*) apparecchio;
(*Tennis*) set *m* inv; (*group of people*) mondo,
ambiente *m*; (*Cinema*) scenario; (*Theatre*:
stage) scene *fpl*; (: *scenery*) scenario; (*Math*)
insieme *m*; (*Hairdressing*) messa in piega
▷ *adj* (*fixed*) stabilito(-a), determinato(-a);
(*ready*) pronto(-a) ▷ *vt* (*place*) posare,
mettere; (*arrange*) sistemare; (*fix*) fissare;
(*adjust*) regolare; (*decide*: *rules etc*) stabilire,
fissare ▷ *vi* (*sun*) tramontare; (*jam*, *jelly*)
rapprendersi; (*concrete*) fare presa; **to be
~ on doing** essere deciso a fare; **to ~ to
music** mettere in musica; **to ~ on fire** dare
fuoco a; **to ~ free** liberare; **to ~ sth going**
mettere in moto qc; **to ~ sail** prendere
il mare; **set aside** *vt* mettere da parte;
set down *vt* (*bus*, *train*) lasciare; **set in**
vi (*infection*) svilupparsi; (*complications*)
intervenire; **the rain has ~ in for the day**
ormai pioverà tutto il giorno; **set off** *vi*
partire ▷ *vt* (*bomb*) far scoppiare; (*cause to
start*) mettere in moto; (*show up well*) dare
risalto a; **set out** *vi* partire ▷ *vt* (*arrange*)
disporre; (*state*) esporre, presentare; **to
~ out to do** proporsi di fare; **set up** *vt*
(*organization*) fondare, costituire; **setback**
n (*hitch*) contrattempo, inconveniente *m*;
set menu *n* menù *m* inv fisso

settee [sɛ'tiː] *n* divano, sofà *m* inv

setting ['sɛtɪŋ] *n* (*background*) ambiente *m*;
(*of controls*) posizione *f*; (*of sun*) tramonto;
(*of jewel*) montatura

settle ['sɛtl] *vt* (*argument*, *matter*)
appianare; (*accounts*) regolare; (*Med*:
calm) calmare ▷ *vi* (*bird*, *dust etc*) posarsi;
(*sediment*) depositarsi; **to ~ for sth**
accontentarsi di qc; **to ~ on sth** decidersi
per qc; **settle down** *vi* (*get comfortable*)
sistemarsi; (*calm down*) calmarsi; (*get back
to normal*: *situation*) tornare alla normalità;
settle in *vi* sistemarsi; **settle up** *vi* **to
~ up with sb** regolare i conti con qn;
settlement *n* (*payment*) pagamento,
saldo; (*agreement*) accordo; (*colony*)
colonia; (*village etc*) villaggio, comunità
f inv

setup ['sɛtʌp] *n* (*arrangement*)
sistemazione *f*; (*situation*) situazione *f*

seven ['sɛvn] *num* sette; **seventeen** *num*
diciassette; **seventeenth** [sɛvn'tiːnθ]
num diciassettesimo(-a); **seventh** *num*
settimo(-a); **seventieth** ['sɛvntɪɪθ] *num*
settantesimo(-a); **seventy** *num* settanta

sever ['sɛvə'] *vt* recidere, tagliare;
(*relations*) troncare

several ['sɛvərl] *adj*, *pron* alcuni(-e),
diversi(-e); **~ of us** alcuni di noi

severe [sɪ'vɪə'] *adj* severo(-a); (*serious*)
serio(-a), grave; (*hard*) duro(-a); (*plain*)
semplice, sobrio(-a)

sew [səʊ] (*pt* **sewed**, *pp* **sewn**) *vt*, *vi* cucire

sewage ['suːɪdʒ] *n* acque *fpl* di scolo

sewer ['suːə'] *n* fogna

sewing ['səʊɪŋ] *n* cucitura; cucito; **sewing
machine** *n* macchina da cucire

sewn [səʊn] *pp* of **sew**

sex [sɛks] *n* sesso; **to have ~ with** avere
rapporti sessuali con; **sexism** ['sɛksɪzə
m] *n* sessismo; **sexist** *adj*, *n* sessista *m*/*f*;
sexual ['sɛksjuəl] *adj* sessuale; **sexual
intercourse** *n* rapporti *mpl* sessuali;
sexuality [sɛksju'ælɪtɪ] *n* sessualità;
sexy ['sɛksɪ] *adj* provocante, sexy *inv*

shabby ['ʃæbɪ] *adj* malandato(-a);
(*behaviour*) vergognoso(-a)

shack [ʃæk] *n* baracca, capanna

shade [ʃeɪd] *n* ombra; (*for lamp*) paralume
m; (*of colour*) tonalità *f* inv; (*small quantity*):
a ~ (more/too large) un po' (di più/
troppo grande) ▷ *vt* ombreggiare, fare
ombra a; **in the ~** all'ombra; **~s** (US) *npl*
(*sunglasses*) occhiali *mpl* da sole

shadow ['ʃædəʊ] *n* ombra ▷ *vt* (*follow*)
pedinare; **shadow cabinet** (BRIT) *n* (*Pol*)
governo *m* ombra *inv*

shady ['ʃeɪdɪ] *adj* ombroso(-a); (*fig*:
dishonest) losco(-a), equivoco(-a)

shaft [ʃɑːft] *n* (*of arrow*, *spear*) asta; (*Aut*,
Tech) albero; (*of mine*) pozzo; (*of lift*)
tromba; (*of light*) raggio

shake [ʃeɪk] (*pt* **shook**, *pp* **shaken**) *vt*
scuotere; (*bottle*, *cocktail*) agitare ▷ *vi*
tremare; **to ~ one's head** (*in refusal*,
dismay) scuotere la testa; **to ~ hands with
sb** stringere *or* dare la mano a qn; **shake
off** *vt* scrollare (via); (*fig*) sbarazzarsi di;
shake up *vt* scuotere; **shaky** *adj* (*hand*,
voice) tremante; (*building*) traballante

shall [ʃæl] *aux vb* **I ~ go** andrò; **~ I open the
door?** apro io la porta?; **I'll get some, ~ I?**
ne prendo un po', va bene?

shallow ['ʃæləʊ] *adj* poco profondo(-a);
(*fig*) superficiale

sham [ʃæm] *n* finzione *f*, messinscena;
(*jewellery*, *furniture*) imitazione *f*

shambles ['ʃæmblz] *n* confusione *f*,
baraonda, scompiglio

shame [ʃeɪm] n vergogna ▷ vt far
vergognare; **it is a ~ (that/to do)** è un
peccato (che + sub/fare); **what a ~!** che
peccato!; **shameful** adj vergognoso(a);
shameless adj sfrontato(-a); (immodest)
spudorato(-a)

shampoo [ʃæmˈpuː] n shampoo m inv ▷ vt
fare lo shampoo a

shandy [ˈʃændɪ] n birra con gassosa

shan't [ʃɑːnt] = **shall not**

shape [ʃeɪp] n forma ▷ vt formare;
(statement) formulare; (sb's ideas)
condizionare; **to take ~** prendere forma

share [ʃeəʳ] n (thing received, contribution)
parte f; (Comm) azione f ▷ vt dividere; (have
in common) condividere, avere in comune;
shareholder n azionista m/f

shark [ʃɑːk] n squalo, pescecane m

sharp [ʃɑːp] adj (razor, knife) affilato(-a);
(point) acuto(-a), acuminato(-a); (nose,
chin) aguzzo(-a); (outline, contrast)
netto(-a); (cold, pain) pungente; (voice)
stridulo(-a); (person: quick-witted)
sveglio(-a); (: unscrupulous) disonesto(-a);
(Mus): **C ~** do diesis m inv ▷ n (Mus) diesis m inv
▷ adv **at 2 o'clock ~** alle due in punto;
sharpen vt affilare; (pencil) fare la punta
a; (fig) acuire; **sharpener** n (also: **pencil
sharpener**) temperamatite m inv; **sharply**
adv (turn, stop) bruscamente; (stand out,
contrast) nettamente; (criticize, retort)
duramente, aspramente

shatter [ˈʃætəʳ] vt mandare in frantumi,
frantumare; (fig: upset) distruggere; (:
ruin) rovinare ▷ vi frantumarsi, andare
in pezzi; **shattered** adj (grief-stricken)
sconvolto(-a); (exhausted) a pezzi,
distrutto(-a)

shave [ʃeɪv] vt radere, rasare ▷ vi radersi,
farsi la barba ▷ n **to have a ~** farsi la barba;
shaver n (also: **electric shaver**) rasoio
elettrico

shaving cream n crema da barba

shaving foam n = **shaving cream**

shavings [ˈʃeɪvɪŋz] npl (of wood etc) trucioli
mpl

shawl [ʃɔːl] n scialle m

she [ʃiː] pron ella, lei; **~-cat** gatta; **~-
elephant** elefantessa

sheath [ʃiːθ] n fodero, guaina;
(contraceptive) preservativo

shed [ʃed] (pt, pp **shed**) n capannone m
▷ vt (leaves, fur etc) perdere; (tears, blood)
versare; (workers) liberarsi di

she'd [ʃiːd] = **she had**; **she would**

sheep [ʃiːp] n inv pecora; **sheepdog** n
cane m da pastore; **sheepskin** n pelle f di
pecora

sheer [ʃɪəʳ] adj (utter) vero(-a)

(e proprio(-a)); (steep) a picco,
perpendicolare; (almost transparent) sottile
▷ adv a picco

sheet [ʃiːt] n (on bed) lenzuolo; (of paper)
foglio; (of glass, ice) lastra; (of metal) foglio,
lamina

sheik(h) [ʃeɪk] n sceicco

shelf [ʃelf] (pl **shelves**) n scaffale m,
mensola

shell [ʃel] n (on beach) conchiglia; (of egg,
nut etc) guscio; (explosive) granata; (of
building) scheletro ▷ vt (peas) sgranare;
(Mil) bombardare

she'll [ʃiːl] = **she will**; **she shall**

shellfish [ˈʃelfɪʃ] n inv (crab etc) crostaceo;
(scallop etc) mollusco; (as food) crostacei;
molluschi

shelter [ˈʃeltəʳ] n riparo, rifugio ▷ vt
riparare, proteggere; (give lodging to) dare
rifugio or asilo a ▷ vi ripararsi, mettersi al
riparo; **sheltered** adj riparato(-a)

shelves [ˈʃelvz] npl of **shelf**

shelving [ˈʃelvɪŋ] n scaffalature fpl

shepherd [ˈʃepəd] n pastore m ▷ vt (guide)
guidare; **shepherd's pie** (BRIT) n timballo
di carne macinata e purè di patate

sheriff [ˈʃerɪf] (US) n sceriffo

sherry [ˈʃerɪ] n sherry m inv

she's [ʃiːz] = **she is**; **she has**

Shetland [ˈʃetlənd] n (also: **the ~s, the ~
Isles**) le isole Shetland, le Shetland

shield [ʃiːld] n (trophy) scudetto;
(protection) schermo ▷ vt **to ~ (from)**
riparare (da), proteggere (da or contro)

shift [ʃɪft] n (change) cambiamento; (of
workers) turno ▷ vt spostare, muovere;
(remove) rimuovere ▷ vi spostarsi,
muoversi

shin [ʃɪn] n tibia

shine [ʃaɪn] (pt, pp **shone**) n splendore m,
lucentezza ▷ vi (ri)splendere, brillare ▷ vt
far brillare, far risplendere; (torch): **to ~ sth
on** puntare qc verso

shingles [ˈʃɪŋglz] n (Med) herpes zoster m

shiny [ˈʃaɪnɪ] adj lucente, lucido(a)

ship [ʃɪp] n nave f ▷ vt trasportare (via
mare); (send) spedire (via mare); **shipment**
n carico; **shipping** n (ships) naviglio;
(traffic) navigazione f; **shipwreck** n relitto;
(event) naufragio ▷ vt **to be shipwrecked**
naufragare, fare naufragio; **shipyard** n
cantiere m navale

shirt [ʃəːt] n camicia; **in ~ sleeves** in
maniche di camicia

shit [ʃɪt] (infl) excl merda (!)

shiver [ˈʃɪvəʳ] n brivido ▷ vi rabbrividire,
tremare

shock [ʃɔk] n (impact) urto, colpo; (Elec)
scossa; (emotional) colpo, shock m inv;

(*Med*) shock ▷ *vt* colpire, scioccare; scandalizzare; **shocking** *adj* scioccante, traumatizzante; scandaloso(-a)

shoe [ʃuː] (*pt, pp* **shod**) *n* scarpa; (*also:* **horse-**) ferro di cavallo ▷ *vt* (*horse*) ferrare; **shoelace** *n* stringa; **shoe polish** *n* lucido per scarpe; **shoeshop** *n* calzoleria

shone [ʃɔn] *pt, pp of* **shine**

shook [ʃuk] *pt of* **shake**

shoot [ʃuːt] (*pt, pp* **shot**) *n* (*on branch, seedling*) germoglio ▷ *vt* (*game*) cacciare, andare a caccia di; (*person*) sparare a; (*execute*) fucilare; (*film*) girare ▷ *vi* (*with gun*) **to ~ (at)** fare fuoco (su); (*with bow*) **to ~ (at)** tirare (su); (*Football*) sparare, tirare (forte); **shoot down** *vt* (*plane*) abbattere; **shoot up** *vi* (*fig*) salire alle stelle; **shooting** *n* (*shots*) sparatoria; (*Hunting*) caccia

shop [ʃɔp] *n* negozio; (*workshop*) officina ▷ *vi* (*also:* **go ~ping**) fare spese; **shop assistant** (*BRIT*) *n* commesso(-a); **shopkeeper** *n* negoziante *m/f*, bottegaio(-a); **shoplifting** *n* taccheggio; **shopping** *n* (*goods*) spesa, acquisti *mpl*; **shopping bag** *n* borsa per la spesa; **shopping centre** (*US* **shopping center**) *n* centro commerciale; **shopping mall** *n* centro commerciale; **shopping trolley** *n* (*BRIT*) carrello del supermercato; **shop window** *n* vetrina

shore [ʃɔːʳ] *n* (*of sea*) riva, spiaggia; (*of lake*) riva ▷ *vt* **to ~ (up)** puntellare; **on ~** a riva

short [ʃɔːt] *adj* (*not long*) corto(-a); (*soon finished*) breve; (*person*) basso(-a); (*curt*) brusco(-a), secco(-a); (*insufficient*) insufficiente ▷ *n* (*also:* **~ film**) cortometraggio; **to be ~ of sth** essere a corto di *o* mancare di qc; **in ~** in breve; **~ of doing** a meno che non si faccia; **everything ~ of** tutto fuorché; **it is ~ for** è l'abbreviazione *o* il diminutivo di; **to cut ~** (*speech, visit*) accorciare, abbreviare; **to fall ~ of** venir meno a; non soddisfare; **to run ~ of** rimanere senza; **to stop ~** fermarsi di colpo; **to stop ~ of** non arrivare fino a; **shortage** *n* scarsezza, carenza; **shortbread** *n* biscotto di pasta frolla; **shortcoming** *n* difetto; **short(crust) pastry** (*BRIT*) *n* pasta frolla; **shortcut** *n* scorciatoia; **shorten** *vt* accorciare, ridurre; **shortfall** *n* deficit *m*; **shorthand** (*BRIT*) *n* stenografia; **short-lived** *adj* di breve durata; **shortly** *adv* fra poco; **shorts** *npl* (*also:* **a pair of shorts**) i calzoncini; **short-sighted** (*BRIT*) *adj* miope; **short-sleeved** [ʃɔːtsliːvd] *adj* a maniche corte; **short story** *n* racconto, novella; **short-tempered** *adj* irascibile;

short-term *adj* (*effect*) di *o* a breve durata; (*borrowing*) a breve scadenza

shot [ʃɔt] *pt, pp of* **shoot** ▷ *n* sparo, colpo; (*try*) prova; (*Football*) tiro; (*injection*) iniezione *f*; (*Phot*) foto *f inv*; **like a ~** come un razzo; (*very readily*) immediatamente; **shotgun** *n* fucile *m* da caccia

should [ʃud] *aux vb* **I ~ go now** dovrei andare ora; **he ~ be there now** dovrebbe essere arrivato ora; **I ~ go if I were you** se fossi in te andrei; **I ~ like to** mi piacerebbe

shoulder [ʃəuldəʳ] *n* spalla; (*BRIT: of road*): **hard ~** banchina ▷ *vt* (*fig*) addossarsi, prendere sulle proprie spalle; **shoulder blade** *n* scapola

shouldn't [ʃudnt] = **should not**

shout [ʃaut] *n* urlo, grido ▷ *vt* gridare ▷ *vi* (*also:* **~ out**) urlare, gridare

shove [ʃʌv] *vt* spingere; (*inf: put*): **to ~ sth in** ficcare qc in

shovel [ʃʌvl] *n* pala ▷ *vt* spalare

show [ʃəu] (*pt* **showed**, *pp* **shown**) *n* (*of emotion*) dimostrazione *f*, manifestazione *f*; (*semblance*) apparenza; (*exhibition*) mostra, esposizione *f*; (*Theatre, Cinema*) spettacolo ▷ *vt* far vedere, mostrare; (*courage etc*) dimostrare, dar prova di; (*exhibit*) esporre ▷ *vi* vedersi, essere visibile; **for ~** per fare scena; **on ~** (*exhibits etc*) esposto(-a); **can you ~ me where it is, please?** può mostrarmi dov'è, per favore?; **show in** *vt* (*person*) far entrare; **show off** *vi* (*pej*) esibirsi, mettersi in mostra ▷ *vt* (*display*) mettere in risalto; (*pej*) mettere in mostra; **show out** *vt* (*person*) accompagnare alla porta; **show up** *vi* (*stand out*) essere ben visibile; (*inf: turn up*) farsi vedere ▷ *vt* mettere in risalto; **show business** *n* industria dello spettacolo

shower [ʃauəʳ] *n* (*rain*) acquazzone *m*; (*of stones etc*) pioggia; (*also:* **~bath**) doccia ▷ *vi* fare la doccia ▷ *vt* **to ~ sb with** (*gifts, abuse etc*) coprire qn di; (*missiles*) lanciare contro qn una pioggia di; **to have a ~** fare la doccia; **shower cap** *n* cuffia da doccia; **shower gel** *n* gel *m* doccia *inv*

showing [ʃəuɪŋ] *n* (*of film*) proiezione *f*

show jumping *n* concorso ippico (di salto ad ostacoli)

shown [ʃəun] *pp of* **show**

show: **show-off** (*inf*) *n* (*person*) esibizionista *m/f*; **showroom** *n* sala d'esposizione

shrank [ʃræŋk] *pt of* **shrink**

shred [ʃred] *n* (*gen pl*) brandello ▷ *vt* fare a brandelli; (*Culin*) sminuzzare, tagliuzzare

shrewd [ʃruːd] *adj* astuto(-a), scaltro(-a)

shriek [ʃriːk] *n* strillo ▷ *vi* strillare

shrimp [ʃrɪmp] *n* gamberetto

shrine [ʃraɪn] n reliquario; (place) santuario
shrink [ʃrɪŋk] (pt **shrank**, pp **shrunk**) vi restringersi; (fig) ridursi; (also: **~ away**) ritrarsi ▷ vt (wool) far restringere ▷ n (inf: pej) psicanalista m/f; **to ~ from doing sth** rifuggire dal fare qc
shrivel ['ʃrɪvl] (also: **~ up**) vt raggrinzare, avvizzire ▷ vi raggrinzirsi, avvizzire
shroud [ʃraʊd] n lenzuolo funebre ▷ vt **~ed in mystery** avvolto(-a) nel mistero
Shrove Tuesday ['ʃrəʊv-] n martedì m grasso
shrub [ʃrʌb] n arbusto
shrug [ʃrʌɡ] n scrollata di spalle ▷ vt, vi **to ~ (one's shoulders)** alzare le spalle, fare spallucce; **shrug off** vt passare sopra a
shrunk [ʃrʌŋk] pp of **shrink**
shudder ['ʃʌdər] n brivido ▷ vi rabbrividire
shuffle ['ʃʌfl] vt (cards) mescolare; **to ~ (one's feet)** strascicare i piedi
shun [ʃʌn] vt sfuggire, evitare
shut [ʃʌt] (pt, pp **shut**) vt chiudere ▷ vi chiudersi, chiudere; **shut down** vt, vi chiudere definitivamente; **shut up** vi (inf: keep quiet) stare zitto(-a), fare silenzio ▷ vt (close) chiudere; (silence) far tacere; **shutter** n imposta; (Phot) otturatore m
shuttle ['ʃʌtl] n spola, navetta; (space shuttle) navetta (spaziale); (also: **~ service**) servizio m navetta inv; **shuttlecock** ['ʃʌtlkɔk] n volano
shy [ʃaɪ] adj timido(-a)
sibling ['sɪblɪŋ] n (formal) fratello/sorella
Sicily ['sɪsɪlɪ] n Sicilia
sick [sɪk] adj (ill) malato(-a); (vomiting): **to be ~** vomitare; (humour) macabro(-a); **to feel ~** avere la nausea; **to be ~ of** (fig) averne abbastanza di; **sickening** adj (fig) disgustoso(-a), rivoltante; **sick leave** n congedo per malattia; **sickly** adj malaticcio(-a); (causing nausea) nauseante; **sickness** n malattia; (vomiting) vomito
side [saɪd] n lato; (of lake) riva; (team) squadra ▷ cpd (door, entrance) laterale ▷ vi **to ~ with sb** parteggiare per qn, prendere le parti di qn; **by the ~ of** a fianco di; (road) sul ciglio di; **~ by ~** fianco a fianco; **from ~ to ~** da una parte all'altra; **to take ~s (with)** schierarsi (con); **sideboard** n credenza; **sideboards** (BRIT), **sideburns** ['saɪdbə:nz] npl (whiskers) basette fpl; **sidelight** n (Aut) luce f di posizione; **sideline** n (Sport) linea laterale; (fig) attività secondaria; **side order** n contorno (pietanza); **side road** n strada secondaria; **side street** n traversa; **sidetrack** vt (fig) distrarre; **sidewalk** (US) n marciapiede m; **sideways** adv (move) di lato, di fianco

siege [si:dʒ] n assedio
sieve [sɪv] n setaccio ▷ vt setacciare
sift [sɪft] vt passare al crivello; (fig) vagliare
sigh [saɪ] n sospiro ▷ vi sospirare
sight [saɪt] n (faculty) vista; (spectacle) spettacolo; (on gun) mira ▷ vt avvistare; **in ~** in vista; **on ~** a vista; **out of ~** non visibile; **sightseeing** n giro turistico; **to go sightseeing** visitare una località
sign [saɪn] n segno; (with hand etc) segno, gesto; (notice) insegna, cartello ▷ vt firmare; (player) ingaggiare; **where do I ~?** dove devo firmare?; **sign for** vt fus (item) firmare per l'accettazione di; **sign in** vi firmare il registro (all'arrivo); **sign on** vi (Mil) arruolarsi; (as unemployed) iscriversi sulla lista (dell'ufficio di collocamento) ▷ vt (Mil) arruolare; (employee) assumere; **sign up** vi (Mil) arruolarsi; (for course) iscriversi ▷ vt (player) ingaggiare; (recruits) reclutare
signal ['sɪgnl] n segnale m ▷ vi (Aut) segnalare, mettere la freccia ▷ vt (person) fare segno a; (message) comunicare per mezzo di segnali
signature ['sɪgnətʃər] n firma
significance [sɪg'nɪfɪkəns] n significato; importanza
significant [sɪg'nɪfɪkənt] adj significativo(-a)
signify ['sɪgnɪfaɪ] vt significare
sign language n linguaggio dei muti
signpost ['saɪnpəʊst] n cartello indicatore
Sikh [si:k] adj, n sikh (m/f) inv
silence ['saɪlns] n silenzio ▷ vt far tacere, ridurre al silenzio
silent ['saɪlnt] adj silenzioso(-a); (film) muto(-a); **to remain ~** tacere, stare zitto
silhouette [sɪlu:'ɛt] n silhouette f inv
silicon chip ['sɪlɪkən-] n piastrina di silicio
silk [sɪlk] n seta ▷ adj di seta
silly ['sɪlɪ] adj stupido(-a), sciocco(-a)
silver ['sɪlvər] n argento; (money) monete da 5, 10, 20 or 50 pence; (also: **~ware**) argenteria ▷ adj d'argento; **silver-plated** adj argentato(-a)
similar ['sɪmɪlər] adj **~ (to)** simile (a); **similarity** [sɪmɪ'lærɪtɪ] n somiglianza, rassomiglianza; **similarly** adv allo stesso modo; così pure
simmer ['sɪmər] vi cuocere a fuoco lento
simple ['sɪmpl] adj semplice; **simplicity** [-'plɪsɪtɪ] n semplicità; **simplify** vt semplificare; **simply** adv semplicemente
simulate ['sɪmjuleɪt] vt fingere, simulare
simultaneous [sɪməl'teɪnɪəs] adj simultaneo(-a); **simultaneously** adv simultaneamente, contemporaneamente
sin [sɪn] n peccato ▷ vi peccare
since [sɪns] adv da allora ▷ prep da ▷ conj

s

(*time*) da quando; (*because*) poiché, dato che; **~ then, ever ~** da allora

sincere [sɪn'sɪəʳ] *adj* sincero(-a); **sincerely** *adv* **yours sincerely** (*in letters*) distinti saluti

sing [sɪŋ] (*pt* **sang**, *pp* **sung**) *vt*, *vi* cantare

Singapore [sɪŋgə'pɔːʳ] *n* Singapore *f*

singer ['sɪŋəʳ] *n* cantante *m/f*

singing ['sɪŋɪŋ] *n* canto

single ['sɪŋgl] *adj* solo(-a), unico(-a); (*unmarried: man*) celibe; (: *woman*) nubile; (*not double*) semplice ▷ *n* (*BRIT: also:* **~ ticket**) biglietto di (sola) andata; (*record*) 45 giri *m*; (*Tennis*) singolo; **single out** *vt* scegliere; (*distinguish*) distinguere; **single bed** *n* letto singolo; **single file** *n* **in single file** in fila indiana; **single-handed** *adv* senza aiuto, da solo(-a); **single-minded** *adj* tenace, risoluto(-a); **single parent** *n* (*mother*) ragazza *f* madre *inv*; (*father*) ragazzo *m* padre *inv*; **single-parent family** famiglia monoparentale; **single room** *n* camera singola

singular ['sɪŋgjuləʳ] *adj* (*exceptional,* Ling) singolare ▷ *n* (Ling) singolare *m*

sinister ['sɪnɪstəʳ] *adj* sinistro(-a)

sink [sɪŋk] (*pt* **sank**, *pp* **sunk**) *n* lavandino, acquaio ▷ *vt* (*ship*) (fare) affondare, colare a picco; (*foundations*) scavare; (*piles etc*): **to ~ sth into** conficcare qc in ▷ *vi* affondare, andare a fondo; (*ground etc*) cedere, avvallarsi; **my heart sank** mi sentii venir meno; **sink in** *vi* penetrare

sinus ['saɪnəs] *n* (*Anat*) seno

sip [sɪp] *n* sorso ▷ *vt* sorseggiare

sir [səʳ] *n* signore *m*; **S~ John Smith** Sir John Smith; **yes ~** sì, signore

siren ['saɪərn] *n* sirena

sirloin ['səːlɔɪn] *n* controfiletto

sister ['sɪstəʳ] *n* sorella; (*nun*) suora; (*BRIT: nurse*) infermiera *f* caposala *inv*; **sister-in-law** *n* cognata

sit [sɪt] (*pt*, *pp* **sat**) *vi* sedere, sedersi; (*assembly*) essere in seduta; (*for painter*) posare ▷ *vt* (*exam*) sostenere, dare; **sit back** *vi* (*in seat*) appoggiarsi allo schienale; **sit down** *vi* sedersi; **sit on** *vt fus* (*jury, committee*) far parte di; **sit up** *vi* tirarsi su a sedere; (*not go to bed*) stare alzato(-a) fino a tardi

sitcom ['sɪtkɔm] *n abbr* (= *situation comedy*) commedia di situazione; (*TV*) telefilm *m inv* comico d'interni

site [saɪt] *n* posto; (*also:* **building ~**) cantiere *m* ▷ *vt* situare

sitting ['sɪtɪŋ] *n* (*of assembly etc*) seduta; (*in canteen*) turno; **sitting room** *n* soggiorno

situated ['sɪtjueɪtɪd] *adj* situato(-a)

situation [sɪtju'eɪʃən] *n* situazione *f*; (*job*)

lavoro; (*location*) posizione *f*; **"~s vacant"** (*BRIT*) "offerte *fpl* di impiego"

six [sɪks] *num* sei; **sixteen** *num* sedici; **sixteenth** [sɪks'tiːnθ] *num* sedicesimo(-a); **sixth** *num* sesto(-a); **sixth form** *n* (*BRIT*) ultimo biennio delle scuole superiori; **sixth-form college** *n* istituto che offre corsi di preparazione all'esame di maturità per ragazzi dai 16 ai 18 anni; **sixtieth** ['sɪkstɪɪθ] *num* sessantesimo(-a) ▷ *pron* (*in series*) sessantesimo(-a); (*fraction*) sessantesimo; **sixty** *num* sessanta

size [saɪz] *n* dimensioni *fpl*; (*of clothing*) taglia, misura; (*of shoes*) numero; (*glue*) colla; **sizeable** *adj* considerevole

sizzle ['sɪzl] *vi* sfrigolare

skate [skeɪt] *n* pattino; (*fish: pl inv*) razza ▷ *vi* pattinare; **skateboard** *n* skateboard *m inv*; **skateboarding** *n* skateboard *m inv*; **skater** *n* pattinatore(-trice); **skating** *n* pattinaggio; **skating rink** *n* pista di pattinaggio

skeleton ['skɛlɪtn] *n* scheletro

skeptical ['skɛptɪkl] (*US*) *adj* = **sceptical**

sketch [skɛtʃ] *n* (*drawing*) schizzo, abbozzo; (*Theatre*) scenetta comica, sketch *m inv* ▷ *vt* abbozzare, schizzare

skewer ['skjuːəʳ] *n* spiedo

ski [skiː] *n* sci *m inv* ▷ *vi* sciare; **ski boot** *n* scarpone *m* da sci

skid [skɪd] *n* slittamento ▷ *vi* slittare

ski: skier ['skiːəʳ] *n* sciatore(-trice); **skiing** ['skiːɪŋ] *n* sci *m*

skilful ['skɪlful] (*US* **skillful**) *adj* abile

ski lift *n* sciovia

skill [skɪl] *n* abilità *f inv*, capacità *f inv*; **skilled** *adj* esperto(-a); (*worker*) qualificato(-a), specializzato(-a)

skim [skɪm] *vt* (*milk*) scremare; (*glide over*) sfiorare ▷ *vi* **to ~ through** (*fig*) scorrere, dare una scorsa a; **skimmed milk** (*US* **skim milk**) *n* latte *m* scremato

skin [skɪn] *n* pelle *f* ▷ *vt* (*fruit etc*) sbucciare; (*animal*) scuoiare, spellare; **skinhead** *n* skinhead *m/f inv*; **skinny** *adj* molto magro(-a), pelle e ossa *inv*

skip [skɪp] *n* saltello, balzo; (*BRIT: container*) benna ▷ *vi* saltare; (*with rope*) saltare la corda ▷ *vt* saltare

ski: ski pass *n* ski pass *m*; **ski pole** *n* racchetta (da sci)

skipper ['skɪpəʳ] *n* (*Naut, Sport*) capitano

skipping rope ['skɪpɪŋ-] (*US* **skip rope**) *n* corda per saltare

skirt [skəːt] *n* gonna, sottana ▷ *vt* fiancheggiare, costeggiare

skirting board (*BRIT*) *n* zoccolo

ski slope *n* pista da sci

ski suit *n* tuta da sci

skull [skʌl] n cranio, teschio

skunk [skʌŋk] n moffetta

sky [skaɪ] n cielo; **skyscraper** n grattacielo

slab [slæb] n lastra; (*of cake, cheese*) fetta

slack [slæk] adj (*loose*) allentato(-a); (*slow*) lento(-a); (*careless*) negligente; **slacks** npl (*trousers*) pantaloni mpl

slain [sleɪn] pp of **slay**

slam [slæm] vt (*door*) sbattere; (*throw*) scaraventare; (*criticize*) stroncare ▷ vi sbattere

slander ['slɑːndər] n calunnia; diffamazione f

slang [slæŋ] n gergo, slang m

slant [slɑːnt] n pendenza, inclinazione f; (*fig*) angolazione f, punto di vista

slap [slæp] n manata, pacca; (*on face*) schiaffo ▷ vt dare una manata a; schiaffeggiare ▷ adv (*directly*) in pieno; **~ a coat of paint on it** dagli una mano di vernice

slash [slæʃ] vt tagliare; (*face*) stregiare; (*fig: prices*) ridurre drasticamente, tagliare

slate [sleɪt] n ardesia; (*piece*) lastra di ardesia ▷ vt (*fig: criticize*) stroncare, distruggere

slaughter ['slɔːtər] n strage f, massacro ▷ vt (*animal*) macellare; (*people*) trucidare, massacrare; **slaughterhouse** n macello, mattatoio

Slav [slɑːv] adj, n slavo(-a)

slave [sleɪv] n schiavo(-a) ▷ vi (*also: ~ away*) lavorare come uno schiavo; **slavery** n schiavitù f

slay [sleɪ] (pt **slew**, pp **slain**) vt (*formal*) uccidere

sleazy ['sliːzɪ] adj trasandato(-a)

sled [slɛd] (us) = **sledge**

sledge [slɛdʒ] n slitta

sleek [sliːk] adj (*hair, fur*) lucido(-a), lucente; (*car, boat*) slanciato(-a), affusolato(-a)

sleep [sliːp] (pt, pp **slept**) n sonno ▷ vi dormire; **to go to ~** addormentarsi; **sleep in** vi (*oversleep*) dormire fino a tardi; **sleep together** vi (*have sex*) andare a letto insieme; **sleeper** (BRIT) n (Rail: on track) traversina; (: train) treno di vagoni letto; **sleeping bag** n sacco a pelo; **sleeping car** n vagone m letto inv, carrozza f letto inv; **sleeping pill** n sonnifero; **sleepover** n notte f che un ragazzino passa da amici; **sleepwalk** vi camminare nel sonno; (*as a habit*) essere sonnambulo(-a); **sleepy** adj assonnato(-a), sonnolento(-a); (*fig*) addormentato(-a)

sleet [sliːt] n nevischio

sleeve [sliːv] n manica; (*of record*) copertina; **sleeveless** adj (*garment*) senza maniche

sleigh [sleɪ] n slitta

slender ['slɛndər] adj snello(-a), sottile; (*not enough*) scarso(-a), esiguo(-a)

slept [slɛpt] pt, pp of **sleep**

slew [sluː] pt of **slay** ▷ vi (BRIT) girare

slice [slaɪs] n fetta ▷ vt affettare, tagliare a fette

slick [slɪk] adj (*skilful*) brillante; (*clever*) furbo(-a) ▷ n (*also*: **oil ~**) chiazza di petrolio

slide [slaɪd] (pt, pp **slid**) n scivolone m; (*in playground*) scivolo; (Phot) diapositiva; (BRIT: also: **hair ~**) fermaglio (per capelli) ▷ vt far scivolare ▷ vi scivolare; **sliding** adj (*door*) scorrevole

slight [slaɪt] adj (*slim*) snello(-a), sottile; (*frail*) delicato(-a), fragile; (*trivial*) insignificante; (*small*) piccolo(-a) ▷ n offesa, affronto; **not in the ~est** affatto, neppure per sogno; **slightly** adv lievemente, un po'

slim [slɪm] adj magro(-a), snello(-a) ▷ vi dimagrire; fare (or seguire) una dieta dimagrante; **slimming** ['slɪmɪŋ] adj (*diet*) dimagrante; (*food*) ipocalorico(-a)

slimy ['slaɪmɪ] adj (*also fig: person*) viscido(-a); (*covered with mud*) melmoso(-a)

sling [slɪŋ] (pt, pp **slung**) n (Med) fascia al collo; (*for baby*) marsupio ▷ vt lanciare, tirare

slip [slɪp] n scivolata, scivolone m; (*mistake*) errore m, sbaglio; (*underskirt*) sottoveste f; (*of paper*) striscia di carta; tagliando, scontrino ▷ vt (*slide*) far scivolare ▷ vi (*slide*) scivolare; (*move smoothly*) **to ~ into/out of** scivolare in/fuori da; (*decline*) declinare; **to ~ sth on/off** infilarsi/togliersi qc; **to give sb the ~** sfuggire qn; **a ~ of the tongue** un lapsus linguae; **slip up** vi sbagliarsi

slipper ['slɪpər] n pantofola

slippery ['slɪpərɪ] adj scivoloso(-a)

slip road (BRIT) n (*to motorway*) rampa di accesso

slit [slɪt] (pt, pp **slit**) n fessura, fenditura; (*cut*) taglio ▷ vt fendere; tagliare

slog [slɔg] (BRIT) n faticata ▷ vi lavorare con accanimento, sgobbare

slogan ['sləugən] n motto, slogan m inv

slope [sləup] n pendio; (*side of mountain*) versante m; (*ski slope*) pista; (*of roof*) pendenza; (*of floor*) inclinazione f ▷ vi **to ~ down** declinare; **to ~ up** essere in salita; **sloping** adj inclinato(-a)

sloppy ['slɔpɪ] adj (*work*) tirato(-a) via; (*appearance*) sciatto(-a)

slot [slɔt] n fessura ▷ vt **to ~ sth into** infilare qc in; **slot machine** n

s

(BRIT: vending machine) distributore m automatico; (for gambling) slot-machine f inv

Slovakia [sləu'vækıə] n Slovacchia

Slovene ['sləuvi:n] adj sloveno(-a) ▷ n sloveno(-a); (Ling) sloveno

Slovenia [sləu'vi:nıə] n Slovenia; **Slovenian** adj, n = **Slovene**

slow [sləu] adj lento(-a); (watch): **to be ~** essere indietro ▷ adv lentamente ▷ vt, vi (also: **~ down, ~ up**) rallentare; **"~"** (road sign) "rallentare"; **slow down** vi rallentare; **slowly** adv lentamente; **slow motion** n **in slow motion** al rallentatore

slug [slʌg] n lumaca; (bullet) pallottola; **sluggish** adj lento(-a); (trading) stagnante

slum [slʌm] n catapecchia

slump [slʌmp] n crollo, caduta; (economic) depressione f, crisi f inv ▷ vi crollare

slung [slʌŋ] pt, pp of **sling**

slur [slə:ᵊ] n (fig): **~ (on)** calunnia (su) ▷ vt pronunciare in modo indistinto

sly [slaɪ] adj (smile, remark) sornione(-a); (person) furbo(-a)

smack [smæk] n (slap) pacca; (on face) schiaffo ▷ vt schiaffeggiare; (child) picchiare ▷ vi **to ~ of** puzzare di

small [smɔ:l] adj piccolo(-a); **small ads** (BRIT) npl piccola pubblicità; **small change** n moneta, spiccioli mpl

smart [smɑ:t] adj elegante; (fashionable) alla moda; (clever) intelligente; (quick) sveglio(-a) ▷ vi bruciare; **smartcard** ['smɑ:tkɑ:d] n smartcard f inv, carta intelligente

smash [smæʃ] n (also: **~-up**) scontro, collisione f; (smash hit) successone m ▷ vt frantumare, fracassare; (Sport: record) battere ▷ vi frantumarsi, andare in pezzi; **smashing** (inf) adj favoloso(-a), formidabile

smear [smɪəᵊ] n macchia; (Med) striscio ▷ vt spalmare; (make dirty) sporcare; **smear test** n (BRIT Med) Pap-test m inv

smell [smɛl] (pt **smelt** or **smelled**) n odore m; (sense) olfatto, odorato ▷ vt sentire (l')odore di ▷ vi (food etc): **to ~ (of)** avere odore (di); (pej) puzzare, avere un cattivo odore; **smelly** adj puzzolente

smelt [smɛlt] pt, pp of **smell** ▷ vt (ore) fondere

smile [smaɪl] n sorriso ▷ vi sorridere

smirk [smə:k] n sorriso furbo; sorriso compiaciuto

smog [smɔg] n smog m

smoke [sməuk] n fumo ▷ vt, vi fumare; **do you mind if I ~?** le dà fastidio se fumo?; **smoke alarm** n rivelatore f di fumo; **smoked** adj (bacon, glass) affumicato(-a);

smoker n (person) fumatore(-trice); (Rail) carrozza per fumatori; **smoking** n fumo; **"no smoking"** (sign) "vietato fumare"; **smoky** adj fumoso(-a); (taste) affumicato(-a)

smooth [smu:ð] adj liscio(-a); (sauce) omogeneo(-a); (flavour, whisky) amabile; (movement) regolare; (person) mellifluo(-a) ▷ vt (also: **~ out**) lisciare, spianare; (: difficulties) appianare

smother ['smʌðəᵊ] vt soffocare

SMS abbr (= short message service) SMS; **SMS message** n SMS m inv, messaggino

smudge [smʌdʒ] n macchia; sbavatura ▷ vt imbrattare, sporcare

smug [smʌg] adj soddisfatto(-a), compiaciuto(-a)

smuggle ['smʌgl] vt contrabbandare; **smuggling** n contrabbando

snack [snæk] n spuntino; **snack bar** n tavola calda, snack bar m inv

snag [snæg] n intoppo, ostacolo imprevisto

snail [sneɪl] n chiocciola

snake [sneɪk] n serpente m

snap [snæp] n (sound) schianto, colpo secco; (photograph) istantanea ▷ adj improvviso(-a) ▷ vt (far) schioccare; (break) spezzare di netto ▷ vi spezzarsi con un rumore secco; (fig: person) parlare con tono secco; **to ~ shut** chiudersi di scatto; **snap at** vt fus (dog) cercare di mordere; **snap up** vt afferrare; **snapshot** n istantanea

snarl [snɑ:l] vi ringhiare

snatch [snætʃ] n (small amount) frammento ▷ vt strappare (con violenza); (fig) rubare

sneak [sni:k] (pt (US) **snuck**) vi **to ~ in/out** entrare/uscire di nascosto ▷ n spione/a; **to ~ up on sb** avvicinarsi quatto quatto a qn; **sneakers** npl scarpe fpl da ginnastica

sneer [snɪəᵊ] vi sogghignare; **to ~ at** farsi beffe di

sneeze [sni:z] n starnuto ▷ vi starnutire

sniff [snɪf] n fiutata, annusata ▷ vi tirare su col naso ▷ vt fiutare, annusare

snigger ['snɪgəᵊ] vi ridacchiare, ridere sotto i baffi

snip [snɪp] n pezzetto; (bargain) (buon) affare m, occasione f ▷ vt tagliare

sniper ['snaɪpəᵊ] n (marksman) franco tiratore m, cecchino

snob [snɔb] n snob m/f inv

snooker ['snu:kəᵊ] n tipo di gioco del biliardo

snoop ['snu:p] vi **to ~ about** curiosare

snooze [snu:z] n sonnellino, pisolino ▷ vi fare un sonnellino

snore [snɔ:ᵊ] vi russare

snorkel ['snɔ:kl] n (of swimmer) respiratore

_m_ a tubo

snort [snɔːt] _n_ sbuffo ▷ _vi_ sbuffare

snow [snəʊ] _n_ neve _f_ ▷ _vi_ nevicare;
snowball _n_ palla di neve ▷ _vi_ (_fig_) crescere
a vista d'occhio; **snowstorm** _n_ tormenta

snub [snʌb] _vt_ snobbare ▷ _n_ offesa,
affronto

snug [snʌg] _adj_ comodo(-a); (_room, house_)
accogliente, comodo(-a)

○ **KEYWORD**

so [səʊ] _adv_ **1** (_thus, likewise_) così; **if so** se è
così, quand'è così; **I didn't do it — you did
so!** non l'ho fatto io — sì che l'hai fatto!;
so do I, so am I _etc_ anch'io; **it's 5 o'clock
— so it is!** sono le 5 — davvero!; **I hope
so** lo spero; **I think so** penso di sì; **so far**
finora, fin qui; (_in past_) fino ad allora
2 (_in comparisons etc: to such a degree_) così;
so big (that) così grande (che); **she's not
so clever as her brother** lei non è (così)
intelligente come suo fratello
3: **so much** _adj_ tanto(-a)
▷ _adv_ tanto; **I've got so much work/
money** ho tanto lavoro/tanti soldi; **I love
you so much** ti amo tanto; **so many**
tanti(-e)
4 (_phrases_): **10 or so** circa 10; **so long!** (_inf:
goodbye_) ciao!, ci vediamo!
▷ _conj_ **1** (_expressing purpose_): **so as to do**
in modo or così da fare; **we hurried so as
not to be late** ci affrettammo per non fare
tardi; **so (that)** affinché + _sub_, perché + _sub_
2 (_expressing result_): **he didn't arrive so I
left** non è venuto così me ne sono andata;
so you see, I could have gone vedi, sarei
potuto andare

soak [səʊk] _vt_ inzuppare; (_clothes_) mettere
a mollo ▷ _vi_ (_clothes etc_) essere a mollo;
soak up _vt_ assorbire; **soaking** _adj_ (_also:
soaking wet) fradicio(-a)

so-and-so ['səʊənsəʊ] _n_ (_somebody_) un
tale; **Mr/Mrs ~** signor/signora tal dei tali

soap [səʊp] _n_ sapone _m_; **soap opera** _n_
soap opera _f inv_; **soap powder** _n_ detersivo

soar [sɔːʳ] _vi_ volare in alto; (_price etc_) salire
alle stelle; (_building_) ergersi

sob [sɔb] _n_ singhiozzo ▷ _vi_ singhiozzare

sober ['səʊbəʳ] _adj_ sobrio(-a); (_not drunk_)
non ubriaco(-a); (_moderate_) moderato(-a);
sober up _vt_ far passare la sbornia a ▷ _vi_
farsi passare la sbornia

so-called ['səʊ'kɔːld] _adj_ cosiddetto(-a)

soccer ['sɔkəʳ] _n_ calcio

sociable ['səʊʃəbl] _adj_ socievole

social ['səʊʃl] _adj_ sociale ▷ _n_ festa, serata;
socialism _n_ socialismo; **socialist** _adj, n_

socialista _m/f_; **socialize** _vi_ **to socialize
(with)** socializzare (con); **social life** _n_
vita sociale; **socially** _adv_ socialmente,
in società; **social security** (_BRIT_) _n_
previdenza sociale; **social services** _npl_
servizi _mpl_ sociali; **social work** _n_ servizio
sociale; **social worker** _n_ assistente _m/f_
sociale

society [sə'saɪətɪ] _n_ società _f inv_; (_club_)
società, associazione _f_; (_also:_ **high ~**) alta
società

sociology [səʊsɪ'ɔlədʒɪ] _n_ sociologia

sock [sɔk] _n_ calzino

socket ['sɔkɪt] _n_ cavità _f inv_; (_of eye_) orbita;
(_BRIT: Elec: also:_ **wall ~**) presa di corrente

soda ['səʊdə] _n_ (_Chem_) soda; (_also:_ **~
water**) acqua di seltz; (_US: also:_ **~ pop**)
gassosa

sodium ['səʊdɪəm] _n_ sodio

sofa ['səʊfə] _n_ sofà _m inv_; **sofa bed** _n_
divano _m_ letto _inv_

soft [sɔft] _adj_ (_not rough_) morbido(-a); (_not
hard_) soffice; (_not loud_) sommesso(-a); (_not
bright_) tenue; (_kind_) gentile; **soft drink**
_n_ analcolico; **soft drugs** _npl_ droghe _fpl_
leggere; **soften** ['sɔfn] _vt_ ammorbidire;
addolcire; attenuare ▷ _vi_ ammorbidirsi;
addolcirsi; attenuarsi; **softly** _adv_
dolcemente; morbidamente; **software**
['sɔftweəʳ] _n_ (_Comput_) software _m_

soggy ['sɔgɪ] _adj_ inzuppato(-a)

soil [sɔɪl] _n_ terreno ▷ _vt_ sporcare

solar ['səʊləʳ] _adj_ solare; **solar power** _n_
energie solare; **solar system** _n_ sistema
_m_ solare

sold [səʊld] _pt, pp of_ **sell**

soldier ['səʊldʒəʳ] _n_ soldato, militare _m_

sold out _adj_ (_Comm_) esaurito(-a)

sole [səʊl] _n_ (_of foot_) pianta (del piede);
(_of shoe_) suola; (_fish: pl inv_) sogliola
▷ _adj_ solo(-a), unico(-a); **solely** _adv_
solamente, unicamente; **I will hold you
solely responsible** la considererò il solo
responsabile

solemn ['sɔləm] _adj_ solenne

solicitor [sə'lɪsɪtəʳ] (_BRIT_) _n_ (_for wills etc_)
≈ notaio; (_in court_) ≈ avvocato

solid ['sɔlɪd] _adj_ solido(-a); (_not hollow_)
pieno(-a); (_meal_) sostanzioso(-a) ▷ _n_
solido

solitary ['sɔlɪtərɪ] _adj_ solitario(-a)

solitude ['sɔlɪtjuːd] _n_ solitudine _f_

solo ['səʊləʊ] _n_ assolo; **soloist** _n_ solista
_m/f_

soluble ['sɔljʊbl] _adj_ solubile

solution [sə'luːʃən] _n_ soluzione _f_

solve [sɔlv] _vt_ risolvere

solvent ['sɔlvənt] _adj_ (_Comm_) solvibile ▷ _n_
(_Chem_) solvente _m_

sombre ['sɔmbər] (US **somber**) adj
scuro(-a); (mood, person) triste

⊙ KEYWORD

some [sʌm] adj 1 (a certain amount or number
of): **some tea/water/cream** del tè/
dell'acqua/della panna; **some children/
apples** dei bambini/delle mele
2 (certain: in contrasts) certo(-a); **some
people say that ...** alcuni dicono che ...,
certa gente dice che ...
3 (unspecified) un(a) certo(-a), qualche;
some woman was asking for you una
tale chiedeva di lei; **some day** un giorno;
some day next week un giorno della
prossima settimana
▷ pron 1 (a certain number) alcuni(-e),
certi(-e); **I've got some** (books etc) ne ho
alcuni; **some (of them) have been sold**
alcuni sono stati venduti
2 (a certain amount) un po'; **I've got some**
(money, milk) ne ho un po'; **I've read some
of the book** ho letto parte del libro
▷ adv **some 10 people** circa 10 persone

some: **somebody** ['sʌmbədɪ] pron
= **someone**; **somehow** ['sʌmhau] adv
in un modo o nell'altro, in qualche modo;
(for some reason) per qualche ragione;
someone ['sʌmwʌn] pron qualcuno;
someplace ['sʌmpleɪs] (US) adv
= **somewhere**; **something** ['sʌmθɪŋ]
pron qualcosa, qualche cosa; **something
nice** qualcosa di bello; **something to do**
qualcosa da fare; **sometime** ['sʌmtaɪm]
adv (in future) una volta o l'altra; (in past):
sometime last month durante il mese
scorso; **sometimes** ['sʌmtaɪmz] adv
qualche volta; **somewhat** ['sʌmwɔt] adv
piuttosto; **somewhere** ['sʌmwɛər] adv in
or da qualche parte

son [sʌn] n figlio
song [sɔŋ] n canzone f
son-in-law ['sʌnɪnlɔː] n genero
soon [suːn] adv presto, fra poco; (early, a
short time after) presto; **~ afterwards** poco
dopo; see also **as**; **sooner** adv (time) prima;
(preference): **I would sooner do** preferirei
fare; **sooner or later** prima o poi
soothe [suːð] vt calmare
sophisticated [səˈfɪstɪkeɪtɪd]
adj sofisticato(-a); raffinato(-a);
complesso(-a)
sophomore ['sɔfəmɔːr] (US) n
studente(-essa) del secondo anno
soprano [səˈprɑːnəu] n (voice) soprano m;
(singer) soprano m/f
sorbet ['sɔːbeɪ] n sorbetto

sordid ['sɔːdɪd] adj sordido(-a)
sore [sɔːr] adj (painful) dolorante ▷ n piaga
sorrow ['sɔrəu] n dolore m
sorry ['sɔrɪ] adj spiacente; (condition,
excuse) misero(-a); **~!** scusa! (or scusi! or
scusate!); **to feel ~ for sb** rincrescersi
per qn
sort [sɔːt] n specie f, genere m; **sort out** vt
(papers) classificare; ordinare; (: letters etc)
smistare; (: problems) risolvere; (Comput)
ordinare
SOS n abbr (= save our souls) S.O.S. m inv
so-so ['səusəu] adv così così
sought [sɔːt] pt, pp of **seek**
soul [səul] n anima
sound [saund] adj (healthy) sano(-a); (safe,
not damaged) solido(-a), in buono stato;
(reliable, not superficial) solido(-a); (sensible)
giudizioso(-a), di buon senso ▷ adv **~
asleep** profondamente addormentato
▷ n suono; (noise) rumore m; (Geo) stretto
▷ vt (alarm) suonare ▷ vi suonare; (fig:
seem) sembrare; **to ~ like** rassomigliare a;
soundtrack n (of film) colonna sonora
soup [suːp] n minestra; brodo; zuppa
sour ['sauər] adj aspro(-a); (fruit)
acerbo(-a); (milk) acido(-a); (fig)
arcigno(-a); acido(-a); **it's ~ grapes** è
soltanto invidia
source [sɔːs] n fonte f, sorgente f; (fig)
fonte
south [sauθ] n sud m, meridione m,
mezzogiorno ▷ adj del sud, sud inv,
meridionale ▷ adv verso sud; **South
Africa** n Sudafrica m; **South African**
adj, n sudafricano(-a); **South America** n
Sudamerica m, America del sud; **South
American** adj, n sudamericano(-a);
southbound ['sauθbaund] adj (gen)
diretto(-a) a sud; (carriageway) sud
inv; **southeastern** [sauθˈiːstən] adj
sudorientale; **southern** ['sʌðən] adj
del sud, meridionale; esposto(-a) a sud;
South Korea n Corea f del Sud; **South
Pole** n Polo Sud; **southward(s)** adv
verso sud; **south-west** n sud-ovest
m; **southwestern** [sauθˈwestən] adj
sudoccidentale
souvenir [suːvəˈnɪər] n ricordo, souvenir
m inv
sovereign ['sɔvrɪn] adj, n sovrano(-a)
sow¹ [səu] (pt **sowed**, pp **sown**) vt
seminare
sow² [sau] n scrofa
soya ['sɔɪə] (US **soy**) n **~ bean** n seme m di
soia; **soya sauce** n salsa di soia
spa [spɑː] n (resort) stazione f termale; (US:
also: **health ~**) centro di cure estetiche
space [speɪs] n spazio; (room) posto;

spazio; (*length of time*) intervallo ▷ *cpd*
spaziale ▷ *vt* (*also*: **~ out**) distanziare;
spacecraft *n inv* veicolo spaziale;
spaceship *n* = **spacecraft**
spacious ['speɪʃəs] *adj* spazioso(-a),
ampio(-a)
spade [speɪd] *n* (*tool*) vanga; pala; (*child's*)
paletta; **~s** *npl* (*Cards*) picche *fpl*
spaghetti [spə'gɛtɪ] *n* spaghetti *mpl*
Spain [speɪn] *n* Spagna
spam [spæm] (*Comput*) *n* spamming ▷ *vt*
to ~ sb inviare a qn messaggi pubblicitari
non richiesti via email
span [spæn] *n* (*of bird, plane*) apertura
alare; (*of arch*) campata; (*in time*) periodo;
durata ▷ *vt* attraversare; (*fig*) abbracciare
Spaniard ['spænjəd] *n* spagnolo(-a)
Spanish ['spænɪʃ] *adj* spagnolo(-a) ▷ *n*
(*Ling*) spagnolo; **the ~** *npl* gli Spagnoli
spank [spæŋk] *vt* sculacciare
spanner ['spænə^r] (*BRIT*) *n* chiave *f* inglese
spare [spɛə^r] *adj* di riserva, di scorta;
(*surplus*) in più, d'avanzo ▷ *n* (*part*) pezzo
di ricambio ▷ *vt* (*do without*) fare a meno
di; (*afford to give*) concedere; (*refrain from
hurting, using*) risparmiare; **to ~** (*surplus*)
d'avanzo; **spare part** *n* pezzo di ricambio;
spare room *n* stanza degli ospiti; **spare
time** *n* tempo libero; **spare tyre** (*US* **spare
tire**) *n* (*Aut*) gomma di scorta; **spare
wheel** *n* (*Aut*) ruota di scorta
spark [spɑ:k] *n* scintilla; **spark(ing) plug**
n candela
sparkle ['spɑ:kl] *n* scintillio, sfavillio ▷ *vi*
scintillare, sfavillare
sparrow ['spærəu] *n* passero
sparse [spɑ:s] *adj* sparso(-a), rado(-a)
spasm ['spæzəm] *n* (*Med*) spasmo; (*fig*)
accesso, attacco
spat [spæt] *pt, pp of* **spit**
spate [speɪt] *n* (*fig*): **~ of** diluvio *or* fiume
m di
spatula ['spætjulə] *n* spatola
speak [spi:k] (*pt* **spoke**, *pp* **spoken**) *vt*
(*language*) parlare; (*truth*) dire ▷ *vi* parlare;
I don't ~ Italian non parlo italiano; **do you
~ English?** parla inglese?; **to ~ to sb/of** *or*
about sth parlare a qn/di qc; **can I ~ to ...?**
posso parlare con...?; **~ up!** parla più forte!;
speaker *n* (*in public*) oratore(-trice);
(*also*: **loudspeaker**) altoparlante *m*; (*Pol*):
the Speaker il presidente della Camera dei
Comuni (*BRIT*) *or* dei Rappresentanti (*US*)
spear [spɪə^r] *n* lancia ▷ *vt* infilzare
special ['spɛʃl] *adj* speciale; **special
delivery** *n* (*Post*): **by special delivery**
per espresso; **special effects** *npl*
(*Cine*) effetti *mpl* speciali; **specialist** *n*
specialista *m/f*; **speciality** [spɛʃɪ'ælɪtɪ]

n specialità *f inv*; **I'd like to try a local
speciality** vorrei assaggiare una specialità
del posto; **specialize** *vi* **to specialize
(in)** specializzarsi (in); **specially** *adv*
specialmente, particolarmente;
special needs *adj* **special needs
children** bambini *mpl* con difficoltà di
apprendimento; **special offer** *n* (*Comm*)
offerta speciale; **special school** *n* (*BRIT*)
scuola speciale (*per portatori di handicap*);
specialty (*US*) *n* = **speciality**
species ['spi:ʃi:z] *n inv* specie *f inv*
specific [spə'sɪfɪk] *adj* specifico(-a),
preciso(-a); **specifically** *adv*
esplicitamente; (*especially*) appositamente
specify ['spɛsɪfaɪ] *vt* specificare, precisare;
unless otherwise specified salvo
indicazioni contrarie
specimen ['spɛsɪmən] *n* esemplare *m*,
modello; (*Med*) campione *m*
speck [spɛk] *n* puntino, macchiolina;
(*particle*) granello
spectacle ['spɛktəkl] *n* spettacolo; **~s**
npl (*glasses*) occhiali *mpl*; **spectacular**
[-'tækjulə^r] *adj* spettacolare
spectator [spɛk'teɪtə^r] *n* spettatore *m*
spectrum ['spɛktrəm] (*pl* **spectra**) *n*
spettro
speculate ['spɛkjuleɪt] *vi* speculare; (*try to
guess*): **to ~ about** fare ipotesi su
sped [spɛd] *pt, pp of* **speed**
speech [spi:tʃ] *n* (*faculty*) parola; (*talk,
Theatre*) discorso; (*manner of speaking*)
parlata; **speechless** *adj* ammutolito(-a),
muto(-a)
speed [spi:d] *n* velocità *f inv*; (*promptness*)
prontezza; **at full** *or* **top ~** a tutta velocità;
speed up *vi, vt* accelerare; **speedboat** *n*
motoscafo; **speeding** *n* (*Aut*) eccesso
di velocità; **speed limit** *n* limite *m* di
velocità; **speedometer** [spɪ'dɔmɪtə^r] *n*
tachimetro; **speedy** *adj* veloce, rapido(-a);
pronto(-a)
spell [spɛl] (*pt, pp* **spelt** (*BRIT*) *or* **spelled**) *n*
(*also*: **magic ~**) incantesimo; (*period of time*)
(*breve*) periodo ▷ *vt* (*in writing*) scrivere
(lettera per lettera); (*aloud*) dire lettera per
lettera; (*fig*) significare; **to cast a ~ on sb**
fare un incantesimo a qn; **he can't ~** fa
errori di ortografia; **spell out** *vt* (*letter by
letter*) dettare lettera per lettera; (*explain*):
to ~ sth out for sb spiegare qc a qn per
filo e per segno; **spellchecker** ['spɛltʃɛkə^r] *n* correttore *m* ortografico; **spelling** *n*
ortografia
spelt [spɛlt] (*BRIT*) *pt, pp of* **spell**
spend [spɛnd] (*pt, pp* **spent**) *vt* (*money*)
spendere; (*time, life*) passare; **spending** *n*
government spending spesa pubblica

spent [spɛnt] *pt, pp of* **spend**
sperm [spə:m] *n* sperma *m*
sphere [sfɪəʳ] *n* sfera
spice [spaɪs] *n* spezia ▷ *vt* aromatizzare
spicy ['spaɪsɪ] *adj* piccante
spider ['spaɪdəʳ] *n* ragno
spike [spaɪk] *n* punta
spill [spɪl] (*pt, pp* **spilt** *or* **spilled**) *vt* versare, rovesciare ▷ *vi* versarsi, rovesciarsi
spin [spɪn] (*pt, pp* **spun**) *n (revolution of wheel)* rotazione *f; (Aviat)* avvitamento; *(trip in car)* giretto ▷ *vt (wool etc)* filare; *(wheel)* far girare ▷ *vi* girare
spinach ['spɪnɪtʃ] *n* spinacio; *(as food)* spinaci *mpl*
spinal ['spaɪnl] *adj* spinale
spin doctor *(inf) n* esperto di comunicazioni responsabile dell'immagine di un partito politico
spin-dryer [spɪn'draɪəʳ] *(BRIT) n* centrifuga
spine [spaɪn] *n* spina dorsale; *(thorn)* spina
spiral ['spaɪərl] *n* spirale *f* ▷ *vi (fig)* salire a spirale
spire ['spaɪəʳ] *n* guglia
spirit ['spɪrɪt] *n* spirito; *(ghost)* spirito, fantasma *m; (mood)* stato d'animo, umore *m; (courage)* coraggio; **~s** *npl (drink)* alcolici *mpl;* **in good ~s** di buon umore
spiritual ['spɪrɪtjuəl] *adj* spirituale
spit [spɪt] (*pt, pp* **spat**) *n (for roasting)* spiedo; *(saliva)* sputo; saliva ▷ *vi* sputare; *(fire, fat)* scoppiettare
spite [spaɪt] *n* dispetto ▷ *vt* contrariare, far dispetto a; **in ~ of** nonostante, malgrado; **spiteful** *adj* dispettoso(-a)
splash [splæʃ] *n* spruzzo; *(sound)* splash *m inv; (of colour)* schizzo ▷ *vt* spruzzare ▷ *vi (also:* **~ about)** sguazzare; **splash out** *(inf) vi (BRIT)* fare spese folli
splendid ['splɛndɪd] *adj* splendido(-a), magnifico(-a)
splinter ['splɪntəʳ] *n* scheggia ▷ *vi* scheggiarsi
split [splɪt] (*pt, pp* **split**) *n* spaccatura; *(fig: division, quarrel)* scissione *f* ▷ *vt* spaccare; *(party)* dividere; *(work, profits)* spartire, ripartire ▷ *vi (divide)* dividersi; **split up** *vi (couple)* separarsi, rompere; *(meeting)* sciogliersi
spoil [spɔɪl] (*pt, pp* **spoilt** *or* **spoiled**) *vt (damage)* rovinare, guastare; *(mar)* sciupare; *(child)* viziare
spoilt [spɔɪlt] *pt, pp of* **spoil**
spoke [spəuk] *pt of* **speak** ▷ *n* raggio
spoken ['spəukn] *pp of* **speak**
spokesman ['spəuksmən] *(irreg) n* portavoce *m inv*
spokesperson ['spəukspə:sn] *n*

portavoce *m/f*
spokeswoman ['spəukswumən] *(irreg) n* portavoce *f inv*
sponge [spʌndʒ] *n* spugna; *(also:* **~ cake)** pan *m* di spagna ▷ *vt* spugnare, pulire con una spugna ▷ *vi* **to ~ off** *or* **on** scroccare a; **sponge bag** *(BRIT) n* nécessaire *m inv*
sponsor ['spɔnsəʳ] *n (Radio, TV, Sport etc)* sponsor *m inv; (Pol: of bill)* promotore(-trice) ▷ *vt* sponsorizzare; *(bill)* presentare; **sponsorship** *n* sponsorizzazione *f*
spontaneous [spɔn'teɪnɪəs] *adj* spontaneo(-a)
spooky ['spu:kɪ] *(inf) adj* che fa accapponare la pelle
spoon [spu:n] *n* cucchiaio; **spoonful** *n* cucchiaiata
sport [spɔ:t] *n* sport *m inv; (person)* persona di spirito ▷ *vt* sfoggiare; **sport jacket** *(US) n* = **sports jacket**; **sports car** *n* automobile *f* sportiva; **sports centre** *(BRIT) n* centro sportivo; **sports jacket** *(BRIT) n* giacca sportiva; **sportsman** *(irreg) n (uomo)* sportivo; **sportswear** *n* abiti *mpl* sportivi; **sportswoman** *(irreg) n* sportiva; **sporty** *adj* sportivo(-a)
spot [spɔt] *n* punto; *(mark)* macchia; *(dot: on pattern)* pallino; *(pimple)* foruncolo; *(place)* posto; *(Radio, TV)* spot *m inv; (small amount):* **a ~ of** un po' di ▷ *vt (notice)* individuare, distinguere; **on the ~** sul posto; *(immediately)* su due piedi; *(in difficulty)* nei guai; **spotless** *adj* immacolato(-a); **spotlight** *n* proiettore *m; (Aut)* faro ausiliario
spouse [spauz] *n* sposo(-a)
sprain [spreɪn] *n* storta, distorsione *f* ▷ *vt* **to ~ one's ankle** storcersi una caviglia
sprang [spræŋ] *pt of* **spring**
sprawl [sprɔ:l] *vi* sdraiarsi (in modo scomposto); *(place)* estendersi (disordinatamente)
spray [spreɪ] *n* spruzzo; *(container)* nebulizzatore *m*, spray *m inv; (of flowers)* mazzetto ▷ *vt* spruzzare; *(crops)* irrorare
spread [sprɛd] (*pt, pp* **spread**) *n* diffusione *f; (distribution)* distribuzione *f; (Culin)* pasta *(da spalmare); (inf: food)* banchetto ▷ *vt (cloth)* stendere, distendere; *(butter etc)* spalmare; *(disease, knowledge)* propagare, diffondere ▷ *vi* stendersi, distendersi; spalmarsi; propagarsi, diffondersi; **spread out** *vi (move apart)* separarsi; **spreadsheet** *n* foglio elettronico ad espansione
spree [spri:] *n* **to go on a ~** fare baldoria
spring [sprɪŋ] (*pt* **sprang**, *pp* **sprung**) *n (leap)* salto, balzo; *(coiled metal)* molla;

(*season*) primavera; (*of water*) sorgente
f ▷ *vi* saltare, balzare; **spring up** *vi*
(*problem*) presentarsi; **spring onion** *n*
(BRIT) cipollina

sprinkle ['sprɪŋkl] *vt* spruzzare; spargere;
to ~ water *etc* **on, ~ with water** *etc*
spruzzare dell'acqua *etc* su

sprint [sprɪnt] *n* scatto ▷ *vi* scattare

sprung [sprʌŋ] *pp of* **spring**

spun [spʌn] *pt, pp of* **spin**

spur [spəːʳ] *n* sperone *m*; (*fig*) sprone *m*,
incentivo ▷ *vt* (*also:* **~ on**) spronare; **on the
~ of the moment** lì per lì

spurt [spəːt] *n* (*of water*) getto; (*of energy*)
scatto ▷ *vi* sgorgare

spy [spaɪ] *n* spia *f* ▷ *vi* **to ~ on** spiare ▷ *vt*
(*see*) scorgere

sq. *abbr* = **square**

squabble ['skwɔbl] *vi* bisticciarsi

squad [skwɔd] *n* (*Mil*) plotone *m*; (*Police*)
squadra

squadron ['skwɔdrn] *n* (*Mil*) squadrone *m*;
(*Aviat, Naut*) squadriglia

squander ['skwɔndəʳ] *vt* dissipare

square [skweəʳ] *n* quadrato; (*in town*)
piazza ▷ *adj* quadrato(-a); (*inf: ideas,
person*) di vecchio stampo ▷ *vt* (*arrange*)
regolare; (*Math*) elevare al quadrato;
(*reconcile*) conciliare; **all ~** pari; **a ~ meal** un
pasto abbondante; **2 metres ~** di 2 metri
per 2; **1 ~ metre** 1 metro quadrato; **square
root** *n* radice *f* quadrata

squash [skwɔʃ] *n* (*Sport*) squash *m*; (BRIT:
drink): **lemon/orange ~** sciroppo di
limone/arancia; (US) zucca; (*Sport*) squash
m ▷ *vt* schiacciare

squat [skwɔt] *adj* tarchiato(-a), tozzo(-a)
▷ *vi* (*also:* **~ down**) accovacciarsi; **squatter**
n occupante *m/f* abusivo(-a)

squeak [skwiːk] *vi* squittire

squeal [skwiːl] *vi* strillare

squeeze [skwiːz] *n* pressione *f*; (*also Econ*)
stretta ▷ *vt* premere; (*hand, arm*) stringere

squid [skwɪd] *n* calamaro

squint [skwɪnt] *vi* essere strabico(-a) ▷ *n*
he has a ~ è strabico

squirm [skwəːm] *vi* contorcersi

squirrel ['skwɪrəl] *n* scoiattolo

squirt [skwəːt] *vi* schizzare; zampillare
▷ *vt* spruzzare

Sr *abbr* = **senior**

Sri Lanka [srɪ'læŋkə] *n* Sri Lanka *m*

St *abbr* = **saint**; **street**

stab [stæb] *n* (*with knife etc*) pugnalata; (*of
pain*) fitta; (*inf: try*): **to have a ~ at (doing)
sth** provare (a fare) qc ▷ *vt* pugnalare

stability [stə'bɪlɪtɪ] *n* stabilità

stable ['steɪbl] *n* (*for horses*) scuderia; (*for
cattle*) stalla ▷ *adj* stabile

stack [stæk] *n* catasta, pila ▷ *vt*
accatastare, ammucchiare

stadium ['steɪdɪəm] *n* stadio

staff [stɑːf] *n* (*work force: gen*) personale
m; (: BRIT: *Scol*) personale insegnante ▷ *vt*
fornire di personale

stag [stæg] *n* cervo

stage [steɪdʒ] *n* palcoscenico; (*profession*):
the ~ il teatro, la scena; (*point*) punto;
(*platform*) palco ▷ *vt* (*play*) allestire,
mettere in scena; (*demonstration*)
organizzare; **in ~s** per gradi; a tappe

stagger ['stægəʳ] *vi* barcollare ▷ *vt* (*person*)
sbalordire; (*hours, holidays*) scaglionare;
staggering *adj* (*amazing*) sbalorditivo(-a)

stagnant ['stægnənt] *adj* stagnante

stag night, stag party *n* festa di addio
al celibato

stain [steɪn] *n* macchia; (*colouring*)
colorante *m* ▷ *vt* macchiare; (*wood*)
tingere; **stained glass** [steɪnd'glɑːs] *n*
vetro colorato; **stainless steel** *n* acciaio
inossidabile

staircase ['steəkeɪs] *n* scale *fpl*, scala

stairs [steəz] *npl* (*flight of stairs*) scale *fpl*,
scala

stairway ['steəweɪ] *n* = **staircase**

stake [steɪk] *n* palo, piolo; (*Comm*)
interesse *m*; (*Betting*) puntata, scommessa
▷ *vt* (*bet*) scommettere; (*risk*) rischiare; **to
be at ~** essere in gioco

stale [steɪl] *adj* (*bread*) raffermo(-a);
(*food*) stantio(-a); (*air*) viziato(-a); (*beer*)
svaporato(-a); (*smell*) di chiuso

stalk [stɔːk] *n* gambo, stelo ▷ *vt* inseguire

stall [stɔːl] *n* bancarella; (*in stable*) box *m
inv* di stalla ▷ *vt* (*Aut*) far spegnere; (*fig*)
bloccare ▷ *vi* (*Aut*) spegnersi, fermarsi; (*fig*)
temporeggiare

stamina ['stæmɪnə] *n* vigore *m*, resistenza

stammer ['stæməʳ] *n* balbuzie *f* ▷ *vi*
balbettare

stamp [stæmp] *n* (*postage stamp*)
francobollo; (*implement*) timbro; (*mark,
also fig*) marchio, impronta; (*on document*)
bollo; timbro ▷ *vi* (*also:* **~ one's foot**)
battere il piede ▷ *vt* battere; (*letter*)
affrancare; (*mark with a stamp*) timbrare;
stamp out *vt* (*fire*) estinguere; (*crime*)
eliminare; (*opposition*) soffocare; **stamped
addressed envelope** *n* (BRIT) busta
affrancata e indirizzata

Be careful not to translate *stamp* the
Italian word by *stampa*.

stampede [stæm'piːd] *n* fuggi fuggi *m inv*

stance [stæns] *n* posizione *f*

stand [stænd] (*pt, pp* **stood**) *n* (*position*)
posizione *f*; (*for taxis*) posteggio; (*structure*)
supporto, sostegno; (*at exhibition*)

S

stand *m inv*; (*in shop*) banco; (*at market*) bancarella; (*booth*) chiosco; (*Sport*) tribuna ▷ *vi* stare in piedi; (*rise*) alzarsi in piedi; (*be placed*) trovarsi ▷ *vt* (*place*) mettere, porre; (*tolerate, withstand*) resistere, sopportare; (*treat*) offrire; **to make a ~** prendere posizione; **to ~ for parliament** (*BRIT*) presentarsi come candidato (per il parlamento); **stand back** *vi* prendere le distanze; **stand by** *vi* (*be ready*) tenersi pronto(-a) ▷ *vt fus* (*opinion*) sostenere; **stand down** *vi* (*withdraw*) ritirarsi; **stand for** *vt fus* (*signify*) rappresentare, significare; (*tolerate*) sopportare, tollerare; **stand in for** *vt fus* sostituire; **stand out** *vi* (*be prominent*) spiccare; **stand up** *vi* (*rise*) alzarsi in piedi; **stand up for** *vt fus* difendere; **stand up to** *vt fus* tener testa a, resistere a

standard ['stændəd] *n* modello, standard *m inv*; (*level*) livello; (*flag*) stendardo ▷ *adj* (*size etc*) normale, standard *inv*; **~s** *npl* (*morals*) principi *mpl*, valori *mpl*; **standard of living** *n* livello di vita

stand-by ['stændbaɪ] *n* riserva, sostituto; **to be on ~** (*gen*) tenersi pronto(-a); (*doctor*) essere di guardia; **stand-by ticket** *n* (*Aviat*) biglietto senza garanzia

standing ['stændɪŋ] *adj* diritto(-a), in piedi; (*permanent*) permanente ▷ *n* rango, condizione *f*, posizione *f*; **of many years' ~** che esiste da molti anni; **standing order** (*BRIT*) *n* (*at bank*) ordine *m* di pagamento (permanente)

stand: **standpoint** ['stændpɔɪnt] *n* punto di vista; **standstill** ['stændstɪl] *n* **at a standstill** fermo(-a); (*fig*) a un punto morto; **to come to a standstill** fermarsi; giungere a un punto morto

stank [stæŋk] *pt of* **stink**

staple ['steɪpl] *n* (*for papers*) graffetta ▷ *adj* (*food etc*) di base ▷ *vt* cucire

star [stɑːʳ] *n* stella; (*celebrity*) divo(-a) ▷ *vi* **to ~ (in)** essere il (o la) protagonista (di) ▷ *vt* (*Cinema*) essere interpretato(-a) da; **the ~s** *npl* (*Astrology*) le stelle

starboard ['stɑːbəd] *n* dritta

starch [stɑːtʃ] *n* amido

stardom ['stɑːdəm] *n* celebrità

stare [steəʳ] *n* sguardo fisso ▷ *vi* **to ~ at** fissare

stark [stɑːk] *adj* (*bleak*) desolato(-a) ▷ *adv* **~ naked** completamente nudo(-a)

start [stɑːt] *n* inizio, (*of race*) partenza; (*sudden movement*) sobbalzo; (*advantage*) vantaggio ▷ *vt* cominciare, iniziare; (*car*) mettere in moto ▷ *vi* cominciare; (*on journey*) partire, mettersi in viaggio; (*jump*) sobbalzare; **when does the film ~?**

a che ora comincia il film?; **to ~ doing** or **to do sth** (in)cominciare a fare qc; **start off** *vi* cominciare; (*leave*) partire; **start out** *vi* (*begin*) cominciare; (*set out*) partire; **start up** *vi* cominciare; (*car*) avviarsi ▷ *vt* iniziare; (*car*) avviare; **starter** *n* (*Aut*) motorino d'avviamento; (*Sport*: *official*) starter *m inv*; (*BRIT*: *Culin*) primo piatto; **starting point** *n* punto di partenza

startle ['stɑːtl] *vt* far trasalire; **startling** *adj* sorprendente

starvation [stɑː'veɪʃən] *n* fame *f*, inedia

starve [stɑːv] *vi* morire di fame; soffrire la fame ▷ *vt* far morire di fame, affamare

state [steɪt] *n* stato ▷ *vt* dichiarare, affermare; annunciare; **the S~s** (*USA*) gli Stati Uniti; **to be in a ~** essere agitato(-a); **statement** *n* dichiarazione *f*; **state school** *n* scuola statale; **statesman** (*irreg*) *n* statista *m*

static ['stætɪk] *n* (*Radio*) scariche *fpl* ▷ *adj* statico(-a)

station ['steɪʃən] *n* stazione *f* ▷ *vt* collocare, disporre

stationary ['steɪʃənəri] *adj* fermo(-a), immobile

stationer's (shop) *n* cartoleria

stationery ['steɪʃnərɪ] *n* articoli *mpl* di cancelleria

station wagon (*US*) *n* giardinetta

statistic [stə'tɪstɪk] *n* statistica; **statistics** *n* (*science*) statistica

statue ['stætjuː] *n* statua

stature ['stætʃəʳ] *n* statura

status ['steɪtəs] *n* posizione *f*, condizione *f* sociale; prestigio; stato; **status quo** [-'kwəu] *n* **the status quo** lo statu quo

statutory ['stætjutrɪ] *adj* stabilito(-a) dalla legge, statutario(-a)

staunch [stɔːntʃ] *adj* fidato(-a), leale

stay [steɪ] *n* (*period of time*) soggiorno, permanenza ▷ *vi* rimanere; (*reside*) alloggiare, stare; (*spend some time*) trattenersi, soggiornare; **to ~ put** non muoversi; **to ~ the night** fermarsi per la notte; **stay away** *vi* (*from person, building*) stare lontano (*from event*) non andare; **stay behind** *vi* restare indietro; **stay in** *vi* (*at home*) stare in casa; **stay on** *vi* restare, rimanere; **stay out** *vi* (*of house*) rimanere fuori (di casa); **stay up** *vi* (*at night*) rimanere alzato(-a)

steadily ['stɛdɪlɪ] *adv* (*firmly*) saldamente; (*constantly*) continuamente; (*fixedly*) fisso; (*walk*) con passo sicuro

steady ['stɛdɪ] *adj* (*not wobbling*) fermo(-a); (*regular*) costante; (*person, character*) serio(-a); (: *calm*) calmo(-a), tranquillo(-a) ▷ *vt* stabilizzare; calmare

steak [steɪk] n (meat) bistecca; (fish) trancia

steal [stiːl] (pt **stole**, pp **stolen**) vt rubare ▷ vi rubare; (move) muoversi furtivamente; **my wallet has been stolen** mi hanno rubato il portafoglio

steam [stiːm] n vapore m ▷ vt (Culin) cuocere a vapore ▷ vi fumare; **steam up** vi (window) appannarsi; **to get ~ed up about sth** (fig) andare in bestia per qc; **steamy** adj (room) pieno(-a) di vapore; (window) appannato(-a)

steel [stiːl] n acciaio ▷ adj di acciaio

steep [stiːp] adj ripido(-a), scosceso(-a); (price) eccessivo(-a) ▷ vt inzuppare; (washing) mettere a mollo

steeple [ˈstiːpl] n campanile m

steer [stɪəʳ] vt guidare ▷ vi (Naut: person) governare; (car) guidarsi; **steering** n (Aut) sterzo; **steering wheel** n volante m

stem [stɛm] n (of flower, plant) stelo; (of tree) fusto; (of glass) gambo; (of fruit, leaf) picciolo ▷ vt contenere, arginare

step [stɛp] n passo; (stair) gradino, scalino; (action) mossa, azione f ▷ vi **to ~ forward/back** fare un passo avanti/indietro; **~s** npl (BRIT) = **stepladder**; **to be in/out of ~ (with)** stare/non stare al passo (con); **step down** vi (fig) ritirarsi; **step in** vi fare il proprio ingresso; **step up** vt aumentare; intensificare; **stepbrother** n fratellastro; **stepchild** n figliastro(-a); **stepdaughter** n figliastra; **stepfather** n patrigno; **stepladder** n scala a libretto; **stepmother** n matrigna; **stepsister** n sorellastra; **stepson** n figliastro

stereo [ˈstɛrɪəu] n (system) sistema m stereofonico; (record player) stereo m inv ▷ adj (also: **~phonic**) stereofonico(-a)

stereotype [ˈstɪərɪətaɪp] n stereotipo

sterile [ˈstɛraɪl] adj sterile; **sterilize** [ˈstɛrɪlaɪz] vt sterilizzare

sterling [ˈstəːlɪŋ] adj (gold, silver) di buona lega ▷ n (Econ) (lira) sterlina; **a pound ~** una lira sterlina

stern [stəːn] adj severo(-a) ▷ n (Naut) poppa

steroid [ˈstɛrɔɪd] n steroide m

stew [stjuː] n stufato ▷ vt cuocere in umido

steward [ˈstjuːəd] n (Aviat, Naut, Rail) steward m inv; (in club etc) dispensiere m; **stewardess** n assistente f di volo, hostess f inv

stick [stɪk] (pt, pp **stuck**) n bastone m; (of rhubarb, celery) gambo; (of dynamite) candelotto ▷ vt (glue) attaccare; (thrust): **to ~ sth into** conficcare or piantare or infiggere qc in; (inf: put) ficcare; (inf: tolerate) sopportare ▷ vi attaccarsi; (remain) restare, rimanere; **stick out** vi sporgere, spuntare; **stick up** vi sporgere, spuntare; **stick up for** vt fus difendere; **sticker** n cartellino adesivo; **sticking plaster** n cerotto adesivo; **stick shift** (US) n (Aut) cambio manuale

sticky [ˈstɪkɪ] adj attaccaticcio(-a), vischioso(-a); (label) adesivo(-a); (fig: situation) difficile

stiff [stɪf] adj rigido(-a), duro(-a); (muscle) legato(-a), indolenzito(-a); (difficult) difficile, arduo(-a); (cold) freddo(-a), formale; (strong) forte; (high: price) molto alto(-a) ▷ adv **bored ~** annoiato(-a) a morte

stifling [ˈstaɪflɪŋ] adj (heat) soffocante

stigma [ˈstɪgmə] n (fig) stigma m

stiletto [stɪˈlɛtəu] (BRIT) n (also: **~ heel**) tacco a spillo

still [stɪl] adj fermo(-a); silenzioso(-a) ▷ adv (up to this time, even) ancora; (nonetheless) tuttavia, ciò nonostante

stimulate [ˈstɪmjuleɪt] vt stimolare

stimulus [ˈstɪmjuləs] (pl **stimuli**) n stimolo

sting [stɪŋ] (pt, pp **stung**) n puntura; (organ) pungiglione m ▷ vt pungere

stink [stɪŋk] (pt **stank**, pp **stunk**) n fetore m, puzzo ▷ vi puzzare

stir [stəːʳ] n agitazione f, clamore m ▷ vt mescolare; (fig) risvegliare ▷ vi muoversi; **stir up** vt provocare, suscitare; **stir-fry** vt saltare in padella ▷ n pietanza al salto

stitch [stɪtʃ] n (Sewing) punto; (Knitting) maglia; (Med) punto (di sutura); (pain) fitta ▷ vt cucire, attaccare; suturare

stock [stɔk] n riserva, provvista; (Comm) giacenza, stock m inv; (Agr) bestiame m; (Culin) brodo; (descent) stirpe f, (Finance) titoli mpl; azioni fpl ▷ adj (fig: reply etc) consueto(-a); classico(-a) ▷ vt (have in stock) avere, vendere; **~s and shares** valori mpl di borsa; **in ~** in magazzino; **out of ~** esaurito(-a), **stockbroker** [ˈstɔkbrəukəʳ] n agente m di cambio; **stock cube** (BRIT) n dado; **stock exchange** n Borsa (valori), **stockholder** [ˈstɔkhəuldəʳ] n (Finance) azionista m/f

stocking [ˈstɔkɪŋ] n calza

stock market n Borsa, mercato finanziario

stole [stəul] pt of **steal** ▷ n stola

stolen [ˈstəuln] pp of **steal**

stomach [ˈstʌmək] n stomaco; (belly) pancia ▷ vt sopportare, digerire; **stomachache** n mal m di stomaco

stone [stəun] n pietra; (pebble) sasso; ciottolo; (in fruit) nocciolo; (Med) calcolo;

(BRIT: *weight*) = 6.348 kg; 14 *libbre* ▷ *adj*
di pietra ▷ *vt* lapidare; (*fruit*) togliere il
nocciolo a

stood [stud] *pt, pp of* **stand**

stool [stuːl] *n* sgabello

stoop [stuːp] *vi* (*also*: **have a ~**) avere una
curvatura; (*also*: **~ down**) chinarsi, curvarsi

stop [stɔp] *n* arresto, fermata; (*stopping place*)
fermata; (*in punctuation*) punto
▷ *vt* arrestare, fermare; (*break off*)
interrompere; (*also*: **put a ~ to**) porre fine
a ▷ *vi* fermarsi; (*rain, noise etc*) cessare,
finire; **to ~ doing sth** cessare *or* finire di
fare qc; **could you ~ here/at the corner?**
può fermarsi qui/all'angolo?; **to ~ dead**
fermarsi di colpo; **stop by** *vi* passare, fare
un salto; **stop off** *vi* sostare brevemente;
stopover *n* breve sosta; (*Aviat*) scalo;
stoppage ['stɔpɪdʒ] *n* arresto, fermata;
(*of pay*) trattenuta; (*strike*) interruzione *f*
del lavoro

storage ['stɔːrɪdʒ] *n* immagazzinamento

store [stɔːʳ] *n* provvista, riserva; (*depot*)
deposito; (BRIT: *department store*) grande
magazzino; (US: *shop*) negozio ▷ *vt*
immagazzinare; **~s** *npl* (*provisions*)
rifornimenti *mpl*, scorte *fpl*; **in ~** di riserva;
in serbo; **storekeeper** (US) *n* negoziante
m/f

storey ['stɔːrɪ] (US **story**) *n* piano

storm [stɔːm] *n* tempesta, temporale
m, burrasca; uragano ▷ *vi* (*fig*) infuriarsi
▷ *vt* prendere d'assalto; **stormy** *adj*
tempestoso(-a), burrascoso(-a)

story ['stɔːrɪ] *n* storia; favola; racconto;
(US) = **storey**

stout [staut] *adj* solido(-a), robusto(-a);
(*friend, supporter*) tenace; (*fat*)
corpulento(-a), grasso(-a) ▷ *n* birra scura

stove [stəuv] *n* (*for cooking*) fornello; (:
small) fornelletto; (*for heating*) stufa

straight [streɪt] *adj* dritto(-a); (*frank*)
onesto(-a), franco(-a); (*simple*) semplice
▷ *adv* diritto; (*drink*) liscio; **to put** *or* **get**
~ mettere in ordine, mettere ordine in; **~**
away, ~ off (*at once*) immediatamente;
straighten *vt* (*also*: **straighten out**)
raddrizzare; **straightforward** *adj*
semplice; onesto(-a), franco(-a)

strain [streɪn] *n* (*Tech*) sollecitazione
f; (*physical*) sforzo; (*mental*) tensione *f*;
(*Med*) strappo; distorsione *f*; (*streak, trace*)
tendenza; elemento ▷ *vt* tendere; (*muscle*)
sforzare; (*ankle*) storcere; (*resources*) pesare
su; (*food*) colare; passare; **strained** *adj*
(*muscle*) stirato(-a); (*laugh etc*) forzato(-a);
(*relations*) teso(-a); **strainer** *n* passino,
colino

strait [streɪt] *n* (*Geo*) stretto; **~s** *npl* **to be**

in dire ~s (*fig*) essere nei guai

strand [strænd] *n* (*of thread*) filo; **stranded**
adj nei guai; senza mezzi di trasporto

strange [streɪndʒ] *adj* (*not known*)
sconosciuto(-a); (*odd*) strano(-a),
bizzarro(-a); **strangely** *adv* stranamente;
stranger *n* sconosciuto(-a); estraneo(-a)

strangle ['stræŋgl] *vt* strangolare

strap [stræp] *n* cinghia; (*of slip, dress*)
spallina, bretella

strategic [strəˈtiːdʒɪk] *adj* strategico(-a)

strategy ['strætɪdʒɪ] *n* strategia

straw [strɔː] *n* paglia; (*drinking straw*)
cannuccia; **that's the last ~!** è la goccia
che fa traboccare il vaso!

strawberry ['strɔːbərɪ] *n* fragola

stray [streɪ] *adj* (*animal*) randagio(-a);
(*bullet*) vagante; (*scattered*) sparso(-a) ▷ *vi*
perdersi

streak [striːk] *n* striscia; (*of hair*) mèche
f inv ▷ *vt* striare, screziare ▷ *vi* **to ~ past**
passare come un fulmine

stream [striːm] *n* ruscello; corrente *f*;
(*of people, smoke etc*) fiume *m* ▷ *vt* (*Scol*)
dividere in livelli di rendimento ▷ *vi*
scorrere; **to ~ in/out** entrare/uscire a fiotti

street [striːt] *n* strada, via; **streetcar** (US)
n tram *m inv*; **street light** *n* lampione *m*;
street map *n* pianta (di una città)

street plan *n* pianta (di una città)

strength [strɛŋθ] *n* forza; **strengthen** *vt*
rinforzare; fortificare; consolidare

strenuous ['strɛnjuəs] *adj* vigoroso(-a),
energico(-a); (*tiring*) duro(-a), pesante

stress [strɛs] *n* (*force, pressure*) pressione *f*;
(*mental strain*) tensione *f*; (*accent*) accento
▷ *vt* insistere su, sottolineare; accentare;
stressed *adj* (*tense: person*) stressato(-a);
(*Ling, Poetry: syllable*) accentato(-a);
stressful *adj* (*job*) difficile, stressante

stretch [strɛtʃ] *n* (*of sand etc*) distesa
▷ *vi* stirarsi; (*extend*) **to ~ to** *or* **as far as**
estendersi fino a ▷ *vt* tendere, allungare;
(*spread*) distendere; (*fig*) spingere (al
massimo); **stretch out** *vi* allungarsi,
estendersi ▷ *vt* (*arm etc*) allungare,
tendere; (*to spread*) distendere

stretcher ['strɛtʃəʳ] *n* barella, lettiga

strict [strɪkt] *adj* (*severe*) rigido(-a),
severo(-a); (*precise*) preciso(-a), stretto(-a);
strictly *adv* severamente; rigorosamente;
strettamente

stride [straɪd] (*pt* **strode**, *pp* **stridden**) *n*
passo lungo ▷ *vi* camminare a grandi passi

strike [straɪk] (*pt, pp* **struck**) *n* sciopero;
(*of oil etc*) scoperta; (*attack*) attacco
▷ *vt* colpire; (*oil etc*) scoprire, trovare;
(*bargain*) fare; (*fig*): **the thought** *or* **it**
~s me that ... mi viene in mente che ...

▷ vi scioperare; (attack) attaccare; (clock) suonare; **on ~** (workers) in sciopero; **to ~ a match** accendere un fiammifero; **striker** n scioperante m/f; (Sport) attaccante m; **striking** adj che colpisce

string [strɪŋ] (pt, pp **strung**) n spago; (row) fila; sequenza; catena; (Mus) corda ▷ vt **to ~ out** disporre di fianco; **to ~ together** (words, ideas) mettere insieme; **the ~s** npl (Mus) gli archi; **to pull ~s for sb** (fig) raccomandare qn

strip [strɪp] n striscia ▷ vt spogliare; (paint) togliere; (also: **~ down**: machine) smontare ▷ vi spogliarsi; **strip off** vt (paint etc) staccare ▷ vi (person) spogliarsi

stripe [straɪp] n striscia, riga; (Mil, Police) gallone m; **striped** adj a strisce or righe

stripper ['strɪpəʳ] n spogliarellista m/f

strip-search ['strɪpsə:tʃ] vt **to ~ sb** perquisire qn facendolo(-a) spogliare ▷ n perquisizione (facendo spogliare il perquisito)

strive [straɪv] (pt **strove**, pp **striven**) vi **to ~ to do** sforzarsi di fare

strode [strəud] pt of **stride**

stroke [strəuk] n colpo; (Swimming) bracciata; (: style) stile m; (Med) colpo apoplettico ▷ vt accarezzare; **at a ~** in un attimo

stroll [strəul] n giretto, passeggiatina ▷ vi andare a spasso; **stroller** (US) n passeggino

strong [strɔŋ] adj (gen) forte; (sturdy: table, fabric etc) robusto(-a); **they are 50 ~** sono in 50; **stronghold** n (also fig) roccaforte f; **strongly** adv fortemente, con forza; energicamente; vivamente

strove [strəuv] pt of **strive**

struck [strʌk] pt, pp of **strike**

structure ['strʌktʃəʳ] n struttura; (building) costruzione f, fabbricato

struggle ['strʌgl] n lotta ▷ vi lottare

strung [strʌŋ] pt, pp of **string**

stub [stʌb] n mozzicone m; (of ticket etc) matrice f, talloncino ▷ vt **to ~ one's toe** urtare or sbattere il dito del piede; **stub out** vt schiacciare

stubble ['stʌbl] n stoppia; (on chin) barba ispida

stubborn ['stʌbən] adj testardo(-a), ostinato(-a)

stuck [stʌk] pt, pp of **stick** ▷ adj (jammed) bloccato(-a)

stud [stʌd] n bottoncino; borchia; (also: **~ earring**) orecchino a pressione; (also: **~ farm**) scuderia, allevamento di cavalli; (also: **~ horse**) stallone m ▷ vt (fig): **~ded with** tempestato(-a) di

student ['stju:dənt] n studente(-essa) ▷ cpd studentesco(-a); universitario(-a); degli studenti; **student driver** (US) n conducente m/f principiante; **students' union** n (BRIT: association) circolo universitario; (: building) sede f del circolo universitario

studio ['stju:dɪəu] n studio; **studio flat** (US **studio apartment**) n monolocale m

study ['stʌdɪ] n studio ▷ vt studiare; esaminare ▷ vi studiare

stuff [stʌf] n roba; (substance) sostanza, materiale m ▷ vt imbottire; (Culin) farcire; (dead animal) impagliare; (inf: push) ficcare; **stuffing** n imbottitura; (Culin) ripieno; **stuffy** adj (room) mal ventilato(-a), senz'aria; (ideas) antiquato(-a)

stumble ['stʌmbl] vi inciampare; **to ~ across** (fig) imbattersi in

stump [stʌmp] n ceppo; (of limb) moncone m ▷ vt **to be ~ed** essere sconcertato(-a)

stun [stʌn] vt stordire; (amaze) sbalordire

stung [stʌŋ] pt, pp of **sting**

stunk [stʌŋk] pp of **stink**

stunned [stʌnd] adj (from blow) stordito(-a); (amazed, shocked) sbalordito(-a)

stunning ['stʌnɪŋ] adj sbalorditivo(-a); (girl etc) fantastico(-a)

stunt [stʌnt] n bravata; trucco pubblicitario

stupid ['stju:pɪd] adj stupido(-a); **stupidity** [-'pɪdɪtɪ] n stupidità f inv, stupidaggine f

sturdy ['stə:dɪ] adj robusto(-a), vigoroso(-a); solido(-a)

stutter ['stʌtəʳ] n balbuzie f ▷ vi balbettare

style [staɪl] n stile m; (distinction) eleganza, classe f; **stylish** adj elegante; **stylist** n **hair stylist** parrucchiere(-a)

sub... [sʌb] prefix sub..., sotto...; **subconscious** adj subcosciente ▷ n subcosciente m

subdued [səb'dju:d] adj pacato(-a); (light) attenuato(-a)

subject [n 'sʌbdʒɪkt, vb səb'dʒɛkt] n soggetto; (citizen etc) cittadino(-a); (Scol) materia ▷ vt **to ~ to** sottomettere a; esporre a; **to be ~ to** (law) essere sottomesso(-a) a; (disease) essere soggetto(-a) a; **subjective** [-'dʒɛktɪv] adj soggettivo(-a); **subject matter** n argomento; contenuto

subjunctive [səb'dʒʌŋktɪv] adj congiuntivo(-a) ▷ n congiuntivo

submarine [sʌbmə'ri:n] n sommergibile m

submission [səb'mɪʃən] n sottomissione f; (claim) richiesta

submit [səb'mɪt] vt sottomettere ▷ vi sottomettersi

subordinate [sə'bɔːdɪnət] *adj, n* subordinato(-a)

subscribe [səb'skraɪb] *vi* contribuire; **to ~ to** (*opinion*) approvare, condividere; (*fund*) sottoscrivere a; (*newspaper*) abbonarsi a; essere abbonato(-a) a

subscription [səb'skrɪpʃən] *n* sottoscrizione *f*; abbonamento

subsequent ['sʌbsɪkwənt] *adj* successivo(-a), seguente; conseguente; **subsequently** *adv* in seguito, successivamente

subside [səb'saɪd] *vi* cedere, abbassarsi; (*flood*) decrescere; (*wind*) calmarsi

subsidiary [səb'sɪdɪərɪ] *adj* sussidiario(-a); accessorio(-a) ▷ *n* filiale *f*

subsidize ['sʌbsɪdaɪz] *vt* sovvenzionare

subsidy ['sʌbsɪdɪ] *n* sovvenzione *f*

substance ['sʌbstəns] *n* sostanza

substantial [səb'stænʃl] *adj* solido(-a); (*amount, progress etc*) notevole; (*meal*) sostanzioso(-a)

substitute ['sʌbstɪtjuːt] *n* (*person*) sostituto(-a); (*thing*) succedaneo, surrogato ▷ *vt* **to ~ sth/sb for** sostituire qc/qn a; **substitution** [sʌbstɪ'tjuːʃən] *n* sostituzione *f*

subtle ['sʌtl] *adj* sottile

subtract [səb'trækt] *vt* sottrarre

suburb ['sʌbəːb] *n* sobborgo; **the ~s** la periferia; **suburban** [sə'bəːbən] *adj* suburbano(-a)

subway ['sʌbweɪ] *n* (US: *underground*) metropolitana; (BRIT: *underpass*) sottopassaggio

succeed [sək'siːd] *vi* riuscire; avere successo ▷ *vt* succedere a; **to ~ in doing** riuscire a fare

success [sək'sɛs] *n* successo; **successful** *adj* (*venture*) coronato(-a) da successo, riuscito(-a); **to be successful (in doing)** riuscire (a fare); **successfully** *adv* con successo

succession [sək'sɛʃən] *n* successione *f*

successive [sək'sɛsɪv] *adj* successivo(-a); consecutivo(-a)

successor [sək'sɛsə'] *n* successore *m*

succumb [sə'kʌm] *vi* soccombere

such [sʌtʃ] *adj* tale; (*of that kind*): **~ a book** un tale libro, un libro del genere; **~ books** tali libri, libri del genere; (*so much*): **~ courage** tanto coraggio ▷ *adv* talmente, così; **~ a long trip** un viaggio così lungo; **~ a lot of** talmente *or* così tanto(-a); **~ as** (*like*) come; **as ~** come *or* in quanto tale; **such-and-such** *adj* tale (*after noun*)

suck [sʌk] *vt* succhiare; (*breast, bottle*) poppare

Sudan [suː'dɑːn] *n* Sudan *m*

sudden ['sʌdn] *adj* improvviso(-a); **all of a ~** improvvisamente, all'improvviso; **suddenly** *adv* bruscamente, improvvisamente, di colpo

sue [suː] *vt* citare in giudizio

suede [sweɪd] *n* pelle *f* scamosciata

suffer ['sʌfə'] *vt* soffrire, patire; (*bear*) sopportare, tollerare ▷ *vi* soffrire; **to ~ from** soffrire di; **suffering** *n* sofferenza

suffice [sə'faɪs] *vi* essere sufficiente, bastare

sufficient [sə'fɪʃənt] *adj* sufficiente; **~ money** abbastanza soldi

suffocate ['sʌfəkeɪt] *vi* soffocare; (*die through lack of air*) asfissiare

sugar ['ʃugə'] *n* zucchero ▷ *vt* zuccherare

suggest [sə'dʒɛst] *vt* proporre, suggerire; indicare; **suggestion** [-'dʒɛstʃən] *n* suggerimento, proposta; indicazione *f*

suicide ['suɪsaɪd] *n* (*person*) suicida *m/f*; (*act*) suicidio; *see also* **commit**; **suicide bombing** *n* attentato suicida

suit [suːt] *n* (*man's*) vestito; (*woman's*) completo, tailleur *m inv*; (*Law*) causa; (*Cards*) seme *m*, colore *m* ▷ *vt* andar bene a *or* per; essere adatto(-a) a *or* per; (*adapt*): **to ~ sth to** adattare qc a; **well ~ed** ben assortito(-a); **suitable** *adj* adatto(-a); appropriato(-a); **suitcase** ['suːtkeɪs] *n* valigia

suite [swiːt] *n* (*of rooms*) appartamento; (*Mus*) suite *f inv*; (*furniture*): **bedroom/ dining room ~** arredo *or* mobilia per la camera da letto/sala da pranzo

sulfur ['sʌlfə'] (US) *n* = **sulphur**

sulk [sʌlk] *vi* fare il broncio

sulphur ['sʌlfə'] (US **sulfur**) *n* zolfo

sultana [sʌl'tɑːnə] *n* (*fruit*) uva (secca) sultanina

sum [sʌm] *n* somma; (*Scol etc*) addizione *f*; **sum up** *vt, vi* riassumere

summarize ['sʌməraɪz] *vt* riassumere, riepilogare

summary ['sʌmərɪ] *n* riassunto

summer ['sʌmə'] *n* estate *f* ▷ *cpd* d'estate, estivo(-a); **summer holidays** *npl* vacanze *fpl* estive; **summertime** *n* (*season*) estate *f*

summit ['sʌmɪt] *n* cima, sommità; (*Pol*) vertice *m*

summon ['sʌmən] *vt* chiamare, convocare

Sun. *abbr* (= *Sunday*) dom.

sun [sʌn] *n* sole *m*; **sunbathe** *vi* prendere un bagno di sole; **sunbed** *n* lettino solare; **sunblock** *n* protezione *f* solare totale; **sunburn** *n* (*painful*) scottatura; **sunburned, sunburnt** *adj* abbronzato(-a); (*painfully*) scottato(-a)

Sunday ['sʌndɪ] *n* domenica

Sunday paper n giornale m della domenica

sunflower ['sʌnflauə'] n girasole m

sung [sʌŋ] pp of **sing**

sunglasses ['sʌnglɑːsɪz] npl occhiali mpl da sole

sunk [sʌŋk] pp of **sink**

sun: **sunlight** n (luce f del) sole m; **sun lounger** n sedia a sdraio; **sunny** adj assolato(-a), soleggiato(-a); (fig) allegro(-a), felice; **sunrise** n levata del sole, alba; **sun roof** n (Aut) tetto apribile; **sunscreen** n (cream) crema solare protettiva; **sunset** n tramonto; **sunshade** n parasole m; **sunshine** n luce f (del) sole m; **sunstroke** n insolazione f, colpo di sole; **suntan** n abbronzatura; **suntan lotion** n lozione f solare; **suntan oil** n olio solare

super ['suːpə'] (inf) adj fantastico(-a)

superb [suː'pəːb] adj magnifico(-a)

superficial [suːpə'fɪʃəl] adj superficiale

superintendent [suːpərɪn'tɛndənt] n direttore(-trice); (Police) ≈ commissario (capo)

superior [su'pɪərɪə'] adj, n superiore m/f

superlative [suː'pəːlətɪv] adj superlativo(-a), supremo(-a) ▷ n (Ling) superlativo

supermarket ['suːpəmɑːkɪt] n supermercato

supernatural [suːpə'nætʃərəl] adj soprannaturale ▷ n soprannaturale m

superpower ['suːpəpauə'] n (Pol) superpotenza

superstition [suːpə'stɪʃən] n superstizione f

superstitious [suːpə'stɪʃəs] adj superstizioso(-a)

superstore ['suːpəstɔː'] n (BRIT) grande supermercato

supervise ['suːpəvaɪz] vt (person etc) sorvegliare; (organization) soprintendere a; **supervision** [-'vɪʒən] n sorveglianza; supervisione f; **supervisor** n sorvegliante m/f; soprintendente m/f; (in shop) capocommesso(-a)

supper ['sʌpə'] n cena

supple ['sʌpl] adj flessibile; agile

supplement [n 'sʌplɪmənt, vb sʌplɪ'mɛnt] n supplemento ▷ vt completare, integrare

supplier [sə'plaɪə'] n fornitore m

supply [sə'plaɪ] vt (provide) fornire; (equip): **to ~ (with)** approvvigionare (di), attrezzare (con) ▷ n riserva, provvista; (supplying) approvvigionamento; (Tech) alimentazione f; **supplies** npl (food) viveri mpl; (Mil) sussistenza

support [sə'pɔːt] n (moral, financial etc) sostegno, appoggio; (Tech) supporto ▷ vt sostenere; (financially) mantenere; (uphold) sostenere, difendere; **supporter** n (Pol etc) sostenitore(-trice), fautore(-trice); (Sport) tifoso(-a)

> Be careful not to translate **support** by the Italian word **sopportare**.

suppose [sə'pəuz] vt supporre; immaginare; **to be ~d to do** essere tenuto(-a) a fare; **supposedly** [sə'pə uzɪdlɪ] adv presumibilmente; **supposing** conj se, ammesso che + sub

suppress [sə'prɛs] vt reprimere; sopprimere; occultare

supreme [su'priːm] adj supremo(-a)

surcharge ['səːtʃɑːdʒ] n supplemento

sure [ʃuə'] adj sicuro(-a); (definite, convinced) sicuro(-a), certo(-a); **~!** (of course) senz'altro!, certo!; **~ enough** infatti; **to make ~ of sth/that** assicurarsi di qc/che; **surely** adv sicuramente; certamente

surf [səːf] n (waves) cavalloni mpl; (foam) spuma

surface ['səːfɪs] n superficie f ▷ vt (road) asfaltare ▷ vi risalire alla superficie; (fig: news, feeling) venire a galla

surfboard ['səːfbɔːd] n tavola per surfing

surfing ['səːfɪŋ] n surfing m

surge [səːdʒ] n (strong movement) ondata; (of feeling) impeto ▷ vi gonfiarsi; (people) riversarsi

surgeon ['səːdʒən] n chirurgo

surgery ['səːdʒərɪ] n chirurgia; (BRIT: room) studio or gabinetto medico, ambulatorio; (: also: **~ hours**) orario delle visite or di consultazione; **to undergo ~** subire un intervento chirurgico

surname ['səːneɪm] n cognome m

surpass [səː'pɑːs] vt superare

surplus ['səːpləs] n eccedenza; (Econ) surplus m inv ▷ adj eccedente, d'avanzo

surprise [sə'praɪz] n sorpresa; (astonishment) stupore m ▷ vt sorprendere; stupire; **surprised** [sə'praɪzd] adj (look, smile) sorpreso(-a); **to be surprised** essere sorpreso, sorprendersi; **surprising** adj sorprendente, stupefacente; **surprisingly** adv (easy, helpful) sorprendentemente

surrender [sə'rɛndə'] n resa, capitolazione f ▷ vi arrendersi

surround [sə'raund] vt circondare; (Mil etc) accerchiare; **surrounding** adj circostante; **surroundings** npl dintorni mpl; (fig) ambiente m

surveillance [sə:'veɪləns] n sorveglianza, controllo

survey [n 'sə:veɪ, vb sə:'veɪ] n quadro generale; (study) esame m; (in housebuying etc) perizia; (of land) rilevamento, rilievo topografico ▷ vt osservare; esaminare; valutare; rilevare; **surveyor** n perito; geometra m; (of land) agrimensore m

survival [sə'vaɪvl] n sopravvivenza; (relic) reliquia, vestigio

survive [sə'vaɪv] vi sopravvivere ▷ vt sopravvivere a; **survivor** n superstite m/f, sopravvissuto(-a)

suspect [adj, n 'sʌspɛkt, vb səs'pɛkt] adj sospetto(-a) ▷ n persona sospetta ▷ vt sospettare; (think likely) supporre; (doubt) dubitare

suspend [səs'pɛnd] vt sospendere; **suspended sentence** n condanna con la condizionale; **suspenders** npl (BRIT) giarrettiere fpl; (US) bretelle fpl

suspense [səs'pɛns] n apprensione f; (in film etc) suspense m; **to keep sb in ~** tenere qn in sospeso

suspension [səs'pɛnʃən] n (gen Aut) sospensione f; (of driving licence) ritiro temporaneo; **suspension bridge** n ponte m sospeso

suspicion [səs'pɪʃən] n sospetto; **suspicious** [səs'pɪʃəs] adj (suspecting) sospettoso(-a); (causing suspicion) sospetto(-a)

sustain [səs'teɪn] vt sostenere; sopportare; (Law: charge) confermare; (suffer) subire

swallow ['swɔləu] n (bird) rondine f ▷ vt inghiottire; (fig: story) bere

swam [swæm] pt of **swim**

swamp [swɔmp] n palude f ▷ vt sommergere

swan [swɔn] n cigno

swap [swɔp] vt **to ~ (for)** scambiare (con)

swarm [swɔ:m] n sciame m ▷ vi (bees) sciamare; (people) brulicare; (place): **to be ~ing with** brulicare di

sway [sweɪ] vi (tree) ondeggiare; (person) barcollare ▷ vt (influence) influenzare, dominare

swear [swɛəʳ] (pt swore, pp sworn) vi (curse) bestemmiare, imprecare ▷ vt (promise) giurare; **swear in** vt prestare giuramento a; **swearword** n parolaccia

sweat [swɛt] n sudore m, traspirazione f ▷ vi sudare

sweater ['swɛtəʳ] n maglione m

sweatshirt ['swɛtʃə:t] n felpa

sweaty ['swɛtɪ] adj sudato(-a), bagnato(-a) di sudore

Swede [swi:d] n svedese m/f

swede [swi:d] n (BRIT) rapa svedese

Sweden ['swi:dn] n Svezia; **Swedish** ['swi:dɪʃ] adj svedese ▷ n (Ling) svedese m

sweep [swi:p] (pt, pp swept) n spazzata; (also: **chimney ~**) spazzacamino ▷ vt spazzare, scopare; (current) spazzare ▷ vi (hand) muoversi con gesto ampio; (wind) infuriare

sweet [swi:t] n (BRIT: pudding) dolce m; (candy) caramella ▷ adj dolce; (fresh) fresco(-a); (fig) piacevole; delicato(-a), grazioso(-a); gentile; **sweetcorn** n granturco dolce; **sweetener** ['swi:tnəʳ] n (Culin) dolcificante m; **sweetheart** n innamorato(-a); **sweetshop** n (BRIT) ≈ pasticceria

swell [swɛl] (pt swelled, pp swollen, swelled) n (of sea) mare m lungo ▷ adj (US: inf: excellent) favoloso(-a) ▷ vt gonfiare, ingrossare; aumentare ▷ vi gonfiarsi, ingrossarsi; (sound) crescere; (also: **~ up**) gonfiarsi; **swelling** n (Med) tumefazione f, gonfiore m

swept [swɛpt] pt, pp of **sweep**

swerve [swə:v] vi deviare; (driver) sterzare; (boxer) scartare

swift [swɪft] n (bird) rondone m ▷ adj rapido(-a), veloce

swim [swɪm] (pt swam, pp swum) n **to go for a ~** andare a fare una nuotata ▷ vi nuotare; (Sport) fare del nuoto; (head, room) girare ▷ vt (river, channel) attraversare or percorrere a nuoto; (length) nuotare; **swimmer** n nuotatore(-trice); **swimming** n nuoto; **swimming costume** n (BRIT) costume m da bagno; **swimming pool** n piscina; **swimming trunks** npl costume m da bagno (da uomo); **swimsuit** n costume m da bagno

swing [swɪŋ] (pt, pp swung) n altalena; (movement) oscillazione f; (Mus) ritmo; swing m ▷ vt dondolare, far oscillare; (also: **~ round**) far girare ▷ vi oscillare, dondolare; (also: **~ round**: object) roteare; (: person) girarsi, voltarsi; **to be in full ~** (activity) essere in piena attività; (party etc) essere nel pieno

swipe card n tessera magnetica

swirl [swə:l] vi turbinare, far mulinello

Swiss [swɪs] adj, n inv svizzero(-a)

switch [swɪtʃ] n (for light, radio etc) interruttore m; (change) cambiamento ▷ vt (change) cambiare; scambiare; **switch off** vt spegnere; **could you ~ off the light?** puoi spegnere la luce?; **switch on**

vt accendere; (*engine, machine*) mettere in moto, avviare; **switchboard** *n* (*Tel*) centralino

Switzerland ['swɪtsələnd] *n* Svizzera
swivel ['swɪvl] *vi* (*also*: **~ round**) girare
swollen ['swəʊlən] *pp of* **swell**
swoop [swu:p] *n* incursione *f* ▷ *vi* (*also*: **~ down**) scendere in picchiata, piombare
swop [swɔp] *n, vt* = **swap**
sword [sɔ:d] *n* spada; **swordfish** *n* pesce *m* spada *inv*
swore [swɔ:ʳ] *pt of* **swear**
sworn [swɔ:n] *pp of* **swear** ▷ *adj* giurato(-a)
swum [swʌm] *pp of* **swim**
swung [swʌŋ] *pt, pp of* **swing**
syllable ['sɪləbl] *n* sillaba
syllabus ['sɪləbəs] *n* programma *m*
symbol ['sɪmbl] *n* simbolo; **symbolic(al)** [sɪm'bɔlɪk(l)] *adj* simbolico(-a); **to be symbolic(al) of sth** simboleggiare qc
symmetrical [sɪ'mɛtrɪkl] *adj* simmetrico(-a)
symmetry ['sɪmɪtrɪ] *n* simmetria
sympathetic [sɪmpə'θɛtɪk] *adj* (*showing pity*) compassionevole; (*kind*) comprensivo(-a); **~ towards** ben disposto(-a) verso

> Be careful not to translate *sympathetic* by the Italian word *simpatico*.

sympathize ['sɪmpəθaɪz] *vi* **to ~ with** (*person*) compatire; partecipare al dolore di; (*cause*) simpatizzare per
sympathy ['sɪmpəθɪ] *n* compassione *f*
symphony ['sɪmfənɪ] *n* sinfonia
symptom ['sɪmptəm] *n* sintomo; indizio
synagogue ['sɪnəgɔg] *n* sinagoga
syndicate ['sɪndɪkɪt] *n* sindacato
syndrome ['sɪndrəum] *n* sindrome *f*
synonym ['sɪnənɪm] *n* sinonimo
synthetic [sɪn'θɛtɪk] *adj* sintetico(-a)
Syria ['sɪrɪə] *n* Siria
syringe [sɪ'rɪndʒ] *n* siringa
syrup ['sɪrəp] *n* sciroppo; (*also*: **golden ~**) melassa raffinata
system ['sɪstəm] *n* sistema *m*; (*order*) metodo; (*Anat*) organismo; **systematic** [-'mætɪk] *adj* sistematico(-a); metodico(-a); **systems analyst** *n* analista *m* di sistemi

t

ta [tɑ:] (BRIT: *inf*) *excl* grazie!
tab [tæb] *n* (*loop on coat etc*) laccetto; (*label*) etichetta; **to keep ~s on** (*fig*) tenere d'occhio
table ['teɪbl] *n* tavolo, tavola; (*Math, Chem etc*) tavola ▷ *vt* (BRIT: *motion etc*) presentare; **a ~ for 4, please** un tavolo per 4, per favore; **to lay** *or* **set the ~** apparecchiare *or* preparare la tavola; **tablecloth** *n* tovaglia; **table d'hôte** [tɑ:bl'dəut] *adj* (*meal*) a prezzo fisso; **table lamp** *n* lampada da tavolo; **tablemat** *n* sottopiatto; **tablespoon** *n* cucchiaio da tavola; (*also*: **tablespoonful**: *as measurement*) cucchiaiata
tablet ['tæblɪt] *n* (*Med*) compressa; (*of stone*) targa
table tennis *n* tennis *m* da tavolo, ping-pong® *m*
tabloid ['tæblɔɪd] *n* (*newspaper*) tabloid *m inv* (*giornale illustrato di formato ridotto*), **the ~s, the ~ press** i giornali popolari
taboo [tə'bu:] *adj, n* tabù *m inv*
tack [tæk] *n* (*nail*) bulletta; (*fig*) approccio ▷ *vt* imbullettare; imbastire ▷ *vi* bordeggiare
tackle ['tækl] *n* attrezzatura, equipaggiamento; (*for lifting*) paranco; (*Football*) contrasto; (*Rugby*) placcaggio ▷ *vt* (*difficulty*) affrontare; (*Football*)

contrastare; (*Rugby*) placcare
tacky ['tækɪ] *adj* appiccicaticcio(-a); (*pej*)
scadente
tact [tækt] *n* tatto; **tactful** *adj*
delicato(-a), discreto(-a)
tactics ['tæktɪks] *n*, *npl* tattica
tactless ['tæktlɪs] *adj* che manca di tatto
tadpole ['tædpəul] *n* girino
taffy ['tæfɪ] (*US*) *n* caramella *f* mou *inv*
tag [tæg] *n* etichetta
tail [teɪl] *n* coda; (*of shirt*) falda ▷ *vt* (*follow*)
seguire, pedinare; **~s** *npl* (*formal suit*) frac
m inv
tailor ['teɪlə'] *n* sarto
Taiwan [taɪ'wɑːn] *n* Taiwan *m*; **Taiwanese**
[taɪwə'niːz] *adj*, *n* taiwanese
take [teɪk] (*pt* **took**, *pp* **taken**) *vt* prendere;
(*gain: prize*) ottenere, vincere; (*require:
effort, courage*) occorrere, volerci; (*tolerate*)
accettare, sopportare; (*hold: passengers etc*)
contenere; (*accompany*) accompagnare;
(*bring, carry*) portare; (*exam*) sostenere,
presentarsi a; **to ~ a photo/a shower**
fare una fotografia/una doccia; **I ~ it**
that suppongo che; **take after** *vt fus*
assomigliare a; **take apart** *vt* smontare;
take away *vt* portare via; togliere; **take
back** *vt* (*return*) restituire; riportare; (*one's
words*) ritirare; **take down** *vt* (*building*)
demolire; (*letter etc*) scrivere; **take in**
vt (*deceive*) imbrogliare, abbindolare;
(*understand*) capire; (*include*) comprendere,
includere; (*lodger*) prendere, ospitare;
take off *vi* (*Aviat*) decollare; (*go away*)
andarsene ▷ *vt* (*remove*) togliere; **take
on** *vt* (*work*) accettare, intraprendere;
(*employee*) assumere; (*opponent*) sfidare,
affrontare; **take out** *vt* portare fuori;
(*remove*) togliere; (*licence*) prendere,
ottenere; **to ~ sth out of sth** (*drawer,
pocket etc*) tirare qc fuori da qc; estrarre qc
da qc; **take over** *vt* (*business*) rilevare ▷ *vi*
to ~ over from sb prendere le consegne
or il controllo da qn; **take up** *vt* (*dress*)
accorciare; (*occupy: time, space*) occupare;
(*engage in: hobby etc*) mettersi a; **to ~ sb
up on sth** accettare qc da qn; **takeaway**
(*BRIT*) *n* (*shop etc*) ≈ rosticceria; (*food*)
pasto per asporto; **taken** *pp of* **take**;
takeoff *n* (*Aviat*) decollo; **takeout** (*US*)
n = **takeaway**; **takeover** *n* (*Comm*)
assorbimento; **takings** ['teɪkɪŋz] *npl*
(*Comm*) incasso
talc [tælk] *n* (*also:* **~um powder**) talco
tale [teɪl] *n* racconto, storia; **to tell ~s** (*fig:
to teacher, parent etc*) fare la spia
talent ['tælnt] *n* talento; **talented** *adj* di
talento
talk [tɔːk] *n* discorso; (*gossip*) chiacchiere

fpl; (*conversation*) conversazione *f*;
(*interview*) discussione *f* ▷ *vi* parlare; **~s** *npl*
(*Pol etc*) colloqui *mpl*; **to ~ about** parlare di;
to ~ sb out of/into doing dissuadere qn
da/convincere qn a fare; **to ~ shop** parlare
di lavoro *or* di affari; **talk over** *vt* discutere;
talk show *n* conversazione *f* televisiva,
talk show *m inv*
tall [tɔːl] *adj* alto(-a); **to be 6 feet ~** ≈ essere
alto 1 metro e 80
tambourine [tæmbə'riːn] *n* tamburello
tame [teɪm] *adj* addomesticato(-a); (*fig:
story, style*) insipido(-a), scialbo(-a)
tamper ['tæmpə'] *vi* **to ~ with**
manomettere
tampon ['tæmpɔn] *n* tampone *m*
tan [tæn] *n* (*also:* **sun~**) abbronzatura
▷ *vi* abbronzarsi ▷ *adj* (*colour*) marrone
rossiccio *inv*
tandem ['tændəm] *n* tandem *m inv*
tangerine [tændʒə'riːn] *n* mandarino
tangle ['tæŋgl] *n* groviglio; **to get into a ~**
aggrovigliarsi; (*fig*) combinare un pasticcio
tank [tæŋk] *n* serbatoio; (*for fish*) acquario;
(*Mil*) carro armato
tanker ['tæŋkə'] *n* (*ship*) nave *f* cisterna *inv*;
(*truck*) autobotte *f*, autocisterna
tanned [tænd] *adj* abbronzato(-a)
tantrum ['tæntrəm] *n* accesso di collera
Tanzania [tænzə'nɪə] *n* Tanzania
tap [tæp] *n* (*on sink etc*) rubinetto; (*gentle
blow*) colpetto ▷ *vt* dare un colpetto a;
(*resources*) sfruttare, utilizzare; (*telephone*)
mettere sotto controllo; **on ~** (*fig:
resources*) a disposizione; **tap dancing** *n*
tip tap *m*
tape [teɪp] *n* nastro; (*also:* **magnetic ~**)
nastro (magnetico); (*sticky tape*) nastro
adesivo ▷ *vt* (*record*) registrare (su nastro);
(*stick*) attaccare con nastro adesivo;
tape measure *n* metro a nastro; **tape
recorder** *n* registratore *m* (a nastro)
tapestry ['tæpɪstrɪ] *n* arazzo; tappezzeria
tar [tɑː'] *n* catrame *m*
target ['tɑːgɪt] *n* bersaglio; (*fig: objective*)
obiettivo
tariff ['tærɪf] *n* tariffa
tarmac ['tɑːmæk] *n* (*BRIT: on road*)
macadam *m* al catrame; (*Aviat*) pista di
decollo
tarpaulin [tɑː'pɔːlɪn] *n* tela incatramata
tarragon ['tærəgən] *n* dragoncello
tart [tɑːt] *n* (*Culin*) crostata; (*BRIT: inf:
pej: woman*) sgualdrina ▷ *adj* (*flavour*)
aspro(-a), agro(-a)
tartan ['tɑːtn] *n* tartan *m inv*
tartar(e) sauce *n* salsa tartara
task [tɑːsk] *n* compito; **to take to ~**
rimproverare

taste [teɪst] n gusto; (flavour) sapore m, gusto; (sample) assaggio; (fig: glimpse, idea) idea ▷ vt gustare; (sample) assaggiare ▷ vi to ~ of or like (fish etc) sapere or avere sapore di; **in good/bad ~** di buon/cattivo gusto; **can I have a ~?** posso assaggiarlo?; **you can ~ the garlic (in it)** (ci) si sente il sapore dell'aglio; **tasteful** adj di buon gusto; **tasteless** adj (food) insipido(-a); (remark) di cattivo gusto; **tasty** adj saporito(-a), gustoso(-a)

tatters ['tætəz] npl **in ~** a brandelli

tattoo [tə'tuː] n tatuaggio; (spectacle) parata militare ▷ vt tatuare

taught [tɔːt] pt, pp of **teach**

taunt [tɔːnt] n scherno ▷ vt schernire

Taurus ['tɔːrəs] n Toro

taut [tɔːt] adj teso(-a)

tax [tæks] n (on goods) imposta; (on services) tassa; (on income) imposte fpl, tasse fpl ▷ vt tassare; (fig: strain: patience etc) mettere alla prova; **tax-free** adj esente da imposte

taxi ['tæksɪ] n taxi m inv ▷ vi (Aviat) rullare; **can you call me a ~, please?** può chiamarmi un taxi, per favore?; **taxi driver** n tassista m/f; **taxi rank** (BRIT) n = **taxi stand**; **taxi stand** n posteggio dei taxi

tax payer n contribuente m/f

TB n abbr = **tuberculosis**

tea [tiː] n tè m inv; (BRIT: snack: for children) merenda; **high ~** (BRIT) cena leggera (presa nel tardo pomeriggio); **tea bag** n bustina di tè; **tea break** (BRIT) n intervallo per il tè

teach [tiːtʃ] (pt, pp **taught**) vt **to ~ sb sth, ~ sth to sb** insegnare qc a qn ▷ vi insegnare; **teacher** n insegnante m/f; (in secondary school) professore(-essa); (in primary school) maestro(-a); **teaching** n insegnamento

tea: tea cloth n (for dishes) strofinaccio; (BRIT: for trolley) tovaglietta da tè; **teacup** ['tiːkʌp] n tazza da tè

tea leaves npl foglie fpl di tè

team [tiːm] n squadra; (of animals) tiro; **team up** vi **to ~ up (with)** mettersi insieme (a)

teapot ['tiːpɒt] n teiera

tear¹ [teə¹] (pt **tore**, pp **torn**) n strappo ▷ vt strappare ▷ vi strapparsi; **tear apart** vt (also fig) distruggere; **tear down** vt +adv (building, statue) demolire; (poster, flag) tirare giù; **tear off** vt (sheet of paper etc) strappare; (one's clothes) togliersi di dosso; **tear up** vt (sheet of paper etc) strappare

tear² [tɪə¹] n lacrima; **in ~s** in lacrime; **tearful** ['tɪəful] adj piangente, lacrimoso(-a); **tear gas** n gas m lacrimogeno

tearoom ['tiːruːm] n sala da tè

tease [tiːz] vt canzonare; (unkindly)

tormentare

tea: teaspoon n cucchiaino da tè; (also: **teaspoonful:** as measurement) cucchiaino; **teatime** n ora del tè; **tea towel** (BRIT) n strofinaccio (per i piatti)

technical ['tɛknɪkl] adj tecnico(-a)

technician [tɛk'nɪʃən] n tecnico(-a)

technique [tɛk'niːk] n tecnica

technology [tɛk'nɒlədʒɪ] n tecnologia

teddy (bear) ['tɛdɪ-] n orsacchiotto

tedious ['tiːdɪəs] adj noioso(-a), tedioso(-a)

tee [tiː] n (Golf) tee m inv

teen [tiːn] adj = **teenage** ▷ n (US) = **teenager**

teenage ['tiːneɪdʒ] adj (fashions etc) per giovani, per adolescenti; **teenager** n adolescente m/f

teens [tiːnz] npl **to be in one's ~** essere adolescente

teeth [tiːθ] npl of **tooth**

teetotal ['tiː'təutl] adj astemio(-a)

telecommunications ['tɛlɪkəmjuːnɪ'keɪʃənz] n telecomunicazioni fpl

telegram ['tɛlɪɡræm] n telegramma m

telegraph pole n palo del telegrafo

telephone ['tɛlɪfəun] n telefono ▷ vt (person) telefonare a; (message) comunicare per telefono; **telephone book** n elenco telefonico; **telephone booth** (BRIT), **telephone box** n cabina telefonica; **telephone call** n telefonata; **telephone directory** n elenco telefonico; **telephone number** n numero di telefono

telesales ['tɛlɪseɪlz] n vendita per telefono

telescope ['tɛlɪskəup] n telescopio

televise ['tɛlɪvaɪz] vt teletrasmettere

television ['tɛlɪvɪʒən] n televisione f; **on ~** alla televisione; **television programme** n programma m televisivo

tell [tɛl] (pt, pp **told**) vt dire; (relate: story) raccontare; (distinguish): **to ~ sth from** distinguere qc da ▷ vi (talk): **to ~ (of)** parlare (di); (have effect) farsi sentire, avere effetto; **to ~ sb to do** dire a qn di fare; **tell off** vt rimproverare, sgridare; **teller** n (in bank) cassiere(-a)

telly ['tɛlɪ] (BRIT: inf) n abbr (= **television**) tivù f inv

temp [tɛmp] n abbr (= **temporary**) segretaria temporanea

temper ['tɛmpə¹] n (nature) carattere m; (mood) umore m; (fit of anger) collera ▷ vt (moderate) moderare; **to be in a ~** essere in collera; **to lose one's ~** andare in collera

temperament ['tɛmprəmənt] n (nature) temperamento; **temperamental** [-'mɛntl] adj capriccioso(-a)

temperature ['tɛmprətʃə¹] n

temperatura; **to have** or **run a ~** avere la febbre

temple ['tɛmpl] n (building) tempio; (Anat) tempia

temporary ['tɛmpərərɪ] adj temporaneo(-a); (job, worker) avventizio(-a), temporaneo(-a)

tempt [tɛmpt] vt tentare; **to ~ sb into doing** indurre qn a fare; **temptation** [-'teɪʃən] n tentazione f; **tempting** adj allettante

ten [tɛn] num dieci

tenant ['tɛnənt] n inquilino(-a)

tend [tɛnd] vt badare a, occuparsi di ▷ vi **to ~ to do** tendere a fare; **tendency** ['tɛndənsɪ] n tendenza

tender ['tɛndəʳ] adj tenero(-a); (sore) dolorante ▷ n (Comm: offer) offerta; (money): **legal ~** moneta in corso legale ▷ vt offrire

tendon ['tɛndən] n tendine m

tenner ['tɛnəʳ] n (BRIT inf) (banconota da) dieci sterline fpl

tennis ['tɛnɪs] n tennis m; **tennis ball** n palla da tennis; **tennis court** n campo da tennis; **tennis match** n partita di tennis; **tennis player** n tennista m/f; **tennis racket** n racchetta da tennis

tenor ['tɛnəʳ] n (Mus) tenore m

tenpin bowling ['tɛnpɪn-] n bowling m

tense [tɛns] adj teso(-a) ▷ n (Ling) tempo

tension ['tɛnʃən] n tensione f

tent [tɛnt] n tenda

tentative ['tɛntətɪv] adj esitante, incerto(-a); (conclusion) provvisorio(-a)

tenth [tɛnθ] num decimo(-a)

tent: **tent peg** n picchetto da tenda; **tent pole** n palo da tenda, montante m

tepid ['tɛpɪd] adj tiepido(-a)

term [təːm] n termine m; (Scol) trimestre m; (Law) sessione f ▷ vt chiamare, definire; **~s** npl (conditions) condizioni fpl; (Comm) prezzi mpl, tariffe fpl; **in the short/long ~** a breve/lunga scadenza; **to be on good ~s with sb** essere in buoni rapporti con qn; **to come to ~s with** (problem) affrontare

terminal ['təːmɪnl] adj finale, terminale; (disease) terminale ▷ n (Elec) morsetto; (Comput) terminale m; (Aviat, for oil, ore etc) terminal m inv; (BRIT: also: **coach ~**) capolinea m

terminate ['təːmɪneɪt] vt mettere fine a

termini ['təːmɪnaɪ] npl of **terminus**

terminology [təːmɪ'nɔlədʒɪ] n terminologia

terminus ['təːmɪnəs] (pl **termini**) n (for buses) capolinea m; (for trains) stazione f terminale

terrace ['tɛrəs] n terrazza; (BRIT: row of houses) fila di case a schiera; **terraced** adj (garden) a terrazze

terrain [tɛ'reɪn] n terreno

terrestrial [tɪ'rɛstrɪəl] adj (life) terrestre; (BRIT: channel) terrestre

terrible ['tɛrɪbl] adj terribile; **terribly** adv terribilmente; (very badly) malissimo

terrier ['tɛrɪəʳ] n terrier m inv

terrific [tə'rɪfɪk] adj incredibile, fantastico(-a); (wonderful) formidabile, eccezionale

terrified ['tɛrɪfaɪd] adj atterrito(-a)

terrify ['tɛrɪfaɪ] vt terrorizzare; **terrifying** adj terrificante

territorial [tɛrɪ'tɔːrɪəl] adj territoriale

territory ['tɛrɪtərɪ] n territorio

terror ['tɛrəʳ] n terrore m; **terrorism** n terrorismo; **terrorist** n terrorista m/f

test [tɛst] n (trial, check: of courage etc) prova; (Med) esame m; (Chem) analisi f inv; (exam: of intelligence etc) test m inv; (: in school) compito in classe; (also: **driving ~**) esame m di guida ▷ vt provare; esaminare; analizzare; sottoporre ad esame; **to ~ sb in history** esaminare qn in storia

testicle ['tɛstɪkl] n testicolo

testify ['tɛstɪfaɪ] vi (Law) testimoniare, deporre; **to ~ to sth** (Law) testimoniare qc; (gen) comprovare or dimostrare qc

testimony ['tɛstɪmənɪ] n (Law) testimonianza, deposizione f

test: **test match** n (Cricket, Rugby) partita internazionale; **test tube** n provetta

tetanus ['tɛtənəs] n tetano

text [tɛkst] n testo; (on mobile phone) SMS m inv, messaggino ▷ vt **to ~ sb** (inf) mandare un SMS a qn; **textbook** n libro di testo

textile ['tɛkstaɪl] n tessile m

text message n (Tel) SMS m inv, messaggino

text messaging [-'mɛsɪdʒɪŋ] n il mandarsi SMS

texture ['tɛkstʃəʳ] n tessitura; (of skin, paper etc) struttura

Thai [taɪ] adj tailandese ▷ n tailandese m/f; (Ling) tailandese m

Thailand ['taɪlænd] n Tailandia

Thames [tɛmz] n **the ~** il Tamigi

than [ðæn, ðən] conj (in comparisons) che; (with numerals, pronouns, proper names) di; **more ~ 10/once** più di 10/una volta; **I have more/less ~ you** ne ho più/meno di te; **I have more pens ~ pencils** ho più penne che matite; **she is older ~ you think** è più vecchia di quanto tu (non) pensi

thank [θæŋk] vt ringraziare; **~ you (very much)** grazie (tante); **~s** npl ringraziamenti mpl, grazie fpl excl grazie!;

~s to grazie a; **thankfully** *adv* con riconoscenza; con sollievo; **thankfully there were few victims** grazie al cielo ci sono state poche vittime; **Thanksgiving (Day)** *n* giorno del ringraziamento

● **THANKSGIVING (DAY)**
●
● Negli Stati Uniti il quarto giovedì di
● novembre ricorre il **Thanksgiving**
● **(Day)**, festa che rievoca la celebrazione
● con cui i Padri Pellegrini, fondatori della
● colonia di Plymouth in Massachusetts,
● ringraziarono Dio del buon raccolto
● del 1621.

🔘 **KEYWORD**

that [ðæt] (*pl* **those**) *adj* (*demonstrative*) quel (quell', quello) *m*; quella (quell') *f*; **that man/woman/book** quell'uomo/quella donna/quel libro; (*not "this"*) quell'uomo/ quella donna/quel libro là; **that one** quello(-a) là
▷ *pron* **1** (*demonstrative*) ciò; (*not "this one"*) quello(-a); **who's that?** chi è?; **what's that?** cos'è quello?; **is that you?** sei tu?; **I prefer this to that** preferisco questo a quello; **that's what he said** questo è ciò che ha detto; **what happened after that?** che è successo dopo?; **that is (to say)** cioè **2** (*relative: direct*) che; (: *indirect*) cui; **the book (that) I read** il libro che ho letto; **the box (that) I put it in** la scatola in cui l'ho messo; **the people (that) I spoke to** le persone con cui *or* con le quali ho parlato **3** (*relative: of time*) in cui; **the day (that) he came** il giorno in cui è venuto
▷ *conj* che; **he thought that I was ill** pensava che io fossi malato
▷ *adv* (*demonstrative*) così; **I can't work that much** non posso lavorare (così) tanto; **that high** così alto; **the wall's about that high and that thick** il muro è alto circa così e spesso circa così

thatched [θætʃt] *adj* (*roof*) di paglia
thaw [θɔː] *n* disgelo ▷ *vi* (*ice*) sciogliersi; (*food*) scongelarsi ▷ *vt* (*food: also:* **~ out**) (fare) scongelare

🔘 **KEYWORD**

the [ðiː, ðə] *def art* **1** (*gen*) il (lo, l') *m*; la (l') *f*; i (gli) *mpl*; le *fpl*; **the boy/girl/ink** il ragazzo/la ragazza/l'inchiostro; **the books/pencils** i libri/le matite; **the history of the world** la storia del mondo; **give it to the postman** dallo al postino;

I haven't the time/money non ho tempo/soldi; **the rich and the poor** i ricchi e i poveri
2 (*in titles*): **Elizabeth the First** Elisabetta prima; **Peter the Great** Pietro il grande
3 (*in comparisons*): **the more he works, the more he earns** più lavora più guadagna

theatre ['θɪətə^r] (*US* **theater**) *n* teatro; (*also:* **lecture ~**) aula magna; (*also:* **operating ~**) sala operatoria
theft [θeft] *n* furto
their [ðɛə^r] *adj* il (la) loro; (*pl*) i (le) loro; **theirs** *pron* il (la) loro; (*pl*) i (le) loro; *see also* **my**; **mine**
them [ðɛm, ðəm] *pron* (*direct*) li (le); (*indirect*) gli (loro *after vb*); (*stressed, after prep: people*) loro; (: *people, things*) essi(-e); *see also* **me**
theme [θiːm] *n* tema *m*; **theme park** *n* parco di divertimenti (*intorno a un tema centrale*)
themselves [ðəm'sɛlvz] *pl pron* (*reflexive*) si; (*emphatic*) loro stessi(-e); (*after prep*) se stessi(-e)
then [ðɛn] *adv* (*at that time*) allora; (*next*) poi, dopo; (*and also*) e poi ▷ *conj* (*therefore*) perciò, dunque, quindi ▷ *adj* **the ~ president** il presidente di allora; **by ~** allora; **from ~ on** da allora in poi
theology [θɪ'ɔlədʒɪ] *n* teologia
theory ['θɪərɪ] *n* teoria
therapist ['θɛrəpɪst] *n* terapista *m/f*
therapy ['θɛrəpɪ] *n* terapia

🔘 **KEYWORD**

there [ðɛə^r] *adv* **1**: **there is, there are** c'è, ci sono; **there are 3 of them** (*people*) sono in 3; (*things*) ce ne sono 3; **there is no-one here** non c'è nessuno qui; **there has been an accident** c'è stato un incidente
2 (*referring to place*) là, lì; **up/in/down there** lassù/là dentro/laggiù; **he went there on Friday** ci è andato venerdì; **I want that book there** voglio quel libro là *or* lì; **there he is!** eccolo!
3: **there, there** (*esp to child*) su, su

there: **thereabouts** [ðɛərə'bauts] *adv* (*place*) nei pressi, da quelle parti; (*amount*) giù di lì, all'incirca; **thereafter** [ðɛər'ɑːftə^r] *adv* da allora in poi; **thereby** [ðɛə'baɪ] *adv* con ciò; **therefore** ['ðɛəfɔː^r] *adv* perciò, quindi; **there's** [ðɛəz] = **there is**; **there has**
thermal ['θəːml] *adj* termico(-a)
thermometer [θə'mɔmɪtə^r] *n*

termometro

thermostat ['θəːməstæt] n termostato
these [ðiːz] pl pron, adj questi(-e)
thesis ['θiːsɪs] (pl **theses**) n tesi f inv
they [ðeɪ] pl pron essi (esse); (people only)
loro; **~ say that** ... (it is said that) si dice
che ...; **they'd = they had**; **they would**;
they'll = they shall; **they will**; **they're
= they are**; **they've = they have**
thick [θɪk] adj spesso(-a); (crowd)
compatto(-a); (stupid) ottuso(-a), lento(-a)
▷ n **in the ~ of** nel folto di; **it's 20 cm ~**
ha uno spessore di 20 cm; **thicken** vi
ispessire ▷ vt (sauce etc) ispessire, rendere
più denso(-a); **thickness** n spessore m
thief [θiːf] (pl **thieves**) n ladro(-a)
thigh [θaɪ] n coscia
thin [θɪn] adj sottile; (person) magro(-a);
(soup) poco denso(-a) ▷ vt **to ~ (down)**
(sauce, paint) diluire
thing [θɪŋ] n cosa; (object) oggetto;
(mania): **to have a ~ about** essere
fissato(-a) con; **~s** npl (belongings) cose fpl;
poor ~ poverino(-a); **the best ~ would be
to** la cosa migliore sarebbe di; **how are ~s?**
come va?
think [θɪŋk] (pt, pp **thought**) vi pensare,
riflettere ▷ vt pensare, credere; (imagine)
immaginare; **to ~ of** pensare a; **what did
you ~ of them?** cosa ne ha pensato?; **to
~ about sth/sb** pensare a qc/qn; **I'll ~
about it** ci penserò; **to ~ of doing** pensare
di fare; **I ~ so/not** penso di sì/no; **to ~ well
of** avere una buona opinione di; **think
over** vt riflettere su; **think up** vt ideare
third [θəːd] num terzo(-a) ▷ n terzo(-a);
(fraction) terzo, terza parte f; (Aut) terza;
(BRIT: Scol: degree) laurea col minimo dei voti;
thirdly adv in terzo luogo; **third party
insurance** (BRIT) n assicurazione f contro
terzi; **Third World** n **the Third World** il
Terzo Mondo
thirst [θəːst] n sete f; **thirsty** adj (person)
assetato(-a), che ha sete
thirteen [θəːˈtiːn] num tredici; **thirteenth**
[-ˈtiːnθ] num tredicesimo(-a)
thirtieth ['θəːtɪɪθ] num trentesimo(-a)
thirty ['θəːtɪ] num trenta

KEYWORD

this [ðɪs] (pl **these**) adj (demonstrative)
questo(-a); **this man/woman/book**
quest'uomo/questa donna/questo libro;
(not "that") quest'uomo/questa donna/
questo libro qui; **this one** questo(-a);
▷ pron (demonstrative) questo(-a); (not "that
one") questo(-a) qui; **who/what is this?**
chi è/che cos'è questo?; **I prefer this to**

that preferisco questo a quello; **this is
where I live** io abito qui; **this is what he
said** questo è ciò che ha detto; **this is Mr
Brown** (in introductions, photo) questo è il
signor Brown; (on telephone) sono il signor
Brown
▷ adv (demonstrative): **this high/long** etc
alto/lungo etc così; **I didn't know things
were this bad** non sapevo andasse così
male

thistle ['θɪsl] n cardo
thorn [θɔːn] n spina
thorough ['θʌrə] adj (search)
minuzioso(-a); (knowledge, research)
approfondito(-a), profondo(-a);
(person) coscienzioso(-a); (cleaning)
a fondo; **thoroughly** adv (search)
minuziosamente; (wash, study) a fondo;
(very) assolutamente
those [ðəʊz] pl pron quelli(-e) ▷ pl adj quei
(quegli) mpl; quelle fpl
though [ðəʊ] conj benché, sebbene ▷ adv
comunque
thought [θɔːt] pt, pp of **think** ▷ n pensiero;
(opinion) opinione f; **thoughtful** adj
pensieroso(-a), pensoso(-a); (considerate)
premuroso(-a); **thoughtless** adj
sconsiderato(-a); (behaviour) scortese
thousand ['θaʊzənd] num mille; **one ~**
mille; **~s of** migliaia di; **thousandth** num
millesimo(-a)
thrash [θræʃ] vt picchiare; bastonare;
(defeat) battere
thread [θrɛd] n filo; (of screw) filetto ▷ vt
(needle) infilare
threat [θrɛt] n minaccia; **threaten** vi
(storm) minacciare ▷ vt **to threaten sb
with/to do** minacciare qn con/di fare;
threatening adj minaccioso(-a)
three [θriː] num tre; **three-
dimensional** adj tridimensionale; (film)
stereoscopico(-a); **three-piece suite**
['θriːpiːs-] n salotto comprendente un
divano e due poltrone; **three-quarters**
npl tre quarti mpl; **three-quarters full**
pieno per tre quarti
threshold ['θrɛʃhəʊld] n soglia
threw [θruː] pt of **throw**
thrill [θrɪl] n brivido ▷ vt (audience)
elettrizzare; **to be ~ed** (with gift etc) essere
elettrizzato(-a); **thrilled** adj **I was thrilled
to get your letter** la tua lettera mi ha
fatto veramente piacere; **thriller** n thriller
m inv; **thrilling** adj (book) pieno(-a) di
suspense; (news, discovery) elettrizzante
thriving ['θraɪvɪŋ] adj fiorente
throat [θrəʊt] n gola; **to have a sore ~**
avere (un or il) mal di gola

throb [θrɔb] vi palpitare; pulsare; vibrare
throne [θrəʊn] n trono
through [θruː] prep attraverso; (time) per, durante; (by means of) per mezzo di; (owing to) a causa di ▷ adj (ticket, train, passage) diretto(-a) ▷ adv attraverso; **to put sb ~ to sb** (Tel) passare qn a qn; **to be ~** (Tel) ottenere la comunicazione; (have finished) essere finito(-a); **"no ~ road"** (BRIT) "strada senza sbocco"; **throughout** prep (place) dappertutto in; (time) per or durante tutto(-a) ▷ adv dappertutto; sempre
throw [θrəʊ] (pt **threw**, pp **thrown**) n (Sport) lancio, tiro ▷ vt tirare, gettare; (Sport) lanciare, tirare; (rider) disarcionare; (fig) confondere; **to ~ a party** dare una festa; **throw away** vt gettare or buttare via; **throw in** vt (Sport: ball) rimettere in gioco; (include) aggiungere; **throw off** vt sbarazzarsi di; **throw out** vt buttare fuori; (reject) respingere; **throw up** vi vomitare
thru [θruː] (US) prep, adj, adv = **through**
thrush [θrʌʃ] n tordo
thrust [θrʌst] (pt, pp **thrust**) vt spingere con forza; (push in) conficcare
thud [θʌd] n tonfo
thug [θʌɡ] n delinquente m
thumb [θʌm] n (Anat) pollice m; **to ~ a lift** fare l'autostop; **thumbtack** (US) n puntina da disegno
thump [θʌmp] n colpo forte; (sound) tonfo ▷ vt (person) picchiare; (object) battere su ▷ vi picchiare; battere
thunder [ˈθʌndəʳ] n tuono ▷ vi tuonare; (train etc): **to ~ past** passare con un rombo; **thunderstorm** n temporale m
Thur(s). abbr (= Thursday) gio.
Thursday [ˈθəːzdɪ] n giovedì m inv
thus [ðʌs] adv così
thwart [θwɔːt] vt contrastare
thyme [taɪm] n timo
Tiber [ˈtaɪbəʳ] n **the ~** il Tevere
Tibet [tɪˈbɛt] n Tibet m
tick [tɪk] n (sound: of clock) tic tac m inv; (mark) segno; spunta; (Zool) zecca; (BRIT: inf): **in a ~** in un attimo ▷ vi fare tic tac ▷ vt spuntare; **tick off** vt spuntare; (person) sgridare
ticket [ˈtɪkɪt] n biglietto; (in shop: on goods) etichetta; (parking ticket) multa; (for library) scheda; **a single/return ~ to ...** un biglietto di sola andata/di andata e ritorno per...; **ticket barrier** n (BRIT: Rail) cancelletto d'ingresso; **ticket collector** n bigliettaio; **ticket inspector** n controllore m; **ticket machine** n distributore m di biglietti; **ticket office** n biglietteria
tickle [ˈtɪkl] vt fare il solletico a; (fig) solleticare ▷ vi **it ~s** mi (or gli etc) fa il

solletico; **ticklish** [-lɪʃ] adj che soffre il solletico; (problem) delicato(-a)
tide [taɪd] n marea; (fig: of events) corso; **high/low ~** alta/bassa marea
tidy [ˈtaɪdɪ] adj (room) ordinato(-a), lindo(-a); (dress, work) curato(-a), in ordine; (person) ordinato(-a) ▷ vt (also: **~ up**) riordinare, mettere in ordine
tie [taɪ] n (string etc) legaccio; (BRIT: also: **neck~**) cravatta; (fig: link) legame m; (Sport: draw) pareggio ▷ vt (parcel) legare; (ribbon) annodare ▷ vi (Sport) pareggiare; **to ~ sth in a bow** annodare qc; **to ~ a knot in sth** fare un nodo a qc; **tie down** vt legare; (to price etc) costringere ad accettare; **tie up** vt (parcel, dog) legare; (boat) ormeggiare; (arrangements) concludere; **to be ~d up** (busy) essere occupato(-a) or preso(-a)
tier [tɪəʳ] n fila; (of cake) piano, strato
tiger [ˈtaɪɡəʳ] n tigre f
tight [taɪt] adj (rope) teso(-a), tirato(-a); (money) poco(-a); (clothes, budget, bend etc) stretto(-a); (control) severo(-a), fermo(-a); (inf: drunk) sbronzo(-a) ▷ adv (squeeze) fortemente; (shut) ermeticamente; **tighten** vt (rope) tendere; (screw) stringere; (control) rinforzare ▷ vi tendersi; stringersi; **tightly** adv (grasp) bene, saldamente; **tights** (BRIT) npl collant m inv
tile [taɪl] n (on roof) tegola; (on wall or floor) piastrella, mattonella
till [tɪl] n registratore m di cassa ▷ vt (land) coltivare ▷ prep, conj = **until**
tilt [tɪlt] vt inclinare, far pendere ▷ vi inclinarsi, pendere
timber [ˈtɪmbəʳ] n (material) legname m
time [taɪm] n tempo; (epoch: often pl) epoca, tempo; (by clock) ora; (moment) momento; (occasion) volta; (Mus) tempo ▷ vt (race) cronometrare; (programme) calcolare la durata di; (fix moment for) programmare; (remark etc) dire (or fare) al momento giusto; **a long ~** molto tempo; **what ~ does the museum/shop open?** a che ora apre il museo/negozio?; **for the ~ being** per il momento; **4 at a ~** 4 per or alla volta; **from ~ to ~** ogni tanto; **at ~s** a volte; **in ~** (soon enough) in tempo; (after some time) col tempo; (Mus) a tempo; **in a week's ~** fra una settimana; **in no ~** in un attimo; **any ~** in qualsiasi momento; **on ~** puntualmente; **5 ~s 5** 5 volte 5, 5 per 5; **what ~ is it?** che ora è?, che ore sono?; **to have a good ~** divertirsi; **time limit** n limite m di tempo; **timely** adj opportuno(-a); **timer** n (time switch) temporizzatore m; (in kitchen) contaminuti m inv; **time-share** adj **time-share apartment/villa** appartamento/villa in

t

multiproprietà; **timetable** n orario; **time zone** n fuso orario

timid ['tɪmɪd] adj timido(-a); (easily scared) pauroso(-a)

timing ['taɪmɪŋ] n (Sport) cronometraggio; (fig) scelta del momento opportuno

tin [tɪn] n stagno; (also: ~ plate) latta; (container) scatola; (BRIT: can) barattolo (di latta), lattina; **tinfoil** n stagnola

tingle ['tɪŋgl] vi pizzicare

tinker ['tɪŋkər]: ~ with vt fus armeggiare intorno a; cercare di riparare

tinned [tɪnd] (BRIT) adj (food) in scatola

tin opener ['-əupnər] (BRIT) n apriscatole m inv

tint [tɪnt] n tinta; **tinted** adj (hair) tinto(-a); (spectacles, glass) colorato(-a)

tiny ['taɪnɪ] adj minuscolo(-a)

tip [tɪp] n (end) punta; (gratuity) mancia; (BRIT: for rubbish) immondezzaio; (advice) suggerimento ▷ vt (waiter) dare la mancia a; (tilt) inclinare; (overturn: also: ~ over) capovolgere; (empty: also: ~ out) scaricare; **how much should I ~?** quanto devo lasciare di mancia?; **tip off** vt fare una soffiata a

tiptoe ['tɪptəu] n **on ~** in punta di piedi

tire ['taɪər] n (US) = **tyre** ▷ vt stancare ▷ vi stancarsi; **tired** adj stanco(-a); **to be tired of** essere stanco or stufo di; **tire pressure** (US) n = **tyre pressure**; **tiring** adj faticoso(-a)

tissue ['tɪʃuː] n tessuto; (paper handkerchief) fazzoletto di carta; **tissue paper** n carta velina

tit [tɪt] n (bird) cinciallegra; **to give ~ for tat** rendere pan per focaccia

title ['taɪtl] n titolo

T-junction ['tiː'dʒʌŋkʃən] n incrocio a T

TM abbr = **trademark**

KEYWORD

to [tuː, tə] prep **1** (direction) a; **to go to France/London/school** andare in Francia/a Londra/a scuola; **to go to Paul's/the doctor's** andare da Paul/dal dottore; **the road to Edinburgh** la strada per Edimburgo; **to the left/right** a sinistra/destra

2 (as far as) (fino) a; **from here to London** da qui a Londra; **to count to 10** contare fino a 10; **from 40 to 50 people** da 40 a 50 persone

3 (with expressions of time): **a quarter to 5** le 5 meno un quarto; **it's twenty to 3** sono le 3 meno venti

4 (for, of): **the key to the front door** la chiave della porta d'ingresso; **a letter to**

his wife una lettera per la moglie

5 (expressing indirect object) a; **to give sth to sb** dare qc a qn; **to talk to sb** parlare a qn; **to be a danger to sb/sth** rappresentare un pericolo per qn/qc

6 (in relation to) a; **3 goals to 2** 3 goal a 2; **30 miles to the gallon** ≈ 11 chilometri con un litro

7 (purpose, result): **to come to sb's aid** venire in aiuto a qn; **to sentence sb to death** condannare a morte qn; **to my surprise** con mia sorpresa

▷ with vb **1** (simple infinitive): **to go/eat** etc andare/mangiare etc

2 (following another vb): **to want/try/ start to do** volere/cercare di/cominciare a fare

3 (with vb omitted): **I don't want to** non voglio (farlo); **you ought to** devi (farlo)

4 (purpose, result) per; **I did it to help you** l'ho fatto per aiutarti

5 (equivalent to relative clause): **I have things to do** ho da fare; **the main thing is to try** la cosa più importante è provare

6 (after adjective etc): **ready to go** pronto a partire; **too old/young to ...** troppo vecchio/giovane per ...

▷ adv **to push the door to** accostare la porta

toad [təud] n rospo; **toadstool** n fungo (velenoso)

toast [təust] n (Culin) pane m tostato; (drink, speech) brindisi m inv ▷ vt (Culin) tostare; (drink to) brindare a; **a piece or slice of ~** una fetta di pane tostato; **toaster** n tostapane m inv

tobacco [tə'bækəu] n tabacco

toboggan [tə'bɔgən] n toboga m inv

today [tə'deɪ] adv oggi ▷ n (also fig) oggi m

toddler ['tɔdlər] n bambino(-a) che impara a camminare

toe [təu] n dito del piede; (of shoe) punta; **to ~ the line** (fig) stare in riga, conformarsi; **toenail** n unghia del piede

toffee ['tɔfɪ] n caramella

together [tə'gɛðər] adv insieme; (at same time) allo stesso tempo; **~ with** insieme a

toilet ['tɔɪlət] n (BRIT: lavatory) gabinetto ▷ cpd (bag, soap etc) da toletta; **where's the ~?** dov'è il bagno?; **toilet bag** n (BRIT) nécessaire m inv da toilette; **toilet paper** n carta igienica; **toiletries** npl articoli mpl da toletta; **toilet roll** n rotolo di carta igienica

token ['təukən] n (sign) segno; (substitute coin) gettone m; **book/record/gift ~** (BRIT) buono-libro/disco/regalo

Tokyo ['təukjəu] n Tokyo f

told [təʊld] *pt, pp of* **tell**

tolerant ['tɒlərnt] *adj* **~ (of)** tollerante (nei confronti di)

tolerate ['tɒləreɪt] *vt* sopportare; (*Med, Tech*) tollerare

toll [təʊl] *n* (*tax, charge*) pedaggio ▷ *vi* (*bell*) suonare; **the accident ~ on the roads** il numero delle vittime della strada; **toll call** (*US*) *n* (*Tel*) (telefonata) interurbana; **toll-free** (*US*) *adj* senza addebito, gratuito(-a) ▷ *adv* gratuitamente; **toll-free number** ≈ numero verde

tomato [tə'mɑːtəʊ] (*pl* **tomatoes**) *n* pomodoro; **tomato sauce** *n* salsa di pomodoro

tomb [tuːm] *n* tomba; **tombstone** ['tuːmstəʊn] *n* pietra tombale

tomorrow [tə'mɒrəʊ] *adv* domani ▷ *n* (*also fig*) domani *m inv*; **the day after ~** dopodomani; **~ morning** domani mattina

ton [tʌn] *n* tonnellata; (*BRIT: 1016 kg: US: 907 kg: metric 1000 kg*): **~s of** (*inf*) un mucchio or sacco di

tone [təʊn] *n* tono ▷ *vi* (*also:* **~ in**) intonarsi; **tone down** *vt* (*colour, criticism, sound*) attenuare

tongs [tɒŋz] *npl* tenaglie *fpl*; (*for coal*) molle *fpl*; (*for hair*) arricciacapelli *m inv*

tongue [tʌŋ] *n* lingua; **~ in cheek** (*say, speak*) ironicamente

tonic ['tɒnɪk] *n* (*Med*) tonico; (*also:* **~ water**) acqua tonica

tonight [tə'naɪt] *adv* stanotte; (*this evening*) stasera ▷ *n* questa notte; questa sera

tonne [tʌn] *n* (*BRIT: metric ton*) tonnellata

tonsil ['tɒnsl] *n* tonsilla; **tonsillitis** [-'laɪtɪs] *n* tonsillite *f*

too [tuː] *adv* (*excessively*) troppo; (*also*) anche; (*also:* **~ much**) ▷ *adv* troppo ▷ *adj* troppo(-a); **~ many** troppi(-e)

took [tʊk] *pt of* **take**

tool [tuːl] *n* utensile *m*, attrezzo; **tool box** *n* cassetta *f* portautensili; **tool kit** *n* cassetta di attrezzi

tooth [tuːθ] *n* (*pl* **teeth**) dente *m*; **toothache** *n* mal *m* di denti; **toothbrush** *n* spazzolino da denti; **toothpaste** *n* dentifricio; **toothpick** *n* stuzzicadenti *m inv*

top [tɒp] *n* (*of mountain, page, ladder*) cima *f*; (*of box, cupboard, table*) sopra *m inv*, parte *f* superiore; (*lid: of box, jar*) coperchio; (: *of bottle*) tappo; (*blouse etc*) sopra *m inv*; (*toy*) trottola ▷ *adj* più alto(-a); (*in rank*) primo(-a); (*best*) migliore ▷ *vt* (*exceed*) superare; (*be first in*) essere in testa a; **on ~ of** sopra, in cima a; (*in addition to*) oltre a; **from ~ to bottom** da cima a fondo;

top up (*US* **top off**) *vt* riempire; (*salary*) integrare; **top floor** *n* ultimo piano; **top hat** *n* cilindro

topic ['tɒpɪk] *n* argomento; **topical** *adj* d'attualità

topless ['tɒplɪs] *adj* (*bather etc*) col seno scoperto

topping ['tɒpɪŋ] *n* (*Culin*) guarnizione *f*

topple ['tɒpl] *vt* rovesciare, far cadere ▷ *vi* cadere; traballare

torch [tɔːtʃ] *n* torcia; (*BRIT: electric*) lampadina tascabile

tore [tɔːʳ] *pt of* **tear**¹

torment [*n* 'tɔːmɛnt, *vb* tɔː'mɛnt] *n* tormento ▷ *vt* tormentare

torn [tɔːn] *pp of* **tear**¹

tornado [tɔː'neɪdəʊ] (*pl* **tornadoes**) *n* tornado

torpedo [tɔː'piːdəʊ] (*pl* **torpedoes**) *n* siluro

torrent ['tɒrnt] *n* torrente *m*; **torrential** [tɔ'rɛnʃl] *adj* torrenziale

tortoise ['tɔːtəs] *n* tartaruga

torture ['tɔːtʃəʳ] *n* tortura ▷ *vt* torturare

Tory ['tɔːrɪ] (*BRIT: Pol*) *adj* dei tories, conservatore(-trice) ▷ *n* tory *m/f inv*, conservatore(-trice)

toss [tɒs] *vt* gettare, lanciare; (*one's head*) scuotere; **to ~ a coin** fare a testa o croce; **to ~ up for sth** fare a testa o croce per qc; **to ~ and turn** (*in bed*) girarsi e rigirarsi

total ['təʊtl] *adj* totale ▷ *n* totale *m* ▷ *vt* (*add up*) sommare; (*amount to*) ammontare a

totalitarian [təʊtælɪ'tɛərɪən] *adj* totalitario(-a)

totally ['təʊtəlɪ] *adv* completamente

touch [tʌtʃ] *n* tocco; (*sense*) tatto; (*contact*) contatto ▷ *vt* toccare; **a ~ of** (*fig*) un tocco di; un pizzico di; **to get in ~ with** mettersi in contatto con; **to lose ~** (*friends*) perdersi di vista; **touch down** *vi* (*on land*) atterrare; **touchdown** *n* atterraggio; (*on sea*) ammaraggio; (*US: Football*) meta; **touched** *adj* commosso(-a); **touching** *adj* commovente; **touchline** *n* (*Sport*) linea laterale; **touch-sensitive** *adj* sensibile al tatto

tough [tʌf] *adj* duro(-a); (*resistant*) resistente

tour ['tʊəʳ] *n* viaggio; (*also:* **package ~**) viaggio organizzato *or* tutto compreso; (*of town, museum*) visita; (*by artist*) tournée *f inv* ▷ *vt* visitare; **tour guide** *n* guida turistica

tourism ['tʊərɪzəm] *n* turismo

tourist ['tʊərɪst] *n* turista *m/f* ▷ *adv* (*travel*) in classe turistica ▷ *cpd* turistico(-a); **tourist office** *n* pro loco *f inv*

tournament ['tuənəmənt] n torneo
tour operator n (BRIT) operatore m
turistico
tow [təu] vt rimorchiare; **"on ~"** (BRIT), **"in ~"** (US) "veicolo rimorchiato"; **tow away** vt rimorchiare
toward(s) [tə'wɔːd(z)] prep verso; (of attitude) nei confronti di; (of purpose) per
towel ['tauəl] n asciugamano; (also: **tea ~**) strofinaccio; **towelling** n (fabric) spugna
tower ['tauə'] n torre f; **tower block** (BRIT) n palazzone m
town [taun] n città f inv; **to go to ~** andare in città; (fig) mettercela tutta; **town centre** n centro (città); **town hall** n ≈ municipio
tow truck (US) n carro m, attrezzi inv
toxic ['tɔksɪk] adj tossico(-a)
toy [tɔɪ] n giocattolo; **toy with** vt fus giocare con; (idea) accarezzare, trastullarsi con; **toyshop** n negozio di giocattoli
trace [treɪs] n traccia ▷ vt (draw) tracciare; (follow) seguire; (locate) rintracciare
track [træk] n (of person, animal) traccia; (on tape, Sport, path: gen) pista; (: of bullet etc) traiettoria; (: of suspect, animal) pista, tracce fpl; (Rail) binario, rotaie fpl ▷ vt seguire le tracce di; **to keep ~ of** seguire; **track down** vt (prey) scovare; snidare; (sth lost) rintracciare; **tracksuit** n tuta sportiva
tractor ['træktə'] n trattore m
trade [treɪd] n commercio; (skill, job) mestiere m ▷ vi commerciare ▷ vt **to ~ sth (for sth)** barattare qc (con qc); **to ~ with/in** commerciare con/in; **trade in** vt (old car etc) dare come pagamento parziale; **trademark** n marchio di fabbrica; **trader** n commerciante m/f; **tradesman** (irreg) n fornitore m; (shopkeeper) negoziante m; **trade union** n sindacato
trading ['treɪdɪŋ] n commercio
tradition [trə'dɪʃən] n tradizione f; **traditional** adj tradizionale
traffic ['træfɪk] n traffico ▷ vi **to ~ in** (pej: liquor, drugs) trafficare in; **traffic circle** (US) n isola rotatoria; **traffic island** n salvagente m, isola f, spartitraffico inv; **traffic jam** n ingorgo (del traffico); **traffic lights** npl semaforo; **traffic warden** n addetto(-a) al controllo del traffico e del parcheggio
tragedy ['trædʒədɪ] n tragedia
tragic ['trædʒɪk] adj tragico(-a)
trail [treɪl] n (tracks) tracce fpl, pista; (path) sentiero; (of smoke etc) scia ▷ vt trascinare,

strascicare; (follow) seguire ▷ vi essere al traino; (dress etc) strusciare; (plant) arrampicarsi; strisciare; (in game) essere in svantaggio; **trailer** n (Aut) rimorchio; (US) roulotte f inv; (Cinema) prossimamente m inv
train [treɪn] n treno; (of dress) coda, strascico ▷ vt (apprentice, doctor etc) formare; (sportsman) allenare; (dog) addestrare; (memory) esercitare; (point: gun etc): **to ~ sth on** puntare qc contro ▷ vi formarsi; allenarsi; **what time does the ~ from Rome get in?** a che ora arriva il treno da Roma?; **is this the ~ for …?** è questo il treno per…?; **one's ~ of thought** il filo dei propri pensieri;
trainee [treɪ'niː] n (in trade) apprendista m/f; **trainer** n (Sport) allenatore(-trice); (: shoe) scarpa da ginnastica; (of dogs etc) addestratore(-trice); **trainers** npl (shoes) scarpe fpl da ginnastica; **training** n formazione f; allenamento; addestramento; **in training** (Sport) in allenamento; **training course** n corso di formazione professionale; **training shoes** npl scarpe fpl da ginnastica
trait [treɪt] n tratto
traitor ['treɪtə'] n traditore m
tram [træm] (BRIT) n (also: **~car**) tram m inv
tramp [træmp] n (person) vagabondo(-a); (inf: pej: woman) sgualdrina
trample ['træmpl] vt **to ~ (underfoot)** calpestare
trampoline ['træmpəliːn] n trampolino
tranquil ['træŋkwɪl] adj tranquillo(-a); **tranquillizer** (US **tranquilizer**) n (Med) tranquillante m
transaction [træn'zækʃən] n transazione f
transatlantic ['trænzət'læntɪk] adj transatlantico(-a)
transcript ['trænskrɪpt] n trascrizione f
transfer [n 'trænsfə', vb træns'fə'] n (gen: also Sport) trasferimento; (Pol: of power) passaggio; (picture, design) decalcomania; (: stick-on) autoadesivo ▷ vt trasferire; passare; **to ~ the charges** (BRIT: Tel) fare una chiamata a carico del destinatario
transform [træns'fɔːm] vt trasformare; **transformation** n trasformazione f
transfusion [træns'fjuːʒən] n trasfusione f
transit ['trænzɪt] n **in ~** in transito
transition [træn'zɪʃən] n passaggio, transizione f
transitive ['trænzɪtɪv] adj (Ling) transitivo(-a)
translate [trænz'leɪt] vt tradurre; **can**

you ~ this for me? me lo può tradurre?;
translation [-'leɪʃən] n traduzione f;
translator n traduttore(-trice)
transmission [trænz'mɪʃən] n
trasmissione f
transmit [trænz'mɪt] vt trasmettere;
transmitter n trasmettitore m
transparent [træns'pærnt] adj
trasparente
transplant [vb træns'plɑ:nt, n
'trænsplɑ:nt] vt trapiantare ▷ n (Med)
trapianto
transport [n 'trænspɔ:t, vb træns'pɔ:
t] n trasporto ▷ vt trasportare;
transportation [-'teɪʃən] n (mezzo di)
trasporto
transvestite [trænz'vɛstaɪt] n
travestito(-a)
trap [træp] n (snare, trick) trappola;
(carriage) calesse m ▷ vt prendere in
trappola, intrappolare
trash [træʃ] (pej) n (goods) ciarpame m;
(nonsense) sciocchezze fpl; **trash can** (US) n
secchio della spazzatura
trauma ['trɔ:mə] n trauma m; **traumatic**
[-'mætɪk] adj traumatico(-a)
travel ['trævl] n viaggio; viaggi mpl ▷ vi
viaggiare ▷ vt (distance) percorrere;
travel agency n agenzia (di) viaggi;
travel agent n agente m di viaggio;
travel insurance n assicurazione f
di viaggio; **traveller** (US **traveler**) n
viaggiatore(-trice); **traveller's cheque**
(US **traveler's check**) n assegno turistico;
travelling (US **traveling**) n viaggi mpl;
travel-sick adj **to get travel-sick** (in
vehicle) soffrire di mal d'auto; (in aeroplane)
soffrire di mal d'aria; (in boat) soffrire di mal
di mare; **travel sickness** n mal m d'auto
(or di mare o d'aria)
tray [treɪ] n (for carrying) vassoio; (on desk)
vaschetta
treacherous ['trɛtʃərəs] adj infido(-a)
treacle ['tri:kl] n melassa
tread [trɛd] (pt **trod**, pp **trodden**) n passo;
(sound) rumore m di passi; (of stairs) pedata;
(of tyre) battistrada m inv ▷ vi camminare;
tread on vt fus calpestare
treasure ['trɛʒər] n tesoro ▷ vt (value)
tenere in gran conto, apprezzare molto;
(store) custodire gelosamente; **treasurer**
['trɛʒərə] n tesoriere(-a)
treasury ['trɛʒərɪ] n **the T~** (BRIT), **the T~**
Department (US) il ministero del Tesoro
treat [tri:t] n regalo ▷ vt trattare; (Med)
curare; **to ~ sb to sth** offrire qc a qn;
treatment ['tri:tmənt] n trattamento
treaty ['tri:tɪ] n patto, trattato
treble ['trɛbl] adj triplo(-a), triplice ▷ vt

triplicare ▷ vi triplicarsi
tree [tri:] n albero
trek [trɛk] n escursione f a piedi;
escursione f in macchina; (tiring walk)
camminata sfiancante ▷ vi (as holiday) fare
dell'escursionismo
tremble ['trɛmbl] vi tremare
tremendous [trɪ'mɛndəs] adj (enormous)
enorme; (excellent) fantastico(-a),
strepitoso(-a)

> Be careful not to translate
> **tremendous** by the Italian word
> **tremendo**.

trench [trɛntʃ] n trincea
trend [trɛnd] n (tendency) tendenza; (of
events) corso; (fashion) moda; **trendy** adj
(idea) di moda; (clothes) all'ultima moda
trespass ['trɛspəs] vi **to ~ on** entrare
abusivamente in; **"no ~ing"** "proprietà
privata", "vietato l'accesso"
trial ['traɪəl] n (Law) processo; (test: of
machine etc) collaudo; **on ~** (Law) sotto
processo; **trial period** n periodo di prova
triangle ['traɪæŋgl] n (Math, Mus)
triangolo
triangular [traɪ'æŋgjulər] adj triangolare
tribe [traɪb] n tribù f inv
tribunal [traɪ'bju:nl] n tribunale m
tribute ['trɪbju:t] n tributo, omaggio; **to**
pay ~ to rendere omaggio a
trick [trɪk] n trucco; (joke) tiro; (Cards) presa
▷ vt imbrogliare, ingannare; **to play a ~**
on sb giocare un tiro a qn; **that should do**
the ~ vedrai che funziona
trickle ['trɪkl] n (of water etc) rivolo;
gocciolio ▷ vi gocciolare
tricky ['trɪkɪ] adj difficile, delicato(-a)
tricycle ['traɪsɪkl] n triciclo
trifle ['traɪfl] n sciocchezza; (BRIT: Culin)
≈ zuppa inglese ▷ adv **a ~ long** un po'
lungo
trigger ['trɪɡər] n (of gun) grilletto
trim [trɪm] adj (house, garden) ben
tenuto(-a); (figure) snello(-a) ▷ n (haircut
etc) spuntata, regolata; (embellishment)
finiture fpl; (on car) guarnizioni fpl ▷ vt
spuntare; (decorate): **to ~ (with)** decorare
(con); (Naut: a sail) orientare
trio ['tri:əu] n trio
trip [trɪp] n viaggio; (excursion) gita,
escursione f; (stumble) passo falso ▷ vi
inciampare; (go lightly) camminare con
passo leggero; **on a ~** in viaggio; **trip up** vi
inciampare ▷ vt fare lo sgambetto a
triple ['trɪpl] adj triplo(-a)
triplets ['trɪplɪts] npl bambini(-e)
trigemini(-e)
tripod ['traɪpɔd] n treppiede m
triumph ['traɪʌmf] n trionfo ▷ vi **to**

~ **(over)** trionfare (su); **triumphant**
[traɪˈʌmfənt] adj trionfante
trivial [ˈtrɪvɪəl] adj insignificante;
(commonplace) banale

Be careful not to translate trivial by
the Italian word triviale.

trod [trɒd] pt of **tread**
trodden [ˈtrɒdn] pp of **tread**
trolley [ˈtrɒlɪ] n carrello
trombone [trɒmˈbəun] n trombone m
troop [tru:p] n gruppo; (Mil) squadrone m;
~**s** npl (Mil) truppe fpl
trophy [ˈtrəufɪ] n trofeo
tropical [ˈtrɒpɪkl] adj tropicale
trot [trɒt] n trotto ▷ vi trottare; **on the** ~
(BRIT: fig) di fila, uno(-a) dopo l'altro(-a)
trouble [ˈtrʌbl] n difficoltà f inv, problema
m; difficoltà fpl, problemi; (worry)
preoccupazione f; (bother, effort) sforzo;
(Pol) conflitti mpl, disordine m; (Med):
stomach etc ~ disturbi mpl gastrici etc
▷ vt disturbare; (worry) preoccupare ▷ vi
to ~ to do disturbarsi a fare; ~**s** npl (Pol
etc) disordini mpl; **to be in** ~ avere dei
problemi; **it's no ~!** di niente!; **what's the**
~? cosa c'è che non va?; **I'm sorry to ~ you**
scusi il disturbo; **troubled** adj (person)
preoccupato(-a), inquieto(-a); (epoch, life)
agitato(-a), difficile; **troublemaker** n
elemento disturbatore, agitatore(-trice);
(child) disloco(-a); **troublesome** adj
fastidioso(-a), seccante
trough [trɒf] n (drinking trough)
abbeveratoio; (also: **feeding** ~) trogolo,
mangiatoia; (channel) canale m
trousers [ˈtrauzəz] npl pantaloni mpl,
calzoni mpl; **short** ~ calzoncini mpl
trout [traut] n inv trota
trowel [ˈtrauəl] n cazzuola
truant [ˈtruənt] (BRIT) n **to play** ~
marinare la scuola
truce [tru:s] n tregua
truck [trʌk] n autocarro, camion m inv;
(Rail) carro merci aperto; (for luggage)
carrello m portabagagli inv; **truck driver** n
camionista m/f
true [tru:] adj vero(-a); (accurate)
accurato(-a), esatto(-a); (genuine) reale;
(faithful) fedele; **to come** ~ avverarsi
truly [ˈtru:lɪ] adv veramente; (truthfully)
sinceramente; (faithfully): **yours** ~ (in letter)
distinti saluti
trumpet [ˈtrʌmpɪt] n tromba
trunk [trʌŋk] n (of tree, person) tronco; (of
elephant) proboscide f; (case) baule m; (us:
Aut) bagagliaio; ~**s** (also: **swimming** ~**s**)
calzoncini mpl da bagno
trust [trʌst] n fiducia; (Law)
amministrazione f fiduciaria; (Comm)

trust m inv ▷ vt (rely on) contare su; (hope)
sperare; (entrust): **to** ~ **sth to sb** affidare qc
a qn; **trusted** adj fidato(-a); **trustworthy**
adj fidato(-a), degno(-a) di fiducia
truth [tru:θ, pl tru:ðz] n verità f inv;
truthful adj (person) sincero(-a);
(description) veritiero(-a), esatto(-a)
try [traɪ] n prova, tentativo; (Rugby) meta
▷ vt (Law) giudicare; (test: also: ~ **out**)
provare; (strain) mettere alla prova ▷ vi
provare; **to have a** ~ fare un tentativo;
to ~ **to do** (seek) cercare di fare; **try on**
vt (clothes) provare; **trying** adj (day,
experience) logorante, pesante; (child)
difficile, insopportabile
T-shirt [ˈti:ʃə:t] n maglietta
tub [tʌb] n tinozza; mastello; (bath)
bagno
tube [tju:b] n tubo; (BRIT: underground)
metropolitana, metrò m inv; (for tyre)
camera d'aria
tuberculosis [tjubə:kjuˈləusɪs] n
tubercolosi f inv
tube station (BRIT) n stazione f della
metropolitana
tuck [tʌk] vt (put) mettere; **tuck away** vt
riporre; (building): **to be** ~**ed away** essere
in un luogo isolato; **tuck in** vt mettere
dentro; (child) rimboccare ▷ vi (eat)
mangiare di buon appetito; abbuffarsi;
tuck shop n negozio di pasticceria (in una
scuola)
Tue(s). abbr (= Tuesday) mar.
Tuesday [ˈtju:zdɪ] n martedì m inv
tug [tʌg] n (ship) rimorchiatore m ▷ vt
tirare con forza
tuition [tju:ˈɪʃən] n (BRIT) lezioni fpl; (:
private tuition) lezioni fpl private; (us: school
fees) tasse fpl scolastiche
tulip [ˈtju:lɪp] n tulipano
tumble [ˈtʌmbl] n (fall) capitombolo ▷ vi
capitombolare, ruzzolare; **to** ~ **to sth**
(inf) realizzare qc; **tumble dryer** (BRIT) n
asciugatrice f
tumbler [ˈtʌmbləʳ] n bicchiere m (senza
stelo)
tummy [ˈtʌmɪ] (inf) n pancia
tumour [ˈtju:məʳ] (us **tumor**) n tumore m
tuna [ˈtju:nə] n inv (also: ~ **fish**) tonno
tune [tju:n] n (melody) melodia, aria
▷ vt (Mus) accordare; (Radio, TV, Aut)
regolare, mettere a punto; **to be in/out**
of ~ (instrument) essere accordato(-a)/
scordato(-a); (singer) essere intonato(-a)/
stonato(-a); **tune in** vi **to** ~ **in (to)**
(Radio, TV) sintonizzarsi (su); **tune up** vi
(musician) accordare lo strumento
tunic [ˈtju:nɪk] n tunica
Tunisia [tju:ˈnɪzɪə] n Tunisia

tunnel ['tʌnl] n galleria ▷ vi scavare una galleria

turbulence ['tə:bjuləns] n (Aviat) turbolenza

turf [tə:f] n terreno erboso; (clod) zolla ▷ vt coprire di zolle erbose

Turin [tjuə'rɪn] n Torino f

Turk [tə:k] n turco(-a)

Turkey ['tə:kɪ] n Turchia

turkey ['tə:kɪ] n tacchino

Turkish ['tə:kɪʃ] adj turco(-a) ▷ n (Ling) turco

turmoil ['tə:mɔɪl] n confusione f, tumulto

turn [tə:n] n giro; (change) cambiamento; (in road) curva; (tendency: of mind, events) tendenza; (performance) numero; (chance) turno; (Med) crisi f inv, attacco ▷ vt girare, voltare; (change): **to ~ sth into** trasformare qc in ▷ vi girare; (person: look back) girarsi, voltarsi; (reverse direction) girare; (change) cambiare; (milk) andare a male; (become) diventare; **a good ~** un buon servizio; **it gave me quite a ~** mi ha fatto prendere un bello spavento; **"no left ~"** (Aut) "divieto di svolta a sinistra"; **it's your ~** tocca a lei; **in ~** a sua volta; a turno; **to take ~s (at sth)** fare (qc) a turno; **~ left/right at the next junction** al prossimo incrocio, giri a sinistra/destra; **turn around** vi (person) girarsi; (rotate) giràre ▷ vt (object) girare; **turn away** vi girarsi (dall'altra parte) ▷ vt mandare via; **turn back** vi ritornare, tornare indietro ▷ vt far tornare indietro; (clock) spostare indietro; **turn down** vt (refuse) rifiutare; (reduce) abbassare; (fold) ripiegare; **turn in** vi (inf: go to bed) andare a letto ▷ vt (fold) voltare in dentro; **turn off** vi (from road) girare, voltare ▷ vt (light, radio, engine etc) spegnere; **I can't ~ the heating off** non riesco a spegnere il riscaldamento; **turn on** vt (light, radio etc) accendere; **I can't ~ the heating on** non riesco ad accendere il riscaldamento; **turn out** vt (light, gas) chiudere; spegnere ▷ vi (voters) presentarsi; **to ~ out to be ...** rivelarsi ..., risultare ...; **turn over** vi (person) girarsi ▷ vt girare; **turn round** vi girare; (person) girarsi; **turn to** vt fus **to ~ to sb** girarsi verso qn; **to ~ to sb for help** rivolgersi a qn per aiuto; **turn up** vi (person) arrivare, presentarsi; (lost object) saltar fuori ▷ vt (collar, sound) alzare; **turning** n (in road) curva; **turning point** n (fig) svolta decisiva

turnip ['tə:nɪp] n rapa

turn: turnout ['tə:naut] n presenza, affluenza; **turnover** ['tə:nəuvə'] n (Comm) turnover m inv; (Culin): **apple etc turnover**
sfogliatella alle mele ecc; **turnstile** ['tə:nstaɪl] n tornella; **turn-up** (BRIT) n (on trousers) risvolto

turquoise ['tə:kwɔɪz] n turchese m ▷ adj turchese

turtle ['tə:tl] n testuggine f; **turtleneck (sweater)** ['tə:tlnɛk-] n maglione m con il collo alto

Tuscany ['tʌskənɪ] n Toscana

tusk [tʌsk] n zanna

tutor ['tju:tə'] n (in college) docente m/f (responsabile di un gruppo di studenti); (private teacher) precettore m; **tutorial** [-'tɔ:rɪəl] n (Scol) lezione f con discussione (a un gruppo limitato)

tuxedo [tʌk'si:dəu] (US) n smoking m inv

TV [ti:'vi:] n abbr (= television) tivù f inv

tweed [twi:d] n tweed m inv

tweezers ['twi:zəz] npl pinzette fpl

twelfth [twelfθ] num dodicesimo(-a)

twelve [twelv] num dodici; **at ~ o'clock** alle dodici, a mezzogiorno; (midnight) a mezzanotte

twentieth ['twɛntɪɪθ] num ventesimo(-a)

twenty ['twɛntɪ] num venti

twice [twaɪs] adv due volte; **~ as much** due volte tanto; **~ a week** due volte alla settimana

twig [twɪg] n ramoscello ▷ vt, vi (inf) capire

twilight ['twaɪlaɪt] n crepuscolo

twin [twɪn] adj, n gemello(-a) ▷ vt **to ~ one town with another** fare il gemellaggio di una città con un'altra; **twin(-bedded) room** n stanza con letti gemelli; **twin beds** npl letti mpl gemelli

twinkle ['twɪŋkl] vi scintillare; (eyes) brillare

twist [twɪst] n torsione f; (in wire, flex) piega; (in road) curva; (in story) colpo di scena ▷ vt attorcigliare; (ankle) slogare; (weave) intrecciare; (roll around) arrotolare; (fig) distorcere ▷ vi (road) serpeggiare

twit [twɪt] (inf) n cretino(-a)

twitch [twɪtʃ] n tiratina; (nervous) tic m inv ▷ vi contrarsi

two [tu:] num due; **to put ~ and ~ together** (fig) fare uno più uno

type [taɪp] n (category) genere m; (model) modello; (example) tipo; (Typ) tipo, carattere m ▷ vt (letter etc) battere (a macchina), dattilografare; **typewriter** n macchina da scrivere

typhoid ['taɪfɔɪd] n tifoidea

typhoon [taɪ'fu:n] n tifone m

typical ['tɪpɪkl] adj tipico(-a); **typically** adv tipicamente; **typically, he arrived**

late come al solito è arrivato tardi
typing ['taɪpɪŋ] *n* dattilografia
typist ['taɪpɪst] *n* dattilografo(-a)
tyre ['taɪəʳ] (*US* **tire**) *n* pneumatico,
gomma; **I've got a flat ~** ho una gomma
a terra; **tyre pressure** *n* pressione *f* (delle
gomme)

UFO ['juːfəu] *n abbr* (= *unidentified flying
object*) UFO *m inv*
Uganda [juː'gændə] *n* Uganda
ugly ['ʌglɪ] *adj* brutto(-a)
UHT *abbr* (= *ultra heat treated*) UHT *inv*, a
lunga conservazione
UK *n abbr* = **United Kingdom**
ulcer ['ʌlsəʳ] *n* ulcera; (*also*: **mouth ~**) afta
ultimate ['ʌltɪmət] *adj* ultimo(-a), finale;
(*authority*) massimo(-a), supremo(-a);
ultimately *adv* alla fine; in definitiva, in
fin dei conti
ultimatum [ʌltɪ'meɪtəm, -tə] (*pl*
ultimatums *or* **ultimata**) *n* ultimatum
m inv
ultrasound [ʌltrə'saund] *n* (*Med*)
ultrasuono
ultraviolet ['ʌltrə'vaɪəlɪt] *adj*
ultravioletto(-a)
umbrella [ʌm'brɛlə] *n* ombrello
umpire ['ʌmpaɪəʳ] *n* arbitro
UN *n abbr* (= *United Nations*) ONU *f*
unable [ʌn'eɪbl] *adj* **to be ~ to** non
potere, essere nell'impossibilità di; essere
incapace di
unacceptable [ʌnək'sɛptəbl] *adj*
(*proposal, behaviour*) inaccettabile; (*price*)
impossibile
unanimous [juː'nænɪməs] *adj* unanime
unarmed [ʌn'ɑːmd] *adj* (*without a weapon*)

disarmato(-a); (*combat*) senz'armi

unattended [ʌnə'tɛndɪd] *adj* (*car, child, luggage*) incustodito(-a)

unattractive [ʌnə'træktɪv] *adj* poco attraente

unavailable [ʌnə'veɪləbl] *adj* (*article, room, book*) non disponibile; (*person*) impegnato(-a)

unavoidable [ʌnə'vɔɪdəbl] *adj* inevitabile

unaware [ʌnə'wɛəʳ] *adj* **to be ~ of** non sapere, ignorare; **unawares** *adv* di sorpresa, alla sprovvista

unbearable [ʌn'bɛərəbl] *adj* insopportabile

unbeatable [ʌn'bi:təbl] *adj* imbattibile

unbelievable [ʌnbɪ'li:vəbl] *adj* incredibile

unborn [ʌn'bɔ:n] *adj* non ancora nato(-a)

unbutton [ʌn'bʌtn] *vt* sbottonare

uncalled-for [ʌn'kɔ:ldfɔ:ʳ] *adj* (*remark*) fuori luogo *inv*; (*action*) ingiustificato(-a)

uncanny [ʌn'kænɪ] *adj* misterioso(-a), strano(-a)

uncertain [ʌn'sə:tn] *adj* incerto(-a); dubbio(-a); **uncertainty** *n* incertezza

unchanged [ʌn'tʃeɪndʒd] *adj* invariato(-a)

uncle ['ʌŋkl] *n* zio

unclear [ʌn'klɪəʳ] *adj* non chiaro(-a); **I'm still ~ about what I'm supposed to do** non ho ancora ben capito cosa dovrei fare

uncomfortable [ʌn'kʌmfətəbl] *adj* scomodo(-a); (*uneasy*) a disagio, agitato(-a); (*unpleasant*) fastidioso(-a)

uncommon [ʌn'kɔmən] *adj* raro(-a), insolito(-a), non comune

unconditional [ʌnkən'dɪʃənl] *adj* incondizionato(-a), senza condizioni

unconscious [ʌn'kɔnʃəs] *adj* privo(-a) di sensi, svenuto(-a); (*unaware*) inconsapevole, inconscio(-a) ▷ *n* **the ~** l'inconscio

uncontrollable [ʌnkən'trəuləbl] *adj* incontrollabile; indisciplinato(-a)

unconventional [ʌnkən'vɛnʃənl] *adj* poco convenzionale

uncover [ʌn'kʌvəʳ] *vt* scoprire

undecided [ʌndɪ'saɪdɪd] *adj* indeciso(-a)

undeniable [ʌndɪ'naɪəbl] *adj* innegabile, indiscutibile

under ['ʌndəʳ] *prep* sotto; (*less than*) meno di; al disotto di; (*according to*) secondo, in conformità a ▷ *adv* (al) disotto; **~ there** là sotto; **~ repair** in riparazione; **undercover** *adj* segreto(-a), clandestino(-a); **underdone** *adj* (*Culin*) al sangue; (*pej*) poco cotto(-a); **underestimate** *vt* sottovalutare; **undergo** *vt* (*irreg*) subire; (*treatment*) sottoporsi a; **undergraduate** *n* studente(-essa) universitario(-a); **underground** *n* (*BRIT*:

railway) metropolitana; (*Pol*) movimento clandestino ▷ *adj* sotterraneo(-a); (*fig*) clandestino(-a) ▷ *adv* sottoterra; **to go underground** (*fig*) darsi alla macchia; **undergrowth** *n* sottobosco; **underline** *vt* sottolineare; **undermine** *vt* minare; **underneath** [ʌndə'ni:θ] *adv* sotto, disotto ▷ *prep* sotto, al di sotto di; **underpants** *npl* mutande *fpl*, slip *m inv*; **underpass** (*BRIT*) *n* sottopassaggio; **underprivileged** *adj* non abbiente; meno favorito(-a); **underscore** *vt* sottolineare; **undershirt** (*US*) *n* maglietta; **underskirt** (*BRIT*) *n* sottoveste *f*

understand [ʌndə'stænd] (*irreg: like* **stand**) *vt, vi* capire, comprendere; **I don't ~** non capisco; **I ~ that ...** sento che ...; credo di capire che ...; **understandable** *adj* comprensibile; **understanding** *adj* comprensivo(-a) ▷ *n* comprensione *f*; (*agreement*) accordo

understatement [ʌndə'steɪtmənt] *n* **that's an ~!** a dire poco!

understood [ʌndə'stud] *pt, pp of* **understand** ▷ *adj* inteso(-a); (*implied*) sottinteso(-a)

undertake [ʌndə'teɪk] (*irreg: like* **take**) *vt* intraprendere; **to ~ to do sth** impegnarsi a fare qc

undertaker ['ʌndəteɪkəʳ] *n* impresario di pompe funebri

undertaking [ʌndə'teɪkɪŋ] *n* impresa; (*promise*) promessa

under: **underwater** [ʌndə'wɔ:təʳ] *adv* sott'acqua ▷ *adj* subacqueo(-a); **underway** [ʌndə'weɪ] *adj* **to be underway** essere in corso; **underwear** ['ʌndəwɛəʳ] *n* biancheria (intima); **underwent** [ʌndə'wɛnt] *vb see* **undergo**; **underworld** ['ʌndəwə:ld] *n* (*of crime*) malavita

undesirable [ʌndɪ'zaɪərəbl] *adj* sgradevole

undisputed [ʌndɪs'pju:tɪd] *adj* indiscusso(-a)

undo [ʌn'du:] *vt* (*irreg*) disfare

undone [ʌn'dʌn] *pp of* **undo**; **to come ~** slacciarsi

undoubtedly [ʌn'dautɪdlɪ] *adv* senza alcun dubbio

undress [ʌn'drɛs] *vi* spogliarsi

unearth [ʌn'ə:θ] *vt* dissotterrare; (*fig*) scoprire

uneasy [ʌn'i:zɪ] *adj* a disagio; (*worried*) preoccupato(-a); (*peace*) precario(-a)

unemployed [ʌnɪm'plɔɪd] *adj* disoccupato(-a) ▷ *npl* **the ~** i disoccupati

unemployment [ʌnɪm'plɔɪmənt] *n* disoccupazione *f*; **unemployment**

u

benefit (*us* **unemployment compensation**) *n* sussidio di disoccupazione

unequal [ʌn'i:kwəl] *adj* (*length, objects*) disuguale; (*amounts*) diverso(-a); (*division of labour*) ineguale

uneven [ʌn'i:vn] *adj* ineguale; irregolare

unexpected [ʌnɪk'spɛktɪd] *adj* inatteso(-a), imprevisto(-a); **unexpectedly** *adv* inaspettatamente

unfair [ʌn'fɛər] *adj* ~ **(to)** ingiusto(-a) (nei confronti di)

unfaithful [ʌn'feɪθful] *adj* infedele

unfamiliar [ʌnfə'mɪlɪər] *adj* sconosciuto(-a), strano(-a); **to be ~ with** non avere familiarità con

unfashionable [ʌn'fæʃnəbl] *adj* (*clothes*) fuori moda; (*district*) non alla moda

unfasten [ʌn'fɑ:sn] *vt* slacciare; sciogliere

unfavourable [ʌn'feɪvərəbl] (*us* **unfavorable**) *adj* sfavorevole

unfinished [ʌn'fɪnɪʃt] *adj* incompleto(-a)

unfit [ʌn'fɪt] *adj* (*ill*) malato(-a), in cattiva salute; (*incompetent*): ~ **(for)** incompetente (in); (: *work, Mil*) inabile (a)

unfold [ʌn'fəuld] *vt* spiegare ▷ *vi* (*story, plot*) svelarsi

unforgettable [ʌnfə'gɛtəbl] *adj* indimenticabile

unfortunate [ʌn'fɔ:tʃnət] *adj* sfortunato(-a); (*event, remark*) infelice; **unfortunately** *adv* sfortunatamente, purtroppo

unfriendly [ʌn'frɛndlɪ] *adj* poco amichevole, freddo(-a)

unfurnished [ʌn'fə:nɪʃt] *adj* non ammobiliato(-a)

unhappiness [ʌn'hæpɪnɪs] *n* infelicità

unhappy [ʌn'hæpɪ] *adj* infelice; ~ **about/with** (*arrangements etc*) insoddisfatto(-a) di

unhealthy [ʌn'hɛlθɪ] *adj* (*gen*) malsano(-a); (*person*) malaticcio(-a)

unheard-of [ʌn'hə:dɔv] *adj* inaudito(-a), senza precedenti

unhelpful [ʌn'hɛlpful] *adj* poco disponibile

unhurt [ʌn'hə:t] *adj* illeso(-a)

unidentified [ʌnaɪ'dɛntɪfaɪd] *adj* non identificato(-a)

uniform ['ju:nɪfɔ:m] *n* uniforme *f*, divisa ▷ *adj* uniforme

unify ['ju:nɪfaɪ] *vt* unificare

unimportant [ʌnɪm'pɔ:tənt] *adj* senza importanza, di scarsa importanza

uninhabited [ʌnɪn'hæbɪtɪd] *adj* disabitato(-a)

unintentional [ʌnɪn'tɛnʃənəl] *adj* involontario(-a)

union ['ju:njən] *n* unione *f*; (*also*: **trade ~**) sindacato ▷ *cpd* sindacale, dei sindacati; **Union Jack** *n* bandiera nazionale britannica

unique [ju:'ni:k] *adj* unico(-a)

unisex ['ju:nɪsɛks] *adj* unisex *inv*

unit ['ju:nɪt] *n* unità *f inv*; (*section: of furniture etc*) elemento; (*team, squad*) reparto, squadra

unite [ju:'naɪt] *vt* unire ▷ *vi* unirsi; **united** *adj* unito(-a); unificato(-a); (*efforts*) congiunto(-a); **United Kingdom** *n* Regno Unito; **United Nations (Organization)** *n* (Organizzazione *f* delle) Nazioni Unite; **United States (of America)** *n* Stati *mpl* Uniti (d'America)

unity ['ju:nɪtɪ] *n* unità

universal [ju:nɪ'və:sl] *adj* universale

universe ['ju:nɪvə:s] *n* universo

university [ju:nɪ'və:sɪtɪ] *n* università *f inv*

unjust [ʌn'dʒʌst] *adj* ingiusto(-a)

unkind [ʌn'kaɪnd] *adj* scortese; crudele

unknown [ʌn'nəun] *adj* sconosciuto(-a)

unlawful [ʌn'lɔ:ful] *adj* illecito(-a), illegale

unleaded [ʌn'lɛdɪd] *adj* (*petrol, fuel*) verde, senza piombo

unleash [ʌn'li:ʃ] *vt* (*fig*) scatenare

unless [ʌn'lɛs] *conj* a meno che (non) + *sub*

unlike [ʌn'laɪk] *adj* diverso(-a) ▷ *prep* a differenza di, contrariamente a

unlikely [ʌn'laɪklɪ] *adj* improbabile

unlimited [ʌn'lɪmɪtɪd] *adj* illimitato(-a)

unlisted [ʌn'lɪstɪd] (*us*) *adj* (*Tel*): **to be ~** non essere sull'elenco

unload [ʌn'ləud] *vt* scaricare

unlock [ʌn'lɔk] *vt* aprire

unlucky [ʌn'lʌkɪ] *adj* sfortunato(-a); (*object, number*) che porta sfortuna

unmarried [ʌn'mærɪd] *adj* non sposato(-a); (*man only*) scapolo, celibe; (*woman only*) nubile

unmistak(e)able [ʌnmɪs'teɪkəbl] *adj* inconfondibile

unnatural [ʌn'nætʃrəl] *adj* innaturale; contro natura

unnecessary [ʌn'nɛsəsərɪ] *adj* inutile, superfluo(-a)

UNO ['ju:nəu] *n abbr* (= *United Nations Organization*) ONU *f*

unofficial [ʌnə'fɪʃl] *adj* non ufficiale; (*strike*) non dichiarato(-a) dal sindacato

unpack [ʌn'pæk] *vi* disfare la valigia (or le valigie) ▷ *vt* disfare

unpaid [ʌn'peɪd] *adj* (*holiday*) non pagato(-a); (*work*) non retribuito(-a); (*bill, debt*) da pagare

unpleasant [ʌn'plɛznt] *adj* spiacevole

unplug [ʌn'plʌg] *vt* staccare

unpopular [ʌn'pɔpjulər] *adj* impopolare

unprecedented [ʌn'prɛsɪdəntɪd] *adj* senza precedenti

unpredictable [ʌnprɪ'dɪktəbl] *adj*
imprevedibile

unprotected ['ʌnprə'tɛktɪd] *adj* (*sex*) non
protetto(-a)

unqualified [ʌn'kwɔlɪfaɪd] *adj* (*teacher*)
non abilitato(-a); (*success*) assoluto(-a),
senza riserve

unravel [ʌn'rævl] *vt* dipanare, districare

unreal [ʌn'rɪəl] *adj* irreale

unrealistic [ʌnrɪə'lɪstɪk] *adj* non
realistico(-a)

unreasonable [ʌn'rɪːznəbl] *adj*
irragionevole

unrelated [ʌnrɪ'leɪtɪd] *adj* **~ (to)** senza
rapporto (con); non imparentato(-a) (con)

unreliable [ʌnrɪ'laɪəbl] *adj* (*person,
machine*) che non dà affidamento; (*news,
source of information*) inattendibile

unrest [ʌn'rɛst] *n* agitazione *f*

unroll [ʌn'rəul] *vt* srotolare

unruly [ʌn'ruːlɪ] *adj* indisciplinato(-a)

unsafe [ʌn'seɪf] *adj* pericoloso(-a),
rischioso(-a)

unsatisfactory ['ʌnsætɪs'fæktərɪ] *adj*
che lascia a desiderare, insufficiente

unscrew [ʌn'skruː] *vt* svitare

unsettled [ʌn'sɛtld] *adj* (*person*)
turbato(-a); indeciso(-a); (*weather*)
instabile

unsettling [ʌn'sɛtlɪŋ] *adj* inquietante

unsightly [ʌn'saɪtlɪ] *adj* brutto(-a),
sgradevole a vedersi

unskilled [ʌn'skɪld] *adj* non
specializzato(-a)

unspoiled ['ʌn'spɔɪld], **unspoilt**
['ʌn'spɔɪlt] *adj* (*place*) non deturpato(-a)

unstable [ʌn'steɪbl] *adj* (*gen*) instabile;
(*mentally*) squilibrato(-a)

unsteady [ʌn'stɛdɪ] *adj* instabile,
malsicuro(-a)

unsuccessful [ʌnsək'sɛsful] *adj* (*writer,
proposal*) che non ha successo; (*marriage,
attempt*) mal riuscito(-a), fallito(-a); **to be ~**
(*in attempting sth*) non avere successo

unsuitable [ʌn'suːtəbl] *adj* inadatto(-a);
inopportuno(-a); sconveniente

unsure [ʌn'ʃuə] *adj* incerto(-a); **to be ~ of
o.s** essere insicuro(-a)

untidy [ʌn'taɪdɪ] *adj* (*room*) in disordine;
(*appearance*) trascurato(-a); (*person*)
disordinato(-a)

untie [ʌn'taɪ] *vt* (*knot, parcel*) disfare;
(*prisoner, dog*) slegare

until [ʌn'tɪl] *prep* fino a; (*after negative*)
prima di ▷ *conj* finché, fino a quando; (*in
past, after negative*) prima che + *sub*, prima
di + *infinitive*; **~ he comes** finché *or* fino a
quando non arriva; **~ now** finora; **~ then**
fino ad allora

untrue [ʌn'truː] *adj* (*statement*) falso(-a),
non vero(-a)

unused [ʌn'juːzd] *adj* nuovo(-a)

unusual [ʌn'juːʒuəl] *adj* insolito(-a),
eccezionale, raro(-a); **unusually** *adv*
insolitamente

unveil [ʌn'veɪl] *vt* scoprire; svelare

unwanted [ʌn'wɔntɪd] *adj* (*clothing*)
smesso(-a); (*child*) non desiderato(-a)

unwell [ʌn'wɛl] *adj* indisposto(-a); **to feel
~** non sentirsi bene

unwilling [ʌn'wɪlɪŋ] *adj* **to be ~ to do** non
voler fare

unwind [ʌn'waɪnd] (*irreg: like* **wind¹**) *vt*
svolgere, srotolare ▷ *vi* (*relax*) rilassarsi

unwise [ʌn'waɪz] *adj* poco saggio(-a)

unwittingly [ʌn'wɪtɪŋlɪ] *adv* senza volerlo

unwrap [ʌn'ræp] *vt* disfare; aprire

unzip [ʌn'zɪp] *vt* aprire (la chiusura lampo
di); (*Comput*) dezippare

🔵 **KEYWORD**

up [ʌp] *prep* **he went up the stairs/the
hill** è salito su per le scale/sulla collina; **the
cat was up a tree** il gatto era su un albero;
they live further up the street vivono un
po' più su nella stessa strada
▷ *adv* **1** (*upwards, higher*) su, in alto; **up in
the sky/the mountains** su nel cielo/in
montagna; **up there** lassù; **up above** su
in alto

2: **to be up** (*out of bed*) essere alzato(-a);
(*prices, level*) essere salito(-a)

3: **up to** (*as far as*) fino a; **up to now** finora

4: **to be up to** (*depending on*): **it's up to
you** sta a lei, dipende da lei; (*equal to*):
he's not up to it (*job, task etc*) non ne è
all'altezza; (*inf: be doing*): **what is he up to?**
cosa sta combinando?
▷ *n* **ups and downs** alti e bassi *mpl*

up-and-coming ['ʌpənd'kʌmɪŋ] *adj*
pieno(-a) di promesse, promettente

upbringing ['ʌpbrɪŋɪŋ] *n* educazione *f*

update [ʌp'deɪt] *vt* aggiornare

upfront [ʌp'frʌnt] *adj* (*inf*) franco(-a),
aperto(-a) ▷ *adv* (*pay*) subito

upgrade [ʌp'greɪd] *vt* (*house, job*)
migliorare; (*employee*) avanzare di grado

upheaval [ʌp'hiːvl] *n* sconvolgimento;
tumulto

uphill [ʌp'hɪl] *adj* in salita; (*fig: task*) difficile
▷ *adv* **to go ~** andare in salita, salire

upholstery [ʌp'həulstərɪ] *n* tappezzeria

upmarket [ʌp'mɑːkɪt] *adj* (*product*) che si
rivolge ad una fascia di mercato superiore

upon [ə'pɔn] *prep* su

upper ['ʌpə'] *adj* superiore ▷ *n* (*of shoe*)

tomaia; **upper-class** *adj* dell'alta
borghesia

upright ['ʌpraɪt] *adj* diritto(-a); verticale;
(*fig*) diritto(-a), onesto(-a)

uprising ['ʌpraɪzɪŋ] *n* insurrezione *f*,
rivolta

uproar ['ʌprɔ:ʳ] *n* tumulto, clamore *m*

upset [*n* 'ʌpsɛt, *vb, adj* ʌp'sɛt] (*irreg:
like* **set**) *n* (*to plan etc*) contrattempo;
(*stomach upset*) disturbo ▷ *vt* (*glass etc*)
rovesciare; (*plan, stomach*) scombussolare;
(*person: offend*) contrariare; (: *grieve*)
addolorare; sconvolgere ▷ *adj*
contrariato(-a), addolorato(-a); (*stomach*)
scombussolato(-a)

upside-down [ʌpsaɪd'daun] *adv*
sottosopra

upstairs [ʌp'stɛəz] *adv, adj* di sopra, al
piano superiore ▷ *n* piano di sopra

up-to-date ['ʌptə'deɪt] *adj* moderno(-a);
aggiornato(-a)

uptown ['ʌptaun] (*US*) *adv* verso i quartieri
residenziali ▷ *adj* dei quartieri residenziali

upward ['ʌpwəd] *adj* ascendente; verso
l'alto; **upward(s)** *adv* in su, verso l'alto

uranium [juə'reɪnɪəm] *n* uranio

Uranus [juə'reɪnəs] *n* (*planet*) Urano

urban ['ə:bən] *adj* urbano(-a)

urge [ə:dʒ] *n* impulso; stimolo; forte
desiderio ▷ *vt* **to ~ sb to do** esortare qn a
fare, spingere qn a fare; raccomandare a
qn di fare

urgency ['ə:dʒənsɪ] *n* urgenza; (*of tone*)
insistenza

urgent ['ə:dʒənt] *adj* urgente; (*voice*)
insistente

urinal ['juərɪnl] *n* (*BRIT: building*)
vespasiano; (: *vessel*) orinale *m*, pappagallo

urinate ['juərɪneɪt] *vi* orinare

urine ['juərɪn] *n* orina

us [ʌs] *pron* ci; (*stressed, after prep*) noi; *see
also* **me**

US(A) *n abbr* (= *United States (of America)*)
USA *mpl*

use [*n* ju:s, *vb* ju:z] *n* uso; impiego,
utilizzazione *f* ▷ *vt* usare, utilizzare,
servirsi di; **in ~** in uso; **out of ~** fuori uso; **to
be of ~** essere utile, servire; **it's no ~** non
serve, è inutile; **she ~d to do it** lo faceva
(una volta), era solita farlo; **to be ~d to**
avere l'abitudine di; **use up** *vt* consumare;
esaurire; **used** *adj* (*object, car*) usato(-a);
useful *adj* utile; **useless** *adj* inutile;
(*person*) inetto(-a); **user** *n* utente *m/f*;
user-friendly *adj* (*computer*) di facile uso

usual ['ju:ʒuəl] *adj* solito(-a); **as ~** come
al solito, come d'abitudine; **usually** *adv*
di solito

utensil [ju:'tɛnsl] *n* utensile *m*; **kitchen ~s**

utensili da cucina

utility [ju:'tɪlɪtɪ] *n* utilità; (*also:* **public ~**)
servizio pubblico

utilize ['ju:tɪlaɪz] *vt* utilizzare; sfruttare

utmost ['ʌtməust] *adj* estremo(-a) ▷ *n* **to
do one's ~** fare il possibile *or* di tutto

utter ['ʌtəʳ] *adj* assoluto(-a), totale ▷ *vt*
pronunciare, proferire; emettere; **utterly**
adv completamente, del tutto

U-turn ['ju:'tə:n] *n* inversione *f* a U

v. *abbr* = **verse**; **versus**; **volt**; (= *vide*) vedi, vedere

vacancy ['veɪkənsɪ] *n* (BRIT: *job*) posto libero; (*room*) stanza libera; **"no vacancies"** "completo"

> Be careful not to translate *vacancy* by the Italian word *vacanza*.

vacant ['veɪkənt] *adj* (*job*, *seat etc*) libero(-a); (*expression*) assente

vacate [və'keɪt] *vt* lasciare libero(-a)

vacation [və'keɪʃən] (*esp* US) *n* vacanze *fpl*; **vacationer** (US **vacationist**) *n* vacanziere(-a)

vaccination [væksɪ'neɪʃən] *n* vaccinazione *f*

vaccine ['væksi:n] *n* vaccino

vacuum ['vækjum] *n* vuoto; **vacuum cleaner** *n* aspirapolvere *m inv*

vagina [və'dʒaɪnə] *n* vagina

vague [veɪg] *adj* vago(-a); (*blurred: photo, memory*) sfocato(-a)

vain [veɪn] *adj* (*useless*) inutile, vano(-a); (*conceited*) vanitoso(-a); **in ~** inutilmente, invano

Valentine's Day ['væləntaɪnzdeɪ] *n* San Valentino *m*

valid ['vælɪd] *adj* valido(-a), valevole; (*excuse*) valido(-a)

valley ['vælɪ] *n* valle *f*

valuable ['væljuəbl] *adj* (*jewel*) di (grande) valore; (*time, help*) prezioso(-a); **valuables** *npl* oggetti *mpl* di valore

value ['vælju:] *n* valore *m* ▷ *vt* (*fix price*) valutare, dare un prezzo a; (*cherish*) apprezzare, tenere a; **~s** *npl* (*principles*) valori *mpl*

valve [vælv] *n* valvola

vampire ['væmpaɪə^r] *n* vampiro

van [væn] *n* (Aut) furgone *m*; (BRIT: *Rail*) vagone *m*

vandal ['vændl] *n* vandalo(-a); **vandalism** *n* vandalismo; **vandalize** *vt* vandalizzare

vanilla [və'nɪlə] *n* vaniglia ▷ *cpd* (*ice cream*) alla vaniglia

vanish ['vænɪʃ] *vi* svanire, scomparire

vanity ['vænɪtɪ] *n* vanità

vapour ['veɪpə^r] (US **vapor**) *n* vapore *m*

variable ['vɛərɪəbl] *adj* variabile; (*mood*) mutevole

variant ['vɛərɪənt] *n* variante *f*

variation [vɛərɪ'eɪʃən] *n* variazione *f*; (*in opinion*) cambiamento

varied ['vɛərɪd] *adj* vario(-a), diverso(-a)

variety [və'raɪətɪ] *n* varietà *f inv*; (*quantity*) quantità, numero

various ['vɛərɪəs] *adj* vario(-a), diverso(-a); (*several*) parecchi(-e), molti(-e)

varnish ['vɑːnɪʃ] *n* vernice *f*; (*nail varnish*) smalto ▷ *vt* verniciare; mettere lo smalto su

vary ['vɛərɪ] *vt*, *vi* variare, mutare

vase [vɑːz] *n* vaso

Vaseline® ['væsɪli:n] *n* vaselina

vast [vɑːst] *adj* vasto(-a); (*amount, success*) enorme

VAT [væt] *n abbr* (= *value added tax*) I.V.A. *f*

Vatican ['vætɪkən] *n* **the ~** il Vaticano

vault [vɔːlt] *n* (*of roof*) volta; (*tomb*) tomba; (*in bank*) camera blindata ▷ *vt* (*also:* **~ over**) saltare (d'un balzo)

VCR *n abbr* = **video cassette recorder**

VDU *n abbr* = **visual display unit**

veal [vi:l] *n* vitello

veer [vɪə^r] *vi* girare; virare

vegan ['vi:gən] *n* vegetaliano(-a)

vegetable ['vɛdʒtəbl] *n* verdura, ortaggio ▷ *adj* vegetale

vegetarian [vɛdʒɪ'tɛərɪən] *adj*, *n* vegetariano(-a); **do you have any ~ dishes?** avete piatti vegetariani?

vegetation [vɛdʒɪ'teɪʃən] *n* vegetazione *f*

vehicle ['vi:ɪkl] *n* veicolo

veil [veɪl] *n* velo

vein [veɪn] *n* vena; (*on leaf*) nervatura

Velcro® ['vɛlkrəu] *n* velcro® *m inv*

velvet ['vɛlvɪt] *n* velluto ▷ *adj* di velluto

vending machine ['vɛndɪŋ-] *n* distributore *m* automatico

vendor ['vɛndə^r] *n* venditore(-trice)

vengeance ['vɛndʒəns] n vendetta; **with a ~** (fig) davvero; furiosamente

Venice ['vɛnɪs] n Venezia

venison ['vɛnɪsn] n carne f di cervo

venom ['vɛnəm] n veleno

vent [vɛnt] n foro, apertura; (in dress, jacket) spacco ▷ vt (fig: one's feelings) sfogare, dare sfogo a

ventilation [vɛntɪ'leɪʃən] n ventilazione f

venture ['vɛntʃəʳ] n impresa (rischiosa) ▷ vt rischiare, azzardare ▷ vi avventurarsi; **business ~** iniziativa commerciale

venue ['vɛnjuː] n luogo (designato) per l'incontro

Venus ['viːnəs] n (planet) Venere m

verb [vəːb] n verbo; **verbal** adj verbale; (translation) orale

verdict ['vəːdɪkt] n verdetto

verge [vəːdʒ] (BRIT) n bordo, orlo; **"soft ~s"** (BRIT: Aut) banchine fpl cedevoli; **on the ~ of doing** sul punto di fare

verify ['vɛrɪfaɪ] vt verificare; (prove the truth of) confermare

versatile ['vəːsətaɪl] adj (person) versatile; (machine, tool etc) (che si presta) a molti usi

verse [vəːs] n versi mpl; (stanza) stanza, strofa; (in bible) versetto

version ['vəːʃən] n versione f

versus ['vəːsəs] prep contro

vertical ['vəːtɪkl] adj verticale ▷ n verticale m

very ['vɛrɪ] adv molto ▷ adj **the ~ book which** proprio il libro che; **the ~ last** proprio l'ultimo; **at the ~ least** almeno; **~ much** moltissimo

vessel ['vɛsl] n (Anat) vaso; (Naut) nave f; (container) recipiente m

vest [vɛst] n (BRIT) maglia; (: sleeveless) canottiera; (US: waistcoat) gilè m inv

vet [vɛt] n abbr (BRIT: = veterinary surgeon) veterinario ▷ vt esaminare minuziosamente

veteran ['vɛtərn] n (also: **war ~**) veterano

veterinary surgeon ['vɛtrɪnərɪ-] (US **veterinarian**) n veterinario

veto ['viːtəu] (pl **vetoes**) n veto ▷ vt opporre il veto a

via ['vaɪə] prep (by way of) via; (by means of) tramite

viable ['vaɪəbl] adj attuabile; vitale

vibrate [vaɪ'breɪt] vi **to ~ (with)** vibrare (di); (resound) risonare (di)

vibration [vaɪ'breɪʃən] n vibrazione f

vicar ['vɪkəʳ] n pastore m

vice [vaɪs] n (evil) vizio; (Tech) morsa; **vice-chairman** (irreg) n vicepresidente m

vice versa ['vaɪsɪ'vəːsə] adv viceversa

vicinity [vɪ'sɪnɪtɪ] n vicinanze fpl

vicious ['vɪʃəs] adj (remark, dog) cattivo(-a); (blow) violento(-a)

victim ['vɪktɪm] n vittima

victor ['vɪktəʳ] n vincitore m

Victorian [vɪk'tɔːrɪən] adj vittoriano(-a)

victorious [vɪk'tɔːrɪəs] adj vittorioso(-a)

victory ['vɪktərɪ] n vittoria

video ['vɪdɪəu] cpd video... ▷ n (video film) video m inv; (also: **~ cassette**) videocassetta; (also: **~ cassette recorder**) videoregistratore m; **video camera** n videocamera; **video (cassette) recorder** n videoregistratore m; **video game** n videogioco; **video shop** n videonoleggio; **video tape** n videotape m inv; **video wall** n schermo m multivideo inv

vie [vaɪ] vi **to ~ with** competere con, rivaleggiare con

Vienna [vɪ'ɛnə] n Vienna

Vietnam [vjɛt'næm] n Vietnam m; **Vietnamese** adj, n inv vietnamita m/f

view [vjuː] n vista, veduta; (opinion) opinione f ▷ vt (look at: also fig) considerare; (house) visitare; **on ~** (in museum etc) esposto(-a); **in full ~ of** sotto gli occhi di; **in ~ of the weather/the fact that** considerato il tempo/che; **in my ~** a mio parere; **viewer** n spettatore(-trice); **viewpoint** n punto di vista; (place) posizione f

vigilant ['vɪdʒɪlənt] adj vigile

vigorous ['vɪgərəs] adj vigoroso(-a)

vile [vaɪl] adj (action) vile; (smell) disgustoso(-a), nauseante; (temper) pessimo(-a)

villa ['vɪlə] n villa

village ['vɪlɪdʒ] n villaggio; **villager** n abitante m/f di villaggio

villain ['vɪlən] n (scoundrel) canaglia; (BRIT: criminal) criminale m; (in novel etc) cattivo

vinaigrette [vɪneɪ'grɛt] n vinaigrette f inv

vine [vaɪn] n vite f; (climbing plant) rampicante m

vinegar ['vɪnɪgəʳ] n aceto

vineyard ['vɪnjɑːd] n vigna, vigneto

vintage ['vɪntɪdʒ] n (year) annata, produzione f ▷ cpd d'annata

vinyl ['vaɪnl] n vinile m

viola [vɪ'əulə] n viola

violate ['vaɪəleɪt] vt violare

violation [vaɪə'leɪʃən] n violazione f; **in ~ of sth** violando qc

violence ['vaɪələns] n violenza

violent ['vaɪələnt] adj violento(-a)

violet ['vaɪələt] adj (colour) viola inv, violetto(-a) ▷ n (plant) violetta; (colour) violetto

violin [vaɪə'lɪn] n violino

VIP n abbr (= very important person) V.I.P. m/f inv

virgin ['vəːdʒɪn] *n* vergine *f* ▷ *adj* vergine *inv*

Virgo ['vəːgəu] *n* (*sign*) Vergine *f*

virtual ['vəːtjuəl] *adj* effettivo(-a), vero(-a); (*Comput, Physics*) virtuale; (*in effect*): **it's a ~ impossibility** è praticamente impossibile; **the ~ leader** il capo all'atto pratico; **virtually** ['vəːtjuəlɪ] *adv* (*almost*) praticamente; **virtual reality** *n* (*Comput*) realtà virtuale

virtue ['vəːtjuː] *n* virtù *f inv*; (*advantage*) pregio, vantaggio, **by ~ of** grazie a

virus ['vaɪərəs] *n* (*also Comput*) virus *m inv*

visa ['viːzə] *n* visto

vise [vaɪs] (*US*) *n* (*Tech*) = **vice**

visibility [vɪzɪ'bɪlɪtɪ] *n* visibilità

visible ['vɪzəbl] *adj* visibile

vision ['vɪʒən] *n* (*sight*) vista; (*foresight, in dream*) visione *f*

visit ['vɪzɪt] *n* visita; (*stay*) soggiorno ▷ *vt* (*person: US: also: ~ with*) andare a trovare; (*place*) visitare; **visiting hours** *npl* (*in hospital etc*) orario delle visite; **visitor** *n* visitatore(-trice); (*guest*) ospite *m/f*; **visitor centre** (*US* **visitor center**) *n* centro informazioni per visitatori di museo, zoo, parco ecc

visual ['vɪzjuəl] *adj* visivo(-a); visuale; ottico(-a); **visualize** ['vɪzjuəlaɪz] *vt* immaginare, figurarsi; (*foresee*) prevedere

vital ['vaɪtl] *adj* vitale

vitality [vaɪ'tælɪtɪ] *n* vitalità

vitamin ['vɪtəmɪn] *n* vitamina

vivid ['vɪvɪd] *adj* vivido(-a)

V-neck ['viːnɛk] *n* maglione *m* con lo scollo a V

vocabulary [vəu'kæbjulərɪ] *n* vocabolario

vocal ['vəukl] *adj* (*Mus*) vocale; (*communication*) verbale

vocational [vəu'keɪʃənl] *adj* professionale

vodka ['vɔdkə] *n* vodka *f inv*

vogue [vəug] *n* moda; (*popularity*) popolarità, voga

voice [vɔɪs] *n* voce *f* ▷ *vt* (*opinion*) esprimere; **voice mail** *n* servizio di segreteria telefonica

void [vɔɪd] *n* vuoto ▷ *adj* (*invalid*) nullo(-a); (*empty*): **~ of** privo(-a) di

volatile ['vɔlətaɪl] *adj* volatile; (*fig*) volubile

volcano [vɔl'keɪnəu] (*pl* **volcanoes**) *n* vulcano

volleyball ['vɔlɪbɔːl] *n* pallavolo *f*

volt [vəult] *n* volt *m inv*; **voltage** *n* tensione *f*, voltaggio

volume ['vɔljuːm] *n* volume *m*

voluntarily ['vɔləntrɪlɪ] *adv* volontariamente; gratuitamente

voluntary ['vɔləntərɪ] *adj* volontario(-a); (*unpaid*) gratuito(-a), non retribuito(-a)

volunteer [vɔlən'tɪər] *n* volontario(-a) ▷ *vt* offrire volontariamente ▷ *vi* (*Mil*) arruolarsi volontario; **to ~ to do** offrire (volontariamente) di fare

vomit ['vɔmɪt] *n* vomito ▷ *vt, vi* vomitare

vote [vəut] *n* voto, suffragio; (*cast*) voto; (*franchise*) diritto di voto ▷ *vt* **to be ~d chairman** *etc* venir eletto presidente *etc*; (*propose*): **to ~ that** approvare la proposta che ▷ *vi* votare; **~ of thanks** discorso di ringraziamento; **voter** *n* elettore(-trice); **voting** *n* scrutinio

voucher ['vautʃər] *n* (*for meal, petrol etc*) buono

vow [vau] *n* voto, promessa solenne ▷ *vt* **to ~ to do/that** giurare di fare/che

vowel ['vauəl] *n* vocale *f*

voyage ['vɔɪɪdʒ] *n* viaggio per mare, traversata

vulgar ['vʌlgər] *adj* volgare

vulnerable ['vʌlnərəbl] *adj* vulnerabile

vulture ['vʌltʃər] *n* avvoltoio

V

waddle ['wɒdl] *vi* camminare come una papera

wade [weɪd] *vi* **to ~ through** camminare a stento in; (*fig: book*) leggere con fatica

wafer ['weɪfə'] *n* (*Culin*) cialda

waffle ['wɒfl] *n* (*Culin*) cialda; (*inf*) ciance *fpl* ▷ *vi* cianciare

wag [wæg] *vt* agitare, muovere ▷ *vi* agitarsi

wage [weɪdʒ] *n* (*also*: **~s**) salario, paga ▷ *vt* **to ~ war** fare la guerra

wag(g)on ['wægən] *n* (*horse-drawn*) carro; (*BRIT*: *Rail*) vagone *m* (merci)

wail [weɪl] *n* gemito; (*of siren*) urlo ▷ *vi* gemere; urlare

waist [weɪst] *n* vita, cintola; **waistcoat** (*BRIT*) *n* panciotto, gilè *m inv*

wait [weɪt] *n* attesa ▷ *vi* aspettare, attendere; **to lie in ~ for** stare in agguato a; **to ~ for** aspettare; **~ for me, please** aspettami, per favore; **I can't ~ to** (*fig*) non vedo l'ora di; **wait on** *vt fus* servire; **waiter** *n* cameriere *m*; **waiting list** *n* lista di attesa; **waiting room** *n* sala d'aspetto *or* d'attesa; **waitress** *n* cameriera

waive [weɪv] *vt* rinunciare a, abbandonare

wake [weɪk] (*pt* **woke, waked**, *pp* **woken, waked**) *vt* (*also*: **~ up**) svegliare ▷ *vi* (*also*: **~ up**) svegliarsi ▷ *n* (*for dead person*) veglia funebre; (*Naut*) scia

Wales [weɪlz] *n* Galles *m*

walk [wɔːk] *n* passeggiata; (*short*) giretto; (*gait*) passo, andatura; (*path*) sentiero; (*in park etc*) sentiero, vialetto ▷ *vi* camminare; (*for pleasure, exercise*) passeggiare ▷ *vt* (*distance*) fare *or* percorrere a piedi; (*dog*) accompagnare, portare a passeggiare; **10 minutes' ~ from** 10 minuti di cammino *or* a piedi da; **from all ~s of life** di tutte le condizioni sociali; **walk out** *vi* (*audience*) andarsene; (*workers*) scendere in sciopero; **walker** *n* (*person*) camminatore(-trice); **walkie-talkie** ['wɔːkɪ'tɔːkɪ] *n* walkie-talkie *m inv*; **walking** *n* camminare *m*; **walking shoes** *npl* pedule *fpl*; **walking stick** *n* bastone *m* da passeggio; **Walkman®** ['wɔːkmən] *n* Walkman® *m inv*; **walkway** *n* passaggio pedonale

wall [wɔːl] *n* muro; (*internal, of tunnel, cave*) parete *f*

wallet ['wɒlɪt] *n* portafoglio; **I can't find my ~** non trovo il portafoglio

wallpaper ['wɔːlpeɪpə'] *n* carta da parati ▷ *vt* (*room*) mettere la carta da parati in

walnut ['wɔːlnʌt] *n* noce *f*; (*tree, wood*) noce *m*

walrus ['wɔːlrəs] (*pl* **walrus** *or* **walruses**) *n* tricheco

waltz [wɔːlts] *n* valzer *m inv* ▷ *vi* ballare il valzer

wand [wɒnd] *n* (*also*: **magic ~**) bacchetta (magica)

wander ['wɒndə'] *vi* (*person*) girare senza meta, girovagare; (*thoughts*) vagare ▷ *vt* girovagare per

want [wɒnt] *vt* volere; (*need*) aver bisogno di ▷ *n* **for ~ of** per mancanza di; **wanted** *adj* (*criminal*) ricercato(-a); **"wanted"** (*in adverts*) "cercasi"

war [wɔː'] *n* guerra; **to make ~ (on)** far guerra (a)

ward [wɔːd] *n* (*in hospital: room*) corsia; (: *section*) reparto; (*Pol*) circoscrizione *f*; (*Law: child: also*: **~ of court**) pupillo(-a)

warden ['wɔːdn] *n* (*of park, game reserve, youth hostel*) guardiano(-a); (*BRIT: of institution*) direttore(-trice); (*BRIT: also*: **traffic ~**) addetto(-a) al controllo del traffico e del parcheggio

wardrobe ['wɔːdrəub] *n* (*cupboard*) guardaroba *m inv*, armadio; (*clothes*) guardaroba; (*Cinema, Theatre*) costumi *mpl*

warehouse ['wɛəhaus] *n* magazzino

warfare ['wɔːfɛə'] *n* guerra

warhead ['wɔːhɛd] *n* (*Mil*) testata

warm [wɔːm] *adj* caldo(-a); (*thanks, welcome, applause*) caloroso(-a); (*person*) cordiale; **it's ~** fa caldo; **I'm ~** ho caldo; **warm up** *vi* scaldarsi, riscaldarsi

▷ vt scaldare, riscaldare; (engine) far scaldare; **warmly** adv (applaud, welcome) calorosamente; (dress) con abiti pesanti; **warmth** n calore m

warn [wɔːn] vt **to ~ sb that/(not) to do/of** avvertire or avvisare qn che/di (non) fare/di; **warning** n avvertimento; (notice) avviso; (signal) segnalazione f; **warning light** n spia luminosa

warrant ['wɔrnt] n (voucher) buono; (Law: to arrest) mandato di cattura; (: to search) mandato di perquisizione

warranty ['wɔrɒntɪ] n garanzia

warrior ['wɔrɪəf] n guerriero(-a)

Warsaw ['wɔːsɔː] n Varsavia

warship ['wɔːʃɪp] n nave f da guerra

wart [wɔːt] n verruca

wartime ['wɔːtaɪm] n **in ~** in tempo di guerra

wary ['wɛərɪ] adj prudente

was [wɒz] pt of **be**

wash [wɒʃ] vt lavare ▷ vi lavarsi; (sea): **to ~ over/against sth** infrangersi su/contro qc ▷ n lavaggio; (of ship) scia; **to give sth a ~** lavare qc, dare una lavata a qc; **to have a ~** lavarsi; **wash up** vi (BRIT) lavare i piatti; (US) darsi una lavata; **washbasin** (US **washbowl**) n lavabo; **wash cloth** (US) n pezzuola (per lavarsi); **washer** n (Tech) rondella; **washing** n (linen etc) bucato; **washing line** n (BRIT) corda del bucato; **washing machine** n lavatrice f; **washing powder** (BRIT) n detersivo (in polvere);

Washington ['wɒʃɪŋtən] n Washington f

wash: **washing-up** n rigovernatura, lavatura dei piatti; **washing-up liquid** n detersivo liquido (per stoviglie); **washroom** n gabinetto

wasn't ['wɒznt] = **was not**

wasp [wɒsp] n vespa

waste [weɪst] n spreco; (of time) perdita; (rubbish) rifiuti mpl; (also: **household ~**) immondizie fpl ▷ adj (material) di scarto; (food) avanzato(-a); (land) incolto(-a) ▷ vt sprecare; **waste ground** (BRIT) n terreno incolto or abbandonato; **wastepaper basket** ['weɪstpeɪpə-] n cestino per la carta straccia

watch [wɒtʃ] n (also: **wrist ~**) orologio (da polso); (act of watching, vigilance) sorveglianza; (guard: Mil, Naut) guardia; (Naut: spell of duty) quarto ▷ vt (look at) osservare; (: match, programme) guardare; (spy on, guard) sorvegliare, tenere d'occhio; (be careful of) fare attenzione a ▷ vi osservare, guardare; (keep guard) fare or montare la guardia; **watch out** vi fare attenzione; **watchdog** n (also fig) cane m da guardia; **watch strap** n cinturino da

orologio

water ['wɔːtəf] n acqua ▷ vt (plant) annaffiare ▷ vi (eyes) lacrimare; (mouth): **to make sb's mouth ~** far venire l'acquolina in bocca a qn; **in British ~s** nelle acque territoriali britanniche; **water down** vt (milk) diluire; (fig: story) edulcorare; **watercolour** (US **watercolor**) n acquerello; **watercress** n crescione m; **waterfall** n cascata; **watering can** n annaffiatoio; **watermelon** n anguria, cocomero; **waterproof** adj impermeabile; **water-skiing** n sci m acquatico

watt [wɒt] n watt m inv

wave [weɪv] n onda; (of hand) gesto, segno; (in hair) ondulazione f; (fig: surge) ondata ▷ vi fare un cenno con la mano; (branches, grass) ondeggiare; (flag) sventolare ▷ vt (hand) fare un gesto con; (handkerchief) sventolare; (stick) brandire; **wavelength** n lunghezza d'onda

waver ['weɪvəf] vi esitare; (voice) tremolare

wavy ['weɪvɪ] adj ondulato(-a); ondeggiante

wax [wæks] n cera ▷ vt dare la cera a; (car) lucidare ▷ vi (moon) crescere

way [weɪ] n via, strada; (path, access) passaggio; (distance) distanza; (direction) parte f, direzione f; (manner) modo, stile m; (habit) abitudine f; **which ~? — this ~** da che parte or in quale direzione? — da questa parte or per di qua; **on the ~** (en route) per strada; **to be on one's ~** essere in cammino or sulla strada; **to be in the ~** bloccare il passaggio; (fig) essere tra i piedi or d'impiccio; **to go out of one's ~ to do** (fig) mettercela tutta or fare di tutto per fare; **under ~** (project) in corso; **to lose one's ~** perdere la strada; **in a ~** in un certo senso; **in some ~s** sotto certi aspetti; **no ~!** (inf) neanche per idea!; **by the ~ ...** a proposito ...; **"~ in"** (BRIT) "entrata", "ingresso"; **"~ out"** (BRIT) "uscita"; **the ~ back** la strada del ritorno; **"give ~"** (BRIT: Aut) "dare la precedenza"

W.C. ['dʌblju:'si:] (BRIT) n W.C. m inv, gabinetto

we [wi:] pl pron noi

weak [wi:k] adj debole; (health) precario(-a); (beam etc) fragile; (tea) leggero(-a); **weaken** vi indebolirsi ▷ vt indebolire; **weakness** n debolezza; (fault) punto debole, difetto; **to have a weakness for** avere un debole per

wealth [welθ] n (money, resources) ricchezza, ricchezze fpl; (of details) abbondanza, profusione f; **wealthy** adj ricco(-a)

weapon ['wepən] n arma; **~s of mass**

w

destruction armi *mpl* di distruzione di massa

wear [wɛəʳ] (*pt* **wore**, *pp* **worn**) *n* (*use*) uso; (*damage through use*) logorio, usura; (*clothing*): **sports/baby ~** abbigliamento sportivo/per neonati ▷ *vt* (*clothes*) portare; (*put on*) mettersi; (*damage: through use*) consumare ▷ *vi* (*last*) durare; (*rub etc through*) consumarsi; **evening ~** abiti *mpl or* tenuta da sera; **wear off** *vi* sparire lentamente; **wear out** *vt* consumare; (*person, strength*) esaurire

weary ['wɪərɪ] *adj* stanco(-a) ▷ *vi* **to ~ of** stancarsi di

weasel ['wi:zl] *n* (*Zool*) donnola

weather ['wɛðəʳ] *n* tempo ▷ *vt* (*storm, crisis*) superare; **What's the ~ like?** che tempo fa?; **under the ~** (*fig: ill*) poco bene; **weather forecast** *n* previsioni *fpl* del tempo, bollettino meteorologico

weave [wi:v] (*pt* **wove**, *pp* **woven**) *vt* (*cloth*) tessere; (*basket*) intrecciare

web [wɛb] *n* (*of spider*) ragnatela; (*on foot*) palma; (*fabric, also fig*) tessuto; **the (World Wide) W~** la Rete; **web page** *n* (*Comput*) pagina *f* web *inv*; **website** *n* (*Comput*) sito (Internet)

wed [wɛd] (*pt, pp* **wedded**) *vt* sposare ▷ *vi* sposarsi

we'd [wi:d] = **we had**; **we would**

Wed. *abbr* (= *Wednesday*) mer.

wedding ['wɛdɪŋ] *n* matrimonio; **wedding anniversary** *n* anniversario di matrimonio; **wedding day** *n* giorno delle nozze *or* del matrimonio; **wedding dress** *n* abito nuziale; **wedding ring** *n* fede *f*

wedge [wɛdʒ] *n* (*of wood etc*) zeppa; (*of cake*) fetta ▷ *vt* (*fix*) fissare con zeppe; (*pack tightly*) incastrare

Wednesday ['wɛnzdɪ] *n* mercoledì *m inv*

wee [wi:] (*Scottish*) *adj* piccolo(-a)

weed [wi:d] *n* erbaccia ▷ *vt* diserbare; **weedkiller** *n* diserbante *m*

week [wi:k] *n* settimana; **a ~ today/on Friday** oggi/venerdì a otto; **weekday** *n* giorno feriale; (*Comm*) giornata lavorativa; **weekend** *n* fine settimana *m or f inv*, weekend *m inv*; **weekly** *adv* ogni settimana, settimanalmente ▷ *adj* settimanale ▷ *n* settimanale *m*

weep [wi:p] (*pt, pp* **wept**) *vi* (*person*) piangere

weigh [weɪ] *vt, vi* pesare; **to ~ anchor** salpare l'ancora; **weigh up** *vt* valutare

weight [weɪt] *n* peso; **to lose/put on ~** dimagrire/ingrassare; **weightlifting** *n* sollevamento pesi

weir [wɪəʳ] *n* diga

weird [wɪəd] *adj* strano(-a), bizzarro(-a);

(*eerie*) soprannaturale

welcome ['wɛlkəm] *adj* benvenuto(-a) ▷ *n* accoglienza, benvenuto *m* ▷ *vt* dare il benvenuto a; (*be glad of*) rallegrarsi di; **thank you — you're ~!** grazie — prego!

weld [wɛld] *n* saldatura ▷ *vt* saldare

welfare ['wɛlfɛəʳ] *n* benessere *m*; **welfare state** *n* stato assistenziale

well [wɛl] *n* pozzo ▷ *adv* bene ▷ *adj* **to be ~** (*person*) stare bene ▷ *excl* allora!; ma!; ebbene!; **as ~** anche; **as ~ as** così come; oltre a; **~ done!** bravo(-a)!; **get ~ soon!** guarisci presto!; **to do ~** andare bene

we'll [wi:l] = **we will**; **we shall**

well: **well-behaved** *adj* ubbidiente; **well-built** *adj* (*person*) ben fatto(-a); **well-dressed** *adj* ben vestito(-a), vestito(-a) bene

wellies (*inf*) ['wɛlɪz] *npl* (BRIT) stivali *mpl* di gomma

well: **well-known** *adj* noto(-a), famoso(-a); **well-off** *adj* benestante, danaroso(-a); **well-paid** [wɛl'peɪd] *adj* ben pagato(-a)

Welsh [wɛlʃ] *adj* gallese ▷ *n* (*Ling*) gallese *m*; **Welshman** (*irreg*) *n* gallese *m*; **Welshwoman** (*irreg*) *n* gallese *f*

went [wɛnt] *pt of* **go**

wept [wɛpt] *pt, pp of* **weep**

were [wəːʳ] *pt of* **be**

we're [wɪəʳ] = **we are**

weren't [wəːnt] = **were not**

west [wɛst] *n* ovest *m*, occidente *m*, ponente *m* ▷ *adj* (a) ovest *inv*, occidentale ▷ *adv* verso ovest; **the W~** l'Occidente *m*; **westbound** ['wɛstbaund] *adj* (*traffic*) diretto(-a) a ovest; (*carriageway*) ovest *inv*; **western** *adj* occidentale, dell'ovest ▷ *n* (*Cinema*) western *m inv*; **West Indian** *adj* delle Indie Occidentali ▷ *n* abitante *m/f* delle Indie Occidentali; **West Indies** [-'ɪndɪz] *npl* Indie *fpl* Occidentali

wet [wɛt] *adj* umido(-a), bagnato(-a); (*soaked*) fradicio(-a); (*rainy*) piovoso(-a) ▷ *n* (BRIT: *Pol*) politico moderato; **to get ~** bagnarsi; **"~ paint"** "vernice fresca"; **wetsuit** *n* tuta da sub

we've [wi:v] = **we have**

whack [wæk] *vt* picchiare, battere

whale [weɪl] *n* (*Zool*) balena

wharf [wɔːf] (*pl* **wharves**) *n* banchina

KEYWORD

what [wɔt] *adj* **1** (*in direct/indirect questions*) che; quale; **what size is it?** che taglia è?; **what colour is it?** di che colore è?; **what books do you want?** quali *or* che libri vuole?

2 (*in exclamations*) che; **what a mess!** che

disordine!
▷ *pron* **1** (*interrogative*) che cosa, cosa, che;
what are you doing? che or (che) cosa
fai?; **what are you talking about?** di
che cosa parli?; **what is it called?** come
si chiama?; **what about me?** e io?; **what
about doing …?** e se facessimo …?
2 (*relative*) ciò che, quello che; **I saw what
you did/was on the table** ho visto quello
che hai fatto/quello che era sul tavolo
3 (*indirect use*) (che) cosa; **he asked me
what she had said** mi ha chiesto che
cosa avesse detto; **tell me what you're
thinking about** dimmi a cosa stai
pensando
▷ *excl* (*disbelieving*) cosa!, come!

whatever [wɔt'ɛvə] *adj* **~ book** qualunque
or qualsiasi libro + *sub* ▷ *pron* **do ~ is
necessary/you want** faccia qualunque
or qualsiasi cosa sia necessaria/lei voglia;
~ happens qualunque cosa accada; **no
reason ~** or **whatsoever** nessuna ragione
affatto or al mondo; **nothing ~** proprio
niente
whatsoever [wɔtsəu'ɛvə] *adj* = **whatever**
wheat [wi:t] *n* grano, frumento
wheel [wi:l] *n* ruota; (*Aut: also*: **steering
~**) volante *m*; (*Naut*) (ruota del) timone *m*
▷ *vt* spingere ▷ *vi* (*birds*) roteare; (*also*: **~
round**) girare; **wheelbarrow** *n* carriola;
wheelchair *n* sedia a rotelle; **wheel
clamp** *n* (*Aut*) morsa che blocca la ruota di
una vettura in sosta vietata
wheeze [wi:z] *vi* ansimare

○ **KEYWORD**

when [wɛn] *adv* quando; **when did it
happen?** quando è successo?
▷ *conj* **1** (*at, during, after the time that*)
quando; **she was reading when I came
in** quando sono entrato lei leggeva; **that
was when I needed you** era allora che
avevo bisogno di te
2 (*on, at which*): **on the day when I met
him** il giorno in cui l'ho incontrato; **one
day when it was raining** un giorno che
pioveva
3 (*whereas*) quando, mentre; **you said I
was wrong when in fact I was right** mi
hai detto che avevo torto, quando in realtà
avevo ragione

whenever [wɛn'ɛvə] *adv* quando mai
▷ *conj* quando; (*every time that*) ogni volta
che
where [wɛəʳ] *adv, conj* dove; **this is ~** è qui
che; **whereabouts** *adv* dove ▷ *n* **sb's**

whereabouts luogo dove qn si trova;
whereas *conj* mentre; **whereby** *pron* per
cui; **wherever** [-'ɛvəʳ] *conj* dovunque +
sub; (*interrogative*) dove mai
whether ['wɛðəʳ] *conj* se; **I don't know ~
to accept or not** non so se accettare o no;
it's doubtful ~ è poco probabile che; **~ you
go or not** che lei vada o no

○ **KEYWORD**

which [wɪtʃ] *adj* **1** (*interrogative· direct,
indirect*) quale; **which picture do you
want?** quale quadro vuole?; **which one?**
quale?; **which one of you did it?** chi di voi
lo ha fatto?
2: **in which case** nel qual caso
▷ *pron* **1** (*interrogative*) quale; **which (of
these) are yours?** quali di questi sono
suoi?; **which of you are coming?** chi di
voi viene?
2 (*relative*) che; (: *indirect*) cui, il (la) quale;
**the apple which you ate/which is on
the table** la mela che hai mangiato/che
è sul tavolo; **the chair on which you are
sitting** la sedia sulla quale or su cui sei
seduto; **he said he knew, which is true**
ha detto che lo sapeva, il che è vero; **after
which** dopo di che

whichever [wɪtʃ'ɛvə] *adj* **take ~ book
you prefer** prenda qualsiasi libro che
preferisce; **~ book you take** qualsiasi libro
prenda
while [waɪl] *n* momento ▷ *conj* mentre;
(*as long as*) finché; (*although*) sebbene + *sub*,
per quanto + *sub*; **for a ~** per un po'
whilst [waɪlst] *conj* = **while**
whim [wɪm] *n* capriccio
whine [waɪn] *n* gemito ▷ *vi* gemere;
uggiolare; piagnucolare
whip [wɪp] *n* frusta; (*for riding*) frustino;
(*Pol: person*) capogruppo (*che sovrintende
alla disciplina dei colleghi di partito*) ▷ *vt*
frustare; (*cream, eggs*) sbattere; **whipped
cream** *n* panna montata
whirl [wə:l] *vt* (*far*) girare rapidamente,
(*far*) turbinare ▷ *vi* (*dancers*) volteggiare;
(*leaves, water*) sollevarsi in vortice
whisk [wɪsk] *n* (*Culin*) frusta; frullino ▷ *vt*
sbattere, frullare; **to ~ sb away** or **off**
portar via qn a tutta velocità
whiskers ['wɪskəz] *npl* (*of animal*) baffi *mpl*;
(*of man*) favoriti *mpl*
whisky ['wɪskɪ] (*us, Ireland* **whiskey**) *n*
whisky *m inv*
whisper ['wɪspəʳ] *n* sussurro ▷ *vt, vi*
sussurrare
whistle ['wɪsl] *n* (*sound*) fischio; (*object*)

fischietto ▷ vi fischiare

white [waɪt] *adj* bianco(-a); (*with fear*) pallido(-a) ▷ *n* bianco; (*person*) bianco(-a); **White House** *n* Casa Bianca; **whitewash** *n* (*paint*) bianco di calce ▷ *vt* imbiancare; (*fig*) coprire

whiting ['waɪtɪŋ] *n inv* (*fish*) merlango

Whitsun ['wɪtsn] *n* Pentecoste *f*

whittle ['wɪtl] *vt* **to ~ away**, **~ down** ridurre, tagliare

whizz [wɪz] *vi* **to ~ past** *or* **by** passare sfrecciando

 KEYWORD

who [hu:] *pron* **1** (*interrogative*) chi; **who is it?, who's there?** chi è? **2** (*relative*) che; **the man who spoke to me** l'uomo che ha parlato con me; **those who can swim** quelli che sanno nuotare

whoever [hu:'ɛvə] *pron* **~ finds it** chiunque lo trovi; **ask ~ you like** lo chieda a chiunque vuole; **~ she marries** chiunque sposerà, non importa chi sposerà; **~ told you that?** chi mai gliel'ha detto?

whole [həul] *adj* (*complete*) tutto(-a), completo(-a); (*not broken*) intero(-a), intatto(-a) ▷ *n* (*all*): **the ~ of** tutto(-a) il (la); (*entire unit*) tutto; (*not broken*) tutto; **the ~ of the town** tutta la città, la città intera; **on the ~**, **as a ~** nel complesso, nell'insieme; **wholefood(s)** *n(pl)* cibo integrale; **wholeheartedly** [həul'hɑː tɪdlɪ] *adv* sentitamente, di tutto cuore; **wholemeal** *adj* (*bread, flour*) integrale; **wholesale** *n* commercio *or* vendita all'ingrosso ▷ *adj* all'ingrosso; (*destruction*) totale; **wholewheat** *adj* = **wholemeal**; **wholly** *adv* completamente, del tutto

 KEYWORD

whom [hu:m] *pron* **1** (*interrogative*) chi; **whom did you see?** chi hai visto?; **to whom did you give it?** a chi lo hai dato? **2** (*relative*) che, *prep* + il (la) quale (*check syntax of Italian verb used*); **the man whom I saw/to whom I spoke** l'uomo che ho visto/al quale ho parlato

whore [hɔ:] (*inf: pej*) *n* puttana

 KEYWORD

whose [hu:z] *adj* **1** (*possessive: interrogative*) di chi; **whose book is this?, whose is this book?** di chi è questo libro?; **whose daughter are you?** di chi sei figlia?

2 (*possessive: relative*): **the man whose son you rescued** l'uomo il cui figlio hai salvato; **the girl whose sister you were speaking to** la ragazza alla cui sorella stavi parlando

▷ *pron* di chi; **whose is this?** di chi è questo?; **I know whose it is** so di chi è

 KEYWORD

why [waɪ] *adv* perché; **why not?** perché no?; **why not do it now?** perché non farlo adesso?

▷ *conj* **I wonder why he said that** mi chiedo perché l'abbia detto; **that's not why I'm here** non è questo il motivo per cui sono qui; **the reason why** il motivo per cui

▷ *excl* (*surprise*) ma guarda un po'!; (*remonstrating*) ma (via)!; (*explaining*) ebbene!

wicked ['wɪkɪd] *adj* cattivo(-a), malvagio(-a); maligno(-a); perfido(-a)

wicket ['wɪkɪt] *n* (*Cricket*) porta; area tra le due porte

wide [waɪd] *adj* largo(-a); (*area, knowledge*) vasto(-a); (*choice*) ampio(-a) ▷ *adv* **to open ~** spalancare; **to shoot ~** tirare a vuoto *or* fuori bersaglio; **widely** *adv* (*differing*) molto, completamente; (*travelled, spaced*) molto; (*believed*) generalmente; **widen** *vt* allargare, ampliare; **wide open** *adj* spalancato(-a); **widespread** *adj* (*belief etc*) molto *or* assai diffuso(-a)

widow ['wɪdəu] *n* vedova; **widower** *n* vedovo

width [wɪdθ] *n* larghezza

wield [wi:ld] *vt* (*sword*) maneggiare; (*power*) esercitare

wife [waɪf] (*pl* **wives**) *n* moglie *f*

wig [wɪg] *n* parrucca

wild [waɪld] *adj* selvatico(-a); selvaggio(-a); (*sea, weather*) tempestoso(-a); (*idea, life*) folle; stravagante; (*applause*) frenetico(-a); **wilderness** ['wɪldə nɪs] *n* deserto; **wildlife** *n* natura; **wildly** *adv* selvaggiamente; (*applaud*) freneticamente; (*hit, guess*) a casaccio; (*happy*) follemente

 KEYWORD

will [wɪl] (*pt, pp* **willed**) *aux vb* **1** (*forming future tense*): **I will finish it tomorrow** lo finirò domani; **I will have finished it by tomorrow** lo finirò entro domani; **will you do it? — yes I will/no I won't** lo farai? — sì

(lo farò)/no (non lo farò)
2 (*in conjectures, predictions*): **he will** or
he'll be there by now dovrebbe essere
arrivato ora; **that will be the postman**
sarà il postino
3 (*in commands, requests, offers*): **will you
be quiet?** vuoi stare zitto?; **will you come?**
vieni anche tu?; **will you help me?** mi
aiuti?, mi puoi aiutare?; **will you have a
cup of tea?** vorrebbe una tazza di tè?; **I
won't put up with it!** non lo accetterò!
▷ *vt* **to will sb to do** volere che qn faccia;
he willed himself to go on continuò
grazie a un grande sforzo di volontà
▷ *n* volontà; testamento

willing ['wɪlɪŋ] *adj* volonteroso(-a); ~
to do disposto(-a) a fare; **willingly** *adv*
volentieri
willow ['wɪləu] *n* salice *m*
willpower ['wɪlpauə'] *n* forza di volontà
wilt [wɪlt] *vi* appassire
win [wɪn] (*pt, pp* **won**) *n* (*in sports etc*)
vittoria ▷ *vt* (*battle, prize, money*) vincere;
(*popularity*) conquistare ▷ *vi* vincere; **win
over** *vt* convincere
wince [wɪns] *vi* trasalire
wind¹ [waɪnd] (*pt, pp* **wound**) *vt*
attorcigliare; (*wrap*) avvolgere; (*clock, toy*)
caricare ▷ *vi* (*road, river*) serpeggiare; **wind
down** *vt* (*car window*) abbassare; (*fig:
production, business*) diminuire; **wind up** *vt*
(*clock*) caricare; (*debate*) concludere
wind² [wɪnd] *n* vento; (*Med*) flatulenza;
(*breath*) respiro, fiato ▷ *vt* (*take breath
away*) far restare senza fiato; ~ **power**
energia eolica
windfall ['wɪndfɔːl] *n* (*money*) guadagno
insperato
winding ['waɪndɪŋ] *adj* (*road*)
serpeggiante; (*staircase*) a chiocciola
windmill ['wɪndmɪl] *n* mulino a vento
window ['wɪndəu] *n* finestra, (*in car, train,
plane*) finestrino; (*in shop etc*) vetrina; (*also:
~ pane*) vetro; **I'd like a ~ seat** vorrei un
posto vicino al finestrino; **window box**
n cassetta da fiori; **window cleaner** *n*
(*person*) pulitore *m* di finestre; **window
pane** *n* vetro; **window seat** *n* posto
finestrino; **windowsill** *n* davanzale *m*
windscreen ['wɪndskriːn] (*US*
windshield) *n* parabrezza *m inv*;
windscreen wiper (*US* **windshield wiper**)
n tergicristallo
windsurfing ['wɪndsəːfɪŋ] *n* windsurf
m inv
windy ['wɪndɪ] *adj* ventoso(-a); **it's** ~ c'è
vento
wine [waɪn] *n* vino; **wine bar** *n* enoteca

(*per degustazione*); **wine glass** *n* bicchiere
m da vino; **wine list** *n* lista dei vini; **wine
tasting** *n* degustazione *f* dei vini
wing [wɪŋ] *n* ala; (*Aut*) fiancata; **wing
mirror** *n* (*BRIT*) specchietto retrovisore
esterno
wink [wɪŋk] *n* ammiccamento ▷ *vi*
ammiccare, fare l'occhiolino; (*light*)
baluginare
winner ['wɪnə'] *n* vincitore(-trice)
winning ['wɪnɪŋ] *adj* (*team, goal*) vincente;
(*smile*) affascinante
winter ['wɪntə'] *n* inverno; **winter sports**
npl sport *mpl* invernali; **wintertime** *n*
inverno, stagione *f* invernale
wipe [waɪp] *n* pulita, passata ▷ *vt* pulire
(*strofinando*); (*erase: tape*) cancellare; **wipe
out** *vt* (*debt*) pagare, liquidare; (*memory*)
cancellare; (*destroy*) annientare; **wipe up**
vt asciugare
wire ['waɪə'] *n* filo; (*Elec*) filo elettrico; (*Tel*)
telegramma *m* ▷ *vt* (*house*) fare l'impianto
elettrico di; (*also:* ~ **up**) collegare,
allacciare; (*person*) telegrafare a
wiring ['waɪərɪŋ] *n* impianto elettrico
wisdom ['wɪzdəm] *n* saggezza; (*of action*)
prudenza; **wisdom tooth** *n* dente *m* del
giudizio
wise [waɪz] *adj* saggio(-a); prudente;
giudizioso(-a)
wish [wɪʃ] *n* (*desire*) desiderio; (*specific
desire*) richiesta ▷ *vt* desiderare, volere;
best ~es (*on birthday etc*) i migliori auguri;
with best ~es (*in letter*) cordiali saluti,
con i migliori saluti; **to ~ sb goodbye**
dire arrivederci a qn; **he ~ed me well** mi
augurò di riuscire; **to ~ to do/sb to do**
desiderare or volere fare/che qn faccia; **to
~ for** desiderare
wistful ['wɪstful] *adj* malinconico(-a)
wit [wɪt] *n* (*also:* ~**s**) intelligenza; presenza
di spirito; (*wittiness*) spirito, arguzia;
(*person*) bello spirito
witch [wɪtʃ] *n* strega

◯ **KEYWORD**

with [wɪð, wɪθ] *prep* **1** (*in the company
of*) con; **I was with him** ero con lui; **we
stayed with friends** siamo stati da amici;
I'll be with you in a minute vengo subito
2 (*descriptive*) con; **a room with a view**
una stanza con vista sul mare (*or* sulle
montagne *etc*); **the man with the grey
hat/blue eyes** l'uomo con il cappello
grigio/gli occhi blu
3 (*indicating manner, means, cause*): **with
tears in her eyes** con le lacrime agli occhi;
red with anger rosso dalla rabbia; **to**

w

shake with fear tremare di paura
4: **I'm with you** (*I understand*) la seguo;
to be with it (*inf: up-to-date*) essere alla
moda; (: *alert*) essere sveglio(-a)

withdraw [wɪð'drɔː] (*irreg: like draw*) *vt*
ritirare; (*money from bank*) ritirare; prelevare
▷ *vi* ritirarsi; **withdrawal** *n* ritiro; prelievo;
(*of army*) ritirata; **withdrawal symptoms**
n (*Med*) crisi *f* di astinenza; **withdrawn** *adj*
(*person*) distaccato(-a)
withdrew [wɪð'druː] *pt of* **withdraw**
wither ['wɪðə'] *vi* appassire
withhold [wɪð'həuld] (*irreg: like hold*)
vt (*money*) trattenere; (*permission*): **to ~
(from)** rifiutare (a); (*information*): **to ~
(from)** nascondere (a)
within [wɪð'ɪn] *prep* all'interno; (*in time,
distances*) entro ▷ *adv* all'interno, dentro; **~
reach (of)** alla portata (di); **~ sight (of)** in
vista (di); **~ a mile of** entro un miglio da; **~
the week** prima della fine della settimana
without [wɪð'aut] *prep* senza; **to go ~ sth**
fare a meno di qc
withstand [wɪð'stænd] (*irreg: like stand*)
vt resistere a
witness ['wɪtnɪs] *n* (*person, also Law*)
testimone *m/f* ▷ *vt* (*event*) essere
testimone di; (*document*) attestare
l'autenticità di
witty ['wɪtɪ] *adj* spiritoso(-a)
wives [waɪvz] *npl of* **wife**
wizard ['wɪzəd] *n* mago
wk *abbr* = **week**
wobble ['wɔbl] *vi* tremare; (*chair*)
traballare
woe [wəu] *n* dolore *m*; disgrazia
woke [wəuk] *pt of* **wake**
woken ['wəukn] *pp of* **wake**
wolf [wulf] (*pl* **wolves**) *n* lupo
woman ['wumən] (*pl* **women**) *n* donna
womb [wuːm] *n* (*Anat*) utero
women ['wɪmɪn] *npl of* **woman**
won [wʌn] *pt, pp of* **win**
wonder ['wʌndə'] *n* meraviglia ▷ *vi* **to ~
whether/why** domandarsi se/perché; **to
~ at** essere sorpreso(-a) di; meravigliarsi
di; **to ~ about** domandarsi di; pensare
a; **it's no ~ that** c'è poco or non c'è da
meravigliarsi che + *sub*; **wonderful** *adj*
meraviglioso(-a)
won't [wəunt] = **will not**
wood [wud] *n* legno; (*timber*) legname *m*;
(*forest*) bosco; **wooden** *adj* di legno; (*fig*)
rigido(-a); inespressivo(-a); **woodwind** *npl*
(*Mus*): **the woodwind** i legni; **woodwork**
n (*craft, subject*) falegnameria
wool [wul] *n* lana; **to pull the ~ over sb's
eyes** (*fig*) imbrogliare qn; **woollen** (*us*

woolen) *adj* di lana; (*industry*) laniero(-a);
woolly (*us* **wooly**) *adj* di lana; (*fig: ideas*)
confuso(-a)
word [wəːd] *n* parola; (*news*) notizie *fpl*
▷ *vt* esprimere, formulare; **in other ~s** in
altre parole; **to break/keep one's ~** non
mantenere/mantenere la propria parola;
to have ~s with sb avere un diverbio con
qn; **wording** *n* formulazione *f*; **word
processing** *n* elaborazione *f* di testi, word
processing *m*; **word processor** *n* word
processor *m inv*
wore [wɔː'] *pt of* **wear**
work [wəːk] *n* lavoro; (*Art, Literature*)
opera ▷ *vi* lavorare; (*mechanism, plan etc*)
funzionare; (*medicine*) essere efficace
▷ *vt* (*clay, wood etc*) lavorare; (*mine etc*)
sfruttare; (*machine*) far funzionare;
(*cause: effect, miracle*) fare; **to be out of
~** essere disoccupato(-a); **~s** *n* (BRIT:
factory) fabbrica *npl* (*of clock, machine*)
meccanismo; **how does this ~?** come
funziona?; **the TV isn't ~ing** la TV non
funziona; **to ~ loose** allentarsi; **work
out** *vi* (*plans etc*) riuscire, andare bene
▷ *vt* (*problem*) risolvere; (*plan*) elaborare;
it ~s out at £100 fa 100 sterline; **worker**
n lavoratore(-trice), operaio(-a); **work
experience** *n* (*previous jobs*) esperienze
fpl lavorative; (*student training placement*)
tirocinio; **workforce** *n* forza lavoro;
working class *n* classe *f* operaia;
working week *n* settimana lavorativa;
workman (*irreg*) *n* operaio; **work of
art** *n* opera d'arte; **workout** *n* (*Sport*)
allenamento; **work permit** *n* permesso
di lavoro; **workplace** *n* posto di lavoro;
workshop *n* officina; (*practical session*)
gruppo di lavoro; **work station** *n* stazione
f di lavoro; **work surface** *n* piano di
lavoro; **worktop** *n* piano di lavoro
world [wəːld] *n* mondo ▷ *cpd* (*champion*)
del mondo; (*power, war*) mondiale; **to
think the ~ of sb** (*fig*) pensare un gran
bene di qn; **World Cup** *n* (*Football*) Coppa
del Mondo; **world-wide** *adj* universale;
World-Wide Web *n* World Wide Web *m*
worm [wəːm] *n* (*also:* **earth~**) verme *m*
worn [wɔːn] *pp of* **wear** ▷ *adj* usato(-a);
worn-out *adj* (*object*) consumato(-a),
logoro(-a); (*person*) sfinito(-a)
worried ['wʌrɪd] *adj* preoccupato(-a)
worry ['wʌrɪ] *n* preoccupazione *f* ▷ *vt*
preoccupare ▷ *vi* preoccuparsi; **worrying**
adj preoccupante
worse [wəːs] *adj* peggiore ▷ *adv, n* peggio;
a change for the ~ un peggioramento;
worsen *vt, vi* peggiorare; **worse off** *adj* in
condizioni (economiche) peggiori

worship ['wəːʃɪp] n culto ▷ vt (God) adorare, venerare; (person) adorare; **Your W~** (BRIT: to mayor) signor sindaco; (: to judge) signor giudice

worst [wəːst] adj il (la) peggiore ▷ adv, n peggio; **at ~** al peggio, per male che vada

worth [wəːθ] n valore m ▷ adj **to be ~ valere; it's ~ it** ne vale la pena; **it is ~ one's while (to do)** vale la pena (fare); **worthless** adj di nessun valore; **worthwhile** adj (activity) utile; (cause) lodevole

worthy ['wəːðɪ] adj (person) degno(-a); (motive) lodevole; **~ of** degno di

---

⭕ **KEYWORD**

would [wud] aux vb **1** (conditional tense): **if you asked him he would do it** se glielo chiedesse lo farebbe; **if you had asked him he would have done it** se glielo avesse chiesto lo avrebbe fatto

2 (in offers, invitations, requests): **would you like a biscuit?** vorrebbe or vuole un biscotto?; **would you ask him to come in?** lo faccia entrare, per cortesia; **would you open the window please?** apra la finestra, per favore

3 (in indirect speech): **I said I would do it** ho detto che l'avrei fatto

4 (emphatic): **it WOULD have to snow today!** doveva proprio nevicare oggi!

5 (insistence): **she wouldn't do it** non ha voluto farlo

6 (conjecture): **it would have been midnight** sarà stato mezzanotte; **it would seem so** sembrerebbe proprio di sì

7 (indicating habit): **he would go there on Mondays** andava lì ogni lunedì

wouldn't ['wudnt] = **would not**

wound¹ [waund] pt, pp of **wind¹**

wound² [wuːnd] n ferita f ▷ vt ferire

wove [wəuv] pt of **weave**

woven ['wəuvn] pp of **weave**

wrap [ræp] vt avvolgere; (pack: also: ~ up) incartare; **wrapper** n (on chocolate) carta; (BRIT: of book) copertina; **wrapping** ['ræpɪŋ] n carta; **wrapping paper** n carta da pacchi; (for gift) carta da regali

wreath [riːθ, pl riːðz] n corona

wreck [rɛk] n (sea disaster) naufragio; (ship) relitto; (pej: person) rottame m ▷ vt demolire; (ship) far naufragare; (fig) rovinare; **wreckage** n rottami mpl; (of building) macerie fpl; (of ship) relitti mpl

wren [rɛn] n (Zool) scricciolo

wrench [rɛntʃ] n (Tech) chiave f; (tug) torsione f brusca; (fig) strazio ▷ vt

strappare; storcere; **to ~ sth from** strappare qc a or da

wrestle ['rɛsl] vi **to ~ (with sb)** lottare (con qn); **wrestler** n lottatore(-trice); **wrestling** n lotta

wretched ['rɛtʃɪd] adj disgraziato(-a); (inf: weather, holiday) orrendo(-a), orribile; (: child, dog) pestifero(-a)

wriggle ['rɪgl] vi (also: ~ about) dimenarsi; (: snake, worm) serpeggiare, muoversi serpeggiando

wring [rɪŋ] (pt, pp **wrung**) vt torcere; (wet clothes) strizzare; (fig): **to ~ sth out of** strappare qc a

wrinkle ['rɪŋkl] n (on skin) ruga; (on paper etc) grinza ▷ vt (nose) torcere; (forehead) corrugare ▷ vi (skin, paint) raggrinzirsi

wrist [rɪst] n polso

write [raɪt] (pt **wrote**, pp **written**) vt, vi scrivere; **write down** vt annotare; (put in writing) mettere per iscritto; **write off** vt (debt, plan) cancellare; **write out** vt mettere per iscritto; (cheque, receipt) scrivere; **write-off** n perdita completa; **writer** n autore(-trice), scrittore(-trice)

writing ['raɪtɪŋ] n scrittura; (of author) scritto, opera; **in ~** per iscritto; **writing paper** n carta da lettere

written ['rɪtn] pp of **write**

wrong [rɔŋ] adj sbagliato(-a); (not suitable) inadatto(-a); (wicked) cattivo(-a); (unfair) ingiusto(-a) ▷ adv in modo sbagliato, erroneamente ▷ n (injustice) torto ▷ vt fare torto a; **I took a ~ turning** ho sbagliato strada; **you are ~ to do it** ha torto a farlo; **you are ~ about that, you've got it ~** si sbaglia; **to be in the ~** avere torto; **what's ~?** cosa c'è che non va?; **to go ~** (person) sbagliarsi; (plan) fallire, non riuscire; (machine) guastarsi; **wrongly** adv (incorrectly, by mistake) in modo sbagliato; **wrong number** n (Tel): **you've got the wrong number** ha sbagliato numero

wrote [rəut] pt of **write**

wrung [rʌŋ] pt, pp of **wring**

WWW n abbr = **World Wide Web**; **the ~** la Rete

w

XL *abbr* = **extra large**

Xmas ['ɛksməs] *n abbr* = **Christmas**

X-ray ['ɛksreɪ] *n* raggio X; (*photograph*)
radiografia ▷ *vt* radiografare

xylophone ['zaɪləfəun] *n* xilofono

yacht [jɔt] *n* panfilo, yacht *m inv*;
yachting *n* yachting *m*, sport *m* della
vela

yard [jɑːd] *n* (*of house etc*) cortile *m*;
(*measure*) iarda (= 914 *mm*; 3 *feet*); **yard sale**
(US) *n* vendita di oggetti usati nel cortile di
una casa privata

yarn [jɑːn] *n* filato; (*tale*) lunga storia

yawn [jɔːn] *n* sbadiglio ▷ *vi* sbadigliare

yd. *abbr* = **yard(s)**

yeah [jɛə] (*inf*) *adv* sì

year [jɪəʳ] *n* anno; (*referring to harvest,
wine etc*) annata; **he is 8 ~s old** ha 8 anni;
an eight-~-old child un(a) bambino(-a)
di otto anni; **yearly** *adj* annuale ▷ *adv*
annualmente

yearn [jəːn] *vi* **to ~ for sth/to do**
desiderare ardentemente qc/di fare

yeast [jiːst] *n* lievito

yell [jɛl] *n* urlo ▷ *vi* urlare

yellow ['jɛləu] *adj* giallo(-a); **Yellow
Pages®** *npl* pagine *fpl* gialle

yes [jɛs] *adv* sì ▷ *n* sì *m inv*; **to say/answer
~** dire/rispondere di sì

yesterday ['jɛstədɪ] *adv* ieri ▷ *n* ieri *m inv*;
~ morning/evening ieri mattina/sera; **all
day ~** ieri per tutta la giornata

yet [jɛt] *adv* ancora; già ▷ *conj* ma,
tuttavia; **it is not finished ~** non
è ancora finito; **the best ~** finora il

migliore; **as ~** finora
yew [juː] *n* tasso (*albero*)
Yiddish ['jɪdɪʃ] *n* yiddish *m*
yield [jiːld] *n* produzione *f*, resa; reddito
▷ *vt* produrre, rendere; (*surrender*)
cedere ▷ *vi* cedere; (*US: Aut*) dare la
precedenza
yob(bo) ['jɔb(əʊ)] *n* (BRIT *inf*) bullo
yoga ['jəʊgə] *n* yoga *m*
yog(h)urt ['jəʊgət] *n* iogurt *m inv*
yolk [jəʊk] *n* tuorlo, rosso d'uovo

◯ **KEYWORD**

you [juː] *pron* **1** (*subject*) tu; (: *polite form*) lei;
(: *pl*) voi; (: *very formal*) loro; **you Italians
enjoy your food** a voi Italiani piace
mangiare bene; **you and I will go** tu ed io
or lei ed io andiamo
2 (*object: direct*) ti; la; vi; loro (*after vb*); (:
indirect) ti; le; vi; loro (*after vb*); **I know you**
ti or la or vi conosco; **I gave it to you** te
l'ho dato; gliel'ho dato; ve l'ho dato; l'ho
dato loro
3 (*stressed, after prep, in comparisons*) te; lei;
voi; loro; **I told you to do it** ho detto a TE
(*or* a LEI *etc*) di farlo; **she's younger than
you** è più giovane di te (*or* lei *etc*)
4 (*impers: one*) si; **fresh air does you good**
l'aria fresca fa bene; **you never know** non
si sa mai

you'd [juːd] = **you had**; **you would**
you'll [juːl] = **you will**; **you shall**
young [jʌŋ] *adj* giovane ▷ *npl* (*of animal*)
piccoli *mpl*; (*people*): **the ~** i giovani, la
gioventù; **youngster** *n* giovanotto,
ragazzo; (*child*) bambino(-a)
your [jɔːʳ] *adj* il (la) tuo(-a) *pl*, i (le) tuoi
(tue); il (la) suo(-a); (*pl*) i (le) suoi (sue); il
(la) vostro(-a); (*pl*) i (le) vostri(-e); il (la)
loro; (*pl*) i (le) loro; *see also* **my**
you're [jʊəʳ] = **you are**
yours [jɔːz] *pron* il (la) tuo(-a); (*pl*) i (le)
tuoi (tue); (*polite form*) il (la) suo(-a); (*pl*)
i (le) suoi (sue); (*pl*) il (la) vostro(-a); (*pl*)
i (le) vostri(-e); (: *very formal*) il (là) loro;
(*pl*) i (le) loro; *see also* **mine**; **faithfully**;
sincerely
yourself [jɔː'sɛlf] *pron* (*reflexive*) ti;
si; (*after prep*) te; sé; (*emphatic*) tu
stesso(-a); lei stesso(-a); **yourselves** *pl
pron* (*reflexive*) vi; si; (*after prep*) voi; loro;
(*emphatic*) voi stessi(-e); loro stessi(-e); *see
also* **oneself**
youth [juːθ, *pl* juːðz] *n* gioventù *f*; (*young
man*) giovane *m*, ragazzo; **youth club** *n*
centro giovanile; **youthful** *adj* giovane;
da giovane; giovanile; **youth hostel** *n*

ostello della gioventù
you've [juːv] = **you have**
Yugoslavia ['juːgəʊ'slaːvɪə] *n* (*Hist*)
Jugoslavia

y

zeal [ziːl] *n* zelo; entusiasmo
zebra ['ziːbrə] *n* zebra; **zebra crossing**
  (BRIT) *n* (passaggio pedonale a) strisce *fpl*,
  zebre *fpl*
zero ['zɪərəu] *n* zero
zest [zɛst] *n* gusto; (*Culin*) buccia
zigzag ['zɪgzæg] *n* zigzag *m inv* ▷ *vi*
  zigzagare
Zimbabwe [zɪm'bɑːbwɪ] *n* Zimbabwe *m*
zinc [zɪŋk] *n* zinco
zip [zɪp] *n* (*also:* **~ fastener**, (US) **zipper**)
  chiusura *f or* cerniera *f* lampo *inv* ▷ *vt* (*also:*
  ~ up) chiudere con una cerniera lampo;
  zip code (US) *n* codice *m* di avviamento
  postale; **zipper** (US) *n* cerniera *f* lampo *inv*
zit [zɪt] *n* brufolo
zodiac ['zəudɪæk] *n* zodiaco
zone [zəun] *n* (*also Mil*) zona
zoo [zuː] *n* zoo *m inv*
zoology [zuː'ɔlədʒɪ] *n* zoologia
zoom [zuːm] *vi* **to ~ past** sfrecciare; **zoom**
  lens *n* zoom *m inv*, obiettivo a focale
  variabile
zucchini [zuː'kiːnɪ] (US) *npl* (*courgettes*)
  zucchine *fpl*